Essentials of
Life-Span Development

SIXTH EDITION

John W. Santrock

University of Texas at Dallas

McGraw Hill Education

ESSENTIALS OF LIFE-SPAN DEVELOPMENT, SIXTH EDITION

Published by McGraw-Hill Education, 2 Penn Plaza, New York, NY 10121. Copyright ©2020 by McGraw-Hill Education. All rights reserved. Printed in the United States of America. Previous editions ©2018, 2016, and 2014. No part of this publication may be reproduced or distributed in any form or by any means, or stored in a database or retrieval system, without the prior written consent of McGraw-Hill Education, including, but not limited to, in any network or other electronic storage or transmission, or broadcast for distance learning.

Some ancillaries, including electronic and print components, may not be available to customers outside the United States.

This book is printed on acid-free paper.

2 3 4 5 6 7 8 9 LMN 21 20

ISBN 978-1-260-05430-9 (bound edition)
MHID 1-260-05430-6 (bound edition)
ISBN 978-1-260-52989-0 (loose-leaf edition)
MHID 1-260-52989-4 (loose-leaf edition)

Portfolio Manager: *Ryan Treat*
Product Development Manager: *Dawn Groundwater*
Product Developer: *Vicki Malinee, Van Brien & Associates*
Marketing Manager: *AJ Laferrera*
Content Project Managers: *Mary E. Powers (Core), Jodi Banowetz (Assessment)*
Buyer: *Samdy Ludovissy*
Design: *Matt Backhaus*
Content Licensing Specialist: *Carrie Burger*
Cover Image: *©Monkey Business Images/Shutterstock (adult couple); ©Oksana Kuzmina/Shutterstock (baby); ©Image Source (boy); ©SpeedKingz/Shutterstock (teenager); ©Rido/Shutterstock (multiethnic family); ©Monkey Business Images/Shutterstock (senior couple); ©wavebreakmedia/Shutterstock (two girls).*
Compositor: *Aptara®, Inc.*

All credits appearing on page or at the end of the book are considered to be an extension of the copyright page.

Library of Congress Cataloging-in-Publication Data

Names: Santrock, John W., author.
Title: Essentials of life-span development / John W. Santrock, University of
  Texas at Dallas.
Description: Sixth edition. | New York, NY : McGraw-Hill Education, [2020] |
  Includes bibliographical references and index.
Identifiers: LCCN 2018035665| ISBN 9781260054309 (alk. paper) | ISBN
  1260054306 (alk. paper)
Subjects: LCSH: Developmental psychology.
Classification: LCC BF713 .S256 2020 | DDC 155—dc23 LC record available at
https://lccn.loc.gov/2018035665

Brief Contents

©Ariel Skelley/Getty Images

©Rob Crandall/Alamy

©Fuse/Getty Images

©Science Photo Library/Getty Images

connect

Contents

©Boris Ryaposov/Shutterstock

©karelnoppe/Getty Images

©amana Images, Inc./Alamy

©Stockbyte/PunchStock

connect McGraw-Hill Education Psychology's APA Documentation Style Guide

How Would You?

About the Author

John W. Santrock

John Santrock received his Ph.D. from the University of Minnesota in 1973. He taught at the University of Charleston and the University of Georgia before joining the Program in Psychology and Human Development at the University of Texas at Dallas, where he currently teaches a number of undergraduate courses and has received the University's Effective Teaching Award. In 2010, he created the UT-Dallas Santrock undergraduate scholarship, an annual award that is given to outstanding undergraduate students majoring in developmental psychology to enable them to attend research conventions.

John has been a member of the editorial boards of *Child Development* and *Developmental Psychology*. His research on the multiple factors involved in how divorce affects children's development is widely cited and used in expert witness testimony to promote flexibility and alternative considerations in custody disputes.

John also has authored these exceptional McGraw-Hill texts: *Children* (14th edition), *Adolescence* (17th edition), *Life-Span Development* (17th edition), *A Topical Approach to Life-Span Development* (9th edition), and *Educational Psychology* (6th edition).

John Santrock (back row middle) with the 2015 recipients of the Santrock Travel Scholarship Award in developmental psychology. Created by Dr. Santrock, this annual award provides undergraduate students with the opportunity to attend a professional meeting. A number of the students shown here attended the Society for Research in Child Development conference.
Courtesy of Jessica Serna

For many years, John was involved in tennis as a player, teaching professional, and coach of professional tennis players. At the University of Miami (FL), the tennis team on which he played still holds the NCAA Division I record for most consecutive wins (137) in any sport. His wife, Mary Jo, has a master's degree in special education and has worked as a teacher and a Realtor. He has two daughters—Tracy, who worked for a number of years as a technology marketing specialist, and Jennifer, who has been a medical sales specialist. However, recently both have followed in their mother's footsteps and are now Realtors. Tracy has run the Boston and New York marathons. Jennifer is a former professional tennis player and NCAA tennis player of the year. John has one granddaughter, Jordan, age 26, who works at Ernst & Young accounting firm, and two grandsons, Alex, age 13, and Luke, age 12. In the last two decades, John also has spent time painting expressionist art.

Dedication:

With special appreciation to my wife, Mary Jo.

Connecting *research* and *results*

As a master teacher, John Santrock connects current research and real-world applications. Through an integrated, personalized digital learning program, students gain the insight they need to study smarter and improve performance.

McGraw-Hill Education Connect is a digital assignment and assessment platform that strengthens the link between faculty, students, and course work, helping everyone accomplish more in less time. Connect for Life-Span Development includes assignable and assessable videos, quizzes, exercises, and interactivities, all associated with learning objectives. Interactive assignments and videos allow students to experience and apply their understanding of psychology to the world with fun and stimulating activities.

Real People, Real World, Real Life

At the higher end of Bloom's taxonomy (analyze, evaluate, create), the McGraw-Hill Education Milestones video series is an observational tool that allows students to experience life as it unfolds, from infancy to late adulthood. This ground-breaking, longitudinal video series tracks the development of real children as they progress through the early stages of physical, social, and emotional development in their first few weeks, months, and years of life. Assignable and assessable within Connect for Life-Span Development, Milestones also includes interviews with adolescents and adults to reflect development throughout the entire life span.

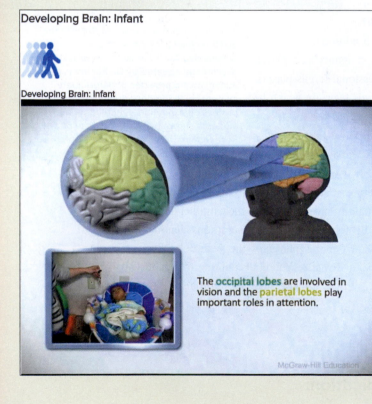

The occipital lobes are involved in vision and the parietal lobes play important roles in attention.

Inform and Engage on Psychological Concepts

At the lower end of Bloom's taxonomy, students are introduced to Concept Clips—the dynamic, colorful graphics and stimulating animations that break down some of psychology's most difficult concepts in a step-by-step manner, engaging students and aiding in retention. They are assignable and assessable in Connect or can be used as a jumping-off point in class. Accompanied by audio narration, Concept Clips cover topics such as object permanence and conservation, as well as theories and theorists like Bandura's social cognitive theory, Vygotsky's sociocultural theory, Buss's evolutionary theory, and Kuhl's language development theory.

Prepare Students for Higher-Level Thinking

Also at the higher end of Bloom's taxonomy, **Power of Process** for Psychology helps students improve critical thinking skills and allows instructors to assess these skills efficiently and effectively in an online environment. Available through Connect, pre-loaded journal articles are available for instructors to assign. Using a scaffolded framework such as understanding, synthesizing, and analyzing, Power of Process moves students toward higher-level thinking and analysis.

Better Data, Smarter Revision, Improved Results

Students helped inform the revision strategy of *Essentials of Life-Span Development.* McGraw-Hill Education's SmartBook® is the first and only adaptive reading and learning experience! SmartBook helps students distinguish the concepts they know from the concepts they don't, while pinpointing the concepts they are about to forget. SmartBook continuously adapts to create a truly personalized learning path. SmartBook's real-time reports help both students and instructors identify the concepts that require more attention, making study sessions and class time more efficient.

Content revisions are informed by data collected anonymously through McGraw-Hill Education's SmartBook.

STEP 1. Over the course of three years, data points showing concepts that caused students the most difficulty were anonymously collected from Connect for Life-Span Development's SmartBook.

STEP 2. The data from SmartBook was provided to the author in the form of a *Heat Map*, which graphically illustrates "hot spots" in the text that affect student learning (see image at right).

STEP 3. The author used the *Heat Map* data to refine the content and reinforce student comprehension in the new edition. Additional quiz questions and assignable activities were created for use in Connect to further support student success.

RESULT: Because the *Heat Map* gave the author empirically based feedback at the paragraph and even sentence level, he was able to develop the new edition using precise student data that pinpointed concepts that gave students the most difficulty.

New to this edition, SmartBook is now optimized for mobile and tablet and is accessible for students with disabilities. Content-wise, it has been enhanced with improved learning objectives that are measurable and observable to improve student outcomes. SmartBook personalizes learning to individual student needs, continually adapting to pinpoint knowledge gaps and focus learning on topics that need the most attention. Study time is more productive and, as a result, students are better prepared for class and coursework. For instructors, SmartBook tracks student progress and provides insights that can help guide teaching strategies.

Powerful Reporting

Whether a class is face-to-face, hybrid, or entirely online, Connect for Life-Span Development provides tools and analytics to reduce the amount of time instructors need to administer their courses. Easy-to-use course management tools allow instructors to spend less time administering and more time teaching, while easy-to-use reporting features allow students to monitor their progress and optimize their study time.

- The At-Risk Student Report provides instructors with one-click access to a dashboard that identifies students who are at risk of dropping out of the course due to low engagement levels.
- The Category Analysis Report details student performance relative to specific learning objectives and goals, including APA outcomes and levels of Bloom's taxonomy.
- Connect Insight is a one-of-a-kind visual analytics dashboard—now available for both instructors and students—that provides at-a-glance information regarding student performance.
- The LearnSmart Reports allow instructors and students to easily monitor progress and pinpoint areas of weakness, giving each student a personalized study plan to achieve success.

Online Instructor Resources

The resources listed here accompany *Essentials of Life-Span Development,* Sixth Edition. Please contact your McGraw-Hill representative for details concerning the availability of these and other valuable materials that can help you design and enhance your course.

Instructor's Manual   Broken down by chapter, this resource provides chapter outlines, suggested lecture topics, classroom activities and demonstrations, suggested student research projects, essay questions, and critical thinking questions.

Test Bank and Computerized Test Bank   This comprehensive Test Bank includes more than 1,500 multiple-choice and approximately 75 essay questions. Organized by chapter, the questions are designed to test factual, applied, and conceptual understanding. All test questions are available within TestGen™ software.

PowerPoint Slides   The PowerPoint presentations, now WCAG compliant, highlight the key points of the chapter and include supporting visuals. All of the slides can be modified to meet individual needs.

The Essential Approach to Life-Span Development

In the view of many instructors who teach the life-span development course, the biggest challenge they face is covering all periods of human development within one academic term. My own teaching experience bears this out. I have had to skip over much of the material in a comprehensive life-span development text in order to focus on key topics and concepts that students find difficult and to fit in applications that are relevant to students' lives. I wrote *Essentials of Life-Span Development* to respond to the need for a shorter text that covers core content in a way that is meaningful to diverse students.

This sixth edition continues my commitment to providing a brief introduction to life-span development—with an exciting difference. Recognizing that most of today's students have grown up in a digital world, I take very seriously the need for communicating content in different ways, online as well as in print. Consequently, I'm enthusiastic about McGraw-Hill's online assignment and assessment platform, **Connect for Life-Span Development,** which incorporates this text, and the captivating **Milestones** video modules. Together, these resources give students and instructors the essential coverage, applications, and course tools they need to tailor the life-span course to meet their specific needs.

The Essential Teaching and Learning Environment

Research shows that students today learn in multiple modalities. Not only do their work preferences tend to be more visual and more interactive, but also their reading and study sessions often occur in short bursts. With shorter chapters and innovative interactive study modules, *Essentials of Life-Span Development* allows students to study whenever, wherever, and however they choose. Regardless of individual study habits, preparation, and approaches to the course, *Essentials* connects with students on a personal, individual basis and provides a road map for success in the course.

Essential Coverage

The challenge in writing *Essentials of Life-Span Development* was determining what comprises the core content of the course. With the help of consultants and instructors who have responded to surveys and reviewed the content at different stages of development, I am able to present all of the core topics, key ideas, and most important research in life-span development that students need to know in a brief format that stands on its own merits.

The 17 brief chapters of *Essentials* are organized chronologically and cover all periods of the human life span, from the prenatal period through late adulthood and death. Providing a broad overview of life-span development, this text especially gives attention to the theories and concepts that students seem to have difficulty mastering.

Essential Applications

Applied examples give students a sense that the field of life-span development has personal meaning for them. In this edition of *Essentials* are numerous real-life applications as well as research applications for each period of the life span.

In addition to applied examples, *Essentials of Life-Span Development* offers applications for students in a variety of majors and career paths.

- *How Would You . . . ?* questions. Given that students enrolled in the life-span course have diverse majors, *Essentials* includes applications that appeal to different interests. The most prevalent areas of specialization are education, human development and family studies, health professions, psychology, and social work. To engage these students and ensure that *Essentials* orients them to concepts that are key to their understanding of life-span development, instructors specializing in these fields contributed *How Would You . . . ?* questions for each chapter. Strategically placed in the margin next to relevant topics, these questions highlight the essential takeaway ideas for these students.

- *Careers in Life-Span Development.* This feature personalizes life-span development by describing an individual working in a career related to the chapter's focus. One example is Jennifer Leonhard, a genetic counselor. The feature describes Ms. Leonhard's education and work setting, discusses various employment options for genetic counselors, and provides resources for students who want to find out more about careers in genetic counseling.

Essential Resources

The following resources accompany *Essentials of Life-Span Development*, 6th edition. Please contact your McGraw-Hill representative for details concerning the availability of these and other valuable materials that can help you design and enhance your course (see page xiv).

- Instructor's Manual
- Test Bank
- WCAG Accessible PowerPoint Slides

Content Revisions

As an indication of the up-to-date nature of this new edition, the text has more than 1,500 citations from 2017, 2018, and 2019. Also, a special effort was made to increase the coverage of the following topics in this new edition: diversity and culture; genetics and epigenetics; neuroscience and the brain; identity issues, especially gender and transgender; health; technology; and successful aging. Following are many of the chapter-by-chapter changes that were made in this new edition of *Essentials of Life-Span Development*.

Chapter 1: Introduction

- Update on life expectancy in the United States (U.S. Census Bureau, 2017)
- New projections on the significant increase in older adults in the world with estimates of a doubling of the population of individuals 60 and over and a tripling or quadrupling of those 80 and over by 2050 (United Nations, 2015)
- New career profile on Gustavo Medrano, clinical psychologist, who works at the Family Institute at Northwestern University
- Updated data on the percentage of U.S. children and adolescents under 18 years of age living in poverty, including data reported separately for African American and Latino families (Jiang, Granja, & Koball, 2017)
- In the discussion of gender, new content on transgender (Budge & Orovecz, 2018; Budge & others, 2018; Savin-Williams, 2017)
- In the section on contemporary topics, a new topic—technology—was added and discussed, including an emphasis on how pervasive it has become in people's lives and how it might influence their development
- In the coverage of cross-cultural studies, a recent study of 26 countries indicating that individuals in Chile had the highest life satisfaction, those in Bulgaria and Spain the lowest (Jang & others, 2017)
- New description of the positive outcomes when individuals have pride in their ethnic group, including recent research (Douglass & Umana-Taylor, 2017; Umana-Taylor & others, 2018)
- New description of emerging adulthood and the dramatic increase in studies on this transitional period between adolescence and adulthood (Arnett, 2016a,b)
- Inclusion of a study involving 17-year survival rates of 20- to 93-year-old Korean adults found that when biological age became greater than chronological age, individuals were less likely to have died (Yoo & others, 2017)
- New content involving how the information processing approach often uses a computer analogy to help explain the connection between cognition and the brain, and how humans process information
- New discussion of artificial intelligence and the new emerging field of developmental robotics that examines various developmental topics and issues using robots, including a new photograph of a "human-like" baby robot (Morse & Cangelosi, 2017)

- Updated and expanded coverage of research methods, including the increased use of eye-tracking to assess infants' perception (van Renswoude & others, 2018), attention (Meng, Uto, & Hashiva, 2017), face processing (Chhaya & others, 2018), autism (Falck-Ytter & others, 2018), and preterm birth effects on language development (Loi & others, 2017)

Chapter 2: Biological Beginnings

- Editing and updating of chapter based on comments by leading expert on prenatal development and birth, Janet DiPietro
- Updated and expanded discussion of genome-wide association studies, including research on autism (Ramswami & Geschwind, 2018), attention deficit hyperactivity disorder (Sanchez-Reige & others, 2018), cancer (Sucheston-Campbell & others, 2018), obesity (Amare & others, 2017), and Alzheimer disease (Liu & others, 2018)
- Updated and expanded research on how exercise, nutrition, and respiration can modify the expression of genes (Kader & others, 2018; Poulsen & others, 2018)
- New coverage of the process of methylation, in which tiny atoms attach themselves to the outside of a gene. Researchers have found that exercise, diet, and tobacco use can change whether a gene is expressed or not through the methylation process (Castellano-Castillo & others, 2018; Martin & Fry, 2018).
- Inclusion of recent research indicating that methylation may be involved in depression (Crawford & others, 2018), breast cancer (Maier & others, 2018), and attention deficit hyperactivity disorder (Kim & others, 2018)
- Updated and expanded research on gene-gene interaction to include alcoholism (Chen & others, 2017), obesity (Bordoni & others, 2017), type 2 diabetes (Saxena, Srivastaya, & Banergee, 2018), cardiovascular disease (De & others, 2017), and Alzheimer disease (Yin & others, 2018)
- Inclusion of recent research in which a higher level maternal responsivity to children with fragile X syndrome's adaptive behavior improved the children's communication skills (Warren & others, 2017)
- New content on the number of children born worldwide with sickle-cell anemia and how stem cell transplantation is being explored in the treatment of infants with sickle-cell anemia (Azar & Wong, 2017)

- Updated description of how research now supports the use of hydroxyurea therapy for infants with sickle cell anemia beginning at 9 months of age (Nevitt, Jones, & Howard, 2017)
- New career profile on Jennifer Leonhard, genetic counselor
- New content on fertility drugs being more likely to produce multiple births than in vitro fertilization (March of Dimes, 2017)
- New coverage of a recent national study in which low birthweight and preterm birth were significantly higher in assisted-reproduction technology conceived infants (Sunderam & others, 2017)
- Updated data on the average length and weight of the fetus at different points in prenatal development, including revisions involving these data in Figure 8
- New commentary about neurogenesis being largely complete by about the end of the fifth month of prenatal development (Keunen, Counsell, & Benders, 2017)
- Discussion of a recent meta-analysis of 15 studies that concluded smoking during pregnancy increases the risk of children having ADHD and that the risk is greater if their mother is a heavy smoker (Huang & others, 2018)
- New content about a recent large-scale U.S. study in which 11.5 percent of adolescent and 8.7 percent of adult pregnant women reported using alcohol in the previous month (Oh & others, 2017)
- Description of recent research in which daughters whose mothers smoked during their pregnancy were more likely to subsequently smoke during their own pregnancy (Ncube & Mueller, 2017)
- Coverage of a recent study that found despite the plethora of negative outcomes for maternal smoking during pregnancy, 23 percent of pregnant adolescents and 15 percent of adult pregnant women reported using tobacco in the previous month (Oh & others, 2017)
- Inclusion of recent research in which cocaine use during pregnancy was associated with impaired connectivity of the thalamus and prefrontal cortex in newborns (Salzwedel & others, 2017)
- Discussion of recent research indicating that cocaine use by pregnant women is linked to self-regulation problems at age 12 (Minnes & others, 2016)
- New research indicating that pregnant women have increased their use of marijuana in recent years (Brown & others, 2016)
- Coverage of the recent concern that marijuana use by pregnant women may further increase given the increasing number of states that are legalizing marijuana (Chasnoff, 2017)
- New section, "Synthetic Opioids and Opiate-Related Pain Killers," that discusses the increasing use of these substances by pregnant women and their possible harmful outcomes for pregnant women and their offspring (Haycraft, 2018; National Institute of Drug Abuse, 2018)

- New description of recent research indicating that prenatal mercury exposure in fish is linked to reduced placental and fetal growth, as well as impaired neuropsychological development (Jeong & others, 2017; Llop & others, 2017; Murcia & others, 2016)
- Revised content on fish consumption by pregnant women, who are now being advised to increase their fish consumption, especially eating more low-mercury-content fish such as salmon, shrimp, tilapia, and cod (American Pregnancy Association, 2018)
- Inclusion of recent research that revealed maternal prenatal stress and anxiety were linked to lower levels of infants' self-regulation (Korja & others, 2017)
- Discussion of a recent study that found when fetuses were exposed to serotonin-based antidepressants, they were more likely to be born preterm (Podrebarac & others, 2017)
- Description of a recent research review that concluded tobacco smoking is linked to impaired male fertility and increases in DNA damage, aneuploidy (abnormal number of chromosomes in a cell), and mutations in sperm (Beal, Yauk, & Marchetti, 2017)
- Discussion of a recent research review in which participation in CenteringPregnancy increased initiation of breast feeding by 53 percent overall and by 71 percent in African American women (Robinson, Garnier-Villarreal, & Hanson, 2018)
- Discussion of a recent study that revealed regular exercise by pregnant women was linked to more advanced development in the neonatal brain (Laborte-Lemoyne, Currier, & Ellenberg, 2017)
- Inclusion of recent research in which two weekly 70-minute yoga sessions reduced pregnant women's stress and enhanced their immune system functioning (Chen & others, 2017)
- New main heading, "Normal Prenatal Development," that includes a description of how most of the time prenatal development occurs in a normal manner
- Coverage of a recent Swedish study that found women who gave birth in water had fewer vaginal tears, shorter labor, needed fewer drugs for pain relief and interventions by medical personnel, and rated their birth experience more positive than women who had conventional spontaneous vaginal births (Ulfsdottir, Saltvedt, & Gerogesson, 2018)
- Inclusion of recent studies in which massage reduced women's pain during labor (Gallo & others, 2018; Shahoei & others, 2018; Unalmis Erdogan, Yanikkerem, & Goker, 2018)
- Update on the percentage of U.S. births that take place in hospitals, at home, and in birthing centers and the percentage of babies born through cesarean delivery (Martin & others, 2017)
- Update on the percentage of births in the United States in which a midwife is involved (Martin & others, 2017)

- New description of global cesarean delivery rates with the Dominican Republic and Brazil having the highest rates (56 percent) and New Zealand and the Czech Republic the lowest (26 percent) (McCullough, 2016). The World Health Organization recommends a cesarean rate of 10 percent or less.
- Revised and updated content on cesarean delivery to include the two most common reasons of why it is carried out: failure to progress through labor and fetal distress
- Updated weights for classification as a low birth weight baby, a very low birth weight baby, and an extremely low birth weight baby
- Updated data on the percentage of births in the United States that are preterm, low birth weight, and cesarean section (Martin & others, 2017)
- Description of recent research indicating that extremely preterm and low birth weight infants have lower executive function, especially in working memory and planning (Burnett & others, 2018)
- Inclusion of recent research that revealed kangaroo care was effective in reducing neonatal pain (Mooney-Leber & Brummelte, 2017)
- Discussion of a longitudinal study in which the nurturing positive effects of kangaroo care with preterm and low birth weight infants at one year of age were still present 20 years later in a number of positive developmental outcomes (Charpak & others, 2018)
- Coverage of a recent study that revealed worsening or minimal improvement in sleep problems from 6 weeks to 7 months postpartum were associated with increased depressive symptoms (Lewis & others, 2018)
- Description of recent research that found women who had a history of depression were 20 times more likely to develop postpartum depression than women who had no history of depression (Silverman & others, 2017)
- Inclusion of recent research in which mothers' postpartum depression, but not generalized anxiety, was linked to their children's emotional negativity and behavior problems at two years of age (Prenoveau & others, 2017)
- Coverage of a recent meta-analysis that concluded that physical exercise during the postpartum period is a safe strategy for reducing postpartum depressive symptoms (Poyatos-Leon & others, 2017)
- Discussion of a recent study that found depressive symptoms in mothers and fathers were linked to impaired bonding with their infant in the postpartum period (Kerstis & others, 2016)

Chapter 3: Physical and Cognitive Development in Infancy

- Revisions based on feedback from leading children's nutrition expert, Maureen Black, and leading children's motor development expert, Karen Adolph
- New discussion of how infant growth is often not smooth and continuous but rather is episodic, occurring in spurts (Adolph, 2018; Lampl & Schoen, 2017)

- Description of a recent study in which sleep sessions lasted approximately 3.5 hours during the first few months and increased to about 10.5 hours from 3 to 7 months (Mindell & others, 2016)
- New commentary about how many mothers today are providing their babies with "tummy time" to prevent a decline in prone skills that can occur because of the "back to sleep movement" to prevent SIDS
- Discussion of a recent research review that revealed a positive link between infant sleeping and cognitive functioning, including memory, language, and executive function (Tham, Schneider, & Broekman, 2017)
- Updated data on the continuing increase in breast feeding by U.S. mothers (Centers for Disease Control and Prevention, 2016)
- Updated support for the role of breastfeeding in reducing a number of disease risks for children and their mothers (Bartick & others, 2017)
- Inclusion of a recent research review indicating that breastfeeding is not associated with a reduced risk of allergies in young children (Heinrich, 2017)
- Description of recent research indicating a reduction in hospitalization for breastfed infants and breastfeeding mothers for a number of conditions (Bartick & others, 2018)
- Discussion of a recent study that found a small increase in intelligence for children who had been breastfed (Bernard & others, 2017)
- Description of recent research in which introduction of vegetables between 4 to 5 months of age was linked with a lower level of infant fussy eating at 4 years of age than when they were introduced after 6 months (de Barse & others, 2017)
- New career profile on Dr. Faize Mustafa-Infante, pediatrician, who especially is passionate about preventing obesity in children
- Discussion of a recent study that examined a number of predictors of motor milestones in the first year (Flensborg-Madsen & Mortensen, 2017)
- Revision of the nature/nurture section in the content on perceptual development to better reflect the Gibsons' view
- Expanded and updated criticism of the innate view of the emergence of infant morality with an emphasis on the importance of infants' early interaction with others and later transformation through language and reflective thought (Carpendale & Hammond, 2016)
- Coverage of a recent study in which hand-eye coordination involving connection of gaze with manual action on objects rather than gaze following alone predicted joint attention (Yu & Smith, 2017)
- New description of Andrew Meltzoff's (2017) view that infants' imitation informs us about their processing of social events and contributes to rapid social learning
- Inclusion of some revisions and updates based on feedback from leading experts Roberta Golinkoff and Virginia Marchman
- Revised definition of infinite generativity to include comprehension as well as production

- New opening commentary about the nature of language learning and how it involves comprehending a sound system (or sign system for individuals who are deaf), the world of objects, actions, and events, and how units such as words and grammar connect sound and world (Israel, 2019; Mithun, 2019)
- Revised definition of infinite generativity to include comprehension as well as production
- Expanded description of how statistical regularity of information is involved in infant word learning (Pace & others, 2016)
- Expanded discussion of statistical learning, including how infants soak up statistical regularities around them merely through exposure to them (Aslin, 2017)
- New research on babbling onset predicting when infants would say their first words (McGillion & others, 2017a)
- New commentary on why gestures such as pointing promote further advances in language development
- New content on the vocabulary spurt and how it involves the increase in the pace at which words are learned
- Expanded descriptions of the functions that child-directed speech serves, including providing infants with information about their native language and heightening differences with speech directed to adults (Golinkoff & others, 2015)
- Coverage of recent research in which child-directed speech in a one-to-one social context for 11- to 14-month-olds was related to productive vocabulary at 2 years of age for Spanish-English bilingual infants for both languages and each language independently (Ramirez-Esparza, Garcia-Sierra, & Kuhl, 2017)
- Inclusion of a recent study that revealed both full-term and preterm infants who heard more caregiver talk based on all-day recordings at 16 months of age had better language skills at 18 months of age (Adams & others, 2018)
- New discussion of recent research in several North American urban areas and the small island of Tanna in the South Pacific Ocean that found that fathers in both types of contexts engaged in child-directed speech with their infants (Broesch & Bryant, 2017)
- New emphasis on the importance of social cues in infant language learning (Ahun & others, 2018; McGillion & others, 2017b; Pace & others, 2016)
- Revised definitions of recasting, expanding, and labeling
- New content on the American Association of Pediatrics (2016) recent position statement on co-viewing of videos indicating that infants can benefit when parents watch videos with them and communicate with them about the videos
- Expanded coverage of how parents can facilitate infants' and toddlers' language development

Chapter 4: Socioemotional Development in Infancy

- Edits made to chapter based on feedback from leading expert Joan Grusec

- Expanded and updated coverage of the brain's role in infant emotional development (Bell & others, 2018; Johnson, 2018; Tottenham, 2017)
- New introductory comments about the important role that cognitive processes, in addition to biological and experiential influences, play in children's emotional development, both in the moment and across childhood (Bell, Diaz, & Liu, 2018)
- Discussion of a recent study in which maternal sensitivity was linked to lower levels of infant fear (Gartstein, Hancock, & Iverson, 2017)
- Description of a recent study that revealed excessive crying in 3-month-olds doubled the risk of behavioral, hyperactive, and mood problems at 5 to 6 years of age (Smarius & others, 2017)
- Inclusion of a recent study in which maternal sensitivity was linked to better emotional self-regulation in 10-month-old infants (Frick & others, 2018)
- Coverage of a recent study that found depressed mothers rocked and touched their crying infants less than non-depressed mothers did (Esposito & others, 2017a)
- New description of a study in which young infants with a negative temperament used fewer attention regulation strategies while maternal sensitivity to infants was linked to more adaptive emotion regulation (Thomas & others, 2017)
- Description of a recent study that revealed if parents had a childhood history of behavioral inhibition, their children who also had a high level of behavioral inhibition were at risk for developing anxiety disorders (Stumper & others, 2017)
- New research that found positive affectivity, surgency, and self-regulation capacity assessed at 4 months of age was linked to school readiness at 4 years of age (Gartstein, Putnam, & Kliewer, 2016)
- Discussion of recent studies indicating a lower level of effortful control and self-regulation capacity in early childhood were linked to a higher level of ADHD symptoms later in childhood (Willoughby, Gottfredson, & Stifter, 2017) and adolescence (Einziger & others, 2017)
- Expanded and updated content on the increasing belief that babies are socially smarter than used to be thought, including information about Amanda Woodward and her colleagues' (Krough-Jespersen & Woodward, 2016; Liberman, Woodward, & Kinzler, 2017) research on how quickly infants understand and respond to others' meaningful intentions
- Discussion of a recent study in which maternal sensitivity and a better home environment in infancy predicted high self-regulation at 4 years of age (Birmingham, Bub, & Vaughn, 2017)
- Inclusion of recent research in Zambia, where siblings were substantially involved in caregiving activities, that revealed infants showed strong attachments to both their mothers and their sibling caregivers with secure attachment being the most frequent attachment classification for both mother-infant and sibling-infant relationships (Mooja, Sichimba, & Bakersman-Kranenburg, 2017)

- Description of a recent study that did not find support for the view that genes influence mother-infant attachment (Leerkes & others, 2017)
- Description of recent research that revealed providing parents who engage in inadequate or problematic caregiving with practice and feedback focused on interacting sensitively enhances parent-infant attachment security (Coyne & others, 2018; Dozier & Bernard, 2017, 2018; Woodhouse, 2018; Woodhouse & others, 2017)
- Discussion of a recent study that found when adults used scaffolding, infants were twice as likely to engage in helping behavior (Dahl & others, 2017)
- Coverage of a recent study of disadvantaged families in which an intervention involving improving early maternal scaffolding was linked to improvement in cognitive skills at 4 years of age (Obradovic & others, 2017)
- New content about mothers playing 3 times more often with children than fathers do (Cabrera & Rossman, 2017)
- Inclusion of recent research with low-income families indicating that fathers' playfulness at 2 years of age was associated with more advanced vocabulary skills at 4 years of age while mothers' playfulness at 2 years of age was linked to a higher level of emotion regulation at 4 years of age (Cabrera & others, 2017)
- Discussion of a recent study that found negative outcomes on cognitive development in infancy when fathers were more withdrawn and depressed and positive outcomes on cognitive development when they were more engaged and sensitive, as well as less controlling (Sethna & others, 2018)

Chapter 5: Physical and Cognitive Development in Early Childhood

- Discussion of a recent study of 4-year-old girls that found a nine-week motor skill intervention improved the girls' ball skills (Veldman & others, 2017)
- Description of recent research indicating that higher motor skill proficiency in preschool was linked to engaging in a higher level of physical activity in adolescence (Venetsanou & Kambas, 2017)
- Inclusion of recent research that found children with a low level of motor competence had a lower motivation for sports participation and lower global self-worth than their counterparts who had a high level of motor competence (Bardid & others, 2018)
- Discussion of a recent study that revealed 2 ½-year-old children's liking for fruits and vegetables was related to their eating more fruits and vegetables at 7 years of age (Fletcher & others, 2018)
- Updated data on the percentage of U.S. 2- to 5-year-old children who are obese, which has recently decreased (Centers for Disease Control and Prevention, 2017)
- New description of the recently devised 5-2-1-0 obesity prevention guidelines for young children: 5 or more servings of fruits and vegetables, no more than 2 hours of screen time, minimum of 1 hour of physical activity, and 0 sugar-sweetened beverages daily (Khalsa & others, 2017)

- New discussion of a longitudinal study that revealed when young children were exposed to environmental tobacco smoke, they were more likely to engage in anti-social behavior at 12 years of age (Pagani & others, 2017)
- Updates and revisions based on feedback from leading expert Megan McClelland
- Updating of recent research on young children's executive function (Blair, 2017; Muller & others, 2017), including a recent study in which young children who showed delayed executive function development had a lower level of school readiness (Willoughby & others, 2017)
- Inclusion of recent research showing the effectiveness of the Tools of the Mind approach in improving a number of cognitive processes and academic skills in young children (Blair & Raver, 2014)
- New research indicating that parental engagement in mind-mindedness advanced preschool children's theory of mind (Hughes, Devine, & Wang, 2017)
- Updated and expanded theory of mind content involving various aspects of social interaction, including secure attachment and mental state talk, parental engagement, peer relations, and living in a higher socioeconomic status family (Hughes, Devine, & Wang, 2018)
- Inclusion of a recent study of 3- to 5-year-old children that revealed earlier development of executive function predicted theory of mind performance, especially for false-belief tasks (Doenyas, Yavuz, & Selcuk, 2017)
- Coverage of a recent study in which theory of mind predicted the severity of autism in children (Hoogenhout & Malcolm-Smith, 2017)
- Revisions to the discussion of young children's language development based on feedback from leading experts Roberta Golinkoff and Virginia Marchman
- Coverage of a recent multigenerational study that found when both Head Start children and their mothers had participated in Head Start, positive cognitive and socioemotional outcomes occurred for the children (Chor, 2018)
- Update on the increase in publicly funded preschool programs that now occurs in 42 states plus the District of Columbia (National Institute for Early Education Research, 2016)
- Description of two recent studies that confirmed the importance of improved parenting engagement and skills in the success of Head Start programs (Ansari & Gershoff, 2016; Roggman & others, 2016)

Chapter 6: Socioemotional Development in Early Childhood

- New emphasis on the importance of how extensively young children can learn by observing the behavior of others, including a recent study in which young children who observed a peer being rewarded for confessing to cheating were more likely to be honest in the future themselves (Ma & others, 2018)

- Inclusion of recent research indicating the broad capacity for self-evaluative emotion was present in the preschool years and was linked to young children's empathetic concern (Ross, 2017)
- Description of a recent study in which young children with higher emotion regulation were more popular with their peers (Nakamichi, 2019)
- New commentary about connections between different emotions and how they may influence development, including a recent study in which participants' guilt proneness combined with their empathy to predict an increase in prosocial behavior (Torstevelt, Sutterlin, & Lugo, 2016)
- Coverage of a recent study in Great Britain in which gender non-conforming boys were most at risk for peer rejection (Braun & Davidson, 2017)
- Inclusion of a recent research review of a large number of studies that found authoritarian parenting was associated with a higher level of externalizing problems (Pinquart, 2017)
- Coverage of a recent study in which an authoritarian style, as well as pressure to eat, were associated with a higher risk for being overweight or obese in young children (Melis Yavuz & Selkuk, 2018)
- Discussion of a recent study that revealed children of authoritative parents engaged in more prosocial behavior than their counterparts whose parents used the other parenting styles discussed in the section (Carlo & others, 2018)
- Description of a recent research review in which authoritative parenting was the most effective parenting style in predicting which children and adolescents would be less likely to be overweight or obese later in their development (Sokol, Qin, & Puti, 2017)
- New commentary about how in many traditional cultures, fathers use an authoritarian style; in such cultures, children benefit more when mothers use an authoritative parenting style
- New section, "Further Thoughts about Parenting Styles," including four factors than can influence how research on parenting styles can be interpreted
- Coverage of a recent review that concluded there is widespread approval of corporal punishment by U.S. parents (Ciocca, 2017)
- Inclusion of a recent research review of risk factors for engaging in child neglect that concluded that most risks involved parental factors, including a history of antisocial behavior/criminal offending, having mental/physical problems, and experiencing abuse in their own childhood (Mulder & others, 2018)
- Discussion of a longitudinal study that found harsh physical punishment in childhood was linked to a higher incidence of intimate partner violence in adulthood (Afifi & others, 2017b)
- Description of a recent Japanese study in which occasional spanking at 3 years of age was associated with a higher level of behavioral problems at 5 years of age (Okunzo & others, 2017)
- Discussion of a recent meta-analysis that found when physical punishment was not abusive, physical punishment was still linked to detrimental child outcomes (Gershoff & Grogan-Kaylor, 2016)
- Coverage of a recent study that found physical abuse was linked to lower levels of cognitive performance and school engagement in children (Font & Cage, 2018)
- Inclusion of a recent study that revealed exposure to either physical or sexual abuse in childhood and adolescence was linked to an increase in 13- to 18-year-olds' suicide ideation, plans, and attempts (Gomez & others, 2017)
- Description of a longitudinal study in which experiencing early abuse and neglect in the first five years of life were linked to having more interpersonal problems and lower academic achievement from childhood through their 30s (Raby & others, 2018)
- Coverage of a large-scale study that found a birth order effect for intelligence, with older siblings having slightly higher intelligence, but no birth order effects for life satisfaction, internal/external control, trust, risk taking, patience, and impulsivity (Rohrer, Egloff, & Schukle, 2017)
- Description of recent research indicating that mothers' and fathers' work-family conflict was linked to 4-year-olds' lower self-control (Ferreria & others, 2018)
- Discussion of a recent study in which experiencing parents' divorce, as well as child maltreatment, in childhood was linked to midlife suicide ideation (Stansfield & others, 2017)
- Inclusion of a recent meta-analysis that revealed when their parents had become divorced, as adults they were more likely to have depression (Sands, Thompson, & Gavsina, 2017)
- Coverage of a recent study that found interparental hostility was a stronger predictor of children's insecurity and externalizing problems than interparental disagreement and low levels of interparental cooperation (Davies & others, 2016)
- Updated data on the percentage of gay and lesbian parents who are raising children
- Inclusion of recent research that revealed no differences in the adjustment of school-aged children adopted in infancy by gay, lesbian, and heterosexual parents (Farr, 2017)
- Description of a recent study of lesbian and gay adoptive families indicated that 98 percent of the parents reported their children had adjusted well to school (Farr, Oakley, & Ollen, 2016)
- Coverage of a longitudinal study that found a multicomponent (school-based educational enrichment and comprehensive family services) preschool-to-third-grade intervention with low-income minority children in Chicago was effective in increasing their high school graduation, as well as undergraduate and graduate school success (Reynolds, Ou, & Temple, 2018)
- Update on the most recent national survey of screen time indicating a dramatic shift to greater use of mobile devices in young children (Common Sense Media, 2013)

- Inclusion of recent research with 2- to 6-year-olds that indicated increased TV viewing on weekends was associated with a higher risk of being overweight or obese (Kondolot & others, 2017)
- Description of a recent meta-analysis that found children's exposure to prosocial media is linked to higher levels of prosocial behavior and empathetic concern (Coyne & others, 2018)

Chapter 7: Physical and Cognitive Development in Middle and Late Childhood

- New coverage of the increase in brain connectivity as children develop and a longitudinal study that found greater connectivity between the prefrontal and parietal regions in childhood was linked to better reasoning ability later in development (Wendelken & others, 2017)
- Discussion of a recent study of elementary school children that revealed 55 minutes or more of daily moderate-to-vigorous physical activity was associated with a lower incidence of obesity (Nemet, 2016)
- Description of a recent meta-analysis that participation in a sustained program of physical activity improved children's attention, executive function, and academic achievement (de Greeff & others, 2018)
- Coverage of a recent study with 7- to 13-year-olds in which a 6-week high-intensity exercise program resulted in improved cognitive control and working memory (Moreau, Kirk, & Waldie, 2018)
- Description of a recent meta-analysis that found children who engage in regular physical activity have better cognitive inhibitory control (Jackson & others, 2016)
- Inclusion of recent research with 8- to 12-year-olds indicating that screen time was associated with lower connectivity between brain regions, as well as lower language skills and cognitive control, while time spent reading was linked to higher levels in these areas (Horowitz-Kraus & Hutton, 2018)
- Updated data on the percentage of 6- to 11-year-old U.S. children who are obese (Ogden & others, 2016)
- Inclusion of a recent Japanese study that revealed the family pattern that was linked to the highest overweight/obesity in children was a combination of irregular mealtimes and the most screen time for both parents (Watanabe & others, 2016)
- Discussion of a recent study in which children were less likely to be obese or overweight when they attended schools in states that had a strong policy emphasis on healthy food and beverage (Datar & Nicosia, 2017)
- Updated statistics on the percentage of U.S. children who have different types of disabilities and revised update of Figure 4 (National Center for Education Statistics, 2016)
- Description of a recent research review that found girls with ADHD had more problematic peer relations than typically developing girls in a number of areas (Kok & others, 2016)

- Coverage of a recent research review that concluded ADHD in childhood is linked to a number of long-term outcomes (Erksine & others, 2016)
- Discussion of a recent study that found childhood ADHD was associated with long-term underachievement in math and reading (Voigt & others, 2017)
- Description of a recent study in which individuals with ADHD were more likely to become parents at 12 to 16 years of age (Ostergaard & others, 2017)
- Coverage of a recent research review that concluded stimulation medications are effective in treating children with ADHD in the short term, but that long-term benefits of such medications are not clear (Rajeh & others, 2017)
- Discussion of a recent meta-analysis that found mindfulness training improved the attention of children with ADHD (Caincross & Miller, 2018)
- Inclusion of a recent meta-analysis that concluded physical exercise is effective in reducing cognitive symptoms of ADHD in individuals 3 to 25 years of age (Tan, Pooley, & Speelman, 2017)
- Coverage of a recent meta-analysis in which exercise was associated with better executive function in children with ADHD (Vysniauske & others, 2018)
- Description of a recent study in which an 8-week yoga program improved the sustained attention of children with ADHD (Chou & Huang, 2017)
- New commentary that despite the recent positive research findings using neurofeedback, mindfulness training, and exercise to improve the attention of children with ADHD, it remains to be determined if they are as effective as stimulant drugs and/or whether they benefit children as add-ons to stimulant drugs (Den Jeijer & others, 2017)
- Updated data on the increasing percentage of children being diagnosed as having autism spectrum disorder (Christensen & others, 2016)
- Inclusion of a recent study that revealed a lower level of working memory was the executive function most strongly associated with autism spectrum disorders (Ziermans & others, 2017)
- New coverage of two recent surveys in which only a minority of parents reported that their child's autism spectrum disorder was identified prior to three years of age and that one-third to one-half of the cases were identified after six years of age (Sheldrick, Maye, & Carter, 2017)
- Discussion of a recent study in which children's verbal working memory was linked to these aspects of both first and second language learners: morphology, syntax, and grammar (Verhagen & Leseman, 2016)
- Inclusion of recent research that found mindfulness-based intervention improved children's attention self-regulation (Felver & others, 2017)
- Description of the most recent revision of the Wechsler Intelligence Scale for Children—V, and its increase in the number of subtests and composite scores (Canivez, Watkins, & Dombrowski, 2017)

- Coverage of recent research that found a significant link between children's general intelligence and their self-control (Meldrum & others, 2017)
- Discussion of a recent two-year intervention study with families living in poverty in which maternal scaffolding and positive home stimulation improved young children's intellectual functioning (Obradovic & others, 2016)
- New content on stereotype threat in the section on cultural bias in intelligence tests (Grand, 2017; Lyons & others, 2018; Williams & others, 2018)
- Update on the percentage of U.S. students who are classified as gifted (National Association for Gifted Children, 2017)
- New commentary that vocabulary development plays an important role in reading comprehension (Vacca & others, 2018)
- Coverage of a recent study of 6- to 10-year-old children that found early bilingual exposure was a key factor in bilingual children outperforming monolingual children on phonological awareness and word learning (Jasinsksa & Petitto, 2018)
- Discussion of research that documented bilingual children were better at theory of mind tasks than were monolingual children (Rubio-Fernandez, 2017)

Chapter 8: Socioemotional Development in Middle and Late Childhood

- New description of recent research studies indicating that children and adolescents who do not have good perspective-taking skills are more likely to have difficulty in peer relations and engage in more aggressive and oppositional behavior (Morosan & others, 2017; Nilsen & Basco, 2017; O'Kearney & others, 2017)
- Inclusion of a longitudinal study that revealed the quality of children's home environment (which involved assessment of parenting quality, cognitive stimulation, and the physical home environment) was linked to their self-esteem in early adulthood (Orth, 2017)
- New discussion of the recent book *Challenging the Cult of Self-Esteem in Education* (Bergeron, 2018) that criticizes education for promising high self-esteem for students, especially those who are impoverished or marginalized
- Coverage of a longitudinal study that found a higher level of self-control in childhood was linked to a slower pace of aging at 26, 32, and 38 years of age (Belsky & others, 2017)
- New description of an app that is effective in improving children's self-control: www.selfregulationstation.com/sr-ipad-app/
- New discussion of a longitudinal study in which a higher level of emotion regulation in early childhood was linked to a higher level of externalizing problems in adolescence (Perry & others, 2017)

- Inclusion of a recent study that revealed females are better than males at facial emotion perception across the life span (Olderbak & others, 2018)
- New section, "Social-Emotional Education Programs," that describes two increasingly implemented programs: 1) Second Step (Committee for Children, 2018) and 2) Collaborative for Academic, Social, and Emotional Learning (CASEL (2018)
- New career profile on Dr. Melissa Jackson, child and adolescent psychiatrist
- Substantial revision of the discussion of Kohlberg's theory of moral development to make it more concise and clear
- New coverage of how we need to make better progress in dealing with an increasing array of temptations and possible wrongdoings in a human social world in which complexity is accumulating over time (Christen, Narvaez, & Gutzwiller, 2018)
- Deletion of the section on Gender Role Classification because of decreasing interest in the topic in recent years
- Discussion of a recent study with eighth grade students in 36 countries that revealed girls had more egalitarian attitudes about gender roles than did boys (Dotti Sani & Uaranta, 2015)
- Description of a recent meta-analysis of attachment in middle/late childhood and adolescence in which parents of children and adolescents who more securely attached were more responsive, more supportive of children's and adolescents' autonomy, used more behavioral control strategies, and engaged in less harsh control strategies (Koehn & Kerns, 2018). Also in this meta-analysis, parents of children and adolescents who showed more avoidant attachment were less responsive and engaged is less behavioral control strategies. Regarding ambivalent attachment, no links to parenting were found.
- Inclusion of recent research indicating that when children have a better parent-child affective relationship with their stepparent, the children have fewer internalizing and externalizing problems (Jensen & others, 2018)
- Coverage of a recent study of young adolescents in which peer rejection predicted increases in aggressive and rule-breaking behavior (Janssens & others, 2017)
- Description of a longitudinal study that revealed children who were bullied at 6 years of age were more likely to have excess weight gain when they were 12 to 13 years old (Sutin & others, 2016)
- Inclusion of a longitudinal study that revealed being a victim of bullying in childhood was linked to increased use of mental health services five decades later (Evans-Lacko & others, 2017)
- Description of recent longitudinal studies that indicated victims bullied in childhood and adolescence have higher rates of agoraphobia, depression, anxiety, panic disorder, and suicidality in the early to mid-twenties (Arseneault, 2017; Copeland & others, 2013)
- Coverage of recent research in which adolescents who were bullied in both a direct way and through

cyberbullying had more behavioral problems and lower self-esteem than their counterparts who were only bullied in one of two ways (Wolke, Lee, & Guy, 2017)

- Inclusion of a 2017/2018 update on the Every Student Succeeds Act (ESSA) with the Trump administration planning to go forward with ESSA but giving states much more flexibility in its implementation (Klein, 2017)
- Coverage of a recent intervention (City Connects program) with first-generation immigrant children attending high-poverty schools that was successful in improving the children's reading and math skills (Dearing & others, 2016)
- Inclusion of a longitudinal study that involved implementation of the Child-Parent Center Program in high-poverty neighborhoods of Chicago that provided school-based educational enrichment and comprehensive family services from 3 to 9 years of age (Reynolds, Ou, & Temple, 2018). Children who participated in the program had higher rates of postsecondary completion, including more years of education, an associate's degree or higher, and a master's degree.
- New coverage of a recent research review that concluded increases in family income for children in poverty was linked to increased achievement in middle school, as well as higher educational attainment in adolescence and emerging adulthood (Duncan, Magnuson, & Votruba-Drzil, 2017)
- New content on Teach for America and its efforts to place college graduates in teaching positions in schools located in low-income areas and a new career profile on Teach for America instructor Ahou Vaziri
- Update on comparisons of U.S. students with their counterparts around the globe in math and science achievement (Desilver, 2017; TIMMS, 2015)
- Coverage of recent research indicating that many parents and teachers with growth mindsets don't have children and adolescents with growth mindsets (Haimovitz & Dweck, 2017)
- New research that indicates the following are what parents and teachers need to do to create growth mindsets in children and adolescents: teach for understanding, provide feedback that improves understanding, give students opportunities to revise their work, communicate how effort and struggle are involved in learning, and function as partners with children and adolescents in the learning process (Hooper & others, 2016; Sun, 2015)
- Inclusion of recent research that found students from lower income families were less likely to have a growth mindset than were students from wealthier families but the achievement of students from lower income families was more likely to be protected if they had a growth mindset (Claro, Paunesku, & Dweck, 2016)
- Discussion of a recent study that revealed having a growth mindset protected women's and minorities' outlook when they chose to confront expressions of bias toward them in the workplace (Rattan & Dweck, 2018)

- Discussion of a recent study in China that found young adolescents with authoritative parents showed better adjustment than their counterparts with authoritarian parents (Zhang & others, 2017)

Chapter 9: Physical and Cognitive Development in Adolescence

- Coverage of a recent study of non-Latino White and African American 12- to 20-year-olds in the United States that found they were characterized much more by positive than problematic development (Gutman & others, 2017). Their engagement in healthy behaviors, supportive relationships with parents and friends, and positive self-conceptions were much stronger than their angry and depressed feelings.
- New discussion of three recent studies in Korea and Japan (Cole & Mori, 2017), China (Song & others, 2017), and Saudi Arabia (Al Alwan & others, 2017), all of which found secular trends of earlier pubertal onset in recent years
- Coverage of a recent U.S study that indicated puberty occurred earlier in girls with a higher body mass index (BMI) (Bratke & others, 2017) and a recent Chinese study revealed similar results (Deng & others, 2018)
- Description of a recent study that revealed child sexual abuse was linked to earlier pubertal onset (Noll & others, 2017)
- New research that revealed young adolescent boys had a more positive body image than their female counterparts (Morin & others, 2017)
- New content on the role of social media and the Internet in influencing adolescents' body images, including one study of U.S. 12- to 14-year-olds that found heavier social media use was associated with body dissatisfaction (Burnette, Kwitowski, & Mazzeo, 2017)
- Inclusion of research in which onset of menarche before 11 years of age was linked to a higher incidence of distress disorders, fear disorders, and externalizing disorders in females (Platt & others, 2017)
- Coverage of a recent study that found early-maturing girls had higher rates of depression and antisocial age as middle-aged adults mainly because their difficulties began in adolescence and did not lessen over time (Mendle & others, 2018)
- Inclusion of a recent study of U.S. college women that found more time on Facebook was related to more frequent body and weight concern comparison with other women, more attention to the physical appearance of others, and more negative feelings about their own bodies (Eckler, Kalyango, Paasch, 2017)
- New research indicating that early-maturing girls are at risk for physical and verbal abuse in dating (Chen, Rothman, & Jaffee, 2018)
- Updated data on the occurrence of various sexual activities engaged in by adolescents according to age, gender, and ethnicity, including updates (Kann & others, 2016a)

- New commentary that while the majority of sexual minority adolescents have competent and successful developmental paths through adolescence, a recent large-scale study revealed that sexual minority youth engage in a higher prevalence of health-risk factors compared to nonsexual minority youth (Kann & others, 2016b)
- Coverage of a recent national study of 7,000 15- to 24-year-olds' engagement in oral sex, including the low percentage of youth who use a condom when having oral sex (Holway & Hernandez, 2018)
- Updated data on the percentage of adolescent males and females who engage in oral sex (Child Trends, 2015)
- Description of a recent study that found that early sexual debut was associated with a number of problems, including sexual risk taking, substance use, violent victimization, and suicidal thoughts and attempts in both sexual minority and heterosexual adolescents (Lowry & others, 2017)
- Discussion of a recent study of Korean girls in which early menarche was associated with earlier initiation of sexual intercourse (Kim & others, 2017)
- Inclusion of recent research in which adolescents who in the eighth grade reported greater parental knowledge and more rules about dating were less likely to initiate sex between the eighth and tenth grade (Ethier & others, 2016)
- Description of a recent study of African American girls that revealed those for whom religion was very or extremely important were much more likely to have a later sexual debut (George Dalmida & others, 2018)
- Updated data on the percentage of adolescents who use contraceptives when they have sexual intercourse (Kann & others, 2016a)
- Updated data on the continued decline in adolescent pregnancy to an historic low in 2015 (Martin & others, 2017)
- Important new section on the increasing number of medical organizations and experts who have recently recommended that adolescents use long-acting reversible contraception (LARC), which consists of intrauterine devices (IUDs) and contraceptive implants (Allen & others, 2017; Deidrich, Klein, & Peipert, 2017; Society for Adolescent Medicine, 2017)
- New research on factors that are linked to repeated adolescent pregnancy (Dee & others, 2017; Maravilla & others, 2017)
- Coverage of recent surveys that find a large percentage of sexual health education programs do not cover birth control (Lindberg & others, 2016) and that sexual health information is more likely to be taught in high school than in middle school (Alan Guttmacher Institute, 2017)
- Inclusion of recent studies and research views that find comprehensive sex education programs and policies are far more effective in pregnancy prevention, reduction of sexually transmitted infections, and delay of sexual intercourse than are abstinence-only programs and policies (Denford & others, 2017; Jaramillo & others, 2017; Santilli & others, 2017)
- New content on the recent increase in abstinence-only-until-marriage (AOUM) policies and programs in the United States that don't seem to recognize that a large majority of adolescents and emerging adults will initiate sexual intercourse, especially given the recent increase in the age at which U.S. males and females get married
- New position of the Adolescent Society of Health and Medicine (2017) that states research clearly indicates that AOUM programs and policies are not effective but, in contrast, research documents that comprehensive sex education programs and policies are effective in delaying sexual intercourse and reducing other sexual risk behaviors
- Updated commentary on the recent concern about the increased government funding of abstinence-only programs (Donovan, 2017)
- New career profile on Dr. Bonnie Halpern-Felsher, University Professor in Pediatrics and Director of Community Efforts to Improve Adolescents' Health
- Updated data on the percentage of U.S. adolescents who are obese (Centers for Disease Control and Prevention, 2016)
- Updated national data on adolescents' exercise patterns, including gender and ethnic variations (Kann & others, 2016a)
- Discussion of a recent study that indicated aerobic exercise reduced the depressive symptoms of adolescents with MDD (Jaworksa & others, 2018)
- Inclusion of a recent large-scale study of Dutch adolescents that revealed physically active adolescents had fewer emotional and peer problems (Kuiper & others, 2018)
- Description of a recent research review that found that among a number of cognitive factors, memory was the factor that was most often improved by exercise in adolescence (Li & others, 2017)
- Coverage of a recent study of U.S. eighth, tenth, and twelfth graders from 1991 to 2016 that found psychological well-being abruptly decreased after 2012 (Twenge, Martin, & Campbell, 2018). In this study, adolescents who spent more on electronic communication and screens and less time on non-screen activities such as exercise had lower psychological well-being.
- Update on the low percentage of adolescents who get 8 hours of sleep or more per night (Kann & others, 2016a)
- Inclusion of a recent national study of more than 10,000 13- to 18-year-olds that revealed that a number of factors involving sleep timing and duration were associated with an increase in anxiety, mood, substance abuse, and behavioral disorders (Zhang & others, 2017)
- Description of a recent study of college students that revealed consistently low sleep duration was associated with less effective attention the next day (Whiting & Murdock, 2016)
- Discussion of a recent study of college students in which a higher level of text messaging activity during

the day and at night was related to a lower level of sleep quality (Murdock, Horissian, & Crichlow-Ball, 2017)

- New content on the increase in adolescents who mix alcohol and energy drinks, which is linked to a higher rate of risky driving (Wilson & others, 2018)
- Updated coverage of the Monitoring the Future study's assessment of drug use by secondary school students with 2017 data on U.S. eighth, tenth, and twelfth graders, including recent increases in marijuana and nicotine vaping use (Johnston & others, 2018)
- Coverage of a recent meta-analysis of parenting factors involved in adolescents' alcohol use that indicated higher levels of parental monitoring, support, and involvement were associated with a lower risk of adolescent alcohol misuse (Yap & others, 2017)
- Discussion of a recent large scale national study in which friends' use was a stronger influence on adolescents' alcohol use than parental use (Deutsch, Wood, & Slutske, 2018)
- New research indicating that having an increase in Facebook friends across two years in adolescence was linked to an enhanced motivation to be thin (Tiggemann & Slater, 2017)
- Coverage of a recent study in which a greater use of social networking sites was linked to being more narcissistic (Gnambs & Appel, 2018)
- Coverage of a recent study in which teacher warmth was higher in the last 4 years of elementary school and then dropped in the middle school years (Hughes & Cao, 2018). The drop in teacher warmth was associated with lower student math scores.
- Inclusion of new information from the Bill and Melinda Gates Foundation's (2017, 2018) indicating that many adolescents graduate from high school without the necessary academic skills to succeed in college or to meet the demands of the modern workplace
- New research on the transition to high school, including the greatest difficulties and factors that provide for improved adaptation to the transition (Benner, Boyle, & Bakhtiari, 2017; Wigfield, Rosenzweig, & Eccles, 2017)

Chapter 10: Socioemotional Development in Adolescence

- New commentary that too little research attention has been given to developmental changes in the specific domains of identity (Galliher, McLean, & Syed, 2017; Vosylis, Erentaite, & Crocetti, 2018)
- New content on the dual cycle identity model that separates out identity development into two processes: 1) A formation cycle and 2) a maintenance cycle (Luyckx & others, 2014, 2017)
- New discussion of parental (Crocetti & others, 2017) and peer/friend (Rivas-Drake & Imana-Taylor, 2018; Santos & others, 2017) influences on adolescent identity development

- Updated description of the positive outcomes when individuals have pride in their ethnic group, including recent research (Anglin & others, 2018; Douglass & Umana-Taylor, 2017; Umana-Taylor & others, 2017)
- New content on identity development and the digital environment that explores the widening audience adolescents and emerging adults have to express their identity and get feedback about it in their daily connections on social media such as Instagram, Snapchat, and Facebook (Davis & Weinstein, 2017; Yau & Reich, 2018)
- Coverage of a recent study of Mexican-origin adolescents that found a positive ethnic identity, social support, and anger suppression helped them cope more effectively with racial discrimination whereas anger expressions reduced their ability to cope with the racial discrimination (Park & others, 2018)
- Inclusion of recent research with fifth and eighth graders in which a higher level of parental monitoring was associated with students' having higher grades (Top, Liew, & Luo, 2017)
- Discussion of a recent study that found better parental monitoring was linked to lower marijuana use by adolescents (Haas & others, 2018) and another study that revealed lower parental monitoring was associated with earlier initiation of alcohol use, binge drinking, and marijuana use in 13- to 14-year-olds (Rusby & others, 2018)
- Inclusion of a recent study that indicated two types of parental media monitoring—active monitoring and connective co-use (engaging in media with the intent to connect with adolescents)—were linked to lower media use by adolescents (Padilla-Walker & others, 2018)
- Discussion of a recent study that revealed from 16 to 20 years of age, adolescents perceived that they had increasing independence and a better relationship with their parents (Hadiwiya & others, 2017)
- Discussion of a recent study of Latino families that revealed a higher level of secure attachment with mothers during adolescence was linked to a lower level of heavy drug use (Gattamorta & others, 2017)
- Coverage of a recent study that revealed when they had grown up in poverty, adolescents engaged in less risk-taking if they had a history of secure attachments to caregivers (Delker, Bernstein, & Laurent, 2018)
- Inclusion of a recent analysis that found secure attachment to the mother and to the father was associated with fewer depressive symptoms in adolescents (Kerstis, Aslund, & Sonnby, 2018)
- Description of a recent study of Chinese American families that found parent-adolescent conflict increased in early adolescence, peaked at about 16 years of age, and then declined through late adolescence and emerging adulthood (Juang & others, 2018)
- New research with Latino families indicating that high parent-adolescent conflict was associated with higher adolescent rates of aggression (Smokowski & others, 2017)
- Inclusion of recent research on adolescent girls that found friends' dieting predicted whether adolescent

girls would engage in dieting or extreme dieting (Balantekin, Birch, & Savage, 2017)

- Discussion of a recent study that indicated that friendship quality was linked to the quality of romantic relationships in adolescence (Kochendorfer & Kerns, 2017)
- Coverage of a recent study that found long-term romantic relationships in adolescence were both supportive and turbulent, characterized by elevated levels of support, negative interactions, higher control, and more jealousy (Lantagne & Furman, 2017)
- New main section, "Socioeconomic Status and Poverty"
- Inclusion of a recent study that found of 13 risk factors, low SES was the most likely to be associated with smoking initiation in fifth graders (Wellman & others, 2017)
- Discussion a recent Chinese study in which adolescents were more likely to have depressive symptoms in low SES families (Zhou, Fan, & Zin, 2017)
- Coverage of a U.S. longitudinal study that revealed low SES in adolescence was linked to having a higher level of depressive symptoms at age 54 for females (Pino & others, 2018). In this study, low SES females who completed college were less likely to have depressive symptoms than low SES females who did not complete college.
- Inclusion of a U.S. longitudinal study that found low SES in adolescence was a risk factor for cardiovascular disease 30 years later (Doom & others, 2017)
- Coverage of a recent study of 12- to 19-year-olds indicating that their perceived well-being was lowest when they had lived in poverty from 0 to 2 years of age (compared to 3 to 5, 6 to 8, and 9 to 11 years of age) and also each additional year lived in poverty was associated with even lower perceived well-being in adolescence (Garipy & others, 2017)
- Description of a recent study that found these four psychological and social factors predicted higher achievement by adolescents living in poverty: 1) academic commitment, 2) emotional control, 3) family involvement, and 4) school climate (Li, Allen, & Casillas, 2017)
- Description of a recent study comparing Asian, Latino, and non-Latino immigrant adolescents in which immigrant Asian adolescents had the highest level of depression, lowest self-esteem, and experienced the most discrimination (Lo & others, 2017)
- Inclusion of a recent study of Mexican origin youth that revealed when adolescents reported a higher level of familism, they engaged in lower levels of risk taking (Wheeler & others, 2017)
- Discussion of a recent study in which heavy media multitaskers were less likely to delay gratification and more likely to endorse intuitive, but wrong, answers on a cognitive reflection task (Schutten, Stokes, & Arnell, 2017)
- Coverage of recent research that found less screen time was linked to adolescents' better health-related quality of life (Yan & others, 2017) and that a higher level of social media use was associated with a higher level of heavy drinking by adolescents (Brunborg, Andreas, & Kvaavik, 2017)

- Discussion of a recent study of 13- to 16-year-olds that found increased night-time mobile phone use was linked to increased externalizing problems and decreased self-esteem (Vernon, Modecki, & Barber, 2018)
- Updated data on the percentage of adolescents who use social networking sites and engage in text messaging daily (Lenhart, 2015; Lenhart & others, 2015)
- Coverage of a recent national study of social media indicating how extensively 18- to 24-year-olds are using various sites such as Snapchat, Instagram, twitter, and YouTube (Smith & Anderson, 2018)
- Updated statistics on the significant decline in juvenile court delinquency caseloads in the United States in recent years (Hockenberry & Puzzanchera, 2017)
- Inclusion of a recent study of more than 10,000 children and adolescence revealing that a family environment characterized by poverty and child maltreatment was linked to entering the juvenile justice system in adolescence (Vidal & others, 2017)
- Description of a recent study of middle school adolescents that found peer pressure for fighting and friends' delinquent behavior were linked to adolescents' aggression and delinquent behavior (Farrell, Thompson, & Mehari, 2017)
- Discussion of a recent study that revealed an increase in the proportion of classmates who engage in delinquent behavior increased the likelihood that other classmates would become delinquents (Kim & Fletcher, 2018)
- Inclusion of a recent study that indicated adolescent delinquents were high on affiliating with deviant peers and engaging in pseudomature behavior and low on peer popularity and school achievement (Gordon Simons & others, 2018)
- Coverage of recent research in which having callous-unemotional traits predicts an increased risk of engaging in delinquency for adolescent males (Ray & others, 2017)
- Description of a recent study of female adolescents in which an increase in their self-control was linked to decreased likelihood of police contact (Hipwell & others, 2018)
- New content indicating that at 12 years of age, 5.2 percent of females compared to 2 percent of males had experienced first-onset depression (Breslau & others, 2017). Also in this study, the cumulative incidence of depression from 12 to 17 years of age was 36 percent for females and 14 percent for boys.
- Recent research that found co-rumination with friends was linked to greater peer stress for adolescent girls (Rose & others, 2017)
- Discussion of recent research indicating that family therapy can be effective in reducing adolescent depression (Poole & others, 2017)
- Inclusion of a recent study that revealed adolescents who were isolated from their peers and whose caregivers emotionally neglected them were at significant risk for developing depression (Christ, Kwak, & Lu, 2017)

- Updated coverage of adolescent suicidal thoughts and behavior in the United States (Kann & others, 2016a)
- Discussion of recent research indicating that the most significant factor in a first suicide attempt during adolescence was a major depressive episode while for children it was child maltreatment (Peyre & others, 2017)
- Coverage of a recent study in which a sense of hopelessness predicted an increase in suicide ideation in depressed adolescents (Wolfe & others, 2018)
- Description of two recent studies that revealed child maltreatment during the childhood years was linked with suicide attempts in adulthood (Park, 2017; Turner & others, 2017)
- Inclusion of a recent study that confirmed childhood sexual abuse was a significant factor in suicide attempts (Ng & others, 2018)
- Discussion of a recent meta-analysis that revealed adolescents who were the victims of cyberbullying were 2½ times more likely to attempt suicide and 2 times more likely to have suicidal thoughts than non-victims (John & others, 2018)

Chapter 11: Physical and Cognitive Development in Early Adulthood

- New section, "The Changing Landscape of Emerging and Early Adulthood," that describes how today's emerging and young adults have very different profiles and experiences than their counterparts from earlier generations in education, work, and lifestyles (Vespa, 2017)
- Inclusion of a recent study with U.S. community college students that found they believe they know when they will be an adult when they can care for themselves and others (Katsiaficas, 2017)
- New coverage of recent trends in first-year college students' increasing motivation to be well-off financially, as well as their increased feeling of being overwhelmed with what they have to do, are depressed, and feel anxious (Eagan & others, 2017)
- Discussion of a recent study in which a higher level of energy drink consumption was linked to more sleep problems in college students (Faris & others, 2017)
- Updated data on the incidence of obesity in U.S. adults (Flegal & others, 2016)
- Discussion of recent international comparisons of 33 countries in which the United States had the highest percentage of obese adults (38 percent) and Japan the lowest percentage (3.7); the average of the countries was 19.5 percent of the population being obese (OECD, 2017)
- Coverage of a recent research review in which moderate and vigorous aerobic exercise resulted in a lower incidence of major depressive disorder (Schuch & others, 2017)
- Inclusion of recent research that revealed a mortality risk reduction for individuals who replaced screen time

with an increase in daily activity levels (Wijndaele & others, 2017)
- Updated data on binge drinking in college and through early adulthood, including new Figure 3 (Schulenberg & others, 2017)
- Updated data on extreme binge drinking in college students, including data on not only 10 or more drinks at one time in the last two weeks, but also 15 or more in the same time frame (Schulenberg & others, 2017)
- Inclusion of a longitudinal study that revealed frequent binge drinking and marijuana use in the freshman year of college predicted delayed college graduation (White & others, 2018)
- Significant updating of the percentage of individuals 18 to 44 years of age in the United States who report they are heterosexual, gay, lesbian, or bisexual, as well as the percentages of these men and women who report about various feelings involving sexual orientation (Copen, Chandra, & Febo-Vazquez, 2016)
- Inclusion of recent research in which sexual activity in adults on day 1 was linked to greater well-being the next day (Kashdan & others, 2018). In this study, higher reported sexual pleasure and intimacy predicted more positive affect and less negative affect the next day.
- New research indicating that suicide ideation was associated with entrance into a friends-with-benefits (FWB) relationship as well as continuation of the FWB relationship (Dube & others, 2017)
- Updated data based on a national survey that found 3.8 percent of U.S. adults reported that they were gay, lesbian, bisexual, or transsexual (Gallup, 2015)
- New commentary that whether an individual is heterosexual, gay, lesbian, or bisexual, the person cannot be talked out of his or her sexual orientation (King, 2017. 2018)
- Updated statistics on HIV/AIDS in the United States (Centers for Disease Control and Prevention, 2018) and around the world (UNAIDS, 2017)
- New discussion of a study that found the search for and presence of meaning was linked to wisdom in emerging adults (Webster & others, 2018)
- Updated data on the percentage of full-time and part-time college students who work, which has slightly decreased in recent years (National Center for Education Statistics, 2017)
- Updated data on the average number of hours U.S. adults work per week (Saad, 2014)
- Updated data from a recent survey that revealed that employers say that 2017 is the best year for recent college graduates to be on the job market since 2007 (CareerBuilder, 2017)
- Inclusion of recent research in which an increase in job strain increased workers' insomnia while a decrease in job strain reduced their insomnia (Halonen & others, 2018)
- Description of a recent study that found depression following job loss predicted increased risk of continued unemployment (Stolove & others, 2017)

- Coverage of a study that revealed heavy drinking from 16 to 30 was linked to higher unemployment in middle age (Berg & others, 2018)

Chapter 12: Socioemotional Development in Early Adulthood

- Inclusion of a longitudinal study from 13 to 72 years of age in which avoidant attachment declined across the life span and being in a relationship predicted lower levels of anxious and avoidant attachment across adulthood (Chopik, Edelstein, & Grimm, 2018)
- Description of a research review that concluded attachment anxious individuals have higher levels of health anxiety (Maunder & others, 2017)
- Coverage of a recent research review that concluded insecure attachment was linked to a higher level of social anxiety in adults (Manning & others, 2017)
- Discussion of recent research that found insecure anxious and insecure avoidant individuals are more likely than securely attached individuals to engage in risky health behaviors, be more susceptible to physical illness, and have poorer disease outcomes (Pietromonaco & Beck, 2018)
- Updated data on the number of Americans who have tried Internet matchmaking and gender differences in the categories males and females lie about in Internet matchmaking (statisticbrain.com, 2017)
- Description of recent research on how romantic relationships change in emerging adulthood, including different characteristics of adolescent and emerging adult romantic relationships (Lantagne & Furman, 2017)
- New section, "Relationship Education for Adolescents and Emerging Adults," that examines the increasing number of relationship education programs for adolescents and emerging adults, describes their main components, and evaluates their effectiveness (Hawkins, 2018; Simpson, Lenohardt, & Hawkins, 2018)
- Update on the increasing percentage of U.S. individuals 18 and older who are single (U.S. Census Bureau, 2017)
- Updated data on the continued increase in being older before getting married in the U.S. with the age for men now at 29.5 years and for women 27.4 years (Livingston, 2017)
- Movement of section on gender and friendships from the section on "Love" to the new section on "Gender and Relationships"
- New section, "Cross-Cultural Differences in Romantic Relationships", that includes comparisons of collectivist and individualist cultures (Gao, 2016) as well as intriguing comparisons of romantic relationships in Japan, Argentina, France, and Qatar (Ansari, 2015)
- Inclusion of data from the recent Match.com 2017 Singles in America national poll that describes Millenials' interest in having sex before a first date, interest in marrying but taking considerable time to get to know someone before committing to a serious relationship,

and males interest in having females initiate the first kiss and asking a guy for his phone number
- Updated data on the percentage of U.S. adults who are cohabiting, which increased to 18 million people in 2016, an increase of 29 percent since 2007 (Stepler, 2017; U.S. Census Bureau, 2016)
- Inclusion of recent research indicating that women who cohabited within the first year of a sexual relationship were less likely to get married than women who waited more than one year before cohabiting (Sassler, Michelmore, & Qian, 2018)
- Coverage of a recent study in which cohabiting individuals were not as mentally healthy as their counterparts in committed marital relationships (Braithwaite & Holt-Lunstad, 2017)
- Description of a recent study of long-term cohabitation (more than 3 years) in emerging adulthood that found emotional distress was higher in long-term cohabitation than in time spent single, with men especially driving the effect (Menitz, 2018). However, heavy drinking was more common in time spent single than in long-term cohabitation.
- New discussion of the marriage paradox including research showing that emerging adults may not be abandoning marriage because they don't like marriage or are disinterested in it, but are delaying marriage because they want to position themselves in the best possible way for developing a healthy marital relationship (Willoughby, Hall, & Goff, 2015; Willoughby & James, 2017)
- Coverage of a recent study of married, divorced, widowed, and single adults that revealed married individuals had the best cardiovascular profile, single men the worst (Manfredni & others, 2017)
- Inclusion of a recent study in Great Britain that found no differences in the causes of breakdowns in marriage and cohabitation (Gravnengen & others, 2017). In this study, "grew apart", "arguments", "unfaithfulness/adultery", "lack of respect, appreciation", and "domestic violence" were the most frequent reasons given for such breakdowns.
- Description of a study of individuals one to 16 years into their marriage that found an increasing trajectory of tension over the course of the marriage was consistently linked to an eventual divorce (Birditt & others, 2017)
- Updated statistics on divorce rates around the world with Russia continuing to have the highest rate (OECD, 2016)
- Coverage of a study that found individuals who were divorced had a higher risk of having alcohol use disorder (Kendler & others, 2017)
- New content indicating that while the divorce rate in first marriages has declined, the divorce rate of remarriages continues to increase (DeLongis & Zwicker, 2017)
- Updated data on the average age at which U.S. women give birth, which occurred more frequently in their 30s than 20s in 2016 for the first time ever, and the average age of a woman giving birth was 27 years of age in 2016 (Centers for Disease Control and Prevention, 2017)
- New research that found the frequency of sexual intercourse in the second to fourteenth years of a marriage

was important to marital satisfaction but that a satisfying sex life and a warm interpersonal relationship were more important (Schoenfeld & others, 2017)

- New main section "Gender Communication, Relationships, and Classification"
- Extensive new content on transgender (Budge & Orovecz, 2018; Budge & others, 2017)
- Discussion of a variety of terms used to describe transgender individuals
- New content indicating that it is much more common to have a transgender identity of being born male but identifying with being a female than the reverse (Zucker & Kreukels, 2016)
- Inclusion of a recent research review that concluded transgender youth have higher rates of depression, suicide attempts, and eating disorders than their non-transgender peers (Connolly & others, 2016)

Chapter 13: Physical and Cognitive Development in Middle Adulthood

- Inclusion of a recent research review that found positive subjective time perceptions were linked to better health and well-being while negative subjective time perceptions were associated with lower levels of health and well-being (Gabrain, Dutt, & Wahl, 2017)
- Description of a recent study in which undergraduate students were shown a computer-generated graph of a person identified as a younger adult, middle-aged adult, or older adult (Kelley, Soborff & Lovaglia, 2017). When asked which person they would choose for a work-related task, they selected the middle-aged adult most often.
- Update on the percentage of adults 40 to 59 years of age classified as obese (40.2 percent) (Centers for Disease Control and Prevention, 2016)
- Coverage of recent research in which an increase in weight gain from early to middle adulthood was linked to an increased risk of major chronic diseases and unhealthy aging (Zheng & others, 2017)
- Inclusion of recent research that revealed greater intake of fruits and vegetables was linked to increased bone density in middle-aged and older adults (Qui & others, 2017)
- Discussion of a Chinese study that found men and women who gained an average of 22 pounds or more from 20 to 45-60 years of age had an increased risk of hypertension and cholesterol, as well as elevated triglyceride levels in middle age (Zhou & others, 2018)
- Description of a recent study that revealed a healthy diet in adolescence was linked to a lower risk of cardiovascular disease in middle-aged women (Dahm & others, 2018)
- New coverage of the American Heart Association's Life's Simple 7—the seven factors that people need to optimize to improve their cardiovascular health
- Description of a study in which optimal Life's Simple 7 at middle age was linked to better cardiovascular

health recovery following a heart attack later in life (Mok & others, 2018)
- Inclusion of a longitudinal study in which increased respiratory fitness from early adulthood to middle adulthood was linked to less decline in lung health over time (Berick others, 2017)
- Discussion of a recent study of young and middle-aged adults that found females had more sleep problems than males (Rossler & others, 2017). However, the good news in this study is that a majority of individuals (72 percent) reported that they did not have any sleep disturbances.
- New research indicating that perceiving one's self as feeling older predicted an increase in sleep difficulties in middle age over time (Stephan & others, 2017)
- New content on the important role of cortisol in stress and health (Leonard, 2018; Wichmann & others, 2017)
- Coverage of a recent study of men and women from 21 to 55 years of age in which married individuals had lower cortisol levels than either their never married or previously married counterparts (Chin & others, 2017)
- Coverage of a recent cross-cultural study in China that found that Mosuo women had fewer negative menopausal symptoms and higher self-esteem that Han Chinese women (Zhang & others, 2016)
- Inclusion of the recent position statement of the North American Menopause Society (2017) regarding the current status of research on various aspects of hormone replacement therapy (HRT)
- Inclusion of a consensus that there is a slight increase in breast cancer for women taking hormone replacement therapy (American Cancer Society, 2017; www.breastcancer.org, 2017)
- Discussion of recent studies and research reviews that indicate testosterone replacement therapy does not increase the risk of prostate cancer (Debruyne & others, 2017; Yassin & others, 2017)
- Description of a recent study in which TRT-related benefits in quality of life and sexual function were maintained for 36 months after initial treatment (Rosen & others, 2017)
- Discussion of a recent study that found the more frequently middle-aged and older adults had sex, the better their overall cognitive functioning was, and especially so in working memory and executive function (Wright, Jenks, & Demeyere, 2018)
- Inclusion of recent research on 24- to 93-year-olds that found everyday problem solving performance increased from early to middle adulthood but began to show a decline at about 50 years of age (Chen, Hertzog, & Park, 2017). In this study, fluid intelligence predicted everyday problem solving performance in young adults, but with increasing age, crystallized intelligence became a better predictor.
- Coverage of a Danish study across 33 years of individuals 20 to 93 years of age that found that those who engaged in a light level of leisure time physical activity lived 2.8 years longer; those who engaged in a moderate

level of leisure time physical activity lived 4.5 years longer; and those who engaged in a high level of leisure time physical activity lived 5.5 years longer (Schnohr & others, 2017)

- Discussion of a recent study that found spiritual well-being predicted which heart failure patients would still be alive five years later (Park & others, 2016)
- New research that indicated adults who volunteered had lower resting pulse rates and their resting pulse rate improved when they were deeply committed to religion (Krause, Ironson, & Hill, 2017)

Chapter 14: Socioemotional Development in Middle Adulthood

- Discussion of a recent study in which participating in an intergenerational civic engagement program enhanced older adults' self-perceptions of generativity (Grunewald & others, 2016)
- Inclusion of recent research that found a higher level of generativity in middle age was linked to greater wisdom in late adulthood (Ardelt, Gerlach, & Vaillant, 2018)
- Coverage of a recent study of gender differences in coping with stress that revealed women were more likely than men to seek psychotherapy, talk to friends about the stress, read a self-help book, take prescription medication, and engage in comfort eating (Liddon, Kingerlee, & Berry, 2017). In this study, when coping with stress, men were more likely than women to attend a support group meeting, have sex or use pornography, try to fix problems themselves, and not admit to having problems.
- Description of recent research that found individuals high in openness to experience have superior cognitive functioning across the life span, have better health and well-being (Strickhouser, Zell, & Krizan, 2017), and are more likely to eat fruits and vegetables (Conner & others, 2017)
- Inclusion of recent research that found conscientiousness was linked to better health and well-being (Strickhouser, Zell, & Krizan, 2017), being more academically successful in medical school (Sobowale & others, 2018), having a lower risk of Internet addiction (Zhou & others, 2017), not being as addicted to Instagram (Kircaburun & Griffiths, 2018), having a lower risk for alcohol addiction (Raketic & others, 2017), and having a lower risk of dementia (Terracciano & others, 2017)
- Coverage of recent research indicating that being optimistic is linked to having better psychological adjustment (Kolokotroni, Anagnostopoulos, & Hantzi, 2018)
- Inclusion of recent research in which more pessimistic college students had more anxious mood and stress symptoms (Lau & others, 2017)
- Discussion of a recent study of married couples that revealed the worst health outcomes occurred when both

spouses decreased their optimism across a four-year period (Chopik, Kim, & Smith, 2018)

- Description of a recent study in which lonely individuals who were optimistic had a lower suicide risk (Chang & others, 2018)
- Inclusion of a recent research review in which the personality trait that changed the most as a result of psychotherapy was emotional stability, followed by extraversion (Roberts & others, 2017). In this study, the personality traits of individuals with anxiety disorders changed the most, those with substance use disorders the least.
- New discussion of the increasing divorce rate in middle-aged adults and the reasons for the increase (Stepler, 2017), as well as the recent labeling of divorce in 50+- year-old adults as "gray divorce" (Crowley, 2018)
- Coverage of a recent study that found the greatest risks for getting divorce in middle adulthood were a shorter duration of marriage, lower marital quality, having financial problems, and not owning a home (Lin & others, 2018). Also in this study, onset of an empty nest, the wife's or husband's retirement, and the wife or husband having a chronic health condition were not related to risk for divorce in middle adulthood.
- Description of a recent Swiss study of middle-aged adults in which single divorcees were more lonely and less resilient than their married and remarried counterparts (Knopfli & others, 2017). Also in this study, single divorcees had the lowest self-reported health.
- New commentary that grandparents especially play important roles in grandchildren's lives when family crises such as divorce, death, illness, abandonment, or poverty occur (Dolbin-McNab & Yancura, 2018)
- New content on how grandparents facilitate women's participation in the labor force in many countries
- Coverage of a recent study of adult grandchildren in which grandparents provided more frequent emotional support to the grandchildren when parents were having life problems and more frequent financial support when parents were unemployed (Huo & others, 2018)

Chapter 15: Physical and Cognitive Development in Late Adulthood

- Update on life expectancy in the United States, which is now at 79 years of age, including the narrowing gender difference (U.S. Census Bureau, 2018)
- Discussion of recent projections for life expectancy in 2030 for 35 developed countries, with the United States increasing in life expectancy but having one of the lowest projected increases of all countries in the study (Kontis & others, 2017). In this study, South Korea is expected to have the highest life expectancy of the 35 countries in 2030, with South Korean women the first group to break the 90-year barrier with a projected life expectancy of 90.8 in 2030.

- Coverage of a recent study of U.S. and Japanese centenarians that found in both countries, health resources (better cognitive function, fewer hearing problems, and positive daily living activities) were linked to a higher level of well-being (Nakagawa & others, 2018)
- Update on gender differences in the oldest people alive in the world today with no men in the oldest 25 individuals
- Description of recent research confirming that shorter telomere length is linked to Alzheimer disease (Scarabino & others, 2017)
- Updated and expanded coverage of the diseases that are linked to mitochondrial dysfunction to include cardiovascular disease (Anupama, Sindhu, & Raghu, 2018), Parkinson disease (Lason, Hanss, & Kruger, 2018), diabetic kidney disease (Forbes & Thorburn, 2018), and impaired liver functioning (Borrelli, 2018)
- Inclusion of recent research in which at-risk overweight and older adults lost significant weight and improved their mobility considerably by participating in a community-based weight reduction program (Rejeski & others, 2017)
- Updated information about some diseases that women are more likely to die from than men are (Ostan & others, 2016)
- Inclusion of a recent study of older adults that revealed walking a dog regularly was associated with better physical health (Curl, Bibbo, & Johnson, 2017)
- Description of a recent study that found a 10-week exercise program improved the physical (aerobic endurance, agility, and mobility) and cognitive (selective attention and planning) functioning of elderly nursing home residents (Pereira & others, 2017)
- Coverage of a recent study in which relative to low physical fitness individuals, those who increased from low to intermediate or high fitness were at a lower risk for all-cause mortality (Brawner & others, 2017)
- Description of a recent study of frail elderly adults in which a high-intensity walking intervention reduced their frailty, increased their walking speed, and improved their mobility (Danilovich, Conroy, & Hornby, 2017)
- Coverage of recent research on older adults that found poorer visual function was associated with cognitive decline (Monge & Madden, 2016; Roberts & Allen, 2016) and having fewer social contacts and engaging in less challenging social/leisure activities (Cimarolli & others, 2017)
- New discussion of a recent Japanese study of older adults (mean age: 76 years) in which having had cataract surgery reduced their risk of developing mild cognitive impairment (Miyata & others, 2018)
- In a recent study of 80- to 106-year-olds, there as a substantial increase in hearing loss in the ninth and then in the tenth decade of life (Wattamwar & others, 2017). In this study, although hearing loss was universal in the 80- to 106-year-olds, only 59 percent of them wore hearing aids.
- New discussion of a recent study of 65-to 85-year-olds that dual sensory loss in vision and hearing was linked to reduced social participation and less social support, as well as increased loneliness (Mick & others, 2018)
- Coverage of a recent study of elderly adults that found those who had a dual sensory impairment involving vision and hearing had functional limitations, experienced cognitive decline, were lonely, and had communication problems (Davidson & Gutherie, 2018)
- New study indicating that older adults with a dual sensory impairment involving vision and hearing had more depressive symptoms (Han & others, 2018)
- Discussion of a recent research review that concluded older adults have a lower pain sensitivity but only for lower pain intensities (Lautenbacher & others, 2017)
- New commentary that although decreased pain sensitivity can help older adults cope with disease and injury, it also can mask injuries and illnesses that need to be treated
- Coverage of a recent study in which a Mediterranean diet reduced the risk for cardiovascular disease in older adults (Nowson & others, 2018)
- Discussion of a recent study that revealed long sleep duration predicted all-cause mortality in individuals 65 years and older (Beydoun & others, 2017)
- Description of a recent Chinese study that found older adults who engaged in a higher level of overall physical activity, leisure-time exercise, and household activity were less likely to have sleep problems (Li & others, 2018)
- Description of a recent study that found older adults' lower level of selective attention was linked to their inferior driving performance (Venkatesan & others, 2018)
- Inclusion of a recent study that found slow processing speed predicted an increase in older adults' falls one year later (Davis & others, 2017)
- Inclusion of a recent study of older adults that found playing processing speed games for five sessions a week across four weeks improved their processing speed (Nouchi & others, 2017)
- Description of a recent experimental study that revealed yoga practice that included postures, breathing, and meditation improved the attention and information processing of older adults (Gothe, Kramer, & McAuley, 2017)
- Coverage of a recent study that found that when older adults regularly engaged in mindfulness mediation, their goal-directed attention improved (Malinowski & others, 2017)
- Description of a recent study that found a mindfulness training program improved older adults' explicit memory (Banducci & others, 2017)
- Coverage of a recent study that revealed imagery strategy training improved older adults' working memory (Borella & others, 2017)
- Inclusion of recent research in which aerobic endurance was linked to better working memory in older adults (Zettel-Watson & others, 2017)
- Discussion of recent research with young, middle-aged, and older adults that found all three age groups' working memory improved with working memory training but that older adults improved less than young adults with the training (Rhodes & Katz, 2017)

- Coverage of a recent study of older adults that found slower processing speed was associated with unsafe driving (Hotta & others, 2018)
- Discussion of a recent experimental study in which high-intensity aerobic training was more effective than moderate aerobic training or resistance training in improving older adults' processing speed (Coetsee & Terblanche, 2017)
- Description of a recent study in which self-reflective exploratory processing of difficult life circumstances was linked to a higher level of wisdom (Westrate & Gluck, 2017)
- Discussion of a recent study of older adults in 10 European countries that revealed improved memory between 2004 and 2013 with the changes more positive for those who had decreases in cardiovascular diseases and increases in exercise and educational achievement (Hessel & others, 2018)
- New coverage of a recent Australian study that found older adults who had retired from occupations that involved higher complexity maintained their cognitive advantage over their counterparts who worked in less complex occupations (Lane & others, 2017)
- New discussion of a recent study of older adults working in low complexity jobs who experienced novelty in their work (assessed through recurrent work-task changes) was linked to better processing speed and working memory (Oltmanns & others, 2017)
- Inclusion of recent research revealed that older adults with type 2 diabetes had greater cognitive impairment than their counterparts who did not have the disease (Bai & others, 2017)
- Inclusion of a recent study that revealed older adults who continued to work in paid jobs had better physical and cognitive functioning than retirees (Tan & others, 2017)
- Coverage of a recent study that found the following were among the most important motives and preconditions to continue working beyond retirement age: financial, health, knowledge, and purpose in life (Sewdas & others, 2017)
- Description of a recent research review in which engaging in low or moderate exercise was linked to improved cognitive functioning in older adults with chronic diseases (Cai & others, 2017)
- Description of recent research in which participating in physical activity in late adulthood was linked to less cognitive decline (Gow, Pattie, & Geary, 2017)
- Coverage of a recent study that found fish oil supplementation improved the working memory of older adults (Boespflug & others, 2016)
- New description of a study that revealed cognitive training using virtual reality-based games with stroke patients improved their attention and memory (Gamito & others, 2017)
- Updated statistics on the percentage of U.S. older adults in different age groups in the work force, including 2017 data (Mislinski, 2017)

- Inclusion of a recent study that revealed baby boomers expect to work longer than their predecessors from prior generations (Dong & others, 2017)
- Updated data (2017) on the percentage of American workers who are very confident that they will have a comfortable retirement (Greenwald, Copeland, & VanDerhei, 2017)
- Updated data on the number of people in the U.S. who currently have Alzheimer disease (5.7 million) (Alzheimer's Association, 2018)
- New content on women being more likely to have the APOE4 gene than men and commentary about the APOE4 gene being the strongest genetic predictor of late-onset (65 years and older) Alzheimer disease (Dubal & Rogine, 2017; Giri & others, 2017)
- New content on APP, PSEN1, and PSEN2 gene mutations being linked to the early onset of Alzheimer disease (Carmona, Hardy, & Guerreiro, 2018)
- Inclusion of new content on how epigenetic factors might influence Alzheimer disease including the role of DNA methylation (Kader & others, 2018; Marioni & others, 2018; Zaghlool & others, 2018)
- Update on drugs that have been approved by the U.S. Food and Drug Administration to treat Alzheimer disease, now totaling five drugs (Almeida, 2018)

Chapter 16: Socioemotional Development in Late Adulthood

- Description of a recent study that supports the activity theory of aging: an activity-based lifestyle was associated with lower levels of depression in older adults (Juang & others, 2017)
- Coverage of a recent study that found a reminiscence intervention improved the coping skills of older adults (Satorres & others, 2018)
- New commentary by Laura Carstensen (2016) that when older adults focus on emotionally meaningful goals, they are more satisfied with their lives, feel better, and experience fewer negative emotions
- New recommendations on ways that older adults can become more socially engaged (Sightlines Project, 2016)
- Inclusion of a recent study of individuals 22 to 94 years of age that revealed on days that middle-aged and older adults, as well as individuals who were less healthy, used more selective optimization with compensation strategies, they reported having a higher level of happiness (Teshale & Lachman, 2016)
- Inclusion of a recent meta-analysis that concluded emotional experiences in older adults are more positive than for younger adults (Laureiro-Martinez, Trujillo, & Unda, 2017). Also, in this review, it was concluded that older adults focus less on negative events in the past than younger adults did.
- New description of a study that found older adults with a higher level of conscientiousness experienced less cognitive decline as they aged (Luchetti & others, 2016)

- In older adults, higher levels of conscientiousness, openness to experience, agreeableness, and extraversion were linked to positive emotions, while neuroticism was associated with negative emotions (Kalbaugh & Huffman, 2017)
- New content indicating that individuals who are extraverted and low in neuroticism are more likely to live longer (Graham & others, 2017)
- Discussion of a recent study of 15- to 105-year-old individuals in 29 European countries that revealed younger individuals engaged in age discrimination more than did older individuals (Bratt & others, 2018)
- Updated data on the significant increase in Internet, smartphone, and social networking use by U.S. older adults (Anderson, 2017)
- Coverage of a recent Hong Kong study that found adults 75 years and older who used smart phones and the Internet to connect with family, friends, and neighbors had a higher level of psychological well-being than their counterparts who did not use this information and communicative technology (Fang & others, 2018)
- Discussion of a recent study in which partnered older adults were more likely to receive Social Security, enjoy relatively higher Social Security benefits, and less likely to live in poverty (Lin, Brown, & Hammersmith, 2017)
- Inclusion of a recent study indicating that the longer older adults had been married, the better their marital quality, owning a home, and being wealthier described older adults who were less likely to get divorced (Lin & others, 2018)
- New discussion of recent research focused on the health and well-being of older adult LGBT individuals, with a focus on comparisons of those who are married, unmarried partnered, and single (Goldsen & others, 2017)
- Updated data on the percentage of men and women 65 years and older who are divorced, which increased dramatically from 1980 to 2015 (U.S. Census Bureau, 2016)
- Updated data on the dramatic increase in older adult men and women who are now cohabiting (Brown & Wright, 2017)
- Coverage of a recent national study of older adults in which among men, cohabitors' psychological well-being fared similarly to married men, better than daters and the unpartnered (Wright & Brown, 2017). In contrast, there were few differences in psychological well-being by partnership status of the women.
- New discussion of research indicating that middle-aged adults feel more positive about providing support for their children than for their aging parents (Birditt & others, 2018)
- Description of a recent study that revealed older adults, compared to younger adults, reported fewer problems with friends, fewer negative friendship qualities, less frequent contact with friends, and more positive friendship qualities with a specific friend (Schlosnagle & Strough, 2017)
- Expanded discussion of socioemotional selectivity theory to include the role of a decreasing amount of time

to live as an explanation of prioritizing meaningful relationships when people get old (Moss & Wilson, 2017)
- Updated data on the number of older adults living in poverty, including the continuing gender difference that a larger percentage of older adult women live in poverty (U.S. Census Bureau, 2018)
- Coverage of a recent 2016 Nielsen survey that found older adults watch a staggering amount of television—51 hours, 32 minutes per week, far more than any other age group (Recode, 2016)
- Description of a longitudinal study from 13 to 72 years of age in which attachment anxiety declined in middle aged and older adults (Chopik, Edelstein, & Grimm, 2018). Also in this study, attachment avoidance decreased in a linear fashion across the life span. Being in a relationship was linked with lower attachment anxiety and attachment avoidance. And men were higher in attachment avoidance throughout the life span.
- Inclusion of a recent study in which 18 percent of older adults stated that they were often or frequently lonely (Due, Sandholt, & Waldorff, 2017)
- Extensive revision and updating of the discussion of volunteering by older adults
- Updated data on the percentage of older adults who engage in volunteering (U.S. Bureau of Labor Statistics, 2016)
- Inclusion of recent research on links between volunteering by older adults and improved health (Burr & others, 2018; Carr, Kail, & Rowe, 2018), better cognitive functioning (Prouix & others, 2018), and less loneliness (Carr & others, 2018)
- Expanded and updating of why volunteering by older adults has positive outcomes for them (Carr, 2018)
- Inclusion of recent research indicating that the life-satisfaction of Latino older adults was higher than for African American and non-Latino older adults (Zhang, Braun, & Wu, 2017)
- Description of a recent study that revealed four factors emerged as best characterizing successful aging: proactive engagement, wellness resources, positive spirit, and valued relationships (Lee, Kahana, & Kahana, 2017)

Chapter 17: Death, Dying, and Grieving

- Inclusion of a recent study in which completion of an advanced directive was associated with a lower probability of receiving life-sustaining treatment (Yen & others, 2017)
- Recent updates on countries that allow assisted suicide (Belgium, Canada, Finland, Luxembourg, the Netherlands, and Switzerland)
- Update on the increasing number of states that allow assisted suicide—California, Colorado, Montana, Oregon, Vermont, and Washington, as well as Washington, DC
- New definition of assisted suicide as a key term and clearer distinctions made between euthanasia, in which the patient self-administers the lethal medication and is

- allowed to decide when and where to do this, and assisted suicide, in which the physician or a third party administers the lethal medication
- Inclusion of a recent Gallup poll in which 69 percent of U.S. adults said that euthanasia should be legal, 51 percent said that they would consider ending their own lives if faced with a terminal illness, and 50 percent reported that physician-assisted suicide is morally acceptable (Swift, 2016)
- New content on recent criticisms of the "good death" concept to move away from focusing on a single event in time to improving people's last years and decades of life (Pollock & Seymour; Smith & Periyakoil, 2018)
- New research on the percentage of adult bereavement cases that involve prolonged grief disorder and ages at which this disorder is more likely to occur (Lundorff & others, 2017)
- Inclusion of a 7-year longitudinal study of older adults in which those experiencing prolonged grief had greater cognitive decline than those with normal grief (Perez & others, 2018)

- Discussion of a recent study that found individuals with complicated grief had a higher level of the personality trait neuroticism (Goetter & others, 2018)
- New research indicating that cognitive behavior therapy reduced prolonged grief symptoms (Bartl & others, 2018)
- Updated statistics on the percentage of widows in the United States (Administration on Aging, 2015)
- Description of a recent cross-cultural study indicating that depression peaked in the first year of widowhood for both men and women, but that depression continued to be present in widowed men for 6 to 10 years post-widowhood (Jadhav & Weir, 2018)
- In a recent study, volunteering reduced widowed older adults' loneliness (Carr & others, 2018)
- Updated data on cremation with an increase to 51.6 deaths followed by cremation in the United States in 2017 with a projected increase to 57.5 percent in 2022 (Cremation Association of North America, 2018). In 2015 in Canada, cremation occurred following 70.5 percent of deaths with a projected increase to 75.1 percent in 2022.

Acknowledgments

The development and writing of *Essentials of Life-Span Development* has been strongly influenced by a remarkable group of consultants, reviewers, and adopters.

Expert Consultants

In writing the sixth edition of *Essentials of Life-Span Development,* I benefitted considerably from the following leading experts who provided detailed feedback in their areas of expertise for *Life-Span Development,* Seventeenth Edition:

William Hoyer, *Syracuse University*

Patricia Miller, *San Francisco State University*

Ross Thompson, *University of California–Davis*

Karen Fingerman, *University of Texas–Austin*

John Richards, *University of South Carolina*

Bonnie Moradi, *University of Florida*

Sheung-Tak Cheng, *Education University of Hong Kong*

Karen Rodrigue, *University of Texas–Dallas*

Applications Contributors

I especially thank the contributors who helped develop the *How Would You . . . ?* questions for students in various majors who are taking the life-span development course:

Michael E. Barber, *Santa Fe Community College*

Maida Berenblatt, *Suffolk Community College*

Susan A. Greimel, *Santa Fe Community College*

Russell Isabella, *University of Utah*

Jean Mandernach, *University of Nebraska–Kearney*

General Reviewers

I gratefully acknowledge the comments and feedback from instructors around the nation who have reviewed *Essentials of Life-Span Development.*

Eileen Achorn, *University of Texas–San Antonio*

Michael E. Barber, *Santa Fe Community College*

Gabriel Batarseh, *Francis Marion University*

Troy E. Beckert, *Utah State University*

Stefanie Bell, *Pikes Peak Community College*

Maida Berenblatt, *Suffolk Community College*

Kathi Bivens, *Asheville Buncombe Technical Community College*

Alda Blakeney, *Kennesaw State University*

Candice L. Branson, *Kapiolani Community College*

Ken Brewer, *Northeast State Technical Community College*

Margaret M. Bushong, *Liberty University*

Krista Carter, *Colby Community College*

Stewart Cohen, *University of Rhode Island*

Rock Doddridge, *Asheville Buncombe Technical Community College*

Laura Duvall, *Heartland Community College*

Jenni Fauchier, *Metro Community College-Omaha*

Richard Ferraro, *University of North Dakota*

Terri Flowerday, *University of New Mexico-Albuquerque*

Laura Garofoli, *Fitchburg State College*

Sharon Ghazarian, *University of North Carolina—Greensboro*

Dan Grangaard, *Austin Community College*

Rodney J. Grisham, *Indian River Community College*

Rea Gubler, *Southern Utah University*

Myra M. Harville, *Holmes Community College*

Brett Heintz, *Delgado Community College*

Sandra Hellyer, *Butler University*

Randy Holley, *Liberty University*

Debra L. Hollister, *Valencia Community College*

Rosemary T. Hornack, *Meredith College*

Alycia Hund, *Illinois State University*

Rebecca Inkrott, *Sinclair Community College-Dayton*

Russell Isabella, *University of Utah*

Alisha Janowsky, *Florida Atlantic University*

Lisa Judd, *Western Technical College*

Tim Killian, *University of Arkansas-Fayetteville*

Shenan Kroupa, *Indiana University-Purdue University Indianapolis*

Pat Lefler, *Bluegrass Community and Technical College*

Jean Mandernach, *University of Nebraska-Kearney*

Carrie Margolin, *Evergreen State College*

Michael Jason McCoy, *Cape Fear Community College*

Carol Miller, *Anne Arundel Community College*

Gwynn Morris, *Meredith College*

Ron Mossler, *Los Angeles Community College*

Bob Pasnak, *George Mason University*

Curtis D. Proctor-Artz, *Wichita State University*

Janet Reis, *University of Illinois-Urbana*

Kimberly Renk, *University of Central Florida*

Vicki Ritts, *St. Louis Community College-Meramec*

Jeffrey Sargent, *Lee University*

James Schork, *Elizabethtown Community and Technical College*

Jason Scofield, *University of Alabama*

Christin E. Seifert, *Montana State University*

Elizabeth Sheehan, *Georgia State University*

Peggy Skinner, *South Plains College*

Christopher Stanley, *Winston-Salem State University*

Wayne Stein, *Brevard Community College-Melbourne*

Rose Suggett, *Southeast Community College*

Kevin Sumrall, *Montgomery College*

Joan Test, *Missouri State University*

Barbara VanHorn, *Indian River Community College*

John Wakefield, *University of North Alabama*

Laura Wasielewski, *St. Anselm College*

Lois Willoughby, *Miami Dade College-Kendall*

Paul Wills, *Kilgore College*

A. Claire Zaborowski, *San Jacinto College*

Pauline Davey Zeece, *University of Nebraska-Lincoln*

Design Reviewers

Cheryl Almeida, *Johnson and Wales University*

Candice L. Branson, *Kapiolani Community College*

Debra Hollister, *Valencia Community College*

Alycia Hund, *Illinois State University*

Jean Mandernach, *University of Nebraska-Kearney*

Michael Jason Scofield, *University of Alabama*

Christin Seifert, *Montana State University*

The McGraw-Hill Education Team

A large number of outstanding professionals at McGraw-Hill Education helped me to produce this edition of *Essentials of Life-Span Development.* I especially want to thank Ryan Treat, Dawn Groundwater, Ann Helgerson, and A.J. Laferrera for their extensive efforts in developing, publishing, and marketing this book. Mary Powers, Vicki Malinee, Janet Tilden, and Jennifer Blankenship were superb in the production and copyediting phases of the text.

1 Introduction

CHAPTER OUTLINE

Stories of Life-Span Development: How Did Ted Kaczynski Become Ted Kaczynski and Alice Walker Become Alice Walker?

Ted Kaczynski sprinted through high school, not bothering with his junior year and making only passing efforts at social contact. Off to Harvard at age 16, Kaczynski was a loner during his college years. One of his roommates at Harvard said that he avoided people by quickly shuffling by them and slamming the door behind him. After obtaining his Ph.D. in mathematics at the University of Michigan, Kaczynski became a professor at the University of California at Berkeley. His colleagues there remember him as hiding from social interaction—no friends, no allies, no networking.

After several years at Berkeley, Kaczynski resigned and moved to a rural area of Montana, where he lived as a hermit in a crude shack for 25 years. Town residents described him as a bearded eccentric. Kaczynski traced his own difficulties to growing up as a genius in a kid's body and sticking out like a sore thumb in his surroundings as a child. In 1996, he was arrested and charged as the notorious Unabomber, America's most wanted killer. Over the course of 17 years, Kaczynski had sent 16 mail bombs that left 23 people wounded or maimed and 3 people dead. In 1998, he pleaded guilty to the offenses and was sentenced to life in prison.

A decade before Kaczynski mailed his first bomb, Alice Walker spent her days battling racism in Mississippi. She had recently won her first writing fellowship, but rather than use the money to follow her dream of moving to Senegal, Africa, she put herself into the heart and heat of the civil rights movement. Walker had grown up knowing the brutal effects of poverty and racism. Born in 1944, she was the eighth child of Georgia sharecroppers who earned $300 a year. When Walker was 8, her brother accidentally shot her in the left eye with a BB gun. Since her parents had no car, it took them a week to get her to a hospital. By the time she received medical care, she was blind in that eye, and it had developed a disfiguring layer of scar tissue. Despite the counts against her, Walker overcame pain and anger and went on to win a Pulitzer Prize for her book *The Color Purple*. She became not only a novelist but also an essayist, a poet, a short-story writer, and a social activist.

What leads one individual, so full of promise, to commit brutal acts of violence and another to turn poverty and trauma into a rich literary harvest? If you have ever wondered why people turn out the way they do, you have asked yourself the central question we will explore in this book.

Essentials of Life-Span Development is a window into the journey of human development—your own and that of every other member of the human species. Every life is distinct, a new biography in the world. Examining the shape of life-span development helps us to understand it better. In this chapter, we explore what it means to take a life-span perspective on development, examine the nature of development, and outline how science helps us to understand it. ∎

The Life-Span Perspective

Each of us develops partly like all other individuals, partly like some other individuals, and partly like no other individual. Most of the time we notice the qualities in an individual that make that person unique. But as humans, we have all traveled some common paths. Each of us—Leonardo da Vinci, Joan of Arc, George Washington, Martin Luther King, Jr., and you—walked at about 1 year, engaged in fantasy play as a young child, and became more independent as a youth. Each of us, if we live long enough, will experience hearing problems and the death of family members and friends. This is the general course of our **development,** the pattern of movement or change that begins at conception and continues through the human life span.

In this section we explore what is meant by the concept of development and why the study of life-span development is important. We outline the main characteristics of the life-span perspective and discuss various influences on development. In addition, we examine some contemporary concerns related to life-span development.

The Importance of Studying Life-Span Development

development The pattern of movement or change that starts at conception and continues through the life span.

How might you benefit from studying life-span development? Perhaps you are, or will be, a parent or teacher. If so, responsibility for children is, or will be, a part of your everyday life. The more you learn about them, the better you can raise them or teach them. Perhaps you hope to gain some insight about your own history—as an infant, a child, an adolescent, or a young adult. Perhaps you want to know more about what your life will be like as you grow through the adult years—as a middle-aged adult, or as an adult in old age, for example. Or perhaps you just stumbled across this course, thinking that it sounded intriguing. Whatever your reasons, you will discover that the study of life-span development addresses some provocative questions about who we are, how we came to be this way, and where our future will take us.

In our exploration of development, we will examine the life span from the point of conception until the time when life (at least, life as we know it) ends. You will see yourself as an infant, as a child, and as an adolescent, and you will learn about how those years influenced the kind of individual you are today. And you will see yourself as a young adult, as a middle-aged adult, and as an adult in old age, and you may be motivated to consider how your experiences will affect your development through the remainder of your adult years.

Characteristics of the Life-Span Perspective

Growth and development are dramatic during the first two decades of life, but development is not something that happens only to children and adolescents. The traditional approach to the study of development emphasizes extensive change from birth to adolescence (especially during infancy), little or no change in adulthood, and decline in old age. Yet a great deal of change does occur in the decades after adolescence. The life-span approach emphasizes developmental change throughout adulthood as well as childhood (Park & Festini, 2018; Schaie & Willis, 2016).

Life Expectancy

Recent increases in human life expectancy have contributed to greater interest in the life-span approach to development. The upper boundary of the human life span (based on the oldest age documented) is 122 years. The maximum life span of humans has not changed since the beginning of recorded history. What has changed is life expectancy, the average number of years that a person born in a particular year can expect to live. In the twentieth century alone, life expectancy increased by 30 years, thanks to improvements in sanitation, nutrition, and medicine (see Figure 1). In 2016, the life expectancy in the United States was 79 years of age (U.S. Census Bureau, 2017). Today, for most individuals in developed countries, childhood and adolescence represent only about one-fourth of their lives.

Laura Carstensen (2015, 2016) recently described the challenges and opportunities involved in this dramatic increase in life expectancy. In her view, the remarkable increase in the number of people living to old age has taken place so quickly that science, technology, and behavioral changes have not kept pace. She proposes that the challenge is to transform a world constructed mainly for young people into a world that is more compatible and supportive for the increasing number of people living to 100 and older.

In further commentary, Carstensen (2015, p. 70) remarked that making this transformation would be no small feat:

> . . . parks, transportation systems, staircases, and even hospitals presume that the users have both strength and stamina; suburbs across the country are built for two parents and their young children, not single people, multiple generations or elderly people who are not able to drive. Our education system serves the needs of young children and young adults and offers little more than recreation for experienced people.

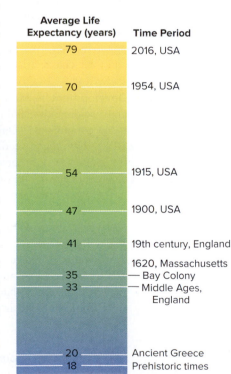

Average Life Expectancy (years)	Time Period
79	2016, USA
70	1954, USA
54	1915, USA
47	1900, USA
41	19th century, England
35	1620, Massachusetts Bay Colony
33	Middle Ages, England
20	Ancient Greece
18	Prehistoric times

Figure 1 Human Life Expectancy at Birth from Prehistoric Time to Contemporary Times
It took 5,000 years to extend human life expectancy from 18 to 41 years of age.

Indeed, the very conception of work as a full-time endeavor ending in the early sixties is ill suited for long lives. Arguably the most troubling aspect of our current perspective on aging is that we fret about ways that older people lack the qualities of younger people rather than exploit a growing new resource right before our eyes: citizens who have deep expertise, emotional balance, and the motivation to make a difference.

Certainly recent progress has been made in improving the lives of older adults. In our discussion of late adulthood, you will read about researchers who are exploring ways to modify the activity of genes related to aging, methods for improving brain functioning in older people, medical discoveries for slowing or even reversing the effects of various chronic diseases, and ways to prepare for a better quality of life when we get old, including strategies for staying cognitively sharp, maintaining our physical fitness, and becoming more satisfied with our lives as older adults. But much more remains to be accomplished, as described earlier by Laura Carstensen (2015, 2016) and others (Adams, 2017; Couch & others, 2017).

Dimensions of the Life-Span Perspective

The belief that development occurs throughout life is central to the life-span perspective on human development, but this perspective has other characteristics as well. According to life-span development expert Paul Baltes (1939–2006), the **life-span perspective** views development as lifelong, multidimensional, multidirectional, plastic, multidisciplinary, and contextual, and as a process that involves growth, maintenance, and regulation of loss (Baltes, 1987, 2003; Baltes, Lindenberger, & Staudinger, 2006). In this view, it is important to understand that development is constructed through biological, sociocultural, and individual factors working together (Baltes, Reuter-Lorenz, & Rösler, 2006). Let's look at each of these characteristics.

Development Is Lifelong In the life-span perspective, early adulthood is not the endpoint of development; rather, no age period dominates development. Researchers increasingly study the experiences and psychological orientations of adults at different points in their lives. Later in this chapter we describe the age periods of development and their characteristics.

Development Is Multidimensional Development consists of biological, cognitive, and socioemotional dimensions. Even within each of those dimensions, there are many components (Dale & others, 2018; Moss & Wilson, 2018; Zammit & others, 2018). The cognitive dimension, for example, includes attention, memory, abstract thinking, speed of processing information, and social intelligence. At every age, changes occur in every dimension. Changes in one dimension also affect development in the other dimensions.

To get an idea of how interactions occur, consider the development of Ted Kaczynski, the so-called Unabomber discussed at the opening of the chapter. When he was 6 months old, he was hospitalized with a severe allergic reaction, and his parents were rarely allowed to visit him. According to his mother, the previously happy baby was never the same after his hospital stay. He became withdrawn and unresponsive. As Ted grew up, he had periodic "shutdowns" accompanied by rage. In his mother's view, events that occurred during her son's infancy warped the development of his mind and emotions.

life-span perspective The perspective that development is lifelong, multidimensional, multidirectional, plastic, multidisciplinary, and contextual; that it involves growth, maintenance, and regulation; and that it is constructed through biological, sociocultural, and individual factors working together.

Development Is Multidirectional Throughout life, some dimensions or components of a dimension expand and others shrink (Kuntzmann, 2019; Mejia & others, 2017; Sternberg & Hagen, 2018; Strandberg, 2019; Yoo & others, 2017). For example, when one language (such as English) is acquired early in development, the capacity for acquiring second and third languages (such as Spanish and Chinese) decreases later in development, especially after early childhood (Levelt, 1989). During adolescence, as individuals establish romantic relationships, their relationships with friends might decrease. During late adulthood, older adults might become wiser by being able to call on experience to guide their intellectual decision making (Hayman, Kerse, & Consedine, 2017; Kuntzmann, 2019; Rakoczy & others, 2018; Thomas & others, 2018), but they perform more poorly on tasks that require speed in processing information (Salthouse, 2017).

Development Is Plastic Even at 10 years old, Ted Kaczynski was extraordinarily shy. Was he destined to remain forever uncomfortable with people? Developmentalists debate how much plasticity people have in various dimensions at different points in their development (Erickson & Oberlin, 2017; Kinugawa, 2019; Park & Festini, 2018). Plasticity means the capacity for change. For example, can you still improve your intellectual skills when you are in your seventies or eighties? Or might these intellectual skills be fixed by the time you are in your thirties so that further improvement is impossible? Researchers have found that the cognitive skills of older adults can be improved through training and developing better strategies (Calero, 2019; Willis & Belleville, 2016). However, possibly we possess less capacity for change when we become old (Salthouse, 2017; Shivarama Shetty & Sajikumar, 2017). The exploration of plasticity and its constraints is a key element on the contemporary agenda for developmental research (Kinugawa, 2019; Puts & others, 2017; Schaie, 2016; Walker, 2019).

Developmental Science Is Multidisciplinary Psychologists, sociologists, anthropologists, neuroscientists, and medical researchers all share an interest in unlocking the mysteries of development through the life span. How do your heredity and health limit your intelligence? Do intelligence and social relationships change with age in the same way around the world? How do families and schools influence intellectual development? These are examples of research questions that cut across disciplines.

Development Is Contextual All development occurs within a **context,** or setting. Contexts include families, schools, peer groups, churches, cities, neighborhoods, university laboratories, countries, and so on. Each of these settings is influenced by historical, economic, social, and cultural factors (Anguiano, 2018; Lubetkin & Jia, 2017; Nair, Roche, & White, 2018).

Contexts, like individuals, change (Matsumoto & Juang, 2017; Taylor, Widaman, & Robins, 2018). Thus, individuals are changing beings in a changing world. As a result of these changes, contexts exert three types of influences (Baltes, 2003): (1) normative age-graded influences, (2) normative history-graded influences, and (3) nonnormative or highly individualized life events. Each of these types can have a biological or environmental impact on development.

Normative age-graded influences are similar for individuals in a particular age group. These influences include biological processes such as puberty and menopause. They also include sociocultural, environmental processes such as beginning formal education (usually at about age 6 in most cultures) and retirement (which takes place during the fifties and sixties in most cultures).

Normative history-graded influences are common to people of a particular generation because of historical circumstances (Heo & others, 2018; Thorvaldsson & others, 2017). For example, in their youth American baby boomers shared the experience of the Cuban missile crisis, the assassination of John F. Kennedy, and the Beatles invasion. Other examples of normative history-graded influences include economic, political, and social upheavals such as the Great Depression in the 1930s, World War II in the 1940s, the civil rights and women's rights movements of the 1960s and 1970s, the terrorist attacks of 9/11/2001, the integration of computers and cell phones into everyday life during the 1990s, and time spent on social media in the twenty-first century (Schaie, 2016; Smith & Anderson, 2018). Long-term changes in the genetic and cultural makeup of a population (due to immigration or changes in fertility rates) are also part of normative historical change.

context The setting in which development occurs, which is influenced by historical, economic, social, and cultural factors.

normative age-graded influences Biological and environmental influences that are similar for individuals in a particular age group.

normative history-graded influences Biological and environmental influences that are associated with history. These influences are common to people of a particular generation.

Nonnormative life events, such as Hurricane Maria in Puerto Rico in 2017, are unusual circumstances that can have a major influence on a person's development.
©Mario Tama/Getty Images

Nonnormative life events are unusual occurrences that have a major impact on the individual's life. These events do not happen to all people, and when they do occur they can influence people in different ways (Fredriksen-Goldsen & others, 2017; Shah & others, 2018). Examples include the death of a parent when a child is young, pregnancy in early adolescence, a fire that destroys a home, winning the lottery, or getting an unexpected career opportunity.

Development Involves Growth, Maintenance, and Regulation of Loss Baltes and his colleagues (2006) assert that the mastery of life often involves conflicts and competition among three goals of human development: growth, maintenance, and regulation of loss. As individuals age into middle and late adulthood, the quest to maintain their capacities and to regulate loss takes center stage away from growth. Thus, a 75-year-old man might aim not to improve his memory or his golf swing but to maintain his independence and to continue playing golf. In other chapters, we will discuss these ideas about maintenance and regulation of loss in greater depth.

How Would You...?

As a **social worker,** how would you explain the importance of considering nonnormative life events when working with a new client?

Development Is a Co-Construction of Biology, Culture, and the Individual Development comes from biological, cultural, and individual factors influencing each other (Baltes, Reuter-Lorenz, & Rösler, 2006; De la Fuente, 2019). For example, the brain shapes culture, but it is also shaped by culture and the experiences that individuals have or pursue. In terms of individual factors, we can go beyond what our genetic inheritance and environment give us. We can create a unique developmental path by actively choosing from the environment the things that optimize our lives (Rathunde & Csikszentmihalyi, 2006).

Contemporary Concerns in Life-Span Development

Pick up a newspaper or magazine and you might see headlines like these: "Technology Threatens Communication Skills," "Political Leanings May Be Written in the Genes," "Mother Accused of Tossing Children into Bay," "Religious Group Protests Transgender Bathrooms," "FDA Warns About Side Effects of ADHD Drug," "Heart Attack Deaths Higher in African American Patients," "Test May Predict Alzheimer Disease." Researchers using the life-span perspective explore these and many other topics of contemporary concern. The roles that health and well-being, parenting, education, sociocultural contexts, and technology play in life-span development, as well as how social policy is related to these issues, are a particular focus of this textbook.

Health and Well-Being

Health professionals today recognize the power of lifestyles and psychological states in health and well-being (Blake, Munoz, & Volpe, 2019; Donatelle, 2019; Hales, 2018; Rolfes, Pinna, & Whitney, 2018). Clinical psychologists are among the health professionals who help people improve their well-being. Read about one clinical psychologist who helps adolescents and adults improve their developmental outcomes in the *Careers in Life-Span Development* profile.

nonnormative life events Unusual occurrences that have a major impact on a person's life. The occurrence, pattern, and sequence of these events are not applicable to many individuals.

Gustavo Medrano, Clinical Psychologist

Gustavo Medrano specializes in helping children, adolescents, and adults of all ages improve their lives when they have problems involving depression, anxiety, emotion regulation, chronic health conditions, and life transitions. He works individually with clients and provides therapy for couples and families. As a native Spanish speaker, he also provides bicultural and bilingual therapy for clients.

Dr. Medrano is a faculty member at the Family Institute at Northwestern University. He obtained his undergraduate degree in psychology at Northwestern and then became a teacher for Teach for America, which involves a minimum of two years spent teaching in a high-poverty area. He received his master's and doctoral degrees in clinical psychology at the University of Wisconsin—Milwaukee. As a faculty member at Northwestern, in addition to doing clinical therapy with clients, he also conducts research with a focus on how family experiences, especially parenting, influence children's and adolescents' coping and pain.

Gustavo Moreno, a clinical psychologist who often works with Spanish-speaking clients.
©Avis Mandel Pictures

Parenting and Education

Can two gay men raise a healthy family? Do children suffer if they grow up in a divorced family? Are U.S. schools failing to teach children how to read and write and calculate adequately? We hear many questions like these related to pressures on the contemporary family and the problems of U.S. schools (Bullard, 2017; Farr & Goldberg, 2018; Lockhart & others, 2017; Trejos-Castillo & Trevino-Schafer, 2018). In later chapters, we analyze child care, the effects of divorce, parenting styles, intergenerational relationships, early childhood education, relationships between childhood poverty and education, children with disabilities; bilingual education, new educational efforts to improve lifelong learning, and many other issues related to parenting and education (Hallahan, Kauffman, & Pullen, 2019; Morrison, 2018; Powell, 2019; Sandler & others, 2017).

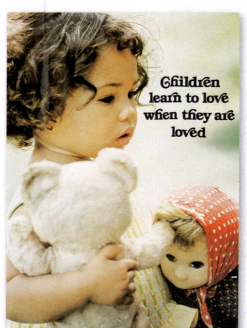

Children learn to love when they are loved

©Robert Maust/Photo Agora

Sociocultural Contexts and Diversity

Health, parenting, and education—like development itself—are all shaped by their sociocultural context (Cummings & others, 2017; Duncan, Magnuson, & Votruba-Drzal, 2017; Lansford & Banati, 2018; Suárez-Orozco & Suárez-Orozco, 2018). To analyze this context, four concepts are especially useful: culture, ethnicity, socioeconomic status, and gender.

Culture encompasses the behavior patterns, beliefs, and all other products of a particular group of people that are passed on from generation to generation. Culture results from the interaction of people over many years (Goldman & others, 2018; Kim & others, 2018; Ragavan & others, 2018). A cultural group can be as large as the United States or as small as an isolated Appalachian town. Whatever its size, the group's culture influences the behavior of its members (Erez,

culture The behavior patterns, beliefs, and all other products of a group that are passed on from generation to generation.

Asian American and Latino children are the fastest-growing immigrant groups in the United States. *How diverse are the students in your life-span development class? How are their experiences in growing up likely similar to or different from yours?*
©Skip O'Rourke/Zuma Press Inc./Alamy

2018; Matsumoto & Juang, 2017). **Cross-cultural studies** compare aspects of two or more cultures. The comparison provides information about the degree to which development is similar, or universal, across cultures, or is instead culture-specific (Duell & others, 2018; Goldman & others, 2018; Shapka & others, 2018; Vignoles & others, 2017). For example, in a recent study of 26 countries, individuals in Chile had the highest life satisfaction, those in Bulgaria and Spain the lowest (Jang & others, 2017).

Ethnicity (the word *ethnic* comes from the Greek word for "nation") is rooted in cultural heritage, nationality, race, religion, and language. African Americans, Latinos, Asian Americans, Native Americans, European Americans, and Arab Americans are a few examples of broad ethnic groups in the United States. Diversity exists within each ethnic group (Hou & Kim, 2018; Kim & others, 2018). In recent years, there has been a growing realization that research on children's and adolescents' development needs to include more children from diverse ethnic groups (Suárez-Orozco, 2018a, b, c). A special concern is the discrimination and prejudice experienced by ethnic minority children (Nieto & Bode, 2018). Recent research indicates that pride in one's ethnic identity group has positive outcomes (Douglass & Umana-Taylor, 2017; Umana-Taylor & others, 2018).

Socioeconomic status (SES) refers to a person's position within society based on occupational, educational, and economic characteristics. Socioeconomic status implies certain inequalities. Differences in the ability to control resources and to participate in society's rewards produce unequal opportunities (Allen & Goldman-Mellor, 2018; Dragoset & others, 2017; Singh & Mukherjee, 2018).

Gender, the characteristics of people as females and males, is another important aspect of sociocultural contexts. Few aspects of our development are more central to our identity and social relationships than gender (Dettori & Rao Gupta, 2018; Ellemers, 2018; Liben, 2017). We discuss sociocultural contexts and diversity in each chapter.

The conditions in which many of the world's women live are a serious concern (UNICEF, 2018). Inadequate educational opportunities, violence, and lack of political access are just some of the problems faced by many women.

Recently, considerable interest has been generated about a category of gender classification, *transgender*, a broad term that refers to individuals who adopt a gender identity that differs from the one assigned to them at birth (Budge & Orovecz, 2018; Budge & others, 2018; Savin-Williams, 2017). For example, individuals may have a female body but identify more strongly with being masculine than being feminine, or have a male body but identify more strongly with being feminine than being masculine. We will have much more to say about gender and transgender later in the text.

Doly Akter, age 17, lives in a slum in Dhaka, Bangladesh, where sewers overflow, garbage rots in the streets, and children are undernourished. Nearly two-thirds of the women in Bangladesh marry before they are 18. Doly organized a club supported by UNICEF in which girls go door-to-door to monitor the hygiene habits of households in their neighborhood, which has led to improved hygiene and health in the families. Also, her group has managed to stop several child marriages by meeting with parents and convincing them that it is not in their daughter's best interests. They emphasize the importance of staying in school and how this will improve their daughter's future. Doly says that the girls in her UNICEF group are far more aware of their rights than their mothers ever were. (UNICEF, 2007).
Courtesy of Naser Siddique/UNICEF Bangladesh

How Would You…?

As a **health-care professional**, how would you explain the importance of examining cross-cultural research when searching for developmental trends in health and wellness?

How Would You…?

As a **psychologist,** how would you explain the importance of examining sociocultural factors in developmental research?

cross-cultural studies Comparisons of one culture with one or more other cultures. These provide information about the degree to which children's development is similar, or universal, across cultures, and the degree to which it is culture-specific.

ethnicity A range of characteristics rooted in cultural heritage, including nationality, race, religion, and language.

socioeconomic status (SES) Refers to the conceptual grouping of people with similar occupational, educational, and economic characteristics.

gender The characteristics of people as females and males.

Family turmoil 45 / 12

Child separation 45 / 14

Exposure to violence 73 / 49

Crowding 16 / 7

Excessive noise 32 / 21

Poor housing quality 24 / 3

Poor children
Middle-income children

Risk factor (stressor)

0 10 20 30 40 50 60 70
Percent of children exposed

Figure 2 **Exposure to Six Stressors Among Children in Poor and Middle-Income Families**
One study analyzed the exposure to six stressors among children in poor and middle-income families (Evans & English, 2002). Poor children were much more likely to face each of these stressors.

Social Policy

Social policy is a government's course of action designed to promote the welfare of its citizens. Values, economics, and politics all shape a nation's social policy. Out of concern that policy makers are doing too little to protect the well-being of children and older adults, life-span researchers are increasingly undertaking studies that they hope will lead to effective social policy (Akinsola & Petersen, 2018; Aspen Institute, 2018; Lerner & others, 2018; Ruck, Peterson-Badali, & Freeman, 2017; Scales & Roehlkepartain, 2018).

Children who grow up in poverty represent a special concern (Duncan, Magnuson, & Votruba-Drzal, 2017; Koller, Santana, & Raffaelli, 2018; Suárez-Orozco, 2018a, b, c; Yoshikawa & others, 2017). In 2015, 19.7 percent of U.S. children under 18 years of age were living in families with incomes below the poverty line, with African American (36 percent) and Latino (30 percent) families with children having especially high rates of poverty (Jiang, Granja, & Koball, 2017). This is an increase from 2001 (16 percent) but slightly down from a peak of 23 percent in 1993. As indicated in Figure 2, one study found that a higher percentage of children in poor families than in middle-income families were exposed to family turmoil, separation from a parent, violence, crowding, excessive noise, and poor housing (Evans & English, 2002).

Developmental psychologists are seeking ways to help families living in poverty improve their well-being, and they have offered many suggestions for improving government policies (Lansford & Banati, 2018; McQueen, 2017; Motti-Stefanidi, 2018; Suárez-Orozco & Suárez-Orozco, 2018). For example, the Minnesota Family Investment Program (MFIP) was designed in the 1990s primarily to influence the behavior of adults—specifically, to move adults off welfare rolls and into paid employment. A key element of the program was its guarantee that adults participating in the program would receive more income if they worked than if they did not. How did the increase in income affect their children? A study of the effects of MFIP found that higher incomes of working poor parents were linked with benefits for their children (Gennetian & Miller, 2002). The children's achievement in school improved, and their behavior problems decreased. A current MFIP study is examining the influence of specific services on low-income families at risk for child maltreatment and other negative outcomes for children (Minnesota Family Investment Program, 2009).

There is increasing interest in developing two-generation educational interventions to improve the academic success of children living in poverty (Gardner, Brooks-Gunn, & Chase-Lansdale, 2016). For example, a recent large-scale effort to help children escape from poverty is the Ascend two-generation educational intervention being conducted by the Aspen Institute (2013, 2018; King, Chase-Lansdale, & Small, 2015). The focus of the intervention emphasizes education (increasing postsecondary education for mothers and improving the quality of their children's early childhood education), economic support (housing, transportation, financial education, health insurance, and food assistance), and social capital (peer support including friends and neighbors; participation in community and faith-based organizations; school and work contacts).

Some children triumph over poverty or other adversities. They show *resilience*. Think back to the chapter-opening story about Alice Walker. In spite of racism, poverty, her low socioeconomic status, and a disfiguring eye injury, she went on to become a successful author and champion for equality.

Are there certain characteristics that make children like Alice Walker resilient? Are there other characteristics that influence children like Ted Kaczynski, who despite his intelligence and education, became a killer? After analyzing research on this topic, Ann Masten and her colleagues

social policy A national government's course of action designed to promote the welfare of its citizens.

(Masten, 2006, 2014, 2015, 2016a, b; 2017; Masten, Burt, & Coatsworth, 2006; Masten & Kalstabakken, 2018; Masten & Palmer, 2018; Motti-Stefanidi & Masten, 2017; Narayan & Masten, 2018; Narayan & others, 2017) have concluded that a number of individual factors, such as good intellectual functioning, influence resiliency. In addition, family and extrafamilial contexts of resilient individuals tend to share certain features. For example, resilient children are likely to have a close relationship to a caring parent figure and bonds to caring adults outside the family.

Ann Masten (*far right*) with a homeless mother and her child who are participating in her research on resilience. She and her colleagues have found that good parenting skills and good cognitive skills (especially attention and self-control) improve the likelihood that children in challenging circumstances will do better when they enter elementary school.
©Dawn Villella Photography

At the other end of the life span, protecting the well-being of older adults also creates policy issues (Burns, Browning, and Kendig, 2017; Jennifer, 2018; Volkwein-Caplan & Tahmaseb-McConatha, 2018). Key concerns are escalating health care costs and the access of older adults to adequate health care (Cunningham, Green, & Braun, 2018; Kane, Saliba, & Hollmann, 2017).

Concerns about the well-being of older adults are heightened by two facts. First, the number of older adults in the United States is growing rapidly. Second, many of these older Americans are likely to need society's help (Andrew & Meeks, 2018; Conway & others, 2018; Shankar & others, 2017).

Not only is the population of older adults growing in the United States, but the world's population of people 60 years and older is projected to increase from 900 million in 2015 to 2.1 billion in 2050 (United Nations, 2015). The global population of individuals 80 years and older is expected to triple or quadruple during the same time frame.

Technology

A final focus in our exploration of contemporary topics is the recent dramatic, almost overwhelming increase in technology at all points in the life span (Lever-Duffy & McDonald, 2018; Vernon, Modecki, & Barber, 2018). When we consider the mid-1950s when television was introduced into people's lives, to the replacement of typewriters with computers that can do far more than just print words, later to the remarkable invention of the Internet and then smartphones, followed by the pervasiveness of social media and even the expanded use of robots that in some areas can do jobs better than humans can, it is obvious that our way of life has been forever changed through technological advances.

We will explore many technology topics in this book. Later in this chapter you will read about the emerging field of developmental robotics in our discussion of information processing as well as coverage of different generations, including the current generation of millennials and their extensive connection with technology. At various points in the book, we explore such topics as whether babies should be watching television and videos, especially how these activities might impair language development; how too much screen time takes away from children's exercise and increases their risk for obesity and cardiovascular disease; how many adolescents spend more time using various media than they do learning in school and whether multitasking with different technology devices is helpful or harmful to academic success; as well as how extensively older adults are adapting to the expanding role of technology in their daily lives, especially since they did not grow up using much technology.

The Nature of Development

In this section we explore what is meant by developmental processes and periods, as well as variations in the way age is conceptualized. We examine some key developmental issues.

If you wanted to describe how and why Alice Walker or Ted Kaczynski developed during their lifetimes, how would you go about it? A chronicle of the events in any person's life can quickly become a confusing and tedious array of details. Two concepts help provide a framework for describing and understanding an individual's development: developmental processes and periods.

Biological, Cognitive, and Socioemotional Processes

At the beginning of this chapter, we defined development as the pattern of change that begins at conception and continues through the life span. The pattern is complex because it is the product of biological, cognitive, and socioemotional processes.

Biological Processes

Biological processes produce changes in an individual's physical nature. Genes inherited from parents, the development of the brain, height and weight gains, changes in motor skills, nutrition, exercise, the hormonal changes of puberty, and cardiovascular decline are all examples of biological processes that affect development.

Cognitive Processes

Cognitive processes refer to changes in an individual's thinking, intelligence, and language. Watching a colorful mobile swinging above the crib, putting together a two-word sentence, memorizing a poem, imagining what it would be like to be a movie star, and solving a crossword puzzle all involve cognitive processes.

Socioemotional Processes

Socioemotional processes involve changes in the individual's relationships with other people, changes in emotions, and changes in personality. An infant's smile in response to a parent's touch, a toddler's aggressive attack on a playmate, a school-age child's development of assertiveness, an adolescent's joy at the senior prom, and the affection of an elderly couple all reflect the role of socioemotional processes in development.

Connecting Biological, Cognitive, and Socioemotional Processes

Biological, cognitive, and socioemotional processes are inextricably intertwined (Diamond, 2013). Consider a baby smiling in response to a parent's touch. This response depends on biological processes (the physical nature of touch and responsiveness to it), cognitive processes (the ability to understand intentional acts), and socioemotional processes (the act of smiling often reflects a positive emotional feeling, and smiling helps to connect us in positive ways with other human beings). Nowhere is the connection across biological, cognitive, and socioemotional processes more obvious than in two rapidly emerging fields:

- *developmental cognitive neuroscience,* which explores links between cognitive processes, development, and the brain (Bell & others, 2018; Lee, Hollarek, & Krabbendam, 2018; Park & Festini, 2018; Reyna & others, 2018)

- *developmental social neuroscience,* which examines connections between socioemotional processes, development, and the brain (Dahl & others, 2018; Steinberg & others, 2018; Suleiman & others, 2017; Sullivan & Wilson, 2018)

biological processes Changes in an individual's physical nature.

cognitive processes Changes in an individual's thought, intelligence, and language.

socioemotional processes Changes in an individual's relationships with other people, emotions, and personality.

In many instances, biological, cognitive, and socioemotional processes are bidirectional. For example, biological processes can influence cognitive processes and vice versa. For the most part, we will study the different processes of development (biological, cognitive, and socioemotional) in separate chapters, but the human being is an integrated individual with a mind and body that are interdependent. Thus, in many places throughout the book we will call attention to the connections between these processes.

Figure 3 Processes Involved in Developmental Changes
Biological, cognitive, and socioemotional processes interact as individuals develop.

Periods of Development

The interplay of biological, cognitive, and socioemotional processes (see Figure 3) over time gives rise to the developmental periods of the human life span. A developmental period is a time frame in a person's life that is characterized by certain features. The most widely used classification of developmental periods involves an eight-period sequence. For the purposes of organization and understanding, this book is structured according to these developmental periods.

The *prenatal period* is the time from conception to birth. It involves tremendous growth—from a single cell to a complete organism with a brain and behavioral capabilities—and takes place in approximately a nine-month period.

Infancy is the developmental period from birth to 18 or 24 months when humans are extremely dependent on adults. During this period, many psychological activities—language, symbolic thought, sensorimotor coordination, and social learning, for example—are just beginning.

Early childhood is the developmental period from the end of infancy to age 5 or 6. This period is sometimes called the "preschool years." During this time, young children learn to become more self-sufficient and to care for themselves. They also develop school readiness skills, such as the ability to follow instructions and identify letters, and they spend many hours playing with peers. First grade typically marks the end of early childhood.

Middle and late childhood is the developmental period from about 6 to 11 years of age, approximately corresponding to the elementary school years. During this period, children master the fundamental skills of reading, writing, and arithmetic. They are formally exposed to the world outside the family and to the prevailing culture. Achievement becomes a more central theme of the child's world, and self-control increases.

Adolescence encompasses the transition from childhood to early adulthood, entered at approximately 10 to 12 years of age and ending at 18 to 22 years of age. Adolescence begins with rapid physical changes—dramatic gains in height and weight, changes in body contour, and the development of sexual characteristics such as enlargement of the breasts, growth of pubic and facial hair, and deepening of the voice. At this point in development, the pursuit of independence and an identity are prominent themes. Thought is more logical, abstract, and idealistic. More time is spent outside the family.

Recently there has been increased interest in the transition between adolescence and adulthood, a transition that has been referred to as *emerging adulthood* (Arnett, 2016a, b). Emerging adulthood occurs approximately from 18 to 25 years of age and is a time of considerable exploration and experimentation, especially in the areas of identity, careers, and lifestyles.

Early adulthood is the developmental period that begins in the late teens or early twenties and lasts through the thirties. For young adults, this is a time for establishing personal and economic independence, becoming proficient in a career, and for many, selecting a mate, learning to live with that person in an intimate way, starting a family, and rearing children.

Middle adulthood is the developmental period from approximately 40 years of age to about 60. It is a time of expanding personal and social involvement and responsibility; of assisting the next generation in becoming competent, mature individuals; and of achieving and maintaining satisfaction in a career.

Late adulthood is the developmental period that begins in the sixties or seventies and lasts until death. It is a time of life review, retirement from the workforce, and adjustment to new social roles involving decreasing strength and health.

Late adulthood potentially lasts longer than any other period of development. Because the number of people in this age group has been increasing dramatically, life-span developmentalists have been paying more attention to differences within late adulthood (Bangerter & others, 2018; Orkaby & others, 2018). According to Paul Baltes and Jacqui Smith (2003), a major change takes place in older adults' lives as they become the "oldest-old," at about 85 years of age. The "young-old" (classified as 65 through 84 in this analysis) have substantial potential for physical and cognitive fitness, retain much of their cognitive capacity, and can develop strategies to cope with the gains and losses of aging. In contrast, the oldest-old (85 and older) show considerable loss in cognitive skills, experience increased chronic stress, and are more frail (Baltes & Smith, 2003). Nonetheless, considerable variation exists in how much of their capabilities the oldest-old retain (Mejia & others, 2017; Park & Festini, 2018; Ribeiro & Araujo, 2019; Robine, 2019; Salthouse, 2017).

Conceptions of Age

In our description of developmental periods, we attached an approximate age range to each period. But we also have noted that there are variations in the capabilities of individuals of the same age, and we have seen how age-related changes can be exaggerated. How important is age when we try to understand an individual?

According to some life-span experts, chronological age is not very relevant to understanding a person's psychological development (Hoyer & Roodin, 2009). Chronological age is the number of years that have elapsed since birth. But time is a crude index of experience, and it does not cause development. Chronological age, moreover, is not the only way of measuring age (MacDonald & Stawski, 2016). Just as there are different domains of development, there are different ways of thinking about age (Fernandez-Ballesteros, 2019).

Four Types of Age

Age has been conceptualized not just as chronological age but also as biological age, psychological age, and social age (Hoyer & Roodin, 2009). *Biological age* is a person's age in terms of biological health. Determining biological age involves knowing the functional capacities of a person's vital organs. One person's vital capacities may be better or worse than those of others of comparable chronological age. The younger the person's biological age, the longer the person is expected to live, regardless of chronological age. A recent study involving 17-year survival rates of 20- to 93-year-old Korean adults found that death rates were higher among individuals whose biological age was greater than their chronological age (Yoo & others, 2017).

(*Left*) Seventy-four year old Barbara Jordan participating in the long jump competition at a Senior Games in Maine; (*right*) A sedentary overweight middle-aged man. *Even though Barbara Jordan's chronological age is older, might her biological age be younger than the middle-aged man's?*
(*Left*) ©John Patriquin/Portland Press Herald/Getty Images; (*right*) ©Owaki-Kulla/Corbis/Getty Images

Psychological age is an individual's adaptive capacities compared with those of other individuals of the same chronological age. Thus, older adults who continue to learn, remain flexible, are motivated, think clearly, and have positive personality traits are engaging in more adaptive behaviors than their chronological age-mates who do not do these things (Bercovitz, Ngnoumen, & Langer, 2019; Fisher & others, 2017; Radoczy & others, 2018; Roberts & others, 2017; Thomas & others, 2018; Westrate & Gluck, 2017). And a recent study found that a higher level of conscientiousness was protective of cognitive functioning in older adults (Wilson & others, 2015).

Social age refers to connectedness with others and the social roles individuals adopt. Individuals who have better social relationships with others are happier and tend to live longer than individuals who are lonely (Antonucci & Webster, 2019; Moss & Wilson, 2018).

From a life-span perspective, an overall age profile of an individual involves not just chronological age but also biological age, psychological age, and social age. For example, a 70-year-old man (chronological age) might be in good physical health (biological age) but might be experiencing memory problems and having trouble coping with the demands placed on him by his wife's recent hospitalization (psychological age) and dealing with a lack of social support (social age).

Three Developmental Patterns of Aging

K. Warner Schaie (2016) recently described three developmental patterns that provide a portrait of how aging can involve individual variations:

- *Normal aging* characterizes most individuals, for whom psychological functioning often peaks in early middle age, remains relatively stable until the late fifties to early sixties, and then shows a modest decline through the early eighties. However, marked decline can occur as individuals near death.

- *Pathological aging* characterizes individuals who show greater than average decline as they age through the adult years. In early old age, they may have mild cognitive impairment, develop Alzheimer disease later on, or have a chronic disease that impairs their daily functioning.

- *Successful aging* characterizes individuals whose positive physical, cognitive, and socioemotional development is maintained longer, declining later in old age than is the case for most people.

For too long, only the declines that occur in late adulthood were highlighted, but recently there has been increased interest in the concept of successful aging (Benetos, 2019; Fernandez-Ballesteros & others, 2019; Alonzo & Molina, 2019; Tanaka, 2017; Tesch-Romer & Wahl, 2017).

Age and Happiness

Is there a best age to be? An increasing number of studies indicate that at least in the United States adults are happier as they age (Stone & others, 2010). Consider also a U.S. study of approximately 28,000 individuals from 18 to 88 that revealed happiness increased with age (Yang, 2008). For example, about 33 percent were very happy at 88 years of age compared with only about 24 percent in their late teens and early twenties. In a recent study of individuals from 22 to 93 years of age, older adults reported having more positive emotional experiences than did young adults (English & Carstensen, 2014).

Why might older people report being happier and more satisfied with their lives than younger people? Despite the increase in physical problems and losses older adults experience, they are more content with what they have in their lives, have better relationships with the people who matter to them, are less pressured to achieve, have more time for leisurely pursuits, and have many years of experience that may help them adapt to their circumstances with greater wisdom than younger adults do (Carstensen, 2015, 2016; Westrate & Gluck, 2017).

Not all studies, though, have found an increase in life satisfaction with age (Steptoe, Deaton, & Stone, 2015). Some studies indicate that the lowest levels of life satisfaction are in middle age, especially from 45 to 54 years of age (OECD, 2014). Other studies

Below are five statements that you may agree or disagree with. Using the 1–7 scale below, indicate your agreement with each item by placing the appropriate number on the line preceding that item. Please be open and honest in your responding.

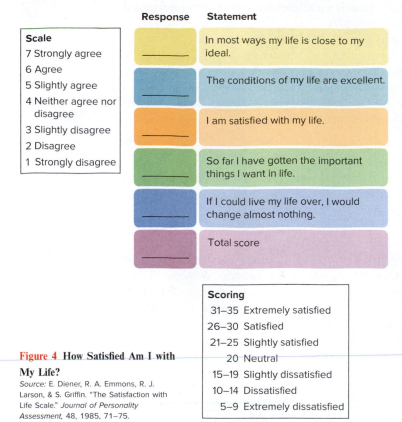

Response	Statement
_____	In most ways my life is close to my ideal.
_____	The conditions of my life are excellent.
_____	I am satisfied with my life.
_____	So far I have gotten the important things I want in life.
_____	If I could live my life over, I would change almost nothing.
_____	Total score

Scoring

31–35	Extremely satisfied
26–30	Satisfied
21–25	Slightly satisfied
20	Neutral
15–19	Slightly dissatisfied
10–14	Dissatisfied
5–9	Extremely dissatisfied

Figure 4 **How Satisfied Am I with My Life?**
Source: E. Diener, R. A. Emmons, R. J. Larson, & S. Griffin. "The Satisfaction with Life Scale." *Journal of Personality Assessment,* 48, 1985, 71–75.

have found that life satisfaction varies across some countries. For example, research with respondents from the former Soviet Union and Eastern Europe, as well as those from South American countries, report a decrease in life satisfaction with advancing age (Deaton, 2008). Further, older adults in poor health, such as those with cardiovascular disease, chronic lung disease, and depression, are less satisfied with their lives than are their healthier older adult counterparts (Wikman, Wardle, & Steptoe, 2011).

Now that you have read about age variations in life satisfaction, think about how satisfied you are with your life. To help you answer this question, complete the items in Figure 4, which presents the most widely used measure in research on life satisfaction (Diener, 2018).

Developmental Issues

Was Ted Kaczynski born a killer, or did the events in his life turn him into one? Kaczynski himself thought that his childhood was the root of his troubles. He said he grew up as a genius in a boy's body and never fit in with other children. Did his early experiences determine his later life? Is your own journey through life marked out ahead of time, or can your experiences change your path? Are the experiences you have early in your journey more important than later ones? Is your journey more like taking an elevator up a skyscraper with distinct stops along the way or more like a cruise down a river with smoother ebbs and flows? These questions point to three issues about the nature of development: the roles played by nature and nurture, stability and change, and continuity and discontinuity.

Nature and Nurture

The **nature-nurture issue** concerns the extent to which development is influenced by nature and by nurture. *Nature* refers to an organism's biological inheritance, *nurture* to its environmental experiences.

According to those who emphasize the role of nature, just as a sunflower grows in an orderly way—unless flattened by an unfriendly environment—so too a human grows in an orderly way. An evolutionary and genetic foundation produces commonalities in growth and development (Mader & Windelspecht, 2019; Starr, Evers, & Starr, 2018). We walk before we talk, speak one word before two words, grow rapidly in infancy and less so in early childhood, experience a rush of sex hormones in puberty, reach the peak

nature-nurture issue The debate about the extent to which development is influenced by nature and by nurture. Nature refers to an organism's biological inheritance, nurture to its environmental experiences.

What are some key developmental issues?
©Rubberball/ PictureQuest

of our physical strength in late adolescence and early adulthood, and then physically decline. Proponents of the importance of nature acknowledge that extreme environments—those≈that are psychologically barren or hostile—can depress development. However, they believe that basic growth tendencies are genetically programmed into humans (Hoefnagels, 2019; Johnson, 2017).

By contrast, other psychologists emphasize the importance of nurture, or environmental experiences, in development (Almy & Cicchetti, 2018; Chen, Lee, & Chen, 2018; Rubin & Barstead, 2018). Experiences run the gamut from the individual's biological environment (nutrition, exercise, medical care, drugs, and physical accidents) to the social environment (family, peers, schools, community, media, and culture) (Kansky, Ruzek, & Allen, 2018; Petersen & others, 2017).

Stability and Change

Is the shy child who hides behind the sofa when visitors arrive destined to become a wallflower at college dances, or might the child become a sociable, talkative individual? Is the fun-loving, carefree adolescent bound to have difficulty holding down a 9-to-5 job as an adult? These questions reflect the **stability-change issue,** involving the degree to which early traits and characteristics persist or change over time.

The roles of early and later experience are an aspect of the stability-change issue that has long been hotly debated (Almy & Cicchetti, 2018; Chatterjee & others, 2018). Some argue that warm, nurturant caregiving during infancy and toddlerhood predicts optimal development later in life (Cassidy, 2016). The later-experience advocates see children as malleable throughout development and believe later sensitive caregiving is just as important as earlier sensitive caregiving (De la Fuente, 2019; Fingerman & others, 2017; Joling & others, 2018; Sawyer & Patton, 2018; Taylor & others, 2018).

Developmentalists who emphasize change take the more optimistic view that later experiences can produce change. Recall that in the life-span perspective, plasticity, the potential for change, exists throughout the life span (Antonucci & Webster, 2019; Blieszner, 2018; Lovden, Backman, & Lindenberger, 2017; Oltmanns & others, 2017; Park & Festini, 2018). Experts such as Paul Baltes (2003) argue that older adults often show less capacity for learning new things than younger adults do. However, many older adults continue to be good at applying what they have learned in earlier times.

Continuity and Discontinuity

When developmental change occurs, is it gradual or abrupt? Think about your own development for a moment. Did you gradually become the person you are today? Or did you experience sudden, distinct changes in your growth? For the most part, developmentalists who emphasize nurture describe development as a gradual, continuous process. Those who emphasize nature often describe development as a series of distinct stages.

The **continuity-discontinuity issue** focuses on the degree to which development involves either gradual, cumulative change (continuity) or distinct stages (discontinuity). In terms of continuity, as the oak grows from a seedling to a giant tree, its development is continuous. Similarly, a child's first word, though seemingly an abrupt, discontinuous event, is actually the result of weeks and months of growth and practice. Puberty might seem abrupt, but it is a gradual process that occurs over several years.

In terms of discontinuity, as an insect grows from a caterpillar to a chrysalis to a butterfly, it passes through a sequence of stages in which change is qualitatively rather than quantitatively different. Similarly, at some point a child moves from not being able to think abstractly about the world to being able to do so. This is a qualitative, discontinuous change in development rather than a quantitative, continuous change.

stability-change issue The debate about the degree to which early traits and characteristics persist through life or change.

continuity-discontinuity issue The debate about the extent to which development involves gradual, cumulative change (continuity) or distinct stages (discontinuity).

Evaluating the Developmental Issues

Developmentalists generally acknowledge that development is not all nature or all nurture, not all stability or all change, and not all continuity or all discontinuity. Nature and nurture, stability and change, continuity and discontinuity characterize development throughout the life span (Kinugawa, 2019; Lindahl-Jacobsen & Christensen, 2019).

Although most developmentalists do not take extreme positions on these three important issues, there is spirited debate regarding how strongly development is influenced by each of these factors (Almy & Cicchetti, 2018; Antonnucci & Webster, 2019; Halldorsdottir & Binder, 2017; Kalat, 2019; Moore, 2017).

Theories of Development

How can we answer questions about the roles of nature and nurture, stability and change, and continuity and discontinuity in development? How can we determine, for example, whether memory loss in older adults can be prevented or whether special care can repair the harm inflicted by child neglect? The scientific method is the best tool we have to answer such questions (Smith & Davis, 2016).

The scientific method is essentially a four-step process: (1) conceptualize a process or problem to be studied, (2) collect research information (data), (3) analyze data, and (4) draw conclusions.

In step 1, when researchers are formulating a problem to study, they often draw on theories and develop hypotheses. A **theory** is an interrelated, coherent set of ideas that helps to explain phenomena and make predictions. It may suggest **hypotheses,** which are specific assertions and predictions that can be tested. For example, a theory on mentoring might state that sustained support and guidance from an adult makes a difference in the lives of children from impoverished backgrounds because the mentor gives the children opportunities to observe and imitate the behavior and strategies of the mentor.

This section outlines five theoretical orientations to development: psychoanalytic, cognitive, behavioral and social cognitive, ethological, and ecological. These theories look at development from different perspectives, and they disagree about certain aspects of development. But many of their ideas are complementary, and each contributes an important piece to the life-span development puzzle. Although the theories disagree about certain aspects of development, many of their ideas are complementary rather than contradictory. Together they let us see the total landscape of life-span development in all its richness.

Psychoanalytic Theories

Psychoanalytic theories describe development primarily in terms of unconscious (beyond awareness) processes that are heavily colored by emotion. Psychoanalytic theorists emphasize that behavior is merely a surface characteristic and that a true understanding of development requires analyzing the symbolic meanings of behavior and the deep inner workings of the mind. Psychoanalytic theorists also stress that early experiences with parents extensively shape development. These characteristics are highlighted in the main psychoanalytic theory, that of Sigmund Freud (1856–1939).

Freud's Theory

Freud was a pioneer in the treatment of psychological problems. Based on his belief that patients who talked about their problems could be restored to psychological health, Freud developed a technique called psychoanalysis. As he listened to, probed, and analyzed his patients, he became convinced that their problems were the result of experiences early in life. He thought that as children grow up, their focus of pleasure and sexual impulses shifts from the mouth to the anus and eventually to the genitals. Consequently, he determined, we pass through five stages of psychosexual development: oral, anal, phallic, latency, and genital (see Figure 5). Our adult personality, Freud (1917) claimed, is determined by the way we resolve conflicts between sources of pleasure at each stage and the demands of reality.

theory A coherent set of ideas that helps to explain data and to make predictions.

hypotheses Assertions or predictions, often derived from theories, that can be tested.

psychoanalytic theories Theories holding that development depends primarily on the unconscious mind and is heavily couched in emotion, that behavior is merely a surface characteristic, that it is important to analyze the symbolic meanings of behavior, and that early experiences are important in development.

Oral Stage	Anal Stage	Phallic Stage	Latency Stage	Genital Stage
Infant's pleasure centers on the mouth.	Child's pleasure focuses on the anus.	Child's pleasure focuses on the genitals.	Child represses sexual interest and develops social and intellectual skills.	A time of sexual reawakening; source of sexual pleasure becomes someone outside the family.
Birth to 1½ Years	1½ to 3 Years	3 to 6 Years	6 Years to Puberty	Puberty Onward

Figure 5 Freudian Stages
Because Freud emphasized sexual motivation, his stages of development are known as psychosexual stages. In his view, if the need for pleasure at any stage is either undergratified or overgratified, an individual may become fixated, or locked in, at that stage of development.

Freud's followers significantly revised his psychoanalytic theory. Many of today's psychoanalytic theorists believe that Freud overemphasized sexual instincts; they place more emphasis on cultural experiences as determinants of an individual's development. Unconscious thought remains a central theme, but conscious thought plays a greater role than Freud envisioned. Next, we will outline the ideas of an important revisionist of Freud's theory—Erik Erikson.

Erikson's Psychosocial Theory

Erik Erikson recognized Freud's contributions but believed that Freud misjudged some important dimensions of human development. For one thing, Erikson (1950, 1968) said we develop in psychosocial stages, rather than the psychosexual stages that Freud described. According to Freud, the primary motivation for human behavior is sexual in nature; according to Erikson, motivation is social and reflects a desire to affiliate with other people. According to Freud, our basic personality is shaped in the first five years of life; according to Erikson, developmental change occurs throughout the life span. Thus, Freud viewed early experiences as far more important than later experiences, whereas Erikson emphasized the importance of both early and later experiences.

In **Erikson's theory,** eight stages of development unfold as we go through life (see Figure 6). At each stage, a unique developmental task confronts individuals with a crisis that must be resolved. According to Erikson, this crisis is not a catastrophe but a turning point marked by both increased vulnerability and enhanced potential. The more successfully an individual resolves these crises, the healthier his or her development will be.

Trust versus mistrust is Erikson's first psychosocial stage, which is experienced in the first year of life. Trust during infancy sets the stage for a lifelong expectation that the world will be a good and pleasant place to live.

Autonomy versus shame and doubt is Erikson's second stage. This stage occurs in late infancy and toddlerhood (1 to 3 years). After gaining trust in their caregivers, infants begin to discover that their behavior is their own. They start to assert their sense of independence or autonomy. They realize their will. If infants and toddlers are restrained too much or punished too harshly, they are likely to develop a sense of shame and doubt.

Initiative versus guilt, Erikson's third stage of development, occurs during the preschool years. As preschool children encounter a widening social world, they face new challenges that require active, purposeful,

Erik Erikson with his wife, Joan, an artist. Erikson generated one of the most important developmental theories of the twentieth century. *Which stage of Erikson's theory are you in? Does Erikson's description of this stage characterize you?*
©Jon Erikson/The Image Works

Erikson's theory A psychoanalytic theory in which eight stages of psychosocial development unfold throughout the life span. Each stage consists of a unique developmental task that confronts individuals with a crisis that must be faced.

responsible behavior. Feelings of guilt may arise, though, if the child is irresponsible and is made to feel too anxious.

Industry versus inferiority is Erikson's fourth developmental stage, occurring approximately in the elementary school years. Children now need to direct their energy toward mastering knowledge and intellectual skills. The negative outcome is that the child may develop a sense of inferiority—feeling incompetent and unproductive.

During the adolescent years individuals face finding out who they are, what they are all about, and where they are going in life. This is Erikson's fifth developmental stage, *identity versus identity confusion.* If adolescents explore roles in a healthy manner and arrive at a positive path to follow in life, then they achieve a positive identity; if not, then identity confusion reigns.

Intimacy versus isolation is Erikson's sixth developmental stage, which individuals experience during early adulthood. At this time, individuals face the developmental task of forming intimate relationships. If young adults form healthy friendships and an intimate relationship with a partner, intimacy will be achieved; if not, isolation will result.

Generativity versus stagnation, Erikson's seventh developmental stage, occurs during middle adulthood. By generativity, Erikson means primarily a concern for helping the younger generation to develop and lead useful lives. The feeling of having done nothing to help the next generation is stagnation.

Integrity versus despair is Erikson's eighth and final stage of development, which individuals experience in late adulthood. During this stage, a person reflects on the past. If the person's life review reveals a life well spent, integrity will be achieved; if not, the retrospective glances likely will yield doubt or gloom—the despair Erikson described.

Evaluating Psychoanalytic Theories

Contributions of psychoanalytic theories like Freud's and Erikson's to life-span development include an emphasis on a developmental framework, family relationships, and unconscious aspects of the mind. These theories have been criticized for a lack of scientific support, too much emphasis on sexual underpinnings, and an image of people that is too negative.

Cognitive Theories

Whereas psychoanalytic theories stress the unconscious, cognitive theories emphasize conscious thoughts. Three important cognitive theories are Piaget's cognitive developmental theory, Vygotsky's sociocultural cognitive theory, and information-processing theory. All three focus on the development of complex thinking skills.

Piaget's Cognitive Developmental Theory

Piaget's theory states that children go through four stages of cognitive development as they actively construct their understanding of the world. Two processes underlie this cognitive construction of the world: organization and adaptation. To make sense of our world, we organize our experiences. For example, we separate important ideas from less important ideas, and we connect one idea to another. In addition to organizing our observations and experiences, we must adjust to changing environmental demands (Miller, 2015).

Piaget's theory The theory that children construct their understanding of the world and go through four stages of cognitive development.

Erikson's Stages	Developmental Period
Integrity versus despair	Late adulthood (60s onward)
Generativity versus stagnation	Middle adulthood (40s, 50s)
Intimacy versus isolation	Early adulthood (20s, 30s)
Identity versus identity confusion	Adolescence (10 to 20 years)
Industry versus inferiority	Middle and late childhood (elementary school years, 6 years to puberty)
Initiative versus guilt	Early childhood (preschool years, 3 to 5 years)
Autonomy versus shame and doubt	Infancy (1 to 3 years)
Trust versus mistrust	Infancy (first year)

Figure 6 Erikson's Eight Life-Span Stages Like Freud, Erikson proposed that individuals go through distinct, universal stages of development. In terms of the continuity-discontinuity issue, both favor the discontinuity side of the debate. Notice that the timing of Erikson's first four stages is similar to that of Freud's stages. *What are the implications of saying that people go through stages of development?*

Sensorimotor Stage	Preoperational Stage	Concrete Operational Stage	Formal Operational Stage
The infant constructs an understanding of the world by coordinating sensory experiences with physical actions. An infant progresses from reflexive, instinctual action at birth to the beginning of symbolic thought toward the end of the stage.	The child begins to represent the world with words and images. These words and images reflect increased symbolic thinking and go beyond the connection of sensory information and physical action.	The child can now reason logically about concrete events and classify objects into different sets.	The adolescent reasons in more abstract, idealistic, and logical ways.
Birth to 2 Years of Age	**2 to 7 Years of Age**	**7 to 11 Years of Age**	**11 Years of Age Through Adulthood**

Figure 7 Piaget's Four Stages of Cognitive Development
According to Piaget, how a child thinks—not how much the child knows—determines the child's stage of cognitive development.
Left to right ©Stockbyte/Getty Images; ©BananaStock/PunchStock; ©image100/Corbis; ©Purestock/Getty Images

Piaget (1954) described four stages in understanding the world (see Figure 7). Each stage is age-related and consists of a distinct way of thinking, a different way of understanding the world. Thus, according to Piaget, the child's cognition is *qualitatively* different in one stage compared with another. What are Piaget's four stages of cognitive development?

The *sensorimotor stage,* which lasts from birth to about 2 years of age, is the first Piagetian stage. In this stage, infants construct an understanding of the world by coordinating sensory experiences (such as seeing and hearing) with physical, motor actions—hence the term *sensorimotor.*

The *preoperational stage,* which lasts from approximately 2 to 7 years of age, is Piaget's second stage. In this stage, children begin to go beyond simply connecting sensory information with physical action and are now able to represent the world with words, images, and drawings. However, according to Piaget, preschool children still lack the ability to perform what he calls *operations,* which are internalized mental actions that allow children to do mentally what they previously could only do physically. For example, if you imagine putting two sticks together to see whether they would be as long as another stick, without actually moving the sticks, you are performing a concrete operation.

The *concrete operational stage,* which lasts from approximately 7 to 11 years of age, is the third Piagetian stage. In this stage, children can perform operations that involve objects, and they can reason logically about specific or concrete examples. Concrete operational thinkers, however, cannot imagine the steps necessary to complete an algebraic equation because doing so would require a level of thinking that is too abstract for this stage of development.

The *formal operational stage,* which appears between the ages of 11 and 15 and continues through adulthood, is Piaget's fourth and final stage. In this stage, individuals move beyond concrete experiences and think in abstract and more logical terms. As part of thinking more abstractly, adolescents develop images of ideal circumstances. They might think about what an ideal

Jean Piaget, the famous Swiss developmental psychologist, changed the way we think about the development of children's minds. *What are some key ideas in Piaget's theory?*
©Yves DeBraine/BlackStar/Stock Photo

parent is like and compare their parents to this ideal standard. They begin to entertain possibilities for the future and are fascinated with what they can become. In solving problems, they become more systematic, developing hypotheses about why something is happening the way it is and then testing these hypotheses. We will examine Piaget's cognitive developmental theory further in other chapters.

Vygotsky's Sociocultural Cognitive Theory

Like Piaget, the Russian developmentalist Lev Vygotsky (1896–1934) reasoned that children actively construct their knowledge. However, Vygotsky (1962) gave social interaction and culture far more important roles in cognitive development than Piaget did.

Vygotsky's theory is a sociocultural cognitive theory that emphasizes how culture and social interaction guide cognitive development. Vygotsky portrayed the child's development as inseparable from social and cultural activities (Daniels, 2017). He stressed that cognitive development involves learning to use the inventions of society, such as language, mathematical systems, and memory strategies. Thus, in one culture children might learn to count with the help of a computer; in another they might learn by using beads. According to Vygotsky, children's social interaction with more-skilled adults and peers is indispensable to their cognitive development (Holzman, 2017). Through this interaction, they learn to use the tools that will help them adapt and be successful in their culture. Later we will examine ideas about learning and teaching that are based on Vygotsky's theory.

Lev Vygotsky was born the same year as Piaget, but he died much earlier, at the age of 37. There is considerable interest today in Vygotsky's sociocultural cognitive theory of child development. *What are some key characteristics of Vygotsky's theory?*
©A.R. Lauria / Dr. Michael Cole, Laboratory of Human Cognition, University of California, San Diego

Information-Processing Theory

Information-processing theory emphasizes that individuals manipulate information, monitor it, and strategize about it. Unlike Piaget's theory but like Vygotsky's theory, information-processing theory does not describe development as stage-like. Instead, according to this theory individuals develop a gradually increasing capacity for processing information, which allows them to acquire increasingly complex knowledge and skills (Chevalier, Dauvier, & Blaye, 2018; Goldstein, 2019).

Robert Siegler (2006, 2017), a leading expert on children's information processing, states that thinking is information processing. In other words, when individuals perceive, encode, represent, store, and retrieve information, they are thinking. Siegler and his colleagues (Braithwaite & Siegler, 2018a, b; Siegler & Braithwaite, 2017; Siegler & Lortie-Forgues, 2017) emphasize that an important aspect of development is learning good strategies for processing information. For example, becoming a better reader might involve learning to monitor the key themes of the material being read.

Siegler (2006, 2017) also argues that the best way to understand how children learn is to observe them while they are learning. He emphasizes the importance of using the *microgenetic method* to obtain detailed information about processing mechanisms as they are occurring moment to moment. Siegler concludes that most research methods indirectly assess cognitive change, being more like snapshots than movies. The microgenetic method seeks to discover not just what children know but the cognitive processes involved in how they acquired the knowledge (Miller, 2015). A number of microgenetic studies have focused on a specific aspect of academic learning, such as how children learn whole number arithmetic, fractions, and other areas of math (Braithwaite & Siegler, 2018a, b; Siegler & Braithwaite, 2017; Siegler & Lortie-Forgues, 2017).

The information processing approach often uses the computer as an analogy to help explain the connection between cognition and the brain

Vygotsky's theory A sociocultural cognitive theory that emphasizes how culture and social interaction guide cognitive development.

information-processing theory A theory emphasizing that individuals manipulate information, monitor it, and strategize about it. The processes of memory and thinking are central.

Figure 8 Comparing the Information Processing of Humans and Computers
Psychologists who study cognition often use a computer analogy to explain how humans process information. The brain is analogous to the computer's hardware and cognition is analogous to the computer's software.
©Creatas/PictureQuest

(Radvansky & Ashcraft, 2018) (see Figure 8). The physical brain is described as the computer's hardware, and cognition as its software. In this analogy, the sensory and perceptual systems provide an "input channel," similar to the way data are entered into the computer. As input (information) comes into the mind, mental processes, or operations, act on it, just as the computer's software acts on the data. The transformed input generates information that remains in memory much in the way a computer stores what it has worked on. Finally, the information is retrieved from memory and "printed out" or "displayed" (so to speak) as an observable response.

Computers provide a logical and concrete, but oversimplified, model of the mind's processing of information. Inanimate computers and human brains function quite differently in some respects. For example, most computers receive information from a human who has already coded the information and removed much of its ambiguity. In contrast, each brain cell, or neuron, can respond to ambiguous information transmitted through sensory receptors such as the eyes and ears.

Computers can do some things better than humans. For instance, computers can perform complex numerical calculations much faster and more accurately than humans could ever hope to. Computers can also apply and follow rules more consistently and with fewer errors than humans and can represent complex mathematical patterns better than humans.

Still, the brain's extraordinary capabilities will probably not be mimicked completely by computers at any time in the near future (Sternberg, 2017). For example, although a computer can improve its ability to recognize patterns or use rules of thumb to make decisions, it does not have the means to develop new learning goals. Furthermore, the human mind is aware of itself; the computer is not. Indeed, no computer is likely to approach the richness of human consciousness.

Nonetheless, the computer's role in cognitive and developmental psychology continues to increase. An entire scientific field called *artificial intelligence (AI)* focuses on creating machines capable of performing activities that require intelligence when they are done by people. And a new field titled *developmental robotics* is emerging that examines various developmental topics and issues using robots, such as motor development, perceptual development, information processing, and language development (Faghihi & Moustafa, 2017; Morse & Cangelosi, 2017). The hope is to build robots that are as much like humans as possible and in doing so to better understand how humans think and develop (Vujovic & others, 2017; Wu & others, 2017).

Evaluating Cognitive Theories

Contributions of cognitive theories include a positive view of development and an emphasis on the active construction of understanding. Criticisms include skepticism about the pureness of Piaget's stages and a belief that too little attention is paid to individual variations.

Above is the humanoid robot iCub created by the Italian Institute of Technology to study such aspects of children's development as perception, cognition, and motor development. In this situation, the robot, the size of a 3.5 year old child, is catching a ball. This robot is being used by more than 20 laboratories worldwide and has 53 motors that move the head, arms and hands, waist, and legs. It also can see and hear, as well as having the sense of proprioception (body configuration) and movement (using gyroscopes).
©Marco Destefanis/Pacific Press/Sipa/Newscom

Behavioral and Social Cognitive Theories

Behavioral and social cognitive theories hold that development can be described in terms of behaviors learned through interactions with our surroundings. Behaviorism essentially holds that we can study scientifically only what can be directly observed and measured. Out of the behavioral tradition grew the belief that development is observable behavior that can be learned through experience with the environment (Maag, 2018). In terms of the continuity-discontinuity issue discussed earlier in this chapter, the behavioral and social cognitive theories emphasize continuity in development and argue that development does not occur in stage-like fashion. Let's explore two versions of behaviorism: Skinner's operant conditioning and Bandura's social cognitive theory.

Skinner's Operant Conditioning

According to B. F. Skinner (1904–1990), through *operant conditioning* the consequences of a behavior produce changes in the probability of the behavior's recurrence. A behavior followed by a rewarding stimulus is more likely to recur, whereas a behavior followed by a punishing stimulus is less likely to recur. For example, when an adult smiles at a child after the child has done something, the child is more likely to engage in that behavior again than if the adult gives the child a disapproving look.

In Skinner's (1938) view, such rewards and punishments shape development. For Skinner the key aspect of development is behavior, not thoughts and feelings. He emphasized that development consists of the pattern of behavioral changes that are brought about by rewards and punishments. For example, Skinner would say that shy people learned to be shy as a result of experiences they had while growing up. It follows that modifications to an environment can help a shy person become more socially oriented.

Bandura's Social Cognitive Theory

Some psychologists agree with the behaviorists' notion that development is learned and is influenced strongly by environmental interactions. However, unlike Skinner, they also see cognition as important in understanding development. **Social cognitive theory** holds that behavior, environment, and person/cognitive factors are the key factors in development.

American psychologist Albert Bandura (born in 1925) is the leading architect of social cognitive theory. Bandura (1986, 2004, 2010a, b, 2012, 2015) emphasizes that cognitive processes have important links with the environment and behavior. His early research program focused heavily on *observational learning* (also called *imitation* or *modeling*), which is learning

behavioral and social cognitive theories Theories holding that development can be described in terms of the behaviors learned through interactions with the environment.

social cognitive theory The theory that behavior, environment, and person/cognitive factors are important in understanding development.

Albert Bandura is one of the leading architects of social cognitive theory. *How does Bandura's theory differ from Skinner's?*
©Dr. Albert Bandura

that occurs through observing what others do. For example, a young boy might observe his father yelling in anger and treating other people with hostility; and then later with his peers, the young boy acts very aggressively, showing the same behavioral characteristics as his father. Social cognitive theorists stress that people acquire a wide range of behaviors, thoughts, and feelings through observing others' behavior and that these observations form an important part of life-span development.

What is *cognitive* about observational learning in Bandura's view? He proposes that people cognitively represent the behavior of others and then sometimes adopt this behavior themselves.

Bandura's (2004, 2010a, b, 2012, 2015) most recent model of learning and development includes three elements: behavior, the person/cognition, and the environment. An individual's confidence in being able to control his or her success is an example of a person factor; strategies for achieving success are an example of a cognitive factor. As shown in Figure 9, influences from behavior, person/cognition, and environment operate interactively.

Figure 9 Bandura's Social Cognitive Model
The arrows illustrate how relations between behavior, person/cognition, and environment are reciprocal rather than one-way. Person/cognition refers to cognitive processes (for example, thinking and planning) and personal characteristics (for example, believing that you can control your experiences).

Evaluating Behavioral and Social Cognitive Theories

Contributions of the behavioral and social cognitive theories include an emphasis on scientific research and environmental determinants of behavior. These theories have been criticized for placing too little emphasis on cognition (Skinner) and giving inadequate attention to developmental changes.

Ethological Theory

Ethology is the study of the behavior of animals in their natural habitat. Ethological theory stresses that behavior is strongly influenced by biology, is tied to evolution, and is characterized by critical or sensitive periods (Bateson, 2015). These are specific time frames during which, according to ethologists, the presence or absence of certain experiences has a long-lasting influence on individuals.

Lorenz's Research with Greylag Geese

European zoologist Konrad Lorenz (1903–1989) helped bring ethology to prominence. In his best-known research, Lorenz (1965) studied the behavior of greylag geese, which follow their mother as soon as they

ethology An approach stressing that behavior is strongly influenced by biology, tied to evolution, and characterized by critical or sensitive periods.

Konrad Lorenz, a pioneering student of animal behavior, is followed through the water by three imprinted greylag geese. Describe Lorenz's experiment with the geese. *Do you think his experiment would have the same results with human babies? Explain.*
©Nina Leen/Time & Life Pictures/Getty Images

hatch. Lorenz separated the eggs laid by one goose into two groups. One group he returned to the goose to be hatched by her. The other group was hatched in an incubator. The goslings in the first group performed as predicted. They followed their mother as soon as they hatched. However, those in the second group, which saw Lorenz when they first hatched, followed him everywhere as though he were their mother. Lorenz marked the goslings and then placed both groups under a box. Mother goose and "mother" Lorenz stood aside as the box was lifted. Each group of goslings went directly to its "mother." Lorenz called this process *imprinting*—the rapid, innate learning that involves attachment to the first moving object seen.

John Bowlby (1969, 1989) illustrated an important application of ethological theory to human development. Bowlby stressed that attachment to a caregiver over the first year of life has important consequences throughout the life span. In his view, if this attachment is positive and secure, the individual will likely develop positively in childhood and adulthood. If the attachment is negative and insecure, development will likely not be optimal. Later we will explore the concept of infant attachment in much greater detail.

In Lorenz's view, imprinting needs to take place at a specific, very early time in the life of the animal, or else it will not take place. This point in time is called a critical period. A related concept is that of a sensitive period, and an example is the time during infancy when, according to Bowlby, attachment should occur in order to promote optimal development of social relationships.

Another theory that emphasizes biological foundations of development—evolutionary psychology—is presented in the chapter on "Biological Beginnings," along with views on the role of heredity in development (Bjorklund, 2018; Lewis & others, 2017; Lickliter, 2018). In addition, we examine a number of biological theories of aging in the chapter on "Physical and Cognitive Development in Late Adulthood" (Falandry, 2019; Jabeen & others, 2018; Jeremic & others, 2018; Kauppila, Kauppila, & Larsson, 2017; Toupance & Benetos, 2019).

Evaluating Ethological Theory

Contributions of ethological theory include a focus on the biological and evolutionary basis of development, and the use of careful observations in naturalistic settings. Criticisms include a belief that it places too much emphasis on biological foundations and that the concept of a critical and sensitive period might be too rigid.

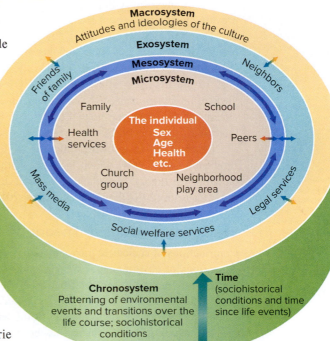

Ecological Theory

While ethological theory stresses biological factors, ecological theory emphasizes environmental factors. One ecological theory that has important implications for understanding life-span development was created by Urie Bronfenbrenner (1917–2005).

Bronfenbrenner's Ecological Theory

Bronfenbrenner's ecological theory (1986, 2004; Bronfenbrenner & Morris, 2006) holds that development reflects the influence of several environmental systems. The theory identifies five environmental systems: microsystem, mesosystem, exosystem, macrosystem, and chronosystem (see Figure 10).

Figure 10 **Bronfenbrenner's Ecological Theory of Development** Bronfenbrenner's ecological theory consists of five environmental systems: microsystem, mesosystem, exosystem, macrosystem, and chronosystem.

How Would You...?

As an **educator,** how might you explain a student's chronic failure to complete homework from the mesosystem level? From the exosystem level?

The *microsystem* is the setting in which the individual lives. These contexts include the person's family, peers, school, and neighborhood. It is in the microsystem that the most direct interactions with social agents take place—with parents, peers, and teachers, for example. The individual is not a passive recipient of experiences in these settings, but someone who helps to construct the settings.

The *mesosystem* involves relations between microsystems or connections between contexts. Examples are the relation of family experiences to school experiences, school experiences to church experiences, and family experiences to peer experiences. For example, children whose parents have rejected them may have difficulty developing positive relations with teachers.

The *exosystem* consists of links between a social setting in which the individual does not have an active role and the individual's immediate context. For example, a husband's or child's experience at home may be influenced by a mother's experiences at work. The mother might receive a promotion that requires more travel, which might increase conflict with the husband and change patterns of interaction with the child.

The *macrosystem* involves the culture in which individuals live. Remember from earlier in the chapter that *culture* refers to the behavior patterns, beliefs, and all other products of a group of people that are passed on from generation to generation. Remember also that cross-cultural studies—the comparison of one culture with one or more other cultures—provide information about the generality of development.

Urie Bronfenbrenner developed ecological theory, a perspective that is receiving increased attention today. His theory emphasizes the importance of both micro and macro dimensions of the environment in which the child lives.
©Cornell University

The *chronosystem* consists of the patterning of environmental events and transitions over the life course, as well as sociohistorical circumstances. For example, divorce is one transition. Researchers have found that the negative effects of divorce on children often peak in the first year after the divorce (Hetherington, 2006). By two years after the divorce, family interaction has become more stable. As an example of sociohistorical circumstances, consider how the opportunities for women to pursue a career have increased since the 1960s.

Responding to growing interest in biological contributions to development, Bronfenbrenner (2004) added biological influences to his theory and relabeled it as a bioecological theory. Nonetheless, it is still dominated by ecological, environmental contexts (Gauvain, 2016; Golinkoff & others, 2017).

Evaluating Ecological Theory

Contributions of ecological theory include its systematic examination of macro and micro dimensions of environmental systems and its attention to connections between environmental systems. A further contribution of Bronfenbrenner's theory is its emphasis on a range of social contexts beyond the family, such as peer relations, neighborhood, religious, school, and workplace environments, as influential in children's and adolescents' development (Cross, 2017). The theory has been criticized for giving inadequate attention to biological factors, as well as placing too little emphasis on cognitive factors.

An Eclectic Theoretical Orientation

No single theory described in this chapter can explain entirely the rich complexity of life-span development, but each has contributed to our understanding of development. Psychoanalytic theory highlights the importance of the unconscious mind. Erikson's theory best describes the changes that occur in adult development. Piaget's, Vygotsky's, and the

THEORY	ISSUES	
	Continuity/discontinuity, early versus later experiences	Biological and environmental factors
Psychoanalytic	Discontinuity between stages—continuity between early experiences and later development; early experiences very important; later changes in development emphasized in Erikson's theory	Freud's biological determination interacting with early family experiences; Erikson's more balanced biological-cultural interaction perspective
Cognitive	Discontinuity between stages in Piaget's theory; continuity between early experiences and later development in Piaget's and Vygotsky's theories; no stages in Vygotsky's theory or information-processing theory	Piaget's emphasis on interaction and adaptation; environment provides the setting for cognitive structures to develop; information-processing view has not addressed this issue extensively but mainly emphasizes biological-environmental interaction
Behavioral and social cognitive	Continuity (no stages); experience at all points of development important	Environment viewed as the cause of behavior in both views
Ethological	Discontinuity but no stages; critical or sensitive periods emphasized; early experiences very important	Strong biological view
Ecological	Little attention to continuity/discontinuity; change emphasized more than stability	Strong environmental view

Figure 11 Summary of Theories and Issues in Life-Span Development

information-processing views provide the most complete description of cognitive development. The behavioral and social cognitive and ecological theories have been the most adept at examining the environmental determinants of development. The ethological theories have drawn attention to biology's role and the importance of sensitive periods in development.

In short, although theories are helpful guides, relying on a single theory to explain development is probably a mistake. Instead, we will take an **eclectic theoretical orientation,** which does not follow any one theoretical approach but rather presents what are considered the best features of each theory. In this way, it represents the study of development as it actually exists—with different theorists making different assumptions, stressing different problems, and using different strategies to discover information. Figure 11 compares the main theoretical perspectives in terms of how they view important issues in life-span development.

Research in Life-Span Development

How do scholars and researchers with an eclectic orientation determine that one theory is somehow better than a different theory? The scientific method discussed earlier in this chapter provides a guide. Through scientific research, theories are tested and refined (Gravetter & Forzano, 2019; Smetana, 2018; Stanovich, 2019).

Generally, research in life-span development is designed to test hypotheses, which may be derived from the theories just described. Through research, theories are modified to reflect new data, and occasionally new theories arise. How are data about life-span development collected? What types of research designs are used to study life-span development? And what are some ethical considerations in conducting research on life-span development?

Methods for Collecting Data

Whether we are interested in studying attachment in infants, the cognitive skills of children, or social relationships in older adults, we can choose from several ways of collecting data (Salkind, 2017). Here we outline the measures most often used, beginning with observation.

eclectic theoretical orientation An approach that selects and uses whatever is considered the best in many theories.

Observation

Scientific observation requires an important set of skills (Stanovich, 2019). For observations to be effective, they must be systematic. We need to have some idea of what we are looking for. We have to know whom we are observing, when and where we will observe, how the observations will be made, and how they will be recorded.

Where should we make our observations? We have two choices: the laboratory and the everyday world.

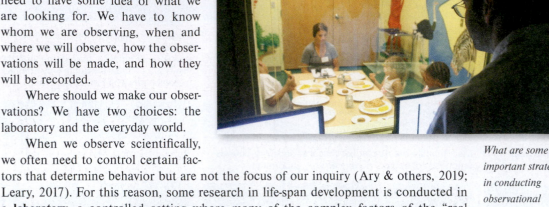

What are some important strategies in conducting observational research with children?
©Charles Fox/
Philadelphia Inquirer/
MCT/Landov

When we observe scientifically, we often need to control certain factors that determine behavior but are not the focus of our inquiry (Ary & others, 2019; Leary, 2017). For this reason, some research in life-span development is conducted in a **laboratory,** a controlled setting where many of the complex factors of the "real world" are absent. For example, suppose you want to observe how children react when they see other people behaving aggressively. If you observe children in their homes or schools, you have no control over how much aggression the children observe, what kind of aggression they see, which people they see acting aggressively, or how other people treat the children. In contrast, if you observe the children in a laboratory, you can control these and other factors and therefore have more confidence about how to interpret your observations.

Laboratory research does have some drawbacks, however, including the following concerns: (1) it is almost impossible to conduct research without the participants' knowing they are being studied; (2) the laboratory setting is unnatural and therefore can cause the participants to behave unnaturally; (3) people who are willing to come to a university laboratory may not fairly represent groups from diverse cultural backgrounds; (4) people who are unfamiliar with university settings, and with the idea of "helping science," may be intimidated by the laboratory setting.

Naturalistic observation provides insights that we sometimes cannot attain in the laboratory (Babbie, 2017). **Naturalistic observation** means observing behavior in real-world settings and making no effort to manipulate or control the situation. Life-span researchers conduct naturalistic observations at sporting events, child-care centers, work settings, malls, and other places people live in and frequent.

Naturalistic observation was used in one study that focused on conversations in a children's science museum (Crowley & others, 2001). When visiting exhibits at the museum with their children, parents were more than three times as likely to engage boys than girls in explanatory talk. The gender difference occurred regardless of whether the father, the mother, or both parents were with the child, although the gender difference was greatest for fathers' science explanations to sons and daughters. This finding suggests a gender bias that encourages boys more than girls to be interested in science.

Survey and Interview

Sometimes the best and quickest way to get information about people is to ask them for it. One technique is to interview them directly. A related method is administering a survey (sometimes referred to as a questionnaire) consisting of a standard set of questions designed to obtain people's self-reported attitudes or beliefs about a particular topic. Surveys are especially useful when information from many people is needed (Ary & others, 2019; Henslin, 2017). In a good survey, the questions are clear and unbiased, allowing respondents to answer unambiguously.

laboratory A controlled setting in which research can take place.

naturalistic observation Observation that occurs in a real-world setting without any attempt to manipulate the situation.

Surveys and interviews can be used to study topics ranging from religious beliefs to sexual habits to attitudes about gun control to beliefs about how to improve schools. Surveys and interviews may be conducted in person, over the telephone, by mail, and over the Internet.

One problem with surveys and interviews is the tendency of participants to answer questions in a way that they think is socially acceptable or desirable rather than to say what they truly think or feel. For example, on a survey or in an interview some individuals might say that they do not take drugs even though they do.

Standardized Test

A **standardized test** has uniform procedures for administration and scoring. Many standardized tests allow performance comparisons; they provide information about individual differences among people (Kaplan & Saccuzzo, 2018). One example is the Stanford-Binet intelligence test, which is discussed in detail later. Your score on the Stanford-Binet test tells you how your performance compares with that of thousands of other people who have taken the test.

One criticism of standardized tests is that they assume a person's behavior is consistent and stable, yet personality and intelligence—two primary targets of standardized testing—can vary with the situation. For example, a person may perform poorly on a standardized intelligence test in an office setting but score much higher at home, where he or she is less anxious.

Case Study

A **case study** is an in-depth look at a single individual. Case studies are performed mainly by mental health professionals when, for either practical or ethical reasons, the unique aspects of an individual's life cannot be duplicated and tested in other individuals. A case study provides information about one person's experiences; it may focus on nearly any aspect of the subject's life that helps the researcher understand the person's mind, behavior, or other attributes. A researcher may gather information for a case study from interviews and medical records. In later chapters we discuss vivid case studies, such as that of Michael Rehbein, who had much of the left side of his brain removed at 7 years of age to end severe epileptic seizures.

A case study can provide a dramatic, in-depth portrayal of an individual's life, but we must be cautious when generalizing from this information. The subject of a case study is unique, with a genetic makeup and personal history that no one else shares. In addition, case studies involve judgments of unknown reliability. Researchers who conduct case studies rarely check to see whether other professionals agree with their observations or findings.

Physiological Measures

Researchers are increasingly using physiological measures when they study development at different points in the life span (Bell & others, 2018; Freberg, 2019; Suleiman & others, 2017; Steinberg & others, 2018). A physiological measure that is increasingly being used is neuroimaging, especially *functional magnetic resonance imaging* (fMRI), in which electromagnetic waves are used to construct images of a person's brain tissue and biochemical activity (Miller & others, 2018; Park & Festini, 2018; Sullivan & Wilson, 2018). Heart rate has been used as an

Mahatma Gandhi was the spiritual leader of India in the mid-twentieth century. Erik Erikson conducted an extensive case study of Gandhi's life to determine what contributed to his identity development. What are some limitations of the case study approach?
©Bettmann/Getty Images

standardized test A test that is given with uniform procedures for administration and scoring.

case study An in-depth examination of an individual.

indicator of infants' and children's development of perception, attention, and memory (Billeci & others, 2018). Further, heart rate has been used as an index of different aspects of emotional development, such as stress, anxiety, and depression (Amole & others, 2017).

Cortisol is a hormone produced by the adrenal gland that is linked to the body's stress level and has been measured in studies of temperament, emotional reactivity, mood, peer relations, and child psychopathology (Bangerter & others, 2018; Jacoby & others, 2016). As puberty unfolds, the blood levels of certain hormones increase. To determine the nature of these hormonal changes, researchers analyze blood samples from adolescent volunteers (Ji & others, 2016).

Sophisticated eye-tracking equipment is now being used to provide more detailed information about infants' perception (Boardman & Fletcher-Watson, 2017; van Renswoude & others, 2018), attention (Meng, Uto, & Hashiya, 2017), face processing (Chhaya & others, 2018), autism (Falck-Ytter & others, 2018; Finke, Wilkinson, & Hickerson, 2017), and preterm birth effects on language development (Loi & others, 2017).

Yet another dramatic change in physiological methods is the advancement in methods to assess the actual units of hereditary information—genes—in studies of biological influences on development (Falandry, 2019; Lai & others, 2017; Toupance & Benetos, 2019; Xing & others, 2018). For example, in the chapter on physical and cognitive development in late adulthood you will read about the role of the ApoE4 gene in Alzheimer disease (Parcon & others, 2018; Park & Festini, 2018).

Research Designs

In addition to a method for collecting data, you also need a research design to study life-span development. There are three main types of research designs: descriptive, correlational, and experimental.

Descriptive Research

All of the data-collection methods that we have discussed can be used in **descriptive research,** which aims to observe and record behavior. For example, a researcher might observe the extent to which people are altruistic or aggressive toward each other. By itself, descriptive research cannot prove what causes some phenomenon, but it can reveal important information about people's behavior and provide a basis for more scientific studies (Ary & others, 2019; Gravetter & Forzano, 2019).

Correlational Research

In contrast with descriptive research, correlational research goes beyond describing phenomena by providing information that helps to predict how people will behave. In **correlational research,** the goal is to describe the strength of the relationship between two or more events or characteristics. The more strongly the two events are correlated (or related or associated), the more effectively we can predict one event from the other (Aron, Coups, & Aron, 2019).

For example, to determine whether children of permissive parents have less self-control than other children, you would need to carefully record observations of parents' permissiveness and their children's self-control. You might observe that the higher a parent was in permissiveness, the lower the child was in self-control. You would then analyze these data statistically to yield a **correlation coefficient,** a number based on a statistical analysis that is used to describe the degree of association between two variables. Correlation coefficients range from −1.00 to +1.00. A negative number means an inverse relation. In the above example, you might find an inverse correlation between permissive parenting and children's self-control, with a coefficient of, say, −.30 meaning that parents who are permissive with their children are likely to have children who have low self-control. By contrast, you might find a positive

descriptive research Type of research that aims to observe and record behavior.

correlational research A type of research that focuses on describing the strength of the relation between two or more events or characteristics.

correlation coefficient A number based on statistical analysis that is used to describe the degree of association between two variables.

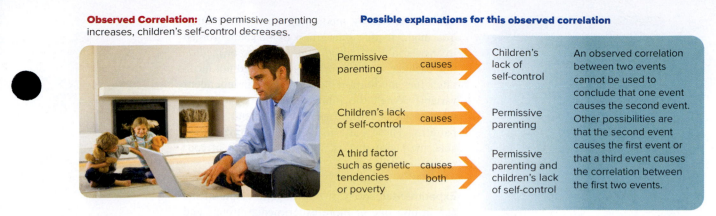

Observed Correlation: As permissive parenting increases, children's self-control decreases.

Possible explanations for this observed correlation

Permissive parenting —**causes**→ Children's lack of self-control

Children's lack of self-control —**causes**→ Permissive parenting

A third factor such as genetic tendencies or poverty —**causes both**→ Permissive parenting and children's lack of self-control

An observed correlation between two events cannot be used to conclude that one event causes the second event. Other possibilities are that the second event causes the first event or that a third event causes the correlation between the first two events.

Figure 12 Possible Explanations for Correlational Data
©Jupiterimages/Getty Images

correlation of $+.30$ between parental monitoring of children and children's self-control, meaning that parents who monitor their children effectively have children with good self-control.

The higher the correlation coefficient (whether positive or negative), the stronger the association between the two variables. A correlation of 0 means that there is no association between the variables. A correlation of $-.40$ is stronger than a correlation of $+.20$ because we disregard whether the correlation is positive or negative in determining the strength of the correlation.

A word of caution is in order, however. Correlation does not equal causation (Aron, Coups, & Aron, 2019; Howell, 2017). The correlational finding just mentioned does not mean that permissive parenting necessarily causes low self-control in children. It could have that meaning, but it also could mean that a child's lack of self-control caused the parents to throw up their arms in despair and give up trying to control the child. It also could mean that other factors, such as heredity or poverty, caused the correlation between permissive parenting and low self-control in children. Figure 12 illustrates these possible interpretations of correlational data.

Experimental Research

To study causality, researchers turn to experimental research. An **experiment** is a carefully regulated procedure in which one or more factors believed to influence the behavior being studied are manipulated while all other factors are held constant. If the behavior under study changes when a factor is manipulated, we say that the manipulated factor has caused the behavior to change. In other words, the experiment has demonstrated cause and effect. The cause is the factor that was manipulated. The effect is the behavior that changed because of the manipulation. Nonexperimental research methods (descriptive and correlational research) cannot establish cause and effect because they do not involve manipulating factors in a controlled way (Gravetter & Forzano, 2019).

Independent and Dependent Variables Experiments include two types of changeable factors: independent and dependent variables. An *independent variable* is a manipulated, influential experimental factor. It is a potential cause. The label "independent" is used because this variable can be manipulated independently of other factors to determine its effect. An experiment may include one independent variable or several of them.

A *dependent variable* is a factor that can change in an experiment, in response to changes in the independent variable. As researchers manipulate the independent variable, they measure the dependent variable for any resulting effect.

For example, suppose that you wanted to study whether pregnant women could change the breathing and sleeping patterns of their

experiment A carefully regulated procedure in which one or more of the factors believed to influence the behavior being studied is manipulated and all other factors are held constant. Experimental research permits the determination of cause.

Independent variable

Dependent variable — Newborns' breathing and sleeping patterns

Figure 13 Principles of Experimental Research
Imagine that you decide to conduct an experimental study of the effects of meditation by pregnant women on their newborns' breathing and sleeping patterns. You randomly assign pregnant women to experimental and control groups. The experimental-group women engage in meditation over a specified number of sessions and weeks. The control group does not. Then, when the infants are born, you assess their breathing and sleeping patterns. If the breathing and sleeping patterns of newborns whose mothers were in the experimental group are more positive than those of the control group, you conclude that meditation caused the positive effects.

newborn babies by meditating during pregnancy. You might require one group of pregnant women to engage in a certain amount and type of meditation each day, while another group would not meditate; the meditation is thus the independent variable. When the infants are born, you would observe and measure their breathing and sleeping patterns. These patterns are the dependent variable, the factor that changes as the result of your manipulation.

Experimental and Control Groups Experiments can involve one or more experimental groups and one or more control groups. An experimental group is a group whose experience is manipulated. A control group is a comparison group that is as much like the experimental group as possible and that is treated in every way like the experimental group except for the manipulated factor (independent variable). The control group serves as a baseline against which the effects of the manipulated condition can be compared.

Random assignment is an important principle for deciding whether each participant will be placed in the experimental group or in the control group. Random assignment means that researchers assign participants to experimental and control groups by chance. It reduces the likelihood that the experiment's results will be due to any preexisting differences between groups. In the example of the effects of meditation by pregnant women on the breathing and sleeping patterns of their newborns, you would randomly assign half of the pregnant women to engage in meditation over a period of weeks (the experimental group) and the other half to not meditate over the same number of weeks (the control group). Figure 13 illustrates the nature of experimental research.

Time Span of Research

Researchers in life-span development have a special concern with the relation between age and some other variable. To explore these relations, researchers can study different individuals of different ages and compare them, or they can study the same individuals as they age over time.

Cross-Sectional Approach

The **cross-sectional approach** is a research strategy that simultaneously compares individuals of different ages. A typical cross-sectional study might include three groups of children: 5-year-olds, 8-year-olds, and 11-year-olds. Another study might include groups of 15-year-olds, 25-year-olds, and 45-year-olds. The groups can be compared with respect to a variety of dependent variables, such as IQ, memory, peer relations, attachment to parents, hormonal changes, and so on. All of this can be accomplished in a short time. In some studies data are collected in a single day. Even in large-scale cross-sectional studies with hundreds of subjects, data collection does not usually take longer than several months to complete.

The main advantage of the cross-sectional study is that the researcher does not have to wait for the individuals to grow up or become older. Despite its efficiency, though, the cross-sectional approach has its drawbacks. It gives no information about how individuals change or about the stability of their characteristics. It can obscure the hills and valleys of growth and development. For example, a cross-sectional study of life satisfaction might reveal average increases and decreases, but it would not show how the life satisfaction of individual adults waxed and waned over the years. It also would not tell us whether

cross-sectional approach A research strategy in which individuals of different ages are compared at one time.

developmental topics and issues using robots, such as motor development, perceptual development, information processing, and language development (Faghihi & Moustafa, 2017; Morse & Cangelosi, 2017). The hope is to build robots that are as much like humans as possible and in doing so to better understand how humans think and develop (Vujovic & others, 2017; Wu & others, 2017).

Evaluating Cognitive Theories

Contributions of cognitive theories include a positive view of development and an emphasis on the active construction of understanding. Criticisms include skepticism about the pureness of Piaget's stages and a belief that too little attention is paid to individual variations.

Behavioral and Social Cognitive Theories

Above is the humanoid robot iCub created by the Italian Institute of Technology to study such aspects of children's development as perception, cognition, and motor development. In this situation, the robot, the size of a 3.5 year old child, is catching a ball. This robot is being used by more than 20 laboratories worldwide and has 53 motors that move the head, arms and hands, waist, and legs. It also can see and hear, as well as having the sense of proprioception (body configuration) and movement (using gyroscopes).
©Marco Destefanis/Pacific Press/Sipa/Newscom

Behavioral and social cognitive theories hold that development can be described in terms of behaviors learned through interactions with our surroundings. Behaviorism essentially holds that we can study scientifically only what can be directly observed and measured. Out of the behavioral tradition grew the belief that development is observable behavior that can be learned through experience with the environment (Maag, 2018). In terms of the continuity-discontinuity issue discussed earlier in this chapter, the behavioral and social cognitive theories emphasize continuity in development and argue that development does not occur in stage-like fashion. Let's explore two versions of behaviorism: Skinner's operant conditioning and Bandura's social cognitive theory.

Skinner's Operant Conditioning

According to B. F. Skinner (1904–1990), through *operant conditioning* the consequences of a behavior produce changes in the probability of the behavior's recurrence. A behavior followed by a rewarding stimulus is more likely to recur, whereas a behavior followed by a punishing stimulus is less likely to recur. For example, when an adult smiles at a child after the child has done something, the child is more likely to engage in that behavior again than if the adult gives the child a disapproving look.

In Skinner's (1938) view, such rewards and punishments shape development. For Skinner the key aspect of development is behavior, not thoughts and feelings. He emphasized that development consists of the pattern of behavioral changes that are brought about by rewards and punishments. For example, Skinner would say that shy people learned to be shy as a result of experiences they had while growing up. It follows that modifications to an environment can help a shy person become more socially oriented.

Bandura's Social Cognitive Theory

Some psychologists agree with the behaviorists' notion that development is learned and is influenced strongly by environmental interactions. However, unlike Skinner, they also see cognition as important in understanding development. **Social cognitive theory** holds that behavior, environment, and person/cognitive factors are the key factors in development.

American psychologist Albert Bandura (born in 1925) is the leading architect of social cognitive theory. Bandura (1986, 2004, 2010a, b, 2012, 2015) emphasizes that cognitive processes have important links with the environment and behavior. His early research program focused heavily on *observational learning* (also called *imitation* or *modeling*), which is learning

behavioral and social cognitive theories Theories holding that development can be described in terms of the behaviors learned through interactions with the environment.

social cognitive theory The theory that behavior, environment, and person/cognitive factors are important in understanding development.

Albert Bandura is one of the leading architects of social cognitive theory. *How does Bandura's theory differ from Skinner's?*
©Dr. Albert Bandura

that occurs through observing what others do. For example, a young boy might observe his father yelling in anger and treating other people with hostility; and then later with his peers, the young boy acts very aggressively, showing the same behavioral characteristics as his father. Social cognitive theorists stress that people acquire a wide range of behaviors, thoughts, and feelings through observing others' behavior and that these observations form an important part of life-span development.

What is *cognitive* about observational learning in Bandura's view? He proposes that people cognitively represent the behavior of others and then sometimes adopt this behavior themselves.

Bandura's (2004, 2010a, b, 2012, 2015) most recent model of learning and development includes three elements: behavior, the person/cognition, and the environment. An individual's confidence in being able to control his or her success is an example of a person factor; strategies for achieving success are an example of a cognitive factor. As shown in Figure 9, influences from behavior, person/cognition, and environment operate interactively.

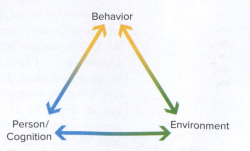

Figure 9 Bandura's Social Cognitive Model The arrows illustrate how relations between behavior, person/cognition, and environment are reciprocal rather than one-way. Person/cognition refers to cognitive processes (for example, thinking and planning) and personal characteristics (for example, believing that you can control your experiences).

Evaluating Behavioral and Social Cognitive Theories

Contributions of the behavioral and social cognitive theories include an emphasis on scientific research and environmental determinants of behavior. These theories have been criticized for placing too little emphasis on cognition (Skinner) and giving inadequate attention to developmental changes.

Ethological Theory

Ethology is the study of the behavior of animals in their natural habitat. Ethological theory stresses that behavior is strongly influenced by biology, is tied to evolution, and is characterized by critical or sensitive periods (Bateson, 2015). These are specific time frames during which, according to ethologists, the presence or absence of certain experiences has a long-lasting influence on individuals.

Lorenz's Research with Greylag Geese

European zoologist Konrad Lorenz (1903–1989) helped bring ethology to prominence. In his best-known research, Lorenz (1965) studied the behavior of greylag geese, which follow their mother as soon as they

ethology An approach stressing that behavior is strongly influenced by biology, tied to evolution, and characterized by critical or sensitive periods.

Konrad Lorenz, a pioneering student of animal behavior, is followed through the water by three imprinted greylag geese. Describe Lorenz's experiment with the geese. *Do you think his experiment would have the same results with human babies? Explain.*
©Nina Leen/Time & Life Pictures/Getty Images

the same adults who had positive or negative perceptions of life satisfaction in early adulthood maintained their relative degree of life satisfaction as they became middle-aged or older adults.

Longitudinal Approach

The **longitudinal approach** is a research strategy in which the same individuals are studied over a period of time, usually several years or more. For example, in a longitudinal study of life satisfaction, the same adults might be assessed periodically over a 70-year time span—at the ages of 20, 35, 45, 65, and 90, for example.

Longitudinal studies provide a wealth of information about vital issues such as stability and change in development and the importance of early experience for later development, but they do have drawbacks (Almy & Cicchetti, 2018; Becht & others, 2018). They are expensive and time-consuming. The longer the study lasts, the more participants drop out—they move, get sick, lose interest, and so forth. The participants who remain may be dissimilar to those who drop out, biasing the outcome of the study. Those individuals who remain in a longitudinal study over a number of years may be more responsible and conformity-oriented than the ones who dropped out, for example, or they might lead more stable lives.

longitudinal approach A research strategy in which the same individuals are studied over a period of time, usually several years or more.

cohort effects Effects that are due to a subject's time of birth or generation but not age.

Cohort Effects

A *cohort* is a group of people who are born at a similar point in history and share similar experiences as a result, such as living through the Vietnam War or growing up in the same city around the same time. These shared experiences may produce a range of differences among cohorts (Ganguli, 2017; Heo & others, 2018; Messerlian & Basso, 2018). For example, people who were teenagers during the Great Depression are likely to differ from people who were teenagers during the booming 1990s in their educational opportunities and economic status, in how they were raised, and in their attitudes toward sex and religion. In life-span development research, **cohort effects** are due to a person's time of birth, era, or generation but not to actual age.

Cohort effects are important because they can powerfully affect the dependent measures in a study ostensibly concerned with age (Bell & others, 2017; Ishtiak-Ahmed & others, 2018). Researchers have shown it is especially important to be aware of cohort effects when assessing adult intelligence (Schaie, 2013, 2016). Individuals born at different points in time—such as 1920, 1940, and 1960—have had varying opportunities for education. Individuals born in earlier years had less access to education, and this fact may have a significant effect on how this cohort performs on intelligence tests. Some researchers have found that cross-sectional studies indicate that more than 90 percent of cognitive decline in aging is due to a slowing of processing speed, whereas longitudinal studies reveal that 20 percent or less of cognitive decline is due to processing speed (MacDonald & others, 2003; MacDonald & Stawski, 2015, 2016; Stawski, Sliwinski, & Hofer, 2013). Another recent example of a cohort effect occurred in a study in which older adults assessed in 2013–2014 engaged in a higher level of abstract reasoning than their counterparts assessed two decades earlier in 1990–1993 (Gerstorf & others, 2015).

Cross-sectional studies can show how different cohorts respond, but they can confuse age changes and cohort effects. Longitudinal studies are effective in studying age changes, but only within one cohort.

Various generations have been given labels by the popular culture. Figure 14 describes the labels of various generations, the historical period for each one, and the reasons for their labels. Consider the following description of the current generation of youth and think about how they differ from earlier youth generations:

How does the youth experienced by today's millennials differ from that of earlier generations?
©Hero Images/Alamy

They are history's first "always connected" generation. Steeped in digital technology and social media, they treat their multi-tasking hand-held gadgets almost like a body part—for better or worse. More than 8-in-10 say they sleep with a cell phone glowing

Generation	Historical Period	Reasons for Label
Millennials	Individuals born in 1980 and later	First generation to come of age and enter emerging adulthood (18 to 25 years of age) in the twenty-first century (the new millennium). Two main characteristics: (1) connection to technology, and (2) ethnic diversity.
Generation X	Individuals born between 1965 and 1980	Described as lacking an identity and savvy loners.
Baby Boomers	Individuals born between 1946 and 1964	Label used because this generation represents the spike in the number of babies born after World War II; the largest generation ever to enter late adulthood in the United States.
Silent Generation	Individuals born between 1928 and 1945	Children of the Great Depression and World War II; described as conformists and civic minded.

Figure 14 Generations, Their Historical Periods, and Characteristics

by the bed, poised to disgorge texts, phone calls, e-mails, songs, news, videos, games, and wake-up jingles. But sometimes convenience yields to temptation. Nearly two-thirds admit to texting while driving (Pew Research Center, 2010, p. 1).

Conducting Ethical Research

Researchers who study human development and behavior confront many ethical issues. For example, a developmentalist who wanted to study aggression in children would have to design the study in such a way that no child would be harmed physically or psychologically, and the researcher would need to get permission from the university to carry out the study. Then the researcher would have to explain the study to the children's parents and obtain consent for the children to participate. Ethics in research may affect you personally if you ever serve as a participant in a study. In that event, you need to know your rights as a participant and the responsibilities of researchers to ensure that these rights are safeguarded.

Today, proposed research at colleges and universities must pass the scrutiny of a research ethics committee before the research can begin. In addition, the American Psychological Association (APA) has developed ethics guidelines for its members. This code of ethics instructs psychologists to protect their research participants from mental and physical harm. The participants' best interests need to be kept foremost in the researcher's mind (Ary & others, 2019; Kazdin, 2017).

APA's guidelines address four important issues:

1. *Informed consent*—All participants must know what their research participation will involve and what risks might develop. Even after informed consent is given, participants must retain the right to withdraw from the study at any time and for any reason.

2. *Confidentiality*—Researchers are responsible for keeping all of the data they gather on individuals completely confidential and, when possible, completely anonymous.

3. *Debriefing*—After the study has been completed, participants should be informed of its purpose and the methods that were used. In most cases, the experimenter also can inform participants in a general manner beforehand about the purpose of the research without leading participants to behave in a way they think that the experimenter is expecting.

4. *Deception*—In some circumstances, telling the participants beforehand what the research study is about substantially alters the participants' behavior and invalidates the researcher's data. In all cases of deception, however, the psychologist must ensure that the deception will not harm the participants and that the participants will be *debriefed* (told the complete nature of the study) as soon as possible after the study is completed.

Summary

The Life-Span Perspective

- Development is the pattern of change that begins at conception and continues through the life span. It includes both growth and decline.
- The life-span perspective includes these basic ideas: development is lifelong, multidimensional, multidirectional, and plastic; its study is multidisciplinary; it is embedded in contexts; it involves growth, maintenance, and regulation; and it is a co-construction of biological, sociocultural, and individual factors.
- Health and well-being, parenting, education, sociocultural contexts and diversity, and social policy are all areas of contemporary concern for those who study life-span development.

The Nature of Development

- Three key developmental processes are biological, cognitive, and socioemotional. Development is influenced by an interplay of these processes.
- The life span is commonly divided into the prenatal period, infancy, early childhood, middle and late childhood, adolescence, early adulthood, middle adulthood, and late adulthood.
- We often think of age only in chronological terms, but a full evaluation of age requires the consideration of biological age, psychological age, and social age as well.
- Three pathways of aging are pathological aging, normal aging, and successful aging.
- In research covering adolescence through late adulthood, many but not all studies find that older adults report the highest level of life satisfaction.
- Three important issues in the study of development are the nature-nurture issue, the continuity-discontinuity issue, and the stability-change issue.

Theories of Development

- According to psychoanalytic theories, including those of Freud and Erikson, development primarily depends on the unconscious mind and is heavily couched in emotion.
- Cognitive theories emphasize thinking, reasoning, language, and other cognitive processes. Three main cognitive theories are Piaget's, Vygotsky's, and information processing.
- Behavioral and social cognitive theories emphasize the environment's role in development. Two key behavioral and social cognitive theories are Skinner's operant conditioning and Bandura's social cognitive theory.
- Lorenz's ethological theory stresses the biological and evolutionary bases of development.
- According to Bronfenbrenner's ecological theory, development predominantly reflects the influence of five environmental systems—the microsystem, mesosystem, exosystem, macrosystem, and chronosystem.
- An eclectic orientation incorporates the best features of different theoretical approaches.

Research in Life-Span Development

- The main methods for collecting data about life-span development are observation, survey (questionnaire) or interview, standardized test, case study, and physiological measures.
- Three basic research designs are descriptive, correlational, and experimental.
- To examine the effects of time and age, researchers can conduct cross-sectional or longitudinal studies. Life-span researchers are especially concerned about cohort effects.
- Researchers have an ethical responsibility to safeguard the well-being of research participants.

Key Terms

behavioral and social cognitive theories
biological processes
Bronfenbrenner's ecological theory
case study
cognitive processes
cohort effects
context
continuity-discontinuity issue
correlation coefficient
correlational research

cross-cultural studies
cross-sectional approach
culture
descriptive research
development
eclectic theoretical orientation
Erikson's theory
ethnicity
ethology
experiment
gender
hypotheses

information-processing theory
laboratory
life-span perspective
longitudinal approach
naturalistic observation
nature-nurture issue
nonnormative life events
normative age-graded influences
normative history-graded influences
Piaget's theory

psychoanalytic theories
social cognitive theory
social policy
socioeconomic status (SES)
socioemotional processes
stability-change issue
standardized test
theory
Vygotsky's theory

©MedicalRF.com/Getty Images

2 Biological Beginnings

Stories of Life-Span Development: The Jim and Jim Twins

Jim Springer and Jim Lewis are identical twins. They were separated at 4 weeks of age and did not see each other again until they were 39 years old. Both worked as part-time deputy sheriffs, vacationed in Florida, drove Chevrolets, had dogs named Toy, and married and divorced women named Betty. One twin named his son James Allan, and the other named his son James Alan. Both liked math but not spelling, enjoyed carpentry and mechanical drawing, chewed their fingernails down to the nubs, had almost identical drinking and smoking habits, had hemorrhoids, put on 10 pounds at about the same point in development, first suffered headaches at the age of 18, and had similar sleep patterns.

Jim and Jim do have some differences. One wears his hair over his forehead, the other slicks it back and has sideburns. One expresses himself best orally; the other is more proficient in writing. But, for the most part, their profiles are remarkably similar.

Another pair of identical twins, Daphne and Barbara, were called the "giggle sisters" by researchers because after being reunited they were always making each other laugh. A thorough search of their adoptive families' histories revealed no gigglers. The giggle sisters ignored stress, avoided conflict and controversy whenever possible, and showed no interest in politics.

Jim and Jim and the giggle sisters were part of the Minnesota Study of Twins Reared Apart, directed by Thomas Bouchard and his colleagues. The study brings identical twins (who are identical genetically because they come from the same fertilized egg) and fraternal twins (who come from different fertilized eggs) from all over the world to Minneapolis to investigate their lives. There the twins complete personality and intelligence tests, and provide detailed medical histories, including information about diet and smoking, exercise habits, chest X-rays, heart stress tests, and EEGs. The twins are asked more than 15,000 questions about their family and childhood, personal interests, vocational orientation, values, and aesthetic judgments (Bouchard & others, 1990).

When genetically identical twins who were separated as infants show such striking similarities in their tastes and habits and choices, can we conclude that their genes must have caused these similarities? Although genes play a role, we also need to consider other possible causes. The twins shared not only the same genes but also some similar experiences. Some of the separated twins lived together for several months prior to their adoption; some had been reunited prior to testing (in some cases, many years earlier); adoption agencies often place twins in similar homes; and even strangers who spend several hours together and start comparing their lives are likely to come up with some coincidental similarities (Joseph, 2006).

The Minnesota study of identical twins points to both the importance of the genetic basis of human development and the need for further research on genetic and environmental factors.

The examples of Jim and Jim and the giggle sisters stimulate us to think about our genetic heritage and the biological foundations of our existence. Organisms are not like billiard balls, moved by simple, external forces to predictable positions on life's pool table. Environmental experiences and biological foundations work together to make us who we are. Our coverage of life's biological beginnings and experiences will emphasize the evolutionary perspective; genetic foundations; the interaction of heredity and environment; and charting growth from conception through the prenatal period, the birth process itself, and the postpartum period that follows birth. ■

The Evolutionary Perspective

From the perspective of evolutionary time, humans are relative newcomers to Earth. As our earliest ancestors left the forest to feed on the savannahs and then to form hunting societies on the open plains, their minds and behaviors changed, and humans eventually became the dominant species on Earth. How did this evolution come about?

Natural Selection and Adaptive Behavior

Charles Darwin (1859) described *natural selection* as the evolutionary process by which those individuals of a species that are best *adapted* to their environment are the ones that are most likely to survive and reproduce. He reasoned that an intense, constant struggle for food, water, and resources must occur among the young of each generation, because many of them do not survive. Those that do survive and reproduce pass on their characteristics to the next generation (Audesirk, Audesirk, & Byers, 2017; Johnson, 2017). Darwin concluded that these survivors are better adapted to their world than are the nonsurvivors. The best-adapted

How does the attachment of this Vietnamese baby to its mother reflect the evolutionary process of adaptive behavior?
©Frans Lemmens/age fotostock

How Would You...?

As a **health-care professional,** how would you explain technology and medicine working against natural selection?

individuals survive and leave the most offspring (Mader & Windelspecht, 2018, 2019; Starr, Evers, & Starr, 2018). Over the course of many generations, organisms with the characteristics needed for survival make up an increased percentage of the population (Hoefnagels, 2018, 2019; Mason & others, 2018; Simon, 2017).

Evolutionary Psychology

Although Darwin introduced the theory of evolution by natural selection in 1859, his ideas have only recently become a popular framework for explaining behavior (Frankenhuis & Tiokhin, 2018; Knapen, Blaker, & Van Vugt, 2018). Psychology's newest approach, **evolutionary psychology,** emphasizes the importance of adaptation, reproduction, and "survival of the fittest" in shaping behavior (Bjorklund, 2018; Legare, Clegg, & Wen, 2018; Szepsenwol & Simpson, 2018). ("Fit" in this sense refers to the ability to bear offspring that survive long enough to bear offspring of their own.) In this view, natural selection favors behaviors that increase reproductive success—that is, the ability to pass your genes to the next generation (Borraz-Leon & others, 2018; Raichlen & Alexander, 2017; Suchow, Bourgin, & Griffiths, 2017).

David Buss (2008, 2012, 2015) argues that just as evolution has contributed to our physical features, such as body shape and height, it also pervasively influences how we make decisions, how aggressive we are, our fears, and our mating patterns. For example, assume that our ancestors were hunters and gatherers on the plains and that men did most of the hunting and women stayed close to home, gathering seeds and plants for food. If you have to travel some distance from your home to track and slay a fleeing animal, you need certain physical traits along with the capacity for certain types of spatial thinking. Men with these traits would be more likely than men without them to survive, to bring home lots of food, and to be considered attractive mates—and thus to reproduce and pass on these characteristics to their children. In other words, if our assumptions were correct, potentially these traits would provide a reproductive advantage for males, and over many generations, men with good spatial thinking skills might become more numerous in the population. Critics point out that this scenario might or might not have actually happened.

Evolutionary Developmental Psychology

There is growing interest in using the concepts of evolutionary psychology to understand human development (Barbaro & others, 2017; Bjorklund, 2018; Lickliter, 2018). Following are some ideas proposed by evolutionary developmental psychologists (Bjorklund & Pellegrini, 2002).

One important concept is that an extended childhood period might have evolved because humans require time to develop a large brain and learn the complexity of human societies. Humans take longer to become reproductively mature than any other primate (see Figure 1). During this extended childhood period, they develop a large brain and have the experiences needed to become competent adults in a complex society.

Another key idea is that many of our evolved psychological mechanisms are *domain-specific*. That is, the mechanisms apply only to a specific aspect of a person's psychological makeup. According to evolutionary psychology, the mind is not a general-purpose device that can be applied equally to a vast array of problems. Instead, as our ancestors dealt with certain recurring problems such as hunting and finding shelter, specialized modules evolved that process information related to those problems: for example, such specialized modules might include a module for physical knowledge for tracking animals, a module for mathematical knowledge for trading, and a module for language.

Evolved mechanisms are not always adaptive in contemporary society. Some behaviors

How Would You...?

As an **educator,** how would you apply the concept of domain-specific psychological mechanisms to explain how a student with a learning disability in reading may perform exceptionally well in math?

evolutionary psychology Emphasizes the importance of adaptation, reproduction, and "survival of the fittest" in shaping behavior.

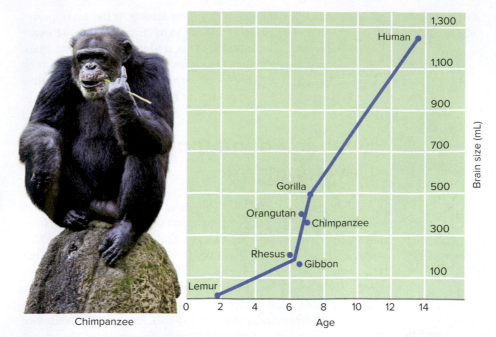

Chimpanzee

Figure 1 **The Brain Sizes of Various Primates and Humans in Relation to the Length of the Juvenile Period**
Compared with other primates, humans have both a larger brain and a longer childhood period.
What conclusions can you draw from the relationship indicated by this graph?
©Getty Images

that were adaptive for our prehistoric ancestors may not serve us well today. For example, the food-scarce environment of our ancestors likely led to humans' propensity to gorge when food is available and to crave high-caloric foods, a trait that might lead to an epidemic of obesity when food is plentiful.

Evaluating Evolutionary Psychology

Although the popular press gives a lot of attention to the ideas of evolutionary psychology, it remains just one theoretical approach. Like the theories described earlier, it has limitations, weaknesses, and critics (Hyde & DeLamater, 2017). One criticism comes from Albert Bandura (1998), whose social cognitive theory was described earlier. Bandura acknowledges the important influence of evolution on human adaptation. However, he rejects what he calls "one-sided evolutionism," which sees social behavior as the product of evolved biological characteristics. An alternative is a *bidirectional view* in which environmental and biological conditions influence each other. In this view, evolutionary pressures created changes in biological structures that allowed the use of tools, which enabled our ancestors to manipulate the environment, constructing new environmental conditions. In turn, environmental innovations produced new selection pressures that led to the evolution of specialized biological systems for consciousness, thought, and language.

In other words, evolution gave us bodily structures and biological potentialities, but it does not dictate behavior. People have used their biological capacities to produce diverse cultures—aggressive and peace-loving, egalitarian and autocratic. As American scientist Stephen Jay Gould (1981) concluded, in most domains of human functioning, biology allows a broad range of cultural possibilities.

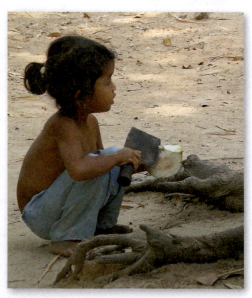

Children in all cultures are interested in the tools that adults in their culture use. For example, this young child is using a machete, near the Angkor Temples in Cambodia. *Might the child's behavior be evolutionary-based or be due to both biological and environmental conditions?*
©Carol Adam/Getty Images

The "big picture" idea of natural selection leading to the development of human traits and behaviors is difficult to refute or test because evolution occurs on a time scale that does not lend itself to empirical study. Thus, studying specific genes in humans and other species—and their links to traits and behaviors—may be the best approach for testing ideas coming out of the evolutionary psychology perspective.

Genetic Foundations of Development

Genetic influences on behavior evolved over time and across many species. Our many traits and characteristics that are genetically influenced have a long evolutionary history that is retained in our DNA (Brooker & others, 2018; Hoefnagels, 2019). In other words, our DNA is not just inherited from our parents; it's also what we've inherited as a species from the species that came before our own. Let's take a closer look at DNA and its role in human development.

How are characteristics that suit a species for survival transmitted from one generation to the next? Darwin did not know the answer to this question because genes and the principles of genetics had not yet been discovered. Each of us carries a human "genetic code" that we inherited from our parents. Because a fertilized egg carries this human code, a fertilized human egg cannot grow into an egret, eagle, or elephant.

Each of us began life as a single cell weighing about one twenty-millionth of an ounce. This tiny piece of matter housed our entire genetic code—instructions that orchestrated growth from that single cell to a person made of trillions of cells, each containing a replica of the original code. That code is carried by our genes. What are genes and what do they do? For the answer, we need to look into our cells.

The nucleus of each human cell contains **chromosomes,** which are threadlike structures made up of deoxyribonucleic acid, or DNA. **DNA** is a complex molecule that has a double helix shape, like a spiral staircase, and contains genetic information. **Genes,** the units of hereditary information, are short segments of DNA, as you can see in Figure 2. They help cells to reproduce themselves and to assemble proteins. Proteins, in turn, are the building blocks of cells as well as the regulators that direct the body's processes (Goodenough & McGuire, 2017; Mason & others, 2018).

Each gene has its own designated place on a particular chromosome. Today, there is a great deal of enthusiasm about efforts to discover the specific locations of genes that are linked to certain functions and developmental outcomes (Hoefnagels, 2018; Johnson, 2017). An important step in this direction was taken when the Human Genome Project and the Celera Corporation completed a preliminary map of the human *genome*—the complete set of developmental instructions for creating proteins that initiate the making of a human organism (Brooker & others, 2018).

Completion of the Human Genome Project has led to use of the *genome-wide association method* to identify genetic variations linked to a particular disease (Yasukochi & others, 2018; Zhu & others, 2018), such as cancer (Sucheston-Campbell & others, 2018); obesity (Amare & others, 2017); cardiovascular disease (Olson & others, 2018); depression (Knowles & others, 2016); suicide (Sokolowski, Wasserman, & Wasserman, 2016); autism (Ramaswami & Geschwind, 2018); attention deficit hyperactivity disorder (Sanchez-Roige & others, 2018); glaucoma (Springelkamp & others, 2017); and Alzheimer disease (Liu & others, 2018). To conduct a genome-wide association study, researchers obtain DNA from individuals

Cell

Nucleus

Chromosome

DNA

Figure 2 Cells, Chromosomes, DNA, and Genes

(*Top*) The body contains trillions of cells. Each cell contains a central structure, the nucleus. (*Middle*) Chromosomes are threadlike structures located in the nucleus of the cell. Chromosomes are composed of DNA. (*Bottom*) DNA has the structure of a spiral staircase. A gene is a segment of DNA.

chromosomes Threadlike structures made up of deoxyribonucleic acid, or DNA.

DNA A complex molecule with a double helix shape that contains genetic information.

genes Units of hereditary information composed of DNA. Genes direct cells to reproduce themselves and manufacture the proteins that maintain life.

who have the disease and those who don't have it. Then, each participant's complete set of DNA, or genome, is purified from the blood or other cells and scanned on machines to determine markers of genetic variation. If the genetic variations occur more frequently in people who have the disease than in those who don't have it, the variations point to the region in the human genome where the disease-causing problem exists.

One of the big surprises of the Human Genome Project was a report indicating that humans have only about 30,000 genes (U.S. Department of Energy, 2001). More recently, the number of human genes has been revised further downward, to approximately 20,700 (Flicek & others, 2013). Further analysis proposes that humans may actually have fewer than 20,000 protein-producing genes (Ezkurdia & others, 2014). Scientists had thought that humans had as many as 100,000 or more genes. They had also believed that each gene programmed just one protein. In fact, humans appear to have far more proteins than they have genes, so there cannot be a one-to-one correspondence between genes and proteins (Commoner, 2002). Each gene is not translated, in automaton-like fashion, into one and only one protein. A gene does not act independently, as developmental psychologist David Moore (2001) emphasized by titling his book *The Dependent Gene*. Rather than being a group of independent genes, the human genome consists of many genes that collaborate both with each other and with nongenetic factors inside and outside the body. The collaboration operates at many points. For example, the cellular "machinery" mixes, matches, and links small pieces of DNA to reproduce the genes, and that machinery is influenced by what is going on around it (Halldorsdottir & Binder, 2017; Moore, 2015, 2017).

Whether a gene is turned "on"—that is, working to assemble proteins—is also a matter of collaboration. The activity of genes (*genetic expression*) is affected by their environment (Gottlieb, 2007; Lickliter, 2018; Moore, 2017). For example, hormones that circulate in the blood make their way into the cell, where they can turn genes "on" and "off." And the flow of hormones can be affected by environmental conditions such as light, day length, nutrition, and behavior.

Numerous studies have shown that external events outside of the original cell and the person, as well as events inside the cell, can excite or inhibit gene expression (Moore, 2017). Recent research has documented that factors such as stress, exercise, nutrition, respiration, radiation, temperature, and sleep can influence gene expression (Giles & others, 2016; Kader, Ghai, & Mahraj, 2018; Mychasiuk, Muhammad, & Kolb, 2016; Poulsen & others, 2018; Stephens & Tsintzas, 2018; Turecki & Meaney, 2016). For example, one study revealed that an increase in the concentration of stress hormones such as cortisol produced a fivefold increase in DNA damage (Flint & others, 2007). Another study also found that exposure to radiation changed the rate of DNA synthesis in cells (Lee & others, 2011). And research indicates that sleep deprivation can affect gene expression in negative ways such as increased inflammation, expression of stress-related genes, and impairment of protein functioning (da Costa Souza & Ribeiro, 2015).

Scientists have found that certain genes become turned on or off as a result of exercise mainly through a process called *methylation*, in which tiny atoms attached themselves to the outside of a gene (Butts & others, 2017; Castellano-Castillo & others, 2018; Marioni & others, 2018). This process makes the gene more or less capable of receiving and responding to biochemical signals from the body (Kader, Ghai, & Mahraj, 2018; Martin & Fry, 2018). In this way the behavior of the gene, but not its structure, is changed. Researchers also have found that diet and tobacco may affect gene behavior through the process of methylation (Chatterton & others, 2017; Zaghlool & others, 2018). Also, recent research indicates that methylation may be involved in depression (Crawford & others, 2018); breast cancer (Parashar & others, 2018); and attention deficit hyperactivity disorder (Kim & others, 2018).

Genes and Chromosomes

Genes are not only collaborative; they are enduring. How do they get passed from generation to generation and end up in all of the trillion cells in the body? Three processes are central to this story: mitosis, meiosis, and fertilization.

(a)

(b)

Figure 3 The Genetic Difference Between Males and Females
Set (a) shows the chromosome structure of a male and set (b) shows the chromosome structure of a female. The last pair of 23 pairs of chromosomes is in the bottom right corner of each set. Notice that the Y chromosome of the male is smaller than the X chromosome of the female. To obtain this kind of chromosomal picture, a cell is removed from a person's body, usually from the inside of the mouth. The chromosomes are stained by chemical treatment, magnified extensively, and then photographed.

Mitosis, Meiosis, and Fertilization

All cells in your body, except the sperm and egg, have 46 chromosomes arranged in 23 pairs. These cells reproduce through a process called **mitosis.** During mitosis, the cell's nucleus—including the chromosomes—duplicates itself and the cell divides. Two new cells are formed, each containing the same DNA as the original cell, arranged in the same 23 pairs of chromosomes.

However, a different type of cell division—**meiosis**—forms eggs and sperm (which also are called *gametes*). During meiosis, a cell of the testes (in men) or ovaries (in women) duplicates its chromosomes but then divides *twice*, thus forming four cells, each of which has only half of the genetic material of the parent cell (Johnson, 2017). By the end of meiosis, each egg or sperm has 23 *unpaired* chromosomes.

During *fertilization*, an egg and a sperm fuse to create a single cell, called a *zygote*. In the zygote, the 23 unpaired chromosomes from the egg and the 23 unpaired chromosomes from the sperm combine to form one set of 23 paired chromosomes—one chromosome of each pair from the mother's egg and the other from the father's sperm. In this manner, each parent contributes half of the offspring's genetic material.

Figure 3 shows 23 paired chromosomes of a male and a female. The members of each pair of chromosomes are both similar and different: Each chromosome in the pair contains varying forms of the same genes, at the same location on the chromosome. A gene that influences hair color, for example, is located on both members of one pair of chromosomes, at the same location on each. However, one of those chromosomes might carry the gene associated with blond hair; the other might carry the gene associated with brown hair.

Do you notice any obvious differences between the chromosomes of the male and those of the female in Figure 3? The difference lies in the 23rd pair. Ordinarily, in females this pair consists of two chromosomes called *X chromosomes;* in males the 23rd pair consists of an X chromosome and a Y chromosome. The presence of a Y chromosome is one factor that makes a person male rather than female.

Sources of Variability

Combining the genes of two parents in their offspring increases genetic variability in the population, which is valuable for a species because it provides more characteristics on which natural selection can operate (Mason & others, 2018; Simon, 2017). In fact, the human genetic process creates several important sources of variability.

First, the chromosomes in the zygote are not exact copies of those in the mother's ovaries and the father's testes. During the formation of the sperm and egg in meiosis, the members of each pair of chromosomes are separated, but which chromosome in the pair goes to the gamete is a matter of chance. In addition, before the pairs separate, pieces of the two chromosomes in each pair are exchanged, creating a new combination of genes on each chromosome. Thus, when chromosomes from the mother's egg and the father's sperm are brought together in the zygote, the result is a truly unique combination of genes.

Another source of variability comes from DNA. Chance events, a mistake by the cellular machinery, or damage caused by an environmental agent such as radiation may produce a *mutated gene*, a permanently altered segment of DNA (Freeman & others, 2017; Hoefnagels, 2019; Mason & others, 2018).

mitosis Cellular reproduction in which the cell's nucleus duplicates itself with two new cells being formed, each containing the same DNA as the parent cell, arranged in the same 23 pairs of chromosomes.

meiosis A specialized form of cell division that occurs to form eggs and sperm (or gametes).

Even when their genes are identical, however, as for the identical twins described at the beginning of the chapter, people vary. The difference between *genotypes* and *phenotypes* helps us understand this source of variability. All of a person's genetic material makes up his or her **genotype**. There is increasing interest in studying *susceptibility genes*, those that make the individual more vulnerable to specific diseases or accelerated aging (J.S. Park & others, 2018; Patel & others, 2018; Scarabino & others, 2017), and *longevity genes,* those that make the individual less vulnerable to certain diseases and more likely to live to an older age (Blankenburg, Pramstaller, & Domingues, 2018; Dato & others, 2017). These are aspects of the individual's genotype.

However, not all of the genetic material is apparent in an individual's observed and measurable characteristics. A **phenotype** consists of observable characteristics, including physical characteristics (such as height, weight, and hair color) and psychological characteristics (such as personality and intelligence).

For each genotype, a range of phenotypes can be expressed, providing another source of variability (Klug & others, 2017). An individual can inherit the genetic potential to grow very large, for example, but good nutrition, among other things, will be essential to achieving that potential.

Genetic Principles

What determines how a genotype is expressed to create a particular phenotype? This question has not yet been fully answered (Lickliter, 2018; Moore, 2015, 2017). However, a number of genetic principles have been discovered, among them those of dominant and recessive genes, sex-linked genes, and polygenically determined characteristics.

Dominant and Recessive Genes

In some cases, one gene of a pair always exerts its effects; in other words, it is *dominant*, overriding the potential influence of the other gene, which is called the *recessive* gene. This is the *dominant-and-recessive genes principle*. A recessive gene exerts its influence only if the two genes of a pair are both recessive. If you inherit a recessive gene for a trait from each of your parents, you will show the trait. If you inherit a recessive gene from only one parent, you may never know that you carry the gene. Brown hair, farsightedness, and dimples override blond hair, nearsightedness, and freckles in the world of dominant and recessive genes. Can two brown-haired parents have a blond-haired child? Yes, they can. Suppose that each parent has a dominant gene for brown hair and a recessive gene for blond hair. Since dominant genes override recessive genes, the parents have brown hair, but both are *carriers* of blondness and pass on their recessive genes for blond hair. With no dominant gene to override them, the recessive genes can make the child's hair blond.

Sex-Linked Genes

Most mutated genes are recessive. When a mutated gene is carried on the X chromosome, the result is called *X-linked inheritance*. It may have implications for males that differ greatly from those for females (Freeman & others, 2017; Mader & Windelspecht, 2018, 2019). Remember that males have only one X chromosome. Thus, if there is an absent or altered, disease-relevant gene on the X chromosome, males have no "backup" copy to counter the harmful gene and therefore may develop an X-linked disease. However, females have a second X chromosome, which is likely to be unchanged. As a result, they are not likely to have the X-linked disease. Thus, most individuals who have X-linked diseases are males. Females who have one abnormal copy of the gene on the X chromosome are known as carriers, and they usually do not show any signs of the X-linked disease. Fragile X syndrome, which we will discuss later in the chapter, is an example of X-linked inheritance (Thurman & others, 2017).

Polygenic Inheritance

Genetic transmission is usually more complex than the simple examples we have examined thus far (Lickliter, 2018). Few characteristics reflect

genotype A person's genetic heritage; the actual genetic material.

phenotype The way an individual's genotype is expressed in observed and measurable characteristics.

the influence of only a single gene or pair of genes. Most are determined by the interaction of many different genes; they are said to be *polygenically* determined (Hill & others, 2018; Zabaneh & others, 2017). Even a simple characteristic such as height reflects the interaction of many genes as well as the influence of the environment. Most diseases, such as cancer and diabetes, develop as a consequence of complex gene interactions and environmental factors (Schaefer, Hornick, & Bovee, 2018).

The term *gene-gene interaction* is increasingly used to describe studies that focus on the interdependent process by which two or more genes influence characteristics, behavior, diseases, and development (Lovely & others, 2017; Yip & others, 2018). For example, recent studies have documented gene-gene interaction in immune system functioning (Heinonen & others, 2015); asthma (Hua & others, 2016); obesity (Bordoni & others, 2017); type 2 diabetes (Saxena, Srivastava, & Banerjee, 2018); alcoholism (Chen & others, 2017); cancer (Su & others, 2018); cardiovascular disease (De & others, 2017); and Alzheimer disease (Yin & others, 2018).

Down syndrome A chromosomally transmitted form of intellectual disability, caused by the presence of an extra copy of chromosome 21.

Chromosome and Gene-Linked Abnormalities

In some (relatively rare) cases, genetic inheritance involves an abnormality. Some of these abnormalities come from whole chromosomes that do not separate properly during meiosis. Others are produced by defective genes.

Chromosome Abnormalities

Sometimes a gamete is formed in which the combined sperm and ovum do not have their normal set of 23 chromosomes. The most notable examples involve Down syndrome and abnormalities of the sex chromosomes. Figure 4 describes some chromosome abnormalities, along with their treatment and incidence.

Down Syndrome Down syndrome is one of the most common genetically linked causes of intellectual disability; it is also characterized by certain physical features (Lewanda & others, 2016; Popadin & others, 2018). An individual with Down syndrome has a round face, a flattened skull, an extra fold of skin over the eyelids, a thickened tongue, short limbs, and delayed development of motor and mental abilities. The syndrome is caused by the presence of an extra copy of chromosome 21. It is not known why the extra chromosome is present, but the health of the male sperm or female ovum may be involved.

Name	Description	Treatment	Incidence
Down syndrome	An extra chromosome causes mild to severe intellectual disabilities and physical abnormalities.	Surgery, early intervention, infant stimulation, and special learning programs	1 in 1,900 births at age 20 1 in 300 births at age 35 1 in 30 births at age 45
Klinefelter syndrome (XXY)	An extra X chromosome causes physical abnormalities.	Hormone therapy can be effective	1 in 1,000 male births
Fragile X syndrome	An abnormality in the X chromosome can cause intellectual disabilities, learning disabilities, or short attention span.	Special education, speech and language therapy	More common in males than in females
Turner syndrome (XO)	A missing X chromosome in females can cause intellectual disabilities and sexual underdevelopment.	Hormone therapy in childhood and puberty	1 in 2,500 female births
XYY syndrome	An extra Y chromosome can cause above-average height.	No special treatment required	1 in 1,000 male births

Figure 4 Some Chromosome Abnormalities
The treatments for these abnormalities do not necessarily erase the problem but may improve the individual's adaptive behavior and quality of life.

How Would You...?

As a **social worker,** how would you respond to a 33-year-old pregnant woman who is concerned about the risk of giving birth to a baby with Down syndrome?

Down syndrome appears approximately once in every 700 live births. Women between the ages of 16 and 34 are less likely to give birth to a child with Down syndrome than are younger or older women. African American children are rarely born with Down syndrome.

These athletes, several of whom have Down syndrome, are participating in a Special Olympics competition. Notice the distinctive facial features of the individuals with Down syndrome, such as a round face and a flattened skull. *What causes Down syndrome?* ©James Shaffer/PhotoEdit

Sex-Linked Chromosome Abnormalities Recall that a newborn normally has either an X and a Y chromosome, or two X chromosomes. Human embryos must possess at least one X chromosome to be viable. The most common sex-linked chromosome abnormalities involve the presence of an extra chromosome (either an X or a Y) or the absence of one X chromosome in females.

Klinefelter syndrome is a chromosomal disorder in which males have an extra X chromosome, making them XXY instead of XY (Skuse, Printzlau, & Wolstencroft, 2018). Males with this disorder have undeveloped testes, and they usually have enlarged breasts and become tall (Belling & others, 2017; Flannigan & Schlegel, 2017). Klinefelter syndrome occurs approximately once in every 1,000 live male births. Only 10 percent of individuals with Klinefelter syndrome are diagnosed before puberty, with the majority not identified until adulthood (Aksglaede & others, 2013).

Fragile X syndrome is a genetic disorder that results from an abnormality in the X chromosome, which becomes constricted and often breaks (Niu & others, 2017). The outcome frequently takes the form of an intellectual disability, autism, a learning disability, or a short attention span (Hall & Berry-Kravis, 2018; Thurman & others, 2017). This disorder occurs more frequently in males than in females, possibly because the second X chromosome in females negates the effects of the other, abnormal X chromosome (Mila & others, 2017). A recent study found that a higher level of maternal responsivity to the adaptive behavior of children with FXS had a positive effect on the children's communication skills (Warren & others, 2017).

Turner syndrome is a chromosomal disorder in females in which either an X chromosome is missing, making the person XO instead of XX, or part of one X chromosome is deleted. Females with Turner syndrome are short in stature and have a webbed neck (Skuse, Printzlau, & Wolstencroft, 2018). In some cases, they are infertile. They have difficulty in mathematics, but their verbal ability is often quite good. Turner syndrome occurs in approximately 1 of every 2,500 live female births (Culen & others, 2017).

XYY syndrome is a chromosomal disorder in which the male has an extra Y chromosome (Tartaglia & others, 2017). Early interest in this syndrome focused on the belief that the extra Y chromosome found in some males contributed to aggression and violence. However, researchers subsequently found that XYY males are no more likely to commit crimes than are XY males (Witkin & others, 1976).

Gene-Linked Abnormalities

Abnormalities can be produced not only by an abnormal number of chromosomes, but also by defective genes. Figure 5 describes some gene-linked abnormalities and outlines their treatment and incidence.

Phenylketonuria (PKU) is a genetic disorder in which the individual cannot properly metabolize phenylalanine, an amino acid that naturally occurs in many food sources. It results from a recessive gene and occurs about once in every 10,000 to 20,000 live births. Today, phenylketonuria is easily detected in infancy, and it is treated by a diet that prevents an excess accumulation of phenylalanine (Medford & others, 2018; Micoch & others, 2018). If phenylketonuria is left untreated, however, excess phenylalanine builds up in the child, producing intellectual disability and hyperactivity. Phenylketonuria accounts for approximately 1 percent of individuals who are institutionalized for intellectual disabilities, and it occurs primarily in Whites.

Name	Description	Treatment	Incidence
Cystic fibrosis	Glandular dysfunction that interferes with mucus production; breathing and digestion are hampered, resulting in a shortened life span.	Physical and oxygen therapy, synthetic enzymes, and antibiotics; most individuals live to middle age.	1 in 2,000 births
Diabetes	Body does not produce enough insulin, which causes abnormal metabolism of sugar.	Early onset can be fatal unless treated with insulin.	1 in 2,500 births
Hemophilia	Delayed blood clotting causes internal and external bleeding.	Blood transfusions/injections can reduce or prevent damage due to internal bleeding.	1 in 10,000 males
Huntington disease	Central nervous system deteriorates, producing problems in muscle coordination and mental deterioration.	Does not usually appear until age 35 or older; death likely 10 to 20 years after symptoms appear.	1 in 20,000 births
Phenylketonuria (PKU)	Metabolic disorder that, left untreated, causes intellectual disability.	Special diet can result in average intelligence and normal life span.	1 in 10,000 to 1 in 20,000 births
Sickle-cell anemia	Blood disorder that limits the body's oxygen supply; it can cause joint swelling, as well as heart and kidney failure.	Penicillin, medication for pain, antibiotics, and blood transfusions.	1 in 400 African American children (lower among other groups)
Spina bifida	Neural tube disorder that causes brain and spine abnormalities.	Corrective surgery at birth, orthopedic devices, and physical/medical therapy.	2 in 1,000 births
Tay-Sachs disease	Deceleration of mental and physical development caused by an accumulation of lipids in the nervous system.	Medication and special diet are used, but death is likely by 5 years of age.	1 in 30 American Jews is a carrier.

Figure 5 Some Gene-Linked Abnormalities

How Would You…?

As a **health-care professional,** how would you explain the heredity-environment interaction to new parents who are upset when they discover that their child has a treatable genetic defect?

Sickle-cell anemia, which occurs most often in African Americans, is a genetic disorder that impairs functioning of the body's red blood cells. More than 300,000 infants worldwide are born with sickle-cell anemia each year (Azar & Wong, 2017). Red blood cells, which carry oxygen to the body's other cells, are usually shaped like a disk. In sickle-cell anemia, a recessive gene causes the red blood cell to become a hook-shaped "sickle" that cannot carry oxygen properly and dies quickly. As a result, the body's cells do not receive adequate oxygen, causing anemia and early death (Patterson & others, 2018; Powell & others, 2018). About 1 in 400 African American babies is affected by sickle-cell anemia. One in 10 African Americans is a carrier, as is 1 in 20 Latin Americans. Recent research strongly supports the use of hydroxyurea therapy for infants with sickle-cell anemia beginning at 9 months of age (Nevitt, Jones, & Howard, 2017). Stem cell transplantation also is being explored as a potential treatment for infants with sickle-cell anemia (Azar & Wong, 2017).

Other diseases that result from genetic abnormalities include cystic fibrosis, some forms of diabetes, hemophilia, Huntington disease, Alzheimer disease, spina bifida, and Tay-Sachs disease. Someday, scientists may be able to determine why these and other genetic abnormalities occur and discover how to cure them (Huang & others, 2017; Wang & others, 2017).

Genetic counselors, usually physicians or biologists who are well-versed in the field of medical genetics, may specialize in providing information to individuals who are at risk of giving birth to children with the kinds of genetic abnormalities just described (Besser & Mounts, 2017; Valiente-Palleja & others, 2018). They can evaluate the degree of risk involved and offer helpful strategies for offsetting some of the effects of these diseases (Jacher & others, 2017; Omaggio, Baker, & Conway, 2018; Sharony & others, 2018; Wang & others, 2018). To read about the career and work of a genetic counselor, see *Careers in Life-Span Development.*

Jennifer Leonhard, Genetic Counselor

Jennifer Leonhard is a genetic counselor at Sanford Bemidji Health Clinic in Bemidji, Minnesota. She obtained an undergraduate degree from Western Illinois University and a master's degree in genetic counseling from the University of Arkansas for Medical Sciences.

Genetic counselors like Jennifer work as members of a health care team, providing information and support to families with birth defects or genetic disorders. They identify families at risk by analyzing inheritance patterns and then explore options with the family. Some genetic counselors, like Leonhard, specialize in prenatal and pediatric genetics, while others focus on cancer genetics or psychiatric genetic disorders.

Genetic counselors hold specialized graduate degrees in medical genetics and counseling. They enter graduate school with undergraduate backgrounds from a variety of disciplines, including biology, genetics, psychology, public health, and social work. There are approximately 30 graduate genetic counseling programs

Jennifer Leonhard (*right*) is a genetic counselor at Sanford Health in Bemidji, Minnesota.
Courtesy of Jennifer Leonhard

in the United States. If you are interested in this profession, you can obtain further information from the National Society of Genetic Counselors at www.nsgc.org.

The Interaction of Heredity and Environment: The Nature-Nurture Debate

Is it possible to untangle the influence of heredity from that of environment and discover the role of each in producing individual differences in development? When heredity and environment interact, how does heredity influence the environment, and vice versa?

Behavior Genetics

Behavior genetics is the field that seeks to discover the influence of heredity and environment on individual differences in human traits and development. Behavior geneticists often study either twins or adoption situations (Charney, 2017; Machalek & others, 2017; Pinheiro & others, 2018; Rana & others, 2018).

In a **twin study,** the behavioral similarities between identical twins (who are genetically identical) are compared with the behavioral similarities between fraternal twins. Recall that although fraternal twins share the same womb, they are no more genetically alike than are non-twin siblings. By comparing groups of identical and fraternal twins, behavior geneticists capitalize on this basic knowledge that identical twins are more similar genetically than are fraternal twins: If they observe that a behavioral trait is more often shared by identical twins than by fraternal twins, they can infer that the trait has a genetic basis (Inderkum & Tarokh, 2018; Li & others, 2016; Rosenstrom & others, 2018; Wertz & others, 2018).

However, several issues complicate the interpretation of twin studies. For example, perhaps the environments of identical twins are more

behavior genetics The field that seeks to discover the influence of heredity and environment on individual differences in human traits and development.

twin study A study in which the behavioral similarity of identical twins is compared with the behavioral similarity of fraternal twins.

similar than those of fraternal twins. Parents and caregivers might stress the similarities of identical twins more than those of fraternal twins, and identical twins might perceive themselves as a "set" and play together more than fraternal twins do. If so, the observed similarities between identical twins might have a significant environmental basis.

In an **adoption study,** investigators seek to discover whether the behavior and psychological characteristics of adopted children are more like those of their adoptive parents, who have provided a home environment, or more like those of their biological parents, who have contributed their heredity (Salvatore & others, 2018). Another form of the adoption study compares adoptees with their adoptive siblings and their biological siblings (Kendler & others, 2016).

adoption study A study in which investigators seek to discover whether, in behavior and psychological characteristics, adopted children are more like their adoptive parents, who provided a home environment, or more like their biological parents, who contributed their heredity. Another form of the adoption study compares adoptive and biological siblings.

Heredity-Environment Correlations

The difficulties that researchers encounter in interpreting the results of twin and adoption studies reflect the complexities of heredity-environment interactions. Some of these interactions are heredity-environment correlations, which means that individuals' genes may influence the types of environments to which they are exposed. In a sense, individuals "inherit" environments that may be related or linked to genetic "propensities." Behavior geneticist Sandra Scarr (1993) described three ways in which heredity and environment are correlated:

- *Passive genotype-environment correlations* occur because biological parents, who are genetically related to the child, provide a rearing environment for the child. For example, the parents might have a genetic predisposition to be intelligent and read skillfully. Because they read well and enjoy reading, they provide their children with books to read. The likely outcome is that their children, given their own inherited predispositions from their parents and their book-filled environment, will become skilled readers.

- *Evocative genotype-environment correlations* occur because a child's characteristics elicit certain types of environments. For example, active, smiling children receive more social stimulation than passive, quiet children do. Cooperative, attentive children evoke more pleasant and instructional responses from the adults around them than uncooperative, distractible children do.

- *Active (niche-picking) genotype-environment correlations* occur when children seek out environments that they find compatible and stimulating. *Niche-picking* refers to finding a setting that is suited to one's abilities. Children select from their surrounding environment specific aspects that they respond to, learn about, or ignore. Their active selections of environments are related to their particular genotype. For example, outgoing children tend to seek out social contexts in which to interact with people, whereas shy children don't. Children who are musically inclined are likely to select musical environments in which they can successfully perform their skills.

The Epigenetic View and Gene × Environment (G × E) Interaction

Notice that Scarr's view gives the preeminent role in development to heredity: her analysis describes how heredity may influence the types of environments that children experience. Critics argue that the concept of heredity-environment correlation gives heredity too great an influence in determining development because it does not consider the role of prior environmental influences in shaping the correlation itself (Moore, 2017). In this section we look at some approaches that place greater emphasis on the role of the environment.

The Epigenetic View

In line with the concept of a collaborative gene, Gilbert Gottlieb (2007) proposed an **epigenetic view,** which states that development is the result of an ongoing, bidirectional interchange between heredity and the environment. Figure 6 compares the heredity-environment correlation and epigenetic views of development.

Let's look at an example that reflects the epigenetic view. A baby inherits genes from both parents at conception. During prenatal development, toxins, nutrition, and stress can influence some genes to stop functioning while others become stronger or weaker. During infancy, additional environmental experiences, such as exposure to toxins, nutrition, stress, learning, and encouragement, continue to modify genetic activity and the activity of the nervous system that directly underlies behavior. Heredity and environment thus operate together—or collaborate—to produce a person's well-being, intelligence, temperament, health, ability to pitch a baseball, ability to read, and so on (Moore, 2017).

Figure 6 Comparison of the Heredity-Environment Correlation and Epigenetic Views

How Would You...?

As a **human development and family studies professional,** how would you apply the epigenetic view to explain why one identical twin can develop alcoholism while the other twin does not?

Gene × Environment (G × E) Interaction

An increasing number of studies are exploring how the interaction between heredity and environment influences development, including interactions that involve specific DNA sequences (Bakusic & others, 2017; Grunblatt & others, 2018; Halldorsdottir & Binder, 2017; Quereshi & Mehler, 2018). The epigenetic mechanisms involve the actual molecular modification of the DNA strand as a result of environmental inputs in ways that alter gene functioning (Knyazev & others, 2018; Rozenblat & others, 2017; Szutorisz & Hurd, 2018).

One study found that individuals who have a short version of a gene labeled 5-HTTLPR (a gene involving the neurotransmitter serotonin) have an elevated risk of developing depression only if they *also* lead stressful lives (Caspi & others, 2003). Thus, the specific gene did not directly cause the development of depression; rather, the gene interacted with a stressful environment in a way that allowed the researchers to predict whether individuals would develop depression. A research meta-analysis indicated that the short version of 5-HTTLPR was linked with higher cortisol stress reactivity (Miller & others, 2013). Researchers also have found support for the interaction between the 5-HTTLPR gene and stress levels in predicting depression in adolescents and older adults (Petersen & others, 2012; Zannas & others, 2012).

Other research involving interaction between genes and environmental experiences has focused on attachment, parenting, and supportive child-rearing environments (Ein-Dor & others, 2018; Labella & Masten, 2018; Naumova & others, 2016). In one study, adults who experienced parental loss as young children were more likely to have unresolved attachment issues as adults only when they had the short version of the 5-HTTLPR gene (Caspers & others, 2009). The long version of the serotonin transporter gene apparently provided some protection and ability to cope better with parental loss. Other studies have found that variations in dopamine-related genes interact with supportive or unsupportive rearing environments to influence children's development (Bakermans-Kranenburg & van IJzendoorn, 2011). The type of research just described is referred to as studies of **gene × environment (G × E) interaction**—the interaction of a specific measured variation in DNA and a specific measured aspect of the environment (Moore, 2017; Samek & others, 2017).

Although there is considerable enthusiasm about the concept of gene × environment interaction (G × E), a research review concluded that this approach is plagued by difficulties in replicating results, inflated claims, and other weaknesses (Manuck & McCaffery, 2014). The science of G × E interaction is very young, and in the next several decades it will likely produce more precise findings (Fumagalli & others, 2018; Marioni & others, 2018).

epigenetic view Emphasizes that development is the result of an ongoing, bidirectional interchange between heredity and environment.

gene × environment (G × E) interaction The interaction of a specified measured variation in DNA and a specific measured aspect of the environment.

Conclusions About Heredity-Environment Interaction

If an attractive, popular, intelligent girl is elected president of her high school senior class, is her success due to heredity or to environment? Of course, the answer is "both."

The relative contributions of heredity and environment are not additive. That is, we can't say that such-and-such a percentage of nature and such-and-such a percentage of experience make us who we are. Nor is it accurate to say that full genetic expression happens once, at the time of conception or birth, after which we carry our genetic legacy into the world to see how far it takes us. Genes produce proteins throughout the life span, in many different environments. Or they don't produce these proteins, depending in part on how harsh or nourishing those environments are.

To what extent are this young girl's piano skills likely due to heredity, environment, or both?
©Francisco Romero/Getty Images

The emerging view is that complex behaviors are influenced by genes in ways that give people a propensity for a particular developmental trajectory (Kalashnikova, Goswami, & Burnham, 2018; Knyazev & others, 2018). However, the individual's actual development requires more: a particular environment. And that environment is complex, just like the mixture of genes we inherit (Almy & Cicchetti, 2018; Tremblay, Vitaro, & Cote, 2018). Environmental influences range from the things we lump together under "nurture" (such as culture, parenting, family dynamics, schooling, and neighborhood quality) to biological encounters (such as viruses, birth complications, and even biological events in cells).

In developmental psychologist David Moore's (2013, 2015, 2017) view, the biological systems that generate behaviors are extremely complex but too often these systems have been described in overly simplified ways that can be misleading. Thus, although genetic factors clearly contribute to behavior and psychological processes, they don't determine these phenotypes independently from the contexts in which they develop. From Moore's (2013, 2015, 2017) perspective, it is misleading to talk about "genes for" eye color, intelligence, personality, or other characteristics. Moore commented that in retrospect we should not have expected to be able to make the giant leap from DNA's molecules to a complete understanding of human behavior any more than we should anticipate being able to easily link air molecules in a concert hall with a full-blown appreciation of a symphony's wondrous experience.

Imagine for a moment that there is a cluster of genes that are somehow associated with youth violence. (This example is hypothetical because we don't know of any such combination.) The adolescent who carries this genetic mixture might experience a world of loving parents, regular nutritious meals, lots of books, and a series of competent teachers. Or the adolescent's world might include parental neglect, a neighborhood in which gunshots and crime are everyday occurrences, and inadequate schooling. In which of these environments are the adolescent's genes likely to manufacture the biological underpinnings of criminality?

If heredity and environment interact to determine the course of development, is that all there is to answering the question of what causes development? Are humans completely at the mercy of their genes and their environment as they develop through the life span? Genetic heritage and environmental experiences are pervasive influences on development. But in thinking about what causes development, recall our discussion of development as the co-construction of biology, culture, *and* the individual. Not only are we the outcomes of our heredity and the environment we experience, but we also can author a unique developmental path by changing our environment. As one psychologist concluded:

> In reality, we are both the creatures and creators of our worlds. We are . . . the products of our genes and environments. Nevertheless, . . . the stream of causation that shapes the future runs through our present choices . . . Mind matters . . . Our hopes, goals, and expectations influence our future. (Myers, 2010, p. 168)

Prenatal Development

germinal period The period of prenatal development that takes place during the first two weeks after conception. It includes the creation of the zygote, continued cell division, and the attachment of the zygote to the uterine wall.

We turn now to a description of how the process of development unfolds from its earliest moment—the moment of conception—when two parental cells, with their unique genetic contributions, merge to create a new individual.

Conception occurs when a single sperm cell from a male unites with an ovum (egg) in a female's fallopian tube in a process called fertilization. Over the next few months the genetic code discussed earlier directs a series of changes in the fertilized egg, but many events and hazards will influence how that egg develops and becomes a person.

The Course of Prenatal Development

Prenatal development lasts approximately 266 days, beginning with fertilization and ending with birth. Pregnancy can be divided into three periods: germinal, embryonic, and fetal.

The Germinal Period

The **germinal period** is the period of prenatal development that takes place in the first two weeks after conception. It includes the creation of the fertilized egg (the zygote), cell division, and the attachment of the multicellular organism to the uterine wall.

Rapid cell division by the zygote begins the germinal period. (Recall from earlier in the chapter that this cell division occurs through a process called mitosis.) Within one week after conception, the differentiation of these cells—their specialization for different tasks—has already begun. At this stage the organism, now called the blastocyst, consists of a hollow ball of cells that will eventually develop into the embryo, and the trophoblast, an outer layer of cells that later provides nutrition and support for the embryo. Implantation, the embedding of the blastocyst in the uterine wall, takes place during the second week after conception. Figure 7 summarizes these significant developments in the germinal period.

Figure 7 Major Developments in the Germinal Period

The Embryonic Period

The **embryonic period** is the period of prenatal development that occurs from two to eight weeks after conception. During the embryonic period, the rate of cell differentiation intensifies, support systems for cells form, and organs develop.

The mass of cells is now called an *embryo*, and three layers of cells form. The embryo's *endoderm* is the inner layer of cells, which will develop into the digestive and respiratory systems. The *ectoderm* is the outermost layer, which will become the nervous system, sensory receptors (ears, nose, and eyes, for example), and skin parts (hair and nails, for example). The *mesoderm* is the middle layer, which will become the circulatory system, bones, muscles, excretory system, and reproductive system. Every body part eventually develops from these three layers. The endoderm primarily produces internal body parts, the mesoderm primarily produces parts that surround the internal areas, and the ectoderm primarily produces surface parts. **Organogenesis** is the name given to the process of organ formation during the first two months of prenatal development. While they are being formed, the organs are especially vulnerable to environmental influences (Rios & Clevers, 2018; Schittny, 2017).

As the embryo's three layers form, life-support systems for the embryo develop rapidly. These systems include the amnion, the umbilical cord (both of which develop from the fertilized egg, not the mother's body), and the placenta. The amnion is like a bag or an envelope; it contains a clear fluid in which the developing embryo floats. The amniotic fluid provides an environment that is temperature- and humidity-controlled, as well as shockproof. The *umbilical cord*, which typically contains two arteries and one vein, connects the baby to the placenta. The *placenta* consists of a disk-shaped group of tissues in which small blood vessels from the mother and the offspring intertwine but do not join.

Very small molecules—oxygen, water, salt, and nutrients from the mother's blood, as well as carbon dioxide and digestive wastes from the baby's blood—pass back and forth between the mother and the embryo or fetus. Large molecules cannot pass through the placental wall; these include red blood cells and some harmful substances, such as most bacteria, maternal wastes, and hormones (Cuffe & others, 2017; Dube, Desparois, & Lafond, 2018). Virtually any drug or chemical substance a pregnant woman ingests can cross the placenta to some degree, unless it is metabolized or altered during passage, or is too large (Burton & Jauniaux, 2015; Koren & Ornoy, 2018).

One study confirmed that ethanol crosses the human placenta and primarily reflects maternal alcohol use (Matlow & others, 2013). Another study revealed that cigarette smoke weakened and increased the oxidative stress of fetal membranes from which the placenta develops (Menon & others, 2011). The stress hormone cortisol also can cross the placenta (Parrott & others, 2014). The mechanisms that govern the transfer of substances across the placental barrier are complex and not yet entirely understood (Huckle, 2017; Jeong & others, 2018; Vaughan & others, 2017; Zhang & others, 2018).

The Fetal Period

The **fetal period**, which lasts about seven months, is the prenatal period that extends from two months after conception until birth in typical pregnancies. Growth and development continue their dramatic course during this time.

Three months after conception (13 weeks), the fetus is about 3 inches long and weighs about four-fifths of an ounce. It has become active, moving its arms and legs, opening and closing its mouth, and moving its head. The face, forehead, eyelids, nose, and chin are distinguishable, as are the upper arms, lower arms, hands, and lower limbs. In most cases, the genitals can be identified as male or female. By the end of the fourth month of pregnancy (17 weeks), the fetus has grown to about 5.5 inches in length and weighs 5 ounces. At this time, a growth spurt occurs in the body's lower parts. For the first time, the mother can feel the fetus move.

By the end of the fifth month (22 weeks), the fetus is about 12 inches long and weighs close to a pound. Structures of the skin have formed—including toenails and fingernails. The fetus is more active, showing a preference for a particular position in the womb. By the end of the sixth month

embryonic period The period of prenatal development that occurs two to eight weeks after conception. During the embryonic period, the rate of cell differentiation intensifies, support systems for the cells form, and organs appear.

organogenesis Organ formation that takes place during the first two months of prenatal development.

fetal period The prenatal period of development that begins two months after conception and usually lasts for seven months.

(26 weeks), the fetus is about 14 inches long and has gained another 6 to 12 ounces. The eyes and eyelids are completely formed, and a fine layer of hair covers the head. A grasping reflex is present and irregular breathing movements occur.

As early as six months of pregnancy (about 24 to 25 weeks after conception), the fetus for the first time has a chance of surviving outside the womb—that is, it is *viable*. Infants that are born early, or between 24 and 37 weeks of pregnancy, usually need help breathing because their lungs are not yet fully mature. By the end of the seventh month, the fetus is about 16 inches long and weighs about 3 pounds.

During the last two months of prenatal development, fatty tissues develop and the functioning of various organ systems—heart and kidneys, for example—steps up. During the eighth and ninth months, the fetus grows longer and gains substantial weight—about 4 more pounds. At birth, the average American baby weighs 8 pounds and is about 20 inches long.

In addition to describing prenatal development in terms of germinal, embryonic, and fetal periods, prenatal development also can be divided into equal three-month periods called *trimesters*. Figure 8 gives an overview of the main events during each

How Would You...?

As a **human development and family studies professional,** how would you characterize the greatest risks at each period of prenatal development?

First trimester (first 3 months)

Conception to 4 weeks
- Is less than 1/10 inch long
- Beginning development of spinal cord, nervous system, gastrointestinal system, heart, and lungs
- Amniotic sac envelops the preliminary tissues of entire body
- Is called a "zygote," then a "blastocyst"

8 weeks
- Is just about .6 inch long
- Face is forming with rudimentary eyes, ears, mouth, and tooth buds
- Arms and legs are moving
- Brain is forming
- Fetal heartbeat is detectable with ultrasound
- Is called an "embryo"

12 weeks
- Is 2 inches long and weighs about .5 ounces
- Can move arms, legs, fingers, and toes
- Fingerprints are present
- Can smile, frown, suck, and swallow
- Sex is distinguishable
- Can urinate
- Is called a "fetus"

Second trimester (middle 3 months)

16 weeks
- Is about 5 inches long and weighs about 3.5 ounces
- Heartbeat is strong
- Skin is thin, transparent
- Downy hair (lanugo) covers body
- Fingernails and toenails are forming
- Has coordinated movements; is able to roll over in amniotic fluid

20 weeks
- Is about 6.5 inches long and weighs about 11 ounces
- Heartbeat is audible with ordinary stethoscope
- Sucks thumb
- Hiccups
- Hair, eyelashes, eyebrows are present

24 weeks
- Is about 12 inches long and weighs about 1.3 pounds
- Skin is wrinkled and covered with protective coating (vernix caseosa)
- Eyes are open
- Waste matter is collected in bowel
- Has strong grip

Third trimester (last 3 months)

28 weeks
- Is about 16 inches long and weighs about 3 pounds
- Is adding body fat
- Is very active
- Rudimentary breathing movements are present

32 weeks
- Is about 17 inches long and weighs about 4 pounds
- Has periods of sleep and wakefulness
- Responds to sounds
- May assume the birth position
- Bones of head are soft and flexible
- Iron is being stored in liver

36 to 38 weeks
- Is 19 to 20 inches long and weighs 6 to 7½ pounds
- Skin is less wrinkled
- Vernix caseosa is thick
- Lanugo is mostly gone
- Is less active
- Is gaining immunities from mother

Figure 8 Growth and Development in the Three Trimesters of Prenatal Development
(*Top*) ©David Spears/PhotoTake, Inc.; (*middle*) ©Neil Bromhall/Science Source; (*bottom*) ©Brand X Pictures/PunchStock

trimester. Remember that the three trimesters are not the same as the three prenatal periods we have discussed. The germinal and embryonic periods occur in the first trimester. The fetal period begins toward the end of the first trimester and continues through the second and third trimesters.

The Brain

One of the most remarkable aspects of the prenatal period is the development of the brain (Andescavage & others, 2017; Ferrazzi & others, 2018). By the time babies are born, they have approximately 100 billion **neurons,** or nerve cells, which handle information processing at the cellular level in the brain. During prenatal development, neurons move to specific locations and start to become connected. The basic architecture of the human brain is assembled during the first two trimesters of prenatal development. In typical development, the third trimester of prenatal development and the first two years of postnatal life are characterized by connectivity and functioning of neurons (Toth & others, 2017; van den Heuvel & others, 2018).

Four important phases of the brain's development during the prenatal period involve (1) formation of the neural tube; (2) neurogenesis; (3) neural migration, and (4) neural connectivity.

As the human embryo develops inside its mother's womb, the nervous system begins forming as a long, hollow tube located on the embryo's back. This pear-shaped *neural tube*, which forms at about 27 days after conception, develops out of the ectoderm (Keunen, Counsell, & Bender, 2017). The tube closes at the top and bottom ends at about 24 days after conception. Figure 9 shows that the nervous system still has a tubular appearance 6 weeks after conception.

Figure 9 Early Formation of the Nervous System
The photograph shows the primitive, tubular appearance of the nervous system at six weeks in the human embryo.
©Claude Edelmann/Science Source

Two birth defects related to a failure of the neural tube to close are anencephaly and spina bifida. When a fetus has anencephaly (that is, when the head end of the neural tube fails to close), the highest regions of the brain fail to develop and the baby dies in the womb, during childbirth, or shortly after birth (Steric & others, 2015). Spina bifida, an incomplete development of the spinal cord, results in varying degrees of paralysis of the lower limbs (Li & others, 2018; Miller, 2018). Individuals with spina bifida usually need assistive devices such as crutches, braces, or wheelchairs. Both maternal diabetes and obesity also place the fetus at risk for developing neural tube defects (McMahon & others, 2013; Yu, Wu, & Yang, 2016). Further, research reveals that a high level of maternal stress during pregnancy is associated with neural tube defects in offspring (Li & others, 2013). A strategy that can help to prevent neural tube defects is for women to take adequate amounts of the B vitamin folic acid (Li & others, 2018; Viswanathan & others, 2017). A recent large-scale study in Brazil found that when flour was fortified with folic acid it produced a significant reduction in neural tube defects (Santos & others, 2016).

In a normal pregnancy, once the neural tube has closed, a massive proliferation of new immature neurons begins to take place about the fifth prenatal week (Zhu & others, 2017). The production of new neurons is called *neurogenesis*, which continues through the remainder of the prenatal period although it is largely complete by the end of the fifth month after conception (Keunen, Counsell, & Benders, 2017). At the peak of neurogenesis, it is estimated that as many as 200,000 neurons are being generated every minute.

At approximately 6 to 24 weeks after conception, *neuronal migration* occurs (Nelson, 2011). Cells begin moving outward from their point of origin to their appropriate locations and creating the different levels, structures, and regions of the brain (Miyazaki, Song, & Takahashi, 2016). Once a cell has migrated to its target destination, it must mature and develop a more complex structure.

neurons Nerve cells that handle information processing at the cellular level in the brain.

At about the 23rd prenatal week, connections between neurons begin to form, a process that continues postnatally (Miller, Huppi, & Mallard, 2016; van den Heuvel & others, 2018). We will have much more to say about the structure of neurons, their connectivity, and the development of the infant brain.

Prenatal Tests

Together with her doctor, a pregnant woman will decide the extent to which she should undergo prenatal testing. A number of tests can indicate whether a fetus is developing normally; these include ultrasound sonography, fetal MRI, chorionic villus sampling, amniocentesis, maternal blood screening, and noninvasive prenatal diagnosis. The decision to have a given test depends on several criteria, such as the mother's age, medical history, and genetic risk factors.

Ultrasound Sonography

An ultrasound test is often conducted seven weeks into a pregnancy and at various times later in pregnancy. *Ultrasound sonography* is a prenatal medical procedure in which high-frequency sound waves are directed into the pregnant woman's abdomen (Tamai & others 2018). The echo from the sounds is transformed into a visual representation of the fetus's inner structures. This technique can detect many abnormalities in the fetus, including microcephaly, in which an abnormally small brain can produce intellectual disability; it can also determine the number of fetuses (that is, detect whether a woman is carrying twins or triplets) and give clues to the baby's sex (Calvo-Garcia, 2016; Larsson & others, 2018). A recent research review concluded that many aspects of the developing prenatal brain can be detected by ultrasound in the first trimester and that about 50 percent of spina bifida cases can be identified at this time, most of these being severe cases (Engels & others, 2016). There is virtually no risk to the woman or fetus in using ultrasound.

A 6-month-old poses with the ultrasound image take four months into the baby's prenatal development. *What is ultrasound sonography and what can it detect?*
©AJ Photo/BSIP/age fotostock

Chorionic Villus Sampling

At some point between the 10th and 12th weeks of pregnancy, chorionic villus sampling may be used to screen for genetic defects and chromosome abnormalities. *Chorionic villus sampling (CVS)* is a prenatal medical procedure in which a tiny tissue sample from the placenta is removed and analyzed (Carlson & Vora, 2017). The results are available in about 10 days.

Amniocentesis

Between the 15th and 18th weeks of pregnancy, *amniocentesis* may be performed. In this procedure, a sample of amniotic fluid is withdrawn by syringe and tested for chromosomal or metabolic disorders (Jung & others, 2017). The later in the pregnancy amniocentesis is performed, the better its diagnostic potential. However, the earlier it is performed, the more useful it is in deciding how to handle a pregnancy when the fetus is found to have a disorder. It may take two weeks for enough cells to grow so that amniocentesis test results can be obtained. Amniocentesis brings a small risk of miscarriage: about 1 woman in every 200 to 300 miscarries after amniocentesis.

Maternal Blood Screening

During the 16th to 18th weeks of pregnancy, maternal blood screening may be performed. *Maternal blood screening* identifies pregnancies that have an elevated risk for birth defects such as spina bifida and Down syndrome (le Ray & others, 2018), as well as congenital heart disease risk for children (Sun & others, 2015). The current blood test is called the *triple screen* because it measures three substances in the mother's blood. After an abnormal triple screen result, the next step is usually an ultrasound examination. If an ultrasound does not explain the abnormal triple screen results, amniocentesis typically is used.

Fetal MRI

The development of brain-imaging techniques has led to increasing use of *fetal MRI* to diagnose fetal malformations (Cheong & Miller, 2018; Choudhri & others, 2018; Ferrazzi & others, 2018; Kang & others, 2017) (see Figure 10). MRI, which stands for magnetic resonance imaging, uses a powerful magnet and radio images to generate detailed images of the body's organs and structures. Currently, high-quality ultrasound is still the first choice in fetal screening, but fetal MRI can provide more detailed images than ultrasound (Griffiths & others, 2018). In many instances, ultrasound will indicate a possible abnormality and fetal MRI will then be used to obtain a clearer, more detailed image (Bernardo & others, 2017). Among the fetal malformations that fetal MRI may be able to detect better than ultrasound sonography are certain abnormalities of the central nervous system, chest, gastrointestinal tract, genital/urinary organs, and placenta (Manganaro & others, 2018). In a recent research review, it was concluded that fetal MRI often does not provide good results in the first trimester of pregnancy because of small fetal structures and movement artifacts (Wataganara & others, 2016). Also, in this review, it was argued that fetal MRI can be especially beneficial in assessing central nervous system abnormalities in the third trimester of pregnancy.

Figure 10 A Fetal MRI.
Increasingly, MRI is being used to diagnose fetal malformations.
©Du Cane Medical Imaging Ltd/
Science Source

Fetal Sex Determination

Chorionic villus sampling has often been used to determine the sex of the fetus at some point between 11 and 13 weeks of gestation. Also, in a recent study, ultrasound accurately identified the sex of the fetus between 11 and 13 weeks of gestation (Manzanares & others, 2016). Recently, though, some noninvasive techniques, such as cell-free DNA analysis in blood plasma, have been able to detect the sex of the fetus at an earlier point (Degrelle & Fournier, 2018; Skrzypek & Hui, 2017). A meta-analysis of studies confirmed that a baby's sex can be detected as early as 7 weeks into pregnancy (Devaney & others, 2011). Being able to detect an offspring's sex as well as the presence of various diseases and defects at such an early stage raises ethical concerns about couples' motivation to terminate a pregnancy (Browne, 2017).

Infertility and Reproductive Technology

Recent advances in biological knowledge have also opened up many choices for infertile people (Dorfeshan & others, 2018; Florencio & others, 2018; Liebermann, 2017; Silber, 2017). Approximately 10 to 15 percent of couples in the United States experience infertility, which is defined as the inability to conceive a child after 12 months of regular intercourse without contraception. The cause of infertility can rest with either the woman or the man, or both (Namgoong & Kim, 2018; Sunderam & others, 2017). The woman may not be ovulating (releasing eggs to be fertilized); she may be producing abnormal ova; her fallopian tubes (by which ova normally reach the womb) may be blocked; or she may have a condition that prevents implantation of the embryo into the uterus. The man may produce too few sperm; the sperm may lack motility (the ability to move adequately); or he may have a blocked passageway (Razavi & others, 2017; Yu & others, 2018; Zalzali & others, 2018).

Surgery can correct some causes of infertility; for others, hormone-based drugs may be effective. Of the 2 million U.S. couples who seek help for infertility every year, about 40,000 try assisted reproduction technologies. *In vitro fertilization (IVF)*, the technique that produced the world's first "test tube baby" in 1978, involves eggs and sperm being combined in a laboratory dish. If any eggs are successfully fertilized, one or more of the resulting fertilized eggs is transferred into the woman's uterus.

How Would You...?

As a **psychologist,** how would you advise a 25-year-old mother who is concerned about the possibility of birth defects but has no genetic history of these types of problems?

Any multiple birth increases the likelihood that the babies will have life-threatening and costly problems, such as extremely low birth weight (March of Dimes, 2018). In a recent national study, low birthweight and preterm birth were significantly higher in infants conceived via assisted-reproduction technology (Sunderam & others, 2017). However, research reviews conclude that children and adolescents conceived through new reproductive technologies—such as in vitro fertilization—are as well-adjusted as their counterparts conceived by natural means (Golombok, 2011a, b, 2017; Golombok & others, 2018).

Hazards to Prenatal Development

For most babies, the course of prenatal development goes smoothly. Their mother's womb protects them as they develop. Despite this protection, however, the environment can affect the embryo or fetus in many well-documented ways.

General Principles

A **teratogen** is any agent that can potentially cause a birth defect or negatively alter cognitive and behavioral outcomes. The field of study that investigates the causes of birth defects is called *teratology* (Boschen & others, 2018; Stancil & others, 2018). Teratogens include drugs, incompatible blood types, environmental pollutants, infectious diseases, nutritional deficiencies, maternal stress, advanced maternal and paternal age, and environmental pollutants.

The dose, genetic susceptibility, and time of exposure to a particular teratogen influence both the severity of the damage to an embryo or fetus and the type of defect:

1. *Dose*—The dose effect is rather obvious—the greater the dose of an agent, such as a drug, the greater the effect.

2. *Genetic susceptibility*—The type or severity of abnormalities caused by a teratogen is linked to the genotype of the pregnant woman and the genotype of the embryo or fetus (Cassina & others, 2017; Middleton & others, 2017).

3. *Time of exposure*—Teratogens do more damage when they occur at some points in development than at others. The probability of a structural defect is greatest early in the embryonic period, when organs are being formed (Feldkamp & others, 2017; Mazzu-Nascimento & others, 2017). After organogenesis is complete, teratogens are less likely to cause anatomical defects. Instead, exposure during the fetal period is more likely to stunt growth or create problems in the way organs function. This is especially true for the developing fetal brain, which continues to form connections throughout pregnancy.

To examine some key teratogens and their effects, let's begin with drugs.

teratogen Any agent that can potentially cause a birth defect or negatively alter cognitive and behavioral outcomes.

Prescription and Nonprescription Drugs

Prescription drugs that can function as teratogens include antibiotics, such as streptomycin and tetracycline; some antidepressants; certain hormones, such as progestin and synthetic estrogen; and Accutane (isotretinoin), often prescribed for acne (Brown & others, 2017; Dathe & Schaefer, 2018). Among the birth defects caused by Accutane are heart defects, eye and ear abnormalities, and brain malformation. In a recent study, Accutane was the fourth most common drug given to female adolescents who were seeking contraception advice from a physician (Stancil & others, 2017). However, physicians did not give the adolescent girls adequate information about the negative effects of Accutane on offspring if the girls become pregnant. Nonprescription drugs that can be harmful include diet pills and high doses of aspirin.

Psychoactive Drugs

Psychoactive drugs act on the nervous system to alter states of consciousness, modify perceptions, and change moods. Examples include caffeine, alcohol, and nicotine, as well as illegal drugs such as cocaine, marijuana, and heroin.

Caffeine People often consume caffeine by drinking coffee, tea, or colas, or by eating chocolate. Research has been mixed on the effects of caffeine intake by pregnant women on the fetus (Chen & others, 2016; De Medeiros & others, 2017). However, the influence of increased consumption of energy drinks that typically have extremely high levels of caffeine on the development of offspring has not yet been studied. The U.S. Food and Drug Administration recommends that pregnant women either not consume caffeine or consume it only sparingly.

Alcohol Heavy drinking by pregnant women can be devastating to offspring (Jacobson & others, 2017). **Fetal alcohol spectrum disorders (FASD)** are a cluster of abnormalities and problems that appear in the offspring of mothers who drink alcohol heavily during pregnancy (Del Campo & Jones, 2017; Helgesson & others, 2018). The abnormalities include facial deformities and defective limbs, face, and heart (Pei & others, 2017). Most children with FASD have learning problems, and many are below average in intelligence; some have an intellectual disability (Khoury & Milligan, 2018). One study revealed that children with FASD have deficiencies in the brain pathways involved in working memory (Diwadkar & others, 2012). A recent research review concluded that FASD is linked to a lower level of executive function in children, especially in planning (Kingdon, Cardoso, & McGrath, 2016). And in a recent study, FASD was associated with both externalized and internalized behavior problems in childhood (Tsang & others, 2016). Also, in a recent study in the United Kingdom, the life expectancy of individuals with FASD was only 34 years of age, about 42 percent of the life expectancy of the general population (Thanh & Jonsson, 2016). In this study, the most common causes of death among individuals with FASD were suicide (15 percent), accidents (14 percent), and poisoning by illegal drugs or alcohol (7 percent). Although mothers of FASD infants are heavy drinkers, many mothers who are heavy drinkers may not have children with FASD or may have one child with FASD and other children who do not have it.

Fetal alcohol spectrum disorders (FASD) are characterized by a number of physical abnormalities and learning problems. Notice the wide-set eyes, flat cheekbones, and thin upper lip in this child with FASD.
©Streissguth, AP, Landesman-Dwyer S, Martin, JC, & Smith, DW (1980). Teratogenic effects of alcohol in humans and laboratory animals. *Science, 209*, 353–361.

What are some guidelines for alcohol use during pregnancy? Even drinking just one or two servings of beer or wine or one serving of hard liquor a few days a week can have negative effects on the fetus, although it is generally agreed that this level of alcohol use will not cause fetal alcohol spectrum disorders (Sarman, 2018). The U.S. Surgeon General recommends that no alcohol be consumed during pregnancy, as does the French Alcohol Society (Rolland & others, 2016). And research suggests that it may not be wise to consume alcohol at the time of conception. Despite such recommendations, a recent large-scale U.S. study found that

11.5 percent of adolescent and 8.7 percent of adult pregnant women reported using alcohol in the previous month (Oh & others, 2017).

Nicotine Cigarette smoking by pregnant women can also adversely influence prenatal development, birth, and postnatal development (Ostfeld & others, 2018). Preterm births and low birth weights, fetal and neonatal deaths, respiratory problems, sudden infant death syndrome (SIDS, also known as crib death), and cardiovascular problems are all more common among the offspring of mothers who smoked during pregnancy (Zhang & others, 2017). Prenatal smoking has been implicated in as many as 25 percent of infants being born with a low birth weight (Brown & Graves, 2013).

Researchers also have found that maternal smoking during pregnancy is a risk factor for the development of attention deficit hyperactivity disorder in offspring (Pohlabein & others, 2017). A recent meta-analysis of 15 studies concluded that smoking during pregnancy increased the risk of children having ADHD and the risk of having ADHD was greater for children whose mothers were heavy smokers (Huang & others, 2018a). Also, in a recent study, maternal cigarette smoking during pregnancy was linked with offspring being more likely to smoke cigarettes at 16 years of age (De Genna & others, 2016). Further, a recent study revealed that daughters whose mothers smoked during their pregnancy were more likely to subsequently smoke during their own pregnancy (Ncube & Mueller, 2017). Another study found that maternal smoking during pregnancy was associated with increased risk of asthma and wheezing of offspring during adolescence (Hollams & others, 2014).

Researchers have documented that environmental tobacco smoke is linked to negative outcomes for offspring (Vardavas & others, 2016). In one study, environmental tobacco smoke led to an increased risk of low birth weight in offspring (Salama & others, 2013) and to diminished ovarian functioning in female offspring (Kilic & others, 2012). Another study revealed that environmental tobacco smoke was associated with 114 deregulations, especially those involving immune functioning, in the fetal cells of offspring (Votavova & others, 2012). Maternal exposure to environmental tobacco smoke during prenatal development also increased the risk of stillbirth (Varner & others, 2014).

Despite the plethora of negative outcomes for maternal smoking during pregnancy, a recent large-scale U.S. study revealed that 23 percent of adolescent and 15 percent of pregnant adult women reported using tobacco in the previous month (Oh & others, 2017). And a final point about nicotine use during pregnancy involves the potential effects of the recent dramatic increase in the use of e-cigarettes (Tegin & others, 2018; Wagner, Camerota, & Propper, 2017).

This baby was exposed to cocaine prenatally. *What are some of the possible effects on development of being exposed to cocaine prenatally?*
©Chuck Nacke/Alamy

Cocaine Does cocaine use during pregnancy harm the developing embryo and fetus? One research study found that cocaine quickly crossed the placenta to reach the fetus (De Giovanni & Marchetti, 2012). The most consistent finding is that cocaine exposure during prenatal development is associated with reduced birth weight, length, and head circumference (Gouin & others, 2011). In other studies, prenatal cocaine exposure has been linked to impaired connectivity of the thalamus and prefrontal cortex in newborns (Salzwedel & others, 2017); impaired motor development at 2 years of age and a slower rate of growth through 10 years of age (Richardson, Goldschmidt, & Willford, 2008); impaired language development and information processing, including attention deficits (especially impulsivity) (Accornero & others, 2006; Richardson & others, 2011); self-regulation problems at age 12 (Minnes & others, 2016); attention deficit hyperactivity disorder (Richardson & others, 2016); increased behavioral problems, especially externalizing problems such as high rates of aggression, oppositional defiant disorder, and delinquency (Minnes & others, 2010; Richardson & others, 2011, 2016); posttraumatic stress disorder (PTSD) (Richardson & others, 2016); and increased likelihood of being in a special education program that involves support services (Levine & others, 2008).

Some researchers argue that these findings should be interpreted cautiously (Accornero & others, 2006). Why? Because other factors in the lives of pregnant women who use cocaine (such as poverty, malnutrition, and other substance abuse) often cannot be ruled out as possible contributors to the problems found in their children (Messiah & others, 2011). For example, cocaine users are more likely than nonusers to smoke cigarettes, use marijuana, drink alcohol, and take amphetamines.

Despite these cautions, the weight of research evidence indicates that children born to mothers who use cocaine are likely to have neurological, medical, and cognitive deficits (Cain, Bornick, & Whiteman, 2013; Field, 2007; Martin & others, 2016; Mayer & Zhang, 2009; Parcianello & others, 2018; Richardson & others, 2011, 2016; Scott-Goodwin, Puerto, & Moreno, 2016). Cocaine use by pregnant women is never recommended.

Marijuana An increasing number of studies find that marijuana use by pregnant women has negative outcomes for offspring (Ruisch & others, 2018). In a recent meta-analysis, marijuana use during pregnancy was linked to offsprings' low birth weight and a greater likelihood of being placed in a neonatal intensive care unit (NICU) (Gunn & others, 2016; Volkow, Compton, & Wargo, 2017). An earlier study revealed that marijuana use by pregnant women was associated with stillbirth (Varner & others, 2014). Another study found that prenatal marijuana exposure was related to lower intelligence in children (Goldschmidt & others, 2008). And yet another study indicated that prenatal exposure to marijuana was linked to marijuana use at 14 years of age (Day, Goldschmidt, & Thomas, 2006). In sum, marijuana use is not recommended for pregnant women.

Despite increasing evidence of negative outcomes, researchers found that marijuana use by pregnant women increased from 2.4 percent in 2002 to 3.85 percent in 2014 (Brown & others, 2016). And there is considerable concern that marijuana use by pregnant women may increase further, given the increasing number of states that have legalized marijuana (Chasnoff, 2017; Hennessy, 2018).

Heroin It is well documented that infants whose mothers are addicted to heroin show several behavioral difficulties at birth (Angelotta & Appelbaum, 2017; National Institute of Drug Abuse, 2018). The difficulties include withdrawal symptoms, such as tremors, irritability, abnormal crying, disturbed sleep, and impaired motor control. Many infants continue to show behavioral problems at their first birthday, and attention deficits may appear later in development. The most common treatment for heroin addiction, methadone, is associated with very severe withdrawal symptoms in newborns (Lai & others, 2017). Increasingly, buprenorphine is being used to treat heroin use during pregnancy (Krans & others, 2016).

Synthetic Opioids and Opiate-Related Pain Killers An increasing number of women are using synthetic opioids, such as fentanyl, and opiate-related pain relievers obtained legally by prescription, such as OxyContin and Vicodin, during their pregnancy (Haycraft, 2018). Infants born to women using these substances during pregnancy are at risk for experiencing opioid withdrawal (Lacaze-Masmonteil & O'Flaherty, 2018). Other possible outcomes for children exposed prenatally to these substances are just beginning to be studied (National Institute of Drug Abuse, 2018). Any prolonged use of synthetic opioids and opiate-related pain relievers is not recommended (Food and Drug Administration, 2018a).

Environmental Hazards

Many aspects of our modern industrial world can endanger the embryo or fetus. Some specific hazards to the embryo or fetus include radiation, toxic wastes, and other environmental pollutants (Sreetharan & others, 2017; Yang, Ren, & Tang, 2017).

X-ray radiation can affect the developing embryo or fetus, especially in the first several weeks after conception, when women do not yet know they are pregnant. Women and their physicians should weigh the risk of an X-ray when the woman is or might be pregnant (Rajaraman & others, 2011). However, a routine diagnostic X-ray of a body area other than the abdomen, with the woman's abdomen protected by a lead apron, is generally considered safe (Brent, 2009, 2011).

Maternal Diseases

Maternal diseases and infections can produce defects in offspring by crossing the placental barrier, or they can cause damage during birth (Cuffe & others, 2017; Koren & Ornoy, 2018). Rubella (German measles) is one disease that can cause prenatal defects. A recent research review concluded that rubella exposure during pregnancy is most likely to cause impairments involving the cardiovascular system and pulmonary system, as well as microcephaly (Yazigi & others, 2017). Women who plan to have children should have a blood test before they become pregnant to determine whether they are immune to the disease (Ogbuanu & others, 2014).

Syphilis (a sexually transmitted infection) is more damaging later in prenatal development—four months or more after conception. Damage includes eye lesions, which can cause blindness, and skin lesions (Braccio, Sharland, & Ladhani, 2016). Penicillin is the only known treatment for syphilis during pregnancy (Moline & Smith, 2016).

Another infection that has received widespread attention is genital herpes. Newborns contract this virus when they are delivered through the birth canal of a mother with genital herpes (Sampath, Maduro, & Schillinger, 2018). About one-third of babies delivered through an infected birth canal die; another one-fourth suffer brain damage. If an active case of genital herpes is detected in a pregnant woman close to her delivery date, a cesarean section can be performed (in which the infant is delivered through an incision in the mother's abdomen) to keep the virus from infecting the newborn (Pinninti & Kimberlin, 2013).

AIDS is a sexually transmitted infection that is caused by the human immunodeficiency virus (HIV), which destroys the body's immune system (Taylor & others, 2017). A mother can infect her offspring with HIV/AIDS in three ways: (1) across the placenta during gestation; (2) through contact with maternal blood or fluids during delivery; and (3) through breast feeding. The transmission of AIDS through breast feeding is a particular problem in many developing countries (UNICEF, 2018). Babies born to HIV-infected mothers can be (1) infected and symptomatic (show HIV symptoms); (2) infected but asymptomatic (not show HIV symptoms); or (3) not infected at all. An infant who is infected and asymptomatic may still develop HIV symptoms up to 15 months of age.

The more widespread disease of diabetes, characterized by high levels of sugar in the blood, also affects offspring (Briana & others, 2018; Haertle & others, 2017; Kaseva & others, 2018). Women who have gestational diabetes (a condition in which women without previously diagnosed diabetes develop high blood glucose levels during pregnancy) have an increased risk of having very large infants (weighing 10 pounds or more), and the infants themselves are at risk for diabetes (Mitanchez & others, 2015) and cardiovascular disease (Amrithraj & others, 2017). Further, a recent study found that maternal diabetes during pregnancy was linked to offspring having an increased risk for fatty liver disease at 18 years of age (Patel & others, 2016).

Other Parental Factors

So far we have discussed a number of drugs, environmental hazards, maternal diseases, and incompatible blood types that can harm the embryo or fetus. Now we will explore other characteristics of the mother and father that can affect prenatal and child development, including nutrition, age, and emotional states and stress.

Maternal Diet and Nutrition A developing embryo or fetus depends completely on its mother for nutrition, which comes from the mother's blood (Kominiarek & Peaceman, 2017). The nutritional status of the embryo or fetus is determined by the mother's total caloric intake as well as her intake of proteins, vitamins, and minerals. Children born to malnourished mothers are more likely than other children to be malformed.

Maternal obesity adversely affects pregnancy outcomes through increased rates of hypertension, diabetes, respiratory complications, infections, and depression in the mother (Baugh & others, 2016; Kumpulainen & others, 2018; Preston, Reynolds, & Pearson, 2018). Research studies have found that maternal obesity is linked to increased risk of stillbirth (Gardosi & others, 2013) or preterm birth (Cnattingius & others, 2013), and increased likelihood that the newborn will be placed in a neonatal intensive care unit (Minsart & others, 2013). A recent study revealed that at 14 weeks following conception, fetuses of obese pregnant women had less efficient cardiovascular functioning than fetuses whose mothers were not obese (Isgut & others, 2017). Further, a longitudinal study revealed that obesity during pregnancy was associated with long-term cardiovascular morbidity in adults (Yaniv-Salem & others, 2016). Further, two recent research reviews concluded that maternal obesity during pregnancy is associated with an increased likelihood of offspring being obese in childhood and adulthood (Pinto Pereira & others, 2016; Santangeli, Sattar, & Huda, 2015). Management of obesity that includes weight loss and increased exercise prior to pregnancy is likely to benefit both the mother and the baby (Aubuchon-Endsley & others, 2018; Dutton & others, 2018).

One aspect of maternal nutrition that is important for normal prenatal development is folic acid, a B-complex vitamin (Li & others, 2018; Viswanathan & others, 2017). A study of more than 34,000 women found that taking folic acid either alone or as part of a multivitamin for at least one year prior to conceiving was linked with a 70 percent lower risk of delivering at 20 to 28 weeks and a 50 percent lower risk of delivering at 28 to 32 weeks (Bukowski & others, 2008). Also, as indicated earlier in the chapter, lack of folic acid is related to neural tube defects in offspring (Kancherla & Oakley, 2018). The U.S. Department of Health and Human Services (2018) recommends that pregnant women consume a minimum of 400 micrograms of folic acid per day (about twice the amount the average woman gets in one day). Orange juice and spinach are examples of foods that are rich in folic acid. Also, a recent research study in China found that folic acid supplementation during pregnancy reduced the risk of preterm birth (X. Liu & others, 2015).

Fish is often recommended as part of a healthy diet and in general fish consumption during pregnancy has positive benefits for children's development (Golding & others, 2016; Julvez & others, 2016). The Food and Drug Administration (2018b) recommends that pregnant women increase their consumption of fish especially because they contain vital nutrients such as omega-3 fatty acids, protein, vitamins, and minerals such as iron. However, pollution has made some kinds of fish a risky choice for pregnant women. Some fish contain high levels of mercury, which is released into the air both naturally and by industrial processes (Wells & others, 2011). Mercury that falls into the water can accumulate in large fish, such as shark, swordfish, king mackerel, and some species of large tuna (American Pregnancy Association, 2018; Mayo Clinic, 2018). Researchers have found that prenatal mercury exposure through consumption of some types of fish during pregnancy is linked to adverse outcomes, including reduced placental and fetal growth, miscarriage, preterm birth, impaired neuropsychological development, and lower intelligence (Jeong & others, 2017; Llop & others, 2017; Murcia & others, 2016; Xue & others, 2007).

Recently, the American Pregnancy Association (2018) revised its conclusions about fish consumption during pregnancy, while continuing to recommend avoidance of high-mercury-content fish such tilefish from

Because the fetus depends entirely on its mother for nutrition, it is important for the pregnant woman to have good nutritional habits. In Kenya, this government clinic provides pregnant women with information about how their diet can influence the health of their fetus and off spring. *What might the information about diet be like?*
©Delphine Bousquet/AFP/Getty Images

the Gulf of Mexico, swordfish, shark, and king mackerel. The association and the FDA now recommend that pregnant women increase their consumption of low-mercury-content fish such as salmon, shrimp, tilapia, and cod.

Maternal Age When possible harmful effects on the fetus and infant are considered, two maternal age categories are of special interest: adolescence and 35 years and older (Gockley & others, 2016; Kawakita & others, 2016; Kingsbury, Plotnikova, & Naiman, 2018; Tearne & others, 2016). The mortality rate of infants born to adolescent mothers is double that of infants born to mothers in their twenties. Adequate prenatal care decreases the probability that a child born to an adolescent girl will have physical problems. However, adolescents are the least likely of women in all age groups to obtain prenatal assistance from clinics and health services.

Maternal age is also linked to the risk that a child will have Down syndrome (Jaruatanasirikul & others, 2017). A baby with Down syndrome rarely is born to a mother 16 to 34 years of age. However, when the mother reaches 40 years of age, the probability is slightly higher than 1 in 100 that a baby born to her will have Down syndrome, and by age 50 it is almost 1 in 10. When mothers are 35 years and older, risks also increase for low birth weight, preterm delivery, and fetal death (Koo & others, 2012). Also, in two studies, very advanced maternal age (40 years and older) was linked to adverse perinatal outcomes, including spontaneous abortion, preterm birth, stillbirth, and fetal growth restriction (Traisrisilp & Tongsong, 2015; Waldenstrom & others, 2015).

We still have much to learn about the role of the mother's age in pregnancy and childbirth. As women remain active, exercise regularly, and are careful about their nutrition, their reproductive systems may remain healthier at older ages than was thought possible in the past.

Emotional States and Stress When a pregnant woman experiences intense fears, anxieties, and other emotions or negative mood states, physiological changes occur that may affect her fetus (Fatima, Srivastav, & Mondal, 2017). A mother's stress may also influence the fetus indirectly by increasing the likelihood that the mother will engage in unhealthy behaviors such as taking drugs and receiving poor prenatal care.

High maternal anxiety and stress during pregnancy can have long-term consequences for the offspring (Isgut & others, 2017; Pinto & others, 2017). One study found that high levels of depression, anxiety, and stress during pregnancy were linked to internalizing problems in adolescence (Betts & others, 2014). A research review indicated that pregnant women with high levels of stress are at increased risk for having a child with emotional or cognitive problems, attention deficit hyperactivity disorder (ADHD), and language delay (Taige & others, 2007). Further, a recent research review concluded that regardless of the form of maternal prenatal stress or anxiety and the prenatal trimester in which the stress or anxiety occurred, during the first two years of life the offspring displayed lower levels of self-regulation (Korja & others, 2017).

Maternal depression also can have an adverse effect on birth outcomes and children's development (M. Park & others, 2018). A research review concluded that maternal depression is linked to preterm birth (Mparmpakas & others, 2013). In one study, researchers discovered that maternal depression during pregnancy was associated with low birth weight in full-term offspring (Chang & others, 2014). There is some concern about pregnant women taking antidepressant medication. For example, a recent study found that taking antidepressants early in pregnancy was linked to an increased risk of miscarriage (Almeida & others, 2016). In another study, when fetuses was exposed to serotonin-based antidepressants, they were more likely to be born preterm (Podrebarac & others, 2017). Further, a recent study revealed that taking antidepressants in the second or third trimester of pregnancy was linked to an increased risk of autism spectrum disorders in children (Boukhris & others, 2016).

How Would You...?

As a **health-care professional,** what advice would you give to an expectant mother who is experiencing extreme psychological stress?

Paternal Factors

In one study, in China, the longer fathers smoked, the higher the risk that their children would develop cancer (Ji & others, 1997). *What are some other paternal factors that can influence the development of the fetus and the child?*
©Ryan Pyle/Corbis/Getty Images

So far, we have discussed how characteristics of the mother—such as drug use, disease, diet and nutrition, age, and emotional states—can influence prenatal development and the development of the child. Might there also be some paternal risk factors? Indeed, there are several (Sigman, 2017). Men's exposure to lead, radiation, certain pesticides, and petrochemicals may cause abnormalities in sperm that lead to miscarriage or diseases such as childhood cancer (Cordier, 2008). The father's smoking during the mother's pregnancy also can cause problems for the offspring (Agricola & others, 2016; Han & others, 2015). A recent research review concluded that tobacco smoking is linked to impaired male fertility, as well as increased DNA damage, aneuploidy (abnormal number of chromosomes in a cell), and mutations in sperm (Beal, Yauk, & Marchetti, 2017). Also, in one study, heavy paternal smoking was associated with an increased risk of early miscarriage (Venners & others, 2005). This negative outcome may be related to the mother's exposure to secondhand smoke. In another study, paternal smoking around the time of the child's conception was linked to an increased risk of the child developing leukemia (Milne & others, 2012). Researchers have found that increasing paternal age decreases the success rate of in vitro fertilization and increases the risk of preterm birth (Sharma & others, 2015). Also, a research review concluded that there is an increased risk of spontaneous abortion, autism, and schizophrenic disorders when the father is 40 years of age and older (Reproductive Endocrinology and Infertility Committee & others, 2012).

Another way that the father can influence prenatal and birth outcomes is through his relationship with the mother. By being supportive, helping with chores, and having a positive attitude toward the pregnancy, the father can improve the physical and psychological well-being of the mother (Molgora & others, 2018). Negative behavior by the father also affects the mother: one study found that intimate partner violence increased the mother's stress level (Fonseca-Machado Mde & others, 2015).

Prenatal Care

Although prenatal care varies enormously from one woman to another, it usually involves a defined schedule of visits for medical care, which typically includes screening for manageable conditions and treatable diseases that can affect the baby or the mother (Flanagan & others, 2018; Goldenberg & McClure, 2018; Jarris & others, 2017). In addition to medical care, prenatal programs often include comprehensive educational, social, and nutritional services (Kroll-Desrosiers & others, 2016; Mazul, Salm Ward, & Ngui, 2017).

Information about pregnancy, labor, delivery, and caring for the newborn can be especially valuable for first-time mothers (Gabbe & others, 2018; Kim & others, 2018; R. Liu & others, 2017). Prenatal care is also very important for women in poverty and immigrant women because it links them with other social services (Mazul, Salm Ward, & Ngui, 2017). A recent study found that inadequate prenatal care was associated with very low birth weight (Xaverius & others, 2016).

An innovative program that is rapidly expanding in the United States is CenteringPregnancy (Barger, Faucher, & Murphy, 2015; Chae & others, 2017; DeCesare & Jackson, 2015; R. Liu & others, 2017). This program is relationship-centered and provides complete prenatal care in a group setting (Heberlein & others, 2016). It replaces traditional 15-minute physician visits with 90-minute peer group support sessions and self-examination led by a physician or certified nurse-midwife. Groups of up to 10 women (and often their partners) meet regularly beginning at 12 to 16 weeks of pregnancy. The sessions emphasize empowering women to play an active role in experiencing a positive pregnancy. Research has revealed that CenteringPregnancy group prenatal care is associated with reduced rates of preterm birth (Novick & others, 2013), as well as reduced rates of low birth weight and placement in a neonatal intensive care unit (Gareau & others, 2016). In another study with adolescent mothers, CenteringPregnancy was successful in getting participants to attend meetings, have appropriate weight gain, increase the use of highly effective contraceptive methods, and increase breast feeding (Trotman & others, 2015). Also, a research review concluded that participation in CenteringPregnancy increased breast-feeding initiation by 53 percent overall and by 71 percent in African American women (Robinson, Garnier-Villarreal, & Hanson, 2018).

The increasingly widespread CenteringPregnancy program alters routine prenatal care by bringing women out of exam rooms and into relationship-oriented groups.
©MBI/Stockbroker/Alamy Stock Photo

Exercise increasingly is recommended as part of a comprehensive prenatal care program (Huang & others, 2018b). Exercise during pregnancy helps prevent constipation, conditions the body, reduces excessive weight gain, lowers the risk of developing hypertension, and is associated with a more positive mental state, including a reduced level of depression (Bacchi & others, 2018; Magro-Malosso & others, 2017). Further, a recent study indicated that pregnant women who did not exercise three or more times a week were more likely to develop hypertension (Barakat & others, 2017). Also, a recent study indicated that two weekly 70-minute yoga sessions reduced pregnant women's stress and enhanced their immune system functioning (Chen & others, 2017). And regular exercise during pregnancy has benefits for the fetus and infant (Newton & May, 2018). For example, a recent study found that women's regular exercise during pregnancy was linked to more advanced development of the neonatal brain (Laborte-Lemoyne, Currier, & Ellenberg, 2017).

Normal Prenatal Development

Much of our discussion so far in this chapter has focused on what can go wrong with prenatal development. Prospective parents should take steps to avoid the vulnerabilities to fetal development that we have described. But it is important to keep in mind that most of the time, prenatal development does not go awry, and development occurs along the positive path that we described at the beginning of the chapter.

Birth and the Postpartum Period

The long wait for the moment of birth is over, and the infant is about to appear. What happens during childbirth, and what can be done to make the experience a positive one?

Nature writes the basic script for how birth occurs, but parents make important choices about the conditions surrounding birth. We look first at the sequence of physical steps through which a child is born.

The Birth Process

The birth process occurs in three stages. It may take place in different contexts and in most cases involves one or more attendants.

Stages of Birth

The first stage of the birth process is the longest. Uterine contractions are 15 to 20 minutes apart at the beginning and last up to a minute each. These contractions cause the woman's cervix to stretch and open. As the first stage progresses, the contractions

After the long journey of prenatal development, birth takes place. During birth the baby is on a threshold between two worlds. *What are the characteristics of the three stages of birth?*
©ERproductions Ltd/Getty Images

come closer together, occurring every two to five minutes. Their intensity increases. By the end of the first stage, contractions dilate the cervix to an opening of about 10 centimeters (4 inches) so that the baby can move from the uterus to the birth canal. For a woman having her first child, the first stage lasts an average of 6 to 12 hours; for subsequent children, this stage typically is much shorter.

The second birth stage begins when the baby's head starts to move through the cervix and the birth canal. It terminates when the baby completely emerges from the mother's body. With each contraction, the mother bears down hard to push the baby out of her body. By the time the baby's head is out of the mother's body, the contractions come almost every minute and last for about a minute. This stage typically lasts approximately 45 minutes to an hour.

Afterbirth is the third stage, during which the placenta, umbilical cord, and other membranes are detached and expelled. This final stage is the shortest of the three birth stages, lasting only minutes.

Childbirth Setting and Attendants

In 2015 in the United States, 98.5 percent of births took place in hospitals (Martin & others, 2017). Of the 1.5 percent of births occurring outside of a hospital, 63 percent took place in homes and almost 31 percent in free-standing birthing centers. The percentage of U.S. births at home is the highest since reporting of this context began in 1989. An increase in home births has occurred mainly among non-Latino White women, especially those who are older and married. For these non-Latino White women, two-thirds of their home births are attended by a midwife.

The person who helps a mother during birth varies across cultures. In U.S. hospitals, it has become the norm for fathers or birth coaches to be with the mother throughout labor and delivery. In the East African Nigoni culture, by contrast, men are completely excluded from the childbirth process. When a woman is ready to give birth, female relatives move into the woman's hut and the husband leaves, taking his belongings (clothes, tools, weapons, and so on) with him. He is not permitted to return until after the baby is born. In some cultures, childbirth is an open, community affair. For example, in the Pukapukan culture in the Pacific Islands, women give birth in a shelter that is open to villagers, who may observe the birth.

Midwives *Midwifery* is a profession that provides health care to women during pregnancy, birth, and the postpartum period (Cohen, Sumersille, & Friedman, 2018; Faucher, 2018). Midwives also may give women information about reproductive health and annual gynecological examinations. They may refer women to general practitioners or obstetricians if a pregnant woman needs medical care beyond a midwife's expertise and skill.

Midwifery is practiced in most countries throughout the world (Arabi & others, 2018; Miyake & others, 2017). In Holland, more than 40 percent of babies are delivered by midwives rather than by doctors. However, in 2015 in the United States only 8 percent of women who delivered a baby were attended by a midwife, a figure that was unchanged since 2000 (Martin & others, 2017). Nevertheless, the 8 percent figure for 2013 represents a substantial increase from less than 1 percent in 1975. A research review concluded that for low-risk women, midwife-led care was characterized by a reduction in procedures during labor and increased satisfaction with care (Sutcliffe & others, 2012). Also, in this study no adverse outcomes were found for midwife-led care compared with physician-led care.

Doulas In some countries, a doula attends a childbearing woman. *Doula* is a Greek word that means "a woman who helps." A *doula* is a caregiver who provides continuous physical, emotional, and educational support for the mother before, during, and after childbirth (Kozhimannil & others, 2016; McLeish & Redshaw, 2018). Doulas remain with the parents throughout labor, assessing and responding to their needs. Researchers have found positive effects when a doula is present at the birth of a child (Wilson & others, 2017). One study also revealed that for Medicaid recipients the odds of having a cesarean delivery were 41 percent lower for doula-supported births in the United States (Kozhimmanil & others, 2013). Thus, increasing doula-supported births could substantially lower the cost of a birth by reducing cesarean rates.

In the United States, most doulas work as independent providers hired by the expectant parents. Doulas typically function as part of a "birthing team," serving as an adjunct to the midwife or the hospital's obstetric staff.

Methods of Childbirth

U.S. hospitals often allow the mother and her obstetrician a range of options regarding their method of delivery. Key choices involve the use of medication, whether to use any of a number of nonmedicated techniques to reduce pain, and when to have a cesarean delivery.

Medication Three basic kinds of drugs that are used for labor are analgesia, anesthesia, and oxytocin/Pitocin.

Analgesia is used to relieve pain. Analgesics include tranquilizers, barbiturates, and narcotics such as Demerol.

Anesthesia is used in late first-stage labor and during delivery to block sensation in an area of the body or to block consciousness. There is a trend toward not using general anesthesia, which blocks consciousness, in normal births because general anesthesia can be transmitted through the placenta to the fetus (Edwards & Jackson, 2017; Wilson & others, 2018). An *epidural block* is regional anesthesia that numbs the woman's body from the waist down.

Oxytocin is a hormone that promotes uterine contractions; a synthetic form called Pitocin™ is widely used to decrease the duration of the first stage of labor. The relative benefits and risks of administering synthetic forms of oxytocin during childbirth continue to be debated (Carlson, Corwin, & Lowe, 2017; Shiner, Many, & Maslovitz, 2016).

Predicting how a drug will affect an individual woman and her fetus is difficult (Eisharkawy, Sonny, & Chin, 2017; Kobayashi & others, 2017). A particular drug might have only a minimal effect on one fetus yet have a much stronger effect on another. The drug's dosage is also a factor (Rankin, 2017). Stronger doses of tranquilizers and narcotics given to decrease the mother's pain potentially have a more negative effect on the fetus than do mild doses. It is important for the mother to assess her level of pain and have a voice in deciding whether she should receive medication.

Natural and Prepared Childbirth For a brief time not long ago, the idea of avoiding all medication during childbirth gained favor in the United States. Instead, many women chose to reduce the pain of childbirth through techniques known as natural childbirth and prepared childbirth. Today, at least some medication is used in the typical childbirth, but elements of natural childbirth and prepared childbirth remain popular (Bacon & Tomich, 2017; London & others, 2017).

Natural childbirth is a childbirth method in which no drugs are given to relieve pain or assist in the birth process. The mother and her partner are taught to use breathing methods and relaxation techniques during delivery. French obstetrician Ferdinand Lamaze developed a method similar to natural childbirth that is known as **prepared childbirth,** or the Lamaze method. It includes a special breathing technique to control pushing in the final stages of labor, as well as more detailed education about anatomy and physiology. The Lamaze method has become very popular in the

natural childbirth A childbirth method in which no drugs are given to relieve pain or assist in the birth process. The mother and her partner are taught to use breathing methods and relaxation techniques during delivery.

prepared childbirth Developed by French obstetrician Ferdinand Lamaze, this childbirth strategy is similar to natural childbirth but includes a special breathing technique to control pushing in the final stages of labor and more detailed anatomy and physiology instruction.

How Would You...?

United States. The pregnant woman's partner usually serves as a coach; the partner attends childbirth classes with her and helps her with her breathing and relaxation during delivery. In sum, proponents of current prepared childbirth methods conclude that when information and support are provided, women *know* how to give birth.

Other Nonmedicated Techniques to Reduce Pain The effort to reduce stress and control pain during labor has recently led to an increase in the use of some older and some newer nonmedicated techniques (Bindler & others, 2017; Cooper, Warland, & McCutcheon, 2018; Lewis & others, 2018a, b). These include waterbirth, massage, and acupuncture.

Waterbirth involves giving birth in a tub of warm water. Some women go through labor in the water and get out for delivery; others remain in the water for delivery. The rationale for waterbirth is that the baby has been in a fluid-filled amniotic sac for many months and that delivery in a similar environment is likely to be less stressful for the baby and the mother (Kavosi & others, 2015; Taylor & others, 2016). An increasing number of studies are either showing no differences in neonatal and maternal outcomes for waterbirth and non-waterbirth deliveries or positive outcomes for waterbirth (Davies & others, 2015; Taylor & others, 2016). For example, in a recent Swedish study, women who gave birth in water had a lower risk of vaginal tears, had a shorter labor, needed fewer drugs for pain relief and fewer interventions for medical problems, and rated their birth experience more positively than women who had conventional spontaneous vaginal births (Ulfsdottir, Saltvedt, & Georgsson, 2018). Also, a recent large-scale study of more than 16,000 waterbirth and non-waterbirth deliveries found fewer negative outcomes for the waterbirth newborns (Bovbjerg, Cheyney, & Everson, 2016). Waterbirth has been practiced more often in European countries such as Switzerland and Sweden in recent decades than in the United States, but is increasingly being included in U.S. birth plans.

Massage is increasingly used during pregnancy, labor, and delivery (Frawley & others, 2017; Withers, Kharazmi, & Lim, 2018). Researchers have found that massage therapy reduces pain during labor (Gallo & others, 2018; Shahoei & others, 2017). For example, a recent study found that lower back massage reduced women's labor pain and increased their satisfaction with the birth experience (Unalmis Erdogan, Yanikkerem, & Goker, 2017).

Acupuncture, the insertion of very fine needles into specific locations in the body, is used as a standard procedure to reduce the pain of childbirth in China, although it only recently has begun to be used for this purpose in the United States (Mollart & others, 2018; Smith, Armour, & Ee, 2016). Research indicates that acupuncture can have positive effects on labor and delivery (Akbarzadeh & others, 2015). For example, in one study acupuncture was successful in reducing labor pain 30 minutes after the intervention (Allameh, Tehrani, & Ghasemi, 2015).

What characterizes the use of waterbirth in delivering a baby?
©Daisy Smith/Alamy

Cesarean Delivery

Normally, the baby's head comes through the vagina first. But if the baby is in a *breech position*, its buttocks are the first part to emerge from the vagina. In 1 of every 25 deliveries, the baby's head is still in the uterus when the rest of the body is out. Because breech births can cause respiratory problems, if the baby is in a breech position a surgical procedure known as a cesarean delivery is usually performed. In a *cesarean delivery* (or cesarean section), the baby is removed from the uterus through an incision made in the mother's abdomen. What are some of the specific causes that influence physicians to perform a cesarean delivery? The most common causes of cesarean delivery are failure to progress through labor (which can be slowed by epidural anesthesia, for example) and fetal distress.

The benefits and risks of cesarean deliveries continue to be debated (Ladewig, London, & Davidson, 2017). Some critics argue that far too many babies are delivered by cesarean section in the United States and around the world (Gibbons & others, 2012). The World Health Organization states that a country's cesarean section rate should be 10 percent or less. The U.S. cesarean birth rate in 2015 was 32 percent, the lowest rate since 2007 (Martin & others, 2017). The highest cesarean rates are in the Dominican Republic and Brazil (56 percent); the lowest in New Zealand and the Czech Republic (26 percent) (McCullogh, 2016).

The Transition from Fetus to Newborn

Much of our discussion of birth so far has focused on the mother. However, birth also involves considerable stress for the baby. If the delivery takes too long, the baby can develop anoxia, a condition in which the fetus or newborn has an insufficient supply of oxygen. Anoxia can cause brain damage.

The baby has considerable capacity to withstand the stress of birth. Large quantities of adrenaline and noradrenaline, hormones that protect the fetus in the event of oxygen deficiency, are secreted in the newborn's body during the birth process.

Immediately after birth, the umbilical cord is cut and the baby is on its own. Before birth, oxygen came from the mother via the umbilical cord, but now the baby can breathe independently.

Almost immediately after birth, a newborn is taken to be weighed, cleaned up, and tested for signs of developmental problems that might require urgent attention. The **Apgar Scale** is widely used to assess the health of newborns at one and five minutes after birth. The Apgar Scale evaluates infants' heart rate, respiratory effort, muscle tone, body color, and reflex irritability. An obstetrician or nurse does the evaluation and gives the newborn a score, or reading, of 0, 1, or 2 on each of these five health signs. A total score of 7 to 10 indicates that the newborn's condition is good. A score of 5 indicates that there may be developmental difficulties. A score of 3 or below signals an emergency and warns that the baby might not survive. The Apgar Scale is especially good at assessing the newborn's ability to cope with the stress of delivery and its new environment (Miyakoshi & others, 2013). It also identifies high-risk infants who need resuscitation. Recent studies have found that low Apgar scores are associated with long-term additional support needs in education and educational attainment (Tweed & others, 2016), risk of developmental vulnerability at 5 years of age (Razaz & others, 2016), and risk of developing ADHD (Hanc & others, 2018).

Nurses often play important roles in the birth of a baby. To read about the work of a nurse who specializes in the care of women during labor and delivery, see *Careers in Life-Span Development*.

Low Birth Weight and Preterm Infants

Three related conditions pose threats to many newborns: low birth weight, preterm birth, and being small for date. *Low birth weight* infants weigh less than 5 pounds and 8 ounces at birth. *Very low birth weight* newborns weigh less than 3 pounds and 4 ounces, and *extremely low birth weight* newborns weigh less than 2 pounds and 3 ounces. Preterm infants are born three weeks or more before the pregnancy has reached its full term—in other words, 35 or fewer weeks after conception. Small for date infants (also called *small for gestational age infants*) have a birth weight that is below normal when the length of the pregnancy is considered. They weigh less than 90 percent of all babies of the same gestational age. Small for date infants may be preterm or full term. One study found that small for date infants have a 400 percent greater risk of death (Regev & others, 2003).

In 2015, 9.6 percent of babies born in the United States were born preterm (Martin & others, 2017). The preterm birth rate was 8.8 percent

Apgar Scale A widely used assessment of the newborn's health at 1 and 5 minutes after birth.

Linda Pugh, Perinatal Nurse

Perinatal nurses work with childbearing women to support health and growth during the childbearing experience. Linda Pugh, Ph.D., R.N.C., is a perinatal nurse on the faculty at The Johns Hopkins University School of Nursing. She is certified as an inpatient obstetric nurse and specializes in the care of women during labor and delivery. She teaches undergraduate and graduate students, educates professional nurses, and conducts research. In addition, Pugh consults with hospitals and organizations about women's health issues and many of the topics we discuss in this chapter.

Pugh's research interests include nursing interventions with low-income breast-feeding women, ways to prevent and ameliorate fatigue during childbearing, and use of breathing exercises during labor.

Linda Pugh (right) with a mother and her newborn.
©Dr. Linda Pugh

for non-Latino White infants, down from 11.4 percent in 2011 (Martin & others, 2017). In 2015, the preterm birth rate was 13.4 percent for African American infants (down from 16.7 percent in 2011) and 9.1 for Latino infants (down from 11.6 percent in 2011) (Martin & others, 2017).

Incidence and Causes of Low Birth Weight

Most, but not all, preterm babies are also low birth weight babies. The incidence of low birth weight varies considerably from country to country. In some countries, such as India and Sudan, where poverty is rampant and the health and nutrition of mothers are poor, the percentage of low birth weight babies reaches as high as 31 percent. In the United States, there has been an increase in low birth weight infants in the last two decades, and the U.S. low birth weight rate of 9.6 percent in 2015 was considerably higher than that of many other developed countries (Martin & others, 2017). For example, only 4 percent of the infants born in Sweden, Finland, Norway, and Korea are low birth weight, and only 5 percent of those born in New Zealand, Australia, and France are low birth weight.

Consequences of Low Birth Weight

The number and severity of health problems increase when infants are born very early and as their birth weight decreases (Linsell & others, 2017; Pascal & others, 2018). Survival rates for infants who are born very early and very small have risen, but with this improved survival rate have come an increased rate of severe brain damage (McNicholas & others, 2014; Rogers & Hintz, 2016) and lower level of executive function, especially in working memory and planning (Burnett & others, 2018).

A "kilogram kid," weighing less than 2.3 pounds at birth. *What are some long-term outcomes of weighing so little at birth?*
©Diether Endlicher/AP Images

For preterm birth, the terms *extremely preterm* and *very preterm* are increasingly used (Kato & others, 2016; Ohlin & others, 2015). *Extremely preterm infants* are born before 28 weeks of gestation, and *very preterm infants* are born before 33 weeks of gestation.

Low birth weight children are more likely than their normal birth weight counterparts to develop a learning disability, attention deficit hyperactivity disorder, autism spectrum disorders, or breathing problems such as asthma (Brinskma & others, 2017; Ng & others, 2017). Also, one study revealed that very preterm, low birth weight infants had abnormal axon development in their brain and impaired cognitive development at 9 years of age (Iwata & others, 2012). Approximately 50 percent of all low birth weight children are enrolled in special education programs.

Nurturing Low Birth Weight and Preterm Infants

Two increasingly used interventions in the neonatal intensive care unit (NICU) are kangaroo care and massage therapy. *Kangaroo care* involves skin-to-skin contact in which the baby, wearing only a diaper, is held upright against the parent's bare chest, much as a baby kangaroo is carried by its mother (Raajashri & others, 2018). Kangaroo care is typically practiced for two to three hours per day over an extended time in early infancy.

Why use kangaroo care with preterm infants? Preterm infants often have difficulty coordinating their breathing and heart rate, and the close physical contact with the parent provided by kangaroo care can help stabilize the preterm infant's heartbeat, temperature, and breathing (Boundy & others, 2018; Furman, 2018). Preterm infants who experience kangaroo care also gain more weight than their counterparts who are not given this care (Faye & others, 2016; Sharma, Murki, & Oleti, 2018). Recent research also revealed that kangaroo care decreased pain in newborns (Mooney-Leber & Brummelte, 2017).

Long-term positive effects of kangaroo care have been shown. For example, one study demonstrated the positive long-term benefits of kangaroo care (Feldman, Rosenthal, & Eidelman, 2014). In this study, maternal-newborn kangaroo care with preterm infants was linked to better respiratory and cardiovascular functioning, sleep patterns, and cognitive functioning from 6 months to 10 years of age. And in a longitudinal study, positive effects of kangaroo care with preterm and low birth weight infants that included higher intelligence and nurturant parenting at one year of age were still present 20 years later in emerging adults, who also showed reduced school absenteeism, reduced hyperactivity, lower aggressiveness, and positive social skills compared with their counterparts who had not received kangaroo care (Charpak & others, 2018).

A new mother practices kangaroo care. *What is kangaroo care? What are some outcomes of kangaroo care?*
©iStockphoto.com/casenbina

A U.S. survey found that mothers had a much more positive view of kangaroo care than did neonatal intensive care nurses and that mothers were more likely to say that it should be provided daily (Hendricks-Munoz & others, 2013). There is concern that kangaroo care is not used more often in neonatal intensive care units (Kymre, 2014; Penn, 2015). Increasingly, kangaroo care is recommended as standard practice for all newborns (Johnston and others, 2017; Smith & others, 2017).

Many adults will attest to the therapeutic effects of receiving a massage. In fact, many will pay a premium to receive one at a spa on a regular basis. But can massage play a role in improving the developmental outcomes for preterm infants? One study found that both kangaroo care and massage therapy were equally effective in improving body weight and reducing length of hospital stay for low birth weight infants (Rangey & Sheth, 2014).

Tiffany Field massages a newborn infant. *What types of infants have massage therapy been shown to help?*
©Dr. Tiffany Field

Many preterm infants experience less touch than full-term infants do because they are isolated in temperature-controlled incubators. Research by Tiffany Field and her colleagues (2001, 2007, 2010a, 2017; Diego, Field, & Hernandez-Reif, 2008, 2014; Field, Diego, & Hernandez-Reif, 2008, 2011) has led to a surge of interest in the role that massage might play in improving developmental outcomes for preterm infants. In Field's first study in this area, massage therapy consisting of firm stroking with the palms of the hands was given three times per day for 15-minute periods to preterm infants (Field & others, 1986). The massage therapy led to 47 percent greater weight gain than did standard medical treatment. The massaged infants also were more active and alert than preterm infants who were not massaged, and they performed better on developmental tests.

In later studies, Field demonstrated the benefits of massage therapy for infants who faced a variety of problems. For example, preterm infants exposed to cocaine in utero who received massage therapy gained weight and improved their scores on developmental tests (Field, 2001). In a review of the use of massage therapy with preterm infants, Field and her colleagues (2004) concluded that the most consistent findings involve two positive results: (1) increased weight gain and (2) discharge from the hospital three to six days earlier. One study revealed that the mechanisms responsible for increased weight gain as a result of massage therapy were stimulation of the vagus nerve (one of 12 cranial nerves leading to the brain) and in turn the release of insulin (a food absorption hormone) (Field, Diego, & Hernandez-Reif, 2011).

How Would You…?

As a **health-care professional,** how would you advise hospital administrators about implementing kangaroo care or massage therapy in the newborn intensive care unit?

Bonding

A special component of the parent-infant relationship is *bonding*, the formation of a connection, especially a physical bond between parents and the newborn in the period shortly after birth. In the mid-twentieth century, U.S. hospitals seemed almost determined to deter bonding. Anesthesia given to the mother during delivery would make the mother drowsy, interfering with her ability to respond to and stimulate the newborn. Mothers and newborns were often separated shortly after delivery, and preterm infants were isolated from their mothers even more than full-term infants were separated from their mothers. In recent decades these practices have changed, but to some extent they are still followed in many hospitals.

Do these practices do any harm? Some physicians believe that during the "critical period" shortly after birth the parents and newborn need to form an emotional attachment as a foundation for optimal development in years to come (Kennell, 2006; Kennell & McGrath, 1999). Although some research supports this bonding hypothesis (Klaus & Kennell, 1976), a body of research challenges the significance of the first few days of life as a critical period (Bakeman & Brown, 1980; Rode & others, 1981). Indeed, the extreme form of the bonding hypothesis—the idea that the newborn *must* have close contact with the mother in the first few days of life to develop optimally—simply is not true.

Nevertheless, the weakness of the bonding hypothesis should not be used as an excuse to keep motivated mothers from interacting with their newborns. Such contact brings pleasure to many mothers and may dispel maternal anxiety about the baby's health and safety. In some cases—including preterm infants, adolescent mothers, and mothers from disadvantaged circumstances—early close contact is key to establishing a climate for improved interaction after the mother and infant leave the hospital.

Many hospitals now offer a *rooming-in* arrangement in which the baby remains in the mother's room most of the time during its hospital stay. However, if parents choose not to use this rooming-in arrangement, the weight of the research suggests that this decision will not harm the infant emotionally (Lamb, 1994).

The Postpartum Period

The weeks after childbirth present challenges for many new parents and their offspring. This is the **postpartum period,** the period after childbirth or delivery that lasts for about six weeks or until the mother's body has completed its adjustment and has returned to a nearly prepregnant state. It is a time when the woman adjusts, both physically and psychologically, to the process of childbearing (Doering & others, 2017).

Physical Adjustments

A woman's body makes numerous physical adjustments in the first days and weeks after childbirth (Doering, Sims, & Miller, 2017). She may have a great deal of energy or feel exhausted and let down. Though these changes are normal, the fatigue can undermine the new mother's sense of well-being and confidence in her ability to cope with a new baby and a new family life.

A concern is the loss of sleep that the primary caregiver experiences in the postpartum period (Thomas & Spieker, 2016). In the 2007 Sleep in America survey, a substantial percentage of women reported loss of sleep during pregnancy and in the postpartum period (National Sleep Foundation, 2007). The loss of sleep can contribute to stress, marital conflict, and impaired decision making (Meerlo, Sgoifo, & Suchecki, 2008). In a recent study, worsening or minimal improvement in sleep problems from 6 weeks to 7 months postpartum were associated with an increase in depressive symptoms (Lewis & others, 2018).

After delivery, the mother's body undergoes sudden and dramatic changes in hormone production. When the placenta is delivered, estrogen and progesterone levels drop steeply and remain low until the ovaries start producing hormones again.

Involution is the process by which the uterus returns to its prepregnant size five or six weeks after birth. Immediately following birth, the uterus weighs 2 to 3 pounds. By the end of five or six weeks, the uterus weighs 2 to 3½ ounces. Nursing the baby helps contract the uterus at a more rapid rate.

Emotional and Psychological Adjustments

Emotional fluctuations are common for mothers in the postpartum period (Pawluski, Lonstein, & Fleming, 2017). For some women, emotional fluctuations decrease within several weeks after the delivery, but other women experience more long-lasting emotional swings (O'Hara & Engeldinger, 2018).

As shown in Figure 11, about 70 percent of new mothers in the United States have what are called the postpartum blues. About two to three days after birth, they begin to feel depressed, anxious, and upset. These feelings may come and go for several months after the birth, often peaking about three to five days after birth. Even without treatment, these feelings usually go away after one or two weeks.

However, some women develop postpartum depression, which involves a major depressive episode that typically occurs about four weeks after delivery (Brummelte & Galea, 2016). In other words, women with postpartum depression have such strong feelings of sadness, anxiety, or despair that for at least a two-week period they have trouble coping with their daily tasks. Without treatment, postpartum depression may become worse and last for many months (Di Florio & others, 2014). And many women with postpartum depression don't seek

Postpartum blues
Symptoms appear 2 to 3 days after delivery and usually subside within 1 to 2 weeks.

Postpartum depression
Symptoms linger for weeks or months and interfere with daily functioning.

No symptoms

Figure 11 Postpartum Blues and Postpartum Depression Among U.S. Women
Some health professionals refer to the postpartum period as the "fourth trimester." Though the time span of the postpartum period does not necessarily cover three months, the term "fourth trimester" suggests continuity and emphasizes the importance of the first several months after birth for the mother.

postpartum period The period after childbirth when the mother adjusts, both physically and psychologically, to the process of childbearing. This period lasts for about six weeks or until her body has completed its adjustment and returned to a nearly prepregnant state.

help. For example, one study found that 15 percent of the women reported postpartum depression symptoms but less than half sought help (McGarry & others, 2009). Estimates indicate that 10 to 14 percent of new mothers experience postpartum depression.

A research review identified the following risk factors for developing postpartum depression: a history of depression, depression and anxiety during pregnancy, neuroticism, low self-esteem, postpartum blues, poor marital relationship, and a low level of social support (O'Hara & McCabe, 2013). And another recent study revealed that women who had a history of depression were 20 times more likely to develop postpartum depression than women who had no history of depression (Silverman & others, 2017).

Several antidepressant drugs are effective in treating postpartum depression and appear to be safe for breast-feeding women (Howard, Mehta, & Powrie, 2017; Latendresse, Elmore, & Deneris, 2017). Psychotherapy, especially cognitive therapy, also is effective in treating postpartum depression for many women (Dennis, 2017; O'Hara & Engeldinger, 2018). In addition, engaging in regular exercise may help to relieve postpartum depression (Gobinath & others, 2018; McCurdy & others, 2017). For example, a recent meta-analysis concluded that physical exercise during the postpartum period is a safe strategy to reduce postpartum depressive symptoms (Poyatos-Leon & others, 2017).

A mother's postpartum depression can affect the way she interacts with her infant (Kleinman & Reizer, 2018; Kerstis & others, 2016). A research review concluded that the interaction difficulties of depressed mothers and their infants occur across cultures and socioeconomic status groups, and encompass less sensitivity of the mothers and less responsiveness on the part of infants (Field, 2010b). Several caregiving activities also are compromised, including feeding, sleep routines, and safety practices. Further, a recent study revealed that mothers' postpartum depression, but not generalized anxiety, were linked to their children's emotional negativity and behavior problems at 2 years of age (Prenoveau & others, 2017).

Fathers also undergo considerable adjustment in the postpartum period, even when they work away from home all day (Shorey & others, 2017; Takehara & others, 2017). Many fathers feel that the baby comes first and gets all of the mother's attention; some feel that they have been replaced by the baby. A recent study found that 5 percent of fathers had depressive symptoms in the first two weeks following delivery (Anding & others, 2016). And a recent study found that depressive symptoms in both the mother and father were associated with impaired bonding with their infant during the postpartum period (Kerstis & others, 2016). The father's support and caring also can play a role in whether the mother develops postpartum depression (Kumar, Oliffe, & Kelly, 2018). One study revealed that higher support by fathers was related to lower incidence of postpartum depression in women (Smith & Howard, 2008).

The postpartum period is a time of considerable adjustment and adaptation for both the mother and the father. Fathers can provide an important support system for mothers, especially in helping mothers care for young infants. *What kinds of tasks might the father of a newborn do to support the mother?*
©Howard Grey/Getty Images

How Would You...?

As a **human development and family studies professional,** how would you talk with mothers and fathers about vulnerabilities in mental health and relationships in the postpartum period?

Summary

The Evolutionary Perspective

- Darwin proposed that natural selection fuels evolution. In evolutionary theory, adaptive behavior is behavior that promotes the organism's survival in a natural habitat.

- Evolutionary psychology holds that adaptation, reproduction, and "survival of the fittest" are important in shaping behavior. Evolutionary developmental psychology emphasizes that humans need an extended "juvenile" period to develop a large brain and learn the complexity of social communities.

Genetic Foundations of Development
- Except in the sperm and egg, the nucleus of each human cell contains 46 chromosomes, which are composed of DNA. Short segments of DNA constitute genes, the units of hereditary information that direct cells to reproduce and manufacture proteins. Genes act collaboratively, not independently.
- Genes are passed on to new cells when chromosomes are duplicated during the processes of mitosis and meiosis.
- Genetic principles include those involving dominant-recessive genes, sex-linked genes, and polygenic inheritance.
- Chromosome abnormalities can produce Down syndrome and other problems; gene-linked disorders, such as PKU, involve defective genes.

The Interaction of Heredity and Environment: The Nature-Nurture Debate
- Behavior geneticists use twin studies and adoption studies to determine the strength of heredity's influence on development.
- In Scarr's heredity-environment correlation view, heredity directs the types of environments that children experience. Scarr identified three types of genotype- environment interactions: passive, evocative, and active (niche-picking).
- The epigenetic view emphasizes that development is the result of an ongoing, bidirectional interchange between heredity and environment. Recently, research interest has focused on how gene interaction influences development.
- The interaction of heredity and environment is complex, but we can create a unique developmental path by changing our environment.

Prenatal Development
- Prenatal development can be divided into three periods: germinal, embryonic, and fetal. The growth of the brain during prenatal development is remarkable.
- A number of prenatal tests, including ultrasound sonography, chorionic villus sampling, amniocentesis, maternal blood screening, and fetal MRI, can reveal whether a fetus is developing normally.

- Approximately 10 to 15 percent of U.S. couples have infertility problems. Assisted reproduction techniques, such as in vitro fertilization, are increasingly being used by infertile couples.
- Some prescription drugs and nonprescription drugs can harm the unborn child. In particular, the psychoactive drugs caffeine, alcohol, nicotine, cocaine, marijuana, heroin, and synthetic opioids as well as opiate-related pain killers can endanger developing offspring. Other potential sources of harmful effects on the fetus include environmental hazards, maternal diseases, maternal diet and nutrition, age, emotional states and stress, and paternal factors.
- Prenatal care usually involves medical care services with a defined schedule of visits and often encompasses educational, social, and nutritional services as well. Inadequate prenatal care may increase the risk of infant mortality and result in low birth weight.
- Although a number of problems that can occur in prenatal development have been described here, most of the time prenatal development does not go awry and occurs in a normal manner.

Birth and the Postpartum Period
- Childbirth occurs in three stages. Childbirth strategies involve the childbirth setting and attendants. In many countries, a midwife attends a childbearing woman. In some countries, a doula helps with the birth. Methods of delivery include medicated, natural and prepared, and cesarean.
- Being born involves considerable stress for the baby, but the baby is well prepared and adapted to handle the stress. Low birth weight, preterm, and small for date infants are at increased risk for developmental problems, although most of these infants are normal and healthy. Kangaroo care and massage therapy have been shown to produce benefits for preterm infants.
- Early bonding has not been found to be critical in the development of a competent infant, but close contact during the first few days after birth may reduce the mother's anxiety and lead to better interaction later.
- The postpartum period lasts for about six weeks after childbirth or until the body has returned to a nearly prepregnant state; postpartum depression is a serious condition that may become worse if not treated.

Key Terms

adoption study	epigenetic view	genes	organogenesis
Apgar Scale	evolutionary psychology	genotype	phenotype
behavior genetics	fetal alcohol spectrum	germinal period	postpartum period
chromosomes	disorders (FASD)	meiosis	prepared childbirth
DNA	fetal period	mitosis	teratogen
Down syndrome	gene × environment (G × E)	natural childbirth	twin study
embryonic period	interaction	neurons	

3 Physical and Cognitive Development in Infancy

©Ariel Skelley/Getty Images

CHAPTER OUTLINE

Stories of Life-Span Development: Newborn Babies in Ghana and Nigeria

Latonya is a newborn baby in Ghana. During her first days of life she has been kept apart from her mother and bottle fed. Manufacturers of infant formula provide free or subsidized milk powder to the hospital where she was born. Latonya's mother has been persuaded to bottle feed rather than breast feed her. When her mother bottle feeds Latonya, she overdilutes the milk formula with unclean water and puts it in bottles that have not been sterilized. Latonya becomes very sick, and she dies before her first birthday.

Ramona was born in Nigeria in a "baby-friendly" program. In this program, babies are not separated from their mothers when they are born, and the mothers are encouraged to breast feed them. The mothers are told of the perils that bottle feeding can cause because of unsafe water and unsterilized bottles. They also are informed about the advantages of breast milk, which include its nutritious and hygienic qualities, its ability to immunize babies against common illnesses, and its role in reducing the mother's risk of breast and ovarian cancer. Ramona's mother is breast feeding her. At 1 year of age, Ramona is very healthy.

For many years, maternity units in hospitals favored bottle feeding and did not give mothers adequate information about the benefits of breast feeding. In recent years, the World Health Organization and UNICEF have tried to reverse the trend toward bottle feeding of infants in many impoverished countries. They instituted the "baby-friendly" program in many countries. They also persuaded the International Association of Infant Formula Manufacturers to stop marketing their baby formulas to hospitals in countries where governments support the baby-friendly initiatives (Grant, 1993). For the hospitals themselves, costs actually were reduced as infant formula, feeding bottles, and separate nurseries became unnecessary. For example, baby-friendly Jose Fabella Memorial Hospital in the Philippines reported saving 8 percent of its annual budget. Still, there are many places in the world where the baby-friendly initiatives have not been implemented.

(*Left*) An HIV-infected mother breast feeding her baby in Nairobi, Africa; (*right*) A Rwandan mother bottle feeding her baby. *What are some concerns about breast versus bottle feeding in impoverished African countries?*
(Left) ©Wendy Stone/Corbis/Getty Images; (right) ©Dave Bartruff/Corbis/Getty Images

The advantages of breast feeding in impoverished countries are substantial (UNICEF, 2018). However, these advantages must be balanced against the risk of passing HIV to the baby through breast milk if the mother has the virus (Croffut & others, 2018; Mnyani & others, 2017; Wojcicki, 2017). The majority of mothers with HIV don't know that they are infected. In some areas of Africa more than 30 percent of mothers have the virus.

In the first two years of life, an infant's body and brain undergo remarkable growth and development. In this chapter we explore how this takes place: through physical growth, motor development, sensory and perceptual development, cognitive development, and language development. ■

Physical Growth and Development in Infancy

At birth, an infant has few of the physical abilities we associate with being human. Its head, which is huge relative to the rest of the body, flops around uncontrollably. Apart from some basic reflexes and the ability to cry, the newborn is unable to perform many actions. Over the next 12 months, however, the infant becomes capable of sitting, standing, stooping, climbing, and usually walking. During the second year, while growth slows, rapid increases in activities such as running and climbing take place. Let's now examine in greater detail the sequence of physical development in infancy.

Patterns of Growth

During prenatal development and early infancy, the head occupies an extraordinary proportion of the total body (see Figure 1). The **cephalocaudal pattern** is the sequence in which the earliest growth always occurs at the top—the head—with physical growth and differentiation of features gradually working their way down from top to bottom (shoulders, middle trunk, and so on). This same pattern occurs in the head area, as the top parts of the head—the eyes and brain—grow faster than the lower parts, such as the jaw.

cephalocaudal pattern Developmental sequence in which the earliest growth always occurs at the top—the head—with physical growth in size, weight, and feature differentiation gradually working from top to bottom.

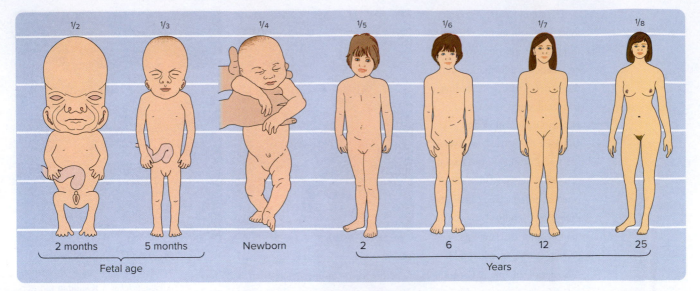

| ½ | ⅓ | ¼ | ⅕ | ⅙ | ⅐ | ⅛ |

| 2 months | 5 months | Newborn | 2 | 6 | 12 | 25 |

Fetal age | Years

Figure 1 Changes in Proportions of the Human Body During Growth. As individuals develop from infancy through adulthood, one of the most noticeable physical changes is that the head becomes smaller in relation to the rest of the body. The fractions listed refer to head size as a proportion of total body length at different ages.

Sensory and motor development generally proceed according to the cephalocaudal pattern. For example, infants see objects before they can control their torso, and they can use their hands long before they can crawl or walk. However, development does not follow a rigid blueprint. One study found that infants reached for toys with their feet four weeks earlier, on average, than they reached for them with their hands (Galloway & Thelen, 2004).

Growth also follows the **proximodistal pattern,** a sequence in which growth starts at the center of the body and moves toward the extremities. For example, infants control the muscles of their trunk and arms before they control their hands, and they use their whole hands before they can control several fingers.

An important point about growth is that it often is not smooth and continuous but rather is *episodic*, occurring in spurts (Adolph, 2018). In infancy, growth spurts may occur in a single day and alternate with long time frames characterized by little or no growth for days and weeks (Lampl & Johnson, 2011; Lampl & Schoen, 2018). In two analyses, in a single day, infants grew seven-tenths of an inch in length in a single day (Lampl, 1993) and their head circumference increased by three-tenths of an inch (Caino & others, 2010).

Height and Weight

The average North American newborn is 20 inches long and weighs 7½ pounds. Ninety-five percent of full-term newborns are 18 to 22 inches long and weigh between 5½ and 10 pounds.

In the first several days of life, most newborns lose 5 to 7 percent of their body weight before they adjust to feeding by sucking, swallowing, and digesting. They then grow rapidly, gaining an average of 5 to 6 ounces per week during the first month. They double their birth weight by the age of 4 months and nearly triple it by their first birthday. Infants grow about 3/4 inch per month during the first year, increasing their birth length by about 40 percent by their first birthday.

Growth slows considerably in the second year of life (London & others, 2017). By 2 years of age, children weigh approximately 26 to 32 pounds, having gained a quarter to half a pound per month during the second year; at this point they have reached about one-fifth of their adult weight. At 2 years of age, the average child is 32 to 35 inches tall, nearly half of his or her eventual adult height.

The Brain

At birth, the infant that began as a single cell has a brain that contains tens of billions of nerve cells, or neurons. Extensive brain development continues after birth, through infancy, and later (Crone, 2017; Sullivan & Wilson, 2018;

proximodistal pattern Developmental sequence in which growth starts at the center of the body and moves toward the extremities.

Figure 2 **Measuring the Activity of the Infant's Brain.**
As shown here, a large number of electrodes are attached to a baby's scalp to measure the brain's activity as part of an EEG assessment.

Vasa & others, 2018). Because the brain is developing so rapidly in infancy, the infant's head should be protected from falls or other injuries and the baby should never be shaken. *Shaken baby syndrome,* which includes brain swelling and hemorrhaging, affects hundreds of babies in the United States each year (Hellgren & others, 2017). One research analysis found that fathers were most often the perpetrators of shaken baby syndrome, followed by child-care providers and boyfriends of the victims' mothers (National Center on Shaken Baby Syndrome, 2012).

Figure 3 **Functional Near-Infrared Spectroscopy (fNRIS).**
This brain-imaging technology is increasingly being used to assess infants' brain activity as they move about their environment.
©Oli Scarff/Getty Images

The Brain's Development

At birth, the brain weighs about 25 percent of its adult weight. By the second birthday, it is about 75 percent of its adult weight. However, the brain's areas do not mature uniformly.

Assessing the infant's brain activity is not as easy as it might seem. Positron-emission tomography (PET) scans pose a radiation risk to babies, and sometimes infants wriggle too much to allow the technician to capture accurate brain images with magnetic resonance imaging (MRI). However, researchers have been successful in using the electroencephalogram (EEG), a measure of the brain's electrical activity, to learn about the brain's development in infancy (Bell & others, 2018; Hari & Puce, 2017) (see Figure 2). For example, a recent study found that higher-quality mother-infant interaction early in infancy predicted higher-quality frontal lobe functioning that was assessed with EEG later in infancy (Bernier, Calkins, & Bell, 2016).

Researchers also are increasingly studying infants' brain activity by using functional near-infrared spectroscopy (fNIRS), which uses very low levels of near-infrared light to monitor changes in blood oxygen (see Figure 3) (de Oliveira & others, 2018; Emberson & others, 2017a, b; Taga, Watanabe, & Homae, 2018). Unlike fMRI, which uses magnetic fields or electrical activity, fNIRS is portable and allows the infants to be assessed as they explore the world around them.

Mapping the Brain

Scientists analyze and categorize areas of the brain in numerous ways (Bell & others, 2018; Dean & others, 2018; Ferjan Ramirez & others, 2017; Xie, Mallin, & Richards, 2018). Of greatest interest is the portion farthest from the spinal cord, known as the *forebrain,* which includes the cerebral cortex and several structures beneath it. The *cerebral cortex* covers the forebrain like a wrinkled cap. It has two halves, or hemispheres. Based on ridges and valleys in the cortex, scientists distinguish four main areas, called lobes, in each hemisphere: the *frontal lobes,* the *occipital lobes,* the *temporal lobes,* and the *parietal lobes* (see Figure 4).

Although these areas are found in the cerebral cortex of each hemisphere, the two hemispheres are not identical in anatomy or function. **Lateralization** is the specialization of function in one hemisphere or the other. Researchers continue to explore the degree to which each hemisphere is involved in various aspects of thinking, feeling, and behavior

Frontal lobe

Parietal lobe

Occipital lobe

Temporal lobe

Figure 4 **The Brain's Four Lobes.**
Shown here are the locations of the brain's four lobes: frontal, occipital, temporal, and parietal.

lateralization Specialization of function in one hemisphere of the cerebral cortex or the other.

(Benjamin & others, 2017; Sidtis & others, 2018). At birth, the hemispheres of the cerebral cortex have already started to specialize: Newborns show greater electrical brain activity in the left hemisphere than in the right hemisphere when listening to speech sounds (Hahn, 1987).

The most extensive research on brain lateralization has focused on language. Speech and grammar are localized in the left hemisphere in most people, but some aspects of language, such as appropriate language use in different contexts and the use of metaphor and humor, involve the right hemisphere (Holler-Wallscheid & others, 2017). Thus, language is not controlled exclusively by the brain's left hemisphere. Further, most neuroscientists agree that complex functions—such as reading, performing music, and creating art—are the outcome of communication between the two sides of the brain (Nora & others, 2017; Raemaekers & others, 2018).

How do the areas of the brain in the newborn and the infant differ from those of an adult, and why do the differences matter? Important differences have been documented at both the cellular and the structural levels.

Changes in Neurons

Within the brain, neurons send electrical and chemical signals, communicating with each other. A *neuron* is a nerve cell that handles information processing (see Figure 5). Extending from the neuron's cell body are two types of fibers, known as *axons* and *dendrites*. Generally, the axon carries signals away from the cell body and dendrites carry signals toward it. A *myelin sheath,* which is a layer of fat cells, encases many axons (see Figure 5). The myelin sheath provides insulation and helps electrical signals travel faster down the axon (Cercignani & others, 2017; van Tilborg & others, 2018). Myelination also is involved in providing energy to neurons and in facilitating communication (Kiray & others, 2016; Saab & Nave, 2017). At the end of the axon are terminal buttons, which release chemicals called *neurotransmitters* into *synapses,* tiny gaps between neurons. Chemical interactions in synapses connect axons and dendrites, allowing information to pass from one neuron to another (Ismail, Fatemi, & Johnston, 2017; Zhou & others, 2018).

Think of the synapse as a river that blocks a road. A grocery truck arrives at one bank of the river, crosses by ferry, and continues its journey to market. Similarly, a message in the brain is "ferried" across the synapse by a neurotransmitter, which pours out information contained in chemicals when it reaches the other side of the river.

Neurons change in two very significant ways during the first years of life. First, *myelination,* the process of encasing axons with fat cells, begins prenatally and continues throughout childhood, even into adolescence (Juraska & Willing, 2017). Second, connectivity among neurons increases, creating new neural pathways (Eggebrecht & others, 2017; Zhou & others, 2018). New dendrites grow, connections among dendrites increase, and synaptic connections between axons and dendrites proliferate. Whereas myelination speeds up neural transmissions, the expansion of dendritic connections facilitates the spreading of neural pathways in infant development.

Researchers have discovered an intriguing aspect of synaptic connections: Nearly twice as many of these connections are made as will ever be used (Huttenlocher & Dabholkar, 1997). The connections that are used become stronger and survive, while the unused ones are replaced by other pathways or disappear. In the language of neuroscience, these connections will be "pruned" (Gould, 2017).

How complex are these neural connections? In a recent analysis, it was estimated that each of the billions of neurons is connected to as many as 1,000 other neurons, producing neural networks with trillions of connections (de Haan, 2015).

(a) Incoming information

Cell body

Nucleus

Axon

Dendrites

(b) Outgoing information

(c) Myelin sheath

(d) Terminal button

To next neuron

Figure 5 **The Neuron.**
(*a*) The dendrites of the cell body receive information from other neurons, muscles, or glands through the axon. (*b*) Axons transmit information away from the cell body. (*c*) A myelin sheath covers most axons and speeds information transmission. (*d*) As the axon ends, it branches out into terminal buttons.

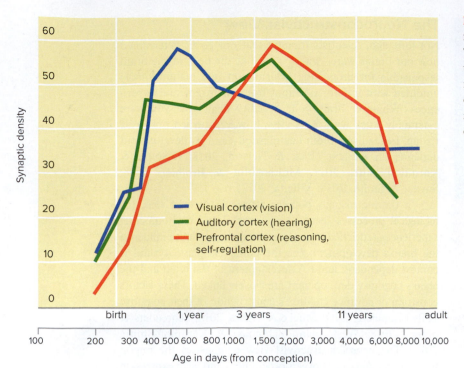

Figure 6 Synaptic Density in the Human Brain from Infancy to Adulthood. The graph shows the dramatic increase and then pruning in synaptic density for three regions of the brain: visual cortex, auditory cortex, and prefrontal cortex. Synaptic density is believed to be an important indication of the extent of connectivity between neurons.

Changes in Regions of the Brain

Figure 6 vividly illustrates the dramatic growth and later pruning of synapses in the visual, auditory, and prefrontal cortex (Huttenlocher & Dabholkar, 1997). Notice that "blooming and pruning" vary considerably by brain region. In the prefrontal cortex, the area of the brain where higher-level thinking and self-regulation occur, the peak of overproduction occurs at just over 3 years of age; it is not until middle to late adolescence that the adult density of synapses is achieved (Crone, 2017). Both heredity and environment are thought to influence the timing and course of synaptic overproduction and subsequent retraction.

Meanwhile, the pace of myelination also varies in different areas of the brain (Croteau-Chonka & others, 2016; Gogtay & Thompson, 2010). Myelination for visual pathways occurs rapidly after birth and is completed in the first six months. Auditory myelination is not completed until 4 or 5 years of age.

Early Experience and the Brain

What determines how these changes in the brain occur? The infant's brain is literally waiting for experiences to determine how connections are made. Before birth, it appears that genes mainly direct how the brain establishes basic wiring patterns; after birth, environmental experiences guide the brain's development. The inflowing stream of sights, sounds, smells, touches, language, and eye contact help shape neural connections (Bick & Nelson, 2018). It may not surprise us, then, that depressed brain activity has been found in children who grow up in a deprived environment (Bick & others, 2017; McLaughlin, Sheridan, & Nelson, 2017). Infants whose caregivers expose them to a variety of stimuli—talking, touching, playing—are most likely to develop to their full potential.

The profusion of neural connections described earlier provides the growing brain with flexibility and resilience (Marrus & others, 2018). As an extreme example, consider 16-year-old Michael Rehbein. When Michael was 4½, he began to experience uncontrollable seizures—from 60 to 400 a day. Doctors said that the only solution was to remove the left hemisphere of his brain, where the seizures were occurring. Michael had his first major surgery at age 7 and another at age 10. Although recovery was slow, his right hemisphere began to reorganize and eventually took over functions, such as speech, that normally occur in the brain's left hemisphere (see Figure 7). Individuals like Michael are living proof of the growing brain's remarkable ability to adapt and recover from a loss of brain tissue.

(a)

(b)

Figure 7 Plasticity in the Brain's Hemispheres.
(*a*) Michael Rehbein at 14 years of age. (*b*)
Brain scans of an intact brain (left) and Michael
Rehbein's brain (right). Michael's right hemisphere has reorganized to take over the language
functions normally carried out by corresponding
areas in the left hemisphere of an intact brain.
However, the right hemisphere is not as efficient
as the left, and more areas of the brain are
recruited to process speech.
Courtesy of The Rehbein Family

The Neuroconstructivist View

Not long ago, scientists thought that our genes determined
how our brains were "wired" and that the cells in the brain
responsible for processing information just maturationally
unfolded with little or no input from environmental experiences. Whatever brain your heredity dealt you, you were
essentially stuck with. This view, however, turned out to be
wrong. Instead, the brain has plasticity and its development
depends on context (Bick & Nelson, 2018; D'Souza &
Karmiloff-Smith, 2018; McLaughlin & Broihier, 2018;
Snyder & Smith, 2018; Villeda, 2017).

In the increasingly popular **neuroconstructivist view,** (a)
biological processes (genes, for example) and environmental
experiences (enriched or impoverished, for example) influence
the brain's development; (b) the brain has plasticity and is
context dependent; and (c) development of the brain and the
child's cognitive development are closely linked. These factors
constrain or advance children's construction of their cognitive
skills (Goldberg, 2017; Mucke & others, 2018; Schreuders &
others, 2018; Westermann, Thomas, & Karmiloff-Smith,
2011). The neuroconstructivist view emphasizes the importance of interactions between experiences and gene expression
in the brain's development, much as the epigenetic view proposes (D'Souza & Karmiloff-Smith, 2018; Moore, 2017).

Sleep

When we were infants, sleep consumed more of our time than
it does now (Dias & others, 2018; Goh & others, 2017). In a
recent study, sleep sessions lasted approximately 3.5 hours
during the first few months and increased to about 10.5 hours
from 3 to 7 months (Mindell & others, 2016). The typical
newborn sleeps 16 to 17 hours a day, but there is considerable
individual variation in how much infants sleep. For newborns,
the range is from about 10 hours to about 21 hours per day.
A research review concluded that infants 0 to 2 years of age
slept an average of 12.8 hours out of the 24, within a range
of 9.7 to 15.9 hours (Galland & others, 2012). One study also
revealed that by 6 months of age the majority of infants slept
through the night, awakening their parents only once or twice
a week (Weinraub & others, 2012).

The most common infant sleep-related problem reported
by parents is nighttime waking (Dias & others, 2018;
Hospital for Sick Children & others, 2010). Surveys indicate
that 20 to 30 percent of infants have difficulty going to sleep at night and staying asleep
until morning (Sadeh, 2008).

REM Sleep

A much greater amount of time is taken up by *REM (rapid eye movement)* sleep in infancy
than at any other point in the life span (Bathory & Tomopoulos, 2017). Unlike adults, who
spend about one-fifth of their night in REM sleep, infants spend about half
of their sleep time in REM sleep, and they often begin their sleep cycle with
REM sleep rather than non-REM sleep. By the time infants reach 3 months
of age, the percentage of time they spend in REM sleep decreases to about
40 percent, and REM sleep no longer begins their sleep cycle.

Why do infants spend so much time in REM sleep? Researchers are
not certain. The large amount of REM sleep may provide infants with

neuroconstructivist view Developmental perspective in which biological processes and environmental
conditions influence the brain's development; the brain has plasticity and
is context dependent; and cognitive
development is closely linked with
brain development.

added self-stimulation, since they spend less time awake than do older children. REM sleep also might promote the brain's development in infancy (Graven, 2006).

SIDS

Sudden infant death syndrome (SIDS) is a condition that occurs when an infant stops breathing, usually during the night, and dies suddenly without an apparent cause. SIDS remains one of the main causes of infant death in the United States, with more than 2,000 infant deaths annually attributed to SIDS (Heron, 2016). Risk of SIDS is highest at 2 to 4 months of age (NICHD, 2018). In 1992, the American Academy of Pediatrics (AAP) began recommending that infants be placed to sleep on their backs to reduce the risk of SIDS, and since then far fewer infants have been placed on their stomachs to sleep (AAP, 2000). Researchers have found that SIDS does indeed decrease when infants sleep on their backs rather than on their stomachs or sides (Bombard & others, 2018; Carlin & Moon, 2017; Sperhake, Jorch, & Bajanowski, 2018). Why? Because sleeping on their backs increases their access to fresh air and reduces their chances of getting overheated.

Is this a good sleep position for infants? Why or why not?
©Maria Teijeiro/Getty Images

SIDS also occurs more often in infants with abnormal brain stem functioning involving the neurotransmitter serotonin (Rognum & others, 2014). Also, heart arrhythmias are estimated to occur in as many as 10 to 15 percent of SIDS cases and research indicates that gene mutations are linked to the occurrence of these arrhythmias in SIDS cases (Sarquella-Brugada & others, 2016). SIDS also is less common in infants who are breast fed (Carlin & Moon, 2017). The risk of SIDS is higher for infants whose mothers smoke and infants who are exposed to secondhand smoke in general (Horne, 2018; Salm Ward & Balfour, 2016). Further, SIDS is more likely to occur in low birth weight infants, African American and Eskimo infants, infants who are passively exposed to cigarette smoke, infants who sleep with their parents in the same bed, infants who don't use a pacifier when they go to sleep, and infants who sleep in a bedroom without a fan (Alm & others, 2016; Carlin & Moon, 2017; Moon & others, 2017). In a recent analysis, it was concluded that after prone sleeping, the two factors that best predict SIDS are (1) maternal smoking, and (2) bed sharing (Mitchell & Krous, 2015).

One concern about the "back to sleep movement" of ensuring that young infants sleep on their back rather than their stomach is delayed acquisition of prone skills. To prevent this delay, many mothers provide their young infants with "tummy time" by periodically placing them on their stomachs when they are awake.

How Would You…?
As a health-care provider, what advice would you provide to parents about preventing SIDS?

Sleep and Cognitive Development

Might infant sleep be linked to children's cognitive development? A recent research review indicated that there is a positive link between infant sleep and cognitive functioning, including memory, language, and executive function (Tham, Schneider, & Broekman, 2017). The link between infant sleep and children's cognitive functioning likely occurs because of sleep's role in brain maturation and memory consolidation, which may improve daytime alertness and learning (Sadeh, 2007). And in a longitudinal study, infants who had more sleep problems were more likely to have emotional dysregulation at 2 to 3 years of age, which in turn was related to poor attention functioning in elementary school (Williams & Sciberras, 2016).

Nutrition

sudden infant death syndrome (SIDS) A condition that occurs when an infant stops breathing, usually during the night, and suddenly dies without an apparent cause.

From birth to 1 year of age, human infants nearly triple their weight and increase their length by 40 percent. What kind of nourishment do they need to sustain this rapid growth?

Breast Feeding Versus Bottle Feeding

For the first four to six months of life, human milk or an alternative formula is the baby's source of nutrients and energy. For years, debate has focused on whether breast feeding is better for the infant than bottle feeding. The growing consensus is that breast feeding is better for the baby's health (Blake, Munoz, & Volpe, 2019: DeBruyne & Pinna, 2017; Thompson & Manore, 2018). Since the 1970s, breast feeding by U.S. mothers has become widespread. In 2016 more than 81 percent of U.S. mothers breast fed their newborns, and 52 percent breast fed their 6-month-olds (Centers for Disease Control and Prevention, 2016). What are some of the benefits of breast feeding? During the first two years of life and beyond, benefits include appropriate weight gain and reduced risk of child and adult obesity (Catalano & Shankar, 2017; Uwaezuoke, Eneh, & Ndu, 2018); reduced risk of SIDS (Carlin & Moon, 2017); fewer gastrointestinal infections (Bartick & others, 2017); and fewer lower respiratory tract infections (Bartick & others, 2017, 2018). Further, a recent study of more than 500,000 Scottish children found that those who were breast fed exclusively at 6 to 8 weeks of age were less likely to have ever been hospitalized through early childhood than their formula-fed counterparts (Ajetunmobi & others, 2015). A recent research review found no support for the hypothesis that breast feeding might reduce the risk of allergies in young children (Heinrich, 2017). Other recent research has found a reduction of hospitalization for breast-fed infants for a number of conditions, including gastrointestinal problems and lower respiratory tract infections, as well as a reduction of hospitalization for breast-feeding mothers for cardiovascular problems and diabetes (Bartick & others, 2018). In a large-scale review, no evidence for the benefits of breast feeding was found for children's cognitive development and cardiovascular functioning (Agency for Healthcare Research and Quality, 2007). However, a recent study did find that breast feeding was associated with a small increase in children's intelligence (Bernard & others, 2017).

Human milk or an alternative formula is a baby's source of nutrients for the first four to six months. The growing consensus is that breast feeding is better for the baby's health, although controversy still swirls about breast versus bottle feeding. *What do research studies indicate are the outcomes of breast feeding for children and mothers?*
©JGI/Blend Images LLC

Benefits of breast feeding for the mother include a lower incidence of breast cancer (Akbari & others, 2011) and a reduction in ovarian cancer (Stuebe & Schwartz, 2010). Many health professionals have argued that breast feeding facilitates the development of an attachment bond between mother and infant (Wittig & Spatz, 2008). However, a research review found that the positive effect of breast feeding on the mother-infant relationship is not supported by research (Jansen, de Weerth, & Riksen-Walraven, 2008). The review concluded that recommending breast feeding should not be based on its role in improving the mother-infant relationship but rather on its positive effects on infant and maternal health.

The American Academy of Pediatrics Section on Breastfeeding (2012) reconfirmed its recommendation of exclusive breast feeding in the first six months followed by continued breast feeding as complementary foods are introduced, and further breast feeding for one year or longer as mutually desired by the mother and infant.

Are there circumstances when mothers should not breast feed? Yes. A mother should not breast feed if she (1) is infected with AIDS or any other infectious disease that can be transmitted through her milk, (2) has active tuberculosis, or (3) is taking any drug that may not be safe for the infant (Brown, 2017; Schultz, Kostic, & Kharasch, 2018).

Some women cannot breast feed their infants because of physical difficulties; others feel guilty if they terminate breast feeding early. Mothers also may worry that they are depriving their infants of important emotional and psychological benefits if they bottle feed rather than breast feed. Some researchers have found, however, that there are few, if any, long-term physical and psychological differences between breast-fed and bottle-fed infants (Colen & Ramey, 2014; Ferguson, Harwood, & Shannon, 1987; Young, 1990).

A further issue in interpreting the benefits of breast feeding was underscored in a large-scale research review (Agency for Healthcare Research and Quality, 2007). While highlighting a number of benefits of breast feeding for children and mothers, the report issued a caution about research on breast feeding: None of the findings imply causality. Breast feeding versus bottle feeding studies are correlational, not experimental, and women who breast feed tend to be wealthier, older, and better educated, and are likely to be more health-conscious than those who bottle feed, which could explain why breast-fed children are healthier.

Nutritional Needs

Individual differences among infants in terms of their nutrient reserves, body composition, growth rates, and activity patterns make it difficult to define actual nutrient needs (Rolfes & Pinna, 2018; Blake, Munoz, & Volpe, 2019). However, because parents need guidelines, nutritionists recommend that infants consume approximately 50 calories per day for each pound they weigh—more than twice an adult's requirement per pound.

A national study of more than 3,000 randomly selected 4- to 24-month-olds documented that many U.S. parents are feeding their babies too few fruits and vegetables and too much junk food (Fox & others, 2004). Up to one-third of the babies ate no vegetables and fruit; almost half of the 7- to 8-month-old babies were fed desserts, sweets, or sweetened drinks. By 15 months, French fries were the most common vegetables the babies ate.

Caregivers play very important roles in infants' early development of eating patterns (Baye, Tariku, & Mouquet-Rivier, 2018; Brown, 2017; Harrison, Brodribb, & Hepworth, 2018). Caregivers who are not sensitive to developmental changes in infants' nutritional needs, neglectful caregivers, and conditions of poverty can contribute to the development of eating problems in infants (Black & Hurley, 2017; Perez-Escamilla & Moran, 2017). One study found that low maternal sensitivity when infants were 15 and 24 months of age was linked to a higher risk of obesity in adolescence (Anderson & others, 2012). And in a recent study, infants who were introduced to vegetables between 4 and 5 months of age showed less fussy eating behavior at 4 years of age than their counterparts who were introduced to vegetables after 6 months (de Barse & others, 2017).

Adequate early nutrition is an important aspect of healthy development (Feldman-Winter & others, 2018; Rolfes & Pinna, 2018). In addition to sound nutrition, children need a nurturing, supportive environment (Black & Hurley, 2017; Blake, Munoz, & Volpe, 2019). One individual who is an ardent advocate of caring for children and is especially passionate about preventing childhood obesity is pediatrician Faize Mustafa-Infante, who is featured in *Careers in Life-Span Development.*

Careers in life-span development

Faize Mustafa-Infante, Pediatric Specialist Focusing on Childhood Obesity

Dr. Mustafa-Infante grew up in Colombia, South America. Her initial profession was teaching elementary school students in Columbia, and then she obtained her medical degree with a specialty in pediatrics. Once she finished her medical training, she moved to San Bernardino, California, where she worked as a health educator with a focus on preventing and treating childhood obesity in low-income communities. Dr. Mustafa-Infante currently works at Mission Pediatrics in Riverside, California, where she mainly treats infants. She continues her effort to prevent obesity in children and also serves as a volunteer for Ayacucho-Medical Mission, a nonprofit organization that provides culturally sensitive medical care for those in greatest need. In regard to her cultural background, she describes herself as a Latino doctor with a Middle Eastern name that reflects her strong family commitments to both heritages. Dr. Mustafa says that hard work and education have been the keys to her success and personal satisfaction.

Motor Development

Meeting infants' nutritional needs helps them to develop the strength and coordination required for motor development. How do infants develop their motor skills, and which skills do they develop at various ages?

Esther Thelen conducts an experiment to discover how infants learn to control their arms to reach and grasp for objects. A computer device monitors the infant's arm movements and tracks muscle patterns. Thelen's research is conducted from a dynamic systems perspective. *What is the nature of this perspective?*
©Dr. David Thelen

Dynamic Systems Theory

Developmentalist Arnold Gesell (1934) thought his painstaking observations had revealed how people develop their motor skills. He had discovered that infants and children develop rolling, sitting, standing, and other motor skills in a fixed order and within specific time frames. These observations, said Gesell, show that motor development comes about through the unfolding of a genetic plan, or maturation.

Later studies, however, demonstrated that the sequence of developmental milestones is not as fixed as Gesell indicated and not due as much to heredity as Gesell argued (Adolph, 2018; Adolph & Hoch, 2019; Adolph & Robinson, 2015). Beginning in the 1980s, the study of motor development underwent a renaissance as psychologists developed new insights about *how* motor skills develop (Adolph, 2018; Kretch & Adolph, 2018; Lee & others, 2019). One increasingly influential perspective is dynamic systems theory, proposed by Esther Thelen (Thelen & Smith, 1998, 2006).

According to **dynamic systems theory,** infants assemble motor skills for perceiving and acting. In other words, perception and action are coupled (Thelen & Smith, 2006). In order to develop motor skills, infants must perceive something in the environment that motivates them to act, then use their perceptions to fine-tune their movements. Motor skills thus represent pathways to the infant's goals (D'Souza & others, 2018).

How is a motor skill developed, according to this theory? When infants are motivated to do something, they might create a new motor behavior. The new behavior is the result of many converging factors: the development of the nervous system, the body's physical properties and its possibilities for movement, the goal the child is motivated to reach, and environmental support for the skill. For example, babies will learn to walk only when their nervous system has matured sufficiently to allow them to control certain leg muscles, when they want to move, when their legs have grown enough to support their weight, and when they have sufficient balance control to support their body on one leg (Adolph, 2018).

Mastering a motor skill requires the infant's active efforts to coordinate several components of the skill (Chen, Jeka, & Clark, 2016; Comalli, Persand, & Adolph, 2017; Franchak, Kretch, & Adolph, 2019; Lee & others, 2019). Infants explore and select possible solutions to the demands of a new task, and they assemble adaptive patterns by modifying their current movement patterns. The first step, for example, occurs when the infant is motivated by a new challenge—such as the desire to cross a room—and initiates this task by taking a few stumbling steps. The infant then "tunes" these movements to make them smoother and more effective. The tuning is achieved through repeated cycles of action and perception of the consequences of that action. According to the dynamic systems view, even universal milestones such as crawling, reaching, and walking are learned through this process of adaptation: Infants modulate their movement patterns to fit a new task by exploring and selecting possible configurations (Adolph, 2018; Adolph, Rachwani, & Hoch, 2018).

Thus, according to dynamic systems theory, motor development is not a passive process in which genes dictate the unfolding of a sequence of skills. Rather, the infant actively puts together a skill in order to achieve a goal within the constraints set by the infant's body and environment.

dynamic systems theory The perspective on motor development that seeks to explain how motor behaviors are assembled for perceiving and acting.

Nature and nurture, the infant and the environment, are all working together as part of an ever-changing system.

As we examine the course of motor development, we will describe how dynamic systems theory applies to some specific skills. First, though, let's examine how the story of motor development begins with reflexes.

Reflexes

The newborn is not completely helpless. Among other things, the newborn has some basic reflexes. Reflexes are built-in reactions to stimuli, and they govern the newborn's movements. Reflexes are genetically carried survival mechanisms that are automatic and involuntary. They allow infants to respond adaptively to their environment before they have had the opportunity to learn. For example, if immersed in water, the newborn automatically holds its breath and contracts its throat to keep water out.

Other important examples are the rooting and sucking reflexes. Both have survival value for newborn mammals, who must find a mother's breast to obtain nourishment. The *rooting reflex* occurs when the infant's cheek is stroked or the side of the mouth is touched. In response, the infant turns its head toward the side that was touched in an apparent effort to find something to suck. The *sucking reflex* occurs when newborns automatically suck an object placed in their mouth. This reflex enables newborns to get nourishment before they have associated a nipple with food.

Another example is the *Moro reflex,* which occurs in response to a sudden, intense noise or movement. When startled, the newborn arches its back, throws back its head, and flings out its arms and legs. Then the newborn rapidly closes its arms and legs. The Moro reflex is believed to be a way of grabbing for support while falling; it would have had survival value for our primate ancestors. An overview of the reflexes we have discussed, along with others, is presented in Figure 8.

Some reflexes—coughing, sneezing, blinking, shivering, and yawning, for example—persist throughout life. They are as important for the adult as they are for the infant.

Reflex	Stimulation	Infant's Response	Developmental Pattern
Blinking	Flash of light, puff of air	Closes both eyes	Permanent
Babinski	Sole of foot stroked	Fans out toes, twists foot in	Disappears after 9 months to 1 year
Grasping	Palms touched	Grasps tightly	Weakens after 3 months, disappears after 1 year
Moro (startle)	Sudden stimulation, such as hearing loud noise or being dropped	Startles, arches back, throws head back, flings out arms and legs and then rapidly closes them to center of body	Disappears after 3 to 4 months
Rooting	Cheek stroked or side of mouth touched	Turns head, opens mouth, begins sucking	Disappears after 3 to 4 months
Stepping	Infant held above surface and feet lowered to touch surface	Moves feet as if to walk	Disappears after 3 to 4 months
Sucking	Object touching mouth	Sucks automatically	Disappears after 3 to 4 months
Swimming	Infant put face down in water	Makes coordinated swimming movements	Disappears after 6 to 7 months
Tonic neck	Infant placed on back	Forms fists with both hands and usually turns head to the right (sometimes called the "fencer's pose" because the infant looks like it is assuming a fencer's position)	Disappears after 2 months

Figure 8 Infant Reflexes

Other reflexes, though, disappear several months after birth, as the infant's brain matures and voluntary control over many behaviors develops. The rooting, sucking, and Moro reflexes, for example, all tend to disappear when the infant is 3 to 4 months old.

The movements of some reflexes eventually become incorporated into more complex, voluntary actions. One important example is the *grasping reflex,* which occurs when something touches the infant's palm. The infant responds by grasping tightly. By the end of the third month, the grasping reflex diminishes, and the infant shows a more voluntary grasp. For example, when an infant sees a mobile turning slowly above a crib, it may reach out and try to grasp it. As its motor development becomes smoother, the infant will grasp objects, carefully manipulate them, and explore their qualities.

The old view of reflexes is that they were exclusively genetic, built-in mechanisms that govern the infant's movements. The new perspective on infant reflexes is that they are not automatic or completely beyond the infant's control. For example, infants can control such movements as alternating their legs to make a mobile jiggle or changing their sucking rate to listen to a recording (Adolph, 2018; Adolph & Berger, 2015).

Gross Motor Skills

Gross motor skills are skills that involve large-muscle activities, such as moving one's arms and walking. Newborn infants cannot voluntarily control their posture. Within a few weeks, though, they can hold their heads erect, and soon they can lift their heads while prone. By 2 months of age, babies can sit while supported on a lap or an infant seat, but they cannot sit independently until they are 6 or 7 months of age. Standing also develops gradually during the first year of life. By about 8 months of age, infants usually learn to pull themselves up and hold on to a chair, and by about 10 to 12 months of age they can often stand alone.

Locomotion and postural control are closely linked, especially in walking upright (Adolph, 2018). To walk upright, the baby must be able both to balance on one leg as the other is swung forward and to shift its weight from one leg to the other (Thelen & Smith, 2006).

Infants must also learn what kinds of places and surfaces are safe for crawling or walking (Adolph & Hoch, 2019; Adolph, Rachwani, & Hoch, 2018). Karen Adolph (1997) investigated how experienced and inexperienced crawling and walking infants go down steep slopes (see Figure 9). Newly crawling infants, who averaged about 8 months in age, rather indiscriminately went down the steep slopes, often falling in the process (with their mothers standing next to the slope to catch them). After weeks of practice, the crawling babies became more adept at judging which slopes were too steep to crawl down and which ones they could navigate safely.

Figure 9 **The Role of Experience in Crawling and Walking Infants' Judgments of Whether to Go Down a Slope**

Karen Adolph (1997) found that locomotor experience rather than age was the primary predictor of adaptive responding on slopes of varying steepness. Newly crawling and walking infants could not judge the safety of the various slopes. With experience, they learned to avoid slopes where they would fall. When expert crawlers began to walk, they again made mistakes and fell, even though they had judged the same slope accurately when crawling. Adolph referred to this as the specificity of learning because it does not transfer across crawling and walking.
©Dr. Karen Adolph, New York University

Newly crawling infant

Experienced walker

You might expect that babies who learned that a slope was too steep for crawling would know when they began walking whether a slope was safe. But Adolph's research indicated that newly walking infants could not judge the safety of the slopes. Only when infants became experienced walkers were they able to accurately match their skills with the steepness of the slopes. They rarely fell downhill, either refusing to go down the steep slopes or going down backward in a cautious manner. Experienced walkers assessed the situation perceptually—looking, swaying, touching, and thinking before they moved down the slope. With experience, both crawlers and walkers learned to avoid the risky slopes where they would fall, integrating perceptual information with the development of a new motor behavior. In this research, we again see the importance of perceptual-motor coupling in the development of motor skills.

Practice is especially important in learning to walk (Kretch & Adolph, 2018; Franchak, Kretch, & Adolph, 2019). Infants and toddlers accumulate an immense number of experiences with balance and locomotion (Cole, Robinson, & Adolph, 2016; Lee & others, 2019). For example, the average toddler traverses almost 40 football fields a day and has 15 falls an hour (Adolph, 2010).

Might the development of walking be linked to advances in other aspects of development? Walking experience leads to being able to gain contact with objects that were previously out of reach and to initiate interaction with parents and other adults, thereby promoting language development (Adolph & Robinson, 2015; He, Walle, & Campos, 2015). Thus, just as with advances in postural skills, walking skills can produce a cascade of changes in the infant's development (Adolph, 2018).

The First Year: Milestones and Variations

Figure 10 summarizes important accomplishments in gross motor skills during the first year, culminating in the ability to walk easily. However, the timing of these milestones, especially the later ones, may vary by as much as two to four months, and experiences can modify the onset of these accomplishments (Adolph, 2018; Adolph & Hoch, 2019).

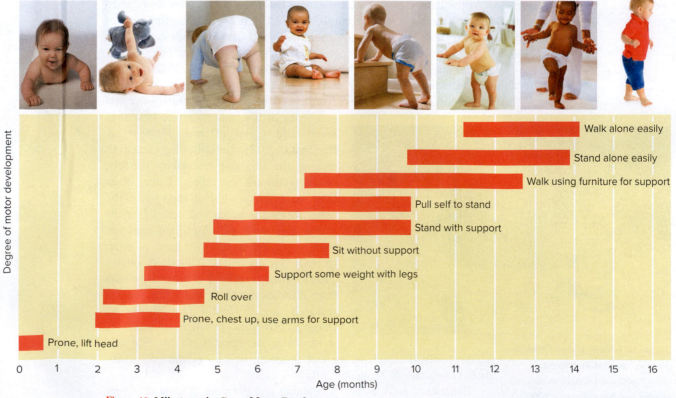

Figure 10 Milestones in Gross Motor Development.
The horizontal red bars indicate the range in which most infants reach various milestones in gross motor development.
(*Left to right*) ©Barbara Penoyar/Getty Images; ©StephaneHachey/Getty Images; ©Image Source/Alamy; ©Victoria Blackie/Getty Images; ©Digital Vision; ©Fotosearch/Getty Images; ©Corbis/PictureQuest; ©amaviael/123RF

How Would You...?

As a **human development and family studies professional,** how would you advise parents who are concerned that their infant is one or two months behind the average gross motor milestones?

In a recent study, a number of factors were linked to the timing of motor development in the first year of life (Flensborg-Madsen & Mortensen, 2017). Twelve developmental milestones were assessed, including grasping, rolling, sitting, and crawling; standing and walking; and overall mean of milestones. A larger size at birth (such as birth weight, birth length, and head circumference) was the aspect of pregnancy and delivery that showed the strongest link to reaching motor milestones earlier. Mother's smoking in the last trimester of prenatal development was associated with reaching the motor milestones later. Also, an increase in size (weight increase, length increase, and head increase) in the first year was related to reaching the motor milestones earlier. Breast feeding also was linked to reaching the milestones earlier.

fine motor skills Motor skills that involve more finely tuned movements, such as finger dexterity.

Development in the Second Year

The motor accomplishments of the first year bring increasing independence, allowing infants to explore their environment more extensively and to initiate interaction with others more readily. In the second year of life, toddlers become more mobile as their motor skills are honed. Child development experts believe that motor activity during the second year is vital to the child's competent development and that few restrictions, except those having to do with safety, should be placed on their adventures (Fraiberg, 1959).

By 13 to 18 months, toddlers can pull a toy attached to a string and use their hands and legs to climb up steps. By 18 to 24 months, toddlers can walk quickly or run stiffly for a short distance, balance on their feet in a squatting position while playing with objects on the floor, walk backward without losing their balance, stand and kick a ball without falling, stand and throw a ball, and jump in place.

Fine Motor Skills

Whereas gross motor skills involve large-muscle activity, **fine motor skills** involve finely tuned movements. Grasping a toy, using a spoon, buttoning a shirt, or doing anything that requires finger dexterity demonstrates fine motor skills. At birth, infants have very little control over fine motor skills, but they do have many components of what will become finely coordinated arm, hand, and finger movements (McCormack, Hoerl, & Butterfill, 2012).

The onset of reaching and grasping marks a significant achievement in infants' ability to interact with their surroundings (Needham & others, 2017). During the first two years of life, infants refine how they reach and grasp (Dosso, Herrera, & Boudreau, 2017). Initially, they reach by moving the shoulder and elbow crudely, swinging toward an object. Later, when they reach for an object they move the wrist, rotate the hand, and coordinate the thumb and forefinger. An infant does not have to see his or her own hand in order to reach for an object (Clifton & others, 1993); rather, reaching is guided by cues from muscles, tendons, and joints. Recent research studies found that short-term training involving practice of reaching movements increased both preterm and full-term infants' reaching for and touching objects (Cunha & others, 2016; Guimaraes & Trudellia, 2015).

Figure 11 Infants' Use of "Sticky Mittens" to Explore Objects. Amy Needham (at right in this photo) and her colleagues (2002) found that "sticky mittens" enhanced young infants' object exploration skills.
©Dr. Amy Needham

Experience plays a role in reaching and grasping (Cunha & others, 2016; Needham & others, 2017). In one study, 3-month-old infants participated in play sessions wearing "sticky mittens"—"mittens with palms that stuck to the edges of toys and allowed the infants to pick up the toys" (Needham, Barrett, & Peterman, 2002, p. 279) (see Figure 11). Infants who participated in sessions with the mittens grasped and manipulated objects earlier in their development than a control group of infants who did not receive the "mitten" experience. The experienced infants looked at the objects longer, swatted at them more during visual contact, and were more likely to mouth the objects. In one study, 5-month-old infants whose parents trained them to use the sticky mittens for 10 minutes a day over a two-week period showed advances in their reaching behavior at the end of the two weeks (Libertus & Needham, 2010).

Rachel Keen (2011; Keen, Lee, & Adolph, 2014) emphasizes that tool use is an excellent context for studying problem solving in infants because tool use provides information about how infants plan to reach a goal. Researchers in this area have studied infants' intentional actions, which range from picking up a spoon in different orientations to retrieving rakes from inside tubes. One study explored motor origins of tool use by assessing developmental changes in banging movements in 6- to 15-month-olds (Kahrs, Jung, & Lockman, 2013). In this study, younger infants were inefficient and variable when banging an object but by 1 year of age infants showed consistent straight up-and-down hand movements that resulted in precise aiming and consistent levels of force.

Just as infants need to exercise their gross motor skills, they also need to exercise their fine motor skills (Cunha & others, 2016; Needham & others, 2017). Especially when they can manage a pincer grip, infants delight in picking up small objects. Many develop the pincer grip and begin to crawl at about the same time, and infants at this time pick up virtually everything in sight, especially on the floor, and put the objects in their mouth. Thus, parents need to be vigilant in monitoring objects within the infant's reach.

Sensory and Perceptual Development

Can a newborn see? If so, what can it perceive? How do sensations and perceptions develop? Can an infant put together information from two modalities, such as sight and sound? These are among the intriguing questions that we explore in this section.

Exploring Sensory and Perceptual Development

How does a newborn know that her mother's skin is soft rather than rough? How does a 5-year-old know what color his hair is? Infants and children "know" these things as a result of information that comes through the senses.

Sensation occurs when information interacts with sensory *receptors*—the eyes, ears, tongue, nostrils, and skin. The sensation of hearing occurs when waves of pulsating air are collected by the outer ear and transmitted through the bones of the inner ear to the auditory nerve. The sensation of vision occurs as rays of light contact the eyes, become focused on the retina, and are transmitted by the optic nerve to the visual centers of the brain.

Perception is the interpretation of what is sensed. The air waves that contact the ears might be interpreted as noise or as musical sounds, for example. The physical energy transmitted to the retina of the eye might be interpreted as a particular color, pattern, or shape, depending on how it is perceived.

The Ecological View

In recent decades, much of the research on perceptual development in infancy has been guided by the ecological view proposed by Eleanor and James J. Gibson (E. Gibson, 1969, 1989, 2001; J. Gibson, 1966, 1979). They argue that we do not have to take bits and pieces of data from sensations and build up representations of the world in our minds. Instead, our perceptual system can select from the rich information that the environment itself provides.

According to the Gibsons' **ecological view,** we directly perceive information that exists in the world around us. Perception brings us into contact with the environment in order to interact with and adapt to it

sensation The product of the interaction between information and the sensory receptors—the eyes, ears, tongue, nostrils, and skin.

perception The interpretation of what is sensed.

ecological view The view that perception functions to bring organisms in contact with the environment and to increase adaptation.

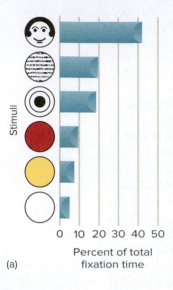

(a)

Stimuli

Percent of total fixation time

(b)

Figure 12 Fantz's Experiment on Infants' Visual Perception.

(*a*) Infants 2 to 3 weeks old preferred to look at some stimuli more than others. In Fantz's experiment, infants preferred to look at patterns rather than at color or brightness. For example, they looked longer at a face, a piece of printed matter, or a bull's-eye than at red, yellow, or white discs. (*b*) Fantz used a "looking chamber" to study infants' perception of stimuli.
©David Linton, Courtesy of the Linton Family

(Franchak, Kretch, & Adolph, 2019). Perception is designed for action. It gives people information such as when to duck, when to turn their bodies as they move through a narrow passageway, and when to put their hands up to catch something (Adolph, 2018).

Studying the Infant's Perception

Studying the infant's perception is not an easy task. Unlike most research participants, infants cannot write, type on a computer keyboard, or speak well enough to explain to an experimenter what their responses are to a given stimulus or condition. Yet scientists have developed several ingenious research methods to examine infants' sensory and perceptual development (Bendersky & Sullivan, 2007).

The Visual Preference Method

Robert Fantz (1963), a pioneer in this effort, made an important discovery: Infants look at different things for different lengths of time. Fantz placed infants in a "looking chamber," which had two visual displays on the ceiling above the infant's head. An experimenter viewed the infant's eyes by looking through a peephole. If the infant was gazing at one of the displays, the experimenter could see the display's reflection in the infant's eyes. This allowed the experimenter to determine how long the infant looked at each display. Fantz (1963) found that infants only 2 days old would gaze longer at patterned stimuli (such as faces or concentric circles) than at red, white, or yellow discs. Similar results were found with infants 2 to 3 weeks old (see Figure 12). Fantz's research method—studying whether infants can distinguish one stimulus from another by measuring the length of time they attend to different stimuli—is referred to as the **visual preference method.**

visual preference method A method developed by Fantz to determine whether infants can distinguish one stimulus from another by measuring the length of time they attend to different stimuli.

habituation Decreased responsiveness to a stimulus after repeated presentations of the stimulus.

dishabituation Recovery of a habituated response after a change in stimulation.

Habituation and Dishabituation Another way in which researchers study infant perception is to present a stimulus (such as a sight or a sound) a number of times. If the infant decreases its response to the stimulus after several presentations, this indicates that the infant is no longer interested in the stimulus. If the researcher now presents a new stimulus, the infant's response will recover—indicating the infant could discriminate between the old and new stimuli (Messinger & others, 2017).

Habituation is the name given to decreased responsiveness to a stimulus after repeated presentations of the stimulus. **Dishabituation** is the recovery of a habituated response after a change in stimulation. Newborn infants can habituate to repeated sights, sounds, smells, or touches (Bendersky & Sullivan, 2007). Among the measures researchers use in habituation studies are sucking behavior (sucking behavior stops when the infant attends to a novel object), heart and respiration rates, and the length of time the infant looks at an object.

Equipment Technology can facilitate the use of most methods for investigating the infant's perceptual abilities. Videotape equipment allows researchers to investigate elusive behaviors. High-speed computers make it possible to perform complex data analysis in minutes. Other equipment records respiration, heart rate, body movement, visual fixation, and sucking behavior, which provide clues to what the infant is perceiving.

Eye Tracking The most important recent advance in measuring infant perception is the development of sophisticated eye-tracking equipment (Boardman & Fletcher-Watson, 2017; Kretch & Adolph, 2017). Eye tracking consists of measuring eye movements that follow (track) a moving object and can be used to evaluate an infant's early visual ability (Bendersky & Sullivan, 2007).

Figure 13 An Infant Wearing Eye-Tracking Headgear
©Dr. Karen Adolph, New York University

Figure 13 shows an infant wearing eye-tracking headgear in a recent study on visually guided motor behavior and social interaction.

One of the main reasons that infant perception researchers are so enthusiastic about the availability of sophisticated eye-tracking equipment is that looking time is among the most important measures of infant perceptual and cognitive development (Aslin, 2012). The new eye-tracking equipment allows for far greater precision in assessing various aspects of infant looking and gaze than is possible with human observation (Boardman & Fletcher-Watson, 2017; Law & others, 2018; van Renswouode & others, 2018). Among the areas of infant perception in which eye-tracking equipment is being used are attention (Meng, Uto, & Hashiya, 2017), memory (Fanning & others, 2018; Kingo & Krojgaard, 2015), and face processing (Chhaya & others, 2018). Further, eye-tracking equipment is improving our understanding of atypically developing infants, such as those who have autism (Falck-Ytter & others, 2018) or were born preterm (Finke, Wilkinson, & Hickerson, 2017; Liberati & others, 2017).

One eye-tracking study shed light on the effectiveness of TV programs and DVDs that claim to educate infants (Kirkorian, Anderson, & Keen, 2012). In this study, 1-year-olds, 4-year-olds, and adults watched *Sesame Street* and the eye-tracking equipment recorded precisely what they looked at on the screen. The 1-year-olds were far less likely to consistently look at the same part of the screen as their older counterparts, suggesting that the 1-year-olds showed little understanding of the Sesame Street video but instead were more likely to be attracted by what was salient than by what was relevant.

Visual Perception

Psychologist William James (1890/1950) called the newborn's perceptual world a "blooming, buzzing confusion." A century later, we can safely say that he was wrong (Damon & others, 2018; Singarajah & others, 2017). Even the newborn perceives a world with some order.

Visual Acuity and Color

Just how well can infants see? The newborn's vision is estimated to be 20/600 on the well-known Snellen eye examination chart (Banks & Salapatek, 1983). This means that an object 20 feet away is only as clear to the newborn's eyes as it would be if it were viewed from a distance of 600 feet by an adult with normal vision (20/20). By 6 months of age, though, an average infant's vision is 20/40 (Aslin & Lathrop, 2008). Figure 14 shows a computer estimation of what a picture of a face looks like to an infant at different ages from a distance of about 6 inches.

Figure 14 **Visual Acuity During the First Months of Life.**
The four photographs represent a computer estimation of what a picture of a face looks like to a
1-month-old, 2-month-old, 3-month-old, and 1-year-old (which approximates the visual acuity of an adult).
©Kevin Peterson/Getty Images/Simulation by Vischeck

Faces are possibly the most important visual stimuli in children's social environment, and it is important that they extract key information from others' faces (Sugden & Moulson, 2017). Infants show an interest in human faces soon after birth (Johnson & Hannon, 2015). Within hours after they are born, research shows that infants prefer to look at faces rather than other objects and to look at attractive faces more than at unattractive ones (Lee & others, 2013).

The infant's color vision also improves. By 8 weeks, and possibly as early as 4 weeks, infants can discriminate among some colors (Kelly, Borchert, & Teller, 1997).

Perceiving Occluded Objects

Take a moment to look at your surroundings. You will likely see that some objects are partly occluded by other objects that are in front of them—possibly a desk behind a chair, some books behind a computer, or a car parked behind a tree. Do infants perceive an object as complete when it is occluded by an object in front of it?

In the first two months of postnatal development, infants do not perceive occluded objects as complete, instead only perceiving what is visible. Beginning at about 2 months of age, infants develop the ability to perceive that occluded objects are whole (Slater, Field, & Hernandez-Reif, 2007). How does perceptual completion develop? In Scott Johnson's (2010, 2011, 2013; Johnson & Hannon, 2015) research, learning, experience, and self-directed exploration via eye movements play key roles in the development of perceptual completion in young infants.

Many objects that are occluded appear and disappear behind closer objects, as when you are walking down the street and see cars appear and disappear behind buildings. Infants develop the ability to track briefly occluded moving objects at about 3 to 5 months (Bertenthal, 2008). One study explored the ability of 5- to 9-month-old infants to track moving objects that disappeared gradually behind an occluded partition, disappeared abruptly, or imploded (shrank quickly) (Bertenthal, Longo, & Kenny, 2007) (see Figure 15). In this study, the infants were more likely to accurately track the moving object when it disappeared gradually than when it vanished abruptly or imploded.

Depth Perception

To investigate whether infants have depth perception, Eleanor Gibson and Richard Walk (1960) constructed a miniature cliff with a drop-off covered by glass. They placed 6- to 12-month-old infants on the edge of this visual cliff and had their mothers coax them to crawl onto the glass (see Figure 16). Most infants would not crawl out on the glass, choosing instead to remain on the shallow side, an indication that they could perceive depth, according to Gibson and Walk. Although researchers do not know exactly how early in life infants can perceive depth, they have found that infants develop the ability to use binocular (two-eyed) cues to depth by about 3 to 4 months of age.

(a) Gradual occlusion

(b) Abrupt occlusion

Figure 16 **Examining Infants' Depth Perception on the Visual Cliff.** Eleanor Gibson and Richard Walk (1960) found that most infants would not crawl out on the glass, which, according to Gibson and Walk, indicated that they had depth perception. However, critics point out that the visual cliff is a better indication of the infant's social referencing and fear of heights than of the infant's perception of depth.
©Mark Richards/PhotoEdit

(c) Implosion

Figure 15 **Infants' Predictive Tracking of a Briefly Occluded Moving Ball.**
The top image shows the visual scene that infants experienced. At the beginning of each event, a multicolored ball bounced up and down with an accompanying bouncing sound, and then rolled across the floor until it disappeared behind the partition. The bottom three images show the three stimulus events that the 5- to 9-month-old infants experienced: (*a*) gradual occlusion—the ball gradually disappears behind the right side of the occluding partition located in the center of the display; (*b*) abrupt occlusion—the ball abruptly disappears when it reaches the location of the white circle and then abruptly reappears 2 seconds later at the location of the second white circle on the other side of the occluding partition; (*c*) implosion—the rolling ball quickly decreases in size as it approaches the occluding partition and rapidly increases in size as it reappears on the other side of the occluding partition.

Other Senses

Other sensory systems besides vision also develop during infancy. In this section, we explore development in hearing, touch and pain, smell, and taste.

Hearing

During the last two months of pregnancy, as the fetus nestles in its mother's womb, it can hear sounds such as the mother's voice (Kisilevsky & others, 2009). In one study, researchers had 16 women read *The Cat in the Hat* aloud to their fetuses during the last months of pregnancy (DeCasper & Spence, 1986). Then, shortly after their babies were born, the mothers read aloud either *The Cat in the Hat* or a story with a different rhyme and pace, *The King, the Mice and the Cheese* (which had not been read during prenatal development). The infants sucked on a nipple in a different way when the mothers read the two stories, suggesting that the infants recognized the pattern and tone of *The Cat in the Hat*. An fMRI study confirmed that a fetus can hear at 33 to 34 weeks into the prenatal period by assessing fetal brain response to auditory stimuli (Jardri & others, 2012).

Newborns are especially sensitive to human speech sounds (Saffran, Werker, & Werner, 2006). Just a few days after birth, newborns will turn toward the sound of a familiar caregiver's voice.

What changes in hearing take place during infancy? They involve perception of a sound's loudness, pitch, and localization. Immediately after birth, infants cannot hear soft sounds quite as well as adults can; a stimulus must be louder for the newborn to hear it (Trehub & others, 1991). By 3 months of age, infants' perception of sounds improves, although some aspects of loudness perception do not reach adult levels until 5 to 10 years of age (Trainor & He, 2013). Infants are also less sensitive to the pitch of a sound than adults are. *Pitch* is the frequency of a sound; a soprano voice sounds high-pitched, a bass voice low-pitched. Infants are less sensitive to low-pitched sounds and are more likely to hear high-pitched sounds (Aslin, Jusczyk, & Pisoni, 1998). By 2 years of age, infants have considerably improved their ability to distinguish sounds with different pitches.

Even newborns can determine the general location from which a sound is coming, but by 6 months they are more proficient at localizing sounds, detecting their origins. The ability to localize sounds continues to improve during the second year (Saffran, Werker, & Werner, 2006).

Touch and Pain

Newborns respond to touch. A touch to the cheek produces a turning of the head; a touch to the lips produces sucking movements. Regular gentle tactile stimulation during prenatal development may have positive developmental outcomes. For example, a recent study found that 3-month-olds who had received regular gentle tactile stimulation as fetuses were more likely to have an easy temperament than their counterparts who had irregular gentle or no tactile stimulation as fetuses (Wang, Hua, & Xu, 2015).

Newborns can also feel pain (Bellini & others, 2016; Jones & others, 2017). The issue of an infant's pain perception often becomes important to parents who give birth to a son and need to consider whether he should be circumcised. An investigation by Megan Gunnar and her colleagues (1987) found that although newborn infant males cry intensely during circumcision, they also display amazing resiliency. Many newly circumcised infants go into a deep sleep not long after the procedure, probably as a coping mechanism. Also, once researchers discovered that newborns feel pain, the practice of operating on newborns without anesthesia began to be reconsidered. Anesthesia is now used in some circumcisions (Morris & others, 2012). And in a recent study, kangaroo care was very effective in reducing neonatal pain, especially indicated by the significantly lower level of crying when the care was instituted after the newborn's blood had been drawn by a heel stick (Seo, Lee, & Ahn, 2016).

Smell

Newborns also can differentiate among odors (Cao Van & others, 2018). For example, the expressions on their faces indicate that they like the scents of vanilla and strawberry but do not like the scent of rotten eggs or fish (Steiner, 1979).

It may take time to develop other odor preferences, however. By the time they were 6 days old, breast-fed infants in one study showed a clear preference for smelling their mother's breast pad rather than a clean breast pad (MacFarlane, 1975). When they were 2 days old they did not show this preference, indicating that they require several days of experience to recognize this scent.

Taste

Sensitivity to taste is present even before birth (De Cosmi, Scaglioni, & Agostini, 2018). In one very early experiment, when saccharin was added to the amniotic fluid of a near-term fetus, swallowing increased (Windle, 1940). In another study, even at only 2 hours of age, babies made different facial expressions when they tasted sweet, sour, and bitter solutions (Rosenstein & Oster, 1988). At about 4 months, infants begin to prefer salty tastes, which as newborns they had found to be aversive (Harris, Thomas, & Booth, 1990).

Intermodal Perception

How do infants put all these stimuli together? Imagine yourself playing basketball or tennis. You are experiencing many visual inputs: the ball coming and going, other players moving around, and so on. However, you are experiencing many auditory inputs as well: the sound of the ball bouncing or being hit, the grunts and groans of the participants, and so on. There is good correspondence between much of the visual and auditory information: When you see the ball bounce, you hear a bouncing sound; when a player stretches to hit a ball, you hear a groan. When you look at and listen to what is going on, you do not experience just the sounds or just the sights; you put all these things together. You experience a unitary episode. This is **intermodal perception,** which involves integrating information from two or more sensory modalities, such as vision and hearing (Bremner & Spence, 2017; Hannon, Schachner, & Nave-Blodgett, 2017). Most perception is intermodal (Bahrick, 2010).

intermodal perception The ability to relate and integrate information from two or more sensory modalities, such as vision and hearing.

Early, exploratory forms of intermodal perception exist even in newborns (Bremner, 2017). For example, newborns turn their eyes and their head toward the sound of a voice or rattle when the sound is maintained for several seconds (Clifton & others, 1981). Intermodal perception becomes sharper with experience in the first year of life (Kirkham & others, 2012). In the first six months, infants have difficulty connecting sensory input from different modes (such as vision and sound), but in the second half of the first year they show an increased ability to make this connection mentally.

Nature, Nurture, and Perceptual Development

Now that we have discussed many aspects of perceptual development, let's explore one of developmental psychology's key issues as it relates to perceptual development: the nature-nurture issue. There has been a longstanding interest in how strongly infants' perception is influenced by nature or nurture (Bremner, 2017; Chen & others, 2017). In the field of perceptual development, those who emphasize nature are referred to as nativists and those who emphasize learning and experience are called empiricists. In the nativist view, the ability to perceive the world in a competent, organized way is inborn or innate. A completely nativist view of perceptual development is no longer accepted in developmental psychology.

The Gibsons argued that a key question in infant perception is what information is available in the environment and how infants learn to generate, differentiate, and discriminate the information—certainly not a nativist view. The Gibsons' ecological view also is quite different from Piaget's constructivist view. According to Piaget, much of perceptual development in infancy must await the development of a sequence of cognitive stages in which infants become able to construct more complex perceptual tasks. Thus, in Piaget's view the ability to perceive size and shape constancy, a three-dimensional world, intermodal perception, and so on develops later in infancy than the Gibsons envision.

The longitudinal research of Daphne Maurer and her colleagues (Chen & others, 2017; Lewis & Maurer, 2005, 2009; Maurer, 2016; Maurer & Lewis, 2013; Maurer & others, 1999) has focused on infants born with cataracts—a thickening of the lens of the eye that causes vision to become cloudy, opaque, and distorted and thus severely restricts these infants' ability to experience their visual world. By studying infants whose cataracts were removed at different points in development, they discovered that those whose cataracts were removed and new lenses placed in their eyes in the first several months after birth showed a normal pattern of visual development. However, the longer the delay in removing the cataracts, the more their visual development was impaired. In their research, Maurer and her colleagues (Maurer, 2016; Maurer, Mondloch, & Leis, 2007) have found that experiencing patterned visual input early in infancy is important for holistic and detailed face processing after infancy. Maurer's research program illustrates how deprivation and experience influence visual development, including an early sensitive period in which visual input is necessary for normal visual development (Maurer & Lewis, 2013).

What roles do nature and nurture play in the infant's perceptual development?
©Boris Ryaposov/ Shutterstock

Today it is clear that an extreme empiricist position on perceptual development is unwarranted. Much of early perception develops from innate (nature) capabilities, and the basic foundation of many perceptual abilities can be detected in newborns, whereas others unfold through maturation (Bornstein, Arterberry, & Mash, 2011). However, as infants develop, environmental experiences (nurture) refine or calibrate many perceptual functions, and they may be the driving force behind some functions (Johnson & Hannon, 2015). The accumulation of experience with and knowledge about their perceptual world contributes to infants' ability to perceive coherent impressions of people and things (Slater & others, 2011). Thus, a full portrait of perceptual development includes the influence of nature, nurture, and a developing sensitivity to information (Bremner & others, 2016; Chen & others, 2017).

Perceptual Motor Coupling

A central theme of the ecological approach is the interplay between perception and action. Action can guide perception, and perception can guide action. Only by moving one's eyes, head, hands, and arms and by moving from one location to another can an individual fully experience his or her environment and learn how to adapt to it. Thus, perception and action are coupled (Adolph, 2018; Franchak, Kretch, & Adolph, 2019).

Babies, for example, continually coordinate their movements with perceptual information to learn how to maintain balance, reach for objects in space, and move across various surfaces and terrains (Adolph & Hoch, 2019; Thelen & Smith, 2006). They are motivated to move by what they perceive. Consider the sight of an attractive toy across the room. In this situation, infants must perceive the current state of their bodies and learn how to use their limbs to reach the toy. Although their movements at first are awkward and uncoordinated, babies soon learn to select patterns that are appropriate for reaching their goals.

Equally important is the other part of the perception-action coupling. That is, action educates perception (Adolph, 2018; Lee & others, 2019). For example, watching an object while exploring it manually helps infants discover its texture, size, and hardness. Moving around in their environment teaches babies about how objects and people look from different perspectives, or whether surfaces will support their weight. In short, infants perceive in order to move and move in order to perceive. Perceptual and motor development do not occur in isolation from each other but instead are coupled.

Cognitive Development

The competent infant not only develops motor and perceptual skills, but also develops cognitive skills. Our coverage of cognitive development in infancy focuses on Piaget's theory and sensorimotor stages as well as on how infants learn, remember, and conceptualize.

Piaget's Theory

Piaget's theory is a general, unifying story of how biology and experience sculpt cognitive development. The Swiss child psychologist Jean Piaget thought that, just as our physical bodies have structures that enable us to adapt to the world, we build mental structures that help us to adapt to the world. *Adaptation* involves adjusting to new environmental demands. Piaget stressed that children actively construct their own cognitive worlds; information is not just poured into their minds from the environment. He sought to discover how children at different points in their development think about the world and how systematic changes in their thinking occur.

Processes of Development

What processes do children use as they construct their knowledge of the world? Piaget developed several concepts to answer this question.

Schemes According to Piaget (1954), as the infant or child seeks to construct an understanding of the world, the developing brain creates **schemes.** These are actions or mental representations that organize knowledge.

schemes In Piaget's theory, actions or mental representations that organize knowledge.

In Piaget's theory, infants create behavioral schemes (physical activities), whereas toddlers and older children create mental schemes (cognitive activities) (Lamb, Bornstein, & Teti, 2002). A baby's schemes are structured by simple actions that can be performed on objects, such as sucking, looking, and grasping. Older children's schemes include strategies and plans for solving problems.

Assimilation and Accommodation To explain how children use and adapt their schemes, Piaget offered two concepts: assimilation and accommodation. **Assimilation** occurs when children use their existing schemes to deal with new information or experiences. **Accommodation** occurs when children adjust their schemes to account for new information and experiences.

Think about a toddler who has learned the word *car* to identify the family's automobile. The toddler might call all moving vehicles on roads "cars," including motorcycles and trucks; the child has assimilated these objects to his or her existing scheme. But the child soon learns that motorcycles and trucks are not cars and fine-tunes the category to exclude those vehicles. The child has accommodated the scheme.

Organization To make sense out of their world, said Piaget, children cognitively organize their experiences. **Organization,** in Piaget's theory, is the grouping of isolated behaviors and thoughts into a higher-order system. Continual refinement of this organization is an inherent part of development. A child who has only a vague idea about how to use a hammer may also have a vague idea about how to use other tools. After learning how to use each one, she relates these uses to one another, thereby organizing her knowledge.

Equilibration and Stages of Development Assimilation and accommodation always take the child to a higher level, according to Piaget. In trying to understand the world, the child inevitably experiences cognitive conflict, or *disequilibrium*. That is, the child is constantly faced with inconsistencies and counterexamples to his or her existing schemes. For example, if a child believes that pouring water from a short, wide container into a tall, narrow container changes the amount of water in the container, the child might wonder where the "extra" water came from and whether there is actually more water to drink. This puzzle creates disequilibrium; and in Piaget's view the resulting search for equilibrium creates motivation for change. The child assimilates and accommodates, adjusting old schemes, developing new schemes, and organizing and reorganizing the old and new schemes. Eventually the organization is fundamentally different from the old organization; it becomes a new way of thinking.

Equilibration is the name Piaget gave to this mechanism by which children shift from one stage of thought to the next. Equilibration does not, however, happen all at once. There is considerable movement between states of cognitive equilibrium and disequilibrium as assimilation and accommodation work in concert to produce cognitive change.

A result of these processes, according to Piaget, is that individuals go through four stages of development. A different way of understanding the world makes one stage more advanced than another. Cognition is *qualitatively* different in one stage compared with another. In other words, the way children reason at one stage is different from the way they reason at another stage. Here our focus is on Piaget's stage of infant cognitive development.

The Sensorimotor Stage

The **sensorimotor stage** lasts from birth to about age 2. In this stage, infants construct an understanding of the world by coordinating sensory experiences (such as seeing and hearing) with physical, motor actions—hence the term *sensorimotor*. At the beginning of this stage, newborns have little more than reflexes to work with. At the end of the sensorimotor

In Piaget's view, what is a scheme? What schemes might this young infant be displaying?
©CSP_NikolayK/age fotostock

accommodation Piagetian concept of adjusting schemes to fit new information and experiences.

assimilation Piagetian concept of using existing schemes to deal with new information or experiences.

organization Piaget's concept of grouping isolated behaviors and thoughts into a higher-order, more smoothly functioning cognitive system.

equilibration A mechanism that Piaget proposed to explain how children shift from one stage of thought to the next.

sensorimotor stage The first of Piaget's stages, which lasts from birth to about 2 years of age; during this stage, infants construct an understanding of the world by coordinating sensory experiences with motoric actions.

stage, 2-year-olds can produce complex sensorimotor patterns and use primitive symbols. We first summarize Piaget's descriptions of how infants develop. Later we consider criticisms of his view.

Object Permanence **Object permanence** is the understanding that objects continue to exist even when they cannot be seen, heard, or touched. Acquiring the sense of object permanence is one of the infant's most important accomplishments, according to Piaget.

How could anyone know whether or not an infant had a sense of object permanence? The principal way in which object permanence is studied is by watching an infant's reaction when an interesting object disappears (see Figure 17). If infants search for the object, it is inferred that they know it continues to exist.

Evaluating Piaget's Sensorimotor Stage Piaget opened up a new way of looking at infants with his view that their main task is to coordinate their sensory impressions with their motor activity. However, the infant's cognitive world is not as neatly packaged as Piaget portrayed it, and some of Piaget's explanations for the cause of change are debated. In the past several decades, there have been many research studies on infant development using sophisticated techniques. Much of the new research suggests that Piaget's view of sensorimotor development needs to be modified (Adolph, 2018; Bell & others, 2018; Bremner & others, 2017; Lee & others, 2019; Van de Vondervoort & Hamlin, 2018).

A-not-B error is the term used to describe the tendency of infants to reach where an object was located earlier rather than where the object was last hidden. Older infants are less likely to make the A-not-B error because their concept of object permanence is more complete.

Figure 17 Object Permanence.
Piaget argued that object permanence is one of infancy's landmark cognitive accomplishments. For this 5-month-old boy, "out of sight" is literally out of mind. The infant looks at the toy monkey (top), but when his view of the toy is blocked (bottom), he does not search for it. Several months later, he will search for the hidden toy monkey, an action reflecting the presence of object permanence.
©Doug Goodman/Science Source

object permanence The Piagetian term for understanding that objects and events continue to exist, even when they cannot directly be seen, heard, or touched.

A-not-B error This term is used to describe the tendency of infants to reach where an object was located earlier rather than where the object was last hidden.

Researchers have found, however, that the A-not-B error does not show up consistently (MacNeill & others, 2018; Sophian, 1985). The evidence indicates that A-not-B errors are sensitive to the delay between hiding the object at B and the infant's attempt to find it (Diamond, 1985). Thus, the A-not-B error might be due to a failure in memory. Another explanation is that infants tend to repeat a previous motor behavior (Clearfield & others, 2006).

Research also suggests that infants develop the ability to understand how the world works at a very early age (Aslin, 2017; Jin & others, 2018; Liu & Spelke, 2017; Stavans & Baillargeon, 2018; Van de Vondervoort & Hamlin, 2018). And a number of theorists, such as Eleanor Gibson (1989) and Elizabeth Spelke (2004, 2011, 2013, 2017), have concluded that infants' perceptual abilities are highly developed very early in life. For example, intermodal perception—the ability to coordinate information from two or more sensory modalities, such as vision and hearing—develops much earlier than Piaget would have predicted (Spelke & Owsley, 1979).

Object permanence also develops earlier than Piaget thought. In his view, object permanence does not develop until approximately 8 to 9 months. However, research by Renée Baillargeon and her colleagues (2004, 2014, 2016; Baillargeon & DeJong, 2017; Baillargeon & others, 2012) documents that infants as young as 3 to 4 months expect objects to be *substantial* (in the sense that other objects cannot move through them) and *permanent* (in the sense that they continue to exist when they are hidden).

Today researchers believe that infants see objects as bounded, unitary, solid, and separate from their background, possibly at birth or shortly thereafter, but definitely by 3 to 4 months, much earlier than Piaget envisioned. Young infants still have much to learn about objects, but the world appears both stable and orderly to them (Bremner, 2017; Liu & Spelke, 2017; Stavans & Baillargeon, 2018).

In considering the big issue of whether nature or nature plays a more important role in infant development, Elizabeth

Spelke (2011, 2013, 2016a, b, 2017; Huang & Spelke, 2015; Liu & Spelke, 2017; Spelke, Bernier, & Snedeker, 2013) comes down clearly on the side of nature. Spelke endorses a **core knowledge approach,** which states that infants are born with domain-specific innate knowledge systems. Among these knowledge systems are those involving space, number sense, object permanence, and language (which we will discuss later in this chapter). Strongly influenced by evolution, the core knowledge domains are theorized to be "prewired" to allow infants to make sense of their world (Coubart & others, 2014; Strickland & Chemla, 2018). After all, Spelke concludes, how could infants possibly grasp the complex world in which they live if they did not come into the world equipped with core sets of knowledge? In this approach, the innate core knowledge domains form a foundation around which more mature cognitive functioning and learning develop. The core knowledge approach argues that Piaget greatly underestimated the cognitive abilities of infants, especially young infants (Spelke, 2017).

Recently, researchers also have explored whether preverbal infants might have a built-in, innate sense of morality (Steckler & Hamlin, 2016; Van de Vondervoort & Hamlin, 2016, 2018). In this research, infants as young as 4 months of age are more likely to make visually guided reaches toward a puppet who has acted as a helper (such as helping someone get up a hill, assisting in opening a box, or giving a ball back) rather than toward a puppet who has hindered others' efforts to achieve such goals (Hamlin, 2013, 2014).

Recently, the view that the emergence of morality in infancy is innate was described as problematic (Carpendale & Hammond, 2016). Instead it was argued that morality may emerge through infants' early interaction with others and undergo later transformation through language and reflective thought.

In criticizing the core knowledge approach, British developmental psychologist Mark Johnson (2008) says that the infants Spelke assesses in her research have already accumulated hundreds, and in some cases even thousands, of hours of experience in grasping what the world is about, which gives considerable room for the environment's role in the development of infant cognition (Highfield, 2008). According to Johnson (2008), infants likely come into the world with "soft biases to perceive and attend to different aspects of the environment, and to learn about the world in particular ways." A major criticism is that nativists completely neglect the infant's social immersion in the world and instead focus only on what happens inside the infant's head apart from the environment (de Haan & Johnson, 2016; Hakuno & others, 2018; Nelson, 2013).

In sum, many researchers conclude that Piaget wasn't specific enough about how infants learn about their world and that infants, especially young infants, are more competent than Piaget thought (Adolph & Hoch, 2019; Aslin, 2017; Bell & others, 2018; Xie, Mallin, & Richards, 2018). As these researchers have examined the specific ways that infants learn, the field of infant cognition has become very specialized. There are many researchers working on different questions, with no general theory emerging that can connect all of the different findings. Their theories often are local theories, focused on specific research questions, rather than grand theories like Piaget's (Kuhn, 1998). Among the unifying themes in the study of infant cognition are seeking to understand more precisely how developmental changes in cognition take place, considering the big issue of nature and nurture, and examining the brain's role in cognitive development. Recall that exploring connections between brain, cognition, and development is the focus of the recently emerging field of *developmental cognitive neuroscience* (Bell & others, 2018; Bick & Nelson, 2018; Gliga & others, 2018; Meltzoff & others, 2018a, b; Saez de Urabain, Nuthmann, & Johnson, 2017).

What are some conclusions that can be reached about infant learning and cognition?
©baobao ou/Getty Images

Learning, Remembering, and Conceptualizing

Earlier we described the behavioral and social cognitive theories, as well as information-processing theory. These theories emphasize that cognitive development does not unfold in a stage-like process as Piaget proposed, but rather advances more gradually (Diamond, 2013). In this section we explore what researchers who are using these approaches can tell us about how infants learn, remember, and conceptualize.

Conditioning

We have discussed Skinner's theory of operant conditioning, in which the consequences of a behavior influence the probability of the behavior's recurrence. Infants can learn through operant conditioning: If an infant's behavior is followed by a rewarding stimulus, the behavior is likely to recur.

Operant conditioning has been especially helpful to researchers in their efforts to determine what infants perceive (Rovee-Collier & Barr, 2010). For example, infants will suck faster on a nipple when the sucking behavior is followed by a visual display, music, or a human voice (Rovee-Collier, 2008).

Carolyn Rovee-Collier (1987) has demonstrated that infants can retain information from the experience of being conditioned. In a characteristic experiment, Rovee-Collier places a 2½-month-old baby in a crib under an elaborate mobile (see Figure 18). She then ties one end of a ribbon to the baby's ankle and the other end to the mobile. Subsequently, she observes that the baby kicks and makes the mobile move. The movement of the mobile is the reinforcing stimulus (which increases the baby's kicking behavior) in this experiment. Weeks later, the baby is returned to the crib, but its foot is not tied to the mobile. The baby kicks, suggesting that it has retained the information that if it kicks a leg, the mobile will move.

Figure 18 The Technique Used in Rovee-Collier's Investigation of Infant Memory.
In Rovee-Collier's experiment, operant conditioning was used to demonstrate that infants as young as 2½ months of age can retain information from the experience of being conditioned. *What did infants recall in Rovee-Collier's experiment?*
©Dr. Carolyn Rovee-Collier

Attention

Attention, the focusing of mental resources on select information, improves cognitive processing on many tasks (Ito-Jager & others, 2017; Posner, 2018a, b; Reynolds & Richards, 2018; Tsurumi, Kanazawa, & Yamaguchi, 2018; Wu & Scerif, 2018; Yu & Smith, 2017). Even newborns can detect a contour and fix their attention on it. Older infants scan patterns more thoroughly. By 4 months, infants can selectively attend to an object. A longitudinal study found that 5-month-olds who were more efficient in processing information quickly had better higher-level cognitive functioning in the preschool years (Cuevas & Bell, 2014).

Closely linked with attention are the processes of habituation and dishabituation, which we discussed earlier in this chapter (Jones & others, 2017). Infants' attention is strongly governed by novelty and habituation (Christodoulou, Leland, & Moore, 2018; Falck-Ytter & others, 2018). When an object becomes familiar, attention becomes shorter, making infants more vulnerable to distraction (Kavsek, 2013).

Another aspect of attention that plays an important role in infant development is **joint attention,** in which individuals focus on the same object or event (Mateus & others, 2018; Urqueta Alfaro & others, 2018). Joint attention requires (1) the ability to track each other's behavior, such as following someone's gaze; (2) one person directing another's attention; and (3) reciprocal interaction. Early in infancy, joint attention usually involves a caregiver pointing or using words to direct an infant's attention. Emerging forms of joint attention occur at about 7 to 8 months, but it is not until 10 to 11 months that joint attention skills are frequently observed (Meltzoff & Brooks, 2009). By their first birthday, infants have begun to direct adults' attention to objects that

attention The focusing of mental resources on select information.

joint attention Process that occurs when (1) individuals focus on the same object and track each other's behavior, (2) one individual directs another's attention, and (3) reciprocal interaction takes place.

capture their interest (Heimann & others, 2006). And one study found that problems in joint attention as early as 8 months of age were linked to a child having been diagnosed with autism by 7 years of age (Veness & others, 2014). Also, a recent study involving the use of eye-tracking equipment with 11- to 24-month-olds revealed that joint attention was predicted by infants' hand-eye coordination involving the connection of gaze with manual actions on objects, rather than by gaze following alone (Yu & Smith, 2017).

Joint attention plays important roles in many aspects of infant development and considerably increases infants' ability to learn from other people (McClure & others, 2018; Yu & Smith, 2017). Nowhere is this more apparent than in observations of interchanges between caregivers and infants as infants are learning language (Mason-Apps & others, 2018; Tomasello, 2014). Researchers have found that joint attention is linked to better sustained attention (Yu & Smith, 2017); memory (Kopp & Lindenberger, 2011); self-regulation (Van Hecke & others, 2012); and executive function (Gueron-Sela & others, 2018).

Imitation

Infant development researcher Andrew Meltzoff and his colleagues (2004, 2007, 2011; Meltzoff & Williamson, 2010, 2013; Meltzoff & others, , 2018a, b; Waismeyer & Meltzoff, 2017) have conducted numerous studies of infants' imitative abilities. Meltzoff sees infants' imitative abilities as biologically based, because infants can imitate a facial expression within the first few days after birth. Meltzoff (2017) also emphasizes that infants' imitation informs us about their processing of social events and contributes to rapid social learning. He also emphasizes that the infant's imitative abilities do not resemble a hardwired response but rather involve flexibility and adaptability. In Meltzoff's observations of infants during the first 72 hours of life, the infants gradually displayed more complete imitation of an adult's facial expression, such as protruding the tongue or opening the mouth wide (see Figure 19).

Meltzoff (2007, 2011; Meltzoff & others, 2018a, b) concludes that infants don't blindly imitate everything they see and often make creative errors. He also argues that beginning at birth there is an interplay between learning by observing and learning by doing (Piaget emphasized learning by doing).

Not all experts on infant development accept Meltzoff's conclusion that newborns are capable of imitation. Some say that these babies were engaging in little more than automatic responses to a stimulus.

Meltzoff (2005, 2011; Meltzoff & Williamson, 2013) has also studied **deferred imitation,** which occurs after a time delay of hours or days. Piaget held that deferred imitation does not occur until about 18 months. Meltzoff's research suggested that it occurs much earlier. In one study, Meltzoff (1988) demonstrated that 9-month-old infants could imitate actions—such as pushing a recessed button in a box, which produced a beeping sound—that they had seen performed 24 hours earlier.

Memory

Meltzoff's studies of deferred imitation suggest that infants have another important cognitive ability: **memory,** which involves the retention of information over time. Sometimes information is retained only for a few seconds, and at other times it is retained for a lifetime. What can infants remember, and when?

Some researchers, such as Rovee-Collier (2008), have concluded that infants as young as 2 to 6 months can remember some experiences through 1½ to 2 years of age. However, critics such as Jean Mandler (2000), a leading

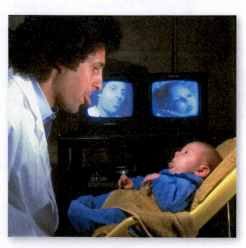

Figure 19 Infant Imitation.
Infant development researcher Andrew Meltzoff protrudes his tongue in an attempt to get an infant to imitate his behavior. *How do Meltzoff's findings about imitation compare with Piaget's descriptions of infants' abilities?*
©Dr. Andrew Meltzoff

deferred imitation Imitation that occurs after a delay of hours or days.

memory A central feature of cognitive development, pertaining to all situations in which an individual retains information over time.

Age Group	Length of Delay
6-month-olds	24 hours
9-month-olds	1 month
10–11-month-olds	3 months
13–14-month-olds	4–6 months
20-month-olds	12 months

Figure 20 **Age-Related Changes in the Length of Time Over Which Memory Occurs**

expert on infant cognition, argue that the infants in Rovee-Collier's experiments are displaying only implicit memory.

Implicit memory refers to memory without conscious recollection—memories of skills and routine procedures that are performed automatically. In contrast, **explicit memory** refers to conscious memory of facts and experiences.

When people think about memory, they are usually referring to explicit memory. Most researchers find that babies do not show explicit memory until the second half of the first year (Bauer, 2013, 2015, 2018; Bauer & Larkina, 2016). Explicit memory improves substantially during the second year of life (Bauer, 2013, 2015, 2018; Bauer & Leventon, 2015). In one longitudinal study, infants were assessed several times during their second year (Bauer & others, 2000). The older infants showed more accurate memory and required fewer prompts to demonstrate their memory than younger infants did. Figure 20 summarizes how long infants of different ages can remember information (Bauer, 2009). As indicated, researchers have documented that 6-month-olds can remember information for 24 hours but 20-month-old infants can remember information they encountered 12 months earlier.

Let's examine another aspect of memory. Do you remember your third birthday party? Probably not. Most adults can remember little, if anything, from the first 3 years of their life. This is called *infantile* or *childhood amnesia*. The few memories that adults are able to report of their life at age 2 or 3 are at best very sketchy (Fivush, 2011; Riggins, 2012).

Patricia Bauer and her colleagues (Bauer, 2015, 2018; Bauer & Larkina, 2016; Pathman, Doydum, & Bauer, 2013) have studied when infantile amnesia begins to occur. In one study, children's memories of events that occurred at 3 years of age were periodically assessed through age 9 (Bauer & Larkina, 2014). By 8 to 9 years of age, children's memories of events that occurred at 3 years of age began to significantly fade away. In Bauer's (2015) view, the processes that account for these developmental changes are early, gradual development of the ability to form, retain, and later retrieve memories of personally relevant past events followed by an accelerated rate of forgetting in childhood.

What is the cause of infantile amnesia? One reason older children and adults have difficulty recalling events from their infant and early childhood years is that during these years the prefrontal lobes of the brain are immature, and this area of the brain is believed to play an important role in storing memories of events (Bauer, 2015, 2018).

In sum, most of young infants' conscious memories appear to be rather fragile and short-lived, although their implicit memory of perceptual-motor actions can be substantial (Bauer, 2015, 2018; Bauer & Fivush, 2014). By the end of the second year, long-term memory is more substantial and reliable (Bauer, 2015, 2018).

implicit memory Memory without conscious recollection; involves skills and routine procedures that are automatically performed.

explicit memory Memory of facts and experiences that individuals consciously know and can state.

concepts Cognitive groupings of similar objects, events, people, or ideas.

Concept Formation and Categorization

Along with attention, imitation, and memory, concepts are a key aspect of infants' cognitive development (Quinn, 2016). **Concepts** are cognitive groupings of similar objects, events, people, or ideas. Without concepts, you would see each object and event as unique; you would not be able to make any generalizations.

Do infants have concepts? Yes, they do, although we do not know just how early concept formation begins (Quinn & Bhatt, 2015). Using habituation experiments like those described earlier in the chapter, some researchers have found that infants as young as 3 months of age can group together objects with similar appearances (Quinn & others, 2013). This research capitalizes on the knowledge that infants are more likely to look at a novel object than at a familiar one.

Jean Mandler (2009) argues that these early categorizations are best described as *perceptual categorization*. That is, the categorizations are based on similar perceptual features of objects, such as size, color, and movement, as well as parts of objects, such as legs for animals. Mandler (2004) concludes that it is not until about 7 to 9 months that infants form *conceptual* categories rather than just making perceptual discriminations between different categories. In one study of 9- to 11-month-olds, infants classified birds as animals and airplanes as vehicles even though the objects were perceptually similar—airplanes and birds with their wings spread (Mandler & McDonough, 1993) (see Figure 21).

Figure 21 Categorization in 9- to 11-Month-Olds.

These are the stimuli used in the study that indicated 9- to 11-month-old infants categorized birds as animals and airplanes as vehicles even though the objects were perceptually similar (Mandler & McDonough, 1993).

In addition to infants categorizing items on the basis of external, perceptual features such as shape, color, and parts, they also may categorize items on the basis of prototypes, or averages, that they extract from the structural regularities of items (Quinn & Bhatt, 2015).

Further advances in categorization occur in the second year of life (Booth, 2006). Many infants' "first concepts are broad and global in nature, such as 'animal' or 'indoor thing.' Gradually, over the first two years these broad concepts become more differentiated into concepts such as 'land animal,' then 'dog,' or to 'furniture,' then 'chair'" (Mandler, 2009, p. 1).

Learning to put things into the correct categories—what makes something one kind of thing rather than another kind of thing, such as what makes a bird a bird, or a fish a fish—is an important aspect of learning (Quinn, 2016). As infant development researcher Alison Gopnik (2010, p. 159) pointed out, "If you can sort the world into the right categories—put things in the right boxes—then you've got a big advance on understanding the world."

How Would You...?

As an **educator,** how would you talk with parents about the importance of concept development in their infants?

In sum, the infant's advances in processing information—through attention, imitation, memory, and concept formation—are much richer, more gradual and less stage-like, and occur earlier than was envisioned by earlier theorists (Bauer, 2018; Meltzoff & others, 2018a, b; Wu & Scerif, 2018; Xie, Mallin, & Richards, 2018). As leading infant researcher Jean Mandler (2004) concluded, "The human infant shows a remarkable degree of learning power and complexity in what is being learned and in the way it is represented" (p. 304).

Language Development

In 1799, villagers in the French town of Aveyron observed a nude boy running through the woods and captured him. Known as the Wild Boy of Aveyron, he was judged to be about 11 years old and believed to have lived in the woods alone for six years (Lane, 1976). When found, he made no effort to communicate, and he never did learn to communicate effectively.

Sadly, a modern-day wild child was discovered in Los Angeles in 1970. Despite intensive intervention, the child, named Genie by researchers, never acquired more than a primitive form of language. Both of these cases—the Wild Boy of Aveyron and Genie—raise questions about the biological and environmental determinants of language, topics that we also examine later in the chapter. First, though, we need to define language.

Defining Language

Language is a form of communication—whether spoken, written, or signed—that is based on a system of symbols. Language consists of the words used by a community and the rules for varying and combining them. All human languages have some common characteristics, such as organizational rules and infinite generativity (Clark, 2017; Genetti, 2019; Ringe, 2019). Rules describe the way the language works. **Infinite generativity** is the ability to produce and comprehend an endless number of meaningful sentences using a finite set of words and rules.

Think how important language is in our everyday lives. We need language to speak with others, listen to others, read, and write. Our language enables us to describe past events in detail and to plan for the future. Language lets us pass down information from one generation to the next and create a rich cultural heritage. Language learning involves comprehending a sound system (or sign system for individuals who are deaf), the world of objects, actions, and events, and how units such as words and grammar connect sound and world (Israel, 2019; Mithun, 2019; van der Hulst, 2017; Wilcox & Occhino, 2017).

language A form of communication, whether spoken, written, or signed, that is based on a system of symbols. Language consists of the words used by a community and the rules for varying and combining them.

infinite generativity The ability to produce and comprehend an endless number of meaningful sentences using a finite set of words and rules.

How Language Develops

Whatever language they learn, infants all over the world follow a similar path in language development. What are some key milestones in this development?

Babbling and Gestures

Babies actively produce sounds from birth onward. The effect of these early communications is to attract attention (Lee & others, 2018; Masapollo, Polka, & Menard, 2016). Babies' sounds and gestures go through the following sequence during the first year:

- *Crying.* Babies cry even at birth. Crying can signal distress, but as we will discuss later, there are different types of cries that signal different things.

- *Cooing.* Babies first coo at about 2 to 4 months. Coos are gurgling sounds that are made in the back of the throat and usually express pleasure during interaction with the caregiver.

- *Babbling.* In the middle of the first year, babies babble—that is, they produce strings of consonant-vowel combinations such as "ba, ba, ba, ba" (Lee & others, 2018). In a recent study, babbling onset predicted when infants would say their first words (McGillion & others, 2017a). Also, in another recent study, a lack of babbling in infants was linked to a risk of having future speech and language problems (Lohmander & others, 2017). And in other research, infants' babbling has been shown to influence the behavior of their caregivers, creating social interaction that facilitates their own language development (Albert, Schwade, & Goldstein, 2018).

- *Gestures.* Infants start using gestures, such as showing and pointing, at about 8 to 12 months (Goldin-Meadow, 2015, 2017a, b; Novack & others, 2018). They may wave bye-bye, nod to mean "yes," and show an empty cup to ask for more milk. Lack of pointing is a significant indicator of problems in the infant's communication system (Cooperrider & Goldin-Meadow, 2017, 2018). Why might gestures such as pointing promote further language development? Infants' gestures advance their language development, since caregivers often talk to them about what they are pointing to. Also, babies' first words often are for things they have previously pointed to.

Recognizing Language Sounds

Long before they begin to learn words, infants can make fine distinctions among the sounds of a language (Kuhl & Damasio, 2012). In Patricia Kuhl's (2000, 2009, 2011, 2012, 2015) research, *phonemes* (the basic sound units of a language) from languages all over the world are piped through a speaker for infants to hear (see Figure 22). A box with a toy bear in it is placed where the infant can see it. A string of identical syllables is played; then the syllables are changed (for example, *ba ba ba ba,* and then *pa pa pa pa*). If the infant turns its head when the syllables change, the box lights up and the bear dances and drums, rewarding the infant for noticing the change.

Kuhl's research has demonstrated that from birth up to about 6 months, infants are "citizens of the world": They can tell when sounds change most of the time no matter what language the syllables come from. But over the next six months, infants get even better at perceiving changes in sounds from their "own" language, the one their parents speak, and gradually lose the ability to recognize differences that are not important in their own language (Kuhl, 2009, 2011, 2012, 2015). Recently, Kuhl (2015) has found that the age at which a baby's brain is most open to learning the sounds of a native language begins at 6 months for vowels and at 9 months for consonants.

Also, in the second half of their first year, infants begin to segment the continuous stream of speech they encounter into words (Ota & Skarabela, 2018; Polka & others, 2018). Initially, they likely rely on statistical information such as the co-occurrence patterns of phonemes and syllables, which allows them to extract potential word forms (Aslin, 2017; Richtsmeier & Goffman, 2017; Saffran & Kirkham, 2018). For example, discovering that the sequence *br* occurs more often at the beginning of words while *nt* is more common at the end of words helps infants detect word boundaries. And as infants extract an increasing number of potential word forms from the speech stream they hear, they begin to associate these with concrete, perceptually available objects in their world (Saffran & Kirkham, 2018; Zamuner, Fais, & Werker, 2014). For example, infants might detect that the spoken word "monkey" has a reliable statistical regularity of occurring in the visual presence of an observed monkey but not in the presence of other animals, such as bears (Pace & others, 2016). Thus, statistical learning involves extracting information from the world to learn about the environment.

Richard Aslin (2017) recently emphasized that statistical learning—which involves no instruction, reinforcement, or feedback—is a powerful learning mechanism in infant development. In statistical learning, infants soak up statistical regularities in the world merely through exposure to them (Lany & others, 2018; Monroy & others, 2018; Saffran & Kirkham, 2018).

Figure 22 From Universal Linguist to Language-Specific Listener. In Patricia Kuhl's research laboratory babies listen to tape-recorded voices that repeat syllables. When the sounds of the syllables change, the babies quickly learn to look at the bear. Using this technique, Kuhl has demonstrated that babies are universal linguists until about 6 months of age, but in the next six months they become language-specific listeners. *Does Kuhl's research give support to the view that either "nature" or "nurture" is the source of language acquisition?*
©Dr. Patricia Kuhl, Institute for Learning and Brain Sciences, University of Washington

First Words

Infants understand words before they can produce or speak them (Pace & others, 2016). For example, as early as 5 months many infants recognize their name. However, the infant's first spoken word, a milestone eagerly anticipated by every parent, usually doesn't occur until 10 to 15 months of age and happens at an average of about 13 months. Yet long before babies say their first words, they have been communicating with their parents, often by gesturing and using their own special sounds. The appearance of first words is a continuation of this communication process.

A child's first words include those that name important people (*dada*), familiar animals (*kitty*), vehicles (*car*), toys (*ball*), food (*milk*), body parts (*eye*), clothes (*hat*), household items (*clock*), and greeting terms (*bye*). Children often express various intentions with their single words, so that "cookie" might mean, "That's a cookie" or "I want a cookie." Nouns are easier to learn because the majority of words in this class are more perceptually accessible than other types of words (Parish-Morris, Golinkoff, & Hirsh-Pasek, 2013). Think how the noun "car" is so much more concrete and

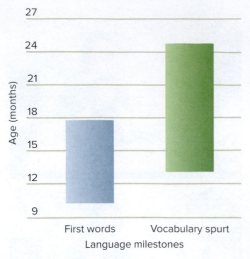

Figure 23 **Variation in Language Milestones.**

What are some possible explanations for variations in the timing of these milestones?

imaginable than the verb "goes," making the word "car" much easier to acquire than the word "goes."

As indicated earlier, children understand their first words earlier than they speak them. On average, infants understand about 50 words at the age of 13 months, but they can't say that many words until about 18 months. Thus, in infancy *receptive vocabulary* (words the child understands) considerably exceeds *spoken vocabulary* (words the child uses). One study revealed that 6-month-olds understand words that refer to body parts, such as "hand" and "feet," but of course, they cannot yet speak these words (Tincoff & Jusczyk, 2012).

The infant's spoken vocabulary rapidly increases once the first word is spoken (Waxman & Goswami, 2012). Whereas the average 18-month-old can speak about 50 words, a 2-year-old can speak about 200 words. This rapid increase in vocabulary that begins at approximately 18 months is called the *vocabulary spurt* (Bloom, Lifter, & Broughton, 1985).

Like the timing of a child's first word, the timing of the vocabulary spurt varies (Dale & Goodman, 2004). Figure 23 shows the range for these two language milestones in 14 children. On average, these children said their first word at 13 months and had a vocabulary spurt at 19 months. However, the ages for the first word of individual children varied from 10 to 17 months and, for their vocabulary spurt, from 13 to 25 months. Also, the spurt actually involves the increase in the rate at which words are learned. That is, early on, a few words are learned every few days, then later on, a few words are learned each day, and eventually many words each day.

Does early vocabulary development predict later language development? A recent study found that infant vocabulary development at 16 to 24 months of age was linked to vocabulary, phonological awareness, reading accuracy, and reading comprehension five years later (Duff & others, 2015).

telegraphic speech The use of short and precise words without grammatical markers such as articles, auxiliary verbs, and other connectives.

Two-Word Utterances

By the time children are 18 to 24 months of age, they usually produce two-word utterances. To convey meaning with just two words, the child relies heavily on gesture, tone, and context. The wealth of meaning children can communicate with a two-word utterance includes the following (Slobin, 1972): identification—"See doggie"; location—"Book there"; repetition—"More milk"; negation—"Not wolf"; possession—"My candy"; attribution—"Big car"; and question—"Where ball?" These examples are from children whose first language is English, German, Russian, Finnish, Turkish, or Samoan.

Notice that two-word utterances omit many parts of speech and are remarkably succinct. In fact, in every language a child's first combinations of words have this economical quality; they are telegraphic. **Telegraphic speech** is the use of short, precise words without grammatical markers such as articles, auxiliary verbs, and other connectives. Telegraphic speech is not limited to two words; "Mommy give ice cream" and "Mommy give Tommy ice cream" are also examples of telegraphic speech.

Around the world, most young children learn to speak in two-word utterances at about 18 to 24 months of age. *What are some examples of these two-word utterances?*
©McPhoto/age fotostock

Typical Age	Language Milestones
Birth	Crying
2 to 4 months	Cooing begins
5 months	Understands first word
6 months	Babbling begins
7 to 11 months	Change from universal linguist to language-specific listener
8 to 12 months	Uses gestures, such as showing and pointing Comprehension of words appears
13 months	First word spoken
18 months	Vocabulary spurt starts
18 to 24 months	Uses two-word utterances Rapid expansion of understanding of words

Figure 24 Some Language Milestones in Infancy.
Despite substantial variations in the language input received by infants, around the world they follow a similar path in learning to speak.

Biological and Environmental Influences

We have discussed a number of language milestones in infancy; Figure 24 summarizes the ages at which infants typically reach these milestones. But what makes this amazing development possible? Everyone who uses language in some way "knows" its rules and has the ability to create an infinite number of words and sentences. Where does this knowledge come from? Is it the product of biology, or is language learned and influenced by experiences?

Biological Influences

The ability to speak and understand language requires a certain vocal apparatus as well as a nervous system with specific capabilities. The nervous system and vocal apparatus of humans' predecessors changed over hundreds of thousands, or millions, of years. With advances in the nervous system and vocal structures, *Homo sapiens* went beyond the grunting and shrieking of other animals to develop speech (Cataldo, Migliano, & Vinicius, 2018; Staes & others, 2017). Although estimates vary, many experts believe that humans acquired language about 100,000 years ago, which in evolutionary time represents a very recent acquisition. It gave humans an enormous edge over other animals and increased the chances of human survival (de Boer & Thompson, 2018; McMurray, 2016; Pinker, 2015).

Some language scholars view the remarkable similarities in how children acquire language all over the world as strong evidence that language has a biological basis. There is evidence that particular regions of the brain are predisposed to be used for language (Coulson, 2018; Schutze, 2017). Two regions involved in language were first discovered in studies of brain-damaged individuals: *Broca's area,* an area in the left frontal lobe of the brain that is involved in producing words (Maher, 2018; Zhang & others, 2017); and *Wernicke's area,* a region of the brain's left hemisphere that is involved in language comprehension (Bruckner & Kammer, 2017; Greenwald, 2018) (see Figure 25). Damage to either of these areas produces types of *aphasia,* a loss or impairment of language processing. Individuals with damage to Broca's area have difficulty producing speech but can comprehend what others say; those with damage to Wernicke's area have poor comprehension and often produce fluent but nonsensical speech.

Linguist Noam Chomsky (1957) proposed that humans are biologically "prewired" to learn language at a certain time and in a certain way. He said that children are born into the world with a **language acquisition device (LAD),** a biological endowment that enables the child to detect the various features and rules of language. Children are prepared by nature with the ability to detect the sounds of

Broca's area   Wernicke's area

Figure 25 Broca's Area and Wernicke's Area.
Broca's area is located in the frontal lobe of the brain's left hemisphere, and it is involved in the control of speech. Wernicke's area is a portion of the left hemisphere's temporal lobe that is involved in understanding language. *How does the role of these areas of the brain relate to lateralization?*

language acquisition device (LAD) Chomsky's term that describes a biological endowment enabling the child to detect the features and rules of language, including phonology, syntax, and semantics.

language, for example, and follow linguistic rules such as those governing how to form plurals and ask questions.

Chomsky's LAD is a theoretical construct, not a physical part of the brain. Is there evidence for the existence of a LAD? Supporters of the LAD concept cite the uniformity of language milestones across languages and cultures, evidence that children create language even in the absence of well-formed input, and the importance of language's biological underpinnings. But as we will see, critics argue that even if infants have something like a LAD, it cannot explain the whole process of language acquisition.

Environmental Influences

Language is not learned in a social vacuum. Most children are bathed in language from a very early age. The support and involvement of caregivers and teachers greatly facilitate a child's language learning (Brown & others, 2018; Clark, 2017; Marchman & others, 2018; Weisleder & others, 2018). Thus, social cues play an important role in infant language learning (Ahun & others, 2018; McGillion & others, 2017b; Pace & others, 2016).

How Would You...?

As a **social worker,** how would you intervene in a family in which a child has lived in social isolation for years?

The support and involvement of caregivers and teachers greatly facilitate a child's language learning (Clark, 2017; Marchman & others, 2018). In one study, both full-term and preterm infants who heard more caregiver talk based on all-day recordings at 16 months of age had better language skills (receptive and expressive language, language comprehension) at 18 months of age (Adams & others, 2018).

Researchers have documented the important effect that early speech input and poverty can have on the development of a child's language skills (Hoff, 2015; NICHD Early Child Care Research Network, 2005). Betty Hart and Todd Risley (1995) observed the language environments of children whose parents were professionals and children whose parents were on welfare. Compared with the professional parents, the parents on welfare talked much less to their young children, talked less about past events, and provided less elaboration. The children of the professional parents had a much larger vocabulary at 36 months than the children of the welfare parents did. Keep in mind, though, that individual variations characterize language development and that some welfare parents do spend considerable time talking to their children.

Given that social interaction is critical for infants to learn language effectively, might they also be able to learn language effectively through television and videos? Researchers have found that infants and young children cannot effectively learn language (phonology or words) from television or videos (Kuhl, 2007; Roseberry & others, 2009). In fact, a study of toddlers found that frequent viewing of television increased the risk of delayed language development (Lin & others, 2015). Thus, just hearing language is not enough even when infants seemingly are fully engaged in the experience. However, another study revealed that Skype provides some improvement in children's language learning over videos and TV (Roseberry & others, 2014), and older children can use information provided from television in their language development.

Also, recently the American Academy of Pediatrics (2016) concluded that when infants are 15 months to 2 years of age, evidence indicates that if parents co-watch educational videos with their infant and communicate with the infant about the information being watched, this interaction can benefit the infant's development. This suggests that when parents treat an educational video or app like a picture book, infants can benefit from it. However, APA still recommends no watching of videos alone for children under 18 months of age.

One intriguing component of the young child's linguistic environment is **child-directed speech** (also referred to as "parentese"), which is language spoken in a higher-than-usual pitch, slower tempo, and exaggerated intonation, with simple words and sentences (Hayashi & Mazuka, 2017). It is hard for most adults to use child-directed speech when not in the presence of a baby. As soon as adults start talking to a baby, though, they often shift into child-directed speech. Much of this is automatic and something most parents are not

child-directed speech Also called parentese, language spoken in a higher pitch, slower tempo, and with more exaggerated intonation than normal, with simple words and sentences.

aware they are doing. Child-directed speech serves the important functions of capturing the infant's attention, maintaining communication and social interaction between infants and caregivers, and providing infants with information about their native language by heightening differences between speech directed to children and adults (Golinkoff & others, 2015). Even 4-year-olds speak in simpler ways to 2-year-olds than to their 4-year-old friends. In recent research, child-directed speech in a one-to-one social context for 11 to 14 years of age was related to productive vocabulary at 2 years of age for Spanish-English bilingual infants across languages and in each individual language (Ramirez-Esparza, Garcia-Sierra, & Kuhl, 2017).

Most research on child-directed speech has involved mothers, but a recent study in several North American urban areas and a small society on the island of Tanna in the South Pacific Ocean found that fathers in both types of contexts engaged in child-directed speech with their infants (Broesch & Bryant, 2018).

Adults often use strategies other than child-directed speech to enhance the child's acquisition of language, including recasting, expanding, and labeling. *Recasting* is when an adult rephrases something the child has said that might lack the appropriate morphology or contain some other error. The adult restates the child's immature utterance in the form of a fully grammatical sentence. For example, when a 2-year-old says, "dog bark," the adult can respond by saying, "Oh, you heard the dog barking!" The adult sentence provides an acknowledgment that the child was heard and then adds the morphology /ing/ and the article (the) that the child's utterance lacked. *Expanding* is adding information to a child's incomplete utterance. For example, a child says, "Doggie eat," and the parent replies, "Yes, the dog is eating his food out of his special dish." *Labeling* is naming objects that children seem interested in. Young children are forever being asked to identify the names of objects. Roger Brown (1958) called this "the original word game." Children want more than the names of objects, though; they often want information about the object too.

Parents use these strategies naturally and in meaningful conversations. Parents do not (and should not) use any deliberate method to teach their children to talk, even with children who are slow in learning language. Children usually benefit when parents guide their discovery of language rather than overloading them; "following in order to lead" helps a child learn language. If children are not ready to take in some information, they are likely to indicate this, perhaps by turning away. Thus, giving the child more information is not always better.

Infants, toddlers, and young children benefit when adults read books to and with them, a process called shared reading (Brown & others, 2018; Marjanovic-Umek, Fekonja-Peklaj, & Socan, 2017; Sinclair & others, 2018). In one study, reading daily to children at 14 to 24 months was positively related to the children's language and cognitive development at 36 months (Raikes & others, 2006).

What are some effective ways that parents can facilitate their children's language development? They include the following strategies (Baron, 1992; Galinsky, 2010; Golinkoff and Hirsh-Pasek, 2000):

Parents should begin talking to their babies at the start. The best language teaching occurs when the talking is begun before the infant becomes capable of intelligible speech. *What are some other guidelines for parents to follow to help their infants and toddlers develop their language skills?*
©John Carter/Science Source

- *Be an active conversational partner.* Initiate conversation with the baby.

- *Narrate your daily activities to the baby as you do them.* For example, talk about how you will put the baby in a high chair for lunch and ask what she would like to eat, and so on.

- *Talk in a slowed-down pace and don't worry about how you sound to other adults when you talk to your baby.* Talking in a slowed-down pace will help your baby detect words in the sea of sounds they experience.

- *Use parent-look and parent-gesture, and name what you are looking at.* When you want your child to pay attention to something, look at it and point to it. Then name it—for example, by saying "Look, Alex, it's an airplane."

- *When you talk with infants and toddlers, be simple, concrete, and repetitive.* Don't try to talk to them in abstract, high-level ways and think you have to say something new or different all of the time. Using familiar words often will help them remember the words.

- *Play games.* Use word games like peek-a-boo and pat-a-cake to help infants learn words.

- *Remember to listen.* Since toddlers' speech is often slow and laborious, parents are often tempted to supply words and thoughts for them. Be patient and let toddlers express themselves.

- *Expand and elaborate language abilities and horizons with infants and toddlers.* Ask questions that encourage answers other than "Yes" and "No." Actively repeat, expand, and recast the utterances. Your toddler might say, "Dada." You could follow with, "Where's Dada?" and then you might continue, "Let's go find him."

How Would You…?

As a **human development and family studies professional,** how would you encourage parents to talk with their infants and toddlers?

An Interactionist View

If language acquisition depended only on biology, Genie and the Wild Boy of Aveyron (discussed earlier in the chapter) should have talked without difficulty. A child's experiences do influence language acquisition (Adams & others, 2018; Pace & others, 2016). But we have seen that language also has strong biological foundations (Dubois & others, 2016); no matter how much you converse with a dog, it won't learn to talk. Unlike dogs, children are biologically equipped to learn language (McMurray, 2016; Pinker, 2015). Children all over the world acquire language milestones at about the same time and in about the same order. An interactionist view emphasizes that both biology and experience contribute to language development (Adams & others, 2017; McGillion & others, 2017b).

This interaction of biology and experience can be seen in variations in the acquisition of language. Children vary in their ability to acquire language, and this variation cannot be completely explained by differences in environmental input alone. However, virtually every child benefits enormously from opportunities to talk and be talked with. Children whose parents and teachers provide them with a rich verbal environment show many positive outcomes (Ahun & others, 2018; Clark, 2017; Marchman & others, 2018; Pickard & others, 2018). Parents and teachers who pay attention to what children are trying to say, expand their children's utterances, read to them, and label things in the environment, are providing valuable, if unintentional, benefits (Capone Singleton, 2018; Weisleder & others, 2018).

Summary

Physical Growth and Development in Infancy
- Most development follows cephalocaudal and proximodistal patterns.
- Physical growth is rapid in the first year, but the rate of growth slows in the second year.
- Dramatic changes characterize the brain's development in the first two years. The neuroconstructivist view is an increasingly popular view of the brain's development.
- Newborns usually sleep 16 to 17 hours a day, but by 4 months many American infants approach adult-like sleeping patterns.

- Sudden infant death syndrome (SIDS) is a condition that occurs when a sleeping infant suddenly stops breathing and dies without an apparent cause.
- Infants need to consume about 50 calories per day for each pound they weigh. The growing consensus is that breast feeding is more beneficial than bottle feeding.

Motor Development
- Dynamic systems theory seeks to explain how motor behaviors are assembled for perceiving and acting. This theory emphasizes that experience plays an important

role in motor development, and that perception and action are coupled.

- Reflexes—automatic movements—govern the newborn's behavior.
- Key gross motor skills, which involve large-muscle activities, developed during infancy include control of posture and walking.
- Fine motor skills involve finely tuned movements. The onset of reaching and grasping marks a significant accomplishment, and this becomes more refined during the first two years of life.

Sensory and Perceptual Development

- Sensation occurs when information interacts with sensory receptors. Perception is the interpretation of sensation.
- Created by the Gibsons, the ecological view states that perception brings people into contact with the environment to interact with and adapt to it.
- The infant's visual acuity increases dramatically in the first year of life. By 3 months of age, infants show size and shape constancy. In Gibson and Walk's classic study, infants had depth perception as young as 6 months of age.
- The fetus can hear several weeks prior to birth. Just after being born, infants can hear but their sensory threshold is higher than that of adults. Newborns can respond to touch, feel pain, differentiate among odors, and may be sensitive to taste at birth.
- A basic form of intermodal perception is present in newborns and sharpens over the first year of life.
- In explaining developments in perception, nature advocates are referred to as nativists and nurture proponents are called empiricists. A strong empiricist approach is unwarranted. A full account of perceptual development includes the roles of nature, nurture, and the infant's developing sensitivity to information.

Cognitive Development

- In Piaget's theory, children construct their own cognitive worlds, building mental structures to adapt to their world. Schemes, assimilation and accommodation, organization, and equilibration are key processes in Piaget's theory. According to Piaget, there are four qualitatively different stages of thought. In sensorimotor thought, the first of Piaget's four stages, the infant organizes and coordinates sensations with physical movements. The stage lasts from birth to about 2 years of age. One key accomplishment of this stage is object permanence. In the past several decades, revisions of Piaget's view have been proposed based on research.
- An approach different from Piaget's focuses on infants' operant conditioning, attention, imitation, memory, and concept formation.

Language Development

- Rules describe the way language works. Language is characterized by infinite generativity.
- Infants reach a number of milestones in development, including first words and two-word utterances.
- Chomsky argues that children are born with the ability to detect basic features and rules of language. However, environmental influences are important, and babies are bathed in language early in their lives.
- How much of language is biologically determined, and how much depends on interaction with others, is a subject of debate among linguists and psychologists. However, all agree that both biological capacity and relevant experience are necessary. Parents should talk extensively with an infant, especially about what the baby is attending to.

Key Terms

A-not-B error
accommodation
assimilation
attention
cephalocaudal pattern
child-directed speech
concepts
core knowledge approach
deferred imitation
dishabituation

dynamic systems theory
ecological view
equilibration
explicit memory
fine motor skills
gross motor skills
habituation
implicit memory
infinite generativity
intermodal perception

joint attention
language
language acquisition device
   (LAD)
lateralization
memory
neuroconstructivist view
object permanence
organization
perception

proximodistal pattern
schemes
sensation
sensorimotor stage
sudden infant death syndrome
   (SIDS)
telegraphic speech
visual preference method

4 Socioemotional Development in Infancy

©Sam Edwards/Getty Images

CHAPTER OUTLINE

EMOTIONAL AND PERSON-ALITY DEVELOPMENT

Emotional Development

Temperament

Personality Development

SOCIAL ORIENTATION AND ATTACHMENT

Social Orientation and Understanding

Attachment

SOCIAL CONTEXTS

The Family

Child Care

Stories of Life-Span Development: Darius and His Father

An increasing number of fathers are staying home to care for their children (Bartel & others, 2018; Dette-Hagenmeyer, Erzinger, & Reichle, 2016). And researchers are finding improved outcomes when fathers are positively engaged with their infants (Alexander & others, 2017; Cabrera & Roggman, 2017; Roopnarine & Yildirim, 2018; Sethna & others, 2018). Consider 17-month-old Darius. On weekdays, Darius' father, a writer, cares for him during the day while his mother works full-time as a landscape architect. Darius' father is doing a great job of caring for him. He keeps Darius nearby while he is writing and spends lots of time talking to him and playing with him. From their interactions, it is clear that they genuinely enjoy each other's company.

Last month, Darius began spending one day a week at a child-care center. His parents selected the center after observing a number of centers and interviewing teachers and center directors. His parents placed him in the center because they wanted him to get some experience with peers and his father to have some time out from caregiving.

Darius' father looks to the future and imagines the Little League games Darius will play in and the many other activities he can enjoy with his son. Remembering how little time his own father spent with him, he is dedicated to making sure that Darius has an involved, nurturing relationship with his father.

How might fathers influence their infants' and children's development?
©Rick Gomez/Corbis/Getty Images

When Darius' mother comes home in the evening, she spends considerable time with him. Darius is securely attached to both his mother and his father.

You have read about how infants perceive, learn, and remember. Infants also are socioemotional beings, capable of displaying emotions and initiating social interaction with people close to them. The main topics that we explore in this chapter are emotional and personality development, attachment, and the social contexts of the family and child care. ■

Emotional and Personality Development

Anyone who has been around infants for even a brief time can tell that they are emotional beings. Not only do infants express emotions, but they also vary in temperament. Some are shy and others are outgoing. Some are active and others much less so. Let's explore these and other aspects of emotional and personality development in infants.

Emotional Development

Imagine what your life would be like without emotion. Emotion is the color and music of life, as well as the tie that binds people together. How do psychologists define and classify emotions, and why are they important to development? How do emotions develop during the first two years of life?

What Are Emotions?

For our purposes, we will define **emotion** as feeling, or affect, that occurs when a person is in a state or an interaction that is important to him or her, especially to his or her well-being. Especially in infancy, emotions have important roles in (1) communication with others and (2) behavioral organization (Ekas, Braungart-Rieker, & Messinger, 2018; Perry & Calkins, 2018). Through emotions, infants communicate such important aspects of their lives as joy, sadness, interest, and fear (Burkitt, 2018; Johnson, 2018; Tottenham, 2017). In terms of behavioral organization, emotions influence infants' social responses and adaptive behavior as they interact with others in their world (Cole, 2016; Cole & Hollenstein, 2018; Hoskin, 2018; Thompson, 2019).

Psychologists classify the broad range of emotions in many ways, but almost all classifications designate an emotion as either positive (pleasant) or negative (unpleasant) (Laurent, Wright, & Finnegan, 2018; Parsons & others, 2017). Positive emotions include happiness, joy, love, and enthusiasm. Negative emotions include anxiety, anger, guilt, and sadness.

Biological and Environmental Influences

Emotions are influenced by biological foundations, cognitive processes, and by a person's experiences (Causadias, Telzer, & Lee, 2017; Cole, Lougheed, & Ram, 2018; Foroughe, 2018; Johnson, 2018; Perry & Calkins, 2018). Certain regions of the brain that develop early in life (such as the brain stem, hippocampus, and amygdala) play a role in distress, excitement, and rage, and even infants display these emotions (van den Boomen, Munsters & Kemner 2018; Tottenham, 2017). But, as we discuss later in the chapter, infants only gradually develop the ability to regulate their emotions, and this ability seems tied to the gradual maturation of the frontal regions of the cerebral cortex that can exert control over other areas of the brain (Bell, Broomell, & Patton, 2018; Bell & others, 2018; Lusby & others, 2016).

Also, cognitive processes, both in immediate "in the moment" contexts and across development, influence infants' and children's emotional development (Bell, Diaz, & Liu, 2018; Jiang & others, 2017). Attention toward or away from an experience can influence infants' and children's emotional responses. For example, children who can distract themselves from a stressful encounter show a lower level of negative affect in the context and less anxiety over time (Crockenberg & Leerkes, 2006).

emotion Feeling, or affect, that occurs when a person is in a state or interaction that is important to them. Emotion is characterized by behavior that reflects (expresses) the pleasantness or unpleasantness of the state a person is in or the transactions being experienced.

Also, as children become older, they develop cognitive strategies for controlling their emotions and become more adept at modulating their emotional arousal (Bell, Diaz, & Liu, 2018; Kaunhoven & Dorjee, 2017).

Cultural experiences and relationships influence emotional development (Bedford & others, 2017; Causaudias, Telzer, & Lee, 2017; Morris & others, 2018; Otto, 2018; Perry & Calkins, 2018). Emotion-linked interchanges provide the foundation for the infant's attachment to the parent (Johnson, 2018). When toddlers hear their parents quarreling, they often react with distress and inhibit their play. Well-functioning families make each other laugh and may develop a light mood to defuse conflicts. One study of 18- to 24-month-olds found that parents' elicitation of talk about emotions was associated with their toddlers' sharing and helping behaviors (Brownell & others, 2013).

How do East Asian mothers handle their infants' and children's emotional development differently from non-Latina White mothers?
©ICHIRO/Getty Images

Emotional development and coping with stress are influenced by whether caregivers have maltreated or neglected children and whether children's caregivers are depressed or not (Almy & Cicchetti, 2018; Thompson, 2019). When infants become stressed, they show better biological recovery from the stressors when their caregivers engage in sensitive caregiving with them (Sullivan & Wilson, 2018; Thompson & Goodvin, 2016).

Display rules—rules governing when, where, and how emotions should be expressed—are not universal. For example, researchers have found that East Asian infants display less frequent and less intense positive and negative emotions than do non-Latino White infants (Cole & Tan, 2007). Throughout childhood, East Asian parents encourage their children to show emotional reserve rather than to be emotionally expressive (Cole, 2016).

Early Emotions

Emotions that infants express in the first six months of life include surprise, interest, joy, anger, sadness, fear, and disgust (see Figure 1). Other emotions that appear in infancy include jealousy, empathy, embarrassment, pride, shame, and guilt; most of these occur for the first time at some point in the second half of the first year or during the second year. These later-developing emotions have been called self-conscious or other-conscious emotions because they involve the emotional reactions of others (Lewis, 2007, 2010, 2015, 2016).

Some experts on infant socioemotional development, such as Jerome Kagan (2010, 2013), conclude that the structural immaturity of the infant brain makes it unlikely

| Joy | Sadness | Fear | Surprise |

Figure 1 Expression of Different Emotions in Infants
(*Left to right*) ©Kozak_O_O/Shutterstock; ©McGraw Hill Companies/Jill Braaten, Photographer; ©Stanislav Photographer/Shutterstock; ©Stockbyte/Getty Images

that emotions that require thought—such as guilt, pride, despair, shame, empathy, and jealousy—can be experienced in the first year. Thus, both Kagan (2010) and Joseph Campos (2009) argue that so-called "self-conscious" emotions don't occur until after the first year, a view that increasingly is shared by most developmental psychologists.

Emotional Expressions and Relationships

Emotional expressions are involved in infants' first relationships. The ability of infants to communicate emotions permits coordinated interactions with their caregivers and the beginning of an emotional bond between them (Thompson, 2015, 2016). Not only do parents change their emotional expressions in response to those of their infants (and each other), but infants also modify their emotional expressions in response to those of their parents (Firk & others, 2018; Johnson, 2018). In other words, these interactions are mutually regulated. Because of this coordination, the interactions between parents and infants are described as *reciprocal,* or *synchronous,* when all is going well. Sensitive, responsive parents help their infants grow emotionally, whether the infants respond in distressed or happy ways (Bell, Broomell, & Patton, 2018; Birmingham, Bub, & Vaughn, 2017). For example, a recent observational study of mother-infant interaction found that maternal sensitivity was linked to a lower level of infant fear (Gartstein, Hancock, & Iverson, 2017).

Crying Cries and smiles are two emotional expressions that infants display when interacting with parents. These are babies' first forms of emotional communication. Crying is the most important mechanism newborns have for communicating with their world. A recent study revealed that depressed mothers rocked and touched their crying infants less than non-depressed mothers (Esposito & others, 2017a). Cries may also provide information about the

What are some different types of cries?
©Design Pics/Don Hammond

health of the newborn's central nervous system. A recent study found that excessive infant crying in 3-month-olds doubled the risk of behavioral, hyperactive, and mood problems at 5 to 6 years of age (Smarius & others, 2017).

Babies have at least three types of cries:

- **Basic cry:** A rhythmic pattern that usually consists of a cry, followed by a briefer silence, then a shorter whistle that is somewhat higher in pitch than the main cry, then another brief rest before the next cry. Some experts believe that hunger is one of the conditions that incite the basic cry.

- **Anger cry:** A variation of the basic cry, with more excess air forced through the vocal cords.

- **Pain cry:** A sudden long, initial loud cry followed by holding of the breath; no preliminary moaning is present. The pain cry may be stimulated by physical pain or by any high-intensity stimulus.

Most adults can determine whether an infant's cries signify anger or pain (Zeskind, Klein, & Marshall, 1992). Parents can distinguish among the various cries of their own baby better than among those of another baby.

Parents of infants want to know whether it is a good idea to respond to their infant cries (Maule & Perren, 2018; Zeifman & St. James-Roberts, 2017). Many developmental

basic cry A rhythmic pattern usually consisting of a cry, a briefer silence, a shorter inspiratory whistle that is higher-pitched than the main cry, and a brief rest before the next cry.

anger cry A cry similar to the basic cry, with more excess air forced through the vocal cords.

pain cry A sudden outburst of loud crying without preliminary moaning, followed by breath holding.

How Would You...?

As a **human development and family studies professional,** how would you respond to the parents of a 13-month-old baby who are concerned because their son has suddenly started crying every morning when they drop him off at child care despite the fact that he has been going to the same child care provider for over six months?

psychologists recommend that parents soothe a crying infant, especially during the first year. This reaction should help infants develop a sense of trust and secure attachment to the caregiver. One study revealed that mothers' negative emotional reactions (anger and anxiety) to crying increased the risk of subsequent attachment insecurity (Leerkes, Parade, & Gudmundson, 2011). Also, another study found that problems in infant soothability at 6 months of age were linked to insecure attachment at 12 months of age (Mills-Koonce, Propper, & Barnett, 2012). And a recent study found that mothers were more likely than fathers to use soothing techniques to reduce infant crying (Dayton & others, 2015).

Smiling Smiling is a critical social skill and a key social signal (Martin & Messinger, 2018). Two types of smiling can be distinguished in infants:

- **Reflexive smile:** A smile that does not occur in response to external stimuli and appears during the first month after birth, usually during sleep.
- **Social smile:** A smile that occurs in response to an external stimulus, typically a face in the case of the young infant. Social smiling occurs as early as 2 months of age.

Researchers have found that smiling and laughter at 7 months of age were associated with self-regulation at 7 years of age (Posner & others, 2014). And one study found that higher maternal effortful control and positive emotionality predicted more initial infant smiling and laughter, while a higher level of parenting stress predicted a lower trajectory of infant smiling and laughter (Bridgett & others, 2013).

Fear One of a baby's earliest emotions is fear, which typically first appears at about 6 months and peaks at about 18 months. However, abused and neglected infants can show fear as early as 3 months (Witherington & others, 2010). The most frequent expression of an infant's fear involves **stranger anxiety,** in which an infant shows fear and wariness of strangers (Van Hulle & others, 2017).

Stranger anxiety usually emerges gradually. It first appears at about 6 months in the form of wary reactions. By 9 months, fear of strangers is often more intense, and it continues to escalate through the infant's first birthday (Emde, Gaensbauer, & Harmon, 1976).

Not all infants show distress when they encounter a stranger. Besides individual variations, whether an infant shows stranger anxiety also depends on the social context and the characteristics of the stranger. Infants show less stranger anxiety when they are in familiar settings. For example, in one study, 10-month-olds showed little stranger anxiety when they met a stranger in their own home but much greater fear when they encountered a stranger in a research laboratory (Sroufe, Waters, & Matas, 1974). Also, infants show less stranger anxiety when they are sitting on their mothers' laps than when they are in an infant seat several feet away from their mothers (Bohlin & Hagekull, 1993). Thus, it appears that when infants feel secure they are less likely to show stranger anxiety.

Who the stranger is and how the stranger behaves also influence stranger anxiety in infants. Infants are less fearful of child strangers than of adult strangers. They also are less fearful of friendly, outgoing, smiling strangers than of passive, unsmiling strangers (Bretherton, Stolberg, & Kreye, 1981).

In addition to stranger anxiety, infants experience fear of being separated from their caregivers. The result is **separation protest**—crying when the caregiver leaves. Separation protest tends to peak at about 15 months among U.S. infants. A study of four different cultures found, similarly, that separation protest peaked at about 13 to 15 months (Kagan, Kearsley, & Zelazo, 1978). Although the percentage of infants who engaged in separation protest varied across cultures, the infants reached a peak of protest at about the same age—just before the middle of the second year.

Social Referencing Infants not only express emotions like fear but also "read" the emotions of other people (Carbajal-Valenzuela &

reflexive smile A smile that does not occur in response to external stimuli. It appears during the first month after birth, usually during sleep.

social smile A smile in response to an external stimulus, which, early in development, typically is a face.

stranger anxiety An infant's fear and wariness of strangers that typically appears in the second half of the first year of life.

separation protest An infant's distressed crying when the caregiver leaves.

others, 2017). **Social referencing** involves "reading" emotional cues in others to help determine how to act in a particular situation. The development of social referencing helps infants interpret ambiguous situations more accurately, as when they encounter a stranger (Stenberg, 2017). By the end of the first year, a parent's facial expression—either smiling or fearful—influences whether an infant will explore an unfamiliar environment.

Infants become better at social referencing in the second year of life. At this age, they tend to "check" with their mother before they act; they look at her to see if she is happy, angry, or fearful.

Emotion Regulation and Coping

During the first year, the infant gradually develops an ability to inhibit, or minimize, the intensity and duration of emotional reactions (Calkins & Perry, 2016; Ekas, Braungart-Rieker, & Messinger, 2018). From early in infancy, babies put their thumbs in their mouths to soothe themselves. In their second year, they may say things to help soothe themselves. When placed in his bed for the night, after a little crying and whimpering, a 20-month-old was overheard saying, "Go sleep, Alex. Okay." But at first, infants depend mainly on caregivers to help them soothe their emotions, as when a caregiver rocks an infant to sleep, sings lullabies, gently strokes the infant, and so on. In a recent study, young infants with a negative temperament used fewer attention regulation strategies, and maternal sensitivity to infants was linked to more adaptive emotion regulation (Thomas & others, 2017). And in another recent study of 10-month-old infants, maternal sensitivity was linked to better emotion regulation in the infants (Frick & others, 2018).

Later in infancy, when they become aroused, infants sometimes redirect their attention or distract themselves in order to reduce their arousal. By age 2, children can use language to define their feeling states and identify the context that is upsetting them (Calkins & Markovitch, 2010). A 2-year-old might say, "Doggy scary." This type of communication may cue caregivers to help the child regulate emotion.

Contexts can influence emotion regulation (Frick & others, 2018; Groh & Haydon, 2018; Morris & others, 2018). Infants are often affected by fatigue, hunger, time of day, which people are around them, and where they are. Infants must learn to adapt to different contexts that require emotion regulation. Further, new demands appear as the infant becomes older and parents modify their expectations. For example, a parent may take it in stride if a 6-month-old infant screams in a restaurant but may react very differently if a 1½-year-old starts screaming.

Temperament

Do you get upset easily? Does it take much to get you angry or to make you laugh? Even at birth, babies seem to have different emotional styles. One infant is cheerful and happy much of the time; another seems to cry constantly. These tendencies reflect **temperament,** or individual differences in behavioral styles, emotions, and characteristic ways of responding. With regard to its link to emotion, temperament refers to individual differences in how quickly the emotion is shown, how strong it is, how long it lasts, and how quickly it fades away (Campos, 2009).

Another way of describing temperament is in terms of predispositions toward emotional reactivity and self-regulation (Bates & Pettit, 2015). *Reactivity* involves variations in the speed and intensity with which an individual responds to situations with positive or negative emotions. *Self-regulation* involves variations in the extent or effectiveness of an individual's control over emotions.

Describing and Classifying Temperament

How would you describe your temperament or the temperament of a friend? Researchers have described and classified the temperaments of individuals in different ways (Abulizi & others, 2017; Gartstein & others, 2017; Janssen & others, 2017; Kagan, 2018). Here we examine three of those ways.

social referencing "Reading" emotional cues in others to help determine how to act in a particular situation.

temperament An individual's behavioral style and characteristic way of responding emotionally.

Chess and Thomas' Classification Psychiatrists Alexander Chess and Stella Thomas (Chess & Thomas, 1977; Thomas & Chess, 1991) identified three basic types, or clusters, of temperament:

- **Easy child:** This child is generally in a positive mood, quickly establishes regular routines in infancy, and adapts easily to new experiences.
- **Difficult child:** This child reacts negatively and cries frequently, engages in irregular daily routines, and is slow to accept change.
- **Slow-to-warm-up child:** This child has a low activity level, is somewhat negative, and displays a low intensity of mood.

In their longitudinal investigation, Chess and Thomas found that 40 percent of the children they studied could be classified as easy, 10 percent as difficult, and 15 percent as slow to warm up. Notice that 35 percent did not fit any of the three patterns. Researchers have found that these three basic clusters of temperament are moderately stable across the childhood years.

One study revealed that young children with a difficult temperament showed more problems when they experienced low-quality child care and fewer problems when they experienced high-quality child care than did young children with an easy temperament (Pluess & Belsky, 2009).

Kagan's Concept of Behavioral Inhibition Another way of classifying temperament focuses on the differences between a shy, subdued, timid child and a sociable, extraverted, bold child. Jerome Kagan (2002, 2010, 2013) regards shyness with strangers (peers or adults) as one feature of a broad temperament category called *inhibition to the unfamiliar*. Inhibited children react to many aspects of unfamiliarity with initial avoidance, distress, or subdued affect, beginning around 7 to 9 months. In one study, having an inhibited temperament at 2 to 3 years of age was related to having social phobia symptoms at 7 years of age (Lahat & others, 2014). And research also indicates that infants and young children who have an inhibited temperament are at risk for developing social anxiety disorder in adolescence and adulthood (Perez-Edgar & Guyer, 2014; Rapee, 2014). Further, recent research indicates that if parents have a childhood history of behavioral inhibition, their children who have a high level of behavioral inhibition are at risk for developing anxiety disorders (Stumper & others, 2017).

Effortful Control (Self-Regulation) Mary Rothbart and John Bates (2006) stress that effortful control (self-regulation) is an important dimension of temperament. Infants who are high in effortful control show an ability to keep their arousal from getting too intense and have strategies for soothing themselves. By contrast, children who

easy child A child who is generally in a positive mood, who quickly establishes regular routines in infancy, and who adapts easily to new experiences.

difficult child A child who tends to react negatively and cry frequently, who engages in irregular daily routines, and who is slow to accept new experiences.

slow-to-warm-up child A child who has a low activity level, is somewhat negative, and displays a low intensity of mood.

What are some ways that developmentalists have classified infants' temperaments? Which classification makes the most sense to you, based on your observations of infants?
©Tom Merton/Getty Images

are low in effortful control are often unable to control their arousal; they are easily agitated and become intensely emotional.

A number of studies have supported the view that effortful control is an important influence on children's development. For example, a study found that young children higher in effortful control were more likely to wait longer to express anger and were more likely to use a self-regulatory strategy, distraction (Tan, Armstrong, & Cole, 2013). Another study revealed that effortful control was a strong predictor of academic success skills in kindergarten children from low-income families (Morris & others, 2013). Further, a recent study revealed that self-regulation capacity at 4 months of age was linked to school readiness at 4 years of age (Gartstein, Putnam, & Kliewer, 2016). And recent studies indicate that lower effortful control and self-regulation capacity in early childhood are linked to a higher risk for developing ADHD in childhood (Willoughby, Gottfredson, & Stifter, 2017) and adolescence (Einziger & others, 2018).

An important point about temperament classifications such as Chess and Thomas' and Rothbart and Bates' is that children should not be pigeonholed as having only one temperament dimension, such as "difficult" or "negative." A good strategy when attempting to classify a child's temperament is to think of temperament as consisting of multiple dimensions (Bates, 2012a, b). For example, a child might be extraverted, show little emotional negativity, and have good self-regulation. Another child might be introverted, show little emotional negativity, and have a low level of self-regulation.

The development of temperament capabilities such as effortful control allows individual differences to emerge (Bates & Pettit, 2015). For example, although maturation

of the brain's prefrontal lobes must occur for any child's attention to improve and the child to achieve effortful control, some children develop effortful control while others do not. And it is these individual differences in children that are at the heart of what temperament is (Bates, 2012a, b).

Biological Foundations and Experience

How does a child acquire a certain temperament? Kagan (2010, 2013) argues that children inherit a physiology that predisposes them to have a particular type of temperament. However, through experience they may learn to modify their temperament to some degree. For example, children may inherit a physiology that predisposes them to be fearful and inhibited but then learn to reduce their fear and inhibition to some degree.

How might caregivers help a child become less fearful and inhibited? An important first step is to find out what frightens the child. Comforting and reassuring the child, and addressing their specific fears, are good strategies.

Biological Influences Specific physiological characteristics have been linked with different temperaments (O'Connor & others, 2017). In particular, an inhibited temperament is associated with a unique physiological pattern that includes a high and stable heart rate, high levels of the hormone cortisol, and high activity in the right frontal lobe of the brain (Kagan, 2013). This pattern may be tied to the excitability of the amygdala, a structure in the brain that plays an important role in fear and inhibition. Twin and adoption studies also suggest that heredity has a moderate influence on differences in temperament within a group of people (Schumann & others, 2017).

Too often the biological foundations of temperament are interpreted as meaning that temperament cannot develop or change. However, important self-regulatory dimensions of temperament such as adaptability, soothability, and persistence look very different in a 1-year-old and a 5-year-old (Thompson, 2015). These temperament dimensions develop and change with the growth of the neurobiological foundations of self-regulation (Calkins & Perry, 2016).

Gender, Culture, and Temperament Gender may be an important factor shaping the context that influences temperament (Korczak & others, 2018; Planalp & others, 2017a). Parents might react differently to an infant's temperament based on whether the baby is a boy or a girl. For example, in one study, mothers were more responsive to the crying of irritable girls than to that of irritable boys (Crockenberg, 1986).

Similarly, the reaction to an infant's temperament may depend in part on culture (Matsumoto & Juang, 2017). For example, an active temperament might be valued in some cultures (such as the United States) but not in others (such as China). Indeed, children's temperament can vary across cultures. For example, behavioral inhibition is valued more highly in China than in North America (Cole, 2016).

In short, many aspects of a child's environment can encourage or discourage the persistence of temperament characteristics (Glynn & others, 2017; Parade & others, 2018; Schumann & others, 2017). One useful way of thinking about these relationships applies the concept of goodness of fit, which we examine next.

Goodness of Fit and Parenting

Goodness of fit refers to the match between a child's temperament and the environmental demands the child must cope with. Suppose Jason is an active toddler who is made to sit still for long periods and Jack is a slow-to-warm-up toddler who is abruptly pushed into new situations on a regular basis. Both Jason and Jack face a lack of fit between their temperament and environmental demands. Lack of fit can produce adjustment problems (Planalp & others, 2017b). In terms of positive goodness of fit, researchers have found that decreases in infants' negative emotionality are linked to higher levels of parental sensitivity, involvement, and responsivity (Wachs & Bates, 2010).

How Would You...?

As a **social worker,** how would you apply information about an infant's temperament to maximize the goodness of fit in a clinical setting?

Many parents don't come to believe in the importance of temperament until the birth of their second child. They viewed their first child's behavior as stemming from how they treated the child. But then they find that some strategies that worked with their first child are not as effective with the second child. Some problems experienced with the first child (such as those associated with feeding, sleeping, and coping with strangers) may not arise with the second child, but new problems arise. Such experiences strongly suggest that children differ from each other very early in life and that these differences have important implications for parent-child interaction (Rothbart, 2011).

What are the implications of temperamental variations for parenting? Decreases in infants' negative emotionality occur when parents are more involved, responsive, and sensitive when interacting with their children (Goodvin, Thompson, & Winer, 2015). Temperament experts Ann Sanson and Mary Rothbart (1995) also recommend the following strategies for temperament-sensitive parenting:

- *Attention to and respect for individuality.* One implication is that it is difficult to generate general prescriptions for "good parenting." A goal might be accomplished in one way with one child and in another

goodness of fit Refers to the match between a child's temperament and the environmental demands with which the child must cope.

way with another child, depending on each child's temperament. Parents need to be flexible and sensitive to the infant's signals and needs.

- *Structuring the child's environment.* Crowded, noisy environments can pose greater problems for some children (such as a "difficult child") than for others (such as an "easy child"). We might also expect that a fearful, withdrawing child would benefit from slower entry into new contexts.

- *Avoid applying negative labels to the child.* Acknowledging that some children are harder to parent than others is often helpful, and advice on how to handle particular kinds of difficult circumstances can be helpful. However, labeling a child "difficult" runs the risk of becoming a self-fulfilling prophecy. That is, if a child is identified as "difficult," people may treat him or her in a way that elicits "difficult" behavior.

What are some good strategies for parents to adopt when responding to their infant's temperament?
©Corbis/age fotostock

A final comment about temperament is that recently the *differential susceptibility model* and the *biological sensitivity to context model* have been proposed and studied (Baptista & others, 2017; Belsky, 2016; Belsky & Pluess, 2016; Belsky & van IJzendoorn, 2017). These models emphasize that certain characteristics—such as a difficult temperament—that render children more vulnerable to difficulty in adverse contexts also make them more susceptible to optimal growth in very supportive conditions. These models may help us see "negative" temperament characteristics in a new light.

Personality Development

Emotions and temperament are key aspects of personality, the enduring personal characteristics of individuals. Let's now examine characteristics that are often thought of as central to personality development during infancy: trust, the development of a sense of self, and progress toward independence.

Trust

According to Erik Erikson (1968), the first year of life is characterized by the trust-versus-mistrust stage of development. Upon emerging from a life of regularity, warmth, and protection in the mother's womb, the infant faces a world that is less secure. Erikson proposed that infants learn trust when they are cared for in a consistently nurturant manner. If the infant is not well fed and kept warm on a consistent basis, a sense of mistrust is likely to develop.

In Erikson's view, the issue of trust versus mistrust is not resolved once and for all in the first year of life. Instead, it arises again at each successive stage of development, and the outcomes can be positive or negative. For example, children who leave infancy with a sense of trust can still have their sense of mistrust activated at a later stage, perhaps if their parents become separated or divorced.

The Developing Sense of Self

It is difficult to study the self in infancy mainly because infants cannot tell us how they experience themselves. Infants cannot verbally express their views of the self. They also cannot understand complex instructions from researchers.

A rudimentary form of self-recognition—being attentive and positive toward one's image in a mirror—appears as early as 3 months (Mascolo & Fischer, 2007; Pipp, Fischer, & Jennings, 1987). However, a central, more complete index of self-recognition—the ability

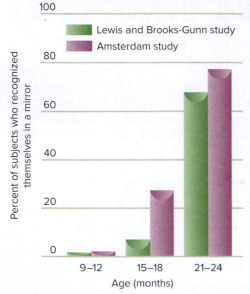

Figure 2 **The Development of Self-Recognition in Infancy**
The graph shows the findings of two studies in which infants less than 1 year of age did not recognize themselves in the mirror. A slight increase in the percentage of infant self-recognition occurred around 15 to 18 months of age. By 2 years of age, a majority of children recognized themselves. *Why do researchers study whether infants recognize themselves in a mirror?*
©Digital Vision/Getty Images

to recognize one's physical features—does not emerge until the second year (Thompson, 2006).

One ingenious strategy to test infants' visual self-recognition is the use of a mirror technique in which an infant's mother first puts a dot of rouge on the infant's nose. Then, an observer watches to see how often the infant touches its nose. Next, the infant is placed in front of a mirror and observers detect whether nose touching increases. Why does this matter? The idea is that increased nose touching indicates that the infant recognizes itself in the mirror and is trying to touch or rub off the rouge because the rouge violates the infant's view of itself; that is, the infant thinks something is not right, since it believes its real self does not have a dot of rouge on it.

Figure 2 displays the results of two investigations that used the mirror technique. The researchers found that before they were 1 year old, infants did not recognize themselves in the mirror (Amsterdam, 1968; Lewis & Brooks-Gunn, 1979). Signs of self-recognition began to appear among some infants when they were 15 to 18 months old. By the time they were 2 years old, most children recognized themselves in the mirror. In sum, infants begin to develop a self-understanding, called self-recognition, at approximately 18 months of age (Hart & Karmel, 1996; Lewis, 2005).

In one study, biweekly assessments of infants from 15 to 23 months of age were conducted (Courage, Edison, & Howe, 2004). Self-recognition emerged gradually over this period, first appearing in the form of mirror recognition, followed by use of the personal pronoun "me" and then by recognizing a photo of themselves. These aspects of self-recognition are often referred to as the first indications of toddlers' understanding of the mental state of "me," "that they are objects in their own mental representation of the world" (Lewis, 2005, p. 363).

Late in the second year and early in the third year, toddlers show other emerging forms of self-awareness that reflect a sense of "me" (Goodvin, Thompson, & Winer, 2015). For example, they refer to themselves by saying "Me big"; they label internal experiences such as emotions; they monitor themselves, as when a toddler says, "Do it myself"; and they announce that things are theirs (Bullock & Lutkenhaus, 1990; Fasig, 2000).

Also, researchers recently have found that the capacity to understand others may begin to develop during infancy (Carpendale & Lewis, 2015; Grossman, 2017). Research indicates that as early as 13 months of age, infants seem to consider another's perspective when predicting that person's actions (Choi & Luo, 2015).

Independence

Not only does the infant develop a sense of self in the second year of life, but independence also becomes a more central theme in the infant's life. Erikson (1968) stressed that independence is an important issue in the second year of life. Erikson's second stage of development is identified as autonomy versus shame and doubt. Autonomy builds as the infant's mental and motor abilities develop. At this point, not only can infants walk, but they can also climb, open and close, drop, push and pull, and hold and let go. Infants feel pride in these new accomplishments and want to do everything themselves, whether the activity is flushing a toilet, pulling the wrapping off a package, or deciding what to eat. It is important to recognize toddlers' motivation to do what they are capable of doing at their own pace. Then they can learn to control their muscles and their impulses themselves. Conversely, when caregivers are impatient and do for toddlers what they are capable of doing themselves, shame and doubt develop. To be sure, every parent has rushed a child from time to time, and one instance of rushing is unlikely to result in impaired development. It is only when parents consistently overprotect toddlers or criticize accidents (wetting, soiling, spilling, or breaking, for example) that children are likely to develop an excessive sense of shame and doubt about their ability to control themselves and their world.

Erikson also argued that the stage of autonomy versus shame and doubt has important implications for the development of independence and identity during adolescence. The development of autonomy during the toddler years gives adolescents the courage to be independent individuals who can choose and guide their own future.

How Would You...?

As a **human development and family studies professional,** how would you work with parents who showed signs of being overly protective or critical to the point of impairing their toddler's autonomy?

Social Orientation and Attachment

So far, we have discussed how emotions and emotional competence change as children develop. We have also examined the role of emotional style; in effect, we have seen how emotions set the tone of our experiences in life. But emotions also write the lyrics because they are at the core of our interest in the social world and our relationships with others.

Social Orientation and Understanding

In Ross Thompson's (2006, 2014, 2015, 2016) view, infants are socioemotional beings who show a strong interest in their social world and are motivated to orient themselves toward it and to understand it. In other chapters we described many of the biological and cognitive foundations that contribute to the infant's development of social orientation and understanding. We will call attention to relevant biological and cognitive factors as we explore social orientation; locomotion; intention, goal-directed behavior and meaningful interactions with others; and social referencing. Discussing biological, cognitive, and social processes together reminds us of an important aspect of development that was pointed out earlier—that these processes are intricately intertwined (Cole, Lougheed, & Ram, 2018; Perry & Calkins, 2018).

Social Orientation

From early in their development, infants are captivated by the social world. Young infants are attuned to the sounds of human voices and stare intently at faces, especially their caregiver's face (Peltola, Strathearn, & Puura, 2018; Sugden & Moulson, 2017). As infants develop, they become adept at interpreting the meaning of facial expressions (Weatherhead & White, 2017). Face-to-face play often begins to characterize caregiver-infant interactions when the infant is about 2 to 3 months of age. Such play reflects many mothers' motivation to create a positive emotional state in their infants (Laible, Thompson, & Froimson, 2015).

Infants also learn about the social world through contexts other than face-to-face play with a caregiver. Even though infants as young as 6 months show an interest in each other, their interaction with peers increases considerably in the latter half of the second year. Between 18 and 24 months, children markedly increase their imitative and reciprocal play—for example, imitating nonverbal actions like jumping and running (Eckerman & Whitehead, 1999). One study involved presenting 1- and 2-year-olds with a simple cooperative task that consisted of pulling a lever to get an attractive toy

Figure 3 The Cooperation Task
The cooperation task consisted of two handles on a box, atop which was an animated musical toy, surreptitiously activated by remote control when both handles were pulled. The handles were placed far enough apart that one child could not pull both handles. The experimenter demonstrated the task, saying, "Watch! If you pull the handles, the doggie will sing" (Brownell, Ramani, & Zerwas, 2006).
©Celia A. Brownell, University of Pittsburgh

(Brownell, Ramani, & Zerwas, 2006) (see Figure 3). Any coordinated actions of the 1-year-olds appeared to be coincidental rather than cooperative, whereas the 2-year-olds' behavior was characterized as active cooperation to reach a goal.

Locomotion

Recall from earlier in the chapter how important independence is for infants, especially in the second year of life. As infants develop the ability to crawl, walk, and run, they are able to explore and expand their social world. These newly developed and self-produced locomotor skills allow the infant to independently initiate social interchanges on a more frequent basis.

Locomotion is also important for its motivational implications (Adolph, 2018; Adolph & Hoch, 2019; Kretch & Adolph, 2018). Once infants have the ability to move in goal-directed pursuits, the rewards gained from these pursuits lead to further efforts to explore and develop skills.

Intention, Goal-Directed Behavior, and Meaningful Interactions with Others

The ability to perceive people as engaging in intentional and goal-directed behavior is an important social-cognitive accomplishment, and this initially occurs toward the end of the first year (Thompson, 2015, 2016). Joint attention and gaze-following help the infant understand that other people have intentions (Gueron-Sela & others, 2018; McClure & others, 2018). By their first birthday, infants have begun to direct their caregiver's attention to objects that capture their interest (Marsh & Legerstee, 2017).

Amanda Woodward and her colleagues (Krogh-Jespersen, Liberman, & Woodward, 2015; Krogh-Jespersen & Woodward, 2016, 2018; Liberman, Woodward, & Kinzler, 2018) argue that infants' ability to understand and respond to others' meaningful intentions is a critical cognitive foundation for effectively engaging in the social world. They especially emphasize that an important aspect of this ability is the capacity to grasp social knowledge quickly in order to make an appropriate social response. Although processing speed is an important contributor to social engagement, other factors are involved such as infants' motivation to interact with someone, the infant's social interactive history with the individual, the interactive partner's social membership, and culturally specific aspects of interaction (Krogh-Jespersen & Woodward, 2016, 2018; Liberman, Woodward, & Kinzler, 2018).

Infants' Social Sophistication and Insight

In sum, researchers are discovering that infants are more socially sophisticated and insightful at younger ages than was previously envisioned (Perry & Calkins, 2018; Steckler & others, 2018; Thompson, 2015, 2016). This sophistication and insight is reflected in infants' perceptions of others' actions as intentionally motivated and goal-directed and their motivation to share and participate in that intentionality by their first birthday (Tomasello, 2014). The more advanced social-cognitive skills of infants could be expected to influence their understanding and awareness of attachment to a caregiver.

Attachment

Attachment is a close emotional bond between two people. There is no shortage of theories about infant attachment. Three theorists—Freud, Erikson, and Bowlby—proposed influential views of attachment.

Freud theorized that infants become attached to the person or object that provides them with oral satisfaction. For most infants, this is the mother, since she is most likely to feed the infant. Is feeding as important as Freud thought? A classic study by Harry Harlow (1958) indicates that the answer is no (see Figure 4).

Harlow removed infant monkeys from their mothers at birth; for six months they were fed by two surrogate (substitute) "mothers." One surrogate mother was made of wire, the other of cloth. Half of the infant monkeys were fed by the wire mother, half by the cloth mother. Periodically, the amount of time the infant monkeys spent with either the wire or the cloth mother was computed. Regardless of which mother fed them, the infant monkeys spent far more time with the cloth mother. Even if the wire mother, but not the cloth mother, provided nourishment, the infant monkeys spent more time with the cloth mother. And when Harlow frightened the monkeys, those who were "raised" by the cloth mother ran to that mother and clung to it; those who were raised by the wire mother did not. Whether the mother provided comfort seemed to determine whether the monkeys associated that mother with security. This study clearly demonstrated that feeding is not the crucial element in the attachment process and that contact comfort is important.

Physical comfort also plays a role in Erik Erikson's (1968) view of the infant's development. Recall Erikson's proposal that during the first year of life infants are in the stage of trust versus mistrust. Physical comfort and sensitive care, according to Erikson (1968), are key to establishing a basic level of trust during infancy. The infant's sense of trust, in turn, is the foundation for attachment and sets the stage for a lifelong expectation that the world will be a good and pleasant place.

The ethological perspective of British psychiatrist John Bowlby (1969, 1989) also stresses the importance of attachment in the first year of life and the responsiveness of the caregiver. Bowlby believed that both the infant and its primary caregivers are biologically predisposed to form attachments. He argued that the newborn is biologically equipped to elicit attachment behavior. The baby cries, clings, coos, and smiles. Later, the infant crawls, walks, and follows the mother. The immediate result is to keep the primary caregiver nearby; the long-term effect is to increase the infant's chances of survival (Thompson, 2006, 2015).

Attachment does not emerge suddenly but rather develops in a series of phases, moving from a baby's general preference for human figures to a partnership with primary caregivers. Following are four such phases based on Bowlby's conceptualization of attachment (Schaffer, 1996):

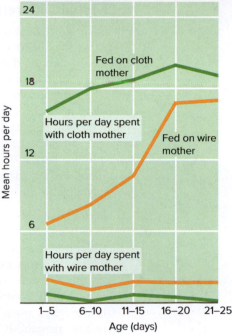

Figure 4 Contact Time with Wire and Cloth Surrogate Mothers
Regardless of whether the infant monkeys were fed by a wire or a cloth mother, they overwhelmingly preferred to spend contact time with the cloth mother. *How do these results compare with what Freud's theory and Erikson's theory would predict about human infants?*
©Martin Rogers/Getty Images

- *Phase 1: From birth to 2 months.* Infants instinctively direct their attachment to human figures. Strangers, siblings, and parents are equally likely to elicit smiling or crying from the infant.

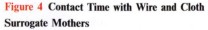

attachment A close emotional bond between two people.

- *Phase 2: From 2 to 7 months.* Attachment becomes focused on one figure, usually the primary caregiver, as the baby gradually learns to distinguish between familiar and unfamiliar people.

- *Phase 3: From 7 to 24 months.* Specific attachments develop. With increased locomotor skills, babies actively seek contact with regular caregivers, such as the mother or father.

- *Phase 4: From 24 months on.* Children become aware of other people's feelings, goals, and plans and begin to take these into account in directing their own actions.

Bowlby argued that infants develop an *internal working model* of attachment, a simple mental model of the caregiver, their relationship to him or her, and the self as deserving of nurturant care. The infant's internal working model of attachment with the caregiver influences the infant's, and later the child's, subsequent responses to other people (Cassidy, 2016; Coyne & others, 2018; Dozier & Bernard, 2018; Hoffman & others, 2017). The internal model of attachment also has played a pivotal role in the discovery of links between attachment and subsequent emotional understanding, conscious development, and self-concept (Bretherton & Munholland, 2016; Vacaru, Sternkenburg, & Schuengel, 2018).

Individual Differences in Attachment

Although attachment to a caregiver intensifies midway through the first year, isn't it likely that the quality of a baby's attachment varies? Mary Ainsworth (1979) thought so. Ainsworth created the **Strange Situation,** an observational measure of infant attachment in which the infant experiences a series of introductions, separations, and reunions with the caregiver and an adult stranger in a prescribed order. In using the Strange Situation, researchers hope that their observations will provide information about the infant's motivation to be near the caregiver and the degree to which the caregiver's presence provides the infant with security and confidence (Brownell & others, 2015; Gaskins & others, 2017; Solomon & George, 2016).

Based on how babies respond in the Strange Situation, they are described as being securely attached or insecurely attached (in one of three ways) to the caregiver:

- **Securely attached babies** use the caregiver as a secure base from which to explore the environment. When they are in the presence of their caregiver, securely attached infants explore the room and examine toys that have been placed in it. When the caregiver departs, securely attached infants might protest mildly; when the caregiver returns, these infants reestablish positive interaction with her, perhaps by smiling or climbing onto her lap. Subsequently, they often resume playing with the toys in the room.

- **Insecure avoidant babies** show insecurity by avoiding the caregiver. In the Strange Situation, these babies engage in little interaction with the caregiver, are not distressed when she leaves the room, usually do not reestablish contact with her upon her return, and may even turn their back on her. If contact is established, the infant usually leans away or looks away.

- **Insecure resistant babies** often cling to the caregiver and then resist her by fighting against the closeness, perhaps by kicking or pushing away. In the Strange Situation, these babies often cling anxiously to the caregiver and don't explore the playroom. When the caregiver leaves, they often cry loudly and then push away if she tries to comfort them upon her return.

Strange Situation An observational measure of infant attachment that requires the infant to move through a series of introductions, separations, and reunions with the caregiver and an adult stranger in a prescribed order.

securely attached babies Babies that use the caregiver as a secure base from which to explore their environment.

insecure avoidant babies Babies that show insecurity by avoiding their mothers.

insecure resistant babies Babies that often cling to the caregiver, then resist her by fighting against the closeness, perhaps by kicking or pushing away.

What is the nature of secure and insecure attachment?
©George Doyle/
Stockbyte/Getty Images

- **Insecure disorganized babies** are disorganized and disoriented. In the Strange Situation, these babies might appear dazed, confused, and fearful. To be classified as disorganized, babies must show strong patterns of avoidance and resistance or display certain specified behaviors, such as extreme fearfulness around the caregiver.

How Would You...?

As a **psychologist,** how would you identify an insecurely attached toddler? How would you encourage a parent to strengthen the attachment bond?

Do individual differences in attachment matter? Ainsworth proposed that secure attachment in the first year of life provides an important foundation for psychological development later in life. The securely attached infant moves freely away from the caregiver but keeps track of where she is through periodic glances. The securely attached infant responds positively to being picked up by others and, when put back down, freely moves away to play. An insecurely attached infant, by contrast, avoids the caregiver or is ambivalent toward her, fears strangers, and is upset by minor, everyday separations.

If early attachment to a caregiver is important, it should set the stage for a child's social behavior later in development. For many children, early attachments seem to foreshadow later functioning (Dozier & others, 2018; Coyne & others, 2018; Finelli, Zeanah, & Smyke, 2018; Sroufe, 2016; Steele & Steele, 2017; Woodhouse, 2018; Woodhouse & others, 2017). In an extensive longitudinal study conducted by Alan Sroufe and his colleagues (2005), early secure attachment (assessed by the behavior during the Strange Situation at 12 and 18 months) was linked with positive emotional health, high self-esteem, self-confidence, and socially competent interaction with peers, teachers, camp counselors, and romantic partners through adolescence. Also, a research meta-analysis found that secure attachment in infancy was linked to social competence with peers in childhood (Groh & others, 2014). Further, a recent study revealed that infant attachment insecurity (especially insecure resistant attachment) and early childhood behavioral inhibition predicted adolescent social anxiety symptoms (Lewis-Morrarty & others, 2015).

Few studies have assessed infants' attachment security to the mother and the father separately. However, one study revealed that infants who were insecurely attached to their mother and father ("double-insecure") at 15 months of age had more externalizing problems (out-of-control behavior, for example) in the elementary school years than their counterparts who were securely attached to at least one parent (Kochanska & Kim, 2013).

An important issue regarding attachment is whether infancy is a critical or sensitive period for development. The studies just described show continuity, with secure attachment in infancy predicting subsequent positive development in childhood and adolescence. For some children, though, there is little continuity. Not all research reveals the power of infant attachment to predict subsequent development (Hudson & others, 2015; Lamb & Lewis, 2015; Roisman & others, 2016; Thompson, 2015, 2016). In one longitudinal study, attachment classification in infancy did not predict attachment classification at 18 years of age (Lewis, Feiring, & Rosenthal, 2000). In this study, the best predictor of an insecure attachment classification at 18 was the occurrence of parental divorce in the intervening years.

Consistently positive caregiving over a number of years is likely to be an important factor in connecting early attachment with the child's functioning later in development. Indeed, researchers have found that early secure attachment and subsequent experiences, especially maternal

To what extent might this adolescent girl's development be linked to how securely or insecurely attached she was during infancy?
(Top) ©Westend61/Getty Images; (bottom) ©iStock.com/RichVintage

insecure disorganized babies
Babies that show insecurity by being disorganized and disoriented.

care and life stresses, are linked with children's later behavior and adjustment (Roisman & Cicchetti, 2017). For example, a longitudinal study revealed that changes in attachment security/insecurity from infancy to adulthood were linked to stresses and supports in socioemotional contexts (Van Ryzin, Carlson, & Sroufe, 2011). These results suggest that attachment continuity may be a reflection of reflect stable social contexts as much as early working models. The study just described (Van Ryzin, Carlson, & Sroufe, 2011) reflects an increasingly accepted view of the development of attachment and its influence on development: the idea that attachment security in infancy does not always by itself produce long-term positive outcomes, but rather is linked to later outcomes through connections with the way children and adolescents subsequently experience various social contexts as they develop.

developmental cascade model Involves connections across domains over time that influence developmental pathways and outcomes.

The Van Ryzin, Carlson, and Sroufe (2011) study reflects a **developmental cascade model,** which involves connections across domains over time that influence developmental pathways and outcomes (Almy & Cicchetti. 2018; Roisman & Cicchetti, 2017). Developmental cascades can include connections between a wide range of biological, cognitive, and socioemotional processes (attachment, for example), and also can involve social contexts such as families, peers, schools, and culture. Further, links can produce positive or negative outcomes at different points in development, such as infancy, early childhood, middle and late childhood, adolescence, and adulthood (Luyten & Fonagy, 2018; Smith & others, 2018).

In addition to challenging whether secure attachment in infancy serves as a critical or sensitive period, some developmentalists argue that the secure attachment concept does not adequately consider certain biological factors in development, such as genes and temperament (Bakermans-Kranenburg & van IJzendoorn, 2016; Belsky & van IJzendoorn, 2017; Esposito & others, 2017b; Kim & others, 2017). For example, Jerome Kagan (1987, 2002) points out that infants are highly resilient and adaptive; he argues that they are evolutionarily equipped to stay on a positive developmental course, even in the face of wide variations in parenting. Kagan and others stress that genetic characteristics and temperament play more important roles in a child's social competence than the attachment theorists, such as Bowlby and Ainsworth, are willing to acknowledge (Bakermans-Kranenburg & van IJzendoorn, 2011). For example, if some infants inherit a low tolerance for stress, this tendency, rather than an insecure attachment bond, may be responsible for an inability to get along with peers. Also, one study found links between disorganized attachment in infancy, a specific gene, and levels of maternal responsiveness (Spangler & others, 2009). In this study, infants with the short version of the gene—serotonin transporter gene 5-HTTLPR—developed a disorganized attachment style only when mothers were slow or inconsistent in responding to them. However, some researchers have not found support for genetic influences on infant-mother attachment (Leerkes & others, 2017) or for gene-environment interactions related to infant attachment (Fraley & others, 2013).

Another criticism of attachment theory is that it ignores the diversity of socializing agents and contexts that exists in an infant's world. A culture's value system can influence the nature of attachment (Matsumoto & Juang, 2017; Otto & Keller, 2018). In northern Germany, for example, expectations for an infant's independence may be responsible for infants showing little distress upon a brief separation from the mother, whereas the Japanese mother's motivation for extremely close proximity to her infant may explain why Japanese infants become upset when they are separated from the mother. Also, in some cultures infants show attachments to many people. Among the Hausa (who live in Nigeria), both grandmothers and siblings provide a significant amount of care for infants (Harkness & Super, 1995). Infants in agricultural societies tend to form attachments to older siblings, who have major responsibility for their younger siblings' care.

In the Hausa culture, siblings and grandmothers provide a significant amount of care for infants. *How might these variations in care affect attachment?*
©Penny Tweedie/The Image Bank/Getty Images

In a recent study in Zambia where siblings were substantially involved in caregiving activities, infants showed strong attachments to both their mothers and their sibling caregivers (Mooya, Sichimba, & Bakersman-Kranenburg, 2016). In this study, secure attachment was the most frequent attachment classification for both mother-infant and sibling-infant relationships.

Researchers recognize the importance of competent, nurturant caregivers in an infant's development (Almy & Cicchetti, 2018; Johnson, 2018). At issue, though, is whether or not secure attachment, especially to a single caregiver, is essential (Roisman & others, 2017).

Despite such criticisms, there is ample evidence that security of attachment is important to development (Coyne & others, 2018; Dozier & Bernard, 2018; Hoffman & others, 2017; Sroufe, 2016; Stevens & N'zi, 2018; Thompson, 2016; Woodhouse, 2018). Secure attachment in infancy reflects a positive parent-infant relationship and provides a foundation that supports healthy socioemotional development in the years that follow.

Caregiving Styles and Attachment

Is the style of caregiving linked with the quality of the infant's attachment? Securely attached babies have caregivers who are sensitive to their signals and are consistently available to respond to the infant's needs (Groh & Haydon, 2018; Woodhouse & others, 2017). These caregivers often let their babies take an active part in determining the onset and pacing of interactions in the first year of life. A recent study revealed that maternal sensitivity and a better home environment in infancy predicted higher self-regulation at 4 years of age (Birmingham, Bub, & Vaughn, 2017). Further, recent research indicates that if parents who engage in inadequate and problematic caregiving are provided with practice and feedback focused on interacting sensitively with their infants, the parent-infant attachment becomes more secure (Coyne & others, 2018; Dozier & Bernard, 2017, 2018; Dozier, Bernard, & Roben, 2017; Woodhouse, 2018; Woodhouse & others, 2017).

How Would You…?

As a **health-care professional,** how would you use an infant's attachment style and/or a parent's caregiving style to determine whether an infant may be at risk for neglect or abuse?

How do the caregivers of insecurely attached babies interact with them? Caregivers of avoidant babies tend to be unavailable or rejecting. They often don't respond to their babies' signals and have little physical contact with them. When they do interact with their babies, they may behave in an angry and irritable way. Caregivers of resistant babies tend to be inconsistent; sometimes they respond to their babies' needs, and sometimes they don't. In general, they tend not to be very affectionate with their babies and show little synchrony when interacting with them. Caregivers of disorganized babies often neglect or physically abuse them (Almy & Cicchetti, 2018).

Social Contexts

Now that we have explored the infant's emotional and personality development and attachment, let's examine the social contexts in which these occur. We begin by studying a number of aspects of the family and then turn to a social context in which infants increasingly spend time: child care.

The Family

The family can be thought of as a constellation of subsystems—a complex whole made up of interrelated, interacting parts—defined in terms of generation, gender, and role. Each family member participates in several subsystems (Chen, Hughes, & Austin, 2017; Solomon-Moore & others, 2018). The father and child represent one subsystem, the mother and father another; the mother, father, and child represent yet another subsystem; and so on.

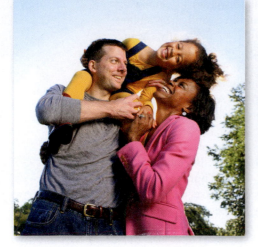

These subsystems have reciprocal influences on each other, as Figure 5 highlights (Maccoby, 2015; Schwartz & Scott, 2018). For example, Jay Belsky (1981) stresses that marital relations, parenting, and infant behavior and development can have both direct and indirect effects on each other. An example of a direct effect is the influence of the parents' behavior on the child. An indirect effect is how the relationship between the spouses mediates the way a parent acts toward the child. For example, marital conflict might reduce the efficiency of parenting, in which case marital conflict would indirectly affect the child's behavior (Dubow & others, 2017; Taylor & others, 2017). The simple fact that two people are becoming parents may have profound effects on their relationship.

The Transition to Parenthood

Whether people become parents through pregnancy, adoption, or stepparenting, they face disequilibrium and must adapt to it (Carlson & VanOrman, 2017). Parents want to develop a strong attachment with their infant, but they also want to maintain strong attachments to their spouse and friends, and possibly to continue their careers. Parents ask themselves how the presence of this new being will change their lives. A baby places new restrictions on partners; no longer will they be able to rush out to a movie at a moment's notice, and money may not be readily available for vacations and other luxuries. Dual-career parents ask, "Will it harm the baby to place her in child care? Will we be able to find responsible baby-sitters?"

In a longitudinal investigation of couples from late pregnancy until three years after the baby was born, couples enjoyed more positive marital relations before the baby was born than afterward (Cowan & Cowan, 2000; Cowan & others, 2005). Still, almost one-third reported an increase in marital satisfaction. Some couples said that the baby had both brought them closer together and moved them farther apart; being parents enhanced their sense of themselves and gave them a new, more stable identity as a couple. Babies opened men up to greater concern with intimate relationships, and the demands of juggling work and family roles stimulated women to manage family tasks more efficiently and pay attention to their own personal growth. The Bringing Home Baby project is a workshop for new parents that emphasizes strengthening their relationship with each other, understanding and becoming acquainted with their baby, resolving conflict, and developing parenting skills (Gottman, 2018). Evaluations of the project revealed that parents who participated became better able to work together as parents; fathers were more involved with their baby and sensitive to the baby's behavior; mothers had fewer symptoms of postpartum depression; and babies showed better overall development than was the case among parents and babies in a control group (Gottman, Gottman, & Shapiro, 2009).

Other recent studies have explored the transition to parenthood (Kuersten-Hogan, 2017). One study revealed that mothers experienced unmet expectations in the transition to parenting, with fathers doing less than their partners had anticipated (Biehle & Mickelson, 2012). And in a study of dual-earner couples, a gender gap was not present prior to the transition to parenthood, but after a child was born, women did more than 2 hours of additional work per day compared with an additional 40 minutes for men (Yavorksy, Dush, & Schoppe-Sullivan, 2015).

Reciprocal Socialization

For many years, socialization was viewed as a one-way process: Children were considered to be the products of their parents' socialization techniques. According to more recent research, however, parent-child interaction is reciprocal (Klein & others, 2017). **Reciprocal socialization** is socialization

Figure 5 Interaction Between Children and Their Parents: Direct and Indirect Effects
©Katrina Wittkamp/Photodisc/Getty Images

reciprocal socialization Socialization that is bidirectional, meaning that children socialize parents, just as parents socialize children.

Caregivers often play games with infants such as peek-a-boo and pat-a-cake. *How is scaffolding involved in these games?*

(*Left*) ©Brand X Pictures/Getty Images; (*right*) ©Stephanie Rausser/The Image Bank/Getty Images

that is bidirectional. That is, children socialize their parents just as parents socialize their children (Maccoby, 2015). The types of behaviors involved in reciprocal socialization in infancy are temporally connected, mutually contingent behaviors such as one partner imitating the sound of another or the mother responding with a vocalization to the baby's arm movements. These reciprocal interchanges and mutual influence processes are sometimes referred to as *transactional* (Sameroff, 2009, 2012).

An important form of reciprocal socialization is **scaffolding,** in which parents time interactions in such a way that the infant experiences turn-taking with the parents. Scaffolding can be used to support children's efforts at any age (Norona & Baker, 2017).

The game peek-a-boo, in which parents initially cover their babies, then remove the covering, and finally register "surprise" at the babies' reappearance, reflects the concept of scaffolding. As infants become more skilled at this game, they gradually do some of the covering and uncovering themselves. Parents try to time their actions in such a way that the infant takes turns with the parent.

How Would You…?

As an **educator,** how would you explain the value of games and the role of scaffolding in the development of infants and toddlers?

Research supports the importance of scaffolding in infant development (Maitre & others, 2017; Mermelshtine, 2017). For example, a recent study found that when adults used explicit scaffolding (encouragement and praise) with 13- and 14-month-old infants they were twice as likely to engage in helping behavior as were their counterparts who did not receive the scaffolding (Dahl & others, 2017). A study involving disadvantaged families revealed that an intervention designed to enhance maternal scaffolding with infants was linked to improved cognitive skills when the children were 4 years old (Obradovic & others, 2016).

Increasingly, genetic and epigenetic factors are being studied to discover not only parental influences on children but also children's influence on parents (Baptista & others, 2017; Lomanowska & others, 2017). Recall that the *epigenetic view* emphasizes that development is the result of an ongoing, bidirectional interchange between heredity and the environment (Moore, 2015, 2017). For example, harsh, hostile parenting is associated with negative outcomes for children, such as being defiant and oppositional (Deater-Deckard, 2013; Thompson & others, 2017). This likely reflects bidirectional influences rather than a unidirectional parenting effect. That is, the parents' harsh, hostile parenting and the children's defiant, oppositional behavior may mutually influence each other. In this bidirectional influence, the parents' and children's behavior may have genetic linkages as well as experiential connections.

Managing and Guiding Infants' Behavior

In addition to sensitive parenting involving warmth and caring that can result in infants being securely attached to their parents, other important aspects of parenting infants involve managing and guiding their behavior in an attempt to reduce or eliminate undesirable behaviors (Holden, Vittrup, & Rosen, 2011). This management process includes (1) being proactive and childproofing the environment so infants won't encounter potentially dangerous objects or situations; and (2) engaging in corrective methods when infants engage in undesirable behaviors such as excessive fussing and crying, throwing objects, and so on.

scaffolding Process in which parents time interactions so that infants experience turn-taking with their parents.

One study assessed discipline and corrective methods that parents had used by the time their infants were 12 and 24 months old (Vittrup, Holden, & Buck, 2006) (see Figure 6). Notice in Figure 6 that the main method parents used by the time infants were 12 months old was diverting the infants' attention, followed by reasoning, ignoring, and negotiating. Also note in Figure 6 that more than one-third of parents had yelled at their infant, about one-fifth had slapped the infant's hands or threatened the infant, and approximately one-sixth had spanked the infant by their first birthday.

As infants move into the second year of life and become more mobile and capable of exploring a wider range of environments, parental management of the toddler's behavior often triggers increased corrective feedback and discipline (Holden, Vittrup, & Rosen, 2011). As indicated in Figure 6, in the study just described, yelling increased from 36 percent at 1 year of age to 81 percent by 2 years of age, slapping the infant's hands increased from 21 percent at 1 year to 31 percent by age 2, and spanking increased from 14 percent at age 1 to 45 percent by age 2 (Vittrup, Holden, & Buck, 2006).

A special concern is that such corrective discipline tactics not become abusive (Almy & Cicchetti, 2018). Too often what starts out as mild to moderately intense discipline on the part of parents can move into highly intense anger. Later in this text, you will read more extensively about the use of punishment with children and child maltreatment.

Method	12 Months	24 Months
Spank with hand	14	45
Slap infant's hand	21	31
Yell in anger	36	81
Threaten	19	63
Withdraw privileges	18	52
Time-out	12	60
Reason	85	100
Divert attention	100	100
Negotiate	50	90
Ignore	64	90

Figure 6 **Parents' Methods for Managing and Correcting Infants' Undesirable Behavior**

Shown here are the percentages of parents who had used various corrective methods by the time the infants were 12 and 24 months old.

Source: Vittrup, B., Holden, G. W., & Buck, M. "Attitudes Predict the Use of Physical Punishment: A Prospective Study of the Emergence of Disciplinary Practices," *Pediatrics,* 117, 2006, 2055–2064.

Maternal and Paternal Caregiving

Much of our discussion of attachment has focused on mothers as caregivers. Do mothers and fathers differ in their caregiving roles? In general, mothers on average still spend considerably more time in caregiving with infants and children than do fathers (Blakemore, Berenbaum, & Liben, 2009). Mothers especially are more likely to engage in the managerial role with their children, coordinating their activities, making sure their health-care needs are met, and so on (Clarke-Stewart & Parke, 2014).

However, an increasing number of U.S. fathers stay home full-time with their children (Bartel & others, 2018; Dette-Hagenmeyer, Erzinger, & Reichle, 2016). The number of stay-at-home dads in the United States was estimated to be 2 million in 2012 (Livingston, 2014). This figure represents a significant increase from 1.6 million in 2004 and 1.1 million in 1989.

A large portion of these full-time fathers have career-focused wives who are the primary providers of family income (O'Brien & Moss, 2010). One study revealed that the stay-at-home fathers were as satisfied with their marriage as traditional parents, although they missed their daily life in the workplace (Rochlen & others, 2008). In this study, the stay-at-home fathers reported that they tended to be ostracized when they took their children to playgrounds and often were excluded from parent groups.

Observations of fathers and their infants suggest that fathers have the ability to act as sensitively and responsively with their infants as mothers do (Cabrera & Roggman, 2017; Lamb & Lewis, 2015). Consider the Aka pygmy culture in Africa, in which fathers spend as much time interacting with their infants as mothers do (Hewlett, 1991, 2000; Hewlett & MacFarlan, 2010). One study also found that marital intimacy and partner support during prenatal development were linked to father-infant attachment following childbirth

(Yu & others, 2012). Remember, however, that although fathers can be active, nurturant, involved caregivers, as in the case of Aka pygmies, in many cultures men have not chosen to follow this pattern.

Do fathers interact with their infants differently from the way mothers do? Maternal interactions usually center on child-care activities—feeding, changing diapers, and bathing. Paternal interactions are more likely to include play, especially rough-and-tumble play (Lamb & Lewis, 2015). Nonetheless, mothers engage in play with their children three times as often as fathers do, and mothers and fathers play differently with their children (Cabrera & Roggman, 2017). Fathers bounce infants, throw them up in the air, tickle them, and so on. Mothers' play is less physical and arousing than that of fathers. In a recent study of low-income families, fathers' playfulness with 2-year-olds was associated with more advanced vocabulary skills at 4 years of age while mothers' playfulness with 2-year-olds was linked to a higher level of emotion regulation at 4 years of age (Cabrera & others, 2017).

An Aka pygmy father with his infant son. In the Aka culture, fathers were observed to be holding or near their infants 47 percent of the time (Hewlett, 1991).
©Nick Greaves/Alamy

However, if fathers have mental health problems, they may not interact as effectively with their infants. For example, in a recent study, children whose fathers' behavior was more withdrawn and depressed at 3 months had a lower level of cognitive development at 24 months of age (Sethna & others, 2018). Also in this study, children whose fathers were more engaged and sensitive, as well as less controlling, at 24 months of age had a higher level of cognitive development at that age.

Do children benefit in other ways when fathers are positively involved in their caregiving? A study of more than 7,000 children who were assessed from infancy to adulthood revealed that those whose fathers were extensively involved in their lives (such as engaging in various activities with them and showing a strong interest in their education) were more successful in school (Flouri & Buchanan, 2004). Further, a recent study revealed that both fathers' and mothers' sensitivity, as assessed when infants were 10 to 12 months old, were linked to children's cognitive development at 18 months and language development at 36 months (Malmberg & others, 2016). Other recent studies indicate that when fathers are positively engaged with their children, developmental outcomes are better (Alexander & others, 2017; Roopnarine & Yildirim, 2018).

Child Care

Many U.S. children today experience multiple caregivers. Most do not have a parent staying home to care for them; instead, the children receive "child care"—that is, some type of care provided by others. Many parents worry that child care will have adverse effects such as reducing their children's emotional attachment to them, constraining their children's cognitive development, failing to teach them how to control anger, or allowing them to be unduly influenced by their peers. Are these concerns justified?

In the United States, approximately 15 percent of children age 5 and younger experience more than one child-care arrangement. One study of 2- and 3-year-old children revealed that an increase in the number of child-care arrangements the children experienced was linked to increased behavioral problems and decreased prosocial behavior (Morrissey, 2009).

Parental Leave

Today far more young children are in child care than at any other time in U.S. history. About 2 million children in the United States currently receive formal, licensed child care, and uncounted millions of children are cared for by unlicensed baby-sitters. In part, these numbers reflect the fact that many U.S. adults do not receive paid leave from their jobs to care for their young children.

Child-care policies around the world vary (Burchinal & others, 2015). Europe has led the way in creating new standards of parental leave: In 1992, the European Union (EU) mandated a paid 14-week maternity leave. In most European countries today, working parents on leave receive 70 to 100 percent of the worker's prior wage, and paid leave averages about 16 weeks (Tolani & Brooks-Gunn, 2008). The United States currently allows up to 12 weeks of unpaid leave for parents who are caring for a newborn.

Most countries restrict eligible benefits to women who have been employed for a minimum length of time prior to childbirth. In Denmark, however, even unemployed mothers are eligible for extended parental leave related to childbirth. In Germany, child-rearing leave is available to almost all parents. The Nordic countries (Denmark, Norway, and Sweden) have extensive gender-equity family leave policies for childbirth that emphasize the contributions of both women and men. For example, in Sweden parents can take an 18-month, job-protected parental leave with benefits to be shared by both parents and applied to full-time or part-time work.

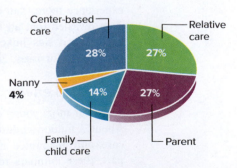

How are child-care policies in many European countries, such as Sweden, different from those in the United States?
©Matilda Lindeblad/Johner Images/Getty Images

Variations in Child Care

Because the United States does not have a policy of paid leave for child care, child care in the United States has become a major national concern (Lamb & Lewis, 2015). Many factors influence the effects of child care, including the age of the child, the type of child care, and the quality of the program.

Child care arrangements vary extensively (Burchinal & others, 2015; Hasbrouck & Pianta, 2016). Child care is provided in large centers with elaborate facilities and in private homes. Some child-care centers are commercial operations; others are nonprofit centers run by churches, civic groups, and employers. Some child-care providers are professionals; others are untrained adults who want to earn extra money. Infants and toddlers are more likely to be found in family child care and informal care settings, while older children are more likely to be in child-care centers and preschool and early education programs. Figure 7 presents the primary care arrangements for U.S. children under age 5 with employed mothers (Clarke-Stewart & Miner, 2008).

Child-care quality makes a difference (Howes, 2016; Vu, 2016). An Australian study revealed that higher-quality child care that included positive child-caregiver relationships at 2 to 3 years of age was linked to children's better self-regulation of attention and emotion at 4 to 5 and 6 to 7 years of age (Gialamas & others, 2014). What constitutes a high-quality child-care program for infants? In high-quality child care (Clarke-Stewart & Miner, 2008, p. 273):

> Caregivers encourage the children to be actively engaged in a variety of activities, have frequent, positive interactions that include smiling, touching, holding, and speaking at the child's eye level, respond properly to the child's questions or requests, and encourage children to talk about their experiences, feelings, and ideas.

High-quality child care also involves providing children with a safe environment, access to age-appropriate toys and participation in age-appropriate activities, and a low caregiver-child ratio that allows caregivers to spend considerable time with children on an individual basis.

Children are more likely to experience poor-quality child care if they come from families with few resources (psychological, social, and economic) (Carta & others, 2012). Many researchers have examined the role of poverty in quality of child care. One study found that extensive child care was harmful to low-income children only when the care was of low quality (Votruba-Drzal, Coley, & Chase-Lansdale, 2004). Even if the child was in child care more than 45 hours a week, high-quality care was associated with fewer internalizing problems (anxiety, for example) and externalizing

Figure 7 Primary Care Arrangements in the United States for Children Under 5 Years of Age with Employed Mothers

How Would You...?

As an **educator,** how would you design the ideal child-care program to promote optimal infant development?

problems (aggressive and destructive behaviors, for example). One study revealed that children from low-income families benefited in terms of school readiness and language development when their parents had access to higher-quality child care (McCartney & others, 2007).

To read about one individual who provides quality child care to individuals from impoverished backgrounds, see *Careers in Life-Span Development.*

Careers in life-span development

Wanda Mitchell, Child-Care Director

Wanda Mitchell is the Center Director at the Hattie Daniels Day Care Center in Wilson, North Carolina. Her responsibilities include directing the operations of the center, which involves creating and maintaining an environment in which young children can learn effectively and ensuring that the center meets state licensing requirements. Wanda obtained her undergraduate degree from North Carolina A&T University, majoring in Child Development. Prior to her current position, she had been an education coordinator for Head Start and an instructor at Wilson Technical Community College. Describing her chosen career, Wanda says, "I really enjoy working in my field. This is my passion. After graduating from college, my goal was to advance in my field."

Wanda Mitchell, child-care director, works with some of the children at her center.
Courtesy of Wanda Mitchell

The National Longitudinal Study of Child Care

In 1991, the National Institute of Child Health and Human Development (NICHD) began a comprehensive longitudinal study of child-care experiences. Data were collected from a diverse sample of almost 1,400 children and their families at 10 locations in the United States across several decades. Researchers used multiple methods (trained observers, interviews, questionnaires, and testing) and measured many facets of children's development, including physical health, cognitive development, and socioemotional development. Following are some of the results of what is now referred to as the NICHD Study of Early Child Care and Youth Development or NICHD SECCYD (NICHD Early Child Care Research Network, 2001, 2002, 2003, 2004, 2005a, b, 2006, 2010).

- *Quality of care.* Evaluations of quality of care were based on characteristics such as group size, child–adult ratio, physical environment, caregiver characteristics (such as formal education, specialized training, and child-care experience), and caregiver behavior (such as sensitivity to children). An alarming conclusion is that a majority of the child care in the first three years of life was of unacceptably low quality. Positive caregiving by nonparents in child-care settings was infrequent—only 12 percent of the children in the study experienced positive nonparental child care (such as positive talk and language stimulation). Further, infants from low-income families experienced lower-quality child care than did infants from higher-income families. When quality of caregivers' care was high, children performed better on cognitive and language tasks, were more cooperative with their mothers during play, showed more positive and skilled interaction with peers, and had fewer behavior problems. Caregiver training and favorable child–staff ratios were linked with higher cognitive and social competence when children were 54 months of age. In research involving the NICHD sample, links were found between nonrelative child care from birth to 4 years of age and adolescent development at 15 years of age (Vandell & others, 2010). In this analysis, better quality of early care was related to a higher level of academic achievement and a lower level of externalizing problems at age 15. In another study, high-quality infant-toddler child care was linked to better memory skills at the end of the preschool years (Li & others, 2013).

What are some important findings from the national longitudinal study of child care conducted by the National Institute of Child Health and Human Development?
©Reena Rose Sibayan/The Jersey Journal/ Landov Images

- *Amount of child care.* The quantity of child care predicted some outcomes (Vandell & others, 2010). When children spent extensive amounts of time in child care beginning in infancy, they experienced fewer sensitive interactions with their mothers, showed more behavior problems, and had higher rates of illness. In general, when children spent 30 hours or more per week in child care, their development was less than optimal. However, a study conducted in Norway (a country that meets or exceeds 8 of 10 UNICEF benchmarks for quality child care) revealed that a high quantity of child care there was not linked to children's externalizing problems (Zachrisson & others, 2013).

- *Family and parenting influences.* The influence of families and parenting was not weakened by extensive child care. Parents played a significant role in helping children regulate their emotions. Especially important parenting influences were being sensitive to children's needs, being involved with children, and providing cognitive stimulation. Indeed, parental sensitivity has been the most consistent predictor of secure attachment (Friedman, Melhuish, & Hill, 2010). An important final point about the extensive NICHD SECCYD research is that findings have consistently shown that family factors are considerably stronger and more consistent predictors of a wide variety of child outcomes than are child-care experiences (quality, quantity, type). The worst outcomes for children occur when both home and child-care settings are of poor quality. For example, a study involving the NICHD SECCYD data revealed that worse socioemotional outcomes (more problem behavior, lower levels of prosocial behavior) for children occurred when they experienced both home and child-care environments that conferred risk (Watamura & others, 2011).

What are some strategies parents can follow in regard to child care? Child-care expert Kathleen McCartney (2003, p. 4) offers this advice:

- *Recognize that the quality of your parenting is a key factor in your child's development.*

- *Make decisions that will improve the likelihood that you will be good parents.* "For some this will mean working full-time"—for personal fulfillment, income, or both. "For others, this will mean working part-time or not working outside the home."

- *Monitor your child's development.* "Parents should observe for themselves whether their children seem to be having behavior problems." They should also talk with child-care providers and their pediatrician about their child's behavior.

- *Take some time to find the best child care.* Observe different child-care facilities and be certain that you like the one you choose. "Quality child care costs money, and not all parents can afford the child care they want."

How Would You...?

As a **psychologist,** based on the findings from the NICHD study, how would you advise parents about their role in their child's development versus the role of nonparental child care?

Summary

Emotional and Personality Development

- Emotion is feeling, or affect, that occurs when a person is in a state or an interaction that is important to them. Infants display a number of emotions early in their development, such as by crying, smiling, and showing fear. Two fears that infants develop are stranger anxiety and fear of separation from a caregiver. As infants develop, it is important for them to increase their ability to regulate their emotions.

- Temperament is an individual's behavioral style and characteristic way of responding emotionally. Chess and Thomas classified infants as (1) easy, (2) difficult, or (3) slow to warm up. Kagan proposed that inhibition to the unfamiliar is an important temperament category. Rothbart and Bates emphasized that effortful control (self-regulation) is an important temperament dimension. Goodness of fit can be an important aspect of a child's adjustment.

- Erikson argued that an infant's first year is characterized by the stage of trust versus mistrust. Independence becomes a central theme in the second year of life, which is characterized by the stage of autonomy versus shame and doubt.

Social Orientation and Attachment

- Infants show a strong interest in their social world and are motivated to understand it. Infants are more socially sophisticated and insightful at an earlier age than was previously thought.

- Attachment is a close emotional bond between two people. In infancy, contact comfort and trust are important in the development of attachment. Securely attached babies use the caregiver, usually the mother, as a secure base from which to explore their environment. Three types of insecure attachment are avoidant, resistant, and disorganized. Caregivers of securely attached babies are more sensitive to the babies' signals and are consistently available to meet their needs.

Social Contexts

- The transition to parenthood requires considerable adaptation and adjustment on the part of parents. Children socialize parents just as parents socialize children. Parents use a wide range of methods to manage and guide infants' behavior. In general, mothers spend more time in caregiving than fathers do; fathers tend to engage in more physical, playful interaction with infants than mothers do.

- The quality of child care is uneven, and child care remains a controversial topic. Quality child care can be achieved and seems to have few adverse effects on children.

Key Terms

anger cry	emotion	reciprocal socialization	social referencing
attachment	goodness of fit	reflexive smile	social smile
basic cry	insecure avoidant babies	scaffolding	Strange Situation
developmental cascade model	insecure disorganized babies	securely attached babies	stranger anxiety
difficult child	insecure resistant babies	separation protest	temperament
easy child	pain cry	slow-to-warm-up child	

5 Physical and Cognitive Development in Early Childhood

©Tim Pannell/Getty Images

CHAPTER OUTLINE

Stories of Life-Span Development: Reggio Emilia's Children

The Reggio Emilia approach is an educational program for young children that was developed in the northern Italian city of Reggio Emilia. Children of single parents and children with disabilities have priority in admission; other children are admitted according to a scale of needs. Parents pay on a sliding scale based on income.

The children are encouraged to learn by investigating and exploring topics that interest them (Bredekamp, 2017). A wide range of stimulating media and materials are available for children to use as they learn music, movement, drawing, painting, sculpting, collage, puppetry, and photography, among other things (Bond, 2015).

In this program, children often explore topics in a group, which fosters a sense of community, respect for diversity, and a collaborative approach to problem solving (Jones & Reynolds, 2011). In this group setting, two co-teachers guide the children in their exploration. The Reggio Emilia teachers treat each project as an adventure. It can start from an adult's suggestion, from a child's idea, or from an unexpected event such as a snowfall. Every project is based on what the children say and do. The teachers allow children enough time to plan and craft a project.

At the core of the Reggio Emilia approach is an image of children who are competent and have rights, especially the right to outstanding care and education. Parent participation is

In a Reggio Emilia classroom, young children explore topics that interest them.
©Ruby Washington/The New York Times/Redux Pictures

considered essential, and cooperation is a major theme in the schools. Many experts on early childhood education believe that the Reggio Emilia approach provides a supportive, stimulating context in which children are motivated to explore their world in a competent and confident manner (Follari, 2019; Morrison, 2017, 2018; Vatalaro, Szente, & Levin, 2015).

Parents and educators who understand how young children develop can play active roles in creating programs that foster children's natural interest in learning, rather than stifling it. In this chapter, the first of two chapters on early childhood (ages 3 to 5), we explore the physical, cognitive, and language changes that typically occur as the toddler develops into the preschooler, and then we look at early childhood education. ■

Physical Changes

Earlier, we described a child's growth in infancy as rapid and following cephalocaudal and proximodistal patterns. Fortunately, the growth rate slows in early childhood; otherwise, we would be a species of giants.

Body Growth and Change

Despite the slowing of growth in height and weight that characterizes early childhood, growth is still the most obvious physical change during this period of development. Yet unseen changes in the brain and nervous system are no less significant in preparing children for advances in cognition and language.

The average child grows 2½ inches in height and gains between 5 and 7 pounds a year during early childhood. As the preschool child grows older, the percentage of increase in height and weight decreases with each additional year (Hockenberry, Wilson, & Rodgers, 2017). Girls are only slightly smaller and lighter than boys during these years, a difference that continues until puberty. In addition, girls have more fatty tissue than boys, and boys have more muscle tissue than girls.

During the preschool years, both boys and girls slim down as the trunk of the body lengthens (Kliegman & others, 2016). Although the head is still somewhat large for the body, by the end of the preschool years most children have lost the top-heavy look they had as toddlers. Body fat also shows a slow, steady decline during the preschool years. The chubby baby often looks much leaner by the end of early childhood.

Growth patterns vary from one individual to another (Grimberg & Allen, 2017). Think back to your preschool years. That was probably the first time you noticed that some children were taller than you, some shorter; some were fatter, some thinner; some were stronger, some weaker. Much of the variation was due to heredity, but environmental experiences were also involved (Hay & others, 2017). A review of the height and weight of children around the world concluded that the two most important contributors to height differences are ethnic origin and nutrition (Meredith, 1978). Urban, middle-socioeconomic status, and firstborn children were taller than rural, lower-socioeconomic status, and later-born children. In the United States, African American children are taller than White children.

The bodies of 5-year-olds and 2-year-olds are different. Notice that the 5-year-old not only is taller and weighs more, but also has a longer trunk and legs than the 2-year-old. *Can you think of some other physical differences between 2- and 5-year-olds?*
©Michael Hitoshi/Getty Images

The Brain

Prefrontal cortex

One of the most important physical developments during early childhood is the continuing development of the brain and other parts of the nervous system (Bell, Broomell, & Patton, 2018; Bell & others, 2018). The increasing maturation of the brain, combined with opportunities to experience a widening world, contribute to children's emerging cognitive abilities. In particular, changes in the brain during early childhood enable children to plan their actions, attend to stimuli more effectively, and make considerable strides in language development.

Although the brain does not grow as rapidly during early childhood as in infancy, it does undergo remarkable changes. By repeatedly obtaining brain scans of the same children for up to four years, researchers have found that children's brains experience rapid, distinct spurts of growth (Gogtay & Thompson, 2010). The overall size of the brain does not increase dramatically from ages 3 to 5; what does change dramatically are local patterns within the brain. The amount of brain material in some areas can nearly double in as little as a year, followed by a dramatic loss of tissue as unneeded cells are pruned and the brain continues to reorganize itself. From 3 to 6 years of age the most rapid growth in the brain takes place in the part of the frontal lobes known as the *prefrontal cortex* (see Figure 1), which plays a key role in planning and organizing new actions and maintaining attention to tasks (Gogtay & Thompson, 2010).

The continuation of two changes that began before birth contributes to the brain's growth during early childhood. First, the number and size of dendrites increase, and second, myelination continues. Recall that **myelination** is the process through which axons (nerve fibers that carry signals away from the cell body) are covered with a layer of fat cells, which increases the speed and efficiency of information traveling through the nervous system. Myelination is important in the development of a number of abilities (Juraska & Willing, 2017; van Tilborg & others, 2018). For example, myelination in the areas of the brain related to hand-eye coordination is not complete until about age 4. Myelination in the areas of the brain related to focusing attention is not complete until the end of middle or late childhood. And myelination of many aspects of the prefrontal cortex, especially those involving higher-level thinking skills, is not completed until late adolescence or emerging adulthood (Bell, Ross, & Patton, 2018; Cohen & Casey, 2017; Dahl & others, 2018). In a recent study, young children with higher cognitive ability showed increased myelination by 3 years of age (Deoni & others, 2016).

Recently, researchers have found that contextual factors such as poverty and parenting quality are linked to the development of the brain (Black & others, 2017; Farah, 2017; Marshall & others, 2018). In one study, children from the poorest homes had significant maturational lags in their frontal and temporal lobes at 4 years of age, and these lags were associated with lower school readiness skills (Hair & others, 2015). In another study, higher levels of maternal sensitivity in early childhood were associated with higher total brain volume (Kok & others, 2015).

Figure 1 The Prefrontal Cortex The brain pathways and circuitry involving the prefrontal cortex (shaded in purple) show significant advances in development during middle and late childhood. *What cognitive processes are linked with these changes in the prefrontal cortex?*

Motor Development

Running as fast as you can, falling down, getting right back up and running just as fast as you can . . . building towers with blocks . . . scribbling, scribbling, and scribbling some more . . . cutting paper with scissors . . . During your preschool years, you probably developed the ability to perform all these activities. What physical changes made this possible?

Gross Motor Skills

The preschool child no longer has to make an effort simply to stay upright and move around. As children move their legs with more confidence and carry themselves more purposefully, moving around in the environment becomes more automatic (Hockenberry, Wilson, & Rodgers, 2017; Perry & others, 2018).

myelination The process by which axons are covered and insulated with a layer of fat cells, which increases the speed at which information travels through the nervous system.

Around age 3, children enjoy simple movements such as hopping, jumping, and running back and forth, just for the sheer delight of performing them. They are eager to demonstrate how they can run across a room and jump all of 6 inches. The run-and-jump will win no Olympic medals, but for the 3-year-old it brings considerable pride and a sense of accomplishment.

At age 4, children are still enjoying the same kinds of activities, but they have become more adventurous. They scramble over low jungle gyms as they display their athletic prowess. Although they have been able to climb stairs with one foot on each step for some time, they are just beginning to be able to come down the same way.

By age 5, children are even more adventuresome than when they were 4. It is not unusual for self-assured 5-year-olds to perform hair-raising stunts on playground equipment. Five-year-olds also run hard and enjoy races with each other and their parents.

How can early childhood educators support young children's motor development? Young children need to practice skills in order to learn them, so instruction should be followed with ample time for practice (Follari, 2019; Morrison, 2017, 2018). A recent study of 4-year-old girls found that a nine-week motor skill intervention improved the girls' ball skills (Veldman & others, 2017).

There can be long-term negative effects for children who fail to develop basic motor skills (Barnett, Salmon, & Hesketh, 2016; Gorgon, 2018). These children will not be as able to join in group games or participate in sports during their school years and in adulthood. In a recent study, children with a low level of motor competence had a lower motivation for sports participation and had lower global self-worth than their counterparts with a high level of motor competence (Bardid & others, 2018). Another recent study found that higher motor proficiency in preschool was linked to engaging in a higher level of physical activity in adolescence (Venetsanou & Kambas, 2017).

Fine Motor Skills

By the time they turn 3, children have had the ability to pick up the tiniest objects between their thumb and forefinger for some time, but they are still somewhat clumsy at it. Three-year-olds can build surprisingly high block towers, each block placed with intense concentration but often not in a completely straight line. When 3-year-olds play with a simple jigsaw puzzle, they are rather rough in placing the pieces. Even when they recognize the hole a piece fits into, they are not very precise in positioning the piece. They often try to force the piece into the hole or pat it vigorously.

By age 4, children's fine motor coordination has improved substantially and is much more precise. Sometimes 4-year-olds have trouble building high towers with blocks because, in their desire to place each of the blocks perfectly, they may upset those already in the stack. Fine motor coordination continues to improve so that by age 5, hand, arm, and body all move together under better command of the eye. Mere towers no longer interest the 5-year-old, who now wants to build a house or a church, complete with steeple, though adults might still need to be told what each finished project is meant to be.

Nutrition and Exercise

Eating habits are important aspects of development during early childhood (Blake, Munoz, & Volpe, 2019; Thompson & Manore, 2018; Wardlaw, Smith, & Collene, 2018). What children eat affects their skeletal growth, body shape, and susceptibility to disease. Exercise and physical activity are also very important aspects of young children's lives (Powers & Dodd, 2017; Powers & Howley, 2018; Walton-Fisette & Wuest, 2018).

Eating Behavior and Overweight Young Children

Young children's eating behavior is strongly influenced by their caregivers' behavior (Black & others, 2017; Lindsay & others, 2018; Scaglioni & others, 2018; Tan & Holub, 2015). Children's eating behavior improves when caregivers eat with children on a predictable schedule, model eating healthy food, make mealtimes pleasant occasions, and engage in certain feeding styles (Daelmans & others, 2017;

What are some trends in the eating habits and weight of young children?
©Lilian Perez/age fotostock

Profili & others, 2017). Distractions created by television, family arguments, and competing activities should be minimized so that children can focus on eating. Experts recommend a sensitive, responsive caregiver feeding style, in which the caregiver is nurturant, provides clear information about what is expected, and responds appropriately to children's cues (Black & Armstrong, 2017; Black & Hurley, 2017). Forceful and restrictive caregiver behaviors are not recommended, as they can lead to excessive weight gain (Rollins & others, 2016).

Being overweight has become a serious health problem in early childhood (Donatelle, 2019; Perry & others, 2017; Roberts, Marx, & Musher-Eizenman, 2018; Smith & Collene, 2019). A national study revealed that 45 percent of children's meals exceed recommendations for saturated and trans fat, which can raise cholesterol levels and increase the risk of heart disease (Center for Science in the Public Interest, 2008). This study also found that one-third of children's daily caloric intake comes from restaurants, twice the percentage consumed away from home in the 1980s. Further, 93 percent of almost 1,500 possible choices at 13 major fast-food chains exceeded 430 calories—one-third of what the National Institute of Medicine recommends that 4- to 8-year-old children consume in a day. Nearly all of the children's meal offerings at KFC, Taco Bell, Sonic, Jack in the Box, and Chick-fil-A were too high in calories. Also, a study of U.S. 2- and 3-year-olds found that French fries and other fried potatoes were the vegetable they were most likely to consume (Fox & others, 2010).

How Would You...?

As a **health-care professional,** how would you work with parents to increase the nutritional value of meals and snacks they provide to their young children?

The Centers for Disease Control and Prevention (2018) has established categories for obesity, overweight, and at risk for being overweight. These categories are determined by body mass index (BMI), which is computed using a formula that takes into account height and weight. Children and adolescents at or above the 97th percentile are classified as obese; those at the 95th or 96th percentile as overweight; and those from the 85th to the 94th percentile as at risk of being overweight.

The percentages of young children who are overweight or at risk of being overweight in the United States have increased dramatically in recent decades, but in the last several years there are indications that fewer preschool children are obese (Wardlaw, Smith, & Collene, 2018). In 2009–2010, 12.1 percent of U.S. 2- to 5-year-olds were classified as obese, compared with 5 percent in 1976–1980 (Ogden & others, 2012). However, in 2013–2014, a substantial drop in the obesity rate of 2- to 5-year-old children occurred in comparison with their counterparts in 2009–2010 (Centers for Disease Control and Prevention, 2018). In 2013–2014, 9.4 percent of 2- to 5-year-olds were obese compared with 12.1 percent in 2004. It is not clear why this drop occurred, but among the possible explanations are families buying lower-calorie foods and being influenced by the Special Supplementation Program for Women, Infants, and Children (which subsidizes food for women and children in low-income families) that emphasizes consuming less fruit juice, cheese, and eggs and more whole fruits and vegetables. In a recent study, 2½-year-olds' liking for fruits and vegetables was related to their eating more fruits and vegetables at 7 years of age (Fletcher & others, 2018).

The risk that overweight children will continue to be overweight when they are older was documented in a U.S. study of nearly 8,000 children (Cunningham, Kramer, & Narayan, 2014). In this study, overweight 5-year-olds were four times more likely to be obese at 14 years of age than their 5-year-old counterparts who began kindergarten at a normal weight. Also, in the study described earlier in which obesity was reduced in preschool children, the children who were obese were five times more likely to be overweight or obese in adulthood (Ogden & others, 2014).

A comparison of 34 countries revealed that the United States had the second highest rate of childhood obesity (Janssen & others, 2005). Childhood obesity contributes to a number of health problems in young children (Eno Persson & others, 2018). For example, physicians are now seeing type 2 (adult-onset) diabetes (a condition directly linked with obesity and a low level of fitness) in children as young as age 5 (Baskaran & Kandemir, 2018). Many aspects of children's lives can contribute to becoming overweight or obese (Labayen Goñi & others, 2018; Sun & others, 2018). Recently, the following 5-2-1-0 obesity prevention guidelines have been established for young children: 5 or more servings of fruits and vegetables, 2 hours or less of screen time, minimum of 1 hour of physical activity, and 0 sugar-sweetened beverages daily (Khalsa & others, 2017). Prevention of obesity in children also includes helping children, parents, and teachers see healthy food as a way to satisfy hunger and meet nutritional needs, not as proof of love or as a reward for good behavior. Routine physical activity should be a daily occurrence (Powers & Howley, 2018). One research study found that viewing as little as one hour of television daily was associated with an increase in body mass index (BMI) between kindergarten and first grade (Peck & others, 2015).

Malnutrition

Poor nutrition affects many young children from low-income families (Lucas, Richter, & Daelmans, 2018; Schiff, 2019). Many of these children do not obtain essential amounts of iron, vitamins, or protein. Poor nutrition is a particular concern for infants from low-income families (Petry & others, 2017).

To address this problem in the United States, the WIC (Women, Infants, and Children) program provides federal grants to states for healthy supplemental foods, health-care referrals, and nutrition education for women from low-income families beginning in pregnancy, and to infants and young children up to 5 years of age who are at nutritional risk (Chang, Brown, & Nitzke, 2017; Gilmore & others, 2017). WIC serves approximately 7,500,000 participants in the United States. Positive influences on infants' and young children's nutrition and health, as well as mothers' health, have been found for participants in WIC (Black & Armstrong, 2017; Chen & others, 2018; Gross & others, 2017; Lee & others, 2017; Martinez-Brockman & others, 2018; McCoy & others, 2018). For example, a multiple-year literacy intervention with Spanish-speaking families in the WIC program in Los Angeles increased literacy resources and activities at home, which in turn led to a higher level of school readiness in children (Whaley & others, 2011). And in longitudinal studies, when mothers participated in WIC programs prenatally and during their children's first five years, young children showed short-term cognitive benefits and longer-term reading and math benefits (Jackson, 2015).

How Would You…?

As a **health-care professional,** how would you advise parents who want to get their talented 4-year-old child into a soccer league for preschool children?

How much physical activity should preschool children engage in per day?
©RubberBall Productions/Getty Images

Exercise

Young children should engage in physical activity every day (Insel & Walton, 2018; Lintu & others, 2017; Walton-Fisette & Wuest, 2018). Expert panels from Australia, Canada, the United Kingdom, and the United States have issued physical activity guidelines for young children that are quite similar (Pate & others, 2015). The guidelines recommend that young children get an average of 15 or more minutes of physical activity per hour over a 12-hour period, or about 3 hours per day total. These guidelines reflect an increase from earlier guidelines (National Association for Sport and Physical Education, 2002). The child's life should center on activities, not meals (Powers & Howley, 2018; Rowland, 2016).

Illness and Death

The vast majority of children in the United States go through the physical changes just described and reach adulthood without serious illness or death. However, some do not. In the United States accidents are the leading cause of death in young children, followed by cancer and cardiovascular disease (National Center for Health Statistics, 2018). In addition to motor vehicle accidents, other accidental deaths in children involve drowning, falls, and poisoning.

Children's safety is influenced not only by their own skills and safety-related behaviors but also by characteristics of their family and home, school and peers, and community (Onders & others, 2018; Saunders & others, 2017). Figure 2 describes steps that can be taken in each of these contexts to enhance children's safety and prevent injury (Sleet & Mercy, 2003).

How Would You...?

As a **health-care professional,** how would you talk with parents about the impact of secondhand smoke on children's health to encourage parents to stop smoking?

One major danger to children is parental smoking (Merianos, Dixon, & Mahabee-Gittens, 2017). An estimated 22 percent of children and adolescents in the United States are exposed to tobacco smoke in the home. An increasing number of studies indicate that children are at risk for health problems when they live in homes in which a parent smokes (Hatoun & others, 2018; Miyahara & others, 2017; Pugmire, Sweeting, & Moore, 2017; Rosen & others, 2018). Children exposed to tobacco smoke in the home are more likely to develop wheezing and asthma than are children in homes where no one smokes (Vo & others, 2017). One study revealed that exposure to secondhand smoke was related to young children's sleep problems, including sleep-disordered breathing (Yolton & others, 2010). Researchers have also found that maternal cigarette smoking and alcohol consumption when children were 5 years of age were linked to early onset of smoking in adolescence (Hayatbakhsh & others, 2013). And a recent study found that young children who were exposed to environmental tobacco smoke were more likely to engage in antisocial behavior when they were 12 years old (Pagani & others, 2017).

Although accidents and serious illnesses such as cancer are the leading causes of death among children in the United States, this is not the case in a number of other countries in the world, where many children die of preventable infectious diseases. Many of the deaths of young children around the world could be prevented by a reduction in poverty and improvements in nutrition, sanitation, education, and health services (UNICEF, 2018). High poverty rates have devastating effects on the health of a country's young children, who are likely to experience hunger, malnutrition, illness, inadequate access to health care, unsafe water, and a lack of protection from harm (Black & others, 2017; UNICEF, 2018). In the last decade, there has been a dramatic increase in the number of young children who have died because HIV/AIDS was transmitted to them by their parents. Deaths of young children due to HIV/AIDS especially occur in countries with high rates of poverty and low levels of education (UNICEF, 2018).

Many children in impoverished countries die before reaching the age of 5 from dehydration and malnutrition brought about by diarrhea. *What are some of the other main causes of death in young children around the world?*
©Kent Page/AP Images

Individual
- Development of social skills and ability to regulate emotions
- Impulse control (such as not darting out into a street to retrieve a ball)
- Frequent use of personal protection (such as bike helmets and safety seats)

Family/Home
- High awareness and knowledge of child management and parenting skills
- Frequent parent protective behaviors (such as use of child safety seats)
- Presence of home safety equipment (such as smoke alarms and cabinet locks)

School/Peers
- Promotion of home/school partnerships
- Absence of playground hazards
- Injury prevention and safety promotion policies and programs

Community
- Availability of positive activities for children and their parents
- Active surveillance of environmental hazards
- Effective prevention policies in place (such as pool fencing)

Figure 2

Characteristics That Enhance Young Children's Safety.

In each context of a child's life, steps can be taken to create conditions that enhance the child's safety and reduce the likelihood of injury. *How are the contexts listed in the figure related to Bronfenbrenner's theory?*

Cognitive Changes

The cognitive world of the preschool child is creative, free, and fanciful. Preschool children's imaginations work overtime, and their mental grasp of the world improves. Our coverage of cognitive development in early childhood focuses on three theories: Piaget's, Vygotsky's, and information processing.

Piaget's Preoperational Stage

Remember that during Piaget's first stage of development, the sensorimotor stage, the infant becomes increasingly able to organize and coordinate sensations and perceptions with physical movements and actions. The **preoperational stage,** which lasts from approximately age 2 to 7, is the second stage in Piaget's theory. In this stage, children begin to represent the world with words, images, and drawings. They form stable concepts and begin to reason. At the same time, the young child's cognitive world is dominated by egocentrism and magical beliefs.

Because Piaget called this stage "preoperational," it might sound like an unimportant waiting period. Not so. However, the label *preoperational* emphasizes that the child does not yet perform **operations,** which are reversible mental actions that allow children to do mentally what before they could do only physically. Mentally adding and subtracting numbers are examples of operations. *Preoperational thought* is the beginning of the ability to reconstruct in thought what has been established in behavior. This stage can be divided into two substages: the symbolic function substage and the intuitive thought substage.

The Symbolic Function Substage

The **symbolic function substage** is the first substage of preoperational thought, occurring roughly between the ages of 2 and 4. In this substage, the young child gains the ability to mentally represent an object that is not present. This ability vastly expands the child's mental world (Lillard & Kavanaugh, 2014). In this substage, children use scribble designs to represent people, houses, cars, clouds, and so on; they begin to use language more effectively and engage in pretend play. However, although young children make distinct progress during this substage, their thinking still has important limitations, two of which are egocentrism and animism.

Egocentrism is the inability to distinguish between one's own perspective and someone else's perspective. The following telephone conversation between 4-year-old Marie, who is at home, and her father, who is at work, typifies Marie's egocentric thought:

Father: Marie, is Mommy there?
Marie silently nods.

Father: Marie, may I speak to Mommy?
Marie nods again, silently.

Marie's response is egocentric in that she fails to consider her father's perspective before replying. A nonegocentric thinker would have responded verbally.

Jean Piaget and Barbel Inhelder (1969) initially studied young children's egocentrism by devising the three mountains task (see Figure 3). The child walks around the model of the mountains and becomes familiar with what the mountains look like from different perspectives, and she can see that there are different objects on the mountains. The child is then seated on one side of the table on which the mountains are placed. The experimenter moves a doll to different locations around the table, and at each location asks the child to select from a series of photos the one that most accurately reflects the view that the doll is seeing. Children in the preoperational stage often pick their own view rather than the doll's view. Preschool children frequently show the ability to take another's perspective on some tasks but not others.

preoperational stage Piaget's second stage, lasting from about 2 to 7 years of age, during which children begin to represent the world with words, images, and drawings, and symbolic thought goes beyond simple connections of sensory information and physical action; stable concepts are formed, mental reasoning emerges, egocentrism is present, and magical beliefs are constructed.

operations In Piaget's theory, these are internalized, reversible sets of actions that allow children to do mentally what they formerly did physically.

symbolic function substage Piaget's first substage of preoperational thought, in which the child gains the ability to mentally represent an object that is not present (between about 2 and 4 years of age).

egocentrism The inability to distinguish between one's own perspective and someone else's (salient feature of the first substage of preoperational thought).

Model of Mountains

C

D ✝ B

A
Child seated here

Photo 1
(View from A)

Photo 2
(View from B)

Photo 3
(View from C)

Photo 4
(View from D)

Figure 3 **The Three Mountains Task**
Photo 1 shows the child's perspective from where he or she is sitting (location A). Photos 2, 3, and 4 show what the mountains would look like to a person sitting at locations B, C, and D, respectively. When asked to choose the photograph that shows what the mountains looks like from position B, the preoperational child selects a photograph taken from location A, the child's view at the time. A child who thinks in a preoperational way cannot take the perspective of a person sitting at another spot.

Animism, another limitation of preoperational thought, is the belief that inanimate objects have lifelike qualities and are capable of action. A young child might show animism by saying, "That tree pushed the leaf off, and it fell down," or "The sidewalk made me mad; it made me fall down." A young child who shows animism fails to distinguish among appropriate and inappropriate occasions for using human perspectives.

The Intuitive Thought Substage

The **intuitive thought substage** is the second substage of preoperational thought, occurring between ages 4 and 7. In this substage, children begin to use primitive reasoning and want to know the answers to all sorts of questions. Consider 4-year-old Terrell, who is at the beginning of the intuitive thought substage. Although he is starting to develop his own ideas about the world he lives in, his ideas are still simple, and he is not very good at thinking things out. He has difficulty understanding events that he knows are taking place but that he cannot see. His fantasized thoughts bear little resemblance to reality. He cannot yet answer the question "What if?" in any reliable way. For example, he has only a vague idea of why he needs to avoid getting hit by a car. He also has difficulty negotiating traffic because he cannot do the mental calculations necessary to estimate whether an approaching car will hit him when he crosses the road.

By age 5 children have just about exhausted the adults around them with "why" questions. The child's questions signal the emergence of interest in reasoning and in figuring out why things are the way they are. Following are some samples of the questions children ask during the intuitive thought substage (Elkind, 1976): "What makes you grow up?" "Why does a woman have to be married to have a baby?" "Who was the mother when everybody was a baby?" "Why do leaves fall?" "Why does the sun shine?"

Piaget called this substage *intuitive* because young children seem so sure about their knowledge and understanding, yet are unaware of how they know what they know. That is, they know something but know it without the use of rational thinking and are sometimes wrong as a result.

Centration and the Limits of Preoperational Thought

Another limitation of preoperational thought is **centration,** a centering of attention on one characteristic to the exclusion of all others. Centration is most clearly evidenced in young children's lack of **conservation;** that is, they lack the awareness that altering an object or substance's appearance does not change its basic properties. For example, to adults it is obvious that a certain

How Would You…?

As a **human development and family studies professional,** how would you explain the child's response in the following scenario: A parent gives a 3-year-old a cookie. The child says, "I want two cookies." The parent breaks the cookie in half and hands the two pieces to the child, who happily accepts them.

animism The belief that inanimate objects have lifelike qualities and are capable of action.

intuitive thought substage Piaget's second substage of preoperational thought, in which children begin to use primitive reasoning and want to know the answers to all sorts of questions (between about 4 and 7 years of age).

centration The focusing of attention on one characteristic to the exclusion of all others.

conservation In Piaget's theory, awareness that altering an object's or a substance's appearance does not change its basic properties.

Figure 4 Piaget's Conservation Task
The beaker test is a well-known Piaget-ian test to determine whether a child can think operationally—that is, can mentally reverse actions and show con-servation of the substance. (a) Two iden-tical beakers, A and B, are presented to the child. Then the experimenter pours the liquid from B into C, which is taller and thinner than A or B. (b) The child is asked if these beakers (A and C) have the same amount of liquid. The preop-erational child says "no." When asked to point to the beaker that has more liquid, the preoperational child points to the tall, thin beaker.
©Tony Freeman/PhotoEdit

amount of liquid remains the same when it is poured from one container to another, regard-less of the containers' shapes. But this is not at all obvious to young children.

The situation that Piaget devised to study conservation is his most famous task. In the conservation task, children are presented with two identical beakers, each filled to the same level with liquid (see Figure 4). They are asked if these beakers contain the same amount of liquid, and they usually say yes. Then the liquid from one beaker is poured into a third beaker, which is taller and thinner than the first two. The children are then asked if the amount of liquid in the tall, thin beaker is equal to that which remains in one of the original beakers. Children who are less than 7 or 8 years old usually say no and justify their answers in terms of the differing height or width of the two beakers. They are typically struck by the height of the liquid in a tall, narrow container and focus on that characteristic to the exclusion of others. Older children usually answer yes and justify their answer appropriately ("If you poured the water back, the amount would still be the same").

In Piaget's theory, failing the conservation of liquid task is a sign that children are at the preoperational stage of cognitive development. The failure demonstrates not only centration but also inability to mentally reverse actions. For example, in the conserva-tion of matter example shown in Figure 5, preoperational children say that the longer shape contains more clay because they assume that "longer is more." Preoperational

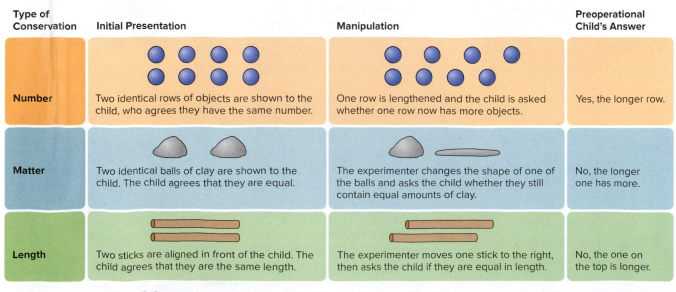

Type of Conservation	Initial Presentation	Manipulation	Preoperational Child's Answer
Number	Two identical rows of objects are shown to the child, who agrees they have the same number.	One row is lengthened and the child is asked whether one row now has more objects.	Yes, the longer row.
Matter	Two identical balls of clay are shown to the child. The child agrees that they are equal.	The experimenter changes the shape of one of the balls and asks the child whether they still contain equal amounts of clay.	No, the longer one has more.
Length	Two sticks are aligned in front of the child. The child agrees that they are the same length.	The experimenter moves one stick to the right, then asks the child if they are equal in length.	No, the one on the top is longer.

Figure 5 Some Dimensions of Conservation: Number, Matter, and Length
What characteristics of preoperational thought do children demonstrate when they fail these conservation tasks?

children cannot mentally reverse the clay-rolling process to see that the amount of clay is the same in both the shorter ball shape and the longer stick shape.

In addition to failing to conserve volume, preoperational children fail to conserve number, matter, length, and area. However, children often vary in their performance on different conservation tasks. Thus, a child might be able to conserve volume but not number.

Some developmental psychologists do not believe that Piaget was entirely correct in his estimate of when children's conservation skills emerge. For example, Rochel Gelman (1969) showed that when children's attention to relevant aspects of the conservation task is improved, they are more likely to conserve. Gelman has also demonstrated that attentional training on one dimension, such as number, improves preschool children's performance on another dimension, such as mass. Thus, Gelman believes that conservation appears earlier than Piaget thought and that attention is especially important in explaining conservation.

Vygotsky's Theory

Like Piaget, Vygotsky was a constructivist, but Vygotsky's theory is a **social constructivist approach,** and it emphasizes the social contexts of learning and the construction of knowledge through social interaction. In Vygotsky's view, children's cognitive development depends on the tools provided by society, and their minds are shaped by the cultural context in which they live (Moura da Costa & Tuleski, 2017; Yu & Hu, 2017). Earlier, we described some basic elements of Vygotsky's theory. Here we expand on his theory, exploring his ideas about the zone of proximal development, scaffolding, and the young child's use of language.

The Zone of Proximal Development and Scaffolding

Vygotsky's belief in the importance of social influences, especially instruction, on children's cognitive development is reflected in his concept of the zone of proximal development. **Zone of proximal development (ZPD)** is Vygotsky's term for the range of tasks that are too difficult for the child to master alone but can be learned with the guidance and assistance of adults or more-skilled children. Thus, the lower limit of the ZPD is the level of skill reached by the child working independently. The upper limit is the level of additional responsibility the child can accept with the assistance of an able instructor (see Figure 6). The ZPD captures the child's cognitive skills that are in the process of maturing and can be accomplished only with the assistance of a more-skilled person (Holzman, 2017). Vygotsky (1962) called these the "buds" or "flowers" of development, to distinguish them from the "fruits" of development, which the child can already accomplish independently.

What are some factors that can influence the effectiveness of the ZPD in children's learning and development? Researchers have found that the ZPD's effectiveness can be enhanced by factors such as the following (Gauvain, 2013): better emotion regulation, secure attachment, absence of maternal depression, and child compliance.

social constructivist approach An approach that emphasizes the social contexts of learning and that knowledge is mutually built and constructed. Vygotsky's theory reflects this approach.

zone of proximal development (ZPD) Vygotsky's term for tasks that are too difficult for children to master alone but can be mastered with assistance.

Upper limit
Level of additional responsibility child can accept with assistance of an able instructor

Zone of proximal development (ZPD)

Lower limit
Level of problem solving reached on these tasks by child working alone

Figure 6 Vygotsky's Zone of Proximal Development
Vygotsky's zone of proximal development has a lower limit and an upper limit. Tasks in the ZPD are too difficult for the child to perform alone. They require assistance from an adult or a more-skilled child. As children experience the verbal instruction or demonstration, they organize the information in their existing mental structures so they can eventually perform the skill or task alone.
©Ariel Skelley/Blend Images

How Would You...?
As an **educator,** how would you apply Vygotsky's ZPD theory and the concept of scaffolding to help a young child complete a puzzle?

Closely linked to the idea of the ZPD is the concept of scaffolding, introduced earlier in the context of parent-infant interaction. *Scaffolding* means changing the level of support. Over the course of a teaching session, a more-skilled person (a teacher or advanced peer) adjusts the amount of guidance to fit the child's current performance (Daniels, 2017). When the student is learning a new task, the skilled person may use direct instruction. As the student's competence increases, less guidance is given.

Language and Thought

According to Vygotsky, children use speech not only for social communication but also to help them solve tasks. Vygotsky (1962) further believed that young children use language to plan, guide, and monitor their behavior. This use of language for self-regulation is called *private speech*. Piaget viewed private speech as egocentric and immature, but Vygotsky saw it as an important tool of thought during the early-childhood years (Lantolf, 2017).

Vygotsky said that language and thought initially develop independently of each other and then merge. He emphasized that all mental functions have external, or social, origins. Children must use language to communicate with others before they can focus inward on their own thoughts. Children also must communicate externally and use language for a long time before they can make the transition from external to internal speech. This transition period occurs between ages 3 and 7 and involves talking to oneself. After a while, self-talk becomes second nature to children, and they can act without verbalizing. When this occurs, children have internalized their egocentric speech in the form of *inner speech*, which becomes their thoughts.

Vygotsky saw children who use a lot of private speech as more socially competent than those who don't. He argued that private speech represents an early transition toward becoming more socially communicative. For Vygotsky, when young children talk to themselves they are using language to govern their behavior and guide themselves. For example, a child working on a puzzle might say to herself, "Which pieces should I put together first? I'll try those green ones first. Now I need some blue ones. No, that blue one doesn't fit there. I'll try it over here." Researchers have found support for Vygotsky's view that private speech plays a positive role in children's development (Winsler, Carlton, & Barry, 2000).

Teaching Strategies Based on Vygotsky's Theory

Vygotsky's theory has been embraced by many teachers and has been successfully applied to education (Adams, 2015; Daniels, 2017; Holtzman, 2017). Here are some ways in which educators can apply Vygotsky's theory:

1. *Assess the child's ZPD.* Like Piaget, Vygotsky did not believe that formal, standardized tests are the best way to assess children's learning. Rather, Vygotsky argued that assessment should focus on determining the child's zone of proximal development. The skilled helper presents the child with tasks of varying difficulty to determine the best level at which to begin instruction.

2. *Use the child's zone of proximal development in teaching.* Teaching should begin near the zone's upper limit, so that the child can reach the goal with help and move to a higher level of skill and knowledge. Offer just enough assistance. You might ask, "What can I do to help you?" Or simply observe the child's intentions and attempts, providing support only when it is needed.

3. *Use more-skilled peers as teachers.* Remember that it is not just adults who are important in helping children learn. Children also benefit from the support and guidance of more-skilled children.

4. *Monitor and encourage children's use of private speech.* Be aware of the developmental change from talking to oneself externally when solving a problem during the preschool years to talking to oneself privately in the early elementary school years. In the elementary school years, encourage children to internalize and self-regulate their talk to themselves.

5. *Place instruction in a meaningful context.* Educators today are moving away from abstract presentations of material, instead providing students with opportunities to experience learning in real-world settings. For example, instead of just memorizing math formulas, students work on math problems that have real-world implications.

With Vygotsky's theory in mind, let's examine an early childhood program that reflects these concepts. Tools of the Mind is an early-childhood education curriculum that emphasizes children's development of self-regulation and the cognitive foundations of literacy. The curriculum was created by Elena Bodrova and Deborah Leong (2007, 2015) and has been implemented in more than 200 classrooms. Most of the children in the Tools of the Mind programs are considered at risk of academic failure because of their living circumstances, which in many instances are characterized by poverty and other difficult conditions such as being homeless and having parents with drug problems.

Tools of the Mind is grounded in Vygotsky's (1962) theory, with special attention to cultural tools and the development of self-regulation, the zone of proximal development, scaffolding, private speech, shared activity, and play as important activity. In a Tools of the Mind classroom, dramatic play has a central role. Teachers guide children in creating themes that are based on the children's interests, such as treasure hunt, store, hospital, and restaurant. Teachers also incorporate field trips, visitor presentations, videos, and books in the development of children's play. They help children develop a play plan, which increases the maturity of their play. Play plans describe what the children expect to do in the play period, including the imaginary context, roles, and props to be used. The play plans increase the quality of their play and self-regulation.

Scaffolding children's writing is another important theme in the Tools of the Mind classroom. Teachers guide children in planning their own message by drawing a line to stand for each word the child says. Children then repeat the message, pointing to each line as they say the word. Then the child writes on the lines, trying to represent each word with some letters or symbols.

Research assessments of children's writing in Tools of the Mind classrooms revealed that they have more advanced writing skills than do children in other early childhood programs (Bodrova & Leong, 2007, 2015). For example, they write more complex messages, use more words, spell more accurately, show better letter recognition, and have a better understanding of the concept of a sentence. The effectiveness of the Tools of the Mind approach also was examined in another study of 29 schools, 79 classrooms, and 759 students (Blair & Raver, 2014). Positive effects of the Tools of the Mind program were found for the cognitive processes of executive function (improved self-regulation, for example) and attention control. Further, the Tools of the Mind program improved children's reading, vocabulary, and mathematics at the end of kindergarten and into the first grade. The most significant improvements occurred in high-poverty schools.

Evaluating Vygotsky's Theory

How does Vygotsky's theory compare with Piaget's? We already have mentioned several comparisons, such as Vygotsky's emphasis on the importance of inner speech in cognitive development and Piaget's view that such speech is immature. Figure 7 compares the two theories. The implication of Piaget's theory for teaching is that children need support to explore their world and discover knowledge. The main implication of Vygotsky's theory is that students need many opportunities to learn with a teacher and more-skilled peers (Gauvain, 2016; Holtzman, 2017). In both theories, teachers serve as facilitators and guides rather than as directors and molders.

Even though their theories were proposed at about the same time, most of the world learned about Vygotsky's theory later than they learned about Piaget's, so Vygotsky's theory has not yet been evaluated as thoroughly. Vygotsky's view of the importance of sociocultural influences on children's development fits with the current belief that it is important to evaluate contextual factors in learning (Yu & Hu, 2017).

Some critics say that Vygotsky was not specific enough about age-related changes (Gauvain & Perez, 2015). Another criticism is that he overemphasized the role of language in thinking. His emphasis on collaboration and guidance also has potential

	Vygotsky	Piaget
Sociocultural Context	Strong emphasis	Little emphasis
Constructivism	Social constructivist	Cognitive constructivist
Stages	No general stages of development proposed	Strong emphasis on stages (sensorimotor, preoperational, concrete operational, and formal operational)
Key Processes	Zone of proximal development, language, dialogue, tools of the culture	Schema, assimilation, accommodation, operations, conservation, classification
Role of Language	A major role; language plays a powerful role in shaping thought	Language has a minimal role; cognition primarily directs language
View on Education	Education plays a central role, helping children learn the tools of the culture	Education merely refines the child's cognitive skills that have already emerged
Teaching Implications	Teacher is a facilitator and guide, not a director; establish many opportunities for children to learn with the teacher and more-skilled peers	Also views teacher as a facilitator and guide, not a director; provide support for children to explore their world and discover knowledge

Figure 7 **Comparison of Vygotsky's and Piaget's Theories**
(*Left*) ©A.R. Lauria/Dr. Michael Cole, Laboratory of Human Cognition, University of California, San Diego; (*right*) ©Bettmann/Getty Images

pitfalls. Might facilitators be too helpful in some cases, as when a parent becomes overbearing and controlling? Further, some children might become lazy and expect help when they could do something on their own.

Information Processing

Piaget's and Vygotsky's theories provided important ideas about how young children think and how their thinking changes. More recently, the information-processing approach has generated research that illuminates how children process information during the preschool years (Braithwaite & Siegler, 2018a, b; Chevalier, Dauvier, & Blaye, 2018). What are the limitations and advances in young children's ability to pay attention to their environment, to remember, to develop strategies and solve problems, and to understand their own mental processes and those of others?

Attention

Recall that we defined *attention* as the focusing of mental resources on select information. The child's ability to pay attention improves significantly during the preschool years (Wu & Scerif, 2018). Toddlers wander around, shift attention from one activity to another, and seem to spend little time focused on any one object or event. By comparison, the preschool child might be observed watching television for half an hour.

Young children especially make advances in two aspects of attention: executive attention and sustained attention (Bell & Cuevas, 2015). **Executive attention** involves planning actions, allocating attention to goals, detecting and compensating for errors, monitoring progress on tasks, and dealing with novel or difficult circumstances (McClelland & others, 2017; Schmitt & others, 2017). **Sustained attention,** also referred to as *vigilance,* is focused and extended engagement with an object, task, event, or other aspect of the environment (Benitez & others, 2017). Research indicates that although older children and adolescents show increases in vigilance, it is during the preschool years that individuals show the greatest increase in vigilance (Rothbart & Posner, 2015).

executive attention Involves planning actions, allocating attention to goals, detecting and compensating for errors, monitoring progress on tasks, and dealing with novel or difficult circumstances.

sustained attention Also referred to as vigilance; involves focused and extended engagement with an object, task, event, or other aspect of the environment.

In at least two ways, however, the preschool child's control of attention is still deficient:

1. *Salient versus relevant dimensions.* Preschool children are likely to pay attention to stimuli that stand out, or are *salient,* even when those stimuli are not relevant to solving a problem or performing a task. For example, if a flashy, attractive clown presents the directions for solving a problem, preschool children are likely to pay more attention to the clown than to the directions. After age 6 or 7, children attend more efficiently to the dimensions of the task that are relevant, such as the directions for solving a problem. This change reflects a shift to cognitive control of attention, so that children act less impulsively and reflect more.

2. *Planfulness.* When experimenters ask children to judge whether two complex pictures are the same, preschool children tend to use a haphazard comparison strategy, not examining all the details before making a judgment. By comparison, elementary-school-age children are more likely to systematically compare the details across the pictures, one detail at a time (Vurpillot, 1968).

What are some advances in children's attention in early childhood?
©Weedezign/Getty Images

In central European countries such as Hungary, kindergarten children participate in exercises designed to improve their attention (Posner & Rothbart, 2007). For example, in one eye-contact exercise, the teacher sits in the center of a circle of children and each child is required to catch the teacher's eye before being permitted to leave the group. In other exercises created to improve attention, teachers have children participate in stop-go activities during which they have to listen for a specific signal, such as a drumbeat or an exact number of rhythmic beats, before stopping the activity.

Computer exercises have been developed to improve children's attention (Rothbart & Posner, 2015; Stevens & Bavelier, 2012). For example, one study revealed that five days of computer exercises that involved learning how to use a joystick, relying on working memory, and resolving conflict improved the attention of 4- to 6-year-old children (Rueda, Posner, & Rothbart, 2005). Although not commercially available, further information about computer exercises for improving children's attention can be downloaded from www.teach-the-brain.org/learn/attention/index.

The ability of preschool children to control and sustain their attention is related to school readiness (Rothbart & Posner, 2015). For example, a study of more than 1,000 children revealed that their ability to sustain their attention at 54 months of age was linked to their school readiness (which included achievement and language skills) (NICHD Early Child Care Research Network, 2005). In another study, the ability to focus attention better at age 5 was linked to a higher level of school achievement at age 9 (Razza, Martin, & Brooks-Gunn, 2012). Also, a recent study found that preschoolers' sustained attention was linked to a greater likelihood of completing college by 25 years of age (McClelland & others, 2013).

Memory

Memory—the retention of information over time—is a central process in children's cognitive development. Most of an infant's memories are fragile and, for the most part, short-lived—except for the memory of perceptual-motor actions, which can be substantial (Bauer, 2018). Thus, to understand the infant's capacity to remember, we need to distinguish *implicit memory* from *explicit memory*. Explicit memory itself, however, comes in many forms (Radvansky & Ashcraft, 2018). One distinction is between relatively permanent or *long-term memory* and short-term memory.

Short-Term Memory In **short-term memory,** individuals retain information for up to 30 seconds if there is no rehearsal of the information. Using *rehearsal* (repeating information after it has been presented), we can keep information in short-term memory for a much longer period. One method of assessing short-term memory is the memory-span task. You hear a short list of

short-term memory The memory component in which individuals retain information for up to 30 seconds, assuming there is no rehearsal of the information.

stimuli—usually digits—presented at a rapid pace (one per second, for example). Then you are asked to repeat the digits.

Research with the memory-span task suggests that short-term memory increases during early childhood. For example, in one investigation memory span increased from about 2 digits in 2- to 3-year-old children to about 5 digits in 7-year-old children, yet between ages 7 and 13 memory span increased by only 1½ digits (Dempster, 1981) (see Figure 8). Keep in mind, though, that memory span varies from one individual to another.

Why does memory span change with age? Rehearsal of information is important; older children rehearse the digits more than younger children do. Also important are efficiency of processing and speed, especially the speed with which memory items can be identified (Schneider, 2011).

The speed-of-processing explanation highlights a key point in the information-processing perspective: The speed with which a child processes information is an important aspect of the child's cognitive abilities, and there is abundant evidence that the speed with which many cognitive tasks are completed improves dramatically during the childhood years (Rose, Feldman, & Jankowski, 2015). One study found that myelination (the process by which the sheath that encases axons helps electrical signals travel faster down the axon) in a number of brain areas was linked to young children's processing speed (Chevalier & others, 2015).

How Accurate Are Young Children's Long-Term Memories? Just as toddlers' short-term memory span increases during the early childhood years, their memory also becomes more accurate. Young children can remember a great deal of information if they are given appropriate cues and prompts (Bruck & Ceci, 2012). Increasingly, young children are even being allowed to testify in court, especially if they are the only witnesses to abuse or a crime (Andrews, Ahern, & Lamb, 2017; Pantell & others, 2018). Several factors can influence the accuracy of a young child's memory, however (Bruck & Ceci, 1999):

- *There are age differences in children's susceptibility to suggestion.* Preschoolers are the most suggestible age group (Lehman & others, 2010). For example, preschool children are more susceptible to believing misleading or incorrect information given after an event (Ghetti & Alexander, 2004). Despite these age differences, there is still concern about the reaction of older children when they are subjected to suggestive interviews (Ahern, Kowalski, & Lamb, 2018; Peixoto & others, 2017).

- *There are individual differences in susceptibility.* Some preschoolers are highly resistant to interviewers' suggestions, whereas others immediately succumb to the slightest suggestion (Ceci, Hritz, & Royer, 2016).

- *Interviewing techniques can produce substantial distortions in children's reports about highly salient events.* Children are suggestible not just about peripheral details but also about the central aspects of an event. In some cases, children's false reports can be tinged with sexual connotations. In laboratory studies, young children have made false claims about "silly events" that involved body contact (such as "Did the nurse lick your knee?" or "Did she blow in your ear?"). A significant number of preschool children have falsely reported that someone touched their private parts, kissed them, or hugged them, when these events clearly did not happen. Nevertheless, young children are capable of recalling much that is relevant about an event (Ahern, Kowalski, & Lamb, 2017). When young children do recall information accurately, the interviewer often has a neutral tone and avoids asking misleading questions, and there is no reason for the child to make a false report.

In sum, the accuracy of a young child's eyewitness testimony may depend on a number of factors, such as the type, number, and intensity of the suggestive techniques

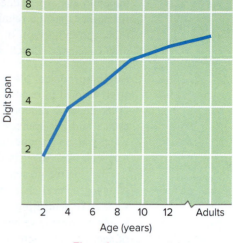

Figure 8 Developmental Changes in Memory Span

In one study, from 2 to 7 years of age children's memory span increased from 2 digits to about 5 digits (Dempster, 1981). Between 7 and 13 years of age, memory span had increased on average only another 1½ digits, to about 7 digits. *What factors might contribute to the increase in memory span during childhood?*

the child has experienced (Andrews, Ahern, & Lamb, 2017; Andrews & Lamb, 2018). It appears that the reliability of young children's reports has as much to do with the skills and motivation of the interviewer as with any natural limitations on young children's memory (Bruck & Ceci, 2012; Ceci, Hritz, & Royer, 2016).

Autobiographical Memory Another aspect of long-term memory that has been extensively studied in regard to children's development is autobiographical memory (Bauer, 2018; Bauer & others, 2017). *Autobiographical memory* involves memory of significant events and experiences in one's life. You are engaging in autobiographical memory when you answer questions such as these: Who was your first-grade teacher and what was s/he like? What is the most traumatic event that happened to you as a child?

During the preschool years, young children's memories increasingly take on more autobiographical characteristics (Bauer, 2018; Bauer & Larkina, 2016). In some areas, such as remembering a story, a movie, a song, or an interesting event or experience, young children have been shown to have reasonably good memories. From 3 to 5 years of age, they (1) increasingly remember events as occurring at a specific time and location, such as "on my birthday at Chuck E. Cheese's last year" and (2) include more elements that are rich in detail in their narratives (Bauer, 2013). In one study, children went from using 4 descriptive items per event at 3½ years of age to 12 such items at 6 years of age (Fivush & Haden, 1997).

Executive Function

Recently, increased interest has been directed toward the development of children's **executive function,** an umbrella-like concept that encompasses a number of higher-level cognitive processes linked to the development of the brain's prefrontal cortex (Knapp & Morton, 2017; Perone, Almy & Zelazo, 2017). Executive function involves managing one's thoughts to engage in goal-directed behavior and exercise self-control. Earlier in this chapter, we described the recent interest in *executive attention*, which comes under the umbrella of executive function.

In early childhood, executive function especially involves developmental advances in cognitive inhibition (such as inhibiting a strong tendency that is incorrect), cognitive flexibility (such as shifting attention to another item or topic), goal-setting (such as sharing a toy or mastering a skill like catching a ball), and delay of gratification (the ability to forego an immediate pleasure or reward for a more desirable one later) (McClelland & others, 2017; Muller & others, 2017). During early childhood, the relatively stimulus-driven toddler is transformed into a child capable of flexible, goal-directed problem solving that characterizes executive function (Zelazo & Muller, 2011).

Researchers have found that advances in executive function during the preschool years are linked with math skills, language development, and school readiness (Blair, 2017; Hoskyn, Iarocci, & Young, 2017; Liu & others, 2018; Muller & others, 2017). One study revealed that executive function skills predicted mathematical gains in kindergarten (Fuhs & others, 2014). Another study of young children also revealed that executive function was associated with emergent literacy and vocabulary development (Becker & others, 2014). And a recent study found that young children who showed delayed development of executive function had a lower level of school readiness (Willoughby & others, 2016).

Walter Mischel and his colleagues (Berman & others, 2013; Mischel, 2014; Mischel, Cantor, & Feldman, 1996; Mischel & Moore, 1980; Mischel & others, 2011; Schlam & others, 2013) have conducted a number of studies of delay of gratification with young children. One way they assess delay of gratification is to place a young child alone in a room with an alluring marshmallow that is within their reach. The children are told that they either can ring a bell at any time and eat the marshmallow or they can wait until the experimenter returns and then receive two marshmallows. For the young children who waited for the experimenter to return, what did they do to help them wait? They engaged in a number of strategies to distract their attention from the marshmallow, including singing songs, picking their noses—anything to keep from looking at the marshmallow. Mischel and his colleagues labeled these strategies "cool thoughts" (that is, doing non-marshmallow-related thoughts and activities), whereas they said the

executive function An umbrella-like concept that consists of a number of higher-level cognitive processes linked to the development of the brain's prefrontal cortex. Executive function involves managing one's thoughts to engage in goal-directed behavior and to use self-control.

young children who looked at the marshmallow were engaging in "hot thoughts." The young children who engaged in cool thoughts were more likely to eat the marshmallow later or wait until the experimenter returned to the room. In one study using the delay of gratification task just described, longer delay of gratification at 4 years of age was linked to a lower body mass index (BMI) three decades later (Schlam & others, 2013).

Researchers have found that advances in executive function in the preschool years are linked with math skills, language development, and school readiness (Blair & Razza, 2007). For example, a recent study found that young children who showed delayed development of executive function had a lower level of school readiness (Willoughby & others, 2016).

Parents and teachers play important roles in the development of executive function (Cheng & others, 2018; Duncan, McClelland, & Acock, 2017). Ann Masten and her colleagues (Labella & others, 2018; Masten, 2013; Masten & others, 2008; Monn & others, 2017) have found that executive function and parenting skills are linked to homeless children's success in school. Masten believes that executive function and good parenting skills are related. In her words, "When we see kids with good executive function, we often see adults around them that are good self-regulators. . . . Parents model, they support, and they scaffold these skills" (Masten, 2012, p. 11). For example, researchers have found that secure attachment to mothers during the toddler years was linked to a higher level of executive function at 5 to 6 years of age (Bernier & others, 2015).

Some developmental psychologists use their training in areas such as cognitive development to pursue careers in applied areas. To read about the work of Helen Hadani, an individual who followed this path, see the *Careers in Life-Span Development* profile.

How did Walter Mischel and his colleagues study young children's delay of gratification? In their research, what later developmental outcomes were linked to the preschoolers' ability to delay gratification?
©Amy Kiley Photography

Careers in life-span development

Helen Hadani, Developmental Psychologist, Toy Designer, and Associate Director of Research for the Center for Childhood Creativity

Helen Hadani obtained a Ph.D. from Stanford University in developmental psychology. As a graduate student at Stanford, she worked part-time for Hasbro Toys and Apple testing children's software and computer products for young children. Her first job after graduate school was with Zowie Intertainment, which was subsequently bought by LEGO. In her work as a toy designer there, Helen conducted experiments and focus groups at different stages of a toy's development and also studied the age-effectiveness of the toy. In Helen's words, "Even in a toy's most primitive stage of development . . . you see children's creativity in responding to challenges, their satisfaction when a problem is solved or simply their delight in having fun" (Schlegel, 2000, p. 50).

More recently, she began working with the Bay Area Discovery Museum's Center for Childhood Creativity (CCC) in Sausalito, California, an education-focused think tank that pioneers new research, thought-leadership, and teacher training programs that advance creative thinking in all children. Helen is currently the Associate Director of Research for the CCC.

Helen Hadani, a developmental psychologist, has worked as a toy designer and is currently directing research on creativity at a children's museum.
©Dr. Helen Hadani

The Child's Theory of Mind

Even young children are curious about the nature of the human mind (Birch & others, 2017; Devine & Hughes, 2018a, b). They have a **theory of mind,** a term that refers to awareness of one's own mental processes and those of others. Studies of theory of mind view the child as "a thinker who is trying to explain, predict, and understand people's thoughts, feelings, and utterances" (Harris, 2006). Children's theory of mind changes as they develop through childhood (Devine & Hughes, 2018a, b; Wellman, 2015). However, whether infants have a theory of mind continues to be questioned by some (Rakoczy, 2012). The consensus is that some changes occur quite early in development, as we see next (Scott & Baillargeon, 2017). The main changes occur at ages 2 to 3, 4 to 5, and beyond age 5.

theory of mind Refers to the awareness of one's own mental processes and the mental processes of others.

Ages 2 to 3 In this time frame, children begin to understand the following three mental states:

1. *Perceptions:* The child realizes that other people see what is in front of their eyes and not necessarily what is in front of the child's eyes.

2. *Emotions:* The child can distinguish between positive and negative emotions. A child might say, "Vic feels bad."

3. *Desires*: The child understands that if someone wants something, he or she will try to get it. A child might say, "I want my mommy."

Children refer to desires earlier and more frequently than they refer to cognitive states such as thinking and knowing (Harris, 2006). Two- to 3-year-olds understand the way desires are related to actions and to simple emotions (Harris, 2006). For example, they understand that people will search for what they want and that if they obtain it, they are likely to feel happy, but if they don't, they will keep searching for it and are likely to feel sad or angry.

Figure 9 Developmental Changes in False-Belief Performance
False-belief performance—the child's understanding that a person has a false belief that contradicts reality—dramatically increases from 2½ years of age through the middle of the elementary school years. In a summary of the results of many studies, 2½-year-olds gave incorrect responses about 80 percent of the time (Wellman, Cross, & Watson, 2001). At 3 years, 8 months, they were correct about 50 percent of the time, and after that, gave increasingly correct responses.

Ages 4 to 5 Children come to understand that the mind can represent objects and events accurately or inaccurately (Tompkins & others, 2017). The realization that people can have *false beliefs*—beliefs that are not true—develops in a majority of children by the time they are 5 years old (Wellman, Cross, & Watson, 2001) (see Figure 9).

In a classic false-belief task, children are told a story about Sally and Anne. In the story, Sally places a toy in a basket and then leaves the room. In her absence, Anne takes the toy from the basket and places it in a box. Children are asked where Sally will look for the toy when she returns. The major finding is that 3-year-olds tend to fail false-belief tasks, saying that Sally will look in the box (even though Sally could not know that the toy has been moved to this new location). Four-year-olds and older children tend to pass the task, correctly saying that Sally will have a "false belief"—she will think the object is in the basket, even though that belief is now false. The conclusion from these studies is that children younger than age 4 do not understand that it is possible to have a false belief.

Beyond Age 5 It is only beyond the preschool years that children have a deepening appreciation of the mind itself rather than just an understanding of mental states (Wellman, 2015). Not until middle and late childhood do children see the mind as an active constructor of knowledge or a processing center (Flavell, Green, & Flavell, 2000). It is only then that they move from understanding that beliefs can be false to realizing that the same event can be open to multiple interpretations (Carpendale & Chandler, 1996).

Individual Differences As in other developmental research, there are individual differences in the ages when children reach certain milestones in their theory of mind (Devine & Hughes, 2018a, b; Wellman, 2015). For example, children who talk with their parents about feelings frequently as 2-year-olds show better performance on theory of mind tasks (Ruffman, Slade, & Crowe, 2002), as do children who frequently engage in pretend play (Harris, 2000).

Executive function, which describes several functions discussed earlier in this chapter, such as planning and inhibition, that are important for flexible, future-oriented behavior, also is connected to theory of mind development (Lecce & others, 2018; Powell & Carey, 2017). Children who perform better at such executive function tasks show a better understanding of theory of mind (Benson & Sabbagh, 2017). For example, in one study of 3- to 5-year-old children, earlier development of executive function predicted theory of mind performance, especially on false belief tasks (Doenyas, Yavuz, & Selcuk, 2018). Language development also likely plays a prominent role in the increasingly reflective nature of theory of mind as children go through the early childhood and middle and late childhood years (Meins & others, 2013). Researchers have found that differences in children's language skills predict performance on theory of mind tasks (Devine & Hughes, 2018a, b). For example, in one study of 3- to 5-year-old children, earlier development of executive function predicted theory of mind performance, especially on false belief tasks (Doenyas, Yavuz, & Selcuk, 2018).

Among other factors that influence children's theory of mind development are advances in prefrontal cortex functioning (Powers, Chavez, & Heatherton, 2016), engaging in make-believe play (Kavanaugh, 2006), and various aspects of social interaction (Hughes, Devine, & Wang, 2017). Among the social interaction factors that advance children's theory of mind are being securely attached to parents who engage children in mental state talk ("That's a good thought you have" or "Can you tell what he's thinking?") (Laranjo & others, 2010), having older siblings and friends who engage in mental state talk (Hughes & others, 2010), and living in a higher-socioeconomic-status family (Devine & Hughes, 2018a). A recent study found that parental engagement in mind-mindedness (viewing children as mental agents by making mind-related comments to them) advanced preschool children's theory of mind (Hughes, Devine, & Wang, 2018). Also, research indicates that children with an advanced theory of mind are more popular with their peers and have better social skills in peer relations (Peterson & others, 2016; Slaughter & others, 2014).

Another individual difference in understanding the mind involves autism (Jones & others, 2018; Leung & others, 2016). Researchers have found that children with autism have difficulty developing a theory of mind, especially in understanding others' beliefs and emotions (Berenguer & others, 2018; Garon, Smith, & Bryson, 2018). Also, a recent study found that theory of mind predicted the severity of autism in children (Hoogenhout & Malcolm-Smith, 2017). Thus, it is not surprising that autistic children have difficulty in interactions with others.

Language Development

Toddlers move rather quickly from producing two-word utterances to creating three-, four-, and five-word combinations. Between ages 2 and 3, they begin the transition from saying simple sentences that express a single proposition to saying complex sentences.

As young children learn the special features of their own language, there are extensive regularities in how they acquire that particular language (Clark, 2017; Litz, Snyder, & Pater, 2017). For example, all children learn the prepositions *on* and *in* before other prepositions. Children learning other languages, such as Russian or Chinese, also acquire the particular features of those languages in a consistent order.

Understanding Phonology and Morphology

Phonology refers to the sound system of a language, including the sounds used and how they may be combined. During the preschool years, most children gradually become more sensitive to the sounds of spoken words

phonology The sound system of a language, including the sounds used and how they may be combined.

and increasingly capable of producing all the sounds of their language (Goad, 2017; Kelly & others, 2018). By their third birthday they can produce all the vowel sounds and most of the consonant sounds (Menn & Stoel-Gammon, 2009). They recognize the sounds before they can produce them, as in the noun "Merry-go-round."

By the time children move beyond two-word utterances, they demonstrate a knowledge of morphology rules (Snyder, 2017). **Morphology** refers to the units of meaning involved in word formation. Children begin using the plural and possessive forms of nouns (such as *dogs* and *dog's*). They put appropriate endings on verbs (such as *-s* when the subject is third-person singular and *-ed* for the past tense). They use prepositions (such as *in* and *on*), articles (such as *a* and *the*), and various forms of the verb *to be* (such as "I *was* going to the store"). Some of the best evidence for changes in children's use of morphological rules occurs in their overgeneralization of the rules, as when a preschool child says "foots" instead of "feet," or "goed" instead of "went."

In a classic experiment that was designed to study children's knowledge of morphological rules, such as how to make a plural, Jean Berko (1958) presented preschool and first-grade children with cards such as the one shown in Figure 10. The children were asked to look at the card while the experimenter read aloud the words on the card. Then the children were asked to supply the missing word. This might sound easy, but Berko was interested in the children's ability to apply the appropriate morphological rule—in this case, to say "wugs" with the *z* sound that indicates the plural.

Although the children's answers were not perfect, they were much better than chance. What makes Berko's study impressive is that most of the words were made up for the experiment. Thus, the children could not base their responses on remembering past instances of hearing the words. That they could make the plurals or past tenses of words they had never heard before was proof that they knew the morphological rules.

Changes in Syntax and Semantics

Preschool children also learn and apply rules of **syntax,** which involves the way words are combined to form acceptable phrases and sentences (Clark, 2017; Tieu & others, 2018). They show a growing mastery of complex rules for how words should be ordered. Consider *wh-* questions, such as "Where is Daddy going?" or "What is that boy doing?" To ask these questions properly, the child must know two important differences between *wh-* questions and affirmative statements (for instance, "Daddy is going to work" and "That boy is waiting for the school bus"). First, a *wh-* word must be added at the beginning of the sentence. Second, the auxiliary verb must be inverted—that is, exchanged with the subject of the sentence. Young children learn quite early where to put the *wh-* word, but they take much longer to learn the auxiliary-inversion rule. Thus, preschool children might ask, "Where Daddy is going?" and "What that boy is doing?"

Gains in **semantics,** the aspect of language that refers to the meaning of words and sentences, also characterize early childhood. Vocabulary development is dramatic (Thornton, 2017). Some experts have concluded that between 18 months and 6 years, young children learn an average of about one new word every waking hour (Gelman & Kalish, 2006)! By the time they enter first grade, it is estimated that children know about 14,000 words (Clark, 1993).

morphology Units of meaning involved in word formation.

syntax The ways words are combined to form acceptable phrases and sentences.

semantics The meaning of words and sentences.

This is a wug.

Now there is another one.
There are two of them.
There are two _____.

Figure 10 **Stimuli in Berko's Study of Young Children's Understanding of Morphological Rules.**
In Jean Berko's (1958) study, young children were presented with cards such as this one with a "wug" on it. Then the children were asked to supply the missing word; in supplying the missing word, they also had to say it correctly. "Wugs" is the correct response here.
Source: Gleason, Jean Berko, "The Child's Learning of English Morphology," *Word,* Vol. 14, 1958, p. 154. Copyright ©1958 by Jean Berko Gleason. All rights reserved. Used with permission.

How can children learn so many new words so quickly? One possible explanation is **fast mapping,** which involves children's ability to make an initial connection between a word and its referent after only limited exposure to the word (McGregor, 2017; van Hout, 2017). Researchers have found that exposure to words on multiple occasions over several days results in more successful word learning than the same number of exposures in a single day (Childers & Tomasello, 2002). Also, fast mapping brings a deeper understanding of word meaning, such as where the word can apply and its nuances.

What are some important aspects of how word learning optimally occurs? Following are six key principles in young children's vocabulary development (Harris, Golinkoff, & Hirsh-Pasek, 2011):

1. *Children learn the words they hear most often.* They learn the words they encounter when interacting with parents, teachers, siblings, and peers, and also from books. They especially benefit from encountering words that they do not know.

2. *Children learn words for things and events that interest them.* Parents and teachers can direct young children to experience words in contexts that interest the children; playful peer interactions are especially helpful in this regard.

3. *Children learn words best in responsive and interactive contexts rather than passive contexts.* Children who experience turn-taking opportunities, joint focusing experiences, and positive, sensitive socializing contexts with adults encounter the scaffolding necessary for optimal word learning. They learn words less effectively when they are passive learners.

4. *Children learn words best in contexts that are meaningful.* Young children learn new words more effectively when new words are encountered in integrated contexts rather than as isolated facts.

5. *Children learn words best when they access clear information about word meaning.* Children whose parents and teachers are sensitive to words the children might not understand and provide support and elaboration with hints about word meaning learn words better than children whose parents and teachers quickly state a new word and don't monitor whether the child understands its meaning.

6. *Children learn words best when grammar and vocabulary are considered.* Children who experience a large number of words and diversity in verbal stimulation develop a richer vocabulary and better understanding of grammar. In many cases, vocabulary and grammar development are connected.

Advances in Pragmatics

Changes in **pragmatics,** the appropriate use of language in different contexts, also characterize young children's language development (Fujiki & Brinton, 2017). A 6-year-old is simply a much better conversationalist than a 2-year-old. What are some of the improvements in pragmatics during the preschool years?

Young children begin to engage in extended discourse (Akhtar & Herold, 2008). For example, they learn culturally specific rules of conversation and politeness, and they become sensitive to the need to adapt their speech to different settings. Their developing linguistic skills and increasing ability to take the perspective of others contribute to their generation of more competent narratives.

As children grow older, they become increasingly able to talk about things that are not here (Grandma's house, for example) and not now (what happened to them yesterday or might happen tomorrow, for example). A preschool child can tell you what she wants for lunch tomorrow, something that would not have been possible at the two-word stage of language development.

Around age 4 or 5, children learn to change their speech style to suit the situation. For example, even 4-year-old children speak to a 2-year-old differently from the way they talk to a same-aged peer; they use shorter sentences with the 2-year-old. They also speak to an adult differently from a same-aged peer, using more polite and formal language with the adult (Shatz & Gelman, 1973).

fast mapping A process that helps to explain how young children learn the connection between a word and its referent so quickly.

pragmatics The appropriate use of language in different contexts.

Young Children's Literacy

Concern about U.S. children's ability to read and write has led to a careful examination of preschool and kindergarten children's experiences, with the hope that a positive orientation toward reading and writing can be developed early in life (Reutzel & Cooter, 2019; Temple & others, 2018). Parents and teachers need to provide young children with a supportive environment for the development of literacy skills (Meyer, 2017). Children should be active participants in a wide range of interesting listening, talking, writing, and reading experiences (Tompkins, 2017, 2019).

Instruction should be built on what children already know about oral language, reading, and writing. Further, early precursors of literacy and academic success include language skills, phonological and syntactic knowledge, letter identification, and enjoyment of books (Temple & others, 2018).

What are some strategies for using books effectively with preschool children? Ellen Galinsky (2010) offers the following recommendations:

- *Use books to initiate conversation with young children.* Ask them to put themselves in the book characters' places and imagine what they might be thinking or feeling.

- *Use what and why questions.* Ask young children to tell you what they think is going to happen next in a story and then to see if it occurs.

- *Encourage children to ask questions about stories.*

- *Choose some books that play with language.* Creative books on the alphabet, including those with rhymes, often interest young children.

Early Childhood Education

How do early education programs treat children, and how do the children fare? Our exploration of early childhood education focuses on variations in programs, education for children who are disadvantaged, and some controversies in early childhood education.

Variations in Early Childhood Education

There are many variations in the way young children are educated (Bredekamp, 2017; Gestwicki, 2017). The foundation of early childhood education is the child-centered kindergarten.

The Child-Centered Kindergarten

Nurturing is a key aspect of the **child-centered kindergarten,** which emphasizes educating the whole child and promoting his or her physical, cognitive, and socioemotional development (Morrison, 2017, 2018). Instruction is organized around the child's needs, interests, and learning styles. Emphasis is on the process of learning, rather than what is learned (Feeney, Moravcik, & Nolte, 2019). The child-centered kindergarten honors three principles: (1) each child follows a unique developmental pattern; (2) young children learn best through firsthand experiences with people and materials; and (3) play is extremely important in the child's total development. *Experimenting, exploring, discovering, trying out, restructuring, speaking,* and *listening* are frequent activities in excellent kindergarten programs. Such programs are closely attuned to the developmental status of 4- and 5-year-old children.

The Montessori Approach

Montessori schools are patterned on the educational philosophy of Maria Montessori (1870–1952), an Italian physician-turned-educator who at the beginning of the twentieth century crafted a revolutionary approach to

child-centered kindergarten Education that involves the whole child by considering both the child's physical, cognitive, and socioemotional development and the child's needs, interests, and learning styles.

young children's education. The **Montessori approach** is a philosophy of education in which children are given considerable freedom and spontaneity in choosing activities. They are allowed to move from one activity to another as they desire, and the teacher acts as a facilitator rather than a director. The teacher shows the child how to perform intellectual activities, demonstrates interesting ways to explore curriculum materials, and offers help when the child requests it (Bahmaee, Saadatmand, & Yarmohammadian, 2016; Taylor, 2017). "By encouraging children to make decisions from an early age, Montessori programs seek to develop self-regulated problem solvers who can make choices and manage their time effectively" (Hyson, Copple, & Jones, 2006, p. 14). The number of Montessori schools in the United States has expanded dramatically in recent years, from one school in 1959 to 355 schools in 1970 and more than 4,000 today.

Some developmental psychologists favor the Montessori approach, but others believe that it neglects children's socioemotional development. For example, although the Montessori approach fosters independence and the development of cognitive skills, it deemphasizes verbal interaction between the teacher and child and between peers. Montessori's critics also argue that it restricts imaginative play and that its heavy reliance on self-corrective materials may not adequately allow for creativity and for a variety of learning styles.

Larry Page and Sergey Brin, founders of the highly successful Internet search engine, Google, said that their early years at Montessori schools were a major factor in their success (International Montessori Council, 2006). During an interview with Barbara Walters, they said they learned how to be self-directed and self-starters at Montessori (ABC News, 2005). They commented that their Montessori experiences encouraged them to think for themselves and allowed them the freedom to develop their own interests.
©James Leynse/Corbis Images/Getty Images

Developmentally Appropriate Education

Many educators and psychologists conclude that preschool and young elementary school children learn best through active, hands-on teaching methods such as games and dramatic play. They believe that schools need to accommodate individual differences in children's development. They also argue that schools should focus on promoting children's socioemotional development as well as their cognitive development. Educators refer to this type of schooling as **developmentally appropriate practice (DAP),** which is based on knowledge of the typical development of children within a particular age span (age-appropriateness), as well as on the uniqueness of the individual child (individual-appropriateness). DAP emphasizes the importance of creating settings that encourage children to be active learners and reflect children's interests and capabilities (Beaver, Wyatt, & Jackman, 2018; Bredekamp, 2017; Morrison, 2017, 2018). Desired outcomes for DAP include thinking critically, working cooperatively, solving problems, developing self-regulatory skills, and enjoying learning. The emphasis in DAP is on the process of learning rather than on its content.

Do developmentally appropriate educational practices improve young children's development? Some researchers have found that young children in developmentally appropriate classrooms are likely to feel less stress, be more motivated, be more socially skilled, have better work habits, be more creative, have better language skills, and demonstrate better math skills than children in developmentally inappropriate classrooms (Hart & others, 2003). However, not all studies find DAP to have significant positive effects (Hyson, Copple, & Jones, 2006). Among the reasons that it is difficult to generalize about research on developmentally appropriate education is

How Would You...?

As an **educator,** how would you design a developmentally appropriate lesson to teach kindergartners the concept of gravity?

Montessori approach An educational philosophy in which children are given considerable freedom and spontaneity in choosing activities and are allowed to move from one activity to another as they desire.

developmentally appropriate practice (DAP) Education that focuses on the typical developmental patterns of children (age appropriateness) and the uniqueness of each child (individual appropriateness).

that individual programs often vary, and developmentally appropriate education is an evolving concept. Recent changes in the concept have given more attention to socio-cultural factors and the teacher's active involvement and implementation of systematic intentions, as well as how strongly academic skills should be emphasized and how they should be taught.

Education for Young Children Who Are Disadvantaged

For many years, U.S. children from low-income families did not receive any education before they entered the first grade. Often when they began first grade they were already several steps behind their classmates in readiness to learn. In the summer of 1965, the federal government began striving to break the cycle of poverty and poor education for young children through **Project Head Start,** a compensatory program designed to give children from low-income families the opportunity to acquire skills and experiences that are important for success in school (Hustedt, Friedman, & Barnett, 2012; Miller, Farkas, & Duncan, 2016; Paschall & Mastergeorge, 2018). More than half a century after the program's inception, Head Start continues to be the largest federally funded program for U.S. children, with almost 1 million children enrolled in it annually (Hagen & Lamb-Parker, 2008). In 2007, 3 percent of Head Start children were 5 years old, 51 percent were 4 years old, 36 percent were 3 years old, and 10 percent were under age 3 (Administration for Children & Families, 2008).

Mixed results have been found for Head Start. A recent study found that one year of Head Start was linked to higher performance in early math, early reading, and receptive vocabulary (Miller, Farkas, & Duncan, 2016). In another study, the best results occurred for Head Start children who had low initial cognitive ability, whose parents had low levels of education, and who attended Head Start more than 20 hours a week (Lee & others, 2014). It is not unusual to find early gains, then see them go away in elementary school. For example, a national evaluation of Head Start revealed that the program had a positive influence on the language and cognitive development of 3- and 4-year-olds (Puma & others, 2010). However, by the end of the first grade, there were few lasting outcomes.

How Would You...?

As a **health-care professional,** how would you explain the importance of including health services as part of an effective Head Start program?

Often the best Head Start results occur when parents make positive contributions to their young children's development (Alarcon, 2017). For example, two recent studies found that improved parenting engagement and skills were linked to the success of children in Head Start programs (Ansari & Gershoff, 2016; Roggman & others, 2016).

Also, one-fourth of Head Start children have mothers who also participated in Head Start. In a multigenerational study, a positive influence on cognitive and socioemotional development (assessed in the third grade) occurred for Head Start children whose mothers had also attended Head Start programs (when compared with Head Start children whose mothers were not in Head Start) (Chor, 2018). This result likely occurred because of improved family resources and home learning environments.

Early Head Start was established in 1995 to serve children from birth to 3 years of age (Burgette & others, 2017). In 2007, half of all new funds appropriated for Head Start programs were used for the expansion of Early Head Start. One study revealed that Early Head Start had a protective effect on risks young children might experience in parenting stress, language development, and self-control (Ayoub, Vallotton, & Mastergeorge, 2011). However, some studies have revealed mixed effects for Early Head Start (Love & others, 2013).

More attention needs to be given to developing consistently high-quality Head Start programs (Faria & others, 2017). One person who is strongly motivated to make Head Start a valuable learning experience for young children from disadvantaged backgrounds is Yolanda Garcia. To read about her work, see *Careers in Life-Span Development.*

Project Head Start A government-funded program that is designed to provide children from low-income families the opportunity to acquire the skills and experiences important for school success.

Yolanda Garcia, Director of Children's Services, Head Start

Yolanda Garcia was the director of the Children's Services Department of the Santa Clara, California, County Office of Education for several decades. As director, she was responsible for managing child development programs for 2,500 3- to 5-year-old children in 127 classrooms. Recently, she became the Director of WestEd's E3 Institute, which focuses on excellence in early childhood education in Santa Clara County.

Her training includes two master's degrees: one in public policy and child welfare from the University of Chicago and another in education administration from San Jose State University.

Garcia has served on many national advisory committees that have produced improvements in the staffing of Head Start programs. Most notably, she served on the Head Start Quality Committee that recommended the development of Early Head Start and revised performance standards for Head Start programs. Garcia currently is a member of the American Academy of Science Committee on the Integration of Science and Early Childhood Education.

Yolanda Garcia, Director of WestEd's E3 Institute, works with a child.
©Yolanda Garcia

One high-quality early childhood education program (although not a Head Start program) is the Perry Preschool program in Ypsilanti, Michigan, a two-year preschool program that includes weekly home visits from program personnel. In analyses of the long-term effects of the program, adults who had been in the Perry Preschool program were compared with a control group of adults from the same background who had not received the enriched early childhood education (Schweinhart & others, 2005; Weikert, 1993). Those who had been in the Perry Preschool program had fewer teen pregnancies and better high school graduation rates, and at age 40 they were more likely to be in the workforce, to own a home, to have a savings account, and to have had fewer arrests.

Controversies in Early Childhood Education

Two current controversies in early childhood education involve (1) what the curriculum for early childhood education should be (Morrison, 2017, 2018) and (2) whether preschool education should be universal in the United States (Zigler, Gilliam, & Barnett, 2011).

Controversy Over Curriculum

A current controversy in early childhood education involves what the curriculum for early childhood education should be (Bredekamp, 2017; Follari, 2019). On one side are those who advocate a child-centered, constructivist approach much like that emphasized by the National Association for the Education of Young Children (NAEYC), along the lines of developmentally appropriate practice. On the other side are those who advocate an academic, direct-instruction approach.

In practice, many high-quality early-childhood education programs include both academic and constructivist approaches. Many education experts, such as Lilian Katz (1999), though, worry about academic approaches that place too much pressure on young children to achieve and don't provide opportunities to actively construct knowledge. Competent early childhood programs also should focus on both cognitive

Stars of the future

What is the curriculum controversy in early childhood education?
©Ronnie Kaufman/ Corbis/Getty Images

development *and* socioemotional development, not exclusively on cognitive development (Feeney, Moravcik, & Nolte, 2019; Follari, 2019).

Universal Preschool Education

Another controversy in early childhood education focuses on whether preschool education should be instituted for all U.S. 4-year-old children. Publicly funded preschool programs now are present in 42 states and the District of Columbia (National Institute for Early Education Research, 2016).

Edward Zigler and his colleagues (2006, 2011) argue that the United States should have universal preschool education. They emphasize that quality preschools prepare children for later academic success. Zigler and his colleagues (2006) cite research showing that quality preschool programs decrease the likelihood that children will be retained in a grade or drop out before graduating from high school. They also point to analyses indicating that universal preschool would bring cost savings on the order of billions of dollars because of a diminished need for remedial and justice services (Karoly & Bigelow, 2005).

Critics of universal preschool education argue that the gains attributed to preschool and kindergarten education are often overstated. They especially stress that research has not proven that nondisadvantaged children benefit from attending a preschool. Thus, the critics say it is more important to improve preschool education for young children who are disadvantaged than to fund preschool education for all 4-year-old children. Some critics, especially homeschooling advocates, emphasize that young children should be educated by their parents, not by schools. Thus, universal preschool education remains a subject of controversy.

How Would You…?
As a **psychologist,** how would you advise preschool teachers to balance the development of young children's skills for academic achievement with opportunities for healthy social interaction?

Summary

Physical Changes
- The average child grows 2½ inches in height and gains between 5 and 7 pounds a year during early childhood, although growth patterns vary from one child to another.
- Some of the brain's growth in early childhood is due to increases in the number and size of dendrites, some to myelination. From ages 3 to 6, the most rapid growth in the brain occurs in the frontal lobes.
- Gross and fine motor skills improve dramatically during early childhood.
- Too many young children in the United States are being raised on diets that are too high in fat. Other nutritional concerns include malnutrition in early childhood and the inadequate diets of many children living in poverty. The child's life should be centered on activities, not meals. Regular exercise should be a part of young children's lives.

- Accidents are the leading cause of death in young children. A special concern is the poor health status of many young children in low-income families. There has been a dramatic increase in HIV/AIDS in young children in developing countries in recent decades.

Cognitive Changes
- According to Piaget, in the preoperational stage children cannot yet perform operations, but they begin to represent the world with symbols, to form stable concepts, and to reason. Preoperational thought is characterized by two substages: symbolic function (2 to 4 years) and intuitive thought (4 to 7 years). Centration and a lack of conservation also characterize the preoperational stage.
- Vygotsky's theory represents a social constructivist approach to development. Vygotsky argues that it is

important to discover the child's zone of proximal development to improve the child's learning.

- Young children make substantial strides in executive and sustained attention. Significant improvement in short-term memory occurs during early childhood. Advances in executive function, an umbrella-like concept that consists of a number of higher-level cognitive processes linked to the development of the prefrontal cortex, occur in early childhood. Theory of mind is the awareness of one's own mental processes and the mental processes of others. Children begin to understand mental states involving perceptions, emotions, and desires at 2 to 3 years of age and at 4 to 5 years of age realize that people can have false beliefs.

Language Development

- Young children increase their grasp of language's rule systems. In terms of phonology, children become more sensitive to the sounds of spoken language. Berko's classic study demonstrated that young children understand morphological rules.
- Preschool children learn and apply rules of syntax, which involves how words should be ordered. In terms of semantics, vocabulary development increases dramatically in early childhood.
- Young children's conversational skills improve in early childhood.
- Early precursors of literacy and academic success develop in early childhood.

Early Childhood Education

- The child-centered kindergarten emphasizes the education of the whole child. The Montessori approach has become increasingly popular. Developmentally appropriate practice focuses on the typical patterns of children (age appropriateness) and the uniqueness of each child (individual appropriateness).
- The U.S. government has tried to break the poverty cycle with programs such as Head Start. Model programs have had positive effects on young children's education.
- Controversy over early childhood education involves what the curriculum should be and whether universal preschool education should be implemented.

Key Terms

animism	executive attention	operations	social constructivist approach
centration	executive function	phonology	sustained attention
child-centered kindergarten	fast mapping	pragmatics	symbolic function substage
conservation	intuitive thought substage	preoperational stage	syntax
developmentally appropriate practice (DAP)	Montessori approach	Project Head Start	theory of mind
egocentrism	morphology	semantics	zone of proximal development (ZPD)
	myelination	short-term memory	

©Rawpixel/Getty Images

6 Socioemotional Development in Early Childhood

CHAPTER OUTLINE

EMOTIONAL AND PERSONALITY DEVELOPMENT

The Self
Emotional Development
Moral Development
Gender

FAMILIES

Parenting
Child Maltreatment
Sibling Relationships and Birth Order
The Changing Family in a Changing Society

PEER RELATIONS, PLAY, AND MEDIA/SCREEN TIME

Peer Relations
Play
Media and Screen Time

Stories of Life-Span Development: Nurturing Socioemotional Development

Like many children, Sarah Newland loves animals. During a trip to the zoo when she was 4 years old, Sarah learned about an animal that was a member of an endangered species, and she became motivated to help. With her mother's guidance, she baked lots of cakes and cookies, then sold them on the sidewalk outside her home. She was excited about making $35 from the cake and cookie sales, and she mailed the money to the World Wildlife Fund. Several weeks later, the fund wrote back to Sarah requesting more money. Sarah was devastated because she thought she had taken care of the animal problem. Her mother consoled her and told her that the endangered animal problem and many others are so big that it takes ongoing help from many people to solve them. Her mother's guidance when Sarah was a young child must have worked because by the end of elementary school, Sarah had begun helping out at a child-care center and working with her mother to provide meals to the homeless.

Sensitive parents like Sarah's mother can encourage young children's sense of morality. Just as parents support and guide their children to become good readers, musicians, or athletes, they also play key roles in promoting young children's socioemotional development. (*Source:* Kantrowitz & Namuth, 1991). ∎

Emotional and Personality Development

Many changes characterize young children's socioemotional development in early childhood. Children's developing minds and social experiences produce remarkable advances in the development of the self, emotional maturity, moral understanding, and gender awareness.

The Self

During the second year of life, children make considerable progress in self-recognition. In the early childhood years, young children develop in many ways that enable them to enhance their self-understanding.

Initiative Versus Guilt

Erik Erikson's (1968) eight developmental stages are encountered during certain time periods in the human life span. Erikson's first stage, trust versus mistrust, describes what he regarded as the main developmental task of infancy. According to Erikson, the psychosocial stage associated with early childhood is *initiative versus guilt*. At this point in development, children have become convinced that they are persons of their own; during early childhood, they begin to discover what kind of person they will become. They identify intensely with their parents, who most of the time appear to them to be powerful and beautiful, though often unreasonable, disagreeable, and sometimes even dangerous. During early childhood, children use their perceptual, motor, cognitive, and language skills to make things happen. They have a surplus of energy that permits them to forget failures quickly and to approach new areas that seem desirable—even if dangerous—with undiminished zest and an increased sense of direction. On their own initiative, then, children at this stage exuberantly move out into a wider social world.

The great governor of initiative is conscience. Children's initiative and enthusiasm may bring them not only rewards but also guilt, which lowers self-esteem.

Self-Understanding and Understanding Others

Research studies have revealed that young children are more psychologically aware—of themselves and others—than was formerly thought (Thompson, 2015). This increased awareness reflects young children's expanding psychological sophistication.

Self-Understanding In Erikson's portrait of early childhood, the young child clearly has begun to develop **self-understanding,** which is the representation of self, the substance and content of self-conceptions (Harter, 2012, 2016). Though not the whole of personal identity, self-understanding provides its rational underpinnings. Mainly through interviews, researchers have probed children's conceptions of many aspects of self-understanding (Harter, 2016).

Early self-understanding involves self-recognition. In early childhood, young children think the self can be described by material characteristics such as size, shape, and color. They distinguish themselves from others through physical and material attributes. Says 4-year-old Sandra, "I'm different from Jennifer because I have brown hair and she has blond hair." Says 4-year-old Ralph, "I am different from Hank because I am taller, and I am different from my sister because I have a bicycle." Physical activities are also a central component of the self in

What characterizes young children's self-understanding?
©Craig G. Bates/Getty Images

self-understanding The child's cognitive representation of self, the substance and content of the child's self-conceptions.

early childhood (Keller, Ford, & Meacham, 1978). For example, preschool children often describe themselves in terms of activities such as play. In sum, in early childhood, children often provide self-descriptions that involve body attributes, material possessions, and physical activities.

Although young children mainly describe themselves in terms of concrete, observable features and activities, at age 4 to 5, as they hear others use psychological trait and emotion terms, they begin to include these in their self-descriptions (Marsh, Ellis, & Craven, 2002). Thus, in a self-description a 4-year-old might say, "I'm not scared. I'm always happy."

Young children's self-descriptions are typically unrealistically positive, as reflected in the comment of the 4-year-old who says he is always happy, which he is not (Harter, 2012, 2016). They express this optimism because they don't yet distinguish between their desired competence and their actual competence, tend to confuse ability and effort (thinking that differences in ability can be changed as easily as can differences in effort), don't engage in spontaneous social comparison of their abilities with those of others, and tend to compare their present abilities with what they could do at an earlier age (which usually makes them look quite good).

Young children are more psychologically aware of themselves and others than used to be thought. Some children are better than others at understanding people's feelings and desires—and, to some degree, these individual differences are influenced by conversations caregivers have with young children about feelings and desires.
©Don Hammond/Design Pics

Understanding Others Children also make advances in their understanding of others (Danovitch & Mills, 2018; Harter, 2016; Landrum, Pflaum, & Mills, 2016; Ma & others, 2018). Young children's theory of mind includes understanding that other people have emotions and desires (Devine & Hughes, 2018a, b). And at age 4 to 5 children not only start describing themselves in terms of psychological traits but also begin to perceive others in terms of psychological traits. Thus, a 4-year-old might say, "My teacher is nice."

An important part of children's socioemotional development is gaining an understanding that people don't always give accurate reports of their beliefs (Mills & Elashi, 2014). Researchers have found that even 4-year-olds understand that people may make statements that aren't true to obtain what they want or to avoid trouble (Lee & others, 2002). Another important aspect of understanding others involves understanding joint commitments. As children approach their third birthday, their collaborative interactions with others increasingly involve obligations to the partner (Tomasello, 2014).

Young children also learn extensively through observing others' behavior. For example, a recent study found that young children who observed a peer being rewarded for confessing to cheating on a task were more likely to be more honest in the future themselves (Ma & others, 2018).

Both the extensive theory of mind research and the recent research on young children's social understanding underscore that young children are not as egocentric as Piaget envisioned (Birch & others, 2017; Devine & Hughes, 2018a, b). Piaget's concept of egocentrism has become so ingrained in people's thinking about young children that too often the current research on social awareness in infancy and early childhood has been overlooked. Research increasingly shows that young children are more socially sensitive and perceptive than previously envisioned, suggesting that parents and teachers can help them to better understand and interact in the social world by how they interact with them (Thompson, 2015). If young children are seeking to better understand various mental and emotional states (intentions, goals, feelings, desires) that they know underlie people's actions, then talking with them about these internal states can improve young children's understanding of them (Thompson, 2015).

However, there is ongoing debate about whether young children are socially sensitive or basically egocentric (Birch & others, 2017). Ross Thompson (2012, 2015) comes down on the side of viewing young children as socially sensitive, while Susan Harter (2012, 2016) argues that there is still evidence to support the conclusion that young children are essentially egocentric.

Emotional Development

The young child's growing awareness of self is linked to the ability to feel an expanding range of emotions. Young children, like adults, experience many emotions during the course of a day. Their emotional development allows them to try to make sense of other people's emotional reactions and to begin to control their own emotions (Blair, 2017; Morris & others, 2018; Rogers & others, 2016).

Expressing Emotions

Recall that even young infants experience emotions such as joy and fear, but to experience *self-conscious emotions* children must be able to refer to themselves and be aware of themselves as distinct from others (Lewis, 2010, 2014, 2015, 2016). Pride, shame, embarrassment, and guilt are examples of self-conscious emotions. These emotions do not appear to develop until self-awareness appears around 18 months of age. In a recent study, the broad capacity for self-evaluative emotion was present in the preschool years and was linked to young children's empathetic concern (Ross, 2017). In this study, young children's moral pride, pride in response to achievement, and resilience to shame were linked to a greater tendency to engage in spontaneous helping.

During the early childhood years, emotions such as pride and guilt become more common. They are especially influenced by parents' responses to children's behavior. For example, a young child may experience shame when a parent says, "You should feel bad about biting your sister." One study revealed that young children's emotional expression was linked to their parents' own expressive behavior (Nelson & others, 2012). In this study, mothers who expressed a high incidence of positive emotions and a low incidence of negative emotions at home had children who were observed to use more positive emotion words during mother-child interactions than did the children of mothers who expressed few positive emotions at home.

Understanding Emotions

Among the most important changes in emotional development in early childhood is an increased understanding of emotions (Calkins & Perry, 2016; Kuhnert & others, 2017; Perry & Calkins, 2018). Young children increasingly understand that certain situations are likely to evoke particular emotions, facial expressions indicate specific emotions, and emotions affect behavior and can be used to influence others. One study found that young children's emotional understanding was linked to an increase in prosocial behavior (Ensor, Spencer, & Hughes, 2011). Also, in a study of 5- to 7-year-olds, understanding others' emotions was related to the children's emotion regulation (Hudson & Jacques, 2014).

Between ages 2 and 4, children considerably increase the number of terms they use to describe emotions. During this time, they are also learning about the causes and consequences of feelings (Denham & others, 2012).

When they are 4 to 5 years old, children show an increased ability to reflect on emotions. They also begin to understand that the same event can elicit different feelings in different people. Moreover, they show growing awareness that they need to manage their emotions to meet social standards. And by age 5 most children can accurately identify emotions that are produced by challenging circumstances and describe strategies they might call on to cope with everyday stress (Cole & others, 2009).

Regulating Emotions

Emotion regulation is an important aspect of development. In particular, it plays a key role in children's ability to manage the demands and conflicts they face in interacting with others (Blair, 2017).

Many researchers consider the growth of emotion regulation in children as fundamental to the development of social competence (Cole, Lougheed, & Ram, 2018; Cole & Hollenstein, 2018; Perry & Calkins, 2018). Emotion regulation can be conceptualized as an important component of self-regulation or of executive function. Recall that executive function is increasingly thought to be a key concept in describing the young child's higher-level cognitive functioning (Cheng & others, 2018; Liu & others, 2018; Muller & others, 2017; Schmitt & others, 2017). Cybelle Raver and her colleagues (Blair, 2017; Blair & Raver, 2012, 2015; Blair, Raver, & Finegood, 2016; Raver & others, 2011, 2012, 2013) are using interventions, such as increasing caregiver emotional expressiveness, to improve young children's emotion regulation and reduce behavior problems in Head Start families.

What are some differences between emotion-coaching and emotion-dismissing parents?
©Jamie Grill/Getty Images

Emotion-Coaching and Emotion-Dismissing Parents Parents can play an important role in helping young children regulate their emotions (Bendezu & others, 2018; Norona & Baker, 2017; Quinones-Camacho & Davis, 2018). Depending on how they talk with their children about emotion, parents can be described as taking an *emotion-coaching* or an *emotion-dismissing* approach (Gottman, 2018). The distinction between these approaches is most evident in the way the parent deals with the child's negative emotions (anger, frustration, sadness, and so on). *Emotion-coaching parents* monitor their children's emotions, view their children's negative emotions as opportunities for teaching, assist them in labeling emotions, and coach them in how to deal effectively with emotions. In contrast, *emotion-dismissing parents* view their role as to deny, ignore, or change negative emotions. Emotion-coaching parents interact with their children in a less rejecting manner, use more scaffolding and praise, and are more nurturant than are emotion-dismissing parents. Moreover, children of emotion-coaching parents are better at soothing themselves when they get upset, are more effective in regulating their negative affect, focus their attention better, and have fewer behavior problems than do children of emotion-dismissing parents. Researchers have found that fathers' emotion coaching is related to children's social competence (Baker, Fenning, & Crnic, 2011) and that mothers' emotion coaching is linked to less oppositional behavior (Dunsmore, Booker, & Ollendick, 2013).

Parents' knowledge of their children's emotional world can help them to guide their children's emotional development and teach them how to cope effectively with problems (Bendezu & others, 2018; Hurrell, Houwing, & Hudson, 2017). For example, one study found that mothers' knowledge about what distresses and comforts their children predicts the children's coping, empathy, and prosocial behavior (Vinik, Almas, & Grusec, 2011).

Regulation of Emotion and Peer Relations Emotions play a strong role in determining the success of a child's peer relationships (Smetana & Ball, 2018). Specifically, the ability to modulate one's emotions is an important skill that benefits children in their relationships with peers. Moody and emotionally negative children are more likely to experience rejection by peers, whereas emotionally positive children are more popular. For example, a recent study found that young children who were more skilled in emotion regulation were more popular with their peers (Nakamichi, 2018).

Moral Development

Unlike a crying infant, a screaming 5-year-old is likely to be considered responsible for making a fuss. The parents may worry about whether the 5-year-old is a "bad" child. Although there are some who view children as innately good, many developmental psychologists believe that just as parents help their children become good readers, musicians, or athletes, parents must nurture goodness and help their children develop morally.

moral development Development that involves thoughts, feelings, and actions regarding rules and conventions about what people should do in their interactions with other people.

heteronomous morality The first stage of moral development in Piaget's theory, occurring from approximately 4 to 7 years of age. Justice and rules are conceived of as unchangeable properties of the world, beyond the control of people.

autonomous morality The second stage of moral development in Piaget's theory, displayed by older children (about 10 years of age and older). The child becomes aware that rules and laws are created by people and that in judging an action, one should consider the actor's intentions as well as the consequences.

Moral development involves the development of thoughts, feelings, and behaviors regarding rules and conventions about what people should do in their interactions with other people. Major developmental theories have focused on different aspects of moral development (Gray & Graham, 2018; Hoover & others, 2018; Killen & Dahl, 2018; Narváez, 2017a, b, 2018; Turiel & Gingo, 2017).

Moral Feelings

Feelings of anxiety and guilt are central to the account of moral development provided by Freud's psychoanalytic theory. According to Freud, children attempt to reduce anxiety, avoid punishment, and maintain parental affection by identifying with their parents and internalizing their standards of right and wrong, thereby developing the *superego,* the moral element of the personality.

Freud's ideas are not backed by research, but guilt certainly can motivate moral behavior. Other emotions, however, also contribute to moral development, including positive feelings. One important example is *empathy,* or responding to another person's feelings with an emotion that echoes those feelings (Kim & Kochanska, 2017).

Infants have the capacity for some purely empathic responses, but empathy often requires the ability to discern another person's emotional states, or what is called *perspective taking.* Learning how to identify a wide range of emotional states in others, and to anticipate what kinds of action will improve another person's emotional state, help to advance children's moral development (Thompson, 2015).

Also, connections between emotions can occur and the connections may influence children's development. For example, in a recent study, participants' guilt proneness combined with their empathy predicted an increase in prosocial behavior (Torstveit, Sutterlin, & Lugo, 2016).

Moral Reasoning

Interest in how children think about moral issues was stimulated by Piaget (1932), who extensively observed and interviewed children from ages 4 through 12. Piaget watched children play marbles to learn how they used and thought about the game's rules. He also asked children about ethical issues—theft, lies, punishment, and justice, for example. He concluded that children go through two distinct stages in how they think about morality:

- From ages 4 to 7, children display **heteronomous morality,** the first stage of moral development in Piaget's theory. Children think of justice and rules as unchangeable properties, beyond the control of people.

- From ages 7 to 10, children are in a period of transition, showing some features of the first stage of moral reasoning and some of the second stage, autonomous morality.

- From about age 10 and older, children show **autonomous morality.** They become aware that rules and laws are created by people, and in judging an action they consider the actor's intentions as well as the action's consequences.

Piaget extensively observed and interviewed 4- to 12-year-old children as they played games to learn how they used and thought about the games' rules.
©Yves De Braine/BlackStar/StockPhoto

How Would You...?

As a **health-care professional,** how would you expect a child in the heteronomous stage of moral development to judge the behaviors of a doctor who unintentionally caused pain to a child during a medical procedure?

Because young children are heteronomous moralists, they judge the rightness or goodness of behavior by considering its consequences, not the intentions of the actor. For example, to the heteronomous moralist, breaking twelve cups accidentally is worse than breaking one cup intentionally. As children develop into moral autonomists, intentions become more important than consequences.

How will this child's moral thinking about stealing a cookie differ according to whether he is in Piaget's heteronomous or autonomous stage?
©Fuse/Getty Images

The heteronomous thinker also believes that rules are unchangeable and are handed down by all-powerful authorities. When Piaget suggested to young children that they use new rules in a game of marbles, they resisted. By contrast, older children—moral autonomists—accept change and recognize that rules are merely conventions that are subject to change.

The heteronomous thinker also believes in **immanent justice,** the concept that if a rule is broken, punishment will be meted out immediately. The young child believes that a violation is followed automatically by its punishment. Thus, young children often look around worriedly after doing something wrong, expecting the inevitable punishment. Immanent justice also implies that if something unfortunate happens to someone, that person must have transgressed earlier. Older children, who are moral autonomists, recognize that punishment occurs only if someone witnesses the wrongdoing and that, even then, punishment is not inevitable.

How do these changes in moral reasoning occur? Piaget argued that as children develop, they become more sophisticated in their thinking about social matters, especially about the possibilities and conditions of cooperation. Piaget stressed that this social understanding comes about through the mutual give-and-take of peer relations. In the peer group, where others have power and status similar to the child's, plans are negotiated and coordinated, and disagreements are reasoned about and eventually settled. Parent-child relations, in which parents have power and children do not, are less likely to advance moral reasoning, because rules are often handed down in an authoritarian manner.

Moral Behavior

The behavioral and social cognitive approach to development focuses on moral behavior rather than moral reasoning. It holds that the processes of reinforcement, punishment, and imitation explain the development of moral behavior. When children are rewarded for behavior that is consistent with laws and social conventions, they are likely to repeat that behavior. When models who behave morally are provided, children are likely to adopt their actions (Ma & others, 2018). And when children are punished for immoral behavior, those behaviors are likely to be reduced or eliminated. However, because punishment may have adverse side effects, it needs to be used judiciously and cautiously.

If a mother has rewarded a 4-year-old boy for telling the truth when he broke a glass at home, does this mean he is likely to tell the truth to his preschool teacher when he knocks over a vase and breaks it? Not necessarily, because the situation influences behavior. More than half a century ago, a comprehensive study of thousands of children in many situations—at home, at school, and at church, for example—found that a totally honest child is virtually nonexistent, as is a child who cheats in all situations (Hartshorne & May, 1928–1930). Behavioral and social cognitive researchers emphasize that what children do in one situation is often only weakly related to what they do in other situations. For example, a child might cheat in class but not in a game, or a child might steal a piece of candy when alone but not when others are present.

Social cognitive theorists also emphasize that the ability to resist temptation is closely tied to the development of self-control (Mischel, 2004), which involves learning to delay gratification. According to social cognitive theorists, cognitive factors are important in the child's development of self-control (Bandura, 2012).

Gender

Gender refers to the characteristics of people as females and males. **Gender identity** is the sense of being male or female, which most children acquire by the time they are 3 years old. **Gender roles** are sets of expectations that prescribe how females or males should think, act, and feel.

immanent justice The expectation that, if a rule is broken, punishment will be meted out immediately.

gender identity The sense of being male or female, which most children acquire by the time they are 3 years old.

gender roles Sets of expectations that prescribe how females or males should think, act, and feel.

During the preschool years, most children increasingly act in ways that match their culture's gender roles.

How do these and other gender differences come about? Biology clearly plays a role. Among the possible biological influences are chromosomes, hormones, and evolution (Antfolk, 2018; Hawley & Bauer, 2018; Li, Kung, & Hines, 2017). However, our focus in this chapter is on the social aspects of gender.

Social Influences

Many social scientists do not locate the cause of psychological gender differences in biological dispositions. Rather, they argue that these differences are due to social experiences (Leaper & Bigler, 2018; Rose & Smith, 2018; Weisgram & Dinella, 2018). Their explanations include both social and cognitive theories.

Social Theories of Gender Three main social theories of gender have been proposed: social role theory, psychoanalytic theory, and social cognitive theory. Alice Eagly (2001, 2010, 2012, 2016, 2017) proposed **social role theory,** which states that gender differences result from the contrasting roles of women and men. In most cultures around the world, women have less power and status than men do, and they control fewer resources (Helgeson, 2017). Compared with men, women perform more domestic work, spend fewer hours in paid employment, receive lower pay, and are more thinly represented in the highest levels of organizations. In Eagly's (2016, 2017) view, as women adapted to roles with less power and less status in society, they showed more cooperative, less dominant profiles than men did. Thus, the social hierarchy and division of labor are important causes of gender differences in power, assertiveness, and nurture (Eagly, 2017; Eagly & Wood, 2017).

The **psychoanalytic theory of gender** stems from Freud's view that the preschool child develops a sexual attraction to the opposite-sex parent. This is the process known as the Oedipus (for boys) or Electra (for girls) complex. At age 5 or 6, the child renounces this attraction because of anxious feelings. Subsequently, the child identifies with the same-sex parent, unconsciously adopting that parent's characteristics. However, developmental psychologists have observed that gender development does not proceed in the manner that Freud proposed (Callan, 2001). Children become gender-typed much earlier than age 5 or 6, and they become masculine or feminine even when the same-sex parent is not present in the family.

The social cognitive approach provides an alternative explanation. According to the **social cognitive theory of gender,** children's gender development occurs through observation and imitation of what other people say and do, and through being rewarded and punished for gender-appropriate and gender-inappropriate behavior (Bussey & Bandura, 1999). From birth onward, males and females are treated differently. When infants and toddlers show gender differences, adults tend to reward them. Parents often use rewards and punishments to teach their daughters to be feminine ("Karen, you are being a good girl when you play gently with your doll") and their sons to be masculine ("Keith, a boy as big as you are is not supposed to cry"). Parents, however, are only one of many sources from which children learn gender roles (Brown & Stone, 2018). Culture, schools, peers, the media, and other family members also provide gender role models (Chen, Lee, & Chen, 2018). For example, children learn about gender by observing other adults in the neighborhood and on television. As children grow older, peers become increasingly important. Let's look more closely at the influence of parents and peers.

Parental Influences

Parents influence their children's gender development by action and by example. (Helgeson, 2017; Leaper & Bigler, 2018). Both mothers and

First imagine that this is a photograph of a baby girl. What expectations would you have of her? Then imagine that this is a photograph of a baby boy. What expectations would you have of him?
©Kwame Zikomo/ Purestock/SuperStock

social role theory A theory that gender differences result from the contrasting roles of men and women.

psychoanalytic theory of gender A theory deriving from Freud's view that the preschool child develops a sexual attraction to the opposite-sex parent, by approximately 5 or 6 years of age renounces this attraction because of anxious feelings, and subsequently identifies with the same-sex parent, unconsciously adopting the same-sex parent's characteristics.

social cognitive theory of gender A theory emphasizing that children's gender development occurs through the observation and imitation of gender behavior and through the rewards and punishments children experience for gender-appropriate and gender-inappropriate behavior.

fathers are psychologically important to their children's gender development (Tenenbaum & May, 2014). Cultures around the world, however, can vary in their role expectations for mother and fathers (Chen, Lee, & Chen, 2018). A research review provided these conclusions (Bronstein, 2006):

How Would You...?

As a **human development and family studies professional,** how would you describe the ways in which parents influence their children's notions of gender roles?

- *Mothers' socialization strategies.* In many cultures, mothers socialize their daughters to be more obedient and responsible than their sons. They also place more restrictions on their daughters' autonomy.

- *Fathers' socialization strategies.* Fathers show more attention to their sons than to their daughters, engage in more activities with their sons, and put forth more effort to promote their sons' intellectual development.

Thus, according to Bronstein (2006, pp. 269–270), "Despite an increased awareness in the United States and other Western cultures of the detrimental effects of gender stereotyping, many parents continue to foster behaviors and perceptions that are consonant with traditional gender role norms."

Peer Influences

Parents provide the earliest discrimination of gender roles, but before long, peers join the process of responding to and modeling masculine and feminine behavior (Brown & Stone, 2018; Rose & Smith, 2018; Zozuls & others, 2016). In fact, peers become so important to gender development that the playground has been described as "gender school" (Luria & Herzog, 1985).

Peers extensively reward and punish gender behavior (Rubin, Bukowski, & Bowker, 2015). For example, when children play in ways that the culture considers sex-appropriate, their peers tend to reward them. But peers often reject children who act in a manner that is considered more characteristic of the other gender (Handrinos & others, 2012). A little girl who brings a doll to the park may find herself surrounded by new friends; a little boy who does the same thing might be jeered at. However, there is greater pressure for boys to conform to a traditional male role than for girls to conform to a traditional female role (Fagot, Rodgers, & Leinbach, 2000). For example, a preschool girl who wants to wear boys' clothing receives considerably more approval than a boy who wants to wear a dress. The very term "tomboy" implies broad social acceptance of girls' adopting traditional male behaviors. In a recent study of 9- to 10-year-olds in Great Britain, gender-nonconforming boys were most at risk for peer rejection (Braun & Davidson, 2017). In this study, gender-nonconforming girls were preferred more than gender-conforming girls, with children most often citing masculine activities as the reason for this choice.

Gender molds important aspects of peer relations (Rubin, Bukowski, & Bowker, 2015). It influences the composition of children's groups, the size of groups, and interactions within a group (Maccoby, 1998, 2002).

- *Gender composition of children's groups.* Around age 3, children already show a preference for spending time with same-sex playmates. This preference increases until around age 12, and during the elementary school years children spend a large majority of their free time with children of their own sex (see Figure 1). Observations of children show that they are more likely to play in same-sex than mixed-sex groups. This tendency increases between 4 and 6 years of age.

- *Group size.* From about age 5, boys are more likely to interact socially in larger clusters than girls are. Boys are also more likely to participate in organized

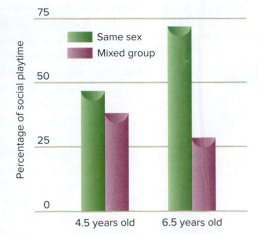

Figure 1

Developmental Changes in Percentage of Time Spent in Same-Sex and Mixed-Sex Group Settings Observations of children show that they are more likely to play in same-sex than mixed-sex groups. This tendency increases between 4 and 6 years of age.

group games than girls are. In one study, same-sex groups of six children were permitted to use play materials in any way they wished (Benenson, Apostolaris, & Parnass, 1997). Girls were more likely than boys to play in dyads or triads, while boys were more likely to interact in larger groups and seek to attain a group goal.

- *Interaction in same-sex groups.* Boys are more likely than girls to engage in rough-and-tumble play, competition, conflict, ego displays, risk taking, and quests for dominance. By contrast, girls are more likely to engage in "collaborative discourse," in which they talk and act in a more reciprocal manner.

Cognitive Influences

Observation, imitation, rewards, and punishment—these are the mechanisms by which gender develops, according to social cognitive theory. Interactions between the child and the social environment are the main keys to gender development. Some critics argue that this explanation pays too little attention to the child's own mind and understanding, and portrays the child as passively acquiring gender roles (Martin & Ruble, 2010).

How Would You...?

As an **educator**, how would you create a classroom climate that promotes healthy gender development for both boys and girls?

One influential cognitive theory is **gender schema theory,** which states that gender typing emerges as children gradually develop gender schemas of what is gender-appropriate and gender-inappropriate in their culture (Halim & others, 2016; Liben, 2017; Liben & others, 2018; Martin & Cook, 2017; Martin, Fabes, & Hanish, 2018). A schema is a cognitive structure, a network of associations that guide an individual's perceptions. A gender schema organizes the world in terms of female and male. Children are internally motivated to perceive the world and to act in accordance with their developing schemas. Bit by bit, children pick up what is gender-appropriate and gender-inappropriate in their culture, developing gender schemas that shape how they perceive the world and what they remember (Conry-Murray, Kim, & Turiel, 2012). Children are motivated to act in ways that conform with these gender schemas. Thus, gender schemas fuel gender typing.

Families

Attachment to a caregiver is a key social relationship during infancy, but some experts maintain that secure attachment and the infant's early experiences have been overdramatized as determinants of life-span development. Social and emotional development is also shaped by other relationships and by temperament, contexts, and social experiences in the early childhood years and later (Almy & Cicchetti, 2018; Gartstein & others, 2017). In this section, we discuss aspects of social relationships in early childhood that go beyond attachment.

Parenting

Some recent media accounts portray many parents as unhappy, feeling little joy in caring for their children. However, researchers have found that parents are more satisfied with their lives than are nonparents, feel relatively better on a daily basis than do nonparents, and have more positive feelings related to caring for their children than to engaging in other daily activities (Nelson & others, 2013).

Good parenting takes time and effort (Grusec, 2017; Lindsay, 2018; Serrano-Villar, Huang, & Calzada, 2017). You can't do it in a minute here and a minute there. You can't do it with CDs or DVDs. Of course, it's not just the quantity of time parents spend with children that is important for children's development—the quality of the parenting is clearly important.

gender schema theory The theory that gender typing emerges as children gradually develop gender schemas of what is gender-appropriate and gender-inappropriate in their culture.

Baumrind's Parenting Styles

Diana Baumrind (1971) stresses that parents should be neither punitive nor aloof. Rather, they should develop rules for their children and be affectionate with them. She has described four parenting styles:

- **Authoritarian parenting** is a restrictive, punitive style in which parents exhort the child to follow their directions and respect their work and effort. The authoritarian parent places firm limits and controls on the child and allows little verbal exchange. For example, an authoritarian parent might say, "You will do it my way or else." Authoritarian parents also might spank the child frequently, enforce rules rigidly but not explain them, and show anger toward the child. Children of authoritarian parents are often unhappy, fearful, and anxious about comparing themselves with others; they also fail to initiate activity and have weak communication skills. Also, a recent research review of a large number of studies concluded that authoritarian parenting is linked to a higher level of externalizing problems (acting out, higher levels of aggression, for example) (Pinquart, 2017).

- **Authoritative parenting** encourages children to be independent but still places limits and controls on their actions. Extensive verbal give-and-take is allowed, and parents are warm and nurturant toward the child. An authoritative parent might put his arm around the child in a comforting way and say, "You know you shouldn't have done that. Let's talk about how you could handle this type of situation better next time." Authoritative parents show pleasure and support in response to their children's constructive behavior. They also expect independent, age-appropriate behavior. Children whose parents are authoritative are often cheerful, self-controlled, self-reliant, and achievement-oriented; they tend to maintain friendly relations with peers, cooperate with adults, and cope well with stress. In a recent study, children of authoritative parents engaged in more prosocial behavior than their counterparts whose parents used the other parenting styles described in this section (Carlo & others, 2017). Also, in a recent research review, authoritative parenting was the most effective parenting style in predicting which children and adolescents would be less likely to be overweight or obese later in their development (Sokol, Qin, & Poti, 2017). Also, a recent study of young children found that an authoritarian parenting style, as well as pressuring the child to eat, were linked to increased risk that the children would be overweight or obese (Melis Yavuz & Selcuk, 2018).

- **Neglectful parenting** is a style in which the parent is uninvolved in the child's life. Children whose parents are neglectful develop the sense that other aspects of the parents' lives are more important than they are. These children tend to be socially incompetent. Many have poor self-control and don't handle independence well. They frequently have low self-esteem, are immature, and may be alienated from the family. In adolescence, they may show patterns of truancy and delinquency. In the recent research review described under authoritarian parenting, neglectful parenting was associated with a higher level of externalizing problems (Pinquart, 2017).

- **Indulgent parenting** is a style in which parents are highly involved with their children but place few demands or controls on them. Such parents let their children do what they want. Some parents deliberately rear their children in this way because they believe the combination of warm involvement and few restraints will produce a creative, confident child. However, children whose parents are indulgent rarely learn respect for others and have difficulty controlling their behavior. They might be domineering, egocentric, and noncompliant, and have unsatisfactory peer relations.

authoritarian parenting A restrictive, punitive style in which parents exhort the child to follow their directions and to respect work and effort. The authoritarian parent places firm limits and controls on the child and allows little verbal exchange. Authoritarian parenting is associated with children's social incompetence.

authoritative parenting A parenting style in which parents encourage their children to be independent but still place limits and controls on their actions. Extensive verbal give-and-take is allowed, and parents are warm and nurturant toward the child. Authoritative parenting is associated with children's social competence.

neglectful parenting A style of parenting in which the parent is very uninvolved in the child's life; it is associated with children's social incompetence, especially a lack of self-control.

indulgent parenting A style of parenting in which parents are highly involved with their children but place few demands or controls on them. Indulgent parenting is associated with children's social incompetence, especially a lack of self-control.

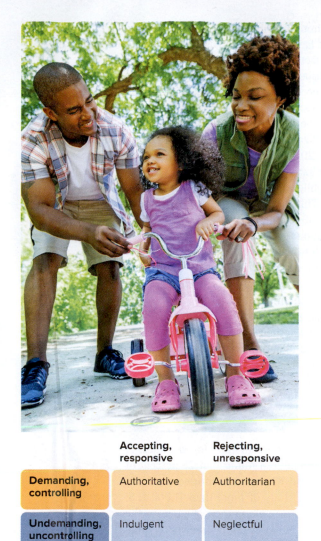

These four classifications of parenting involve combinations of acceptance and responsiveness on the one hand and demand and control on the other (Maccoby & Martin, 1983). How these dimensions combine to produce authoritarian, authoritative, neglectful, and indulgent parenting is shown in Figure 2.

	Accepting, responsive	Rejecting, unresponsive
Demanding, controlling	Authoritative	Authoritarian
Undemanding, uncontrolling	Indulgent	Neglectful

Figure 2 Classification of Parenting Styles
The four types of parenting styles (authoritative, authoritarian, indulgent, and neglectful) involve the dimensions of acceptance and responsiveness, on the one hand, and demand and control on the other. For example, authoritative parenting involves being both accepting/responsive and demanding/controlling.
©Steve Debenport/Getty Images

How Would You...?

As a **human development and family studies professional,** how would you characterize the parenting style that prevails within your own family?

Parenting Styles in Context

Among Baumrind's four parenting styles, authoritative parenting clearly conveys the most benefits to the child and to the family as a whole. Do the benefits of authoritative parenting transcend the boundaries of ethnicity, socioeconomic status, and household composition? Although some exceptions have been found, evidence linking authoritative parenting with competence on the part of the child occurs in research across a wide range of ethnic groups, social strata, cultures, and family structures (Steinberg, 2014).

Nevertheless, researchers have found that in some ethnic groups, aspects of the authoritarian style may be associated with more positive outcomes than Baumrind predicts (Pinquart & Kauser, 2018). In the Arab world, many families are very authoritarian, dominated by the father's rule, and children are taught strict codes of conduct and family loyalty (Booth, 2002). As another example, Asian American parents often continue aspects of traditional Asian child-rearing practices that have sometimes been described as authoritarian. The parents exert considerable control over their children's lives. However, Ruth Chao (2001, 2005, 2007; Chao & Otsuki-Clutter, 2011; Chao & Tseng, 2002) argues that the style of parenting used by many Asian American parents is distinct from the domineering control that is characteristic of the authoritarian style. Instead, Chao argues that it reflects concern and involvement in children's lives and is best conceptualized as a type of training. The high academic achievement of many Asian American children may be a consequence of their parents' "training" (Stevenson & Zusho, 2002).

Further Thoughts on Parenting Styles

First, keep in mind that research on parenting styles and children's development is correlational, not causal, in nature. Thus, if a study reveals that authoritarian parenting is linked to higher levels of aggression in children, it may be just as likely that aggressive children elicited authoritarian parenting as it is that authoritarian parenting produced aggressive children. Also recall that a third factor may influence the correlation between two factors. Thus, in the example of the correlation between authoritarian parenting and aggressive

How Would You...?

As a **psychologist,** how would you use the research on parenting styles to design a parent education class that teaches effective skills for interacting with young children?

According to Ruth Chao, which type of parenting style do many Asian American parents use?
©Blend Images/ SuperStock

children, possibly authoritarian parents (first factor) and aggressive children (second factor) share genes (third factor) that predispose them to behave in ways that produced the correlation.

Second, parenting styles do not capture the important themes of reciprocal socialization and synchrony (Cox & others, 2018). Remember that children socialize parents, just as parents socialize children (Klein & others, 2018).

Third, many parents use a combination of techniques rather than a single technique, although one technique may be dominant. Consistent parenting is usually recommended, yet a wise parent may sense the importance of being more permissive in certain situations, more authoritarian in others, and more authoritative in yet other circumstances.

Fourth, much of the parenting style research has involved mothers but not fathers. In many families, mothers will use one style, fathers another style. Especially in traditional cultures, fathers have an authoritarian style and mothers a more permissive, indulgent style. It has often been said that it is beneficial for parents to engage in a consistent parenting style; however, if fathers are authoritarian and aren't willing to change, children benefit when mothers use an authoritative style.

Punishment

Use of corporal (physical) punishment is legal in every state in the United States. A national survey of U.S. parents with 3- and 4-year-old children found that 26 percent of parents reported spanking their children frequently, and 67 percent reported yelling at their children frequently (Regalado & others, 2004). A study of more than 11,000 U.S. parents indicated that 80 percent of the parents reported spanking their children by the time they reached kindergarten (Gershoff & others, 2012). Another recent research review concluded that there is widespread approval of corporal punishment by U.S. parents (Chiocca, 2017). A cross-cultural comparison found that individuals in the United States and Canada were among those who held the most favorable attitudes toward corporal punishment and were most likely to remember it being used by their parents (see Figure 3) (Curran & others, 2001). Physical punishment is outlawed in 41 countries, with a number of countries increasing the ban on physical punishment mainly to promote children's rights to protection from abuse and exploitation (Committee on the Rights of the Child, 2014).

What are some reasons for avoiding spanking or similar punishments? They include the following:

- When adults punish a child by yelling, screaming, or spanking, they are presenting children with out-of-control models for handling stressful situations. Children may imitate this behavior.

- Punishment can instill fear, rage, or avoidance. For example, spanking the child may cause the child to avoid being near the parent and to fear the parent.

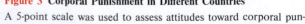

Figure 3 Corporal Punishment in Different Countries
A 5-point scale was used to assess attitudes toward corporal punishment, with scores closer to 1 indicating an attitude against its use and scores closer to 5 suggesting an attitude favoring its use. *Why are studies of corporal punishment correlational studies, and how does that affect their usefulness?*

- Punishment tells children what not to do rather than what to do. Children should be given constructive feedback, such as "Why don't you try this?"
- Parents might unintentionally become so angry when they are punishing the child that they become abusive.

Most child psychologists recommend handling misbehavior by reasoning with the child, especially explaining the consequences of the child's actions for others. *Time out*, in which the child is removed from a setting that offers positive reinforcement, can also be effective. For example, when the child has misbehaved, a parent might forbid TV viewing for a specified time.

Debate about the effects of punishment on children's development continues (Afifi & others, 2017a, b; Ferguson, 2013; Gershoff & Grogan-Kaylor, 2016; Gershoff, Lee, & Durrant, 2017; Grusec & others, 2013; Holden & others, 2017; Laible, Thompson, & Froimson, 2015). Several longitudinal studies have found that physical punishment of young children is associated with higher levels of aggression later in childhood and adolescence (Gershoff & others, 2012; Thompson & others, 2017). An in one longitudinal study, harsh physical punishment in childhood was linked to a higher incidence of intimate partner violence in adulthood (Afifi & others, 2017b).

However, a meta-analysis that focused on longitudinal studies revealed that the negative outcomes of punishment on children's internalizing and externalizing problems were minimal (Ferguson, 2013). A research review of 26 studies also concluded that only severe or predominant use of spanking, not mild spanking, compared unfavorably with alternative discipline practices (Larzelere & Kuhn, 2005). Nonetheless, in a recent meta-analysis, when physical punishment was not abusive it still was linked to detrimental child outcomes (Gershoff & Grogan-Kaylor, 2016). And in a recent Japanese study, occasional spanking at 3 years of age was associated with a higher level of behavioral problems at 5 years of age (Okuzono & others, 2017).

In sum, in the view of some experts, it is still difficult to determine whether the effects of physical punishment are harmful to children's development, although such a view might be distasteful to some individuals (Ferguson, 2013). Also, as with other research on parenting, research on punishment is correlational in nature, making it difficult to discover causal factors. Also, consider the concept of reciprocal socialization (discussed in the chapter on socioemotional development in infancy and earlier in this chapter), which emphasizes bidirectional child and parent influences.

Nonetheless, a large majority of leading experts on parenting conclude that physical punishment has harmful effects on children and should not be used (Afifi & others, 2017a, b; Gershoff, Lee, & Durrant, 2017; Holden & others, 2017). Also, in a research review, Elizabeth Gershoff (2013) concluded that the defenders of spanking have not produced any evidence that spanking produces positive outcomes for children, while negative outcomes of spanking have been replicated in many studies. Further, physical punishment that involves abuse can be very harmful to children's development, as discussed later in this chapter (Almy & Cicchetti, 2018).

Coparenting

Coparenting refers to the support that parents give each other in raising a child. Poor coordination between parents, undermining of one parent by the other, lack of cooperation and warmth, and aloofness by one parent are conditions that place children at risk (Bertoni & others, 2018; Lam & others, 2018; Latham, Mark, & Oliver, 2018; Pruett & others, 2017; Reader, Teti, & Cleveland, 2017). In addition, one study revealed that coparenting is more beneficial than either maternal or paternal parenting in helping children to development self-control (Karreman & others, 2008). Another study found that greater father involvement in young children's play was linked to an increase in supportive coparenting (Jia & Schoppe-Sullivan, 2011).

Parents who do not spend enough time with their children or who have problems in child rearing can benefit from counseling and therapy. To read about the work of marriage and family counselor Darla Botkin, see *Careers in Life-Span Development*.

Darla Botkin, Marriage and Family Therapist

Darla Botkin is a marriage and family therapist who teaches, conducts research, and engages in marriage and family therapy. She is on the faculty of the University of Kentucky. Botkin obtained a bachelor's degree in elementary education with a concentration in special education, and she went on to receive a master's degree in early childhood education. She spent the next six years working with children and their families in a variety of settings, including child care, elementary school, and Head Start. These experiences led her to recognize the interdependence of the developmental settings

Darla Botkin (*left*) conducts a family therapy session.
©Dr. Darla Botkin

that children and their parents experience (such as home, school, and work). She returned to graduate school and obtained a Ph.D. in family studies from the University of Tennessee. She then became a faculty member in the Family Studies program at the University of Kentucky. Completing further coursework and clinical training in marriage and family therapy, she became certified as a marriage and family therapist.

Botkin's current interests include working with young children in family therapy, exploring gender and ethnic issues in family therapy, and understanding the role of spirituality in family wellness.

Child Maltreatment

Unfortunately, punishment sometimes leads to the abuse of infants and children (Cicchetti, 2017; Doyle & Cicchetti, 2018). In 2013, 679,000 U.S. children were found to be victims of child abuse at least once during that year (U.S. Department of Health and Human Services, 2015). Ninety-one percent of these children were abused by one or both parents. Laws in many states now require physicians and teachers to report suspected cases of child abuse, yet many cases go unreported, especially those involving battered infants.

Types of Child Maltreatment

The four main types of child maltreatment are physical abuse, child neglect, sexual abuse, and emotional abuse (National Clearinghouse on Child Abuse and Neglect, 2013):

- *Physical abuse* is characterized by the infliction of physical injury as a result of punching, beating, kicking, biting, burning, shaking, or otherwise harming a child. The parent or other person may not intend to hurt the child; the injury may result from excessive physical punishment (Lo & others, 2017; Smith & others, 2018).

- *Child neglect* is characterized by failure to provide for the child's basic needs. Neglect can be physical (abandonment, for example), educational (allowing chronic truancy, for example), or emotional (marked inattention to the child's needs, for example) (Naughton & others, 2017). Child neglect is by far the most common form of child maltreatment. In every country where relevant data have been collected, neglect occurs up to three times as often as abuse (Read & others, 2018). A recent research review of risk factors for engaging in child neglect found that most risks

Eight-year-old Donnique Hein lovingly holds her younger sister, 6-month-old Maria Paschel, after a meal at Laura's Home, a crisis shelter in suburban Cleveland run by the City Mission.
©Joshua Gunter/The Plain Dealer/Landov Images

involved parent factors, including a history of antisocial behavior/criminal offending, having mental/physical problems, and experiencing abuse in their own childhood (Mulder & others, 2018).

- *Sexual abuse* includes fondling of genitals, intercourse, incest, rape, sodomy, exhibitionism, and commercial exploitation through prostitution or production of pornographic materials (Beier, 2018; Oates, 2018).

- *Emotional abuse (psychological/verbal abuse/mental injury)* includes acts or omissions by parents or other caregivers that have caused, or could cause, serious behavioral, cognitive, or emotional problems (Hagborg, Tidefors, & Fahlke, 2017; Prino, Longobadi, & Setanni, 2018).

Although any of these forms of child maltreatment may be found separately, they often occur in combination. Emotional abuse is almost always present when other forms are identified.

The Context of Abuse

No single factor causes child maltreatment (Cicchetti & Toth, 2016; Doyle & Cicchetti, 2018). A combination of factors, including cultural norms, characteristics of the family, and developmental characteristics of the child, likely contribute to child maltreatment (Cicchetti, 2018). Among the family and family-associated characteristics that may contribute to child maltreatment are parenting stress, substance abuse, social isolation, single parenting, and socioeconomic difficulties (especially poverty) (Almy & Cicchetti, 2018). The interactions among all family members need to be considered, regardless of who performs violent acts against the child. For example, even though the father may be the one who physically abuses the child, the behavior of the mother, the child, and siblings should also be evaluated.

Developmental Consequences of Abuse

Among the consequences of maltreatment in childhood and adolescence are poor emotion regulation, attachment problems, problems in peer relations, difficulty in adapting to school, and other psychological problems, such as depression, delinquency, and substance abuse (Almy & Cicchetti, 2018; Bell & others, 2018; Handley, Rogosch, & Cicchetti, 2018). For example, a recent study also found that physical abuse was linked to lower levels of cognitive development and school engagement in children (Font & Cage, 2018). Also, compared with their peers, adolescents who experienced abuse or neglect as children are more likely to engage in violent romantic relationships, delinquency, sexual risk taking, and substance abuse (Trickett & others, 2011). And a recent study found that exposure to either physical or sexual abuse in childhood and adolescence was linked to an increase in 13- to 18-year-olds' suicidal ideation, plans, and attempts (Gomez & others, 2017).

During their adult years, individuals who were maltreated as children are more likely to experience physical illness, mental illness, and sexual problems (Brown & others, 2018; Gekker & others, 2018). As adults, maltreated children are also at higher risk for violent behavior toward other adults—especially dating partners and marital partners—as well as for substance abuse, anxiety, and depression (Miller-Perrin, Perrin, & Kocur, 2009). Also,

How Would You...?

As a **health-care professional,** how would you work with parents during infant and early childhood checkups to prevent child maltreatment?

in a longitudinal study, experiencing early abuse and neglect in the first five years of life were linked to having more interpersonal problems and lower academic achievement from childhood through their thirties (Raby & others, 2018). Further, a 30-year longitudinal study found that middle-aged adults who had experienced maltreatment during childhood were at increased risk for diabetes, lung disease, malnutrition, and vision problems (Widom & others, 2012). However, this study also found that 75 percent of parents who had experienced maltreatment during childhood had never abused their own children. Thus, it is important to note that the majority of people who were abused in childhood are unlikely to abuse their own children.

How Would You...?

As an **educator,** how would you explain the potential impact of maltreatment at home on a child's performance in school?

An important research agenda is to discover how to prevent child maltreatment or intervene in children's lives when they have been maltreated (Almy & Cicchetti, 2018; Cozza & others, 2018; McCarroll & others, 2017; Weiller & Taussig, 2018). In one study of maltreating mothers and their 1-year-old children, two treatments were effective in reducing child maltreatment: (1) home visitation that emphasized improved parenting, coping with stress, and increasing support for the mother; and (2) parent-infant psychotherapy that focused on improving maternal-infant attachment (Cicchetti, Toth, & Rogosch, 2005).

Sibling Relationships and Birth Order

How do developmental psychologists characterize sibling relationships? And how does birth order influence behavior, if at all?

Sibling Relationships

Approximately 80 percent of American children have one or more siblings—that is, sisters and brothers (Dunn, 2015; Fouts & Bader, 2017). If you grew up with siblings, you probably have rich memories of your relationships with them. Two- to 4-year-old siblings in each other's presence have a conflict once every 10 minutes, on average; the rate of conflict declines somewhat from ages 5 to 7 (Kramer, 2006). What do parents do when they encounter siblings having a verbal or physical confrontation? One study revealed that they do one of three things: (1) intervene and try to help them resolve the conflict, (2) admonish or threaten them, or (3) do nothing at all (Kramer & Perozynski, 1999). Of interest is the fact that in families with two siblings ages 2 to 5 the most frequent parental reaction to sibling conflict is to do nothing at all.

Laurie Kramer (2006), who has conducted a number of research studies on siblings, says that not intervening and letting sibling conflict escalate are not good strategies. She developed a program titled "More Fun with Sisters and Brothers" that teaches 4- to 8-year-old siblings social skills for developing positive interactions (Kramer & Radey, 1997). Among the skills taught in the program are how to appropriately initiate play, how to accept and refuse invitations to play, how to take another person's perspective, how to deal with angry feelings, and how to manage conflict.

However, conflict is only one of the many dimensions of sibling relations (McHale, Updegraff, & Whiteman, 2013; Pike & Oliver, 2017). Sibling relations also include helping, sharing, teaching, compromising, and playing, and siblings can act as emotional supports and communication partners as well as rivals. A research review concluded that sibling relationships in adolescence are not as close, are less intense, and are more egalitarian than in childhood (East, 2009).

Do parents usually favor one sibling over others—and if so, does it make a difference in a child's development? One study of 384 sibling pairs revealed that 65 percent of their mothers and 70 percent of their fathers showed favoritism toward one sibling (Shebloski, Conger, & Widaman, 2005). When favoritism of one sibling occurred, it was linked to lower self-esteem and sadness in the less-favored sibling. Indeed, equality and fairness are major concerns in regard to siblings' relationships with each other and how they are treated by their parents (Aldercotte, White, & Hughes, 2016; Campione-Barr, Greer, & Kruse, 2013).

Judy Dunn (2007, 2015), a leading expert on sibling relationships, described three important characteristics of sibling relationships:

1. *The emotional quality of the relationship.* Siblings often express intense emotions—both positive and negative—toward each other. Many children and adolescents have mixed feelings toward their siblings.

What characterizes children's sibling relationships?
©RubberBall Productions/ Getty Images

2. *The familiarity and intimacy of the relationship.* Siblings typically know each other very well, and this intimacy suggests that they can either provide support or tease and undermine each other, depending on the situation.

3. *The variation in sibling relationships.* Some siblings describe their relationships more positively than others do. Thus, there is considerable variation in sibling relationships. We just noted that many siblings have mixed feelings about each other, but some children and adolescents describe their siblings mainly in warm, affectionate ways, whereas others primarily talk about how irritating and mean a sibling is.

Birth Order

Whether a child has older or younger siblings has been linked to the development of certain personality characteristics. For example, one research review concluded that "firstborns are the most intelligent, achieving, and conscientious, while later-borns are the most rebellious, liberal, and agreeable" (Paulhus, 2008, p. 210). Compared with later-born children, firstborn children have also been described as more adult-oriented, helpful, conforming, and self-controlled. However, when actual birth-order differences are reported, they often are small.

What accounts for differences related to birth order? Proposed explanations usually point to variations in interactions associated with a particular position in the family. In one study, mothers became more negative, coercive, and restraining and played less with the firstborn following the birth of a second child (Dunn & Kendrick, 1982).

What about children who don't have siblings? The popular conception is that an only child is a "spoiled brat" with undesirable characteristics such as dependency, lack of self-control, and self-centered behavior. But researchers present a more positive portrayal in which only children are often achievement-oriented and display desirable personality characteristics, especially in comparison with later-borns and children from large families (Falbo & Poston, 1993; Jiao, Ji, & Jing, 1996).

So far, our discussion suggests that birth order might be a strong predictor of behavior. However, an increasing number of family researchers stress that when all the factors that influence behavior are considered, birth order by itself has limited accuracy as a predictor of behavior. Indeed, in a recent large-scale study, a birth order effect occurred for intelligence, with firstborns having slightly higher intelligence, but there were no birth order effects for life satisfaction, internal/external control, trust, risk taking, patience, and impulsivity (Rohrer, Egloff, & Schmukle, 2017). Think about some of the other important factors in children's lives that influence their behavior. They include heredity, models of competency or incompetency that parents present to children on a daily basis, peer and school influences, socioeconomic and sociohistorical factors, and cultural variations. When someone says that firstborns are always like this but last-borns are always like that, he or she is making overly simplistic statements that do not adequately take into account the complexity of influences on a child's development.

The Changing Family in a Changing Society

Beyond variations in number of siblings, the families that children experience differ in many important ways (Hardy, Smeeding, & Ziliak, 2018; Parke, 2017; Patterson & others, 2018). As shown in Figure 4, the United States has one of the highest percentages of single-parent families in the world. Among two-parent families, there are those in which both parents work, those in which parents have found new spouses after divorce, and those in which the parents are gay or lesbian. Differences in culture and socioeconomic status (SES) also influence families. How do these variations in families affect children?

Working Parents

More than half of U.S. mothers with a child under age 5 are in the labor force, as are more than two-thirds with a child 6 to 17 years old. Maternal employment is a part of modern life, but its effects are still being debated.

Parental employment can have both positive and negative effects on parenting (O'Brien & others, 2014). Research indicates that what matters for children's

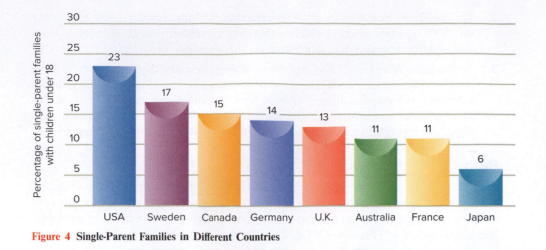

Figure 4 **Single-Parent Families in Different Countries**

development is the nature of the parents' work rather than whether or not both parents work outside the home (Clarke-Stewart & Parke, 2014; Goldberg & Lucas-Thompson, 2008). For example, a study of almost 3,000 adolescents found a negative association of the father's, but not the mother's, unemployment on the adolescents' health (Bacikova-Sleskova, Benka, & Orosova, 2015). Also, a recent study found that mothers' and fathers' work-family conflict was linked to lower self-control in 4-year-old children (Ferreira & others, 2018).

Ann Crouter (2006) described how parents bring their experiences at work into their homes. She concluded that parents who experience poor working conditions, such as long hours, overtime work, high levels of stress, and lack of autonomy at work, are likely to be more irritable at home and engage in less effective parenting than their counterparts who experience better working conditions. A consistent finding is that children (especially girls) whose mothers are employed engage in less gender stereotyping and have more egalitarian views of gender than do children whose mothers do not work outside the home (Goldberg & Lucas-Thompson, 2008).

How does work affect parenting?
©Keith Brofsky/Photodisc/Getty Images

Children in Divorced Families

Divorce rates changed rather dramatically in the United States and many countries around the world in the late twentieth century (Braver & Lamb, 2013). The U.S. divorce rate increased dramatically in the 1960s and 1970s but has declined since the 1980s. However, the divorce rate in the United States is still much higher than in most other countries.

It is estimated that 40 percent of children born to married parents in the United States will experience their parents' divorce (Hetherington & Stanley-Hagan, 2002). Let's examine some important questions about children in divorced families:

- *Are children better adjusted in intact, never-divorced families than in divorced families?* Most researchers agree that children from divorced families show poorer adjustment than their counterparts in never-divorced families (Amato & Anthony, 2014; Arkes, 2015; Hetherington, 2006; Weaver & Schofield, 2015) (see Figure 5). Those who have experienced multiple divorces are at greater risk. Children in divorced

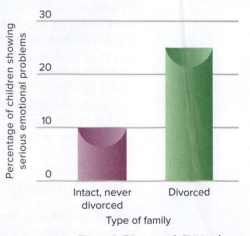

Figure 5 **Divorce and Children's Emotional Problems**

In Hetherington's research, 25 percent of children from divorced families showed serious emotional problems, compared with only 10 percent of children from intact, never-divorced families. However, keep in mind that a substantial majority (75 percent) of the children from divorced families did not show serious emotional problems.

families are more likely than those in never-divorced families to have academic problems, to exhibit externalized problems (such as acting out and delinquency) and experience internalized problems (such as anxiety and depression), to be less socially responsible, to have less competent intimate relationships, to drop out of school, to become sexually active at an earlier age, to take drugs, to associate with antisocial peers, to have low self-esteem, and to be less securely attached to their partners as young adults (Lansford, 2012, 2013). In a recent study, both parental divorce and child maltreatment were linked to midlife suicidal ideation (Stansfield & others, 2017). Also, a recent meta-analysis found that when their parents had been divorced, adults were more likely to have depression (Sands, Thompson, & Gaysina, 2017).

What concerns are involved in whether parents should stay together for the sake of the children or become divorced?
©Image Source/PunchStock

- *Should parents stay together for the sake of the children?* Whether parents should stay in an unhappy or conflictual marriage for the sake of their children is one of the most commonly asked questions about divorce (Hetherington, 2006; Morrison, Fife, & Hertlein, 2017). If the stresses and disruptions in family relationships associated with an unhappy marriage that erode the well-being of children are reduced by the move to a divorced, single-parent family, divorce can be advantageous. However, if the diminished resources and increased risks associated with divorce are accompanied by inept parenting and sustained or increased conflict, not only between the divorced couple but also among the parents, children, and siblings, the best choice for the children would be for an unhappy marriage to be continued (Hetherington & Stanley-Hagan, 2002). It is difficult to determine how these "ifs" will play out when parents either remain together in an acrimonious marriage or become divorced.

- Many of the problems experienced by children of divorced parents begin during the predivorce period, a time when parents often are in active conflict. Thus, when children of divorced parents show problems, the problems may be due not only to the divorce itself but also to the marital conflict that led to it (Cummings & others, 2017; Davies, Martin, & Cummings, 2018; Davies, Martin & Sturge-Apple, 2016). E. Mark Cummings and his colleagues (2017; Cummings & Miller, 2015; Cummings & Valentino, 2015) have proposed emotion security theory, which has its roots in attachment theory and states that children appraise marital conflict in terms of their sense of security and safety in the family. These researchers make a distinction between marital conflict that is negative for children (such as hostile emotional displays and destructive conflict tactics) and marital conflict that can be positive for children (such as marital disagreement that involves calmly discussing each person's perspective and then working together to find a solution). In a recent study, intensification of interparental conflict in the early elementary school years predicted increases in emotional insecurity five years late in early adolescence, which in turn predicted decreases in adolescent friendship affiliation, and this friendship decrease was linked to a downturn in social competence (Davies, Martin, & Cummings, 2018).

- *How much do family processes matter after a divorce?* They matter a great deal (Bastaitis, Pasteels, & Mortelmans, 2018; Demby, 2016). When divorced parents' relationship with each other is harmonious and when they use authoritative parenting, children's adjustment improves (Hetherington, 2006). A number of researchers have shown that a disequilibrium, which includes diminished parenting skills, occurs in the first year following the divorce—but by two years after the divorce, restabilization has occurred and parenting skills have improved (Hetherington, 1989). When the divorced parents can agree on childrearing strategies and can maintain a cordial relationship with each other, frequent visits by the noncustodial parent usually benefit the child (Fabricius

& others, 2010). Following a divorce, father involvement with children drops off more than mother involvement, especially for fathers of girls. Further, a recent study of non-residential fathers in divorced families indicated that high father-child involvement and low interparental conflict were linked to positive child outcomes (Flam & others, 2016). Also, a recent research review concluded that co-parenting (co-parental support, cooperation, and agreement) following divorce was related to positive child outcomes such as lower anxiety and depression, as well as higher self-esteem and academic performance (Lamela & Figueiredo, 2016).

- *What factors influence an individual child's vulnerability to suffering negative consequences as a result of divorce?* Among the factors involved are the parent's and child's adjustment prior to the divorce, as well as the child's personality and temperament, gender, and custody situation (Hetherington, 2006). In one study, a higher level of predivorce maternal sensitivity and child IQ served as protective factors in reducing children's problems after the divorce (Weaver & Schofield, 2015). Children whose parents later divorce show poorer adjustment before the breakup (Lansford, 2012, 2013). Children who are socially mature and responsible, who show few behavioral problems, and who have an easy temperament are better able to cope with their parents' divorce. Children with a difficult temperament often have problems coping with their parents' divorce (Hetherington, 2006). Joint custody also works best for children when the parents can get along with each other (Clarke-Stewart & Parke, 2014).

- *What role does socioeconomic status play in the lives of children whose parents have divorced?* Mothers who have custody of their children experience the loss of about one-fourth to one-half of their predivorce income, compared with a loss of only one-tenth by fathers who have custody. This income loss for divorced mothers is accompanied by increased workloads, high rates of job instability, and residential moves to less desirable neighborhoods with inferior schools (Lansford, 2009).

Gay and Lesbian Parents

Increasingly, gay and lesbian couples are creating families that include children (Farr, 2017; Oakley, Farr, & Scherer, 2017; Simon & others, 2018). Data indicate that approximately 20 percent of same-sex couples are raising children under the age of 18 in the United States (Gates, 2013).

Like heterosexual couples, gay and lesbian parents vary greatly. They may be single, or they may have same-gender partners. Many lesbian mothers and gay fathers are noncustodial parents because they lost custody of their children to heterosexual spouses after a divorce.

Parenthood among lesbians and gay men is controversial. Opponents claim that being raised by gay or lesbian parents harms the child's development. But researchers have found few differences between children growing up with lesbian mothers or gay fathers on the one hand, and children growing up with heterosexual parents on the other (Farr & Goldberg, 2018; Golombok, 2011a, b; Patterson, Farr, & Hastings, 2015). For example, children raised by gay or lesbian parents are just as popular with their peers, and no differences are found in the adjustment and mental health of children living in these families in comparison with children raised by heterosexual parents (Farr & others, 2018; Patterson, Farr, & Hastings, 2015). For example, in a recent study, the adjustment of school-aged children adopted during infancy by gay, lesbian, and heterosexual parents showed no differences (Farr, 2017). Rather, children's behavior patterns and family functioning were predicted by earlier child adjustment issues and parental stress. In another recent study of lesbian and gay adoptive parents, 98 percent of the adoptive parents reported that their children had

What are the research findings regarding the development and psychological well-being of children raised by gay and lesbian couples?
©Creatas/Getty Images

adjusted well to school (Farr, Oakley, & Ollen, 2016). Contrary to the once-widespread expectation that being raised by a gay or lesbian parent would result in the child's growing up to be gay or lesbian, in reality the overwhelming majority of children from gay or lesbian families have a heterosexual orientation (Golombok, 2011a, b).

Also, one study compared the incidence of coparenting in adoptive heterosexual, lesbian, and gay couples with preschool-aged children (Farr & Patterson, 2013). Both self-reports and observations found that lesbian and gay couples shared child care more than heterosexual couples did, with lesbian couples being the most supportive and gay couples the least supportive. Further, researchers have found more positive parenting in adoptive gay father families and fewer child externalizing problems in these families than in heterosexual families (Golombok & others, 2014).

Cultural, Ethnic, and Socioeconomic Variations

Parenting can be influenced by culture, ethnicity, and socioeconomic status (Nieto & Bode, 2018; White & others, 2013). Recall from Bronfenbrenner's ecological theory that a number of social contexts influence the child's development. In Bronfenbrenner's theory, culture, ethnicity, and socioeconomic status are classified as part of the macrosystem because they represent broader societal contexts.

Cross-Cultural Studies Different cultures often give different answers to such basic questions as what the father's role in the family should be, what support systems are available to families, and how children should be disciplined (Matsumoto & Juang, 2017; Suh & others, 2017). There are important cross-cultural variations in parenting. In some cultures, such as rural areas of many countries, authoritarian parenting is widespread (Smetana & Ball, 2018).

Cultural change, brought about by factors such as increasingly frequent international travel, the Internet and electronic communications, and economic globalization, is affecting families in many countries around the world (Eo & Kim, 2018). There are trends toward greater family mobility, migration to urban areas, and separation as some family members work in cities or countries far from their homes. Other trends include smaller families, fewer extended-family households, and increased rates of maternal employment (Brown & Larson, 2002). These trends can change the nature of the resources available to children. For example, when several generations no longer live in close proximity, children may lose the support and guidance of grandparents, aunts, and uncles. On the positive side, smaller families may produce more openness and communication between parents and children.

Ethnicity Families within various ethnic groups in the United States differ in their typical size, structure, composition, reliance on kinship networks, and levels of income and education (Nieto & Bode, 2018). Large and extended families are more common among minority groups than among the non-Latino White majority. For example, 19 percent of Latino families have three or more children, compared with 14 percent of African American and 10 percent of White families. African American and Latino children interact more with grandparents, aunts, uncles, cousins, and more distant relatives than do non-Latino White children.

Single-parent families are more common among African Americans and Latinos than among non-Latino White Americans. In comparison with two-parent households, single parents often have more limited resources in terms of time, money, and energy (Koppelman, 2017). Ethnic minority parents also tend to be less educated and are

What are some characteristics of families within different ethnic groups?
©Bill Aron/PhotoEdit

What are some of the stressors that immigrant families experience when they come to the United States?
©J. Emilio Flores/Corbis/Getty Images

more likely to live in low-income circumstances than their non-Latino White counterparts. Still, many impoverished ethnic minority families manage to find ways to raise competent children.

Of course, individual families vary, and how ethnic minority families deal with stress depends on many factors (Derlan & others, 2018; Yoshikawa & others, 2017). Whether the parents are native-born or immigrants, how long the family has been in this country, its socioeconomic status, and its national origin all make a difference (Giuntella, 2017). The characteristics of the family's social context also influence its adaptation. What are the attitudes toward the family's ethnic group within its neighborhood or city? Can the family's children attend good schools? Are there community groups that welcome people from the family's ethnic group? Do members of the family's ethnic group form community groups of their own?

A major change in families in the last several decades has been the dramatic increase in the immigration of Latino and Asian families into the United States (Anguiano & others, 2018; Bas-Sarmiento & others, 2017; Non & others, 2018; Umana-Taylor & Douglass, 2017). Immigrant families often experience stressors uncommon to or less prominent among long-time residents, such as language barriers, dislocations and separations from support networks, the dual struggle to preserve identity and to acculturate, and changes in SES status (Gangamma & Shipman, 2018; Nair, Roche, & White, 2018; Wang & Palacios, 2017).

Many members of families that have recently immigrated to the United States adopt a bicultural orientation, selecting characteristics of the U.S. culture that help them to survive and advance, while still retaining aspects of their culture of origin. In adopting characteristics of the U.S. culture, Latino families are increasingly embracing the importance of education. Although their school dropout rates have remained higher than the rates for other ethnic groups, toward the end of the first decade of the twenty-first century they declined considerably (National Center for Education Statistics, 2017). However, while many ethnic/immigrant families adopt a bicultural orientation, parenting in many ethnic minority families also focuses on issues associated with promoting children's ethnic pride, knowledge of their ethnic group, and awareness of discrimination (McDermott & others, 2018; Umana-Taylor & Douglass, 2017: Umana-Taylor & others, 2018).

Socioeconomic Status Low-income families have less access to resources than do higher-income families (Singh & Mukherjee, 2018; Yoshikawa & others, 2017). The resources in question include nutrition, health care, protection from danger, and enriching educational and socialization opportunities, such as tutoring and lessons in various activities (Coley & others, 2018). These differences are compounded in low-income families characterized by long-term poverty (Nieto & Bode, 2018). A longitudinal study found that a multicomponent (school-based educational enrichment and comprehensive family services) preschool to third-grade intervention with low-income minority children in Chicago was effective in increasing their rate of high school graduation, as well as undergraduate and graduate school success (Reynolds, Qu, & Temple, 2018).

In the United States and most Western cultures, researchers have identified differences in child-rearing practices among groups of varying socioeconomic status (SES) (Hoff, Laursen, & Tardif, 2002, p. 246):

- "Lower-SES parents (1) are more concerned that their children conform to society's expectations, (2) create a home atmosphere in which it is clear that parents have authority over children," (3) are more likely to use physical punishment in disciplining their children, and (4) are more directive and less conversational with their children.

- "Higher-SES parents (1) are more concerned with developing children's initiative" and their capacity to delay gratification, (2) "create a home atmosphere in which children are more nearly equal participants and in which rules are discussed as opposed to being laid down" in an authoritarian manner, (3) are less likely to use physical punishment, and (4) "are less directive and more conversational" with their children.

Peer Relations, Play, and Media/Screen Time

The family is an important social context for children's development. However, children's development also is strongly influenced by what goes on in other social contexts, such as in peer groups and when children are playing or using various media (Bukowski, Laursen, & Rubin, 2018; Rose & Smith, 2018).

Peer Relations

As children grow older, they spend an increasing amount of time with their peers—children of about the same age or maturity level.

What are the functions of a child's peer group? One of its most important functions is to provide a source of information and comparison about the world outside the family. Children receive feedback about their abilities from their peer group. They evaluate what they can do in terms of whether it is better than, as good as, or worse than what other children can do. It is hard to make these judgments at home because siblings are usually older or younger.

Good peer relations promote normal socioemotional development (Bukowski, Laursen, & Rubin, 2018). Special concerns in peer relations focus on children who are withdrawn or aggressive (Rubin & others, 2018). Withdrawn children who are rejected by peers or are victimized and feel lonely are at increased risk for depression (Coplan & others, 2018). Children who are aggressive with their peers are at increased risk for developing a number of problems, including delinquency and dropping out of school (Vitaro, Boivin, & Poulin, 2018).

Good peer relations can be necessary for normal socioemotional development (Prinstein & others, 2018). Recall from our discussion of gender that by about age 3, children already prefer to spend time with same-sex rather than opposite-sex playmates, and this preference increases in early childhood. During these same years, the frequency of peer interactions, both positive and negative, picks up considerably (Cillessen & Bukowski, 2018). Although aggressive interactions and rough-and-tumble play increase, the proportion of aggressive exchanges, compared with friendly exchanges, decreases. Many preschool children spend considerable time in peer interaction just conversing with playmates about such matters as "negotiating roles and rules in play, arguing, and agreeing" (Rubin, Bukowski, & Parker, 2006).

Parents may influence their children's peer relations in many ways, both direct and indirect (Booth-Laforce & Groh, 2018). Parents affect their children's peer relations through their interactions with their children, how they manage their children's lives, and the opportunities they provide to their children (Brown & Bakken, 2011). For example, when mothers coached their preschool daughters about the negative aspects of peer conflicts involving relational aggression (harming someone by manipulating relationships), the daughters engaged in lower rates of relational aggression (Werner & others, 2014).

What are some characteristics of young children's peer relations?
©INSADCO Photography/Alamy Stock Photo

Play

An extensive amount of peer interaction during childhood involves play, but social play is only one type of play. Play is a pleasurable activity that is engaged in for its own sake, and its functions and forms vary.

Functions of Play

Play is an important aspect of children's development (Bergen, 2015; Clark, 2016; Taggart, Eisen, & Lillard, 2018). Theorists have focused on different aspects of play and highlighted a long list of functions (Henricks, 2015a, b).

According to Freud and Erikson, play helps the child master anxieties and conflicts (Demanchick, 2015). Because pent-up tensions are released through play, the child can cope better with life's problems. Therapists use *play therapy* both to allow the child to work off frustrations and to analyze the child's conflicts and ways of coping with them (Clark, 2015, 2016). Children may feel less threatened and be more likely to express their true feelings in the context of play.

Play is also an important context for cognitive development (Taggart, Eisen, & Lillard, 2018). Both Piaget and Vygotsky concluded that play is the child's work. Piaget (1962) maintained that play advances children's cognitive development. At the same time, he said that children's cognitive development constrains the way they play. Play permits children to practice their competencies and acquired skills in a relaxed, pleasurable way. Piaget thought that cognitive structures need to be exercised, and play provides the perfect setting for this exercise (DeLisi, 2015).

Vygotsky (1962) also considered play to be an excellent setting for cognitive development. He was especially interested in the symbolic and make-believe aspects of play, as when a child substitutes a stick for a horse and rides the stick as if it were a horse. For young children, the imaginary situation is real (Bodrova & Leong, 2015). Parents should encourage such imaginary play because it advances the child's cognitive development, especially creative thought.

Daniel Berlyne (1960) described play as exciting and pleasurable in itself because it satisfies our exploratory drive. This drive involves curiosity and a quest for information about something new or unusual. Play encourages exploratory behavior by offering children the possibilities of novelty, complexity, uncertainty, surprise, and incongruity.

More recently, play has been described as an important context for the development of language and communication skills (Taggart, Eisen, & Lillard, 2018). Language and communication skills may be enhanced through discussions and negotiations regarding roles and rules in play as young children practice various words and phrases. These types of social interactions during play can benefit young children's literacy skills (Bredekamp, 2017; Follari, 2019). And play is a central focus of the child-centered kindergarten and is thought to be an essential aspect of early childhood education (Feeney, Moravcik, & Nolte, 2019; Morrison, 2017, 2018).

Types of Play

The contemporary perspective on play emphasizes both the cognitive and the social aspects of it (Loizou, 2017; Sim & Xu, 2017). Among the most widely studied types of children's play are sensorimotor and practice play, pretense/symbolic play, social play, constructive play, and games (Bergen, 1988).

Sensorimotor and Practice Play Sensorimotor play is behavior that allows infants to derive pleasure from exercising their sensorimotor schemes. The development of sensorimotor play follows Piaget's description of sensorimotor thought. Infants begin to engage in exploratory and playful visual and motor transactions during the second quarter of the first year of life. By the age of 9 months, many infants can select novel objects for exploration and play, especially responsive objects such as toys that make noise or bounce.

Practice play involves the repetition of behavior when new skills are being learned or when physical or mental mastery and coordination of

sensorimotor play Behavior engaged in by infants to derive pleasure from exercising their existing sensorimotor schemes.

practice play Play that involves repetition of behavior when new skills are being learned or when physical or mental mastery and coordination of skills are required for games or sports.

A preschool "superhero" at play.
©RichVintage/Getty Images

skills are required for games or sports. Sensorimotor play, which often involves practice play, is primarily confined to infancy, whereas practice play can continue to occur throughout life. During the preschool years, children often engage in practice play.

Pretense/Symbolic Play Pretense/symbolic play occurs when the child transforms the physical environment into a symbol (Taggart, Eisen, & Lillard, 2018). Between 9 and 30 months, children increasingly use objects in symbolic play. They learn to transform objects—substituting them for other objects and acting toward them as if they were these other objects. For example, a preschool child may treat a table as if it were a car and say, "I'm fixing the car" as he grabs a leg of the table.

Many experts on play consider the preschool years the "golden age" of pretense/symbolic play that is dramatic or sociodramatic in nature. This type of make-believe play often appears at about 18 months and reaches a peak at ages 4 to 5, then gradually declines.

Some child psychologists believe that pretend play is an important aspect of young children's development and often reflects advances in their cognitive development, especially as an indication of symbolic understanding (Taggart, Eisen, & Lillard, 2018). For example, Catherine Garvey (2000) and Angeline Lillard (2006, 2015) emphasize that hidden in young children's pretend-play narratives are remarkable capacities for role-taking, balancing of social roles, metacognition (thinking about thinking), testing of the distinction between reality and pretense, and numerous nonegocentric capacities that reveal young children's remarkable cognitive skills.

Social Play Social play is play that involves interaction with peers. It increases dramatically during the preschool years. For many children, social play is the main context for their social interactions with peers (Solovieva & Quintanar, 2017). Social play includes varied interchanges such as turn taking, conversations about numerous topics, social games and routines, and physical play. It often provides a high degree of pleasure to the participants.

Constructive Play Constructive play combines sensorimotor/practice play with symbolic representation. It occurs when children engage in the self-regulated creation of a product or solution. Constructive play increases in the preschool years as symbolic play increases and sensorimotor play decreases. Constructive play is also a frequent form of play in the elementary school years, both in and out of the classroom.

Games Games are activities that are engaged in for pleasure and have rules. Often they involve competition. Preschool children may begin to participate in social games that involve simple rules of reciprocity and turn taking. However, games take on a much stronger role in the lives of elementary school children. In one study, the highest incidence of game playing occurred between ages 10 and 12 (Eiferman, 1971). After age 12, games decline in popularity (Bergen, 1988).

pretense/symbolic play Play in which the child transforms the physical environment into a symbol.

social play Play that involves social interactions with peers.

constructive play Play that combines sensorimotor and repetitive activity with symbolic representation of ideas. Constructive play occurs when children engage in self-regulated creation or construction of a product or a problem solution.

games Activities engaged in for pleasure that include rules and often involve competition between two or more individuals.

How Would You...?

As an **educator,** how would you integrate play into the learning process?

Trends in Play

Kathy Hirsh-Pasek, Roberta Golinkoff, and Dorothy Singer (Hirsh-Pasek & others, 2009; Singer, Golinkoff, & Hirsh-Pasek, 2006) are concerned about the reduced amount of free play time that young children have, reporting that it has declined considerably in recent decades. They especially are worried about young children's play time being restricted at home and school so they can spend more time on academic subjects. They also point out that many schools have eliminated recess. And it is not just the decline in free play time that bothers them. They underscore that learning in playful contexts captivates children's minds in ways that enhance their cognitive and socioemotional development—Singer, Golinkoff, and Hirsh-Pasek's (2006) first book on play was titled *Play = Learning*. Among the cognitive benefits of play they described are these skills: creative; abstract thinking; imagination; attention, concentration, and persistence; problem-solving; social cognition, empathy, and perspective taking; language; and mastering new concepts. Among the socioemotional experiences and development they believe play promotes are enjoyment, relaxation, and self-expression; cooperation, sharing, and turn-taking; anxiety reduction; and self-confidence. With so many positive cognitive and socioemotional outcomes of play, clearly it is important that we find more time for play in young children's lives (Taggart, Eisen, & Lillard, 2018).

What are some concerns of Hirsh-Pasek and her colleagues about trends in children's play?
©ONOKY Photononstop/Alamy

Media and Screen Time

Few developments in society in the second half of the twentieth century had a greater impact on children than television. Television continues to have a strong influence on children's development, but children's use of other media and information/communication devices has led to the use of the term *screen time,* which encompasses the time individuals spend watching/using television, DVDs, and computers; playing video games; and using hand-held electronic devices such as smartphones (Gebremariam & others, 2017; Li & others, 2017). In a national survey, there was a dramatic increase in young children's use of mobile devices in just two years from 2011 to 2013 (Common Sense Media, 2013). In this survey, playing games was the most common activity they performed using mobile devices, followed by using apps, watching videos, and watching TV/movies.

Despite the move to mobile devices, television is still a strong influence in young children's media life, with 2- to 4-year-old children watching TV approximately 2 to 4 hours per day (Common Sense Media, 2013). In a national survey, 50 percent of U.S. children's screen time was spent in front of TV sets (Common Sense Media, 2013). Compared with their counterparts in other developed countries, children in the United States watch television for considerably longer periods. The American Association of Pediatrics (2016) recommends that 2- to 5-years olds watch no more than one hour of TV a day. The AAP also recommends that they view only high-quality programs such as Sesame Street and other PBS shows for young children.

Some types of TV shows are linked to positive outcomes for children. For example, a recent meta-analysis found that children's exposure to prosocial media is linked to higher levels of prosocial behavior and empathetic concern (Coyne, Padilla-Walker, & Holmgren, 2018). And a meta-analysis of studies in 14 countries found three categories of positive outcomes from watching the TV show *Sesame Street*: cognitive, learning about the world, and social reasoning and attitudes toward outgroups (Mares & Pan, 2013).

What are some concerns about young children's media and screen time?
©karelnoppe/Getty Images

However, too much screen time can have a negative influence on children by making them passive learners, distracting them from doing homework, teaching them stereotypes, providing them with violent models of aggression, and presenting them with unrealistic views of the world (Calvert, 2015; Picherot & others, 2018). Among other concerns about young children engaging in so much screen time are decreased time spent in play, less time interacting with peers, reduced physical activity, poor sleep habits, increased risk of being overweight or obese, and higher rates of aggression (Berglind & others, 2018; Hale & others, 2018; Lissak, 2018). A research review concluded that higher levels of screen time (mostly involving TV viewing) were associated with lower levels of cognitive development in early childhood (Carson & others, 2015). Also, a study of preschool children found that each additional hour of screen time was linked to less nightly sleep, later bedtimes, and reduced likelihood of sleeping 10 or more hours per night (Xu & others, 2016). Further, researchers have found that a high level of TV viewing is linked to a greater incidence of obesity in children and adolescents. For example, a recent study of 2- to 6-year-olds indicated that increased TV viewing time on weekends was associated with a higher risk of being overweight or obese (Kondolot & others, 2017). Indeed, viewing as little as one hour of television daily was associated with an increase in body mass index (BMI) between kindergarten and first grade (Peck & others, 2015).

The extent to which children are exposed to violence and aggression on television raises special concerns (Calvert, 2015). For example, Saturday morning cartoon shows average more than 25 violent acts per hour. In a study of children, greater exposure to TV violence, video game violence, and music video violence was independently associated with a higher level of physical aggression (Coker & others, 2015).

Parents play an important role in children's media use. One study found that a higher degree of parental monitoring of children's media use was linked to a number of positive outcomes in children's lives (more sleep, better school performance, less aggressive behavior, and more prosocial behavior) (Gentile & others, 2014). Another study found that when parents reduced their own screen time, their children's screen time also decreased (Xu, Wen, & Rissel, 2014).

How Would You...?

As a **human development and family studies professional,** how would you talk with parents about strategies for reducing young children's screen time?

Summary

Emotional and Personality Development

- In Erikson's theory, early childhood is a period when development involves resolving the conflict of initiative versus guilt. Young children improve their self-understanding and understanding of others.

- Young children's range of emotions expands during early childhood as they increasingly experience self-conscious emotions such as pride, shame, and guilt. Children benefit from having emotion-coaching parents.

- Moral development involves thoughts, feelings, and actions regarding rules and regulations about what people should do in their interactions with others. Piaget proposed cognitive changes in children's moral reasoning. Behavioral and social cognitive theorists argue that there is considerable situational variability in moral behavior.

- Gender refers to the social and psychological dimensions of being male or female. Both psychoanalytic theory and social cognitive theory emphasize the adoption of parents' gender characteristics. Peers are especially adept at rewarding gender-appropriate behavior. Gender schema theory emphasizes the role of cognition in gender development.

Families

- Authoritarian, authoritative, neglectful, and indulgent parenting styles produce different results. Authoritative parenting is the style most often associated with children's social competence. Ethnic variations characterize parenting styles. Physical punishment is widely used by U.S. parents, but there are a number of reasons why it is not a good choice. Coparenting has positive effects on children's development.

- Child maltreatment may take the form of physical abuse, child neglect, sexual abuse, and emotional abuse.

- Siblings interact with each other in positive and negative ways. Birth order is related in certain ways to child characteristics, but by itself it is not a good predictor of behavior.

- In general, having both parents employed full-time outside the home has not been shown to have negative effects on children. If divorced parents develop a harmonious relationship and practice authoritative parenting, children's adjustment improves. Researchers have found few differences between children growing up in gay or lesbian families and children growing up in heterosexual families. Culture, ethnicity, and socioeconomic status are linked to a number of aspects of children's development.

Peer Relations, Play, and Media/Screen Time

- Peers are powerful socialization agents. Peers provide a source of information and comparison about the world outside the family.
- Play's functions include affiliation with peers, tension release, advances in cognitive development, exploration, and provision of a safe haven. The contemporary perspective on play emphasizes both the cognitive and the social aspects of play. Among the most widely studied types of children's play are sensorimotor play, practice play, pretense/symbolic play, social play, constructive play, and games.
- There are serious concerns about the extensive amount of time young children are spending with various media. Watching TV violence and playing violent video games have been linked to children's aggressive behavior.

Key Terms

authoritarian parenting
authoritative parenting
autonomous morality
constructive play
games
gender identity

gender roles
gender schema theory
heteronomous morality
immanent justice
indulgent parenting
moral development

neglectful parenting
practice play
pretense/symbolic play
psychoanalytic theory of
  gender
self-understanding

sensorimotor play
social cognitive theory of
  gender
social play
social role theory

7 Physical and Cognitive Development in Middle and Late Childhood

©Digital Vision/Getty Images

Stories of Life-Span Development: Angie and Her Weight

Angie, an elementary-school-age girl, offered the following comments about facing her weight problem and dealing with it effectively:

> When I was eight years old, I weighed 125 pounds. My clothes were the size that large teenage girls wear. I hated my body, and my classmates teased me all the time. I was so overweight and out of shape that when I took a P.E. class my face would get red and I had trouble breathing. I was jealous of the kids who played sports and weren't overweight like I was.
>
> I'm nine years old now and I've lost 30 pounds. I'm much happier and proud of myself. How did I lose the weight? My mom said she had finally decided enough was enough. She took me to a pediatrician who specializes in helping children lose weight and keep it off. The pediatrician counseled my mom about my eating and exercise habits, then had us join a group that he had created for overweight children and their parents. My mom and I go to the group once a week, and we've now been participating in the program for six months. I no longer eat fast-food meals, and my mom is cooking more healthy meals. Now that I've lost weight, exercise is not as hard for me, and I don't get teased by the kids at school. My mom's pretty happy, too, because she's lost 15 pounds herself since we've been in the counseling program.

Not all overweight children are as successful as Angie at reducing their weight. Indeed, being overweight in childhood has become a major national health concern in the United States. Later in the chapter, we further explore the problems associated with being overweight in childhood.

During the middle and late childhood years, which last from approximately 6 years of age to 10 or 11 years of age, children grow taller, heavier, and stronger, and become more adept at using their physical skills. During these years, disabilities may emerge that call for special attention and intervention. It is also during this age period that children's cognitive abilities increase dramatically. Their command of grammar becomes proficient, they learn to read, and they may acquire a second language. ■

Physical Changes and Health

Continued growth and change in proportions characterize children's bodies during middle and late childhood. During this time period, some important changes in the brain also take place and motor skills improve. Developing a healthy lifestyle that includes regular exercise and good nutrition is a key aspect of making sure these years are a time of healthy growth and development.

Body Growth and Change

The period of middle and late childhood involves slow, consistent growth (Hockenberry, Wilson, & Rodgers, 2017). This is a period of calm before the rapid growth spurt of adolescence. During the elementary school years, children grow an average of 2 to 3 inches a year until, at the age of 11, the average girl is 4 feet, 10¼ inches tall, and the average boy is 4 feet, 9 inches tall. During middle and late childhood, children gain about 5 to 7 pounds a year. The weight increase is due mainly to increases in the size of the skeletal and muscular systems, as well as the size of some body organs.

Proportional changes are among the most pronounced physical changes in middle and late childhood (Kliegman & others, 2016). Head and waist circumference decrease in relation to body height. A less noticeable physical change is that bones continue to ossify during middle and late childhood, although they still yield to pressure and pull more than do mature bones.

Muscle mass and strength gradually increase during these years as "baby fat" decreases (Perry & others, 2018). The loose movements and knock-knees of early childhood give way to improved muscle tone. Thanks both to heredity and to exercise, children double their strength capabilities during these years. Because of their greater number of muscle cells, boys are usually stronger than girls.

The Brain

Total brain volume stabilizes by the end of late childhood, but significant changes in various structures and regions of the brain continue to occur (Wendelken & others, 2016, 2017). As children develop, activation in some brain areas increases while it decreases in other areas (Denes, 2016; Khundrakpam & others, 2018; Mah, Geeraert, & Lebel, 2017). One shift in activation that occurs is from diffuse, larger areas to more focal, smaller areas (Turkeltaub & others, 2003). This shift is characterized by synaptic pruning, in which areas of the brain not being used lose synaptic connections and those areas being used show increased connections. In one study, researchers found less diffusion and more focal activation in the prefrontal cortex from 7 to 30 years of age (Durston & others, 2006). This shift in activation was accompanied by increased efficiency in cognitive performance, especially cognitive control, which involves effective control and flexibility in a number of areas (Markant & Thomas, 2013).

What characterizes physical growth during middle and late childhood?
©Chris Windsor/Digital Vision/Getty Images

Leading researchers in developmental cognitive neuroscience have proposed that the prefrontal cortex likely orchestrates the functions of many other brain regions during development (de Haan & Johnson, 2016). As part of this organizational role, the prefrontal cortex may provide an advantage to neural networks and connections that include the prefrontal cortex. In this view, the prefrontal cortex coordinates which neural connections are the most effective for solving a problem at hand.

Connectivity between brain regions increases as children develop (Faghiri & others, 2018). In a longitudinal study that followed individuals from 6 to 22 years of age, connectivity between the prefrontal and parietal lobes in childhood was linked to better reasoning ability later in development (Wendelken & others, 2017).

Motor Development

During middle and late childhood, children's motor skills become much smoother and more coordinated than they were in early childhood (Hockenberry, Wilson, & Rodgers, 2017). For example, only one child in a thousand can hit a tennis ball over the net at the age of 3, yet by the age of 10 or 11 most children can learn to play the sport. Running, climbing, skipping rope, swimming, bicycling, and skating are just a few of the many physical skills elementary school children can master. In gross motor skills that involve large muscle activity, boys usually outperform girls.

Increased myelination of the central nervous system is reflected in the improvement of fine motor skills during middle and late childhood. Children can more adroitly use their hands as tools. Six-year-olds can hammer, paste, tie shoes, and fasten clothes. By 7 years of age, children's hands have become steadier. At this age, children prefer a pencil to a crayon for printing, and they reverse letters less often. Printing becomes smaller. At 8 to 10 years of age, they can use their hands independently with more ease and precision. Fine motor coordination develops to the point at which children can write rather than print words. Cursive letter size becomes smaller and more even. At 10 to 12 years of age, children begin to show manipulative skills similar to the abilities of adults. They can master the complex, intricate, and rapid movements needed to produce fine-quality crafts or to play a difficult piece on a musical instrument. Girls usually outperform boys in their use of fine motor skills.

Exercise

American children and adolescents are not getting enough exercise (Dumuid & others, 2017; Walton-Fisette & Wuest, 2018). Increasing children's exercise levels has positive outcomes (Powers & Dodd, 2017; Powers & Howley, 2018).

An increasing number of studies document the positive impact of exercise on children's physical development (Dowda & others, 2017; Martin & others, 2018; Yan & others, 2018). A recent study of more than 6,000 elementary school children revealed that 55 minutes or more of moderate-to-vigorous physical activity daily was associated with a lower incidence of obesity (Nemet, 2016). Researchers also have found that aerobic exercise benefits children's attention, memory, effortful and goal-directed thinking and behavior, creativity, and academic success (Ludyga & others, 2017; Martin & others, 2018). A recent meta-analysis concluded that sustained physical activity programs were linked to improvements in children's attention, executive function, and academic achievement (de Greeff & others, 2018). Also, a recent study found that a 6-week high-intensity exercise program with 7- to 13-year-olds improved their cognitive control and working memory (Moreau, Kirk, & Waldie, 2018). Further, a recent meta-analysis concluded that children who engage in regular physical activity have better cognitive inhibitory control (Jackson & others, 2016).

Parents and schools play important roles in determining children's exercise levels (Brusseau & others, 2018; de Heer & others, 2017; Lind & others, 2018; Lo & others, 2018a; Solomon-Moore & others, 2018). Growing up with parents who exercise regularly provides positive models of exercise for children (Crawford & others, 2010). Also,

How Would You...?

As an **educator,** how would you structure the curriculum to ensure that elementary school students are getting adequate physical activity throughout the day?

in one study, a school-based physical activity was successful in improving children's fitness and lowering their fat content (Kriemler & others, 2010).

Some of the ways children spend their time can have negative consequences. For example, the total amount of time that children and adolescents spend in front of a television or computer screen daily places them at risk for reduced activity and being overweight (Taverno Ross & others, 2013). In other studies, excessive screen time has been linked to lower levels of physical activity, increased rates of obesity, worse sleep patterns, and lower brain and cognitive functioning in children (Biddle, Pearson, & Salmon, 2018; Dumuid & others, 2017; Xu & others, 2016). Also, a recent study of 8- to 12-year-olds found that large amounts of screen time were associated with lower connectivity between brain regions, as well as lower levels of language skills and cognitive control (Horowitz-Kraus & Hutton, 2018). In this study, time spend reading was linked to higher levels of functioning in these areas.

Health, Illness, and Disease

For the most part, middle and late childhood is a time of excellent health. Disease and death are less prevalent at this time than during other periods in childhood and in adolescence. However, many children in middle and late childhood face health problems that threaten their development (Blake, Munoz, & Volpe, 2019).

Overweight Children

Being overweight is an increasingly prevalent health problem in children (Thompson & Manore, 2018; Wardlaw, Smith, & Collene, 2018). Over the last three decades, the percentage of U.S. children who are at risk for being overweight has increased dramatically. Recently there has been a decrease in the percentage of 2- to 5-year-old children who are obese, which dropped from 12.1 percent in 2009–2010 to 9.4 percent in 2013–2014 (Ogden & others, 2016). In 2013–2014, 17.4 percent of 6- to 11-year-old U.S. children were classified as obese, a rate that was essentially unchanged from 2009–2010 (Ogden & others, 2016).

It is not just in the United States that more children are becoming overweight (Zhou & others, 2017). One study found that general and abdominal obesity in Chinese children increased significantly from 1993 to 2009 (Liang & others, 2012).

What are some concerns about overweight children?
©Image Source/Getty Images

Causes of Being Overweight During Childhood Heredity and environmental contexts are related to being overweight in childhood (Insel & Roth, 2018; Yanovski & Yanovski, 2018). Recent genetic analysis indicates that heredity is an important factor in children becoming overweight (Donatelle, 2019). Overweight parents tend to have overweight children (Pufal & others, 2012). Environmental factors that influence whether children become overweight include availability of food (especially food high in fat content), energy-saving devices, declining physical activity, parents' eating habits and monitoring of children's eating habits, the context in which a child eats, and heavy screen time (Ren & others, 2017; Valgarda, 2018). In a recent Japanese study, the family pattern that was linked to the highest rates of overweight/obesity in children was a combination of irregular mealtimes and the most screen time for both parents (Watanabe & others, 2016). Further, a recent study found that children were less likely to be obese or overweight when they attended schools in states that had a strong policy emphasis on healthy foods and beverages (Datar & Nicosia, 2017). Also, in a 14-year longitudinal study, parental weight change predicted children's weight change (Andriani, Liao, & Kuo, 2015). As described earlier, a recent study of more than 6,000 elementary school children revealed that 55 minutes or more of moderate-to-vigorous physical activity daily was associated with a lower incidence of obesity (Nemet, 2016).

Consequences of Being Overweight During Childhood

The increasing number of overweight children in recent decades is cause for great concern because being overweight raises the risk for many medical and psychological problems (Powers & Dodd, 2017; Schiff, 2019). Diabetes, hypertension (high blood pressure), and elevated blood cholesterol levels are common in children who are overweight (Chung, Onuzuruike, & Magge, 2018; Martin-Espinosa & others, 2017). Research reviews have concluded that obesity was linked with low self-esteem in children (Gomes & others, 2011; Moharei & others, 2018).

Intervention Programs A combination of diet, exercise, and behavior modification is often recommended to help children lose weight (Martin & others, 2018). Intervention programs that emphasize getting parents to engage in healthier lifestyles themselves, as well as to offer their children healthier food choices and persuade them to exercise more, can produce weight reduction in overweight and obese children (Yackobovitch & others, 2018).

Child life specialists are among the health professionals who strive to reduce stress in children who have health issues. To read about the work of child life specialist Sharon McLeod, see *Careers in Life-Span Development.*

Careers in life-span development

Sharon McLeod, Child Life Specialist

Sharon McLeod is a child life specialist who is clinical director of the Child Life and Recreational Therapy Department at the Children's Hospital Medical Center in Cincinnati. Under McLeod's direction, the goals of the Child Life Department are to promote children's optimal growth and development, reduce the stress of health-care experiences, and provide support to child patients and their families. These goals are accomplished through therapeutic play and developmentally appropriate activities, educating and psychologically preparing children for medical procedures, and serving as a resource for parents and other professionals regarding children's development and health-care issues, including problems related to being overweight.

McLeod says that human growth and development provides the foundation for her profession as a child life specialist. She also describes her best times as a student as those when she conducted fieldwork, had an internship, and experienced hands-on applications of theories and concepts she learned in her courses.

Sharon McLeod, child life specialist, works with a child at Children's Hospital Medical Center in Cincinnati.
©Sharon McLeod

Children with Disabilities

The elementary school years are a time when disabilities become prominent for some children. What are some of the disabilities that children have? What characterizes the educational issues facing children with disabilities?

Disability	Percentage of All Children in Public Schools
Learning disabilities	4.6
Speech or hearing impairments	2.7
Autism	1.0
Intellectual disabilities	0.9
Emotional disturbance	0.7

Figure 1 U.S. Children with a Disability Who Receive Special Education Services

Figures are for the 2012–2013 school year and represent the four categories with the highest numbers and percentages of children. Both learning disability and attention deficit hyperactivity disorder are combined in the learning disabilities category (Condition of Education, 2016).

Source: US Department of Education. *The Condition of Education: Participation in Education.* Washington, DC: U.S. Office of Education, 2016.

Figure 2 Brain Scans and Learning Disabilities
An increasing number of studies are using MRI brain scans to examine the brain pathways involved in learning disabilities. Shown here is 9-year-old Patrick Price, who has dyslexia. Patrick is going through an MRI scanner disguised by drapes to look like a child-friendly castle. Inside the scanner, children must lie virtually motionless as words and symbols flash on a screen, and they are asked to identify them by clicking different buttons.
©Manuel Balce Ceneta/AP Images

The Scope of Disabilities

Of all children in the United States, 12.9 percent from 3 to 21 years of age received special education or related services in 2012–2013, an increase of 3 percent since 1980–1981 (Condition of Education, 2016). As indicated in Figure 1, students with a learning disability were by far the largest group of students with a disability who received special education, followed by children with speech or language impairments, autism, intellectual disabilities, and emotional disturbance. Note that the U.S. Department of Education includes both students with a learning disability and students with ADHD in the category of learning disability.

Learning Disabilities

The U.S. government uses the following definition to determine whether a child should be classified as having a learning disability: A child with a **learning disability** has difficulty in learning that involves understanding or using spoken or written language, and the difficulty can appear in listening, thinking, reading, writing, and spelling. A learning disability also may involve difficulty in doing mathematics. To be classified as a learning disability, the learning problem is not primarily the result of visual, hearing, or motor disabilities; intellectual disability; emotional disorders; or environmental, cultural, or economic disadvantage.

About three times as many boys as girls are classified as having a learning disability. Among the explanations for this gender difference are a greater biological vulnerability among boys and referral bias. That is, boys are more likely than girls to be referred by teachers for treatment because of troublesome behavior.

Approximately 80 percent of children with a learning disability have a reading problem (Shaywitz, Gruen, & Shaywitz, 2007). Three types of learning disabilities are dyslexia, dysgraphia, and dyscalculia:

- *Dyslexia* is a category reserved for individuals who have a severe impairment in their ability to read and spell (Nergard-Nilssen & Eklund, 2018).

- *Dysgraphia* is a learning disability that involves difficulty in handwriting (Hook & Haynes, 2017). Children with dysgraphia may write very slowly, their writing products may be virtually illegible, and they may make numerous spelling errors because of their inability to match up sounds and letters.

- *Dyscalculia*, also known as developmental arithmetic disorder, is a learning disability that involves difficulty in math computation (McCaskey & others, 2018; Nelson & Powell, 2018).

The precise causes of learning disabilities have not yet been determined (Friend, 2018). To reveal any regions of the brain that might be involved in learning disabilities, researchers use brain-imaging techniques such as magnetic resonance imaging (Ramus & others, 2018) (see Figure 2). This research indicates that it is unlikely learning disabilities reside in a single, specific brain location. More likely, learning disabilities

learning disability Describes a child who has difficulty understanding or using spoken or written language or doing mathematics. To be classified as a learning disability, the problem is not primarily the result of visual, hearing, or motor disabilities; intellectual disability; emotional disorders; or due to environmental, cultural, or economic disadvantage.

How Would You…?
As an **educator,** how would you explain the nature of learning disabilities to a parent whose child has recently been diagnosed with a learning disability?

are due to problems integrating information from multiple brain regions or subtle difficulties in brain structures and functions.

Interventions with children who have a learning disability often focus on improving reading ability (Cunningham, 2017; Temple & others, 2018). Intensive instruction over a period of time by a competent teacher can help many children (Tompkins, 2018).

Attention Deficit Hyperactivity Disorder (ADHD)

Attention deficit hyperactivity disorder (ADHD) is a disability in which children consistently show one or more of these characteristics over a period of time: (1) inattention, (2) hyperactivity, and (3) impulsivity. Children who are inattentive have such difficulty focusing on any one thing that they may get bored with a task after only a few minutes—or even seconds. Children who are hyperactive show high levels of physical activity, seeming to be almost constantly in motion. Children who are impulsive have difficulty curbing their reactions; they do not do a good job of thinking before they act. Depending on the characteristics that children with ADHD display, they can be diagnosed as (1) ADHD with predominantly inattention; (2) ADHD with predominantly hyperactivity/impulsivity; or (3) ADHD with both inattention and hyperactivity/impulsivity.

The number of children diagnosed and treated for ADHD has increased substantially in recent decades, by some estimates doubling in the 1990s. The American Psychiatric Association (2013) reported in the *DSM-V* that 5 percent of children have ADHD, although estimates are higher in community samples. For example, the Centers for Disease Control and Prevention (2017) estimates that ADHD continues to increase in 4- to 17-year-old children, going from 8 percent in 2003 to 9.5 percent in 2007 and to 11 percent in 2016. According to the Centers for Disease Control and Prevention, 13.2 percent of U.S. boys and 5.6 of U.S. girls have ever been diagnosed with ADHD. The disorder is diagnosed four to nine times more often in boys than in girls.

Many children with ADHD show impulsive behavior, such as this boy reaching to pull a girl's hair. *How would you handle this situation if you were a teacher in this classroom?*
©Nicole Hill/Rubberball/Getty Images

There is controversy, however, about the reasons for the increased diagnosis of ADHD (Hallahan, Kauffman, & Pullen, 2019; Turnbull & others, 2016). Some experts attribute the increase mainly to heightened awareness of the disorder; others are concerned that many children might be incorrectly diagnosed (Watson & others, 2014).

Adjustment and optimal development also are difficult for children who have ADHD, so it is important that the diagnosis be accurate (Hallahan, Kauffman, & Pullen, 2019; Hechtman & others, 2016). Children who are diagnosed with ADHD have an increased risk of lower academic achievement, problematic peer relations, school dropout, adolescent pregnancy, substance use problems, and antisocial behavior (Machado & others, 2018). A recent study found that childhood ADHD was associated with long-term underachievement in math and reading (Voigt & others, 2017). Also, a recent research review concluded that in comparison with typically developing girls, girls with ADHD had more problems with friendship, peer interaction, social skills, and peer victimization (Kok & others, 2016). Further, a recent research review concluded that ADHD in childhood was linked to the following long-term outcomes: failure to complete high school, other mental and substance use disorders, criminal activity, and unemployment (Erskine & others, 2016). And a recent study revealed that individuals with ADHD were more likely to become parents at 12 to 16 years of age (Ostergaard & others, 2017).

Definitive causes of ADHD have not been found. However, a number of causes have been proposed (Mash & Wolfe, 2019; Smith & others, 2018). Some children may

How Would You...?

As a **health-care professional,** how would you respond to this comment from a parent? "I do not believe that ADHD is a real disorder. Children are supposed to be active."

inherit a tendency to develop ADHD from their parents (Hess & others, 2018). Other children likely develop ADHD because of damage to their brain during prenatal or postnatal development (Hinshaw, 2018). Among early possible contributors to ADHD are cigarette and alcohol exposure, as well as a high level of maternal stress and depression during prenatal development and low birth weight (Weissenberger & others, 2017; Wolford & others, 2017).

As with learning disabilities, the development of brain-imaging techniques is leading to a better understanding of ADHD (Riaz & others, 2018; Sun & others, 2018). One study revealed that peak thickness of the cerebral cortex occurred three years later (10.5 years) in children with ADHD than in children without ADHD (peak at 7.5 years) (Shaw & others, 2007). The delay was more prominent in the prefrontal regions of the brain that are especially important in attention and planning (see Figure 3). Another study also found delayed development in the brain's frontal lobes among children with ADHD, which likely was due to delayed or decreased myelination (Nagel & others, 2011). Researchers also are exploring the roles that various neurotransmitters, such as serotonin and dopamine, might play in ADHD (Ledonne & Mercuri, 2017; Vanicek & others, 2017).

The delays in brain development just described are in areas linked to executive function (Munroe & others, 2018). An increasing focus of interest in the study of children with ADHD is their difficulty on tasks involving executive function, such as behavioral inhibition when necessary, use of working memory, and effective planning (Krieger &Amador-Campos, 2018). Researchers also have found deficits in theory of mind in children with ADHD (Maoz & others, 2018; Mary & others, 2016). Children diagnosed with ADHD have an increased risk of school dropout, adolescent pregnancy, substance use problems, and antisocial behavior (Machado & others, 2018; Regnart, Truter, & Meyer, 2017).

Prefrontal cortex Prefrontal cortex

■ Greater than 2 years delay
■ 0 to 2 years delay

Figure 3 Regions of the Brain in Which Children with ADHD Had a Delayed Peak in the Thickness of the Cerebral Cortex
Note: The greatest delays occurred in the prefrontal cortex.

How Would You...?
As a **human development and family studies professional,** how would you advise parents who are hesitant about medicating their child who was recently diagnosed with a mild form of ADHD?

Stimulant medication such as Ritalin or Adderall (which has fewer side effects than Ritalin) is effective in improving the attention of many children with ADHD, but it usually does not improve their attention to the same level as in children who do not have ADHD (Sclar & others, 2012). A recent research review also concluded that stimulant medications are effective in treating ADHD during the short term but that longer-term benefits of stimulant medications are not clear (Rajeh & others, 2017). Researchers have often found that a combination of medication (such as Ritalin) and behavior management improves the behavior of children with ADHD better than medication alone or behavior management alone, although this treatment does not work in all cases (Parens & Johnston, 2009).

Recently, researchers have been exploring the possibility that three types of training exercises might reduce ADHD symptoms. First, *neurofeedback* can improve the attention of children with ADHD (Goode & others, 2018; Thibault & others, 2018). Neurofeedback trains individuals to become more aware of their physiological responses so they can attain better control over their brain's prefrontal cortex, where executive control primarily occurs. Second, *mindfulness training* also has been found to decrease ADHD symptoms in children (Lo & others, 2018b). For example, a recent meta-analysis concluded that mindfulness training significantly improved the attention of children with ADHD (Cairncross & Miller, 2018). Also, a recent study confirmed that an 8-week yoga program was effective in improving the sustained attention of children with ADHD (Chou & Huang, 2017). And, third, physical exercise also is being investigated as a possible treatment for children with ADHD (Den Heijer & others, 2017; Pan & others, 2018). For example, a recent meta-analysis concluded that physical exercise is effective in reducing cognitive symptoms of ADHD in individuals 3 to 25 years of age (Tan, Pooley & Speelman, 2016). Another meta-analysis concluded that short-term aerobic exercise is effective in reducing symptoms such as inattention, hyperactivity, and impulsivity (Cerillo-Urbina & others, 2015). And a third recent meta-analysis indicated that exercise is associated with better executive function in children with ADHD (Vysniauske & others, 2018).

Despite the encouraging recent studies of using neurofeedback, mindfulness training, and exercise to improve the attention of children with ADHD, it has not yet been determined whether these non-drug therapies are as effective as stimulant drugs and/ or whether they benefit children as add-ons to stimulant drugs to provide a combination treatment (Den Heijer & others, 2017).

Autism Spectrum Disorders

Autism spectrum disorders (ASD), also called pervasive developmental disorders, range from the more severe disorder called *autistic disorder* to the milder disorder called *Asperger syndrome*. Autism spectrum disorders are characterized by problems in social interaction, problems in verbal and nonverbal communication, and repetitive behaviors (Boutot, 2017; Gerenser & Lopez, 2017; Jones & others, 2018). Children with these disorders may also show atypical responses to sensory experiences (National Institute of Mental Health, 2018). Autism spectrum disorders can often be detected in children as young as 1 to 3 years of age.

Recent estimates of autism spectrum disorders indicate that they are dramatically increasing in occurrence or are increasingly being detected. Once thought to affect only 1 in 2,500 children decades ago, they were estimated to be present in about 1 in 150 children in 2002 (Centers for Disease Control and Prevention, 2007). In the most recent survey, the estimated percentage of 8-year-old children with autism spectrum disorders had increased to 1 in 68 (Christensen & others, 2016). In the recent surveys, autism spectrum disorders were identified five times more often in boys than in girls, and 8 percent of individuals aged 3 to 21 with these disorders were receiving special education services (Centers for Disease Control and Prevention, 2017).

What characterizes autism spectrum disorders?
©Rob Crandall/Alamy

Autism is usually identified during early or middle childhood rather than during infancy. In recent surveys, only a minority of parents reported that their child's autism spectrum disorder was identified prior to 3 years of age, and one-third to one-half of the cases were identified after 6 years of age (Sheldrick, Maye, & Carter, 2017). However, researchers are conducting studies that seek to find earlier determinants of autism spectrum disorders (Reiersen, 2017).

Autistic disorder is a severe developmental autism spectrum disorder that has its onset during the first three years of life and includes deficiencies in social relationships; abnormalities in communication; and restricted, repetitive, and stereotyped patterns of behavior.

Asperger syndrome is a relatively mild autism spectrum disorder in which the child has relatively good verbal language skills, milder nonverbal language problems, and a restricted range of interests and relationships (Boutot, 2017). Children with Asperger syndrome often engage in obsessive, repetitive routines and preoccupations with a particular subject. For example, a child may be obsessed with baseball scores or YouTube videos.

Children with autism have deficits in cognitive processing of information (Jones & others, 2018). For example, a recent study found that a lower level of working memory was the executive function most strongly associated with autism spectrum disorders (Ziermans & others, 2017). Children with these disorders may also show atypical responses to sensory experiences (National Institute of Mental Health, 2018). Intellectual disability is present in some children with autism; others show average or above-average intelligence (Volkmar & others, 2014).

autism spectrum disorders (ASD)
Also called pervasive developmental disorders, they range from the severe disorder labeled autistic disorder to the milder disorder called Asperger syndrome. These disorders are characterized by problems in social interaction, verbal and nonverbal communication, and repetitive behaviors.

What causes autism spectrum disorders? The current consensus is that autism is a brain dysfunction characterized by abnormalities in brain structure and neurotransmitters (Fernandez, Mollinedo-Gajate, & Penagarikano, 2018). Recent interest has focused on a lack of connectivity between brain regions as a key factor in autism (Abbott & others, 2018; Nair & others, 2018; Nunes & others, 2018). Genetic factors also likely play a role in the development of autism spectrum disorders (Valiente-Palleja & others, 2018;

Yuan & others, 2017), but there is no evidence that family socialization causes autism. Intellectual disability is present in some children with autism, while others show average or above-average intelligence (Memari & others, 2012).

Children with autism benefit from a well-structured classroom, individualized teaching, and small-group instruction (Mastropieri & Scruggs, 2018). Behavior modification techniques are sometimes effective in helping autistic children learn (Alberto & Troutman, 2017).

Educational Issues

Until the 1970s most U.S. public schools either refused enrollment to children with disabilities or inadequately served them. This changed in 1975, when *Public Law 94-142*, the Education for All Handicapped Children Act, required that all students with disabilities be given a free, appropriate public education. In 1990, Public Law 94-142 was recast as the Individuals with Disabilities Education Act (IDEA). IDEA was amended in 1997 and then reauthorized in 2004 and renamed the Individuals with Disabilities Education Improvement Act.

IDEA spells out broad mandates for providing educational services to children with disabilities of all kinds (Heward, Alber-Morgan, & Konrad, 2017; Smith & others, 2018). These services include evaluation and eligibility determination, appropriate education and an individualized education plan (IEP), and education in the least restrictive environment (LRE) (Cook & Richardson-Gibbs, 2018).

An **individualized education plan (IEP)** is a written statement that spells out a program that is specifically tailored for a student with a disability (Hallahan, Kauffman, & Pullen, 2019). The **least restrictive environment (LRE)** is a setting that is as similar as possible to the one in which children who do not have a disability are educated. This provision of the IDEA has given a legal basis to efforts to educate children with a disability in the regular classroom. The term **inclusion** describes educating a child with special educational needs full-time in the regular classroom (Lewis, Wheeler, & Carter, 2017). In 2014, 61 percent of U.S. students with a disability spent more than 80 percent of their school day in a general classroom (compared with only 33 percent in 1990) (Condition of Education, 2016).

Many legal changes regarding children with disabilities have been extremely positive (Smith & others, 2016). Compared with several decades ago, far more children today are receiving competent, specialized services. For many children, inclusion in the regular classroom, with modifications or supplemental services, is appropriate (Mastropieri & Scruggs, 2018). However, some leading experts on special education argue that some children with disabilities may not benefit from inclusion in the regular classroom. James Kauffman and his colleagues, for example, advocate a more individualized approach that does not necessarily involve full inclusion but allows options such as special education outside the regular classroom with trained professionals and adapted curricula (Kauffman, McGee, & Brigham, 2004). They go on to say, "We sell students with disabilities short when we pretend that they are not different from typical students. We make the same error when we pretend that they must not be expected to put forth extra effort if they are to learn to do some things—or learn to do something in a different way" (p. 620). Like general education, special education should challenge students with disabilities "to become all they can be."

individualized education plan (IEP) A written statement that spells out a program tailored to a child with a disability.

least restrictive environment (LRE) The concept that a child with a disability should be educated in a setting that is as similar as possible to the one in which children who do not have a disability are educated.

inclusion Educating a child who requires special education full-time in the regular classroom.

IDEA mandates free, appropriate education for all children. *What services does IDEA mandate for children with disabilities?*
©Bill Aron/PhotoEdit

Cognitive Changes

It is the wisdom of the human life span that at no time are children more ready to learn than during the period of expansive imagination at the end of early childhood. Do children enter a new stage of cognitive development in middle and late childhood?

Piaget's Cognitive Developmental Theory

According to Piaget (1952), the preschool child's thought is preoperational. Preschool children can form stable concepts, and they have begun to reason, but their thinking is flawed by egocentrism and magical belief systems. As we discussed in the chapter on physical and cognitive development in early childhood, however, Piaget may have underestimated the cognitive skills of preschool children. Some researchers argue that under the right conditions, young children may display abilities that are characteristic of Piaget's next stage of cognitive development, the stage of concrete operational thought (Gelman, 1969). Here we will cover the characteristics of concrete operational thought and evaluate Piaget's portrait of this stage.

The Concrete Operational Stage

Piaget proposed that the *concrete operational stage* lasts from approximately 7 to 11 years of age. In this stage, children can perform concrete operations, and they can reason logically as long as reasoning can be applied to specific or concrete examples. Remember that *operations* are mental actions that are reversible, and *concrete operations* are operations that are applied to real, concrete objects.

The conservation tasks described in the chapter on physical and cognitive development in early childhood indicate whether children are capable of concrete operations. For example, recall that in one task involving conservation of matter, the child is presented with two identical balls of clay. The experimenter rolls one ball into a long, thin shape; the other remains in its original ball shape. The child is then asked if there is more clay in the ball or in the long, thin piece of clay. By the time children reach the age of 7 or 8, most answer that the amount of clay is the same. To answer this problem correctly, children have to imagine the clay rolling back into a ball. This type of imagination involves a reversible mental action applied to a real, concrete object. Concrete operations allow the child to consider several characteristics rather than focus on a single property of an object. In the clay example, the preoperational child is likely to focus on height or width. The concrete operational child coordinates information about both dimensions.

What other abilities are characteristic of children who have reached the concrete operational stage? One important skill is the ability to classify or divide things into different sets or subsets and to consider their interrelationships. Consider the family tree of four generations that is shown in Figure 4 (Furth & Wachs, 1975). This family tree suggests that the grandfather (A) has three children (B, C, and D), each of whom has two children (E through J), and that one of these children (J) has three children (K, L, and M). A child who comprehends the classification system can move up and down a level, across a level, and up and down and across within the system. The concrete operational child understands that person J can at the same time be father, brother, and grandson, for example.

Children who have reached the concrete operational stage are also capable of **seriation**, which is the ability to order stimuli along a quantitative dimension (such as length). To see if students can serialize, a teacher might haphazardly place eight sticks of different lengths on a table. The teacher then asks the students to order the sticks by length. Many young children end up with two or three small groups of "big" sticks or "little" sticks, rather than a correct ordering of all eight sticks. Another ineffective strategy they use is to line up the tops of the sticks evenly but ignore the bottoms. The concrete operational thinker simultaneously understands that each stick must be longer than the one that precedes it and shorter than the one that follows it.

Another aspect of reasoning about the relations between classifications is **transitivity**, which is the ability to logically

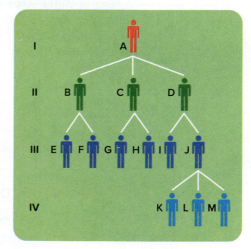

Figure 4 Classification: An Important Ability in Concrete Operational Thought

A family tree of four generations (I to IV): The preoperational child has trouble classifying the members of the four generations; the concrete operational child can classify the members vertically, horizontally, and obliquely (up and down and across). For example, the concrete operational child understands that a family member can be a son, a brother, and a father, all at the same time.

seriation The concrete operation that involves ordering stimuli along a quantitative dimension (such as length).

transitivity The ability to logically combine relations to understand certain conclusions.

How Would You…?

As a **psychologist,** how would you characterize the contribution Piaget made to our current understanding of cognitive development in childhood?

combine relations to understand certain conclusions. In this case, consider three sticks (A, B, and C) of differing lengths. A is the longest, B is intermediate in length, and C is the shortest. Does the child understand that if A is longer than B and B is longer than C, then A is longer than C? In Piaget's theory, concrete operational thinkers do; preoperational thinkers do not.

Evaluating Piaget's Concrete Operational Stage

Has Piaget's portrait of the concrete operational child stood the test of research? According to Piaget, various aspects of a stage should emerge at the same time. In fact, however, some concrete operational abilities do not appear in synchrony. For example, children do not learn to conserve at the same time they learn to cross-classify.

Furthermore, education and culture exert stronger influences on children's development than Piaget reasoned (Feeney, Moravcik, & Nolte, 2019; Follari, 2019; Morrison, 2018; Roberts & others, 2018). Some preoperational children can be trained to reason at a concrete operational stage. And the age at which children acquire conservation skills is related to how much practice their culture provides in these skills.

Thus, although Piaget was a giant in the field of developmental psychology, his conclusions about the concrete operational stage have been challenged. Later, after examining the final stage in his theory of cognitive development, we will further evaluate Piaget's contributions and consider criticisms of his theory.

Neo-Piagetians argue that Piaget got some things right but that his theory needs considerable revision. They give more emphasis to how children use attention, memory, and strategies to process information (Case & Mueller, 2001). They especially believe that a more accurate portrayal of children's thinking requires attention to children's strategies, the speed at which children process information, the particular task involved, and the division of problems into smaller, more precise steps (Morra & others, 2008). These issues are addressed by the information-processing approach, and we will discuss some of them later in this chapter.

An outstanding teacher and education in the logic of science and mathematics are important cultural experiences that promote the development of operational thought. *Might Piaget have underestimated the roles of culture and schooling in children's cognitive development?*
©Majority World/Getty Images

Information Processing

If we examine how children handle information during middle and late childhood instead of analyzing the type of thinking they display, what do we find? During these years, most children dramatically improve their ability to sustain and control attention (Posner, 2018a, b; Wu & Scerif, 2018). Other changes in information processing during middle and late childhood involve memory, thinking, and metacognition (Braithwaite & Siegler, 2018; Meltzer, 2018).

Memory

Short-term memory increases considerably during early childhood but after the age of 7 does not show as much increase. British cognitive psychologist Alan Baddeley (1990, 2001, 2007, 2010, 2012, 2013, 2015, 2018a, b) defines **working memory** as a kind of mental "workbench" where individuals manipulate and assemble information when they make decisions, solve problems, and comprehend written and spoken language. Working memory is described as being more active and powerful in modifying information than short-term memory. Working memory involves bringing information to

neo-Piagetians Developmentalists who have elaborated on Piaget's theory, giving more emphasis to how children use attention, memory, and strategies to process information.

working memory A mental "workbench" where individuals manipulate and assemble information when making decisions, solving problems, and comprehending written and spoken language.

mind and mentally working with or updating it, as when you link one idea to another and relate what you are reading now to something you read earlier.

Working memory develops slowly. Even by 8 years of age, children can only hold in memory half the items that adults can remember (Kharitonova, Winter, & Sheridan, 2015). Working memory is linked to many aspects of children's development (Baddeley & others, 2018a, b; Nicolaou & others, 2018; Sanchez-Perez & others, 2018; Swanson, 2017). For example, children who have better working memory are more advanced in language comprehension, math skills, problem solving, and reasoning than their counterparts with less effective working memory (Ogino & others, 2017; Simms, Frausel, & Richland, 2018; Tsubomi & Watanabe, 2017). Also, in a recent study, children's verbal working memory was linked to acquisition of the following skills in both first- and second-language learners: morphology, syntax, and grammar (Verhagen & Leseman, 2016).

Long-term memory, a relatively permanent and unlimited type of memory, increases with age during middle and late childhood. In part, improvements in memory reflect children's increased knowledge and their increased use of strategies. Keep in mind that it is important not to view memory in terms of how children add something to it but rather to underscore how children actively construct their memory (Bauer & others, 2017; Radvansky & Ashcraft, 2018).

Knowledge and Expertise Much of the research on the role of knowledge in memory has compared experts and novices. Experts have acquired extensive knowledge about a particular content area; this knowledge influences what they notice and how they organize, represent, and interpret information (Ericsson & others, 2018; Varga & others, 2018). This in turn affects their ability to remember, reason, and solve problems. When individuals have expertise about a particular subject, their memory also tends to be good regarding material related to that subject (Staszewski, 2013).

For example, one study found that 10- and 11-year-olds who were experienced chess players ("experts") were able to remember more information about chess pieces than college students who were not chess players ("novices") (Chi, 1978). In contrast, when the college students were presented with other stimuli, they were able to remember them better than the children were. Thus, the children's expertise in chess gave them superior memories, but only regarding chess.

There are developmental changes in expertise (Ericsson & others, 2018). Older children usually have more expertise about a subject than younger children do, which can contribute to their better memory for the subject.

Strategies Long-term memory depends on the learning activities individuals engage in when learning and remembering information. **Strategies** consist of deliberate mental activities to improve the processing of information. They do not occur automatically but require effort and work (Braithwaite & Siegler, 2018; Chu & others, 2018; Graham & others, 2018; Harris & others, 2018). Following are some effective strategies for adults to use in helping children improve their memory skills:

- *Guide children to elaborate about the information they are to remember.* **Elaboration** involves more extensive processing of the information, such as thinking of examples or relating the information to one's own life. Elaboration makes the information more meaningful.

- *Encourage children to engage in mental imagery.* Mental imagery can help even young school children to remember visuals. However, for remembering verbal information, mental imagery works better for older children than for younger children.

- *Motivate children to remember material by understanding it rather than by memorizing it.* Children will remember information better over the long term if they understand the information rather than just rehearse and memorize it. Rehearsal works well for encoding information into short-term memory, but when children need to retrieve the information from long-term memory, rehearsal is much less efficient. For most information, encourage children to understand it, give it meaning, elaborate on it, and personalize it.

long-term memory A relatively permanent type of memory that holds huge amounts of information for a long period of time.

strategies Deliberate mental activities designed to improve the processing of information.

elaboration An important strategy that involves engaging in more extensive processing of information.

- *Repeat and vary instructional information and link it to other information early and often.* These recommendations improve children's consolidation and reconsolidation of the information they are learning (Bauer, 2009). Varying the themes of a lesson increases the number of associations in memory storage, and linking the information expands the network of associations in memory storage; both strategies expand the routes for retrieving information from storage in the brain.

- *Embed memory-relevant language when instructing children.* Teachers who use mnemonic devices and metacognitive questions that encourage children to think about their thinking can improve student performance.

Fuzzy Trace Theory Might something other than knowledge and strategies be responsible for the improvement in memory during the elementary school years? Charles Brainerd and Valerie Reyna (2014) argue that fuzzy traces account for much of this improvement. Their **fuzzy trace theory** states that memory is best understood by considering two types of memory representations: (1) verbatim memory trace and (2) gist. The *verbatim memory trace* consists of the precise details of the information, whereas *gist* refers to the central idea of the information. When gist is used, fuzzy traces are built up. Although individuals of all ages extract gist, young children tend to store and retrieve verbatim traces. At some point during the early elementary school years, children begin to use gist more, and according to the theory, this contributes to the improved memory and reasoning of older children because fuzzy traces are more enduring and less likely to be forgotten than verbatim traces.

Thinking

Thinking involves manipulating and transforming information in memory. Two important aspects of thinking are being able to think critically and creatively.

Critical Thinking Currently there is considerable interest among psychologists and educators regarding critical thinking (Bonney & Sternberg, 2017). **Critical thinking** involves thinking reflectively and productively and evaluating evidence. In this book, the *"How Would You . . . ?"* questions challenge you to think critically about a topic or an issue related to the discussion.

Jacqueline and Martin Brooks (2001) lament that few schools really teach students to think critically and develop a deep understanding of concepts. Deep understanding occurs when students are stimulated to rethink previously held ideas. In Brooks and Brooks' view, schools spend too much time getting students to give a single correct answer in an imitative way, rather than encouraging them to expand their thinking by coming up with new ideas and rethinking earlier conclusions. They observe that too often teachers ask students to recite, define, describe, state, and list, rather than to analyze, infer, connect, synthesize, criticize, create, evaluate, think, and rethink. Many successful students complete their assignments, do well on tests and get good grades, yet they don't ever learn to think critically and deeply. They think superficially, staying on the surface of problems rather than stretching their minds and becoming deeply engaged in meaningful thinking.

Robert Roeser and his colleagues (Roeser & Eccles, 2015; Roeser & Zelazo, 2012; Roeser & others, 2014) have emphasized that mindfulness is an important mental process that children can engage in to improve a number of cognitive and socioemotional skills, such as executive function, focused attention, emotion regulation, and empathy. *Mindfulness* involves paying careful attention to your thoughts, feelings, and environment (Hudziak & Archangeli, 2017). It has been proposed that mindfulness training could be implemented in schools through practices such as using age-appropriate activities that increase children's reflection on moment-to-moment experiences and result in improved self-regulation (Roeser & Eccles, 2015). For example, a training program in mindfulness and caring for others was effective in improving the cognitive control of fourth- and fifth-graders (Schonert-Reichl & others, 2015). In other recent research, mindfulness training has been found to improve children's attention and self-regulation (Poehlmann-Tynan & others, 2016); achievement (Singh & others, 2016); and coping strategies in stressful situations (Dariotis & others, 2016).

fuzzy trace theory States that memory is best understood by considering two types of memory representations: (1) verbatim memory trace and (2) gist. In this theory, older children's better memory is attributed to the fuzzy traces created by extracting the gist of information.

thinking Manipulating and transforming information in memory.

critical thinking Thinking reflectively and productively, as well as evaluating the evidence.

For example, in a recent study, mindfulness training improved children's self-regulation of attention (Felver & others, 2017). In addition to mindfulness, activities such as yoga, meditation, and tai chi have been recently suggested as candidates for improving children's cognitive and socioemotional development (Felver & others, 2017). Together these activities are being grouped under the topic of *contemplative science*, a cross-disciplinary term that involves the study of how various types of mental and physical training might enhance children's development (Roeser & Eccles, 2015).

Creative Thinking Cognitively competent children not only think critically, but also creatively (Renzulli, 2018; Sternberg, 2018e, f; Sternberg & Kaufman, 2018b; Sternberg & Sternberg, 2017). **Creative thinking** is the ability to think in novel and unusual ways and to come up with unique solutions to problems. Thus, intelligence and creativity are not the same thing. This difference was recognized by J. P. Guilford (1967), who distinguished between **convergent thinking,** which produces one correct answer and characterizes the kind of thinking that is required on conventional tests of intelligence, and **divergent thinking,** which produces many different answers to the same question and characterizes creativity. For example, a typical item on a conventional intelligence test is "How many quarters will you get in return for 60 dimes?" In contrast, the following question has many possible answers: "What images come to mind when you hear the phrase 'sitting alone in a dark room' or 'some unique uses for a paper clip'?"

It is important to recognize that children will show more creativity in some domains than others (Sternberg, 2018e, f). A child who shows creative thinking skills in mathematics may not exhibit these skills in art, for example. An important goal is to help children learn to think creatively.

A special concern today is that the creative thinking of children in the United States appears to be declining. A study of approximately 300,000 U.S. children and adults found that creativity scores rose until 1990, but since then have steadily declined (Kim, 2010). Among the likely causes of this decline are the amount of time U.S. children spend watching TV and playing video games instead of engaging in creative activities, as well as the lack of emphasis on creative thinking skills in schools (Beghetto & Kaufman, 2017; Renzulli, 2017, 2018; Sternberg, 2018e, f). In some countries, though, there has been increasing emphasis on creative thinking in schools. For example, historically, creative thinking has typically been discouraged in Chinese schools. However, Chinese educators are now encouraging teachers to spend more classroom time on creative activities (Plucker, 2010).

Metacognition

Metacognition is cognition about cognition, or knowing about knowing (Flavell, 2004; Norman, 2017). Many studies classified as "metacognitive" have focused on *metamemory*, or knowledge about memory. This includes general knowledge about memory, such as knowing that recognition tests are easier than recall tests. It also encompasses knowledge about one's own memory, such as a student's ability to monitor whether she has studied enough for a test that is coming up next week (Dimmitt & McCormick, 2012). Conceptualization of metacognition consists of several dimensions of executive function, such as planning (deciding how much time to spend focusing on a task, for example) and self-regulation (modifying strategies as work on a task progresses, for example) (Allen & others, 2017; Fergus & Bardeen, 2018). Researchers have found that metacognition involves children's confidence in their eyewitness judgments (Buratti, Allwood, & Johansson, 2014).

Young children do have some general knowledge about memory (Lukowski & Bauer, 2014). By 5 or 6 years of age, children usually already know that familiar items are easier to learn than unfamiliar ones, that short lists are easier to memorize than long ones, that recognition is easier than recall, and that forgetting is more likely to occur over time (Lyon & Flavell, 1993). However, in other ways young children's metamemory is limited. They don't understand

creative thinking The ability to think in novel and unusual ways and to come up with unique solutions to problems.

convergent thinking The type of thinking that produces one correct answer and is typically assessed by standardized intelligence tests.

divergent thinking Thinking that produces many answers to the same question and is characteristic of creativity.

metacognition Cognition about cognition, or knowing about knowing.

that related items are easier to remember than unrelated ones and that remembering the gist of a story is easier than remembering information verbatim (Kreutzer, Leonard, & Flavell, 1975). By the fifth grade, children do understand that gist recall is easier than verbatim recall.

Young children also have only limited knowledge about their own memory. They have an inflated opinion of their memory abilities. For example, in one study a majority of young children predicted that they would be able to recall all 10 items on a list of 10 items. When tested for this, however, none of the young children managed this feat (Flavell, Friedrichs, & Hoyt, 1970). As they move through the elementary school years, children can give more realistic evaluations of their memory skills.

In addition to metamemory, metacognition includes knowledge about memory strategies (Graham, 2018a, b; Harris & others, 2018). In the view of Michael Pressley (2007), the key to education is helping students learn a rich repertoire of strategies that produce solutions to problems. Good thinkers routinely use strategies and effective planning to solve problems. Good thinkers also know when and where to use strategies. Understanding when and where to use strategies often results from monitoring the learning situation.

Cognitive developmentalist John Flavell is a pioneer in providing insights about children's thinking. Among his many contributions are establishing the field of metacognition and conducting numerous studies in this area, including metamemory and theory of mind studies.
Courtesy of Dr. John Flavell

How Would You...?

As an **educator,** how would you advise teachers and parents about ways to improve children's metacognitive skills?

Executive Function

Earlier you read about executive function and its characteristics in early childhood (Bervoets & others, 2018; Gordon & others, 2018). Some of the cognitive topics we already have discussed in this chapter—working memory, critical thinking, creative thinking, and metacognition—can be considered under the umbrella of executive function and linked to the development of the brain's prefrontal cortex (Knapp & Morton, 2017; Muller & others, 2017).

Also, earlier in this chapter in the coverage of brain development in middle and late childhood, you read about the increase in cognitive control, which involves flexible and effective control in a number of areas such as focusing attention, reducing interfering thoughts, inhibiting motor actions, and exercising flexibility in deciding between competing choices (Perone, Palanisamy, & Carlson, 2018).

Adele Diamond and Kathleen Lee (2011) highlighted the following dimensions of executive function that they conclude are the most important for 4- to 11-year-old children's cognitive development and school success:

What are some changes in executive function from 4 to 11 years of age?
©Hero Images/Corbis/ Glow Images

- *Self-control/inhibition.* Children need to develop self-control that will allow them to concentrate and persist on learning tasks, to inhibit their tendencies to repeat incorrect responses, and to resist the impulse to do something that they later would regret.

- *Working memory.* Children need an effective working memory to mentally work with the masses of information they will encounter as they go through school and beyond.

- *Flexibility.* Children need to be flexible in their thinking so as to consider different strategies and perspectives.

Researchers have found that executive function is a better predictor of school readiness than general IQ (Blair & Razza, 2007). A number of diverse activities have been found to increase children's executive function, such as computerized training that uses games to improve working memory (Cogmed, 2013); aerobic exercise (Kvalo & others, 2017); mindfulness (Gallant, 2016); scaffolding of self-regulation (Bodrova & Leong, 2015); and some types of school curricula (the Montessori curriculum, for example) (Diamond & Lee, 2011).

Intelligence

How can intelligence be defined? **Intelligence** is the ability to solve problems and to adapt and learn from experiences. Interest in intelligence has often focused on individual differences and assessment. *Individual differences* are the stable, consistent ways in which people differ from each other (Sackett & others, 2017). We can talk about individual differences in personality or any other domain, but it is in the domain of intelligence that the most attention has been directed at individual differences (Estrada & others, 2017). For example, an intelligence test purports to inform us about whether a student can reason better than others who have taken the test. Let's go back in history and see what the first intelligence test was like.

The Binet Tests

In 1904, the French Ministry of Education asked psychologist Alfred Binet to devise a method of identifying children who were unable to learn in school. School officials wanted to reduce crowding by placing students who did not benefit from regular classroom teaching in special schools. Binet and his student Theophile Simon developed an intelligence test to meet this request. The test is called the *1905 Scale*. It consists of 30 questions on topics ranging from the ability to touch one's ear to the ability to draw designs from memory and define abstract concepts.

Binet developed the concept of **mental age (MA),** an individual's level of mental development relative to others. A few years later, in 1912, William Stern created the concept of **intelligence quotient (IQ),** a person's mental age divided by chronological age (CA) and multiplied by 100. That is, IQ = MA/CA × 100. If mental age is the same as chronological age, then the person's IQ is 100. If mental age is above chronological age, then IQ is more than 100. If mental age is below chronological age, then IQ is less than 100.

The Binet test has been revised many times to incorporate advances in the understanding of intelligence and intelligence tests. These revisions are called the *Stanford-Binet tests* (Stanford University is where the revisions have been done). In 2004, the test—now called the *Stanford-Binet 5*—was revised to analyze an individual's response in five content areas: fluid reasoning, knowledge, quantitative reasoning, visual-spatial reasoning, and working memory. A general composite score also is still obtained.

By administering the test to large numbers of people of different ages (from preschool through late adulthood) from different backgrounds, researchers have found that scores on the Stanford-Binet approximate a normal distribution (see Figure 5). A **normal distribution**

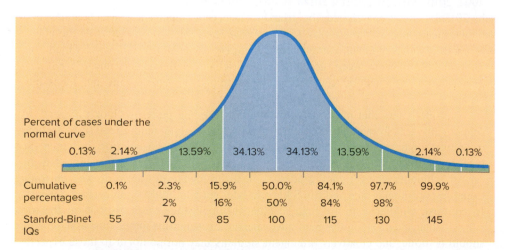

Figure 5 The Normal Curve and Stanford-Binet IQ Scores
The distribution of IQ scores approximates a normal curve. Most of the population falls in the middle range of scores. Notice that extremely high and extremely low scores are very rare. Slightly more than two-thirds of the scores fall between 85 and 115. Only about 1 in 50 individuals has an IQ of more than 130, and only about 1 in 50 individuals has an IQ of less than 70.

is symmetrical, with a majority of the scores falling in the middle of the possible range of scores and few scores appearing toward the extremes of the range.

The Wechsler Scales

Another set of tests widely used to assess students' intelligence is called the Wechsler scales, developed by psychologist David Wechsler. They include the Wechsler Preschool and Primary Scale of Intelligence–Fourth Edition (WPPSI-IV) to test children from 2.5 years to 7.25 years of age; the Wechsler Intelligence Scale for Children–Fifth Edition (WISC-V) for children and adolescents 6 to 16 years of age; and the Wechsler Adult Intelligence Scale–Fourth Edition (WAIS-IV).

The WISC-V now not only provides an overall IQ score but also yields five composite scores (Verbal Comprehension, Working Memory, Processing Speed, Fluid Reasoning, and Visual Spatial) (Canivez, Watkins, & Dombowski, 2017). These allow the examiner to quickly see whether the individual is strong or weak in different areas of intelligence. The Wechsler also include 16 verbal and nonverbal subscales. Three of the Wechsler subscales are shown in Figure 6.

Types of Intelligence

Is it more appropriate to think of a child's intelligence as a general ability or as a number of specific abilities? Robert Sternberg and Howard Gardner have proposed influential theories that reflect this second viewpoint.

Sternberg's Triarchic Theory Robert J. Sternberg (1986, 2004, 2010, 2011, 2012, 2013, 2014a, b, 2015, 2016a, b, 2017a, b; 2018a, b, c, d) developed the **triarchic theory of intelligence,** which states that intelligence comes in three forms: (1) *analytical intelligence*, which refers to the ability to analyze, judge, evaluate, compare, and contrast; (2) *creative intelligence*, which consists of the ability to create, design, invent, originate, and imagine; and (3) *practical intelligence*, which involves the ability to use, apply, implement, and put ideas into practice.

Sternberg says that children with different triarchic patterns "look different" in school (2017a, b, 2018a, b, c, d). Students with high analytic ability tend to be favored in conventional schooling. They often do well under direct instruction, in which the teacher lectures and gives students objective tests. They often are considered to be "smart" students who get good grades, show up in high-level tracks, do well on traditional tests of intelligence and the SAT, and later get admitted to competitive colleges. In contrast, children who are high in creative intelligence often are not on the top rung of their class. Many teachers have specific expectations about how assignments should be done, and creatively intelligent students may not conform to those expectations. Instead of giving conformist answers, they give unique answers, for which they might get reprimanded or marked down. No teacher wants to discourage creativity, but Sternberg stresses that too often a teacher's desire to increase students' knowledge suppresses the development of creative thinking.

triarchic theory of intelligence
Sternberg's theory that intelligence consists of analytical intelligence, creative intelligence, and practical intelligence.

Similarities

A child must think logically and abstractly to answer a number of questions about how things might be similar.

Example: "In what way are a lion and a tiger alike?"

Comprehension

This subscale is designed to measure an individual's judgment and common sense.

Example: "What is the advantage of keeping money in a bank?"

Nonverbal Subscales

Block Design

A child must assemble a set of multicolored blocks to match designs that the examiner shows. Visual-motor coordination, perceptual organization, and the ability to visualize spatially are assessed.

Example: "Use the four blocks on the left to make the pattern on the right."

Figure 6 Sample Subscales of the Wechsler Intelligence Scale for Children–Fifth Edition (WISC-V)
Three of the WISC subscales are shown here. The simulated items are similar to those found in the Wechsler Intelligence Scale for Children–Fifth Edition.
Source: Wechsler Intelligence Scale for Children, Fifth Edition (WISC-V), Upper Saddle River, NJ: Pearson Education, Inc., 2014.

Like children high in creative intelligence, children who are practically intelligent often do not relate well to the demands of school. However, many of these children do well outside of the classroom's walls. They may have excellent social skills and good common sense. As adults, some become successful managers, entrepreneurs, or politicians in spite of having undistinguished school records.

Gardner's Eight Frames of Mind Howard Gardner (1983, 1993, 2002, 2016) suggests there are eight types of intelligence, or "frames of mind." These are described here, with examples of the types of vocations in which they represent strengths (Campbell, Campbell, & Dickinson, 2004):

- *Verbal*: The ability to think in words and use language to express meaning. Occupations: Authors, journalists, speakers.
- *Mathematical*: The ability to carry out mathematical operations. Occupations: Scientists, engineers, accountants.
- *Spatial*: The ability to think three-dimensionally. Occupations: Architects, artists, sailors.
- *Bodily-kinesthetic*: The ability to manipulate objects and be physically adept. Occupations: Surgeons, craftspeople, dancers, athletes.
- *Musical*: A sensitivity to pitch, melody, rhythm, and tone. Occupations: Composers, musicians, and sensitive listeners.
- *Interpersonal*: The ability to understand and interact effectively with others. Occupations: Successful teachers, mental health professionals.
- *Intrapersonal*: The ability to understand oneself. Occupations: Theologians, psychologists.
- *Naturalist*: The ability to observe patterns in nature and understand natural and human-made systems. Occupations: Farmers, botanists, ecologists, landscapers.

According to Gardner, everyone has all of these intelligences to varying degrees. As a result, we prefer to learn and process information in specific ways. People learn best when they can do so in a way that uses their stronger intelligences.

How Would You...?

As a **psychologist,** how would you use Gardner's theory of multiple intelligences to respond to children who are distressed by their below-average score on a traditional intelligence test?

Evaluating the Multiple-Intelligences Approaches Sternberg's and Gardner's approaches have much to offer. They have stimulated teachers to think more broadly about what makes up children's competencies (Gardner, 2016; Gardner, Kornhaber, & Chen, 2018; Sternberg, 2017a, b, 2018a, b, c). And they have motivated educators to develop programs that instruct students in multiple domains. These approaches have also contributed to interest in assessing intelligence and classroom learning in innovative ways, such as by evaluating student portfolios (Gardner, 2016; Gardner, Kornhaber, & Chen, 2018).

Still, doubts about multiple-intelligences approaches persist and many psychologists endorse the general intelligence approach (Hagmann-von Arx, Lemola, & Grob, 2018). Some argue that a research base to support the three intelligences of Sternberg or the eight intelligences of Gardner has not yet emerged. One expert on intelligence, Nathan Brody (2007), observes that people who excel at one type of intellectual task are likely to excel in others. Thus, individuals who do well at memorizing lists of digits are also likely to be good at solving verbal problems and spatial layout problems. If musical skill reflects a distinct type of intelligence, ask other critics, why not label the skills of outstanding chess players, prizefighters, painters, and poets as types of intelligence?

Advocates of the concept of general intelligence point to its accuracy in predicting school and job success. For example, scores on tests of general intelligence are substantially correlated with school grades and achievement test performance, both at the time of the test and years later (Cucina & others, 2016; Strenze, 2007). For example, a meta-analysis of 240 independent samples and more than 100,000 individuals found a correlation of +.54 between intelligence and school grades (Roth & others, 2015). Also, a recent study found a significant link between children's general intelligence and their self-control (Meldrum & others, 2017).

The argument between those who support the concept of general intelligence and those who advocate the multiple-intelligences view is ongoing (Gardner, 2016; Gardner, Kornhaber, & Chen, 2018; Hagmann-von Arx, Lemola, & Grob, 2017). Sternberg (2017a, b, 2018b, c) actually accepts that there is a general intelligence for the kinds of analytical tasks that traditional IQ tests assess but thinks that the range of tasks those tests measure is far too narrow.

Culture and Intelligence

Differing conceptions of intelligence occur not only among psychologists but also among cultures (Sternberg, 2018f). What is viewed as intelligent in one culture may not be thought of as intelligent in another. For example, people in Western cultures tend to view intelligence in terms of reasoning and thinking skills, whereas people in Eastern cultures see intelligence as a way for members of a community to engage successfully in social roles (Nisbett, 2003).

Interpreting Differences in IQ Scores

The IQ scores that result from tests such as the Stanford-Binet and Wechsler scales provide information about children's mental abilities. However, interpretation of scores on intelligence tests is a controversial topic.

The Influence of Genetics How strong is the effect of genetics on intelligence? Some researchers argue that heredity plays a strong role in intelligence, but this assertion is difficult to prove because teasing apart the influences of heredity and environment is virtually impossible. Also, most research on heredity and environment does not include environments that differ radically. Thus, it is not surprising that many genetic studies show environment to be a fairly weak influence on intelligence.

Have scientists been able to pinpoint specific genes that are linked to intelligence? A research review concluded that there may be more than 1,000 genes that affect intelligence, each possibly having a small influence on an individual's intelligence (Davies & others, 2011). Thus, some scientists argue that there is a strong genetic component to intelligence (Hill & others, 2018; Rimfeld & others, 2017). One strategy for examining the role of heredity in intelligence is to compare the IQs of identical and fraternal twins. Recall that identical twins have exactly the same genetic makeup but fraternal twins do not. If intelligence is genetically determined, say some investigators, identical twins' IQs should be more similar than those of fraternal twins. A research review of many studies found that the difference in the average correlation of intelligence between identical and fraternal twins was 0.15, suggesting a relatively low correlation between genetics and intelligence (Grigorenko, 2000) (see Figure 7).

Today, most researchers agree that genetics and environment interact to influence intelligence. For most people, this means that modifications in environment can change their IQ scores considerably. Although genetic endowment may always influence a person's intellectual ability, the environmental influences and opportunities we provide children and adults do make a difference (Sternberg, 2017a, b; 2018a, b, c).

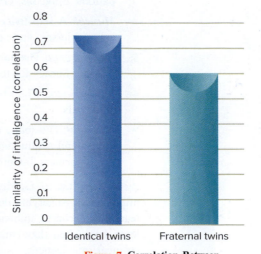

Figure 7 Correlation Between Intelligence Test Scores and Twin Status
The graph represents a summary of research findings that have compared the intelligence test scores of identical and fraternal twins. An approximate .15 difference in correlation has been found, with a higher correlation for identical twins (.75) and a lower correlation for fraternal twins (.60).

Environmental Influences The environment's role in intelligence is reflected in the 12- to 18-point increase in IQ when children are adopted from lower-SES to middle-SES homes (Nisbett & others, 2012). Environmental influences on intelligence also involve schooling (Gustafsson, 2007). The biggest effects have been found when large groups of children have been deprived of formal education for an extended period, resulting in lower intelligence (Ceci & Gilstrap, 2000). Another possible effect of education can be seen in rapidly increasing IQ test scores around the world (Flynn, 1999, 2007, 2011, 2013). IQ scores have been increasing so fast that a high percentage of people regarded as having average intelligence at the turn of the century would be considered below average in intelligence today (see Figure 8). If a representative sample of people today took the Stanford-Binet test version used in 1932, about 25 percent would be defined as having very superior intelligence, a label usually accorded to fewer than 3 percent of the population. Because the increase has taken place in a relatively short time, it can't be due to heredity, but rather may be due to increasing levels of education attained by a much greater percentage of the world's population, or to other environmental factors such as the explosion of information to which people are exposed (Laciga & Cigler, 2017; Shenk, 2017; Weber, Dekhtyar, & Herlitz, 2017). The worldwide increase in intelligence test scores that has occurred over a short time frame has been called the *Flynn effect* after the Australian researcher who discovered it, James Flynn.

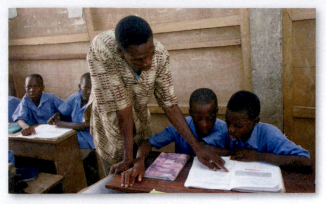

Students in an elementary school in South Africa. *How might schooling influence the development of children's intelligence?* ©Owen Franken/Corbis/Getty Images

Researchers are increasingly concerned about improving the early environment of children who are at risk for impoverished intelligence (Hardy, Smeeding, & Ziliak, 2018; Yoshikawa & others, 2017). For various reasons, many low-income parents have difficulty providing an intellectually stimulating environment for their children. Programs that educate parents to be more sensitive caregivers and better teachers, as well as access to support services such as quality child-care programs, can make a difference in a child's intellectual development (Follari, 2019; Morrison, 2018). In a recent two-year intervention study with families living in poverty, maternal scaffolding and positive home stimulation improved young children's intellectual functioning (Obradovic & others, 2016). Thus, the efforts to counteract a deprived early environment's effect on intelligence emphasize prevention rather than remediation.

In sum, there is a consensus among psychologists that both heredity and environment influence intelligence (Sauce & Matzel, 2018; Sternberg, 2017a, 2018a). This consensus reflects the nature-nurture issue, which focuses on the extent to which

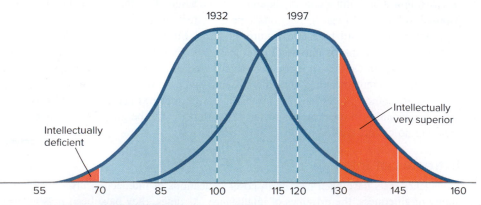

Figure 8 **The Increase in IQ Scores from 1932 to 1997**

As measured by the Stanford-Binet intelligence test, American children seem to be getting smarter. Scores of a group tested in 1932 fell along a bell-shaped curve with half below 100 and half above. Studies show that if children took that same test today, half would score above 120 on the 1932 scale. Very few of them would score in the "intellectually deficient" end on the left side, and about one-fourth would rank in the "very superior" range.

development is influenced by nature (heredity) and nurture (environment). Although psychologists agree that intelligence is the product of both nature and nurture, there is still disagreement about how strongly each influences intelligence.

Group Differences On average, African American schoolchildren in the United States score 10 to 15 points lower on standardized intelligence tests than non-Latino White American schoolchildren do (Brody, 2000). Children from Latino families also score lower than non-Latino White children. These are *average scores*, however; there is significant overlap in the distribution of scores. About 15 to 25 percent of African American schoolchildren score higher than half of White schoolchildren do, and many White schoolchildren score lower than most African American schoolchildren. As African Americans have gained social, economic, and educational opportunities, the gap between African Americans and Whites on standardized intelligence tests has begun to narrow. This gap especially narrows in college, where African American and White students often experience more similar environments than in the elementary and high school years (Myerson & others, 1998). Further, a study using the Stanford Binet Intelligence Scales found no differences in overall intellectual ability between non-Latino White and African American preschool children when the children were matched on age, gender, and parental education level (Dale & others, 2014). Nonetheless, a research analysis concluded that the underrepresentation of African Americans in STEM (science, technology, engineering, and math) subjects and careers is linked to practitioners' expectations that they have less innate talent than non-Latino Whites (Leslie & others, 2015).

One potential influence on intelligence test performance is **stereotype threat,** the anxiety that one's behavior might confirm a negative stereotype about one's group, such as an ethnic group (Grand, 2017; Williams & others, 2018). For example, when African Americans take an intelligence or achievement test, they may experience anxiety about confirming the old stereotype that Blacks are "intellectually inferior." Research studies have confirmed the existence of this type of stereotype threat (Lyons & others, 2018; Wegmann, 2017). Also, African American students do more poorly on standardized tests if they perceive that they are being evaluated. If they think the test doesn't count, they perform as well as White students (Steele, Spencer, & Aronson, 2002). However, some critics argue that the extent to which stereotype threat explains the testing gap has been exaggerated (Sackett, Borneman, & Connelly, 2009).

Creating Culture-Fair Tests Culture-fair tests are tests of intelligence that are intended to be free of cultural bias. Two types of culture-fair tests have been devised. The first includes items that are familiar to children from all socioeconomic and ethnic backgrounds, or items that at least are familiar to the children taking the test. For example, a child might be asked how a bird and a dog are different, on the assumption that all children have been exposed to birds and dogs. The second type of culture-fair test has no verbal questions.

Why is it so hard to create culture-fair tests? Most tests tend to reflect what the dominant culture thinks is important (Sternberg, 2018f). If tests have time limits, that will bias the test against groups not concerned with time. If languages differ, the same words might have different meanings for different language groups. Even pictures can produce bias because some cultures have less experience with drawings and photographs. Because of such difficulties in creating culture-fair tests, Robert Sternberg (2018f) concludes that there are no culture-fair tests, only culture-reduced tests.

Extremes of Intelligence

Intelligence tests have been used to discover indications of intellectual disability or giftedness, the extremes of intelligence. At times, they have been misused for this purpose. Keeping in mind the theme that an intelligence test should not be used as the sole indicator of intellectual disability or giftedness, we will explore the nature of these intellectual extremes.

Intellectual Disability Intellectual disability is a condition of limited mental ability in which an individual has a low IQ, usually below 70 on a traditional intelligence test, and has difficulty adapting to the demands of everyday life

stereotype threat Anxiety that one's behavior might confirm a negative stereotype about one's group, such as an ethnic group.

culture-fair tests Tests of intelligence that are designed to be free of cultural bias.

intellectual disability A condition of limited mental ability in which an individual has a low IQ, usually below 70 on a traditional test of intelligence, and has difficulty adapting to the demands of everyday life.

(Heward, Alber-Morgan, & Konrad, 2017). About 5 million Americans fit this definition of intellectual disability.

About 89 percent of the individuals with an intellectual disability fall into the mild intellectual disability category, with IQs of 55 to 70; most of them are able to live independently as adults and work at a variety of jobs. About 6 percent are classified as having a moderate intellectual disability, with IQs of 40 to 54; these people can attain a second-grade level of skills and may be able to support themselves as adults through some types of labor. About 3.5 percent are in the severe category, with IQs of 25 to 39; these individuals learn to talk and accomplish very simple tasks but require extensive supervision. Less than 1 percent have IQs below 25; they fall into the profoundly disabled classification and need constant supervision.

Intellectual disability can have an organic cause, or it can be social and cultural in origin:

What causes a child to develop Down syndrome?
©Stockbyte/Veer

- **Organic intellectual disability** is intellectual disability that is caused by a genetic disorder or by brain damage; the word *organic* refers to the tissues or organs of the body, indicating physical damage. Most people who suffer from organic intellectual disability have IQs that range between 0 and 50. However, children with Down syndrome have an average IQ of approximately 50. As discussed earlier, Down syndrome is caused by an extra copy of chromosome 21.

- **Cultural-familial intellectual disability** is a mental deficit in which no evidence of organic brain damage can be found; individuals' IQs generally range from 50 to 70. Psychologists suspect that such mental deficits result from the normal variation that distributes people along the range of intelligence scores combined with growing up in a below-average intellectual environment.

Giftedness There have always been people whose abilities and accomplishments outshine those of others—the whiz kid in class, the star athlete, the natural musician. People who are **gifted** have above-average intelligence (an IQ of 130 or higher) or superior talent for something, or both.

When it comes to programs for the gifted, most school systems select children who have intellectual superiority and academic aptitude, whereas children who are talented in the visual and performing arts (arts, drama, dance, music), athletics, or other special aptitudes tend to be overlooked (Olszewski-Kubilius & Thomson, 2013). There also are increasing calls to further expand the criteria for giftedness to include such factors as creativity and commitment (Sternberg, 2017c; Sternberg & Kaufman, 2018a).

Estimates vary but indicate that approximately 6 to 10 percent of U.S. students are classified as gifted (National Association for Gifted Children, 2017). This percentage is likely conservative because it focuses more on children who are gifted intellectually and academically, often failing to include those who are gifted in creative thinking or the visual and performing arts (Ford, 2012). Also, African American, Latino, and Native American children are underrepresented in gifted programs (Ford, 2015a, b, 2016). Much of the underrepresentation involves the lower test scores for these children compared with non-Latino White and Asian American children, which may be due to a number of reasons such as test bias and fewer opportunities to develop language skills such as vocabulary and comprehension (Ford, 2016).

What are the characteristics of children who are gifted? Despite speculation that giftedness is linked with having a mental disorder, no relation between giftedness and mental disorder has been found. Similarly, the idea that gifted children are maladjusted is a myth, as Lewis Terman (1925) found when he conducted an extensive study of 1,500 children whose Stanford-Binet IQ scores averaged 150. The children in Terman's study were socially

organic intellectual disability Intellectual disability that involves some physical damage and is caused by a genetic disorder or brain damage.

cultural-familial intellectual disability Intellectual disability in which there is no evidence of organic brain damage, but the individual's IQ generally is between 50 and 70.

gifted Having above-average intelligence (an IQ of 130 or higher) and/or superior talent for something.

well adjusted, and many went on to become successful doctors, lawyers, professors, and scientists. Studies support the conclusion that gifted people tend to be more mature than others, have fewer emotional problems than average, and grow up in a positive family climate (Feldman, 2001). For example, one study revealed that parents and teachers identified elementary school children who are not gifted as having more emotional and behavioral risks than children who are gifted (Eklund & others, 2015). In this study, when children who are gifted did have problems, they were more likely to be internalized problems, such as anxiety and depression, than externalized problems, such as acting out and high levels of aggression.

Ellen Winner (1996) described three criteria that characterize gifted children, whether in art, music, or academic domains:

1. *Precocity*. Gifted children are precocious. They begin to master an area earlier than their peers. Learning in their domain is more effortless for them than for ordinary children. In most instances, these gifted children are precocious because they have an inborn high ability in a particular domain or domains.

2. *Marching to a different drummer*. Gifted children learn in a qualitatively different way from ordinary children. One way that they march to a different drummer is that they need minimal help, or scaffolding, from adults to learn. In many instances, they resist any kind of explicit instruction. They often make discoveries on their own and solve problems in unique ways.

3. *A passion to master*. Gifted children are driven to understand the domain in which they have high ability. They display an intense, obsessive interest and an ability to focus. They motivate themselves, says Winner, and do not need to be "pushed" by their parents.

4. *Information-processing skills*. Researchers have found that children who are gifted learn at a faster pace, process information more rapidly, are better at reasoning, use superior strategies, and monitor their understanding better than their nongifted counterparts (Ambrose & Sternberg, 2016).

At 2 years of age, art prodigy Alexandra Nechita colored in coloring books for hours and also took up pen and ink. She had no interest in dolls or friends. By age 5 she was using watercolors. Once she started school, she would paint as soon as she got home. At age 8, she saw the first public exhibit of her work. Since then, working quickly and impulsively on canvases as large as 5 feet by 9 feet, she has completed hundreds of paintings, some of which sell for close to $100,000 apiece. She continues to paint today—relentlessly and passionately. It is, she says, what she loves to do. *What are some characteristics of children who are gifted?*
©Koichi Kamoshida/Newsmakers/Getty Images

Is giftedness a product of heredity or environment? The answer is likely both (Sternberg & Kaufman, 2018a). Individuals who are gifted recall that they had signs of high ability in a particular area at a very young age, prior to or at the beginning of formal training (Howe & others, 1995). This suggests the importance of innate ability in giftedness. However, researchers have also found that individuals with world-class status in the arts, mathematics, science, and sports all report strong family support and years of training and practice (Bloom, 1985). Deliberate practice is an important characteristic of individuals who become experts in a particular domain. For example, in one study, the best musicians engaged in twice as much deliberate practice over their lives as did the least successful ones (Ericsson, Krampe, & Tesch-Romer, 1993).

Individuals who are highly gifted are typically not gifted in many domains, and research on giftedness is increasingly focused on domain-specific developmental paths (Sternberg & Kaufman, 2018a). During the childhood years, the domain(s) in which individuals are gifted usually emerges. Thus, at some point in the childhood years, the child who will become a gifted artist or the child who will become a gifted mathematician begins to show expertise in that domain. Regarding domain-specific giftedness, software genius Bill Gates (1998), the founder of Microsoft and one of the world's richest people, commented that when you are good at something, you may have to resist the urge to think that you will be good at everything. Because he has been so successful at software development, he has found that people also expect him to be brilliant in other domains in which he is far from gifted.

How Would You...?

As an **educator,** how would you structure educational programs for children who are gifted that would challenge and expand their talents?

An increasing number of experts argue that the education of children who are gifted in the United States requires a significant overhaul (Renzulli, 2017, 2018). Ellen Winner (1996, 2009) argues that too often children who are gifted are socially isolated and underchallenged in the classroom. It is not unusual for other students to label them "nerds" or "geeks." Many eminent adults report that school was a negative experience for them, that they were bored and sometimes knew more than their teachers (Bloom, 1985). Winner argues that American students will benefit more from their education when standards are raised for all children. She recommends that some underchallenged students be allowed to attend advanced classes in their domain of exceptional ability, such as allowing some precocious middle school students to take college classes in their area of expertise. For example, at age 13, Bill Gates took college math classes and hacked a computer security system; Yo-Yo Ma, famous cellist, graduated from high school at 15 and attended Juilliard School of Music in New York City.

A young Bill Gates, founder of Microsoft and now one of the world's richest people. Like many highly gifted students, Gates was not especially fond of school. He hacked a computer security system when he was 13 and as a high school student, he was allowed to take some college math classes. He dropped out of Harvard University and began developing a plan for what was to become Microsoft Corporation. *What are some ways that schools can enrich the education of highly talented students like Gates to make it a more challenging, interesting, and meaningful experience?*
©Deborah Feingold/Getty Images

Language Development

Children gain new skills as they enter school that make it possible for them to learn to read and write (Fox & Alexander, 2017; Graham, 2018a, b; Reutzel & Cooter, 2019). These include increased use of language to talk about things that are not physically present, learning what a word is, and learning how to recognize and talk about sounds (Berko Gleason, 2003). Children also learn the *alphabetic principle*—that the letters of the alphabet represent sounds of the language.

Vocabulary, Grammar, and Metalinguistic Awareness

During middle and late childhood, changes occur in the way children's mental vocabulary is organized. When asked to say the first word that comes to mind when they hear a word, preschool children typically provide a word that often follows the word in a sentence. For example, when asked to respond to "dog" the young child may say "barks," or to the word "eat" respond with "lunch." At about 7 years of age, children begin to respond with a word that is the same part of speech as the stimulus word. For example, a child may now respond to the word "dog" with "cat" or "horse." To "eat," they now might say "drink." This is evidence that children of this age have begun to categorize their vocabulary by parts of speech (Berko Gleason, 2003).

The process of categorizing becomes easier as children increase their vocabulary (Clark, 2017). Children's vocabulary increases from an average of about 14,000 words at age 6 to an average of about 40,000 words by age 11.

Children make similar advances in grammar (Behrens, 2012; Clark, 2017). During the elementary school years, children's improvement in logical reasoning and analytical skills helps them understand such constructions as the appropriate use of comparatives (*shorter, deeper*) and subjectives ("If you were president . . . "). During the elementary school years, children become increasingly able to understand and use complex grammar, such as the following sentence: *The boy who kissed his mother wore a hat*. They also learn to use language in a more connected way, producing connected discourse. They become able to relate sentences to one another to produce descriptions, definitions, and narratives that make sense. Children must be able to do these things orally before they can be expected to deal with them in written assignments.

These advances in vocabulary and grammar during the elementary school years are accompanied by the development of **metalinguistic awareness,** which is knowledge about language, such as knowing what a preposition is or being able to discuss the sounds of a language (Schiff, Nuri Beh-Shushan, & Ben-Artzi, 2017; Yeon, Bae, & Joshi, 2017). Metalinguistic awareness allows children "to think about their language, understand what words are, and even define them" (Berko Gleason, 2009, p. 4). It improves considerably during the elementary school years (Pan & Uccelli, 2009). Defining words becomes a regular part of classroom discourse, and children increase their knowledge of syntax as they study and talk about the components of sentences, such as subjects and verbs (Crain, 2012). And reading also feeds into metalinguistic awareness as children try to comprehend written text.

Children also make progress in understanding how to use language in culturally appropriate ways—a process called pragmatics (Beguin, 2016). By the time they enter adolescence, most children know the rules for the use of language in everyday contexts—that is, what is appropriate and inappropriate to say.

Reading

Before learning to read, children learn to use language to talk about things that are not present; they learn what a word is; and they learn how to recognize sounds and talk about them. Children who begin elementary school with a robust vocabulary have an advantage when it comes to learning to read. Vocabulary development plays an important role in reading comprehension (Vacca & others, 2018).

How should children be taught to read? One debate has focused on the whole-language approach versus the phonics approach (Fox & Alexander, 2017).

The **whole-language approach** stresses that reading instruction should parallel children's natural language learning. In some whole-language classes, beginning readers are taught to recognize whole words or even entire sentences, and to use the context of what they are reading to guess at the meaning of words. Reading materials that support the whole-language approach are whole and meaningful—that is, children are given material in its complete form, such as stories and poems, so that they learn to understand language's communicative function. Reading is connected with listening and writing skills. Although there are variations in whole-language programs, most share the premise that reading should be integrated with other skills and subjects, such as science and social studies, and that it should focus on real-world material. Thus, a class might read newspapers, magazines, or books, and then write about and discuss what they have read.

A teacher helps a student sound out words. Researchers have found that phonics instruction is a key aspect of teaching students to read, especially beginning readers and students with weak reading skills.
©Gideon Mendel/Corbis/Getty Images

In contrast, the **phonics approach** emphasizes that reading instruction should teach basic rules for translating written symbols into sounds. Early phonics-centered reading instruction should involve simplified materials. Only after children have learned correspondence rules that relate spoken phonemes to the alphabet letters that are used to represent them should they be given complex reading materials, such as books and poems.

Which approach is better? Research suggests that children can benefit from both approaches, but instruction in phonics needs to be emphasized (Reutzel & Cooter, 2019; Tompkins, 2018). An increasing number of experts in the field of reading now conclude that direct instruction in phonics is a key aspect of learning to read (Cunningham, 2017; Fox & Alexander, 2017).

metalinguistic awareness Refers to knowledge about language, such as knowing what a preposition is or being able to discuss the sounds of a language.

whole-language approach An approach to reading instruction based on the idea that instruction should parallel children's natural language learning. Reading materials should be whole and meaningful.

phonics approach The idea that reading instruction should teach the basic rules for translating written symbols into sounds.

Beyond the phonics/whole language issue in learning to read, becoming a good reader includes learning to read fluently (Stevens, Walker, & Vaughn, 2017). Many beginning or poor readers do not recognize words automatically. Their processing capacity is consumed by the demands of word recognition, so they have less comprehension of groupings of words as phrases or sentences. As their processing of words and passages becomes more automatic, it is said that their reading becomes more fluent. Also, children's vocabulary development plays an important role in the development of their reading comprehension (Vacca & others, 2018). And metacognitive strategies, such as learning to monitor one's reading progress, getting the gist of what is being read, and summarizing also are important in becoming a good reader (Schiff, Nuri Ben-Shushan, & Ben-Artzi, 2017).

Second-Language Learning and Bilingual Education

Are there sensitive periods in learning a second language? That is, if individuals want to learn a second language, how important is the age at which they begin to learn it? What is the best way for U.S. schools to teach children who come from homes in which English is not the primary language?

Second-Language Learning

For many years, it was claimed that if individuals did not learn a second language prior to puberty they would never reach native-language learners' proficiency in the second language (Johnson & Newport, 1991). However, recent research indicates a more complex conclusion: There are sensitive periods for learning a second language. Additionally, these sensitive periods likely vary across different areas of language systems (Thomas & Johnson, 2008). For example, late language learners, such as adolescents and adults, may learn new vocabulary more easily than new sounds or new grammar (Neville, 2006). Also, children's ability to pronounce words with a native-like accent in a second language typically decreases with age, with an especially sharp drop occurring after the age of about 10 to 12. Adults tend to learn a second language faster than children, but their level of second-language mastery is not as high as children's. And the way children and adults learn a second language differs somewhat. Compared with adults, children are less sensitive to feedback, less likely to use explicit strategies, and more likely to learn a second language from large amounts of input (Thomas & Johnson, 2008).

Students in the United States are far behind their counterparts in many developed countries in learning a second language. For example, in Russia, schools have 10 grades, called *forms*, which roughly correspond to the 12 grades in American schools. Russian children begin school at age 7 and begin learning English in the third form. Because of this emphasis on teaching English, most Russian citizens under the age of 40 today are able to speak at least some English. The United States is the only technologically advanced Western nation that does not have a national foreign language requirement at the high school level, even for students in rigorous academic programs.

U.S. students who do not learn a second language may be missing more than the chance to acquire a skill. *Bilingualism*—the ability to speak two languages—has a positive effect on children's cognitive development (Tompkins, 2015). Children who are fluent in two languages perform better than their single-language counterparts on tests of control of attention, concept formation, analytical reasoning, cognitive flexibility, and cognitive complexity (Bialystok, 2001, 2007, 2011, 2014, 2015, 2017; Bialystok & Craik, 2010; Sullivan & others, 2014). Recent research also documented that bilingual children are better at theory of mind tasks (Rubio-Fernandez, 2017). They also are more conscious of the structure of spoken and written language and better at noticing errors of grammar and meaning, skills that benefit their reading ability (Bialystok, 1997; Kuo & Anderson, 2012). A recent study of 6- to 10-year-olds found that early bilingual exposure was a key factor in bilingual children outperforming monolingual children on phonological awareness and word learning (Jasinska & Petitto, 2018).

Overall, bilingualism is linked to positive outcomes for both children's language and cognitive development (Antovich & Graf Estes, 2018; Singh & others, 2018; Yow &

others, 2018). An especially important developmental question that many parents of infants and young children have is whether they should teach them two languages simultaneously or whether doing this would confuse them. The answer is that teaching infants and young children two languages simultaneously (as when a mother's native language is English and her husband's is Spanish) has numerous benefits and few drawbacks (Bialystok, 2014, 2015, 2017).

In the United States, many immigrant children go from being monolingual in their home language to bilingual in that language and in English, only to end up as monolingual speakers of English. This is called *subtractive bilingualism*, and it can have negative effects on children, who often become ashamed of their home language.

How Would You...?

As a **human development and family studies professional,** how would you describe the advantages of promoting bilingualism in the home for school-age children in the United States who come from families whose first language is not English?

Bilingual Education

A current controversy related to bilingualism involves the millions of U.S. children who come from homes in which English is not the primary language (Diaz-Rico, 2018; Echevarria, Vogt, & Short, 2017; Esposito & others, 2018; Peregoy & Boyle, 2017). What is the best way to teach these English language learners (ELLs)?

ELLs have been taught in one of two main ways: (1) instruction in English only, or (2) a *dual-language* (used to be called bilingual) approach that involves instruction in their home language and English (Diaz-Rico, 2018). In a dual-language approach, instruction is given in both the ELL child's home language and English for varying amounts of time at certain grade levels. One of the arguments for the dual-language approach is the research discussed earlier demonstrating that bilingual children have more advanced information-processing skills than monolingual children do.

If a dual-language strategy is used, too often it has been thought that immigrant children need only one or two years of this type of instruction. However, in general it takes immigrant children approximately three to five years to develop speaking proficiency and seven years to develop reading proficiency in English (Hakuta, Butler, & Witt, 2000). Also, immigrant children vary in their ability to learn English (Esposito & others, 2018). Children who come from lower socioeconomic backgrounds have more difficulty than those from higher socioeconomic backgrounds (Hakuta, 2001). Thus, especially for immigrant children from low socioeconomic backgrounds, more years of dual-language instruction may be needed than they currently are receiving.

A first- and second-grade bilingual English-Cantonese teacher instructing students in Chinese in Oakland, California. *What have researchers found about the effectiveness of bilingual education?*
©Elizabeth Crews

What have researchers found regarding outcomes of ELL programs? Drawing conclusions about the effectiveness of ELL programs is difficult because of variations across programs in the number of years they are in effect, type of instruction, quality of schooling other than ELL instruction, teachers, children, and other factors. Further, no effective experiments have been conducted that compare bilingual education with English-only education in the United States (Snow & Kang, 2006). Some experts have concluded that the quality of instruction is more important in determining outcomes than the language in which it is delivered (Lesaux & Siegel, 2003).

Nonetheless, other experts, such as Kenji Hakuta (2001, 2005), support the combined home language and English approach because (1) children have difficulty learning a subject when it is taught in a language they do not understand; and (2) when both languages are integrated in the classroom, children learn the second language more readily and participate more actively. In support of Hakuta's view, most large-scale studies have found that the academic achievement of ELLs is higher in dual-language programs than English-only programs (Genesee & Lindholm-Leary, 2012).

Summary

Physical Changes and Health

- The period of middle and late childhood involves slow, consistent growth.
- Changes in the brain in middle and late childhood include advances in functioning in the prefrontal cortex, which is associated with an increase in cognitive control.
- Motor development becomes much smoother and more coordinated. Boys usually are better at gross motor skills, girls at fine motor skills.
- Most U.S. children do not get nearly enough exercise.
- For the most part, middle and late childhood is a time of excellent health. However, being overweight in childhood poses serious health risks.

Children with Disabilities

- Approximately 13 percent of U.S. children from 3 to 21 years of age receive special education or related services. Approximately 80 percent of children with a learning disability have a reading problem. The number of children diagnosed with ADHD has been increasing. Autism spectrum disorders recently have been estimated to characterize 1 in 88 U.S. children.
- U.S. legislation requires that all children with disabilities be given a free, appropriate public education. Increasingly, this education has involved full inclusion.

Cognitive Changes

- Piaget theorized that the stage of concrete operational thought characterizes children from about 7 to 11 years of age. During this stage children are capable of concrete operations, conservation, classification, seriation, and transitivity. Criticisms of Piaget's theory have been proposed.
- Changes in these aspects of information occur in middle and late childhood: attention, memory, critical thinking, creative thinking, metacognition, and executive function.
- Widely used intelligence tests today include the Stanford-Binet test and Wechsler scales. Sternberg proposed that intelligence comes in three main forms, whereas Gardner said there are eight types of intelligence. Intelligence is influenced by heredity and environment. Extremes of intelligence include intellectual disability and giftedness.

Language Development

- In the elementary school years, improvements in children's language development include vocabulary, grammar, and metalinguistic awareness.
- Both the phonics and whole-language approaches to reading instruction can benefit children, but experts increasingly view phonics instruction as critical in learning to read.
- Recent research indicates a complex conclusion about whether there are sensitive periods in learning a second language. Bilingual children are characterized by a number of cognitive advantages. Bilingual education in the United States aims to teach academic subjects to immigrant children in their native language while gradually adding English instruction.

Key Terms

attention deficit hyperactivity disorder (ADHD)
autism spectrum disorders (ASD)
convergent thinking
creative thinking
critical thinking
cultural-familial intellectual disability
culture-fair tests

divergent thinking
elaboration
fuzzy trace theory
gifted
inclusion
individualized education plan (IEP)
intellectual disability
intelligence
intelligence quotient (IQ)

learning disability
least restrictive environment (LRE)
long-term memory
mental age (MA)
metacognition
metalinguistic awareness
neo-Piagetians
normal distribution
organic intellectual disability

phonics approach
seriation
stereotype threat
strategies
thinking
transitivity
triarchic theory of intelligence
whole-language approach
working memory

8 Socioemotional Development in Middle and Late Childhood

©FatCamera/Getty Images

CHAPTER OUTLINE

EMOTIONAL AND PERSONALITY DEVELOPMENT
The Self
Emotional Development
Moral Development
Gender

FAMILIES
Developmental Changes in Parent-Child Relationships
Parents as Managers
Attachment
Stepfamilies

PEERS
Developmental Changes
Peer Status

Social Cognition
Bullying
Friends

SCHOOLS
Contemporary Approaches to Student Learning
Socioeconomic Status, Ethnicity, and Culture

Stories of Life-Span Development: Learning in Troubled Schools

In *The Shame of the Nation,* Jonathan Kozol (2005) described his visits to 60 U.S. schools in urban low-income areas in 11 states. He saw many schools in which the minority population was 80 to 90 percent. Kozol observed numerous inequities—unkempt classrooms, hallways, and restrooms; inadequate textbooks and supplies; and lack of resources. He also saw teachers mainly instructing students to memorize material by rote, especially as preparation for mandated tests, rather than stimulating them to engage in higher-level thinking. Kozol also frequently observed teachers using threatening disciplinary tactics to control the classroom.

However, some teachers Kozol observed were effective in educating children in these undesirable conditions. At P.S. 30 in the South Bronx, Mr. Bedrock teaches fifth grade. One student in his class, Serafina, recently lost her mother to AIDS. When Kozol visited the class, he was told that two other children had taken the role of "allies in the child's struggle for emotional survival" (Kozol, 2005, p. 291). Textbooks are in short supply for the class, and the social studies text is so out of date it claims that Ronald Reagan is the country's president. But Mr. Bedrock told Kozol that it's a "wonderful" class this year. About their teacher, 56-year-old Mr. Bedrock, one student said, "He's getting old . . . but we love him anyway" (p. 292). Kozol found the students orderly, interested, and engaged.

What are some of the challenges faced by children growing up in the South Bronx?
©Andy Levin/Science Source

The years of middle and late childhood bring many changes to children's social and emotional lives. The development of their self-conceptions, moral reasoning, and gendered behavior is significant. Transformations in their relationships with parents and peers occur, and schooling takes on a more academic flavor. ▪

Emotional and Personality Development

In this section, we explore how the self continues to develop during middle and late childhood and we trace the emotional changes that take place during these years. We also discuss children's moral development and many aspects of the role that gender plays in their development in middle and late childhood.

The Self

What is the nature of the child's self-understanding, understanding of others, and self-esteem during the elementary school years? What roles do self-efficacy and self-regulation play in children's achievement?

The Development of Self-Understanding

In middle and late childhood, especially from 8 to 11 years of age, children increasingly describe themselves with psychological characteristics and traits rather than the more concrete self-descriptions of younger children. Older children are more likely to describe themselves as *"popular, nice, helpful, mean, smart,* and *dumb"* (Harter, 2006, p. 526).

In addition, during the elementary school years, children become more likely to recognize social aspects of the self (Harter, 2012, 2013, 2016). They include references to social groups in their self-descriptions, such as referring to themselves as a Girl Scout, a Catholic, or someone who has two close friends (Livesly & Bromley, 1973).

Children's self-understanding in the elementary school years also includes increasing reference to social comparison (Harter, 2012, 2013, 2016). At this point in development, children are more likely to distinguish themselves from others in comparative rather than in absolute terms. That is, elementary-school-age children are no longer as likely to think about what they do or do not do, but are more likely to think about what they can do in comparison with others.

Consider a series of studies in which Diane Ruble (1983) investigated children's use of social comparison in their self-evaluations. Children were given a difficult task and then offered feedback on their performance as well as information about the performances of other children their age. The children were then asked for self-evaluations. Children younger than 7 made virtually no reference to the information about other children's performances. However, many children older than 7 included socially comparative information in their self-descriptions.

How Would You...?

As a **psychologist,** how would you explain the role of social comparison for the development of a child's sense of self?

Understanding Others

Earlier we described the advances and limitations of young children's social understanding. In middle and late childhood, **perspective taking,** the social cognitive process involved in assuming the perspective of others and understanding their thoughts and feelings, improves. Executive function is at work in perspective taking. Among the executive functions called on when children engage in perspective taking are cognitive inhibition (controlling one's own thoughts to consider the perspective of others) and cognitive flexibility (seeing situations in different ways). Recent research indicates that children and adolescents who do not have good perspective taking skills are more likely to have difficulty in peer relations and engage

perspective taking The social cognitive process involved in assuming the perspective of others and understanding their thoughts and feelings.

in more aggressive and oppositional behavior (Morosan & others, 2017; Nilsen & Bacso, 2017; O'Kearney & others, 2017).

In middle and late childhood, children also become more skeptical of others' claims (Heyman, Fu, & Lee, 2013). They become increasingly skeptical of some sources of information about psychological traits. A recent study of 6- to 9-year-olds revealed that older children were less trusting and more skeptical of others' distorted claims than were younger children (Mills & Elashi, 2014).

What are some changes in children's understanding of others in middle and late childhood?
©asiseeit/E+/Getty Images

Self-Esteem and Self-Concept

High self-esteem and a positive self-concept are important characteristics of children's well-being (Miller & Cho, 2018; Oberle, 2018). Investigators sometimes use the terms *self-esteem* and *self-concept* interchangeably or do not precisely define them, but there is a meaningful difference between them (Harter, 2013, 2016). **Self-esteem** refers to global evaluations of the self; it is also called *self-worth* or *self-image*. For example, a child may perceive that she is not merely a person but a *good* person. **Self-concept** refers to domain-specific evaluations of the self. Children can make self-evaluations in many domains of their lives—academic, athletic, appearance, and so on. In sum, *self-esteem* refers to global self-evaluations, *self-concept* to domain-specific evaluations.

The foundations of self-esteem and self-concept emerge from the quality of parent-child interaction in infancy and early childhood (Miller & Cho, 2018). Thus, if children have low self-esteem in middle and late childhood, they may have experienced neglect or abuse in relationships with their parents earlier in development. Children with high self-esteem are more likely to be securely attached to their parents and have parents who engage in sensitive caregiving (Lockhart & others, 2017; Thompson, 2016). And in a longitudinal study, the quality of children's home environment (which involved assessment of parenting quality, cognitive stimulation, and the physical home environment) was linked to their self-esteem in early adulthood (Orth & others, 2017).

Self-esteem reflects perceptions that do not always match reality (Cramer, 2017). A child's self-esteem might reflect a belief about whether he or she is intelligent and attractive, for example, but that belief is not necessarily accurate. Thus, high self-esteem may refer to accurate, justified perceptions of one's worth as a person and one's successes and accomplishments, but it can also refer to an arrogant, grandiose, unwarranted sense of superiority over others (Lavner & others, 2016). In the same manner, low self-esteem may reflect either an accurate perception of one's shortcomings or a distorted, even pathological insecurity and inferiority.

Variations in self-esteem have been linked with many aspects of children's development. However, much of the research is *correlational* rather than *experimental*. Recall that correlation does not equal causation. Thus, if a correlational study finds an association between children's low self-esteem and low academic achievement, low academic achievement could cause the low self-esteem as much as low self-esteem could cause low academic achievement. A recent longitudinal study explored whether self-esteem is a cause or consequence of social support in youth (Marshall & others, 2014). In this study, self-esteem predicted subsequent changes in social support but social support did not predict subsequent changes in self-esteem.

What are the consequences of low self-esteem? Low self-esteem has been implicated in overweight and obesity, anxiety, depression, suicide, drug use, and delinquency (Orth & others, 2017; Paxton & Damiano, 2017; Stadelmann & others, 2017). One study revealed that youth with low self-esteem had lower life satisfaction at 30 years of age (Birkeland & others, 2012). Another study found that low and decreasing self-esteem in adolescence was linked to adult depression two decades later (Steiger & others, 2014).

Researchers have found only moderate correlations between school performance and self-esteem, and these correlations do not suggest that high self-esteem produces better school performance (Baumeister, 2013). In fact, efforts to increase students'

How Would You...?

As an **educator,** how would you work with children to improve their self-esteem in relation to their academic ability?

self-esteem have not always led to improved school performance (Davies & Brember, 1999).

Children with high self-esteem have greater initiative, but this can produce positive or negative outcomes. For example, children with high self-esteem are prone to both prosocial and antisocial actions (Krueger, Vohs, & Baumeister, 2008).

In addition, a current concern is that too many of today's children grow up receiving praise for mediocre or even poor performance and as a consequence have inflated self-esteem (Stipek, 2005). They may have difficulty handling competition and criticism. This theme is vividly captured by the title of a book, *Dumbing Down Our Kids: Why American Children Feel Good About Themselves But Can't Read, Write, or Add* (Sykes, 1995). A similar theme—the promise of high self-esteem for students in education, especially those who are impoverished or marginalized—characterized a more recent book *Challenging the Cult of Self-Esteem in Education* (Bergeron, 2018). In a series of studies, researchers found that inflated praise, although well intended, may cause children with low self-esteem to avoid important learning experiences such as tackling challenging tasks (Brummelman & others, 2014). Another study found that narcissistic parents especially overvalue their children's talents (Brummelman & others, 2015).

What are the best strategies for improving children's self-esteem? Teachers, social workers, health-care professionals, and others are often concerned about low self-esteem in the children they serve. Researchers have suggested several strategies to improve self-esteem in at-risk children (Bednar, Wells, & Peterson, 1995; Harter, 2006, 2012, 2016).

- *Identify the causes of low self-esteem.* Intervention should target the causes of low self-esteem. Children have the highest self-esteem when they perform competently in domains that are important to them. Therefore, it is helpful to encourage children to identify and value their areas of competence, such as academic skills, athletic skills, physical attractiveness, and social acceptance.

- *Provide emotional support and social approval.* Some children with low self-esteem come from conflictual families or conditions of abuse or neglect—situations in which emotional support is unavailable. In some cases, alternative sources of support can be arranged either informally through the encouragement of a teacher, a coach, or another significant adult, or more formally through programs such as Big Brothers and Big Sisters.

- *Help children achieve.* Achievement also can improve children's self-esteem. For example, the straightforward teaching of real skills to children often results in increased achievement and thus in enhanced self-esteem. Children develop higher self-esteem when they know which tasks will achieve their goals and when they have successfully performed them or similar tasks.

- *Help children cope.* Self-esteem can be built when a child faces a problem and tries to cope with it, rather than avoiding it. If coping rather than avoidance prevails, children often face problems realistically, honestly, and nondefensively. This produces favorable self-evaluative thoughts, which lead to the self-generated approval that raises self-esteem.

How can parents help children develop higher self-esteem?
©Roberto Westbrook/ Getty Images

Self-Efficacy

Self-efficacy is the belief that one can master a situation and produce favorable outcomes. Albert Bandura (2001, 2006, 2010a, 2012, 2016), whose social cognitive theory was described earlier, states that self-efficacy is a critical factor in whether or not students achieve. Self-efficacy is the belief that "I can"; helplessness is the belief that "I cannot." Students with high self-efficacy endorse such statements as "I know that I will be able to learn the material in this class" and "I expect to be able to do well at this activity."

Dale Schunk (2016) has applied the concept of self-efficacy to many aspects of students' achievement. In his view, self-efficacy influences a student's choice of activities. Students with low self-efficacy for learning may avoid many learning tasks, especially those that are challenging. By contrast,

self-efficacy The belief that one can master a situation and produce favorable outcomes.

EMOTIONAL AND PERSONALITY DEVELOPMENT   **229**

children with high self-efficacy eagerly work at learning tasks (Schunk, 2016). Students with high self-efficacy are more likely to expend effort and persist longer at a learning task than students with low self-efficacy.

How Would You...?

As an **educator,** how would you encourage enhanced self-efficacy in a student who says, "I can't do this work"?

Self-Regulation

One of the most important aspects of the self in middle and late childhood is the increased capacity for self-regulation (Blair, 2017; Galinsky & others, 2017; Schunk & Greene, 2018; Usher & Schunk, 2018; Winne, 2018). This increased capacity is characterized by deliberate efforts to manage one's behavior, emotions, and thoughts that lead to increased social competence and achievement (Schunk & Greene, 2018). In a recent study, higher levels of self-control assessed at 4 years of age were linked to improvements in the math and reading achievement of early elementary school children living in predominantly rural and low-income contexts (Blair & others, 2015). Also, a study of almost 17,000 3- to 7-year-old children revealed that self-regulation was a protective factor for children growing up in low-socioeconomic-status (SES) conditions (Flouri, Midouhas, & Joshi, 2014).

Some researchers emphasize the early development of self-regulation in childhood and adolescence as a key contributor to adult health and even longevity (Eisenberg, Spinrad, & Valiente, 2016; Llewellyn & others, 2017). For example, Nancy Eisenberg and her colleagues (2014) concluded that research indicates self-regulation fosters conscientiousness later in life, both directly and through its link to academic motivation/success and internalized compliance with norms. Further, a longitudinal study found that a higher level of self-control in childhood was linked to a slower pace of aging (assessed with 18 biomarkers—cardiovascular and immune system, for example) at 26, 32, and 38 years of age (Belsky & others, 2017). Also, an app for iPads has been developed to help children improve their self-regulation (for more information, go to www.selfregulationstation.com/sr-ipad-app/).

Industry Versus Inferiority

Earlier we described Erik Erikson's (1968) eight stages of human development. His fourth stage, industry versus inferiority, appears during middle and late childhood. The term *industry* expresses a dominant theme of this period: Children become interested in how things are made and how they work. When children are encouraged in their efforts to make, build, and work—whether building a model airplane, constructing a tree house, fixing a bicycle, solving an addition problem, or cooking—their sense of industry increases. Conversely, parents who see their children's efforts at making things as "mischief" or "making a mess" will tend to foster a sense of inferiority in their children.

Emotional Development

Preschoolers become more adept at talking about their own and others' emotions. They also show a growing awareness of the need to control and manage their emotions to meet social standards. In middle and late childhood, children further develop their understanding and self-regulation of emotion (Calkins & Perry, 2016; Cole & Hollenstein, 2018; Cole, Lougheed, & Ram, 2018; Morris & others, 2018). In a recent study, a low level of emotion regulation in childhood was especially important in predicting a higher level of externalizing problems in adolescence (Perry & others, 2017).

Developmental Changes

Developmental changes in emotions during middle and late childhood include the following (Calkins & Perry, 2016; Denham, Bassett, & Wyatt, 2015; Goodvin, Thompson, & Winer, 2015; Kuebli, 1994; Perry & Calkins, 2018):

- *Improved emotional understanding.* Children in elementary school develop an increased ability to understand such complex emotions as pride and shame. These emotions become less tied to the reactions of other people; they become more self-generated and integrated with a sense of personal responsibility. Also, during middle and late childhood as part of their understanding of emotions, children can engage in "mental time travel," in which they anticipate and recall the cognitive and emotional aspects of events (Hjortsvang & Lagattuta, 2017; Kramer & Lagattuta, 2018; Lagattuta, 2014a, b; Lagattuta & others, 2015).

- *Increased understanding that more than one emotion can be experienced in a particular situation.* A third-grader, for example, may realize that achieving something might involve both anxiety and joy.

- *Increased tendency to be aware of the events leading to emotional reactions.* A fourth-grader may become aware that her sadness today is influenced by her friend moving to another town last week.

- *Ability to suppress or conceal negative emotional reactions.* A fifth-grader has learned to tone down his anger better than he used to when one of his classmates irritates him.

- *The use of self-initiated strategies for redirecting feelings.* In the elementary school years, children become more reflective about their emotional lives and increasingly use strategies to control their emotions. They become more effective at cognitively managing their emotions, such as soothing themselves after an upset.

- *A capacity for genuine empathy.* A fourth-grader, for example, feels sympathy for a distressed person and experiences vicariously the sadness the distressed person is feeling.

Social-Emotional Education Programs

An increasing number of social-emotional educational programs have been developed to improve many aspects of children's and adolescents' lives. Two such programs are the Second Step program created by the Committee for Children (2018) and the Collaborative for Academic, Social, and Emotional Learning (CASEL, 2018). Many social-emotional education programs only target young children, but Second Step can be implemented in pre-K through eighth grade and CASEL can used with pre-K through twelfth-grade students.

- *Second Step* focuses on these aspects of social-emotional learning from pre-K through the eighth grade: (1) pre-K: self-regulation and executive function skills that improve their attention and help them control their behavior; (2) K–grade 5: making friends, self-regulation of emotion, and solving problems; and (3) grades 6–8: communication skills, coping with stress, and decision making to avoid engaging in problem behaviors.

Children engaging in an activity in a Second Step socio-emotional program.
©Elizabeth D. Herman/The New York Times/Redux

- *CASEL* targets five core social and emotional learning domains: (1) self-awareness (recognizing one's emotions and how they affect behavior, for example); (2) self-management (self-control, coping with stress, and impulse control, for example); (3) social awareness (perspective taking and empathy, for example); (4) relationship skills (developing positive relationships and communicating effectively with individuals from diverse backgrounds, for example); and (5) responsible decision making (engaging in ethical behavior, and understanding the consequences of one's actions, for example).

Coping with Stress

An important aspect of children's emotional lives is learning how to cope with stress (Masten, 2018a, b; Masten & Palmer, 2018). As children get older, they more accurately appraise a stressful situation and determine how much control they have over it (Almy & Cicchetti, 2018; Masten, 2017, 2018a, b; Masten & Kalstabakken, 2018). Older children generate more coping alternatives to stressful conditions and use more cognitive coping strategies (Saarni & others, 2006). They are better than younger children at intentionally shifting their thoughts to something that is less stressful; and at reframing, or changing their perception of a stressful situation. For example, a younger child may be very disappointed that a teacher did not say hello when the child arrived in the classroom. An older child may reframe the situation and think, "My teacher may have been busy with other things and just forgot to say hello."

By 10 years of age, most children are able to use cognitive strategies to cope with stress (Saarni, 1999). However, in families that have not been supportive and are characterized by turmoil or trauma, children may be so overwhelmed by stress that they do not use such strategies (Klingman, 2006).

Disasters, such as the bombing of the World Trade Center in New York City in September 2001 or Hurricane Sandy in 2012, can especially harm children's development and produce adjustment problems (Masten & Kalstabakken, 2018; Narayan & Masten, 2019; Narayan & others, 2017). Among the outcomes for children who experience disasters are acute stress reactions, depression, panic disorder, and post-traumatic stress disorder (Danielson & others, 2017; Lieber, 2017). The likelihood that a child will face these problems following a disaster depends on factors such as the nature and severity of the disaster and the type of support available to the child (Masten & Kalstabakken, 2018; Narayan & Masten, 2019). Also, children who have developed a number of coping techniques have the best chance of adapting and functioning competently in the face of disasters and trauma (Ungar, 2015).

Children grieve at a memorial near the Sandy Hook Elementary School in Newtown, Connecticut, following the shooting in December 2012 that left 26 people dead, 20 of them young children. *What are some effective strategies that adults can use to help children cope with traumatic events?*
©Gordon M. Grant/Alamy

In research on disasters and trauma, the term *dose-response effects* is often used. A widely supported finding in this research area is that the more severe the disaster or trauma (dose), the worse the adaptation and adjustment (response) following the event (Masten, 2017; Narayan & Masten, 2019).

Researchers have offered some recommendations for parents, teachers, and other adults caring for children after a disaster (Gurwitch & others, 2001):

How Would You…?

As a **social worker,** how would you counsel a child who has been exposed to a traumatic event?

- Reassure children (numerous times, if necessary) of their safety and security.

- Allow children to retell events and be patient in listening to them.

- Encourage children to talk about any disturbing or confusing feelings, reassuring them that such feelings are normal after a stressful event.

- Protect children from re-exposure to frightening situations and reminders of the trauma—for example, by limiting discussion of the event in front of the children.

- Help children make sense of what happened, keeping in mind that children may misunderstand what took place. For example, young children "may blame themselves, believe things happened that did not happen, believe that terrorists are in the school, etc. Gently help children develop a realistic understanding of the event" (p. 10).

Child and adolescent psychiatrists are among the mental health professionals who help youth cope with stress, including traumatic experiences. To read about a child psychiatrist who treats children and adolescents, see *Careers in Life-Span Development.*

Moral Development

Recall that Piaget proposed that younger children are characterized by heteronomous morality but that by 10 years of age they have moved into a higher stage called autonomous morality. According to Piaget, older children consider the intentions of the individual, believe that rules are subject to change, and are aware that punishment does not always follow wrongdoing.

A second major perspective on moral development was proposed by Lawrence Kohlberg (1958, 1986). Piaget's cognitive stages of development serve as the underpinnings

Melissa Jackson, Child Psychiatrist

Dr. Melissa Jackson is a child and adolescent psychiatrist in Miami, Florida. She obtained a medical degree from the University of Florida and then completed an internship and residency in psychiatry at Advocate Lutheran General Hospital in Chicago, followed by a fellowship in child and adolescent psychiatry at the University of Southern California. Among the problems and disorders that Dr. Jackson treats are post-traumatic stress disorder, ADHD, anxiety, autism, depression, and a number of behavioral issues. In addition to her psychiatric treatment of children, she founded Health for Honduras, which includes trips to Honduras to provide services to children in orphanages.

To become a child and adolescent psychiatrist like Melissa Jackson requires completing an undergraduate degree, then obtaining a medical degree, followed by a three- to four-year residency in general psychiatry, and finally a two-year fellowship in the subspecialty of child and adolescent psychiatry. An important aspect of being a psychiatrist is that psychiatrists can prescribe medication, while psychologists cannot.

for Kohlberg's theory, but Kohlberg proposed three levels of moral development, which he believed are universal. Development from one level to another, said Kohlberg, is fostered by opportunities to take the perspective of others and to experience conflict between one's current level of moral thinking and the reasoning of someone at a higher level.

The Kohlberg Levels

Kohlberg identified the following levels of moral thinking:

- **Preconventional reasoning** is Kohlberg's lowest level of moral reasoning. At this level, children interpret good and bad in terms of external rewards and punishments. For example, children and adolescents obey adults because adults tell them to obey. Or they might be nice to others so that others will be nice to them. This earliest level has sometimes been described as "What's in it for me?"

- **Conventional reasoning** is the second, or intermediate, level in Kohlberg's theory of moral development. At this level, individuals apply certain standards, but they are the standards set by others, such as parents or the government.

- **Postconventional reasoning** is the highest level in Kohlberg's theory of moral development. At this level, the individual recognizes alternative moral courses, explores the options, and then decides on a personal moral code. In postconventional reasoning, individuals engage in deliberate checks on their reasoning to ensure that it meets high ethical standards.

Kohlberg believed that these levels occur in a sequence and are age related: Before age 9, most children use level 1, preconventional reasoning based on external rewards and punishments. By early adolescence, moral reasoning is increasingly based on level 2, the application of standards set by others. Not everyone progresses beyond level 2 even in adulthood, but by early adulthood a small number of individuals reason in postconventional ways (level 3).

Influences on the Kohlberg Levels

What factors influence movement through Kohlberg's stages? Although moral reasoning at each level presupposes a certain level of cognitive development, Kohlberg argued that advances in children's cognitive development did not ensure development of moral reasoning. Instead, moral reasoning also reflects children's experiences in dealing with moral questions and moral conflict.

Several investigators have tried to advance children's levels of moral development by having a model present arguments that reflect moral thinking above the child's established level. This approach applies Vygotsky's principle of scaffolding; it also applies the concepts of equilibrium and conflict that Piaget used to explain cognitive development. By presenting

preconventional reasoning The lowest level in Kohlberg's theory of moral development. The individual's moral reasoning is controlled primarily by external rewards and punishment.

conventional reasoning The second, or intermediate, level in Kohlberg's theory of moral development. At this level, individuals abide by certain standards, but they are the standards of others, such as parents or the laws of society.

postconventional reasoning The highest level in Kohlberg's theory of moral development. At this level, the individual recognizes alternative moral courses, explores the options, and then decides on a personal moral code.

arguments slightly beyond a child's current level of moral reasoning, the researchers created a disequilibrium that motivated the children to restructure their moral thought. The upshot of studies using this approach is that virtually any discussion about the child's current level seems to promote more advanced moral reasoning (Walker, 1982).

Kohlberg believed that peer interaction is a critical part of the social stimulation that challenges children to change their moral reasoning. Whereas adults characteristically impose rules and regulations on children, the give-and-take among peers gives children an opportunity to take the perspective of another person and to generate rules democratically. Kohlberg stressed that encounters with peers can produce perspective-taking opportunities that may advance a child's moral reasoning.

Kohlberg's Critics

Kohlberg's theory has provoked debate, research, and criticism (Gray & Graham, 2018; Hoover & others, 2018; Killen & Dahl, 2018; Narváez, 2016, 2017a, b, 2018; Turiel & Gingo, 2017). Key criticisms involve the relative importance of moral thought and moral behavior, whether moral reasoning is conscious/deliberative or unconscious/ automatic, the roles of culture and the family in moral development, and the significance of concern for others.

Moral Thought and Moral Behavior Kohlberg's theory has been criticized for placing too much emphasis on moral thought and not enough emphasis on moral behavior (Walker, 2004). Moral reasons can sometimes be used as a shelter for immoral behavior (Bandura, 2016). Corrupt CEOs and politicians have often endorsed the loftiest of moral virtues in public before their own immoral behavior is exposed. Whatever the type of public scandal, you will probably find that the culprits expressed virtuous thoughts but engaged in immoral behavior. No one wants a nation of cheaters and thieves who can reason at the postconventional level and who may know what is right yet still do what is wrong.

Conscious/Deliberate Versus Unconscious/Automatic Social psychologist Jonathan Haidt (2006, 2013, 2017) argues that a major flaw in Kohlberg's theory is his view that moral thinking is deliberative and that individuals go around all the time contemplating and reasoning about morality. Haidt believes that moral thinking is more often an intuitive gut reaction, with deliberative moral reasoning serving as an after-the-fact justification. Thus, in his view, much of morality begins with rapid evaluative judgments of others rather than with strategic reasoning about moral circumstances.

Culture and Moral Reasoning Kohlberg emphasized that his levels of moral reasoning are universal, but some critics claim his theory is culturally biased (Graham & others, 2017; Gray & Graham, 2018). For example, Kohlberg's level 3 moral thinking has not been found in all cultures (Gibbs & others, 2007; Snarey, 1987).

Cohort effects regarding moral reasoning have occurred (Narváez & Gleason, 2013). In recent years, postconventional moral reasoning has been declining in college students, not down to the next level (conventional), but to the lowest level (personal interests) (Thoma & Bebeau, 2008). Some moral development researchers conclude that prosocial behavior has declined in recent years and that humans, especially those living in Western cultures, are "on a fast train to demise" (Narváez & Gleason, 2013). They emphasize that the solution to improving people's moral lives lies in better child-rearing strategies and social supports for families and children. Further, recently it has been argued that we need better progress in dealing with an increasing array of temptations and possible wrongdoings in a human social world in which complexity is accumulating over time (Christen, Narváez, & Gutzwiller, 2018).

In sum, although Kohlberg's approach does capture much of the moral reasoning used in various cultures around the world, his approach misses or misconstrues some important moral concepts in particular cultures (Gibbs, 2014; Gray & Graham, 2018).

Families and Moral Development Kohlberg argued that family processes are essentially unimportant in children's moral development. As noted earlier, he argued that parent-child relationships usually provide children with little opportunity for give-and-take or perspective taking. Rather, Kohlberg said that such opportunities are more likely to be provided by children's peer relations.

Did Kohlberg underestimate the contribution of family relationships to moral development? Most experts on children's moral development conclude that parents' moral values and actions influence children's development of moral thoughts (Carlo & others, 2017). Nonetheless, most developmentalists agree with Kohlberg and Piaget that peers play an important role in the development of moral reasoning.

Gender and the Care Perspective The most publicized criticism of Kohlberg's theory has come from Carol Gilligan (1982, 1996), who argues that Kohlberg's theory reflects a gender bias. According to Gilligan, Kohlberg's theory is based on a male norm that puts abstract principles above relationships and concern for others and sees the individual as standing alone and independently making moral decisions. It puts justice at the heart of morality. In contrast with Kohlberg's **justice perspective,** Gilligan argues for a **care perspective,** which is a moral perspective that views people in terms of their connectedness with others and emphasizes interpersonal communication, relationships with others, and concern for others. According to Gilligan, Kohlberg greatly underplayed the care perspective, perhaps because he was a male, because most of his research was with males rather than females, and because he used male responses as a model for his theory.

However, questions have been raised about Gilligan's gender conclusions (Walker & Frimer, 2011). For example, a meta-analysis casts doubt on Gilligan's claim of substantial gender differences in moral judgment (Jaffee & Hyde, 2000). And a review concluded that girls' moral orientations are "somewhat more likely to focus on care for others than on abstract principles of justice, but they can use both moral orientations when needed (as can boys . . .)" (Blakemore, Berenbaum, & Liben, 2009, p. 132).

Domain Theory: Moral, Social Conventional, Personal Reasoning

The **domain theory of moral development** states that there are different domains of social knowledge and reasoning, including moral, social conventional, and personal domains. In domain theory, children's and adolescents' moral, social conventional, and personal knowledge and reasoning emerge from their attempts to understand and deal with different forms of social experience (Jambon & Smetana, 2018; Killen & Dahl, 2018; Turiel & Gingo, 2017).

Social conventional reasoning focuses on conventional rules that have been established by social consensus in order to control behavior and maintain the social system. The rules themselves are arbitrary, such as raising your hand in class before speaking, using one staircase at school to go up and the other to go down, not cutting in front of someone standing in line to buy movie tickets, and stopping at a stop sign when driving. There are sanctions if we violate these conventions, although the rules can be changed by consensus.

In contrast, moral reasoning focuses on ethical issues and rules of morality. Unlike conventional rules, moral rules are not arbitrary. They are obligatory, widely accepted, and somewhat impersonal (Turiel & Gingo, 2017). Rules pertaining to lying, cheating, stealing, and physically harming another person are moral rules because violation of these rules affronts ethical standards that exist apart from social consensus and convention. Moral judgments involve concepts of justice, whereas social conventional judgments are concepts of social organization. Violating moral rules is usually more serious than violating conventional rules.

The social conventional approach is a serious challenge to Kohlberg's approach because Kohlberg argued that social conventions are a stop-over on the road to higher moral sophistication. For social conventional reasoning advocates, social conventional reasoning is not lower than postconventional reasoning but rather something that needs to be disentangled from the moral thread (Killen & Dahl, 2018).

Recently, a distinction also has been made between moral and conventional issues, which are viewed as legitimately subject to adult social regulation, and personal issues, which are more likely subject to the

justice perspective A moral perspective that focuses on the rights of the individual; individuals independently make moral decisions.

care perspective The moral perspective of Carol Gilligan, which views people in terms of their connectedness with others and emphasizes interpersonal communication, relationships with others, and concern for others.

domain theory of moral development Theory that identifies different domains of social knowledge and reasoning, including moral, social conventional, and personal domains. These domains arise from children's and adolescents' attempts to understand and deal with different forms of social experience.

social conventional reasoning Thoughts about social consensus and convention, in contrast with moral reasoning, which stresses ethical issues.

child's or adolescent's independent decision making and personal discretion (Jambon & Smetana, 2018). Personal issues include control over one's body, privacy, and choice of friends and activities. Thus, some actions belong to a *personal* domain not governed by moral strictures or social norms.

Prosocial Behavior

Whereas Kohlberg's and Gilligan's theories have focused primarily on the development of moral reasoning, the study of prosocial moral behavior has placed more emphasis on the behavioral aspects of moral development (Carlo & others, 2018; Dirks, Dunfield & Recchia, 2018; Eisenberg & Spinrad, 2016; Laible & others, 2017). Children engage in both immoral antisocial acts, such as lying and cheating, and prosocial moral behavior, such as showing empathy or helping others altruistically. Even during the preschool years, children may care for others or comfort someone in distress, but prosocial behavior is more prevalent in adolescence than in childhood (Eisenberg & Spinrad, 2016). Parents can be especially helpful in guiding children to engage in prosocial behavior (Carlo & others, 2018).

How does children's sharing change from the preschool to the elementary school years?
©Ariel Skelley/age fotostock

Sharing is one aspect of prosocial behavior that researchers have studied. Children's sharing comes to reflect a more complex sense of what is just and right during middle and late childhood. By the start of the elementary school years, children begin to express objective ideas about fairness (Eisenberg, Fabes, & Spinrad, 2006). It is common to hear 6-year-old children use the word *fair* as synonymous with *equal* or *same*. By the middle to late elementary school years, children come to believe that equity can also mean that people with special merit or special needs deserve special treatment.

Gender

Gilligan's claim that Kohlberg's theory of moral development reflects gender bias reminds us of the pervasive influence of gender on development. Long before elementary school, boys and girls show preferences for different toys and activities (Leaper & Bigler, 2018), As we discussed in the chapter on socioemotional development in early childhood, preschool children display a gender identity and gender-typed behavior that reflects biological, cognitive, and social influences. Here we examine gender stereotypes, gender similarities and differences, and gender-role classification.

Gender Stereotypes

In the past, a well-adjusted boy was supposed to be independent, aggressive, and powerful. A well-adjusted girl was supposed to be dependent, nurturing, and uninterested in power. These notions reflect **gender stereotypes,** which are broad categories that encompass general impressions and beliefs about females and males.

Recent research has found that gender stereotypes are, to a great extent, still present in today's world, influencing the lives of both children and adults (Biernat, 2017; Ellemers, 2018; Hyde, 2017; Liben, 2017). Gender stereotyping continues to change during middle and late childhood and adolescence (Blakemore, Berenbaum, & Liben, 2009; Brannon, 2017). During the elementary school years, children have considerable knowledge about which activities are linked with being male or female. For example, a study of 6- to 10-year-olds revealed gender stereotyping in math—both boys and girls indicated math is for boys (Cvencek, Meltzoff, & Greenwald, 2011). Researchers also have found that boys' gender stereotypes are more rigid than those of girls (Blakemore, Berenbaum, & Liben, 2009).

Gender Similarities and Differences

What is the reality behind gender stereotypes? Let's examine some of the similarities and differences between boys and girls, keeping in mind that (1) the differences are averages—not characteristics of all boys versus all girls; (2) even when differences are reported, there is considerable gender

gender stereotypes Broad categories that reflect society's impressions and beliefs about females and males.

overlap; and (3) the differences may be due primarily to biological factors, sociocultural factors, or both. First, we examine physical similarities and differences, and then we turn to cognitive and socioemotional similarities and differences.

Physical Development Women have about twice the body fat of men, with most of it concentrated around the breasts and hips. In males, fat is more likely to go to the abdomen. On average, males grow to be 10 percent taller than females. Other physical differences are less obvious. From conception onward, females have a longer life expectancy than males, and females are less likely than males to develop physical or mental disorders. Males have twice the risk of coronary disease that females do.

Does gender matter when it comes to brain structure and function? Human brains are much alike, whether the brain belongs to a male or a female (Halpern & others, 2007). However, researchers have found some differences in the brains of males and females (Hofer & others, 2007). Female brains are approximately 10 percent smaller than male brains (Giedd, 2012). However, female brains have more folds; the larger number of folds (called convolutions) allows more surface brain tissue within the skulls of females than males (Luders & others, 2004). An area of the parietal lobe that functions in visuospatial skills is larger in males than females (Frederikse & others, 2000). And the areas of the brain involved in emotional expression show more metabolic activity in females than males (Gur & others, 1995).

Although some differences in brain structure and function have been found, many of these differences are small and research often is inconsistent regarding the differences. Also, when sex differences in the brain have been revealed, in many cases they have not been directly linked to psychological differences (Blakemore, Berenbaum, & Liben, 2009).

Although research on sex differences in the brain is still in its infancy, it is likely that there are far more similarities than differences in the brains of females and males. A further point is worth noting: Anatomical sex differences in the brain may be due to the biological origins of these differences, behavioral experiences (which underscores the brain's continuing plasticity), or a combination of these factors.

Cognitive Development and Achievement No gender differences in general intelligence have been revealed, but gender differences have been found in some cognitive areas (Blakemore, Berenbaum, & Liben, 2009). Research has shown that in general girls and women have slightly better verbal skills than boys and men, although in some verbal skill areas the differences are substantial (Blakemore, Berenbaum, & Liben, 2009).

There is strong evidence that females outperform males in reading and writing. In national studies, girls have had higher reading achievement than have boys (National Assessment of Educational Progress, 2012). A recent international study in 65 countries found that girls had higher reading achievement than did boys in every country (Reilly, 2012). In this study, the gender difference in reading was stronger in countries with less gender equity and lower economic prosperity. In the United States, girls also have consistently outperformed boys in writing skills in the National Assessment of Educational Progress in fourth-, eighth-, and twelfth-grade assessments.

Are there gender differences in math competence? A very large-scale study of more than 7 million U.S. students in grades 2 through 11 revealed no differences in math scores for boys and girls (Hyde & others, 2008). And a recent meta-analysis found no gender differences in math scores for adolescents (Lindberg & others, 2010). A recent research review concluded that girls have more negative math attitudes and that parents' and teachers' expectancies for children's math competence are often gender-biased in favor of boys (Gunderson & others, 2012).

One area of math that has been examined for possible gender differences is visuospatial skills, which include being able to rotate objects mentally and determine what they would look like when rotated (Halpern, 2012). These types of skills are important in courses such as plane and solid geometry and geography. A research review revealed that boys have better visuospatial skills than girls (Halpern & others, 2007). For example, despite equal participation in the National Geography Bee, in most years all 10 finalists are boys (Liben, 1995). However, some experts argue that the gender difference in visuospatial skills is small (Hyde & Else-Quest, 2013).

Are there gender differences in school contexts and achievement? In regard to school achievement, girls earn better grades, complete high school at a higher rate, and are less likely to drop out of school than boys (Halpern, 2012). Males are more likely than females to be assigned to special/remedial education classes. Girls are more likely than boys to be engaged with academic material, be attentive in class, put forth more academic effort, and participate more in class (DeZolt & Hull, 2001).

Keep in mind that measures of achievement in school or scores on standardized tests may reflect many factors besides cognitive ability. For example, performance in school may in part reflect attempts to conform to gender roles or differences in motivation, self-regulation, or other socioemotional characteristics (Klug & others, 2016; Martin & others, 2016; Wentzel & Miele, 2016; Wigfield & others, 2015).

Socioemotional Development Three areas of socioemotional development in which gender similarities and differences have been studied extensively are aggression, emotion, and prosocial behavior.

One of the most consistent gender differences is that boys are more physically aggressive than girls are (Hyde, 2017). The difference occurs in all cultures and appears very early in children's development (Dayton & Malone, 2017). The physical aggression difference is especially pronounced when children are provoked. Both biological and environmental factors have been proposed to account for gender differences in aggression. Biological factors include heredity and hormones. Environmental factors include cultural expectations, adult and peer models, and social agents that reward aggression in boys and punish aggression in girls.

Although boys are consistently more physically aggressive than girls, might girls show as much or more verbal aggression, such as yelling, than boys? When verbal aggression is examined, gender differences often disappear; sometimes, though, verbal aggression is more pronounced in girls (Eagly & Steffen, 1986).

Recently, increased interest has been shown in *relational aggression*, which involves harming someone by manipulating a relationship (Casper & Card, 2017; Eisman & others, 2018). Relational aggression includes such behaviors as trying to make others dislike a certain individual by spreading malicious rumors about the person (Orpinas, McNicholas, & Nahapetyan, 2015). Relational aggression increases in middle and late childhood (Dishion & Piehler, 2009). Mixed findings have characterized research on whether girls show more relational aggression than boys, but one consistent finding is that relational aggression comprises a greater percentage of girls' overall aggression than it does for boys (Putallaz & others, 2007). One research review revealed that girls engage in more relational aggression than boys in adolescence but not in childhood (Smith, Rose, & Schwartz-Mette, 2010).

Gender differences occur in some aspects of emotion (Brody, Hall, & Stokes, 2018; Connolly & others, 2018). Females express emotion more than males do, are better than males at decoding emotion, smile more, cry more, and are happier. Males report experiencing and expressing more anger than females do (Kring, 2000). And a meta-analysis found that females are better than males at recognizing nonverbal displays of emotion (Thompson & Voyer, 2014). Also, a recent study revealed that females are better than males at facial emotion perception across the life span (Olderbak & others, 2018).

An important skill is to be able to regulate and control one's emotions and behavior (Berke, Reidy, & Zeichner, 2018; Usher & Schunk, 2018). Males usually show less self-regulation of emotion than females do, and this lower level of self-control can translate into behavioral problems (Schunk & Greene, 2018).

Are there gender differences in prosocial behavior? Across childhood and adolescence, females engage in more prosocial behavior than males do (Hastings, Miller, & Troxel, 2015). Females also view themselves as more empathetic than males do (Eisenberg & Spinrad, 2016). There is a small difference between boys and girls in the extent to which they share, with girls sharing slightly more than boys. However, the greatest gender difference in prosocial behavior occurs with kind and considerate behavior, which females engage in more often than males.

How Would You...?

As a **psychologist,** how would you discuss gender similarities and differences with a parent or teacher who is concerned about a child's academic progress and social skills?

Gender in Context

The importance of considering gender in context is nowhere more apparent than when examining what is culturally prescribed behavior for females and males in different countries around the world (UNICEF, 2018). Although there has been greater acceptance of similarities in male and female behavior in recent decades in the United States, in many countries gender roles have remained gender-specific. For example, in many Middle Eastern and some Asian countries, the division of labor between males and females is dramatic. Males are socialized and schooled to work in the public sphere, females in the private world of home and child rearing. In Iran, the dominant view is that the man's duty is to provide for his family and the woman's is to care for her family and household. China also has been a male-dominant culture. Although women have made some strides in China, especially in urban areas, the male role is still dominant. Most males in China do not accept gender equity.

In a recent study of eighth-grade students in 36 countries, in every country girls had more egalitarian attitudes about gender roles than boys did (Dotti Sani & Quaranta, 2015). In this study, girls had more egalitarian gender attitudes in countries with higher levels of societal gender equality. In another recent study of 15- to 19-year-olds in the country of Qatar, males had more negative views of gender equality than females did (Al-Ghanim & Badahdah, 2017).

In China, females and males are usually socialized to behave, feel, and think differently. The old patriarchal traditions of male supremacy have not been completely uprooted. Chinese women still make considerably less money than Chinese men do. In rural China, male supremacy still governs many women's lives.
©Diego Azubel/EPA/Newscom

Families

Our discussion of parenting and families in this section focuses on how parent-child interactions typically change in middle and late childhood, how parents act as managers, the role of attachment, and how children are affected by living with stepparents.

Developmental Changes in Parent-Child Relationships

As children move into the middle and late childhood years, parents spend considerably less time with them (Grusec, 2017; Pomerantz & Grolnick, 2017). In one study, parents spent less than half as much time with their children aged 5 to 12 in caregiving, instruction, reading, talking, and playing as they did when the children were younger (Hill & Stafford, 1980). However, parents continue to be extremely important in their children's lives. One analysis concluded: "Parents serve as gatekeepers and provide scaffolding as children assume more responsibility for themselves and . . . regulate their own lives" (Huston & Ripke, 2006, p. 422).

What are some changes in the focus of parent-child interaction in middle and late childhood?
©wavebreakmediamicro/123RF

Parents especially play an important role in supporting and stimulating children's academic achievement in middle and late childhood (Lansford & others, 2018; Longo, McPherran Lombardi, & Dearing, 2017). The value parents place on education can make a difference in whether children do well in school. Parents not only influence children's in-school achievement, but they also make decisions about children's out-of-school activities. Whether children participate in sports, music, and other activities is heavily influenced by the extent to which parents sign up children for such activities and encourage their participation (Simpkins & others, 2006).

Elementary school children tend to receive less physical discipline than preschoolers do. Instead of spanking or coercive holding, their parents are more likely to use deprivation of privileges, appeals to the child's self-esteem, comments designed to increase the child's sense of guilt, and statements that the child is responsible for his or her actions. During middle and late childhood, some control is transferred from parent to child. A gradual process, it produces *coregulation* rather than control by either the child or the parent alone (Maccoby, 1984). Parents continue to exercise general supervision and control, while children are allowed to engage in moment-to-moment self-regulation. The major shift to autonomy does not occur until about the age of 12 or later. A key developmental task as children move toward autonomy is learning to relate to adults outside the family on a regular basis—adults such as teachers who interact with the child much differently from the way parents do.

Parents as Managers

Parents can play important roles as managers of children's opportunities, as monitors of their behavior, and as social initiators and arrangers (Longo, McPherran Lombardi, & Dearing, 2017). Mothers are more likely than fathers to engage in a managerial role in parenting.

Family management practices are positively related to students' grades and self-responsibility, and negatively to school-related problems (Eccles, 2007). Among the most important practices are maintaining a structured and organized family environment, such as establishing routines for homework, chores, bedtime, and so on, and effectively monitoring the child's behavior. A research review of the influence of family functioning on African American students' academic achievement found that when parents monitored their son's academic achievement by ensuring that homework was completed, restricted time spent on nonproductive distractions (such as video games and TV), and participated in a consistent, positive dialogue with teachers and school officials, their son's academic achievement benefited (Mandara, 2006).

Attachment

Earlier you read about the importance of secure attachment in infancy and the role of sensitive parenting in attachment (Coyne & others, 2018; Hoffman & others, 2017; Roisman & Cicchetti, 2017; Thompson, 2016; Woodhouse, 2018). During middle and late childhood, attachment becomes more sophisticated. As children's social worlds expand to include peers, teachers, and others, they typically spend less time with parents. Kathryn Kerns and her colleagues (Brumariu & others, 2018a, b; Kerns & Brumariu, 2016; Kerns & Seibert, 2012; Koehn & Kerns, 2018) have studied links between attachment to parents and various child outcomes in the middle and late childhood years and found that secure attachment is associated with a lower level of internalized symptoms, anxiety, and depression in children. One study revealed that children who were less securely attached to their mothers reported having more anxiety (Brumariu, Kerns, & Seibert, 2012). Also in this study, secure attachment was linked to a higher level of children's emotion regulation and less difficulty in identifying emotions. And in a recent meta-analysis of attachment in middle/late childhood and adolescence, parents of children and adolescents who were more securely attached were more responsive, more supportive of children's and adolescents' autonomy, used more behavioral control strategies, and engaged in less harsh control strategies (Koehn & Kerns, 2018). Also in this meta-analysis, parents of children and adolescents who showed more avoidant attachment were less responsive and used fewer behavioral control strategies; regarding ambivalent attachment, no links to parenting were found.

Stepfamilies

Not only has divorce become commonplace in the United States, so has getting remarried (Ganong, Coleman, & Russell, 2015; Papernow, 2018). It takes time to marry, have children, get divorced, and then remarry. Consequently, there are far more elementary and secondary school children than infants or preschool children living in stepfamilies. The number of remarriages involving children has grown steadily in recent years. Also, divorces occur at a 10 percent higher rate in remarriages than in first marriages (Cherlin & Furstenberg, 1994). About half of all children whose parents divorce will have a stepparent within four years after the separation.

How Would You...?

As a **human development and family studies professional,** what advice would you offer to divorced parents who want to ease their children's adjustment to remarriage?

Remarried parents face unique tasks. The couple must define and strengthen their marriage while renegotiating the biological parent-child relationships and establishing stepparent-stepchild and stepsibling relationships (Ganong, Coleman, & Russell, 2015). The complex histories and multiple relationships make adjustment difficult (Dodson & Davies, 2014). Only one-third of stepfamily couples stay remarried.

Most stepfamilies are preceded by divorce rather than death of a spouse (Pasley & Moorefield, 2004). Three common types of stepfamily structure are (1) stepfather, (2) stepmother, and (3) blended or complex. In stepfather families, the mother typically had custody of the children and remarried, introducing a stepfather into her children's lives. In stepmother families, the father usually had custody and remarried, introducing a stepmother into his children's lives. In a blended or complex stepfamily, both parents bring children from previous marriages.

In E. Mavis Hetherington's (2006) longitudinal analyses, children and adolescents who had been in a simple stepfamily (stepfather or stepmother) for a number of years were adjusting better than in the early years of the remarried family and were functioning well in comparison with children and adolescents in conflictual families that had not gone through a divorce, and children and adolescents in complex (blended) stepfamilies. More than 75 percent of the adolescents in long-established simple stepfamilies described their relationships with their stepparents as "close" or "very close." Hetherington (2006) concluded that in long-established simple stepfamilies adolescents seem to eventually benefit from the presence of a stepparent and the resources provided by the stepparent.

Children often have better relationships with their custodial parents (mothers in stepfather families, fathers in stepmother families) than with stepparents (Antfolk & others, 2017; Santrock, Sitterle, & Warshak, 1988). Also, children in simple stepfamilies (stepmother, stepfather) often show better adjustment than their counterparts in complex (blended) families (Hetherington, 2006).

As in divorced families, children in stepfamilies show more adjustment problems than children in never-divorced families (Hetherington, 2006)—academic problems and lower self-esteem, for example (Anderson & others, 1999). However, it is important to recognize that a majority of children in stepfamilies do not have adjustment problems. In one analysis, 25 percent of children from stepfamilies showed adjustment problems, compared with 10 percent in intact, never-divorced families (Hetherington & Kelly, 2002). Further, a recent study found that when children have a better parent-child affective relationship with their stepparent, the children have fewer internalizing and externalizing problems (Jensen & others, 2018).

Peers

Having positive relationships with peers is especially important in middle and late childhood (Nesi & others, 2017; Rubin & Barstead, 2018; Witkow, Rickert, & Cullen, 2017). Engaging in positive interactions with peers, resolving conflicts in nonaggressive ways, and having quality friendships not only bring positive outcomes at this time in children's lives, but also are linked to more positive relationships in adolescence and adulthood (Kindermann & Gest, 2018; Laursen, 2018; Laursen & Adams, 2018; Vitaro, Boivin, & Poulin, 2018). In one longitudinal study, being popular with peers and engaging in low levels of aggression at 8 years of age were related to higher levels of occupational status at 48 years of age (Huesmann & others, 2006). Another study found that peer competence (a composite measure that included social contact with peers, popularity with peers, friendship, and social skills) in middle and late childhood was linked to having better relationships with coworkers in early adulthood (Collins & van Dulmen, 2006). And a recent study indicated that low peer status in childhood (low acceptance/likeability) was linked to increased probability of being unemployed and having mental health problems in adulthood (Almquist & Brannstrom, 2014).

Developmental Changes

As children enter the elementary school years, reciprocity becomes especially important in peer interchanges. Researchers estimate that the percentage of time spent in social interaction with peers increases from approximately 10 percent at 2 years of age to more than 30 percent in middle and late childhood (Rubin, Bukowski, & Parker, 2006). In an early classic study, a typical day in elementary school included approximately 300 episodes with peers (Barker & Wright, 1951). As children move through middle and late childhood, the size of their peer group increases, and peer interaction is less closely supervised by adults (Rubin & others, 2015). Until about 12 years of age, children's preference for same-sex peer groups increases.

Peer Status

Which children are likely to be popular with their peers and which ones tend to be disliked? Developmentalists address this and similar questions by examining *sociometric status,* a term that describes the extent to which children are liked or disliked by their peer group (Cillessen & Bukowski, 2018). Sociometric status is typically assessed by asking children to rate how much they like or dislike each of their classmates. Status may also be assessed by asking children to nominate the children they like the most and those they like the least.

What are some key aspects of peer relationships in middle and late childhood?
©Shutterstock/Monkey Business Images

How Would You…?

As a **social worker,** how would you help a rejected child develop more positive relationships with peers?

Developmentalists have distinguished five peer statuses:

- **Popular children** are frequently nominated as a best friend and are rarely disliked by their peers.

- **Average children** receive an average number of both positive and negative nominations from their peers.

- **Neglected children** are infrequently nominated as a best friend but are not disliked by their peers.

- **Rejected children** are infrequently nominated as someone's best friend and are actively disliked by their peers.

- **Controversial children** are frequently nominated both as someone's best friend and as being disliked.

Popular children have many social skills that contribute to their being well liked (McDonald & Asher, 2018). They give out reinforcements, listen carefully, maintain open lines of communication with peers, are happy, control their negative emotions, show enthusiasm and concern for others, and are self-confident without being conceited (Hartup, 1983).

Rejected children often have significant adjustment problems (Prinstein & others, 2018). For example, one study revealed a link between peer rejection and depression in adolescence (Platt, Kadosh, & Lau, 2013). Researchers also have found that peer rejection consistently is linked to the development and maintenance of conduct problems (Prinstein & others, 2018). For example, in a recent study of young adolescents, peer rejection predicted increases in aggressive and rule-breaking behavior (Janssens & others, 2017).

popular children Children who are frequently nominated as a best friend and are rarely disliked by their peers.

average children Children who receive an average number of both positive and negative nominations from their peers.

neglected children Children who are infrequently nominated as a best friend but are not disliked by their peers.

rejected children Children who are infrequently nominated as a best friend and are actively disliked by their peers.

controversial children Children who are frequently nominated both as someone's best friend and being disliked.

John Coie (2004, pp. 252–253) provided three reasons why aggressive, peer-rejected boys have problems in social relationships:

- "First, the rejected, aggressive boys are more impulsive and have problems sustaining attention. As a result, they are more likely to be disruptive of ongoing activities in the classroom and in focused group play.

- Second, rejected, aggressive boys are more emotionally reactive. They are aroused to anger more easily and probably have more difficulty calming down once aroused. Because of this they are more prone to become angry at peers and attack them verbally and physically. . . .

- Third, rejected children have fewer social skills in making friends and maintaining positive relationships with peers."

Social Cognition

Social cognition involves thoughts about social matters, such as an aggressive boy's interpretation of an encounter as hostile and his classmates' perception of his behavior as inappropriate (Carpendale & Lewis, 2015). Children's social cognition about their peers becomes increasingly important for understanding peer relationships in middle and late childhood. Of special interest are the ways in which children process information about peer relations and their social knowledge (Dodge, 2011).

Kenneth Dodge (1983) argues that children go through six steps in processing information about their social world. They selectively attend to social cues, attribute intent, generate goals, access behavioral scripts from memory, make decisions, and enact behavior. Dodge has found that aggressive boys are more likely to perceive another child's actions as hostile when the child's intention is ambiguous. Furthermore, when aggressive boys search for cues to determine a peer's intention, they respond more rapidly, less efficiently, and less reflectively than do nonaggressive children. These are among the social cognitive factors believed to be involved in children's conflicts.

Social knowledge also is involved in children's ability to get along with peers. They need to know what goals to pursue in poorly defined or ambiguous situations, how to initiate and maintain a social bond, and what scripts to follow to get other children to be their friends. For example, as part of the script for getting friends, it helps to know that saying nice things, regardless of what the peer does or says, will make the peer like the child more.

How Would You...?

As a **psychologist,** how would you characterize differences in the social cognition of aggressive children compared with children who behave in less hostile ways?

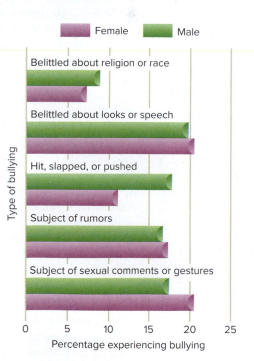

Figure 1 Bullying Behaviors Among U.S. Youth
This graph shows the types of bullying most often experienced by U.S. youth. The percentages reflect the extent to which bullied students said that they had experienced a particular type of bullying. In terms of gender, note that when they were bullied, boys were more likely to be hit, slapped, or pushed than girls were.

Bullying

Significant numbers of students are victimized by bullies (Beltran-Catalan & others, 2018; Hall, 2017; Lee & Vaillancourt, 2018; Muijs, 2017; Salmivalli & Peets, 2018). In a survey of 15,000 students in grades 6 through 10, nearly one-third said that they had experienced occasional or frequent involvement as a victim or perpetrator in bullying (Nansel & others, 2001). Bullying was defined as verbal or physical behavior intended to disturb someone less powerful (see Figure 1). Boys are more likely to be bullies than girls, but gender differences regarding victims of bullies are less clear (Peets, Hodges, & Salmivalli, 2011). In the study, boys and younger middle school students were most likely to be bullied (Nansel & others, 2001). Bullied children reported more loneliness and difficulty in making friends, while those who did the bullying were more likely to have low grades and to smoke and drink alcohol.

Anxious, socially withdrawn, and aggressive children are often the victims of bullying (Coplan & others, 2018; Rubin & Barstead, 2018). Anxious and socially withdrawn children may be victimized because they are nonthreatening and unlikely to retaliate if bullied, whereas aggressive children may be the targets of bullying because their behavior is irritating to bullies. One study revealed that having supportive friends was linked to a lower level of bullying and victimization (Kendrick, Jutengren, & Stattin, 2012).

Social contexts also influence bullying (Prinstein & others, 2018; Troop-Gordon, 2017). Seventy to 80 percent of victims and their bullies are in the same classroom (Salmivalli, Peets, & Hodges, 2011). Classmates are often aware of and may witness bullying. The larger social context of the peer group plays an important role in bullying. Bullies often torment victims to gain higher status in the peer group and need others to witness their power displays. Many bullies are not rejected by the peer group.

What are the outcomes of bullying? Children who are bullied are more likely to experience depression, engage in suicidal ideation, and attempt suicide than their counterparts who have not been the victims of bullying (Eastman & others, 2018; Salmivalli & Peets, 2018). A longitudinal study found that children who were bullied at 6 years of age were more likely to have excess weight gain when they were 12 to 13 years of age (Sutin & others, 2016). Further, a longitudinal study of 6,000 children found that children who were the victims of peer bullying from 4 to 10 years of age were more likely to engage in suicidal ideation at 11½ years of age (Winsper & others, 2012). And a recent analysis concluded that bullying can have long-term effects, including difficulty in forming lasting relationships and getting along with coworkers (Wolke & Lereya, 2015).

Longitudinal studies have indicated that victims bullied in childhood and adolescence have higher rates of agoraphobia (an abnormal fear of being in public, open, and crowded places), depression, anxiety, panic disorder, and suicidality in their early to mid-twenties compared with those who have not been bullied in childhood and adolescence (Arseneault, 2017; Copeland & others, 2013). In addition, another recent study revealed that being a victim of bullying in childhood was linked to increased use of mental health services by the victims five decades later (Evans-Lacko & others, 2017).

How Would You...?

As a **health-care professional,** how would you characterize the health risks that bullying poses to the victims of bullying?

An increasing concern is peer bullying and harassment on the Internet (called *cyberbullying*) (Holfeld & Mishna, 2018; Laftman & others, 2018; Wolke, Lee, & Guy, 2017). One study involving third- to sixth-graders revealed that engaging in cyber aggression was related to loneliness, lower self-esteem, fewer mutual friendships, and lower peer popularity (Schoffstall & Cohen, 2011). Another recent study revealed that cyberbullying contributed to depression and suicidal ideation above and beyond the contribution of involvement in traditional types of bullying (physical and verbal bullying in school and in neighborhood contexts, for example) (Bonanno & Hymel, 2013). And a recent meta-analysis concluded that being the victim of cyberbullying was linked to stress and suicidal ideation (Kowalski & others, 2014). Further, a longitudinal study found that adolescents experiencing social and emotional difficulties were more likely to be both cyberbullied and traditionally bullied than traditionally bullied only (Cross, Lester, & Barnes, 2015). In this study, adolescents targeted in both ways stayed away from school more than their counterparts who were traditionally bullied only. And a recent study revealed that adolescents who were bullied both in a direct way and through cyberbullying had more behavioral problems and lower self-esteem than adolescents who were only bullied in one of these two ways (Wolke, Lee, & Guy, 2017). Information about preventing cyberbullying can be found at www.stopcyberbullying.org/.

What characterizes bullying? What are some strategies to reduce bullying?
©Photodisc/Getty Images

Extensive interest has been directed toward finding ways to prevent and treat bullying and victimization (Gower, Cousin, & Borowsky, 2017; Hall, 2017; Menesini & Salmivalli, 2017; Muijs, 2017; Salmivallli & Peets, 2018; Wojcik & Helka, 2018). A research review revealed mixed results for school-based intervention (Vreeman & Carroll, 2007). School-based interventions vary greatly, ranging from involving the whole school in an antibullying campaign to providing individualized social skills training. One of the most promising bullying intervention programs has been created by Dan Olweus. This program focuses on 6- to 15-year-olds with the goal of decreasing opportunities and rewards for bullying. School staff is instructed in ways to improve peer relations and make schools safer. When properly implemented, the program reduces bullying by 30 to 70 percent (Olweus, 2003). A recent research review concluded that interventions focused on the whole school, such as Olweus', are more effective than interventions involving classroom curricula or social skills training (Cantone & others, 2015).

Friends

Friendship is an important aspect of children's lives in middle and late childhood (Bagwell & Bukowski, 2018). Like adult friendships, children's friendships are typically characterized by similarity. Throughout childhood, friends are more similar than dissimilar in terms of age, sex, race, and many other factors. Friends often have similar attitudes toward school, similar educational aspirations, and closely aligned achievement orientations.

Willard Hartup (1983, 1996, 2009) has studied peer relations and friendship for more than three decades and has concluded that friends can be cognitive and emotional resources from childhood through old age, fostering self-esteem and a sense of well-being. More specifically, children's friendships can serve six functions (Gottman & Parker, 1987):

- *Companionship*. Friendship provides children with a familiar partner and playmate, someone who is willing to spend time with them and join in collaborative activities.

How Would You...?

As an **educator,** how would you design and implement a bullying reduction program at your school?

- *Stimulation*. Friendship provides children with interesting information, excitement, and amusement.

- *Physical support*. Friendship provides time, resources, and assistance.

- *Ego support*. Friendship provides the expectation of support, encouragement, and feedback, which helps children maintain an impression of themselves as competent, attractive, and worthwhile individuals.

- *Social comparison*. Friendship provides information about where the child stands vis-à-vis others and whether the child is doing okay.

- *Affection and intimacy*. Friendship provides children with a warm, close, trusting relationship with another individual. Intimacy in friendships is characterized by self-disclosure and the sharing of private thoughts. Research reveals that intimate friendships may not appear until early adolescence (Berndt & Perry, 1990).

Although having friends can bring developmental advantages, not all friendships are alike (de la Haye & others, 2017; Zhang & others, 2018). People differ in the company they keep—that is, who their friends are. Developmental advantages occur when children have friends who are socially skilled and supportive (Laursen, 2018). However, it is not developmentally advantageous to have coercive and conflict-ridden friendships (Bagwell & Bukowski, 2018).

Friendship also plays an important role in children's emotional well-being and academic success (Ryan & Shin, 2018). Students with friends who are academically oriented are more likely to achieve success in school themselves (Wentzel & Ramani, 2016).

What are some characteristics of children's friendships?
©Image Source/Alamy

Schools

For most children, entering the first grade signals new obligations. They form new relationships and develop new standards by which to judge themselves. School provides children with a rich source of new ideas to shape their sense of self. They will spend many years in schools as members of small societies in which there are tasks to be accomplished, people to socialize with and be socialized by, and rules that define and limit behavior, feelings, and attitudes. By the time students graduate from high school, they will have spent 12,000 hours in the classroom.

Contemporary Approaches to Student Learning

Because there are so many different educational approaches, controversy swirls about the best way to teach children (Borich, 2017; Powell, 2019). There also is considerable interest in finding the best way to hold schools and teachers accountable for whether children are learning (McMillan, 2018).

Constructivist and Direct Instruction Approaches

The **constructivist approach** is learner centered and emphasizes the importance of individuals actively constructing their knowledge and understanding with guidance from the teacher. In the constructivist view, teachers should not attempt to simply pour information into children's minds. Rather, children should be encouraged to explore their world, discover knowledge, reflect, and think critically with careful monitoring and meaningful guidance from the teacher (Brophy & Alleman, 2018; Orlich & Harder, 2018). The constructivist belief is that for too long in American education children have been required to sit still, be passive learners, and rotely memorize irrelevant as well as relevant information (Johnson & others 2018). Today, constructivism may include an emphasis on collaboration—children working with each other in their efforts to know and understand (Daniels, 2017). A teacher with a constructivist instructional philosophy would not have children memorize information rotely but would guide their learning while giving them opportunities to meaningfully construct their knowledge and deepen their understanding of the material.

By contrast, the **direct instruction approach** is structured and teacher centered. It is characterized by teacher direction and control, high teacher expectations for students' progress, maximum time spent by students on academic tasks, and efforts by the teacher to keep negative affect to a minimum. An important goal in the direct instruction approach is maximizing student learning time (Powell, 2019; Webb & Metha, 2017).

Advocates of the constructivist approach argue that the direct instruction approach turns children into passive learners and does not adequately challenge them to think in critical and creative ways. The direct instruction enthusiasts say that the constructivist approaches do not give enough attention to the content of a discipline, such as history or science. They also believe that the constructivist approaches are too relativistic and vague.

Some experts believe that many effective teachers use both a constructivist *and* a direct instruction approach rather than relying on either approach exclusively (Bransford & others, 2006; Johnson & others, 2018). Some circumstances may call more for a constructivist approach, others for direct instruction. For example, experts increasingly recommend an explicit, intellectually engaging direct instruction approach when teaching students who have a learning disability involving reading or writing (Cunningham, 2017; Temple & others, 2018).

Accountability

Since the 1990s, the U.S. public and governments at every level have demanded increased accountability from schools. One result has been the spread of state-mandated tests to measure what students have or have not learned (Martin, Sargrad, & Batel, 2017; McMillan, 2018; Popham, 2017). Many states have identified objectives for students in

constructivist approach A learner-centered approach that emphasizes the importance of individuals actively constructing their knowledge and understanding with guidance from the teacher.

direct instruction approach A structured, teacher-centered approach that is characterized by teacher direction and control, high teacher expectations for students' progress, maximum time spent by students on learning tasks, and efforts by the teacher to keep negative affect to a minimum.

their state and created tests to measure whether students were meeting those objectives. This approach became national policy in 2002 when the No Child Left Behind (NCLB) legislation was signed into law.

No Child Left Behind (NCLB) Advocates argue that statewide standardized testing will have a number of positive effects. These include improved student performance; more time teaching the subjects that are tested; high expectations for all students; identification of poorly performing schools, teachers, and administrators; and improved confidence in schools as test scores rise.

Is this classroom more likely constructivist or direct instruction? Explain.
©Elizabeth Crews

Critics argue that the NCLB legislation is doing more harm than good (Ladd, 2017; Sadker & Zittleman, 2016). One criticism stresses that using a single test as the sole indicator of students' progress and competence presents a very narrow view of students' skills (Lewis, 2007). This criticism is similar to the one leveled at IQ tests. To assess student progress and achievement, many psychologists and educators emphasize that a number of measures should be used, including tests, quizzes, projects, portfolios, classroom observations, and so on. Also, the tests used as part of NCLB don't measure creativity, motivation, persistence, flexible thinking, and social skills (Stiggins, 2008). Teachers may end up spending far too much class time "teaching to the test" by drilling students and having them memorize isolated facts rather than focusing on thinking skills needed for success in life (Ladd, 2017). Also, some individuals are concerned that gifted students are neglected as schools focus on raising the achievement level of students who are not doing well (Ballou & Springer, 2017).

Each state is allowed to have different criteria for what constitutes passing or failing grades on tests designated for NCLB inclusion. An analysis of NCLB data indicated that almost every fourth-grade student in Mississippi knows how to read but only half of Massachusetts' students do (Birman & others, 2007). Clearly, Mississippi's standards for passing the reading test are far below those of Massachusetts. Many states have taken the safe route and kept the standard for passing low. Thus, while one of NCLB's goals was to raise standards for achievement in U.S. schools, apparently allowing states to set their own standards likely has lowered achievement standards.

Common Core In 2009, the Common Core State Standards Initiative was endorsed by the National Governors Association in an effort to implement more rigorous state guidelines for educating students. The Common Core Standards specify what students should know and the skills they should develop at each grade level in various content areas (Common Core State Standards Initiative, 2018). A large majority of states have agreed to implement the Standards but they have generated considerable controversy, with some critics arguing that they are simply a further effort by the federal government to control education and that they emphasize a "one-size-fits-all" approach that pays little attention to individual variations in students. Supporters say that the Standards provide much-needed detailed guidelines and important milestones for students to achieve.

Every Student Succeeds Act (ESSA) The most recent accountability initiative is the *Every Student Succeeds Act (ESSA)*, which was passed into law in December 2015. In 2018, the Trump administration was planning to go forward with ESSA but to give states much more flexibility in implementing the law (Klein, 2018). The law replaced *No Child Left Behind*, in the process modifying but not completely eliminating standardized testing. ESSA retains annual testing for reading and writing in grades 3 to 8, then once more in high school. The new law also allows states to scale back the role that tests have in holding schools accountable for student achievement. And schools must use at least one nonacademic factor—such as student engagement—when tracking schools' success.

The new law continues to require states and districts to improve their lowest-performing schools and to increase their effectiveness in teaching historically underperforming students, such as English-language learners, ethnic minority students, and students with a disability. Also, states and districts are required to put in place challenging academic standards, although they can opt out of state standards involving Common Core.

Socioeconomic Status, Ethnicity, and Culture

Children from low-income, ethnic minority backgrounds have more difficulties in school than do their middle-socioeconomic-status, White counterparts. Why? Critics argue that schools have not done a good job of assisting low-income, ethnic minority students to overcome the barriers to their achievement (Coley & others, 2018; Rosen & others, 2018; Duncan, Magnuson, & Votruba-Drzal, 2017). And comparisons of student achievement indicate that U.S. students have lower achievement in math and science than students in a number of other countries, especially those in eastern Asia (Desilver, 2017).

The Education of Students from Low-Income Backgrounds

Many children in poverty face problems that present barriers to their learning (Nieto & Bode, 2018; Sawyer & others, 2018; Watson, 2018). They might have parents who don't set high educational standards for them, who are incapable of reading to them, or who can't afford educational materials and experiences such as books and trips to zoos and museums. They might be malnourished or live in areas with high levels of crime and violence. One study revealed that neighborhood disadvantage (involving such characteristics as low neighborhood income and high unemployment) was linked to less

consistent, less stimulating, and more punitive parenting, and ultimately to negative child outcomes such as behavioral problems and low verbal ability (Kohen & others, 2008). Another study revealed that the longer children experienced poverty, the more detrimental the poverty was to their cognitive development (Najman & others, 2009).

The schools that children from impoverished backgrounds attend often have fewer resources than schools in higher-income neighborhoods. Compared with schools in higher-income areas, schools in low-income areas are more likely to have more students with low achievement test scores, low graduation rates, and smaller percentages of students going to college; they are more likely to have young teachers with less experience; and they are more likely to encourage rote learning than to work with children to improve their thinking skills (Banks, 2015; Bennett, 2015). Many of the school buildings and classrooms are old and crumbling. These are the types of undesirable conditions Jonathan Kozol (2005) observed in many inner-city schools. In sum, far too many schools in low-income neighborhoods provide students with environments that are not conducive to effective learning (Nieto & Bode, 2018; Sawyer & others, 2018; Watson, 2018).

In a recent research review, it was concluded that increases in family income for children in poverty were associated with increased achievement in middle school as well as greater educational attainment in adolescence and emerging adulthood (Duncan, Magnuson, & Votruba-Drzal, 2017).

In *The Shame of the Nation*, Jonathan Kozol (2005) criticized the inadequate quality and lack of resources in many U.S. schools, especially those in the poverty areas of inner cities that have high concentrations of ethnic minority children. Kozol praises teachers like Angela Lively (*above*), who keeps a box of shoes in her Indianapolis classroom for students in need.
©Michael Conroy/AP Images

How Would You...?

As a **health-care professional,** how would you advise school administrators about health and nutrition challenges faced by low-income students that may influence their performance on achievement tests?

Schools and school programs are the focus of some poverty interventions (Dragoset & others, 2017). In a recent intervention with first-generation immigrant children attending high-poverty schools, the City Connects program was successful in improving children's math and reading achievement at the end of elementary school (Dearing & others, 2016). The program is directed by a full-time school counselor or social worker in each school. Annual reviews of children's needs are conducted during the first several months of the school year. Then site coordinators and teachers collaborate to develop a student support plan that might include an after-school program, tutoring, mentoring, or family counselling. For children identified as having intense needs (about 8 to 10 percent of the children), a wider team of professionals becomes involved, possibly including school psychologists, principals, nurses, and/or community agency staff, to create additional supports. In another longitudinal study, an intervention called a Child-Parent Center Program provided school-based educational enrichment and comprehensive family services to families with children from 3 to 9 years of age in high-poverty neighborhoods in Chicago. The program was linked to higher rates of postsecondary degree completion, including more years of education, completion of an associate's degree or higher, and attainment of a master's degree (Reynolds, Ou, & Temple, 2018).

Another important effort to improve the education of children growing up in low-income conditions is Teach for America (2018), a nonprofit organization that recruits and selects college graduates from universities to serve as teachers. The selected members commit to teaching for two years in a public school in a low-income community. Since the program's inception in 1990, more than 42,000 individuals have taught more than 50,000 students for Teach for America. These teachers can be, but don't have to be, education majors. In the summer before beginning to teach, they attend an intensive training program. To read about one individual who became a Teach for America instructor, see the *Careers in Life-Span Development* profile.

Ethnicity in Schools

More than one-third of African American and almost one-third of Latino students attend schools in the 47 largest city school districts, compared with only 5 percent of White and

Careers in life-span development

Ahou Vaziri, Teach for America Instructor

Ahou Vaziri was a top student in author John Santrock's educational psychology course at the University of Texas at Dallas where she majored in Psychology and Child Development. The following year she served as a teaching intern for the educational psychology course, then submitted an application to join Teach for America and was accepted. Ahou was assigned to work in a low-income area of Tulsa, Oklahoma, where she taught English to seventh- and eighth-graders. In her words, "The years I spent in the classroom for Teach for America were among the most rewarding experiences I have had thus far in my career. I was able to go home every night after work knowing that I truly made a difference in the lives of my students."

After her two-year teaching experience with Teach for America, Ahou continued to work for the organization in their recruitment of college students to become Teach for America instructors. Subsequently, she moved into a role that involved developing curricula for Teach for America. Recently she completed a graduate degree in counseling from Southern Methodist University, and she is continuing her work in improving children's lives.

Ahou Vaziri interacting with students in her Teach for America class in Tulsa, Oklahoma
Courtesy of Ahou Vaziri

22 percent of Asian American students. Many of these inner-city schools are still segregated, are grossly underfunded, and do not provide adequate opportunities for children to learn effectively. Thus, the effects of low socioeconomic status (SES) and of ethnicity are often intertwined (Nieto & Bode, 2018).

How Would You…?

As an **educator,** how would you structure a lesson plan using the jigsaw strategy?

The school experiences of students from different ethnic groups vary considerably (Loria & Caughy, 2017; Suárez-Orozco, 2018; Suárez-Orozco & Suárez-Orozco, 2018). African American and Latino students are much less likely than non-Latino White or Asian American students to be enrolled in college preparatory programs and more likely to be enrolled in remedial and special education programs. Asian American students are far more likely to take advanced math and science courses in high school. African American students are twice as likely as Latinos, Native Americans, or non-Latino Whites to be suspended from school.

The comparisons just described do not address the reasons for the educational disparities. For the ethnic minority students, such as African American and Latino students, many have grown up in poverty conditions, less well-funded schools, and experienced discrimination, bias, and prejudice (U.S. Department of Education, Office of Civil Rights, 2018). For example, in regard to African American students being suspended from school more than other ethnic groups, a recent study found that African American students are more likely to be perceived as troublemakers and be given more severe punishment than non-Latino White students (Jarvis & Okonofua, 2020). However, diversity characterizes every ethnic group (Sawyer & others, 2018).

For example, the higher percentage of Asian American students in advanced classes mainly applies to students from Chinese, Taiwanese, Japanese, Korean, and East Indian cultural backgrounds; students with Hmong and Vietnamese cultural backgrounds have had less academic success. Following are some strategies for improving relationships among ethnically diverse students:

- *Turn the class into a jigsaw classroom.* When Eliot Aronson was a professor at the University of Texas at Austin, the school system contacted him for ideas on how to reduce the increasing racial tension in classrooms. Aronson (1986) developed the concept of a "jigsaw classroom" in which students from different cultural backgrounds are placed in a cooperative group in which they have to construct different parts of a project to reach a common goal. Aronson used the term *jigsaw* because he saw the technique as much like a group of students cooperating to put different pieces together to complete a jigsaw puzzle. How might this work? Team sports, drama productions, and music performances are examples of contexts in which students participate cooperatively to reach a common goal; however, the jigsaw technique also lends itself to group science projects, history reports, and other learning experiences involving a variety of subject matter.

- *Encourage students to have positive personal contact with diverse other students.* Mere contact does not do the job of improving relationships with diverse others. For example, busing ethnic minority students to predominantly White schools, or vice versa, has not reduced prejudice or improved interethnic relations. What matters is what happens after children get to school. Especially beneficial in improving interethnic relations is sharing one's worries, successes, failures, coping strategies, interests, and other personal information with people of other ethnicities. When this happens, people tend to look at others as individuals rather than as members of a homogeneous group.

- *Reduce bias.* Teachers can reduce bias by displaying images of children from diverse ethnic and cultural groups, selecting play materials and classroom activities that encourage cultural understanding, helping students resist stereotyping, and working with parents to reduce children's exposure to bias and prejudice at home.

James Comer, with some of the inner-city children who attend a school that became a better learning environment because of Comer's intervention.
©Chris Volpe

Three important aspects of the Comer Project for Change are (1) a governance and management team that develops a comprehensive school plan, assessment strategy, and staff development plan; (2) a mental health or school support team; and (3) a parents' program. Comer believes that the entire school community should have a cooperative rather than an adversarial attitude. The Comer program is currently operating in more than 600 schools in 26 states.

Cross-Cultural Comparisons

International assessments indicate that the United States has not fared well in comparisons with many other countries in the areas of math and science achievement (Desilver, 2017). In a recent assessment of fourth- and eighth-grade students on the Trends in International Mathematics and Science Study (TIMSS), U.S. fourth-grade students placed eleventh out of 48 countries in math and eighth in science (TIMSS, 2015). Also in the TIMSS study, U.S. eighth-grade students placed eighth in math and eighth in science among the 37 countries studied. The top five spots in the international assessments mainly go to East Asian countries, especially Singapore, China, and Japan. The only two non-Asian countries to crack the top five in recent years for math and science are Finland and Estonia.

Despite the recent gains by U.S. elementary school students, it is disconcerting that in most comparisons, the rankings for U.S. students in reading, math, and science compared with students in other countries decline as they go from elementary school to high school. Also, U.S. students' achievement scores in math and science are still far below those of students in many East Asian countries.

Harold Stevenson's (1995, 2000; Stevenson, Hofer, & Randel, 1999; Stevenson & others, 1990) research explores reasons for the poor performance of U.S. students compared with students in selected Asian countries. Stevenson and his colleagues have completed five cross-cultural comparisons of students in the United States, China, Taiwan, and Japan. In these studies, Asian students consistently outperform American students. And the longer the students are in school, the wider the gap becomes between Asian and American students—the lowest difference is in the first grade, the highest in the eleventh grade (the highest grade studied). Stevenson and his colleagues spent thousands of hours observing in classrooms, as well as interviewing and surveying teachers, students, and parents. They found that the Asian teachers spent more of their time teaching math than the U.S. teachers did. More than one-fourth of total classroom time in the first grade was spent on math instruction in Japan, compared with only one-tenth of the time in the U.S. first-grade classrooms. Also, the Asian students were in school an average of 240 days a year, compared with 178 days in the United States.

Differences were also found between the Asian and American parents. The U.S. parents had much lower expectations for their children's education and achievement than did the Asian parents. Also, the U.S. parents were more likely to believe that their children's math achievement was due to innate ability, while the Asian parents were more likely to say that their children's math achievement was the consequence of effort and training (see Figure 2). The Asian students were more likely to do math homework than were the U.S. students, and the Asian parents were far more likely to help their children with their math homework than were the U.S. parents (Chen & Stevenson, 1989). A recent study examined factors that might account for the superior academic performance of Asian American children (Hsin & Xie, 2014). In this study, the Asian American advantage was mainly due to children exerting greater academic effort and not to advantages in tested cognitive abilities or sociodemographic factors.

There is rising concern that U.S. children are not reaching their full potential, which ultimately will reduce the capacity of the United States to compete globally (Pomerantz, 2018). Researchers are interested in determining how parents can

How do U.S. students fare against Asian students in math and science achievement? What were some findings in Stevenson's research that might explain the results of those international comparisons?
©amana Images, Inc./Alamy

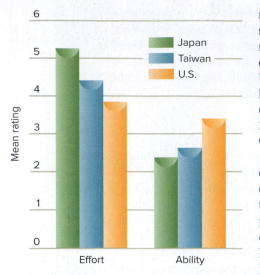

Figure 2 Mothers' Beliefs About the Factors Responsible for Children's Math Achievement in Three Countries

In one study, mothers in Japan and Taiwan were more likely to believe that their children's math achievement was due to effort rather than innate ability, while U.S. mothers were more likely to believe their children's math achievement was due to innate ability (Stevenson, Lee, & Stigler, 1986). If parents believe that their children's math achievement is due to innate ability and their children are not doing well in math, the implication is that they are less likely to think their children will benefit from putting forth more effort.

maximize their children's motivation and achievement in school while also maintaining positive emotional adjustment. To this end, Eva Pomerantz and her colleagues are conducting research with children and their parents in the United States and China, where children often attain higher levels of achievement than their U.S. counterparts (Pomerantz, Cheung, & Qin, 2012; Pomerantz & Grolnick, 2017; Pomerantz & Kempner, 2013; Pomerantz, Kim, & Cheung, 2012; Qu & others, 2016).

Compared with U.S. parents, East Asian parents spend considerably more time helping their children with homework (Chen & Stevenson, 1989). Pomerantz's research indicates that East Asian parental involvement in children's learning is present as early as the preschool years and continues throughout the elementary school years (Cheung & Pomerantz, 2012; Ng, Pomerantz, & Deng, 2014; Ng, Pomerantz, & Lam, 2013). In East Asia, children's learning is considered to be a far greater responsibility of parents than it is in the United States (Ng, Pomerantz, & Lam, 2013; Pomerantz, 2018; Pomerantz, Kim, & Cheung, 2012).

Pomerantz and her colleagues also are conducting research on the role of parental control in children's achievement. In a recent study in which the title of the resulting article included the phrase "My Child Is My Report Card," Chinese mothers exerted more control (especially psychological control) over their children than did U.S. mothers (Ng, Pomerantz, & Deng, 2014). Chinese mothers' self-worth was more contingent on their children's achievement than was the case for U.S. mothers. Pomerantz's research reflects a variation of authoritarian parenting in which the parenting strategy of many Asian parents is to train their children to achieve high levels of academic success. Amy Chua's 2011 book, *Battle Hymn of the Tiger Mother,* sparked considerable interest in the role of parenting in children's achievement. Chua uses the term "Tiger Mother" to mean a mother who engages in strict disciplinary practices. In another recent book, *Tiger Babies Strike Back*, Kim Wong Keltner (2013) argues that the Tiger Mother parenting style can be so demanding and confining that being an Asian American child is like being in an "emotional jail." She says that the Tiger Mother authoritarian style does provide some advantages for children, such as emphasizing the value of going for what you want and not taking no for an answer, but that too often the outcome is not worth the emotional costs that accompany it.

Recent research on Chinese-American immigrant families with first- and second-grade children has found that children with authoritarian (highly controlling) parents are more aggressive, are more depressed, have a higher anxiety level, and show poorer social skills than children whose parents engage in non-authoritarian styles (Zhou & others, 2013). Qing Zhou (2013), lead author on the study just described and the director of the University of California's Culture and Family Laboratory, is conducting workshops to teach Chinese mothers positive parenting strategies such as using listening skills, praising their children for good behavior, and spending more time with their children in fun activities. Also, in a recent study in China, young adolescents with authoritative parents showed better adjustment than their counterparts with authoritarian parents (Zhang & others, 2017).

In sum, while an authoritarian, psychologically controlling style of parenting may be associated with higher levels of achievement, especially in Asian children, there are concerns that an authoritarian, highly controlling style also may produce more emotional difficulties in children (Pomerantz, 2018).

Related to the differences in the attitudes of Asian and U.S. parents involving explanations of effort and ability, Carol Dweck (2006, 2015, 2016; Dweck & Molden, 2017) described the importance of children's **mindset,** which she defines as the cognitive view individuals develop for themselves. She concludes that individuals have one of two mindsets: (1) a *fixed mindset,* in which they believe that their qualities are carved in stone and cannot change; or (2) a *growth mindset,* in which they believe their qualities can change and improve through their effort. Dweck (2006, 2015, 2016)

mindset the cognitive view that individuals develop for themselves.

argues that individuals' mindsets influence whether they will be optimistic or pessimistic, what their goals will be and how hard they will strive to reach those goals, and their achievement.

Dweck says that mindsets begin to be shaped in childhood as children interact with parents, teachers, and coaches, who themselves have either a fixed mindset or a growth mindset. However, recent research indicates that many parents and teachers with growth mindsets don't always instill them in children and adolescents (Haimovitz & Dweck, 2016, 2017). The following strategies have been found to increase adolescents' growth mindset: teach for understanding; provide feedback that improves understanding; give students opportunities to revise their work; communicate how effort and struggling are involved in learning; and function as a partner with children and adolescents in the learning process (Haimovitz & Dweck, 2017; Hooper & others, 2016; Sun, 2015).

In recent research by Dweck and her colleagues, students from lower-income families were less likely to have a growth mindset than their counterparts from wealthier families (Claro, Paunesku, & Dweck, 2016). However, the achievement of students from lower-income families who did have a growth mindset was more likely to be protected from the negative effects of poverty.

Dweck and her colleagues (Blackwell & Dweck, 2008; Blackwell, Trzesniewski, & Dweck, 2007; Dweck, 2015, 2016; Dweck & Master, 2009; Dweck & Molden, 2017) have incorporated information about the brain's plasticity into their efforts to improve students' motivation to achieve and succeed. In one study, they assigned two groups of students to eight sessions of either (1) study skills instruction, or (2) study skills instruction plus information about the importance of developing a growth mindset (Blackwell, Trzesniewski, & Dweck, 2007). One of the exercises in the growth-mindset group, titled "You Can Grow Your Brain," emphasized that the brain is like a muscle that can get stronger as it is exercised and develops new connections. Students were informed that the more you challenge your brain to learn, the more your brain cells grow. Both groups had a pattern of declining math scores prior to the intervention. Following the intervention, scores for the group that received only the study skills instruction continued to decline, but the group that received the combination of study skills instruction plus the growth-mindset emphasis improved their math achievement. In a recent study conducted by Dweck and her colleagues (Paunesku & others, 2015), underachieving high school students read online modules about how the brain changes when people learn and study hard. Following the online exposure to information about the brain and learning, the underachieving students improved their grade point averages.

Dweck has also created a computer-based workshop, "Brainology," to teach students that their intelligence can change (Blackwell & Dweck, 2008) (see Figure 3). The workshop includes six modules about how the brain works and discussion about how students can make their brain improve. After the workshop was tested in 20 New York City schools, students strongly endorsed the value of the computer-based brain modules. Said

How Would You...?

As an **educator**, how would incorporate the concept of mindset into your classroom as a teacher?

Figure 3 A Screen from Carol Dweck's Brainology Program, Which Is Designed to Cultivate Children's Growth Mindset
Courtesy of Dr. Carol S. Dweck

one student, "I will try harder because I know that the more you try, the more your brain knows" (Dweck & Master, 2009, p. 137).

Dweck and her colleagues also have found that a growth mindset can prevent negative stereotypes from undermining achievement. For example, believing that math ability can be learned helped to protect females from negative gender stereotyping about math (Good, Rattan, & Dweck, 2012). Also, in recent research, having a growth mindset helped to protect women's and minorities' outlook when they chose to confront expressions of bias toward them (Rattan & Dweck, 2018).

Summary

Emotional and Personality Development

- Self-descriptions increasingly involve psychological and social characteristics in middle and late childhood. Perspective taking increases in middle and late childhood. Self-concept refers to domain-specific evaluations of the self. Self-esteem refers to global evaluations of the self and is also referred to as self-worth or self-image. Self-efficacy and self-regulation are linked to children's competence and achievement. Erikson's fourth stage of development, industry versus inferiority, characterizes the middle and late childhood years.
- Emotional development occurs in middle and late childhood. As children get older, they use a greater variety of coping strategies and more cognitive strategies.
- Kohlberg argued that moral development consists of three levels—preconventional, conventional, and postconventional. Criticisms of Kohlberg's theory have been made, especially by Gilligan. The domain theory of moral development states that there are different domains of social knowledge and reasoning, including moral, social conventional, and personal. Prosocial behavior involves positive moral behaviors such as sharing.
- Gender stereotyping is present in children's lives, and research indicates that it increases during middle and late childhood. A number of physical differences exist between males and females. Some experts argue that cognitive differences between males and females have been exaggerated. In terms of socioemotional differences, males are more physically aggressive than females, whereas females regulate their emotions better and engage in more prosocial behavior than males do.

Families

- Parents spend less time with children during middle and late childhood than in early childhood. New parent-child issues emerge and discipline changes. Control is more coregulatory.

- Parents can play important roles as managers of children's opportunities.
- Secure attachment to parents is linked to lower levels of internalized symptoms, anxiety, and depression in children during middle and late childhood.
- Children living in stepparent families have more adjustment problems than their counterparts in never-divorced families.

Peers

- A number of developmental changes in peer relations occur in middle and late childhood.
- Peer statuses—popular children, neglected children, rejected children, controversial children, and average children—are important in middle and late childhood.
- Social information processing and social knowledge are two important dimensions of social cognition.
- Significant numbers of children are bullied, and this can result in negative developmental outcomes for victims as well as bullies.
- Children who are friends tend to be similar to each other. Children's friendships serve a number of functions.

Schools

- Contemporary approaches to student learning include constructivism and direct instruction. In the United States, standardized testing of elementary school students has been mandated to improve accountability of schools.
- Children in poverty face many barriers to learning at school as well as at home. Low expectations for ethnic minority children represent one of the barriers to their learning.
- U.S. children are more achievement-oriented than children in many countries but perform more poorly in math and science than many children in Asian countries. Fixed or growth mindset is the cognitive view that individuals develop for themselves.

Key Terms

average children	domain theory of moral	perspective taking	rejected children
care perspective	development	popular children	self-concept
constructivist approach	gender stereotypes	postconventional	self-efficacy
controversial children	justice perspective	reasoning	self-esteem
conventional reasoning	mindset	preconventional	social conventional
direct instruction approach	neglected children	reasoning	reasoning

9 Physical and Cognitive Development in Adolescence

CHAPTER OUTLINE

Stories of Life-Span Development: Annie, Arnie, and Katie

Fifteen-year-old Annie developed a drinking problem, and recently she was kicked off the cheerleading squad at her school for missing practice so often—but that didn't stop her drinking. She and her friends began skipping school regularly so they could drink.

Fourteen-year-old Arnie is a juvenile delinquent. Last week he stole a TV set, struck his mother and bloodied her face, broke some streetlights in the neighborhood, and threatened a boy with a wrench and hammer.

Twelve-year-old Katie, more than just about anything else, wanted a playground in her town. She knew that other kids also wanted one, so she put together a group that generated funding ideas for the playground. They presented their ideas to the town council. Her group got more youth involved, and they raised money by selling candy and sandwiches door-to-door. The playground became a reality, a place where, as Katie says, "People can have picnics and make friends." Katie's advice: "You won't get anywhere if you don't try."

Adolescents like Annie and Arnie are the ones we hear about the most. But there are many adolescents like Katie who contribute in positive ways to their community, and competently make the transition through adolescence. Indeed, for most young people, adolescence is not a time of rebellion, crisis, pathology, and deviance. A far more accurate vision of adolescence is of a time of evaluation, of decision making, of commitment, of carving out a place in the world. Most of the problems of today's youth are not with the youth themselves. What adolescents need is access to a range of legitimate opportunities and to long-term support from adults who care deeply about them (Lerner & others, 2018; Lovell & White, 2019; Ogden & Hagen, 2019).

Adolescence is a transitional period in the human life span, entered at approximately 10 to 12 years of age and exited at about 18 to 22 years of age. We begin this chapter by examining some general characteristics of adolescence, then turn our attention to major physical changes and health issues of adolescence. Next, we describe the significant cognitive changes that take place during adolescence. Last, we consider various aspects of schools for adolescents. ■

The Nature of Adolescence

There is a long history of worrying about how adolescents will "turn out." In 1904, G. Stanley Hall proposed the "storm-and-stress" view that adolescence is a turbulent time charged with conflict and mood swings. However, when Daniel Offer and his colleagues (1988) studied the self-images of adolescents in a number of countries, at least 73 percent of the adolescents displayed a healthy self-image rather than attitudes of storm-and-stress.

In matters of taste and manners, the young people of every generation have seemed unnervingly radical and different from adults—different in how they look, in how they behave, in the music they enjoy, in their hairstyles, and in the clothing they choose. It would be an enormous error, though, to confuse adolescents' enthusiasm for trying on new identities and enjoying moderate amounts of outrageous behavior with hostility toward parental and societal standards. Acting out and boundary testing are time-honored ways in which adolescents move toward accepting, rather than rejecting, parental values.

Katie (*front*) and some of her volunteers.
©Ronald Cortes

Negative stereotyping of adolescence has been extensive (Jiang & others, 2018; Petersen & others, 2017). However, much of the negative stereotyping has been fueled by media reports of a visible minority of adolescents. In the last decade there has been a call for adults to have a more positive attitude toward youth and emphasize their positive development. Indeed, researchers have found that a majority of adolescents are making the transition from childhood through adolescence to adulthood in a positive way (Seider, Jayawickreme, & Lerner, 2017). For example, a recent study of non-Latino White and African American 12- to 20-year-olds in the United States found that they were characterized much more by positive than problematic development, even during their most vulnerable times (Gutman & others, 2017). Their engagement in healthy behaviors, supportive relationships with parents and friends, and positive self-perceptions were much stronger than their angry and depressed feelings.

Although most adolescents negotiate the lengthy path to adult maturity successfully, too large a group does not (Frydenberg, 2019). Ethnic, cultural, gender, socioeconomic, age, and lifestyle differences influence the actual life trajectory of each adolescent (Rojas-Flores & others, 2017). Different portrayals of adolescence emerge, depending on the particular group of adolescents being described. Today's adolescents are exposed to a complex menu of lifestyle options through the media, and many face the temptations of drug use and sexual activity at increasingly young ages. Too many

Growing up has never been easy. However, adolescence is not best viewed as a time of rebellion, crisis, pathology, and deviance. A far more accurate vision of adolescence describes it as a time of evaluation, decision making, commitment, and carving out a place in the world. Most of the problems of today's youth are not with the youth themselves. What adolescents need is access to a range of legitimate opportunities and to long-term support from adults who care deeply about them. *What might be some examples of such support and caring?*
©Regine Mahaux/The Image Bank/Getty Images

adolescents are not provided with adequate opportunities and support to become competent adults (Lovell & White, 2019; Ogden & Haden, 2019).

Peter Benson and his colleagues (Benson, 2010; Benson, Roehlkepartain, & Scales, 2012; Benson & Scales, 2009, 2011) argue that the United States has a fragmented social policy for youth that too often has focused only on the negative developmental deficits of adolescents, especially health-compromising behaviors such as drug use and delinquency, and not enough on positive, strength-based approaches. According to Benson and his colleagues (2004, p. 783), a strength-based approach to social policy for youth

> adopts more of a wellness perspective, places particular emphasis on the existence of healthy conditions, and expands the concept of health to include the skills and competencies needed to succeed in employment, education, and life. It moves beyond the eradication of risk and deliberately argues for the promotion of well-being.

Physical Changes

One father remarked that the problem with his teenage son was not that he grew, but that he did not know when to stop growing. In addition to pubertal changes, other physical changes we will explore involve sexuality and the brain.

Puberty

Puberty is not the same as adolescence. For most of us, puberty ends long before adolescence does, although puberty is the most important marker of the beginning of adolescence.

Puberty is a brain-neuroendocrine process occurring primarily in early adolescence that provides stimulation for the rapid physical changes that take place during this period of development (Cicek & others, 2018; Shalitin & Kiess, 2017). Puberty is not a single, sudden event. We know whether a young boy or girl is going through puberty, but pinpointing puberty's beginning and end is difficult. Among the most noticeable changes are signs of sexual maturation and increases in height and weight.

Sexual Maturation, Height, and Weight

Think back to the onset of your puberty. Of the striking changes that were taking place in your body, what was the first to occur? Researchers have found that male pubertal characteristics typically develop in this order: increase in penis and testicle size, appearance of straight pubic hair, minor voice change, first ejaculation (which usually occurs through masturbation or a wet dream), appearance of kinky pubic hair, onset of maximum growth in height and weight, growth of hair in armpits, more detectable voice changes, and, finally, growth of facial hair.

What is the order of appearance of physical changes in females? First, either the breasts enlarge or pubic hair appears. Later, hair appears in the armpits. As these changes occur, the female grows in height and her hips become wider than her shoulders. **Menarche**—a girl's first menstruation—comes rather late in the pubertal cycle.

Marked weight gains coincide with the onset of puberty. During early adolescence, girls tend to outweigh boys, but by about age 14 boys begin to surpass girls. Similarly, at the beginning of the adolescent period, girls tend to be as tall as or taller than boys of their age, but by the end of the middle school years most boys have caught up, or, in many cases, surpassed girls in height.

As indicated in Figure 1, the growth spurt occurs approximately two years earlier for girls than for boys. The mean age at the beginning of the growth spurt in girls is 9; for boys, it is 11. The peak rate of pubertal change occurs at 11½ years for girls and 13½ years for boys. During their growth spurt, girls increase in height about 3½ inches per year, boys about 4 inches. Boys and girls who are shorter or taller than their peers before adolescence are likely to remain so during adolescence.

puberty A brain-neuroendocrine process occurring primarily in early adolescence that provides stimulation for the rapid physical changes that occur in this period of development.

menarche A girl's first menstruation.

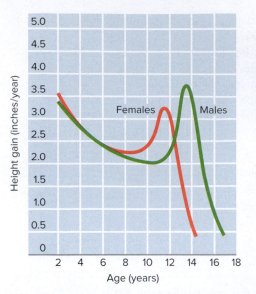

Hormonal Changes

Behind the first whisker in boys and the widening of hips in girls is a flood of **hormones,** powerful chemical substances secreted by the endocrine glands and carried through the body by the bloodstream (Herting & Sowell, 2017; Nguyen, 2018). The endocrine system's role in puberty involves the interaction of the hypothalamus, the pituitary gland, and the gonads. The **hypothalamus** is a structure in the brain that monitors eating and sex. The **pituitary gland** is an important endocrine gland that controls growth and regulates other glands; among these, the **gonads**—the testes in males, the ovaries in females—are particularly important in giving rise to pubertal changes in the body.

The concentrations of certain hormones increase dramatically during adolescence (Novello & Speiser, 2018; Piekarski & others, 2017; Rovner & others, 2018). *Testosterone* is a hormone associated in boys with the development of genitals, an increase in height, and a change in voice (Giri & others, 2017; Werenga & others, 2018). *Estradiol* is a type of estrogen; in girls it is associated with breast, uterine, and skeletal development (Ding & others, 2018). In one study, testosterone levels increased eighteen-fold in boys but only two-fold in girls during puberty; estradiol increased eight-fold in girls but only two-fold in boys (Nottelmann & others, 1987). Thus, both testosterone and estradiol are present in the hormonal makeup of both boys and girls, but testosterone dominates in male pubertal development, estradiol in female pubertal development (Benyi & Sävendahl, 2017; Hsueh & He, 2018). The same influx of hormones that grows hair on a male's chest and increases the fatty tissue in a female's breasts may also contribute to psychological development in adolescence.

However, one research review concluded that there is insufficient quality research to confirm that changing testosterone levels during puberty are linked to mood and behavior in adolescent males (Duke, Balzer, & Steinbeck, 2014). Thus, hormonal effects by themselves do not account for adolescent development (Susman & Dorn, 2013). For example, in one study, social factors accounted for two to four times as much variance as did hormonal factors in young adolescent girls' depression and anger (Brooks-Gunn & Warren, 1989). Behavior and moods also can affect hormones. Stress, eating patterns, exercise, sexual activity, tension, and depression can activate or suppress various aspects of the hormonal system. In sum, the hormone-behavior link is complex (Susman & Dorn, 2013).

Timing and Variations in Puberty

In the United States—where children mature up to a year earlier than children in European countries—the average age of menarche has declined significantly since the mid-nineteenth century. Also, recent studies in Korea and Japan (Cole & Mori, 2018), China (Song & others, 2016), and Saudi Arabia (Al Alwan & others, 2017) found that pubertal onset has been occurring earlier in recent years. Fortunately, however, we are unlikely to see pubescent toddlers, since what has happened in the past century is likely the result of improved nutrition and health (Herman-Giddens, 2007).

Why do the changes of puberty occur when they do, and how can variations in their timing be explained? The basic genetic program for puberty is wired into the species (Howard & Dunkel, 2018; Toro, Aylwin, & Lomniczi, 2018), but nutrition, health, family stress, and other environmental factors also affect puberty's timing and makeup (Villamor & Jansen, 2016). A number of studies have found that higher weight, especially obesity, is linked to earlier pubertal development (Shailtin & Kiess, 2017). For example, a recent study concluded that

hormones Powerful chemical substances secreted by the endocrine glands and carried through the body by the bloodstream.

hypothalamus A structure in the higher portion of the brain that monitors eating and sex.

pituitary gland An important endocrine gland that controls growth and regulates other glands, including the gonads.

gonads The sex glands—the testes in males and the ovaries in females.

How Would You...?
As a **psychologist,** how would you explain the link between biological/physical changes and adolescent mood swings?

earlier pubertal onset occurred in girls with a higher body mass index (BMI) (Bratke & others, 2017). Further, a recent Chinese study also revealed that a higher BMI was associated with earlier pubertal onset (Deng & others, 2018). Also, puberty comes earlier when girls and boys experience considerable stress and conflict. For example, a recent study found that child sexual abuse was linked to earlier pubertal onset (Noll & others, 2017).

For most boys, the pubertal sequence may begin as early as age 10 or as late as 13½ and may end as early as age 13 or as late as 17. Thus, the normal range is wide enough that, given two boys of the same chronological age, one might complete the pubertal sequence before the other one has begun it. For girls, menarche is considered within the normal range if it appears between the ages of 9 and 15.

What are some of the differences in the ways girls and boys experience pubertal growth?
©Fuse/Getty Images

Body Image

One psychological aspect of physical change in puberty is certain: Adolescents are preoccupied with their bodies and develop images of what their bodies are like (Hoffman & Warschburger, 2018; Senin-Calderon & others, 2017). One study revealed that adolescents with the most positive body images engaged in health-enhancing behaviors, especially regular exercise (Frisen & Holmqvist, 2010).

The recent dramatic increase in Internet use, particularly social media platforms, has raised concerns about their influence on adolescents' body images (Saul & Rodgers, 2018). For example, a recent study of U.S. 12- to 14-year-olds found that heavier social media use was associated with body dissatisfaction (Burnette, Kwitowski, & Mazzeo, 2017). Also, in a recent study of U.S. college women, spending more time on Facebook was related to more frequent body and weight concern comparisons with other women, more attention to the physical appearance of others, and more negative feelings about their own bodies (Eckler, Kalyango, & Paasch, 2017). In sum, various aspects of exposure to the Internet and social media are increasing the body dissatisfaction of adolescents and emerging adults, especially females.

How Would You…?

As a **human development and family studies professional,** how would you counsel parents about communicating with their adolescent daughter regarding changes in her behavior that likely reflect a declining body image?

Gender differences characterize adolescents' perceptions of their bodies (Hoffman & Warschburger, 2017, 2018; Mitchison & others, 2017). In general, girls are less happy with their bodies and have more negative body images than boys throughout puberty (Bearman & others, 2006). Girls' more negative body images may be due to media portrayals of the attractiveness of being thin, coupled with the increased levels of body fat in girls during puberty (Griffiths & others, 2017). In a recent U.S. study of young adolescents, boys had a more positive body image than girls did (Morin & others, 2017). Also, another study found that both boys' and girls' body images became more positive as they moved from the beginning to the end of adolescence (Holsen, Carlson Jones, & Skogbrott Birkeland, 2012).

Early and Late Maturation

You may have entered puberty earlier or later than average, or perhaps you were right on time. Adolescents who mature earlier or later than their peers perceive themselves differently (Selkie, 2018; Ullsperger & Nikolas, 2017). In the Berkeley Longitudinal Study some years ago, early-maturing boys perceived themselves more positively and had more successful peer relations than did their late-maturing counterparts (Jones, 1965). When the late-maturing boys were in their thirties, however, they had developed a stronger sense of identity than the early-maturing boys had (Peskin, 1967). This may have occurred because the late-maturing boys had more time to explore life's options, or because the early-maturing boys continued to focus on their advantageous physical status instead of on career development and achievement. More recent research confirms, though, that at least during adolescence it is advantageous to be an early-maturing rather than a late-maturing boy (Graber, Brooks-Gunn, & Warren, 2006).

By contrast, an increasing number of researchers have found that early maturation increases girls' vulnerability to a number of problems (Black & Rofey, 2018; Hamilton & others, 2014; Selkie, 2018). Early-maturing girls are more likely to smoke, drink, be depressed, have an eating disorder, struggle for earlier independence from their parents, and have older friends; and their bodies are likely to elicit responses from males that lead to earlier dating and earlier sexual experiences (Baker & others, 2012; Negriff, Susman, & Trickett, 2011; Rudolph & others, 2014; Selkie, 2018; Wang & others, 2018). In a recent study, onset of menarche before 11 years of age was linked to a higher incidence of distress disorders, fear disorders, and externalizing disorders in females (Platt & others, 2017). Further, researchers recently found that early-maturing girls had higher rates of depression and antisocial behavior as middle-aged adults mainly because their difficulties began in adolescence and did not lessen over time (Mendle, Ryan, & McKone, 2018). In another study, early menarche was associated with risky sexual behavior in Korean females (Cheong & others, 2015). Researchers also have found that early-maturing girls tend to engage in sexual intercourse earlier and have more unstable sexual relationships (Moore, Harden, & Mendle, 2014). Further, a study revealed that early-maturing Chinese girls and boys engaged in delinquency more than their on-time or late-maturing counterparts (Chen & others, 2015). Another study found that early maturation predicted a stable higher level of depression for adolescent girls (Rudolph & others, 2014). Also, a recent study indicated that early-maturing girls are at increased risk for physical and verbal abuse in dating (Chen, Rothman, & Jaffee, 2018). In addition, early-maturing girls are less likely to graduate from high school, and they tend to cohabit and marry earlier (Cavanagh, 2009).

How Would You...?

As a **health-care professional,** how would you use your knowledge of puberty to reassure adolescents who are concerned that they are maturing more slowly than their friends?

The Brain

Along with the rest of the body, the brain is changing during adolescence, but the study of adolescent brain development is in its infancy. As advances in technology take place, significant strides will also likely be made in charting developmental changes in the adolescent brain (Dahl & others, 2018; Goddings & Mills, 2017; Juraska & Willing, 2017; Sherman, Steinberg, & Chein, 2018; Vijayakumar & others, 2018). What do we know now?

The dogma of the unchanging brain has been discarded, and researchers are mainly focused on context-induced plasticity of the brain over time (Duell & others, 2018; Tamnes & others, 2018; Zanolie & Crone, 2018). The development of the brain mainly changes in a bottom-up, top-down sequence, with sensory, appetitive (eating, drinking), sexual, sensation-seeking, and risk-taking brain linkages maturing first and higher-level brain linkages such as self-control, planning, and reasoning maturing later (Zelazo, 2013).

Recall that researchers have discovered that nearly twice as many synaptic connections are made as we will ever use (Huttenlocher & Dabholkar, 1997). The connections that we do use are strengthened and survive, while the unused ones are replaced by other pathways or disappear. That is, in the language of neuroscience, these connections will be "pruned." As a result of this pruning, by the end of adolescence individuals have "fewer, more selective, more effective neuronal connections than they did as children" (Kuhn, 2009, p. 153). And this pruning indicates that the activities adolescents choose to engage in and not to engage in influence which neural connections will be strengthened and which will disappear (Juraska & Willing, 2017).

Using fMRI brain scans, scientists have discovered that adolescents' brains undergo significant structural changes (Crone, 2017; Crone, Peters, & Steinbeis, 2018; Dahl & others, 2018; Lebel & Deoni, 2018; Reyna, 2018). The **corpus callosum,** where nerve fibers connect the brain's

corpus callosum The location where nerve fibers connect the brain's left and right hemispheres.

left and right hemispheres, thickens in adolescence, and this improves adolescents' ability to process information (Chavarria & others, 2014). Earlier we described advances in the development of the prefrontal cortex—the highest level of the frontal lobes involved in reasoning, decision making, and self-control. However, the prefrontal cortex doesn't finish maturing until the emerging adult years—approximately 18 to 25 years of age—or later (Goddings & Mills, 2017; Sousa & others, 2018).

At a lower, subcortical level, the **limbic system,** which is the seat of emotions and where rewards are experienced, matures much earlier than the prefrontal cortex and is almost completely developed by early adolescence (Cohen & Casey, 2017). The limbic system structure that is especially involved in emotion is the **amygdala.** Figure 2 shows the locations of the corpus callosum, prefrontal cortex, and the limbic system.

With the onset of puberty, the levels of neurotransmitters change (Crone, 2017). For example, an increase in the neurotransmitter dopamine occurs in both the prefrontal cortex and the limbic system during adolescence (Dahl & others, 2018). Increases in dopamine have been linked to increased risk taking and use of addictive drugs (Gulick & Gamsby, 2018; Webber & others, 2017). Researchers have also found that dopamine plays an important role in reward seeking during adolescence (Dubol & others, 2018).

Earlier we described the increased focal activation that is linked to synaptic pruning in a specific region, such as the prefrontal cortex. In middle and late childhood, while there is increased focal activation within a specific brain region such as the prefrontal cortex, there also are only limited connections across distant brain regions. By the time individuals reach emerging adulthood, there are increased connections across brain areas (Dahl & others, 2018; Lebel & Deoni, 2018; Sousa & others, 2018). The increased connectedness (referred to as brain networks) is especially prevalent across more distant brain regions. Thus, as children and adolescents mature, greater efficiency and focal activation occurs in local areas of the brain, and simultaneously there is an increase in brain networks across different brain regions (de Haan & Johnson, 2016). In a recent study, reduced connectivity between the brain's frontal lobes and amygdala during adolescence was linked to increased depression (Scheuer & others, 2017).

Many of the changes in the adolescent brain that have been described involve the rapidly emerging field of *developmental social neuroscience,* which involves connections between development, the brain, and socioemotional processes (Dahl & others, 2018; Sherman, Steinberg, & Chein, 2018; Telzer, Rogers, & Van Hoorn, 2017; Zanolie & Crone, 2018). For example, consider leading researcher Charles Nelson's (2003) view that, although adolescents are capable of very strong emotions, their prefrontal cortex hasn't adequately developed to the point at which they can control these passions. It is as if their brain doesn't have the brakes to slow down their emotions. Or consider this interpretation of the development of emotion and cognition in adolescents: "early activation of strong 'turbo-charged' feelings with a relatively un-skilled set of 'driving skills' or cognitive abilities to modulate strong emotions and motivations" (Dahl, 2004, p. 18).

Prefrontal cortex
This "judgment" region reins in intense emotions but doesn't finish developing until at least emerging adulthood.

Corpus callosum
These nerve fibers connect the brain's two hemispheres; they thicken in adolescence to process information more effectively.

Amygdala
Limbic system structure especially involved in emotion.

Limbic system
A lower, subcortical system in the brain that is the seat of emotions and experience of rewards. This system is almost completely developed by early adolescence.

Figure 2 The Changing Adolescent Brain: Prefrontal Cortex, Limbic System, and Corpus Callosum

limbic system A lower, subcortical system in the brain that is the seat of emotions and experience of rewards.

amygdala The region of the brain that is the seat of emotions.

Of course, a major issue is which comes first: biological changes in the brain or experiences that stimulate these changes (Lerner, Boyd, & Du, 2008). In a longitudinal study, 11- to 18-year-olds who lived in poverty conditions had diminished brain functioning at 25 years of age (Brody & others, 2017). However, the adolescents from poverty backgrounds whose families participated in a supportive parenting intervention did not show this diminished brain functioning in adulthood. Another study found that the prefrontal cortex thickened and more brain connections formed when adolescents resisted peer pressure (Paus & others, 2007). Scientists have yet to determine whether the brain changes come first or whether the brain changes result from experiences with peers, parents, and others. Once again, we encounter the nature/nurture issue that is so prominent in an examination of development through the life span.

In closing this section on the development of the brain in adolescence, a further caution is in order. Much of the research on neuroscience and the development of the brain in adolescence is correlational in nature, and thus causal statements need to be scrutinized (de Haan & Johnson, 2016). This caution, of course, applies to any period in the human life span.

Adolescent Sexuality

Not only are adolescents characterized by substantial changes in physical growth and the development of the brain, but adolescence also is a bridge between the asexual child and the sexual adult. Adolescence is a time of sexual exploration and experimentation, of sexual fantasies and realities, of incorporating sexuality into one's identity.

Developing a Sexual Identity

Mastering emerging sexual feelings and forming a sense of sexual identity is a multifaceted and lengthy process (Diamond & Alley, 2018; Savin-Williams, 2017, 2018). It involves learning to manage sexual feelings (such as sexual arousal and attraction), developing new forms of intimacy, and learning the skills to regulate sexual behavior to avoid undesirable consequences.

An adolescent's sexual identity involves activities, interests, styles of behavior, and an indication of sexual orientation (whether an individual has same-sex or other-sex attractions) (Goldberg & Halpern, 2017). For example, some adolescents have a high anxiety level about sex, others a low level. Some adolescents are strongly aroused sexually, others less so. Some adolescents are very active sexually, others not at all (Carroll, 2018; Hyde & DeLamater, 2017). Some adolescents are sexually inactive in response to their strong religious upbringing; others go to church regularly, yet their religious training does not inhibit their sexual activity.

It is commonly believed that most gay and lesbian individuals quietly struggle with same-sex attractions in childhood, do not engage in heterosexual dating, and gradually recognize that they are gay or lesbian in middle to late adolescence. Many youths do follow this developmental pathway, but others do not (Diamond & Alley, 2018). For example, many people have no recollection of early same-sex attractions and experience a more abrupt sense of their same-sex attraction in late adolescence. Researchers also have found that the majority of adolescents with same-sex attractions also experience some degree of other-sex attractions. Even though some adolescents who are attracted to individuals of their own sex fall in love with these individuals, others claim that their same-sex attractions are purely physical (Savin-Williams, 2017, 2018).

In sum, gay and lesbian youth have diverse patterns of initial attraction, often have bisexual attractions, and may have physical or emotional attraction to same-sex individuals but do not always fall in love with them (Savin-Williams, 2017, 2018). Further, the majority of sexual minority (gay, lesbian, and bisexual) adolescents have competent and successful paths of development through adolescence and become healthy and productive adults. However, in a recent large-scale study, sexual minority adolescents were more likely to engage in health-risk behaviors (greater drug use and sexual risk taking, for example) than heterosexual adolescents (Kann & others, 2016b).

The Timing of Adolescent Sexual Behaviors

What is the current profile of sexual activity of adolescents? In a U.S. national survey conducted in 2015, 58 percent of twelfth-graders reported having experienced sexual intercourse, compared with 24 percent of ninth-graders (Kann & others, 2016a). By age 20, 77 percent of U.S. youth report having engaged in sexual intercourse (Dworkin & Santelli, 2007). Nationally, 46 percent of twelfth-graders, 33.5 percent of eleventh-graders, 25.5 percent of tenth-graders, and 16 percent of ninth-graders recently reported that they were currently sexually active (Kann & others, 2016a).

What trends in adolescent sexual activity have occurred in recent decades? From 1991 to 2015, fewer adolescents reported any of the following: ever having had sexual intercourse, currently being sexually active, having had sexual intercourse before the age of 13, and having had sexual intercourse with four or more persons during their lifetime (Kann & others, 2016a).

Sexual initiation varies by ethnic group in the United States (Kann & others, 2016a). African Americans are likely to engage in sexual behaviors earlier than other ethnic groups, whereas Asian Americans are likely to engage in them later (Feldman, Turner, & Araujo, 1999). In a more recent national U.S. survey of ninth- to twelfth-graders, 48.5 percent of African Americans, 42.5 percent of Latinos, and 39.9 percent of non-Latino Whites said they had experienced sexual intercourse (Kann & others, 2016a). In this study, 8 percent of African Americans (compared with 5 percent of Latinos and 2.5 percent of non-Latino Whites) said they had their first sexual experience before 13 years of age.

Research indicates that oral sex is now a common occurrence among U.S. adolescents (Holway, 2015). In a recent national survey of more than 7,000 15- to 24-year-olds, 58.6 percent of the females reported ever having performed oral sex and 60.4 percent said that they had ever received oral sex (Holway & Hernandez, 2018). Also, in a previous survey, 51 percent of U.S. 15- to 19-year-old boys and 47 percent of girls in the same age range said they had engaged in oral sex (Child Trends, 2015). One study also found that among female adolescents who reported having vaginal sex first, 31 percent reported having a teen pregnancy, whereas among those who initiated oral-genital sex first, only 8 percent reported having a teen pregnancy (Reese & others, 2013). Thus, how adolescents initiate their sex lives may have positive or negative consequences for their sexual health (Goldstein & Halpern-Felsher, 2018; Kahn & Halpern, 2018).

Risk Factors in Adolescent Sexuality

Many adolescents are not emotionally prepared to handle sexual experiences, especially in early adolescence (Charlton & others, 2018; Ihongbe, Cha, & Masho, 2017; Weisman & others, 2018). A recent study found that early sexual debut (first sexual intercourse before age 13) was associated with sexual risk taking, substance use, violent victimization, and suicidal thoughts/attempts in both sexual minority (gay, lesbian, and bisexual adolescents) and heterosexual youth (Lowry & others, 2017). Also, in a recent study of Korean adolescent girls, early menarche was linked with earlier initiation of sexual intercourse (Kim & others, 2017).

A number of family factors are associated with sexual risk taking (Ashcraft & Murray, 2017; Ruiz-Casares & others, 2017). For example, one study found that difficulties and disagreements between Latino adolescents and their parents were linked to the adolescents' early sexual initiation (Cordova & others, 2014). Also, a recent study revealed that adolescents who reported greater parental knowledge of their whereabouts and more family rules about dating in the eighth grade were less likely to initiate sex from the eighth to tenth grade (Ethier & others, 2016). And a recent study revealed that of a number of parenting practices, the factor that best predicted a lower level of risky sexual behavior by adolescents was supportive parenting (Simons & others, 2016).

What are some risk factors for adolescent sexual problems?
©Jacob Lund/Shutterstock

Socioeconomic status, peer relations, school performance, sports participation, and religious orientation provide further information about sexual risk taking by adolescents (Choukas-Bradley & Prinstein, 2016; Warner, 2018; Widman & others, 2016). For example, the percentage of sexually active young adolescents is higher in low-income areas of inner cities (Morrison-Beedy & others, 2013). Also, one study found that adolescents who associated with more deviant peers in early adolescence were likely to have had more sexual partners by age 16 (Lansford & others, 2010). And a research review found that school connectedness was linked to positive sexuality outcomes (Markham & others, 2010). Also, a study of middle school students revealed that better academic achievement was a protective factor in delaying initiation of sexual intercourse (Laflin, Wang, & Barry, 2008). Further, a recent study found that adolescent males who play sports engage in a higher level of sexual risk taking, while adolescent females who play sports engage in a lower level of sexual risk taking (Lipowski & others, 2016). And a recent study of African American adolescent girls indicated that those who reported that religion was of low or moderate importance to them had a much earlier sexual debut that their counterparts who said that religion was very or extremely important to them (George Dalmida & others, 2018).

Contraceptive Use

Sexual activity brings considerable risks if appropriate safeguards are not taken (Carroll, 2019; Chandra-Mouli & others, 2018; King & Regan, 2018). Youth encounter two kinds of risks: unintended, unwanted pregnancy and sexually transmitted infections. Both of these risks can be reduced significantly if condoms are used.

Too many sexually active adolescents still do not use contraceptives, use them inconsistently, or use contraceptive methods that are less effective than others (Apter, 2018; Diedrich, Klein, & Peipert, 2017). In 2015, 14 percent of sexually active adolescents did not use any contraceptive method the last time they had sexual intercourse (Kann & others, 2016a). Researchers have found that U.S. adolescents are less likely to use condoms than their European counterparts (Jorgensen & others, 2015).

Recently, a number of leading medical organizations and experts have recommended that adolescents use long-acting reversible contraception (LARC) (Fridy & others, 2018). These include the Society for Adolescent Health and Medicine (2017), the American Academy of Pediatrics and American College of Obstetrics and Gynecology (Allen & Barlow, 2017), and the World Health Organization (2018). LARC consists of the use of intrauterine devices (IUDs) and contraceptive implants, which have much lower rates of unwanted pregnancy than birth control pills and condoms (Diedrich, Klein, & Peipert, 2017; Society for Adolescent Health and Medicine, 2017).

Sexually Transmitted Infections

Some forms of contraception, such as birth control pills or implants, do not protect against sexually transmitted infections, or STIs. **Sexually transmitted infections (STIs)** are contracted primarily through sexual contact, including oral-genital and anal-genital contact. Every year more than 3 million American adolescents (about one-fourth of those who are sexually experienced) acquire an STI (Centers for Disease Control and Prevention, 2018). In a single act of unprotected sex with an infected partner, a teenage girl has a 1 percent risk of getting HIV, a 30 percent risk of acquiring genital herpes, and a 50 percent chance of contracting gonorrhea (Glei, 1999). Other very widespread STIs are chlamydia and human papillomavirus (HPV). Later we will discuss these and other sexually transmitted infections.

Adolescent Pregnancy

Adolescent pregnancy is a problematic outcome of sexuality in adolescence that requires major efforts to reduce its occurrence (Brindis, 2017; Romero & others, 2017; Tevendale & others, 2017). In cross-cultural comparisons, the

sexually transmitted infections (STIs) Infections contracted primarily through sexual contact, including oral-genital and anal-genital contact.

United States continues to have some of the highest rates of adolescent pregnancy and childbearing in the industrialized world, despite a considerable decline in the 1990s. The U.S. adolescent pregnancy rate is eight times as high as that in the Netherlands. Although U.S. adoles-

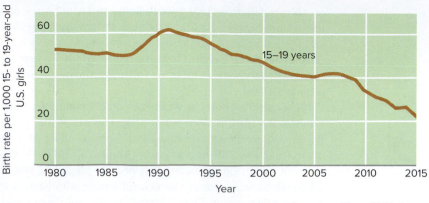

Figure 3 Birth Rates for U.S. 15- to 19-Year-Old Girls from 1980 to 2015
Source: Martin, J. A. et al. "Births: Final data for 2015." *National Vital Statistics Reports*, 66 (1), 2017, 1.

cents are no more sexually active than their counterparts in the Netherlands, their adolescent pregnancy rate is dramatically higher. In the United States, 82 percent of pregnancies to mothers 15 to 19 years of age are unintended (Koh, 2014). A cross-cultural comparison found that among 21 countries, the United States had the highest adolescent pregnancy rate among 15- to 19-year-olds and Switzerland the lowest (Sedgh & others, 2015).

Despite the negative comparisons of the United States with many other developed countries, there have been some encouraging trends in U.S. adolescent pregnancy rates. In 2015, the U.S. birth rate for 15- to 19-year-olds was 22.3 births per 1,000 females, the lowest rate ever recorded, which represents a dramatic decrease from the 61.8 births per 1,000 females in the same age range in 1991, and down even 4 percent since 2014 (Martin & others, 2017) (see Figure 3). There also has been a substantial decrease in adolescent pregnancies across ethnic groups in recent years. Reasons for the decline include school/community health classes, increased contraceptive use, and fear of sexually transmitted infections such as AIDS.

Ethnic variations characterize birth rates for U.S. adolescents. Latina adolescents are more likely than African American and non-Latina White adolescents to have a child (Martin & others, 2015). Latina and African American adolescent girls who have a child are also more likely to have a second child than are non-Latina White adolescent girls (Rosengard, 2009).

What are some consequences of adolescent pregnancy?
©Geoff Manasse/Getty Images

Indeed, a special concern is repeated adolescent pregnancy. In a recent national study, the percentage of teen births that were repeat births decreased from 2004 (21 percent) to 2015 (17 percent) (Dee & others, 2017). In a recent meta-analysis, use of effective contraception, especially LARC, and education-related factors (higher level of education and school continuation) resulted in a lower incidence of repeated teen pregnancy, while depression and a history of abortion were linked to a higher percentage of repeated teen pregnancy (Maravilla & others, 2017).

Outcomes Adolescent pregnancy creates health risks for both the baby and the mother (Barnes & others, 2017; Khatun & others, 2017; SmithBattie & others, 2017). Infants born to adolescent mothers are more likely to have low birth weights—a prominent factor in infant mortality—as well as neurological problems and childhood illness (Khashan, Baker, & Kenny, 2010). Adolescent mothers are more likely to be depressed and to drop out of school than their peers (Siegel & Brandon, 2014). Although many adolescent mothers resume their education later in life, they generally never catch up economically with women who postpone childbearing until their twenties. Also, a study of African American urban youth found that at 32 years of age, women who had been teenage mothers were more likely to be unemployed, live in poverty, depend on welfare, and not have completed college than were women who had not been teenage mothers (Assini-Meytin & Green, 2015). In this study, at 32 years of age, men who had been teenage fathers were more likely to be unemployed than were men who had not been teenage fathers.

Though the consequences of America's high adolescent pregnancy rate are cause for great concern, it often is not pregnancy alone that leads to negative consequences for an adolescent mother and her offspring. Adolescent mothers are more likely to come from low-SES backgrounds (Mollborn, 2017). Many adolescent mothers also were not good students before they became pregnant (Malamitsi-Puchner & Boutsikou, 2006). However, not every adolescent female who bears a child lives a life of poverty and low achievement. Thus, although adolescent pregnancy is a high-risk circumstance and adolescents who do not become pregnant generally fare better than those who do, some adolescent mothers do well in school and have positive outcomes (Schaffer & others, 2012).

Serious, extensive efforts are needed to help pregnant adolescents and young mothers enhance their educational and occupational opportunities (Finley & others, 2018; Leftwich & Alves, 2017; SmithBattle & others, 2017). Adolescent mothers also need help in obtaining competent child care and in planning for the future.

Adolescents can benefit from age-appropriate family life education. Family and consumer science educators teach life skills, such as effective decision making, to adolescents. The *Careers in Life-Span Development* profile describes the work of one family and consumer science educator.

Careers in life-span development

Lynn Blankinship, Family and Consumer Science Educator

Lynn Blankinship is a family and consumer science educator. She has an undergraduate degree in this area from the University of Arizona and has taught for more than 20 years, the last 14 at Tucson High Magnet School.

Lynn received the Tucson Federation of Teachers Educator of the Year Award for 1999–2000 and was honored as the Arizona Teacher of the Year in 1999.

Lynn especially enjoys teaching life skills to adolescents. One of her favorite activities is having students care for an automated baby that imitates the needs of real babies. She says that this program has a profound impact on students because the baby must be cared for around the clock for the duration of the assignment. Lynn also coordinates real-world work experiences and training for students in several child-care facilities in the Tucson area.

Family and consumer science educators like Lynn Blankinship may specialize in early childhood education or instruct middle and high school students about such matters as nutrition, interpersonal relationships, human sexuality, parenting, and human development. Hundreds of colleges and

Lynn Blankinship (*center*) teaches life skills to students.
Courtesy of Lynn Blankinship

universities throughout the United States offer two- and four-year degree programs in family and consumer science. These programs usually require an internship. Additional education courses may be needed to obtain a teaching certificate. Some family and consumer science educators go on to graduate school for further training, which provides a background for possible jobs in college teaching or research.

Reducing Adolescent Pregnancy Girls Inc. offers four programs that are intended to increase adolescent girls' motivation to avoid pregnancy until they are mature enough to make responsible decisions about motherhood (Roth & others, 1998). Growing Together, a series of five two-hour workshops for adolescent girls and their mothers, and Will Power/Won't Power, a series of six two-hour sessions that focus on assertiveness training, are designed for 12- to 14-year-old girls. For older adolescent girls, Taking Care of Business provides nine sessions that emphasize career planning and provide information about sexuality, reproduction, and contraception. The program Health Bridge coordinates health and educational services—girls can participate in this program as one of their Girls Inc. club activities. Girls who participated in these programs were less likely to get pregnant than girls who did not participate (Girls Inc., 1991).

How Would You...?

As an **educator**, how would you incorporate sex education throughout the curriculum to encourage adolescents' healthy, responsible sexual development?

What percentage of U.S. adolescents receive formal instruction in sexual health? In 2011 to 2013, more than 80 percent of 15- to 19-year-olds were given information about STIs, HIV/AIDS, or how to say no to sex (Lindberg, Maddow-Zimet, & Boonstra, 2016). However, only 55 percent of males and 60 percent of females in this age range had received information about birth control. Sexual health information also is more likely to be taught in high school than in middle school (Alan Guttmacher Institute, 2017).

Currently, a major controversy in sex education is whether schools should have an abstinence-only program or a program that emphasizes contraceptive knowledge (MacKenzie, Hedge, & Enslin, 2017). Recent research reviews have concluded that abstinence-only programs do not delay the initiation of sexual intercourse and do not reduce HIV risk behaviors (Denford & others, 2017; Jaramillo & others, 2017; Santelli & others, 2017). Recently there has been an increased emphasis on abstinence-only-until-marriage (AOUM) policies and programs in many U.S. schools. However, a major problem with such policies and programs is that a very large majority of individuals engage in sexual intercourse at some point in adolescence or emerging adulthood, while the average age when people marry for the first time continues to go up (currently 27 for females, 29 for males in the United States). The Society for Adolescent Health and Medicine (2017) recently released a policy position that states research evidence indicates that many comprehensive sex education programs successfully delay initiation of sexual intercourse and reduce rates of sexually transmitted infections. The Society's position also states that research indicates AOUM programs are ineffective in delaying sexual intercourse and reducing other sexual risk behaviors.

Some sex-education programs are starting to include abstinence-plus sexuality by promoting abstinence as well as providing instructions for contraceptive use (Barr & others, 2014). However, despite the evidence that favors comprehensive sex education, there recently has been an increase in government funding for abstinence-only programs (Donovan, 2017). Also, in some states (Texas and Mississippi, for example), many students still either get abstinence-only instruction or no sex education at all.

Adolescent Health

Adolescence is a critical juncture in the adoption of behaviors that are relevant to health (Devenish, Hooley, & Mellor, 2017; Yap & others, 2017). Many of the behaviors that are linked to poor health habits and early death in adults begin during adolescence (Backman & others, 2018; Hodder & others, 2018). Conversely, the early formation of healthy behavior patterns, such as regular exercise and a preference for foods low in fat and cholesterol, not only has immediate health benefits but helps in adulthood to delay or prevent disability and mortality from heart disease, stroke, diabetes, and cancer (Blake, 2017; Donatelle, 2019).

Bonnie Halpern-Felsher, University Professor in Pediatrics and Director of Community Efforts to Improve Adolescents' Health

Dr. Halpern-Felsher recently became a professor in the Department of Pediatrics at Stanford University after holding this position for a number of years at the University of California–San Francisco. Her work exemplifies how some professors not only teach and conduct research in a single discipline, like psychology, but do work in multiple disciplines and also work outside their university in the community to improve the lives of youth. Dr. Halpern-Felsher is a developmental psychologist with additional training in adolescent health. She is especially interested in understanding why adolescents engage in risk-taking behavior and using this research to develop intervention programs for improving adolescents' lives.

In particular, she has studied adolescent sexual decision-making and reproductive health, including cognitive and socio-emotional predictors of sexual behavior. Her research has included influences of parenting and peer relationships on adolescent sexual behavior. Dr. Halpern-Felsher has served as a consultant for a number of community-based adolescent health promotion campaigns, and she has been involved in community-based efforts to reduce substance abuse among adolescents. For example, recently she worked with the state of California to

Dr. Bonnie Halpern-Felsher (2nd from left) with some of the students she is mentoring in the STEP-UP program
Courtesy of Dr. Bonnie Halpern-Felsher

implement new school-based tobacco prevention and educational materials. As a further indication of her strong commitment to improving adolescents' lives, Dr. Halpern-Felsher coordinates the STEP-UP program (Short-Term Research Experience for Underrepresented Persons) in which she has personally mentored and supervised 22 to 25 middle and high school students every year since 2007.

To read about an individual who has made a number of contributions to a better understanding of adolescents' health and ways to improve their health, see the *Careers in Life-Span Development* profile.

Nutrition and Exercise

Concerns are growing about adolescents' nutrition and exercise habits (Donatelle & Ketcham, 2018; Schiff, 2019; Walton-Fisette & Wuest, 2018).

Nutrition

The eating habits of many adolescents are health-compromising, and an increasing number of adolescents have an eating disorder (Insel & Roth, 2018; Smith & Collene, 2019; Stice & others, 2017). National data indicate that the percentage of overweight U.S. 12- to 19-year-olds increased from 11 percent in the early 1990s to 20.5 percent in 2014 (Centers for Disease Control and Prevention, 2016). In another study, 12.4 percent of U.S. kindergarten children were obese and by 14 years of age, 20.8 percent were obese (Cunningham, Kramer, & Narayan, 2014).

Being obese in adolescence predicts obesity in emerging adulthood. For example, a longitudinal study of more than 8,000 adolescents found that obese adolescents were more likely to develop severe obesity in emerging adulthood than were overweight or normal-weight adolescents (The & others, 2010). In another longitudinal study, the percentage of overweight individuals increased from 20 percent at 14 years of age to 33 percent at 24 years of age (Patton & others, 2011).

Exercise

What are some characteristics of adolescents' exercise patterns?
©Tom Stewart/Corbis/Getty Images

Researchers have found that individuals become less active as they reach and progress through adolescence (Alberga & others, 2012). A national study revealed that only 48.6 percent of U.S. adolescents met the federal government's exercise recommendations (a minimum of 60 minutes of moderate to vigorous exercise per day) (Kann & others, 2016a). This national study also found that adolescent girls were much less likely to engage in 60 minutes or more of vigorous exercise per day in five of the last seven days (42 percent) than were boys (61 percent) (Kann & others, 2016b). Ethnic differences in exercise participation rates of U.S. adolescents also occur, and these rates vary by gender. In the national study just mentioned, non-Latino White boys exercised the most, African American and Latino girls the least (Kann & others, 2016a).

Exercise is linked to a number of positive physical outcomes in adolescence (Janz & Baptista, 2018; Owen & others, 2018; Powers & Howley, 2018; Walton-Fisette & Wuest, 2018). Regular exercise has a positive effect on adolescents' weight status (Kuzik & others, 2017; Medrano & others, 2018). Other positive health outcomes of exercise in adolescence are reduced triglyceride levels, lower blood pressure, and a lower incidence of type II diabetes (Barton & others, 2017; Rowland, 2018). Also in a recent study, an exercise program of 180 minutes per week improved the sleep patterns of obese adolescents (Mendelson & others, 2016). Further, a recent study of adolescents with major depressive disorder (MDD) revealed that engaging in aerobic exercise for 12 weeks lowered their depressive symptoms (Jaworska, Broer, & van der Wouden, 2018). And in a recent large-scale study of Dutch adolescents, physically active adolescents had fewer emotional and peer problems (Kuiper & others, 2018). Further, in a recent research review, among a number of cognitive factors, memory was the factor that most often was improved by exercise in adolescence (Li & others, 2017).

Adolescents' exercise levels are increasingly being found to be associated with parenting, peer relationships, and screen-based activity (Foster & others, 2018; Mason & others, 2017; Michaud & others, 2017). One study revealed that family meals during adolescence reduced the likelihood of being overweight or obese in adulthood (Berge & others, 2015). Peers often influence adolescents' physical activity (Chung, Ersig, & McCarthy, 2017). For example, researchers found that female adolescents' physical activity was linked to their male and female friends' physical activity, while male adolescents' physical activity was associated with their female friends' physical activity (Sirard & others, 2013). Higher screen time is also linked to adolescents engaging in less exercise as well as being overweight or obese (Pearson & others, 2017). Further, a recent study of U.S. eighth-, tenth-, and twelfth-graders from 1991 to 2016 found that psychological well-being (assessed with indicators of self-esteem, life satisfaction, and happiness) abruptly decreased after 2012 (Twenge, Martin, & Campbell, 2018). In this study, adolescents who spent more time on electronic communication devices and screens (social media, the Internet, texting, and gaming) and less time on nonscreen activities (in-person social interaction, sports/exercise, homework, and attending religious services) had lower psychological well-being.

How Would You...?

As a **health-care professional,** how would you explain the benefits of physical fitness in adolescence to adolescents, parents, and teachers?

Sleep Patterns

Like nutrition and exercise, sleep is an important influence on well-being. Might changing sleep patterns in adolescence contribute to adolescents' health-compromising behaviors? Recently there has been a surge of interest in adolescent sleep patterns (Fatima,

Doi, & Al Mamun, 2018; Hoyt & others, 2018a, b; Meltzer, 2017; Palmer & others, 2018; Wheaton & others, 2018). A longitudinal study in which adolescents completed daily diaries during 14-day periods in ninth, tenth, and twelfth grades found that regardless of how much students studied each day, when the students sacrificed sleep time to study more than usual, they had difficulty understanding what was taught in class and were more likely to struggle with class assignments the next day (Gillen-O'Neel, Huynh, & Fuligni, 2013). Researchers also have found that adolescents who get less than 7.7 hours of sleep per night on average have more emotional and peer-related problems, higher anxiety, and a higher level of suicidal ideation (Sarchiapone & others, 2014). And a recent national study of more than 10,000 13- to 18-year-olds revealed that later weeknight bedtime, shorter week-night sleep duration, greater weekend bedtime delay, and both short and long periods of weekend oversleep were linked to increased rates of anxiety, mood, substance abuse, and behavioral disorders (Zhang & others, 2017).

In a national survey of youth, only 27 percent of U.S. adolescents got eight or more hours of sleep on an average school night, 5 percent less than just 2 years earlier (Kann & others, 2016a). In this study, the percentage of adolescents getting this much sleep on an average school night decreased as they got older. The National Sleep Foundation (2006) conducted a U.S. survey of 1,602 caregivers and their 11- to 17-year-olds. Forty-five percent of the adolescents got inadequate sleep on school nights (less than eight hours). Older adolescents (ninth- to twelfth-graders) got markedly less sleep on school nights than younger adolescents (sixth- to eighth-graders)—62 percent of the older adolescents got inadequate sleep compared with 21 percent of the younger adolescents. Adolescents who got inadequate sleep (less than eight hours) on school nights were more likely to feel tired, cranky, and irritable; to fall asleep in school; to be in a depressed mood; and to drink caffeinated beverages than their counterparts who got optimal sleep (nine or more hours).

Mary Carskadon (2006, 2011a, b; Jenni & Carskadon, 2007) has conducted a number of research studies on adolescent sleep patterns. She has found that when given the opportunity, adolescents will sleep an average of 9 hours and 25 minutes a night. Most get considerably less than 9 hours of sleep, however, especially during the week. This shortfall creates a sleep deficit, which adolescents often attempt to make up on the weekend. She also found that older adolescents tend to be sleepier during the day than younger adolescents are. Carskadon theorized that this sleepiness was not due to academic work or social pressures. Rather, her research suggests that adolescents' biological clocks undergo a shift as they get older, delaying their period of wakefulness by about one hour. A delay in the nightly release of the sleep-inducing hormone melatonin, which is produced in the brain's pineal gland, seems to underlie this shift. Melatonin is secreted at about 9:30 p.m. in younger adolescents and approximately an hour later in older adolescents.

Carskadon concludes that early school starting times may cause grogginess, inattention in class, and poor performance on tests. Based on her research, school officials in Edina, Minnesota, decided to start classes at 8:30 a.m. rather than the usual 7:25 a.m. Since the later start time went into effect, there have been fewer referrals for discipline problems, and the number of students who report being ill or depressed has decreased. The school system reports that test scores have improved for high school students but not for middle school students. This finding supports Carskadon's suspicion that early start times are likely to be more stressful for older than for younger adolescents.

One study found that just a 30-minute delay in school start time was linked to improvements in adolescents' sleep, alertness, mood, and health (Owens, Belon, & Moss, 2010). In another study, early school start times were linked to a higher vehicle crash rate in adolescent

In Mary Carskadon's sleep laboratory at Brown University, an adolescent girl's brain activity is being monitored. Carskadon (2006) says that in the morning, sleep-deprived adolescents' "brains are telling them it's night time . . . and the rest of the world is saying it's time to go to school" (p. 19).
©Jim LoScalzo

drivers (Vorona & others, 2014). The American Academy of Pediatrics has recommended that schools institute start times from 8:30 to 9:30 a.m. to improve adolescents' academic performance and quality of life (Adolescent Sleep Working Group, AAP, 2014).

Do sleep patterns change in emerging adulthood? Research indicates that they do (Galambos, Howard, & Maggs, 2011; Kloss & others, 2016). One study revealed that more than 60 percent of college students were categorized as poor-quality sleepers (Lund & others, 2010). In this study, the weekday bedtimes and rise times of first-year college students were approximately 1 hour and 15 minutes later than those of seniors in high school (Lund & others, 2010). However, the first-year college students had later bedtimes and rise times than third- and fourth-year college students, indicating that at about 20 to 22 years of age, a reverse shift in the timing of bedtimes and rise times occurs. In another study, consistently low sleep duration in college students was associated with less effective attention the next day (Whiting & Murdock, 2016). Also, in a recent study of college students, a higher level of text messaging (greater number of daily texts, awareness of nighttime cell phone notifications, and compulsion to check nighttime notifications) was linked to a lower level of sleep quality (Murdock, Horissian, & Crichlow-Ball, 2017).

Leading Causes of Death in Adolescence

The three leading causes of death in adolescence are unintentional injuries, homicide, and suicide (National Center for Health Statistics, 2018). Almost half of all deaths occurring from 15 to 24 years of age are due to unintentional injuries, the majority of them involving motor vehicle accidents.

Risky driving habits, such as speeding, tailgating, and driving under the influence of alcohol or other drugs, may be more important contributors to these accidents than lack of driving experience (White & others, 2018; Williams & others, 2018). In about 50 percent of motor vehicle fatalities involving adolescents, the driver has a blood alcohol level of 0.10 percent—twice the level needed to be designated as "under the influence" in some states. An increasing concern is the growing number of adolescents who mix alcohol and energy drinks, a practice that is linked with risky driving (Wilson & others, 2018). A high rate of intoxication is also found in adolescents who die as pedestrians or while using recreational vehicles.

Homicide is the second-leading cause of death in adolescence (National Center for Health Statistics, 2018), especially among African American male adolescents. The rate of the third-leading cause, adolescent suicide, has tripled since the 1950s. Suicide accounts for 6 percent of deaths in the 10-to-14 age group and 12 percent of deaths in the 15-to-19 age group.

Substance Use and Abuse

In the University of Michigan study, the use of drugs among U.S. secondary school students declined in the 1980s but began to increase in the early 1990s, only to later decline in the early part of the first decade of the twenty-first century. However, from 2006 through 2017, overall use of illicit drugs began increasing again, due mainly to an increase in marijuana use by adolescents. In 2006, 36.5 percent of twelfth-graders reported annual use of an illicit drug, but in 2017 that figure had increased to 39.9 percent. However, if marijuana use is subtracted from the annual use figures, there has been a significant decline in drug use by adolescents. When marijuana use is deleted, in 2006, 19.2 percent of twelfth graders used an illicit drug annually, but that figure showed a significant decline to 13.3 percent in 2017 (Johnston & others, 2018). Marijuana is the most widely used illicit drug by adolescents.

The United States continues to have one of the highest rates of adolescent drug use of any industrialized nation. Because of the increased legalization of marijuana use for adults in a number of states, youth are likely to have easier access to the drug and usage rates among adolescents are expected to increase in the future.

In the twenty-first century, alcohol and cigarette use have decreased in U.S. adolescents (Johnston & others, 2018). However, a substantial number of U.S. adolescents are vaping. In the 2017 national study just described, 19 percent of twelfth-graders, 16 percent of tenth-graders, and 8 percent of eighth-graders vaped nicotine.

A special concern involves adolescents who begin to use drugs early in adolescence or even in childhood. A longitudinal study of individuals from 8 to 42 years of age found that early onset of drinking was linked to increased risk of heavy drinking in middle age (Pitkänen, Lyrra, & Pulkkinen, 2005). Another study revealed that the onset of alcohol use before age 11 was linked to a higher risk for alcohol dependence in early adulthood (Guttmannova & others, 2012). Further, a longitudinal study found that earlier age at first use of alcohol was linked to risk of heavy alcohol use in early adulthood (Liang & Chikritzhs, 2015). And another study indicated that early- and rapid-onset trajectories of alcohol, marijuana, and substance use were associated with substance abuse in early adulthood (Nelson, Van Ryzin, & Dishion, 2015).

Parents play an important role in preventing adolescent drug abuse (Chan & others, 2017; Cruz & others, 2018; Estrada & others, 2017; Eun & others, 2018; Garcia-Huidobro & others, 2018). Researchers have found that parental monitoring is linked with a lower incidence of problem behavior by adolescents, including substance abuse (Wang & others, 2014). In a recent meta-analysis of parenting factors involved in adolescent alcohol use, higher levels of parental monitoring, support, and involvement were associated with a lower risk of adolescent alcohol misuse (Yap & others, 2017). Further, a research review found that when adolescents ate dinner more often with their families they were less likely to have problems such as substance abuse (Sen, 2010). And research revealed that authoritative parenting was linked to lower rates of adolescent alcohol consumption (Piko & Balazs, 2012), while parent-adolescent conflict was related to higher levels of adolescent alcohol use (Chaplin & others, 2012).

How Would You...?

As a **human development and family studies professional,** how would you explain to parents the importance of parental monitoring in preventing adolescent substance abuse?

Along with parents, peers play a very important role in adolescent substance use (Strong & others, 2017). When adolescents' peers and friends use drugs, the adolescents are more likely to also use drugs (Cambron & others, 2018). A large-scale national study of adolescents indicated that friends' use of alcohol was a stronger influence on alcohol use than parental use (Deutsch, Wood, & Slutske, 2018).

Educational success is also a strong buffer against the emergence of drug problems in adolescence (Kendler & others, 2018). In one study, early educational achievement considerably reduced the likelihood that adolescents would develop drug problems, including alcohol abuse, smoking, and abuse of various illicit drugs (Bachman & others, 2008).

Eating Disorders

Earlier in the chapter under the topic of nutrition and exercise, we described the increasing numbers of adolescents who are overweight. Let's now examine two different eating problems—anorexia nervosa and bulimia nervosa—that are far more common in adolescent girls than boys.

Anorexia Nervosa

Although most U.S. girls have been on a diet at some point, slightly less than 1 percent ever develop anorexia nervosa. **Anorexia nervosa** is an eating disorder that involves the relentless pursuit of thinness through starvation. It is a serious disorder that can lead to death (Brockmeyer & others, 2018; Pinhas & others, 2017). According to the psychiatric classification system, DSM-5, individuals have anorexia nervosa when there is: 1) a restriction in energy intake leading to significantly low body weight; 2) a presence of intense fear of gaining weight or becoming fat or a persistent behavior that interferes with gaining weight; and 3) a disturbance in how body weight or shape is experienced or lack of recognition of how serious the current low weight is. Obsessive thinking about

anorexia nervosa An eating disorder that involves the relentless pursuit of thinness through starvation.

weight and compulsive exercise also are linked to anorexia nervosa (Smith, Mason, & Lavender, 2018). Even when they are extremely thin, individuals with this eating disorder see themselves as too fat (Cornelissen & others, 2015). They never think they are thin enough, especially in the abdomen, buttocks, and thighs. They usually weigh themselves frequently, often take their body measurements, and gaze critically at themselves in mirrors.

Anorexia nervosa typically begins in the early to middle adolescent years, often following an episode of dieting and some type of life stress (Fitzpatrick, 2012). It is about 10 times more likely to occur in females than males. When anorexia nervosa does occur in males, the symptoms and other characteristics (such as a distorted body image and family conflict) are usually similar to those reported by females who have the disorder (Ariceli & others, 2005).

Although anorexia nervosa can be present in individuals from any ethnic group, most individuals with anorexia are non-Latina White adolescent or young adult females from well-educated, middle- and upper-income families and are competitive and high-achieving (Darcy, 2012). Individuals with anorexia nervosa often set high standards, become stressed about not being able to reach these standards, and are intensely concerned about how others perceive them (Murray & others, 2017; Stice & others, 2017). Unable to meet these high expectations, they turn to something they can control—their weight. Offspring of mothers with anorexia nervosa are at risk for becoming anorexic themselves (Machado & others, 2014). Problems in family functioning are increasingly being found to be linked to the appearance of anorexia nervosa in adolescent girls (Dimitropoulos & others, 2018), and family therapy is often recommended as an effective treatment for adolescent girls with anorexia nervosa (Ganci, Pradel, & Hughes, 2018; Hail & Le Grange, 2018; Hughes & others, 2018).

Biology and culture are involved in anorexia nervosa. Genes play an important role in anorexia nervosa (Baker, Schaumberg, & Munn-Chernoff, 2017; Meyre & others, 2018; Werenga & others, 2018). Also, the physical effects of dieting may change neural networks and thus sustain the disordered pattern (Sciafe & others, 2017). The U.S. perception that thinness is fashionable likely contributes to the incidence of anorexia nervosa. The media portray thin as beautiful in their choice of fashion models, whom many adolescent girls strive to emulate (Cazzato & others, 2016). Social media also influence the pursuit of thinness. A recent study found that having an increase in Facebook friends across two years was linked to enhanced motivation to be thin (Tiggemann & Slater, 2017).

Anorexia nervosa has become an increasing problem for adolescent girls and young adult women. *What are some possible causes of anorexia nervosa?* ©Ian Thraves/Alamy

Bulimia Nervosa

Whereas people with anorexia control their eating by restricting it, most individuals with bulimia cannot. **Bulimia nervosa** is an eating disorder in which the individual consistently follows a binge-and-purge pattern, periodically overeating and then engaging in self-induced vomiting or use of laxatives. According to the DSM-5 classification system, an individual with bulimia nervosa is characterized by: 1) eating in a specific amount of time (such as within a 2-hour time frame) an amount of food that is larger than what most people would eat in a similar period in similar circumstances, and 2) a lack of control over eating during an episode. Although many people binge and purge occasionally, a person is considered to have a serious bulimic disorder if the episodes occur at least twice a week for three months (Castillo & Weiselberg, 2017).

Most people with bulimia are preoccupied with food, have a strong fear of becoming overweight, are depressed or anxious, and have a distorted body image (Murray & others, 2017; Smith, Mason, & Lavender, 2018; Stice & others, 2017). Bulimics may have difficulty controlling their emotions (Lavender & others, 2014). Unlike people who have anorexia, people who binge and purge typically fall within a normal weight range, which makes bulimia more difficult to detect.

One to 2 percent of U.S. women develop bulimia nervosa, and about 90 percent of people with bulimia are women. Bulimia nervosa typically begins in late adolescence or early

How Would You...?

As a **health-care professional,** how would you educate parents to identify the signs and symptoms that may signal an eating disorder?

bulimia nervosa An eating disorder in which the individual consistently follows a binge-and-purge pattern.

adulthood. Many women who develop bulimia nervosa were somewhat over-weight before the onset of the disorder, and the binge eating often began during an episode of dieting. About 70 percent of individuals who develop bulimia nervosa eventually recover from the disorder (Agras & others, 2004). Like anorexics, bulimics are highly perfectionistic (Lampard & others, 2012). Drug therapy and psychotherapy have been effective in treating bulimia nervosa (Agras, Fitzsimmons-Craft, & Wilfley, 2017), and cognitive behavior therapy has been especially helpful (de Abreu & Cangelli Filho, 2017; Forrest & others, 2018; Peterson & others, 2017).

hypothetical-deductive reasoning Piaget's formal operational concept that adolescents have the cognitive ability to develop hypotheses, or best guesses, about ways to solve problems.

Adolescent Cognition

Adolescents' developing power of thought opens up new cognitive and social horizons. Let's examine what their developing power of thought is like, beginning with the per-spective provided by Piaget's theory (1952).

Piaget's Theory

Piaget proposed that around 7 years of age children enter the concrete operational stage of cognitive development. They can reason logically about concrete events and objects, and they make gains in their ability to classify objects and to reason about the relationships between classes of objects. Around age 11, according to Piaget, the fourth and final stage of cognitive development—the formal operational stage—begins.

The Formal Operational Stage

Formal operational thought is more abstract than concrete operational thought. Adolescents are no longer limited to actual, concrete experiences as anchors for thought. They can con-jure up make-believe situations, abstract propositions, and events that are purely hypothetical, and can try to reason logically about them. The abstract quality of thinking during the formal operational stage is evident in the adolescent's verbal problem-solving ability. The concrete operational thinker needs to see the concrete elements A, B, and C to be able to make the logical inference that if A = B and B = C, then A = C, whereas the formal operational thinker can solve this problem merely through verbal presentation.

Another indication of the abstract quality of adolescents' thought is their increased tendency to think about thought itself. One adolescent commented, "I began thinking about why I was thinking what I was. Then I began thinking about why I was thinking about what I was think-ing about what I was." If this sounds abstract, it is, and it characterizes the adolescent's enhanced focus on thought and its abstract qualities.

Accompanying the abstract nature of for-mal operational thought is thought full of ideal-ism and possibilities, especially at the beginning of the formal operational stage. Adolescents engage in extended speculation about ideal characteristics—qualities they desire in themselves and in others. Such thoughts often lead adoles-cents to compare themselves with others in regard to such ideal standards. And their thoughts are often fantasy flights into future possibilities.

Adolescents also think more logically. Children are likely to solve problems through trial and error, while adolescents begin to think more as a scientist does, devising plans to solve problems and systematically testing solutions. This type of problem solving requires **hypothetical-deductive reasoning,** which involves creating a hypothesis and deducing its implications, which provides ways to

Might adolescents' ability to reason hypo-thetically and to evaluate what is ideal ver-sus what is real lead them to engage in demonstrations, such as this one supporting the value of public education? What other causes might be attractive to adolescents' newfound cognitive abilities of hypothetical-deductive reasoning and idealistic thinking?
©Jim West/Alamy

test the hypothesis. Thus, formal operational thinkers develop hypotheses about ways to solve problems and then systematically deduce the best path to follow to solve the problem.

Evaluating Piaget's Theory

Researchers have challenged some of Piaget's ideas regarding the formal operational stage (Reyna & Zayas, 2014). Among their findings is that there is much more individual variation than Piaget envisioned: Only about one in three young adolescents is a formal operational thinker, and many American adults never become formal operational thinkers; neither do many adults in other cultures.

Furthermore, education in the logic of science and mathematics promotes the development of formal operational thinking. This point recalls a criticism of Piaget's theory: Culture and education exert stronger influences on cognitive development than Piaget argued (Petersen & others, 2017; Wagner, 2018).

Piaget's theory of cognitive development has been challenged on other points as well (Kuhn, 2013; Reyna, 2018; Romer, Reyna, & Satterthwaite, 2017). Piaget conceived of stages as unitary structures of thought, with various aspects of a stage emerging at the same time. However, most contemporary developmentalists agree that cognitive development is not as stage-like as Piaget thought (Braithwaite & Siegler, 2018; Wu & Scerif, 2018). Furthermore, children can be trained to reason at a higher cognitive stage, and some cognitive abilities emerge earlier than Piaget thought (Johnson & Hannon, 2015). For instance, some understanding of the conservation of number has been demonstrated as early as age 3, although Piaget did not think it emerged until age 7. Other cognitive abilities can emerge later than Piaget thought (Kuhn, 2013).

Despite these challenges to Piaget's ideas, we owe him a tremendous debt (Miller, 2011). Piaget was the founder of the present field of cognitive development, and he developed a long list of masterful concepts of enduring power and fascination: assimilation, accommodation, object permanence, egocentrism, conservation, and others. Psychologists also owe him the current vision of children as active, constructive thinkers. And they are indebted to him for creating a theory that has generated a huge volume of research on children's cognitive development.

Piaget was a genius when it came to observing children. His careful observations demonstrated inventive ways to discover how children act on, and adapt to, their world. Children need to make their experiences fit their schemes yet simultaneously adapt their schemes to reflect their experience. Piaget revealed how cognitive change is likely to occur if the context is structured to allow gradual movement to the next higher level. Concepts do not emerge suddenly, full-blown, but instead develop through a series of partial accomplishments that lead to increasingly comprehensive understanding (Sloutsky, 2015).

Adolescent Egocentrism

Adolescent egocentrism is the heightened self-consciousness of adolescents. David Elkind (1976) maintains that adolescent egocentrism has two key components—the imaginary audience and personal fable. The **imaginary audience** is adolescents' belief that others are as interested in them as they themselves are, as well as attention-getting behavior—attempts to be noticed, visible, and "on stage." For example, an eighth-grade boy might walk into the classroom thinking that all eyes are riveted on his spotty complexion. Adolescents sense that they are "on stage" in early adolescence, believing they are the main actors and all others are the audience.

The **personal fable** is the part of adolescent egocentrism involving a sense of uniqueness and invincibility (or invulnerability). For example, a

Many adolescent girls spend long hours in front of the mirror, depleting cans of hairspray, tubes of lipstick, and jars of cosmetics. *How might this behavior be related to changes in adolescent cognitive and physical development?*
©Image Source/Jupiter Images

13-year-old says about herself: "No one understands me, particularly my parents. They have no idea of what I am feeling." Adolescents' sense of personal uniqueness makes them believe that no one can understand how they really feel. As part of their effort to retain a sense of personal uniqueness, they might craft a story about the self that is filled with fantasy in a world that is far removed from reality. Personal fables frequently show up in adolescent diaries.

Adolescents also often show a sense of invincibility or invulnerability. For example, during a conversation with another girl, 14-year-old Margaret says, "Are you kidding? I won't get pregnant." This sense of invincibility may lead adolescents to believe that they are invulnerable to dangers and catastrophes (such as deadly car wrecks) that happen to other people. As a result, some adolescents engage in risky behaviors such as drag racing, drug use, and having sexual intercourse without using contraceptives or barriers against STIs (Alberts, Elkind, & Ginsberg, 2007). However, some research studies suggest that rather than perceiving themselves to be invulnerable, adolescents tend to portray themselves as vulnerable to experiencing a premature death (Fischhoff & others, 2010; Reyna & Rivers, 2008).

Might social media such as Facebook serve as an amplification tool for adolescent egocentrism? One study found that Facebook usage does indeed increase self-interest (Chiou, Chen, & Liao, 2014). A recent meta-analysis concluded that a greater use of social networking sites was linked to a higher level of narcissism (Gnambs & Appel, 2018).

Information Processing

Deanna Kuhn (2009) discussed some important characteristics of adolescents' information processing and thinking. In her view, in the later years of childhood and continuing in adolescence, individuals approach cognitive levels that may or may not be achieved, in contrast with the largely universal cognitive levels that young children attain. By adolescence, considerable variation in cognitive functioning is present across individuals. This variability supports the argument that adolescents are producers of their own development to a greater extent than are children. That is, adolescents are more likely than children to initiate changes in thinking rather than depend on others, such as parents and teachers, to direct their thinking.

Executive Function

Kuhn (2009) argues that the most important cognitive change in adolescence is improvement in *executive function,* an umbrella-like concept that consists of a number of higher-level cognitive processes linked to the development of the prefrontal cortex (Bernstein & Waber, 2018; Crone, Peters, & Steinbeis, 2018; Gerst & others, 2017). Executive function involves managing one's thoughts to engage in goal-directed behavior and to exercise self-control (Bardikoff & Sabbagh, 2017; Knapp & Morton, 2017; Meltzer, 2018; Wiebe & Karbach, 2018). Our further coverage of executive function in adolescence focuses on cognitive control and decision making.

Cognitive Control Cognitive control involves effective control in a number of areas, including controlling attention, reducing interfering thoughts, and being cognitively flexible (Breiner & others, 2018; Stewart & others, 2017). Cognitive control continues to increase in adolescence and emerging adulthood (Chevalier, Dauvier, & Blaye, 2018; Romer, Reyna, & Satterthwaite, 2017). Think about all the times adolescents need to engage in cognitive control, such as the following situations (Galinsky, 2010):

- making a real effort to stick with a task, avoiding interfering thoughts or environmental events, and instead doing what is most effective;
- stopping and thinking before acting to avoid blurting out something that a minute or two later they will wish they hadn't said;
- continuing to work on something that is important but boring when there is something a lot more fun to do, inhibiting their behavior and doing the boring but important task, saying to themselves, "I have to show the self-discipline to finish this."

Controlling attention is a key aspect of learning and thinking in adolescence and emerging adulthood (Lau & Waters, 2017; Mueller & others, 2017; Wu & Scerif, 2018). Distractions that can interfere with attention come from the external environment (such as other students talking while the student is trying to listen to a lecture, or the student turning on a laptop or phone during a lecture to look at Facebook, for example) or intrusive distractions from competing thoughts in the individual's mind. Self-oriented thoughts, such as worrying, self-doubt, and intense emotionally laden thoughts may interfere with focusing attention on thinking tasks (Walsh, 2011).

Decision Making Adolescence is a time of increased decision making—which friends to choose; which person to date; whether to have sex, buy a car, go to college, and so on (Helm, McCormick, & Reyna, 2018; Helm & Reyna, 2018; Meschkow & others, 2018; Reyna, 2018; Reyna & others, 2018; Steinberg & others, 2018). How competent are adolescents at making decisions? Older adolescents are described as more competent than younger adolescents, who in turn are more competent than children (Keating, 1990). Compared with children, young adolescents are more likely to generate different options, examine a situation from a variety of perspectives, anticipate the consequences of decisions, and consider the credibility of sources. In risky situations it is important for an adolescent to quickly get the *gist,* or meaning, of what is happening and glean that the situation is a dangerous context, which can cue personal values that will protect the adolescent from making a risky decision (Reyna & Zayas, 2014).

How do emotions and social contexts influence adolescents' decision making?
©JodiJacobson/Getty Images

Most people make better decisions when they are calm than when they are emotionally aroused (Crone & Konijn, 2018). That may especially be true for adolescents, who have a tendency to be emotionally intense. The same adolescent who makes a wise decision when calm may make an unwise decision when emotionally aroused (Steinberg & others, 2018).

How Would You...?

As an **educator,** how would you incorporate decision-making exercises into the school curriculum for adolescents?

The social context plays a key role in adolescent decision making (Breiner & others, 2018; Sherman, Steinberg, & Chein, 2018; Silva & others, 2017; Steinberg & others, 2018). Adolescents' willingness to make risky decisions is more likely to occur in contexts where substances and other temptations are readily available (Reyna & Zayas, 2014). And the presence of peers in risk-taking situations increases the likelihood that adolescents will make risky decisions (Albert & Steinberg, 2011a, b). In a recent study, adolescents took greater risks and showed stronger preference for immediate rewards when they were with three same-aged peers than when they were alone (Silva, Chein, & Steinberg, 2016).

Adolescents need more opportunities to practice and discuss realistic decision making. Many real-world decisions on matters such as sex, drugs, and daredevil driving occur in an atmosphere of stress that includes time constraints and emotional involvement. One strategy for improving adolescent decision making is to provide more opportunities for them to engage in role playing and peer-group problem solving.

Schools

Our discussion of adolescents' schooling will focus on the transition from elementary to middle or junior high school, the characteristics of effective schools for adolescents, aspects of high school life that interfere with learning, and how adolescents can benefit from engaging in service learning.

The Transition to Middle or Junior High School

The first year of middle school or junior high school can be difficult for many students (Madjar, Cohen, & Shoval, 2018; Wigfield & others, 2015). In one study of the transition from sixth grade in an elementary school to seventh grade in a junior high school, adolescents' perceptions of the quality of their school life plunged in the seventh grade (Hirsch & Rapkin, 1987). Compared with their earlier feelings as sixth-graders, the seventh-graders were less satisfied with school, were less committed to school, and liked their teachers less. This occurred regardless of how academically successful the students were. Further, a recent study found that teacher warmth was higher in the last four years of elementary school and then dropped in the middle school years (Hughes & Cao, 2018). The drop in teacher warmth was associated with lower student math scores.

The transition to middle or junior high school takes place at a time when many changes—in the individual, the family, school—are occurring simultaneously (Wigfield, Rosenzweig, & Eccles, 2017; Wigfield, Tonks, & Klauda, 2016). These changes include puberty and concerns about body image; the emergence of at least some aspects of formal operational thought, including changes in social cognition; increased responsibility and decreased dependency on parents; change to a larger, more impersonal school structure; change from one teacher to many teachers and from a small, homogeneous set of peers to a larger, more heterogeneous set; and an increased focus on achievement and performance. Moreover, when students make the transition to middle or junior high school, they experience the **top-dog phenomenon,** moving from being the oldest, biggest, and most powerful students in the elementary school to being the youngest, smallest, and least powerful students.

The transition from elementary to middle or junior high school occurs at the same time as a number of other developmental changes. What are some of these other developmental changes? ©Will & Deni McIntyre/Corbis/Getty Images

How Would You...?

As an **educator,** how would you design school programs to enhance students' smooth transition into middle school?

There can also be positive aspects to this transition. Students are more likely to feel grown up, have more subjects from which to select, feel more challenged intellectually by academic work, have more opportunities to spend time with peers and locate compatible friends, and enjoy increased independence from direct parental monitoring.

Effective Schools for Young Adolescents

There are continuing calls for improving middle school education (Rajan & others, 2017). Educators and psychologists worry that junior high and middle schools have become watered-down versions of high schools, mimicking their curricular and extracurricular schedules. Critics argue that these schools should offer activities that reflect a wide range of individual differences in biological and psychological development among young adolescents. Expressing these concerns, the Carnegie Council on Adolescent Development (1989) issued an extremely negative evaluation of U.S. middle schools. It concluded that most young adolescents attended massive, impersonal schools; were taught from irrelevant curricula; trusted few adults in school; and lacked access to health care and counseling. It recommended that the nation develop smaller "communities" or "houses" to lessen the impersonal nature of large middle schools, maintain lower student-to-counselor ratios (10 to 1 instead of several hundred to 1), involve parents and community leaders in schools, develop new curricula, have teachers team teach in more flexibly designed curriculum blocks that integrate several disciplines, boost students' health and fitness with more in-school programs, and help students who need public health care to get it. Almost three decades later, experts were still finding that middle schools throughout the nation would require a major redesign to become effective in educating adolescents (Roeser, 2016; Wigfield & others, 2015).

top-dog phenomenon The circumstance of moving from the top position in elementary school to the lowest position in middle or junior high school.

High School

Just as there are concerns about U.S. middle school education, so are there concerns about U.S. high school education (Eccles & Roeser, 2015; Kitsantas & Cleary, 2016). A recent analysis indicated that only 25 percent of U.S. high school graduates have the academic skills to succeed in college (Bill & Melinda Gates Foundation, 2017). Not only are many high school graduates poorly prepared for college, they also are poorly prepared for the demands of the modern, high-performance workplace (Bill & Melinda Gates Foundation, 2018).

Critics stress that many high schools have low expectations for success and inadequate standards for learning. Critics also argue that too often high schools foster passivity instead of creating a variety of pathways for students to achieve an identity. Many students graduate from high school with inadequate reading, writing, and mathematical skills—including many who go on to college and must enroll in remediation classes to complete their coursework. Other students drop out of high school and do not have skills that will allow them to obtain decent jobs, much less to be informed citizens.

The transition to high school can have problems, just as the transition to middle school can. These problems may include the following (Benner, Boyle, & Bakhtiari, 2017; Eccles & Roeser, 2015; Wigfield, Rosenzweig, & Eccles, 2017): high schools are often even larger, more bureaucratic, and more impersonal than middle schools are; there isn't much opportunity for students and teachers to get to know each other, which can lead to distrust; and teachers too infrequently make content relevant to students' interests. Such experiences likely undermine the motivation of students.

Robert Crosnoe's (2011) book, *Fitting In, Standing Out,* highlighted another major problem with U.S. high schools: how the negative social aspects of adolescents' lives undermine their academic achievement. Adolescents become immersed in complex peer group cultures that demand conformity. High school is supposed to be about getting an education, but in reality for many youth it is more about navigating the social worlds of peer relations that may or may not value education and academic achievement. Adolescents who fail to fit in, especially those who are obese or gay, become stigmatized. Crosnoe recommends increased school counseling services, expanded extracurricular activities, and improved parental monitoring to reduce such problems. One study revealed that immigrant adolescents who participated in extracurricular activities improved their academic achievement and increased their school engagement (Camacho & Fuligni, 2015).

Yet another concern about U.S. high schools involves students dropping out of school (Bill & Melinda Gates Foundation, 2018). In the last half of the twentieth century and the first decade of the twenty-first century, U.S. high school dropout rates declined (National Center for Education Statistics, 2017). In the 1940s, more than half of U.S. 16- to 24-year-olds had dropped out of school; by 2015, this figure had decreased to 5.9 percent. The dropout rate of Latino adolescents remains high, although it has been decreasing considerably in the twenty-first century (from 27.8 percent in 2000 to 9.2 percent in 2016). The lowest dropout rate in 2015 was for Asian American adolescents (2.1 percent), followed by non-Latino White adolescents (4.6 percent), African American adolescents (6.5 percent), and Latino adolescents (9.2 percent) (National Center for Education Statistics, 2017). Gender differences in U.S. school dropout rates have been narrowing, but males were still slightly more likely to drop out than females in 2015 (6.3 percent versus 5.4 percent) (National Center for Education Statistics, 2017).

Students at the Ahfachkee School located on the Seminole Tribe's Big Cypress Reservation in Florida. An important education goal is to increase the high school graduation rate of Native American adolescents.
©J.Albert Diaz/Miami Herald/MCT/Getty Images

National data on Native American adolescents are inadequate because statistics have been collected sporadically and/or from small samples. However, there are some indications that this group may have the highest dropout rate. Also, the average U.S. high school

service learning A form of education that promotes social responsibility and service to the community.

dropout rates mask some very high dropout rates in low-income areas of inner cities. For example, in Detroit, Cleveland, and Chicago, dropout rates are higher than 50 percent. Also, the percentages cited earlier are for 16- to 24-year-olds. When dropout rates are calculated in terms of students who do not graduate from high school within four years, the percentages are much higher. Thus, in considering high school dropout rates, it is important to examine age, the number of years it takes to complete high school, and various contexts including ethnicity, gender, and location.

Students drop out of school for many reasons (Dupere & others, 2015; Schoeneberger, 2012). In one study, almost 50 percent of the dropouts cited school-related reasons for leaving school, such as not liking school or being expelled or suspended (Rumberger, 1983). Twenty percent of the dropouts (but 40 percent of the Latino students) cited economic reasons for leaving school. One-third of the female students dropped out for personal reasons such as pregnancy or marriage.

According to a research review, the most effective programs to discourage dropping out of high school provide early reading support, tutoring, counseling, and mentoring (Lehr & others, 2003). Clearly, then, early detection of children's school-related difficulties and getting children engaged with school in positive ways are important strategies for reducing the dropout rate (Bill & Melinda Gates Foundation, 2018; Crosnoe, Bonazzo, & Wu, 2015).

Service Learning

Service learning is a form of education that promotes social responsibility and service to the community. Adolescents engage in activities such as tutoring, helping older adults, working in a hospital, assisting at a child-care center, or cleaning up a vacant lot to make it into a play area. An important goal of service learning is to encourage adolescents to become less self-centered and more strongly motivated to help others (Hart & Van Goethem, 2017). Service learning is often more effective when two conditions are met (Nucci, 2006): (1) giving students some degree of choice in the service activities in which they participate, and (2) providing students with opportunities to reflect about their participation.

A key feature of service learning is that it benefits not only adolescents but also the recipients of their help. One eleventh-grade student worked as a reading tutor for students from low-income backgrounds with reading skills well below their grade levels. Until she did the tutoring, she had not realized how many students had not experienced the same opportunities that she had when she was growing up. An especially rewarding moment was when one young girl told her, "I want to learn to read like you so I can go to college when I grow up."

What are some of the positive effects of service learning?
©Ariel Skelley/Blend Images/Getty Images

How Would You...?

As an **educator,** how would you devise a program to increase adolescents' motivation to participate in service learning?

Researchers have found that service learning also benefits adolescent development in other ways, including higher grades in school, increased goal setting, higher self-esteem, an improved sense of being able to make a difference for others, and an increased likelihood that the adolescents will serve as volunteers in the future (Hart, Goel, & Atkins, 2017; Hart & van Goethem, 2017; Hart & others, 2017). One study found that adolescent girls participated in service learning more than did adolescent boys (Webster & Worrell, 2008).

Summary

The Nature of Adolescence

- Many stereotypes of adolescents are too negative. Most adolescents today successfully negotiate the path from childhood to adulthood. However, too many of today's adolescents are not provided with adequate

opportunities and support to become competent adults. It is important to view adolescents as a heterogeneous group because different portraits of adolescents emerge, depending on the particular set of adolescents being described.

Physical Changes

- Puberty's determinants include nutrition, health, and heredity. Hormonal changes occurring in puberty are substantial. Puberty occurs approximately two years earlier for girls than for boys. Individual variation in pubertal changes is substantial. Adolescents show considerable interest in their body image, with girls having more negative body images than boys. Early-maturing girls are vulnerable to a number of risks.
- Changes in the brain during adolescence involve the thickening of the corpus callosum and a gap in maturation between the limbic system, which is the seat of emotions, and the prefrontal cortex, which functions in reasoning and self-regulation.
- Adolescence is a time of sexual exploration and sexual experimentation. About one in four sexually experienced adolescents acquires a sexually transmitted infection (STI). America's adolescent pregnancy rate has declined since the 1990s but is still higher than that of other industrialized nations.

Adolescent Health

- Adolescence is a critical juncture in health. Poor nutrition and lack of exercise are special concerns.
- Many adolescents stay up later than when they were children and are getting less sleep than they need.
- Accidents are the leading cause of death in adolescence.
- Although drug use in adolescence has declined in recent years, it still is a major concern.

- Eating disorders have increased in adolescence, with a substantial increase in the percentage of adolescents who are overweight. Two eating disorders that may emerge in adolescence are anorexia nervosa and bulimia nervosa.

Adolescent Cognition

- In Piaget's formal operational stage, thought is more abstract, idealistic, and logical than during the concrete operational stage. However, many adolescents are not formal operational thinkers.
- Adolescent egocentrism, which involves a heightened self-consciousness, reflects another cognitive change in adolescence in addition to Piaget's description of three cognitive stages.
- Changes in information processing in adolescence are mainly reflected in improved executive function, which includes advances in cognitive control and decision making.

Schools

- The transition to middle or junior high school is often stressful. One source of stress is the move from the top-dog to the lowest position in school.
- Some critics argue that a major redesign of U.S. middle schools is needed.
- The overall U.S. high school dropout rate declined considerably in the last half of the twentieth century, but the dropout rates for Native American and Latino adolescents remain very high.
- Service learning is linked to a number of positive benefits for adolescents.

Key Terms

adolescent egocentrism	gonads	imaginary audience	puberty
amygdala	hormones	limbic system	service learning
anorexia nervosa	hypothalamus	menarche	sexually transmitted infections
bulimia nervosa	hypothetical-deductive	personal fable	(STIs)
corpus callosum	reasoning	pituitary gland	top-dog phenomenon

10 Socioemotional Development in Adolescence

©Huntstock, Inc./Alamy

CHAPTER OUTLINE

IDENTITY
What Is Identity?
Erikson's View
Developmental Changes
Ethnic Identity

FAMILIES
Parental Management and Monitoring
Autonomy and Attachment
Parent-Adolescent Conflict

PEERS
Friendships
Peer Groups
Dating and Romantic Relationships

CULTURE AND ADOLESCENT DEVELOPMENT
Cross-Cultural Comparisons
Socioeconomic Status and Poverty

Ethnicity
Media and Screen Time

ADOLESCENT PROBLEMS
Juvenile Delinquency
Depression and Suicide
The Interrelation of Problems and Successful Prevention/Intervention Programs

Stories of Life-Span Development: Jewel Cash, Teen Dynamo

The mayor of the city says she is "everywhere." She persuaded the city's school committee to consider ending the practice of locking tardy students out of their classrooms. She also swayed a neighborhood group to support her proposal for a winter jobs program. According to one city council-man, "People are just impressed with the power of her arguments and the sophistication of the argument" (Silva, 2005, pp. B1, B4). She is Jewel E. Cash, and she did all these things while she was a teenager attending the prestigious Boston Latin Academy.

Jewel was raised in one of Boston's housing projects by her mother, a single parent. During high school she was a member of the Boston Student Advisory Council, mentored children, volunteered at a women's shelter, managed and danced in two troupes, and participated in a neighborhood watch group—among other activities. Jewel is far from typical, but her activities illustrate that cognitive and socioemotional development allows

Jewel Cash, seated next to her mother, participates in a crime watch meeting at a community center.
©Matthew J. Lee/The Boston Globe/Getty Images

adolescents—even those from disadvantaged backgrounds—to be capable, effective individuals. As an adult, Jewel works with a public consulting group and has continued helping others as a mentor and community organizer.

Significant changes characterize socioemotional development in adolescence. These changes include searching for identity. Changes also take place in the social contexts of adolescents' lives, with transformations occurring in relationships with families and peers in cultural contexts. Adolescents also may develop socioemotional problems such as delinquency and depression. ■

Identity

Jewel Cash told an interviewer from the *Boston Globe,* "I see a problem and I say, 'How can I make a difference?'. . . I can't take on the world, even though I can try. . . . I'm moving forward but I want to make sure I'm bringing people with me" (Silva, 2005, pp. B1, B4). Jewel's confidence and positive identity sound at least as impressive as her activities. This section examines how adolescents develop characteristics like these. How well did you understand yourself during adolescence, and how did you acquire the stamp of your identity? Is your identity still developing?

What Is Identity?

Questions about identity surface as common, virtually universal, concerns during adolescence. Some decisions made during adolescence might seem trivial: whom to date, whether or not to break up, which major to study, whether to study or play, whether or not to be politically active, and so on. Over the years of adolescence and emerging adulthood, however, such decisions begin to form the core of what the individual is all about as a human being—what is called his or her identity.

When identity has been conceptualized and researched, it typically is explored in a broad sense. However, identity is a self-portrait that is composed of many pieces and domains:

- The career and work path the person wants to follow (vocational/career identity)
- Whether the person is conservative, liberal, or middle-of-the-road (political identity)
- The person's spiritual beliefs (religious identity)
- Whether the person is single, married, divorced, and so on (relationship identity)
- The extent to which the person is motivated to achieve and is intellectually oriented (achievement, intellectual identity)
- Whether the person is heterosexual, homosexual, bisexual, or transgendered (sexual identity)
- Which part of the world or country a person is from and how intensely the person identifies with his or her cultural heritage (cultural/ethnic identity)
- The kinds of things a person likes to do, which can include sports, music, hobbies, and so on (interests)
- The individual's personality characteristics, such as being introverted or extraverted, anxious or calm, friendly or hostile, and so on (personality)
- The individual's body image (physical identity)

What are some important dimensions of identity?
©JGI/Jamie Grill/Getty Images

Currently, too little research attention has been given to developmental changes in specific domains of identity (Galliher, McLean, & Syed, 2017; Negru-Subtirica & Pop, 2018; Vosylis, Erentaite, & Crocetti, 2018).

Synthesizing the identity components can be a long-drawn-out process, with many negations and affirmations of various roles and faces (Meeus, 2017; Reece & others, 2017). Identity development takes place in bits and pieces. Decisions are not made once and for all, but have to be made again and again. Identity development does not happen neatly, and it does not happen cataclysmically (Adler & others, 2017; Hatano, Sugimura, & Schwartz, 2018; van Doeselaar & others, 2018).

Erikson's View

It was Erik Erikson (1950, 1968) who first understood that questions about identity are central to understanding adolescent development. Today, as a result of Erikson's masterful thinking and analysis, identity is considered a key aspect of adolescent development.

Recall that in Erikson's theory, his fifth developmental stage, which individuals experience during adolescence, is *identity versus identity confusion*. During this time, said Erikson, adolescents are faced with deciding who they are, what they are all about, and where they are going in life.

The search for an identity during adolescence is aided by a *psychosocial moratorium,* which is Erikson's term for the gap between childhood security and adult autonomy. During this period, society leaves adolescents relatively free of responsibilities and able to try out different identities. Adolescents in effect search their culture's identity files, experimenting with different roles and personalities. They may want to pursue one career one month (lawyer, for example) and another career the next month (doctor, actor, teacher, social worker, or astronaut, for example). They may dress neatly one day, sloppily the next. This experimentation is a deliberate effort on the part of adolescents to find out where they fit into the world. Most adolescents eventually discard undesirable roles.

Developmental Changes

Although questions about identity may be especially important during adolescence and emerging adulthood, identity formation neither begins nor ends during these years. It begins with the appearance of attachment, the development of the sense of self, and the emergence of independence in infancy; the process reaches its final phase with a life review and integration in old age. What is important about identity development in late adolescence and emerging adulthood is that for the first time, physical development, cognitive development, and socioemotional development advance to the point at which the individual can begin to sort through and synthesize childhood identities and identifications to construct a viable path toward adult maturity.

How do individual adolescents go about the process of forming an identity? Eriksonian researcher James Marcia (1980, 1994) believes that Erikson's theory of identity development encompasses four *statuses* of identity, or ways of resolving the identity crisis: identity diffusion, identity foreclosure, identity moratorium, and identity achievement. What determines an individual's identity status? Marcia classifies individuals based on the existence or extent of their crisis or commitment (see Figure 1). **Crisis** is defined as a period of identity development during which the individual is exploring alternatives. Most researchers use the term *exploration* rather than crisis. **Commitment** is personal investment in identity.

The four statuses of identity are described as follows:

- **Identity diffusion** is the status of individuals who have not yet experienced a crisis or made any commitments. Not only are they undecided about occupational and ideological choices, they are also likely to show little interest in such matters.

- **Identity foreclosure** is the status of individuals who have made a commitment but have not experienced a crisis. This occurs most often when parents hand down commitments to their adolescents, usually in an authoritarian way, before adolescents have had a chance to explore different approaches, ideologies, and vocations on their own.

crisis Marcia's term for a period of identity development during which the adolescent is exploring alternatives.

commitment Marcia's term for the part of identity development in which adolescents show a personal investment in forming an identity.

identity diffusion Marcia's term for adolescents who have not yet experienced a crisis (explored meaningful alternatives) or made any commitments.

identity foreclosure Marcia's term for adolescents who have made a commitment but have not experienced a crisis.

Position on Occupation and Ideology	Identity Status			
	Identity Diffusion	Identity Foreclosure	Identity Moratorium	Identity Achievement
Crisis	Absent	Absent	Present	Present
Commitment	Absent	Present	Absent	Present

Figure 1 Marcia's Four Statuses of Identity
According to Marcia, an individual's status in developing an identity can be described as identity diffusion, identity foreclosure, identity moratorium, or identity achievement. The status depends on the presence or absence of (1) a crisis or exploration of alternatives and (2) a commitment to an identity. *What is the identity status of most young adolescents?*

- **Identity moratorium** is the status of individuals who are in the midst of a crisis but whose commitments are either absent or are only vaguely defined.

- **Identity achievement** is the status of individuals who have undergone a crisis and have made a commitment.

Some critics argue that the identity status approach does not produce enough depth in understanding identity development (Landberg, Dimitrova, & Syed, 2018; Meeus, 2017; Syed, Juang, & Svensson, 2018; Vosylis, Erentaite, & Crocetti, 2018). The newer *dual cycle identity model* separates identity development into two processes: (1) a formation cycle that relies on exploration in breadth and identification with commitment; and (2) A maintenance cycle that involves exploration in depth as well as reconsideration of commitments (Luyckz & others, 2014, 2017).

One way that researchers are now examining identity changes in depth is to use a *narrative approach*. This involves asking individuals to tell their life stories and evaluate the extent to which their stories are meaningful and integrated (Maher, Winston, & Ur, 2017; McLean & others, 2018; Sauchelli, 2018; Svensson, Berne, & Syed, 2018). The term *narrative identity* "refers to the stories people construct and tell about themselves to define who they are for themselves and others. Beginning in adolescence and young adulthood, our narrative identities are the stories we live by" (McAdams, Josselson, & Lieblich, 2006, p. 4).

A recent study used both identity status and narrative approaches to examine college students' identity domains. In both approaches, the interpersonal domain was most frequently described (McLean & others, 2016). In the interpersonal domain, dating and friendships were frequently mentioned, although there was no mention of gender roles. In the narrative domain, family stories were common.

Researchers are developing a consensus that the key changes in identity are most likely to take place in emerging adulthood, the period from about 18 to 25 years of age (Landberg, Dimitrova, & Syed, 2018; Layland, Hill, & Nelson, 2018). For example, from the years preceding high school through the last few years of college, the number of individuals who are identity achieved increases, whereas the number of individuals who are identity diffused decreases (Waterman, 1985, 1992). Many young adolescents are identity diffused. College upperclassmen are more likely than high school students or college freshmen to be identity achieved.

Why might college produce some key changes in identity? Increased complexity in the reasoning skills of college students combined with a wide range of new experiences that highlight contrasts between home and college and between themselves and others stimulate them to reach a higher level of integrating various dimensions of their identity. College contexts serve as a virtual "laboratory" for identity development through such experiences as diverse coursework and exposure to peers from diverse backgrounds. Also, one of emerging adulthood's key themes is not having many social commitments, which gives individuals considerable independence in developing a life path (Arnett, 2015).

How Would You…?

As a **psychologist,** how would you apply Marcia's theory of identity formation to describe your current identity status or that of adolescents you know?

identity moratorium Marcia's term for adolescents who are in the midst of a crisis, but their commitments are either absent or vaguely defined.

identity achievement Marcia's term for adolescents who have undergone a crisis and have made a commitment.

Resolution of the identity issue during adolescence and emerging adulthood does not mean that identity will be stable through the remainder of life (McLean & others, 2018). Many individuals who develop positive identities follow what are called "MAMA" cycles; that is, their identity status changes from *moratorium* to *achievement* to *moratorium* to *achievement* (Marcia, 1994). These cycles may be repeated throughout life (Francis, Fraser, & Marcia, 1989). Marcia (2002) points out that the first identity is just that—it is not, and should not be regarded as, the final product.

Researchers have explored how parents and peers might influence an adolescent's identity development (Quimby & others, 2018; Rivas-Drake & Umana-Taylor, 2018). Parents are important figures in the adolescent's development of identity (Cooper, 2011; Crocetti & others, 2017). In a meta-analysis, securely attached adolescents were far more likely to be identity achieved than their counterparts who were identity diffused or identity foreclosed (Arseth & others, 2009). Recent longitudinal studies also have documented that the ethnic identity of adolescents is influenced by positive and diverse friendships (Rivas-Drake & others, 2017; Santos & others, 2017).

For today's adolescents and emerging adults, the contexts involving the digital world, especially social media platforms such as Instagram, Snapchat, and Facebook, have introduced new ways for youth to express and explore their identity (Davis & Weinstein, 2017). Adolescents and emerging adults often cast themselves as positively as they can on their digital devices—posting their most attractive photos and describing themselves in idealistic ways, continually editing and reworking their online self-portraits to enhance them (Yau & Reich, 2018). Adolescents' and emerging adults' online world provides extensive opportunities for both expressing their identity and getting feedback about it. Of course, such feedback is not always positive, just as in their offline world.

Ethnic Identity

Throughout the world, ethnic minority groups have struggled to maintain their ethnic identities while blending in with the dominant culture (Erikson, 1968). **Ethnic identity** is an enduring aspect of the self that includes a sense of membership in an ethnic group, along with the attitudes and feelings related to that membership (Adams & others, 2018; Polenova & others, 2018; White & others, 2018; Yoon & others, 2017). Most adolescents from ethnic minorities develop a *bicultural identity*. That is, they identify in some ways with their ethnic group and in other ways with the majority culture (Abu-Rayya & others, 2018; Douglass & Umana-Taylor, 2017; Meeus, 2017).

For ethnic minority individuals, adolescence and emerging adulthood are often special junctures in their development (Butler-Barnes & others, 2018; Cheon & others, 2018; Espinosa & others, 2017). Although children are aware of some ethnic and cultural differences, individuals consciously confront their ethnicity for the first time in adolescence or emerging adulthood. Unlike children, adolescents and emerging adults have the ability to interpret ethnic and cultural information, to reflect on the past, and to speculate about the future. With their advancing cognitive skills of abstract thinking and self-reflection, adolescents (especially older adolescents) increasingly consider the meaning of their ethnicity and also have more ethnic-related experiences.

Recent research indicates that adolescents' pride in their ethnic identity group has positive outcomes (Anglin & others, 2018; Douglass & Umana-Taylor, 2017; Umana-Taylor & Douglass, 2017; Umana-Taylor & others, 2018). For example, in a recent study, strong ethnic group affiliation and connection served a protective function in reducing risk for psychiatric

ethnic identity An enduring, basic aspect of the self that includes a sense of membership in an ethnic group and the attitudes and feelings related to that membership.

One adolescent girl, 16-year-old Michelle Chinn, made these comments about ethnic identity development: "My parents do not understand that teenagers need to find out who they are, which means a lot of experimenting, a lot of mood swings, a lot of emotions and awkwardness. Like any teenager, I am facing an identity crisis. I am still trying to figure out whether I am a Chinese American or an American with Asian eyes."
©Red Chopsticks/Getty Images

How Would You...?

As a **human development and family studies professional,** how would you design a community program that assists ethnic minority adolescents to develop a healthy bicultural identity?

problems (Anglin & others, 2018). In another study, Asian American adolescents' ethnic identity was associated with high self-esteem, positive relationships, academic motivation, and lower levels of depression over time (Kiang, Witkow, & Champagne, 2013). And in a recent study of Mexican-origin adolescents, a positive ethnic identity, social support, and anger suppression helped them cope more effectively with racial discrimination, whereas anger expression reduced their ability to cope with the discrimination (Park & others, 2018).

The indicators of identity change often differ for each succeeding generation (Phinney & Vedder, 2013). First-generation immigrants are likely to be secure in their identities and unlikely to change much; they may or may not develop a new identity. The degree to which they begin to feel "American" appears to be related to whether or not they learn English, develop social networks beyond their ethnic group, and become culturally competent in their new country. Second-generation immigrants are more likely to think of themselves as "American," possibly because citizenship is granted at birth. Their ethnic identity is likely to be linked to retention of their ethnic language and social networks. In the third and later generations, the issues become more complex. Historical, contextual, and political factors that are unrelated to acculturation may affect the extent to which members of this generation retain their ethnic identities. For non-European ethnic groups, racism and discrimination influence whether ethnic identity is retained.

Families

Adolescence typically alters the relationship between parents and their children. Among the most important aspects of family relationships in adolescence are those that involve parental management and monitoring, autonomy and attachment, and parent-adolescent conflict.

Parental Management and Monitoring

A key aspect of the managerial role of parenting is effective monitoring, which is especially important as children move into the adolescent years (Bendezu & others, 2018; Lindsay & others, 2018; Rusby & others, 2018). Monitoring includes supervising adolescents' choice of social settings, activities, and friends, as well as their academic efforts. In a recent study of fifth- to eighth-graders, a higher level of parental monitoring was associated with students having higher grades (Top, Liew, & Luo, 2017). A research meta-analysis also found that a higher level of parental monitoring and rule enforcement were linked to later initiation of sexual intercourse and increased use condoms by adolescents (Dittus & others, 2015). Also, a recent study revealed that better parental monitoring was linked to lower rates of marijuana use by adolescents (Haas & others, 2018), and in another recent study, lower parental monitoring was associated with earlier initiation of alcohol use, binge drinking, and marijuana use in 13- to 14-year-olds (Rusby & others, 2018). Further, a recent study revealed that two types of parental media monitoring (active monitoring and connective co-use (engaging in media with the intent to connect with adolescents) were linked to lower media use by adolescents (Padilla-Walker & others, 2018).

A current interest involving parental monitoring focuses on adolescents' management of their parents' access to information, especially strategies for disclosing or concealing information about their activities (Rote & Smetana, 2016). When parents engage in positive parenting practices, adolescents are more likely to disclose information. For example, disclosure increases when parents ask adolescents questions and when adolescents' relationship with parents is characterized by a high level of trust, acceptance, and quality (McElvaney, Greene, & Hogan, 2014). Researchers have found that adolescents' disclosure to parents about their whereabouts, activities, and friends is linked to positive adolescent adjustment (Cottrell & others, 2017). A study of 10- to 18-year-olds found that lower adolescent disclosure to parents was linked to antisocial behavior (Criss & others, 2015).

Three ways that parents can engage in parental monitoring are (1) solicitation (asking questions); (2) control (enforcing disclosure rules); and (3) when youth don't comply, snooping. In one study, snooping was perceived by both adolescents and parents as the most likely of these three strategies to violate youths' privacy rights (Hawk, Becht, & Branje, 2016). Also, in this study, snooping was a relatively infrequent parental monitoring tactic but was a better indicator of problems in adolescent and family functioning than were solicitation and control.

What kinds of strategies can parents use to guide adolescents in effectively handling their increased motivation for autonomy?
©Hero Images/Getty Images

Autonomy and Attachment

With most adolescents, parents are likely to find themselves engaged in a delicate balancing act, weighing competing needs for autonomy and control, for independence and connection.

The Push for Autonomy

The typical adolescent's push for autonomy and responsibility puzzles and angers many parents. As parents see their teenager slipping from their grasp, they may have an urge to take stronger control. Heated emotional exchanges may ensue, with either side calling names, making threats, and doing whatever seems necessary to gain control. Parents may feel frustrated because they *expect* their teenager to heed their advice, to want to spend time with the family, and to grow up to do what is right. Most parents anticipate that their teenager will have some difficulty adjusting to the changes that adolescence brings, but few parents imagine and predict just how strong an adolescent's desires will be to spend time with peers or how intensely adolescents will want to show that it is they—not their parents—who are responsible for their successes and failures.

Adolescents' ability to attain autonomy and gain control over their behavior is facilitated by appropriate adult reactions to their desire for control (McElhaney & Allen, 2012). At the onset of adolescence, the average individual does not have the knowledge to make appropriate or mature decisions in all areas of life. As the adolescent pushes for autonomy, the wise adult relinquishes control in those areas where the adolescent can make reasonable decisions, but continues to guide the adolescent to make reasonable decisions in areas in which the adolescent's knowledge is more limited. Gradually, adolescents acquire the ability to make mature decisions on their own. A recent study also found that from 16 to 20 years of age, adolescents perceived that they had increasing independence and improved relationships with their parents (Hadiwijaya & others, 2017).

Gender differences characterize autonomy-granting in adolescence. Boys are given more independence than girls. In one study, this was especially true in U.S. families with a traditional gender-role orientation (Bumpus, Crouter, & McHale, 2001). Also, Latino parents protect and monitor their daughters more closely than is the case for non-Latino parents (Romo, Mireles-Rios, & Lopez-Tello, 2014). Although Latino cultures may place a stronger emphasis on parental authority and restrict adolescent autonomy, one study revealed that regardless of where they were born, Mexican-origin adolescent girls living in the United States expected autonomy at an earlier age than their mothers preferred (Bamaca-Colbert & others, 2012).

The Role of Attachment

Recall that one of the most widely discussed aspects of socioemotional development in infancy is secure attachment to caregivers (Hoffman & others, 2017; Meins, Bureau, & Ferryhough, 2018). In the past decade, researchers have explored whether secure attachment also might be an important concept in adolescents' relationships with their parents (Arriaga & others, 2018; Delker, Bernstein, & Laurent, 2018; Hocking & others, 2018; Kerstis, Aslund, & Sonnby, 2018; Lockhart & others, 2017; Straus, 2018). Researchers have found that securely attached adolescents are less likely than those who are insecurely attached to have emotional difficulties and to engage in problem behaviors such as juvenile delinquency and drug abuse (Allen & Tan, 2016). A study involving adolescents and emerging adults from 15 to 20 years of age found that insecure attachment to mothers was linked to becoming depressed and remaining depressed (Agerup & others, 2015). In a longitudinal study, Joseph Allen and colleagues (2009) found that secure attachment at 14 years of age was linked to a number of positive outcomes at 21 years of age, including relationship competence, financial/career competence, and fewer problematic behaviors. Further, in a recent study of Latino families, a higher level of secure attachment with mothers was associated with less heavy drug use by adolescents (Gattamorta & others, 2017). And in a research review, the most consistent outcomes of secure attachment in adolescence involved positive peer relations and development of the adolescent's capacity to regulate emotions (Allen & Miga, 2010).

Parent-Adolescent Conflict

Although parent-adolescent conflict increases in early adolescence, it does not reach the tumultuous proportions G. Stanley Hall envisioned at the beginning of the twentieth century (Bornstein, Jager, & Steinberg, 2013). Rather, much of the conflict involves the everyday events of family life, such as keeping a bedroom clean, dressing neatly, getting home by a certain time, and not talking endlessly on the phone. The conflicts rarely involve major dilemmas such as drugs or delinquency.

We indicated above that conflict with parents escalates in early adolescence. Does the conflict decrease later in adolescence? A research review concluded that parent-adolescent conflict decreases from early adolescence through late adolescence (Laursen, Coy, & Collins, 1998). And in a recent study of Chinese American families, parent-adolescent conflict increased in early adolescence, peaked at about 16 years of age, and then decreased through late adolescence and emerging adulthood (Juang & others, 2018). Parent-adolescent relationships also become more positive if adolescents go away to college than if they attend college while living at home (Sullivan & Sullivan, 1980).

The everyday conflicts that characterize parent-adolescent relationships may actually serve a positive developmental function. These minor disputes and negotiations facilitate the adolescent's transition from being dependent on parents to becoming an autonomous individual. Recognizing that conflict and negotiation can serve a positive developmental function can tone down parental hostility.

The old model of parent-adolescent relationships suggested that as adolescents mature they detach themselves from parents and move into a world of autonomy apart from parents. The old model also suggested that parent-adolescent conflict is intense and stressful throughout adolescence. The new model emphasizes that parents serve as important attachment figures and support systems while adolescents explore a wider, more complex social world. The new model also emphasizes that in most families, parent-adolescent conflict is moderate rather than severe and that the everyday negotiations and minor disputes not only are normal but also can serve the positive developmental function of helping the adolescent make the transition from childhood dependency to adult independence (see Figure 2).

Still, a high degree of conflict characterizes some parent-adolescent relationships (Smokowski & others, 2017). And this prolonged, intense conflict is associated with various adolescent problems: movement out of the home, juvenile delinquency, school

According to one adolescent girl, Stacey Christensen, age 16: "I am lucky enough to have open communication with my parents. Whenever I am in need or just need to talk, my parents are there for me. My advice to parents is to let your teens grow at their own pace, be open with them so that you can be there for them. We need guidance; our parents need to help but not be too overwhelming."
©Stockbyte/Getty Images

How Would You…?

As a **social worker,** how would you counsel a mother who is experiencing stress because of increased conflict with her young adolescent daughter?

dropout, pregnancy and early marriage, membership in religious cults, and drug abuse (Brook & others, 1990). For example, a recent study found that a higher level of parent-adolescent conflict was associated with higher adolescent anxiety, depression, and aggression, and lower self-esteem (Smokowski & others, 2016). Another study found that high parent-adolescent conflict was associated with a lower level of empathy in adolescents throughout the six years of the study from 13 to 18 years of age (Van Lissa & others, 2015). Further, in another recent study of Latino families, parent-adolescent conflict was linked to adolescents' higher level of aggressive behavior (Smokowski & others, 2017).

When families emigrate to another country, adolescents typically acculturate more quickly to the norms and values of their new country than do their parents (Fuligni, 2012). This likely occurs because of immigrant adolescents' exposure in school to the language and culture of the host country. The norms and values immigrant adolescents experience are especially likely to diverge from those of their parents in areas such as autonomy and romantic relationships. Such divergences are likely to increase parent-adolescent conflict in immigrant families. In a recent study of Chinese American families, parent-adolescent conflict was linked to a sense of alienation between parents and adolescents, which in turn was related to more depressive symptoms, delinquent behavior, and lower academic achievement (Hou, Kim, & Wang, 2016).

Peers

Peers play powerful roles in the lives of adolescents (Bukowski, Laursen, & Rubin, 2018; Gordon Simons & others, 2018; Vitaro, Boivin, & Poulin, 2018). When you think back to your own adolescent years, you probably recall many of your most enjoyable moments as experiences shared with peers. Peer relations undergo important changes in adolescence, including changes in friendships, peer groups, and the beginning of romantic relationships (Furman, 2018; Martin, Fabes, & Hanish, 2018; Nishina & Bellmore, 2018).

Friendships

For most children, being popular with their peers is a strong motivator. Beginning in early adolescence, however, teenagers typically prefer to have a smaller number of friendships that are more intense and intimate than those of young children.

Harry Stack Sullivan (1953) was the most influential theorist to discuss the importance of adolescent friendships. In contrast with other psychoanalytic theorists who focused almost exclusively on parent-child relationships, Sullivan argued that friends are also important in shaping the development of children and adolescents. Everyone, said Sullivan, has basic social needs, such as the need for tenderness (secure attachment), playful companionship, social acceptance, intimacy, and sexual relations. Whether or not these needs are fulfilled largely determines our emotional well-being. For example, if the need for playful companionship goes unmet, then we become bored and depressed; if the need for social acceptance is not met, we suffer a diminished sense of self-worth.

During adolescence, said Sullivan, friends become increasingly important in meeting social needs. In particular, Sullivan argued that the need for intimacy intensifies during early adolescence, motivating teenagers to seek out close friends. If adolescents fail to forge such close friendships, they experience loneliness and a reduced sense of

Old Model

Autonomy, detachment from parents; parent and peer worlds are isolated

Intense, stressful conflict throughout adolescence; parent-adolescent relationships are filled with storm and stress on virtually a daily basis

New Model

Attachment and autonomy; parents are important support systems and attachment figures; adolescent-parent and adolescent-peer worlds have some important connections

Moderate parent-adolescent conflict is common and can serve a positive developmental function; conflict greater in early adolescence

Figure 2 Old and New Models of Parent-Adolescent Relationships
©Martin Barraud/Caia Image/Glow Images

self-worth. The nature of relationships with friends during adolescence can foreshadow the quality of romantic relationships in emerging adulthood. For example, a longitudinal study revealed that having more secure relationships with close friends at age 16 was linked with more positive romantic relationships at age 20 to 23 (Simpson & others, 2007).

Many of Sullivan's ideas have withstood the test of time. For example, adolescents report disclosing intimate and personal information to their friends more often than do younger children (Buhrmester, 1998) (see Figure 3). Adolescents also say they depend more on friends than on parents to satisfy their needs for companionship, reassurance of worth, and intimacy. The ups and downs of experiences with friends shape adolescents' well-being (Bagwell & Bukowski, 2018; Nesi & others, 2017). Adolescent girls are more likely to disclose information about problems to a friend than are adolescent boys (Rose & Smith, 2018).

Although having friends can be a developmental advantage, not all friendships are alike and the quality of friendship matters (Bagwell & Bukowski, 2018). People differ in the company they keep—that is, who their friends are. It is a developmental disadvantage to have coercive, conflict-ridden, and poor-quality friendships (Raudsepp & Riso, 2017; Rubin & Barstead, 2018; Rubin & others, 2018). One study revealed that having friends who engage in delinquent behavior is associated with early onset and more persistent delinquency (Evans, Simons, & Simons, 2016). Another study found that adolescents adapted their smoking and drinking behavior to that of their best friends (Wang & others, 2016). Further, a recent study of adolescent girls revealed that friends' dieting predicted whether adolescent girls would engage in dieting or extreme dieting (Balantekin, Birch, & Savage, 2018).

What changes take place in friendship during the adolescent years?
©SW Productions/Getty Images

Although most adolescents develop friendships with individuals who are close to their own age, some adolescents become best friends with younger or older individuals. Adolescents who interact with older youth engage in deviant behavior more frequently, but it is not known whether the older youth guide younger adolescents toward deviant behavior or whether the younger adolescents were already prone to deviant behavior before they developed friendships with older youth.

Peer Groups

How extensive is peer pressure in adolescence? What roles do cliques and crowds play in adolescents' lives? As we see next, researchers have found that the standards of peer groups and the influence of crowds and cliques become increasingly important during adolescence.

Peer Pressure

Young adolescents conform more to peer standards than children do (Choukas-Bradley & Prinstein, 2016; Nesi & others, 2017). Around the eighth and ninth grades, conformity to peers—especially to their antisocial standards—peaks (Brown & Larson, 2009). At this point, adolescents are most likely to go along with a peer to steal hubcaps off a car, paint graffiti on a wall, or steal cosmetics from a store counter. One study found that U.S. adolescents are more likely than Japanese adolescents to put pressure on their peers to resist parental influence (Rothbaum & others, 2000).

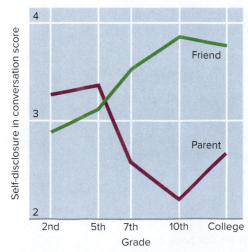

Figure 3 Developmental Changes in Self-Disclosing Conversations
Self-disclosing conversations with friends increased dramatically in adolescence while declining in an equally dramatic fashion with parents. However, self-disclosing conversations with parents began to pick up somewhat during the college years. The measure of self-disclosure involved a 5-point rating scale completed by the children and youth, with a higher score representing greater self-disclosure. The data shown represent the means for each age group.

Adolescents are more likely to conform to their peers when they are uncertain about their social identity and when they are in the presence of someone they perceive to have higher status than they do (Prinstein & Giletta, 2016). Also, a recent study found that boys were more likely to be influenced by peer pressure involving sexual behavior than were girls (Widman & others, 2016).

Cliques and Crowds

Cliques and crowds assume more important roles during adolescence than during childhood (Brown, 2011; Ellis & Zarbatany, 2018). **Cliques** are small groups that range from 2 to about 12 individuals and average about 5 or 6 individuals. The clique members are usually of the same sex and about the same age.

Cliques can form because adolescents engage in similar activities, such as being in a club or on a sports team. Some cliques also form because of friendship. Several adolescents may form a clique because they have spent time with each other, share mutual interests, and enjoy each other's company. Not necessarily friends to start with, they often develop a friendship if they stay in the clique. What do adolescents do in cliques? They share ideas and hang out together. Often they develop an in-group identity in which they believe that their clique is better than other cliques.

Crowds are larger than cliques and less personal. Adolescents are usually members of a crowd based on reputation, and they may or may not spend much time together. Many crowds are defined by the activities adolescents engage in (such as "jocks" who are good at sports or "druggies" who take drugs).

What characterizes peer pressure in adolescence?
©Christin Rose/Getty Images

Dating and Romantic Relationships

Adolescents spend considerable time either dating or thinking about dating (Furman, 2018; Lantagne & Furman, 2017). Dating can be a form of recreation, a source of status, a setting for learning about close relationships, and a way to find a mate.

Developmental Changes in Dating and Romantic Relationships

Three stages characterize the development of romantic relationships in adolescence (Connolly & McIsaac, 2009):

1. *Entering into romantic attractions and affiliations at about age 11 to 13.* This initial stage is triggered by puberty. From age 11 to 13, adolescents become intensely interested in romance and it dominates many conversations with same-sex friends. Developing a crush on someone is common, and the crush often is shared with a same-sex friend. Young adolescents may or may not interact with the individual who is the object of their infatuation. When dating occurs, it usually takes place in a group setting.

2. *Exploring romantic relationships at approximately age 14 to 16.* At this point in adolescence, two types of romantic involvement occur: (a) *Casual dating* emerges between individuals who are mutually attracted. These dating experiences are often short-lived, last a few months at best, and usually endure no longer than a few weeks. (b) *Dating in groups* is common and reflects the importance of peers in adolescents' lives. A friend often acts as a third-party facilitator of a potential dating relationship by communicating their friend's romantic interest and determining whether the other person feels a similar attraction.

3. *Consolidating dyadic romantic bonds at about age 17 to 19.* At the end of the high school years, more serious romantic relationships develop. This stage is characterized by the formation of strong emotional bonds more closely resembling those in adult romantic relationships. These bonds often are more stable and enduring than earlier bonds, typically lasting one year or more.

clique A small group that ranges from 2 to about 12 individuals, averaging about 5 or 6 individuals, and often consists of adolescents who engage in similar activities.

crowd A larger group structure than a clique, a crowd is usually formed based on reputation, and members may or may not spend much time together.

Two variations on these stages in the development of romantic relationships in adolescence involve early and late bloomers (Connolly & McIsaac, 2009). *Early bloomers* include 15 to 20 percent of 11- to 13-year-olds who say that they currently are in a romantic relationship and 35 percent who indicate that they have had some prior experience in romantic relationships. *Late bloomers* comprise approximately 10 percent of 17- to 19-year-olds who say that they have had no experience with romantic relationships and another 15 percent who report that they have not engaged in any romantic relationships that lasted more than four months. One study found that early bloomers externalized problem behaviors through adolescence more than their on-time and late-bloomer counterparts (Connolly & others, 2013).

What are some developmental changes in dating and romantic relationships in adolescence?
©Digital Vision/Getty Images

How do romantic relationships further change through adolescence? Short-term romantic relationships were increasingly supportive in late adolescence (Lantagne & Furman, 2017). Long-term adolescent relationships were both supportive and turbulent, characterized by elevated levels of support, negative interactions, higher control, and more jealousy.

Dating in Gay and Lesbian Youth

Recently, researchers have begun to study romantic relationships among gay and lesbian youth (Diamond & Alley, 2018; Savin-Williams, 2017). Many sexual minority youth date other-sex peers, which can help them to clarify their sexual orientation or disguise it from others (Savin-Williams, 2018). Most gay and lesbian youth have had some same-sex sexual experience, often with peers who are "experimenting," and then go on to a primarily heterosexual orientation (Savin-Williams, 2017, 2018).

Sociocultural Contexts and Dating

The sociocultural context exerts a powerful influence on adolescents' dating patterns (Furman, 2018; Moosmann & Roosa, 2015). This influence may be seen in differences in dating patterns among ethnic groups within the United States. Values, religious beliefs, and traditions often dictate the age at which dating begins, how much freedom in dating is allowed, whether dates must be chaperoned by adults or parents, and the roles of males and females in dating. For example, Latino and Asian American cultures have more conservative standards regarding adolescent dating than does the Anglo-American culture. Dating may become a source of conflict within a family if the parents grew up in cultures where dating began at a late age, little freedom in dating was allowed, dates were chaperoned, and dating was especially restricted for adolescent girls. A recent study found that mother-daughter conflict in Mexican American families was linked to an increase in daughters' romantic involvement (Tyrell & others, 2016). When immigrant adolescents choose to adopt the ways of the dominant U.S. culture (such as unchaperoned dating), they often clash with parents and extended-family members who have more traditional values.

Dating and Adjustment

Researchers have linked dating and romantic relationships with various measures of how well adjusted adolescents are (Davila, Capaldi, & La Greca, 2016; Furman, 2018; Yoon & others, 2017). For example, one study of 200 tenth-graders revealed that the more romantic experiences they had had, the more likely they were to report high levels of social acceptance, friendship competence, and romantic competence; however, having more romantic experience also was linked to a higher level of substance use, delinquency, and sexual behavior (Furman, Low, & Ho, 2009).

Dating and romantic relationships at an early age can be especially problematic (Furman, 2018). One study found that romantic activity was linked to depression in early adolescent girls (Starr & others, 2012). Researchers also have found that early dating and "going with" someone are linked with adolescent pregnancy and problems at home and school (Florsheim, Moore, & Edgington, 2003).

However, in some cases, romantic relationships in adolescence are associated with positive developmental changes. For example, in a recent study, having a supportive romantic relationship in adolescence was linked to positive outcomes for adolescents who had a negative relationship with their mother (Szwedo, Hessel, & Allen, 2017). In another study, adolescents who engaged in a higher level of intimate disclosure at age 10 reported a higher level of companionship in romantic relationships at 12 and 15 years of age (Kochendorfer & Kerns, 2017). In this study, those who reported more conflict in friendships had a lower level of companionship in romantic relationships at 15 years of age.

How Would You...?

As a **psychologist,** how would you explain the risks of dating and romantic relationships during early adolescence?

Culture and Adolescent Development

We live in an increasingly diverse world, one that includes more extensive contact between adolescents from different cultures and ethnic groups. In this section, we explore these differences as they relate to adolescents. We explore how adolescents in various cultures spend their time, and some of the rites of passage they undergo. Further, we discuss the many challenges faced by adolescents who grow up in families that are struggling financially. We also examine how ethnicity and the media affect U.S. adolescents and influence their development.

Cross-Cultural Comparisons

What traditions remain for adolescents around the globe? What circumstances are changing adolescents' lives?

Traditions and Changes in Adolescence Around the Globe

Depending on the culture being observed, adolescence may involve many different experiences (Chen, Lee, & Chen, 2018; Matsumoto & Juang, 2017).

Health Adolescent health and well-being have improved in some respects but not in others. Overall, fewer adolescents around the world die from infectious diseases and malnutrition now than in the past (UNICEF, 2018). However, a number of adolescent health-compromising behaviors (especially illicit drug use and unprotected sex) are increasing in frequency. Extensive increases in the rates of HIV in adolescents have occurred in many sub-Saharan countries (UNICEF, 2018).

Gender Around the world, the experiences of male and female adolescents continue to be quite different. Except in a few regions such as Japan, the Philippines, and Western countries, males have far greater access to educational opportunities than females do (UNICEF, 2018). In many countries, adolescent females have less freedom than males to pursue a variety of careers and engage in various leisure activities. Gender differences in sexual expression are widespread, especially in India, Southeast Asia, Latin America, and Arab countries where there are far more restrictions on the sexual activity of adolescent females than on that of males. These gender differences do appear to be narrowing over time, however. In some countries, educational and career opportunities for women are expanding, and control over adolescent girls' romantic and sexual relationships is weakening.

How Would You...?

As a **health-care professional,** how would you explain to policy makers and insurance providers the importance of cultural context when creating guidelines for adolescent health coverage?

Family In some countries, adolescents grow up in closely knit families with extensive extended-kin networks that retain a traditional way of life. For example, in Arab countries, "adolescents are taught strict codes of conduct and loyalty" (Brown & Larson, 2002, p. 6). However, in Western countries such as the United States, parenting is less authoritarian than in the past, and much larger numbers of adolescents are growing up in divorced families and stepfamilies.

In many countries around the world, current trends "include greater family mobility, migration to urban areas, family members working in distant cities or countries, smaller families, fewer extended-family households, and increases in mothers' employment" (Brown & Larson, 2002, p. 7). Unfortunately, many of these changes may reduce the ability of families to spend time with their adolescents.

Asian Indian adolescents in a marriage ceremony.
©Prakash Hatvalne/AP Images

Peers Some cultures give peers a stronger role in adolescence than other cultures do (Brown & Larson, 2002). In most Western nations, peers figure prominently in adolescents' lives, in some cases taking on roles that would otherwise be assumed by parents. Among street youth in South America, the peer network serves as a surrogate family that supports survival in dangerous and stressful settings. In other regions of the world, such as in Arab countries, peer relations are restricted, especially for girls (Booth, 2002).

Adolescents' lives, then, are shaped by a combination of change and tradition. Researchers have found both similarities and differences in the experiences of adolescents in different countries (Larson & Dawes, 2015).

Muslim school in Middle East with boys only.
©Yvan Cohen/LightRocket/Getty Images

Rites of Passage

Another variation in the experiences of adolescents in different cultures is whether the adolescents go through a rite of passage. Some societies have elaborate ceremonies that signal the adolescent's move to maturity and achievement of adult status (Ember, Ember, & Peregrine, 2015; Miller, 2017). A **rite of passage** is a ceremony or ritual that marks an individual's transition from one status to another. Most rites of passage focus on the transition to adult status. In many primitive cultures, rites of passage are the avenue through which adolescents gain access to sacred adult practices, to knowledge, and to sexuality. These rites often involve dramatic practices intended to facilitate the adolescent's separation from the immediate family, especially the mother. The transformation is usually characterized by some form of ritual death and rebirth, or by means of contact with the spiritual world. Bonds are forged between the adolescent and the adult instructors through shared rituals, hazards, and secrets to allow the adolescent to enter the adult world. This kind of ritual provides a forceful and discontinuous entry into the adult world at a time when the adolescent is perceived to be ready for the change.

An especially rich tradition of rites of passage for adolescents has prevailed in African cultures, especially sub-Saharan Africa. Under the influence of Western industrialized culture, many of these rites are disappearing today, although they are still prevalent in locations where formal education is not readily available.

Do we have such rites of passage for American adolescents? We certainly do not have universal formal ceremonies that mark the passage from adolescence to adulthood. Certain religious and social groups do,

Street youth in Rio de Janeiro.
©Tom Stoddart/Getty Images

How Would You...?

As an **educator,** how would you modify high school graduation to make it a more meaningful rite of passage for adolescents in the United States?

rite of passage A ceremony or ritual that marks an individual's transition from one status to another. Most rites of passage focus on the transition to adult status.

These Congolese Kota boys painted their faces as part of a rite of passage to adulthood. *What rites of passage do American adolescents have?*
©Daniel Laine/Gamma Rapho

however, have initiation ceremonies that indicate that an advance in maturity has been reached: the Jewish bar and bat mitzvah, the Catholic confirmation, and social debuts, for example. School graduation ceremonies come the closest to being culture-wide rites of passage in the United States. The high school graduation ceremony has become nearly universal for middle-class adolescents and increasing numbers of adolescents from low-income backgrounds.

Socioeconomic Status and Poverty

In the chapter on "Socioemotional Development in Middle and Late Childhood," we described many aspects of the challenges facing children who live in low-income and impoverished families. Here we focus on these challenges associated with economic hardship.

Adolescents from low-SES backgrounds are at risk for experiencing low achievement and emotional problems, as well as lower occupational attainment in adulthood (Chaudry & others, 2017; Coley & others, 2018; Pulcini & others, 2018; Rosen & others, 2018). Psychological problems such as smoking, depression, and juvenile delinquency, as well as health problems, are more prevalent among low-SES adolescents than among economically advantaged adolescents (Simon & others, 2017). For example, a recent study found that of 13 risk factors, low SES was most likely to be associated with smoking initiation in fifth-graders (Wellman & others, 2018). Also, in a recent Chinese study, adolescents in low-income families were more likely to have depressive symptoms than adolescents in families with average or high incomes (Zhou, Fan, & Yin, 2017). Further, in a U.S. longitudinal study, low SES in adolescent females was linked to having a higher level of depressive symptoms at age 54 (Pino & others, 2018). And in this study, low-SES females who completed college were less likely to have depressive symptoms at age 54 than low-SES females who did not complete college. In another longitudinal study, low SES in adolescence was a risk factor for having cardiovascular disease 30 years later (Doom & others, 2017). In this study, the following factors were found to be involved in the pathway to cardiovascular disease for low-SES individuals: health-compromising behaviors, financial stress, inadequate medical care, and lower educational attainment.

Are there psychological and social factors that predict higher achievement for adolescents living in poverty? A recent study found that higher levels of the following four factors assessed at the beginning of the sixth grade were linked to higher grade point averages at the end of the seventh grade: (1) academic commitment, (2) emotional control, (3) family involvement and (4) school climate (Li, Allen, & Casillas, 2017).

When poverty is persistent and long-standing, it can have especially damaging effects on adolescents (Chaudry & others, 2017; Duncan, Magnuson, & Votruba-Drzal, 2017; Green & others, 2018). A recent study found that 12- to 19-year-olds' perceived well-being was lowest when they had lived in poverty from birth to 2 years of age (compared with 3 to 5, 6 to 8, and 9 to 11 years of age) and also each additional year lived in poverty was associated with even lower perceived well-being (Gariepy & others, 2017).

Ethnicity

Earlier in this chapter we explored the identity development of ethnic minority adolescents. Here, we further examine immigration and the relationship between ethnicity and socioeconomic status.

Immigration

Relatively high rates of immigration are contributing to the growing proportion of ethnic minority adolescents and emerging adults in the United States (Calzada & others, 2018; Titzmann & Gniewosz, 2018; Yoon & others, 2017). Immigrant families are those in which at least one of the parents was born outside the country of residence. Variations in immigrant families involve whether one or both parents are foreign born, whether the child was born in the host country, and the ages at which immigration took place for both the parents and the children (Kim & others, 2018).

What are some of the circumstances immigrants face that challenge their adjustment? Immigrants often experience stressors uncommon to or less prominent among longtime residents, such as language barriers, dislocations and separations from support networks, the dual struggle to preserve identity and to acculturate, and changes in SES status (Brietzke & Perreira, 2017; Hou & Kim, 2018; Suárez-Orosco, 2018a, b, c; Yoshikawa & others, 2017). In a recent study comparing Asian, Latino, and non-Latino White immigrants' adolescents, immigrant Asian adolescents had the highest level of depression, the lowest self-esteem, and were the most likely to report experiencing discrimination (Lo & others, 2017).

What are some cultural adaptations these Mexican American girls likely have made as immigrants to the United States?
©Caroline Woodham/Getty Images

Many individuals in immigrant families are dealing with the problem of being undocumented (Beck & others, 2017; Rojas-Flores & others, 2017). Living in an undocumented family can affect children's and adolescents' developmental outcomes through parents being unwilling to sign up for services for which they are eligible, through conditions linked to low-wage work and lack of benefits, through stress, and through a lack of cognitive stimulation in the home. Consequently, when working with adolescents and their immigrant families, counselors need to adapt intervention programs to optimize cultural sensitivity (Calzada & others, 2018; Suárez-Orosco & Suárez-Orosco, 2018).

The ways in which ethnic minority families deal with stress depend on many factors (Davis & others, 2018; Gonzales-Backen & others, 2017; Lorenzo-Blanco & others, 2018). Whether the parents are native-born or immigrants, how long the family has been in the United States, its socioeconomic status, family values, how competently parents rear their children and adolescents, and their national origin all make a difference (Hou & Kim, 2018; Kim & others, 2018). A recent study of Mexican-origin youth found that when adolescents reported a higher level of familism (giving priority to one's family), they engaged in lower levels of risk taking (Wheeler & others, 2017). Another study revealed that parents' education before migrating was strongly linked to their children's academic achievement (Pong & Landale, 2012).

Ethnicity and Socioeconomic Status

Much of the research on ethnic minority adolescents has failed to tease apart the influences of ethnicity and socioeconomic status (SES). These factors can interact in ways that exaggerate the influence of ethnicity because ethnic minority individuals are overrepresented in the lower socioeconomic levels of American society (Nieto & Bode, 2018). Consequently, researchers too often have given ethnic explanations for aspects of adolescent development that were largely attributable to SES.

Not all ethnic minority families are poor. However, poverty contributes to the stressful life experiences of many ethnic minority adolescents (Berman & others, 2018; Duncan, Magnuson, & Votruba-Drzal, 2017; Taylor, Widaman, & Robins, 2018). Thus, many ethnic minority adolescents experience a double disadvantage: (1) prejudice, discrimination, and bias because of their ethnic minority status; and (2) the stressful effects of poverty (Kimmel & Aronson, 2018).

Although some ethnic minority youth come from middle-income backgrounds, economic advantage does not entirely enable them to escape the prejudice, discrimination, and bias associated with being a member of an ethnic minority group (Gollnick & Chinn, 2017). Even Japanese Americans, who are often characterized as a "model minority" because of their strong achievement orientation and family cohesiveness, still experience stress associated with ethnic minority status.

Media and Screen Time

What are some trends in adolescent media use and screen time?
©Brendan O'Sullivan/ Getty Images

The culture adolescents experience involves not only cultural values, SES, and ethnicity, but also media and screen time influences (Guadagno, 2018; Lever-Duffy & McDonald, 2018; Maloy & others, 2017; Roblyer & Hughes, 2019; Smaldino & others, 2019). Television continues to have a strong influence on children's and adolescent's development, but children's use of other media and information/ communication devices has led to the use of the term *screen time,* which includes how much time individuals spend watching television or DVDs, playing video games, and using computers or mobile media such as iPhones (Lissak, 2018; Ngantcha & others, 2018; Poulain & others, 2018; Yan, 2018). A recent study revealed that less screen time was associated with adolescents having a better quality of life (Yan & others, 2017). A recent study found that nighttime mobile phone use and poor sleep behavior increased from 13 to 16 years of age (Vernon, Modecki, & Barber, 2018). In this study, increased nighttime mobile phone use was linked to increases in externalizing problems as well as decreases in self-esteem and coping.

To better understand various aspects of U.S. adolescents' media use, the Kaiser Family Foundation funded national surveys in 1999, 2004, and 2009. The 2009 survey documented that adolescent media use had increased dramatically in the previous decade (Rideout, Foehr, & Roberts, 2010). Today's youth live in a world in which they are encapsulated by media. In the 2009 survey, 8- to 11-year-olds used media 5 hours and 29 minutes a day, but 11- to 14-year-olds used media an average of 8 hours and 40 minutes a day, and 15- to 18-year-olds an average of 7 hours and 58 minutes a day. Thus, media use jumps more than 3 hours in early adolescence! Adding up the daily media use figures to obtain weekly media use leads to the staggering levels of more than 60 hours a week of media use by 11- to 14-year-olds and almost 56 hours a week by 15- to 18-year-olds!

A major trend in the use of technology is the dramatic increase in media multitasking (Edwards & Shin, 2017; Hadington & Murphy, 2018; Steinborn & Huestegge, 2017). In the 2009 survey, when the amount of time spent multitasking was included in computing media use, 11- to 14-year-olds spent nearly 12 hours a day (compared with almost 9 hours a day when multitasking was not included) exposed to media (Rideout, Foehr, & Roberts, 2010)! One study of 8- to 12-year-old girls also found that a higher level of media multitasking was linked to negative social well-being while a higher level of face-to-face communication was associated with positive social well-being indicators, such as greater social success, feeling more normal, and having fewer friends whom parents thought were a bad influence (Pea & others, 2012). In another study, heavy media multitaskers were more likely to be depressed and have social anxiety than their counterparts who engaged in a lower incidence of media multitasking (Becker, Alzahabi, & Hopwood, 2013). Also, in a recent study, heavy multimedia multitaskers were less likely than light media multitaskers to delay gratification and more likely to endorse intuitive, but wrong, answers on a cognitive reflection task (Schutten, Stokes, & Arnell, 2017). And in a recent research review, a higher level of media multitasking was linked to lower levels of school achievement, executive function, and growth mindset in adolescents (Cain & others, 2016).

In some cases, media multitasking—such as text messaging, listening to an iPod, and updating a YouTube site simultaneously—is engaged in while doing homework. It is hard to imagine that this allows a student to do homework efficiently, although there is little research on media multitasking. A research review concluded that at a general level, using digital technologies (surfing the Internet, texting someone) while engaging in a learning task (reading, listening to a lecture) distracts learners and impairs performance on many tasks (Courage & others, 2015). Also in this research, it was concluded that when driving subtasks such as various perceptual-motor activities (steering control, changing lanes, maneuvering through traffic, braking, and acceleration) and ongoing cognitive tasks (planning, decision making, or maintaining a conversation with a passenger) are combined with interactive in-vehicle devices (phones, navigation aids, portable music devices), the task of driving becomes more complex and the potential for distraction high.

Mobile media, such as cell phones and iPads, are mainly driving the increased media use by adolescents (Yan, 2018). For example, in 2004, 39 percent of adolescents owned a cell phone, a figure that jumped to 66 percent in 2009 and then to 87 percent in 2016 with a prediction of 92 percent in 2019 (eMarketeer.com, 2016; Rideout, Foehr, & Roberts, 2010).

A national survey revealed dramatic increases in U.S. adolescents' use of social media and text messaging (Lenhart, 2015). In 2015, 92 percent of U.S. 13- to 17-year-olds reported using social networking sites daily. Twenty-four percent of the adolescents said they go online almost constantly. Much of this increase in going online has been fueled by smartphones and mobile devices. Also, in a recent national survey, 78 percent of 18- to 24-year-olds reported that they use Snapchat, 71 percent said they use Instagram, 68 percent said they use Facebook, and almost half (45 percent) indicated they use Twitter (Smith & Anderson, 2018). And in this recent survey, a whopping 94 percent in this age group said they use YouTube. A recent study indicated that a higher level of social media use was associated with a higher frequency of heavy drinking by adolescents (Brunborg, Andreas, & Kvaavik, 2017).

Text messaging has become the main way that adolescents connect with their friends, surpassing face-to-face contact, e-mail, instant messaging, and voice calling (Lenhart, 2015; Lenhart & others, 2015). In the national survey and a further update (Lenhart & others, 2015), daily text messaging increased from 38 percent who texted friends daily in 2008 to 55 percent in 2015. However, voice mail was the primary way that most adolescents preferred to connect with parents.

Adolescent Problems

Earlier we described several adolescent problems: substance abuse, sexually transmitted infections, and eating disorders. In this chapter, we examine the problems of juvenile delinquency, depression, and suicide. We also explore interrelationships among adolescent problems and discuss how such problems can be prevented or remedied.

Juvenile Delinquency

The label **juvenile delinquent** is applied to an adolescent who breaks the law or engages in behavior that is considered illegal. Like other categories of disorders, juvenile delinquency is a broad concept; legal infractions range from littering to murder. Because the adolescent technically becomes a juvenile delinquent only after being judged guilty of a crime by a court of law, official records do not accurately reflect the number of illegal acts juvenile delinquents commit.

Males are more likely to engage in delinquency than are females—in 2014, 72 percent of delinquency cases in the United States involved males, 28 percent females (Hockenberry & Puzzanchera, 2017). Since 2008, delinquency cases have dropped more for males than for females.

Delinquency rates among youths from minority groups and low-SES families are especially high compared with the overall proportions of these groups in the general population. However, such groups have less influence over the judicial decision-making process in the United States and therefore may be judged delinquent more readily than their non-Latino White, middle-SES counterparts.

One issue in juvenile justice is whether an adolescent who commits a crime should be tried as an adult (Fine & others, 2017). Some psychologists have proposed that individuals 12 and under should not be evaluated under adult criminal laws and that those 17 and older should be (Cauffman & others, 2015). They also recommend that individuals 13 to 16 years of age be given some type of individualized assessment to determine whether they will be tried in a juvenile court or an adult criminal court.

juvenile delinquent An adolescent who breaks the law or engages in behavior that is considered illegal.

Causes of Delinquency

What causes delinquency? Many reasons have been proposed, including heredity, identity problems, community influences, and family experiences. Erik Erikson (1968), for example, argues that adolescents whose development has restricted them from acceptable social roles, or made them feel that they cannot measure up to the demands placed on them, may choose a negative identity. Adolescents with a negative identity may find support for their delinquent image among peers, reinforcing the negative identity. For Erikson, delinquency is an attempt to establish an identity, even if it is a negative one.

What are some factors that are linked to whether adolescents will engage in delinquent acts?
©Bill Aron/PhotoEdit

Although delinquency is less exclusively a phenomenon of lower socioeconomic status (SES) than it was in the past, some characteristics of lower-SES culture might promote delinquency (Dawson-McClure & others, 2015). A recent study of more than 10,000 children and adolescents found that family environment characterized by poverty and child maltreatment was linked to entering the juvenile justice system in adolescence (Vidal & others, 2017). The norms of many lower-SES peer groups and gangs are antisocial, or counterproductive to the goals and norms of society at large. Getting into or staying out of trouble are prominent features of life for some adolescents in low-income neighborhoods. One study found that youth whose families had experienced repeated poverty were more than twice as likely to be delinquent at 14 and 21 years of age (Najman & others, 2010).

Certain characteristics of family support systems are also associated with delinquency (Muftic & others, 2018; Ray & others, 2017). Parental monitoring of adolescents is especially important in determining whether an adolescent becomes a delinquent (Bendezu & others, 2018). And one study found that low rates of delinquency from 14 to 23 years of age were associated with an authoritative parenting style (Mann & others, 2015). Further, research indicates that family therapy is often effective in reducing delinquency (Darnell & Schuler, 2015). An increasing number of studies have found that siblings can influence whether an adolescent becomes a delinquent (Laursen & others, 2017; Wallace, 2017). Peer relations also can influence delinquency (Kim & Fletcher, 2018; Prinstein & others, 2018). A recent study revealed that having friends who engage in delinquency was associated with early onset and more persistent delinquency (Evans, Simons, & Simons, 2016). And in a recent study of middle school adolescents, peer pressure for fighting and friends' delinquent behavior were linked to adolescents' aggression and delinquent behavior (Farrell, Thompson, & Mehari, 2017).

How Would You...?

As a **social worker,** how would you apply your knowledge of juvenile delinquency and adolescent development to improve the juvenile justice system?

Lack of academic success is associated with delinquency (Mercer & others, 2016). And a number of cognitive factors such as low self-control, low intelligence, and lack of sustained attention are linked to delinquency (Fine & others, 2016; Guo, 2018; Hipwell & others, 2018). Further, recent research indicates that having callous-unemotional personality traits predicts an increased risk of engaging in delinquency for adolescent males (Ray & others, 2017).

Rodney Hammond is an individual whose goal is to help at-risk adolescents, such as juvenile delinquents, cope more effectively with their lives. Read about his work in the *Careers in Life-Span Development* profile.

Depression and Suicide

What is the nature of depression in adolescence? What causes an adolescent to commit suicide?

Depression

Rates of ever experiencing major depressive disorder range from 15 to 20 percent for adolescents (Graber & Sontag, 2009). Adolescents who are experiencing a high level of stress and/or a loss of some type are at increased risk for developing depression

Rodney Hammond, Health Psychologist

In describing his college experiences, Rodney Hammond said:

> When I started as an undergraduate at the University of Illinois, Champaign-Urbana, I hadn't decided on my major. But to help finance my education, I took a part-time job in a child development research program sponsored by the psychology department. There, I observed inner-city children in settings designed to enhance their learning. I saw firsthand the contribution psychology can make, and I knew I wanted to be a psychologist. (American Psychological Association, 2003, p. 26)

Rodney Hammond went on to obtain a doctorate in school and community psychology with a focus on children's development. For a number of years he trained clinical psychologists at Wright State University in Ohio and directed a program to reduce violence in ethnic minority youth. There, he and his associates taught at-risk youth how to use social skills to effectively manage conflict and to recognize situations that could lead to violence. Rodney became the first Director of Violence Prevention at the Centers for Disease Control and Prevention in Atlanta, Georgia.

Rodney says that if you are interested in people and problem solving, psychology is a wonderful way to put these subjects

Rodney Hammond counsels an adolescent girl about the risks of adolescence and how to effectively cope with them.
Courtesy of Dr. Rodney Hammond

together. Following his recent retirement from the Centers for Disease Control and Prevention, he is now Adjunct Professor of Human Development and Counseling at the University of Georgia.

(Cohen & others, 2018; Luyten & Fonagy, 2018; Teivaanmaki & others, 2018). Also, a recent study found that adolescents who became depressed were characterized by a sense of hopelessness (Weersing & others, 2016).

Adolescent females are far more likely to develop depression than are their male counterparts. In a recent study, at 12 years of age, 5.2 percent of females compared with 2 percent of males had experienced first-onset depression (Breslau & others, 2017). In this study, the cumulative incidence of depression from 12 to 17 years of age was 36 percent for females and 14 percent for males. Among the reasons for this gender difference are that females tend to ruminate in their depressed mood and amplify it; females' self-images, especially their body images, are more negative than males'; females face more discrimination than males do; and puberty occurs earlier for girls than for boys (Kouros, Morris, & Garber, 2016). As a result, girls experience a confluence of changes and life experiences in the middle school years that can increase depression (Chen & others, 2015).

Is adolescent depression linked to problems in emerging and early adulthood? One study initially assessed U.S. adolescents when they were 16 to 17 years of age and then again every two years until they were 26 to 27 years of age (Naicker & others, 2013). In this study, significant effects that persisted after 10 years were depression recurrence, stronger depressive symptoms, migraine headaches, poor self-rated health, and low levels of social support. Adolescent depression was not associated with employment status, personal income, marital status, and educational attainment a decade later.

Genes are linked to adolescent depression (Hannigan, McAdams, & Eley, 2017; Van Assche & others, 2017). One study found that certain dopamine-related genes were associated with depressive symptoms in adolescents (Adkins & others, 2012). Another study revealed that the link between adolescent girls' perceived stress and depression occurred only when the girls had the short version of the serotonin-related gene—5HTTLPR (Beaver & others, 2012).

Poor relationships are linked to adolescent depression. A recent study found that adolescents who were isolated from their peers and whose caregivers emotionally neglected them were at significant risk for developing depression (Christ, Kwak, & Lu, 2017). Certain family factors place adolescents at risk for developing depression (Bleys & others, 2018; Dardas, van de Water, & Simmons, 2018; Oppenheimer, Hankin, & Young, 2018; Possel & others, 2018). These include having a depressed parent, emotionally unavailable parents, parents who have high marital conflict, and parents with financial problems. One study also revealed that mother-adolescent co-rumination, especially when focused on the mother's problems, was linked to adolescents' depression (Waller & Rose, 2010). Also, another study found that positive parenting characteristics such as emotional and educational support were associated with less depression in adolescents (Smokowski & others, 2015).

Poor peer relationships also are associated with adolescent depression (Rose & Smith, 2018; Siennick & others, 2017). Not having a close relationship with a best friend, having less contact with friends, having friends who are depressed, and experiencing peer rejection all increase depressive tendencies in adolescents (Platt, Kadosh, & Lau, 2013). Also, in a recent study, co-rum ination with friends was linked to greater peer stress for adolescent girls (Rose & others, 2017). Further, problems in romantic relationships can produce adolescent depression (Furman, 2018).

A research review concluded that drug therapy using serotonin reuptake inhibitors, cognitive behavioral therapy, and interpersonal therapy are effective in treating adolescent depression (Maalouf & Brent, 2012). However, the most effective treatment was a combination of drug therapy and cognitive behavioral therapy. Another research review concluded that Prozac and other SSRIs (selective serotonin reuptake inhibitors) show clinical benefits for adolescents at risk for moderate and severe depression (Cousins & Goodyer, 2015). Other recent research indicates that family therapy also can be effective in reducing adolescent depression (Poole & others, 2018).

Suicide

Suicide behavior is rare in childhood but escalates in adolescence and then increases further in emerging adulthood (Park & others, 2006). Suicide is the third-leading cause of death in 10- to 19-year-olds today in the United States (Centers for Disease Control and Prevention, 2018).

Although a suicide threat should always be taken seriously, far more adolescents contemplate or attempt it unsuccessfully than actually commit it (Castellvi & others, 2017). In the last two decades there has been a considerable decline in the percentage of adolescents who think seriously about committing suicide, although from 2009 to 2015 this percentage increased from 14 to 18 percent (Kann & others, 2016a). In this national study, in 2015, 8.6 percent attempted suicide and 2.8 percent engaged in suicide attempts that required medical attention.

Females are more likely to attempt suicide than males, but males are more likely to succeed in committing suicide (Ivey-Stephenson & others, 2017). Males use more lethal means, such as guns, in their suicide attempts, whereas adolescent females are more likely to cut their wrists or take an overdose of sleeping pills—methods that are less likely to result in death.

Suicidal adolescents often have depressive symptoms (Lee & Ham, 2018). Although not all depressed adolescents are suicidal, depression is the most frequently cited factor associated with adolescent suicide (Thompson & Swartout, 2017). In a recent study, the most significant factor in a first suicide attempt during adolescence was a major depressive episode, while for children it was child maltreatment (Peyre & others, 2017). Also, in another recent study, a sense of hopelessness predicted an increase in suicidal ideation in depressed adolescents (Wolfe & others, 2018).

Both earlier and later experiences are linked to suicide attempts, and these can involve family relationships (Bjorkenstam, Kosidou, & Bjorkenstam, 2017; King & others, 2017; Lee & others, 2018). One study found that family discord and negative relationships with parents were associated with increased suicide attempts by depressed adolescents (Consoli & others, 2013). In two recent studies, child maltreatment during

What are some characteristics of adolescents who become depressed? What are some factors that are linked with suicide attempts by adolescents?
©Science Photo Library/ age fotostock

How Would You…?

As a **psychologist,** how would you talk with an adolescent who has just threatened suicide?

the childhood years was linked with suicide attempts in adulthood (Park, 2017; Turner & others, 2017). Also, a recent study confirmed that early sexual abuse is linked to suicidal behavior (Ng & others, 2018). Further, a recent study indicated that adolescents who were being treated in a suicide clinic experienced lower family cohesion than non-clinical adolescents and adolescents being treated at a general psychiatric clinic (Jakobsen, Larsen, & Horwood, 2017). Recent and current stressful circumstances, such as getting poor grades in school or experiencing the breakup of a romantic relationship, also may trigger suicide attempts (Im, Oh, & Suk, 2017).

Further, being victimized by bullying is associated with suicide-related thoughts and behavior (Barzilay & others, 2017; Pham & Adesman, 2018). A recent meta-analysis revealed that adolescents who were the victims of cyberbullying were 2½ times more likely to have suicidal thoughts than nonvictims (John & others, 2018). Cyberbullying has been found to be more strongly associated with suicidal ideation than traditional bullying (van Geel, Vedder, & Tanilon, 2014).

The Interrelation of Problems and Successful Prevention/Intervention Programs

The four problems that affect the most adolescents are (1) drug abuse, (2) juvenile delinquency, (3) sexual problems, and (4) school-related problems (Dryfoos, 1990; Dryfoos & Barkin, 2006). The adolescents most at risk have more than one of these problems.

Researchers are increasingly finding that problem behaviors in adolescence are interrelated. For example, heavy substance abuse is related to early sexual activity, lower grades, dropping out of school, and delinquency (Belenko & others, 2017). Early initiation of sexual activity is associated with the use of cigarettes and alcohol, the use of marijuana and other illicit drugs, lower grades, dropping out of school, and delinquency (Lowry & others, 2017). Delinquency is related to early sexual activity, early pregnancy, substance abuse, and dropping out of school (Marotta, 2017; Rioux & others, 2018). As many as 10 percent of adolescents in the United States have been estimated to engage in all four of these problem behaviors (for example, adolescents who have dropped out of school are behind in their grade level, are users of heavy drugs, regularly use cigarettes and marijuana, and are sexually active but do not use contraception). In 1990, it was estimated that another 15 percent of high-risk youth engaged in two or three of the four main problem behaviors (Dryfoos, 1990). More recently, this estimate was increased from the 15 percent figure in 1990 to 20 percent of all adolescents in 2006 (Dryfoos & Barkin, 2006).

A review of the programs that have been successful in preventing or reducing adolescent problems found these common components (Dryfoos, 1990; Dryfoos & Barkin, 2006):

1. *Intensive individualized attention.* In successful programs, high-risk adolescents are attached to a responsible adult who gives the adolescent attention and deals with the adolescent's specific needs (Crooks & others, 2017; Plourde & others, 2017). This theme occurs in a number of programs. In a successful substance-abuse program, for example, a student assistance counselor is available full-time for individual counseling and referral for treatment.

2. *Community-wide multiagency collaborative approaches.* The basic philosophy of community-wide programs is that a number of different programs and services have to be in place (Trude & others, 2018). In one successful substance-abuse program, a community-wide health promotion campaign has been implemented that uses local media and community education in concert with a substance-abuse curriculum in the schools.

What are some strategies for preventing and intervening in adolescent problems?
©Image Source/Alamy

3. *Early identification and intervention.* Reaching younger children and their families before children develop problems, or at the onset of their problems, is a successful strategy (Almy & Cicchetti, 2018; Mash & Wolfe, 2019). One preschool program serves as an excellent model for the prevention of delinquency, pregnancy, substance abuse, and dropping out of school. Operated by the High/Scope Foundation in Ypsilanti, Michigan from 1962 to 1967, the Perry Preschool has had a long-term positive impact on its students. This enrichment program, directed by David Weikart, served disadvantaged African American children. They attended a high-quality, two-year preschool program and received weekly home visits from program personnel. Based on official police records, by age 19, individuals who had attended the Perry Preschool program were less likely to have been arrested and reported fewer adult offenses than a control group did. The Perry Preschool students also were less likely to drop out of school, and teachers rated their social behavior as more competent than that of a control group who had not received the enriched preschool experience (High/Scope Resource, 2005).

Summary

Identity
- Identity is a self-portrait composed of many pieces.
- Identity versus identity confusion is Erikson's fifth stage of the human life span, which individuals experience during adolescence.
- James Marcia proposed four identity statuses—diffusion, foreclosure, moratorium, and achievement—that are based on crisis (exploration) and commitment. Increasingly, experts argue that the main changes in identity occur in emerging adulthood rather than adolescence.
- Ethnicity is an important influence on identity.

Families
- A key aspect of the managerial role of parenting in adolescence is effectively monitoring the adolescent's development. Adolescents' disclosure to parents about their whereabouts is linked to positive adolescent adjustment.
- The adolescent's push for autonomy is one of the hallmarks of adolescence. Attachment to parents increases the probability that an adolescent will be socially competent.
- Parent-adolescent conflict increases in adolescence. The conflict is usually moderate rather than severe.

Peers
- Harry Stack Sullivan argued that there is a dramatic increase in the psychological importance and intimacy of close friends in early adolescence. Peer conformity and cliques and crowds assume more importance in adolescence.
- Three stages characterize adolescent dating and romantic relationships. Many gay and lesbian youth date other-sex peers. Culture can exert a powerful influence on adolescent dating. Some aspects of dating and romantic relationships are linked to adjustment difficulties.

Culture and Adolescent Development
- Adolescent development varies across cultures, and rites of passage still characterize adolescents in some cultures.
- Low socioeconomic status and poverty can have extremely negative effects on adolescents' development, including lower achievement, lower occupational attainment, and psychological problems.
- Immigration is an important aspect of many ethnic adolescents' lives. Although not all ethnic minority families are poor, poverty contributes to the stress experienced by many ethnic minority adolescents.
- There has been a dramatic increase in adolescents' media multitasking and use of the Internet for social connections.

Adolescent Problems
- Juvenile delinquency is a major problem in adolescence. Numerous causes have been proposed to explain delinquency.
- Adolescents have a higher rate of depression than children, and females have a much higher rate of depression than males do. Adolescent suicide is the third leading cause of death in U.S. adolescents, and numerous factors are linked to suicide.
- Researchers are increasingly finding that problem behaviors in adolescence are interrelated, and common components characterize successful programs designed to prevent or reduce adolescent problems.

Key Terms

clique	crowd	identity diffusion	juvenile delinquent
commitment	ethnic identity	identity foreclosure	rite of passage
crisis	identity achievement	identity moratorium	

11

Physical and Cognitive Development in Early Adulthood

©Sam Edwards/Caiaimage/Getty Images

CHAPTER OUTLINE

Stories of Life-Span Development: Dave Eggers, Pursuing a Career in the Face of Stress

He was a senior in college when both of his parents died of cancer within five weeks of each other. What would he do? He and his 8-year-old brother left Chicago to live in California, where his older sister was entering law school. Dave would take care of his younger brother, but he needed a job. That first summer, he took a class in furniture painting; then he worked for a geological surveying company, re-creating maps on a computer. Soon, though, he did something very different: With friends from high school, Dave Eggers started *Might,* a satirical magazine for twenty-somethings. It was an edgy, highly acclaimed publication, but not a moneymaker. After a few years, Eggers had to shut down the magazine, and he abandoned California for New York.

This does not sound like a promising start for a career. But within a decade after his parents' death, Eggers had not only raised his young brother but had also founded a quarterly journal and Web site,

Dave Eggers, talented and insightful author.
©Cosima Scavolini/LaPresse/Zumapress.com/Newscom

McSweeney's, and had written a best-seller, *A Heartbreaking Work of Staggering Genius,* which received the National Book Critics Circle Award and was nominated for a Pulitzer Prize. It is a slightly fictionalized account of Eggers' life as he helped care for his dying mother, raised his brother, and searched for his own place in the world. Despite the pain of his loss and the responsibility for his brother, Eggers quickly built a record of achievement as a young adult. ∎

The Transition from Adolescence to Adulthood

When does an adolescent become an adult? It is not easy to tell when a girl or a boy enters adolescence. The task of determining when an individual becomes an adult is even more difficult.

Becoming an Adult

For most individuals, becoming an adult involves a lengthy transition period. The transition from adolescence to adulthood has been referred to as **emerging adulthood,** which occurs from approximately 18 to 25 years of age (Arnett, 2006, 2010, 2012, 2015). Experimentation and exploration characterize the emerging adult. At this point in their development, many individuals are still exploring which career path they want to follow, what they want their identity to be, and which lifestyle they want to adopt (for example, being single, cohabiting, or getting married) (Jensen, 2018; Padilla-Walker & Nelson, 2017).

Key Features of Emerging Adulthood

Jeffrey Arnett (2006) has concluded that five key features characterize emerging adulthood:

- *Identity exploration, especially in love and work.* Emerging adulthood is the time during which key changes in identity take place for many individuals (Layland, Hill, & Nelson, 2018; Vosylis, Erentaite, & Crocetti, 2018).

- *Instability.* Residential changes peak during early adulthood, a time during which there also is often instability in love, work, and education.

- *Self-focused.* According to Arnett (2006, p. 10), emerging adults "are self-focused in the sense that they have little in the way of social obligations, little in the way of duties and commitments to others, which leaves them with a great deal of autonomy in running their own lives."

- *Feeling in-between.* Many emerging adults don't consider themselves adolescents or full-fledged adults.

- *The age of possibilities, a time when individuals have an opportunity to transform their lives.* Arnett (2006) describes two ways in which emerging adulthood is the age of possibilities: (1) many emerging adults are optimistic about their future; and (2) for emerging adults who have experienced difficult times while growing up, emerging adulthood presents an opportunity to reorient their lives in a more positive direction.

Research indicates that these five aspects characterize not only individuals in the United States as they make the transition from adolescence to early adulthood, but also their counterparts in European countries and Australia (Arnett, 2012, 2015; Buhl & Lanz, 2007; Sirsch & others, 2009). Although emerging adulthood does not characterize development in all cultures, it does appear to occur in those where assuming adult roles and responsibilities is postponed (Kins & Beyers, 2010). Critics of the concept of emerging adulthood argue that

How Would You...?

As a **social worker,** how would you apply your knowledge of contemporary society to counsel a client making the transition into adulthood?

emerging adulthood A period of transition from adolescence to adulthood (approximately 18 to 25 years of age) that involves experimentation and exploration.

it applies mainly to privileged adolescents and is not always a self-determined choice for many young people, especially those in limiting socioeconomic conditions (Cote & Bynner, 2008). One study revealed that U.S. at-risk youth entered emerging adulthood slightly earlier than the general population of youth (Lisha & others, 2012).

The Changing Landscape of Emerging and Early Adulthood

In earlier generations, by their mid-twenties at the latest, individuals were expected to have finished college, obtained a full-time job, and establish their own household, most often with a spouse and a child. However, individuals are now taking much longer to reach these developmental milestones, many of which they are not experiencing until their late twenties or even thirties (Vespa, 2017). It is not surprising that their parents recall having had a much earlier timetable of reaching these developmental milestones.

Consider that for the first time in the modern era, in 2014, living with parents was the most frequent living arrangement for 18- to 34-year-olds (Fry, 2016). Dating all the way back to 1880, living with a romantic partner, whether a spouse or a significant other, was previously the most common living arrangement for emerging and young adults. In 2014, 32.1 percent of 18- to 34-year-olds lived with their parents, followed by 31.6 percent who lived with a spouse or partner in their own home, while 14 percent headed the household in which they lived alone. The remaining 22 percent lived in another family member's home, with a non-relative, or in group quarters (college dorm, for example).

In terms of education, today's emerging and young adults are better educated than their counterparts in the 1970s (Vespa, 2017). For example, they are much more likely to have a college degree today. The biggest reason for this educational improvement since the 1970s, though, is a gender difference reversal. In 1975, more young men had college degrees, but today there are more young women than young men who have a college degree.

In terms of work, more young adults are working today than in 1975 (Vespa, 2017). The main reason for this increase also involves a gender change—the significant rise of young women in the workforce, which has increased from slightly below 50 percent to more than two-thirds of young women in the workforce today. In 1975, almost all of the women who were not in the workforce indicated the reason this was the case is that they were taking care of their home and children. However, in 2016, less than 50 percent of the women who were not in the workforce were homemakers.

We will further discuss these lifestyle changes in the chapter on "Socioemotional Development in Early Adulthood."

Markers of Becoming an Adult

In the United States, the most widely recognized marker of entry into adulthood is holding a more or less permanent, full-time job, which usually happens when an individual finishes school—high school for some, college for others, graduate or professional school for still others. However, other criteria are far from clear. Economic independence is one marker of adult status, but achieving it is often a long process. College graduates are increasingly returning to live with their parents as they attempt to establish themselves economically. A longitudinal study found that at age 25 only slightly more than half of the participants were fully financially independent of their family of origin (Cohen & others, 2003). The most dramatic findings in this study, though, involved the extensive variability in the individual trajectories of adult roles across ten years from 17 to 27 years of age; many of the participants moved back and forth between increasing and decreasing economic dependency. One study revealed that continued co-residence with parents during emerging adulthood slowed down the process of becoming a self-sufficient and independent adult (Kins & Beyers, 2010).

Other studies show that taking responsibility for oneself is likely an important marker of adult status for many individuals (Smith & others, 2017). In one study, both parents and college students agreed that taking responsibility for one's actions and developing emotional control are important aspects of becoming an adult (Nelson & others, 2007). And in a study of Danish emerging adults, the most

How Would You...?

As a **psychologist,** how would you offer guidance to emerging adults who are concerned because they have not yet settled into a career and a long-term relationship?

widely described markers of emerging adulthood were accepting self-responsibility, making independent decisions, and becoming financially independent (Arnett & Padilla-Walker, 2015). In this study the least-described markers were the traditional transition events of getting married and avoiding getting drunk. Also, a recent U.S. study of community college students found that they believed they would reach adulthood when they could care for themselves and others (Katsiaficas, 2017).

What we have discussed about the markers of adult status mainly characterizes individuals in industrialized societies, especially Americans. In developing countries, marriage is more often a significant marker for entry into adulthood, and this usually occurs much earlier than the adulthood markers in the United States (Arnett, 2015). In one study, the majority of 18- to 26-year-olds in India felt that they had achieved adulthood (Seiter & Nelson, 2010).

The Transition from High School to College

For many individuals in developed countries, going from high school to college is an important aspect of the transition to adulthood (Eagan & others, 2017; Staley, 2019). Just as the transition from elementary school to middle or junior high school involves change and possible stress, so does the transition from high school to college. The two transitions have many parallels. Going from being a senior in high school to being a freshman in college replays the top-dog phenomenon of transferring from the oldest and

most powerful group of students to the youngest and least powerful group of students that occurred earlier as adolescence began. For many students, the transition from high school to college involves movement to a larger, more impersonal school structure; interaction with peers from more diverse geographical and sometimes more diverse ethnic backgrounds; and increased focus on achievement and its assessment. And like the transition from elementary to middle or junior high school, the transition from high school to college can involve positive features. Students are more likely to feel grown up, have more subjects from which to select, have more time to spend with peers, have more opportunities to explore different lifestyles and values, enjoy greater independence from parental monitoring, and be challenged intellectually by academic work (Halonen & Santrock, 2013).

The transition from high school to college often involves positive as well as negative features. In college, students are likely to feel grown up, spend more time with peers, have more opportunities to explore different lifestyles and values, and enjoy greater freedom from parental monitoring. However, college involves a larger, more impersonal school structure and an increased focus on achievement and its assessment. *What was your transition to college like?*
©Stockbyte/PunchStock

Over the past three decades, the Higher Education Research Institute at UCLA has surveyed first-year college students' backgrounds, experiences, and views on a number of topics. In recent years, traditional-aged college students have shown an increased concern for personal well-being and a decreased concern for the well-being of others, especially for the disadvantaged (Eagan & others, 2017). Today's college freshmen are more strongly motivated to be well-off financially and less motivated to develop a meaningful philosophy of life than were their counterparts of 40 years ago. In 2016, 82.4 percent of students (the highest percent ever in this survey) viewed becoming well-off financially as an "essential" or a "very important" objective compared with only 42 percent in 1971.

There are, however, some signs that U.S. college students are shifting toward a stronger interest in the welfare of society. In the survey

How Would You...?
As an **educator,** how would you prepare high school students to ease the transition to college?

just described, U.S. college freshmen's interest in developing a meaningful philosophy of life increased from 39 percent in 2001 to 46.8 percent in 2016 (Eagan & others, 2017).

An increasing number of first-year college students also report having higher levels of stress and depression. In the national survey just described, 41 percent of first-year college students said they frequently or occasionally felt overwhelmed with all they had to do, 12 percent indicated they were depressed, and 34.5 percent reported feeling anxious (Eagan & others, 2017).

College counselors can provide good information about coping with stress and academic matters. To read about the work of college counselor Grace Leaf, see *Careers in Life-Span Development*.

Careers in life-span development

Grace Leaf, College/Career Counselor and College Administrator

For many years, Grace Leaf was a counselor at Spokane Community College in Washington. In 2014, she became Vice President of Instruction at Lower Columbia College in Spokane. She has a master's degree in educational leadership and is working toward a doctoral degree in educational leadership at Gonzaga University in Washington. In her job as a college counselor, she provided orientation sessions for international students, individual and group advising, and individual and group career planning. Grace tries to connect students with their goals and values and helps them design educational programs that fit their needs and visions.

College counselors help students to cope with adjustment problems, identify their abilities and interests, develop academic plans, and explore career options. Some have an undergraduate

Grace Leaf *(center)* counsels college students at Spokane Community College about careers.
Courtesy of Grace Leaf

degree, others a master's degree like Grace Leaf. Some college counselors have a graduate degree in counseling; others may have an undergraduate degree in psychology or another discipline.

Physical Development

As emerging and young adults learn more about healthy lifestyles and how they contribute to a longer life span, they are increasingly interested in monitoring their physical performance, health, nutrition, exercise, and substance use.

Physical Performance and Development

Most of us reach our peak physical performance before the age of 30, often between the ages of 19 and 26. This peak of physical performance occurs not only for the average young adult, but for outstanding athletes as well. Even though athletes as a group keep getting better than their predecessors—running faster, jumping higher, and lifting more weight—the age at which they reach their peak performance has remained virtually unchanged.

Different types of athletes, however, reach their peak performances at different ages. Most swimmers and gymnasts peak in their late teens. Golfers and marathon runners tend to peak in their late twenties. In other areas of athletics, peak performance often occurs in the early to mid-twenties.

Not only do we reach our peak in physical performance during early adulthood, it is also during this age period that we begin to decline in physical performance. Muscle tone and strength usually begin to show signs of decline around the age of 30. Sagging chins and protruding abdomens also may begin to appear for the first time. The lessening of physical abilities is a common complaint among the just-turned thirties. Sensory systems show little change in early adulthood, but the lens of the eye loses some of its elasticity and becomes less able to change shape and focus on near objects. Hearing peaks in adolescence, remains constant in the first part of early adulthood, and then begins to decline in the last part of early adulthood. And in the middle to late twenties, the body's fatty tissue increases.

Health

Emerging adults have more than twice the mortality rate of adolescents (Park & others, 2006). As indicated in Figure 1, males are mainly responsible for the higher mortality rate of emerging adults.

Figure 1 **Mortality Rates of U.S. Adolescents and Emerging Adults**

Although emerging adults have a higher death rate than adolescents, emerging adults have few chronic health problems, and they have fewer colds and respiratory problems than they did when they were children (Rimsza & Kirk, 2005). Although most college students know how to prevent illness and promote health, they don't fare very well when it comes to applying this information to themselves (Lau & others, 2013). In many cases, emerging adults are not as healthy as they seem (Fatusi & Hindin, 2010).

A longitudinal study revealed that most bad health habits that were engaged in during adolescence increased in emerging adulthood (Harris & others, 2006). Inactivity, poor food choices, obesity, substance use, reproductive health care, and health-care access worsened in emerging adulthood. For example, when they were 12 to 18 years of age, only 5 percent reported no weekly exercise, but when they became 19 to 26 years of age, 46 percent said they did not exercise during a typical week. And another study found that rates of being overweight or obese increased from 25.6 percent for college freshmen to 32 percent for college seniors (Nicoteri & Miskovsky, 2014).

Why might it be easy to develop bad health habits in emerging and early adulthood?
©BananaStock/Getty Images

In emerging and early adulthood, few individuals stop to think about how their personal lifestyles will affect their health later in their adult lives. As emerging adults, many of us develop a pattern of not eating breakfast, not eating regular meals, relying on snacks as our main food source during the day, eating excessively to the point where we exceed the normal weight for our age, smoking moderately or excessively, drinking moderately or excessively, failing to exercise, getting only a few hours of sleep at night, and engaging in risky sexual behavior (Donatelle, 2019; Hales, 2018; Lipson & Sonneville, 2017; Schlarb, Friedrich, & Clausen, 2017; Schulenberg & others, 2017).

Research indicates that 70 percent of college students do not get adequate sleep and that 50 percent report daytime sleepiness (Hershner & Chervin, 2015). In a recent study, higher consumption of energy drinks was linked to more sleep problems in college students (Faris & others, 2017). Emerging adults are not the only ones who are getting inadequate sleep. Many adults in their late twenties and thirties don't get enough either (Brimah &

others, 2013). A statement by the American Academy of Sleep Medicine and Sleep Research Society (Luyster & others, 2012) emphasized that chronic sleep deprivation may contribute to cardiovascular disease, a shortened life span, and cognitive and motor impairment that increase the risk of motor vehicle crashes and work-related accidents.

The lifestyles just described are associated with poor health, which in turn reduces life satisfaction (Insel & Roth, 2018; Kilwein & Looby, 2017; Powers & Haley, 2018). In the Berkeley Longitudinal Study—in which individuals were evaluated over a period of 40 years—physical health at age 30 predicted life satisfaction at age 70, more so for men than for women (Mussen, Honzik, & Eichorn, 1982). Another study explored links between health behavior and life satisfaction of more than 17,000 individuals who were 17 to 30 years old in 21 countries (Grant, Wardle, & Steptoe, 2009). The young adults' life satisfaction was positively related to not smoking, exercising regularly, using sun protection, eating fruit, and limiting fat intake, but it was not related to alcohol consumption and fiber intake.

Eating and Weight

Obesity is a serious and pervasive health problem for many individuals (Blake, 2017; Schiff, 2019; Smith & Collene, 2019). In a recent U.S. survey in 2013-2014, 37.7 percent of adults were classified as obese (35 percent of men; 40 percent of women) (Flegal & others, 2016). In this survey, 34 percent of adults from 20 to 39 years old were obese. Also, analysts have predicted that by 2030, 42 percent of U.S. adults will be obese (Finkelstein & others, 2012). In a recent international comparison of 33 countries, the United States had the highest percentage of obese adults (38.2 percent) and Japan the lowest percentage (3.7); the average of the countries was 19.5 percent of the population being obese (OECD, 2017).

Being overweight or obese is linked to increased risk of hypertension, diabetes, and cardiovascular disease (Aune & others, 2018; Young & others, 2018). Overweight and obesity also are associated with mental health problems (Hong & Hur, 2017; Rajan & Menon, 2017; Zhang & others, 2018). For example, in one study, overweight/obese adults who were depressed were more likely to be characterized by atypical features of depression such as rejection sensitivity and leaden paralysis (a sense of heaviness in arms and legs) than normal-weight depressed adults (Lojko & others, 2015).

One thing we know about losing weight is that the most effective programs include exercise (Walton-Fisette & Wuest, 2018). A research review concluded that adults who engaged in diet-plus-exercise programs lost more weight than those who followed diet-only programs (Wu & others, 2009). Also, a study of approximately 2,000 U.S. adults found that exercising 30 minutes a day, planning meals, and weighing themselves daily were the strategies used more often by successful dieters than by unsuccessful dieters (Kruger, Blanck, & Gillespie, 2006) (see Figure 2).

Regular Exercise

One of the main reasons that health experts want people to exercise is that it helps to prevent diseases, such as heart disease and diabetes (Walton-Fisette & Wuest, 2018). Many health experts recommend that young adults engage in 30 minutes or more of aerobic exercise daily. **Aerobic exercise** is sustained exercise—jogging, swimming, or cycling, for example—that stimulates heart and lung activity. Most health experts recommend exercising vigorously enough to raise your heart rate to at least 60 percent of your maximum heart rate. Only about one-fifth of adults, however, meet these recommended levels of physical activity.

A national poll in the United States found that 51.6 percent of individuals 18 years and older exercised for 30 or more minutes 3 or more

Figure 2

Comparison of Strategies Used by Successful and Unsuccessful Dieters
©iStockphoto.com/Ljupco

aerobic exercise Sustained exercise (such as jogging, swimming, or cycling) that stimulates heart and lung activity.

days a week (Gallup, 2013). In this survey, young adults 18 to 29 years of age (56.8 percent) were the most likely to exercise of all adult age groups. Also in this survey, men were more likely to exercise than women.

Researchers have found that exercise benefits not only physical health, but mental health as well (Netz, 2017). For example, in recent research, moderate to vigorous aerobic exercise was effective in reducing major depressive disorder (Schuch & others, 2017; Paolucci & others, 2018; Werneck, Oyeyemi, & Silva, 2018). Also, in a daily diary study on days when emerging adult (18 to 25 years of age) college students engaged in more physical activity they reported greater satisfaction with life (Maher & others, 2013). And yet another study found a reduction in mortality risk when screen time was replaced by increased physical activity (Wijndaele & others, 2017).

How Would You...?

As a **health-care professional,** how would you design a community education program to emphasize the importance of regular exercise for young adults?

Substance Abuse

Earlier we explored substance abuse in adolescence. One study revealed that only 20 percent of college students reported abstaining from drinking alcohol (Huang & others, 2009). Fortunately, by the time individuals reach their mid-twenties, many have reduced their use of alcohol and drugs (Schulenberg & others, 2017). As in adolescence, male college students and young adults are more likely to take drugs than their female counterparts (Johnston & others, 2015).

Heavy binge drinking often occurs in college, and it can take its toll on students (Wombacher & others, 2018). In 2016, 32 percent of U.S. college students reported having had five or more drinks in a row at least once in the last two weeks (Schulenberg & others, 2017). The term *extreme binge drinking* (also called high-intensity drinking) describes individuals who had 10 or more drinks in a row or 15 or more drinks in a row in the last

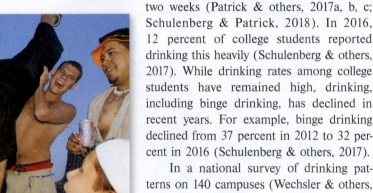

What kinds of problems are associated with binge drinking in college?
©Joe Raedle/Newsmakers/Getty Images

two weeks (Patrick & others, 2017a, b, c; Schulenberg & Patrick, 2018). In 2016, 12 percent of college students reported drinking this heavily (Schulenberg & others, 2017). While drinking rates among college students have remained high, drinking, including binge drinking, has declined in recent years. For example, binge drinking declined from 37 percent in 2012 to 32 percent in 2016 (Schulenberg & others, 2017).

In a national survey of drinking patterns on 140 campuses (Wechsler & others, 1994), almost half of the binge drinkers reported problems that included missing classes, sustaining physical injuries, experiencing troubles with police, and having unprotected sex. For example, binge-drinking college students were 11 times more likely to fall behind in school, 10 times more likely to drive after drinking, and twice as likely to have unprotected sex in comparison with college students who did not binge drink. And a longitudinal study revealed that frequent binge drinking and marijuana use during the freshman year of college predicted delayed college graduation (White & others, 2018).

When does binge drinking peak during development? A longitudinal study revealed that binge drinking peaks at about 21 to 22 years of age and then declines through the remainder of the twenties (Schulenberg & others, 2017) (see Figure 3). Recent data from the Monitoring the Future study at the University of Michigan also indicate that binge drinking peaked at 21 to 22 years of age, with 38 percent reporting that they had engaged in binge drinking at least once in the last 2 weeks (Schulenberg & others, 2017).

How Would You...?

As a **social worker,** how would you apply your understanding of binge drinking to develop a program to encourage responsible alcohol use on college campuses?

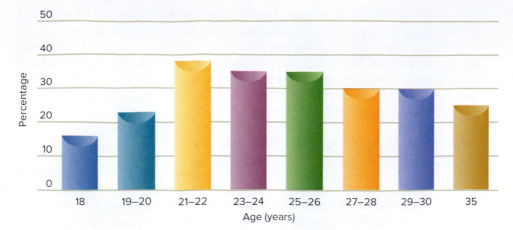

Figure 3 Binge Drinking in the Adolescence–Early Adulthood Transition
Note that the percentage of individuals engaging in binge drinking peaked at 21 or 22 years of age, remained high through the mid-twenties, then began to decline in the late twenties. Binge drinking was defined as having five or more alcoholic drinks in a row in the previous two weeks.
Source: Schulenberg, J., et al. *Monitoring the Future*, Figure 4-20b, 2017.

Sexuality

We have explored how adolescents develop a sexual identity and become sexually active. What happens to their sexuality in adulthood?

Sexual Activity in Emerging Adulthood

At the beginning of emerging adulthood (age 18), surveys indicate that slightly more than 60 percent of individuals have experienced sexual intercourse, but by the end of emerging adulthood (age 25), most individuals have had sexual intercourse (Lefkowitz & Gillen, 2006). Also, the average age of marriage in the United States is currently 29.5 for males and 27.4 for females (Livingston, 2017). Thus, emerging adulthood is a time during which most individuals are both sexually active and unmarried (Waterman & Lefkowitz, 2018).

Casual sex is more common in emerging adulthood than it is during the late twenties (Waterman & Lefkowitz, 2018; Wesche & Lefkowitz, 2019; Wesche & others, 2018). A recent trend has involved "hooking up" to have non-relationship sex (from kissing to intercourse) (Blayney & others, 2018; Penhollow, Young, & Nnaka, 2017; Sullivan & others, 2018). One study revealed that 20 percent of first-year college women on one large university campus had engaged in at least one hook-up over the course of the school year (Fielder & others, 2013). In this study, impulsivity, sensation seeking, and alcohol use were among the predictors of a higher likelihood of hooking up. Further, another study indicated that 40 percent of 22-year-olds reporting having had a recent casual sexual partner (Lyons & others, 2015). And one study of more than 3,900 18- to 25-year-olds indicated that having casual sex was negatively linked to well-being and positively related to psychological distress (Bersamin & others, 2014).

In addition to hooking up, another type of casual sex that has increased among emerging adults is "friends with benefits (FWB)," which involves a relationship formed by the integration of friendship and sexual intimacy without an explicit commitment characteristic of an exclusive romantic relationship (Weger, Cole, & Akbulut, 2018). A recent study found that suicidal ideation was associated with entrance into a friends-with-benefits relationship as well as continuation of the FWB relationship (Dube & others, 2017).

Sexual Orientation and Behavior

A national study of sexual behavior in the United States among adults 25 to 44 years of age found that 98 percent of the women and 97 percent of the men said that they had ever engaged in vaginal intercourse (Chandra & others, 2011). Also in this study, 89 percent of the women and 90 percent of the men reported that they had ever had oral sex with an opposite-sex partner, and 36 percent of the women and 44 percent of the men stated that they had ever had anal sex with an opposite-sex partner.

Detailed information about various aspects of sexual activity in adults of different ages comes from the 1994 Sex in America survey. In this study Robert Michael and his colleagues (1994) interviewed more than 3,000 people from 18 to 59 years of age who were randomly selected, in sharp contrast with earlier samples that were based on unrepresentative groups of volunteers.

Heterosexual Attitudes and Behavior

Here are some of the key findings from the 1994 Sex in America survey:

- Americans tend to fall into three categories: One-third have sex twice a week or more, one-third a few times a month, and one-third a few times a year or not at all.

- Married (and cohabiting) couples have sex more often than noncohabiting couples (see Figure 4).

- Most Americans do not engage in kinky sexual acts. When asked about their favorite sexual acts, the vast majority (96 percent) said that vaginal sex was "very" or "somewhat" appealing. Oral sex was in third place, after an activity that many have not labeled a sexual act—watching a partner undress.

- Adultery is clearly the exception rather than the rule. Nearly 75 percent of the married men and 85 percent of the married women in the survey indicated that they had never been unfaithful.

- Men think about sex far more often than women do—54 percent of the men said they thought about it every day or several times a day, whereas 67 percent of the women said they thought about it only a few times a week or a few times a month.

In sum, one of the most powerful messages in the 1994 survey was that Americans' sexual lives are more conservative than was previously believed. Although 17 percent of the men and 3 percent of the women said they had had sex with at least 21 partners, the overall impression from the survey was that sexual behavior is ruled by marriage and monogamy for most Americans.

How extensive are gender differences in sexuality? An analysis of almost 8,000 emerging adults found that males had stronger permissive attitudes, especially about sex in casual

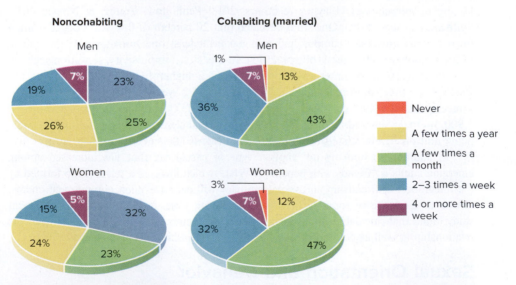

Figure 4 The Sex in America Survey
The percentages show noncohabiting and cohabiting (married) males' and females' responses to the question "How often have you had sex in the past year?" in a 1994 survey (Michael & others, 1994).
What was one feature of the Sex in America survey that made it superior to most surveys of sexual behavior?
Source: Michael, R. T., Gagnon, J. H., Laumann, E. O., & Kolata, G. *Sex in America.* Boston: Little, Brown, 1994.

relationships, than did females (Sprecher, Treger, & Sakaluk, 2013). Also, a meta-analysis revealed that men reported having slightly more sexual experiences and more permissive attitudes than women for most aspects of sexuality (Petersen & Hyde, 2010). For the following factors, stronger differences were found: Men said that they engaged more often in masturbation, pornography use, and casual sex, and had more permissive attitudes about casual sex than their female counterparts did.

Given all the media and public attention focusing on the negative aspects of sexuality—such as adolescent pregnancy, sexually transmitted infections, rape, and so on—it is important to underscore that research strongly supports the role of sexuality in well-being (King, 2017, 2018). For example, in a Swedish study frequency of sexual intercourse was strongly linked to life satisfaction for both women and men (Brody & Costa, 2009). And in a recent study, sexual activity in adults on day 1 was linked to greater well-being the next day (Kashdan & others, 2018). Also in this study, higher reported sexual pleasure and intimacy predicted more positive affect and less negative affect the next day.

Sources of Sexual Orientation

Until the end of the nineteenth century, it was generally believed that people were either heterosexual or homosexual. Today, the more accepted view of sexual orientation depicts it not as an either/or proposition but as a continuum from exclusive male-female relations to exclusive same-sex relations (King, 2017, 2018). Some individuals are bisexual, being sexually attracted to people of both sexes.

People sometimes think that bisexuality is simply a stepping stone to same-sex sexuality, while others view it as a sexual orientation itself or as an indicator of sexual fluidity (King, 2017, 2018). Evidence supports the notion that bisexuality is a stable orientation that involves attraction to both sexes (Lippa, 2013).

Compared with men, women are more likely to change their sexual patterns and desires (Knight & Hope, 2012). Women are more likely than men to have sexual experiences with same- and opposite-sex partners, even if they identify themselves strongly as being heterosexual or lesbian (King, 2017, 2018). Also, women are more likely than men to identify themselves as bisexual (Gates, 2011).

In the Sex in America survey, 2.7 percent of the men and 1.3 percent of the women reported having had same-sex relations in the past year (Michael & others, 1994). However, in a national survey a higher percentage (3.8 percent) of U.S. adults reported that they were gay, lesbian, bisexual, or transsexual (Gallup, 2015). In the most recent national survey of sexual orientation that included men and women from 18 to 44 years of age, almost three times as many women (17.4 percent) as men (6.2 percent) reported having had same-sex contact (Copen, Chandra, & Febo-Vasquez, 2018). Feelings of attraction only to the opposite sex were more frequent for men (92.1 percent) than for women (81 percent). Also in this study, 92.3 percent of women and 95.1 percent of men described themselves as heterosexual or straight. Further, 1.3 percent of women and 1.9 percent of men said they were homosexual, gay, or lesbian. Also, 5.5 percent of women and 2 percent of men reported that they were bisexual.

What likely determines an individual's sexual orientation? (Top) ©Laurence Mouton/Getty Images; (middle & bottom) ©2009 JupiterImages Corporation

Why are some individuals lesbian, gay, or bisexual (LGB) and others heterosexual? Speculation surrounding this question has been extensive (Savin-Williams, 2017, 2018).

All people, regardless of their sexual orientation, have similar physiological responses during sexual arousal and seem to be aroused by the same types of tactile stimulation. Investigators typically find no differences between LGBs and heterosexuals in a wide range of attitudes, behaviors, and adjustments (Fingerhut & Peplau, 2013).

Recently, researchers have explored the possible biological basis of same-sex relations. The results of hormone studies have been inconsistent. If gay males are given male sex hormones (androgens), their sexual orientation doesn't change. Their sexual desire merely increases. A very early prenatal critical period might influence sexual orientation (Berenbaum & Beltz, 2011). If this critical-period hypothesis turns out to be correct, it would explain why clinicians have found that sexual orientation is difficult, if not impossible, to modify.

Researchers have also examined genetic influences on sexual orientation by studying twins. A Swedish study of almost 4,000 twins found that only about 35 percent of the variation in homosexual behavior in men and 19 percent in women were explained by genetic differences (Langstrom & others, 2010). This result suggests that although genes likely play a role in sexual orientation, they are not the only factor involved (King, 2017, 2018).

An individual's sexual orientation—same-sex, heterosexual, or bisexual—is most likely determined by a combination of genetic, hormonal, cognitive, and environmental factors (King, 2017, 2018). Most experts on same-sex relations believe that no one factor alone causes sexual orientation and that the relative weight of each factor can vary from one individual to the next. That said, it has become clear that whether heterosexual, gay, lesbian, or bisexual, a person cannot be talked out of his or her sexual orientation (King, 2017, 2018).

Attitudes and Behavior of Lesbians and Gay Males

Many gender differences that appear in heterosexual relationships occur in same-sex relationships (Diamond & Alley, 2018; Savin-Williams, 2017, 2018). For example, lesbians have fewer sexual partners than gays, and lesbians have less permissive attitudes about casual sex outside a primary relationship than gays do (Fingerhut & Peplau, 2013).

Sexually Transmitted Infections

Sexually transmitted infections (STIs) are diseases that are primarily contracted through sexual relations—intercourse as well as oral-genital and anal-genital sex. STIs affect about one of every six U.S. adults (National Center for Health Statistics, 2018). Among the most prevalent STIs are bacterial infections—such as gonorrhea, syphilis, and chlamydia—and STIs caused by viruses—such as AIDS (acquired immune deficiency syndrome), genital herpes, and genital warts. Figure 5 describes these sexually transmitted infections.

No single disease has had a greater impact on sexual behavior, or created more public fear in the last several decades, than infection with the human immunodeficiency virus (HIV) (Crooks & Baur, 2017). HIV is a virus that destroys the body's immune system. Once a person is infected with HIV, the virus breaks down and overpowers the immune system, which leads to AIDS. An individual sick with AIDS has such a weakened immune system that a common cold can be life-threatening.

In 2015, approximately 1.1 million people in the United States were living with an HIV infection (Centers for Disease Control and Prevention, 2018). In 2015, male-male sexual contact continued to be the most frequent AIDS transmission category. Because of education and the development of more effective drug treatments, deaths due to HIV/AIDS have begun to decline in the United States. Globally, the total number of individuals living with HIV was 36.7 million in 2016, with 25.7 million of these individuals with HIV living in sub-Saharan Africa (UNAIDS, 2017). Currently, only about 60 percent of individuals with HIV know they have the disease (UNAIDS, 2017). Approximately half of all new HIV infections around the world occur in the 15- to 24-year-old age category. In one study, only 49 percent of 15- to 24-year-old females in low- and middle-income countries knew that using a condom helps to prevent HIV infection, compared with 74 percent of young males (UNAIDS, 2011). The good news is that global rates of HIV infection fell by 35 percent from 2000 to 2014 (UNAIDS, 2015).

What are some good strategies for protecting against HIV and other sexually transmitted infections? They include the following:

- *Knowing your own and your partner's risk status.* Anyone who has had previous sexual activity with another person might have contracted an STI without being aware of it. Spend time getting to know a

sexually transmitted infections (STIs) Diseases that are contracted primarily through sexual contact.

STI	Description/cause	Incidence	Treatment
Gonorrhea	Commonly called the "drip" or "clap." Caused by the bacterium *Neisseria gonorrhoeae*. Spread by contact between infected moist membranes (genital, oral-genital, or anal-genital) of two individuals. Characterized by discharge from penis or vagina and painful urination. Can lead to infertility.	500,000 cases annually in U.S.	Penicillin, other antibiotics
Syphilis	Caused by the bacterium *Treponema pallidum*. Characterized by the appearance of a sore where syphilis entered the body. The sore can be on the external genitals, vagina, or anus. Later, a skin rash breaks out on palms of hands and bottom of feet. If not treated, can eventually lead to paralysis or even death.	100,000 cases annually in U.S.	Penicillin
Chlamydia	A common STI named for the bacterium *Chlamydia trachomatis*, an organism that spreads by sexual contact and infects the genital organs of both sexes. A special concern is that females with chlamydia may become infertile. It is recommended that adolescent and young adult females have an annual screening for this STI.	About 3 million people in U.S. annually	Antibiotics
Genital herpes	Caused by a family of viruses with different strains. Involves an eruption of sores and blisters. Spread by sexual contact.	One of five U.S. adults	No known cure but antiviral medications can shorten outbreaks
AIDS	Caused by a virus, the human immunodeficiency virus (HIV), which destroys the body's immune system. Semen and blood are the main vehicles of transmission. Common symptoms include fevers, night sweats, weight loss, chronic fatigue, and swollen lymph nodes.	More than 300,000 cumulative cases of HIV virus in U.S. 25–34-year-olds; epidemic incidence in sub-Saharan countries	New treatments have slowed the progression from HIV to AIDS; no cure
Genital warts	Caused by the human papillomavirus, which does not always produce symptoms. Usually appear as small, hard painless bumps in the vaginal area, or around the anus. Very contagious. Certain high-risk types of this virus cause cervical cancer and other genital cancers. May recur despite treatment. A new HPV preventive vaccine, Gardasil, has been approved for girls and women 9–26 years of age.	About 5.5 million new cases annually; considered the most common STI in the U.S.	A topical drug, freezing, or surgery

Figure 5 Sexually Transmitted Infections

prospective partner before you have sex. Use this time to inform the other person of your STI status and inquire about your partner's. Remember that many people lie about their STI status.

- *Obtaining medical examinations.* Many experts recommend that couples who want to begin a sexual relationship have a medical checkup to rule out STIs before engaging in sex. If cost is an issue, contact your campus health service or a public health clinic.

- *Having protected, not unprotected, sex.* When correctly used, latex condoms help to prevent many STIs from being transmitted. Condoms are most effective in preventing gonorrhea, syphilis, chlamydia, and HIV. They are less effective against the spread of herpes.

- *Not having sex with multiple partners.* One of the best predictors of getting an STI is having sex with multiple partners. Having more than one sex partner elevates the likelihood of encountering an infected partner.

How Would You...?

As a **health-care professional,** what advice would you give to a patient who is sexually active, does not use condoms, and does not want to be tested for any sexually transmitted infections?

Cognitive Development

Are there changes in cognitive performance during these years? To explore the nature of cognition in early adulthood, we focus on issues related to cognitive stages and creative thinking.

Cognitive Stages

Are young adults more advanced in their thinking than adolescents are? Let's examine how Piaget and others have answered this intriguing question.

Piaget's View

Piaget concluded that an adolescent and an adult think qualitatively in the same way. That is, Piaget argued that at approximately 11 to 15 years of age, adolescents enter the formal operational stage, which is characterized by more logical, abstract, and idealistic thinking than the concrete operational thinking of 7- to 11-year-olds. Piaget did believe that young adults are more quantitatively advanced in their thinking in the sense that they have more knowledge than adolescents possess. He also believed, as do information-processing psychologists, that adults especially increase their knowledge in a specific area, such as a physicist's understanding of physics or a financial analyst's knowledge about finance. According to Piaget, however, formal operational thought is the final stage in cognitive development, and it characterizes adults as well as adolescents.

What are some ways that young adults might think differently from adolescents?
©Yuri Arcurs/Alamy

Some developmentalists theorize it is not until adulthood that many individuals consolidate their formal operational thinking. That is, they may begin to plan and hypothesize about intellectual problems in adolescence, but they become more systematic and sophisticated at this as young adults. Nonetheless, even many adults do not think in formal operational ways at all (Kuhn, 2009).

Postformal Thought

It has been proposed that the idealism of Piaget's formal operational stage declines in young adults and is replaced by more realistic, pragmatic thinking. It also has been proposed that young adults move into a new qualitative stage of cognitive development called postformal thought (Sinnott, 2003). **Postformal thought** is:

> ## How Would You...?
> As an **educator**, how would you characterize the differences in the cognitive development of adolescents and adults? How would this distinction influence your approach to teaching these different populations?

- *Reflective, relativistic, and contextual.* As young adults engage in solving problems, they might think deeply about many aspects of work, politics, relationships, and other areas of life (Labouvie-Vief, 1986). They find that what might be the best solution to a problem at work (with a boss or co-worker) might not be the best solution at home (with a romantic partner). Thus, postformal thought holds that the correct answer to a problem requires reflective thinking and may vary from one situation to another. Some psychologists argue that reflective thinking continues to increase and becomes more internal and less contextual in middle age (Labouvie-Vief, Gruhn, & Studer, 2010; Mascalo & Fischer, 2010).

- *Provisional.* Many young adults also become more skeptical about the truth and seem unwilling to accept an answer as final. Thus, they come to see the search for truth as an ongoing and perhaps never-ending process.

- *Realistic.* Young adults understand that thinking can't always be abstract. In many instances, it must be realistic and pragmatic.

- *Recognized as being influenced by emotion.* Emerging and young adults are more likely than adolescents to understand that their thinking is influenced by emotions (Girgis & others, 2018; Labouvie-Vief, 2009). However, too often negative emotions produce thinking that is distorted and self-serving at this point in development.

postformal thought Thinking that is reflective, relativistic, and contextual; provisional; realistic; and influenced by emotions.

In addition to the characteristics just described for a possible fifth, postformal stage, a recent study explored wisdom and meaning as important developments in emerging adulthood (Webster & others, 2018). In this study, it was found that the search for and presence of meaning was linked to wisdom, which was assessed with five components: critical life experiences, reminiscence/reflectiveness, openness to experience, emotional regulation, and humor. We will further explore meaning in life in the chapter on "Socioemotional Development in Middle Adulthood" and wisdom in the chapter on "Cognitive Development in Late Adulthood."

Creativity

Early adulthood is a time of great creativity for some people. At the age of 30, Thomas Edison invented the phonograph, Hans Christian Andersen wrote his first volume of fairy tales, and Mozart composed *The Marriage of Figaro*. One early study of creativity found that individuals' most creative products were generated in their thirties, and that 80 percent of the most important creative contributions were completed by age 50 (Lehman, 1960). Even though a decline in creative contributions is often found in the fifties and later, the decline is not as great as was commonly thought.

Any consideration of decline in creativity with age must take into account the field of creativity involved (Kandler & others, 2016). In fields such as philosophy and history, older adults often show as much creativity as they did when they were in their thirties and forties. By contrast, in fields such as lyric poetry, abstract math, and theoretical physics, the peak of creativity is often reached in the twenties or thirties.

Researchers have found that personality traits are linked to creativity (Feist, 2018; Kandler & others, 2016). In one recent study, the personality trait of openness to experience predicted creativity in the arts, while intellectual capacity predicted creativity in the sciences (Kaufman & others, 2016).

Can you make yourself more creative? Mihaly Csikszentmihalyi (1995) interviewed 90 leading figures in art, business, government, education, and science to learn how creativity works. He discovered that creative people regularly experience a state he calls *flow,* a heightened state of pleasure experienced when we are engaged in mental and physical challenges that absorb us. Csikszentmihalyi (2000) believes everyone is capable of achieving flow. Based on his interviews with some of the most creative people in the world, the first step toward a more creative life is cultivating your curiosity and interest. How can you do this?

- Try to be surprised by something every day. Maybe it is something you see, hear, or read about. Become absorbed in a lecture or a book. Be open to what the world is telling you. Life is a stream of experiences. Swim widely and deeply in it, and your life will be richer.

- Try to surprise at least one person every day. In a lot of things you do, you have to be predictable and patterned. Do something different for a change. Ask a question you normally would not ask. Invite someone to go to a show you haven't seen or a museum you never have visited.

How Would You...?

As an **educator,** how would you use your understanding of creativity to become a more effective teacher?

- Write down each day what surprised you and how you surprised others. Most creative people keep a diary, notes, or lab records to ensure that their experience is not fleeting or forgotten. Start with a specific task. Each evening, record the most surprising event that occurred that day and your most surprising action. After a few days, reread your notes and reflect on your past experiences. After a few weeks, you might see a pattern of interest emerging in your notes, one that might suggest an area you can explore in greater depth.

- When something sparks your interest, follow it. Usually when something captures your attention, it is short-lived—an idea, a song, a flower. Too often we are too busy to explore the idea, song, or flower further. Or we think these areas are none of our business because we are not experts about them. Yet the world is our business. We can't know which part of it is best suited to our interests until we make a serious effort to learn as much about as many aspects of it as possible.

Mihaly Csikszentmihalyi, in the setting where he gets his most creative ideas. *When and where do you get your most creative thoughts?*
Courtesy of Dr. Mihaly Csiksentmihalyi

- Wake up in the morning with a specific goal to look forward to. Creative people wake up eager to start the day. Why? Not necessarily because they are cheerful, enthusiastic types but because they know that there is something meaningful to accomplish each day, and they can't wait to get started.

- Spend time in settings that stimulate your creativity. In Csikszentmihalyi's (1995) research, he gave people an electronic pager and beeped them randomly at different times of the day. When he asked them how they felt, they reported the highest levels of creativity when walking, driving, or swimming. I (your author) do my most creative thinking when I'm jogging. These activities are semiautomatic in that they take a certain amount of attention while leaving some time free to make connections among ideas. Another setting in which highly creative people report coming up with novel ideas is the sort of half-asleep, half-awake state we are in when we are deeply relaxed or barely awake.

Careers and Work

Earning a living, choosing an occupation, establishing a career, and developing in a career—these are important themes of early adulthood. Let's consider some of the factors that go into choosing a career and a job and examine how work typically affects the lives of young adults.

Careers

What are some developmental changes young adults experience as they choose a career? How effectively are individuals finding a path to purpose today?

Developmental Changes

Many children have idealistic fantasies about what they want to be when they grow up. For example, many young children want to be superheroes, sports stars, or movie stars. In the high school years, they often begin to think about careers in a somewhat less idealistic way. In their late teens and early twenties, their career decision making has usually turned more serious as they explore different career possibilities and zero in on the career they want to enter. In college, this often means choosing a major or specialization that is designed to lead to work in a particular field. By their early and mid-twenties, many individuals have completed their education or training and entered a full-time occupation. From the mid-twenties through the remainder of early adulthood, individuals often seek to establish their emerging career in a particular field. They may work hard to move up the career ladder and improve their financial standing.

Phyllis Moen (2009a) described the career mystique, which includes ingrained cultural beliefs that engaging in hard work for long hours through adulthood will produce a path to status, security, and happiness. That is, many individuals have an idealized concept of a career path toward achieving the American dream of upward mobility by climbing occupational ladders. However, the lockstep career mystique has never been a reality for many individuals, especially ethnic minority individuals, women, and poorly educated adults. Further, the career mystique has increasingly become a myth for many individuals in middle-income occupations as global outsourcing of jobs and widespread layoffs during the 2007–2009 recession have led to reduced job security for millions of Americans.

Finding a Path to Purpose

In his book *The Path to Purpose: Helping Our Children Find Their Calling in Life*, William Damon (2008) suggested that purpose is a missing ingredient in many adolescents' and emerging adults' achievement and career development. Too many youth drift aimlessly through their high school and college years, Damon says, engaging in behavior that places them at risk for not fulfilling their potential and not finding a life pursuit that energizes them.

In interviews with 12- to 22-year-olds, Damon found that only about 20 percent had a clear vision of where they wanted to go in life, what they wanted to achieve, and why. The largest percentage—about 60 percent—had engaged in some potentially purposeful activities, such as service learning or fruitful discussions with a career counselor—but they still did not have a real commitment or any reasonable plans for reaching their goals. And slightly more than 20 percent expressed no aspirations and, in some instances, said they didn't see any reason to have aspirations.

Damon concludes that most teachers and parents communicate the importance of achieving goals such as studying hard and getting good grades, but rarely discuss the purpose of these goals and where they might lead young adults. Damon emphasizes that too often students focus only on short-term goals and don't explore the big, long-term picture of what they want to do with their life. The following interview questions that Damon (2008, p. 135) has used in his research are good springboards for getting individuals to reflect on their purpose:

Hari Prabhakar (*in rear*) at a screening camp in India that he created as part of his Tribal India Health Foundation. Hari reflects William Damon's concept of finding a path to purpose. His ambition is to become an international health expert. A 2006 graduate from Johns Hopkins University (with a double major in public health and writing and a 3.9 GPA), he pursued many activities outside the classroom, in the health field. As he transitioned from high school to college, Hari created the Tribal India Health Foundation (www.tihf.org), which provides assistance in bringing low-cost health care to rural areas in India. Juggling roles as a student and as the foundation's director, Hari spent 15 hours a week leading Tribal India Health during his undergraduate years. Hari said (Johns Hopkins University, 2006): "I have found it very challenging to coordinate the international operation. . . . It takes a lot of work, and there's not a lot of free time. But it's worth it when I visit our patients and see how they and the community are getting better."
Courtesy of Hari Prabhakar

- What's most important to you in your life?
- Why do you care about those things?
- Do you have any long-term goals?
- Why are these goals important to you?
- What does it mean to have a good life?
- What does it mean to be a good person?
- If you were looking back on your life now, how would you like to be remembered?

Recent research has provided support for the importance of purpose in people's lives. In one study, purpose predicted emerging adults' well-being (Hill & others, 2016). In another study, a high sense of purpose in life was associated with a lower incidence of cardiovascular disease and a longer life (Cohen, Bavishi, & Rozanski, 2016).

Work

In this final section, we'll examine how work affects people's lives, the role of work in college, the occupational outlook, unemployment, dual-earner couples, and diversity in the workplace.

The Impact of Work

Work defines people in fundamental ways (Adler & Elmhurst, 2019; Hsieh & Huang, 2017). It is an important influence on their financial standing, housing, the way they spend their time, where they live, their friendships, and their health. Some people define their identity through their work. Work also creates a structure and rhythm to life that is often missed when individuals do not work for an extended period. When they are unable to work, many individuals experience emotional distress and low self-esteem.

Most individuals spend about one-third of their lives at work. In one survey, U.S. individuals 18+ years old who were employed full-time worked an average of 47 hours per week, almost a full work day longer than the standard 9 to 5 five days a week schedule

(Saad, 2014). In this survey, half of all individuals working full-time reported that they work more than 40 hours a week and nearly 40 percent said they work 50 hours a week or more. Only 8 percent indicated they worked less than 40 hours per week.

The U.S. job market for college graduates has been improving recently. According to a recent survey, 74 percent of employers reported that they were planning to hire recent college graduates in 2017, up from 67 percent in 2016 (CareerBuilder, 2017). The 74 percent figure is the best job outlook for recent college graduates since 2007. Also good news for recent college graduates is that in 2017, employers said they were planning to pay new employees more than they did in 2016.

A trend in the U.S. workforce is the disappearing long-term career for an increasing number of adults, especially men in private-sector jobs (Hollister, 2011). Among the reasons for the reduced number of long-term jobs is the dramatic increase in technology and cheaper labor in other countries.

Many young and older adults are working at a series of jobs, and many work in short-term jobs (Greenhaus, 2013). Early careers are especially unstable as some young workers move from "survival jobs" to "career jobs" in the process of finding a job that matches their personal interests and goals (Staff, Mont'Alvao, & Mortimer, 2015). A study of more than 1,100 individuals from 18 to 31 years of age revealed that maintaining a high aspiration and certainty over career goals better insulated individuals against unemployment during the severe economic recession that began in 2007 (Vuolo, Staff, & Mortimer, 2012).

An important consideration regarding work is how stressful it is (Dragano & others, 2017; Hassard & others, 2018; Mayerl & others, 2017). In a national survey of U.S. adults, 55 percent indicated they were less productive because of stress (American Psychological Association, 2007). In this study, 52 percent reported that they had considered or made a career decision, such as looking for a new job, declining a promotion, or quitting a job, because of stress in the workplace. In this survey, main sources of stress included low salaries (44 percent), lack of advancement opportunities (42 percent), uncertain job expectations (40 percent), and long hours (39 percent). One study revealed that stressors at work were linked to arterial hypertension in employees (Lamy & others, 2014). A recent study indicated that increases in job strain increased workers' insomnia, while decreases in job strain reduced their insomnia (Halonen & others, 2018).

How Would You...?

As an **educator,** what advice would you give to a student who has a full-time job while taking college classes?

Many adults hold changing expectations about work, yet employers often aren't meeting their expectations (Hall & Mirvis, 2013). For example, current policies and practices were designed for a single-breadwinner (male) workforce and an industrial economy, making these policies and practices out of step with a service-oriented workforce of women and men, and of single parents and dual earners. Many workers today want flexibility and greater control over the time and timing of their work, yet most employers offer little flexibility, even if policies like flextime are "on the books."

Work During College

The percentage of full-time U.S. college students who also held jobs increased from 34 percent in 1970 to 47 percent in 2008, then declined to 43 percent in in 2015 (down from a peak of 52 percent in 2000) (National Center for Education Statistics, 2017). In 2015, 78 percent of part-time U.S. college students were employed, up from 74 percent in 2011 but slightly down from 81 percent in 2008.

Figure 6 **The Relation of Hours Worked Per Week in College to Grades**

Among college students working to pay for school expenses, 16 percent of those working 1 to 15 hours per week reported that working had a negative impact on their grades (National Center for Education Statistics, 2002). Thirty percent of college students who worked 16 to 20 hours a week said the same, as did 48 percent who worked 35 hours or more per week.

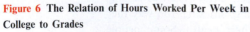
Source: National Center for Education Statistics. *The Condition of Education: Work During College.* Washington, DC: U.S. Office of Education, 2002.

Working can pay for schooling or help offset some of its costs, but working also can restrict students' opportunities to learn. For those who identified themselves primarily as students, one national study found that as the number of hours worked per week increased, their grades suffered (National Center for Education Statistics, 2002) (see Figure 6). Thus, college students need to carefully examine whether the number of hours they work is having a negative impact on their college success.

Monitoring the Occupational Outlook

As you explore the type of work you are likely to enjoy and in which you can succeed, it is important to be knowledgeable about different fields and companies. Occupations may have many job openings one year but few in another year as economic conditions change. Thus, it is critical to keep up with the occupational outlook in various fields. An excellent resource for doing this is the U.S. government's *Occupational Outlook Handbook,* which is revised every two years.

According to the 2016–2017 handbook, the job categories of wind turbine service technicians, occupational therapy assistants, physical therapist assistants, physical therapist aides, home health aides, commercial drivers, nurse practitioners, physical therapists, and statisticians are projected to be the fastest-growing through 2024. Projected job growth varies widely by educational requirements. Jobs that require a college degree are expected to grow the fastest. Most of the highest-paying occupations require a college degree.

Unemployment

Unemployment produces stress regardless of whether the job loss is temporary, cyclical, or permanent (Frasquilho & others, 2016). Researchers have linked unemployment to physical problems (such as heart attack and stroke), emotional problems (such as depression and anxiety), marital difficulties, and homicide (Rizvi & others, 2015; Yoo & others, 2016). One study revealed that 90 or more days of unemployment was associated with subsequent cardiovascular disease across an 8-year follow-up period (Lundin & others, 2014). A research review concluded that unemployment was associated with an increased mortality risk for individuals in the early and middle stages of their careers, but the link was weaker for those in the later years of their career (Roelfs & others, 2011). In a recent study, depression following job loss predicted increased risk of continued unemployment (Stolove, Galatzer-Levy, & Bonanno, 2017). And one study found that involuntary job loss was linked to increased rates of attempted suicide and suicide (Milner & others, 2014). Also, in another study, unemployment was associated with higher mortality and the link was higher for those who were unmarried (Van Hedel & others, 2015).

Might unemployment be linked to certain characteristics in childhood and adolescence? Longitudinal data revealed that low self-control in childhood was linked to the emergence and persistence of unemployment from 21 to 50 years of age (Daly & others, 2015). Further, a recent study found that heavy drinking from 16 to 30 years of age was linked to higher unemployment in middle age (Berg & others, 2018).

Stress from unemployment comes not only from a loss of income and the resulting financial hardships but also from decreased self-esteem (Howe & others, 2012). Individuals who cope best with unemployment have financial resources to rely on, often savings or the earnings of other family members. Emotional support from understanding, adaptable family members also helps individuals to cope with unemployment. Job counseling and self-help groups can provide practical advice on job searching, résumé writing, and interviewing skills, and also can lend emotional support (van Hooft, 2014).

The economic recession that hit in 2007 resulted in millions of Americans losing their jobs, such as these individuals who are waiting in line to apply for unemployment benefits in Chicago. *What are some of the potential negative outcomes of the stress caused by job loss?* ©Scott Olson/Getty Images

Dual-Earner Couples

Dual-earner couples may have special problems finding a balance between work and the rest of life (Schooreel & Verbruggen, 2016; Sun & others, 2017). If both partners are working, who cleans the house or calls the repairman or takes care of the other endless details involved in maintaining a home? If the couple has children, who is responsible for being sure that the children get to school or to piano lessons on time, and who writes the notes to approve field trips or meets the teacher or makes the dental appointments?

Many dual-earner couples engage in a range of adaptive strategies to coordinate their work and manage the family side of the work-family equation (Flood & Genadek, 2016). Researchers have found that even though couples may strive for gender equality in dual-earner families, gender inequalities persist (Cunningham, 2009). For example, women still do not earn as much as men in the same jobs, and this inequity contributes to gender divisions in how much time each partner spends in paid work, homemaking, and caring for children. Thus, the decisions that dual-earner couples often make are in favor of men's greater earning power and women spending more time than men in homemaking and caring for children (Moen, 2009b). One study indicated that women reported more family interference from work than did men (Allen & Finkelstein, 2014). Another study found that partner coping, having a positive attitude toward multiple roles, using planning and management skills, and not having to cut back on professional responsibilities were linked to better relationships between dual earners (Matias & Fontaine, 2015).

Summary

The Transition from Adolescence to Adulthood

- Emerging adulthood, the time of transition from adolescence to adulthood, is characterized by experimentation and exploration. Today's emerging and young adults are experiencing emerging and early adulthood quite differently from their counterparts in earlier generations.
- The transition from high school to college can involve both positive and negative features.

Physical Development

- Peak physical performance is often reached between 19 and 26 years of age. Then, toward the latter part of early adulthood, a detectable slowdown in physical performance is apparent for most individuals.
- Health problems in emerging and young adults may include obesity, a serious problem throughout the United States. Binge drinking is a special problem among U.S. college students, but by the mid-twenties alcohol and drug use often decreases.

Sexuality

- Patterns of sexual activity change during emerging adulthood.
- An individual's sexual orientation likely stems from a combination of genetic, hormonal, cognitive, and environmental factors.
- Sexually transmitted infections, also called STIs, are contracted primarily through sexual contact.

Cognitive Development

- It has been proposed that the idealism of Piaget's formal operational stage declines in young adults and is replaced by more realistic, pragmatic thinking. A qualitatively different, fifth cognitive stage called postformal thought also has been proposed.
- Creativity peaks in adulthood, often in the forties, and then declines. Csikszentmihalyi proposed that the first step toward living a creative life is to cultivate curiosity and interest.

Careers and Work

- Thoughts about career choice for adolescents and young adults reflect developmental changes. Damon argues that too many individuals have difficulty finding a path to purpose today.
- Work defines people in fundamental ways and is a key aspect of their identity. Working during college can have a positive outcome, but it may also have a negative impact on grades. Jobs that require a college education will be the fastest-growing and highest-paying careers in the United States during the next decade.
- As the number of women working outside the home has increased, new issues involving work and family have arisen.

Key Terms

aerobic exercise	emerging adulthood	postformal thought	sexually transmitted infections (STIs)

12 Socioemotional Development in Early Adulthood

©Ariel Skelley/Blend Images/Corbis

CHAPTER OUTLINE

Stories of Life-Span Development: Gwenna's Pursuit and Greg's Lack of Commitment

Commitment is an important issue in a romantic relationship for most individuals. Consider Gwenna, who decides that it is time to have a talk with Greg about his commitment to their relationship (Lerner, 1989, pp. 44–45):

> She shared her perspective on both the strengths and weaknesses of their relationship and what her hopes were for the future. She asked Greg to do the same. Unlike earlier conversations, this one was conducted without her pursuing him, pressuring him, or diagnosing his problems with women. At the same time, she asked Greg some clear questions, which exposed his vagueness.
>
> "How will you know when you are ready to make a commitment? What specifically would you need to change or be different than it is today?"
>
> "I don't know," was Greg's response. When questioned further, the best he could come up with was that he'd just feel it.
>
> "How much more time do you need to make a decision one way or another?"
>
> "I'm not sure," Greg replied. "Maybe a couple of years, but I really can't answer a question like that. I can't predict my feelings."
>
> And so it went.

Gwenna really loved this man, but two years (and maybe longer) was longer than she could comfortably wait. So, after much thought, she told Greg that she would wait till fall (about ten months), but that she would move on if he couldn't commit himself to marriage by then. She was open about her wish to marry and have a family with him, but she was equally clear that her first priority was a mutually committed relationship. If Greg had not reached that point by fall, then she would end the relationship—painful though it would be.

During the waiting period, Gwenna was able to not pursue him and not get distant or otherwise reactive to his expressions of ambivalence and doubt. In this way she gave Greg emotional space to struggle with his dilemma, and the relationship had its best chance of succeeding. Her bottom-line position ("a decision by fall") was not a threat or an attempt to rope Greg in, but rather a clear statement of what was acceptable to her.

When fall arrived, Greg told Gwenna he needed another six months to make up his mind. Gwenna deliberated a while and decided she could live with that. But when the six months were up, Greg was uncertain and asked for more time. It was then that Gwenna took the painful but ultimately empowering step of ending their relationship.

Love is of central importance in each of our lives, as it is in Gwenna's and Greg's lives. Shortly, we discuss the many faces of love, as well as the diversity of adult lifestyles, aspects of marriage and the family, and the role of gender in relationships. To begin, though, we will return to an issue we initially raised in the introductory chapter of this text: stability and change. ▪

Stability and Change from Childhood to Adulthood

For adults, socioemotional development revolves around adaptively integrating our emotional experiences into enjoyable relationships with others on a daily basis. Young adults like Gwenna and Greg face choices and challenges in adopting lifestyles that will be emotionally satisfying, predictable, and manageable for them. Clearly they do not come to these tasks as blank slates, but do their decisions and actions simply reflect the persons they had already become when they were 5 years old or 10 years old or 20 years old?

Current research shows that the first 20 years of life lay the foundation for an adult's socioemotional development (Almy & Cicchetti, 2018; Goodnight & others, 2017). And there is also every reason to believe that experiences in the early adult years are important in determining what the individual will be like later in adulthood. A common finding is that the smaller the time intervals over which we measure socioemotional characteristics, the more similar an individual will look from one measurement to the next. Thus, if we measure an individual's self-concept at the age of 20, and then again at the age of 30, we will probably find more stability than if we measured the individual's self-concept at the age of 10 and then again at the age of 30.

In trying to understand the young adult's socioemotional development, it would be misleading to look at an adult's life only in the present, ignoring the unfolding of social relationships and emotions (Bain & Durbach, 2018; Dowling & others, 2017). So, too, it would be a mistake to search only through a 30-year-old's first five to ten years of life in trying to understand why he or she is having difficulty in a close relationship. To further explore stability and change, let's examine attachment.

Attachment appears during infancy and plays an important part in socioemotional development (Leerkes & others, 2017; Mesman, 2018). We've discussed its role in infancy and adolescence. How do these earlier patterns of attachment and adults' attachment styles influence the lives of adults?

Although relationships with romantic partners differ from those with parents, romantic partners fulfill some of the same needs for adults as parents do for their children (Arriaga & others, 2018; Gewirtz-Meydan & Finzi-Dottan, 2018; Simpson & Rholes, 2017).

How are attachment patterns in childhood linked to relationships in emerging and early adulthood?
(*left*) ©BLOOMimage/Getty Images; (*right*) ©Jade/Getty Images

How Would You...?

As a human development and family studies professional, how would you help individuals understand how early relationship experiences might influence their close relationships in adulthood?

Recall that *securely attached* infants are defined as those who use the caregiver as a secure base from which to explore the environment. Similarly, adults may count on their romantic partner to be a secure base to which they can return and obtain comfort and security during stressful times (Mikulincer & Shaver, 2016).

Do adult attachment patterns with partners reflect childhood attachment patterns with parents and parental sensitivity in infancy? In a retrospective study, Cindy Hazan and Phillip Shaver (1987) revealed that young adults who were securely attached in their romantic relationships were more likely to describe their early relationship with their parents as securely attached. In a longitudinal study, infants who were securely attached at age 1 were securely attached 20 years later in their adult romantic relationships (Steele & others, 1998). Also, a longitudinal study revealed that securely attached infants were in more stable romantic relationships in adulthood than their insecurely attached counterparts (Salvatore & others, 2011). A longitudinal study found that insecure avoidant attachment at 8 years of age was linked to a lower level of social initiative and prosocial behavior and a higher level of social anxiety and loneliness at 21 years of age (Fransson & others, 2016). And in a longitudinal study from 13 to 72 years of age, avoidant attachment declined across the lifespan and being in a relationship predicted lower levels of anxious and avoidant attachment across adulthood (Chopik, Edelstein, & Grimm, 2018). However, in another longitudinal study, links between early attachment styles and later attachment styles were lessened by stressful and disruptive experiences such as the death of a parent or instability of caregiving (Lewis, Feiring, & Rosenthal, 2000).

Adults' attachment can be categorized as secure, avoidant, or anxious:

- **Secure attachment style.** Securely attached adults have positive views of relationships, find it easy to get close to others, and are not overly concerned with or stressed out about their romantic relationships. These adults tend to enjoy sexuality in the context of a committed relationship and are less likely than others to have one-night stands.

- **Avoidant attachment style.** Avoidant individuals are hesitant about getting involved in romantic relationships, and once they are in a relationship, they tend to distance themselves from their partner.

- **Anxious attachment style.** These individuals demand closeness, are less trusting, and are more emotional, jealous, and possessive.

secure attachment style An attachment style that describes adults who have positive views of relationships, find it easy to get close to others, and are not overly concerned or stressed out about their romantic relationships.

avoidant attachment style An attachment style that describes adults who are hesitant about getting involved in romantic relationships and once they are in a relationship tend to distance themselves from their partner.

anxious attachment style An attachment style that describes adults who demand closeness, are less trusting, and are more emotional, jealous, and possessive.

What are some key dimensions of attachment in adulthood, and how are they related to relationship patterns and well-being?
©Fuse/Getty Images

The majority of adults (about 60 to 80 percent) describe themselves as securely attached, and not surprisingly adults prefer having a securely attached partner (Zeifman & Hazan, 2008). Researchers are studying links between adults' current attachment styles and various aspects of their lives (Dagan, Facompre, & Bernard, 2018; Huelsnitz & others, 2018; Pepping & MacDonald, 2018; Umemura & others, 2018). For example, securely attached adults are more satisfied with their close relationships than insecurely attached adults, and the relationships of securely attached adults are more likely to be characterized by trust, commitment, and longevity. A recent research review concluded that attachment-anxious individuals have higher levels of health anxiety (Maunder & others, 2017). Another recent research review concluded that insecure attachment was linked to a higher level of social anxiety in adults (Manning & others, 2017). In another study, young adults with an anxious attachment style were more likely to be characterized by higher negative affect, stress, and perceived social rejection; those with an avoidant attachment style were more likely to be characterized by less desire to be with others when alone (Sheinbaum & others, 2015). Further, researchers recently have found that insecure anxious and insecure avoidant individuals are more likely than securely attached individuals to engage in risky health behaviors, are more susceptible to physical illness, and have poorer disease outcomes (Pietromonaco & Beck, 2018). And a meta-analysis of 94 samples of U.S. college students from 1988 to 2011 found that the percentage of students with a secure attachment style had decreased in recent years while the percentage of students with insecure attachment styles had increased (Konrath & others, 2014).

If you have an insecure attachment style, are you stuck with it and does it doom you to have problematic relationships? Attachment categories are somewhat stable in adulthood, but adults do have the capacity to change their attachment thinking and behavior (Mikulincer & Shaver, 2016). Although attachment insecurities are linked to relationship problems, attachment style is only one factor that contributes to relationship functioning; other factors also contribute to relationship satisfaction and success. Later in the chapter, we will discuss some of these factors in our coverage of marital relationships.

Love and Close Relationships

Love refers to a vast and complex territory of human behavior, spanning a range of relationships that includes friendship, romantic love, affectionate love, and consummate love (Berscheid, 2010; Blieszner & Ogletree, 2017, 2018; Lantagne, Furman, & Novak, 2017; Sternberg & Sternberg, 2018). In most of these types of love, one recurring theme is intimacy.

Intimacy

Self-disclosure and the sharing of private thoughts are hallmarks of intimacy (Williams, Sawyer, & Wahlstrom, 2017). Adolescents have an increased need for intimacy. At the same time, they are engaged in the essential tasks of developing an identity and establishing their independence from their parents. Juggling the competing demands of intimacy, identity, and independence also becomes a central task of adulthood.

Recall that Erik Erikson (1968) argues that identity versus identity confusion—pursuing who we are, what we are all about, and where we are going in life—is the most important issue to be negotiated in adolescence. In early adulthood, according to Erikson, after individuals are well on their way to establishing stable and successful identities, they enter the sixth developmental stage, which is intimacy versus isolation. Erikson describes intimacy as finding one-self while losing oneself in another person, and it requires a commitment to another person.

Development in early adulthood often involves balancing intimacy and commitment on the one hand, and independence and freedom on the other. At the same time that individuals are trying to establish an identity, they face the challenges of increasing their independence from their parents, developing an intimate relationship with another individual, and continuing their friendship commitments. They also face the task of making decisions for themselves instead of relying on what others say or do.

Why is intimacy an important aspect of early adulthood?
©Peeter Viisimaa/Getty Images

Friendship

Increasingly, researchers are finding that friendship plays an important role in development throughout the life span (Blieszner, 2017; Blieszner & Ogletree, 2017, 2018). Most U.S. men and women have a best friend. Ninety-two percent of women and 88 percent of men have a best friend of the same sex (Blieszner, 2009). Many friendships are long-lasting, as 65 per-cent of U.S. adults have known their best friend for at least 10 years and only 15 percent have known their best friend for less than 5 years. Adulthood brings opportunities for new friendships; when individuals move to new locations, they may establish new friendships in their neighborhood or at work (Blieszner, 2016; Blieszner & Ogletree, 2017, 2018).

Romantic and Affectionate Love

Although friendship is included in some conceptualizations of love, when we think about what love is, other types of love typically come to mind. In this section we explore two widely recognized types of love: romantic love and affectionate love.

Romantic Love

Some friendships evolve into **romantic love,** which is also called passionate love, or *eros.* Romantic love has strong components of sexuality and infatuation, and as well-known love researcher Ellen Berscheid (2010) has found, it often predominates in the early part of a love relationship. A meta-analysis found that males show higher avoid-ance and lower anxiety about romantic love than females do (Del Giudice, 2011).

A complex intermingling of different emotions goes into romantic love—including passion, fear, anger, sexual desire, joy, and jealousy. Sexual desire is the most important ingredient of romantic love (Berscheid, 2010). Obviously, some of these emotions are a source of anguish, which can lead to other issues such as depression. One study found that a relationship between romantic lovers was more likely than a relationship between friends to be a cause of depression (Berscheid & Fei, 1977). Another study revealed that a heightened state of romantic love in young adults was linked to stronger depression and anxiety symptoms but better sleep quality (Bajoghli & others, 2014). Other research-ers found that declaring a relationship status on Facebook was associated with both romantic love and jealousy (Orosz & others, 2015).

Online Romantic Attraction Recently, romantic attraction has not only taken place in person but also over the Internet (Fullwood & Attrill-Smith, 2018; Jung & others, 2017). In one U.S. survey, 10 percent of 18- to

romantic love Also called passion-ate love, or *eros;* romantic love has strong sexual and infatuation compo-nents and often predominates in the early period of a love relationship.

Manti Te'o.
©John Biever/Sports
Illustrated/Getty Images

24-year-olds, 22 percent of 25- to 34-year-olds, and 17 percent of 35- to 44-year-olds reported that they had used online dating sites or apps (Pew Research Center, 2015). In their twenties, women have more online pursuers than men, but in their forties men have more online pursuers. When online dating began in 2005 it was viewed by most people as not being a good way to meet people, but in a national survey ten years later a majority of Americans said that online dating is a good way to meet people (Pew Research Center, 2015).

Is looking for love and a marital partner online likely to work out? It didn't work out well in 2012 for Notre Dame linebacker Manti Te'o, whose online girlfriend turned out to be a "catfish," someone who fakes an identity online. However, online dating sites claim that their sites often have positive outcomes. A poll commissioned by Match.com in 2009 reported that twice as many marriages occurred between individuals who met through an online dating site as between people who met at bars, clubs, and other social events.

One problem with online matchmaking is that many individuals misrepresent their characteristics, such as how old they are, how attractive they are, and their occupation. Recent data indicate that men lie most about their age, height, and income; women lie most about their weight, physical build, and age (statisticbrain.com, 2017). Despite such dishonesty, some researchers have found that romantic relationships initiated on the Internet are more likely than relationships established in person to last for more than two years (Bargh & McKenna, 2004). And a national study of more than 19,000 individuals found that more than one-third of marriages now begin online (Cacioppo & others, 2013). Also in this study, marriages that began online were slightly less likely to break up and were characterized by slightly higher marital satisfaction than those that started in traditional offline contexts.

Romantic Relationship Changes in Emerging Adulthood How do romantic relationships change in emerging adulthood? In a recent study across 10 years, short-term relationships were supported more as individuals moved into emerging adulthood (Lantagne, Furman, & Novak, 2017). Long-term adolescent relationships were both supportive and turbulent, characterized by elevated levels of support, negative interactions, higher control, and more jealousy. In emerging adulthood, long-term relationships continued to provide high levels of support, while negative interactions, control, and jealousy decreased.

Relationship Education for Adolescents and Emerging Adults Programs in relationship education have mainly focused on helping committed adult couples to strengthen their relationships. Recently, though, an increasing number of relationship education programs have been developed for adolescents and emerging adults (Hawkins, 2018). *Relationship education* consists of interventions to provide individuals and couples with information and skills that produce positive romantic relationships and marriages. These interventions are diverse and include instruction in basic relationship knowledge and skills to youth in a classroom setting, helping unmarried couple learn more about relationships in small-group settings, and premarital education for engaged couples.

How Would You...?

As a **health-care professional,** how would you advise individuals who are concerned about their sexual functioning because their romantic relationship seems to be losing its spark?

A recent meta-analysis of 30 studies of relationship education for adolescents and emerging adults found a positive effect of the programs (Simpson, Leonhardt, & Hawkins, 2018). The skills most often assessed in these studies are interpersonal communication, problem-solving and conflict strategies, and self-regulation (Simpson, Leonhardt, & Hawkins, 2018). The positive effects of relationship education were stronger for emerging adults than adolescents. They also were stronger for more disadvantaged participants than more advantaged participants.

Affectionate Love

Love is more than just passion. **Affectionate love,** also called companionate love, is the type of love that occurs when someone desires to have the other person near and has a deep, caring affection for the person (Sternberg & Sternberg, 2018; Youyou & others, 2017).

affectionate love In this type of love, also called companionate love, an individual desires to have the other person near and has a deep, caring affection for the other person.

The early stages of love have more romantic love ingredients—but as love matures, passion tends to give way to affection (Berscheid, 2010). Phillip Shaver (1986) proposed a developmental model of love in which the initial phase of romantic love is fueled by a mixture of sexual attraction and gratification, a reduced sense of loneliness, uncertainty about the security of developing another attachment, and excitement from exploring the novelty of another human being. With time, he says, sexual attraction wanes, attachment anxieties either lessen or produce conflict and withdrawal, novelty is replaced with familiarity, and lovers find themselves either securely attached in a deeply caring relationship or distressed—feeling bored, disappointed, lonely, or hostile, for example. In the latter case, one or both partners may eventually end the relationship and then move on to another relationship.

Consummate Love

So far we have discussed two forms of love: romantic (or passionate) and affectionate (or companionate). According to Robert J. Sternberg (1988; Sternberg & Sternberg, 2018), these are not the only forms of love. Sternberg proposed that love can be thought of as a triangle with three main dimensions—passion, intimacy, and commitment. Passion involves physical and sexual attraction to another. Intimacy relates to the emotional feelings of warmth, closeness, and sharing in a relationship. Commitment is the cognitive appraisal of the relationship and the intent to maintain the relationship even in the face of problems.

In Sternberg's theory, the strongest, fullest form of love is *consummate love,* which involves all three dimensions (see Figure 1). If passion is the only ingredient in a relationship (with intimacy and commitment low or absent), we are merely *infatuated.* An example might be an affair or a fling in which there is little intimacy and even less commitment. A relationship marked by intimacy and commitment but low or lacking in passion is called *affectionate love,* a pattern often found among couples who have been married for many years. If passion and commitment are present but intimacy is not, Sternberg calls the relationship *fatuous love,* as when one person worships another from a distance. But if couples share all three dimensions—passion, intimacy, and commitment—they experience consummate love (Sternberg & Sternberg, 2018).

Cross-Cultural Variations in Romantic Relationships

Culture has strong influences on many aspects of human development, and romantic relationships are no exception (Gao, 2016). In collectivist countries like China and Korea, intimacy is more diffused in love because of the strong group emphasis on connections outside of a romantic love relationship. By contrast, in individualistic countries such as the United States and most European countries, intimacy is often more intensified because an individual's social network is likely to be smaller and less group oriented

Types of Love	Passion	Intimacy	Commitment
Infatuation	Present	Absent or low	Absent or low
Affectionate love	Absent or low	Present	Present
Fatuous love	Present	Absent or low	Present
Consummate love	Present	Present	Present

Present   Absent or low

Figure 1 Sternberg's Triangle of Love Sternberg identified three dimensions of love: passion, intimacy, and commitment. Various combinations of these dimensions result in infatuation, affectionate love, fatuous love, and consummate love.

(Gao, 2016). Also, research indicates that greater passion characterizes U.S. romantic relationships than Chinese romantic relationships (Gao, 2001). And researchers have found that self-disclosure is more common in U.S. romantic relationships than Japanese romantic relationships (Kito, 2005). Feelings of commitment are stronger in Chinese romantic relationships than in U.S. romantic relationships (Dion & Dion, 1993).

In an exploration of cross-cultural variations, romantic relationships were examined in three countries—Japan, France, and Argentina (Ansari, 2015). In Japan, the marriage rate is rapidly decreasing to the point that the Japanese government is very concerned about how this decline could lead to a considerable drop in Japan's population. In 2013, 45 percent of Japanese women 16 to 24 years of age reported that they were not interested in or despised having sexual contact. Also, the percentage of Japanese men and women who aren't involved in any romantic relationship has increased significantly in recent years.

In Argentina, romantic interest is much stronger than in Japan (Ansari, 2015). Sexual and romantic flirtation is a way of life for many Argentinians. Online dating is not nearly as frequent as in the United States, apparently because men are so forward in their romantic pursuits in person.

In France, as in Argentina, interest in passionate love is strong. However, in the three-country comparison, one aspect of French interest in romantic relationships stood out—their affinity for having extramarital affairs. In one comparison, only 47 percent of those surveyed in France reported that having an extramarital affair is morally wrong, compared with 69 percent in Japan and 72 percent in Argentina (Wike, 2014). In this survey, 84 percent of people in the United States said infidelity was morally wrong. In sum, there are striking cultural variations in many aspects of romantic relationships.

Also in this exploration of romantic relationships in different countries, the Middle Eastern country of Qatar was studied (Ansari, 2015). In Qatar, casual dating is forbidden and public displays of affection can be punished with prison time. However, recently with the advent of smartphones, social media, and the Internet, young adults in Qatar are contacting each other about co-ed parties in hotel rooms, a private way to hang out away from the monitoring of parents, neighbors, and government officials.

Adult Lifestyles

A striking social change in recent decades has been the decreased stigma attached to individuals who do not maintain what were long considered conventional families. Adults today choose many lifestyles and form many types of families (Schwartz & Scott, 2018). They live alone, cohabit, marry, divorce, or live with someone of the same sex.

In his book *The Marriage-Go-Round* sociologist Andrew Cherlin (2009) concluded that the United States has more marriages and remarriages, more divorces, and more short-term cohabiting (living together) relationships than most countries. Combined, these lifestyles create more turnover and movement in and out of relationships in the United States than in virtually any other country. Let's explore these varying relationship lifestyles.

Single Adults

Recent decades have seen a dramatic rise in the percentage of single adults. In 2016, 45.2 percent of individuals 18 years and older were single (U.S. Census Bureau, 2017). The increasing number of single adults reflects rising rates of cohabitation and a trend toward postponing marriage. The United States has a lower percentage of single adults than many other countries such as Great Britain, Germany, and Japan. The fastest growth in adopting a single adult lifestyle is occurring in rapidly developing countries such as China, India, and Brazil (Klinenberg, 2013).

Common challenges faced by single adults may include forming intimate relationships with other adults, confronting loneliness, and finding a niche in a society that is marriage-oriented. Bella DePaulo (2006, 2011) argues that society has a widespread bias against unmarried adults that is seen in everything from missed perks in jobs to deep social and financial prejudices.

Advantages of being single include having time to make decisions about one's life course, time to develop personal resources to meet goals, freedom to make autonomous decisions and pursue one's own schedule and interests, opportunities to explore new places and try out new experiences, and privacy.

In a recent national survey, millennials were far more likely than older generations to want to find romance and commitment (Match.com, 2017). In this recent survey, 40 percent of actively dating single adults have dated someone they met online, while only 24 percent met through a friend. Also in this study, millennials were 48 percent more likely than older generations to have sex before the first date. This "fast sex, slow love" pattern may reflect how millennials want to know as much about someone as possible before committing to a serious relationship (Fisher, 2017). Also in the recent survey, among single men 18 to 70+, 95 percent of single men favor women initiating the first kiss and also asking for a man's phone number, but only 29 percent of single women actually follow the first kiss pattern and only 13 percent actually ask for a man's phone number (Match.com, 2017).

Cohabiting Adults

Cohabitation refers to living together in a sexual relationship without being married. Cohabitation has undergone considerable changes in recent years (Perelli-Harris & others, 2017; Sassler, Michelmore, & Qian, 2018; Thorsen, 2017). Cohabitation rates in the United States continue to rise (Stepler, 2017). In a recent national poll, the number of cohabiting adults increased 29 percent from 2007 to 2016, reaching a figure of 18 million adults in a cohabiting relationship (U.S. Census Bureau, 2016). In 2016, 14 percent of U.S. adults 25 to 34 and 10 percent who were 18 to 24 years old were cohabiting. Cohabitation rates are even higher in some countries—in Sweden, for example, cohabitation before marriage is virtually universal (Stokes & Raley, 2009).

A number of couples view their cohabitation not as a precursor to marriage but as an ongoing lifestyle (Klinenberg, 2013). These couples do not want the official aspects of marriage. In the United States, cohabiting arrangements tend to be short-lived, with one-third lasting less than a year (Hyde & DeLamater, 2017). Fewer than 1 out of 10 lasts five years. Of course, it is easier to dissolve a cohabitation relationship than a marriage.

Couples who cohabit face certain problems (Braithwaite & Holt-Lunstad, 2017; Fincham & May, 2017). Disapproval by parents and other family members can place emotional strain on the cohabiting couple. Some cohabiting couples have difficulty owning property jointly. Legal rights on the dissolution of the relationship are less certain than in a divorce.

If a couple live together before they marry, does cohabiting help or harm their chances of later having a stable and happy marriage? The majority of studies have found lower rates of marital satisfaction and higher rates of divorce in couples who lived together before getting married (Copen, Daniels, & Mosher, 2013; Whitehead & Popenoe, 2003). However, research indicates that the link between marital cohabitation and marital instability in first marriages has weakened (Smock & Gupta, 2013). Further, in a recent large-scale study, women who cohabited within the first year of a sexual relationship were less likely to get married than women who waited more than one year before cohabiting (Sassler, Michelmore, & Qian, 2018).

What are some potential advantages and disadvantages of cohabitation?
©Image Source/Corbis

What might explain the finding that cohabiting is linked with divorce more than not cohabiting? The most frequently given explanation is that the less traditional lifestyle of cohabitation may attract less conventional individuals who are not great believers in marriage in the first place (Whitehead & Popenoe, 2003). An alternative explanation is that the experience of cohabiting changes people's attitudes and habits in ways that increase their likelihood of divorce.

Researchers also have found that cohabiting individuals are not as mentally healthy as their counterparts in committed marital relationships (Braithwaite & Holt-Lunstad, 2017; Fincham & May, 2017). In a recent study of long-term cohabitation (more than three years) in emerging adulthood, emotional distress was higher in long-term cohabitation than during time spent single, with men especially driving the effect (Memitz, 2018). However, heavy drinking was more common during time spent being single than in long-term cohabitation.

How Would You...?

As a **psychologist,** how would you counsel a couple deciding whether to cohabit before marriage?

Research has provided clarification of cohabitation outcomes. One meta-analysis found the negative link between cohabitation and marital instability did not hold up when only cohabitation with the eventual marital partner was examined, indicating that these cohabitors may attach more long-term positive meaning to living together (Jose, O'Leary, & Moyer, 2010). Also, one study found that cohabiting did not have a negative effect on marriage if the couple did not have any previous live-in lovers and did not have children prior to the marriage (Cherlin, 2009). Another study concluded that the risk of marital dissolution between cohabitors (compared with individuals who married without cohabiting) was much smaller when they cohabited in their mid-twenties and later (Kuperberg, 2014).

Married Adults

Until about 1930, stable marriage was widely accepted as the endpoint of adult development. In the last 70 to 80 years, however, personal fulfillment both inside and outside marriage has emerged as a goal that competes with marital stability. The changing norm of male-female equality in marriage and increasingly high expectations for what a marital relationship should be have produced marital relationships that are more fragile and intense than they were for earlier generations (Schwartz & Scott, 2018). A study of 502 newlyweds found that nearly all couples had optimistic forecasts of how their marriage would change over the next four years (Lavner & Bradbury, 2013). Despite their optimistic forecasts, their marital satisfaction declined across this time frame. Wives with the most optimistic forecasts showed the steepest declines in marital satisfaction.

©Shutterstock/Luca Santilli

Some characteristics of marital partners predict whether the marriage will last longer. Two such characteristics are education and ethnicity. A survey of more than 22,000 women found that both women and men with a bachelor's degree were more likely to delay marriage but were also more likely to eventually get married and stay married for more than 20 years (Copen, Daniels, & Mosher, 2013). Also in this study, Asian American women were the most likely of all ethnic groups to be in a first marriage that lasted at least 20 years—70 percent were in a first marriage that lasted this long, compared with 54 percent for non-Latino White women, 53 percent for Latino women, and 37 percent for African American women.

Marital Trends

In 2016, 50 percent of adults in the United States were married, down from 72 percent in 1960 (Parker & Stepler, 2017). Also, in 2016, the U.S. average age for a first marriage had climbed to 29.5 years for men and 27.4 years for women, higher than at any other point in history (Livingston, 2017). In 1960, the average age for a first marriage in the United States was 23 years for men and 20 years for women. In addition, the increased cohabitation rate in the United States has contributed to the lower percentage of adults who are married (Wang & Parker, 2014). Also, a higher percentage of U.S. adults never marry—in 2014, a record percentage (23 percent of men, 17 percent of women) of persons 25 years and older had never married. Nevertheless, the United States is still a marrying society, with 78.5 percent of U.S. adults 25 years and older having been married at some point in their lives in 2016.

Although marriage rates are declining and the average age of marriage is going up, research with emerging and young adults indicates that they view marriage as a very important life pursuit. Indeed, in one study of young adults, they predicted that marriage would be more important in their life than parenting, careers, or leisure activities (Willoughby, Hall, & Goff, 2015). In a recent book, *The Marriage Paradox* (Willoughby & James, 2017), it was concluded that the importance of marriage to emerging and young adults may be what is encouraging them to first build better a better career and financial foundation to increase the likelihood their marriage will be successful later. In this perspective, emerging and young adults may not be abandoning marriage because they don't like it or are uninterested in it, but rather because they want to position themselves in the best possible way for developing a healthy marital relationship.

One study explored what U.S. never-married men and women are looking for in a potential spouse (Wang, 2014). Following are the percentages who reported that various factors would be very important for them:

Factor	Men	Women
Similar ideas about having and raising children	62	70
A steady job	46	78
Same moral and religious beliefs	31	38
At least as much education	26	28
Same racial or ethnic background	7	10

Thus, in this study, never-married men said that the most important characteristic of a potential spouse was similar ideas about having and raising children, but never-married women placed greater importance on having a partner with a steady job.

Is there a best age to get married? Marriages in adolescence are more likely to end in divorce than marriages in adulthood (Copen & others, 2012). However, researchers have not been able to pin down a specific age range for getting married that is most likely to result in a successful marriage (Furstenberg, 2007).

The Benefits of a Good Marriage

Are there any benefits to having a good marriage? Individuals who are happily married live longer, healthier lives than either divorced individuals or those who are unhappily married (Lo, Cheng, & Simpson, 2016). In one research review, it was concluded that the experience of divorce or separation confers risk for poor health outcomes, including a 23 percent higher mortality rate (Sbarra, 2015). A survey of U.S. adults 50 years and older also revealed that a lower portion of adult life spent in marriage was linked to an increased likelihood of dying at an earlier age (Henretta, 2010). Also, in a large-scale study in the United States and six European countries, not being in the labor force was associated with higher mortality but marriage attenuated the increased mortality risk linked to labor force inactivity (Van Hedel & others, 2015). And a recent research review of individuals who were married, divorced, widowed, and single found that married individuals had the best cardiovascular profile and single men the worst (Manfredini & others, 2017). Further, an unhappy marriage can shorten a person's life by an average of four years (Gove, Style, & Hughes, 1990).

What are the reasons for the benefits of a happy marriage? People in happy marriages are likely to feel less stressed physically and emotionally, which puts less wear and tear on a person's body. Such wear and tear can lead to numerous physical ailments, such as high blood pressure and heart disease, as well as psychological problems such as anxiety, depression, and substance abuse.

Divorced Adults

In the 1980s divorce reached epidemic proportions in the United States (Braver & Lamb, 2013). However, the divorce rate declined in recent decades, peaking at 5.1 divorces per 1,000 people in 1981 and declining to 3.2 divorces per 1,000 people in 2014 (OECD, 2016). The 2014 divorce rate of 3.2 compares with a marriage rate of 6.9 per 1,000 people in 2014.

Although the divorce rate has dropped, the United States still has one of the highest divorce rates in the world. Russia has the highest divorce rate (4.7 divorces per 1,000 people in a single year) (OECD, 2016). Individuals in some groups have higher rates of divorce (Perelli-Harris & others, 2017). Youthful marriage, low educational level, low income, not having a religious affiliation, having parents who are divorced, and having a baby before marriage are factors that are associated with increases in divorce (Hoelter, 2009). And certain characteristics of one's partner increase the likelihood of divorce: alcoholism, psychological problems, domestic violence, infidelity, and inadequate division of household labor (Affleck, Carmichael, & Whitley, 2018; Perelli-Harris & others, 2017).

Earlier, we indicated that researchers have not been able to pin down a specific age that is the best time to marry so that the marriage will be less likely to end in a divorce. However, if a divorce is going to occur, it usually takes place early in a marriage, most often between the fifth and tenth years of marriage (National Center for Health Statistics, 2000) (see Figure 2). For example, one study found that divorce peaked in Finland approximately five to seven years into the marriage, and then the rate of divorce gradually declined (Kulu, 2014). This timing may reflect an effort by partners in troubled marriages to stay in the marriage and try to work things out. If after several years these efforts have not improved the relationship, the couple may then seek a divorce.

What causes people to get divorced? A recent study in Great Britain found no differences in the causes of breakdowns in marriage and cohabitation (Gravningen & others, 2017). In this study, the following percentages cited these reasons: "grew apart" (men 39 percent, women 36 percent), "arguments" (men 27 percent, women 30 percent), "unfaithfulness/adultery" (men 18 percent, women 24 percent), "lack of respect, appreciation" (men 17 percent, women 25 percent), and "domestic violence" (men 4 percent, women 16 percent).

Both partners experience challenges after a marriage dissolves (Sbarra, Hasselmo, & Bourassa, 2015). Divorced adults have higher rates of depression, anxiety, physical

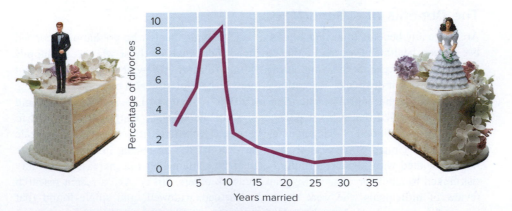

Figure 2 **The Divorce Rate in Relation to Number of Years Married**
Shown here is the percentage of divorces as a function of how long couples have been married. Notice that most divorces occur in the early years of marriage, peaking in the fifth to tenth years of marriage.
©Digital Vision/Getty Images

illnesses, suicide, motor vehicle accidents, alcoholism, and mortality (Braver & Lamb, 2013). In a recent study, individuals who were divorced had a higher risk of having alcohol use disorder (Kendler & others, 2017). Also, both divorced women and divorced men complain of loneliness, diminished self-esteem, anxiety about the unknowns in their lives, and difficulty in forming satisfactory new intimate relationships (Sbarra & Borelli, 2018). One research review concluded that both divorced men and women are more likely to commit suicide than their married counterparts (Yip & others, 2015). And in another study, both divorced men and women had a higher risk for having a heart attack than those who were married, but the risk for this cardiovascular disease was higher for divorced women than for divorced men (Dupre & others, 2015).

There are gender differences in the process and outcomes of divorce (Braver & Lamb, 2013; Daoulah & others, 2017). A recent study of couples who had been married from one to sixteen years found that wives' increased tension over the course of a marriage was a factor that was consistently linked to an eventual divorce (Birditt & others, 2017). Women are more likely to sense that something is wrong with the marriage and are more likely to seek a divorce than are men. Women also show better emotional adjustment and are more likely to perceive divorce as a "second chance" to increase their happiness, improve their social lives, and seek better work opportunities. However, divorce typically has a more negative economic impact on women than it does on men.

Remarried Adults

Adults who remarry usually do so rather quickly, with approximately 50 percent remarrying within three years after they initially divorce (Sweeney, 2009, 2010). Men remarry sooner than women. Men with higher incomes are more likely to remarry than their counterparts with lower incomes. Remarriage occurs sooner for partners who initiate a divorce (especially in the first several years after divorce and for older women) than for those who do not initiate it (Sweeney, 2009, 2010). And some remarried individuals are more adult-focused, responding more to the concerns of their partner, while others are more child-focused, responding more to the concerns of their children (Anderson & Greene, 2011).

Statistical data indicate that the remarriage rate in the United States has declined, going from 50 of every 1,000 divorced or widowed Americans in 1990 to 28 of every 1,000 in 2013 (Payne, 2015). One reason for the decline is the dramatic increase in cohabitation in recent years. Men are more likely to get remarried than women; in 2013, the remarriage rate was almost twice as high for men as for women (40 per 1,000 for men and 21 per 1,000 for women in that year) (Livingston, 2017). Thus, men are either more eager or more able to find new spouses than are women.

Remarried adults often find it difficult to stay remarried. While the divorce rate in first marriages has declined, the divorce rate of remarriages continues to increase (DeLongis & Zwicker, 2017). Why? For one thing, many remarry not for love but for financial reasons, for help in rearing children, and to reduce loneliness. They also might carry into the stepfamily negative patterns that produced failure in an earlier marriage. Remarried couples also experience more stress in rearing children than parents in never-divorced families (Ganong & Coleman, 2018). One study revealed that positive attitudes about divorce, low marital quality, and divorce proneness were more common among remarried persons than among their counterparts in first marriages (Whitton & others, 2013). Another study found that remarried adults had less frequent sex than those in their first marriage (Stroope, McFarland, & Uecker, 2015).

Gay and Lesbian Adults

Until recently, the legal context of marriage created barriers to breaking up that did not exist for same-sex partners. However, the legalization of same-sex marriage in all 50 states in 2015 extended this barrier to same-sex partners (Diamond, 2017; Holley, 2017). In many additional ways, researchers have found that gay and lesbian relationships are similar—in their satisfactions, loves, joys, and conflicts—to heterosexual relationships (Balsam, Rostosky, & Riggle, 2017). For example, like heterosexual couples, gay and lesbian couples need to find a balance of romantic love, affection, autonomy, and equality that is acceptable to both partners (Hope, 2009). An increasing number of gay and lesbian couples are creating families that include children (Farr & Goldberg, 2018; Sumontha, Farr, & Patterson, 2018).

Data from the American Community Survey conducted in 2006–2010 indicate that among same-sex couples in the United States, lesbian couples are approximately five times more likely to be raising children than are gay couples (Miller & Price, 2013). An increasing number of same-sex couples are adopting children (Farr, Oakley, & Ollen, 2016). The percentage of same-sex couples who had adopted children increased dramatically from 10 percent in 2000 to 19 percent in 2009 (DiBennardo & Gates, 2014). Also, research indicates that lesbian and gay couples share child care more than heterosexual couples do, with lesbian couples being the most supportive and gay couples the least supportive (Farr & Patterson, 2013). Also, one survey found that a greater percentage of same-sex, dual-earner couples than different-sex couples said they share laundry (44 versus 31 percent), household repairs (33 versus 15 percent), and routine (74 versus 38 percent) and sick (62 versus 32 percent) child care responsibilities (Matos, 2015).

There are a number of misconceptions about gay and lesbian couples (Farr, 2017; Simon & others, 2018). Contrary to stereotypes, one partner is masculine and the other feminine in only a small percentage of gay and lesbian couples. Only a small segment of the gay population has a large number of sexual partners, and this is uncommon among lesbians. Furthermore, researchers have found that gay and lesbian couples prefer long-term, committed relationships (Fingerhut & Peplau, 2013). About half of committed gay couples do have an open relationship that allows the possibility of sex (but not affectionate love) outside of the relationship. Lesbian couples usually do not have an open relationship.

A special concern is the stigma, prejudice, and discrimination that lesbian, gay, and bisexual individuals experience because of widespread social devaluation of same-sex relationships (Conlin, Douglass, & Ouch, 2018; Holley, 2017; Valdiserri & others, 2018). However, researchers have found that many individuals in these relationships see stigma as bringing them closer together and strengthening their relationship (Frost, 2011).

Challenges in Marriage, Parenting, and Divorce

No matter what lifestyles young adults choose, their choices will bring certain challenges. Because many choose the lifestyle of marriage, we'll consider some of the challenges in marriage and describe elements of successful marriages. We also examine some challenges in parenting and trends in childbearing. Given the statistics about divorce rates in the previous section, we'll then consider how to deal with divorce.

Making Marriage Work

John Gottman (1994, 2006, 2011; Gottman & Gottman, 2009; Gottman & Silver, 2000) uses many methods to analyze what makes marriages work. He interviews couples about the history of their marriage, their philosophy about marriage, and how they view their parents' marriages. He videotapes them talking to each other about how their day went and evaluates what they say about the good and bad times of their marriages. Gottman also uses physiological measures to chart their heart rate, blood

What makes marriages work? What are the benefits of having a good marriage?
©Image Source Pink/ Alamy

flow, blood pressure, and immune functioning moment by moment. In addition, he checks back with the couples every year to see how their marriage is faring. Gottman's research represents the most extensive assessment of marital relationships available. Currently, he and his colleagues are following 700 couples in seven studies.

Among the principles Gottman has found that determine whether a marriage will work are the following:

- *Establishing love maps.* Individuals in successful marriages have personal insights and detailed maps of each other's life and world. They aren't psychological strangers. In good marriages, partners are willing to share their feelings with each other. They use these "love maps" to express not only their understanding of each other but also their fondness and admiration.

- *Nurturing fondness and admiration.* In successful marriages, partners sing each other's praises. More than 90 percent of the time, when couples put a positive spin on their marriage's history, the marriage is likely to have a positive future.

- *Turning toward each other instead of away.* In good marriages, spouses are adept at turning toward each other regularly. They see each other as friends. This friendship doesn't keep arguments from occurring, but it can prevent differences from overwhelming the relationship. In these good marriages, spouses respect each other and appreciate each other's point of view despite disagreements.

- *Letting your partner influence you.* Bad marriages often involve one spouse who is unwilling to share power with the other. Although power-mongering is more common in husbands, some wives also show this trait. A willingness to share power and to respect the other person's view is a prerequisite to compromising.

- *Creating shared meaning.* The more partners can speak candidly and respectfully with each other, the more likely they are to create shared meaning in their marriage. This also includes sharing goals with one's spouse and working together to achieve each other's goals.

In a provocative book titled *Marriage, a History: How Love Conquered Marriage,* Stephanie Coontz (2005) concluded that marriages in America today are fragile not because Americans have become self-centered and career-minded but because expectations for marriage have become unrealistically high compared with previous generations. To make a marriage work, Coontz emphasizes like Gottman that partners need to develop a deep friendship, show respect for each other, and embrace commitment.

How Would You...?

As a **human development and family studies professional,** how would you counsel a newly married couple seeking advice on how to make their marriage work?

How important is the sexual aspect of a relationship in the couple's marital satisfaction? A recent study of couples in their second to fourteenth years of marriage found that frequency of engaging in sexual intercourse was linked to a couple's marital satisfaction, but that a satisfying sex life and a warm interpersonal relationship were more important than frequency (Schoenfeld & others, 2017).

Becoming a Parent

For many young adults, parental roles are well planned, coordinated with other roles in life, and developed with the individual's economic situation in mind. For others, the discovery that they are about to become parents is a startling surprise. In either event, the prospective parents may have mixed emotions and romantic illusions about having a child (Florsheim, 2014).

Parenting requires a number of interpersonal skills and imposes emotional demands, yet there is little in the way of formal education for this task. Most parents learn parenting practices from their own parents—some they accept, some they discard. Unfortunately, when parenting practices are passed on from one generation to the next, both desirable and undesirable practices are perpetuated. Adding to the challenges of the task of parenting, husbands and wives may bring different parenting practices to

Janis Keyser, Parent Educator

Janis Keyser is a parent educator who teaches in the Department of Early Childhood Education at Cabrillo College in California. In addition to teaching college classes and conducting parenting workshops, she has co-authored a book with Laura Davis (1997): *Becoming the Parent You Want to Be: A Sourcebook of Strategies for the First Five Years.*

Keyser co-authors a nationally syndicated parenting column, "Growing Up, Growing Together." She is the mother of three, stepmother of five, grandmother of twelve, and great-grandmother of six.

Parent educators may have different educational backgrounds and occupational profiles. Janis Keyser has a background in early childhood education and, as just indicated, teaches at a college. Many parent educators have majored in areas such as child development as an undergraduate and/or taken a specialization of parenting and family courses in a master's or doctoral degree program in human development and family studies, clinical psychology, counseling psychology, or social work. As part of, or in addition

Janis Keyser (*right*) conducts a parenting workshop.
Courtesy of Janis Keyser

to, their work in colleges and clinical settings, they may conduct parent education groups and workshops.

---

the marriage (Huston & Holmes, 2004). The parents, then, may disagree about which is a better way to interact with a child.

Parent educators seek to help individuals become better parents. To read about the work of one parent educator, see *Careers in Life-Span Development.*

Like the age when individuals first marry, the age at which individuals have children has been increasing (Baca Zinn, Eitzen, & Wells, 2016; Schwartz & Scott, 2018). The age at which women gave birth occurred more frequently in their thirties than in their twenties in 2016 for the first time ever, although the average age overall was 27 years of age (Centers for Disease Control and Prevention, 2017). As the use of contraception has become widespread, many individuals consciously choose when they will have children and how many children they will rear. The number of one-child families is increasing, for example, and U.S. women overall are having fewer children. These childbearing results are creating several trends:

What are some trends in having children?
©Ryan McVay/Getty Images

- By giving birth to fewer children and reducing the demands of child care, women free up a significant portion of their life spans for other endeavors.

- As working women increase in number, they invest less actual time in the child's development.

- Men are apt to invest a greater amount of time in fathering.

- Parental care is often supplemented by institutional care (child care, for example).

How Would You...?

As a **human development and family studies professional,** how would you advise a young woman who is inquiring about the best age to have children?

As more women show an increased interest in developing a career, they are not only marrying later, but also having fewer children and having them later in life. What are some of the advantages of having children early or late? Some of the advantages of having children early (in the twenties) are that the parents are likely to have more physical energy (for example, they can cope better with such matters as getting up in the middle of the night with infants and waiting up until adolescents come home at night); the mother is likely to have fewer medical problems with pregnancy and childbirth; and the parents may be less likely to build up expectations for their children, as do many couples who have waited many years to have children.

There are also advantages to having children later (in the thirties). These parents have had more time to consider and achieve some of their goals in life and to determine what they want from their family and career roles. Older parents also are more mature and able to benefit from their life experiences to engage in more competent parenting, and they are more securely established in their careers and tend to have more income for child-rearing expenses than younger parents do.

Dealing with Divorce

If a marriage doesn't work, what happens after divorce? Psychologically, one of the most common characteristics of divorced adults is difficulty trusting someone else in a romantic relationship. Following a divorce, though, people's lives can take diverse turns (Perelli-Harris & others, 2017). For example, in one research study 20 percent of the divorced group became more competent and better adjusted following their divorce (Hetherington & Kelly, 2002).

Strategies for divorced adults include the following (Hetherington & Kelly, 2002):

- Think of divorce as a chance to grow personally and to develop more positive relationships.

- Make decisions carefully, realizing that the consequences of your decisions regarding work, lovers, and children may last a lifetime.

- Focus more on the future than the past. Think about what is most important for you going forward in your life, set some challenging goals, and plan how to reach them.

- Use your strengths and resources to cope with difficulties.

- Don't expect to be successful and happy in everything you do. The path to a more enjoyable life will likely have a number of twists and turns, and moving forward will require considerable effort and resilience.

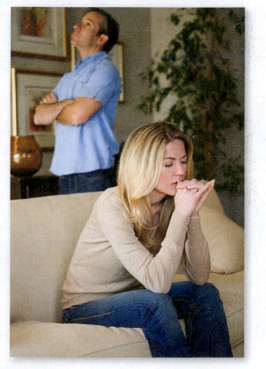

What are some strategies for coping with divorce?
©Image Source/Getty Images

Gender and Communication Styles, Relationships, and Classification

In our discussion of children's socioemotional development, we described many aspects of gender development. Gender continues to be a very important aspect of adults' lives and their development. Here we discuss the communication styles of males and females, how males and females relate to others, and how gender is classified including the recent interest in transgender.

Gender and Communication Styles

Stereotypes about differences in men's and women's attitudes toward communication and about differences in how they communicate with each other have spawned countless cartoons and jokes. Are the supposed differences real?

Men's and Women's Styles of Communication

When Deborah Tannen (1990) analyzed the talk of women and men, she found that many wives complained about their husbands by saying, "He doesn't listen to me anymore" and "He doesn't talk to me anymore." Lack of communication, although high on women's lists of reasons for divorce, is mentioned much less often by men.

What are some differences in women's and men's communication styles?
©Onoky/SuperStock

Communication problems between men and women may come in part from differences in their preferred ways of communicating. Tannen distinguishes *rapport talk* from *report talk*. **Rapport talk** is the language of conversation; it is a way of establishing connections and negotiating relationships. **Report talk** is talk that is designed to give information; this category of communication includes public speaking. According to Tannen, women enjoy rapport talk more than report talk, and men's lack of interest in rapport talk bothers many women. In contrast, men prefer to engage in report talk. Men hold center stage through verbal performances such as telling stories and jokes. They learn to use talk as a way to get and keep attention.

How extensive are gender differences in communication? Research has yielded somewhat mixed results, but some gender differences have been found (Anderson, 2006). One study of a sampling of students' e-mails found that people could guess the writer's gender two-thirds of the time (Thompson & Murachver, 2001). Another study revealed that women make 63 percent of phone calls and when talking to another woman stay on the phone longer (7.2 minutes) than men do when talking with other men (4.6 minutes) (Smoreda & Licoppe, 2000). However, meta-analyses suggest that overall gender differences in communication are small in both children and adults (Hyde, 2014; Leaper & Smith, 2004).

Gender and Relationships

As in the childhood and adolescent years, there are gender differences in adult friendship (Blieszner & Ogletree, 2017). Compared with men, women have more close friends and their friendships involve more self-disclosure and exchange of mutual support (Dow & Wood, 2006). Women are more likely to listen at length to what a friend has to say and be sympathetic, and women have been labeled as "talking companions" because talk is so central to their relationships (Gouldner & Strong, 1987). Women's friendships tend to be characterized not only by depth but also by breadth: Women share many aspects of their experiences, thoughts, and feelings (Helgeson, 2012). When female friends get together, they like to talk, but male friends are more likely to engage

rapport talk Use of conversation to establish connections and maintain relationships.

report talk Talk that is designed to convey information.

How is adult friendship different among female friends, male friends, and cross-gender friends?
©PhotoAlto

in activities, especially outdoors. Thus, the adult male pattern of friendship often involves keeping one's distance while sharing useful information. Men are less likely than women to talk about their weaknesses with their friends, and men seek practical solutions to their problems rather than sympathy (Tannen, 1990). Also, adult male friendships are more competitive than those of women (Helgeson, 2012).

What are some characteristics of female-male friendships? Cross-gender friendships are more common among adults than children but less common than same-gender friendships in adulthood (Blieszner, 2009). Cross-gender friendships can provide both opportunities and problems (Helgeson, 2012). The opportunities involve learning more about common feelings and interests and shared characteristics, as well as acquiring knowledge and understanding of beliefs and activities that historically have been typical of the other gender.

Problems can arise in cross-gender friendships because of different expectations. One problem that can plague an adult cross-gender friendship is unclear sexual boundaries, which can produce tension and confusion (Hart, Adams, & Tullett, 2016).

Gender Classification

Gender can be classified in multiple ways. In recent years, emphasis has been placed on flexibility and equality in gender roles (Leaper, 2017; Mehta & Keener, 2017).

Transgender is a broad term that refers to individuals who adopt a gender identity that differs from the one assigned to them at birth (Budge & Orovecz, 2018; Budge & others, 2018a, b; Katz-Wise & others, 2018; King, 2017, 2019). For example, an individual may have a female body but identify more strongly with being masculine than being feminine, or have a male body but identify more strongly with being feminine than masculine. A transgender identity of being born male but identifying with being a female is much more common than the reverse (Zucker, Lawrence, & Kreukels, 2016). Transgender persons also may not want to be labeled "he" or "she" but prefer a more neutral label such as "they" or "ze" (Scelfo, 2015).

Because of the nuances and complexities involved in such gender categorizations, some experts have recently argued that a better overarching umbrella term might be *trans* to identify a variety of gender identities and expressions different from the gender identity they were assigned at birth (Moradi & others, 2016). The variety of gender identities might include transgender, gender queer (also referred to as gender expansive, this broad gender identity category encompasses individuals who are not exclusively masculine or exclusively feminine), and gender nonconforming (individuals whose behavior/appearance does not conform to social expectations for what is appropriate for their gender). Another recently generated term, *cisgender,* can be used to describe individuals whose gender identity and expression corresponds with the gender identity assigned at birth (Moradi & others, 2016).

What characterizes transgender individuals?
©FatCamera/Getty Images

Transgender individuals can be straight, gay, lesbian, or bisexual. A recent research review concluded that transgender youth have higher rates of depression, suicide attempts, and eating disorders than their cisgender peers (Connolly & others, 2016). Among the explanations for this higher rate of disorders are the distress of living in the wrong body and the discrimination and misunderstanding they experience as a gender minority individual (Budge & others, 2018a, b).

Among individuals who identify themselves as transgender persons, the majority eventually adopt a gender identity in line with the body into which they were born (Byne & others, 2012; King, 2019). Some transgender individuals seek transsexual surgery to go from a male body to a female body or vice versa, but most do not. Some choose just to have hormonal treatments, such as biological females who use testosterone to enhance their masculine

transgender A broad term that refers to individuals whose gender identity or behavior is either completely or partially at odds with the sex into which they were born.

characteristics, or biological males who use estrogen to increase their feminine characteristics. Yet other transgender individuals opt for another, broader strategy that involves choosing a lifestyle that challenges the traditional view of having a gender identity that does not fit within one of two opposing categories (King, 2017, 2019; Savin-Williams, 2017). Because trans individuals experience considerable discrimination, it is important that society provide a more welcoming and accepting attitude toward them.

Summary

Stability and Change from Childhood to Adulthood

- The first 20 years are important in predicting an adult's personality, but so are ongoing experiences in the adult years. Attachment styles, for example, reflect childhood patterns and continue to influence relationships in adulthood. Adult attachments are categorized as secure, avoidant, or anxious. A secure attachment style is linked with positive aspects of relationships.

Love and Close Relationships

- Erikson theorized that intimacy versus isolation is the key developmental issue in early adulthood.
- Friendship plays an important role in adult development, especially in terms of emotional support.
- Romantic love, also called passionate love, includes passion, sexuality, and a mixture of emotions, not all of which are positive. Affectionate love, also called companionate love, usually becomes more important as relationships mature.
- Sternberg proposed a triarchic model of love: passion, intimacy, and commitment. If all three qualities are present, the result is consummate love.

Adult Lifestyles

- Being single has become an increasingly prominent lifestyle. Autonomy is one of its advantages. Challenges faced by single adults include achieving intimacy, coping with loneliness, and finding a positive identity in a marriage-oriented society.
- Cohabitation, an increasingly popular lifestyle, does not lead to greater marital happiness but sometimes is linked to possible negative consequences if a cohabiting couple marries.
- The age at which individuals marry in the United States is increasing. Though marriage rates have declined, a large percentage of Americans still marry. The benefits of marriage include better physical and mental health and a longer life.

- The U.S. divorce rate increased dramatically in the middle of the twentieth century but began to decline in the 1980s.
- Divorce is a complex and emotional experience.
- Stepfamilies are complex, and adjustment is difficult. Evidence on the benefits of remarriage after divorce is mixed.
- One of the most striking research findings about gay and lesbian couples is how similar their relationships are to heterosexual couples' relationships.

Challenges in Marriage, Parenting, and Divorce

- Gottman's research indicates that couples in successful marriages establish love maps, nurture fondness and admiration, turn toward each other, accept the influence of the partner, and create shared meaning.
- Families are becoming smaller, and many women are delaying childbirth until they have become well established in a career.
- Divorced adults often have difficulty trusting someone else in a romantic relationship. Certain strategies are effective in dealing with divorce.

Gender and Communication Styles, Relationships, and Classification

- Tannen distinguishes between report talk, which many men prefer, and rapport talk, which many women prefer; however, meta-analyses have found only small gender differences in overall communication.
- Gender differences characterize adult friendships. Female friends tend to share their experiences, thoughts, and feelings, while male friends tend to be more competitive and to keep some emotional distance while sharing useful information.
- In recent years, emphasis has been placed on flexibility and equality in gender roles. Transgender individuals adopt a gender identity different from the one assigned to them at birth.

Key Terms

affectionate love	avoidant attachment style	report talk	secure attachment style
anxious attachment style	rapport talk	romantic love	transgender

13 Physical and Cognitive Development in Middle Adulthood

©Tomas Rodriguez/Corbis/Getty Images

CHAPTER OUTLINE

Stories of Life-Span Development: Changing Perceptions of Time

Our perception of time depends on where we are in the life span. We are more concerned about time at some points in life than others (Hoppmann & others, 2017; MacDonald, DeCarlo, & Dixon, 2011). Pink Floyd, in their song "Time," described how when people are young life seems longer and time passes more slowly, but when we get older, time seems to pass much more quickly.

In middle adulthood, individuals increasingly think about time-left-to-live instead of time-since-birth (Brothers & others, 2016; Kotter-Gruhn & Smith, 2011; Setterson, 2009; Strough & others, 2016). Middle-aged adults begin to look back to where they have been, reflecting on what they have done with the time they have had. They look toward the future in terms of how much time remains to accomplish what they hope to do with their lives. Older adults look backward even more than middle-aged adults, which is not surprising given the shorter future that awaits them. Also not surprisingly, given the many years they still have to live, emerging adults and young adults are more likely to look forward in time than backward in time.

A recent research review examined subjective time in middle and late adulthood, including such components as future time perspective, personal goals, and autobiographical memories (Gabrian, Dutt, & Wahl, 2017). The review concluded that positive subjective time perceptions (such as an expanded view of the future, a focus on positive past and future life content, and favorable time-related evaluations) were linked to better health and well-being, while negative subjective time perceptions were associated with lower levels of health and well-being.

In this chapter on middle adulthood, we discuss physical changes; cognitive changes; changes in careers, work, and leisure. We will also discuss the importance of religion and meaning in life. To begin, though, we explore how middle age is changing. ∎

The Nature of Middle Adulthood

Is midlife experienced the same way today as it was 100 years ago? How can middle adulthood be defined, and what are some of its main characteristics?

Changing Midlife

Many of today's 50-year-olds are in better shape, more alert, and more productive than their 40-year-old counterparts from a generation or two earlier. As more people lead healthier lifestyles and medical discoveries help to slow down the aging process, the boundaries of middle age are being pushed upward. It seems that middle age is starting later and lasting longer for increasing numbers of active, healthy, and productive people. A current saying is "60 is the new 40," implying that many 60-year-olds today are living a life that is as active, productive, and healthy as earlier generations did in their forties.

Questions such as, "To which age group do you belong?" and "How old do you feel?" reflect the concept of *age identity*. A consistent finding is that as adults become older their age identity is younger than their chronological age (Setterson & Trauten, 2009; Westerhof, 2009). One study found that almost half of the individuals 65 to 69 years of age considered themselves middle-aged (National Council on Aging, 2000), and another study found a similar pattern: Half of the 60- to 75-year-olds viewed themselves as middle-aged (Lachman, Maier, & Budner, 2000). And a British survey of people over 50 years of age revealed that they perceived middle age to begin at 53 (Beneden Health, 2013). In this study, respondents said that being middle-aged is characterized by enjoying afternoon naps, groaning when you bend down, and preferring a quiet night in rather than a night out. Also, some individuals consider the upper boundary of midlife as the age when they make the transition from work to retirement.

When Carl Jung studied midlife transitions early in the twentieth century, he referred to midlife as "the afternoon of life" (Jung, 1933). Midlife serves as an important preparation for late adulthood, "the evening of life" (Lachman, 2004, p. 306). But "midlife" came much earlier in Jung's time. In 1900 the average life expectancy was only 47 years of age; only 3 percent of the population lived past 65. Today, the average life expectancy is 79, and 12 percent of the U.S. population is older than 65 (U.S. Census Bureau, 2015). As a much greater percentage of the population lives to older ages, the midpoint of life and what constitutes middle age or middle adulthood are getting harder to pin down (Cohen, 2012). Statistically, the middle of life today is about 39.5 years of age, but most 39-year-olds don't want to be called "middle-aged." What we think of as middle age comes later—anywhere from 40 or 45 to about 60 or 65 years of age. And as more people live longer, the upper boundary of middle age will likely be nudged higher still.

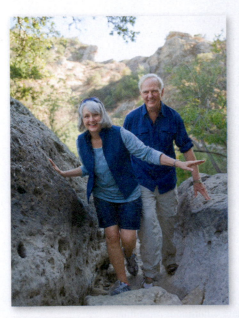

How is midlife changing?
©Siri Stafford/Getty Images

In comparison with previous decades and centuries, an increasing percentage of today's population is made up of middle-aged and older adults. In the past, the age structure of the population could be represented by a pyramid, with the largest percentage of the population in the childhood years. Today, the percentages of people at different ages in the life span are more similar, creating what is called the "rectangularization" of the age distribution (a vertical rectangle) (Himes, 2009).

Compared to late adulthood, far less research attention has been given to middle adulthood (Elliot & others, 2018; Lachman, Teshale, & Agrigoroaei, 2015). In a U.S. Census Bureau (2012) assessment, more than 102,713,000 people in the U.S. were 40 to 64 years of age, which accounts for 33.2 percent of the U.S. population. Given the large percentage of people in middle adulthood and the key roles that individuals in midlife play in families, the workplace, and the community, researchers need to give greater attention to this age period.

Also, too often middle-age has been described more negatively than it should be. Indeed, in a recent study, undergraduate college students were shown a computer-generated graphic of a person identified as a younger adult, middle-aged adult, or older adult (Kelley, Soboroff, & Lovaglia, 2017). When asked which person they would choose for a work-related task, they selected the middle-aged adult most often.

Defining Middle Adulthood

Although the age boundaries are not set in stone, we will consider **middle adulthood** to be the developmental period that begins at approximately 40 years of age and extends to about 60 to 65 years of age. For many people, middle adulthood is a time of declining physical skills and expanding responsibility; a period in which people become more conscious of the young-old polarity and the shrinking amount of time left in life; a point when individuals seek to transmit something meaningful to the next generation; and a time when people reach and maintain satisfaction in their careers.

In sum, middle adulthood involves "balancing work and relationship responsibilities in the midst of the physical and psychological changes associated with aging" (Lachman, 2004, p. 305).

In midlife, as in other age periods, individuals make choices, selecting what to do, deciding how to invest time and resources, and evaluating what aspects of their lives they need to change (Robinson & Lachman, 2017). In midlife, "a serious accident, loss, or illness" may be a "wake-up call" that produces "a major restructuring of time and a reassessment" of life's priorities (Lachman, 2004, p. 310).

What are the main characteristics of middle adulthood? What differentiates early and late midlife?
©kali9/Getty Images

For many increasingly healthy adults, middle age is lasting longer. Indeed, a growing number of experts on middle adulthood describe the age period of 55 to 65 as *late midlife* (Deeg, 2005). Compared with earlier midlife, late midlife is more likely to be characterized by the death of a parent, the last child leaving the parental home, becoming a grandparent, preparing for retirement, and in most cases actual retirement. Many people in this age range experience their first confrontation with health problems. Overall, then, although gains and losses may balance each other in early midlife, losses may begin to outweigh gains for many individuals in late midlife (Baltes, Lindenberger, & Staudinger, 2006). Margie Lachman and her colleagues (2015) describe middle age as a pivotal period because it is a time of balancing growth and decline, linking earlier and later periods of development, and connecting younger and older generations.

Keep in mind, though, that midlife is characterized by individual variations (Robinson & Lachman, 2017). As life-span expert Gilbert Brim (1992) commented, middle adulthood is full of changes, twists, and turns; the path is not fixed. People move in and out of states of success and failure.

middle adulthood The developmental period beginning at approximately 40 years of age and extending to about 60 to 65 years of age.

Physical Development

What physical changes accompany the change to middle adulthood? How healthy are middle-aged adults? How sexually active are they?

Physical Changes

Although everyone experiences some physical changes due to aging in the middle adulthood years, the speed of the aging process varies considerably from one individual to another. Genetic makeup and lifestyle factors play important roles in whether chronic disease will appear and when (Kiviniemi & others, 2017; Pazoki & others, 2018). Middle age is a window through which we can glimpse later life while there is still time to engage in prevention and to influence some of the course of aging (Robinson & Lachman, 2017).

Visible Signs

One of the most visible signs of change in middle adulthood is physical appearance. The first outwardly noticeable signs of aging usually are apparent by the forties or fifties. The skin begins to wrinkle and sag because of a loss of fat and collagen in underlying tissues (Cole & others, 2018; Czekalla & others, 2017). Small, localized areas of pigmentation in the skin produce age spots, especially in areas that are exposed to sunlight, such as the hands and face. For most people, their hair becomes thinner and grayer. Fingernails and toenails develop ridges and become thicker and more brittle.

Since a youthful appearance is valued in our culture, many individuals whose hair is graying, whose skin is wrinkling, whose bodies are sagging, and whose teeth are yellowing strive to make themselves look younger. Undergoing cosmetic surgery, dyeing hair, wearing wigs, enrolling in weight-reduction programs, participating in exercise regimens, and taking heavy doses of vitamins are common in middle age. Many baby boomers have shown a strong interest in plastic surgery and Botox, which may reflect their desire to take control of the aging process (Harii & others, 2017; Lim & others, 2018).

Height and Weight

Individuals lose height in middle age, and many gain weight (Lebenbaum & others, 2018; Yang & others, 2017). On average, from 30 to 50 years of age, men lose about half an inch in height; they may lose another 3/4 inch from 50 to 70 years of age (Hoyer & Roodin, 2009). The height loss for women can be as much as 2 inches over a 50-year span from 25 to 75 years of age. Note that there are large variations in the extent to which individuals become shorter with aging. The decrease in height is due to bone loss in the vertebrae.

On average, body fat accounts for about 10 percent of body weight in adolescence; it makes up 20 percent or more in middle age. Obesity increases from early to middle adulthood (Nevalainen & others, 2017). In a national U.S. survey in 2014, 40.2 percent of U.S. adults 40 to 59 years of age were classified as obese compared with 32 percent of younger adults (Centers for Disease Control and Prevention, 2016). Being overweight is a critical health problem in middle adulthood and increases the risk that individuals will develop a number of other health problems such as hypertension and diabetes (Forrest, Leeds, & Ufelle, 2017; Jia, Hill, & Sowers, 2018;

Famous actor Sean Connery as a young adult in his twenties (*top*) and as a middle-aged adult in his fifties (*bottom*). *What are some of the most outwardly noticeable signs of aging in middle adulthood?*
(*Top*) ©Bettmann/Getty Images; (*bottom*) ©Time & Life Pictures/Getty Images

How Would You...?

As a **human development and family studies professional,** how would you characterize the impact of the media in shaping middle-aged adults' expectations about their changing physical appearance?

Petrie, Guzik, & Touyz, 2018; Wedell-Neergaard & others, 2018). Also, a recent study revealed that an increase in weight gain from early adulthood to middle adulthood was linked to an increased risk of major chronic diseases and unhealthy aging (Zheng & others, 2017).

Strength, Joints, and Bones

Maximum physical strength often is attained in the twenties. The term *sarcopenia* refers to age-related loss of muscle mass and strength (Landi & others, 2018). Muscle loss with age occurs at a rate of approximately 1 to 2 percent per year past the age of 50 (Marcell, 2003). A loss of strength especially occurs in the back and legs. Obesity is a risk factor for sarcopenia (Albar-Almazan & others, 2018; Cruz-Jentoft & others, 2017). Recently, researchers have increasingly used the term "sarcopenic obesity" to describe individuals who have sarcopenia and are obese (Yang & others, 2017; Xiao & others, 2018). In a recent study sarcopenic obesity was associated with a 24 percent increase in risk for all-cause mortality, with a higher risk of mortality for men than for women (Tian & Xu, 2016).

Peak functioning of the body's joints also usually occurs in the twenties. The cartilage that cushions the movement of bones and other connective tissues, such as tendons and ligaments, become less efficient in the middle-adult years, a time when many individuals experience joint stiffness and greater difficulty in movement.

Maximum bone density occurs by the mid- to late thirties, from which point there is a progressive loss of bone. The rate of this bone loss begins slowly but accelerates during the fifties (Locquet & others, 2018). Women lose bone mass about twice as quickly as men. By the end of midlife, bones break more easily and heal more slowly (de Villiers, 2018; Gulsahi, 2015). A recent study found that greater intake of fruits and vegetables was linked to increased bone density in middle-aged and older adults (Qiu & others, 2017).

Vision and Hearing

Accommodation of the eye—the ability to focus and maintain an image on the retina—declines sharply between 40 and 59 years of age. In particular, middle-aged individuals begin to have difficulty viewing close objects, which means that many individuals have to wear glasses with bifocal lenses—lenses with two sections that enable the wearer to see items at different distances (Schieber, 2006). Also, there is some evidence that the retina becomes less sensitive to low levels of illumination. Laser surgery and implantation of intraocular lenses have become routine procedures for correcting vision in middle-aged adults (Arba-Mosquera, Vinciguerra, & Verma, 2018).

Hearing also can start to decline by the age of 40 (Roring, Hines, & Charness, 2007). Sensitivity to high pitches usually declines first. The ability to hear low-pitched sounds does not seem to decline much in middle adulthood, though. Men usually lose their sensitivity to high-pitched sounds sooner than women do. However, this gender difference might be due to men's greater exposure to noise in occupations such as mining, automobile work, and so on (Scialfa & Kline, 2007). Also, recent advances in the effectiveness of hearing aids are dramatically improving the hearing of many aging adults (Courtois & others, 2018). However, even with the advent of technologically sophisticated hearing devices, many people don't always wear them, or wear them inappropriately.

Cardiovascular System

Midlife is the time when high blood pressure and high cholesterol take many individuals by surprise. Cardiovascular disease increases considerably in middle age (Kanesarajah & others, 2018; Mok & others, 2018).

The level of cholesterol in the blood increases through the adult years and in midlife begins to accumulate on the artery walls, increasing the risk of cardiovascular disease (Choi & Lee, 2017; Mok & others, 2018; Pirillo & others, 2018; Talbot & others, 2018). High blood pressure (hypertension), too, often occurs in the forties and fifties (Mrowka, 2017). One study found that uncontrolled hypertension can damage the brain's structure

How Would You...?

As a **social worker,** how would you apply information on weight and health to promote healthier lifestyles for middle-aged adults?

and function as early as the late thirties and early forties (Maillard & others, 2012). Another study revealed that hypertension in middle age was linked to risk of cognitive impairment in late adulthood (23 years later) (Virta & others, 2013). Also, a recent Chinese study revealed that men and women who gained an average of 22 pounds or more from 20 to 45–60 years of age had an increased risk of hypertension and cholesterol, as well as elevated triglyceride levels in middle age (Zhou & others, 2017). And risk factors for cardiovascular disease in middle adulthood can show up even earlier in development. A recent study indicated that a healthy diet in adolescence was linked to a lower risk of cardiovascular disease in middle-aged women (Dahm & others, 2018).

Exercise, weight control, and a diet rich in fruits, vegetables, and whole grains can often help to stave off many cardiovascular problems in middle age (de Gregorio, 2018; Kim & others, 2017). In a recent study, a high level of physical activity was associated with a lower risk of cardiovascular disease in the three weight categories studied (normal, overweight, and obese) (Carlsson & others, 2016). Another study found that having an unhealthy diet was a strong predictor of cardiovascular disease (Menotti & others, 2015). Further, the health benefits of cholesterol-lowering and hypertension-lowering drugs are a major factor in improving the health of many middle-aged adults and increasing their life expectancy (Svatikova & Kopecky, 2017; Talbot & others, 2018).

Members of the Masai tribe in Kenya, Africa, can stay on a treadmill for a long time because of their active lives. Incidence of heart disease is extremely low in the Masai tribe, which also can be attributed to their energetic lifestyle.
Courtesy of The Family of Dr. George V. Mann

As reflected in the research we have just described, the American Heart Association has proposed "Life's Simple 7": a list of strategies for improving cardiovascular health. The seven strategies are (1) manage blood pressure; (2) control cholesterol; (3) reduce blood sugar; (4) get active; (5) eat better; (6) lose weight; and (7) quit smoking. In a recent study, optimal performance on Life's Simple 7 at middle age was linked to better cardiovascular health recovery following a heart attack in later in life (Mok & others, 2018).

Lungs

There is little change in lung capacity through most of middle adulthood. However, at about the age of 55, the proteins in lung tissue become less elastic. This change, combined with a gradual stiffening of connective tissues in the chest wall, decreases the lungs' capacity to shuttle oxygen from the air people breathe to the blood in their veins. The lung capacity of individuals who are smokers drops precipitously in middle age, but if the individuals quit smoking their lung capacity improves, although not to the level of individuals who have never smoked. A longitudinal study also found that increased cardiorespiratory fitness from early adulthood to middle adulthood was linked to less decline in lung health over time (Benck & others, 2017).

Sleep

Some aspects of sleep become more problematic in middle age (Muller & others, 2017). The total number of hours slept usually remains the same as in early adulthood, but beginning in the forties, wakeful periods are more frequent and there is less of the deepest type of sleep (stage 4). The amount of time spent lying awake in bed at night begins to increase in middle age, and this can produce a feeling of being less rested in the morning. One study revealed that poor sleep quality in middle adulthood was linked to cognitive decline (Waller & others, 2016). And a Korean study found that these factors were linked to sleep problems in middle age: unemployment, being unmarried, currently being a smoker, lack of exercise, having irregular meals, and frequently experiencing stressful events (Yoon & others, 2015). Further, in a recent study of young and middle-aged adults, females had more severe sleep problems than males (Rossler & others, 2017). However, in this study the good news is that a majority of individuals (72 percent) reported no sleep disturbances.

Health and Disease

In middle adulthood, the frequency of accidents declines, and individuals are less susceptible to colds and allergies than in childhood, adolescence, or early adulthood. Indeed, many individuals live through middle adulthood without having a disease or persistent health problem. For others, however, disease and persistent health problems become more common in middle adulthood than in earlier life stages (Koyanagi & others, 2018).

Stress is increasingly being identified as a factor in disease (Berntson, Patel, & Stewart, 2017; Yu & others, 2018). The cumulative effect of chronic stress often takes a toll on the health of individuals by the time they reach middle age. Chronic stressors have been linked to a downturn in immune system functioning in a number of contexts, including worries about living next to a damaged nuclear reactor; failures in close relationships (divorce, separation, and marital distress) (Kiecolt-Glaser & Wilson, 2017); depression; loneliness; and burdensome caregiving for a family member with progressive illness (Bennett, Fagundes, & Kiecolt-Glaser, 2016; Fagundes & others, 2016; Jaremka, Derry, & Kiecolt-Glaser, 2016). Research indicates that stress-reducing activities such as yoga, relaxation, and hypnosis have positive influences on immune system functioning (Derry & others, 2015; Kiecolt-Glaser & others, 2014).

An important aspect of understanding stress and disease are stress hormones (Fali, Vallet, & Sauce, 2018). One hormone in particular, *cortisol*, has been labeled the stress hormone because elevated cortisol levels are linked to physical health problems such as lower immune system functioning and higher blood pressure, cholesterol, and cardiovascular disease, as well as to higher levels of mental health problems such as anxiety and depressive disorders (Leonard, 2018; Wichmann & others, 2017). A recent study of men and women from 21 to 55 years of age found that married individuals had lower cortisol levels than either their never-married or previously married counterparts (Chin & others, 2017).

How individuals react to stressors is linked to health outcomes. In one study, how people reacted to daily stressors in their lives was linked to future chronic health problems (Piazza & others, 2013). Also, in a recent study, adults who did not maintain positive affect when confronted with minor stressors in everyday life had elevated levels of IL-6, an inflammation marker (Sin & others, 2017). And in another study, a greater decrease in positive affect in response to daily stressors was associated with earlier death (Mroczek & others, 2015).

Mortality Rates

Infectious disease was the main cause of death until the middle of the twentieth century. As infectious disease rates declined and more individuals lived through middle age, chronic disorders increased. These are characterized by a slow onset and a long duration (Kelley-Moore, 2009). Chronic disorders account for 86 percent of total health-care spending in the United States (Qin & others, 2015).

In middle age, many deaths are caused by a single, readily identifiable condition, whereas in old age, death is more likely to result from the combined effects of several chronic conditions. For many years heart disease was the leading cause of death in middle adulthood, followed by cancer; however, since 2005 more individuals 45 to 64 years of age in the United States died of cancer, followed by cardiovascular disease (Centers for Disease Control and Prevention, 2015). The gap between cancer and the second leading cause of death widens as individuals age from 45 to 54 and from 55 to 64 years of age. In 2013, about 46,000 45- to 54-year-olds died of cancer and about 35,000 died of cardiovascular disease; about 113,000 55- to 64-year-olds died of cancer and about 73,000 died of cardiovascular disease (Centers for Disease Control and Prevention, 2015). Men have higher mortality rates than women for all of the leading causes of death (Kochanek & others, 2011).

climacteric The midlife transition in which fertility declines.

menopause The complete cessation of a woman's menstrual cycles, which usually occurs in the late forties or early fifties.

Sexuality

What kinds of changes characterize the sexuality of women and men as they go through middle age? **Climacteric** is a term used to describe the midlife transition during which fertility declines. Let's explore the substantial differences in the climacteric of women and men during middle adulthood.

Menopause

Menopause is the time in middle age, usually in the late forties or early fifties, when a woman's menstrual periods cease completely. The average age at which women have their last period is 51 (Wise, 2006). However, there is large variation in the age at which menopause occurs—from 39 to 59 years of age. Later menopause is linked with increased risk of breast cancer (Mishra & others, 2009).

Researchers have found that almost 50 percent of Canadian and American menopausal women have occasional hot flashes, but only one in seven Japanese women do (Lock, 1998). *What factors might account for these variations?*
©BLOOMimage/Getty Images

In menopause, production of estrogen by the ovaries declines dramatically, and this decline produces uncomfortable symptoms in some women—"hot flashes," nausea, fatigue, and rapid heartbeat, for example (Chiaramonte, Ring, & Locke, 2017; Noble, 2018). However, cross-cultural studies reveal wide variations in the menopause experience (Sievert, 2014). For example, hot flashes are uncommon in Mayan women (Beyene, 1986). Asian women report fewer hot flashes than women in Western societies (Payer, 1991). In a recent study in China, Mosuo women (Mosuo is a matriarchal tribe in southern China where women have the dominant role in society, don't marry, and can take on as many lovers as they desire) had fewer negative menopausal symptoms, higher self-esteem, and better family support than Han Chinese women (the majority ethnic group in China) (Zhang & others, 2016). It is difficult to determine the extent to which these cross-cultural variations are due to genetic, dietary, reproductive, or cultural factors.

Menopause overall is not the negative experience for most women that it was once thought to be (Brown & others, 2018; Henderson, 2011). Most women do not have severe physical or psychological problems related to menopause. For example, a research review concluded that there is no clear evidence that depressive disorders occur more often during menopause than at other times in a woman's reproductive life (Judd, Hickey, & Bryant, 2012).

Hormone replacement therapy (HRT) augments the declining levels of reproductive hormone production by the ovaries (Anderson, Borgquist, & Jirstrom, 2018; Langer, 2017; Lobo, 2017). HRT can consist of various forms of estrogen, usually in combination with a progestin.

In a recent position statement by leading experts of the North American Menopause Society (2017), the following conclusions were reached about HRT:

- Hormone replacement therapy is most favorable in reducing negative menopausal symptoms and reducing bone loss or fracture for women 60 years and younger who are within 10 years of menopausal onset.

- Hormone replacement therapy is less favorable for women who are more than 10 or more years from menopausal onset or are 60 years and older, because of greater risk for cardiovascular disease and Alzheimer disease.

How Would You...?

As a **human development and family studies professional,** how would you counsel middle-aged women who voice the belief that hormone replacement therapy will help them to "stay young"?

Further, research indicates that hormone replacement therapy is linked to a slightly higher risk of breast cancer and the longer HRT is taken, the greater the risk of breast cancer (American Cancer Society, 2018; breastcancer.org, 2018).

The National Institutes of Health recommends that women who have not had a hysterectomy and who are currently taking hormones consult with their doctor to determine whether they should continue the treatment. If they are taking HRT for short-term relief of menopausal symptoms, the benefits may outweigh the risks. Many middle-aged women are seeking alternatives to HRT such as regular exercise, dietary supplements, herbal remedies, relaxation therapy, acupuncture, and nonsteroidal medications (Goldstein & others, 2017; Woyka, 2017).

Hormonal Changes in Middle-Aged Men

Do men go through anything like the menopause that women experience? In other words, is there a male menopause? During middle adulthood, most men do not lose their capacity to father children, although there usually is a modest decline in their sexual hormone level and activity (Blumel & others, 2014; Jannini & Nappi, 2018). They experience hormonal changes in their fifties and sixties, but nothing like the dramatic drop in estrogen that women experience. Testosterone production begins to decline about 1 percent per year during middle adulthood, and sperm count usually shows a slow decline, but men do not lose their fertility in middle age. The term *male hypogonadism* is used to describe a condition in which the body does not produce enough testosterone (Mayo Clinic, 2018).

Recently, there has been a dramatic surge of interest in *testosterone replacement therapy (TRT)* (Gilbert & others, 2017). Research indicates that TRT can improve sexual functioning, muscle strength, and bone health (Ismaeel & Wang, 2017; Mayo Clinic, 2018). A recent study found that TRT was associated with increased longevity in men with a low level of testosterone (Comhaire, 2016). Another recent study indicated that TRT-related benefits in quality of life and sexual function were maintained for 36 months after initial treatment (Rosen & others, 2017). Also, recent research indicates that testosterone replacement therapy is associated with a reduced incidence of heart attack or stroke, as well as a reduction in all-cause mortality (Jones & Kelly, 2018; Sharma & others, 2015).

©McGraw-Hill Education/Suzie Ross, photographer

The gradual decline in men's testosterone levels in middle age can reduce their sexual drive (O'Connor & others, 2011). Their erections are less full and less frequent, and men require more stimulation to achieve them. Researchers once attributed these changes to psychological factors, but increasingly they find that as many as 75 percent of the erectile dysfunctions in middle-aged men stem from physiological problems. Smoking, diabetes, hypertension, elevated cholesterol levels, and obesity are at fault in many erectile problems in middle-aged men (Schulster, Liang, & Najari, 2017; Sgro & Di Luigi, 2017).

Erectile dysfunction (ED), difficulty in attaining or maintaining an erection, is present in approximately 50 percent of men 40 to 70 years of age (Mola, 2015). A low level of testosterone and cardiovascular problems can contribute to erectile dysfunction (Hackett & Kirby, 2018). The main treatment for erectile dysfunction has not focused on TRT but on the drug Viagra and on similar drugs such as Levitra and Cialis (Bennett, 2018; Gesser-Edelsburg & Hijazi, 2018; Melehan & others, 2018; Ozcan & others, 2018; Peng & others, 2017). Viagra works by allowing increased blood flow into the penis, which produces an erection. Its success rate is in the 60 to 85 percent range (Claes & others, 2010).

Sexual Attitudes and Behavior

Although the ability of men and women to function sexually shows little biological decline in middle adulthood, sexual activity usually occurs less frequently than in early adulthood (Fileborn & others, 2017; Rees & others, 2018). Career interests, family matters, diminishing energy levels, and routine may contribute to this decline (Avis & others, 2009).

In the Sex in America survey, the frequency of sexual activity was greatest for individuals 25 to 29 years old (47 percent had sex twice a week or more) and dropped off for individuals in their fifties (23 percent of 50- to 59-year-old males said they had sex twice a week or more, while only 14 percent of the females in this age group reported this frequency) (Michael & others, 1994). Note, though, that the Sex in America survey may underestimate the frequency of sexual activity of middle-aged adults because the data were collected prior to the widespread use of erectile dysfunction drugs such as Viagra. In a recent study, higher frequency of sexual activity in middle-aged and older adults was linked to better overall cognitive functioning, especially in working memory and executive function (Wright, Jenks, & Demeyere, 2018).

Living with a spouse or partner makes all the difference in whether people engage in sexual activity, especially for women over 40 years of age. In one study conducted as part of the Midlife in the United States Study (MIDUS), 95 percent of women in their forties with partners said that they had been sexually active in the last six months, compared with only 53 percent of those without partners (Brim, 1999). By their fifties, 88 percent of women living with a partner had been sexually active in the last six months, but only 37 percent of those who were neither married nor living with someone said they had been sexually active in the last six months.

How does the pattern of sexual activity change when individuals become middle-aged?
©Image Source/PunchStock

A large-scale study of U.S. adults 40 to 80 years of age found that early ejaculation (26 percent) and erectile difficulties (22 percent) were the most common sexual problems of older men (Laumann & others, 2009). In this study, the most common sexual problems of women were lack of sexual interest (33 percent) and lubrication difficulties (21 percent).

A person's health in middle age is a key factor in sexual activity in middle age (Almont & others, 2017; Rees & others, 2018). A study of adults 55 years and older revealed that their level of sexual activity was associated with their physical and mental health (Bach & others, 2013).

How Would You...?

As a **psychologist,** how would you counsel a couple about the ways that the transition to middle adulthood might affect their sexual relationship?

Cognitive Development

We have seen that middle-aged adults may not see as well, run as fast, or be as healthy as they were in their twenties and thirties. We've also seen a decline in their sexual activity. What about their cognitive skills? Do these skills decline as we enter and move through middle adulthood? To answer this question, we will explore the possibility of age-related changes in intelligence and information processing.

Intelligence

Our exploration of possible changes in intelligence in middle adulthood focuses on the concepts of fluid and crystallized intelligence, cohort effects, and the Seattle Longitudinal Study.

Fluid and Crystallized Intelligence

John Horn argues that some abilities begin to decline in middle age, whereas others increase (Horn & Donaldson, 1980). He argues that **crystallized intelligence,** an individual's accumulated information and verbal

crystallized intelligence Accumulated information and verbal skills, which increase in middle age, according to Horn.

skills, continues to increase in middle adult-hood, whereas **fluid intelligence,** one's ability to reason abstractly, begins to decline during middle adulthood (see Figure 1).

Horn's data were collected in a cross-sectional manner. Recall that a cross-sectional study assesses individuals of different ages at the same point in time. For example, a cross-sectional study might assess the intelligence of different groups of 40-, 50-, and 60-year-olds in a single evaluation, such as in 1980. The 40-year-olds in the study would have been born in 1940 and the 60-year-olds in 1920—different eras that offered different economic and educational opportunities. The 60-year-olds likely had fewer educational opportunities as they grew up. Thus, if we find differences between 40- and 60-year-olds on intelligence tests when they are assessed cross-sectionally, these differences might be due to cohort effects related to educational differences rather than to age.

By contrast, recall that in a longitudinal study, the same individuals are studied over a period of time. Thus, a longitudinal study of intelligence in middle adulthood might consist of giving the same intelligence test to the same individuals when they are 40, then 50, and then 60 years of age. As we see next, whether data on intelligence are collected cross-sectionally or longitudinally can make a difference in what is found about changes in crystallized and fluid intelligence and about intellectual decline.

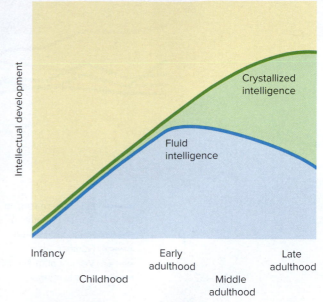

Figure 1 **Fluid and Crystallized Intelligence Across the Life Span** According to Horn, crystallized intelligence (based on cumulative learning experiences) increases throughout the life span, but fluid intelligence (the ability to perceive and manipulate information) steadily declines from middle adulthood onward.

How Would You...?

As an **educator,** how would you explain how changes in fluid and crystallized intelligence might influence the way middle-aged adults learn?

The Seattle Longitudinal Study

K. Warner Schaie (1996, 2005, 2010, 2011, 2013) is conducting an extensive study of intellectual abilities in adulthood. Five hundred individuals initially were tested in 1956. New waves of participants are added periodically. The main focus in the Seattle Longitudinal Study has been on individual change and stability in intelligence. The main mental abilities tested are *verbal comprehension* (ability to understand ideas expressed in words); *verbal memory* (ability to encode and recall meaningful language units, such as a list of words); *numeric ability* (ability to perform simple mathematical computations such as addition, subtraction, and multiplication); *spatial orientation* (ability to visualize and mentally rotate stimuli in two- and three-dimensional space); *inductive reasoning* (ability to recognize and understand patterns and relationships in a problem and use this understanding to solve other instances of the problem); and *perceptual speed* (ability to quickly and accurately make simple discriminations in visual stimuli).

The highest level of functioning for four of the six intellectual abilities occurred during middle adulthood (Schaie, 2013) (see Figure 2). For both women and men, peak performance on verbal ability, verbal memory, inductive reasoning, and spatial orientation was attained in middle age. Only two of the six abilities—numeric ability and perceptual speed—showed a decline in middle age. Perceptual speed showed the earliest decline, actually beginning in early adulthood. Interestingly, in terms of John Horn's ideas that were discussed earlier, for the participants in the Seattle Longitudinal Study, middle age was a time of peak performance for some aspects of both crystallized intelligence (verbal ability) and fluid intelligence (spatial orientation and inductive reasoning).

Notice in Figure 2 that declines in functioning for most cognitive abilities began in the sixties, although verbal comprehension did not drop until the mid-seventies. From the mid-seventies through the mid-nineties, all cognitive abilities showed considerable decline.

fluid intelligence The ability to reason abstractly, which steadily declines from middle adulthood on, according to Horn.

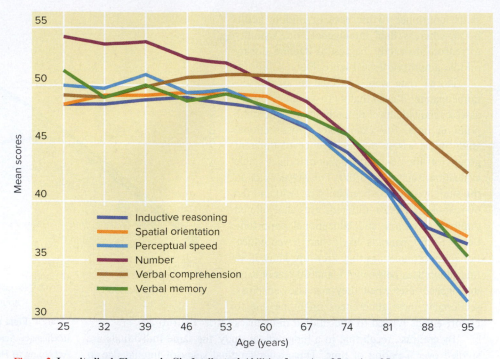

Figure 2 Longitudinal Changes in Six Intellectual Abilities from Age 25 to Age 95
Source: Schaie, K. W. "Longitudinal Changes in Six Intellectual Abilities from Age 25 to Age 95." Figure 5.7a, *in Developmental Influences on Intelligence: The Seattle Longitudinal Study*, (2nd rev edit.) 2013, p. 162.

When Schaie (1994) assessed intellectual abilities both cross-sectionally and longitudinally, he found declines more often in the cross-sectional than in the longitudinal assessments. For example, as shown in Figure 3, when assessed cross-sectionally, inductive reasoning showed a consistent decline during middle adulthood. In contrast, when assessed longitudinally, inductive reasoning increased until toward the end of middle adulthood, when it began to show a slight decline. In Schaie's (2009, 2010, 2011, 2013, 2016) view, it is during middle adulthood, not early adulthood, that people reach a peak in their cognitive functioning for many intellectual skills.

Such differences across generations involve *cohort effects*. In a recent analysis, Schaie (2013, 2016) concluded that the advances in cognitive functioning in middle age that have occurred in recent decades are likely due to a combination of factors: increased educational attainment, different occupational structures (increasing numbers of workers in professional occupations with greater work complexity), changes in health care and lifestyles, immigration, and social interventions in poverty. The impressive gains in cognitive functioning in recent cohorts have been documented more clearly for fluid intelligence than for crystallized intelligence (Schaie, 2013).

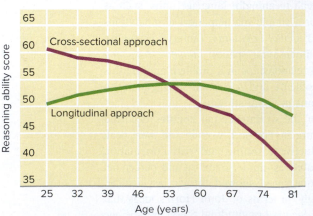

Figure 3 Cross-Sectional and Longitudinal Comparisons of Intellectual Change in Middle Adulthood

Why do you think reasoning ability peaks during middle adulthood?

Some researchers disagree with Schaie that middle adulthood is the time when the level of functioning in a number of cognitive domains is maintained or even increases (Finch, 2009). For example, Timothy Salthouse (2009, 2012, 2018) has emphasized that a lower level of cognitive functioning in middle adulthood is likely due to age-related neurobiological decline. Salthouse (2014, 2016) also argues that a main reason for different trends in longitudinal and cross-sectional comparisons of cognitive functioning is that prior experience with tests increases scores the next time a test is taken.

Information Processing

As we saw in the coverage of theories of development and of cognitive development from infancy through adolescence, the information-processing approach provides another way to examine cognitive abilities (Braithwaite & Siegler, 2018; Braithwaite, Tian, & Siegler, 2018). Among the information-processing changes that take place in middle adulthood are those involved in speed of processing information, memory, and expertise.

Speed of Information Processing

As we just discussed, in Schaie's (1996, 2013) Seattle Longitudinal Study, perceptual speed begins declining in early adulthood and continues to decline in middle adulthood. A common way to assess speed of information processing is through a reaction-time task, in which individuals simply press a button as soon as they see a light appear. Middle-aged adults are slower to push the button when the light appears than young adults are (Salthouse, 2009, 2012, 2018). However, keep in mind that the decline is not dramatic—less than 1 second in most investigations. Also, in a longitudinal study, a smaller decline in processing speed in middle and late adulthood was one of the key predictors of living longer (Aichele, Rabbitt, & Ghisletta, 2016).

Memory

In Schaie's (1994, 1996, 2013) Seattle Longitudinal Study, verbal memory peaked in the fifties. However, in some other studies, verbal memory has shown a decline in middle age, especially when assessed in cross-sectional studies (Salthouse, 2018). For example, when asked to remember lists of words, numbers, or meaningful prose, younger adults outperformed middle-aged adults (Salthouse & Skovronek, 1992). Although there still is some controversy about whether memory declines during middle adulthood, most experts conclude that it does decline, at least in late middle age (Ferreira & others, 2015; Salthouse, 2018).

Aging and cognition expert Denise Park (2001) argues that starting in late middle age, more time is needed to learn new information. The slowdown in learning new information has been linked to changes in **working memory,** the mental "workbench" where individuals manipulate and assemble information when making decisions, solving problems, and comprehending written and spoken language (Baddeley, 2007, 2012, 2015, 2018a, b). In this view, in late middle age, working memory capacity—the amount of information that can be immediately retrieved and used—becomes more limited.

Memory decline is more likely to occur among individuals who don't use effective memory strategies, such as organization and imagery (Hoyer & Roodin, 2009). By organizing lists of phone numbers into different categories or imagining the phone numbers as representing different objects around the house, many people can improve their memory in middle adulthood.

Expertise

Because it takes so long to attain, expertise often shows up more in middle adulthood than in early adulthood (Charness & Krampe, 2008). Recall that *expertise* involves having extensive, highly organized knowledge and understanding of a particular domain. Developing expertise and becoming an "expert" in a field usually is the result of many years of experience, learning, and effort (Ericsson, 2017; Ericsson & others, 2016, 2018).

Adults in middle age who have become experts in their fields are likely to do the following: rely on their accumulated experience to solve problems; process information automatically and analyze it more efficiently when solving a problem; devise better strategies and shortcuts to solving problems; and be more creative and flexible in solving problems.

working memory Closely related to short-term memory but places more emphasis on mental work. Working memory is like a mental "workbench" where individuals can manipulate and assemble information when making decisions, solving problems, and deciphering written and spoken language.

Careers, Work, and Leisure

What are some issues that workers face in midlife? What role does leisure play in the lives of middle-aged adults?

Work in Midlife

The role of work, whether one works in a full-time career, at a part-time job, as a volunteer, or as a homemaker, is central during the middle years (Cahill, Giandrea, & Quinn, 2016; Wang & Shi, 2016). Middle-aged adults may reach their peak in position and earnings. They may also be saddled with multiple financial burdens including rent or mortgage payments, medical bills, home repairs, college tuition, loans to family members, or bills from nursing homes for aging parents. One study found that difficulty managing different job demands was associated with poor health in middle-aged adults (Nabe-Nielsen & others, 2014).

What characterizes work in middle adulthood?
©Ariel Skelley/Getty Images

In 2015 in the United States, 79.4 percent of 45- to 54-year-olds were in the workforce (a decrease of 3.4 percent since 2000) and 64.1 percent of 55- to 64-year-olds were in the workforce (an increase of 8 percent since 2000) (Short, 2015). Later in the text we will describe various aspects of workforce participation among individuals age 65 and over in the United States, which has increased by a remarkable 50 percent since 2000 (Short, 2015).

Do middle-aged workers perform their work as competently as younger adults? Age-related declines occur in some occupations, such as air traffic controllers and professional athletes, but for most jobs, no differences have been found in the work performance of young adults and middle-aged adults (Salthouse, 2012). However, leading Finnish researcher Clas-Hakan Nygard (2013) concludes from his longitudinal research that the ability to work effectively peaks during middle age because of increased motivation, work experience, employer loyalty, and better strategic thinking. Nygard also has found that the quality of work done by middle-aged employees is linked to how much their work is appreciated and how well they get along with their immediate supervisors. And Nygard and his colleagues discovered that work ability in middle age was linked to mortality and disability 28 years later (von Bonsdorff & others, 2011, 2012).

For many people, midlife is a time of evaluation, assessment, and reflection in terms of the work they are doing and want to do in the future (Cahill, Giandrea, & Quinn, 2016). Among the work issues that some people face in midlife are recognizing limitations in career progress, deciding whether to change jobs or careers, deciding whether to rebalance family and work, and planning for retirement (Sterns & Huyck, 2001).

Career Challenges and Changes

The current middle-aged worker faces several important challenges in the twenty-first century (Brand, 2014). These include the globalization of work, rapid developments in information technologies, downsizing of organizations, pressure to choose early retirement, and concerns about pensions and health care.

Globalization has replaced what was once a primarily non-Latino White male workforce in the United States with employees of different ethnic and national backgrounds who have emigrated from different parts of the world. To improve profits, many companies are restructuring, downsizing, and outsourcing jobs. One of the outcomes of this change has been for companies to offer incentives to middle-aged employees who choose to retire early—in their fifties, or in some cases even forties, rather than their sixties.

The decline in defined-benefit pensions and increased uncertainty about the fate of health insurance are eroding the sense of personal control among middle-aged workers. As a consequence, many are delaying their retirement from work.

Some midlife career changes are self-motivated, while others are the consequence of losing one's job (Moen, 2009a, b). Some individuals in middle age decide that they don't want to continue doing the same work for the rest of their working lives (Hoyer & Roodin, 2009). One aspect of middle adulthood involves adjusting idealistic hopes to reflect realistic possibilities in light of how much time individuals have before they retire and how quickly they are reaching their occupational goals (Levinson, 1978). Individuals could become motivated to change jobs if they perceive that they are behind schedule, if their goals are

How Would You...?

As a **social worker,** what advice would you offer to middle-aged adults who are dissatisfied with their careers?

unrealistic, if they don't like the work they are doing, or if their job has become too stressful.

A final point to make about career development in middle adulthood is that cognitive factors earlier in development are linked to occupational attainment in middle age. In one study, task persistence at 13 years of age was related to occupational success in middle age (Andersson & Bergman, 2011).

leisure The pleasant times after work when individuals are free to pursue activities and interests of their own choosing.

Leisure

As adults, not only must we learn how to work well, but we also need to learn how to relax and enjoy leisure (Finkel, Andel, & Pedersen, 2018). **Leisure** refers to the pleasant times after work when individuals are free to pursue activities and interests of their own choosing—hobbies, sports, or reading, for example. In one analysis of research on what U.S. adults regret the most, not engaging in more leisure-time pursuits was one of the top six regrets (Roese & Summerville, 2005). A Finnish study found that engaging in little leisure-time activity in middle age was linked to risk of cognitive impairment in late adulthood (23 years later) (Virta & others, 2013). Another study revealed that middle-aged individuals who engaged in high levels of leisure-time physical activity were less likely to have Alzheimer disease 28 years later (Tolppanen & others, 2015).

Also, different types of leisure activities may be linked to different outcomes (Hagnas & others, 2018). A recent study found that engaging in higher complexity of work before retirement was associated with less cognitive decline during retirement (Andel, Finkel, & Pedersen, 2016). However, when those who had worked in occupations with fewer cognitive challenges prior to retirement engaged in physical (sports, walking) and cognitive (reading books, doing puzzles, and playing chess) leisure activities during retirement, they showed less cognitive decline. Also, a Danish longitudinal study of 20- to 93-year-olds found that those who engaged in a light level of leisure-time physical activity lived 2.8 years longer, those who engaged in a moderate level of leisure-time physical activity lived 4.5 years longer, and those who engaged in high level of leisure-time physical activity lived 5.5 years longer (Schnohr & others, 2017). Further, a study revealed that middle-aged adults who engaged in active leisure-time pursuits had higher levels of cognitive performance in late adulthood (Ihle & others, 2015). And in another study, individuals who engaged in a greater amount of sedentary screen-based leisure time activity (TV, video games, computer use) had shorter telomere length (telomeres cover the end of chromosomes, and as people age their telomeres become shorter and this shorter telomere length is linked to earlier mortality) (Loprinzi, 2015).

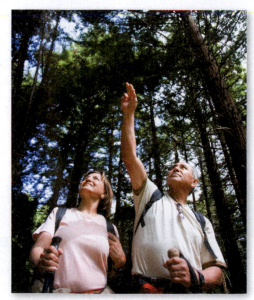

Leisure can be an especially important aspect of middle adulthood (Parkes, 2006). By middle adulthood, more money may be available to many individuals, and there may be more free time and paid vacations. In short, midlife changes may produce expanded opportunities for leisure. For many individuals, middle adulthood is the first time in their lives when they have the opportunity to explore their leisure-time interests.

Adults in midlife need to begin preparing psychologically for retirement. Developing constructive and fulfilling leisure-time activities in middle adulthood is an important part of this preparation (Gibson, 2009). If an

Sigmund Freud once commented that the two things adults need to do well to adapt to society's demands are to work and to love. To his list we add "and to play." In our fast-paced society, it is all too easy to get caught up in the frenzied, hectic pace of our achievement-oriented work world and ignore leisure and play. Imagine your life as a middle-aged adult. What would be the ideal mix of work and leisure? *What leisure activities do you want to enjoy as a middle-aged adult?*

©Digital Vision/Getty Images

How Would You...?

As a **psychologist,** how would you explain the link between leisure and stress reduction to a middle-aged individual?

adult chooses activities that can be continued into retirement, the transition from work to retirement can be less stressful.

Religion and Meaning in Life

What role does religion play in our development as adults? Is discovering the meaning of life an important theme for many middle-aged adults?

Religion and Adult Lives

In research that was part of the Midlife in the United States Study (MIDUS), more than 70 percent of U.S. middle-aged adults said that they are religious and that they consider spirituality a major part of their lives (Brim, 1999). In thinking about religion and adult development, it is important to consider the role of individual differences. Religion is a powerful influence in some adults' lives, whereas it plays little or no role in others' lives (Krause & Hayward, 2016). In a longitudinal study of individuals from their early thirties through their late sixties and early seventies, a significant increase in spirituality occurred between late middle (mid-fifties/early sixties) and late adulthood (Wink & Dillon, 2002) (see Figure 4). In one survey, 77 percent of 30- to 49-year-olds and 84 percent of 50- to 64-year-olds reported having a religious affiliation (compared with 67 percent of 18- to 29-year-olds and 90 percent of adults 90 years of age and older) (Pew Research Center, 2012).

Females have consistently shown a stronger interest in religion than males have (Bijur & others, 1993). Compared with men, they participate more in both organized and personal forms of religion, are more likely to believe in a higher power or presence, and are more likely to feel that religion is an important dimension of their lives. In the longitudinal study just described, the spirituality of women increased more than that of men during the second half of life (Wink & Dillon, 2002).

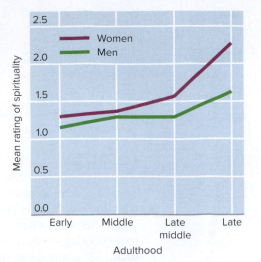

Figure 4 Levels of Spirituality in Four Adult Age Periods
In a longitudinal study, the spirituality of individuals in four different adult age periods—early (thirties), middle (forties), late middle (mid-fifties/early sixties), and late (late sixties/early seventies) adulthood—was assessed (Wink & Dillon, 2002). Based on responses to open-ended questions in interviews, the spirituality of the individuals was coded on a five-point scale with 5 being the highest level of spirituality and 1 the lowest.

Religion and Health

What might be some of the effects of religion on physical health? Some cults and religious sects encourage behaviors that are damaging to health, such as ignoring sound medical advice. For individuals in the religious mainstream, however, researchers are increasingly finding positive links between religion and physical health (Dimaghani, 2018; Krause & Hayward, 2016; Park & Ono, 2018). In a recent study, spiritual well-being predicted which heart failure patients would still be alive five years later (Park & others, 2016). In another study, adults who volunteered had lower resting pulse rates and their resting pulse rates improved if they were more deeply committed to religion (Krause, Ironson, & Hill, 2017). And in an analysis of a number of studies, adults with a higher level

What roles do religion and spirituality play in the lives of middle-aged adults? Why might religion promote health?
©Erik S. Lesser/Newscom

of spirituality/religion had an 18 percent increase in longevity (Lucchetti, Lucchetti, & Koenig, 2011). In this analysis, a high level of spirituality/religion was more closely tied to longevity than 60 percent of 25 other health interventions (such as eating fruits and vegetables and taking statin drugs for cardiovascular disease).

Why might religion promote physical health? There are several possible answers (Holt & others, 2017; Park & others, 2017). First, there are *lifestyle issues*—for example, religious individuals have lower rates of drug use than their nonreligious counterparts (Gartner, Larson, & Allen, 1991). Second are *social networks*—the degree to which individuals are connected to others affects their health. Well-connected individuals have fewer health problems (Hill & Pargament, 2003). Religious groups, meetings, and activities provide social connectedness for individuals. A third answer involves *coping with stress*—religion offers a source of comfort and support when individuals are confronted with stressful events. One study revealed that highly religious individuals were less likely than their moderately religious, somewhat religious, and non-religious counterparts to be psychologically distressed (Park, 2013).

Religious counselors often advise people about mental health and coping. To read about the work of one religious counselor, see *Careers in Life-Span Development.*

Careers in life-span development

Gabriel Dy-Liacco, University Professor and Pastoral Counselor

Gabriel Dy-Liacco currently is a professor in religious and pastoral counseling at Regent University in the Virginia Beach, Virginia, area. He obtained his Ph.D. in pastoral counseling from Loyola College in Maryland and also has worked as a psychotherapist in mental health settings such as a substance-abuse program, military family center, psychiatric clinic, and community mental health

center. Earlier in his career he was a pastoral counselor at the Pastoral Counseling and Consultation Centers of Greater Washington, DC, and taught at Loyola University in Maryland. As a pastoral counselor, he works with adolescents and adults in the aspects of their lives that they show the most concern about—psychological, spiritual, or the interface of both. Having lived in Peru, Japan, and the Philippines, he brings considerable multicultural experience to teaching and counseling settings.

Meaning in Life

Austrian psychiatrist Viktor Frankl's mother, father, brother, and wife died in the concentration camps and gas chambers in Auschwitz, Poland, during World War II. Frankl survived the concentration camp and went on to write about the search for meaning in life. In his book, *Man's Search for Meaning,* Frankl (1984) emphasized each person's uniqueness and the finiteness of life. He believed that examining the finiteness of our existence and the certainty of death adds meaning to life. If life were not finite, said Frankl, we could spend our life doing just about whatever we pleased because our time would be unlimited.

Frankl said that the three most distinctly human qualities are spirituality, freedom, and responsibility. Spirituality, in his view, does not have a religious underpinning. Rather, it refers to a human being's uniqueness of spirit, philosophy, and mind. Frankl proposed that people ask themselves questions about why they exist, what they want from life, and what their lives mean.

It is in middle adulthood that individuals begin to face death more often, especially the deaths of parents and other older relatives. As they become increasingly aware of the diminishing number of years ahead of them, many individuals in middle age begin to ask and evaluate the questions that Frankl proposed. And meaning-making coping is especially helpful in times of chronic stress and loss.

What characterizes the search for meaning in life?
©Eric Audras/Getty Images

Researchers are increasingly studying the factors involved in a person's exploration of meaning in life and exploring whether developing a sense of meaning in life is linked to positive developmental outcomes (Ahmadi & others, 2017; Park, 2010, 2012; Sloan &

others, 2017; Zhang, 2018). In research studies, many individuals state that religion played an important role in increasing their exploration of meaning in life (Krause, 2008, 2009; Krause & Hayward, 2016). Studies also suggest that individuals who have found a sense of meaning in life are physically healthier and happier, and experience less depression, than their counterparts who report that they have not discovered meaning in life (Krause, 2009; Zhang, 2018).

Having a sense of meaning in life can lead to clearer guidelines for living one's life and enhanced motivation to take care of oneself and reach goals. A higher level of meaning in life also is linked to a higher level of psychological well-being and physical health (Park, 2012).

Summary

The Nature of Middle Adulthood
- As more people live to older ages, what we think of as middle age is starting later and lasting longer.
- Middle age involves extensive individual variation. For most people, middle adulthood involves declining physical skills, expanding responsibility, awareness of the young-old polarity, motivation to transmit something meaningful to the next generation, and reaching and maintaining career satisfaction. Increasingly, researchers are distinguishing between early and late midlife.

Physical Development
- The physical changes of midlife are usually gradual. Decline occurs in a number of aspects of physical development.
- In middle adulthood, the frequency of accidents declines and individuals are less susceptible to colds. Stress can be a factor in disease.
- Until recently, cardiovascular disease was the leading cause of death in middle age, but now cancer is the leading cause of death in this age group.
- Most women do not have serious physical or psychological problems related to menopause. Sexual behavior occurs less frequently in middle adulthood than early adulthood.

Cognitive Development
- Horn argued that crystallized intelligence continues to increase in middle adulthood, whereas fluid intelligence

declines. Schaie found that declines in cognitive development are less likely to occur when longitudinal rather than cross-sectional studies are conducted. He also discovered that the highest levels of a number of intellectual abilities occur in middle age.
- Working memory declines in late middle age. Memory is more likely to decline in middle age when individuals don't use effective memory strategies. Expertise often increases in middle adulthood.

Careers, Work, and Leisure
- Midlife is often a time to reflect on career progress and prepare for retirement.
- Today's middle-aged workers face a number of challenges.
- In preparing for late adulthood, adults in midlife not only need to learn to work well, but also discover how to enjoy leisure.

Religion and Meaning in Life
- The majority of middle-aged adults say that spirituality is a major part of their lives.
- In mainstream religions, religion is positively linked to physical health. Religion can play an important role in coping for some individuals.
- Many middle-aged individuals reflect on life's meaning.

Key Terms

climacteric	fluid intelligence	menopause	working memory
crystallized intelligence	leisure	middle adulthood	

Socioemotional Development in Middle Adulthood

CHAPTER OUTLINE

PERSONALITY THEORIES AND DEVELOPMENT
Adult Stage Theories
The Life-Events Approach
Stress and Personal Control in Midlife

STABILITY AND CHANGE
Longitudinal Studies
Conclusions

CLOSE RELATIONSHIPS
Love and Marriage at Midlife
The Empty Nest and Its Refilling
Sibling Relationships and Friendships
Grandparenting
Intergenerational Relationships

Stories of Life-Span Development: Sarah and Wanda, Middle-Age Variations

Forty-five-year-old Sarah feels tired, depressed, and angry when she looks back on the way her life has gone. She became pregnant when she was 17 and married Ben, the baby's father. They stayed together for three years after their son was born, and then Ben left her for another woman. Sarah went to work as a salesclerk to make ends meet. Eight years later, she married Alan, who had two children of his own from a previous marriage. Sarah stopped working for several years to care for the children. Then, like Ben, Alan started cheating on her. She found out about it from a friend. Nevertheless, Sarah stayed with Alan for another year. Finally, he was gone so much that she could not take it anymore and decided to divorce him. Sarah went back to work again as a salesclerk; she has been in the same position for 16 years now. During those 16 years, she has dated a number of men, but the relationships never seemed to work out. Her son never finished high school and has drug problems. Her father died last year, and Sarah is trying to help her mother financially, although she can barely pay her own bills. Sarah looks in the mirror and does not like what she sees. She sees her past as a shambles, and the future does not look rosy, either.

Forty-five-year-old Wanda feels energetic, happy, and satisfied. As a young woman, she graduated from college and worked for three years as a high school math teacher. She married Andy, who had just finished law school. One year later, they had their first child, Josh. Wanda stayed home with Josh for two years and then returned to her job as a math teacher. Even during her pregnancy, Wanda stayed active and exercised regularly, playing tennis almost every day. After her pregnancy, she kept up her exercise habits. Wanda and Andy had another child, Wendy. Now, as they move into their middle-age years, their children are both in college, and Wanda and Andy are enjoying spending more time with each other. Last weekend they visited Josh at his college, and the weekend before they visited Wendy at her college. Wanda continued working as a high school math teacher until six years ago. She had developed computer skills as part of her job and taken some computer courses at a nearby college, doubling up during the summer months. She resigned her math teaching job and took a job with a computer company, where she has already worked her way into management. Wanda looks in the mirror and likes what she sees. She sees her past as enjoyable, although not without hills and valleys, and she looks to the future with zest and enthusiasm.

As with Sarah and Wanda, there are individual variations in the way people experience middle age. To begin the chapter, we examine personality theories and development in middle age, including ideas about individual variation. Then we turn our attention to how much individuals change or stay the same as they go through the adult years, and finally we explore a number of aspects of close relationships during middle adulthood. ■

Personality Theories and Development

What is the best way to conceptualize middle age? Is it a stage or a crisis? How extensively is middle age influenced by life events? Do middle-aged adults experience stress differently from younger and older adults? Is personality linked with contexts such as the point in history in which individuals go through midlife, their culture, and their gender?

Adult Stage Theories

A number of adult stage theories have been proposed and have contributed to the view that midlife brings a crisis in development. Two prominent theories that define stages of adult development are Erik Erikson's life-span view and Daniel Levinson's seasons of a man's life.

Erikson's Stage of Generativity Versus Stagnation

Erikson (1968) proposed that middle-aged adults face a significant issue—generativity versus stagnation, which is the name Erikson gave to the seventh stage in his life-span theory. **Generativity** encompasses adults' desire to leave legacies of themselves to the next generation. Through these legacies adults achieve a kind of immortality. By contrast, **stagnation** (sometimes called "self-absorption") develops when individuals sense that they have done little or nothing for the next generation.

How Would You...?

As an **educator,** how would you describe ways in which the profession of teaching might establish generativity for someone in middle adulthood?

Generative adults commit themselves to the continuation and improvement of society as a whole through their connection to the next generation. Generative adults develop a positive legacy of the self and then offer it as a gift to the next generation (Grossman & Gruenwald, 2017; Serrat & others, 2018). Middle-aged adults can achieve generativity in a number of ways (Kotre, 1984). Through biological generativity, adults have offspring. Through parental generativity, adults nurture and guide children. Through work generativity, adults develop skills that are passed down to others. And through cultural generativity, adults create, renovate, or conserve some aspect of culture that ultimately survives (Lewis & Allen, 2017).

generativity Adults' desire to leave legacies of themselves to the next generation; the positive side of Erikson's middle adulthood stage of generativity versus stagnation.

stagnation Sometimes called "self-absorption," this state of mind develops when individuals sense that they have done little or nothing for the next generation; this is the negative side of Erikson's middle adulthood stage of generativity versus stagnation.

Through generativity, adults promote and guide the next generation by parenting, teaching, leading, and doing things that benefit the community (Russo-Netzer & Moran, 2018; Serrat & others, 2018). One of the participants in a study of aging said: "From twenty to thirty I learned how to get along with my wife. From thirty to forty I learned how to be a success at my job, and at forty to fifty I worried less about myself and more about the children" (Vaillant, 2002, p. 114).

Does research support Erikson's theory that generativity is an important dimension of middle age? Yes, it does (Dunlop, Bannon, & McAdams, 2017). In one study, Carol Ryff (1984) examined the views of women and men at different ages and found that middle-aged adults especially were concerned about generativity. In a longitudinal study of Smith College women, the desire for generativity increased as the participants aged from their thirties to their fifties (Stewart, Ostrove, & Helson, 2001). In another study, generativity was strongly linked to middle-aged adults' positive social engagement in contexts such as family life and community activities (Cox & others, 2010). And in one study of males, achievement of generativity in middle age was related to better health in late adulthood (Landes & others, 2014). In another study, participating in an intergenerational civic engagement program enhanced older adults' perceptions of generativity (Grunewald & others, 2016). Further, in another study, a higher level of generativity in midlife was linked to greater wisdom in late adulthood (Ardelt, Gerlach, & Vaillant, 2018).

How Would You...?

As a **human development and family studies professional,** how would you advise a middle-aged woman who never had children and now fears she has little opportunity to leave a legacy to the next generation?

Levinson's Seasons of a Man's Life

In *The Seasons of a Man's Life*, clinical psychologist Daniel Levinson (1978) reported the results of extensive interviews with 40 middle-aged men. The interviews were conducted with hourly workers, business executives, academic biologists, and novelists. Levinson bolstered his conclusions with information from the biographies of famous men and the development of memorable characters in literature. Although Levinson's major interest focused on midlife change in men, he described a number of stages and transitions during the period from 17 to 65 years of age, as shown in Figure 1. Levinson emphasizes that developmental tasks must be mastered at each stage.

At the end of one's teens, according to Levinson, a transition from dependence to independence should occur. This transition is marked by the formation of a dream—an image of the kind of life the youth wants to have, especially in terms of a career and marriage. Levinson sees the twenties as a *novice phase* of adult development. It is a time of reasonably free experimentation and of testing the dream in the real world. In early adulthood, the two major tasks to be mastered are exploring the possibilities for adult living and developing a stable life structure.

From about age 28 to 33, the man goes through a transition period in which he must face the more serious question of determining his goals.

Era of late adulthood: 60 to ?

Late adult transition: Age 60 to 65

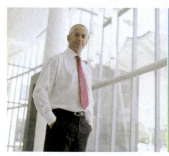

Culminating life structure for middle adulthood: 55 to 60

Age 50 transition: 50 to 55

Entry life structure for middle adulthood: 45 to 50

Middle adult transition: Age 40 to 45

Culminating life structure for early adulthood: 33 to 40

Age 30 transition: 28 to 33

Entry life structure for early adulthood: 22 to 28

Early adult transition: Age 17 to 22

Figure 1 Levinson's Periods of Adult Development

According to Levinson, adulthood for men has three main stages, which are surrounded by transition periods. Specific tasks and challenges are associated with each stage.

(*Top*) ©Amos Morgan/Getty Images; (*middle*) ©Sam Edwards/age fotostock; (*bottom*) ©image100 Ltd

During his thirties, he usually focuses on family and career development. In the later years of this period, he enters a phase of *Becoming One's Own Man* (or BOOM, as Levinson calls it). By age 40, he has reached a stable point in his career, has outgrown his earlier, more tenuous attempts at learning to become an adult, and now must look forward to the kind of life he will lead as a middle-aged adult.

According to Levinson, the transition to middle adulthood lasts about five years (ages 40 to 45) and requires the adult male to come to grips with four major conflicts that have existed in his life since adolescence: (1) being young versus being old, (2) being destructive versus being constructive, (3) being masculine versus being feminine, and (4) being attached to others versus being separated from them. Seventy to 80 percent of the men Levinson interviewed found the midlife transition tumultuous and psychologically painful, as many aspects of their lives came into question. According to Levinson, the success of the midlife transition rests on how effectively the individual reduces the polarities and accepts each of them as an integral part of his being.

Because Levinson interviewed middle-aged males, we can consider the data about middle adulthood more valid than the data about early adulthood. When individuals are asked to remember information about earlier parts of their lives, they may distort and forget things. The original Levinson data included no females, although Levinson (1996) reported that his stages, transitions, and the crisis of middle age apply to females as well as males. Levinson's work included no statistical analysis. However, the quality and quantity of the Levinson biographies make them outstanding examples of the clinical tradition.

How Pervasive Are Midlife Crises?

©John Simmons/Alamy

Levinson (1978) views midlife as a crisis, believing that the middle-aged adult is suspended between the past and the future, trying to cope with this gap that threatens life's continuity. George Vaillant (1977) has a different view. Vaillant's study—called the "Grant Study"—involved men who were in their early thirties and in their late forties who initially had been interviewed as undergraduates at Harvard University. He concludes that just as adolescence is a time for detecting parental flaws and discovering the truth about childhood, the forties are a decade of reassessing and recording the truth about adolescence and adulthood. However, whereas Levinson sees midlife as a crisis, Vaillant maintains that only a minority of adults experience a midlife crisis.

Today, adult development experts are virtually unanimous in their belief that midlife crises have been exaggerated (Lachman, Teshale, & Agrigoroaei, 2015). Further, happiness and positive affect have an upward trajectory from early adulthood to late adulthood (Carstensen, 2015; Sims, Hogan, & Carstensen, 2015).

The Life-Events Approach

Age-related stages represent one major way to examine adult personality development. A second major way to conceptualize adult personality development is to focus on life events (Kok & others, 2017; Oren & others, 2017; Patrick, Carney, & Nehrkorn, 2017). In the early version of the life-events approach, life events were viewed as taxing circumstances for individuals, forcing them to change their personality (Holmes & Rahe, 1967). Such events as the death of a spouse, divorce, marriage, and so on were believed to involve varying degrees of stress and therefore likely to influence the individual's development. One study found that stressful life events were associated with cardiovascular disease in middle-aged women (Kershaw & others, 2014). And a research meta-analysis found an association between stressful life events and autoimmune diseases such as arthritis and psoriasis (Porcelli & others, 2016).

Today's life-events approach is more sophisticated. The **contemporary life-events approach** emphasizes that how life events influence the individual's

contemporary life-events approach An approach emphasizing that how a life event influences the individual's development depends not only on the life event itself but also on mediating factors, the individual's adaptation to the life event, the life-stage context, and the sociohistorical context.

development depends not only on the life event itself but also on mediating factors (physical health, family supports, for example), the individual's adaptation to the life event (appraisal of the threat, coping strategies, for example), the life-stage context, and the sociohistorical context (see Figure 2). For example, if individuals are in poor health and have little family support, life events are likely to be more stressful. Whatever the context or mediating variables, however, one individual may perceive a life event as highly stressful, whereas another individual may perceive the same event as a challenge.

Although the life-events approach is a valuable addition to understanding adult development, it has its drawbacks. One significant drawback is that the life-events approach places too much emphasis on change. Another drawback is its failure to recognize that our daily experiences may be the primary sources of stress in our lives (Du, Derks, & Bakker, 2018; Keles & others, 2016; Koffer & others, 2018; Louch & others, 2017). Enduring a boring but tense job, staying in an unsatisfying marriage, or living in poverty do not show up on scales of major life events. Yet the everyday pounding we take from these living conditions can add up to a highly stressful life and eventually lead to illness (Sarid & others, 2018; Scott & others, 2018; Smyth & others, 2018). One study found that stressful daily hassles were linked to increased anxiety and decreased physical well-being (Falconier & others, 2015).

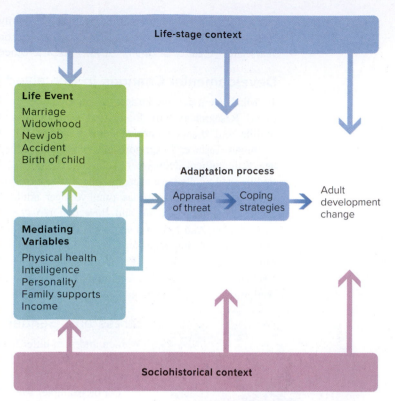

Figure 2 A Contemporary Life-Events Framework for Interpreting Adult Developmental Change According to the contemporary life-events approach, the influence of a life event depends on the event itself, on mediating variables, on the life-stage and sociohistorical context, and on the individual's appraisal of the event and coping strategies.

Stress and Personal Control in Midlife

Margie Lachman and her colleagues (2015) have described how personal control changes when individuals move into middle age. In their view, middle age is a time when a person's sense of control is frequently challenged by many demands and responsibilities, as well as physical and cognitive aging. By contrast, young people are more likely to have a sense of invulnerability, an unrealistic view of their personal control, and a lack of awareness regarding the aging process. Many young people focus primarily on self-pursuits and don't need to worry much about taking responsibility for others. But in middle age, less attention is given to self-pursuits and more to responsibility for others, including family members who are younger and older than they are. According to Lachman and her colleagues (2015), how middle adulthood plays out is largely in one's own hands, which can be stressful as individuals are faced with taking on and juggling responsibilities in different areas of their lives.

One study in which participants kept daily diaries over a one-week period found that both young and middle-aged adults had more stressful days than older adults (Almeida & Horn, 2004). In this study, although young adults experienced daily stressors more frequently than middle-aged adults did, middle-aged adults experienced more "overload" stressors that involved juggling too many activities at once. In another study, healthy older adult women 63 to 93 years of age reported their daily experiences over the course of one week (Charles & others, 2010). In this study, the older the women were, the fewer stressors and less frequent negative emotions they reported. Also, in other research, greater emotional reactivity to daily stressors was linked to increased risk of reporting a chronic physical health condition and anxiety/mood disorders 10 years later (Charles & others, 2013; Piazza & others, 2013).

Developmental Changes in Perceived Personal Control

To what extent do middle-aged adults perceive that they can control what happens to them? Researchers have found that on average a sense of personal control peaks in midlife and then declines (Lachman, 2006; Lachman, Agrigoroaei, & Hahn, 2016; Lachman, Teshale, & Agrigoroaei, 2015). Some aspects of personal control increase with age while others decrease (Lachman, Neupert, & Agrigoroaei, 2011). For example, middle-aged adults have a greater sense of control over their finances, work, and marriage than younger adults but less control over their sex life and their children (Lachman & Firth, 2004). And having a sense of control in middle age is one of the most important modifiable factors in delaying the onset of diseases in middle adulthood and reducing the frequency of diseases in late adulthood (Lachman, Neupert, & Agrigoroaei, 2011; Robinson & Lachman, 2017).

How Would You...?

As a **health-care professional,** how would you convince a company that it should sponsor a stress-reduction program for its middle-aged employees?

How do women and men differ in the way they experience and respond to stressors?
©Altrendo images/Getty Images

Stress and Gender

Women and men differ in the way they experience and respond to stressors (Taylor, 2015, 2018). Women are more vulnerable to social stressors such as those involving romance, family, and work. For example, women experience higher levels of stress when things go wrong in romantic and marital relationships. Women also are more likely than men to become depressed when they encounter stressful life events such as a divorce or the death of a friend. And a recent study found that in coping with stress, women were more likely than men to seek psychotherapy, talk to friends about the stress, read a self-help book, take prescription medication, and engage in comfort eating (Liddon, Kingerlee, & Barry, 2017). In this study, in coping with stress men were more likely than women to attend a support group meeting, have sex or use pornography, try to fix problems themselves, and not admit to having problems.

When men face stress, they are likely to respond in a **fight-or-flight** manner—become aggressive, withdraw from social contact, or drink alcohol. By contrast, according to Shelley Taylor (2011a, b, c, 2015, 2018), when women experience stress, they are more likely to engage in a **tend-and-befriend** pattern, seeking social alliances with others, especially friends. Taylor argues that when women experience stress, their bodies produce elevated levels of the hormone *oxytocin*, which is linked to nurturing in animals.

Stability and Change

Questions about stability and change are an important issue in life-span development. One of the main ways that stability and change are assessed is through longitudinal studies that assess the same individuals at different points in their lives.

Longitudinal Studies

A number of longitudinal studies have assessed stability and change in the personalities of individuals at different points in their lives (Borghuis & others, 2017; Chopik & Kitayama, 2018; Fajkowska, 2018; Graham & others, 2017; Hengartner & Yamanaka-Altenstein, 2017). Here, we will examine three longitudinal studies to help us understand the extent to which there is stability or change in adult personality development: Costa and McCrae's Baltimore Study, the Berkeley Longitudinal Studies, and Vaillant's studies.

fight-or-flight The view that when men experience stress, they are more likely to become aggressive, withdraw from social contact, or drink alcohol.

tend-and-befriend Taylor's view that when women experience stress, they are more likely to seek social alliances with others, especially female friends.

O	C	E	A	N
Openness	**C**onscientiousness	**E**xtraversion	**A**greeableness	**N**euroticism (emotional stability)
• Imaginative or practical	• Organized or disorganized	• Sociable or retiring	• Softhearted or ruthless	• Calm or anxious
• Interested in variety or routine	• Careful or careless	• Fun-loving or somber	• Trusting or suspicious	• Secure or insecure
• Independent or conforming	• Disciplined or impulsive	• Affectionate or reserved	• Helpful or uncooperative	• Self-satisfied or self-pitying

Figure 3 **The Big Five Factors of Personality**
Each of the broad supertraits encompasses more narrow traits and characteristics. Use the acronym OCEAN to remember the Big Five personality factors (openness, conscientiousness, extraversion, agreeableness, neuroticism).

Costa and McCrae's Baltimore Study

A major study of adult personality development continues to be conducted by Paul Costa and Robert McCrae (1998; McCrae & Costa, 2006). They focus on what are called the **Big Five factors of personality,** which are openness to experience, conscientiousness, extraversion, agreeableness, and neuroticism (emotional stability); these factors are described in Figure 3. (Notice that if you create an acronym from these factor names, you will get the word OCEAN.) A number of research studies point to these factors as important dimensions of personality (Graham & others, 2017; Hampson & Edmonds, 2018; Roberts & Damian, 2018; Roberts & others, 2017; Strickhouser, Zell, & Krizan, 2017).

Using their five-factor personality test, Costa and McCrae (1998, 2000) studied approximately one thousand college-educated men and women aged 20 to 96, assessing the same individuals over many years. Data collection began in the 1950s to mid-1960s and is ongoing. Costa and McCrae concluded that considerable stability exists across the adult years for the five personality factors.

However, more recent research indicates greater developmental changes in the five personality factors in adulthood (Roberts & others, 2017). For example, one study found that emotional stability, extraversion, openness, and agreeableness were lower in early adulthood, peaked between 40 and 60 years of age, and decreased in late adulthood, while conscientiousness showed a continuous increase from early adulthood to late adulthood (Specht, Egloff, & Schukle, 2011). Most research studies find that the greatest changes in personality occur in early adulthood (Roberts & Damian, 2018).

Further evidence supporting the importance of the Big Five factors indicates that they are related to major aspects of a person's life such as health, intelligence, achievement, and relationships (Roberts & Hill, 2017). The following research supports these links:

- *Openness to experience.* Individuals high in openness to experience are more likely to have superior cognitive functioning, achievement, and IQ across the life span (Briley, Domiteaux, & Tucker-Drob, 2014); show creative achievement in the arts (Kaufman & others, 2016); experience less negative affect to stressors (Leger & others, 2016); have better health and well-being (Strickhouser, Zell, & Krizan, 2017); and are more likely to eat fruits and vegetables (Conner & others, 2017).

- *Conscientiousness.* Individuals high in conscientiousness are more likely to live longer (Graham & others, 2017); have better health and less stress; are less likely to have an alcohol addiction (Raketic & others, 2017); experience less cognitive decline in aging (Luchetti & others, 2016); are less likely to be characterized by Internet addiction (Zhou & others, 2017); are more successful at accomplishing goals (McCabe & Fleeson, 2016); are more likely to perform well academically in medical school (Sobowale & others, 2018); and are less likely to be addicted to Instagram (Kircaburun & Griffiths, 2018).

- *Extraversion.* Individuals high in extraversion are more likely than others to be satisfied in relationships (Toy, Nai, & Lee, 2016); show less negative affect to stressors (Leger & others, 2016); and have a more positive sense of well-being in the future (Soto, 2015).

Big Five factors of personality
Emotional stability (neuroticism), extraversion, openness to experience, agreeableness, and conscientiousness.

- *Agreeableness*. People who are high in agreeableness tend to live longer (Graham & others, 2017); are more likely to be generous and altruistic (Caprara & others, 2010); have more satisfying romantic relationships (Donnellan, Larsen-Rife, & Conger, 2005); engage in more positive affect to stressors (Leger & others, 2016); and have a lower risk of dementia (Terracciano & others, 2017).

- *Neuroticism*. People high in neuroticism are more likely to die at a younger age than average (Graham & others, 2017); have worse health and report having more health complaints (Strickhouser, Zell, & Krizan, 2017); are more likely to be drug dependent (Valero & others, 2014); have a higher risk of coronary heart disease (Lee & others, 2014); and have a lower sense of well-being 40 years later (Gale & others, 2013).

Researchers increasingly are finding that optimism is linked to better adjustment, improved health, and increased longevity (Boelen, 2015; Kolokotroni, Anagnostopoulos, & Hantzi, 2018). A recent study revealed that college students who were more pessimistic had more anxious mood and stress symptoms (Lau & others, 2017). A study involving adults 50 years of age and older revealed that being optimistic and having an optimistic spouse were both associated with better health and physical functioning (Kim, Chopik, & Smith, 2014). Further, another study of married couples found that the worst health outcomes occurred when both spouses decreased in optimism across a four-year time frame (Chopik, Kim, & Smith, 2018). In another study, a higher level of optimism following an acute coronary event was linked to engaging in more physical activity and having fewer cardiac readmissions (Huffman & others, 2016). Also, in a recent study, lonely individuals who were optimistic had a lower suicide risk than their counterparts who were more pessimistic (Chang & others, 2018). And a research review concluded that the positive influence of optimism on outcomes for people with chronic diseases (such as cancer, cardiovascular disease, and respiratory disease) may reflect either or both of the following factors: (a) a direct effect on the neuroendocrine system and on immune system function; and (b) an indirect effect on health outcomes as a result of protective health behaviors, adaptive coping strategies, and enhanced positive mood (Avvenuti, Baiardini, & Giardini, 2016).

Berkeley Longitudinal Studies

In the Berkeley Longitudinal Studies, more than 500 children and their parents were initially studied in the late 1920s and early 1930s. The book *Present and Past in Middle Life* (Eichorn & others, 1981) profiles these individuals as they became middle-aged. The results from early adolescence through a portion of midlife did not support either extreme in the debate over whether personality is characterized by stability or change. Some characteristics were more stable than others, however. The most stable characteristics were the degree to which individuals were intellectually oriented, self-confident, and open to new experiences. The characteristics that changed the most included the extent to which the individuals were nurturant or hostile and whether they had strong or weak self-control.

George Vaillant's Studies

Longitudinal studies by George Vaillant explore a question that differs somewhat from the studies described so far: Does personality at middle age predict what a person's life will be like in late adulthood? Vaillant (2002) has conducted three longitudinal studies of adult development and aging: (1) a sample of 268 socially advantaged Harvard graduates born about 1920 (called the Grant Study); (2) a sample of 456 socially disadvantaged inner-city men born about 1930; and (3) a sample of 90 middle-SES, intellectually gifted women born about 1910. These individuals have been assessed numerous times (in most cases, every two years), beginning in the 1920s to 1940s and continuing today for those still living. The main assessments involve extensive interviews with the participants, their parents, and teachers.

Vaillant categorized 75- to 80-year-olds as "happy-well," "sad-sick," or "dead." He used data collected from these individuals when they were 50 years of age to predict which categories they were likely to end up in at 75 to 80 years of age. Alcohol abuse and smoking at age 50 were the best predictors of which individuals would be dead at 75 to 80 years of age. Other factors at age 50 were linked with being in the "happy-well" category at 75 to 80 years of age: getting regular exercise, avoiding being overweight, being well-educated, having a stable marriage, being future-oriented, being thankful and forgiving, empathizing with others, being active with other people, and having good coping skills.

Wealth and income at age 50 were not linked with being in the "happy-well" category at 75 to 80 years of age. Generativity in middle age (defined in this study as "taking care of the next generation") was more strongly related than intimacy to whether individuals would have an enduring and happy marriage at 75 to 80 years of age (Vaillant, 2002).

The results for one of Vaillant's studies, the Grant Study of Harvard men, indicated that when individuals at 50 years of age were not heavy smokers, did not abuse alcohol, had a stable marriage, exercised, maintained a normal weight, and had good coping skills, they were more likely to be alive and happy at 75 to 80 years of age.

How Would You...?

As a **health-care professional,** how would you use the results of Vaillant's research to advise a middle-aged adult patient who abuses alcohol and smokes?

Conclusions

What can be concluded about stability and change in personality development during the adult years? Avshalom Caspi and Brent Roberts (2001) concluded that the evidence does not support the view that personality traits become completely fixed at a certain age in adulthood. However, they argue that change is typically limited, and in some cases the changes in personality are small. They also say that age is positively related to stability and that stability peaks in the fifties and sixties. That is, people show greater stability in their personality when they reach midlife than when they were younger adults (Hill & Roberts, 2016; Nye & others, 2016). These findings support what is called a **cumulative personality model** of development, which states that with time and age, people become more adept at interacting with their environment in ways that promote stability of personality.

This does not mean that change is absent throughout midlife. Ample evidence shows that social contexts, new experiences, and sociohistorical changes can affect personality development (Ayoub & Roberts, 2018; Lachman, Teshale, & Agrigoroaei, 2015; Mroczek, Spiro, & Griffin, 2006). However, Caspi and Roberts (2001) concluded that as people get older, stability increasingly outweighs change. In a recent research review, the personality trait that changed the most as a result of psychotherapy intervention was emotional stability, followed by extraversion (Roberts & others, 2017). In this review, the personality traits of individuals with anxiety disorders changed the most and those with substance use disorders the least.

In general, changes in personality traits across adulthood also occur in a positive direction. Over time, "people become more confident, warm, responsible, and calm" (Roberts & Mroczek, 2008, p. 33). Such positive changes equate with becoming more socially mature.

In sum, recent research contradicts the old view that stability in personality begins to set in at about 30 years of age (Chopik & Kitayama, 2018; Roberts & Damian, 2018; Roberts & others, 2017). Although there are some consistent developmental changes in the personality traits of large numbers of people, at the individual level people can show unique patterns of personality traits—and these patterns often reflect life experiences related to themes of their particular developmental period (Roberts & Mroczek, 2008). For example, researchers have found that individuals who are in a stable marriage and on a solid career track become more socially dominant, conscientious, and emotionally stable as they go through early adulthood (Roberts & Wood, 2006). And, for some of these individuals, there is greater change in their personality traits than for other individuals (McAdams & Olson, 2010).

cumulative personality model The principle that with time and age, people become more adept at interacting with their environment in ways that promote stability of personality.

Close Relationships

There is a consensus among middle-aged Americans that a major component of well-being involves positive relationships with others, especially parents, spouse, and off-spring (Lachman, Teshale, & Agrigoroaei, 2015). To begin our examination of midlife relationships, let's explore love and marriage in middle-aged adults.

Love and Marriage at Midlife

Two major forms of love are romantic love and affectionate love. The fires of romantic love burn strongly in early adulthood. Affectionate, or companionate, love increases during middle adulthood. That is, physical attraction, romance, and passion are more important in new relationships, especially those begun in early adulthood. Security, loyalty, and mutual emotional interest become more important as relationships mature, especially in middle adulthood (Crowley, 2018).

Marriage

One study revealed that marital satisfaction increased in middle age (Gorchoff, John, & Helson, 2008). Even some marriages that were difficult and rocky during early adulthood become more stable during middle adulthood. Although the partners may have lived through a great deal of turmoil, they eventually discover a deep and solid foundation on which to anchor their relationship. In middle adulthood, the partners may have fewer financial worries, less housework and chores, and more time with each other. Middle-aged partners are more likely to view their marriage as positive if they engage in mutual activities. One study found that middle-aged married individuals had a lower likelihood of work-related health limitations (Lo, Cheng, & Simpson, 2016). Another study of middle-aged adults revealed that positive marital quality was linked to better health for both spouses (Choi, Yorgason, & Johnson, 2016).

Most individuals in midlife who are married voice considerable satisfaction with being married. In a large-scale study of individuals in middle adulthood, 72 percent of those who were married said their marriage was either "excellent" or "very good" (Brim, 1999). Possibly by middle age, many of the worst marriages already have dissolved. A longitudinal study of African American and non-Latino White men who were initially assessed when they were 51 to 62 years of age and then followed for 18 years found that the longevity gap that favors non-Latino White men was linked to their higher rate of marriage (Su, Stimpson, & Wilson, 2015).

What characterizes marriage in middle adulthood?
©shapecharge/Getty Images

Divorce

What trends characterize divorce in U.S. middle-aged adults? In a recent analysis that compared divorce rates for different age groups in 1990 to 2015, the divorce rate had gone down for young adults but increased for middle-aged adults (Stepler, 2017):

25 to 39 years	40 to 49 years	50+ years
−21 percent	+14 percent	+109 percent

The trend toward increasing rates of divorce after age 50 has led researchers to use the term "gray divorce" in reference to marital breakups that occur in this age group (Crowley, 2018; Lin & others, 2018). What accounts for this increase in middle-age divorce? One explanation is the changing view of women, who initiate approximately 60 percent of the divorces after 40 years of age. Compared with earlier decades, divorce has less stigma for women and they are more likely to leave an unhappy marriage. Also compared with earlier decades, more women are employed and are less dependent on their husband's income. Another explanation involves the increase in remarriages, in which the divorce rate is 2½ times as high as it is for those in first marriages.

A survey by AARP (2004) of 1,148 40- to 79-year-olds who were divorced at least once in their forties, fifties, or sixties found that staying married because of their children was by far the main reason many people took a long time to become divorced. Despite the worry and stress involved in going through a divorce, three-fourths of the divorcees

How Would You…?

As a **social worker,** how would you describe the different reasons for divorce in young and middle-aged couples?

said they had made the right decision to dissolve their marriage and reported a positive outlook on life. Sixty-six percent of the divorced women said they had initiated the divorce, compared with only 41 percent of the divorced men. The divorced women were much more afraid of having financial problems (44 percent) than the divorced men were (11 percent).

Following are the main reasons that middle-aged and older adults cited for their divorce:

Main Causes for Women	Main Causes for Men
1. Verbal, physical, or emotional abuse (23 percent)	1. No obvious problems, just fell out of love (17 percent)
2. Alcohol or drug abuse (18 percent)	2. Cheating (14 percent)
3. Cheating (17 percent)	3. Different values, lifestyles (14 percent)

In a recent study of the antecedents of "gray divorce," factors traditionally associated with divorce in young adults also were reflected in divorces among adults 50 years and older (Lin & others, 2018). Divorce was more likely to occur in these older adults' lives when they had been married fewer years, their marriage was of lower quality (less marital satisfaction, for example), they did not own a home, and they had financial problems. Factors that were not linked to divorce in these older adults were the onset of an empty nest, the wife's or husband's retirement, and whether the wife or husband had a chronic health condition.

Also, in a recent Swiss study of middle-aged adults, single divorcees were more lonely and less resilient than their married and remarried counterparts (Knopfli & others, 2016). And in this study, single divorcees had the lowest self-rated health.

The Empty Nest and Its Refilling

An important event in a family is the launching of a child into adult life. Parents face new adjustments as a result of the child's absence. College students usually think that their parents suffer from their absence. In fact, parents who live vicariously through their children might experience the **empty nest syndrome,** which includes a decline in marital satisfaction after children leave the home. For most parents, however, marital satisfaction does not decline after children have left home. Rather, for most parents, marital satisfaction increases during the years after child rearing has ended (Fingerman & Baker, 2006). With their children gone, marital partners have more time to pursue careers and other interests and more time for each other. One study revealed that the transition to an empty nest increased marital satisfaction and that this improvement was linked to an increase in the quality of time—but not the quantity of time—spent with partners (Gorchoff, John, & Helson, 2008).

What are some ways that divorce might be more positive or more negative in middle adulthood than in early adulthood?
©Stock4B/Getty Images

In today's uncertain economic climate, the refilling of the empty nest is becoming a common occurrence as adult children return to the family home after several years of college, after graduating from college, or to save money after taking a full-time job (Merrill, 2009). Young adults also may move back in with their parents after an unsuccessful career or a divorce. And some individuals don't leave home at all until their middle to late twenties because they cannot financially support themselves. Numerous labels have been applied to these young adults who return to their parents' homes to live, including "boomerang kids" and "B2B" (or Back-to-Bedroom) (Furman, 2005).

empty nest syndrome A term used to indicate a decrease in marital satisfaction after children leave home.

How Would You...?

As a **psychologist,** how would you counsel parents of adult children who return to the family home for a few years following their college graduation?

What are some strategies that can help parents and their young adult children get along better?
©Fuse/Getty Images

The middle generation has always provided support for the younger generation, even after the nest is bare. Through loans and monetary gifts for education, and through emotional support, the middle generation has helped the younger generation. Adult children appreciate the financial and emotional support their parents provide at a time when they often feel considerable stress about their career, work, and lifestyle. And parents feel good that they can provide this support.

However, as with most family living arrangements, there are both pluses and minuses when adult children live with their parents. One of the most common complaints voiced by both adult children and their parents is a loss of privacy. The adult children complain that their parents restrict their independence, cramp their sex lives, reduce their rock music listening, and treat them as children rather than adults. Parents often complain that their quiet home has become noisy, that they stay up late worrying until their adult children come home, that meals are difficult to plan because of conflicting schedules, that their relationship as a married couple has been invaded, and that they have to shoulder too much responsibility for their adult children. In sum, when adult children return home to live, it causes a disequilibrium in family life that requires considerable adaptation on the part of parents and their adult children.

When adult children ask to return home to live, parents and their adult children should agree on the conditions and expectations beforehand. For example, they might discuss and agree on whether the young adults will pay rent, wash their own clothes, cook their own meals, do any household chores, pay their phone bills, come and go as they please, be sexually active or drink alcohol at home, and so on. If these conditions aren't negotiated at the beginning, conflict often results because the expectations of parents and young adult children will likely be violated.

Sibling Relationships and Friendships

Sibling relationships persist over the entire life span for most adults (Whiteman, McHale, & Soli, 2011). Eighty-five percent of today's adults have at least one living sibling. Sibling relationships in adulthood may be extremely close, apathetic, or highly rivalrous (Bedford, 2009). The majority of sibling relationships in adulthood are close (Cicirelli, 2009). Those siblings who are psychologically close to each other in adulthood tended to be that way in childhood. It is rare for sibling closeness to develop for the first time in adulthood (Dunn, 1984). One study revealed that adult siblings often provide practical and emotional support to each other (Voorpostel & Blieszner, 2008). Another study revealed that men who had poor sibling relationships in childhood were more likely to develop depression by age 50 than men who had more positive sibling relationships as children (Waldinger, Vaillant, & Orav, 2007).

Friendships continue to be important in middle adulthood, just as they were in early adulthood. It takes time to develop intimate friendships, so friendships that have endured over the adult years are often deeper than those that have just been formed in middle adulthood.

Grandparenting

The increase in longevity is influencing the nature of grandparenting (Hayslip, Fruhauf, & Dolbin-MacNab, 2018; Huo & Fingerman, 2018; Huo & others, 2018). In 1900, only 4 percent of 10-year-old children had four living grandparents, but by 2000 that figure had risen to more than 40 percent. And in 1990 only about 20 percent of people 30 years of age had living grandparents, a figure that is projected to increase to 80 percent in 2020 (Hagestad & Uhlenberg, 2007). Further increases in longevity are likely to support this trend in the future, although the current trend toward delayed childbearing is likely to undermine it.

Grandparent Roles

Grandparents play important roles in the lives of many grandchildren (Bol & Kalmijn, 2016; Hayslip, Fruhauf, & Dolbin-MacNab, 2018). Grandparents especially play important roles in grandchildren's lives when family crises such as divorce, death, illness, abandonment, or poverty occur (Dolbin-MacNab & Yancura, 2018). In many countries around the world, grandparents facilitate women's participation in the labor force by providing child care. Some estimates suggest that worldwide more than 160 million grandparents are raising grandchildren (Leinaweaver, 2014).

What are some changes that are occurring in grandparents' roles?
©JGI/Jamie Grill/Getty Images

Many adults become grandparents for the first time during middle age. Researchers have consistently found that grandmothers have more contact with grandchildren than do grandfathers (Watson, Randolph, & Lyons, 2005). Perhaps women tend to define their role as grandmothers as part of their responsibility for maintaining ties between family members across generations. Men may have fewer expectations about the grandfather role and see it as more voluntary.

Most research on grandparents has focused on grandchildren as children or adolescents, but a recent study focused on grandparents and adult grandchildren (Huo & others, 2018). In this study, grandparents' affective connections with their adult grandchildren involved frequent listening, emotional support, and companionship. Also in this study, grandparents provided more frequent emotional support to their adult grandchildren when parents were having life problems and more frequent financial support when parents were unemployed.

In 2014, 10 percent (7.4 million) of children in the United States lived with at least one grandparent, a dramatic increase since 1981 when 4.7 million children were living with at least one grandparent (U.S. Census Bureau, 2015). Divorce, adolescent pregnancies, and drug use by parents are the main reasons that grandparents are thrust back into the "parenting" role they thought they had shed. One study revealed that grandparent involvement was linked with better adjustment when it occurred in single-parent and stepparent families than in two-parent biological families (Attar-Schwartz & others, 2009). Also, in many countries, when grandparents help take care of their grandchildren, it often facilitates their daughters' participation in the labor force.

Grandparents who are full-time caregivers for grandchildren are at elevated risk for health problems, depression, and stress (Hayslip, Fruhauf, & Dolbin-MacNab, 2018; Silverstein, 2009). A research review concluded that grandparents raising grandchildren are especially at risk for developing depression (Hadfield, 2014). Caring for grandchildren is linked with these problems in part because full-time grandparent caregivers are often characterized by low-income, minority status and by not being married (Minkler & Fuller-Thompson, 2005). Grandparents who are part-time caregivers are less likely to have the negative health portrait that full-time grandparent caregivers have

How Would You…?

As a **human development and family studies professional,** how would you educate parents about the mutual benefits of grandparents being actively involved in children's lives?

As divorce and remarriage have become more common, a special concern of grandparents is visitation privileges with their grandchildren. In the last 10 to 15 years, more states have passed laws giving grandparents the right to petition a court for visitation privileges with their grandchildren, even if a parent objects. Whether such forced visitation rights for grandparents are in the child's best interest is still being debated.

Intergenerational Relationships

Family is important to most people. When 21,000 adults aged 40 to 79 in 21 countries were asked, "When you think of who you are, you think mainly of _____," 63 percent said "family," 9 percent said "religion," and 8 percent said "work" (HSBC Insurance, 2007). In this study, in all 21 countries, middle-aged and older adults expressed a strong feeling of responsibility between generations in their family, with the strongest intergenerational ties indicated in Saudi Arabia, India, and Turkey. More than 80 percent of the middle-aged and older adults reported that adults have a duty to care for their parents (and parents-in-law) in time of need later in life.

Adults in midlife play important roles in the lives of the young and the old (Antonucci & others, 2016; Birditt & others, 2016; Fingerman & others, 2018; Polenick, Birditt, & Zarit, 2018; Polenick & others, 2018; Sechrist & Fingerman, 2018). Middle-aged adults share their experience and transmit values to the younger generation. They may be launching children and experiencing the empty nest, adjusting to having grown children return home, or becoming grandparents. They also may be giving or receiving financial assistance, caring for a widowed or sick parent, or adapting to being the oldest generation after both parents have died.

Middle-aged and older adults around the world show a strong sense of family responsibility. A study of middle-aged and older adults in 21 countries revealed the strongest intergenerational ties in Saudi Arabia.
©Reza/National Geographic/Getty Images

Middle-aged adults have been described as the "sandwich," "squeezed," or "overload" generation because of the responsibilities they have for their adolescent and young adult children on the one hand and their aging parents on the other (Etaugh & Bridges, 2010). However, an alternative view is that in the United States, a "sandwich" generation, in which the middle generation cares for both grown children and aging parents simultaneously, occurs less often than a "pivot" generation, in which the middle generation alternates attention between the demands of grown children and aging parents (Sechrist & Fingerman, 2018). By middle age, more than 40 percent of adult children (most of them daughters) provide care for aging parents or parents-in-law (National Alliance for Caregiving, 2009). However, two studies revealed that middle-aged parents are more likely to provide support to their grown children than to their parents (Fingerman & others, 2011, 2012). When middle-aged adults have a parent with a disability, their support for that parent increases (Fingerman & others, 2011b). This support might involve locating a nursing home and monitoring its quality, procuring medical services, arranging public service assistance, and handling finances. In some cases, adult children provide direct assistance with daily living, including such activities as eating, bathing, and dressing. Even less severely impaired older adults may need help with shopping, housework, transportation, home maintenance, and bill paying.

Some researchers have found that relationships between aging parents and their children are often characterized by ambivalence (Antonucci & others, 2016; Sechrist & Fingerman, 2018). Perceptions include love, reciprocal help, and shared values on the positive side and isolation, family conflicts and problems, abuse, neglect, and caregiver stress on the negative side. One study found that middle-aged adults positively supported family responsibility to emerging adult children but were more ambivalent about providing care for aging parents, viewing it as both a joy and a burden (Igarashi & others, 2013).

With each new generation, personality characteristics, attitudes, and values are replicated or changed (Antonucci & others, 2016). As older family members die, their biological, intellectual, emotional, and personal legacies are carried on in the next generation. Their children become the oldest generation and their grandchildren the second

How Would You...?

As a **health-care professional,** how would you advise a family contemplating the potential challenges of having a middle-aged family member take on primary responsibility for the daily care of a chronically ill parent?

generation. As adult children become middle-aged, they often develop more positive perceptions of their parents (Field, 1999). Both similarity and dissimilarity across generations are found. For example, similarity between parents and an adult child is most noticeable in religion and politics, least in gender roles, lifestyle, and work orientation.

Gender differences also characterize intergenerational relationships (Antonucci & others, 2016; Sechrist & Fingerman, 2018). Women play an especially important role in maintaining family relationships across generations. Women's relationships across generations are typically closer than other family bonds (Merrill, 2009). In one study, mothers and their adult daughters had much closer relationships than mothers and sons, fathers and daughters, and fathers and sons (Rossi, 1989). Also in this study, married men were more involved with their wives' kin than with their own. And maternal grandmothers and maternal aunts were cited twice as often as their counterparts on the paternal side of the family as the most important or loved relative. Another study revealed that mothers' intergenerational ties were more influential for grandparent-grandchild relationships than fathers' were (Monserud, 2008).

What is the nature of intergenerational relationships?
©Steve Casimiro/The Image Bank/Getty Images

Summary

Personality Theories and Development

- Erikson says that the seventh stage of the human life span, generativity versus stagnation, occurs in middle adulthood. Levinson concluded that a majority of Americans, especially men, experience a midlife crisis. Research, though, indicates that midlife crises are not pervasive.
- In the contemporary version of the life-events approach, how life events influence the individual's development depends not only on the life event but also on mediating factors, adaptation to the event, the life-stage context, and the sociohistorical context.
- Young and middle-aged adults experience more stress than do older adults, and as adults become older, they report less control over some areas of their lives and more control over other areas.

Stability and Change

- In Costa and McCrae's Baltimore Study, the Big Five personality factors showed considerable stability. In the Berkeley Longitudinal Studies, the extremes in the stability-change argument were not supported. George Vaillant's

research revealed links between a number of characteristics at age 50 and health and well-being at 75 to 80 years of age.
- Some researchers suggest that personality stability peaks in the fifties and sixties, others say that it begins to stabilize at about age 30, and still others argue that limited personality changes continue during midlife.

Close Relationships

- Affectionate love increases in midlife for many couples.
- Rather than reducing marital satisfaction as was once thought, the empty nest increases it for most parents. Growing numbers of young adults are returning home to live with their middle-aged parents.
- Sibling relationships continue throughout life, and friendships continue to be important in middle age.
- Depending on the family's culture and situation, grandparents assume different roles. The profile of grandparents is changing.
- Family members usually maintain contact across generations. The middle-aged generation plays an important role in linking generations.

Key Terms

Big Five factors of personality
contemporary life-events approach
cumulative personality model
empty nest syndrome
fight-or-flight
generativity
stagnation
tend-and-befriend

15 Physical and Cognitive Development in Late Adulthood

©Rod Porteous/Robert Harding/Alamy

Stories of Life-Span Development: Learning to Age Successfully

In 2010, 90-year-old Helen Small completed her master's degree at the University of Texas at Dallas. The topic of her master's degree research project was romantic relationships in late adulthood. Helen said that she had interviewed only one individual who was older than she was—a 92-year-old man.

I (your author, John Santrock) first met Helen when she took my undergraduate course in life-span development in 2006. After the first test, Helen stopped showing up and I wondered what had happened to her. It turned out that she had broken her shoulder when she tripped over a curb while hurrying to class. The next semester, she took my class again and did a great job in it, even though the first several months she had to take notes with her left hand (she was right-handed) because of her lingering shoulder problem.

Helen grew up in the Great Depression and first went to college in 1938 at the University of Akron, which she attended for only one year. She got married and her marriage lasted 62 years. After her husband's death, Helen went back to college in 2002, first at Brookhaven Community College and then at UT-Dallas. When I interviewed her, she told me that she had promised her mother that she would finish college. Her most important advice for college students was "Finish college and be persistent. When you make a commitment, always see it through. Don't quit. Go after what you want in life."

Helen not only was cognitively fit, she also was physically fit. She worked out three times a week for about an hour each time—aerobically on a treadmill for about 30 minutes and then on six different weight machines.

What struck me most about Helen when she took my undergraduate course in life-span development was how appreciative she was of the opportunity to learn and how passionately she pursued studying and doing well in the course. Helen was quite popular with the younger students in the course and she was a terrific role model for them.

After her graduation, I asked her what she planned to do during the next few years and she responded, "I've got to figure out what I'm going to do with the rest of my life." For several years, Helen came each semester to my course in life-span development when we were discussing cognitive aging. She wowed the class and was an inspiration to all who came in contact with her.

What kinds of things did Helen do to stay cognitively fit? She worked as a public ambassador for Dr. Denise Park's Center for Vital Longevity at UT-Dallas, regularly served as a volunteer guide for Dallas' new Perot Science Museum, and worked on archival materials for the UT-Dallas library. Also, in 2015, she began teaching English to immigrant bilingual adults. Helen also published her first book: *Why Not? My Seventy Year Plan for a College Degree* (Small, 2011). It's a wonderful, motivating invitation to live your life fully and reach your potential no matter what your age. Following an amazing, fulfilling life, Helen Small passed away in 2017 at the age of 97.

The story of Helen Small's physical and cognitive well-being in late adulthood raises some truly fascinating questions about life-span development, which we explore in this chapter. They include: Why do we age, and what, if anything, can we do to delay the aging process? What chance do you have of living to be 100? How does the body change in old age? How well do older adults function cognitively? What roles do work and retirement play in older adults' lives? ▪

Helen Small with the author of your text, John Santrock, in his undergraduate course on life-span development at the University of Texas at Dallas in spring 2012. After she graduated, Helen returned each semester to talk with students in the class about cognitive aging.
(Top) Courtesy of Helen Small; *(bottom)* Courtesy of Dr. John Santrock

Longevity, Biological Aging, and Physical Development

What do we really know about longevity? What are the current biological theories about why we age? How does our brain change during this part of our life span? What happens to us physically? Does our sexuality change?

Longevity

The United States is no longer a youthful society. As more individuals are living past age 65, the proportion of individuals at different ages has become increasingly similar. Indeed, the concept of a period called "late adulthood," beginning in the sixties or seventies and lasting until death, is relatively new. Before the twentieth century, most individuals died before they reached 65.

Life Span and Life Expectancy

Since the beginning of recorded history, **life span,** the maximum number of years an individual can live, has remained steady at approximately 120 to 125 years of age. But since 1900 improvements in medicine, nutrition, exercise, and life-style have increased our life expectancy by an average of 31 years.

Recall that **life expectancy** is the number of years that the average person born in a particular year will probably live. The average life expectancy of individuals born in 2017 in the United States was 79 years (U.S. Census Bureau, 2018). Sixty-five-year-olds in the United States today can expect to live an average of 19.5 more years (20.6 for females, 18.4 for males) (U.S. Department of Health and Human Services, 2018). People who are 100 years of age can only expect to live an average of 2.3 years longer (U.S. Census Bureau, 2013).

Differences in Life Expectancy

How does the United States fare in life expectancy, compared with other countries around the world? We do considerably better than some and somewhat worse than others. In 2015, Monaco had the highest estimated life expectancy at birth (90 years), followed by Japan, Singapore, and Macau (a region of China near Hong Kong) (85 years) (Central Intelligence Agency, 2015). Of 224 countries, the United States ranked 43rd at 79 years. The lowest estimated life expectancy in 2015 occurred in the African countries of Chad and Guinea-Bissau (50) and Swaziland and Afghanistan (51 years). Differences in life expectancies across countries are due to factors such as health conditions and medical care throughout the life span.

©Comstock/PunchStock

In a recent analysis, projections of life expectancy in 2030 were made for 35 developed countries (Kontis & others, 2017). It was predicted that life expectancy in the United States would increase to 83.3 years for women and 79.5 years for men by 2030. However, the United States, although expected to increase in life expectancy, had one of the lowest growth rates in life expectancy for all of the countries in the study. South Korea is projected to have the highest life expectancy in 2030, with South Korean women predicted to have an average life expectancy of 90.8, the first nation to break the 90-year life expectancy barrier. So why the lower growth in life expectancy for the United States and the very high growth for South Korea? The United States has the highest child and maternal mortality rates, homicide rate, and body-mass index of high-income countries in the world. In South Korea, delayed onset of chronic diseases is occurring and children's nutrition is improving. South Korea also has a low rate of obesity, and blood pressure is not as high as it is in most countries.

In 2017, the overall life expectancy for women was 81 years of age, and for men it was 77 years of age (U.S Census Bureau, 2018). The gender gap in longevity decreased from 7.8 years in 1979 to 4 years in 2017. Beginning in the mid-thirties, women outnumber men; this gap widens during the remainder of the adult years. By the time adults are 75 years of age, more than 61 percent are female; for those 85 and over, the figure is almost 70 percent female. A recent list (2017) of the oldest people alive today in the world had no men in the top 25.

Why can women expect to live longer than men? Social factors such as health attitudes, habits, lifestyles, and occupation are probably important (Saint-Onge, 2009). Men are more likely than women to die from most of the leading causes of death, including cancer of the respiratory system, motor vehicle accidents, cirrhosis of the liver, emphysema, and coronary heart disease (Alfredsson & others, 2018; Dao-Fu & others, 2016; Pedersen & others, 2016). These causes of death are associated with lifestyle. For example, the sex difference in deaths due to lung cancer and emphysema occurs because men are heavier smokers than women. However, women are more likely than men to die from some diseases such as Alzheimer disease and some aspects of cardiovascular disease, such as hypertension-related problems (Ostan & others, 2016).

life span The upper boundary of life, which is the maximum number of years an individual can live. The maximum life span of human beings is about 120 to 125 years of age.

life expectancy The number of years that will probably be lived by the average person born in a particular year.

The sex difference in longevity also is influenced by biological factors (Alfredsson & others, 2018; Beltran-Sanchez, Finch, & Crimmins, 2015; Crimmins & Levine, 2016). In virtually all species, females outlive males. Women have more resistance to infections and degenerative diseases (Pan & Chang, 2012). For example, the female's estrogen production helps to protect her from arteriosclerosis (hardening of the arteries) (Valera & others, 2015). And the additional X chromosome that women carry in comparison with men may be associated with the production of more antibodies to fight off disease. The sex difference in mortality is still present in late adulthood but less pronounced than earlier in adulthood, and it is especially linked to the higher level of cardiovascular disease in men than women (Alfredsson & others, 2018; Yang & Kozloski, 2011).

Centenarians

In the United States, there were only 15,000 centenarians in 1980, but that number rose to 50,000 in 2000 and to 72,000 in 2014 (Xu, 2016). The number of U.S. centenarians is projected to reach 600,000 by 2050 (U.S. Census Bureau, 2011).

Many people expect that "the older you get, the sicker you get." However, researchers are finding that this is not true for some centenarians (Revelas & others, 2018; Willcox, Scapagnini, & Willcox, 2014). A study of 93 centenarians revealed that despite some physical limitations, they had a low rate of age-associated diseases and most had good mental health (Selim & others, 2005). And a study of centenarians from 100 to 119 years of age found that the older the age group (110 to 119—referred to as *supercentenarians*—compared with 100 to 104, for example), the later the onset of diseases such as cancer and cardiovascular disease, as well as functional decline (Andersen & others, 2012). The research just described was carried out as part of the New England Centenarian Study (NECS) conducted by Thomas Perls and his colleagues. Perls has a term for this process of staving off high-mortality chronic diseases until much later ages than is usually the case in the general population: he calls it the *compression of morbidity* (Sebastiani & Perls, 2012). Further, there are far more female supercentenarians than males—a list (2015) of the oldest people who have ever lived had only two men (number 11 and number 17) in the top 25.

Among the factors that are associated with living to be 100 are longevity genes and the ability to cope effectively with stress (Blankenburg, Pramstaller, & Domingues, 2018; Muntane & others, 2018; Revelas & others, 2018). NECS researchers also have discovered a strong genetic component to living to be 100 that consists of many genetic links, each with modest effects but collectively having a strong influence (Sebastiani & others, 2013). Other characteristics of centenarians in the NECS study include the following: few of the centenarians are obese, habitual smoking is rare, and only a small percentage (less than 15 percent) have had significant changes in their thinking skills (disproving the belief that most centenarians likely would develop Alzheimer disease). And in a recent study of U.S. and Japanese centenarians, in both countries, health resources (better cognitive function, fewer hearing problems, and positive activities in daily living) were linked to a higher level of well-being (Nakagawa & others, 2018).

Jeanne Louise Calment, celebrating her 117th birthday. She was the world's oldest living person, dying at age 122. She said reasons she had lived so long included not worrying about things she couldn't do anything about; enjoying an occasional glass of port wine; having a diet rich in olive oil; and laughing often. Regarding her longevity, she once said that God must have forgotten about her. On her 120th birthday, she was asked her what kind of future she anticipated. Calment replied, "A very short one." Becoming accustomed to the media attention she received, at 117 she stated, "I wait for death . . . and journalists." Calment walked, biked, and began taking fencing lessons at age 85 and rode a bicycle until she was 100.
©Jean-Pierre Fizet/Sygma/Getty Images

Biological Theories of Aging

Even if we stay remarkably healthy, we begin to age at some point. Four biological theories provide intriguing explanations of why we age: evolutionary, cellular clock, free-radical, and hormonal stress.

Evolutionary Theory

In the **evolutionary theory of aging,** natural selection has not eliminated many harmful conditions and nonadaptive characteristics in older adults (Greenberg & Vatolin, 2018; Yanai & others, 2017). Why? Because natural selection is linked to reproductive fitness, which is present only in the earlier part of adulthood. For example, consider Alzheimer disease, an irreversible brain disorder, which does not appear until late middle adulthood or late adulthood. According to evolutionary theory, possibly if Alzheimer disease occurred earlier in development, it might have been eliminated many centuries ago. Evolutionary theory has its critics (Cohen, 2015). One criticism is that the "big picture" idea of natural selection leading to the development of human traits and behaviors is difficult to refute or test because evolution occurs on a time scale that does not lend itself to empirical study. Another criticism is the failure of evolutionary theory to account for cultural influences (Singer, 2016).

evolutionary theory of aging The view that natural selection has not eliminated many harmful conditions and nonadaptive characteristics in older adults.

cellular clock theory Leonard Hayflick's theory that the maximum number of times human cells can divide is about 75 to 80. As we age, our cells become increasingly less capable of dividing.

Genetic/Cellular Process Theories

One recent view stated that aging is best explained by cellular maintenance requirements and evolutionary constraints (Vanhaelen, 2015). In recent decades, there has been a significant increase in research on genetic and cellular processes involved in aging (Benetos & others, 2019; Falandry, 2019; Hernandez-Segura, Nehme, & Demaria, 2018; Ong & Ramasamy, 2018). Five such advances involve telomeres, free radicals, mitochondria, sirtuins, and the mTOR pathway.

Cellular Clock Theory **Cellular clock theory** is Leonard Hayflick's (1977) theory that cells can divide a maximum of about 75 to 80 times and that as we age our cells become less capable of dividing. Hayflick found that cells extracted from adults in their fifties to seventies divided fewer than 75 to 80 times. Based on the ways cells divide, Hayflick places the upper limit of human life-span potential at about 120 to 125 years of age.

In the last decade, scientists have tried to fill in a gap in cellular clock theory (Nene & others, 2018; Toupance & Benetos, 2019; Zgheib & others, 2018). Hayflick did not know why cells die. The answer may lie at the tips of chromosomes (Gorenjak & others, 2018).

Each time a cell divides, *telomeres,* which are DNA sequences that cap chromosomes, become shorter and shorter (Chang & Blau, 2018) (see Figure 1). After about 70 or 80 replications, the telomeres are dramatically reduced, and the cell no longer can reproduce. One study revealed that healthy centenarians had longer telomeres than unhealthy centenarians (Terry & others, 2008). Further, a recent study confirmed that shorter telomere length was linked to Alzheimer disease (Scarabino & others, 2017).

Injecting the enzyme *telomerase* into human cells grown in the laboratory can substantially extend the life of the cells beyond the approximately 70 to 80 normal cell divisions (Harrison, 2012). However, telomerase is present in approximately 85 to 90 percent of cancerous cells and thus may not produce healthy life extension of cells (Cleal, Norris, & Baird, 2018).

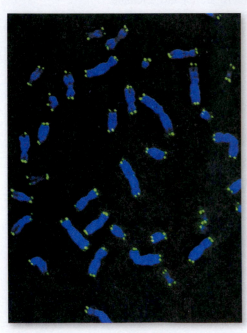

Figure 1

Telomeres and Aging

The photograph shows actual telomeres lighting up the tips of chromosomes.
Courtesy of Dr. Jerry Shay

To capitalize on the high presence of telomerase in cancerous cells, researchers currently are investigating gene therapies that inhibit telomerase and lead to the death of cancerous cells while keeping healthy cells alive (de Vitis, Berardinelli, & Sgura, 2018; Haraguchi & others, 2017; Ozturk, Li, & Tergaonkar, 2018). A recent focus of these gene therapies is on stem cells and their renewal (Li & Denchi, 2018; Liu, 2017). Telomeres and telomerase are increasingly thought to be key components of the stem cell regeneration process, providing a possible avenue to restrain cancer and delay aging (Gunes, Avila, & Rudolph, 2018; Li & others, 2017; Marion & others, 2017; Zhou & others, 2018).

Free-Radical Theory A third theory of aging is **free-radical theory,** which states that people age because when cells metabolize energy, the by-products include unstable oxygen molecules known as *free radicals*. The free radicals ricochet around the cells, damaging DNA and other cellular structures (Guillaumet-Adkins & others, 2017; Jabeen & others, 2018; Jeremic & others, 2018). The damage can lead to a range of disorders, including cancer and arthritis (Hegedus & others, 2018; Phull & others, 2018; Saha & others, 2017). Overeating is linked with an increase in free radicals, and researchers have found that calorie restriction—a diet low in calories but adequate in proteins, vitamins, and minerals—reduces the oxidative damage created by free radicals (Kalsi, 2015). In addition to diet, researchers also are exploring the role that exercise might play in reducing oxidative damage in cells (Robinson & others, 2017). A study of obese men found that endurance exercise reduced their oxidative damage (Samjoo & others, 2013).

Mitochondrial Theory **Mitochondrial theory** is a theory of aging that emphasizes the decay of *mitochondria*—tiny bodies within cells that supply essential energy for function, growth, and repair—that is primarily due to oxidative damage and loss of critical micronutrients supplied by the cell (Hamilton & Miller, 2017; Zole & Ranka, 2018). Energy sensing and apoptosis (programmed cell death) also have been emphasized as key aspects of the mitochondrial theory of aging (Gonzalez-Freire & others, 2015).

The mitochondrial damage may lead to a range of disorders, including cardiovascular disease (Anupama, Sindhu, & Raghu, 2018); neurodegenerative diseases such as Alzheimer disease (Birnbaum & others, 2018); Parkinson disease (Larson, Hanss, & Kruger, 2018); diabetic kidney disease (Forbes & Thorburn, 2018); and impaired liver functioning (Borrelli & others, 2018). However, it is not known whether the defects in mitochondria cause aging or merely accompany the aging process.

Sirtuin Theory **Sirtuins** are a family of proteins that have been linked to longevity, regulation of mitochondria functioning in energy, possible benefits of calorie restriction, stress resistance, and a lower incidence of cardiovascular disease and cancer (Ansari & others, 2017; Blank & Grummt, 2017; Sanikhani & others, 2018; Wood & others, 2018). One of the sirtuins, SIRT 1, has been connected to DNA repair and aging (Kida & Goligorsky, 2016).

How Would You...?

As an **educator,** how would you use a biological perspective to explain changes in learning as people age?

mTOR Pathway Theory The **mTOR pathway** is a cellular pathway that involves the regulation of growth and metabolism. TOR stands for "target of rapamycin," and in mammals it is called mTOR. Rapamycin is a naturally derived antibiotic and immune system suppressant/modulator, first discovered in the 1960s on Easter Island. It has been commonly used and is FDA approved for preventing organ rejection and in bone-marrow transplants. Recently, proposals have been made that the mTOR pathway has a central role in the life of cells, acting as a cellular router for growth, protein production/metabolism, and stem cell functioning (Houssaini & others, 2018; Kraig & others, 2018; Lim & others, 2017; Zhang & others, 2017). Some scientists also argue that the pathway is linked to longevity, the successful outcomes of calorie restriction, and reductions in cognitive decline, and may influence the course of a number of diseases, including cancer, cardiovascular disease, and Alzheimer disease (Maid & Power, 2018; Tramultola, Lanzillotta, & Di Domenico, 2017; Van Skike & others, 2018). Rapamycin has not been approved as an anti-aging drug and has some serious side effects, including increased risk of infection and lymphoma, a deadly cancer.

Some critics argue that scientific support for sirtuins and the mTOR pathway as key causes of aging in humans has not been found and that research has not adequately documented the effectiveness of using drugs such as rapamycin to slow the aging process or extend the human life span (Ehninger, Neff, & Xie, 2014).

free-radical theory A theory of aging proposing that people age because normal cell metabolism produces unstable oxygen molecules known as free radicals. These molecules ricochet around inside cells, damaging DNA and other cellular structures.

mitochondrial theory The theory that aging is caused by the decay of mitochondria, tiny cellular bodies that supply energy for function, growth, and repair.

sirtuins A family of proteins that have been linked to longevity, regulation of mitochondrial functioning in energy, potential benefits of calorie restriction, resistance to stress, and a reduced risk of cardiovascular disease and cancer.

mTOR pathway A cellular pathway involving the regulation of growth and metabolism that has been proposed as a key aspect of longevity

Hormonal Stress Theory

Cellular clock and free radical theories attempt to explain aging at the cellular level. In contrast, **hormonal stress theory** argues that aging in the body's hormonal system can lower resistance to stress and increase the likelihood of disease. Normally, when people experience stressors, the body responds by releasing certain hormones. As people age, the hormones stimulated by stress remain at elevated levels longer than when people were younger (Gekle, 2017; Kim, Jee, & Pikhart, 2018). These prolonged, elevated levels of stress-related hormones are associated with increased risks for many diseases, including cardiovascular disease, cancer, diabetes, and hypertension (Burleson, 2017; Castagne & others, 2018; Steptoe & others, 2017). Researchers are exploring stress-buffering strategies, including exercise, in an effort to find ways to attenuate some of the negative effects of stress on the aging process (Gomes & others, 2017; Kim, Jee, & Pikhart, 2018; Niraula, Sheridan, & Godbout, 2017).

Recently, a variation of hormonal stress theory has emphasized the contribution of a decline in immune system functioning with aging (Fulop & others, 2019; Garschall & Flatt, 2018; Jasiulionis, 2018; Masters & others, 2017). In a recent study, the percentage of T cells (a type of white blood cell essential for immunity) decreased in older adults in their seventies, eighties, and nineties (Valiathan, Ashman, & Asthana, 2016). Aging contributes to immune system deficits that give rise to infectious diseases in older adults (Le Page & others, 2018; Song & others, 2018). The extended duration of stress and diminished restorative processes in older adults may accelerate the effects of aging on immunity.

hormonal stress theory The theory that aging in the body's hormonal system can lower resilience under stress and increase the likelihood of disease.

Conclusions

Which of these biological theories best explains aging? That question has not yet been answered. It likely will turn out that more than one—or perhaps all—of these biological processes contribute to aging. In a recent analysis, it was concluded that aging is a very complex process involving multiple degenerative factors, including interacting cell- and organ level communications (de Magalhaes & Tacutu, 2016). Although there are some individual aging triggers such as telomere shortening, a complete picture of biological aging involves multiple processes operating at different biological levels.

The Aging Brain

How does the brain change during late adulthood? Does it retain plasticity? As we will see, the brain shrinks and slows but still has considerable adaptive ability.

The Shrinking, Slowing Brain

On average, the brain loses 5 to 10 percent of its weight between the ages of 20 and 90. Brain volume also decreases (Liu & others, 2016; Peng & others, 2016). One study found a decrease in total brain volume and volume in key brain structures such as the frontal lobes and hippocampus from 22 to 88 years of age (Sherwood & others, 2011). Also, recent analyses concluded that in healthy aging the decrease in brain volume is due mainly to shrinkage of neurons, lower numbers of synapses, reduced length and complexity of axons, and reduced tree-like branching in dendrites, but only to a minor extent attributable to neuron loss (Penazzi, Bakota, & Brandt, 2016; Skaper & others, 2017). Of course, for individuals with disorders such as Alzheimer disease, neuron loss occurs (Moore & Murphy, 2016; Poulakis & others, 2018). Further, in a recent study, global brain volume predicted mortality in a large population of stroke-free community-dwelling adults (Van Elderen & others, 2016).

Some brain areas shrink more than others with aging (Moore & Murphy, 2016). The prefrontal cortex is one area that shrinks, and research has linked this shrinkage with a decrease in working memory and other cognitive activities in older adults (Hoyer, 2015). The sensory regions of the brain—such as the primary visual cortex, primary motor cortex, and somatosensory cortex—are less vulnerable to the aging process (Rodrique & Kennedy, 2011). A general slowing of function in the brain and spinal cord begins in middle adulthood and accelerates in late adulthood (Salthouse, 2017).

Both physical coordination and intellectual performance are affected. For example, after age 70 many adults no longer show a knee-jerk reflex, and by age 90 most reflexes are much slower (Spence, 1989). Slowing of the brain can impair the performance of older adults on intelligence tests, especially timed tests (Lu & others, 2011).

Aging also has been linked to a decline in the production of some neurotransmitters. Reduction in acetylcholine is linked to memory loss, especially in people with Alzheimer disease (Jensen & others, 2015). Severe reductions in dopamine are involved in a reduction in motor control in Parkinson disease (Ruitenberg & others, 2015).

Historically, as in the research just discussed, much of the focus on links between brain functioning and aging has been on volume of brain structures and regions. Currently, however, increased emphasis is being given to changes in myelination and neural networks (Anthony & Lin, 2018; Grady, 2017; Habeck & others, 2018; Madden & Parks, 2017). Research indicates that demyelination (deterioration in the myelin sheath that encases axons and is associated with information processing) occurs with aging in the brains of older adults (Callaghan & others, 2014; Rodrique & Kennedy, 2011).

The Adaptive Brain

The human brain has remarkable repair capability (Erickson & Oberlin, 2017; Garaschuk, Semchyshyn, & Lushchak, 2018; Ishi & others, 2018; Kinugawa, 2019). Even in late adulthood, the brain loses only a portion of its ability to function, and the activities older adults engage in can still influence the brain's development (Borsa & others, 2018; Lovden, Backman, & Lindenberger, 2017; Reuter-Lorenz & Lustig, 2017). For example, in an fMRI study, higher levels of aerobic fitness were linked with greater volume in the hippocampus, which translates into better memory (Erickson & others, 2011).

Can adults, even aging adults, generate new neurons? Researchers have found that *neurogenesis*, the generation of new neurons, does occur in lower mammalian species, such as mice (Adlof & others, 2017; O'Leary & others, 2018). Also, research indicates that exercise and an enriched, complex environment can generate new brain cells in rats and mice, and that stress reduces their survival rate (Abbink & others, 2017; Park & others, 2018; Ruitenberg & others, 2017; Zhang & others, 2018). For example, in a recent study, mice in an enriched environment learned more flexibly because of adult hippocampal neurogenesis (Garthe, Roeder, & Kempermann, 2016). One study revealed that coping with stress stimulated hippocampal neurogenesis in adult monkeys (Lyons & others, 2010). And researchers have discovered that if rats are cognitively challenged to learn something, new brain cells survive longer (Shors, 2009).

It also is now accepted that neurogenesis can occur in human adults (Horgusluoglu & others, 2017; Shohayeb & others, 2018; Su, Dhananjaya, & Tarn, 2018). However, researchers have documented neurogenesis in only two brain regions: the hippocampus, which is involved in memory (Olesen & others, 2017), and the olfactory bulb, which is involved in smell (Bonzano & De Marchis, 2017). It also is not known what functions these new brain cells perform, and at this point researchers have documented that they last for only several weeks (Nelson, 2008).

Researchers currently are studying factors that might inhibit and promote neurogenesis, including various drugs, stress, and exercise (Liu & Nusslock, 2018; Tharmaratnam & others, 2017; Zhou & others, 2017). They also are examining how the grafting of neural stem cells to various regions of the brain, such as the hippocampus, might increase neurogenesis (Akers & others, 2018; Zhang & others, 2017). And increasing attention is being given to the possible role neurogenesis might play in neurodegenerative diseases, such as Alzheimer disease, Parkinson disease, and Huntington disease (Ma & others, 2017; Shohayeb & others, 2018; Zheng & others, 2017).

Dendritic growth can occur in human adults, possibly even in older adults (Eliasieh, Liets, & Chalupa, 2007). Recall that dendrites are the receiving portion of the neuron. One study compared the brains of adults at various ages (Coleman, 1986). From the forties through the seventies, the growth of dendrites increased. However, in people in their nineties, dendritic growth no longer occurred.

Changes in lateralization may provide one type of adaptation in aging adults (Hong & others, 2015). Recall that lateralization is the specialization of function in one hemisphere of the brain or the other. Using neuroimaging techniques, researchers found that brain activity in the prefrontal cortex is lateralized less in older adults than in younger adults when they are engaging in cognitive tasks (Cabeza, 2002; Cabeza & Dennis, 2013; Park & Farrell, 2016; Sugiura, 2016). For example, Figure 2 shows that when younger adults are given the task of recognizing words they have previously seen, they process the information primarily in the right hemisphere; older adults are more likely to use both hemispheres (Madden & others, 1999). The decrease in lateralization in older adults might play a compensatory role in the aging brain. That is, using both hemispheres may improve the cognitive functioning of older adults.

Figure 2 The Decrease in Brain Lateralization in Older Adults
Younger adults primarily used the right prefrontal region of the brain (*top left photo*) during a recall memory task, whereas older adults used both the left and right prefrontal regions (*bottom two photos*).
Courtesy of Dr. Roberto Cabeza

The Nun Study

The Nun Study, directed by David Snowdon, is an intriguing ongoing investigation of aging in 678 nuns, many of whom are from the convent of the Sisters of Notre Dame in Mankato, Minnesota (Pakhomov & Hemmy, 2014; Snowdon, 2003; Tyas & others, 2007). They lead an intellectually challenging life, and brain researchers conclude that this contributes to their quality of life as older adults and possibly to their longevity. All of the 678 nuns agreed to participate in annual assessments of their cognitive and physical functioning. They also agreed to donate their brains for scientific research when they die, and they are the largest group of brain donors in the world. Examination of the nuns' donated brains, as well as others', has led neuroscientists to believe that the brain has a remarkable capacity to change and grow, even in old age.

Top: Sister Marcella Zachman (*left*) finally stopped teaching at age 97. Now, at 99, she helps ailing nuns exercise their brains by quizzing them on vocabulary or playing a card game called Skip–Bo, at which she deliberately loses. Sister Mary Esther Boor (*right*), also 99 years of age, is a former teacher who stays alert by doing puzzles and volunteering to work the front desk. *Bottom*: A technician holds the brain of a deceased Mankato nun. The nuns donate their brains for research that explores the effects of stimulation on brain growth.
©James Balog

Physical Development

Physical decline is inevitable if we manage to live to an old age, but the timing of physical problems related to aging is not uniform. Let's examine some physical changes that occur as we age, including changes in physical appearance and movement, some of the senses, and our circulation and lungs.

Physical Appearance and Movement

In late adulthood, the changes in physical appearance that began occurring during middle age become more pronounced. Wrinkles and age spots are the most noticeable changes. We also get shorter as we get older. Both men and women become shorter in late adulthood because of bone loss in their vertebrae (Hoyer & Roodin, 2009).

Our weight usually drops after we reach 60 years of age. This likely occurs because we lose muscle, which also gives our bodies a "sagging" look (Evans, 2010). One study found that long-term aerobic exercise was linked with greater muscle strength in 65- to 86-year-olds (Crane, Macneil, & Tarnopolsky, 2013).

Older adults move more slowly than young adults, and this slowing occurs for many types of movement with a wide range of difficulty (Davis & others, 2013). Adequate mobility is an important aspect of maintaining an independent and active lifestyle in late adulthood (Danilovich & others, 2018;

Gray-Miceli, 2017). Recent research indicates that obesity is linked to mobility limitation in older adults (Anson & others, 2018). In another study, at-risk overweight and obese older adults lost significant weight and improved their mobility considerably by participating in a community-based weight reduction program (Rejeski & others, 2017).

Exercise benefits frail elderly adults. In a recent study, high-intensity walking training reduced the older adults' frailty, increased their walking speed, and improved their balance (Danilovich, Conroy, & Hornby, 2017). And in another recent study, a 10-week exercise program improved the physical (aerobic endurance, agility, and mobility) and cognitive function (selective attention and planning) of elderly nursing home residents (Pereira & others, 2018).

The risk of falling in older adults increases with age and is greater for women than for men (JafariNasabian & others, 2017). Falls are the leading cause of injury deaths among adults who are 65 years and older (National Center for Health Statistics, 2018). Each year, approximately 200,000 adults over the age of 65 (many of them women) fracture a hip in a fall. Half of these older adults die within 12 months, frequently from pneumonia. A research meta-analysis found that exercise reduces falls in adults 60 years of age and older (Stubbs, Brefka, & Denkinger, 2015).

Sensory Development

Seeing, hearing, and other aspects of sensory functioning are linked with our ability to perform everyday activities, and sensory functioning declines in older adults (Hochberg & others, 2012). For example, researchers have found that visual decline in late adulthood is linked to (a) cognitive decline (Monge & Madden, 2016; Roberts & Allen, 2016), as well as (b) having fewer social contacts and engaging in less challenging social/leisure activities (Cimarolli & others, 2017).

Vision In late adulthood, the decline in vision that began for most adults in early or middle adulthood becomes more pronounced (Jensen & Tubaek, 2018). The eye does not adapt as quickly when moving from a well-lighted place to one of semidarkness. The tolerance for glare also diminishes. The area of the visual field becomes smaller, and events that occur away from the center of the visual field sometimes are not detected (Scialfa & Kline, 2007). All of these changes can make night driving especially difficult (Kimlin, Black, & Wood, 2017).

Depth perception typically declines in late adulthood, which can make it difficult for older adults to determine how close or far away or how high or low something is (Bian & Anderson, 2008). A decline in depth perception can make steps or street curbs difficult to navigate.

Three diseases that can impair the vision of older adults are cataracts, glaucoma, and macular degeneration:

How Would You...?

As a **health-care professional,** how would you respond to an older adult who shows signs of impaired vision but denies, or is unaware of, the problem?

- **Cataracts** involve a thickening of the lens of the eye that causes vision to become cloudy and distorted (Radhakrishnan & others, 2018). By age 70, approximately 30 percent of individuals experience a partial loss of vision due to cataracts. Initially, cataracts can be treated by glasses; if they worsen, a simple surgical procedure can replace the natural lenses with artificial ones (Jiang & others, 2018; Singh, Dohlman, & Sun, 2017). A recent Japanese study found that older adults (mean age: 76 years) who had cataract surgery were less likely to develop mild cognitive impairment than their counterparts who had not had the surgery (Miyata & others, 2018).

- **Glaucoma** involves damage to the optic nerve because of the pressure created by a buildup of fluid in the eye (Jiang & others, 2018; Koh & others, 2017). Approximately 1 percent of individuals in their seventies and 10 percent of those in their nineties have glaucoma, which can be treated with eye drops. If left untreated, glaucoma can ultimately destroy a person's vision.

cataracts Involve a thickening of the lens of the eye that causes vision to become cloudy and distorted.

glaucoma Damage to the optic nerve because of the pressure created by a buildup of fluid in the eye.

- **Macular degeneration** is a disease that involves deterioration of the *macula* of the retina, which corresponds to the focal center of the visual field. Individuals with macular degeneration may have relatively normal peripheral vision but be unable to see clearly what is right in front of them (Hernandez-Zimbron & others, 2018; Owsley & others, 2016) (see Figure 3). This condition affects 1 in 25 individuals from age 66 to 74 and 1 in 6 of those age 75 and older. There is increased interest in using stem-cell based therapy to treat macular degeneration (Apatoff & others, 2018; Bakondi & others, 2017).

Hearing For hearing as for vision, it is important to determine the degree of decline in the aging adult (Johnson, Xu, & Cox, 2017). A national survey revealed that 63 percent of adults 70 years and older had a hearing loss, defined as an inability to hear sounds softer than 25 dB with their better ear (Lin & others, 2011). In this study, hearing aids were used by 40 percent of those with moderate hearing loss. Also, a recent study of 80- to 106-year-olds found a substantial increase in hearing loss in the ninth and then in the tenth decades of life (Wattamwar & others, 2017). In this study, although hearing loss was virtually universal in the 80- to 106-year-olds, only 59 percent of them wore hearing aids. Research has found that older adults' hearing problems are associated with less time spent out of home and in leisure activities (Mikkola & others, 2016), an increase in falls (Gopinath & others, 2012), reduction in cognitive functioning (Golub, 2017), and loneliness (Mick & others, 2018).

Figure 3 Macular Degeneration
This simulation of the effect of macular degeneration shows how individuals with this eye disease can see their peripheral field of vision but can't clearly see what is in their central visual field.
©Cordelia Molloy/Science Source

How Would You…?

As an **educator,** how would you structure your classroom and plan class activities to accommodate the sensory decline of older adult students?

What outcomes occur when older adults have dual sensory loss in vision and hearing? In a recent study of 65- to 85-year-olds, dual sensory loss in vision and hearing was linked to reduced social participation and less social support, as well as increased loneliness (Mick & others, 2018). In another recent study, this type of dual sensory loss in older adults (mean age of 82 years) involved greater functional limitations, increased loneliness, cognitive decline, and communication problems (Davidson & Gutherie, 2018). And in another recent study, older adults who had a dual sensory impairment involving vision and hearing had more depressive symptoms (Han & others, 2018).

Smell and Taste Most older adults lose some of their sense of smell or taste, or both (Correia & others, 2016). A recent national study of community-dwelling older adults revealed that 74 percent had impaired taste and 22 percent had impaired smell (Correia & others, 2016). These losses often begin around 60 years of age (Hawkes, 2006). A majority of individuals 80 years of age and older experience a significant reduction in smell (Lafreniere & Mann, 2009). Researchers have found that older adults show a greater decline in their sense of smell than in their taste (Schiffman, 2007). Smell and taste decline less in healthy older adults than in their less healthy counterparts.

Touch and Pain Changes in touch and pain are also associated with aging (Kemp & others, 2014). A recent national study of community-dwelling older adults revealed that 70 percent of older adults had impaired touch (Correia & others, 2016). For most older adults, a decline in touch sensitivity is not problematic (Hoyer & Roodin, 2009).

macular degeneration A disease that involves deterioration of the macula of the retina, which corresponds to the focal center of the visual field.

An estimated 60 to 75 percent of older adults report at least some persistent pain (Molton & Terrill, 2014). The most frequent pain complaints of older adults involve back pain (40 percent), peripheral neuropathic pain (35 percent), and chronic joint pain (15 to 25 percent) (Denard & others, 2010). The presence of pain increases with age in older adults, and women are more likely to report having pain than are men (Tsang & others, 2008). In a recent research review, it was concluded that older adults have lower pain sensitivity than their younger counterparts but only for lower pain intensities (Lautenbacher & others, 2017). Although decreased sensitivity to pain can help older adults cope with disease and injury, it can also mask injuries and illnesses that need to be treated.

The Circulatory System and Lungs

Cardiovascular disorders increase in late adulthood (Lind & others, 2018). In older adults, 64 percent of men and 69 percent of women 65 to 74 years of age have hypertension (high blood pressure) (Centers for Disease Control and Prevention, 2018). Consistent blood pressures above 120/80 should be treated to reduce the risk of heart attack, stroke, or kidney disease. Various drugs, a healthy diet, and exercise can reduce the risk of cardiovascular disease in older adults (Cheng & others, 2017; Kantoch & others, 2018). In a study of older adults, a faster exercise walking pace, not smoking, modest alcohol intake, and avoiding obesity were associated with a lower risk of heart failure (Del Gobbo & others, 2015). And in a recent study of adults age 65 and over, a Mediterranean diet lowered their risk of cardiovascular problems (Nowson & others, 2018).

Lung capacity drops 40 percent between the ages of 20 and 80, even without disease (Fozard, 1992). Lungs lose elasticity, the chest shrinks, and the diaphragm weakens (Skloot, 2017). The good news, though, is that older adults can improve lung functioning with diaphragm-strengthening exercises.

Sleep

Approximately 50 percent of older adults complain of having difficulty sleeping (Farajinia & others, 2014). Researchers have found that older adults' sleep is lighter and more disruptive (takes longer to fall asleep and also involves more awakenings and greater difficulty in going back to sleep) (McRae & others, 2016). Poor sleep is a risk factor for falls, obesity, and earlier death and is linked to a lower level of cognitive functioning (Onen & Onen, 2018).

Many of the sleep problems of older adults are associated with health problems (Brewster, Riegel, & Gehrman, 2018; Dean & others, 2017; Li, Vitiello, & Gooneratne, 2018). Recent research indicates that when older adults sleep less than seven hours or more than nine hours a night, their cognitive functioning is harmed (Devore, Grodstein, & Schemhammer, 2016; Lo & others, 2016). And a recent Chinese study revealed that older adults who engaged in a higher level of overall physical activity, leisure-time exercise, and household activity were less likely to have sleep problems (Li & others, 2018).

Sexuality

In the absence of two circumstances—disease and the belief that old people are or should be asexual—sexuality can be lifelong (Corona & others, 2013). Aging, however, does induce some changes in human sexual performance, more so in the male than in the female (Estill & others, 2018). Orgasm becomes less frequent in males with age, occurring in every second to third attempt rather than every time. More direct stimulation usually is needed to produce an erection.

Many older adults are sexually active as long as they are healthy (Thomas, Hess, & Thurston, 2015). However, in one study, sexual activity did decline through the later years of life: 73 percent of 57- to 64-year-olds, 53 percent of 65- to 74-year-olds, and 26 percent of 75- to 85-year-olds

What are some characteristics of sexuality in older adults? How does sexuality change as older adults go through the late adulthood period?
©Image Source/Getty Images

reported that they were sexually active (Lindau & others, 2007). Nonetheless, with recent advances in erectile dysfunction medications, such as Viagra, an increasing number of older men, especially the young-old, are able to have an erection (Bennett, 2018; Constantinescu & others, 2017; Gesser-Edelsburg & Hijazi, 2018; Ozcan & others, 2018). Also, recent research suggests that declining levels of serum testosterone, which is linked to erectile dysfunction, can be treated with testosterone replacement therapy to improve sexual functioning in males (Hackett & Kirby, 2018; Hackett & others, 2017; Jones & Kelly, 2018; Mayo Clinic, 2018). However, the benefit-risk ratio of testosterone replacement therapy is uncertain for older males (Isidori & others, 2014).

Health

What types of health problems do people have in late adulthood, and what can be done to maintain or improve their health and ability to function in everyday life?

Health Problems

As we age, it becomes increasingly likely that we will have some disease or illness (Baker & Petersen, 2018; Benetos & others, 2019). The majority of adults still alive at 80 years of age or older have some type of impairment. Chronic diseases (those with a slow onset and a long duration) are rare in early adulthood, increase in middle adulthood, and become more common in late adulthood (Hirsch & Sirois, 2016).

Arthritis is the most common chronic disorder in late adulthood, followed by hypertension. Older women have a higher incidence of arthritis, hypertension, and visual problems but a lower incidence of hearing problems than older men do.

Low income is also strongly related to health problems in late adulthood (Boylan, Cundiff, & Matthews, 2018; Caplan, Washington, & Swanner, 2017). Approximately three times as many poor as non-poor older adults report that chronic disorders limit their activities.

Causes of Death in Older Adults

Nearly 60 percent of U.S. adults 65 to 74 years old die of cancer or cardiovascular disease. Cancer recently replaced cardiovascular disease as the leading cause of death in U.S. middle-aged adults. However, cardiovascular disease is the leading cause of death in U.S. 65- to 74-year-olds (Centers for Disease Control and Prevention, 2018). And in the 75-to-84 and 85-and-over age groups, cardiovascular disease also is the leading cause of death (Centers for Disease Control and Prevention, 2018). As individuals age through the late adult years, they become more and more likely to die from cardiovascular disease than from cancer.

Arthritis

Arthritis is an inflammation of the joints accompanied by pain, stiffness, and movement problems. This incurable disorder can affect hips, knees, ankles, fingers, and vertebrae. Individuals with arthritis often experience difficulty moving about and performing routine daily activities. Arthritis is especially prevalent in older adults (Daien & others, 2017; Koyanagi & others, 2018). Recent research documents the benefits of exercise in older adults with arthritis (AbouAssi & others, 2017; Allen & others, 2018). A recent study of women found that leisure-time physical inactivity was found to be a risk factor for subsequent development of arthritis (Di Giuseppe & others, 2015). In this study, women engaging in the most vigorous category of leisure-time activities were the least likely to develop arthritis.

How Would You…?

As a **health-care professional,** how would you educate older adults on the range of chronic diseases that are common for this age group?

arthritis Inflammation of the joints that is accompanied by pain, stiffness, and movement problems; especially common in older adults.

Osteoporosis

Normal aging brings some loss of bone tissue, but for some individuals loss of bone tissue becomes severe (Fougare & Cesari, 2019). **Osteoporosis** involves an extensive loss of bone tissue and is the main reason many older adults walk with a marked stoop (JafariNasabian & others, 2017). Women are especially vulnerable to osteoporosis, which is the leading cause of broken bones in women (Ballane & others, 2017; Madrasi & others, 2018). Approximately 80 percent of osteoporosis cases in the United States occur in females, 20 percent in males. Almost two-thirds of women over the age of 60 are affected by osteoporosis. It is more common in non-Latina White, thin, and small-framed women.

Osteoporosis is related to deficiencies in calcium, vitamin D, and estrogen, and to lack of exercise (Kemmler, Engelke, & von Stengel, 2016). To prevent osteoporosis, young and middle-aged women should eat foods rich in calcium, exercise regularly, and avoid smoking (Garcia-Gomariz & others, 2018; Giangregorio & El-Kotob, 2017; Kemmler, Kohl, & von Stengel, 2017; Varahra & others, 2018). Drugs such as Fosamax can be used to reduce the risk of osteoporosis (Tu & others, 2018).

osteoporosis A chronic condition that involves an extensive loss of bone tissue and is the main reason many older adults walk with a marked stoop. Women are especially vulnerable to osteoporosis.

Exercise, Nutrition, and Weight

Although we may be in the evening of our lives in late adulthood, we are not meant to live out our remaining years passively. Everything we know about older adults suggests they are healthier and happier the more active they are (Cho, Post, & Kim, 2018; Erickson & Oberlin, 2017; Henderson & others, 2018; Strandberg, 2019). Can regular exercise lead to a healthier late adulthood and increase longevity? How does eating a calorie-restricted diet and controlling weight also contribute to living longer?

Exercise

In one study, exercise literally made the difference between life and death for middle-aged and older adults (Blair, 1990). More than 10,000 men and women were divided into categories of low fitness, medium fitness, and high fitness (Blair & others, 1989). Then they were studied over a period of eight years. As shown in Figure 4, sedentary participants (low fitness) were more than twice as likely to die during the eight-year time span of the study as those who were moderately fit and more than three times as likely to die as those who were highly fit. The positive effects of being physically fit occurred for both men and women in this study. Further, in a recent study, relative to individuals with low physical fitness, those who increased from low to intermediate or high fitness were at a lower risk for all-cause mortality (Brawner & others, 2017).

Gerontologists increasingly recommend strength training in addition to aerobic activity and stretching for older adults (Falck & others, 2017; Grgic & others, 2018). Resistance exercise can preserve and possibly increase muscle mass in older adults (Grgic & others, 2018; Nordheim & others, 2018). One study found that core resistance and balance training improved older adult women's balance, trunk muscle strength, leg power, and body composition better than Pilates training (Markovic & others, 2015).

Exercise is an excellent way to maintain physical and cognitive skills as well as mental health (Brawner & others, 2017; Erickson & Oberlin, 2017; Frith & Loprinzi, 2018; Strandberg, 2019). The current recommendations for older adults' physical activity are 2 hours and 30 minutes of moderate-intensity aerobic activity (brisk walking, for example) per week and muscle strengthening activities on 2 or more days a week (Centers

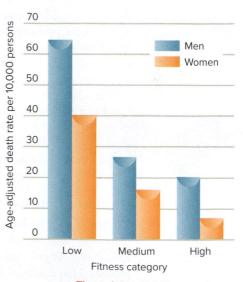

Figure 4 Physical Fitness and Mortality

In this study of middle-aged and older adults, being moderately fit or highly fit meant that individuals were less likely to die over a period of eight years than their less fit (more sedentary) counterparts (Blair & others, 1989).

Source: Blair, S. N., & others. "Physical fitness and all-cause mortality: A prospective study of healthy men and women." *Journal of the American Medical Association*, 262, 1989, 2395–2401.

In 1991 Johnny Kelley ran his sixtieth Boston Marathon, and in 2000 he was named "Runner of the Century" by *Runner's World* magazine. At 70 years of age, Kelley was still running 50 miles a week. At that point in his life, Kelley said, "I'm afraid to stop running. I feel so good. I want to stay alive." He lived 27 more years and died at age 97 in 2004.
©Charles Krupa/AP Images

for Disease Control and Prevention, 2018). In the recent recommendations, even greater benefits can be attained with 5 hours of moderate-intensity aerobic activity per week as well as walking on a regular basis. For example, a recent study of older adults found that walking a dog regularly was associated with better physical health (Curl, Bibbo, & Johnson, 2017).

Exercise helps people to live independent lives with dignity in late adulthood (Henderson & others, 2018; Marzetti & others, 2017; Strasser & others, 2018). At age 80, 90, and even 100, exercise can help prevent older adults from falling down or even being institutionalized (Hill & others, 2018). One study found that an exercise program reduced the number of falls in older adults with dementia (Burton & others, 2015). Exercise also is linked to the prevention or delayed onset of chronic diseases, such as cardiovascular disease, type 2 diabetes, and obesity, as well as improvement in the treatment of these diseases (Jaul & Barron, 2017; Mora & Valencia, 2018; Preston, Reynolds, & Pearson, 2018; Scott & others, 2018). Researchers also increasingly are finding that exercise improves cellular functioning in older adults. For example, researchers have discovered that aerobic exercise is linked to greater telomere length in older adults (Loprinzi & Loenneke, 2016).

Exercise improves older adults' brain and cognitive functioning (Coetsee & Terblanche, 2018; Smith, Hendy, & Tempest, 2018). For example, a research review concluded that more physically fit and active older adults have greater prefrontal cortex and hippocampal volume, a higher level of brain connectivity, and more efficient brain activity (Erickson, Hillman, & Kramer, 2015). Older adults who exercise regularly not only show better brain functioning, they also process information more effectively than older adults who are more sedentary (Erickson & Oberlin, 2017). In the research review on brain functioning, the researchers also found that more physically fit and active older adults show have superior memory functioning and a higher level of executive function (Erickson, Hillman, & Kramer, 2015).

Exercise also is linked to increased longevity. Energy expenditure during exercise of at least 1,000 kcal/week reduces mortality by about 30 percent, while 2,000 kcal/week reduces mortality by about 50 percent (Lee & Skerrett, 2001). One study of older adults found that total daily physical activity was linked to increased longevity across a four-year period (Buchman & others, 2012).

Nutrition and Weight

Scientists have accumulated considerable evidence that calorie restriction (CR) in laboratory animals can increase the animals' life spans (Someya & others, 2017). Research indicates that calorie restriction (CR) slows RNA decline during the aging process (Hou & others, 2016). Animals that are fed diets restricted in calories, although adequate in protein, vitamins, and minerals, live as much as 40 percent longer than animals that have unlimited access to food (Jolly, 2005). And chronic problems such as cardiovascular, kidney, and liver disease appear at a later age (Tanajak & others, 2017). Also, research indicates that CR may provide neuroprotection for an aging central nervous system (White & others, 2017). One study found that CR maintained more youthful functioning in the hippocampus, which is an important brain structure for memory (Schafer & others, 2015).

No one knows for certain how CR works to increase the life span of animals. Some scientists suggest that CR might lower the level of free radicals and reduce oxidative stress in cells (Tanajak & others, 2017). Others argue that CR might trigger a state of emergency called "survival mode" in which the body eliminates all unnecessary functions to focus only on staying alive (Schreiber, O'Leary, & Kennedy, 2016).

Whether similar very low-calorie diets can stretch the human life span is not known (Locher & others, 2016). In some instances, the animals in these studies received 40 percent less calories than normal. In humans, a typical level of calorie restriction involves a 30 percent decrease, which translates to about 1,120 calories a day for the average woman and 1,540 for the average man.

Health Treatment

About 3 percent of adults age 65 and older in the United States reside in a nursing home at some point in their lives. As older adults age, however, their probability of being in a nursing home or other extended-care facility increases. Twenty-three percent of adults aged 85 and older live in nursing homes or other extended-care facilities.

The quality of nursing homes and other extended-care facilities for older adults varies enormously and is a source of national concern (Kim, 2016; Marshall & Hale, 2018; Wangmo, Nordstrom, & Kressig, 2017). More than one-third are seriously deficient. They fail federally mandated inspections because they do not meet the minimum standards for physicians, pharmacists, and various rehabilitation specialists (occupational and physical therapists). Further concerns focus on the patient's right to privacy, access to medical information, safety, and lifestyle freedom within the individual's range of mental and physical capabilities.

Because of the inadequate quality and the escalating costs of many nursing homes, many specialists in the health problems of the aged stress that home health care, elder-care centers, and preventive medicine clinics are good alternatives (Kim, 2016). They are potentially less expensive than hospitals and nursing homes (Rotenberg & others, 2018). They also are less likely to engender the feelings of depersonalization and dependency that occur so often in residents of institutions. Currently, there is an increased demand for, and a shortage of, home care workers because of the increasing number of older adults and their preference to stay out of nursing homes (Franzosa, Tsui, & Baron, 2018).

In a classic study, Judith Rodin and Ellen Langer (1977) found that an important factor related to health, and even survival, in a nursing home is the patient's feelings of control and self-determination. One group was encouraged to make more day-to-day choices and thus to feel they had more control over their lives. They began to decide such matters as what they ate, when their visitors could come, what movies they saw, and who could come to their rooms. Another group in the same nursing home was told by the administrator how caring the nursing home staff was and how much they wanted to help, but these residents were given no added responsibility over their lives. Eighteen months later, the residents who had been given extra responsibility were healthier, happier, and more alert and active than the residents who had not received added responsibility. Even more important was the finding that after 18 months only half as many nursing home residents in the "responsibility" group had died as in the "dependent" group (see Figure 5). Perceived control over one's environment, then, can literally be a matter of life and death.

Geriatric nurses can be especially helpful in improving health treatment. To read about the work of one geriatric nurse, see *Careers in Life-Span Development*.

How Would You...?

As a **health-care professional,** how would you use your understanding of development in late adulthood to advocate for improved access to quality medical care for older adults?

How Would You...?

As a **psychologist,** how would you structure the environment of a nursing home to produce maximum health and psychological benefits for the residents?

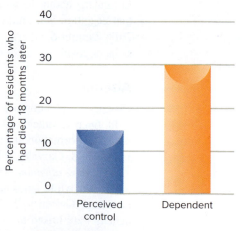

Figure 5 Perceived Control and Mortality
In the study by Rodin and Langer (1977), nursing home residents who were encouraged to feel more in control of their lives were more likely to be alive 18 months later than those who were treated as more dependent on the nursing home staff..
Source: Rodin, J., & Langer, E. J. "Long term effects of a control-relevant intervention with the institutionalized aged." *Journal of Personality and Social Psychology*, 35, 1977, 397–402.

Sarah Kagan, Geriatric Nurse

Sarah Kagan is a professor of nursing at the University of Pennsylvania School of Nursing. She provides nursing consultation to patients, their families, nurses, and physicians regarding the complex needs of older adults related to their hospitalization. She also consults on research and the management of patients who have head and neck cancers. Sarah teaches in the undergraduate nursing program, where she directs a course on "Nursing Care in the Older Adult." In 2003, she was awarded a MacArthur Fellowship for her work in the field of nursing.

Geriatric nurses like Sarah Kagan seek to prevent or intervene in the chronic or acute health problems of older adults. They may work in hospitals, nursing homes, schools of nursing, or with geriatric medical specialists or psychiatrists in a medical clinic or in private practice. Like pediatric nurses, geriatric nurses take courses in a school of nursing and obtain a degree in nursing, which takes from two to five years. They complete courses in

Sarah Kagan with a patient.
©Jacqueline Larma/AP Images

biological sciences, nursing care, and mental health as well as supervised clinical training in geriatric settings. They also may obtain a master's or doctoral degree in their specialty.

Cognitive Functioning

At age 89, the great pianist Arthur Rubinstein gave one of his best performances at New York's Carnegie Hall. When Pablo Casals was 95, a reporter asked him, "Mr. Casals, you are the greatest cellist who ever lived. Why do you still practice six hours a day?" Mr. Casals replied, "Because I feel like I am making progress" (Canfield & Hansen, 1995).

Multidimensionality and Multidirectionality

In thinking about the nature of cognitive change in adulthood, it is important to consider that cognition is a multidimensional concept (Kinugawa, 2019; Silverman & Schmeidler, 2018; Zammit & others, 2018). It is also important to consider that, although some dimensions of cognition might decline as we age, others might remain stable or even improve.

Attention

Changes in attention are important aspects of cognitive aging (Bechi Gabrielli & others, 2018; Oren & others, 2018). In many contexts older adults may not be able to focus on relevant information as effectively as younger adults can (Gilsoul & others, 2018; Ziegler, Janowich, & Gazzaley, 2018).

Selective attention, which consists of focusing on a specific aspect of experience that is relevant while ignoring others that are irrelevant, generally decreases in older adults (Zanto & Gazzaley, 2017). For example, a recent study found that selective attention deficits were linked to older adults' less competent driving (Venkatesan & others, 2018). However, on simple tasks involving a search for a feature, such as determining whether a target item is present on a computer screen, age differences are minimal when individuals are given sufficient practice. In one study, 10 weeks of speed of processing training improved the selective attention of older adults (O'Brien & others, 2013). Another study revealed that older adults who participated in 20 one-hour video game training sessions with a commercially available program (Lumosity) showed a significant reduction in distraction and increased alertness (Mayas & others, 2014). The Lumosity program sessions focus on problem solving, mental calculation, working memory, and attention.

Sustained attention is the ability to focus attention on a selected stimulus for a prolonged period of time. Researchers have found that older adults often perform as well as middle-aged and younger adults on measures of sustained attention (Berardi, Parasuraman, & Haxby, 2001). However, consistency of attention is important. A study of older adults found that the greater the variability in their sustained attention (vigilance), the more likely they were to experience falls (O'Halloran & others, 2011).

Researchers are exploring ways that older adults' attention might be improved. For example, in a recent experimental study, yoga practice that included postures, breathing, and meditation improved the attention and information processing of older adults (Gothe, Kramer, & McAuley, 2017). Also, another recent study found that when older adults regularly engaged in mindfulness meditation their goal-directed attention improved (Malinowski & others, 2017).

What are some developmental changes in attention in late adulthood?
©Digital Vision/PunchStock

Memory

Memory does change during aging, but not all types of memory change with age in the same way. We will begin by exploring possible changes in explicit and implicit memory.

Explicit and Implicit Memory Researchers have found that aging is linked with a decline in explicit memory (Reuter-Lorenz & Lustig, 2017). **Explicit memory** is memory of facts and experiences that individuals consciously know and can state. Explicit memory also is sometimes called *declarative memory*. Examples of explicit memory include recounting the plot of a movie you have seen or being at a grocery store and remembering what you wanted to buy. **Implicit memory** is memory without conscious recollection; it involves skills and routine procedures, such as driving a car or typing on a computer keyboard, that you perform without having to consciously think about what you are doing. Implicit memory is less likely to be adversely affected by aging than explicit memory is (Norman, Holmin, & Bartholomew, 2011).

Episodic and Semantic Memory Episodic and semantic memory are viewed as forms of explicit memory. **Episodic memory** is the retention of information about the where and when of life's happenings. For example, what was the color of the walls in your bedroom when you were a child? What did you eat for breakfast this morning?

Younger adults have better episodic memory than older adults have (Allen & others, 2018; Despres & others, 2017; Siegel & Castel, 2018). Also, older adults think that they can remember long-ago events better than more recent events. However, researchers consistently have found that the older the memory is, the less accurate it is in older adults (Smith, 1996). Also, one study found that episodic memory performance predicted which individuals would develop dementia 10 years prior to the clinical diagnosis of the disease (Boraxbekk & others, 2015). Further, in a recent study, a mindfulness training program was effective in improving episodic memory recall in older adults (Banducci & others, 2017).

Semantic memory is a person's knowledge about the world. It includes a person's fields of expertise, general academic knowledge of the sort learned in school, and "everyday knowledge" about the meanings of words, important places, and common things. Older adults often take longer to retrieve semantic information, but usually they can ultimately retrieve it. However, the ability to retrieve very specific information (such as names) usually declines in older adults (Hoffman & Morcom, 2018). For the most part, episodic memory declines more than semantic memory in older adults (Allen & others, 2018; Reuter-Lorenz & Lustig, 2017; Siegel & Castel, 2018).

Cognitive Resources: Working Memory and Perceptual Speed Two important cognitive resource mechanisms are working memory and

explicit memory Memory of facts and experiences that individuals consciously know and can state.

implicit memory Memory without conscious recollection; involves skills and routine procedures that are automatically performed.

episodic memory The retention of information about the where and when of life's happenings.

semantic memory A person's knowledge about the world—including a person's fields of expertise, general academic knowledge of the sort learned in school, and "everyday knowledge."

perceptual speed (Salthouse, 2017; Zammit & others, 2018). Recall that *working memory* is closely linked to short-term memory but places more emphasis on memory as a place for mental work (Baddeley, 2015, 2018a, b). Researchers have found declines in working memory during late adulthood (Dai, Thomas, & Taylor, 2018; Kilic, Sayali, & Oztekin, 2017; Nissim & others, 2017; Lopez-Higes & others, 2018). One study revealed that working memory continued to decline from 65 to 89 years of age (Elliott & others, 2011). Explanation of the decline in working memory in older adults focuses on their less efficient inhibition in preventing irrelevant information from entering working memory and their increased distractibility (Reuter-Lorenz & Lustig, 2017).

Is there plasticity in the working memory of older adults? Researchers have found that older adults' working memory can be improved through training (Cantarella & others, 2017). For example, researchers have found that strategy training improved the working memory of older adults (Bailey, Dunlosky, & Hertzog, 2014). Further, in a recent study, aerobic endurance was linked to better working memory in older adults (Zettel-Watson & others, 2017). In addition, a recent study revealed that imagery strategy training improved the working memory of older adults (Borella & others, 2017). Thus, there appears to be some plasticity in the working memory of older adults (Oh & others, 2018). However, a recent study of young, middle-aged, and older adults found that all age groups' working memory improved with working memory training, but the older adults had less improvement with training than the younger adults did (Rhodes & Katz, 2017).

Perceptual speed is another cognitive resource that has been studied by researchers on aging. Perceptual speed is the amount of time it takes to perform simple perceptual-motor tasks such as deciding whether pairs of two-digit or two-letter strings are the same, or how long it takes someone to step on the brakes when the car directly ahead stops. Perceptual speed shows considerable decline in late adulthood, and it is strongly linked with decline in working memory (Salthouse, 2017; Wilson & others, 2018). A recent study of older adults revealed that slower processing speed was associated with unsafe driving acts (Hotta & others, 2018). Another recent study found that slow processing speed predicted an increase in older adults' falls one year later (Davis & others, 2017). Also, in a 20-year longitudinal study of 42- to 97-year-olds, greater declines in processing speed were linked to increased mortality risk (Aichele, Rabbitt, & Ghisletta, 2015).

Recent research has included an effort to improve older adults' processing speed through exercise interventions. For example, a recent experimental study found that high-intensity aerobic training was more effective than moderate-intensity aerobic training or resistance training in improving older adults' processing speed (Coetsee & Terblanche, 2018). And in a recent study of older adults, playing processing speed games for five sessions a week over four weeks improved their processing speed (Nouchi & others, 2016).

Executive Function

We discussed executive function in a number of chapters earlier in the text. Recall that *executive function* is an umbrella-like concept that consists of a number of higher-level cognitive processes linked to the development of the brain's prefrontal cortex. Executive function involves managing one's thoughts to engage in goal-directed behavior and to exercise self-control (Perone, Almy & Zelazo, 2017).

How does executive function change in late adulthood? Earlier in this chapter, you read that the prefrontal cortex is one area of the brain that shrinks with aging, and recent research has linked this shrinkage with a decrease in working memory and other cognitive activities in older adults (Reuter-Lorenz & Lustig, 2017) Older adults are less effective in performing tasks involving executive function and have less effective cognitive control than younger adults do (Gaillardin & Baudry, 2018; Zammit & others, 2018). For example, in terms of cognitive flexibility, older adults don't perform as well as younger adults at switching back and forth between tasks or mental sets (Chiu & others, 2018). And in terms of cognitive inhibition, older adults are less effective than younger adults at inhibiting dominant or automatic responses (Lopez-Higes & others, 2018; Reuter-Lorenz & Lustig, 2017).

Although in general aspects of executive function decline in late adulthood, there is considerable variability in executive function among older adults. For example, some older adults have a better working memory and are more cognitively flexible than other older adults (McGough & others, 2018). And there is increasing research evidence that being physically active and engaging in aerobic exercise improves executive function in older adults (Eggenberger & others, 2015). For example, one study found that more physically fit older adults were more cognitively flexible than their less physically fit counterparts (Berryman & others, 2013). And a recent study of older adults revealed that across a 10-year period physically active women experienced less decline in executive function (Hamer, Muniz Terrera,& Demakokos, 2018).

Executive function increasingly is thought to be involved not only in cognitive performance but also in health, emotion regulation, adaptation to life's challenges, motivation, and social functioning. In one study, executive function but not memory predicted a higher risk of coronary heart disease and stroke three years later in older adults (Rostamian & others, 2015).

Wisdom

Does wisdom, like good wine, improve with age? What is this thing we call "wisdom"? **Wisdom** is expert knowledge about the practical aspects of life that permits excellent judgment about important matters. This practical knowledge involves exceptional insight into human development and interactions, good judgment, and an understanding of how to cope with difficult life problems. Thus, wisdom, more than standard conceptions of intelligence, focuses on life's pragmatic concerns and human conditions (Kuntzmann, 2019; Sternberg & Glueck, 2018; Sternberg & Hagen, 2018). A recent study found that self-reflective exploratory processing of difficult life experiences (meaning-making and personal growth) was linked to a higher level of wisdom (Westrate & Gluck, 2017).

In regard to wisdom, Paul Baltes and his colleagues (Baltes & Kunzmann, 2007; Baltes & Smith, 2008) have reached the following conclusions: (1) *High levels of wisdom are rare.* Few people, including older adults, attain a high level of wisdom. That only a small percentage of adults show wisdom supports the contention that it requires experience, practice, or complex skills. (2) *Factors other than age are critical for wisdom to develop to a high level.* For example, certain life experiences, such as being trained and working in a field involving difficult life problems and having wisdom-enhancing mentors, contribute to higher levels of wisdom. Also, people higher in wisdom have values that are more likely to consider the welfare of others than their own happiness. (3) *Personality-related factors, such as openness to experience, generativity, and creativity, are better predictors of wisdom than cognitive factors such as intelligence.*

Education, Work, and Health

Education, work, and health are three important influences on the cognitive functioning of older adults (Calero, 2019; Walker, 2019). They are also three of the most important factors involved in understanding why cohort effects need to be taken into account in studying the cognitive functioning of older adults. Indeed, cohort effects are very important considerations in the study of cognitive aging (Schaie, 2013, 2016). One study found that older adults assessed in 2013–2014 engaged in a higher level of abstract reasoning than their counterparts who had been assessed two decades earlier (Gerstorf & others, 2015). And a recent study of older adults in 10 European countries revealed improved memory between 2004 and 2013, with the changes more positive for older adults who had decreases in cardiovascular disease and increases in exercise and educational achievement (Hessel & others, 2018).

Education Successive generations in America's twentieth century were better educated, and this trend continues in the twenty-first century (Schaie, 2013, 2016). Educational experiences are positively correlated with scores on intelligence tests and information-processing tasks, such as memory exercises (Steffener & others, 2014). Also, one study found that older adults with a higher level of education had better cognitive functioning (Rapp & others, 2013).

wisdom Expert knowledge about the practical aspects of life that permits excellent judgment about important matters.

Work Successive generations have also had work experiences that included a stronger emphasis on cognitively oriented labor. Our great-grandfathers and grandfathers were more likely to be manual laborers than were our fathers, who are more likely to be involved in cognitively oriented occupations.

Researchers have found that when older adults engage in complex working tasks and challenging daily work activities their cognitive functioning shows less age-related decrease (Fisher & others, 2017; Lovden, Backman, & Lindenberger, 2017; Wang & Shi, 2016). For example, in a recent Australian study, older adults who had retired from occupations that involved higher complexity maintained their cognitive advantage over their counterparts whose occupations had involved lower complexity (Lane & others, 2017). And in another recent study of older adults working in low-complexity jobs, experiencing novelty in their work (assessed through recurrent work-task changes) was linked with better processing speed and working memory (Oltmanns & others, 2017).

Health Successive generations have also been healthier in late adulthood as more effective treatments for a variety of illnesses (such as hypertension) have been developed. Many of these illnesses, such as stroke, heart disease, and diabetes, have a negative impact on intellectual performance (Hagenaars & others, 2018; Li, Huang, & Gao, 2017; Loprinzi, Crush, & Joyner, 2017; van der Flier & others, 2018). Further, in a recent study of the oldest-old Chinese, early-stage chronic kidney disease was associated with cognitive decline (Bai & others, 2017). Researchers also have found age-related cognitive decline in adults with mood disorders such as depression (Bourassa & others, 2017; Farioli-Vecchioli & others, 2018; Knight, Rastegar, & Kim, 2016). Thus, some of the decline in intellectual performance found for older adults is likely due to health-related factors rather than to age per se (Drew & others, 2017; Koyanagi & others, 2018).

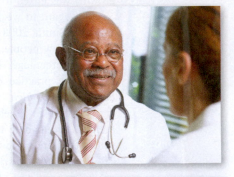

Use It or Lose It

Changes in cognitive activity patterns might result in disuse and consequent atrophy of cognitive skills (Calero, 2019; Kinugawa, 2019; Kuntzmann, 2019; Lovden, Backman, & Lindenberger, 2017; Oltmanns & others, 2017). This concept is captured in the phrase "Use it or lose it." The mental activities that are likely to benefit the maintenance of cognitive skills in older adults include activities such as reading books, doing crossword puzzles, and going to lectures and concerts. In one study, reading daily was linked to reduced mortality in men in their seventies (Jacobs & others, 2008). In another study, 75- to 85-year-olds were assessed for an average of five years (Hall & others, 2009). At the beginning of the research, the older adults indicated how often they participated in six activities on a daily basis: reading, writing, doing crossword puzzles, playing cards or board games, having group discussions, and playing music. For each additional activity the older adult engaged in, the onset of rapid memory loss was delayed by 0.18 year. For older adults who participated in 11 activities per week compared with their counterparts who engaged in only 4 activities per week, the point at which accelerated memory decline occurred was delayed by 1.29 years. And in an analysis of older adults over a 12-year period, those who reduced their cognitive lifestyle activities (such as using a computer or playing bridge)

How are education, work, and health linked to cognitive functioning in older adults?
(*Top*) ©Silverstock/Getty Images; (*middle*) ©Kurt Paulus/ Getty Images; (*bottom*) ©Tom Grill/Corbis RF

subsequently showed declines in verbal speed, episodic memory, and semantic memory (Small & others, 2012). These declines in cognitive functioning were linked to subsequent lower engagement in social activities.

Training Cognitive Skills

If older adults are losing cognitive skills, can these skills be regained through training? An increasing number of research studies indicate that cognitive skills can be restored to a degree (Bonfiglio & others, 2018; Calero, 2019; Cantarella & others, 2017; Gmiat & others, 2018; Kinugawa, 2019; Lopez-Higes & others, 2018; Reuter-Lorenz & Lustig, 2017).

Consider a study of 60- to 90-year-olds which found that sustained engagement in cognitively demanding, novel activities improved the older adults' episodic memory (Park & others, 2014). To produce this result, the older adults spent an average of 16.5 hours a week for three months learning how to quilt or use digital photography. In a more recent study, 60- to 90-year-olds who participated in iPad training 15 hours a week for 3 months improved their episodic memory and processing speed compared with their counterparts who engaged in social or non-challenging activities (Chan & others, 2016).

Members of the Young@Heart chorus have an average age of 80. Young@Heart became a hit documentary in 2008. The documentary displays the singing talents, energy, and optimism of a remarkable group of older adults, who clearly are on the "use it" side of "use it or lose it."
©Everett Collection, Inc./Alamy

Two key conclusions can be derived from research in this area: (1) training can improve the cognitive skills of many older adults, but (2) there is some loss in plasticity in late adulthood, especially in those who are 85 and older (Baltes, Lindenberger, & Staudinger, 2006).

Meta-examinations of four longitudinal observational studies (Long Beach Longitudinal Study; Origins of Variance in the Oldest-old [Octo-Twin] Study in Sweden; Seattle Longitudinal Study; and Victoria Longitudinal Study in Canada) of older adults' naturalistic cognitive activities found that changes in cognitive activity predicted cognitive outcomes as long as two decades later (Brown & others, 2012; Lindwall & others, 2012; Mitchell & others, 2012; Rebok & others, 2014). However, the hypothesis that engaging in cognitive activity at an earlier point in development might have improved older adults' ability to later withstand cognitive decline was not supported. On a positive note, when older adults continued to increase their engagement in cognitive and physical activities, they were better able to maintain their cognitive functioning in late adulthood.

The Stanford Center for Longevity (2011) and together the Stanford Center for Longevity and the Max Planck Institute for Human Development (2014) reported information based on a consensus of leading scientists in the field of aging on how successfully the cognitive skills of older adults can be improved. One of their concerns is the misinformation given to the public touting products to improve the functioning of the mind for which there is no scientific evidence. For example, nutritional supplements have been advertised as "magic bullets" to slow the decline of mental functioning and improve the mental ability of older adults. Some of the claims are reasonable but not scientifically tested, while others are unrealistic and implausible (Willis & Belleville, 2016).

A research review of dietary supplements and cognitive aging did indicate that ginkgo biloba was linked with improvements in some aspects of attention in older adults and that omega-3 polyunsaturated fatty acids (fish oil) was related to reduced risk of age-related cognitive decline (Gorby, Brownawell, & Falk, 2010). In this research review, there was no evidence of cognitive improvements in aging adults who took supplements containing ginseng and glucose. Also, an experimental study with 50- to 75-year-old females found that those who took fish oil for 26 weeks had improved executive function and beneficial effects in a number of areas of brain functioning compared with their female counterparts who took a placebo pill (Witte & others, 2014). In another study, fish oil supplement use was linked to higher cognitive scores and less atrophy in one or more brain regions (Daiello & others, 2015). And in a recent study, fish oil supplementation improved the working memory of older adults (Boespflug & others, 2016). Overall, though, research has not provided consistent plausible evidence that dietary supplements can accomplish major cognitive goals in aging adults over a number of years.

How Would You...?

As a **psychologist,** how would you design activities and interventions to elicit and maintain cognitive vitality in older adults?

However, some software-based cognitive training games have been found to improve older adults' cognitive functioning (Gillian & others, 2019; Ordonez & others, 2017; West & others, 2017). For example, a study of 60- to 85-year-olds found that a multitasking video game that simulates day-to-day driving experiences (NeuroRacer) improved cognitive control skills, such as sustained attention and working memory, immediately after training on the video game and six months later (Anguera & others, 2013). In another recent study, computerized cognitive training slowed the decline in older adults' overall memory performance, an outcome that was linked to enhanced connectivity between the hippocampus and prefrontal cortex (Suo & others, 2016). And in another recent study, cognitive training using virtual reality-based games with stroke patients improved their attention and memory (Gamito & others, 2017). Nonetheless, it is possible that the training games may improve cognitive skills in a laboratory setting but not generalize to gains in the real world.

Also, recall our discussion earlier in the chapter that indicated regular exercise can improve the cognitive functioning of older adults. For example, a recent research review concluded that engaging in low or moderate levels of exercise was linked to improved cognitive functioning in older adults with chronic diseases (Coetsee & Terblanche, 2018; Erickson & Oberlin, 2017; Gmiat & others, 2018; Strandberg, 2019; Walker, 2019). Also, in a recent study, engagement in physical activity in late adulthood was linked to less cognitive decline (Gow, Pattie, & Deary, 2017).

In sum, improvements in the cognitive vitality of older adults can be accomplished through some types of cognitive, physical fitness, and nutritional interventions (Farioli-Vecchioli & others, 2018; Gillian & others, 2019; Perkisas & Vandewoude, 2019; Reuter-Lorenz & Lustig, 2017; Strandberg, 2019). However, benefits have not been observed in all studies (Salthouse, 2017). An important finding in the meta-analysis of four longitudinal studies was that older adults were better able to maintain their cognitive functioning over a prolonged period of time when increasing their engagement in cognitive and physical activities (Rebok & others, 2014). Further research is needed to determine more precisely which cognitive improvements occur in older adults as a result of training (Salthouse, 2017).

Cognitive Neuroscience and Aging

On several occasions in this chapter, we have noted that certain regions of the brain are involved in links between aging and cognitive functioning. In this section, we further explore the brain's role in aging and cognitive functioning. The field of *cognitive neuroscience* has emerged as the major discipline that studies links between brain activity and cognitive functioning (Kennedy & others, 2017; Kinugawa, 2019; Park & Festini, 2018). This field especially relies on brain-imaging techniques, such as fMRI, PET, and DTI (diffusion tensor imaging) to reveal the areas of the brain that are activated when individuals engage in certain cognitive activities (Madden & Parks, 2017; Park & Festini, 2017). For example, as an older adult is asked to encode and then retrieve verbal materials or images of scenes, the older adult's brain activity will be monitored by an fMRI brain scan.

Changes in the brain can influence cognitive functioning, and changes in cognitive functioning can influence the brain (Kinugawa, 2019). For example, aging of the brain's prefrontal cortex may produce a decline in working memory (Reuter-Lorenz & Lustig, 2017). And, when older adults do not regularly use their working memory (recall the section "Use It or Lose It"), neural connections in the prefrontal lobe may atrophy.

Further, cognitive interventions that activate older adults' working memory may increase these neural connections.

Although in its infancy as a field, the cognitive neuroscience of aging is beginning to uncover some important links between aging, the brain, and cognitive functioning (Ezaki & others, 2018; Kinugawa, 2019; Rugg, 2017). These include the following:

- Neural circuits in specific regions of the brain's prefrontal cortex decline, and this decline is linked to poorer performance by older adults on tasks involving complex reasoning, working memory, and episodic memory (Grady, 2017; Reuter-Lorenz & Lustig, 2017) (see Figure 6).

- Recall from earlier in the chapter that older adults are more likely than younger adults to use both hemispheres of the brain to compensate for age-related declines in attention, memory, and language (Davis & others, 2012; Reuter-Lorenz, Festini, & Jantz, 2016). Two neuroimaging studies revealed that better memory performance in older adults was linked to higher levels of activity in both hemispheres of the brain during information processing (Angel & others, 2011; Manenti, Cotelli, & Miniussi, 2011).

- Functioning of the hippocampus declines but to a lesser degree than the functioning of the frontal lobes in older adults (Antonenko & Floel, 2014). In K. Warner Schaie's (2013) recent research, individuals whose memory and executive function declined in middle age had more hippocampal atrophy in late adulthood, but those whose memory and executive function improved in middle age did not show a decline in hippocampal functioning in late adulthood.

- Patterns of neural decline with aging are more noticeable for retrieval than for encoding (Gutchess & others, 2005).

- Compared with younger adults, older adults often show greater activity in the frontal and parietal lobes of the brain on simple tasks, but as attentional demands increase, older adults display less effective functioning in the frontal and parietal lobes of the brain that involve cognitive control (Campbell & others, 2012).

- Cortical thickness in the frontoparietal network predicts executive function in older adults (Schmidt & others, 2016).

- Younger adults have better connectivity between brain regions than older adults (Damoiseaux, 2017; Madden & Parks, 2017).

- An increasing number of cognitive and fitness training studies include brain imaging techniques such as fMRI to assess the results of such training on brain functioning (Kinugawa, 2019; Walker, 2019). In one study, older adults who walked one hour a day three days a week for six months showed increased volume in the frontal and temporal lobes of the brain (Colcombe & others, 2006).

Figure 6 The Prefrontal Cortex Advances in neuroimaging are allowing researchers to make significant progress in connecting changes in the brain with cognitive development. Shown here is an fMRI of the brain's prefrontal cortex. *What links have been found between the prefrontal cortex, aging, and cognitive development?*
Courtesy of Dr. Sam Gilbert, Institute of Cognitive Neuroscience, UK

Work and Retirement

What percentage of older adults continue to work? How productive are they? Who adjusts best to retirement? These are some of the questions we will examine in this section.

Work

In 2000, 23 percent of U.S. 65- to 69-year-olds were in the work force; in 2015, this percentage had jumped to 32 percent (Short, 2018). For 70- to 74-year-olds, in 2000, 13 percent were in the workforce, but this percentage had increased to 19 percent in 2015. This increase has occurred more for women than men. For example, labor force participation by 75-and-over women has risen 87 percent since 2000, while participation in the work force by 75-and-over men has increased 45 percent (Short, 2018). A recent study found that older workers worked beyond retirement age to improve their financial status, health, knowledge levels, and sense of purpose (Sewdas & others, 2017).

Since the mid-1990s, a significant shift has occurred in the percentage of older adults working part-time or full-time (U.S. Bureau of Labor Statistics, 2008). After 1995, of the adults 65 and older in the workforce, those engaging in full-time work rose substantially and those working part-time decreased considerably. This significant rise in full-time employment likely reflects the increasing number of older adults who realize that they may not have adequate money to fund their retirement (Rix, 2011). One survey revealed that 47 percent of Americans 50 years and older now expect to retire later than they had previously envisioned (Associated Press–NORC Center for Public Affairs Research, 2013). Seventy-eight percent of the workers cited financial reasons, with many responding that they had less money available for retirement than they had before the 2008 recession. A recent study found that baby boomers expect to work longer than their predecessors in prior generations (Dong & others, 2017).

Older workers have lower rates of absenteeism, fewer accidents, and increased job satisfaction compared with their younger counterparts (Warr, 2004). This means that older workers can be of considerable value to a company, above and beyond their cognitive competence. Changes in federal law now allow individuals over the age of 65 to continue working in most jobs.

An increasing number of middle-aged and older adults are embarking on a second or a third career (Cahill & others, 2018). In some cases, this is an entirely different type of work or a continuation of previous work but at a reduced level. Many older adults also participate in unpaid work as volunteers or as active participants in a voluntary association. These options afford older adults opportunities for productive activity, social interaction, and a positive identity (Topa, Depolo, & Alcover, 2018).

Several studies have found that older adults who continue to work have better physical and cognitive profiles that those who retire. For example, one study found that physical functioning declined faster in retirement than in full-time work for employees 65 years of age and older, with the difference not explained by absence of chronic diseases and lifestyle risks (Stenholm & others, 2014). And in another recent study of older adults, those who continued to work in paid jobs had better physical and cognitive functioning than retirees (Tan & others, 2017).

Ninety-two-year-old Russell "Bob" Harrell (right) puts in 12-hour days at Sieco Consulting Engineers in Columbus, Indiana. A highway and bridge engineer, he designs and plans roads. James Rice (age 48), a vice president of client services at Sieco, says that Harrell wants to learn something new every day and that he has learned many life lessons from being around him. Harrell says he is not planning to retire. *What are some variations in work and retirement in older adults?*
©Greg Sailor

Adjustment to Retirement

In the past, when most people reached an accepted retirement age, usually in their sixties, retirement meant a one-way exit from full-time work to full-time leisure (Wang & Shi, 2016). Increasingly, individuals are delaying retirement and moving into and out of work (Cahill & others, 2018; Kojola & Moen, 2016). Currently, there is no single dominant pattern to retirement but rather a diverse mix of pathways involving occupational identities, finances, health, and expectations and perceptions of retirement (Kojola & Moen, 2016). Leading expert Phyllis Moen (2007) described how today, when people

What are some keys to adjusting effectively in retirement?
©Bronwyn Kidd/Getty Images

reach their sixties, the life path they follow is less clear: (1) some individuals don't retire from their careers; (2) some retire from their career work and then take up a new and different job; (3) some retire from career jobs but do volunteer work; (4) some retire from a post-retirement job and go on to yet another job; (5) some move in and out of the workforce, so they never really have a "career" job from which they retire; (6) some individuals who are in poor health move to a disability status and eventually into retirement; and (7) some who are laid off define it as "retirement."

How Would You...?

As a **psychologist,** how would you assist older adults in making appropriate adjustments and preparations for a psychologically satisfying retirement?

A 2017 survey indicated that only 18 percent of American workers feel very confident that they will have enough money to have a comfortable retirement (Greenwald, Copeland, & VanDerhei, 2017). However, 60 percent said they feel somewhat or very confident they will have enough money to live a comfortable retirement. In this survey, 30 percent of American workers reported that preparing for retirement made them feel mentally or emotionally distressed. In regard to retirement income, the two main worries of individuals as they approach retirement are: (1) having to draw retirement income from savings, and (2) paying for health-care expenses (Yakoboski, 2011).

Older adults who adjust best to retirement are healthy, have adequate income, are active, are educated, have an extended social network including both friends and family, and usually were satisfied with their lives before they retired (Ilmakunnas & Ilmakunnas, 2018; Miller, 2018). Older adults who have inadequate income and are in poor health, and who must adjust to other stress that occurs at the same time as retirement, such as the death of a spouse, have the most difficult time adjusting to retirement (Biro & Elek, 2018; Mossburg, 2018).

Mental Health

Although a substantial portion of the population can now look forward to a longer life, that life may be hampered by a mental disorder in old age (Brown & Wolf, 2018; Bruce & Sirey, 2018; Guo & others, 2018; Szanto & others, 2018; van den Brink & others, 2018)—a troubling prospect to individuals and their families and costly to society. Mental disorders make individuals increasingly dependent on the help and care of others. The cost of disorders such as dementia in older adults is estimated at more than $40 billion per year in the United States. More important, though, is the loss of human potential and the suffering involved (Frank & others, 2018; Wolff & others, 2017). Although mental disorders in older adults are a major concern, however, older adults do not have a higher overall incidence of mental disorders than younger adults do (Busse & Blazer, 1996).

Dementia and Alzheimer Disease

Among the most debilitating of mental disorders in older adults are the dementias. In recent years, extensive attention has been focused on the most common dementia, Alzheimer disease.

Dementia

Dementia is a global term for any neurological disorder in which the primary symptoms involve a deterioration of mental functioning. Individuals with dementia often lose the ability to care for themselves and may become unable to recognize familiar surroundings and people—including family members (Brown & Wolf, 2018). It is estimated that 23 percent of women and 17 percent of men 85 years and older are at risk for developing dementia (Alzheimer's Association, 2014). However, these estimates may be high because of the Alzheimer's Association's lobbying efforts to increase funding for research and treatment facilities. Dementia is a broad category, and it is important that every effort is made to narrow the older adult's disorder and

dementia A global term for any neurological disorder in which the primary symptoms involve a deterioration of mental functioning.

Alzheimer disease A progressive, irreversible brain disorder characterized by a gradual deterioration of memory, reasoning, language, and eventually physical function.

determine a specific cause of the deteriorating mental functioning (Dooley, Bass, & McCabe, 2018; MacNeil Vroomen & others, 2018; Mao & others, 2018; Morikawa & others, 2017; Wolters & others, 2018).

Alzheimer Disease

One form of dementia is **Alzheimer disease**—a progressive, irreversible brain disorder that is characterized by a gradual deterioration of memory, reasoning, language, and eventually, physical function. In 2018, an estimated 5.7 million adults in the United States had Alzheimer disease, and it is projected that 10 million baby boomers will develop Alzheimer disease (Alzheimer's Association, 2018). Ten percent of individuals 65 and older have Alzheimer disease. The percentage of individuals with Alzheimer disease increases dramatically at older ages: 3 percent of 65- to 74-year-olds, 17 percent of 75- to 84-year-olds, and 32 percent of people 85 and older (Alzheimer's Association, 2018).

Women are more likely than men to develop Alzheimer disease because they live longer than men and their longer life expectancy increases the number of years during which they can develop it. It is estimated that Alzheimer disease triples the health-care costs of Americans 65 years of age and older (Alzheimer's Association, 2018). Because of the increasing prevalence of Alzheimer disease, researchers have stepped up their efforts to discover the causes of the disease and to find more effective ways to treat it (Di Domenico & others, 2018; Lin & others, 2017; Lin, Zheng, & Zhang, 2018; Perneczky, 2018; Wolters & others, 2018).

Causes and Risk Factors Once destruction of brain tissue occurs from Alzheimer disease, it is unlikely that treatment of the disease will reverse the damage, at least based on the state of research now and in the foreseeable future. Alzheimer disease involves a deficiency in the brain messenger chemical *acetylcholine,* which plays an important role in memory (Kamal & others, 2017; Karthivashan & others, 2018; Kumar & others, 2018). Also, as Alzheimer disease progresses, the brain shrinks and deteriorates (see Figure 7). This deterioration is characterized by the formation of *amyloid plaques* (dense deposits of protein that accumulate in the blood vessels) (Kocahan & Dogan, 2017; Morbelli & Bauckneht, 2018) and *neurofibrillary tangles* (twisted fibers that build up in neurons) (Villemagne & others, 2018; Xiao & others, 2017). Neurofibrillary tangles consist mainly of a protein called *tau* (Islam & others, 2017; Kuznetsov & Kuznetsov, 2018). Currently, there is considerable research interest in the roles that amyloid and tau play in Alzheimer disease (Di Domenico & others, 2018; Michalicova & others, 2017; Park & Festini, 2018; Timmers & others, 2018).

Until recently, neuroimaging of plaques and tangles had not been developed. However, new neuroimaging techniques have been developed that can detect these key indicators of Alzheimer disease in the brain (Park & Festini, 2018). This imaging breakthrough is providing scientists with an improved opportunity to identify the transition from healthy cognitive functioning to the earliest indication of Alzheimer disease (Morbelli & Bauckneht, 2018).

Figure 7 Two Brains: Normal Aging and Alzheimer Disease The photograph on the left shows a slice of a normal aging brain, while the photograph on the right shows a slice of a brain ravaged by Alzheimer disease. Notice the deterioration and shrinking in the Alzheimer disease brain.
©Alfred Pasieka/Science Source

There is increasing interest in the role that oxidative stress might play in Alzheimer disease (Butterfield, 2018; D'Acunto & others, 2018; Mantzavinosa & others, 2017). Oxidative stress occurs when the body fails to defend itself against free-radical attacks and oxidation (Chhetri, King, & Gueven, 2018; Feltosa, 2018). Recall from earlier in the chapter that free-radical theory is a major theory of aging.

Although scientists are not certain what causes Alzheimer disease, age is an important risk factor and genes also are likely to play an important role (Del-Aguila & others, 2018; Lane-Donovan & Herz, 2017). The number of individuals with Alzheimer disease doubles for every five years after the age of 65. A gene called *apolipoprotein E (ApoE)* is linked to an increasing presence of plaques and tangles in the brain. Special attention has focused on an allele (an alternative form of a gene) labeled ApoE4 that is a strong risk factor for Alzheimer disease (Carmona, Hardy, & Guerreiro, 2018; Fladby & others, 2017). More than 60 percent of individuals with Alzheimer disease have at least one ApoE4 allele, and females are more likely to have this allele than males (Dubal & Rogine, 2017). Indeed, the ApoE4 gene is the strongest genetic predictor of late-onset (65 years and older) Alzheimer disease (Giri & others, 2017). Despite links between the presence of the ApoE4 gene and Alzheimer disease, less than 50 percent of individuals who carry the ApoE4 gene develop dementia in old age. Advances as a result of the Human Genome Project have recently allowed identification of other genes that are risk factors for Alzheimer disease, although they are not as strongly linked to the disease as the ApoE4 gene is (Costa & others, 2017; Shi & others, 2017). APP, PSEN1, and PSEN2 also are gene mutations that are linked to early-onset Alzheimer disease (Carmona, Hardy, & Guerreiro, 2018).

Although individuals with a family history of Alzheimer disease are at greater risk, the disease is complex and likely to be caused by a number of factors, including lifestyles (Shackleton, Crawford, & Bachmeier, 2017). Researchers are increasingly interested in exploring how epigenetics may improve understanding of Alzheimer disease (Gangisetty, Cabrera, & Murugan, 2018; Sharma, Raghuraman, & Sajikumar, 2018). A particular focus is DNA methylation, which we discussed in the chapter on "Biological Beginnings." Recall that DNA methylation involves tiny atoms attaching themselves to the outside of a gene, a process that is increased through exercise and healthy diet but reduced by tobacco use (Marioni & others, 2018; Zaghlool & others, 2018). Thus, lifestyles likely interact with genes to influence Alzheimer disease (Kader, Ghai, & Mahraj, 2018; Shackleton, Crawford, & Bachmeier, 2017).

For many years, scientists have known that a healthy diet, exercise, and weight control can lower the risk of cardiovascular disease. Now, they are finding that these healthy lifestyle factors may lower the risk of Alzheimer disease as well (Bleckwenn & others, 2017; Wolters & others, 2018). Recently, a number of cardiac risk factors have been implicated in Alzheimer disease—obesity, smoking, hypertension, arteriosclerosis, high cholesterol, lipids, and permanent atrial fibrillation (Falsetti & others, 2018; Ihara & Washida, 2018; Rodrique & Bischof, 2017). One of the best strategies for intervening in the lives of people who are at risk for Alzheimer disease is to improve their cardiac functioning through diet, drugs, and exercise (Law & others, 2018; McLimans & others, 2017; Pedrinolla, Schena, & Venturelli, 2018).

A meta-analysis of modifiable risk factors in Alzheimer disease found that some medical exposures (estrogen, statins, and nonsteroidal anti-inflammatory drugs) and some dietary factors (folate, vitamin E/C, and coffee) were linked to a reduced incidence of Alzheimer disease (Xu & others, 2015). Also in this meta-analysis, some preexisting diseases (arteriosclerosis and hypertension) as well as depression increased the risk of developing Alzheimer disease. Further, cognitive activity and low-to-moderate alcohol use decreased the risk of developing Alzheimer disease.

Mild Cognitive Impairment *Mild cognitive impairment (MCI)* represents a transitional state between the cognitive changes of normal aging and very early Alzheimer disease and other dementias (Cespedes & others, 2017; Gasquoine, 2018). MCI is increasingly recognized as a risk factor for Alzheimer disease. Estimates indicate that as many as 10 to 20 percent of

How Would You...?

As a **health-care professional,** how would you respond to an older adult who is concerned that her declining short-term memory is an early symptom of Alzheimer disease?

individuals age 65 and older have MCI (Alzheimer's Association, 2017). Some individuals with MCI do not go on to develop Alzheimer disease, but MCI is a risk factor for Alzheimer disease. One study revealed that individuals with mild cognitive impairment who developed Alzheimer disease had at least one copy of the ApoE4 gene (Alegret & others, 2014). In this study, the extent of memory impairment was the key factor that was linked to the speed of decline from mild cognitive impairment to Alzheimer disease. Distinguishing between individuals who merely have age-associated declines in memory and those with MCI is difficult, as is predicting which individuals with MCI will subsequently develop Alzheimer disease (Eliassen & others, 2017; Mendoza Laiz & others, 2018).

Drug Treatment of Alzheimer Disease Five drugs have been approved by the U.S. Food and Drug Administration (FDA) for the treatment of Alzheimer disease (Almeida, 2018). Three of the medications, Aricept (donepezil), Razadyne (galantamine), and Exelon (rivastigmine), are cholinesterase inhibitors designed to improve memory and other cognitive functions by increasing levels of acetylcholine in the brain (Gareri & others, 2017). A fourth drug, Namenda (memantine), regulates the activity of glutamate, which is involved in processing information. Namzatric, a combination of memantine and donepezil, is the fifth approved medicine to treat Alzheimer disease; this medicine is designed to improve cognition and overall mental ability (Almeida, 2018). A research review concluded that cholinesterase inhibitors do not reduce progression to dementia from mild cognitive impairment (Masoodi, 2013). Also, keep in mind that the current drugs used to treat Alzheimer disease only slow the downward progression of the disease; they do not address its cause (Boccardi & others, 2017). Also, no drugs have yet been approved by the Food and Drug Administration (FDA) for the treatment of MCI (Alzheimer's Association, 2018).

Caring for Individuals with Alzheimer Disease A special concern is caring for Alzheimer patients (Alzheimer's Association, 2018; Callahan & others, 2017; Merlo & others, 2018; Wolff & others, 2018). Health-care professionals believe that the family can be an important support system for the Alzheimer patient, but this support can have costs for family members, who can become emotionally and physically drained by the extensive care required for a person with Alzheimer disease (Wawrziczny & others, 2017; White & others, 2018). A recent study confirmed that family caregivers' health-related quality of life in the first three years after they began caring for a family member with Alzheimer disease deteriorated more than that of their counterparts of the same age and gender who were not caring for an Alzheimer patient (Valimaki & others, 2016). Another study compared family members' perceptions of caring for someone with Alzheimer disease, cancer, or schizophrenia (Papastavrou & others, 2012). In this study, the highest perceived burden was reported for Alzheimer disease.

Respite care (services that provide temporary relief to those who are caring for individuals with disabilities, illnesses, or the elderly) has been developed to help people who have to meet the day-to-day needs of Alzheimer patients. This type of care provides much-needed breaks from the burden of providing chronic care (Washington & Tachman, 2017; Wolff & others, 2018).

Parkinson Disease

Another type of dementia is **Parkinson disease,** a chronic, progressive disorder characterized by muscle tremors, slowing of movement, and partial facial paralysis. Parkinson disease is triggered by degeneration of dopamine-producing neurons in the brain (Chung & others, 2018; Goldstein & others, 2018; Rastedt, Vaughan, & Foster, 2017). Dopamine is a neurotransmitter that is necessary for normal brain functioning. Why these neurons degenerate is not known.

The main treatment for Parkinson disease involves administering drugs that enhance the effect of dopamine (dopamine agonists) in the disease's earlier stages and later administering the drug L-dopa, which is converted by the brain into dopamine (Juhasz & others, 2017; Radhakrishnan & Goval, 2018). However, it is difficult to determine the correct level of dosage

Parkinson disease A chronic, progressive disease characterized by muscle tremors, slowing of movement, and partial facial paralysis.

of L-dopa, and the medication loses its efficacy over time (Nomoto & others, 2009). Another treatment for advanced Parkinson disease is deep brain stimulation (DBS), which involves implantation of electrodes within the brain (Krishnan & others, 2018; Singh & others, 2018; Stefani & others, 2017). The electrodes are then stimulated by a pacemaker-like device. Stem cell transplantation and gene therapy also offer hope for treating Parkinson disease (Choi & others, 2017; Parmar, 2018).

Summary

Longevity, Biological Aging, and Physical Development

- Life expectancy has increased dramatically, but life span has not. In the United States, the number of people living to age 100 or older is increasing.
- Biological theories of aging include evolutionary theory, cellular clock theory, free-radical theory, mitochondrial theory, sirtuin theory, the mTOR pathway theory, and hormonal stress theory.
- The aging brain retains considerable plasticity and adaptability.
- Among physical changes that accompany aging are slower movement and the appearance of wrinkled skin and age spots on the skin. There are also declines in perceptual abilities, cardiovascular functioning, and lung capacity. Many older adults' sleep difficulties are linked to health problems.
- Although sexual activity declines in late adulthood, many individuals continue to be sexually active as long as they are healthy.

Health

- The probability of disease or illness increases with age. Chronic disorders, such as arthritis and osteoporosis, become more common in late adulthood. Cancer and cardiovascular disease are the leading causes of death in late adulthood.
- The physical benefits of exercise have been clearly demonstrated in older adults. Leaner adults, especially women, live longer, healthier lives.
- The quality of nursing homes varies enormously. Alternatives include home health care, elder-care centers, and preventive medicine clinics.

Cognitive Functioning

- Although older adults are not as adept as middle-aged and younger adults at complicated tasks that involve selective

and divided attention, they perform just as well on measures of sustained attention. Some aspects of memory, such as episodic memory, decline in older adults. Components of executive function—such as cognitive control and working memory—decline in late adulthood, although there is individual variation in older adults' executive function. Wisdom has been theorized to increase in older adults, but researchers have not consistently documented this increase.
- Older adults who engage in cognitive activities, especially challenging ones, have higher cognitive functioning than those who don't use their cognitive skills.
- Cognitive and fitness training can improve some cognitive skills of older adults, but there is some loss of plasticity in late adulthood.
- There is considerable interest in the cognitive neuroscience of aging. A consistent finding is a decline in the functioning of the prefrontal cortex in late adulthood, which is linked to poorer performance in complex reasoning and aspects of memory.

Work and Retirement

- Increasing numbers of older adults engage in part-time work or volunteer work and continue being productive throughout late adulthood.
- Healthy, economically stable, educated, satisfied individuals with an extended social network adjust best to retirement.

Mental Health

- Individuals with dementias, such as Alzheimer disease, often lose the ability to care for themselves. Alzheimer disease is by far the most common dementia.
- Parkinson disease is a chronic, progressive disease characterized by muscle tremors, slowing of movement, and facial tremors.

Key Terms

Alzheimer disease
arthritis
cataracts
cellular clock theory
dementia
episodic memory

evolutionary theory of aging
explicit memory
free-radical theory
glaucoma
hormonal stress theory
implicit memory

life expectancy
life span
macular degeneration
mitochondrial theory
mTOR pathway
osteoporosis

Parkinson disease
semantic memory
sirtuins
wisdom

16 Socioemotional Development in Late Adulthood

CHAPTER OUTLINE

THEORIES OF SOCIOEMOTIONAL DEVELOPMENT

Erikson's Theory

Activity Theory

Socioemotional Selectivity Theory

Selective Optimization with Compensation Theory

PERSONALITY AND SOCIETY

Personality

Older Adults in Society

FAMILIES AND SOCIAL RELATIONSHIPS

Lifestyle Diversity

Attachment

Older Adult Parents and Their Adult Children

Friendship

Social Support and Social Integration

Altruism and Volunteerism

ETHNICITY, GENDER, AND CULTURE

Ethnicity

Gender

Culture

SUCCESSFUL AGING

Stories of Life-Span Development: Bob Cousy, Adapting to Life as an Older Adult

Bob Cousy was a star player on Boston Celtics teams that won numerous National Basketball Association championships. In recognition of his athletic accomplishments, Cousy was honored by ESPN as one of the top 100 athletes of the twentieth century. After he retired from basketball, he became a college basketball coach and then into his seventies was a broadcaster of Boston Celtics basketball games. Now in his eighties, Cousy has retired from broadcasting but continues to play golf and tennis on a regular basis. He has enjoyed a number of positive social relationships, including his marriage, children and grandchildren, and many friends. In 2013, after 63 years of marriage, Cousy said a last goodbye to his wife, who had dementia and died. After she developed dementia, he cared for her in their home on a daily basis as she slowly succumbed to the deterioration of her mind and body. Since her death, when he goes to bed each night, he tells her he loves her (Williamson, 2013).

As is the case with many famous people, Cousy's awards reveal little about his personal life and contributions. In addition to his extensive provision of care for his wife in her last years, two other examples illustrate his humanitarian efforts to help others (McClellan, 2004). First, when Cousy played for the Boston Celtics, his African American teammate, Chuck Cooper, was refused a hotel room on a road trip because of his race. Cousy expressed anger to his coach about the situation and then accompanied an appreciative Cooper on a train back to Boston. Second, the Bob Cousy Humanitarian Fund "honors individuals who have given their lives to using the game of basketball as a medium to help others" (p. 4). The Humanitarian Fund reflects Cousy's motivation to care for others, be appreciative and give something back, and make the world less self-centered.

Bob Cousy's active, involved life as an older adult reflects some of

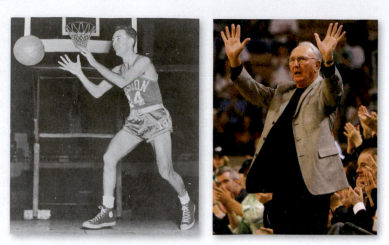

Bob Cousy, as a Boston Celtics star when he was a young adult (*left*) and as an older adult (*right*). *What are some changes he has made in his life as an older adult?*
(*Left*) ©Hulton Archive/Getty Images; (*right*) ©Charles Krupa/AP Images

the themes of socioemotional development in older adults, including the important role that being active plays in life satisfaction, how people adapt to changing skills, and the positive role of close relationships with friends and family in an emotionally fulfilling life. Our coverage of socioemotional development in late adulthood describes a number of theories about the socioemotional lives of older adults; the older adult's personality and roles in society; the importance of family ties and social relationships; the social contexts of ethnicity, gender, and culture; and the increasing attention on elements of successful aging. ■

Theories of Socioemotional Development

In this section, we explore four main theories of socioemotional development that focus on late adulthood: Erikson's theory, activity theory, socioemotional selectivity theory, and selective optimization with compensation theory.

Erikson's Theory

Earlier we described Erik Erikson's (1968) eight stages of the human life span and, as we explored different periods of development, we examined the stages in more detail. **Integrity versus despair** is Erikson's eighth and final stage of development, which individuals experience during late adulthood. This stage involves reflecting on the past and either piecing together a positive review or concluding that one's life has not been well spent. Through many different routes, the older adult may have developed a positive outlook in each of the preceding periods. If so, retrospective glances and reminiscences will reveal a picture of a life well spent, and the older adult will be satisfied (integrity). But if the older adult resolved one or more of the earlier stages in a negative way (being socially isolated in early adulthood or stagnating in middle adulthood, for example), retrospective glances about the total worth of his or her life might be negative (despair).

What characterizes a life review in late adulthood?
©PeopleImages/Getty Images

integrity versus despair Erikson's eighth and final stage of development, which individuals experience in late adulthood. This involves reflecting on the past and either piecing together a positive review or concluding that one's life has not been well spent.

Life review is prominent in this final stage. It involves looking back at one's life experiences and evaluating, interpreting, and often reinterpreting them (Hitchcock & others, 2017; Zhang & Ho, 2017). Distinguished aging researcher Robert Butler (2007) argues that the life review is set in motion by looking forward to death. Sometimes the life review proceeds quietly; at other times it is intense, requiring considerable work to achieve some sense of personality integration. The life review may be observed initially in stray and insignificant thoughts about oneself and one's life history. These thoughts may continue to emerge in brief intermittent spurts or become essentially continuous.

How Would You...?

As a **psychologist,** how would you explain to an older adult the benefits of engaging in a life review?

One aspect of life review involves identifying and reflecting on not only the positive aspects of one's life but also regrets as part of developing a mature wisdom and self-understanding (Korte & others, 2014; Randall, 2013). The hope is that by examining both positive experiences and things an individual regrets doing, a more accurate vision of the complexity of one's life and possibly increased life satisfaction will be attained (King & Hicks, 2007).

Although thinking about regrets can be helpful as part of a life review, research indicates that older adults should not dwell on regrets, especially since opportunities to undo regrettable actions decline with age (Suri & Gross, 2012). One study revealed that an important factor in the outlook of older adults who showed a higher level of emotion regulation and successful aging was reduced responsiveness to regrets (Brassen & others, 2012).

In working with older clients, some clinicians use *reminiscence therapy*, which involves discussing past activities and experiences with another individual or group (Woods & others, 2018; Wu & others, 2018). Therapy may include the use of photographs, familiar items, and video/audio recordings. Reminiscence therapy can improve the mood and quality of life of older adults, including those with dementia (Han & others, 2017; Siverova & Buzgova, 2018; Yen & Lin, 2018). In a study with older adults who had dementia, reminiscence therapy reduced their depressive symptoms and improved their self-acceptance and positive relations with others (Gonzalez & others, 2015). Another recent study found that a reminiscence intervention improved the coping skills of older adults (Satorres & others, 2018). Further, in a version of reminiscence therapy, *attachment-focused* reminiscence therapy reduced depressive symptoms, perceived stress, and emergency room visits in older African Americans (Sabir & others, 2016).

Activity Theory

Activity theory states that the more active and involved older adults are, the more likely they are to be satisfied with their lives. Researchers have found that when older adults are active, energetic, and productive, they age more successfully and are happier than they are if they disengage from society (Antonucci & Webster, 2019; Duggal & others, 2018; Strandberg, 2019; Walker, 2019). A recent study found that older adults who increased their leisure-time activity levels were three times more likely to have a slower progression to having a functional disability (Chen & others, 2016). Also, a study of Canadian older adults revealed that those who were more physically active had higher life satisfaction and greater social interaction than their physically inactive counterparts (Azagba & Sharaf, 2014). And a recent study indicated that an activity-based lifestyle was linked to lower levels of depression in older adults (Juang & others, 2018).

Activity theory suggests that many individuals will achieve greater life satisfaction if they continue their middle-adulthood roles into late adulthood (Walker, 2019). If these roles are stripped from them (as in early retirement), it is important for them to find substitute roles that keep them active and involved.

activity theory Theory that the more active and involved older adults are, the more likely they are to be satisfied with their lives.

socioemotional selectivity theory The theory that older adults become more selective about their social networks. Because they place a high value on emotional satisfaction, older adults often prefer to spend time with familiar individuals with whom they have had rewarding relationships.

Socioemotional Selectivity Theory

Socioemotional selectivity theory states that older adults become more selective about their social networks. Because they place a high value on emotional satisfaction, older adults spend more time with familiar individuals

Should adults stay active or become more disengaged as they become older? Explain.
©Chuck Savage/Getty Images

with whom they have had rewarding relationships. Developed by Laura Carstensen (1998, 2006, 2008, 2010, 2014, 2015; Carstensen & DeLiema, 2018; Carstensen & others, 2015), this theory argues that older adults deliberately withdraw from social contact with individuals peripheral to their lives while they maintain or increase contact with close friends and family members with whom they have had enjoyable relationships. This selective narrowing of social interaction maximizes positive emotional experiences and minimizes emotional risks as individuals become older. The fact that older adults have a decreasing number of years to live likely increases their emphasis on prioritizing meaningful relationships (Moss & Wilson, 2018).

Socioemotional selectivity theory challenges the stereotype that the majority of older adults are in emotional despair because of their social isolation (Carstensen, 2014, 2015; Carstensen & others, 2015). Rather, older adults consciously choose to decrease the total number of their social contacts in favor of spending increased time in emotionally rewarding moments with friends and family. That is, they systematically prune their social networks so that available social partners satisfy their emotional needs (Carstensen & others, 2015; Sims, Hogan, & Carstensen, 2015). Not surprisingly, older adults have far smaller social networks than younger adults do (Carstensen & Fried, 2012). In a study of individuals from 18 to 94 years of age, as they grew older they had fewer peripheral social contacts but retained close relationships with people who provided them with emotional support (English & Carstensen, 2014).

However, when the Stanford Center on Longevity conducted a recent large-scale examination of healthy living in different age groups called the Sightlines Project, social engagement with individuals and communities appeared to be weaker today than it was 15 years ago for 55- to 64-year-olds (Parker, 2016). Many of these individuals, who are about to reach retirement age, had weaker relationships with spouses, partners, family, friends, and neighbors than their counterparts of 15 years ago. The Sightlines Project (2016) recommends implementing the following strategies to increase the social engagement of older adults: employer wellness programs that strengthen support networks, environmental design that improves neighborhood and community life, technologies that improve personal relationships, and opportunities for volunteerism.

Socioemotional selectivity theory also focuses on the types of goals that individuals are motivated to achieve (Sims, Hogan, & Carstensen, 2015). Two important classes of goals are (1) knowledge-related and (2) emotion-related. The trajectory of motivation for knowledge-related goals starts relatively high in the early years of life, peaks in adolescence and early adulthood, and then declines in middle and late adulthood. The emotion-related trajectory is high during infancy and early childhood, declines from middle childhood through early adulthood, and increases in middle and late adulthood. In a recent commentary, Laura Carstensen (2016) noted that when older adults focus on emotionally meaningful goals, they are more satisfied with their lives, feel better, and experience fewer negative emotions.

In general, compared with younger adults, the feelings of older adults mellow. Emotional life is on a more even keel, with fewer highs and lows. It may be that although older adults have less extreme joy, they have more contentment, especially when they are connected in positive ways with friends and family. Older adults react less strongly to negative circumstances, are better at ignoring irrelevant negative information, and remember more positive than negative information (Mather, 2012; Paul, 2019). And in a recent study, older adults reacted with less anger about a personal memory than younger adults did (Kunzmann & others, 2017).

In other research, positive emotions increased and negative emotions (except for sadness) decreased from 50 years of age through the mid-eighties (Stone & others, 2010). In this study, older adults reported experiencing more positive emotions than younger adults did. Other research also indicates that happier people live longer (Frey, 2011). Also, in a recent meta-analysis of 72 studies of more than 19,000 individuals in 19 countries, it was concluded that emotional experiences are

Laura Carstensen (*right*), in a caring relationship with an older woman. Her theory of socioemotional selectivity is gaining recognition as an explanation for changes in social networks as people age.
Courtesy of Dr. Laura Carstensen

How Would You...?

As a **health-care professional,** how would you assess whether an older adult's limited social contacts signal unhealthy social isolation or healthy socioemotional selectivity?

more positive in late adulthood than in early adulthood (Laureiro-Martinez, Trujillo, & Unda, 2017). Also, in this review, it was concluded that older adults focus less on negative events in their past than younger adults do. In sum, the emotional life of older adults is more positive and less negative than stereotypes suggest (Carstensen, 2016; Sims, Hogan, & Carstensen, 2015).

Selective Optimization with Compensation Theory

Selective optimization with compensation theory states that successful aging is linked with three main factors: selection, optimization, and compensation (SOC). The theory describes how people can produce new resources and allocate them effectively to the tasks they want to master (Alonso-Fernandez & others, 2016; Baltes, Lindenberger, & Staudinger, 2006; Freund & Hennecke, 2015; Freund, Nikitin, & Riediger, 2013; Nikitin & Freund, 2019). *Selection* is based on the concept that older adults have a reduced capacity and loss of functioning, which require a reduction in performance in most life domains. *Optimization* suggests that it is possible to maintain performance in some areas through continued practice and the use of new technologies. *Compensation* becomes relevant when life tasks require a level of capacity beyond the current level of the older adult's performance potential. In a recent study of individuals from 22 to 94 years of age, on days when middle-aged and older adults, as well as individuals who were less healthy, used more selective optimization with compensation strategies, they reported a higher level of happiness (Teshale & Lachman, 2016).

Older adults especially need to compensate in circumstances involving high mental or physical demands, such as when thinking about and memorizing new material in a very short period of time, reacting quickly when driving a car, or playing a competitive game of tennis. When older adults develop an illness, the need for compensation is obvious.

In the view of Paul Baltes and his colleagues (2006), the selection of domains and life priorities is an important aspect of development. Life goals and personal life investments likely vary across the life course for most people. For many individuals, it is not just the sheer attainment of goals, but rather the attainment of *meaningful* goals, that makes life satisfying. In one cross-sectional study, the personal life investments of 25- to 105-year-olds were assessed (Staudinger, 1996) (see Figure 1). From 25 to 34 years of age,

Figure 1 Degree of Personal Life Investment at Different Points in Life
Shown here are the top four domains of personal life investment at different points in life. The highest degree of investment is listed at the top (for example, work was the highest personal investment from 25 to 34 years of age, family from 35 to 84, and health from 85 to 105).
Left to right: ©Ryan McVay/Getty Images; ©image100/PunchStock; ©Image Source/Getty Images; ©Fuse/Getty Images; ©Image Source/Getty Images

participants said that they personally invested more time in work, friends, family, and independence, in that order. From 35 to 54 and 55 to 65 years of age, family became more important than friends in terms of their personal investment. Little changed in the rank ordering of persons 70 to 84 years old, but for participants 85 to 105 years old, health became the most important personal investment. Thinking about life showed up for the first time on the most important list for those who were 85 to 105 years old.

Personality and Society

Is personality linked to mortality in older adults? How are older adults perceived and treated by society?

Personality

In the chapter on "Socioemotional Development in Middle Adulthood," we described the Big Five factors of personality: openness to experience, conscientiousness, extraversion, agreeableness, and neuroticism. (Recall that combining the first letter of each factor creates the word OCEAN.) Several of the Big Five factors of personality continue to change in late adulthood (Graham & others, 2017; Hill & Roberts, 2016; Hampson & Edmonds, 2018; Roberts & others, 2017). For example, in one study, older adults were more conscientious and agreeable than middle-aged and younger adults (Allemand, Zimprich, & Hendriks, 2008). Another study examined developmental changes in the components of conscientiousness (Jackson & others, 2009). In this study, the transition into late adulthood was characterized by increases in the following aspects of conscientiousness: impulse control, reliability, and conventionality.

Conscientiousness is associated with a number of other positive outcomes for older adults. For example, older adults with a higher level of conscientiousness experience less cognitive decline as they age (Luchetti & others, 2016). Also, in older adults, higher levels of conscientiousness, openness to experience, agreeableness, and extraversion were linked to positive emotions, while neuroticism was associated with negative emotions (Kahlbaugh & Huffman, 2017).

Some personality traits are associated with the mortality of older adults (Hill & Roberts, 2016; Roberts & others, 2017). Having a higher level of conscientiousness has been linked to living a longer life than the other four factors (Jackson & Roberts, 2016; Graham & others, 2017; Roberts & Damian, 2018). Also, individuals who are extraverted live longer, as do individuals who are low on neuroticism (Graham & others, 2017). Affect and outlook on life are linked to mortality in older adults (Carstensen, 2014, 2015; Carstensen & others, 2015). Older adults characterized by negative affect don't live as long as those who display more positive affect, and optimistic older adults who have a positive outlook on life live longer than their pessimistic and negative counterparts (Kolokotroni, Anagnostopoulos & Hantzi, 2018; Reed & Carstensen, 2015).

Older Adults in Society

Does society negatively stereotype older adults? What are some social policy issues in an aging society? What role does technology play in the lives of older adults?

Stereotyping of Older Adults

Social participation by older adults is often discouraged by **ageism,** which is prejudice against others because of their age, especially prejudice against older adults (Avalon, 2018; Avalon & Tesch-Romer, 2017; Gendron, Inker, & Welleford, 2018; Harris & others, 2018; Lytle, Levy, & Meeks, 2018). They are often perceived as incapable of thinking clearly, learning new things, enjoying sex, contributing to the community, or holding responsible jobs. Many older adults face painful discrimination and might be too polite and timid to attack it. Because of

ageism Prejudice against people because of their age, especially prejudice against older adults.

their age, older adults might not be hired for new jobs or might be eased out of old ones; they might be shunned socially; and they might be edged out of their family life.

Ageism is widespread (de Leo, 2018; O'Connor & Kelson, 2018; Sao Jose & Amado, 2017; Sargent-Cox, 2017; Wilson & Roscigno, 2018). One study found that men were more likely to negatively stereotype older adults than were women (Rupp, Vodanovich, & Crede, 2005). The most frequent form of ageism is disrespect for older adults, followed by assumptions about ailments or frailty caused by age (Palmore, 2004). Also, a recent study in 29 European countries examined age discrimination among individuals from 15 to 115 years of age (Bratt & others, 2018). In this study, younger individuals showed more age discrimination toward older adults than did older individuals.

How Would You…?

As a **human development and family studies professional,** how would you design a public awareness campaign to reduce ageism?

Policy Issues in an Aging Society

The aging society and older persons' status in this society raise policy issues about the well-being of older adults (Fernandez-Ballesteros, 2019; Mendoza-Nunez & de la Luz Martinez-Maldonado, 2019; Moon, 2016). These include the status of the economy and income, provision of health care, and eldercare, each of which we consider in turn.

Status of the Economy and Income Many older adults are concerned about their ability to have enough money to live a comfortable life as older adults (Cahill, Giandrea, & Quinn, 2016). An important issue is whether our economy can bear the burden of so many older persons, who by reason of their age alone are usually consumers rather than producers. Especially troublesome is the low rate of savings among U.S. adults, which has contributed to the financial problems of some older adults since the recent economic downturn (Topa, Lunceford, & Boyatzis, 2018; Williamson & Beland, 2016). Surveys indicate that Americans' confidence in their ability to retire comfortably has reached all-time lows in recent years (Helman, Copeland, & VanDerhei, 2012).

Of special concern are older adults who are poor (Domenech-Abella & others, 2018; George & Ferraro, 2016). One study found that cognitive processing speed was slower in older adults living in poverty (Zhang & others, 2015). Researchers also have found that poverty in late adulthood is linked to an increase in physical and mental health problems (Domenech-Abella & others, 2018; George & Ferraro, 2016). Also, one study revealed that low SES increases the risk of earlier death in older adults (Krueger & Chang, 2008).

Census data suggest that the overall number of older people living in poverty has declined since the 1960s, but in 2016, 9.3 percent of older adults in the United States still were living in poverty (U.S. Census Bureau, 2018). In 2016, U.S. women 65 years and older (10.6 percent) were much more likely to live in poverty than their male counterparts (7.6 percent) (U.S. Census Bureau, 2018). Nineteen percent of single, divorced, or widowed women 65 years and older lived in poverty. There is a special concern about poverty among older women and considerable discussion about the role of Social Security in providing a broad economic safety net for them (Couch & others, 2017).

Poverty rates among older adults who belong to ethnic minorities are much higher than the rate for non-Latino Whites. In 2015, 24.1 percent of African American older adults and 21.1 percent of Latino older adults lived in poverty, compared with 11.6 percent of non-Latino Whites (U.S. Census Bureau, 2016).

Health Care An aging society also brings with it various problems involving health care, especially those involving chronic diseases (Onder & others, 2018; Papanicolas, Wolski, & Jha, 2018), including escalating costs (Bail & others, 2018; Hudson, 2016; Roohan, 2018). Approximately one-third of total health-care expenses in the United States involve the care of adults 65 and over, who comprise only 12 percent of the population. Medicare is the program that provides health-care insurance to adults over 65 under the Social Security system (Trivedi, 2016). Until the Affordable

How Would You…?

As a **health-care professional,** how would you recommend addressing the medical community's emphasis on "cure" rather than "care" when treating chronic illness in older adults?

Care Act was enacted, the United States was the only developed country that did not have a national health care system.

Technology The Internet plays an increasingly important role in providing access to information and communication for adults as well as youth (Gavett & others, 2017; Gillain & others, 2019; Ware & others, 2017). In 2016, 67 percent of U.S. adults 65 and over used the Internet, up from 59 percent in 2013 and 14 percent in 2000 (Anderson, 2017). Among the general U.S. population, 90 percent are Internet users. Younger seniors use the Internet more than older seniors do (82 percent of 65- to 69-year-olds, compared with 44 percent of people 80 and older. Increasing numbers of older adults use e-mail and smartphones to communicate, especially with friends and relatives (Gillain & others, 2019). In 2016, approximately 40 percent of U.S. adults 65 and over were smartphone users, up 24 percent from 2013 (Anderson, 2017). In this survey, 59 percent of 65- to 69-year-olds but only 17 percent of people 80 and over used smartphones. Lower-SES older adults use smartphones and the Internet much less than middle- and upper-SES older adults do.

Are older adults keeping up with changes in technology?
©Paul Sutherland/Getty Images

Older adults also are using social media more today than in the past. In 2016, 34 percent of U.S. adults 65 and over reported using social networking sites like Facebook and Twitter, 7 percent higher than in 2013 (Anderson, 2017).

A recent study in Hong Kong found that adults 75 and older who used smartphones and the Internet to connect with family, friends, and neighbors had a higher level of psychological well-being than their counterparts who did not use this information and communicative technology (Fang & others, 2018). Also, as with children and younger adults, cautions about verifying the accuracy of information—especially on topics involving health care—on the Internet should always be kept in mind (Miller & Bell, 2012).

Although computers, smartphones, and the Internet are now playing more important roles in the lives of people of all ages, people continue to watch extensive amounts of television, especially in late adulthood. In a 2016 Nielsen survey, adults age 65 and older watched television an average of 51 hours, 32 minutes per week (Recode, 2016). That 51+ hours per week is far more than any other age group—25 to 34 years (23 hrs, 26 min), 35 to 49 years (32 hrs, 7 min), and 50 to 64 years (44 min, 6 sec). The staggering number of hours older adults watch television each week raises concerns about how such lengthy sedentary behavior might interfere with engaging in adequate amounts of physical exercise and social activities, which are linked to healthy development.

Families and Social Relationships

Are the close relationships of older adults different from those of younger adults? What are the lifestyles of older adults like? What characterizes the relationships of older adult parents and their adult children? What benefits do friendships and social networks contribute to the lives of older adults? How might older adults' altruism and volunteerism contribute to positive outcomes?

Lifestyle Diversity

The lifestyles of older adults are changing. Formerly, the later years of life were likely to consist of marriage for men and widowhood for women. With demographic shifts toward marital dissolution characterized by divorce, one-third of adults can now expect to marry, divorce, and remarry during their lifetime.

Married Older Adults

In 2016, 57.8 percent of U.S. adults over 65 years of age were married (U.S. Census Bureau, 2017). Older men were far more likely to be married than older women. In 2016, 24 percent of U.S. adults over 65 years of age were widowed (U.S. Census

Bureau, 2017). There were more than four times as many widows as widowers.

Individuals who are in a marriage or a partnership in late adulthood are usually happier, feel less distressed, and live longer than those who are single (Blieszner, 2018). A longitudinal study of adults 75 years of age and older revealed that individuals who were married were less likely to die during a seven-year time span (Rasulo, Christensen, & Tomassini, 2005).

In late adulthood, married individuals are more likely to find themselves having to care for a sick partner with a limiting health condition (Blieszner & Ogletree, 2017, 2018; Monin & others, 2018). The stress of caring for a spouse who has a chronic disease can place demands on intimacy (Polenick & DePasquale, 2018).

How might marriage affect the health and well-being of LGBT older adults? In a recent study, 24 percent of LGBT individuals 50 years and older, 24 percent were legally married, 26 percent unmarried and partnered, and 50 percent single (Goldsen & others, 2017). In this study, couples who were legally married reported having a better quality of life and more economic and social resources than unmarried couples. And those who were single reported having poorer health and fewer resources than legally married or unmarried couples.

What are some adaptations that many married older adults need to make?
©Thinkstock/Getty Images

Divorced and Remarried Older Adults

An increasing number of older adults are divorced (Lin & others, 2018; Suitor, Gilligan, & Pillemer, 2016). In a recent comparison, in 1980, 3 percent of women 65 years and older were divorced but that rate increased to 13 percent in 2015; for men, in 1980 4 percent of those 65 and older were divorced but that rate increased to 11 percent in 2015 (U.S. Census Bureau, 2017). Many of these individuals were divorced or separated before they entered late adulthood.

The majority of divorced older adults are women due to their greater longevity, and men are more likely to remarry, thus removing themselves from the pool of divorced older adults (Peek, 2009). Divorce is far less common among older adults than younger adults, likely reflecting cohort effects rather than age effects since divorce was somewhat rare when current cohorts of older adults were young (Peek, 2009).

In a recent study, many of the same factors traditionally associated with divorce in younger adults were also likely to occur in older adults (Lin & others, 2018). The longer older adults had been married, the more likely they were to have better marital quality, own a home, and be wealthy, and the less likely they were to become divorced. Another recent study found that partnered older adults were more likely to receive relatively high Social Security benefits and less likely to live in poverty (Lin, Brown, & Hammersmith, 2017).

In sum, there are social, financial, and physical consequences of divorce for older adults (Butrica & Smith, 2012). Divorce can weaken kinship ties when it occurs in later life, especially in the case of older men. Divorced older women are less likely to have adequate financial resources than married older women, and divorce is linked to higher rates of health problems in older adults (Bennett, 2006).

How Would You...?

As a psychologist, how would you assist older adults in coping with the unique challenges faced by divorcées at this age?

Rising divorce rates, increased longevity, and better health have led to an increase in remarriage by older adults (Ganong, Coleman, & Sanner, 2018; Koren & others, 2016; Papernow, 2018). What happens when an older adult wants to remarry or does remarry? Some older adults perceive negative social pressure about their decision to remarry. These negative sanctions range from raised eyebrows to rejection by adult children (Ganong & Coleman, 2018). However, the majority of adult children support the decision of their older adult parents to remarry.

Adult children can be personally affected by remarriage between older adults. Researchers have found that remarried parents and stepparents provide less support to adult stepchildren than do parents in first marriages (Ganong, Coleman, & Sanner, 2018).

Cohabiting Older Adults

An increasing number of older adults cohabit (Wu, Schimmele, & Quellet, 2015). In 2016, cohabitation levels more than doubled for older men from 1990 (1.5 percent) to 2015 (3.8 percent) and increased for older women in the same time frame from less than 1 percent to 2.6 percent (Brown & Wright, 2017). These percentages are expected to continue increasing in the next decade. In many cases, the cohabiting is more for companionship than for love. In other cases, such as when one partner faces the potential need for expensive care, a couple may decide to maintain their assets separately and thus not marry. One study found that older adults who cohabited had a more positive, stable relationship than younger adults who cohabited, although cohabiting older adults were less likely to have plans to marry their partner than younger ones were (King & Scott, 2005). Other research also has revealed that middle-aged and older adult cohabiting men and women reported higher levels of depression than their married counterparts (Brown, Bulanda, & Lee, 2005). And in a recent national study of older adults, among men, cohabitors' psychological well-being (lower levels of depression, stress, and loneliness) fared similarly to married men and better than daters and the unpartnered (Wright & Brown, 2017). In contrast, there were few differences related to partnership status in the psychological well-being of women.

Attachment

Far less research has been conducted on how attachment affects aging adults than on attachment in children, adolescents, and young adults (Freitas & Rahioul, 2017; Homan, 2018). However, it has been found that older adults have fewer attachment relationships than younger adults (Cicirelli, 2010). Also, in a longitudinal study from 13 to 72 years of age, attachment anxiety declined in middle-aged and older adults (Chopik, Edelstein, & Grimm, 2018). Attachment avoidance decreased in a linear fashion across the life span. Being in a relationship was linked to lower attachment anxiety and attachment avoidance across adulthood. And men were higher in attachment avoidance throughout the life span.

Older Adult Parents and Their Adult Children

Approximately 80 percent of older adults have living children, many of whom are middle-aged. About 10 percent of older adults have children who are 65 years or older. Adult children are an important part of the aging parent's social network. Older adults with children have more contacts with relatives than do those without children.

Increasingly, diversity characterizes older adult parents and their adult children (Antonucci & others, 2016; Birditt & others, 2018; Huo & others, 2018a, b; Lowenstein, Katz, & Tur-Sanai, 2019; Sechrist & Fingerman, 2018). Divorce, cohabitation, and nonmarital childbearing are more common in the history of older adults today than in the past.

Gender plays an important role in relationships involving older adult parents and their children (Antonucci & others, 2016). Adult daughters are more likely than adult sons to be involved in the lives of aging parents. For example, adult daughters are three times more likely than adult sons to give parents assistance with daily living activities (Dwyer & Coward, 1991).

A valuable task that adult children can perform is to coordinate and monitor services for an aging parent (or other relative) who becomes disabled (Huo & others, 2018b). This might involve locating a nursing home and monitoring its quality, procuring medical services, arranging public service assistance, and handling finances. In some cases, adult children provide direct assistance with activities of daily living such as eating, bathing, and dressing. Even less severely impaired older adults may need help with shopping, housework, transportation, home maintenance, and bill paying. Also, some researchers have found that relationships between aging parents and their children are usually characterized by ambivalence (Birditt & others, 2018; Sechrist & Fingerman, 2018). For example, researchers have found that middle-aged adults feel more positive about providing support for their children than their aging parents (Birditt & others, 2018).

Friendship

In early adulthood, friendship networks expand as new social connections are made away from home. In late adulthood, new friendships are less likely to be forged, although some adults do seek out new friendships, especially following the death of a spouse (Adams, Hahmann, & Blieszner, 2017; Blieszner, & Ogletree, 2017, 2018). Aging expert Laura Carstensen (2006) concluded that people choose close friends over new friends as they grow older. And as long as they have several close people in their network, they seem content, says Carstensen.

In a recent study, compared with younger adults, older adults reported fewer problems with friends, fewer negative friendship qualities, less frequent contact with friends, and more positive friendship qualities with a specific friend (Schlosnagle & Strough, 2017). In another study of married older adults, women were more depressed than men if they did not have a best friend, and women who did have a friend reported lower levels of depression (Antonucci, Lansford, & Akiyama, 2001). Similarly, women who did not have a best friend were less satisfied with life than women who did have a best friend. And a longitudinal study of adults 75 years of age and older revealed that individuals who maintained close ties with friends were less likely to die across a seven-year age span (Rasulo, Christensen, & Tomassini, 2005). These findings were stronger for women than for men.

How Would You...?

As a **human development and family studies professional,** how would you characterize the importance of friendships for older adults?

Social Support and Social Integration

Social support and social integration play important roles in the physical and mental health of older adults (Antonucci & Webster, 2019; Howard & others, 2017; Smith & others, 2018; Tkatch & others, 2017). In the *social convoy* model of social relations, individuals go through life embedded in a personal network of individuals to whom they give, and from whom they receive, social support (Antonucci & others, 2016; Antonucci & Webster, 2019). Social support can help individuals of all ages cope more effectively with life's challenges. For older adults, social support is related to their physical health, mental health, and life satisfaction (Antonucci & other, 2016). For example, a recent study found that a higher level of social support was associated with older adults' increased life satisfaction (Dumitrache, Rubio, & Rubio-Herrera, 2017). Social support also decreases the probability that an older adult will be institutionalized or become depressed (Heard & others, 2011). Further, one study revealed that older adults who experienced a higher level of social support showed later cognitive decline than their counterparts with a lower level of social support (Dickinson & others, 2011). In recent analyses, it was concluded that 80 percent of the supportive care for older adults with some form of limitation was provided by family members or other informal caregivers, which places an enormous burden on the caregiver (Antonucci & others, 2016; Antonucci & Webster, 2019; Sherman, Webster, & Antonucci, 2016).

Social integration also plays an important role in the lives of many older adults (Antonucci & others, 2016; Antonucci & Webster, 2019; Hawkley & Kocherginsky, 2018). Remember from our earlier discussion of socioemotional selectivity theory that many older adults choose to have fewer peripheral social contacts and more emotionally positive contacts with friends and family (Carstensen & others, 2011). Thus, a decrease in the overall social activity of many older adults may reflect their greater interest in spending more time in a small circle of friends and family members where they are less likely to have negative emotional experiences (Blieszner & Ogletree, 2017, 2018). And one study found that increased use of the Internet by older adults was associated with having more opportunities to meet new people, feeling less isolated, and feeling more connected with friends and family (Cotten, Anderson, & McCullough, 2013).

Older adults tend to report being less lonely than younger adults and less lonely than would be expected based on their circumstances (Schnittker, 2007). This likely reflects their more selective social networks and greater acceptance of loneliness in their lives (Koropeckyj-Cox, 2009; Antonucci & Webster, 2019). In a recent study, 18 percent of older adults stated they were often or frequently lonely (Due, Sandholdt, & Waldorff, 2018). In this study, the most important predictors of feeling lonely were anxiety and depressive symptoms, living alone, and low social participation.

Altruism and Volunteerism

Are older adults more altruistic than younger adults? In one investigation, older adults' strategies were more likely to be aimed at contributing to the public good while younger adults' strategies were more likely to focus on optimizing personal financial gain (Freund & Blanchard-Fields, 2014). Also, a national survey found that 24 percent of U.S. adults 65 years and older engaged in volunteering in 2015 (U.S. Bureau of Labor Statistics, 2016). In this survey, the highest percentage of volunteering occurred between 35 and 44 years of age (31.8 percent).

A common perception is that older adults need to be given help rather than give help themselves. However, one study found that older adults perceived their well-being as better when they provided social support to others than when they received it, except when social support was provided by a spouse or sibling (Thomas, 2010). And a 12-year longitudinal study revealed that older adults who had persistently low or declining feelings of usefulness to others had an increased risk of earlier death (Gruenewald & others, 2009).

Volunteering is associated with a number of positive outcomes for aging adults (Carr, 2018; Guiney & Machado, 2018). Recent studies have found that when aging adults volunteer they have better health (Burr & others, 2018; Carr, Kail, & Rowe, 2018), have better cognitive functioning (Proulx, Curl, & Ermer, 2018), and are less lonely (Carr & others, 2018). And, in a meta-analysis, older adults who engaged in organizational volunteering had a lower mortality risk than those who did not (Okun, Yeung, & Brown, 2013).

Why might volunteering be linked to these positive outcomes for aging adults? Among the reasons for the positive outcomes of volunteering are increased opportunities to engage in constructive physical, cognitive, and social activities that convey meaning and purpose to one's life. And such benefits may spill over to other aspects of older adults' lives (Carr, 2018). For example, volunteering may lead to increased socializing with others outside of the volunteering activity. This social engagement may help to reduce time spent in sedentary activities such as watching television.

Ninety-eight-year-old volunteer Iva Broadus plays cards with 10-year-old DeAngela Williams in Dallas, Texas. Iva was recognized as the oldest volunteer in the Big Sister program in the United States. Iva says that card-playing helps to keep her memory and thinking skills sharp and can help DeAngela's as well.
©Dallas Morning News, photographer Jim Mahoney

How Would You…?

As an **educator,** how would you persuade the school board to sponsor a volunteer program to bring older adults into the school system to work with elementary students?

Ethnicity, Gender, and Culture

How is ethnicity linked to aging? Do gender roles change in late adulthood? What are some of the social aspects of aging in different cultures?

Ethnicity

Ethnic minority older adults, especially African Americans and Latinos, are overrepresented in poverty statistics (Antonucci & others, 2016). Comparative information about African Americans, Latinos, and non-Latino Whites indicates a possible double jeopardy for elderly ethnic minority individuals who face problems related to *both* ageism and racism (Allen, 2016; McCluney & others, 2018). They also are more likely to have a history of less education, longer periods of unemployment, worse housing conditions, and shorter life expectancies (Treas & Gubernskaya, 2016). In recent analyses, non-Latino White men and women with 16 years or more of schooling had a life expectancy that was 14 years higher than that of African Americans with fewer than 12 years of education (Antonucci & others, 2016).

Norma Thomas, Social Work Professor and Administrator

Dr. Norma Thomas has worked for more than three decades in the field of aging. She obtained her undergraduate degree in social work from Pennsylvania State University and her doctoral degree in social work from the University of Pennsylvania. Thomas' activities are varied. Earlier in her career when she was a social work practitioner, she provided services to older adults of color in an effort to improve their lives. She currently is a professor and academic administrator at Widener University in Chester, Pennsylvania, a fellow of the Institute of Aging at the University of Pennsylvania, and the chief executive officer and co-founder of the Center on Ethnic and Minority Aging (CEMA). CEMA was formed to provide research, consultation, training, and services to benefit aging individuals of color, their families, and their communities. Thomas has created numerous community service events that benefit older adults of color, especially African Americans and Latinos. She has also been a consultant to various national, regional, and state agencies in her effort to improve the lives of aging adults of color.

Norma Thomas.
Courtesy of Dr. Norma Thomas

Despite the stress and discrimination older ethnic minority individuals face, many of these older adults have developed coping mechanisms that allow them to survive in the dominant non-Latino White world. Extension of family networks helps older minority group individuals cope with the bare essentials of living and gives them a sense of being loved. Churches in African American and Latino communities provide avenues for meaningful social participation, feelings of power, and a sense of internal satisfaction (Hill & others, 2005). To read about one individual who is providing help for aging minorities, see *Careers in Life-Span Development*.

Gender

Many older women face the burden of both ageism and sexism (Angel, Mudrazija, & Benson, 2016) and also racism for female ethnic minorities (Hinze, Lin, & Andersson, 2012). The poverty rate for older adult females is almost double that of older adult males.

Culture

Six factors are most likely to predict high status for older adults in a culture (Sangree, 1989):

- Older persons have valuable knowledge.
- Older persons control key family/community resources.
- Older persons are permitted to engage in useful and valued functions as long as possible.
- Age-related role changes involve greater responsibility, authority, and advisory capacity.
- The extended family is a common family arrangement in the culture, and the older person is integrated into the extended family.
- In general, respect for older adults is greater in collectivistic cultures (such as China and Japan) than in individualistic cultures (such as the United States). However, some researchers are finding that this collectivistic/individualistic difference in respect for older adults is not as strong as it used to be and that, in some cases, older adults in individualistic cultures receive considerable respect (Antonucci, Vandewater, & Lansford, 2000).

Cultures vary in the prestige they give to older adults. In the Navajo culture, older adults are especially treated with respect because of their wisdom and extensive life experiences. *What are some other factors that are linked with respect for older adults in a culture?*
©Alison Wright/Corbis/Getty Images

Successful Aging

As we have discussed aging, it should be apparent that there are large individual differences in the patterns of change for older adults. The most common pattern is *normal aging*, which characterizes most individuals (Schaie, 2016). Their psychological functioning often peaks in early midlife, plateaus until the late fifties to early sixties, then modestly declines through the early eighties, although marked decline often occurs prior to death. Another pattern involves *pathological aging*, which characterizes individuals who in late adulthood show greater than average decline. These individuals may have mild cognitive impairment in early old age, develop Alzheimer disease later, or have chronic disease that impairs their daily functioning. A third pattern of change in old age is *successful aging*, which characterizes individuals whose physical, cognitive, and socioemotional development is maintained longer than for most individuals and declines later than for most people.

For too long successful aging has been ignored (Docking & Stock, 2018; Fernandez-Ballesteros, 2019; Robine, 2019). Throughout this edition, we have called attention to the positive aspects of aging. With a proper diet, an active lifestyle, mental stimulation and flexibility, positive coping skills, good social relationships and support, and the absence of disease, many abilities can be maintained or in some cases even improved as we get older (Amano, Park, & Morrow-Howell, 2018; Antonucci & Webster, 2019; Caprara & Mendoza-Ruvalcaba, 2019; Loprinzi & Crush, 2018; Marquez-Gonzalez, Cheng, & Losada, 2019; Strandberg, 2019). Even when individuals develop a disease, improvements in medicine and lifestyle modifications mean that increasing numbers of older adults can continue to lead active, constructive lives (Batis & Zagaria, 2018; Orkaby & others, 2018; Santacreu, Rodriguez, & Molina, 2019). A Canadian study found that the predicted self-rated probability of aging successfully was 41 percent for those 65 to 74, 33 percent for those 75 to 84, and 22 percent for those 85+ years of age (Meng & D'Arcy, 2014). In this study, being younger, married, a regular drinker, in better health (self-perceived), and satisfied with life were associated with successful aging. Presence of disease was linked to a significant decline in successful aging. In a more recent study, the following four factors emerged as best characterizing successful aging: proactive engagement, wellness resources, positive spirit, and valued relationships (Lee, Kahana, & Kahana, 2017).

Being active and engaged is an especially important aspect of successful aging (Carr, 2018; Walker, 2019). Older adults who exercise regularly, attend meetings, participate in church activities, and go on trips are more satisfied with their lives than their counterparts who disengage from society (Arrieta & others, 2018; Strandberg, 2019). Older adults who engage in challenging cognitive activities are more likely to retain their cognitive skills for a longer period of time (Calero, 2019; Kinugawa, 2019; Kunzmann, 2019; Reuter-Lorenz & Lustig, 2017). Older adults who are emotionally selective, optimize their choices, and compensate effectively for losses increase their chances of aging successfully (Carstensen, 2015; Moss & Wilson, 2018; Nikitin & Freund, 2019; Paul, 2019). Also, a study of 90- to 91-year-olds found that living circumstances, especially owning one's own home and living there as long as possible; independence in various aspects of life; good health; and a good death were described as important themes of successful aging (Nosraty & others, 2015). In this study, social and cognitive aspects were thought to be more important than physical health.

Successful aging also involves perceived control over the environment (Bercovitz, Ngnoumen, & Langer, 2019; Robinson & Lachman, 2017). In the chapter on "Physical and Cognitive Development in Late Adulthood," we described how perceived control over the environment had a positive effect on nursing home residents' health and longevity. In recent years, the term *self-efficacy* has often been used to describe perceived control over the environment and the ability to produce positive outcomes (Bandura, 2010, 2012).

Examining the positive aspects of aging is an important trend in life-span development that is likely to benefit future generations of older adults (Calero, 2019; Fernandez-Ballesteros, 2019; Reed & Carstensen, 2015; Strandberg, 2019). And a very important agenda is to continue to improve our understanding of how people can live longer, healthier, more productive and satisfying lives (Antonucci & Webster, 2019; Docking & Stock, 2018; Dombrowsky, 2018; Walker, 2019).

In the "Introduction" chapter, we described Laura Carstensen's (2015) perspective on the challenges and opportunities involved in the dramatic increase in life expectancy that has been occurring and continues to occur. In her view, the remarkable increase in the number of people living to older ages has occurred in such a short time that science, technology, and behavioral adaptations have not kept pace. She proposes that the challenge is to change a world constructed mainly for young people to a world that is more compatible and supportive for the increasing number of people living to 100 and older.

In further commentary, Carstensen (2015, p. 70) remarked that making such changes would be no small feat:

> . . . parks, transportation systems, staircases, and even hospitals presume that the users have both strength and stamina; suburbs across the country are built for two parents and their young children, not single people, multiple generations or elderly people who are not able to drive. Our education system serves the needs of young children and young adults and offers little more than recreation for experienced people.

Indeed, the very conception of work as a full-time endeavor ending in the early sixties is ill suited for long lives. Arguably the most troubling aspect of our attitude toward aging is that we fret about ways that older people lack the qualities of younger people rather than exploit a growing new resource right before our eyes: citizens who have deep expertise, emotional balance, and the motivation to make a difference.

Summary

Theories of Socioemotional Development

- Erikson's eighth stage of development is called integrity versus despair. Life review is an important theme during this stage.
- Older adults who are active are more likely to be satisfied with their lives.
- Older adults are more selective about their social networks than are younger adults. Older adults also experience more positive emotions and less negative emotions than younger adults.
- Successful aging involves selection, optimization, and compensation.

Personality and Society

- Some of the Big Five factors of personality, such as conscientiousness, extraversion, and openness, are linked to well-being and mortality in older adults.
- Ageism, which is prejudice against others because of their age, is widespread. Social policy issues in an aging society include the status of the economy and income, as well as provision of health care. Older adults are the fastest-growing segment of Internet users.

Families and Social Relationships

- Married older adults are often happier than single older adults. Divorce and remarriage present challenges to older adults. An increasing number of older adults cohabit.
- Older adults have fewer attachment relationships than younger adults; attachment anxiety decreases with increasing age; attachment security is linked to psychological and physical well-being in older adults.
- Approximately 80 percent of older adults have adult children who are an important part of their social network.
- Older adults tend to choose long-term friends over new friends.
- Social support is linked to improved physical and mental health in older adults. Older adults who participate in more organizations live longer than their counterparts who have low participation rates.
- Altruism and volunteering are associated with positive benefits for older adults.

Ethnicity, Gender, and Culture

- Aging minorities in the United States face the double burden of ageism and racism.
- Many women face the burden of both ageism and sexism.
- Factors that predict high status for the elderly across cultures range from value placed on their accumulated knowledge to integration into the extended family.

Successful Aging

- Three patterns of aging are normal, pathological, and successful. Increasingly, the positive aspects of older adulthood are being studied. Factors that are linked with successful aging include an active lifestyle, positive coping skills, good social relationships and support, and the absence of disease.

Key Terms

activity theory
ageism

integrity versus
despair

selective optimization with
compensation theory

socioemotional selectivity
theory

17

Death, Dying, and Grieving

©Fuse/Getty Images

Stories of Life-Span Development: Paige Farley-Hackel and Ruth McCourt, 9/11/2001

Paige Farley-Hackel and her best friend Ruth McCourt teamed up to take McCourt's 4-year-old daughter, Juliana, to Disneyland. They were originally booked on the same flight from Boston to Los Angeles, but McCourt decided to use her frequent flyer miles and go on a different airplane. Both their flights exploded 17 minutes apart after terrorists hijacked them, then rammed them into the twin towers of the World Trade Center in New York City on 9/11/2001.

Forty-six-year-old Farley-Hackel was a writer, motivational speaker, and spiritual counselor who lived in Newton, Massachusetts. She was looking forward to the airing of the first few episodes of her new radio program, *Spiritually Speaking,* and wanted to eventually be on *The Oprah Winfrey Show,* said her husband, Allan Hackel. Following 9/11, Oprah televised a memorial tribute to Farley-Hackel, McCourt, and Juliana.

Forty-five-year-old Ruth McCourt was a homemaker from New London, Connecticut, who met Farley-Hackel at a day spa she used to own in Boston. McCourt gave up the business when she got married, but the friendship between the two women lasted. They often traveled together and shared their passion for reading, cooking, and learning.

In this chapter, we explore many aspects of death and dying. Among the questions that we will ask are: How can death be defined? How is death viewed in other cultures? How do people face their own death? How do people cope with the death of someone they love? ▪

Defining Death and Life/Death Issues

Is there one point in the process of dying that is *the* point at which death takes place, or is death a more gradual process? What are some decisions individuals can make about life, death, and health care?

Determining Death

Twenty-five years ago, determining whether someone was dead was simpler than it is today. The end of certain biological functions—such as breathing and blood pressure—and the rigidity of the body (rigor mortis) were considered to be clear signs of death. Defining death today is more complex (Ganapathy, 2018; Hammand & others, 2017; Johnson, 2017).

Brain death is a neurological definition of death which states that a person is brain dead when all electrical activity of the brain has ceased for a specified period of time. A flat EEG (electroencephalogram) recording for a specified period of time is one criterion of brain death. The higher portions of the brain often die sooner than the lower portions. Because the brain's lower portions monitor heartbeat and respiration, individuals whose higher brain areas have died may continue to breathe and have a heartbeat (MacDougall & others, 2014). The definition of brain death currently followed by most physicians includes the death of both the higher cortical functions and the lower brain stem functions (Oliva & others, 2017; Waweru-Siika & others, 2017).

What are some issues in determining death?
©Dario Mitidieri/Getty Images

Some medical experts argue that the criteria for death should include only higher cortical functioning. If the cortical death definition were adopted, then physicians could claim a person is dead who has no cortical functioning, even if the lower brain stem is functioning. Supporters of the cortical death policy argue that the functions we associate with being human, such as intelligence and personality, are located in the higher cortical part of the brain. They believe that when these functions are lost, the "human being" is no longer alive.

How Would You...?

As a **health-care professional,** how would you explain "brain death" to the family of an individual who has suffered a severe head injury in an automobile accident?

Decisions Regarding Life, Death, and Health Care

In cases of catastrophic illness or accidents, patients might not be able to respond adequately to participate in decisions about their medical care. To prepare for this situation, some individuals make choices earlier.

Advance Care Planning

Advance care planning refers to the process of patients thinking about and communicating their preferences regarding end-of-life care (Pereira-Salgado & others, 2018; Rietjens & others, 2017; Sulmasy, 2018). For many patients in a coma, it is not clear what their wishes regarding termination of treatment might be if they still were conscious (Abu Snineh, Camicioli, & Miyasaki, 2017). In one study, researchers found that advance care planning decreased life-sustaining treatment, increased hospice use, and decreased hospital use (Brinkman-Stoppelenburg, Rietjens, & van der Heide, 2014). A recent study revealed that completion of an advance directive was associated

brain death A neurological definition of death. A person is brain dead when all electrical activity of the brain has ceased for a specified period of time. A flat EEG recording is one criterion of brain death.

with a lower probability of receiving life-sustaining treatments (Yen & others, 2018). Recognizing that some terminally ill patients might prefer to die rather than linger in a painful or vegetative state, the organization "Choice in Dying" created the *living will*, a legal document that reflects the patient's advance care planning. One study of older adults found that advance care planning was associated with improved quality of care at the end of life, including less in-hospital death and greater use of hospice care (Bischoff & others, 2013).

euthanasia The act of painlessly ending the lives of persons who are suffering from incurable diseases or severe disabilities; sometimes called "mercy killing."

passive euthanasia Withholding available treatments, such as the use of life-sustaining devices, and allowing a person to die.

active euthanasia Death induced deliberately, as when a physician or a third party ends the patient's life by administering a lethal dose of a drug.

Physicians' concerns over malpractice suits and the efforts of people who support the living will concept have produced natural death legislation. Laws in all 50 states now accept an *advance directive,* such as a living will (Olsen, 2016). An advance directive states such preferences as whether life-sustaining procedures should or should not be used to prolong the life of an individual when death is imminent. An advance directive must be signed while the individual still is able to think clearly (Myers & others, 2018; Shin & others, 2016). A study of end-of-life planning revealed that only 15 percent of patients 18 years of age and older had a living will (Clements, 2009). Almost 90 percent of the patients reported that it was important to discuss health-care wishes with their family, but only 60 percent of them had done so. A research review concluded that physicians have a positive attitude toward advance directives (Coleman, 2013).

How Would You…?

As a **social worker,** how would you explain to individuals the advantages of engaging in advance care planning?

Available or being considered in 34 states, Physician Orders for Life-Sustaining Treatment (POLST) is a more specific document that involves the health-care professional and the patient or surrogate in stating the wishes of the patient (Hopping-Winn & others, 2018; Lammers & others, 2018; Moss & others, 2017; Struck, Brown & Madison, 2017). POLST translates treatment preferences into medical orders such as those involving cardiopulmonary resuscitation, extent of treatment, and artificial nutrition via a tube (Mayoral & others, 2018; Stuart & Thielke, 2017).

Euthanasia

Euthanasia ("easy death") is the act of painlessly ending the lives of individuals who are suffering from an incurable disease or severe disability (Kanniyakonil, 2018; Miller, Dresser, & Kim, 2018; Preston, 2018; Savulescu, 2018). Sometimes euthanasia is called "mercy killing." Distinctions are made between two types of euthanasia: passive and active. **Passive euthanasia** occurs when a person is allowed to die by withholding available treatment, such as withdrawing a life-sustaining device. For example, this might involve turning off a respirator or a heart-lung machine. **Active euthanasia** occurs when death is deliberately induced, as when a physician or a third party ends the patient's life by administering a lethal dose of a drug.

Terri Schiavo (*right*) shown with her mother. *What issues did the Terri Schiavo case raise?*
©Stringer/Getty Images

Technological advances in life-support devices raise the issue of quality of life (Dean, 2017; Goligher & others, 2017; Jouffre & others, 2018; Lum & others, 2017). Nowhere was this more apparent than in the highly publicized case of Terri Schiavo, who suffered severe brain damage related to cardiac arrest and a lack of oxygen to the brain. She went into a coma and spent 15 years in a vegetative state. Across the 15 years, the question of whether passive euthanasia should be implemented, or whether she should be kept in the vegetative state with the hope that her condition might change for the better, was debated between family

How Would You...?

As a **psychologist**, how would you counsel the family of a brain-dead patient on the topic of euthanasia when there is no living will or advance directive for guidance?

members and eventually at a number of levels in the judicial system. At one point toward the end of her life, a judge ordered that her feeding tube be removed. However, subsequent appeals led to its reinsertion twice. The feeding tube was removed a third and final time on March 18, 2005, and she died 13 days later from passive euthanasia.

Should individuals like Terri Schiavo be kept alive in a vegetative state? The trend is toward acceptance of passive euthanasia in the case of terminally ill patients (Hurst & Mauron, 2017; Sannita, 2017).

The most widely publicized cases of active euthanasia involve "assisted suicide." In **assisted suicide,** a physician supplies the information and/or the means of committing suicide (such as giving the patient a prescription for a lethal dose of sleeping pills) but requires the patient to self-administer the lethal medication and to determine when and where to do this. Thus, assisted suicide differs from active euthanasia, in which a physician causes the death of an individual through a direct action in response to a request by the person (Hosie, 2018; Miller & Appelbaum, 2018; Vandenberghe, 2018). The most widely publicized incidents of assisted suicide and active euthanasia were carried out by Michigan physician Jack Kevorkian, who assisted terminally ill patients in ending their lives. After a series of trials, Kevorkian was convicted of second-degree murder and served eight years in prison for his actions. In 2007 he was released from prison at age 79 for good behavior and promised not to participate in any further assisted suicides. Kevorkian died at the age of 83.

Assisted suicide is legal in Belgium, Canada, Finland, Luxembourg, the Netherlands, and Switzerland. The U.S. government has no official policy on assisted suicide and leaves the decision up to each of the states. Currently, six states allow assisted suicide—California, Colorado, Montana, Oregon, Vermont, and Washington, as well as Washington DC. In states where assisted suicide is illegal, the crime is typically considered manslaughter or a felony.

In one research review, the percentage of physician-assisted deaths ranged from 0.1 to 0.2 percent in the United States and Luxembourg to 1.8 to 2.9 percent in the Netherlands (Steck & others, 2013). In this review, the percentage of assisted suicide cases reported to authorities has increased in recent years and the individuals who die through assisted suicide are most likely to be males from 60 to 75 years of age.

To what extent do people in the United States think euthanasia and assisted suicide should be legal? A recent Gallup poll found that 69 percent of U.S. adults said euthanasia should be legal, 51 percent said they would consider ending their own lives if faced with a terminal illness, and 50 percent reported that physician-assisted suicide is morally acceptable (Swift, 2016).

Why is euthanasia so controversial? Those in favor of euthanasia argue that death should be calm and dignified, not a painful and prolonged ordeal (Jouffre & others, 2018; Lum & others, 2017; Porteri, 2018). Those against euthanasia stress that it is a criminal act of murder in most states in the United States and in most other countries. Many religious individuals, especially Christians, say that taking a life for any reason is against God's will and is an act of murder.

Needed: Better Care for Dying Individuals

Too often, death in America is lonely, prolonged, and painful. Scientific advances sometimes have made dying harder by delaying the inevitable. Also, even though painkillers are available, too many people experience severe pain during their last days and months of life (Buiting & de Graas, 2018; Chi & others, 2018; Hughes, Volicer, & van der Steen, 2018; Montague & others, 2017). One study found that 61 percent of dying patients were in pain in the last year of life and that nearly one-third had symptoms of depression and confusion prior to death (Singer & others, 2015).

Care providers are increasingly interested in helping individuals experience a "good death" (Flaskerud, 2017; Tenzek & Depner, 2017) that involves physical comfort, support from loved ones, acceptance, and

assisted suicide Involves a physician supplying the information and/or the means of committing suicide but requiring the patient to self-administer the lethal medication and to decide when and where to do this.

appropriate medical care. For some individuals, a good death involves accepting one's impending death and not feeling like a burden to others (Krishnan, 2017). Three frequent themes identified in articles on a good death involve (1) preference for dying process (94 percent of reports), (2) pain-free status (81 percent), and (3) emotional well-being (64 percent) (Meier & others, 2016).

Recent criticisms of the "good death" concept emphasize that death itself has shifted from being an event at a single point in time to being a process that takes place over years and even decades (Pollock & Seymour, 2018; Smith & Periyakoil, 2018). Thus, say the critics, we need to move away from the concept of a "good death" as a specific event for an individual person to a larger vision of a world that not only meets the needs of individuals at their moment of death but also focuses on making their lives better during the last years and decades of their lives.

Hospice is a program committed to making the end of life as free from pain, anxiety, and depression as possible (Fridman & others, 2018; Wang & others, 2017). Traditionally, a hospital's goal has been to cure illness and prolong life (Koksvik, 2018). In contrast, hospice care emphasizes **palliative care,** which involves reducing pain and

hospice A program committed to making the end of life as free from pain, anxiety, and depression as possible. The goals of hospice care contrast with those of a hospital, which are to cure disease and prolong life.

palliative care Emphasized in hospice care; involves reducing pain and suffering and helping individuals die with dignity.

How Would You...?

As a **human development and family studies professional,** how would you advocate for a terminally ill person's desire for hospice care?

suffering and helping individuals die with dignity (Bangerter & others, 2018; Chi & others, 2018; Nilsen & others, 2018; Pidgeon & others, 2018). However, U.S. hospitals recently have rapidly expanded their provision of palliative care. More than 85 percent of mid- to large-size U.S. hospitals have a palliative care team (Morrison, 2013). Hospice-care professionals work together to treat the dying person's symptoms, make the individual as comfortable as possible, show interest in the person and the person's family, and help everyone involved cope with death (Bogusz, Pekacka-Falkowska, & Magowska, 2018; Stiel & others, 2018; Wise, 2017).

Today more hospice programs are home-based, a blend of institutional and home care designed to humanize the end-of-life experience for the dying person. To read about the work of a home hospice nurse, see the *Careers in Life-Span Development* profile.

Careers in life-span development

Kathy McLaughlin, Home Hospice Nurse

Kathy McLaughlin is a home hospice nurse in Alexandria, Virginia. She provides care for individuals with terminal cancer, Alzheimer disease, and other illnesses. There currently is a shortage of home hospice nurses in the United States.

Kathy says that she has seen too many people dying in pain, away from home, hooked up to needless machines. In her work as a home hospice nurse, she comments, "I know I'm making a difference. I just feel privileged to get the chance to meet this person who is not going to be around much longer. I want to enjoy the moment with this person. And I want them to enjoy the moment. They have great stories. They are better than novels" (McLaughlin, 2003, p. 1).

Kathy McLaughlin with her hospice patient.
Courtesy of The Family of Mary Monteiro

Hospice nurses like Kathy McLaughlin care for terminally ill patients and seek to make their remaining days of life as pain-free and comfortable as possible. They typically spend several hours a day in the terminally ill patient's home, serving not just as a medical caregiver but also as an emotional caregiver. Hospice nurses usually coordinate the patient's care through an advising physician.

Hospice nurses must be registered nurses (RNs) and also be certified for hospice work. Educational requirements are an undergraduate degree in nursing; some hospice nurses also have graduate degrees in nursing. Certification as a hospice nurse requires a current license as an RN, a minimum of two years of experience as an RN in hospice-nursing settings, and achievement of a passing score on an exam administered by the National Board for the Certification of Hospice Nurses.

Death and Sociohistorical, Cultural Contexts

Today in the United States, the deaths of older adults account for approximately two-thirds of the 2 million deaths that occur each year. Thus, what we know about death, dying, and grieving mainly is based on information about older adults. Youthful death is far less common. When, where, and how people die have changed historically in the United States. Also, attitudes toward death vary across cultures.

Changing Historical Circumstances

We have already described one of the historical changes involving death—the increasing complexity of determining when someone is truly dead. Another involves the age group in which death most often strikes. Two hundred years ago, almost one of every two children died before the age of 10, and often one parent died before children grew up. Today, death occurs most often among older adults. In the United States, life expectancy has increased from 47 years for a person born in 1900 to 79 years for someone born today (U.S. Census Bureau, 2018). Today, the life expectancy in the United States for women is 81, for men 76. In 1900, most people died at home, cared for by their family. As our population has aged and become more mobile, growing numbers of older adults die apart from their families. More than 80 percent of all U.S. deaths occur in institutions or hospitals. The care of a dying older person has shifted away from the family and minimized our exposure to death and its painful surroundings.

Death in Different Cultures

Cultural variations characterize the experience of death and attitudes about death (Guilbeau, 2018; Miller, 2016; Prince, 2018; Wang & others, 2018; Whitehouse, 2018). Individuals are more conscious of death in times of war, famine, and plague. Most societies throughout history have had philosophical or religious beliefs about death, and most societies have a ritual that deals with death (see Figure 1). Death may be seen as a punishment for one's sins, an act of atonement, or a judgment of a just God. For some, death means loneliness; for others, death is a quest for happiness. For still others, death represents redemption, a relief from the trials and tribulations of the earthly world. Some embrace death and welcome it; others abhor and fear it. Death may be seen as the fitting end to a fulfilled life. From this perspective, how we depart from earth is influenced by how we have lived.

In most societies, death is not viewed as the end of existence—although the biological body has died, the spirit is believed to live on (Hamilton & others, 2018; Jones & Nie, 2018; Pun & others, 2018). This religious perspective is favored by most Americans as well. Cultural variations in attitudes toward death include belief in reincarnation, which is an important aspect of the Hindu and Buddhist religions. In the Gond culture of India, death is believed to be caused by magic and demons.

Figure 1 A Ritual Associated with Death
Family memorial day at the national cemetery in Seoul, South Korea.
©Ahn Young-joon/AP Images

In many ways, we in the United States are death avoiders and death deniers (Norouzieh, 2005). This denial can take many forms: the tendency of the funeral industry to gloss over death and fashion lifelike qualities in the dead; the persistent search for a "fountain of youth"; the rejection and isolation of the aged, who may remind us of death; and the medical community's emphasis on prolonging biological life rather than on diminishing human suffering.

Facing One's Own Death

Most dying individuals want an opportunity to make some decisions regarding their own life and death (Kastenbaum, 2012). Some individuals want to complete unfinished business; they want time to resolve problems and conflicts and to put their affairs in order. As individuals face death, a majority prefer to be at home when they are near death. A Canadian study found that 71 percent wanted to be at home when they die, 15 percent preferred to be in a hospice/palliative care facility, 7 percent wanted to be in a hospital, and only 2 percent preferred to be in a nursing home (Wilson & others, 2013).

Kübler-Ross' Stages of Dying

Elisabeth Kübler-Ross (1969) divided the behavior and thinking of dying persons into five stages: denial and isolation, anger, bargaining, depression, and acceptance.

Denial and isolation is Kübler-Ross' first stage of dying, in which the person denies that death is really going to take place. The person may say, "No, this can't happen to me. It's not possible." This is a common reaction to terminal illness. However, denial is usually only a temporary defense. It is eventually replaced with increased awareness when the person is confronted with such matters as financial considerations, unfinished business, and worry about the well-being of surviving family members.

Anger is the second stage of dying, in which the dying person recognizes that denial can no longer be maintained. Denial often gives way to anger, resentment, rage, and envy. The dying person's question is "Why me?" At this point, the person becomes increasingly difficult to care for as anger may become displaced and projected onto physicians, nurses, family members, and even God. The realization of loss is great, and those who symbolize life, energy, and competent functioning are especially salient targets of the dying person's resentment and jealousy.

Bargaining is the third stage of dying, in which the person develops the hope that death can somehow be postponed or delayed. Some persons enter into a bargaining or negotiation— often with God—as they try to delay their death. Psychologically, the person is saying, "Yes, me, but . . ." In exchange for a few more days, the person promises to lead a reformed life dedicated to God or to the service of others.

Depression is the fourth stage of dying, in which the dying person comes to accept the certainty of death. A period of depression or preparatory grief may appear. The dying person may become silent, refuse visitors, and spend much of the time crying or grieving. This behavior is normal and is an effort to disconnect the self from love objects. Attempts to cheer up the dying person at this stage should be discouraged, says Kübler-Ross, because the dying person has a need to contemplate impending death.

Acceptance is the fifth stage of dying, in which the person develops a sense of peace, an acceptance of his or her fate, and in many cases, a desire to be left alone. Feelings and physical pain may be virtually absent. Kübler-Ross describes this stage as the end of the dying struggle, the final resting stage before death. Figure 2 is a summary of Kübler-Ross' dying stages.

denial and isolation Kübler-Ross' first stage of dying, in which the dying person denies that she or he is really going to die.

anger Kübler-Ross' second stage of dying, in which the dying person's denial often gives way to anger, resentment, rage, and envy.

bargaining Kübler-Ross' third stage of dying, in which the dying person develops the hope that death can somehow be postponed.

depression Kübler-Ross' fourth stage of dying, in which the dying person begins to acknowledge the certainty of her or his death. A period of depression or preparatory grief may appear.

acceptance Kübler-Ross' fifth stage of dying, in which the dying person develops a sense of peace, an acceptance of her or his fate, and in many cases, a desire to be left alone.

Denial and isolation

Anger

Bargaining

Depression

Acceptance

Figure 2 Kübler-Ross' Stages of Dying
According to Elisabeth Kübler-Ross, we go through five stages of dying: denial and isolation, anger, bargaining, depression, and acceptance. *Does everyone go through these stages, or go through them in the same order?* Explain.
©Science Photo Library/Getty Images

According to Robert Kastenbaum (2009, 2012), there are some problems with Kübler-Ross' approach. For example, the existence of the five-stage sequence has not been demonstrated by either Kübler-Ross or independent research. Also, the stage interpretation neglects variations in patients' situations, including relationship support, specific effects of illness, family obligations, and the institutional climate in which they were interviewed. However, Kübler-Ross' pioneering efforts were important in calling attention to those who are attempting to cope with life-threatening illnesses. She did much to encourage attention to the quality of life for dying persons and their families.

Perceived Control and Denial

How Would You...?

As a **human development and family studies professional,** how would you advise family members to empower dying loved ones to feel they have more control over the end of their lives?

Perceived control may work as an adaptive strategy for some older adults who face death. When individuals are led to believe they can influence and control events—such as prolonging their lives—they may become more alert and cheerful. As discussed in the chapter on "Socioemotional Development in Late Adulthood," nursing home residents who were given options for control felt better and lived longer than their counterparts who had no control over their environment or activities (Rodin & Langer, 1977).

Denial also may be a fruitful way for some individuals to approach death. It can be adaptive or maladaptive (Cottrell & Duggleby, 2016). Denial can be used to avoid the destructive impact of shock by delaying the necessity of dealing with one's death. Denial can insulate the individual from having to cope with intense feelings of anger and hurt; however, if denial keeps us from having a life-saving operation, it clearly is maladaptive. Denial is neither good nor bad; its adaptive qualities need to be evaluated on an individual basis.

Coping with the Death of Someone Else

Loss can come in many forms in our lives—divorce, the death of a pet, being fired from a job, losing a limb—but no loss is greater than that which comes through the death of someone we love and care for—a parent, sibling, spouse, relative, or friend. In the ratings of life's stresses that require the most adjustment, death of a spouse is given the highest number. How should we communicate with a dying individual? How does grieving help us cope with the death of someone we love? How do we make sense of the world when a loved one has passed away? How are people affected by losing a life partner? And what are some forms of mourning and funeral rites?

Communicating with a Dying Person

Most psychologists believe that dying individuals should know they are dying and significant others know that their loved one is dying, so they can interact and communicate with each other on the basis of this mutual knowledge (Banja, 2005). What are some of the advantages of this open awareness for the dying individual? First, dying individuals can close their lives in accord with their own ideas about proper dying. Second, they may be able to complete some plans and projects, make arrangements for survivors, and participate in decisions about a funeral and burial. Third, dying individuals have the opportunity to reminisce, to converse with others who have been important to them, and to end life conscious of their unique struggles and accomplishments. And fourth, dying individuals have more understanding of what is happening within their bodies and what the medical staff is doing for them (Kalish, 1981).

In addition, some experts believe that conversation should not focus on mental pathology or preparation for death but instead on strengths of the individual and preparation for the remainder of life. Because external accomplishments are not possible, communication should be directed more at internal growth. Important support for a dying individual may come not only from mental health professionals but also from nurses, physicians, a spouse, or intimate friends (DeSpelder & Strickland, 2005). Effective strategies for communicating with a dying person include the following:

What are some good strategies for communicating with a dying person?
©Stockbroker/Photolibrary

1. Establish your presence, be at the same eye level; don't be afraid to touch the dying person—dying individuals are often starved for human touch.

2. Eliminate distractions—for example, ask if it is okay to turn off the TV. Realize that excessive small talk can be a distraction.

3. Dying individuals who are very frail often have little energy. If the dying person you are visiting is very frail, you may want to keep your visit short.

4. Don't insist that the dying person feel acceptance about death if the dying person wants to deny the reality of the situation; on the other hand, don't insist on denial if the dying individual indicates acceptance.

5. Allow the dying person to express guilt or anger; encourage the expression of feelings.

6. Ask the person what the expected outcome for the illness is. Discuss alternatives and unfinished business.

7. Sometimes dying individuals have limited access to other people. Ask the dying person if there is anyone he or she would like to see that you can contact.

8. Encourage the dying individual to reminisce, especially if you have memories in common.

9. Talk with the individual when she or he wishes to talk. If this is impossible, make an appointment for a later time, and keep it.

10. Express your regard for the dying individual. Don't be afraid to express love, and don't be afraid to say good-bye.

Grieving

Grief is a complex emotional state that is an evolving process with multiple dimensions. Our exploration of grief focuses on dimensions of grieving and how coping may vary with the type of death.

Dimensions of Grieving

Grief is the emotional numbness, disbelief, separation anxiety, despair, sadness, and loneliness that accompany the loss of someone we love (Bui & Okereke, 2018). An important dimension of grief is pining for the lost person. Pining or yearning reflects an intermittent, recurrent wish or need to recover the lost person. Another important dimension of grief is separation anxiety, which not only includes pining and preoccupation with thoughts of the deceased person but also focuses on places and things associated with the deceased, as well as crying or sighing (Sirrine, Salloum, & Boothroyd, 2017). Grief may also involve despair and sadness, including a sense of hopelessness and defeat, depressive symptoms, apathy, loss of meaning for activities that used to involve the person who is gone, and growing desolation (Milic & others, 2018; Schwartz, Howell, & Jamison, 2018). One study found that older adults who were bereaved had more dysregulated cortisol patterns, indicative of the intensity of their stress (Holland & others, 2014). Another study found that college students who lost someone close to them in campus shootings and had

grief The emotional numbness, disbelief, separation anxiety, despair, sadness, and loneliness that accompany the loss of someone we love.

complicated grief or prolonged grief disorder Grief that involves enduring despair and remains unresolved over an extended period of time.

experienced severe posttraumatic stress symptoms four months after the shootings were more likely to have severe grief one year after the shootings (Smith & others, 2015).

These feelings occur repeatedly shortly after a loss. As time passes, pining and protest over the loss tend to diminish, although episodes of depression and apathy may remain or increase. The sense of separation anxiety and loss may continue to the end of one's life, but most of us emerge from grief's tears, turning our attention once again to productive tasks and regaining a more positive view of life (Mendes, 2016).

The grieving process is more like a roller-coaster ride than an orderly progression of stages with clear-cut time frames. The ups and downs of grief often involve rapidly changing emotions, meeting the challenges of learning new skills, detecting personal weaknesses and limitations, creating new patterns of behavior, and forming new friendships and relationships. For most individuals, grief becomes more manageable over time, with fewer abrupt highs and lows. But many grieving spouses report that even though time has brought some healing, they have never gotten over their loss. They have just learned to live with it. However, even six months after their loss, some individuals have difficulty moving on with their life. They feel numb or detached, believe their life is empty without the deceased, and feel that the future has no meaning. This type of grief reaction has been labeled as **complicated grief or prolonged grief disorder** (Breen & others, 2018; Li, Tendeiro, & Stroebe, 2018; Maciejewski & Prigerson, 2017; Tsai & others, 2018). Approximately 7 to 10 percent of bereaved individuals experience prolonged or complicated grief (Maccalum & Bryant, 2013). In a recent meta-analysis, 9.8 percent of adult bereavement cases were classified as characterized by prolonged grief disorder (Lundorff & others, 2017). In this study, the older individuals were, the more likely prolonged grief disorder was present. A person who loses someone on whom he or she was emotionally dependent is often at greatest risk for developing prolonged grief (Rodriguez Villar & others, 2012). A recent study revealed that individuals with complicated grief had a higher level of the personality trait of neuroticism (Goetter & others, 2018).

How Would You...?

As a **social worker,** how would you respond to bereaved clients who ask, "What is normal grieving?" as they attempt to cope with the death of a loved one?

Complicated grief usually has negative consequences for physical and mental health (Djelantik & others, 2017; Tang & Chow, 2017; Trevino & others, 2018). A recent 7-year longitudinal study of older adults found that those experiencing prolonged grief had greater cognitive decline than their counterparts with normal grief (Perez & others, 2018). Recent research indicates that cognitive-behavior therapy reduced prolonged grief symptoms (Bartl & others, 2018).

Another type of grief is *disenfranchised grief,* which describes an individual's grief over a deceased person that is a socially ambiguous loss that can't be openly mourned or supported (Patlamazoglou, Simmonds, & Snell, 2018; Tullis, 2017). Examples of disenfranchised grief include a relationship that isn't socially recognized such as an ex-spouse, a hidden loss such as an abortion, and circumstances of the death that are stigmatized such as death because of AIDS. Disenfranchised grief may intensify an individual's grief because it cannot be publicly acknowledged. This type of grief may be hidden or repressed for many years, only to be reawakened by later deaths.

Coping and Type of Death

The impact of death on surviving individuals is strongly influenced by the circumstances under which the death occurs (Lovgren & others, 2018; Tobin, Lambert, & McCarthy, 2018). Deaths that are sudden, untimely, violent, or traumatic are likely to have more intense and prolonged effects on surviving individuals and make the coping process more difficult for them (Creighton & others, 2018; Feigelman & others, 2018; Pitman & others, 2018). Such deaths often are accompanied by post-traumatic stress disorder (PTSD) symptoms, such as intrusive thoughts, flashbacks, nightmares, sleep disturbances, or problems in concentrating. The death of a child can be especially devastating and extremely difficult for parents (Eskola & others, 2017; Fu & others, 2018; Keim & others, 2017).

Making Sense of the World

Not only do many individuals who face death search for meaning in life, so do many bereaved individuals (Breen & others, 2018; Steffen & Coyle, 2017). One beneficial aspect of grieving is that it stimulates many individuals to try to make sense of their world (Bianco, Sambin, & Palmieri, 2017; Breen & others, 2018). Many grieving persons ruminate on the events that led up to the death of their loved one. In the days and weeks after the death, the closest family members share memories with each other, sometimes reminiscing about family experiences. One study examined meaning-making following a child's death (Meert & others, 2015). From 8 to 20 weeks following the child's death, the child's intensive care physician conducted a bereavement meeting with 53 parents of 35 children who had died. Four meaning-making processes were identified in the meetings: (1) sense making (seeking biomedical explanations for the death, revisiting parents' prior decisions and roles, and assigning blame); (2) benefit finding (exploring possible positive consequences of the death such as ways to help others, providing feedback to the hospital, and making donations); (3) continuing bonds (reminiscing about the child, sharing photographs, and holding community events to honor the child); and (4) identity reconstruction (changes in the parents' sense of self, including changes in relationships, work, and home).

These restaurant workers, who lost their jobs on 9/11/01, made a bittersweet return with a New York restaurant they call their own. Colors, named for the many nationalities and ethnic groups among its owners, is believed to be the city's first cooperative restaurant. World-famous restaurant Windows on the World was destroyed and 73 workers killed when the Twin Towers were destroyed by terrorists. The former Windows survivors at the new venture planned to split 60 percent of the profits between themselves and to donate the rest to a fund to open other cooperative restaurants.
©Thomas Hinton/Splash News/Newscom

When a death is caused by an accident or a disaster, the effort to make sense of it is pursued more vigorously (Park, 2016). As added pieces of news come trickling in, they are integrated into the puzzle. The bereaved want to put the death into a perspective that they can understand—divine intervention, a curse from a neighboring tribe, a logical sequence of cause and effect, or whatever it may be. A study of more than 1,000 college students found that making sense was an important factor in their grieving of a violent loss by accident, homicide, or suicide (Currier, Holland, & Neimeyer, 2006).

Losing a Life Partner

In 2015 in the United States, 14 percent of 65- to 74-year-olds, 31 percent of 75-to 84-year-olds, and 59 percent of those 85 and over were widowed (Administration on Aging, 2015). Approximately three times as many women as men are widowed. Those left behind after the death of an intimate partner often suffer profound grief and may endure financial loss, loneliness, increased physical illness, and psychological disorders such as depression (Daoulah & others, 2017; Siflinger, 2017). In one study, becoming widowed was associated with a 48 percent increase in risk of mortality (Sullivan & Fenelon, 2014). Mortality risk increased for men if their wives' deaths were not expected, but for women the unexpected death of a husband mattered less in terms of their mortality risk. In another study, Mexican American older adults experienced a significant increase in depressive symptoms during the transition to widowhood (Monserud & Markides, 2017). Frequent church attendance was a protective factor against increases in depressive symptoms. Also, in a recent cross-cultural study in the United States, England, Europe, Korea, and China, depression peaked in the first year of widowhood for men and women (Jadhav & Weir, 2018). In this study, women recovered to levels comparable to married individuals in all countries, but widowed men continued to have high levels of depression 6 to 10 years post-bereavement everywhere except in Europe.

How surviving spouses cope varies considerably (Hasmanova Marhankova, 2016). Becoming widowed is likely to be especially difficult when individuals have been happily married for a number of decades. In such circumstances, losing your spouse, who may

How Would You...?

As a **social worker,** how would you help a widow or widower to connect with a support group to deal with the death of a loved one?

also be your best friend and with whom you have lived a deeply connected life, can be extremely emotional and difficult to cope with. A six-year longitudinal study of individuals aged 80 and older found that the loss of a spouse, especially in men, was related to a lower level of life satisfaction over time (Berg & others, 2009). Another study revealed that widowed persons who did not expect to be reunited with their loved ones in the afterlife reported more depression, anger, and intrusive thoughts at 6 and 18 months after their loss (Carr & Sharp, 2014).

Many widows are lonely. The poorer and less educated they are, the lonelier they tend to be. The bereaved are also at increased risk for many health problems (Jadhav & Weir, 2018). For either widows or widowers, social support helps them adjust to the death of a spouse (Dahlberg, Agahi, & Lennartsson, 2018; Hendrickson & others, 2018; Huang & others, 2017). The Widow-to-Widow program, begun in the 1960s, provides support for newly widowed women. Volunteer widows reach out to other widows, introducing them to others who may have similar problems, leading group discussions, and organizing social activities. The program has been adopted by AARP and disseminated throughout the United States as the Widowed Persons Service. The model has since been adopted by numerous community organizations to provide support for those going through a difficult transition. Also, in recent research, when widows engaged in volunteering to help others, it reduced their loneliness (Carr & others, 2018).

Forms of Mourning

One decision facing the bereaved is what to do with the body. In the United States in 2017, 51.6 percent of deaths were followed by cremation—a significant increase from 14 percent in 1985 and 27 percent in 2000 (Cremation Association of North America, 2018). In 2017 in Canada, 70.5 percent of deaths were followed by cremation. Projections indicate that in 2022, 57.5 percent of U.S. deaths will be followed by cremation while the cremation rate in Canada will increase to 75.1 percent. Cremation is more popular in the Pacific region of the United States and less popular in the South. It is more popular in Canada than in the United States and most popular of all in Japan and other Asian countries.

The funeral industry has been a target of controversy in recent years. Funeral directors and their supporters argue that the funeral provides a form of closure to the relationship with the deceased, especially when there is an open casket. Their critics claim that funeral directors are just trying to make money and that embalming is grotesque. One way to avoid being exploited during bereavement is to purchase funeral arrangements in advance.

The family and the community have important roles in mourning in some cultures. One of those cultures is the Amish, a conservative group with approximately 80,000 members in the United States, Ontario, and several small settlements in South and Central America. The Amish live in a family-oriented society in which family and community support are essential for survival. At the time of death, close neighbors assume the responsibility of notifying others of the death. The Amish community handles virtually all aspects of the funeral.

The funeral service is held in a barn in warmer months and in a house during colder months. Calm acceptance of death, influenced by a deep religious

A funeral procession of horse-drawn buggies on their way to the burial of five young Amish girls who were murdered in October 2006. A remarkable aspect of their mourning involved the outpouring of support and forgiveness they gave to the widow of the murderer.
©Glenn Fawcett/Baltimore Sun/MCT/Getty Images

faith, is an integral part of the Amish culture. Following the funeral, a high level of support is given to the bereaved family for at least a year. Visits to the family, special scrapbooks and handmade items for the family, new work projects started for the widow, and quilting days that combine fellowship and productivity are among the supports given to the bereaved family.

We have arrived at the end of this edition. Our study of the human life span has been long and complex. You have read about many physical, cognitive, and socioemotional changes that take place from conception through death. This is a good time to reflect on what you have learned. Which theories, studies, and ideas were especially interesting to you? What did you learn about your own development?

I hope this edition and course have been a window to the life span of the human species and a window to your own personal journey in life. I wish you all the best in the remaining years of your journey through the human life span.

John W. Santrock

Summary

Defining Death and Life/Death Issues

- Most physicians today agree that the higher and lower portions of the brain must stop functioning in order for an individual to be considered *brain dead.*
- Decisions regarding life, death, and health care can involve a number of circumstances and issues, and individuals can use a living will to make these choices while they can still think clearly. Hospice care emphasizes reducing pain and suffering rather than prolonging life.

Death and Sociohistorical, Cultural Contexts

- Over the years, the circumstances of when, where, and why people die have changed. Throughout history, most societies have had philosophical or religious beliefs about death, and most societies have rituals that deal with death.
- The United States has been described as a death-denying and death-avoiding culture.

Facing One's Own Death

- Kübler-Ross proposed five stages of facing death, and although her view has been criticized, her efforts were

important in calling attention to the experience of coping with life-threatening illness.

- Perceived control over events and denial may work together as an adaptive orientation for a dying individual.

Coping with the Death of Someone Else

- Most psychologists recommend an open communication system with a dying person and his or her significant others.
- Grief is multidimensional and in some cases may last for years. Complicated grief or prolonged grief disorder and disenfranchised grief are especially challenging.
- The grieving process may stimulate individuals to strive to make sense out of the world.
- Usually the most difficult loss is the death of a spouse. The bereaved are at increased risk for health problems.
- Forms of mourning vary across cultures.

Key Terms

acceptance	bargaining	denial and isolation	hospice
active euthanasia	brain death	depression	palliative care
anger	complicated grief or prolonged	euthanasia	passive euthanasia
assisted suicide	grief disorder	grief	

A

A-not-B error This term is used to describe the tendency of infants to reach where an object was located earlier rather than where the object was last hidden.

acceptance Kübler-Ross' fifth stage of dying, in which the dying person develops a sense of peace, an acceptance of her or his fate, and in many cases, a desire to be left alone.

accommodation Piagetian concept of adjusting schemes to fit new information and experiences.

active euthanasia Death induced deliberately, as when a physician or a third party ends the patient's life by administering a lethal dose of a drug.

activity theory Theory that the more active and involved older adults are, the more likely they are to be satisfied with their lives.

adolescent egocentrism The heightened self-consciousness of adolescents.

adoption study A study in which investigators seek to discover whether, in behavior and psychological characteristics, adopted children are more like their adoptive parents, who provided a home environment, or more like their biological parents, who contributed their heredity. Another form of the adoption study compares adoptive and biological siblings.

aerobic exercise Sustained exercise (such as jogging, swimming, or cycling).

affectionate love In this type of love, also called companionate love, an individual desires to have the other person near and has a deep, caring affection for the other person.

ageism Prejudice against people because of their age, especially prejudice against older adults.

Alzheimer disease A progressive, irreversible brain disorder characterized by a gradual deterioration of memory, reasoning, language, and eventually physical function.

amygdala The region of the brain that is the seat of emotions.

anger Kübler-Ross' second stage of dying, in which the dying person's denial often gives way to anger, resentment, rage, and envy.

anger cry A cry similar to the basic cry, with more excess air forced through the vocal cords.

animism The belief that inanimate objects have lifelike qualities and are capable of action.

anorexia nervosa An eating disorder that involves the relentless pursuit of thinness through starvation.

anxious attachment style An attachment style that describes adults who demand closeness, are less trusting, and are more emotional, jealous, and possessive.

Apgar Scale A widely used assessment of the newborn's health at 1 and 5 minutes after birth.

arthritis Inflammation of the joints that is accompanied by pain, stiffness, and movement problems; especially common in older adults.

assimilation Piagetian concept of using existing schemes to deal with new information or experiences.

assisted suicide Involves a physician supplying the information and/or the means of committing suicide but requiring the patient to self-administer the lethal medication and to decide when and where to do this.

attachment A close emotional bond between two people.

attention The focusing of mental resources on select information.

attention deficit hyperactivity disorder (ADHD) A disability in which children consistently show one or more of the following characteristics: (1) inattention, (2) hyperactivity, and (3) impulsivity.

authoritarian parenting A restrictive, punitive style in which parents exhort the child to follow their directions and to respect work and effort. The authoritarian parent places firm limits and controls on the child and allows little verbal exchange. Authoritarian parenting is associated with children's social incompetence.

authoritative parenting A parenting style in which parents encourage their children to be independent but still place limits and controls on their actions. Extensive verbal give-and-take is allowed, and parents are warm and nurturant toward the child. Authoritative parenting is associated with children's social competence.

autism spectrum disorders (ASD) Also called pervasive developmental disorders, they range from the severe disorder labeled autistic disorder to the milder disorder called Asperger syndrome. These disorders are characterized by problems in social interaction, verbal and nonverbal communication, and repetitive behaviors.

autonomous morality The second stage of moral development in Piaget's theory, displayed by older children (about 10 years of age and older). The child becomes aware that rules and laws are created by people and that in judging an action, one should consider the actor's intentions as well as the consequences.

average children Children who receive an average number of both positive and negative nominations from their peers.

avoidant attachment style An attachment style that describes adults who are hesitant about getting involved in romantic relationships and once they are in a relationship tend to distance themselves from their partner.

B

bargaining Kübler-Ross' third stage of dying, in which the dying person develops the hope that death can somehow be postponed.

basic cry A rhythmic pattern usually consisting of a cry, a briefer silence, a shorter inspiratory whistle that is higher-pitched than the main cry, and a brief rest before the next cry.

behavior genetics The field that seeks to discover the influence of heredity and environment on individual differences in human traits and development.

behavioral and social cognitive theories Theories holding that development can be described in terms of the behaviors learned through interactions with the environment.

Big Five factors of personality Emotional stability (neuroticism), extraversion, openness to experience, agreeableness, and conscientiousness.

biological processes Changes in an individual's physical nature.

brain death A neurological definition of death. A person is brain dead when all electrical activity of the brain has ceased for a specified period of time. A flat EEG recording is one criterion of brain death.

Bronfenbrenner's ecological theory Bronfenbrenner's environmental systems theory, which focuses on five environmental systems: microsystem, mesosystem, exosystem, macrosystem, and chronosystem.

bulimia nervosa An eating disorder in which the individual consistently follows a binge-and-purge pattern.

C

care perspective The moral perspective of Carol Gilligan, which views people in terms of their connectedness with others and emphasizes interpersonal communication, relationships with others, and concern for others.

case study An in-depth examination of an individual.

cataracts Involve a thickening of the lens of the eye that causes vision to become cloudy and distorted.

cellular clock theory Leonard Hayflick's theory that the maximum number of times human cells can divide is about 75 to 80. As we age, our cells become increasingly less capable of dividing.

centration The focusing of attention on one characteristic to the exclusion of all others.

cephalocaudal pattern Developmental sequence in which the earliest growth always occurs at the top—the head—with physical growth in size, weight, and feature differentiation gradually working from top to bottom.

child-centered kindergarten Education that involves the whole child by considering both the child's physical, cognitive, and socioemotional development and the child's needs, interests, and learning styles.

child-directed speech Also called parentese, language spoken in a higher pitch, slower tempo, and with more exaggerated intonation than normal, with simple words and sentences.

chromosomes Threadlike structures made up of deoxyribonucleic acid, or DNA.

climacteric The midlife transition in which fertility declines.

clique A small group that ranges from 2 to about 12 individuals, averaging about 5 or 6 individuals, and often consists of adolescents who engage in similar activities.

cognitive processes Changes in an individual's thought, intelligence, and language.

cohort effects Effects that are due to a subject's time of birth or generation but not age.

commitment Marcia's term for the part of identity development in which adolescents show a personal investment in forming an identity.

complicated grief or prolonged grief disorder Grief that involves enduring despair and remains unresolved over an extended period of time.

concepts Cognitive groupings of similar objects, events, people, or ideas.

conservation In Piaget's theory, awareness that altering an object's or a substance's appearance does not change its basic properties.

constructive play Play that combines sensorimotor and repetitive activity with symbolic representation of ideas. Constructive play occurs when children engage in self-regulated creation or construction of a product or a problem solution.

constructivist approach A learner-centered approach that emphasizes the importance of individuals actively constructing their knowledge and understanding with guidance from the teacher.

contemporary life-events approach An approach emphasizing that how a life event influences the individual's development depends not only on the life event itself but also on mediating factors, the individual's adaptation to the life event, the life-stage context, and the sociohistorical context.

context The setting in which development occurs, which is influenced by historical, economic, social, and cultural factors.

continuity-discontinuity issue The debate about the extent to which development involves gradual, cumulative change (continuity) or distinct stages (discontinuity).

controversial children Children who are frequently nominated both as someone's best friend and as being disliked.

conventional reasoning The second, or intermediate, level in Kohlberg's theory of moral development. At this level, individuals abide by certain standards, but they are the standards of others, such as parents or the laws of society.

convergent thinking The type of thinking that produces one correct answer and is typically assessed by standardized intelligence tests.

core knowledge approach Theory that infants are born with domain-specific innate knowledge systems.

corpus callosum The location where nerve fibers connect the brain's left and right hemispheres.

correlation coefficient A number based on statistical analysis that is used to describe the degree of association between two variables.

correlational research A type of research that focuses on describing the strength of the relation between two or more events or characteristics.

creative thinking The ability to think in novel and unusual ways and to come up with unique solutions to problems.

crisis Marcia's term for a period of identity development during which the adolescent is exploring alternatives.

critical thinking Thinking reflectively and productively, as well as evaluating the evidence.

cross-cultural studies Comparisons of one culture with one or more other cultures. These provide information about the degree to which children's development is similar, or universal, across cultures, and the degree to which it is culture-specific.

cross-sectional approach A research strategy in which individuals of different ages are compared at one time.

crowd A larger group structure than a clique, a crowd is usually formed based on reputation, and members may or may not spend much time together.

crystallized intelligence Accumulated information and verbal skills, which increase in middle age, according to Horn.

cultural-familial intellectual disability Intellectual disability in which there is no evidence of organic brain damage, but the individual's IQ generally is between 50 and 70.

culture The behavior patterns, beliefs, and all other products of a group that are passed on from generation to generation.

culture-fair tests Tests of intelligence that are designed to be free of cultural bias.

cumulative personality model The principle that with time and age, people become more adept at interacting with their environment in ways that promote stability of personality.

D

deferred imitation Imitation that occurs after a delay of hours or days.

dementia A global term for any neurological disorder in which the primary symptoms involve a deterioration of mental functioning.

denial and isolation Kübler-Ross' first stage of dying, in which the dying person denies that she or he is really going to die.

depression Kübler-Ross' fourth stage of dying, in which the dying person begins to acknowledge the certainty of her or his death. A period of depression or preparatory grief may appear.

descriptive research Type of research that aims to observe and record behavior.

development The pattern of movement or change that starts at conception and continues through the life span.

developmental cascade model Involves connections across domains over time that influence developmental pathways and outcomes.

developmentally appropriate practice (DAP) Education that focuses on the typical developmental patterns of children (age appropriateness) and the uniqueness of each child (individual appropriateness).

difficult child A child who tends to react negatively and cry frequently, who engages in irregular daily routines, and who is slow to accept new experiences.

direct instruction approach A structured, teacher-centered approach that is characterized by teacher direction and control, high teacher expectations for students' progress, maximum time spent by students on learning tasks, and efforts by the teacher to keep negative affect to a minimum.

dishabituation Recovery of a habituated response after a change in stimulation.

divergent thinking Thinking that produces many answers to the same question and is characteristic of creativity.

DNA A complex molecule with a double helix shape that contains genetic information.

domain theory of moral development Theory that identifies different domains of social knowledge and reasoning, including moral, social conventional, and personal domains. These domains arise from children's and adolescents' attempts to understand and deal with different forms of social experience.

Down syndrome A chromosomally transmitted form of intellectual disability, caused by the presence of an extra copy of chromosome 21.

dynamic systems theory The perspective on motor development that seeks to explain how motor behaviors are assembled for perceiving and acting.

E

easy child A child who is generally in a positive mood, who quickly establishes regular routines in infancy, and who adapts easily to new experiences.

eclectic theoretical orientation An approach that selects and uses whatever is considered the best in many theories.

ecological view The view that perception functions to bring organisms in contact with the environment and to increase adaptation.

egocentrism The inability to distinguish between one's own perspective and someone else's (salient feature of the first substage of preoperational thought).

elaboration An important strategy that involves engaging in more extensive processing of information.

embryonic period The period of prenatal development that occurs two to eight weeks after conception. During the embryonic period, the rate of cell differentiation intensifies, support systems for the cells form, and organs appear.

emerging adulthood A period of transition from adolescence to adulthood (approximately 18 to 25 years of age) that involves experimentation and exploration.

emotion Feeling, or affect, that occurs when a person is in a state or interaction that is important to them. Emotion is characterized by behavior that reflects (expresses) the pleasantness or unpleasantness of the state a person is in or the transactions being experienced.

empty nest syndrome A term used to indicate a decrease in marital satisfaction after children leave home.

epigenetic view Emphasizes that development is the result of an ongoing, bidirectional interchange between heredity and environment.

episodic memory The retention of information about the where and when of life's happenings.

equilibration A mechanism that Piaget proposed to explain how children shift from one stage of thought to the next.

Erikson's theory A psychoanalytic theory in which eight stages of psychosocial development unfold throughout the life span. Each stage consists of a unique developmental task that confronts individuals with a crisis that must be faced.

ethnic identity An enduring, basic aspect of the self that includes a sense of membership in an ethnic group and the attitudes and feelings related to that membership.

ethnicity A range of characteristics rooted in cultural heritage, including nationality, race, religion, and language.

ethology An approach stressing that behavior is strongly influenced by biology, tied to evolution, and characterized by critical or sensitive periods.

euthanasia The act of painlessly ending the lives of persons who are suffering from incurable diseases or severe disabilities; sometimes called "mercy killing."

evolutionary psychology Emphasizes the importance of adaptation, reproduction, and "survival of the fittest" in shaping behavior.

evolutionary theory of aging The view that natural selection has not eliminated many harmful conditions and nonadaptive characteristics in older adults.

executive attention Involves planning actions, allocating attention to goals, detecting and compensating for errors, monitoring progress on tasks, and dealing with novel or difficult circumstances.

executive function An umbrella-like concept that consists of a number of higher-level cognitive processes linked to the development of the brain's prefrontal cortex. Executive function involves managing one's thoughts to engage in goal-directed behavior and to use self-control.

experiment A carefully regulated procedure in which one or more of the factors believed to influence the behavior being studied is manipulated and all other factors are held constant. Experimental research permits the determination of cause.

explicit memory Memory of facts and experiences that individuals consciously know and can state.

F

fast mapping A process that helps to explain how young children learn the connection between a word and its referent so quickly.

fetal alcohol spectrum disorders (FASD) A cluster of abnormalities that appears in the offspring of mothers who drink alcohol heavily during pregnancy.

fetal period The prenatal period of development that begins two months after conception and usually lasts for seven months.

fight-or-flight The view that when men experience stress, they are more likely to become aggressive, withdraw from social contact, or drink alcohol.

fine motor skills Motor skills that involve more finely tuned movements, such as finger dexterity.

fluid intelligence The ability to reason abstractly, which steadily declines from middle adulthood on, according to Horn.

free-radical theory A theory of aging proposing that people age because normal cell metabolism produces unstable oxygen molecules known as free radicals. These molecules ricochet around inside cells, damaging DNA and other cellular structures.

fuzzy trace theory States that memory is best understood by considering two types of memory representations: (1) verbatim memory trace and (2) gist. In this theory, older children's better memory is attributed to the fuzzy traces created by extracting the gist of information.

G

games Activities engaged in for pleasure that include rules and often involve competition between two or more individuals.

gender The characteristics of people as females and males.

gender identity The sense of being male or female, which most children acquire by the time they are 3 years old.

gender roles Sets of expectations that prescribe how females or males should think, act, and feel.

gender schema theory The theory that gender typing emerges as children gradually develop gender schemas of what is gender-appropriate and gender-inappropriate in their culture.

gender stereotypes Broad categories that reflect society's impressions and beliefs about females and males.

gene × environment (G × E) interaction The interaction of a specified measured variation in DNA and a specific measured aspect of the environment.

generativity Adults' desire to leave legacies of themselves to the next generation; the positive side of Erikson's middle adulthood stage of generativity versus stagnation.

genes Units of hereditary information composed of DNA. Genes direct cells to reproduce themselves and manufacture the proteins that maintain life.

genotype A person's genetic heritage; the actual genetic material.

germinal period The period of prenatal development that takes place during the first two weeks after conception. It includes the creation of the zygote, continued cell division, and the attachment of the zygote to the uterine wall.

gifted Having above-average intelligence (an IQ of 130 or higher) and/or superior talent for something.

glaucoma Damage to the optic nerve because of the pressure created by a buildup of fluid in the eye.

gonads The sex glands—the testes in males and the ovaries in females.

goodness of fit Refers to the match between a child's temperament and the environmental demands with which the child must cope.

grief The emotional numbness, disbelief, separation anxiety, despair, sadness, and loneliness that accompany the loss of someone we love.

gross motor skills Motor skills that involve large-muscle activities, such as walking.

H

habituation Decreased responsiveness to a stimulus after repeated presentations of the stimulus.

heteronomous morality The first stage of moral development in Piaget's theory, occurring from approximately 4 to 7 years of age. Justice and rules are conceived of as unchangeable properties of the world, beyond the control of people.

hormonal stress theory The theory that aging in the body's hormonal system can lower resilience under stress and increase the likelihood of disease.

hormones Powerful chemical substances secreted by the endocrine glands and carried through the body by the bloodstream.

hospice A program committed to making the end of life as free from pain, anxiety, and depression as possible. The goals of hospice care contrast with those of a hospital, which are to cure disease and prolong life.

hypothalamus A structure in the higher portion of the brain that monitors eating and sex.

hypotheses Assertions or predictions, often derived from theories, that can be tested.

hypothetical-deductive reasoning Piaget's formal operational concept that adolescents have the cognitive ability to develop hypotheses, or best guesses, about ways to solve problems.

I

identity achievement Marcia's term for adolescents who have undergone a crisis and have made a commitment.

identity diffusion Marcia's term for adolescents who have not yet experienced a crisis (explored meaningful alternatives) or made any commitments.

identity foreclosure Marcia's term for adolescents who have made a commitment but have not experienced a crisis.

identity moratorium Marcia's term for adolescents who are in the midst of a crisis, but their commitments are either absent or vaguely defined.

imaginary audience Involves adolescents' belief that others are as interested in them as they themselves are; attention-getting behavior motivated by a desire to be noticed, visible, and "on stage."

immanent justice The expectation that, if a rule is broken, punishment will be meted out immediately.

implicit memory Memory without conscious recollection; involves skills and routine procedures that are automatically performed.

inclusion Educating a child who requires special education full-time in the regular classroom.

individualized education plan (IEP) A written statement that spells out a program tailored to a child with a disability.

indulgent parenting A style of parenting in which parents are highly involved with their children but place few demands or controls on them. Indulgent parenting is associated with children's social incompetence, especially a lack of self-control.

infinite generativity The ability to produce and comprehend an endless number of meaningful sentences using a finite set of words and rules.

information-processing theory A theory emphasizing that individuals manipulate information, monitor it, and strategize about it. The processes of memory and thinking are central.

insecure avoidant babies Babies that show insecurity by avoiding their mothers.

insecure disorganized babies Babies that show insecurity by being disorganized and disoriented.

insecure resistant babies Babies that often cling to the caregiver, then resist her by fighting against the closeness, perhaps by kicking or pushing away.

integrity versus despair Erikson's eighth and final stage of development, which individuals experience in late adulthood. This involves reflecting on the past and either piecing together a positive review or concluding that one's life has not been well spent.

intellectual disability A condition of limited mental ability in which an individual has a low IQ, usually below 70 on a traditional test of intelligence, and has difficulty adapting to the demands of everyday life.

intelligence Problem-solving skills and the ability to learn from, and adapt to, the experiences of everyday life.

intelligence quotient (IQ) A person's mental age divided by chronological age and multiplied by 100.

intermodal perception The ability to relate and integrate information from two or more sensory modalities, such as vision and hearing.

intuitive thought substage Piaget's second substage of preoperational thought, in which children begin to use primitive reasoning and want to know the answers to all sorts of questions (between about 4 and 7 years of age).

J

joint attention Process that occurs when (1) individuals focus on the same object and track each other's behavior, (2) one individual directs another's attention, and (3) reciprocal interaction takes place.

justice perspective A moral perspective that focuses on the rights of the individual; individuals independently make moral decisions.

juvenile delinquent An adolescent who breaks the law or engages in behavior that is considered illegal.

L

laboratory A controlled setting in which research can take place.

language A form of communication, whether spoken, written, or signed, that is based on a system of symbols. Language consists of the words used by a community and the rules for varying and combining them.

language acquisition device (LAD) Chomsky's term that describes a biological endowment enabling the child to detect the features and rules of language, including phonology, syntax, and semantics.

lateralization Specialization of function in one hemisphere of the cerebral cortex or the other.

learning disability Describes a child who has difficulty understanding or using spoken or written language or doing mathematics. To be classified as a learning disability, the problem is not primarily the result of visual, hearing, or motor disabilities; intellectual disability; emotional disorders; or due to environmental, cultural, or economic disadvantage.

least restrictive environment (LRE) The concept that a child with a disability should be educated in a setting that is as similar as possible to the one in which children who do not have a disability are educated.

leisure The pleasant times after work when individuals are free to pursue activities and interests of their own choosing.

life expectancy The number of years that will probably be lived by the average person born in a particular year.

life span The upper boundary of life, which is the maximum number of years an individual can live. The maximum life span of human beings is about 120 to 125 years of age.

life-span perspective The perspective that development is lifelong, multidimensional, multidirectional, plastic, multidisciplinary, and contextual; that it involves growth, maintenance, and regulation; and that it is constructed through biological, sociocultural, and individual factors working together.

limbic system A lower, subcortical system in the brain that is the seat of emotions and experience of rewards.

long-term memory A relatively permanent type of memory that holds huge amounts of information for a long period of time.

longitudinal approach A research strategy in which the same individuals are studied over a period of time, usually several years or more.

M

macular degeneration A disease that involves deterioration of the macula of the retina, which corresponds to the focal center of the visual field.

meiosis A specialized form of cell division that occurs to form eggs and sperm (or gametes).

memory A central feature of cognitive development, pertaining to all situations in which an individual retains information over time.

menarche A girl's first menstruation.

menopause The complete cessation of a woman's menstrual cycles, which usually occurs in the late forties or early fifties.

mental age (MA) Binet's measure of an individual's level of mental development, compared with that of others.

metacognition Cognition about cognition, or knowing about knowing.

metalinguistic awareness Refers to knowledge about language, such as knowing what a preposition is or being able to discuss the sounds of a language.

middle adulthood The developmental period beginning at approximately 40 years of age and extending to about 60 to 65 years of age.

mindset The cognitive view that individuals develop for themselves.

mitochondrial theory The theory that aging is caused by the decay of mitochondria, tiny cellular bodies that supply energy for function, growth, and repair.

mitosis Cellular reproduction in which the cell's nucleus duplicates itself with two new cells being formed, each containing the same DNA as the parent cell, arranged in the same 23 pairs of chromosomes.

Montessori approach An educational philosophy in which children are given considerable freedom and spontaneity in choosing activities and are allowed to move from one activity to another as they desire.

moral development Development that involves thoughts, feelings, and actions regarding rules and conventions about what people should do in their interactions with other people.

morphology Units of meaning involved in word formation.

mTOR pathway A cellular pathway involving the regulation of growth and metabolism that has been proposed as a key aspect of longevity

myelination The process by which axons are covered and insulated with a layer of fat cells, which increases the speed at which information travels through the nervous system.

N

natural childbirth A childbirth method in which no drugs are given to relieve pain or assist in the birth process. The mother and her partner are taught to use breathing methods and relaxation techniques during delivery.

naturalistic observation Observation that occurs in a real-world setting without any attempt to manipulate the situation.

nature-nurture issue The debate about the extent to which development is influenced by nature and by nurture. Nature refers to an organism's biological inheritance, nurture to its environmental experiences.

neglected children Children who are infrequently nominated as a best friend but are not disliked by their peers.

neglectful parenting A style of parenting in which the parent is very uninvolved in the child's life; it is associated with children's social incompetence, especially a lack of self-control.

neo-Piagetians Developmentalists who have elaborated on Piaget's theory, giving more emphasis to how children use attention, memory, and strategies to process information.

neuroconstructivist view Developmental perspective in which biological processes and environmental conditions influence the brain's development; the brain has plasticity and is context dependent; and cognitive development is closely linked with brain development.

neurons Nerve cells that handle information processing at the cellular level in the brain.

nonnormative life events Unusual occurrences that have a major impact on a person's life. The occurrence, pattern, and sequence of these events are not applicable to many individuals.

normal distribution A symmetrical distribution with most scores falling in the middle of the possible range of scores and few scores appearing toward the extremes of the range.

normative age-graded influences Biological and environmental influences that are similar for individuals in a particular age group.

normative history-graded influences Biological and environmental influences that are associated with history. These influences are common to people of a particular generation.

O

object permanence The Piagetian term for understanding that objects and events continue to exist, even when they cannot directly be seen, heard, or touched.

operations In Piaget's theory, these are internalized, reversible sets of actions that allow children to do mentally what they formerly did physically.

organic intellectual disability Intellectual disability that involves some physical damage and is caused by a genetic disorder or brain damage.

organization Piaget's concept of grouping isolated behaviors and thoughts into a higher-order, more smoothly functioning cognitive system.

organogenesis Organ formation that takes place during the first two months of prenatal development.

osteoporosis A chronic condition that involves an extensive loss of bone tissue and is the main reason many older adults walk with a marked stoop. Women are especially vulnerable to osteoporosis.

P

pain cry A sudden outburst of loud crying without preliminary moaning, followed by breath holding.

palliative care Emphasized in hospice care; involves reducing pain and suffering and helping individuals die with dignity.

Parkinson disease A chronic, progressive disease characterized by muscle tremors, slowing of movement, and partial facial paralysis.

passive euthanasia Withholding available treatments, such as the use of life-sustaining devices, and allowing a person to die.

perception The interpretation of what is sensed.

personal fable The part of adolescent egocentrism that involves an adolescent's sense of uniqueness and invincibility (or invulnerability).

perspective taking The social cognitive process involved in assuming the perspective of others and understanding their thoughts and feelings.

phenotype The way an individual's genotype is expressed in observed and measurable characteristics.

phonics approach The idea that reading instruction should teach the basic rules for translating written symbols into sounds.

phonology The sound system of a language, including the sounds used and how they may be combined.

Piaget's theory The theory that children construct their understanding of the world and go through four stages of cognitive development.

pituitary gland An important endocrine gland that controls growth and regulates other glands, including the gonads.

popular children Children who are frequently nominated as a best friend and are rarely disliked by their peers.

postconventional reasoning The highest level in Kohlberg's theory of moral development. At this level, the individual recognizes alternative moral courses, explores the options, and then decides on a personal moral code

postformal thought Thinking that is reflective, relativistic, and contextual; provisional; realistic; and influenced by emotions.

postpartum period The period after childbirth when the mother adjusts, both physically and psychologically, to the process of childbearing. This period lasts for about six weeks or until her body has completed its adjustment and returned to a nearly prepregnant state.

practice play Play that involves repetition of behavior when new skills are being learned or when physical or mental mastery and coordination of skills are required for games or sports.

pragmatics The appropriate use of language in different contexts.

preconventional reasoning The lowest level in Kohlberg's theory of moral development. The individual's moral reasoning is controlled primarily by external rewards and punishment.

preoperational stage Piaget's second stage, lasting from about 2 to 7 years of age, during which children begin to represent the world with words, images, and drawings, and symbolic thought goes beyond simple connections of sensory information and physical action; stable concepts are formed, mental reasoning emerges, egocentrism is present, and magical beliefs are constructed.

prepared childbirth Developed by French obstetrician Ferdinand Lamaze, this childbirth strategy is similar to natural childbirth but includes a special breathing technique to control pushing in the final stages of labor and more detailed anatomy and physiology instruction.

pretense/symbolic play Play in which the child transforms the physical environment into a symbol.

Project Head Start A government-funded program that is designed to provide children from low-income families the opportunity to acquire the skills and experiences important for school success.

proximodistal pattern Developmental sequence in which growth starts at the center of the body and moves toward the extremities.

psychoanalytic theories Theories holding that development depends primarily on the unconscious mind and is heavily couched in emotion, that behavior is merely a surface characteristic, that it is important to analyze the symbolic meanings of behavior, and that early experiences are important in development.

psychoanalytic theory of gender A theory deriving from Freud's view that the preschool child develops a sexual attraction to the opposite-sex parent, by approximately 5 or 6 years of age renounces this attraction because of anxious feelings, and subsequently identifies with the same-sex parent, unconsciously adopting the same-sex parent's characteristics.

puberty A brain-neuroendocrine process occurring primarily in early adolescence that provides stimulation for the rapid physical changes that occur in this period of development.

R

rapport talk Use of conversation to establish connections and maintain relationships.

reciprocal socialization Socialization that is bidirectional, meaning that children socialize parents, just as parents socialize children.

reflexive smile A smile that does not occur in response to external stimuli. It appears during the first month after birth, usually during sleep.

rejected children Children who are infrequently nominated as a best friend and are actively disliked by their peers.

report talk Talk that is designed to convey information.

rite of passage A ceremony or ritual that marks an individual's transition from one status to another. Most rites of passage focus on the transition to adult status.

romantic love Also called passionate love, or *eros;* romantic love has strong sexual and infatuation components and often predominates in the early period of a love relationship.

S

scaffolding Process in which parents time interactions so that infants experience turn-taking with their parents.

schemes In Piaget's theory, actions or mental representations that organize knowledge.

secure attachment style An attachment style that describes adults who have positive views of relationships, find it easy to get close to others, and are not overly concerned or stressed out about their romantic relationships.

securely attached babies Babies that use the caregiver as a secure base from which to explore their environment.

selective optimization with compensation theory The theory that successful aging involves three main factors: selection, optimization, and compensation.

self-concept Domain-specific evaluations of the self.

self-efficacy The belief that one can master a situation and produce favorable outcomes.

self-esteem The global evaluative dimension of the self. Self-esteem is also referred to as self-worth or self-image.

self-understanding The child's cognitive representation of self, the substance and content of the child's self-conceptions.

semantic memory A person's knowledge about the world—including a person's fields of expertise, general academic knowledge of the sort learned in school, and "everyday knowledge."

semantics The meaning of words and sentences.

sensation The product of the interaction between information and the sensory receptors—the eyes, ears, tongue, nostrils, and skin.

sensorimotor play Behavior engaged in by infants to derive pleasure from exercising their existing sensorimotor schemes.

sensorimotor stage The first of Piaget's stages, which lasts from birth to about 2 years of age; during this stage, infants construct an understanding of the world by coordinating sensory experiences with motoric actions.

separation protest An infant's distressed crying when the caregiver leaves.

seriation The concrete operation that involves ordering stimuli along a quantitative dimension (such as length).

service learning A form of education that promotes social responsibility and service to the community.

sexually transmitted infections (STIs) Infections contracted primarily through sexual contact, including oral-genital and anal-genital contact.

short-term memory The memory component in which individuals retain information for up to 30 seconds, assuming there is no rehearsal of the information.

sirtuins A family of proteins that have been linked to longevity, regulation of mitochondrial functioning in energy, potential benefits of calorie restriction, resistance to stress, and a reduced risk of cardiovascular disease and cancer.

slow-to-warm-up child A child who has a low activity level, is somewhat negative, and displays a low intensity of mood.

social cognitive theory The theory that behavior, environment, and person/cognitive factors are important in understanding development.

social cognitive theory of gender A theory emphasizing that children's gender development occurs through the observation and imitation of gender behavior and through the rewards and punishments children experience for gender-appropriate and gender-inappropriate behavior.

social constructivist approach An approach that emphasizes the social contexts of learning and that knowledge is mutually built and constructed. Vygotsky's theory reflects this approach.

social conventional reasoning Thoughts about social consensus and convention, in contrast with moral reasoning, which stresses ethical issues.

social play Play that involves social interactions with peers.

social policy A national government's course of action designed to promote the welfare of its citizens.

social referencing "Reading" emotional cues in others to help determine how to act in a particular situation.

social role theory A theory that gender differences result from the contrasting roles of men and women.

social smile A smile in response to an external stimulus, which, early in development, typically is a face.

socioeconomic status (SES) Refers to the conceptual grouping of people with similar occupational, educational, and economic characteristics.

socioemotional processes Changes in an individual's relationships with other people, emotions, and personality.

socioemotional selectivity theory The theory that older adults become more selective about their social networks. Because they place a high value on emotional satisfaction, older adults often prefer to spend time with familiar individuals with whom they have had rewarding relationships.

stability-change issue The debate about the degree to which early traits and characteristics persist through life or change.

stagnation Sometimes called "self-absorption," this state of mind develops when individuals sense that they have done little or nothing for the next generation; this is the negative side of Erikson's middle adulthood stage of generativity versus stagnation.

standardized test A test that is given with uniform procedures for administration and scoring.

stereotype threat Anxiety that one's behavior might confirm a negative stereotype about one's group, such as an ethnic group.

Strange Situation An observational measure of infant attachment that requires the infant to move through a series of introductions, separations, and reunions with the caregiver and an adult stranger in a prescribed order.

stranger anxiety An infant's fear and wariness of strangers that typically appears in the second half of the first year of life.

strategies Deliberate mental activities designed to improve the processing of information.

sudden infant death syndrome (SIDS) A condition that occurs when an infant stops breathing, usually during the night, and suddenly dies without an apparent cause.

sustained attention Also referred to as vigilance; involves focused and extended engagement with an object, task, event, or other aspect of the environment.

symbolic function substage Piaget's first substage of preoperational thought, in which the child gains the ability to mentally represent an object that is not present (between about 2 and 4 years of age).

syntax The ways words are combined to form acceptable phrases and sentences.

T

telegraphic speech The use of short and precise words without grammatical markers such as articles, auxiliary verbs, and other connectives.

temperament An individual's behavioral style and characteristic way of responding emotionally.

tend-and-befriend Taylor's view that when women experience stress, they are more likely to seek social alliances with others, especially female friends.

teratogen Any agent that can potentially cause a birth defect or negatively alter cognitive and behavioral outcomes.

theory A coherent set of ideas that helps to explain data and to make predictions.

theory of mind Refers to the awareness of one's own mental processes and the mental processes of others.

thinking Manipulating and transforming information in memory.

top-dog phenomenon The circumstance of moving from the top position in elementary school to the lowest position in middle or junior high school.

transgender A broad term that refers to individuals whose gender identity or behavior is either completely or partially at odds with the sex into which they were born.

transitivity The ability to logically combine relations to understand certain conclusions.

triarchic theory of intelligence Sternberg's theory that intelligence consists of analytical intelligence, creative intelligence, and practical intelligence.

twin study A study in which the behavioral similarity of identical twins is compared with the behavioral similarity of fraternal twins.

V

visual preference method A method developed by Fantz to determine whether infants can distinguish one stimulus from another by measuring the length of time they attend to different stimuli.

Vygotsky's theory A sociocultural cognitive theory that emphasizes how culture and social interaction guide cognitive development.

W

whole-language approach An approach to reading instruction based on the idea that instruction should parallel children's natural language learning. Reading materials should be whole and meaningful.

wisdom Expert knowledge about the practical aspects of life that permits excellent judgment about important matters.

working memory Closely related to short-term memory but places more emphasis on mental work. Working memory is like a mental "workbench" where individuals can manipulate and assemble information when making decisions, solving problems, and deciphering written and spoken language.

Z

zone of proximal development (ZPD) Vygotsky's term for tasks that are too difficult for children to master alone but can be mastered with assistance.

A

AAP (2000). Changing concepts of sudden infant death syndrome. *Pediatrics, 105,* 650–656.

AARP (2004). The divorce *experience: A study of divorce at midlife and beyond.* Washington, DC: AARP.

Abbink, M.R., & others (2017). Early-life stress diminishes the increase in neurogenesis after exercise in adult female mice. *Hippocampus, 8,* 839–844.

Abbott, A.E., & others (2018). Repetitive behaviors in autism are linked to the imbalance of corticostriatal connectivity: A functional connectivity MRI study. *Social Cognitive and Affective Neuroscience, 13,* 32–42.

ABC News (2005, December 12). *Larry Page and Sergey Brin.* Retrieved from http://abcnews.go.com?Entertainment/12/8/05

AbouAssi, H., & others (2017). Does a lack of physical activity explain the rheumatoid arthritis lipid profile? *Lipids in Health and Disease, 16*(1), 39.

Abu Snineh, M., Camicioli, R., & Miyasaki, J.M. (2017). Decisional capacity for advance care directives in Parkinson's disease with cognitive concerns. *Parkinsonism and Related Diseases, 39,* 77–79.

Abulizi, X., & others (2017). Temperament in infancy and behavioral and emotional problems at age 5.5: The EDEN mother-child cohort. *PLoS One, 12*(2), 0171971.

Abu-Rayya, H.M., & others (2018). Comparative associations between achieved bicultural identity, achieved ego identity, and achieved religious identity, and adaptation among Australian adolescent Muslims. *Psychological Reports, 12,* 324–333.

Accornero, V.H., Anthony, J.C., Morrow, C.E., Xue, L., & Bandstra, E.S. (2006). Prenatal cocaine exposure: An examination of childhood externalizing and internalizing behavior problems at age 7 years. *Epidemiology, Psychiatry, and Society, 15,* 20–29.

Adams, A. (2015). A cultural historical theoretical perspective of discourse and design in the science classroom. *Cultural Studies of Science Education, 10,* 329–338.

Adams, B.G., & others (2018). When there are only minorities. *Emerging Adulthood, 6,* 7–16.

Adams, K.A., & others (2018, in press). Caregiver talk and medical risk as predictors of language outcomes in full-term and preterm toddlers. *Child Development.*

Adams, M.L. (2017). Differences between young and older U.S. adults with multiple chronic conditions. *Preventing Chronic Disease.*

Adams, R.G., Hahmann, J., & Blieszner, R. (2017). Interactive motifs and processes in old age. In M. Hojjat & A. Moyer (Eds.), *Psychology of friendship.* Thousand Oak, CA: Sage.

Adkins, D.E., Daw, J.K., McClay, J.L., & van den Oord, E.J. (2012). The influence of five monoamine genes on trajectories of depressive symptoms across adolescence and young adulthood. *Development and Psychopathology, 24,* 267–285.

Adler, J.M., & others (2017). Research methods in studying narrative identity: A primer. *Social Psychology and Personality Science, 8,* 519–527.

Adler, R., & Elmhurst, J.M. (2019). *Communicating at work* (12th ed.). New York: McGraw-Hill.

Adlof, E.W., & others (2017). Adult-born neurons modify excitatory transmission to existing neurons. *Elife, 6:* 1986.

Administration for Children & Families (2008). *Statistical fact sheet fiscal year 2008.* Washington, DC: Author.

Administration on Aging (2015). *A profile of older Americans: 2015.* Washington, DC: U.S. Department of Health and Human Services.

Adolescent Sleep Working Group, AAP (2014). School start times for adolescents. *Pediatrics, 134,* 642–649.

Adolph, K.E. (1997). Learning in the development of infant locomotion. *Monographs of the Society for Research in Child Development,* 62(3, Serial No. 251).

Adolph, K.E. (2010). *Perceptual learning.* Retrieved January 10, 2010, from http://www.psych.nyu.edu/adolph/research1.php

Adolph, K.E. (2018). Motor development. In M.H. Bornstein (Ed.), *SAGE encyclopedia of lifespan human development.* Thousand Oaks, CA: Sage.

Adolph, K.E., & Berger, S.E. (2015). Physical and motor development. In M.H. Bornstein & M.E. Lamb (Eds.), *Developmental science* (7th ed.). New York: Psychology Press.

Adolph, K.E., & Hoch, J.E. (2019, in press). Motor development embodied, embedded, enculturated, and enabling. *Annual Review of Psychology.*

Adolph, K.E., Rachwani, J., & Hoch, J.E. (2018, in press). Motor and physical development: Locomotion. *Neuroscience and Biobehavioral Psychology.*

Adolph, K.E., & Robinson, S.R.R. (2015). Motor development. In R. Lerner (Ed.), *Handbook of child psychology and developmental science* (7th ed.). New York: Wiley.

Affleck, W., Carmichael, V., & Whitley, R. (2018, in press). Men's mental health: Social determinants and its implications for services. *Canadian Journal of Psychiatry.*

Afifi, T.O., & others (2017a). Spanking and adult mental health impairment: The case for the designation of spanking as an adverse childhood experience. *Child Abuse and Neglect, 11,* 24–31.

Afifi, T.O., & others (2017b). The relationships between harsh physical punishment and child maltreatment in childhood and intimate partner violence in adulthood. *BMC Public Health, 17*(1), 493.

Agency for Healthcare Research and Quality (2007*). Evidence report/Technology assessment Number 153: Breastfeeding and maternal and infant health outcomes in developed countries.* Rockville, MD: U.S. Department of Health and Human Services.

Agerup, T., Lydersen, S., Wallander, J., & Sund, A.M. (2015). Associations between parental attachment and course of depression between adolescence and young adulthood. *Child Psychiatry and Human Development, 46,* 632–642.

Agras, W.S., Fitzsimmons-Craft, E.E., & Wilfley, D.E. (2017). Evolution of cognitive-behavior therapy for eating disorders. *Behavior Research and Therapy, 88,* 26–36.

Agras, W.S., & others (2004). Report of the National Institutes of Health workshop on overcoming barriers to treatment research in anorexia nervosa. *International Journal of Eating Disorders, 35,* 509–521.

Agricola, E., & others (2016). Investigating paternal preconception risk factors for adverse pregnancy outcomes in a population of Internet users. *Reproductive Health, 13,* 37.

Ahern, E., Kowalski, M., & Lamb, M.E. (2018, in press). A case study perspective: The experiences of young persons testifying to child sexual exploitation in British Criminal Court. *Journal of Child Sexual Abuse.*

Ahmadi, F., & others (2017). Meaning-making coping among cancer patients in Sweden and South Korea: A comparative perspective. *Journal of Religion and Health, 56,* 1794–1811.

Ahun, M.N., & others (2018). Child development in rural Ghana between cognitive/language milestones and indicators of nutrition and stimulation of children under two years of age. *Canadian Journal of Public Health, 108,* e578–e585.

Aichele, S., Rabbitt, P., & Ghisletta, P. (2015). Life span decrements in fluid intelligence and processing speed predict mortality risk. *Psychology and Aging, 30,* 598–612.

Aichele, S., Rabbitt, P., & Ghisletta, P. (2016). Think fast, feel fine, live long: A 29-year study of cognition, health, and survival in middle-aged and older adults. *Psychological Science, 27,* 518–529.

Ainsworth, M.D.S. (1979). Infant-mother attachment. *American Psychologist, 34,* 932–937.

Ajetunmobi, O.M., & others (2015). Breastfeeding is associated with reduced childhood hospitalization: Evidence from a Scottish birth cohort (1997–2009). *Journal of Pediatrics, 166,* 620–625.

Akbari, A., & others (2011). Parity and breastfeeding are preventive measures against breast cancer in Iranian women. *Breast Cancer, 18,* 51–55.

Akbarzadeh, M., Masoudi, Z., Zare, N., & Vazin, F. (2015). Comparison of the effects of doula supportive care and acupressure at the BL32 point on the mother's anxiety level and delivery outcome. *Iranian Journal of Nursing and Midwifery Research, 20,* 239–246.

Akers, K.G., & others (2018, in press). Regulatory influence of sleep and epigenetics on adult hippocampal neurogenesis and cognitive and emotional function. *Stem Cells.*

Akhtar, N., & Herold, K. (2008). Pragmatic development. In M.M. Haith & J.B. Benson (Eds.), *Encyclopedia of infant and early childhood development.* Oxford, UK: Elsevier.

Akinsola, E.F., & Petersen, A.C. (2018). Adolescent development and capacity building. In J.E. Lansford & P. Banati (Eds.), *Handbook of adolescent development research and its impact on global policy.* New York: Oxford University Press.

Aksglaede, L., & others (2013). 47, XXY Klinefelter syndrome: Clinical characteristics and age-specific recommendations for medical management. *American Journal of Medical Genetics C: Seminars in Medical Genetics, 163,* 55–63.

Al Alwan, I.A., & others (2017). Decline in menarcheal age among Saudi girls. *Saudi Medical Journal, 36,* 1324–1328.

Alan Guttmacher Institute (2017 September). *American adolescents' sources of sexual health information.* New York: Author.

Alarcon, C. (2017). Parent education in the home. *NAMTA Journal, 42,* 155–167.

Albar-Almazan, A., & others (2018). Sarcopenia and sarcopenic obesity in Spanish community-dwelling middle-aged and older women: Association with balance and confidence, fear of falling, and risk. *Maturitas, 107,* 26–32.

Alberga, A.S., & others (2012). Healthy eating, aerobic and resistance training in youth (HEARTY): Study rationale, design, and methods. *Contemporary Clinical Trials, 33,* 839–847.

Albert, D., & Steinberg, L. (2011a). Judgment and decision making in adolescence. *Journal of Research on Adolescence, 21,* 211–224.

Albert, D., & Steinberg, L. (2011b). Peer influences on adolescent risk behavior. In M. Bardo, D. Fishbein, & R. Milich (Eds.), *Inhibitory control and drug abuse prevention: From research to translation.* New York: Springer.

Albert, R.R., Schwade, J.A., & Goldstein, M.H. (2018, in press). The social functions of babbling: Acoustic and contextual characteristics that facilitate maternal responsiveness. *Developmental Science.*

Alberto, P.A., & Troutman, A.C. (2017). *Applied behavior analysis for teachers* (9th ed.). Upper Saddle River, NJ: Pearson.

Alberts, E., Elkind, D., & Ginsberg, S. (2007). The personal fable and risk taking in early adolescence. *Journal of Youth and Adolescence, 36,* 71–76.

Aldercotte, A., White, N., & Hughes, C. (2016). Sibling and peer relationships in early childhood. In L. Balter & C.S. Tamis-Lemonda (Eds.), *Child psychology* (3rd ed.). New York: Routledge.

Alegret, M., & others (2014). Cognitive, genetic, and brain perfusion factors associated with four-year incidence of Alzheimer's disease from mild cognitive impairment. *Journal of Alzheimer's Disease, 41,* 739-748.

Alexander, C.P., & others (2017). Fathers make a difference: Positive relationships with mother and baby in relation to infant colic. *Child Care, Health, and Development, 43,* 687-696.

Alfredsson, J., & others (2018, in press). Sex differences in management and outcomes of patients with type 2 diabetes and cardiovascular disease: A report from TECOS. *Diabetes, Obesity, and Metabolism.*

Al-Ghanim, & Badahdah, A.M. (2017). Gender roles in the Arab world: Development and psychometric properties of the Arab Adolescents Gender Roles Attitude Scale. *Sex Roles, 77,* 165-177.

Allameh, Z., Tehrani, H.G., & Ghasemi, M. (2015). Comparing the impact of acupuncture and pethidine on reducing labor pain. *Advanced Biomedical Research, 4,* 46.

Allemand, M., Zimprich, D., & Hendriks, A.A.J. (2008). Age differences in five personality domains across the life span. *Developmental Psychology, 44,* 758-770.

Allen, A.P., & others (2018). Autobiographical memory, the aging brain, and mechanisms of psychological interventions. *Aging Research Reviews, 42,* 100-111.

Allen, J.O. (2016). Ageism as a risk factor for chronic disease. *Gerontologist, 56,* 610-614.

Allen, J.P., & Miga, E.M. (2010). Attachment in adolescence: A move to the level of emotion regulation. *Journal of Social and Personal Relationships, 27,* 226-234.

Allen, J.P., & Tan, J. (2016). The multiple facets of attachment in adolescence. In J. Cassidy & P.R. Shaver (Eds.), *Handbook of attachment* (3rd ed.). New York: Guilford.

Allen, J.P., & others (2009, April). *Portrait of the secure teen as an adult.* Paper presented at the meeting of the Society for Research in Child Development, Denver.

Allen, K., & Goldman-Mellor, S. (2018, in press). Neighborhood characteristics and adolescent suicidal behavior: Evidence from a population-based study. *Suicide and Life-Threatening Behavior.*

Allen, K.D., & others (2018, in press). Physical therapy vs. Internet-based exercise training for patients with knee osteoarthritis: Results of a randomized controlled trial. *Osteoarthritis and Cartilage.*

Allen, M., & others (2017). Metacognitive ability correlates with hippocampal and prefrontal microstructure. *NeuroImage, 149,* 415-423.

Allen, S., & Barlow, E. (2017). Long-acting reversible contraception: An essential guide for pediatric primary care. *Pediatric Clinics of North America, 64,* 359-369.

Allen, T.D., & Finkelstein, L.M. (2014). Work-family conflict among members of full-time dual-earner couples: An examination of family life stage, gender, and age. *Journal of Occupational Health Psychology, 19,* 376-384.

Alm, B., Wennergren, G., Mollborg, P., & Lagercrantz, H. (2016). Breastfeeding and dummy use have a protective effect on sudden infant death syndrome. *Acta Paediatrica, 105,* 31-38.

Almeida, D.M., & Horn, M.C. (2004). Is daily life more stressful during middle adulthood? In C.D. Ryff & R.C. Kessler (Eds.), *A portrait of midlife in the United States.* Chicago: University of Chicago Press.

Almeida, M.J. (2018). *Approved drugs for Alzheimer's disease.* Retrieved March 1, 2018, from https://alzheimersnewstoday.com/alzheimers-disease-treatment/approved-drugs/

Almeida, N.D., & others (2016). Risk of miscarriage in women receiving antidepressants in early pregnancy, correcting for induced abortions. *Epidemiology, 27,* 538-546.

Almont, T., & others (2017). Sexual quality of life and needs for sexology care of cancer patients admitted for radiotherapy: A 3-month cross-sectional study in a regional comprehensive reference cancer center. *Journal of Sexual Medicine, 14,* 566-576.

Almquist, Y.B., & Brannstrom, L. (2014). Childhood peer status and the clustering of social, economic, and health-related circumstances in adulthood. *Social Science & Medicine, 105,* 67-75.

Almy, B., & Cicchetti, D. (2018). Developmental cascades. In M.H. Bornstein (Ed.), *SAGE encyclopedia of lifespan human development.* Thousand Oaks, CA: Sage.

Alonzo, M., & Molina, M.A. (2019). Behavioral health. In R. Fernandez-Ballesteros & others (Eds.), *Cambridge handbook of successful aging.* New York: Cambridge University Press.

Alonzo-Fernandez, M., & others (2016). Acceptance and commitment therapy and selective optimization with compensation for institutionalized older people with chronic pain. *Pain Medicine, 17,* 264-277.

Alzheimer's Association (2014). *2014 Alzheimer's disease facts and figures.* Chicago: Alzheimer's Association.

Alzheimer's Association (2018). *2018 Alzheimer's disease facts and figures.* Chicago: Alzheimer's Association.

Amano, T., Park, S., & Morrow-Howell, N. (2018). The association between cognitive impairment and patterns of activity engagement among older adults. *Research on Aging, 40,* 645-667.

Amare, A.T., & others (2017). The genetic overlap between mood disorders and cardiometabolic disease: A systematic review of genome wide and candidate gene studies. *Translational Psychiatry, 7,* e1007.

Amato, P.R., & Anthony, C.J. (2014). Estimating the effects of parental divorce and death with fixed effects models. *Journal of Marriage and the Family, 76,* 370-386.

Ambrose, D., & Sternberg, R.J. (2016). *Giftedness and talent in the 21st century.* Rotterdam, The Netherlands: Sense Publishers.

American Academy of Pediatrics (2016). *American Academy of Pediatrics announces new recommendations for children's media use.* Elk Grove Village, IL: AAP.

American Academy of Pediatrics Section on Breastfeeding (2012). Breastfeeding and the use of human milk. *Pediatrics, 129,* e827-e841.

American Cancer Society (2018). *Information and resources for cancer.* Retrieved February 15, 2018, from http:www.cancer.org

American Pregnancy Association (2018). *Promoting pregnancy wellness.* Retrieved January 18, 2018, from www.americanpregnancy.org

American Psychiatric Association (2013). *DSM-V.* Arlington, VA: Author.

American Psychological Association (2003). *Psychology: Scientific problem solvers.* Washington, DC: Author.

American Psychological Association (2007). *Stress in America.* Washington, DC: American Psychological Association.

Amole, M.C., & others (2017). Depression impacts the physiological responsiveness of mother-daughter dyads during social interaction. *Depression and Anxiety, 34,* 118-126.

Amrithraj, A.I., & others (2017). Gestational diabetes alters functions in offspring's umbilical cord cells with implications for cardiovascular health. *Endocrinology, 158,* 2102-2112.

Amsterdam, B.K. (1968). *Mirror behavior in children under two years of age.* Unpublished doctoral dissertation, University of North Carolina, Chapel Hill.

Andel, R., Finkel, D., & Pedersen, N.L. (2016). Effects of preretirement work complexity and postretirement leisure activity on cognitive aging. *Journals of Gerontology B: Psychological Sciences and Social Sciences, 71,* 849-858.

Andersen, S.L., Sebastiani, P., Dworkis, D.A., Feldman, L., & Perls, T.T. (2012). Health span approximates life span among many supercentenarians: Compression of morbidity at the approximate limit of life span. *Journals of Gerontology A: Biological Sciences and Medical Sciences, 67A,* 395-405.

Anderson, E., Greene, S.M., Hetherington, E.M., & Clingempeel, W.G. (1999). The dynamics of parental remarriage. In E.M. Hetherington (Ed.), *Coping with divorce, single parenting, and remarriage.* Mahwah, NJ: Erlbaum.

Anderson, E.R., & Greene, S.M. (2011). "My child and I are a package deal": Balancing adult and child concerns in repartnering after divorce. *Journal of Family Psychology, 25,* 741-750.

Anderson, M.A. (2017, May 17). *Technology use among seniors.* Washington, DC: Pew Research Center.

Anderson, P.A. (2006). The evolution of biological sex differences in communication. In K. Dindia & D.J. Canary (Eds.), *Sex differences and similarities in communication.* Mahwah, NJ: Erlbaum.

Anderson, S.E., Gooze, R.A., Lemeshow, S., & Whitaker, R.C. (2012). Quality of early maternal-child relationship and risk of adolescent obesity. *Pediatrics, 129,* 132-140.

Andersson, G., Borgquist, S., & Jirstrom, K. (2018, in press). Hormonal factors and pancreatic cancer risk in women: The Malmo Diet and Cancer Study. *International Journal of Cancer.*

Andersson, H., & Bergman, L.R. (2011). The role of task persistence in young adolescence for successful educational and occupational attainment in middle adulthood. *Developmental Psychology, 47,* 950-960.

Andescavage, N.N., & others (2017). Complex trajectories of brain development in the healthy human fetus. *Cerebral Cortex, 27,* 5274-5283.

Anding, J.E., & others (2016). Couple comorbidity and correlates of postnatal depressive symptoms in mothers and fathers in the first two weeks following delivery. *Journal of Affective Disorders, 190,* 300-309.

Andrew, N., & Meeks, S. (2018). Fulfilled preferences, perceived control, life satisfaction, and loneliness in elderly long-term care residents. *Aging and Mental Health, 22,* 183-189.

Andrews, S.J., Ahern, E.C., & Lamb, M.E. (2017). Children's uncertain responses when testifying about alleged sexual abuse in Scottish courts. *Behavioral Sciences & the Law, 35,* 204-224.

Andrews, S.J., & Lamb, M.E. (2018, in press). Lawyers' question repetition and children's responses in Scottish courts. *Journal of Interpersonal Violence.*

Andriani, H., Liao, C.Y., & Kuo, H.W. (2015). Parental weight changes as key predictors of child weight changes. *BMC Public Health, 15,* 645.

Angel, J.L., Mudrazija, S., & Benson, R. (2016). Racial and ethnic inequalities in health. In L.K. George & K.F. Ferraro (Eds.), *Handbook of aging and the social sciences* (8th ed.). New York: Elsevier.

Angel, L., Fay, S., Bouazzaoui, B., & Isingrini, M. (2011). Two hemispheres for better memory in old age: Role of executive functioning. *Journal of Cognitive Neuroscience, 23,* 3767-3777.

Angelotta, C., & Appelbaum, P.S. (2017). Criminal charges for harm from substance use in pregnancy. *Journal of the American Academy of Psychiatry and the Law, 45,* 193-203.

Anglin, D.M., & others (2018, in press). Ethnic identity, racial discrimination, and attenuated psychotic symptoms in an urban population of emerging adults. *Early Intervention in Psychiatry.*

Anguera, J.A., & others (2013). Video game training enhances cognitive control in older adults. *Nature, 501,* 97-101.

Anguiano, R.M., & others (2018). Language brokering among Latino immigrant families: Moderating variables and youth outcomes. *Journal of Youth and Adolescence, 47,* 222-242.

Ansari, A. (2015). *Modern romance.* New York: Penguin.

Ansari, A., & Gershoff, E. (2016). Parent involvement in Head Start and children's development: Indirect effects through parenting. *Journal of Marriage and the Family, 76,* 562-579.

Ansari, A., & others (2017). Function of the SIRT3 mitochondrial deacetylase in cellular physiology, cancer, and neurodegenerative disease. *Aging Cell, 16,* 4-16.

Anson, E., & others (2018, in press). Influences of age, obesity, and adverse drug effects on balance and mobility testing scores in ambulatory older adults. *Journal of Geriatric Physical Therapy.*

Antfolk, J. (2018, in press). Age limits. *Evolutionary Psychology.*

Antfolk, J., & others (2017). Willingness to invest in children: Psychological kinship estimates and emotional closeness. *Evolutionary Psychology, 15*(2), 1474704917705730.

Anthony, M., & Lin, F. (2018, in press). A systematic review for functional neuroimaging studies of cognitive reserve across the cognitive aging spectrum. *Archives of Clinical Neuropsychology.*

Antonenko, D., & Floel, A. (2014). Healthy aging by staying selectively connected: A mini-review. *Gerontology, 60*(1), 3–9.

Antonucci, T.C., Lansford, J.E., & Akiyama, H. (2001). The impact of positive and negative aspects of marital relationships and friendships on the well-being of older adults. In J.P. Reinhardt (Ed.), *Negative and positive support.* Mahwah, NJ: Erlbaum.

Antonucci, T.C., Vandewater, E.A., & Lansford, J.E. (2000). Adulthood and aging: Social processes and development. In A. Kazdin (Ed.), *Encyclopedia of psychology.* Washington, DC, and New York: American Psychological Association and Oxford University Press.

Antonucci, T.C., & Webster, N.J. (2019, in press). Involvement with life and social networks. In R. Fernandez-Ballesteros & others (Eds.), *Cambridge handbook of successful aging.* New York: Cambridge University Press.

Antonucci, T.C., & others (2016). Society and the individual at the dawn of the twenty-first century. In K.W. Schaie & S.L. Willis (Eds.), *Handbook of the psychology of aging* (8th ed.). New York: Elsevier.

Antovich, D.M., & Graf Estes, K. (2018, in press). Learning across languages: Bilingual experience supports dual language statistical word segmentation. *Developmental Science.*

Anupama, N., Sinhu, G., & Raghu, K.G. (2018). Significance of mitochondria on cardiometabolic syndromes. *Fundamental and Clinical Pharmacology, 32,* 346–356.

Apatoff, M.B.L., & others (2018). Autologous stem cell therapy for inherited and acquired retinal disease. *Regenerative Medicine, 13,* 89–96.

Apter, D. (2018). Contraception options: Aspects unique to adolescent and young adult. *Best Practices and Research: Clinical Obstetrics and Gynecology, 48,* 115–127.

Arabi, A.M.E., & others (2018). Perinatal outcomes following Helping Babies Breathe training and regular peer-peer skills practice among village midwives in Sudan. *Archives of Disease in Childhood, 103,* 24–27.

Arba-Mosquera, S., Vinciguerra, P., & Verma, S. (2018). Review of technological advancements in calibration systems for laser vision correction. *Journal of Biomedical Optics, 23*(2), 1–8.

Ardelt, M., Gerlach, K.R., & Vaillant, G.E. (2018, in press). Early and midlife predictors of wisdom and subjective well-being in old age. *Journals of Gerontology B: Psychological Sciences and Social Sciences.*

Ariceli, G., Castro, J., Cesena, J., & Toro, J. (2005). Anorexia nervosa in male adolescents: Body image, eating attitudes, and psychological traits. *Journal of Adolescent Health, 36,* 221–226.

Arkes, J. (2015). The temporal effects of divorces and separations on children's academic achievement and problem behavior. *Journal of Divorce and Remarriage, 56,* 25–42.

Arnett, J.J. (2006). Emerging adulthood: Understanding the new way of coming of age. In J.J. Arnett & J.L. Tanner (Eds.), *Emerging adults in America.* Washington, DC: American Psychological Association.

Arnett, J.J. (2010). Oh, grow up! Generational grumbling and the new life stage of emerging adulthood—Commentary on Trzesniewski & Donnellan (2010). *Perspectives on Psychological Science, 5,* 89–92.

Arnett, J.J. (2015). *Emerging adulthood* (2nd ed.). New York: Oxford University Press.

Arnett, J.J. (2016a). Does emerging adulthood theory apply across social classes? National data on a persistent question. *Emerging Adulthood, 4,* 227–235.

Arnett, J.J. (2016b). Emerging adulthood and social class: Rejoinder to Furstenberg, Silva, and du Bois-Reymond. *Emerging Adulthood, 4,* 244–247.

Arnett, J.J. (Ed.) (2012). *Adolescent psychology around the world.* New York: Psychology Press.

Arnett, J.J., & Padilla-Walker, L.M. (2015). Brief report: Danish emerging adults' conceptions of adulthood. *Journal of Adolescence, 38,* 39–44.

Aron, A., Coups, E.J., & Aron, E.N. (2019). *Statistics for psychology, brief course* (6th ed.). Upper Saddle River, NJ: Pearson.

Aronson, E. (1986, August). *Teaching students things they think they already know about: The case of prejudice and desegregation.* Paper presented at the meeting of the American Psychological Association, Washington, DC.

Arriaga, X.B., & others (2018). Revising working models across time: Relationship situations that enhance attachment security. *Personality and Social Psychology Review, 22,* 71–96.

Arrieta, H., & others (2018). A multicomponent exercise program improves physical function in long-term nursing home residents: A randomized controlled trial. *Experimental Gerontology, 103,* 94–100.

Arseneault, L. (2017). The long-term impact of bullying victimization on mental health. *World Psychiatry, 16,* 27–28.

Arseth, A., Kroger, J., Martinussen, M., & Marcia, J.E. (2009). Meta-analytic studies of identity status and the relational issues of attachment and intimacy. *Identity, 9,* 1–32.

Ary, D., & others (2019). *Introduction to research in education* (10th ed.). Boston: Cengage.

Ashcraft, A.M., & Murray, P.J. (2017). Talking to parents about adolescent sexuality. *Pediatric Clinics of North America, 64,* 305–320.

Aslin, R. (2017). Statistical learning: A powerful mechanism that operates by mere exposure. *Wiley Interdisciplinary Reviews: Cognitive Science, 8,* 1–2.

Aslin, R.N. (2012). Infant eyes: A window on cognitive development. *Infancy, 17,* 126–140.

Aslin, R.N., Jusczyk, P.W., & Pisoni, D.B. (1998). Speech and auditory processing during infancy: Constraints on and precursors to language. In W. Damon (Ed.), *Handbook of child psychology* (5th ed., Vol. 2). New York: Wiley.

Aslin, R.N., & Lathrop, A.L. (2008). Visual perception. In M. Haith & J. Benson (Eds.), *Handbook of infant and early childhood development.* London: Elsevier.

Aspen Institute (2013). *Two generations, one future.* Washington, DC: Aspen Institute.

Aspen Institute (2018). *Making tomorrow better together.* Washington, DC: Aspen Institute.

Assini-Meytin, L.C., & Green, K.M. (2015). Long-term consequences of adolescent parenthood among African-American youth: A propensity score matching approach. *Journal of Adolescent Health, 56,* 529–535.

Associated Press–NORC Center for Public Affairs Research (2013). *Survey on later-life work.* Chicago: NORC Center for Public Affairs, University of Chicago.

Attar-Schwartz, S., Tan, J.P., Buchanan, A., Flouri, E., & Griggs, J. (2009). Grandparenting and adolescent development in two-parent biological, lone-parent, and step-families. *Journal of Family Psychology, 23,* 67–75.

Aubuchon-Endsley, N., & others (2018, in press). Maternal pre-pregnancy obesity and gestational weight gain influence neonatal neurobehavior. *Maternal and Child Nutrition.*

Audesirk, G., Audesirk, T., & Byers, B.E. (2017). *Biology* (11th ed.). Upper Saddle River, NJ: Pearson.

Aune, D., & others (2018, in press). Body mass index, abdominal fatness, and the risk of sudden cardiac death: A systematic review and dose-response meta-analysis of prospective studies. *European Journal of Epidemiology.*

Avalon, L. (2018, in press). Are older adults perceived as a threat to society? Exploring age-based threats in 29 nations. *Journals of Gerontology B: Psychological Sciences and Social Sciences.*

Avalon, L., & Tesch-Romer, C. (2017). Taking a closer look at ageism: Self- and other-directed ageist attitudes and discrimination. *European Journal of Aging, 14,* 1–4.

Avis, N.E., & others (2009). Longitudinal changes in sexual functioning as women transition through menopause: Results from the Study of Women's Health Across the Nation. *Menopause, 16,* 442–452.

Avvenuti, G., Baiardini, I., & Giardini, A. (2016). Optimism's explicative role for chronic diseases. *Frontiers in Psychology, 7,* 295.

Ayoub, C., Vallotton, C.D., & Mastergeorge, A.M. (2011). Developmental pathways to integrated social skills: The role of parenting and early intervention. *Child Development, 82,* 583–600.

Ayoub, M., & Roberts, B.W. (2018). Environmental conditions and the development of personality. In V. Hill & T.K. Shackelford (Eds.), *Encyclopedia of personality and individual differences.* New York: Springer.

Azagba, S., & Sharaf, M.F. (2014). Physical inactivity among older Canadian adults. *Journal of Physical Activity and Health, 11*(1), 99–108.

Azar, S., & Wong, T.E. (2017). Sickle cell disease: A brief update. *Medical Clinics of North America, 101,* 375–393.

B

Babbie, E.R. (2017). *The basics of social research* (7th ed.). Boston: Cengage.

Baca Zinn, M., Eitzen, D.S., & Wells, B. (2016). *REVEL for diversity in families* (10th ed.). Upper Saddle River, NJ: Pearson.

Bacchi, M., & others (2018). Aquatic activities during pregnancy prevent excessive maternal weight gain and preserve birthweight. *American Journal of Health Promotion, 32,* 729–735.

Bach, L.E., Mortimer, J.A., Vandeweerd, C., & Corvin, J. (2013). The association of physical and mental health with sexual activity in older adults in a retirement community. *Journal of Sexual Medicine, 10*(11), 2671–2678.

Bachman, J.G., & others (2008). *The education-drug use connection.* Clifton, NJ: Psychology Press.

Bacikova-Sleskova, M., Benka, J., & Orosova, O. (2015). Parental employment status and adolescents' health: The role of financial situation, parent-adolescent relationship, and adolescents' resilience. *Psychology and Health, 30,* 400–422.

Backman, H., & others (2018). Interpersonal relationships as protective and risk factors for psychopathy: A follow-up study of adolescent offenders. *Journal of Youth and Adolescence, 47,* 1022–1036.

Bacon, J.L., & Tomich, P. (2017). *Obstetrics and gynecology.* New York: Elsevier.

Baddeley, A.D. (1990). *Human memory: Theory and practice.* Boston: Allyn & Bacon.

Baddeley, A.D. (2001). *Is working memory still working?* Paper presented at the meeting of the American Psychological Association, San Francisco.

Baddeley, A.D. (2007). *Working memory, thought, and action.* New York: Oxford University Press.

Baddeley, A.D. (2010). Working memory. *Current Biology, 20,* 136–140.

Baddeley, A.D. (2012). Working memory: Theories, models, and controversies. *Annual Review of Psychology* (Vol. 63). Palo Alto, CA: Annual Reviews.

Baddeley, A.D. (2013). On applying cognitive psychology. *British Journal of Psychology, 104,* 443–456.

Baddeley, A.D. (2015). Origins of the multicomponent working memory model. In M. Eysenck & D. Groome (Eds.), *Cognitive psychology: Revisiting the classic studies.* Thousand Oaks, CA: Sage.

Baddeley, A.D. (2018a, in press). Exploring the sentence advantage in working memory: Insights from serial recall and recognition. *Quarterly Journal of Experimental Psychology.*

Baddeley, A.D. (2018b, in press). Modularity, working memory, and language acquisition. *Second Language Research.*

Bagwell, C.L., & Bukowski, W.M. (2018). Friendship in childhood and adolescence. In W.M. Bukowski & others (Eds.), *Handbook of peer interactions, relationships, and groups* (2nd ed.). New York; Guilford.

Bahmaee, A.B., Saadatmand, Z., & Yarmohammadian, M.H. (2016). Principle elements of curriculum in the preschool pattern of Montessori. *International Education Studies, 9,* 148–153.

Bahrick, L.E. (2010). Intermodal perception and selective attention to intersensory redundancy: Implications for social development and autism. In J.G. Bremner & T.D. Wachs (Eds.), *Wiley-Blackwell handbook of infant development* (2nd ed.). New York: Wiley.

Bai, K., & others (2017). Kidney function and cognitive decline in an oldest-old Chinese population. *Clinical Interventions in Aging, 12,* 1049–1054.

Bail, K., & others (2018). Predicting excess cost for older inpatients with clinical complexity: A retrospective cohort study examining cognition, comorbidities, and complications. *PLoS One, 13*(2), e0193319.

Bailey, H.R., Dunlosky, J., & Hertzog, C. (2014). Does strategy training reduce age-related deficits in working memory? *Gerontology, 60,* 346–356.

Baillargeon, R. (2004). The acquisition of physical knowledge in infancy: A summary in eight lessons. In U. Goswami (Ed.), *Blackwell handbook of childhood cognitive development.* Malden, MA: Blackwell.

Baillargeon, R. (2014). Cognitive development in infancy. *Annual Review of Psychology* (Vol. 65). Palo Alto, CA: Annual Reviews.

Baillargeon, R. (2016). Cognitive development in infancy. *Annual Review of Psychology* (Vol. 67). Palo Alto, CA: Annual Reviews.

Baillargeon, R., & DeJong, G.F. (2017). Explanation-based reasoning in infancy. *Psychonomic Bulletin and Review, 24,* 1511–1526.

Baillargeon, R., & others (2012). Object individuation and physical reasoning in infancy: An integrative account. *Language, Learning, and Development, 8,* 4–46.

Bain, K., & Durbach, C. (2018, in press). Adaptation, resilience, and secure attachment states of mind in young South African female students exposed to intimate partner violence in childhood. *Journal of Interpersonal Violence.*

Bajoghli, H., & others (2014). "I love you more than I can stand!"—romantic love, symptoms of depression and anxiety, and sleep complaints are related among young adults. *International Journal of Psychiatry in Clinical Practice, 18,* 169–174.

Bakeman, R., & Brown, J.V. (1980). Early interaction: Consequences for social and mental development at three years. *Child Development, 51,* 437–447.

Baker, D.J., & Petersen, R.C. (2018). Cellular senescence in brain aging and neurodegenerative diseases: Evidence and perspectives. *Journal of Clinical Investigation, 128,* 1208–1216.

Baker, J.H., Schaumberg, K., & Munn-Chernoff, M.A. (2017). Genetics of anorexia nervosa. *Current Psychiatry Reports, 19*(11), 84.

Baker, J.H., Thorton, L.M., Lichtenstein, P., & Bulik, C.M. (2012). Pubertal development predicts eating behaviors in adolescents. *International Journal of Eating Disorders, 45*(7), 819–826.

Baker, J.K., Fenning, R.M., & Crnic, K.A. (2011). Emotion socialization by mothers and fathers: Coherence among behaviors and associations with parent attitudes and children's competence. *Social Development, 20,* 412–430.

Bakermans-Kranenburg, M.J., & van IJzendoorn, M.H. (2011). Differential susceptibility to rearing environment depending on dopamine-related genes: New evidence and a meta-analysis. *Development and Psychopathology, 23,* 39–52.

Bakermans-Kranenburg, M.J., & van IJzendoorn, M.H. (2016). Attachment, parenting, and genetics. In J. Cassidy & P.R. Shaver (Eds.), *Handbook of parenting* (3rd ed.). New York: Guilford.

Bakondi, B., Girman, S., Lu, B., & Wang, S. (2017). Multimodal delivery of isogenic mesenchymal stem cells yields synergistic protection from retinal degeneration and vision loss. *Stem Cells Translational Medicine, 6,* 444–457.

Bakusic, J., & others (2017). Stress, burnout, and depression: A systematic review on DNA methylation mechanisms. *Journal of Psychosomatic Research, 92,* 34–44.

Balantekin, K.N., Birch, L.L., & Savage, J.S. (2018, in press). Family, friend, and media factors are associated with patterns of weight-control behavior among adolescent girls. *Eating and Weight Disorders.*

Ballane, G., & others (2017). Worldwide prevalence and incidence of osteoporotic vertebral fractures. *Osteoporosis International, 28,* 1531–1542.

Ballou, D., & Springer, M.G. (2017). Has NCLB encouraged educational triage? Accountability and the distribution of achievement gains. *Education Finance and Policy, 12,* 77–106.

Balsam, K.F., Rostosky, S.S., & Riggle, E.D. (2017). Breaking up is hard to do: Women's experience of dissolving their same-sex relationship. *Journal of Lesbian Studies, 21,* 30–46.

Baltes, P.B. (1987). Theoretical propositions of life-span developmental psychology: On the dynamics between growth and decline. *Developmental Psychology, 23,* 611–626.

Baltes, P.B. (2003). On the incomplete architecture of human ontogeny: Selection, optimization, and compensation as foundation of developmental theory. In U.M. Staudinger & U. Lindenberger (Eds.), *Understanding human development.* Boston: Kluwer.

Baltes, P.B., & Kunzmann, U. (2007). Wisdom and aging: The road toward excellence in mind and character. In D.C. Park & N. Schwarz (Eds.), *Cognitive aging: A primer* (2nd ed.). Philadelphia: Psychology Press.

Baltes, P.B., Lindenberger, U., & Staudinger, U. (2006). Life span theory in developmental psychology. In W. Damon & R. Lerner (Eds.), *Handbook of child psychology* (6th ed.). New York: Wiley.

Baltes, P.B., Reuter-Lorene, P., & Rösler, F. (Eds.). (2006). *Lifespan development and the brain.* New York: Cambridge University Press.

Baltes, P.B., & Smith, J. (2003). New frontiers in the future of aging: From successful aging of the young to the dilemmas of the fourth age. *Gerontology, 49,* 123–135.

Baltes, P.B., & Smith, J. (2008). The fascination of wisdom: Its nature, ontogeny, and function. *Perspectives in Psychological Sciences, 3,* 56–64.

Bamaca-Colbert, M., Umana-Taylor, A.J., Espinosa-Hernandez, G., & Brown, A.M. (2012). Behavioral autonomy expectations among Mexican- origin mother-daughter dyads: An examination of within-group variability. *Journal of Adolescence, 35,* 691–700.

Banducci, S.E., & others (2017). Active experiencing training improves episodic memory recall in older adults. *Frontiers in Aging Neuroscience, 9,* 133.

Bandura, A. (1986). *Social foundations of thought and action: A social cognitive theory.* Englewood Cliffs, NJ: Prentice Hall.

Bandura, A. (1998, August). *Swimming against the mainstream: Accentuating the positive aspects of humanity.* Paper presented at the meeting of the American Psychological Association, San Francisco.

Bandura, A. (2001). Social cognitive theory. *Annual Review of Psychology.* Palo Alto, CA: Annual Reviews.

Bandura, A. (2004, May). *Toward a psychology of human agency.* Paper presented at the meeting of the American Psychological Society, Chicago.

Bandura, A. (2006). Toward a psychology of human agency. *Perspectives on Psychological Science, 1,* 164–180.

Bandura, A. (2010a). Self-efficacy. In D. Matsumoto (Ed.), *Cambridge dictionary of psychology.* New York: Cambridge University Press.

Bandura, A. (2010b). Vicarious learning. In D. Matsumoto (Ed.), *Cambridge dictionary of psychology.* New York: Cambridge University Press.

Bandura, A. (2012). Social cognitive theory. *Annual Review of Clinical Psychology* (Vol. 8). Palo Alto, CA: Annual Reviews.

Bandura, A. (2016). *Moral disengagement: How people do harm and live with themselves.* New York: Worth.

Bangerter, L.R., & others (2018, in press). Everyday support for aging parents: Links to middle-aged children's diurnal cortisol and daily mood. *Gerontologist.*

Bangerter, L.R., & others (2018, in press). Recommendation from the Salzburg Global Seminar on Rethinking Care Toward the End of Life. *International Journal for Quality Health Care.*

Banja, J. (2005). Talking to the dying. *Case Manager, 16,* 37–39.

Banks, J.A. (2015). *Cultural diversity and education* (6th ed.). Upper Saddle River, NJ: Pearson.

Banks, M.S., & Salapatek, P. (1983). Infant visual perception. In P.H. Mussen (Ed.), *Handbook of child psychology* (4th ed., Vol. 2). New York: Wiley.

Baptista, J., & others (2017). Serotonin transporter polymorphism moderates the effects of caregiver intrusiveness on ADHD symptoms among institutionalized preschoolers. *European Child and Adolescent Psychiatry, 26,* 303–313.

Barakat, R., & others (2017). Influence of land and water exercise in pregnancy on outcomes: A cross-sectional study. *Medicine & Science in Sports and Exercise, 49,* 1397–1403.

Barbaro, N., Boutwell, B.B., Barnes, J.C., & Shackelford, T.K. (2017). Rethinking the transmission gap: What behavioral genetics and evolutionary psychology mean for attachment theory: A comment on Verhage et. al. (2016). *Psychological Bulletin, 143,* 107–113.

Bardid, F., & others (2018, in press). Configurations of actual and perceived motor competence among children: Associations with motivation for sports and global self-worth. *Human Movement Science.*

Bardikoff, N., & Sabbagh, M. (2017). The differentiation of executive function over development: Insights from developmental cognitive neuroscience. In N. Budwig, E. Turiel, & P.D. Zelazo (Eds.), *New perspectives on human development.* New York: Cambridge University Press.

Barger, M., Faucher, M.A., & Murphy, P.A. (2015). Part II: The CenteringPregnancy model of group prenatal care. *Journal of Midwifery and Women's Health, 60,* 211–213.

Bargh, J.A., & McKenna, K.Y.A. (2004). The Internet and social life. *Annual Review of Psychology* (Vol. 55). Palo Alto, CA: Annual Reviews.

Barker, R., & Wright, H.F. (1951). *One boy's day.* New York: Harper & Row.

Barnes, J., & others (2017). Randomized controlled trial and economic evaluation of nurse-led group support for young mothers during pregnancy and the first year postpartum versus traditional care. *Trials, 18*(1), 508.

Barnett, L.M., Salmon, J., & Hesketh, K.D. (2016). More active pre-school children have better motor coordination at school starting age: An observational cohort study. *BMC Public Health, 16,* 1068.

Baron, N.S. (1992). *Growing up with language.* Reading, MA: Addison-Wesley.

Barr, E.M., & others (2014). New evidence: Data documenting parental support for earlier sexuality education. *Journal of School Health, 84,* 10–17.

Bartel, A.P., & others (2018). Paid family leave, fathers' leave taking, and leave-sharing in dual-family households. *Journal of Policy Analysis and Management, 37,* 10–37.

Bartick, M.C., & others (2017). Disparities in breast-feeding: Impact of maternal and child health outcomes and costs. *Journal of Pediatrics, 181,* 49-55.

Bartick, M.C., & others (2018, in press). Suboptimal breastfeeding in the United States: Maternal and pediatric health outcomes and costs. *Maternal and Child Nutrition.*

Bartl, H., & others (2018, in press). Does prolonged grief treatment foster posttraumatic growth? Secondary results from a treatment study with long-term follow-up and mediation analysis. *Psychology and Psychotherapy.*

Barton, M., & others (2017). Better health-related fitness in youth: Implications for public health guidelines. *International Journal of Exercise Science, 10,* 379-389.

Barzilay, S., & others (2017). Bullying victimization and suicide ideation and behavior among adolescents in Europe: A 10-country study. *Journal of Adolescent Health, 61,* 179-186.

Baskaran, C., & Kandemir, N. (2018). Update on endo-crine aspects of childhood obesity. *Current Opinion in Endocrinology, Diabetes, and Obesity, 25,* 55-60.

Bas-Sarmiento, P., & others (2017). Mental health in immigrants versus native population: A systematic review of the literature. *Archives of Psychiatric Nursing, 31,* 111-121.

Bastaitis, K., Pasteels, I., & Mortelmans, D. (2018). How do post-divorce parental and maternal family trajectories related to adolescents' subjective well-being? *Journal of Adolescence, 64,* 98-108.

Bates, J.E. (2012a). Temperament as a tool in pro-moting early childhood development. In S.L. Odom, E.P. Pungello, & N. Gardner-Neblett (Eds.), *Infants, toddlers, and families in poverty.* New York: Guilford University Press.

Bates, J.E. (2012b). Behavioral regulation as a product of temperament and environment. In S.L. Olson & A.J. Sameroff (Eds.), *Biopsychosocial regulatory processes in the development of childhood behavioral problems.* New York: Cambridge University Press.

Bates, J.E., & Pettit, G.S. (2015). Temperament, par-enting, and social development. In J.E. Grusec & P.D. Hastings (Eds.), *Handbook of socialization* (2nd ed.). New York: Guilford.

Bateson, P. (2015). Human evolution and development: An ethological perspective. In R.M. Lerner (Ed.), *Hand-book of child psychology and developmental science* (7th ed.). New York: Wiley.

Bathory, E., & Tomopoulos, S. (2017). Sleep regulation, physiology, and development, sleep duration and pat-terns, and sleep hygiene in infants, toddlers, and pre-school children. *Current Problems in Pediatric and Adolescent Health Care, 47,* 29-42.

Batis, J.A., & Zagaria, A.B. (2018). Addressing obesity in aging patients. *Medical Clinics of North America, 102,* 65-85.

Bauer, P.J. (2009). Learning and memory: Like a horse and carriage. In A. Woodward & A. Needham (Eds.), *Learning and the infant mind.* New York: Oxford University Press.

Bauer, P.J. (2013). Memory. In P.D. Zelazo (Ed.), *Oxford handbook of developmental psychology.* New York: Oxford University Press.

Bauer, P.J. (2015). A complementary processes account of the development of childhood amnesia and a personal past. *Psychological Review, 122,* 204-231.

Bauer, P.J. (2018). Memory development. In J. Rubenstein & P. Rakic (Eds.), *Neural circuit development and function in the healthy and diseased brain* (2nd ed.). New York: Elsevier.

Bauer, P.J., & Fivush, R. (Eds.) (2014). *Wiley-Blackwell handbook of children's memory.* New York: Wiley.

Bauer, P.J., & Larkina, M. (2014). The onset of child-hood amnesia in childhood: A prospective investigation of the course and determinants of forgetting of early-life events. *Memory, 22,* 907-924.

Bauer, P.J., & Larkina, M. (2016). Childhood amnesia in the making: Different distributions of autobiographi-cal memories in children and adolescents. *Journal of Experimental Psychology: General, 143,* 597-611.

Bauer, P.J., & Leventon, S.J. (2015). The development of declarative memory in infancy and implications for social learning. In S.D. Calkins (Ed.), *Handbook of biopsychosocial development.* New York: Guilford.

Bauer, P.J., Wenner, J.A., Dropik, P.I., & Wewerka, S.S. (2000). Parameters of remembering and forgetting in the transition from infancy to early childhood. *Mono-graphs of the Society for Research in Child Development, 65*(4, Serial No. 263).

Bauer, P.J., & others (2017). Neural correlates of auto-biographical memory retrieval in children and adults. *Memory, 25,* 450-466.

Baugh, N., & others (2016). The impact of maternal obesity and excessive gestational weight gain on maternal and infant outcomes in Maine: Analysis of pregnancy risk assessment monitoring results from 2000 to 2010. *Journal of Pregnancy, 2016,* 58711313.

Baumeister, R.F. (2013). Self-esteem. In E. Anderson (Ed.), *Psychology of classroom learning: An encyclopedia.* Detroit: Macmillan.

Baumrind, D. (1971). Current patterns of parental author-ity. *Developmental Psychology Monographs, 4*(1, Pt. 2).

Baye, K., Tariku, A., & Mouquet-River, C. (2018, in press). Caregiver-infant's feeding behaviors are associ-ated with energy intake of 9-11-month-old infants in rural Ethiopia. *Maternal and Child Nutrition.*

Beal, M.A., Yauk, C.L., & Marchetti, F. (2017). From sperm to offspring: Assessing the heritable genetic con-sequences of paternal smoking and potential public health impacts. *Mutation, 773,* 26-50.

Bearman, S.K., Presnall, K., Martinez, E., & Stice, E. (2006). The skinny on body dissatisfaction: A longitudi-nal study of adolescent girls and boys. *Journal of Youth and Adolescence, 35,* 217-229.

Beaver, K.M., Vaughn, M.G., Wright, J.P., & Delisi, M. (2012). An interaction between perceived stress and 5HTTLPR genotype in the prediction of stable depres-sive symptomatology. *American Journal of Orthopsychiatry, 82,* 260-266.

Beaver, N., Wyatt, S., & Jackman, H. (2018). *Early education curriculum* (7th ed.). Boston: Cengage.

Bechi Gabrielli, G., & others (2018, in press). When divided attention fails to enhance memory encoding: The attentional boost effect is eliminated in young-old adults. *Psychology and Aging.*

Becht, A.I., & others (2018, in press). Goal-directed correlates and neurobiological underpinnings of adoles-cent identity: A multimethod multisample longitudinal approach. *Child Development.*

Beck, T.L., Le, T.K., Henry-Okator, Q., & Shah, M.K. (2017). Medical care for undocumented immigrants: National and international issues. *Primary Care, 44,* e1-e13.

Becker, D.R., Miao, A., Duncan, R., & McClelland, M.M. (2014). Behavioral self-regulation and executive function both predict visuomotor skills and early academic achievement. *Early Childhood Research Quarterly, 29,* 411-424.

Becker, M.W., Alzahabi, R., & Hopwood, C.J. (2013). Media multitasking is associated with symptoms of depression and social anxiety. *Cyberpsychology, Behavior, and Social Networking, 16,* 132-136.

Bedford, R., & others (2017). The role of infants' mother-directed gaze, maternal sensitivity, and emotion regulation in childhood. *European Child and Adolescent Psychiatry, 26,* 947-956.

Bednar, R.L., Wells, M.G., & Peterson, S.R. (1995). *Self-esteem* (2nd ed.). Washington, DC: American Psychological Association.

Beghetto, R.A., & Kaufman, J.C. (Eds.) (2017). *Nurtur-ing creativity in the classroom* (2nd ed.). New York: Cambridge University Press.

Beguin, M. (2016). Object pragmatics and language development. *Integrative Psychological and Behavioral Science, 50,* 603-620.

Behrens, H. (2012). Grammatical categories. In E.L. Bavin (Ed.), *Cambridge handbook of child language.* New York: Cambridge University Press.

Beier, K.M. (2018, in press). Preventing child sexual abuse—The Prevention Project Dunkelfeld. *Journal of Sexual Medicine.*

Belenko, S., & others (2017). The juvenile justice behavioral health services cascade: A new framework for measuring unmet substance use treatment services needs among adolescent defenders. *Journal of Substance Abuse Treatment, 74,* 80-91.

Bell, M.A., Broomell, A.P.R., & Patton, L.K. (2018). Brain development. In M.H. Bornstein (Ed.), *SAGE encyclopedia of lifespan human development.* Thousand Oaks, CA: Sage.

Bell, M.A., Broomell, A.P.R., & Patton, L.K. (2018). Emotion regulation. In M.H. Bornstein (Ed.), *SAGE encyclopedia of lifespan human development.* Thousand Oaks, CA: Sage.

Bell, M.A., & Cuevas, K. (2015). Psychobiology of executive function in early development. In J.A. Griffin, L.S. Freund, & P. McCardle (Eds.), *Executive function in preschool children.* Washington, DC: American Psycho-logical Association.

Bell, M.A., Diaz, A., & Liu, R. (2018, in press). Cognition-emotion interactions. In V. LaBue & others (Eds.), *Handbook of emotional development.* New York: Springer.

Bell, M.A., Ross, A.P., & Patton, L.K. (2018). Emotion regulation. In M.H. Bornstein (Ed.), *SAGE encyclopedia of lifespan human development.* Thousand Oaks, CA: Sage.

Bell, M.F., & others (2018). School readiness and maltreated children: Associations of timing, type, and chronicity of maltreatment. *Child Abuse and Neglect, 76,* 426-439.

Bell, S.P., & others (2017). Late-life body mass index, rapid weight loss, Apolipoprotein e4 and the risk of cog-nitive decline and incident dementia. *Journal of Nutri-tion, Health, and Aging, 21,* 1259-1267.

Belling, K., & others (2017). Klinefelter syndrome comorbidities linked to increased X chromosome gene dosage and altered protein interactome activity. *Human Molecular Genetics, 28,* 1219-1229.

Bellini, C.V., & others (2016). How painful is a heelprick or a venipuncture in a newborn? *Journal of Maternal-Fetal and Neonatal Medicine, 29,* 202-206.

Belsky, D.W., & others (2017). Impact of early personal-history characteristics on the pace of aging: Implications for clinical trials of therapies to slow aging and extend healthspan. *Aging Cell, 16,* 644-651.

Belsky, J. (1981). Early human experience: A family perspective. *Developmental Psychology, 17,* 3-23.

Belsky, J. (2016). The differential susceptibility hypothesis: Sensitivity to the environment for better or for worse. *JAMA Pediatrics, 170,* 321-322.

Belsky, J., & Pluess, M. (2016). Differential susceptibility to context: Implications for developmental psychopathology. In D. Cicchetti (Ed.), *Developmental psychopathology* (3rd ed.). New York: Wiley.

Belsky, J., & van IJzendoorn, M.H. (2017). Genetic differential susceptibility to the effects of parenting. *Current Opinion in Psychology, 15,* 125-130.

Beltran-Catalan, M., & others (2018). Victimization through bullying and cyberbullying: Emotional intel-ligence, severity of victimization, and technology use in different types of victims. *Psicothema, 30,* 183-188.

Beltran-Sanchez, H., Finch, C.E., & Crimmins, E.M. (2015). Twentieth-century surge of excess adult male mortality. *Proceedings of the National Academy of Sciences U.S.A., 112,* 8993-8998.

Benck, L.R., & others (2017). Association between cardiorespiratory fitness and lung health from young adulthood to middle age. *American Journal of Respiratory and Critical Care Medicine, 195,* 1236-1243.

Bendersky, M., & Sullivan, M.W. (2007). Basic meth-ods in infant research. In A. Slater & M. Lewis (Eds.), *Introduction to infant development* (2nd ed.). New York: Oxford University Press.

Bendezu, J.J., & others (2018, in press). Child lan-guage and parenting antecedents and externalizing outcomes of emotion regulation pathways across early childhood: A person-centered approach. *Development and Psychopathology.*

Bendezu, J.J., & others (2018, in press). Longitudinal relations among parental monitoring strategies, knowledge, and adolescent delinquency in a racially diverse at-risk sample. *Journal of Clinical Child and Adolescent Psychology.*

Beneden Health (2013). *Middle age survey.* Unpublished data, Beneden Health, York, England.

Benenson, J.F., Apostolaris, N.H., & Parnass, J. (1997). Age and sex differences in dyadic and group interaction. *Developmental Psychology, 33,* 538–543.

Benetos, A. (2019). The biomedical bases of successful aging. In R. Fernandez-Ballesteros & others (Eds.), *Cambridge handbook of successful aging.* New York: Cambridge University Press.

Benetos, A., & others (2019, in press). Arterial stiffness and blood pressure during the aging process. In R. Fernandez-Ballesteros & others (Eds.), *Cambridge handbook of successful aging.* New York: Cambridge University Press.

Benitez, V.L., & others (2017). Sustained selective attention predicts flexible switching in preschoolers. *Journal of Experimental Child Psychology, 156,* 29–42.

Benjamin, C.F., & others (2017). Presurgical language fMRI: Mapping of six critical regions. *Human Brain Mapping, 38,* 4239–4255.

Benner, Boyle, & Bakhtiari, F. (2017). Understanding students' transition to high school: Demographic variation and the role of supportive relationships. *Journal of Youth and Adolescence, 46,* 2129–2142.

Bennett, C.I. (2015). *Comprehensive multicultural education* (8th ed.). Upper Saddle River, NJ: Pearson.

Bennett, J.M., Fagundes, C.P., & Kiecolt-Glaser, J.K. (2016). The chronic stress of caregiving accelerates the natural aging of the immune system. In A.C. Phillips, J.M. Lord, & J.A. Bosch (Eds.), *Immunosenescence: Psychological and behavioral determinants.* New York: Springer.

Bennett, K.M. (2006). Does marital status and marital status change predict physical health in older adults? *Psychological Medicine, 36,* 1313–1320.

Bennett, N. (2018). Sexual dysfunction: Behavioral, medical, and surgical treatment. *Medical Clinics of North America, 102,* 349–360.

Benson, J.E., & Sabbagh, M.A. (2017). Executive function helps children think about and learn about others' mental states. In M.J. Hoskyns & others (Eds.), *Executive functions in children's everyday lives.* New York: Oxford University Press.

Benson, P.L. (2010). *Parent, teacher, mentor, friend: How every adult can change kids' lives.* Minneapolis: Search Institute Press.

Benson, P.L., Mannes, M., Pittman, K., & Ferber, T. (2004). Youth development, developmental assets, and public policy. In R. Lerner & L. Steinberg (Eds.), *Handbook of adolescent psychology* (2nd ed.). New York: Wiley.

Benson, P.L., Roehlkepartain, E.C., & Scales, P.C. (2012). Spirituality and positive youth development. In L. Miller (Ed.), *Oxford handbook of spirituality and consciousness.* New York: Oxford University Press.

Benson, P.L., & Scales, P.C. (2009). The definition and preliminary measurement of thriving in adolescence. *Journal of Positive Psychology, 4,* 85–104.

Benson, P.L., & Scales, P.C. (2011). Thriving and sparks: Development and emergence of new core concepts in positive youth development. In R.J.R. Levesque (Ed.), *Encyclopedia of adolescence.* Berlin: Springer.

Benyi, E., & Sävendahl, L. (2017). The physiology of childhood growth: Hormonal regulation. *Hormone Research in Pediatrics, 88,* 6–14.

Berardi, A., Parasuraman, R., & Haxby, J.V. (2001). Overall vigilance and sustained attention decrements in healthy aging. *Experimental Aging Research, 27,* 19–39.

Bercovitz, K.E., Ngnoumen, C., & Langer, E.J. (2019, in press). Personal control and aging. In R. Fernandez-

Ballesteros & others (Eds.), *Cambridge handbook of successful aging.* New York: Cambridge University Press.

Berenbaum, S.A., & Beltz, A.M. (2011). Sexual differentiation of human behavior: Effects of prenatal and pubertal organization hormones. *Frontiers in Neuroscience, 32,* 183–200.

Berenguer, C., & others (2018). Contribution of theory of mind, executive functioning, and pragmatics to socialization behaviors of children with high-functioning autism. *Journal of Autism and Developmental Disorders, 48,* 430–441.

Berg, A.I., Hoffman, L., Hassing, L.B., McClearn, G.E., & Johansson, B. (2009). What matters, and what matters most, for change in life satisfaction in the oldest old? A study over 6 years among individuals 80+. *Aging and Mental Health, 13,* 191–201.

Berg, N., & others (2018). Associations between unemployment and heavy episodic drinking from adolescence to midlife in Sweden and Finland. *European Journal of Public Health, 28,* 258–263.

Berge, J.M., & others (2015). The protective role of family meals for youth obesity: 10-year longitudinal associations. *Journal of Pediatrics, 166,* 296–301.

Bergen, D. (1988). Stages of play development. In D. Bergen (Ed.), *Play as a medium for learning and development.* Portsmouth, NH: Heinemann.

Bergen, D. (2015). Psychological approaches to the study of play. In J.E. Johnson & others (Eds.), *Handbook of the study of play.* Blue Ridge Summit, PA: Rowman & Littlefield.

Bergeron, K.E. (2018). *Challenging the cult of self-esteem in education.* New York: Routledge.

Berglind, D., Ljung, R., Tynelius, P., & Brooke, H.L. (2018, in press). Cross-sectional and prospective associations of meeting 24-h movement guidelines with overweight and obesity in preschool children. *Pediatric Obesity.*

Berke, D.S., Reidy, D., & Zeichner, A. (2018, in press). Masculinity, emotion regulation, and psychopathology: A critical review and integrated model. *Clinical Psychology Review.*

Berko, J. (1958). The child's learning of English morphology. *Word, 14,* 150–177.

Berko Gleason, J. (2003). Unpublished review of J.W. Santrock's *Life-span development* (9th ed.). New York: McGraw-Hill.

Berko Gleason, J. (2009). The development of language: An overview. In J. Berko Gleason & N.B. Ratner (Eds.), *The development of language* (7th ed.). Boston: Allyn & Bacon.

Berlyne, D.E. (1960). *Conflict, arousal, and curiosity.* New York: McGraw-Hill.

Berman, M.G., & others (2013). Dimensionality of brain networks linked to life-long individual differences in self-control. *Nature Communications, 4,* 1373.

Berman, R.S., & others (2018). Screening for poverty and poverty-related social determinants of health. *Pediatric Review, 39,* 235–246.

Bernard, J.Y., & others (2017). Breastfeeding, polyunsaturated fatty acid levels in colostrum and child intelligent quotient at age 5-6 years. *Journal of Pediatrics, 183,* 43–50.

Bernardo, S., & others (2017). MRI and US in the evaluation of fetal anomalies: The need to work together. *Prenatal Diagnosis, 37,* 1343–1349.

Berndt, T.J., & Perry, T.B. (1990). Distinctive features and effects of early adolescent friendships. In R. Montemayor (Ed.), *Advances in adolescent research.* Greenwich, CT: JAI Press.

Bernier, A., Beauchamp, M.H., Carlson, S.M., & Lalonde, G. (2015). A secure base from which to regulate: Attachment security in toddlerhood is a predictor of executive functioning at school entry. *Developmental Psychology, 51,* 1177–1189.

Bernier, A., Calkins, S.D., & Bell, M.A. (2016). Longitudinal associations between the quality of mother-infant interactions and brain development across infancy. *Child Development, 87,* 1159–1174.

Bernstein, J.H., & Waber, D.P. (2018). Executive capacities from a developmental perspective. In N. L. Meltzer (Ed.), *Executive function in education* (2nd ed.). New York: Guilford.

Berntson, J., Patel, J.S., & Stewart, J.C. (2017). Number of recent stressful life events and incident cardiovascular disease: Moderation by lifetime depressive disorder. *Journal of Psychosomatic Research, 99,* 149–154.

Berryman, N., & others (2013). Executive functions, physical fitness, and mobility in well-functioning older adults. *Experimental Gerontology, 48,* 1402–1409.

Bersamin, M.M., & others (2014). Risky business: Is there an association between casual sex and mental health among emerging adults? *Journal of Sex Research, 51,* 43–51.

Berscheid, E. (2010). Love in the fourth dimension. *Annual Review of Psychology* (Vol. 61). Palo Alto, CA: Annual Reviews.

Berscheid, E., & Fei, J. (1977). Sexual jealousy and romantic love. In G. Clinton & G. Smith (Eds.), *Sexual jealousy.* Englewood Cliffs, NJ: Prentice Hall.

Bertenthal, B.I. (2008). Perception and action. In M.M. Haith & J.B. Benson (Eds.), *Infant and early childhood development.* Oxford, UK: Elsevier.

Bertenthal, B.I., Longo, M.R., & Kenny, S. (2007). Phenomenal permanence and the development of predictive tracking in infancy. *Child Development, 78,* 350–363.

Bertoni, A., & others (2018, in press). The associations of separated parents in Italy: Their role for parents' well-being and coparenting. *Health & Social Care in the Community.*

Bervoets, J., & others (2018). Enhancing executive functions among Dutch elementary school children using the Train Your Mind program: Protocol for a cluster randomized trial. *JMIR Research Protocols, 7*(6), e144.

Besser, A.G., & Mounts, E.L. (2017). Counseling considerations for chromosomal mosaicism detected by preimplantation genetic screening. *Reproductive Biomedicine Online. 45,* 369–374.

Betts, K.S., Williams, G.M., Najman, J.M., & Alati, R. (2014). Maternal depressive, anxious, and stress symptoms during pregnancy predict internalizing problems in adolescence. *Depression and Anxiety, 31,* 9–18.

Beyene, Y. (1986). Cultural significance and physiological manifestations of menopause: A biocultural analysis. *Culture, Medicine and Psychiatry, 10,* 47–71.

Bialystok, E. (1997). Effects of bilingualism and biliteracy on children's emerging concepts of print. *Developmental Psychology, 33,* 429–440.

Bialystok, E. (2001). *Bilingualism in development: Language, literacy, and cognition.* New York: Cambridge University Press.

Bialystok, E. (2007). Acquisition of literacy in preschool children. A framework for research. *Language Learning, 57,* 45–77.

Bialystok, E. (2011, April). *Becoming bilingual: Emergence of cognitive outcomes of bilingualism in immersion education.* Paper presented at the meeting of the Society for Research in Child Development, Montreal.

Bialystok, E. (2014). Language experience changes language and cognitive ability: Implications for social policy. In B. Spolsky, O. Inbar-Lourie, & M. Tannenbaum (Eds.), *Challenges for language education and policy.* New York: Routledge.

Bialystok, E. (2015). The impact of bilingualism on cognition. In R. Scott & S. Kosslyn (Eds.), *Emerging trends in the social and behavioral sciences.* New York: Wiley.

Bialystok, E. (2017). The bilingual adaptation: How minds accommodate experience. *Psychological Bulletin, 143,* 233–262.

Bialystok, E., & Craik, F.I.M. (2010). Cognitive and linguistic processing in the bilingual mind. *Current Directions in Psychological Science, 19,* 19–23.

Bian, Z., & Anderson, G.J. (2008). Aging and the perceptual organization of 3-D scenes. *Psychology and Aging, 23,* 342–352.

Bianco, S., Sambin, M., & Palmieri, A. (2017). Meaning making after a near-death experience: The relevance of intrapsychic and interpersonal dynamics. *Death Studies, 41,* 562–573.

Bick, J., & Nelson, C.A. (2018, in press). Early experience and brain development. *Wiley Interdisciplinary Review of Cognitive Science.*

Bick, J., & others (2017). Early deprivation, atypical brain development, and internalizing symptoms in late childhood. *Neuroscience, 342,* 140–153.

Biddle, S.J.H., Pearson, N., & Salmon, J. (2018). Sedentary behaviors and adiposity in young people: Causality and conceptual model. *Exercise and Sport Sciences Reviews, 46,* 18–25.

Biehle, S.N., & Mickelson, K.D. (2012). First-time parents' expectations about the division of childcare and play. *Journal of Family Psychology, 26,* 36–45.

Biernat, M. (2017). Gender stereotyping, prejudice, and shifting standards. In C.B. Travis & J.W. White (Eds.), *APA handbook of the psychology of women.* Washington, DC: American Psychological Association.

Bijur, P.E., Wallston, K.A., Smith, C.A., Lifrak, S., & Friedman, S.B. (1993, August). *Gender differences in turning to religion for coping.* Paper presented at the meeting of the American Psychological Association, Toronto.

Bill and Melinda Gates Foundation (2017). *K-12 education.* Retrieved March 28, 2017, from www.gatesfoundation.org/What-We-Do/US-Programs/K-12-Edu. . .

Bill and Melinda Gates Foundation (2018). *All lives have equal value.* Retrieved November 10, 2017, from www.gatesfoundation.org

Billeci, L., & others (2018). Heart rate variability during a joint attention task in toddlers with autism spectrum disorders. *Frontiers in Physiology, 9,* 467.

Bindler, R.C., & others (2017). *Clinical manual for maternity and pediatric nursing* (5th ed.). Upper Saddle River, NJ: Pearson.

Birch, S.A., & others (2017). Perspectives on perspective taking: How children think about the minds of others. *Advances in Child Development and Behavior, 52,* 185–226.

Birditt, K.S., & others (2016). Daily interactions in the parent-adult child tie: Links between children's problems and parents' diurnal cortisol rhythms. *Psychoneuroendocrinology, 63,* 208–216.

Birditt, K.S., & others (2017). The development of marital tension: Implications for divorce among married couples. *Developmental Psychology, 53,* 1995–2006.

Birditt, K.S., & others (2018, in press). Conflict strategies in the parent-adult child tie: Generation differences and implications for well-being. *Journals of Gerontology B: Psychological Sciences and Social Sciences.*

Birkeland, M.S., Melkevick, O., Holsen, I., & Wold, B. (2012). Trajectories of global self-esteem development during adolescence. *Journal of Adolescence, 35,* 43–54.

Birman, B.F., & others (2007). *State and local implementation of the "No Child Left Behind" act. Volume II—Teacher quality under "NCLB": Interim report.* Jessup, MD: U.S. Department of Education.

Birmingham, R.S., Bub, K.L., & Vaughn, B.E. (2017). Parenting in infancy and self-regulation in preschool: An investigation of the role of attachment history. *Attachment and Human Development, 19,* 107–129.

Birnbaum, J.H., & others (2018). Oxidative stress and altered mitochondrial protein expression in the absence of amyloid-B and tau pathology in iPAC-derived neurons from sporadic Alzheimer's disease patients. *Stem Cell Research, 27,* 121–130.

Biro, A., & Elek, P. (2018, in press). How does retirement affect healthcare expenditures? Evidence from a change in the retirement age. *Health Economics.*

Bischoff, K.E., Sudore, R., Miao, Y., Boscardin, W.J., & Smith, A.K. (2013). Advance care planning and the quality of end-of-life care in older adults. *Journal of the American Geriatrics Society, 61,* 209–214.

Bjorkenstam, C., Kosidou, K., & Bjorkenstam, E. (2017). Childhood adversity and risk of suicide: Cohort study

of 548,721 adolescents and young adults in Sweden. *BMJ, 357,* 1334.

Bjorklund, D.F. (2018, in press). A metatheory for cognitive development (or "Piaget is dead" revisited). *Child Development.*

Bjorklund, D.F., & Pellegrini, A.D. (2002). *The origins of human nature.* New York: Oxford University Press.

Black, J.J., & Rofey, D.L. (2018). An overview of common psychiatric problems among adolescent and young adult females: Focus on mood and anxiety. *Best Practices in Research and Clinical Obstetrics and Gynecology, 48,* 165–173.

Black, M.M., & Armstrong, B. (2017). Building healthy development and behavior among WIC participants. *Journal of Developmental and Behavioral Pediatrics, 38,* 347–348.

Black, M.M., & Hurley, K.M. (2017). Responsive feeding: Strategies to promote healthy mealtime interactions. *Nestle Nutrition Institute Workshop Series, 87,* 153–165.

Black, M.M., & others (2017). Early childhood development coming of age: Science through the life course. *Lancet, 389*(10064), 77–90.

Blackwell, L.S., & Dweck, C.S. (2008). *The motivational impact of a computer-based program that teaches how the brain changes with learning.* Unpublished manuscript, Department of Psychology, Stanford University, Palo Alto, CA.

Blackwell, L.S., Trzesniewski, K.H., & Dweck, C.S. (2007). Implicit theories of intelligence predict achievement across an adolescent transition: A longitudinal study and an intervention. *Child Development, 78,* 246–263.

Blair, C. (2017). A bidirectional theory of executive functions and self-regulation. In K. Vohs & R. Baumeister (Eds.), *Handbook of self-regulation* (3rd ed.). New York: Guilford.

Blair, C. (2017). Educating executive function. *Wiley Interdisciplinary Reviews. Cognitive Science, 8,* 1–2.

Blair, C., & others (2015). Multiple aspects of self-regulation uniquely predict mathematics but not letter-word knowledge in the early elementary grades. *Developmental Psychology, 5,* 459–472.

Blair, C., & Raver, C.C. (2012). Child development in the context of poverty: Experiential canalization of brain and behavior. *American Psychologist, 67,* 309–318.

Blair, C., & Raver, C.C. (2014). Closing the achievement gap through modification and neuroendocrine function: Results from a cluster randomized controlled trial of an innovative approach for the education of children in kindergarten. *PLoS One, 9*(11), e112393.

Blair, C., & Raver, C.C. (2015). School readiness and self-regulation: A developmental psychobiological approach. *Annual Review of Psychology* (Vol. 66). Palo Alto, CA: Annual Reviews.

Blair, C., Raver, C.C., & Finegood, E.D. (2016). Self-regulation and developmental psychopathology: Experiential canalization of brain and behavior. In D. Cicchetti (Ed.), *Developmental psychopathology* (3rd ed.). New York: Wiley.

Blair, C., & Razza, R.P. (2007). Relating effortful control, executive functioning, and false belief understanding to emerging math and literacy ability in kindergarten. *Child Development, 78,* 647–663.

Blair, M., & Somerville, S.C. (2009). The importance of differentiation in young children's acquisition of expertise. *Cognition, 112,* 259–280.

Blair, S.N. (1990). Personal communication. Dallas: Cooper Aerobics Center.

Blair, S.N., & others (1989). Physical fitness and all-cause mortality: A prospective study of healthy men and women. *Journal of the American Medical Association, 262,* 2395–2401.

Blake, J.S. (2017). *Nutrition and you* (4th ed.). Upper Saddle River, NJ: Pearson.

Blake, J.S., Munoz, K.D., & Volpe, S. (2019). *Nutrition* (4th ed.). Upper Saddle River, NJ: Pearson.

Blakemore, J.E.O., Berenbaum, S.A., & Liben, L.S. (2009). *Gender development.* Clifton, NJ: Psychology Press.

Blank, M.F., & Grummt, I. (2017). The seven faces of SIRT7. *Transcription, 8,* 67–74.

Blankenburg, H., Pramstaller, P.P., & Domingues, F.S. (2018). A network-based meta-analysis for characterizing the genetic landscape of aging. *Biogerontology, 19,* 81–94.

Blayney, J.A., & others (2018, in press). Examining the influence of gender and sexual motivation in college hookups. *Journal of American College Health.*

Bleckwenn, M., & others (2017). Impact of coronary heart disease on cognitive decline in Alzheimer's disease: A prospective longitudinal cohort study in primary care. *British Journal of General Practice, 67,* e111–e117.

Bleys, D., & others (2018, in press). Parental psychological control, adolescent self-criticism, and adolescent depressive symptoms: A latent change modeling approach to Belgian adolescents. *Journal of Clinical Psychology.*

Blieszner, R.A. (2009). Friendship, adulthood. In D. Carr (Ed.), *Encyclopedia of the life course and human development.* Boston: Gale Cengage.

Blieszner, R.A. (2016). Friendships. In S.K. Whitbourne (Ed.), *Encyclopedia of adulthood and aging* (Vol. 2). New York: Wiley.

Blieszner, R.A. (2018). Family life cycle. In M.H. Bornstein (Ed.), *SAGE encyclopedia of lifespan human development.* Thousand Oaks, CA: Sage.

Blieszner, R.A., & Ogletree, A.M. (2017). We get by with a little help from our friends. *Generations, 41,* 55–62.

Blieszner, R.A., & Ogletree, A.M. (2018). Relationships in middle and late adulthood. In D.A. Vangelisti & D. Perlman (Eds.), *Cambridge handbook of personal relationships* (2nd ed.). New York: Cambridge University Press.

Bloom, B. (1985). *Developing talent in young people.* New York. Ballantine.

Bloom, L., Lifter, K., & Broughton, J. (1985). The convergence of early cognition and language in the second year of life: Problems in conceptualization and measurement. In M. Barrett (Ed.), *Single word speech.* London: Wiley.

Blumel, J.E., Lavin, P., Vellejo, M.S., & Sarra, S. (2014). Menopause or climacteric, just a semantic discussion or has it clinical implications? *Climacteric, 17,* 235–241.

Boardman, J.P., & Fletcher-Watson, S. (2017). What can eye-tracking tell us? *Archives of Disease in Childhood, 102,* 301–302.

Boccardi, V., & others (2017). Anticholinergic burden and functional status in older people with cognitive impairment: Results from the Regal Project. *Journal of Nutrition, Health, and Aging, 21,* 389–396.

Bodrova, E., & Leong, D.J. (2007). *Tools of the mind* (2nd ed.). Geneva, Switzerland: International Bureau of Education, UNESCO.

Bodrova, E., & Leong, D.J. (2015). Vygotskian and post-Vygotskian views of children's play. *American Journal of Play, 7,* 371–388.

Boelen, P.A. (2015). Optimism in prolonged grief and depression following loss: A three-wave longitudinal study. *Psychiatry Research, 227,* 313–317.

Boespflug, E.L., & others (2016). Fish oil supplementation increases event-related posterior cingulate activation in older adults with subjective memory impairment. *Journal of Nutritional Health and Aging, 20,* 161–169.

Bogusz, H., Pekacka-Falkowska, K., & Magowska, A. (2018, in press). Under the British roof: The British contribution to the development of hospice and palliative care in Poland. *Journal of Palliative Care.*

Bohlin, G., & Hagekull, B. (1993). Stranger wariness and sociability in the early years. *Infant Behavior and Development, 16,* 53–67.

Bol, T., & Kalmijn, M. (2016). Grandparents' resources and grandchildren's schooling: Does grandparental involvement moderate the grandparent effect? *Social Science Research, 55,* 155–170.

Bombard, J.M., & others (2018). Vital signs: Trends and disparities in infant safe sleep practices—United States, 2009–2015. *MMWR Morbidity and Mortality Weekly Report, 67*(1), 39–46.

Bonanno, R.A., & Hymel, S. (2013). Cyber bullying and internalizing difficulties: Above and beyond the impact of traditional forms of bullying. *Journal of Youth and Adolescence, 42,* 685–697.

Bond, V.L. (2015). Sounds to share: The state of music education in three Reggio Emilia inspired North American preschools. *Journal of Research in Music Education, 62,* 462–484.

Bonfiglio, T., Vergassola, M., Olivero, G., & Pittaluga, A. (2018, in press). Environmental training and synaptic functions in young and old brain: A presynaptic perspective. *Current Medicinal Chemistry.*

Bonney, C.R., & Sternberg, R.J. (2017). Learning to think critically. In R.E. Mayer & P.A. Alexander (Eds.), *Handbook of learning and instruction* (2nd ed.). New York: Routledge.

Bonzano, S., & De Marchis, S. (2017). Detecting neuronal differentiation markers in newborn cells of the adult brain. *Methods in Molecular Biology, 1560,* 163–177.

Booth, A. (2006). Object function and categorization in infancy: Two mechanisms of facilitation. *Infancy, 10,* 145–169.

Booth, M. (2002). Arab adolescents facing the future: Enduring ideals and pressures to change. In B.B. Brown, R.W. Larson, & T.S. Saraswathi (Eds.), *The world's youth.* New York: Cambridge University Press.

Booth-Laforce, C., & Groh, A.M. (2018). Parent-child attachment and peer relations. In W.M. Bukowski & others (Eds.), *Handbook of peer interaction, relationships, and groups.* New York: Guilford.

Boraxbekk, C.J., & others (2015). Free recall episodic memory performance predicts dementia ten years prior to clinical diagnosis: Findings from the Betula Longitudinal Study. *Dementia and Geriatric Cognitive Disorders Extra, 5,* 191–202.

Bordoni, L., & others (2017). Obesity-related genetic polymorphisms and adiposity indices in a young Italian population. *IUBMB Life, 69,* 98–105.

Borella, E., & others (2017). Training working memory in older adults: Is there an advantage of using strategies? *Psychology and Aging, 32,* 178–191.

Borghuis, J., & others (2017). Big Five personality stability, change, and codevelopment across adolescence and early adulthood. *Journal of Personality and Social Psychology, 113,* 641–657.

Borich, G.D. (2017). *Effective teaching methods* (9th ed.). Upper Saddle River, NJ: Pearson.

Bornstein, M.H., Arterberry, M.E., & Mash, C. (2011). Perceptual development. In M.H. Bornstein & M.E. Lamb (Eds.), *Developmental psychology: An advanced textbook* (6th ed.). New York: Psychology Press.

Bornstein, M.H., Jager, J., & Steinberg, L. (2013). Adolescents, parents/friends/peers: A relationship model. In I. Weiner & others (Eds.), *Handbook of psychology* (2nd ed., Vol. 6). New York: Wiley.

Borraz-Leon, J.I., & others (2018, in press). Choosing fighting competitors among men: Testosterone, personality, and motivations. *Evolutionary Psychology.*

Borrelli, A., & others (2018). Role of gut microbiota and oxidative stress in the progression of non-alcoholic fatty liver disease to hepatocarcinoma: Current and innovative therapeutic approaches. *Redox Biology, 15,* 467–479.

Borsa, V.M., & others (2018). Bilingualism and healthy aging: Aging effects and neural maintenance. *Neuropsychologia, 111,* 151–161.

Boschen, K.E., Keller, S.M., Roth, T.L., & Klintsova, L.Y. (2018). Epigenetic mechanisms in alcohol- and adversity-induced developmental origins of neurobehavioral functioning. *Neurotoxicology, 66,* 63–79.

Bouchard, T.J., Lykken, D.T., McGue, M., Segl, N.L., & Tellegen, A. (1990). Source of human psychological differences. *The Minnesota Study of Twins Reared Apart. Science, 250,* 223–228.

Boukhris, T., Sheehy, O., Mottron, L., & Bérard, A. (2016). Antidepressant use during pregnancy and the risk of autism spectrum disorder in children. *JAMA Pediatrics, 170,* 117–124.

Boundy, E.O., & others (2018, in press). Kangaroo care and neonatal outcomes: A meta-analysis. *Pediatrics.*

Bourassa, K.J., & others (2017). Social participation predicts cognitive functioning in aging adults over time: Comparisons with physical health, depression, and physical activity. *Aging and Mental Health, 21,* 133–146.

Boutot, E.A. (2017). *Autism spectrum disorders* (2nd ed.). Upper Saddle River, NJ: Pearson.

Bovbjerg, M.L., Cheyney, M., & Everson, C. (2016). Maternal and newborn outcomes following waterbirth: The Midwives Alliance of North America Statistics Project, 2004 to 2009 cohort. *Journal of Midwifery and Women's Health, 61,* 11–20.

Bowlby, J. (1969). *Attachment and loss* (Vol. 1). London: Hogarth Press.

Bowlby, J. (1989). *Secure and insecure attachment.* New York: Basic Books.

Boylan, J.M., Cundiff, J.M., & Matthews, K.A. (2018, in press). Socioeconomic status and cardiovascular responses to standardized stressors: A systematic review and meta-analysis. *Psychosomatic Medicine.*

Braccio, S., Sharland, M., & Ladhani, S.N. (2016). Prevention and treatment of mother-to-child syphilis. *Current Opinion in Infectious Diseases, 29,* 268–274.

Brainerd, C.J., & Reyna, V.E. (2014). Dual processes in memory development: Fuzzy-trace theory. In P. Bauer & R. Fivush (Eds.), *Wiley-Blackwell handbook of children's memory.* New York: Wiley.

Braithwaite, D.W., & Sieger, R.S. (2018a, in press). Developmental changes in whole number bias. *Developmental Science.*

Braithwaite, D.W., & Siegler, R.S. (2018b, in press). Children learn spurious associations in their math textbooks: Examples from fraction arithmetic. *Journal of Experimental Psychology: Learning, Memory, and Cognition.*

Braithwaite, D.W., Tian, J., & Siegler, R.S. (2018, in press). Do children understand fraction addition? *Developmental Science.*

Braithwaite, S., & Holt-Lunstad, J. (2017). Romantic relationships and mental health. *Current Opinion in Psychology, 13,* 120–125.

Brand, J. (2014). Social consequences of job loss and unemployment. *Annual Review of Sociology* (Vol. 40). Palo Alto, CA: Annual Reviews.

Brannon, L. (2017). *Gender.* New York: Routledge.

Bransford, J., & others (2006). Learning theories in education. In P.A. Alexander & P.H. Winne (Eds.), *Handbook of educational psychology* (2nd ed.). Mahwah, NJ: Erlbaum.

Brassen, S., & others (2012). Don't look back in anger! Responsiveness to missed chances in successful and unsuccessful aging. *Science, 336,* 612–614.

Bratke, H., & others (2017). Timing of menarche in Norwegian girls: Associations with body mass, waist circumference, and skinfold thickness. *BMC Pediatrics, 17,* 138.

Bratt, C., & others (2018). Perceived age discrimination across age in Europe: From an aging society to a society for all ages. *Developmental Psychology, 54,* 167–180.

Braun, S.S., & Davidson, A.J. (2017). Gender (non) conformity in middle childhood: A mixed methods approach to understanding gender-typed behavior, friendship, and peer preference. *Sex Roles, 71,* 16–29.

Braver, S.L., & Lamb, M.E. (2013). Marital dissolution. In G.W. Peterson & K.R. Bush (Eds.), *Handbook of marriage and the family* (3rd ed.). New York: Springer.

Brawner, C.A., & others (2017). Change in maximal exercise capacity is associated with survival in men and women. *Mayo Clinic Proceedings, 92,* 383–390.

Bredekamp, S. (2017). *REVEL for effective practices in early childhood* (3rd ed.). Upper Saddle River, NJ: Pearson.

Breen, L.J., & others (2018). Differences in meanings made according to prolonged grief symptomatology. *Death Studies, 42,* 69–78.

Breiner, K., & others (2018). Combined effects of peer presence, social cues, and rewards on cognitive control in adolescence. *Developmental Psychobiology, 60,* 292–302.

Bremner, A.J. (2017). Multisensory development: Calibrating a coherent sensory milieu in early life. *Current Biology, 27,* R305–R307.

Bremner, A.J., & Spence, C. (2017). The development of tactile perception. *Advances in Child Development and Behavior, 52,* 227–268.

Bremner, J.G., & others (2016). Limits of object persistence: Young infants perceive continuity of vertical and horizontal trajectories but not 45-degree oblique trajectories. *Infancy, 44,* 240–248.

Brent, R.L. (2009). Saving lives and changing family histories: Appropriate counseling of pregnant women and men and women of reproductive age concerning the risk of diagnostic radiation exposure during and before pregnancy. *American Journal of Obstetrics and Gynecology, 200,* 4–24.

Brent, R.L. (2011). The pulmonologist's role in caring for pregnant women with regard to reproductive risks of diagnostic radiological studies or radiation therapy. *Clinics in Chest Medicine, 32,* 33–42.

Breslau, J., & others (2017). Sex differences in recent first-onset depression in an epidemiological sample of adolescents. *Translational Psychiatry, 7*(5), e1139.

Bretherton, I., & Munholland, K.A. (2016). The internal working model construct in light of contemporary neuroimaging research. In J. Cassidy & P.R. Shaver (Ed.), *Handbook of attachment* (3rd ed.). New York: Guilford.

Bretherton, I., Stolberg, U., & Kreye, M. (1981). Engaging strangers in proximal interaction: Infants' social initiative. *Developmental Psychology, 17,* 746–755.

Brewster, G.S., Riegel, B., & Gehrman, P.R. (2018), Insomnia in the older adult. *Sleep Medicine Clinics, 13,* 13–19.

Briana, D.D., & others (2018). Differential expression of cord blood neurotrophins in gestational diabetes: The impact of fetal growth abnormalities. *Journal of Maternal-Fetal and Neonatal Medicine, 31,* 278–283.

Bridgett, D.J., Laake, L.M., Gartstein, M.A., & Dorn, D. (2013). Development of infant positive emotionality: The contribution of maternal characteristics and effects on subsequent parenting. *Infant and Child Development, 22*(4), 362–382.

Brietzke, M., & Perreira, K. (2017). Stress and coping: Latino youth coming of age in a new Latino destination. *Journal of Adolescent Research, 32,* 407–432.

Briley, D.A., Domiteaux, M., & Tucker-Drob, E.M. (2014). Achievement-relevant personality: Relations with the Big Five and validation of an efficient instrument. *Learning and Individual Differences, 32,* 26–39.

Brim, G. (1992, December 7). Commentary, *Newsweek,* p. 52.

Brim, O. (1999). *The MacArthur Foundation study of midlife development.* Vero Beach, FL: MacArthur Foundation.

Brimah, P., & others (2013). Sleep duration and reported functional capacity among black and white U.S. adults. *Journal of Sleep Medicine, 9,* 605–609.

Brindis, C.D. (2017). Advancing the field of teenage pregnancy prevention through community-wide pregnancy prevention initiatives. *Journal of Adolescent Health, 60*(Suppl. 3), S1–S2.

Brinkman-Stoppelenburg, A., Rietjens, J.A., & van der Heide, A. (2014). The effects of advance care planning on end-of-life care: A systematic review. *Palliative Medicine, 28,* 1000–1025.

Brinskma, D.M., & others (2017). Age-dependent role of pre- and perinatal factors in interaction with genes on ADHD symptoms across adolescence. *Journal of Psychiatric Research, 90,* 110–117.

Brockmeyer, T., & others (2018). Body image related negative interpretation bias in anorexia nervosa. *Behavior Research and Therapy, 104,* 69–73.

Brody, G.H., & others (2017). Protective prevention effects on the association of poverty with brain development. *JAMA Pediatrics, 17,* 46–52.

Brody, L.R., Hall, J.A., & Stokes, L.R. (2018). Gender and emotion: Theory, findings, and content. In L.F. Barrett & others (Eds.), *Handbook of emotion* (4th ed.). New York: Guilford.

Brody, N. (2000). Intelligence. In A. Kazdin (Ed.), *Encyclopedia of psychology.* Washington, DC, & New York: American Psychological Association and Oxford University Press.

Brody, N. (2007). Does education influence intelligence? In P.C. Kyllonen, R.D. Roberts, & L. Stankov (Eds.), *Extending intelligence.* Mahwah, NJ: Erlbaum.

Brody, R.M., & Costa, R.M. (2009). Satisfaction (sexual, life, relationship, and mental health) is associated directly with penile-vaginal intercourse, but inversely related to other sexual behavior frequencies. *Journal of Sexual Medicine, 6,* 1947–1954.

Broesch, T., & Bryant, G.A. (2018, in press). Fathers' infant-directed speech in a small-scale society. *Child Development.*

Bronfenbrenner, U. (1986). Ecology of the family as a context for human development: Research perspectives. *Developmental Psychology, 22,* 723–742.

Bronfenbrenner, U. (2004). *Making human beings human.* Thousand Oaks, CA: Sage.

Bronfenbrenner, U., & Morris, P.A. (2006). The ecology of developmental processes. In W. Damon & R. Lerner (Eds.), *Handbook of child psychology* (6th ed.). New York: Wiley.

Bronstein, P. (2006). The family environment: Where gender role socialization begins. In J. Worell & C.D. Goodheart (Eds.), *Handbook of girls' and women's psychological health.* New York: Oxford University Press.

Brook, J.S., Brook, D.W., Gordon, A.S., Whiteman, M., & Cohen, P. (1990). The psychological etiology of adolescent drug use: A family interactional approach. *Genetic Psychology Monographs, 116*(2).

Brooker, R., & others (2018). *Principles of biology* (2nd ed.). New York: McGraw-Hill.

Brooks, J.G., & Brooks, M.G. (2001). *The case for constructivist classrooms* (2nd ed.). Upper Saddle River, NJ: Erlbaum.

Brooks-Gunn, J., & Warren, M.P. (1989). The psychological significance of secondary sexual characteristics in 9- to 11-year-old girls. *Child Development, 59,* 161–169.

Brophy, J., & Alleman, J. (2018). *Powerful social studies for elementary students* (4th ed.). Boston: Cengage.

Brothers, A., Gabrian, M., Wahl, H.W., & Diehl, M. (2016). Future time perspective and awareness of age-related change: Examining their role in predicting psychological well-being. *Psychology and Aging, 31,* 605–617.

Brown, B.B. (2011). Popularity in peer group perspective: The role of status in adolescent peer systems. In A.H.N. Cillessen, D. Schwartz, & L. Mayeux (Eds.), *Popularity in the peer system.* New York: Guilford.

Brown, B.B., & Bakken, J.P. (2011). Parenting and peer relationships: Reinvigorating research on family-peer linkages in adolescence. *Journal of Research on Adolescence, 21,* 153–165.

Brown, B.B., & Larson, J. (2009). Peer relationships in adolescence. In R.M. Lerner & L. Steinberg (Eds.), *Handbook of adolescent development* (3rd ed.). New York: Wiley.

Brown, B.B., & Larson, R.W. (2002). The kaleidoscope of adolescence: Experiences of the world's youth at the beginning of the 21st century. In B.B. Brown, R.W. Larson, & T.S. Saraswathi (Eds.), *The world's youth.* New York: Cambridge University Press.

Brown, C.L., & others (2012). Social activity and cognitive functioning over time: A coordinated analysis of four longitudinal studies. *Journal of Aging Research, 2012,* Article ID 287438.

Brown, C.S., & Stone, E.A. (2018). Environmental and social contributions to children's gender-typed toy play: The role of family, peers, and the media. In E.S. Weisgram & L.M. Dinella (Eds.), *Gender typing of children's play.* Washington, DC: APA Books.

Brown, H.L., & Graves, C.R. (2013). Smoking and marijuana in pregnancy. *Clinical Obstetrics and Gynecology, 56,* 107–113.

Brown, J.E. (2017). *Nutrition through the life cycle* (6th ed.). Boston: Cengage.

Brown, L., & others (2018, in press). It's not as bad as you think: Menopausal representations are more positive in postmenopausal women. *Journal of Psychosomatic Obstetrics and Gynecology.*

Brown, M.I., & others (2018, in press). Promoting language and social communication development in babies through an early storybook reading intervention. *International Journal of Speech-Language Pathology.*

Brown, M.T., & Wolf, D.A. (2018). Estimating the prevalence of serious mental illness and dementia diagnoses among Medicare beneficiaries in the Health and Retirement Study. *Research on Aging, 40,* 668–686.

Brown, Q.L., & others (2016). Trends in marijuana use among pregnant and non-pregnant reproductive-aged women, 2002–2014. *JAMA, 317,* 207–209.

Brown, R. (1958). *Words and things.* Glencoe, IL: Free Press.

Brown, R.C., & others (2018). The impact of child maltreatment on non-suicidal self-injury: Data from a representative sample of the general population. *BMC Psychiatry, 18*(1), 181.

Brown, S.L., Bulanda, J.R., & Lee, G.R. (2005). The significance of nonmarital cohabitation: Marital status and mental health benefits among middle-aged and older adults. *Journals of Gerontology B: Psychological Sciences and Social Sciences, 60,* S21–S29.

Brown, S.L., & Wright, M.W. (2017). Marriage, cohabitation, and divorce in later life. *Innovations in Aging, 1*(2).

Brown, S.M., & others (2017). Systematic medications used in treatment of common dermatological conditions: Safety profile with respect to pregnancy, breast feeding, and content in seminal fluid. *Journal of Dermatological Treatment, 16,* 1–53.

Browne, T.K. (2017). Why parents should not be told the sex of their fetus. *Journal of Medical Ethics, 43,* 5–10.

Brownell, C.A., Lemerise, E.A., Pelphrey, K.A., & Roisman, G.I. (2015). Measuring socioemotional behavior and development. In R.M. Lerner (Ed.), *Handbook of child psychology and developmental science* (7th ed.). New York: Wiley.

Brownell, C.A., Ramani, G.B., & Zerwas, S. (2006). Becoming a social partner with peers: Cooperation and social understanding in one- and two-year-olds. *Child Development, 77,* 803–821.

Brownell, C.A., Svetlova, M., Anderson, R., Nichols, S.R., & Drummond, J. (2013). Socialization of early prosocial behavior: Parents' talk about emotions is associated with sharing and helping in toddlers. *Infancy, 18,* 91–119.

Bruce, M.L., & Sirey, J.A. (2018, in press). Integrated care for depression in older primary care patients. *Canadian Journal of Psychiatry.*

Bruck, M., & Ceci, S.J. (1999). The suggestibility of children's memory. *Annual Review of Psychology* (Vol. 50). Palo Alto, CA: Annual Reviews.

Bruck, M., & Ceci, S.J. (2012). Forensic developmental psychology in the courtroom. In D. Faust & M. Ziskin (Eds.), *Coping with psychiatric and psychological testimony.* New York: Cambridge University Press.

Bruckner, S., & Kammer, T. (2017). Both anodal and cathodal transcranial direct current stimulation improves semantic processing. *Neuroscience, 343,* 269–275.

Brumariu, L.E., Kerns, K.A., & Seibert, A.C. (2012). Mother-child attachment, emotion regulation, and anxiety symptoms in middle childhood. *Personal Relationships, 19*(3), 569–585.

Brumariu, L.E., & others (2018a, in press). The Security Scale as a measure of attachment: Meta-analytic evidence of validity. *Attachment and Human Development.*

Brumariu, L.E., & others (2018b, in press). Middle childhood attachment strategies: Validation of an observational measure. *Attachment and Human Development.*

Brummelman, J.E., & others (2014). "That's not beautiful—That's incredibly beautiful!" The adverse impact of inflated praise on children with low self-esteem. *Psychological Science, 25,* 728–735.

Brummelman, J.E., & others (2015). My child is God's gift to humanity: Development and validation of the Parental Overvaluation Scale (POS). *Journal of Personality and Social Psychology, 108,* 665–679.

Brummelte, S., & Galea, L.A. (2016). Postpartum depression: Etiology, treatment, and consequences for maternal care. *Hormones and Behavior, 77,* 153–166.

Brunborg, G.S., Andreas, J.B., & Kvaavik, E. (2017). Social media use and episodic heavy drinking among adolescents. *Psychological Reports, 120,* 475–490.

Brusseau, T.A., & others (2018, in press). Trends in physical activity, health-related fitness, and gross motor skills in children during a two-year comprehensive school physical activity program. *Journal of Science and Medicine in Sport.*

Buchman, A.S., Yu, L., Boyle, P.A., Shah, R.C., & Bennett, D.A. (2012). Total daily physical activity and longevity in old age. *Archives of Internal Medicine, 172,* 444–446.

Budge, S.L., & Orovecz, J.J. (2018). Gender fluidity. In K. Nadal (Ed.), *SAGE encyclopedia of psychology and gender.* Thousand Oaks, CA: Sage.

Budge, S.L., & others (2018a, in press). The relationship between conformity to gender norms, sexual orientation, and gender identity for sexual minorities. *Counseling Psychology Quarterly.*

Budge, S.L., & others (2018b, in press). Trans individuals' facilitative coping: An analysis of internal and external processes. *Journal of Counseling Psychology.*

Buhl, H.M., & Lanz, M. (2007). Emerging adulthood in Europe: Common traits and variability across five European countries. *Journal of Adolescent Research, 22,* 439–443.

Buhrmester, D. (1998). Need fulfillment, interpersonal competence, and the developmental contexts of early adolescent friendship. In W.M. Bukowski & A.F. Newcomb (Eds.), *The company they keep: Friendship in childhood and adolescence.* New York: Cambridge University Press.

Bui, E., & Okereke, O. (2018). From bereavement to grief to cognitive decline: A call for novel treatment and prevention approaches. *American Journal of Geriatric Psychiatry, 26,* 481–482.

Buiting, H.M., & de Graas, T. (2018, in press). Possible underestimation of the provision of palliative care. *JAMA Oncology.*

Bukowski, R., & others (2008, January). *Folic acid and preterm birth.* Paper presented at the meeting of the Society for Maternal-Fetal Medicine, Dallas.

Bukowski, W.M., Laursen, B., & Rubin, K.H. (Eds.) (2018). *Handbook of peer interaction, relationships, and groups* (2nd ed.). New York: Guilford.

Bullard, J. (2017). *Creating environments for learning: Birth to eight* (3rd ed.). Upper Saddle River, NJ: Pearson.

Bullock, M., & Lutkenhaus, P. (1990). Who am I? Self-understanding in toddlers. *Merrill Palmer Quarterly, 36,* 217–238.

Bumpus, M.F., Crouter, A.C., & McHale, S.M. (2001). Parental autonomy granting during adolescence: Gender differences in context. *Developmental Psychology, 37,* 163–173.

Buratti, S., Allwood, C.M., & Johansson, M. (2014). Stability in the metamemory realism of eyewitness confidence judgments. *Cognitive Processing, 15,* 39–53.

Burchinal, M., Magnuson, K., Powell, D., & Hong, S.S. (2015). Early child care and education. In R.M. Lerner (Ed.), *Handbook of child psychology and developmental science* (7th ed.). New York: Wiley.

Burgette, J.M., & others (2017). Impact of Early Head Start in North Carolina on dental care use among children younger than 3 years. *American Journal of Public Health, 107,* 614–620.

Burkitt, I. (2018). Decentering emotion regulation: From emotion regulation to relational emotion. *Emotion Review, 10,* 167–173.

Burleson, G.R. (2017). Immunological variation due to genetics of inflammatory SNPs and age and impact of disease manifestation. *Toxicology Pathology, 45,* 146–149.

Burnett, A.C., & others (2018, in press). Trends in executive functioning in extremely preterm children across 3 birth eras. *Pediatrics.*

Burnette, C.B., Kwitowski, M.A., & Mazzeo, S.E. (2017). "I don't need people to tell me I'm pretty on social media": A qualitative study of social media and body image in early adolescent girls. *Body Image, 23,* 114–125.

Burns, R.A., Browning, C., & Kendig, H.L. (2017). Living well with chronic disease for those older adults living in the community. *International Psychogeriatrics, 29,* 835–843.

Burr, J.A., & others (2018). Health benefits associated with three helping behaviors: Evidence for incident cardiovascular disease. *Journals of Gerontology B: Psychological Sciences and Social Sciences. 83,* 492–500.

Burton, E., & others (2015). Effectiveness of exercise programs to reduce falls in older people with dementia living in the community: A systematic review and meta-analysis. *Clinical Interventions in Aging, 9,* 421–434.

Burton, G.J., & Jauniaux, E. (2015). What is the placenta? *American Journal of Obstetrics and Gynecology, 213*(Suppl. 4), S6.e1–e4.

Buss, D.M. (2008). Evolutionary psychology (3rd ed.). Boston: Allyn & Bacon.

Buss, D.M. (2012). Evolutionary psychology (4th ed.). Boston: Allyn Bacon.

Buss, D.M. (2015). Evolutionary psychology (5th ed.). Upper Saddle River, NJ: Pearson.

Busse, E.W., & Blazer, D.G. (1996). *The American Psychiatric Press textbook of geriatric psychiatry* (2nd ed.). Washington, DC: American Psychiatric Press.

Bussey, K., & Bandura A. (1999). Social cognitive theory of gender development and differentiation. *Psychological Review, 106,* 676–713.

Butler, R.N. (2007). Life review. In J.E. Birren (Ed.), *Encyclopedia of gerontology* (2nd ed.). San Diego: Academic Press.

Butler-Barnes, S.T., & others (2018, in press). Promoting resilience in African American girls: Racial identity as a protective factor. *Child Development.*

Butrica, B.A., & Smith, K.E. (2012). The retirement prospects of divorced women. *Social Security Bulletin, 72,* 11–22.

Butterfield, D.A. (2018, in press). Perspectives on oxidative stress in Alzheimer's disease and predictions of future research emphases. *Journal of Alzheimer's Disease.*

Butts, B., & others (2017). ASC methylation and interleukin-1*B* are associated with aerobic capacity in heart failure. *Medicine and Science in Sports and Exercise. 49,* 1072–1078.

Byne, W., & others (2012). Report of the American Psychiatric Association Task Force on the treatment of gender identity disorder. *Archives of Sexual Behavior, 41,* 759–796.

C

Cabeza, R. (2002). Hemispheric asymmetry reduction in older adults: The HAROLD model. *Psychology and Aging, 17,* 85–100.

Cabeza, R., & Dennis, N.A. (2013). Frontal lobes and aging: Deterioration and compensation. In D.T. Stuss & R.T. Knight (Eds.), *Principles of frontal lobe function* (2nd ed.). New York: Oxford University Press.

Cabrera, N.J., & Roggman, L. (2017). Father play: Is it special? *Infant Mental Health Journal, 38,* 706–708.

Cabrera, N.J., & others (2017). The magic of play: Low-income mothers' and fathers' playfulness and children's emotion regulation and vocabulary skills. *Infant Mental Health Journal, 38,* 757–771.

Cacioppo, J.T., Cacioppo, S., Gonzaga, G.C., Ogburn, E.L., & VanderWheele, T.J. (2013). Marital satisfaction and break-ups differ across on-line and off-line meeting venues. *Proceedings of the National Academy of Sciences, 110* (25), 10135–10140.

Cahill, K.E., Giandrea, M.D., & Quinn, J.F. (2016). Evolving patterns of work and retirement. In L.K. George & K.F. Ferraro (Eds.), *Handbook of aging and the social sciences* (8th ed.). New York: Elsevier.

Cahill, M., & others (2018, in press). The transition to retirement experiences of academics in "higher education": A meta-ethnography. *Gerontologist.*

Cain, M.A., Bornick, P., & Whiteman, V. (2013). The maternal, fetal, and neonatal effects of cocaine exposure in pregnancy. *Clinical Obstetrics and Gynecology, 56,* 124–132.

Cain, M.S., Leonard, J.A., Gabriel, J.D., & Finn, A.S. (2016). Media multitasking in adolescence. *Psychonomic Bulletin and Review, 23,* 1932–1941.

Caino, S., & others (2010). Short-term growth in head circumference and its relationship with supine length in healthy infants. *Annals of Human Biology, 37,* 108–116.

Cairncross, M., & Miller, C.J. (2018, in press). The effectiveness of mindfulness-based therapies for ADHD: A meta-analytic review. *Journal of Attention Disorders.*

Calero, M.D. (2019, in press). Effects of environmental enrichment and training across the life span in cognition. In R. Fernandez-Ballesteros & others (Eds.), *Cambridge handbook of successful aging.* New York: Cambridge University Press.

Calkins, S.D., & Markovitch, S. (2010). Emotion regulation and executive functioning in early development: Integrating mechanisms of control supporting adaptive functioning. In S.D. Calkins & M.A. Bell (Eds.), *Child development at the intersection of emotion and cognition.* Washington, DC: American Psychological Association.

Calkins, S.D., & Perry, N.B. (2016). The development of emotion regulation. In D. Cicchetti (Ed.), *Developmental psychopathology* (3rd ed.). New York: Wiley.

Callaghan, M.E., & others (2014). Widespread age-related differences in the human brain microstructure revealed by quantitative magnetic resonance imaging. *Neurobiology of Aging, 35,* 1862–1872.

Callahan, C.M., & others (2017). Targeting functional decline in Alzheimer disease: A randomized trial. *Annals of Internal Medicine, 166,* 164–171.

Callan, J.E. (2001). Gender development: Psychoanalytic perspectives. In J. Worrel (Ed.). *Encyclopedia of women and gender.* San Diego: Academic Press.

Calvert, S.L. (2015). Children and digital media. In R.M. Lerner (Ed.), *Handbook of child psychology and developmental science* (7th ed.). New York: Wiley.

Calvo-Garcia, M.A. (2016). Guidelines for scanning twins and triplets with US and MRI. *Pediatric Radiology, 46,* 156–166.

Calzada, E.J., & others (2018). Mental health issues in Latino populations. In A.D. Martinez & S.D. Rhodes (Ed.), *New and emerging issues in Latina/o families.* New York: Springer.

Camacho, D.E., & Fuligni, A.J. (2015). Extracurricular participation among adolescents from immigrant families. *Journal of Youth and Adolescence, 44,* 1251–1262.

Cambron, C., & others (2018). Neighborhood, family, and peer factors associated with early adolescent smoking and alcohol use. *Journal of Youth and Adolescence, 47,* 369–382.

Campbell, K.L., Grady, C.L., Ng, C., & Hasher, L. (2012). Age differences in the frontoparietal cognitive control network: Implications for distractibility. *Neuropsychologia, 50*(9), 2212–2223.

Campbell, L., Campbell, B., & Dickinson, D. (2004). *Teaching and learning through multiple intelligences* (3rd ed.). Boston: Allyn & Bacon.

Campione-Barr, N., Greer, K.B., & Kruse, A. (2013). Differential associations between domains of sibling conflict and adolescent emotional adjustment. *Child Development, 84,* 938–954.

Campos, J. (2009). Unpublished review of J.W. Santrock's *Life-span development* (13th ed.). New York: McGraw-Hill.

Canfield, J., & Hansen, M.V. (1995). *A second helping of chicken soup for the soul.* Deerfield Beach, FL: Health Communications.

Canivez, G.L., Watkins, M.W., & Dombrowski, S.C. (2017). Structural validity of the Wechsler Intelligence Scale for Children—Fifth Edition: Confirmatory factor analyses with the 16 primary and secondary subtests. *Psychological Assessment, 29,* 458–472.

Cantarella, A., & others (2017). Benefits in tasks related to everyday life competencies after working memory training in older adults. *International Journal of Geriatric Psychiatry, 32,* 86–93.

Cantone, E., & others (2015). Interventions on bullying and cyberbullying in schools: A systematic review. *Clinical Practice and Epidemiology in Mental Health, 11*(Suppl. 1), S58–S76.

Cao Van, H., & others (2018). Olfactory stimulation may promote oral feeding in immature newborn: A randomized controlled trial. *European Archives of Otorhinolaryngology, 275,* 125–129.

Caplan, M.A., Washington, T.R., & Swanner, L. (2017). Beyond income: A social justice approach to assessing poverty among older adults with chronic kidney disease. *Journal of Gerontological Social Work, 60,* 553–568.

Capone Singleton, N. (2018). Late talkers: Why the wait-and-see approach is outdated. *Pediatric Clinics of North America, 65,* 13–29.

Caprara, G.V., & others (2010). The contributions of agreeableness and self-efficacy beliefs to prosociality. *European Journal of Personality, 24,* 36–55.

Caprara, M.G., & Mendoza-Ruvalcaba, N. (2019, in press). Promoting successful aging: A psychosocial perspective. In R. Fernandez-Ballesteros & others (Eds.), *Cambridge handbook of successful aging.* New York: Cambridge University Press.

Carbajal-Valenzuela, C.C., & others (2017). Development of emotional face processing in premature and full-term infants. *Clinical EEG and Neuroscience, 48,* 88–95.

CareerBuilder (2017). *2017 college grads: You're entering the best job market in 10 years.* Retrieved from www.careerbuilder.com/advice/2017

Carlin, R.E., & Moon, R.Y. (2017). Risk factors, protective factors, and current recommendations to reduce sudden infant death syndrome: A review. *JAMA Pediatrics, 17,* 175–180.

Carlo, G., & others (2018, in press). Longitudinal relations among parenting styles, prosocial behaviors, and academic outcomes in U.S. Mexican adolescents. *Child Development.*

Carlson, M., & Vora, N.L. (2017). Prenatal diagnosis: Screening and diagnostic tools. *Obstetrics and Gynecology Clinics of North America, 44,* 245–256.

Carlson, M.J., & VanOrman, A.G. (2017). Trajectories of relationship supportiveness after childbirth: Does marriage matter? *Social Science Research, 66,* 102–117.

Carlson, N.S., Corwin, E.J., & Lowe, N.K. (2017). Oxytocin augmentation in spontaneously laboring, nulliparous women. *Biological Research in Nursing, 19,* 382–392.

Carlsson, A.C., & others (2016). Physical activity, obesity, and risk of cardiovascular disease in middle-aged men during a median of 30 years of follow-up. *European Journal of Preventive Cardiology, 23,* 359–365.

Carmona, S., Hardy, J., & Guerreiro, R. (2018). The genetic landscape of Alzheimer's disease. *Handbook of Clinical Neurology, 148,* 395–408.

Carnegie Council on Adolescent Development (1989). *Turning points: Preparing American youth for the twenty-first century.* New York: Carnegie Foundation.

Carpendale, J.I., & Chandler, M.J. (1996). On the distinction between false belief understanding and subscribing to an interpretive theory of mind. *Child Development, 67,* 1686–1706.

Carpendale, J.I., & Hammond, S.I. (2016). The development of moral sense and moral thinking. *Current Opinion in Pediatrics, 28,* 743–747.

Carpendale, J.I.M., & Lewis, C. (2015). The development of social understanding. In R.M. Lerner (Ed.), *Handbook of child psychology and developmental science* (7th ed.). New York: Wiley.

Carr, D. (2018). Volunteering among older adults: Life course correlates and consequences. *Journals of Gerontology B: Psychological Sciences and Social Sciences. 73.* 479–481.

Carr, D., Kail, B.L., & Rowe, J.W. (2018). The relation of volunteering and subsequent changes in physical disability in older adults. *Journals of Gerontology B: Psychological Sciences and Social Sciences, 73,* 511–521.

Carr, D., & Sharp, S. (2014). Do afterlife beliefs affect psychological adjustment to late-life spousal loss? *Journals of Gerontology B: Psychological Sciences and Social Sciences, 69B*(1), 103–112.

Carr, D., & others (2018). Does becoming a volunteer attenuate loneliness among recently widowed older adults? *Journals of Gerontology B: Psychological Sciences and Social Sciences, 73,* 501–510.

Carroll, J.L. (2019). *Sexuality now* (6th ed.). Boston: Cengage.

Carskadon, M.A. (2006, March). *Too little, too late: Sleep bioregulatory processes across adolescence.* Paper presented at the meeting of the Society for Research on Adolescence, San Francisco.

Carskadon, M.A. (2011a). Sleep in adolescents: The perfect storm. *Pediatric Clinics of North America, 58,* 637–647.

Carskadon, M.A. (2011b). Sleep's effects on cognition and learning in adolescence. *Progress in Brain Research, 190,* 137–143.

Carson, V., & others (2015). Systematic review of sedentary behavior and cognitive development in early childhood. *Preventive Medicine, 78,* 15–22.

Carstensen, L.L. (1998). A life-span approach to social motivation. In J. Heckhausen & C. Dweck (Eds.), *Motivation and self-regulation across the life span.* New York: Cambridge University Press.

Carstensen, L.L. (2006). The influence of a sense of time on human development. *Science, 312,* 1913–1915.

Carstensen, L.L. (2008, May). *Long life in the 21st century.* Paper presented at the meeting of the Association of Psychological Science, Chicago.

Carstensen, L.L. (2010). Social and emotional aging. *Annual Review of Psychology,* 2009 (Vol. 61). Palo Alto, CA: Annual Reviews.

Carstensen, L.L. (2014). Our aging population may just save us all. In P. Irving (Ed.), *The upside of aging.* New York: Wiley.

Carstensen, L.L. (2015, February). The new age of much older age. *Time Magazine, 185*(6), 68–70.

Carstensen, L.L. (2016, February). The new age of aging. *Time, 186*(2), 22–29.

Carstensen, L.L., & DeLiema, M. (2018). The positivity effect: A negativity bias in youth fades with age. *Current Opinion in Behavioral Sciences, 19,* 7–12.

Carstensen, L.L., & Fried, L.P. (2012). The meaning of old age. *Global population aging: Peril or promise?* Geneva, Switzerland: World Economic Forum.

Carstensen, L.L., Rosenberger, M.E., Smith, K., & Modrek, S. (2015). Optimizing health in aging societies. *Public Policy and Aging Report, 25,* 38–42.

Carstensen, L.L., & others (2011). Emotional experience improves with age: Evidence based on over 10 years of sampling. *Psychology and Aging, 26,* 21–33.

Carta, J.J., Greenwood, C., Baggett, K., Buzhardt, J., & Walker, D. (2012). Research-based approaches for individualizing caregiving and educational interventions for infants and toddlers in poverty. In S.L. Odom, E.P.

Pungello, & N. Gardner-Neblett (Eds.), *Infants, toddlers, and families in poverty.* New York: Guilford.

Case, R., & Mueller, M.R. (2001). Differentiation, integration, and covariance mapping as fundamental processes in cognitive and neurological growth. In J.L. McClelland & R.S. Slegler (Eds.), *Mechanisms of cognitive development.* Mahwah, NJ: Erlbaum.

CASEL (2018). *Collaborative for Academic, Social, and Emotional Learning.* Retrieved January 3, 2018, from www.casel.org

Casper, D.M., & Card, N.A. (2017). Overt and relational victimization: A meta-analytic review of their overlap and associations with social-psychological adjustment. *Child Development, 88,* 466–483.

Caspers, K.M., & others (2009). Association between the serotonin transporter polymorphism (5-HTTLPR) and adult unresolved attachment. *Developmental Psychology, 45,* 64–76.

Caspi, A., & Roberts, B.W. (2001). Personality development across the life course: The argument for change and continuity. *Psychological Inquiry, 12,* 49–66.

Caspi, A., & others (2003). Influence of life stress on depression: Moderation by a polymorphism in the 5-HTT gene. *Science, 301,* 386–389.

Cassidy, J. (2016). The nature of the child's ties. In J. Cassidy & P.R. Shaver (Eds.), *Handbook of attachment* (3rd ed.). New York: Guilford.

Cassina, M., & others (2017). Human teratogens and genetic phenocopies: Understanding pathogenesis through human genes mutation. *European Journal of Medical Genetics, 60,* 22–31.

Castagne, R., & others (2018, in press). Allostatic load and subsequent all-cause mortality: Which biological markers drive the relationship? Findings from a UK birth cohort. *European Journal of Epidemiology.*

Castellano-Castillo, D., & others (2018). Adipose tissue LPL methylation is associated with triglyceride concentrations in the metabolic syndrome. *Clinical Chemistry, 64,* 210–218.

Castellvi, P., & others (2017). Longitudinal association between self-injurious thoughts and behaviors and suicidal behavior in adolescents and young adults: A systematic review and meta-analysis. *Journal of Affective Disorders, 215,* 37–48.

Castillo, M., & Weiselberg, E. (2017). Bulimia nervosa/purging disorder. *Current Problems in Pediatric and Adolescent Health Care, 47,* 85–94.

Catalano, P.M., & Shankar, K. (2017). Obesity and pregnancy: Mechanisms of short term and long term adverse consequences for mother and child. *BMJ, 356,* 1.

Cataldo, D.M., Migliano, A.B., & Vinicius, L. (2018). Speech, stone tool-making, and the evolution of language. *PLoS One, 13*(1), e019071.

Cauffman, E., Shulman, E., Bechtold, J., & Steinberg, L. (2015). Children and the law. In R.M. Lerner (Ed.), *Handbook of child psychology* (7th ed.). New York: Wiley.

Causadias, J.M., Telzer, E.H., & Lee, R.M. (2017). Culture and biology interplay: An introduction. *Cultural Diversity and Ethnic Minority Psychology, 23,* 1–4.

Cavanagh, S.E. (2009). Puberty. In D. Carr (Ed.), *Encyclopedia of the life course and human development.* Boston: Gale Cengage.

Cazzato, V., & others (2016). The effects of body exposure on self-body image and esthetic appreciation in anorexia nervosa. *Experimental Brain Research, 234,* 695–709.

Ceci, S.J., & Gilstrap, L.L. (2000). Determinants of intelligence: Schooling and intelligence. In A. Kazdin (Ed.), *Encyclopedia of psychology.* Washington, DC, & New York: American Psychological Association and Oxford University Press.

Ceci, S.J., Hritz, A., & Royer, C.E. (2016). Understanding suggestibility. In W. O'Donohue & M. Fanetti (Eds.), *A guide to evidence-based practice.* New York: Springer.

Center for Science in the Public Interest (2008). *Obesity on the kids' menu at top chains.* Retrieved October 24, 2008, from www.cspinet.org/new/200808041.html

Centers for Disease Control and Prevention (2007). *Autism and developmental disabilities monitoring (ADDM) network.* Atlanta: Author.

Centers for Disease Control and Prevention (2015). *National Health Interview Survey 2014.* Atlanta: Author.

Centers for Disease Control and Prevention (2016). *Breastfeeding report card, United States 2016.* Atlanta: Author.

Centers for Disease Control and Prevention (2016). *Child obesity facts.* Atlanta: Author.

Centers for Disease Control and Prevention (2016). *Prevalence of obesity among adults: United States: 2016.* Atlanta: Author.

Centers for Disease Control and Prevention (2017). *Autism spectrum disorders.* Atlanta: Author.

Centers for Disease Control and Prevention (2017). *Births, marriages, divorces, and deaths.* Atlanta: Author.

Centers for Disease Control and Prevention (2018). *Body mass index for children and teens.* Atlanta: Author.

Centers for Disease Control and Prevention (2018). *Deaths.* Atlanta: Author.

Centers for Disease Control and Prevention (2018). *High blood pressure facts.* Atlanta; Author.

Centers for Disease Control and Prevention (2018). *HIV/AIDS.* Atlanta: Author.

Centers for Disease Control and Prevention (2018). *How much physical activity do older adults need?* Atlanta: Author.

Centers for Disease Control and Prevention (2018). *Sexually transmitted disease surveillance.* Atlanta: Author.

Centers for Disease Control and Prevention (2018). *Suicide.* Atlanta: Author.

Central Intelligence Agency (2015). *The world factbook: Life expectancy at birth.* Washington, DC: CIA.

Cercignani, M., & others (2017). Characterizing axonal myelination within the healthy population: A tract-by-tract mapping of effects of age and gender on the fiber-g ratio. *Neurobiology of Aging, 49,* 109–118.

Cerillo-Urbina, A.J., & others (2015). The effects of physical exercise in children with attention deficit hyperactivity disorder: A systematic review and meta-analysis of randomized controlled trials. *Child Care, Health, and Development, 41,* 779–788.

Cespedes, M.I., & others (2017). Comparisons of neurodegeneration over time between healthy aging and Alzheimer's disease cohorts via Bayesian inference. *BMJ Open, 7*(2), e012174.

Chae, S.Y., & others (2017). Promoting improved social support and quality of life with the CenteringPregnancy group model of prenatal care. *Archives of Women's Mental Health, 20,* 209–220.

Chan, G.C., & others (2017). Peer drug use and adolescent polysubstance use: Do parenting and school factors moderate this association? *Addictive Behaviors, 64,* 78–81.

Chan, M.Y., Haber, S., Drew, L.M., & Park, D.C. (2016). Training older adults to use tablet computers: Does it enhance cognitive function? *Gerontologist, 56,* 475–484.

Chandra, A., Mosher, W.D., Copen, C., & Sionean, C. (2011, March 3). Sexual behavior, sexual attraction, and sexual identity in the United States: Data from the 2006–2008 National Survey of Family Growth. *National Health Statistics Reports, 36,* 1–28.

Chandra-Mouli, V., & others (2018). 38.8 million additional modern contraceptive users: This, in fact, is "a never-before opportunity to strengthen investment and action on adolescent contraception." *Reproductive Health, 15*(1), 17.

Chang, A.C.Y., & Blau, H.M. (2018). Short telomeres—a hallmark of heritable cardiomyopathies. *Differentiation, 100,* 31–36.

Chang, E.C., & others (2018). Does optimism weaken the negative effects of being lonely on suicide risk? *Death Studies, 42,* 63–68.

Chang, H.Y., & others (2014). Prenatal maternal depression is associated with low birth weight through shorter gestational age in term infants in Korea. *Early Human Development, 90,* 15–20.

Chang, M.W., Brown, R., & Nitzke, S. (2017). Results and lessons learned from a prevention of weight gain program for low-income overweight and obese young mothers: Mothers in motion. *BMC Public Health, 17,* 182.

Chao, R.K. (2001). Extending research on the consequences of parenting style for Chinese Americans and European Americans. *Child Development, 72,* 1832–1843.

Chao, R.K. (2005, April). *The importance of Guan in describing control of immigrant Chinese.* Paper presented at the meeting of the Society for Research in Child Development, Atlanta.

Chao, R.K. (2007, March). *Research with Asian Americans: Looking back and moving forward.* Paper presented at the meeting of the Society for Research in Child Development, Boston.

Chao, R.K., & Otsuki-Clutter, M. (2011). Racial and ethnic differences: Sociocultural and contextual explanations. *Journal of Research on Adolescence, 21,* 47–60.

Chao, R.K., & Tseng, V. (2002). Parenting of Asians. In M.H. Bornstein, *Handbook of parenting* (2nd ed., Vol. 4). Mahwah: NJ: Erlbaum.

Chaplin, T.M., & others (2012). Parent-adolescent conflict interactions and adolescent alcohol use. *Addictive Behaviors, 37,* 605–612.

Charles, S.T., Piazza, J.R., Mogle, J., Sliwinski, M.J., & Almedia, D.M. (2013). The wear and tear of daily stressors on mental health. *Psychological Science, 24,* 733–741.

Charles, S.T., & others (2010). Fewer ups and downs: Daily stressors mediate age differences in negative affect. *Journals of Gerontology B: Psychological Sciences and Social Sciences, 65B,* 279–286.

Charlton, B.M., & others (2018, in press). Teen pregnancy risk factors among young women of diverse sexual orientations. *Pediatrics.*

Charness, N., & Krampe, R.T. (2008). Expertise and knowledge. In D.F. Alwin & S.M. Hofer (Eds.), *Handbook on cognitive aging.* Thousand Oaks, CA: Sage.

Charney, E. (2017). Genes, behavior, and behavior genetics. *Wiley Interdisciplinary Reviews. Cognitive Science, 8,* 1–2.

Charpak, N., & other (2018, in press). Twenty-year follow-up of kangaroo mother care versus traditional care. *Pediatrics.*

Chasnoff, I.J. (2017). Medical marijuana laws and pregnancy: Implications for public health policy. *American Journal of Obstetrics and Gynecology, 16,* 27–30.

Chatterjee, D., & others (2018, in press). Adverse childhood experiences and early initiation of marijuana and alcohol use: The potential moderating effects of internal assets. *Substance Use and Misuse.*

Chatterton, Z., & others (2017). In utero exposure to maternal smoking is associated with DNA methylations and reduced neuronal content in the developing fetal brain. *Epigenetics and Chromatin, 10,* 4.

Chaudry, A., & others (2017). *Cradle to kindergarten: A new plan to combat inequality.* New York: Russell Sage Foundation.

Chavarria, M.C., & others (2014). Puberty in the corpus callosum. *Neuroscience, 265,* 1–8.

Chen, C., & Stevenson, H.W. (1989). Homework: A cross-cultural comparison. *Child Development, 60,* 551–561.

Chen, F.R., Rothman, E.F., & Jaffee, S.R. (2018, in press). Early puberty, friendship, group characteristics, and dating abuse in U.S. girls. *Pediatrics.*

Chen, J., Yu, J., Wu, Y., & Zhang, J. (2015). The influence of pubertal timing and stressful life events on depression and delinquency among Chinese adolescents. *Psychology Journal, 4,* 88–97.

Chen, L.C., Jeka, J., & Clark, J.E. (2016). Development of adaptive sensorimotor control in infant sitting posture. *Gait and Posture, 45,* 157–163.

Chen, L.W., & others (2016). Maternal caffeine intake during pregnancy and risk of pregnancy loss: A categorical and dose-response meta-analysis of prospective studies. *Public Health Nutrition, 19,* 1233–1244.

Chen, L.W., & others (2018). Measuring the cost and value of quality improvement initiatives for local health departments. *Journal of Public Health Management and Practice, 24,* 164–171.

Chen, P.J., & others (2017). Effects of prenatal yoga on women's stress and immune function across pregnancy: A randomized controlled trial. *Complementary Therapies in Medicine, 31,* 109–117.

Chen, R., Hughes, A.C., & Austin, J.P. (2017). The use of theory in family therapy research: Content analysis. *Journal of Marital and Family Therapy, 43,* 514–525.

Chen, X., Lee, J., & Chen, L. (2018). Culture and peer relationships. In W.M. Bukowski & others (Eds.), *Handbook of peer interactions, relationships, and groups* (2nd ed.). New York: Guilford.

Chen, Y.M., & others (2016). Trajectories of older adults' leisure-time activity and functional disability: A 12-year follow-up. *International Journal of Behavioral Medicine, 23,* 697–706.

Chen, Y-C., & others (2017). Early binocular input is critical for development of audiovisual but not visuotactile simultaneity perception. *Current Biology, 27,* 583–589.

Cheng, H.M., & others (2017). Vascular aging and hypertension: Implications for the clinical application of central blood pressure. *International Journal of Cardiology, 230,* 209–213.

Cheng, N., & others (2018). Quality of maternal parenting of 9-month-old infants predicts executive function performance at 2 and 3 years of age. *Frontiers in Psychology, 8,* 2293.

Cheon, Y.M., & others (2018, in press). The development of ethnic/racial self-labeling: Individual differences in context. *Journal of Youth and Adolescence.*

Cheong, J.I., & others (2015). The effect of early menarche on the sexual behaviors of Korean female adolescents. *Annals of Pediatric Endocrinology and Metabolism, 20,* 130–135.

Cheong, J.L.Y., & Miller, S.P. (2018). Imaging the neonatal brain in the 21st century: Why, when, and how? *Archives of Disease in Childhood. Fetal and Neonatal Edition, 103,* F4–F5.

Cherlin, A.J. (2009). *The marriage-go-round.* New York: Random House.

Cherlin, A.J., & Furstenberg, F.F. (1994). Stepfamilies in the United States: A reconsideration. In J. Blake & J. Hagen (Eds.), *Annual review of sociology.* Palo Alto, CA: Annual Reviews.

Chess, S., & Thomas, A. (1977). Temperamental individuality from childhood to adolescence. *Journal of Child Psychiatry, 16,* 218–226.

Cheung, C., & Pomerantz, E.M. (2012). Why does parents' involvement in children's learning enhance children's achievement? The role of parent-oriented motivation. *Journal of Educational Psychology. 104*(3), 820–832.

Chevalier, N., Dauvier, B., & Blaye, A. (2018, in press). From prioritizing objects to prioritizing cues: A developmental shift for cognitive control. *Developmental Science.*

Chevalier, N., & others (2015). Myelination is associated with processing speed in early childhood: Preliminary insights. *PLoS One, 10,* e0139897.

Chhaya, R., & others (2018, in press). The feasibility of an automated eye-tracking-modified Fagan test of memory for human faces in young Ugandan HIV-exposed children. *Child Neuropsychology.*

Chhetri, J., King, A.E., & Gueven, N. (2018). Alzheimer's disease and NQO1: Is there a link? *Current Alzheimer Research, 15,* 56–66.

Chi, M.T. (1978). Knowledge structures and memory development. In R.S. Siegler (Ed.), *Children's thinking: What develops?* Hillsdale, NJ: Erlbaum.

Chi, N.C., & others (2018). Pain management concerns from the hospice family caregivers' perspective. *American Journal of Hospice and Palliative Care, 35,* 601–611.

Chiaramonte, D., Ring, M., & Locke, A.M. (2017). Integrative women's health. *Medical Clinics of North America, 101,* 955–975.

Child Trends (2015, November). *Oral sex behaviors among teens.* Washington, DC: Child Trends.

Childers, J.B., & Tomasello, M. (2002). Two-year-olds learn novel nouns, verbs, and conventional actions from massed or distributed exposures. *Developmental Psychology, 38,* 967–978.

Chin, B., & others (2017). Marital status as a predictor of diurnal salivary cortisol levels and slopes in a community sample of healthy adults. *Psychoneuroendocrinology, 78,* 68–75.

Chiocca, E.M. (2017). American parents' attitudes and beliefs about corporal punishment: An integrative literature review. *Journal of Pediatric Health Care, 31,* 372–383.

Chiou, W.B., Chen, S.W., & Liao, D.C. (2014). Does Facebook promote self-interest? Enactment of indiscriminate one-to-many communication on online social networking sites decreases prosocial behavior. *Cyberpsychology, Behavior, and Social Networking, 17,* 68–73.

Chiu, H.L., & others (2018, in press). Effectiveness of executive function training on mental set shifting, working memory, and inhibition in healthy older adults: A double-blind randomized controlled trial. *Journal of Advanced Nursing.*

Cho, D., Post, J., & Kim, S.K. (2018, in press). Comparison of passive and active leisure activities and life satisfaction with aging. *Geriatrics and Gerontology International.*

Choi, D.H., & others (2017). Therapeutic potential of induced neural stem cells for Parkinson's disease. *International Journal of Molecular Science, 25,* 1404–1414.

Choi, H., Yorgason, J.B., & Johnson, D.R. (2016). Marital quality and health in middle and later adulthood: Dyadic associations. *Journals of Gerontology B: Psychological Sciences and Social Sciences, 7,* 154–164.

Choi, Y., & Lee, H.J. (2017). Do regular cholesterol screenings lead to lower cholesterol levels and better health behaviors for all? Spotlight on middle-aged and older adults in the United States. *Journal of Aging and Health, 29,* 389–414.

Choi, Y.J., & Luo, Y. (2015). 13-month-olds' understanding of social interaction. *Psychological Science, 26,* 274–283.

Chomsky, N. (1957). *Syntactic structures.* The Hague: Mouton.

Chopik, W.J., Edelstein, R.S., & Grimm, K.J. (2018, in press). Longitudinal changes in attachment orientation over a 59-year period. *Journal of Personality and Social Psychology.*

Chopik, W.J., Kim, E.S., & Smith, J. (2018). An examination of dyadic changes in optimism and physical health over time. *Health Psychology, 37,* 42–50.

Chopik, W.J., & Kitayama, S. (2018, in press). Personality change across the life span: Insights from a cross-cultural, longitudinal study. *Journal of Personality.*

Chor, E. (2018). Multigenerational Head Start participation: An unexpected marker of progress. *Child Development, 89,* 264–279.

Chou, C.C., & Huang, C.J. (2017). Effects of an 8-week yoga program on sustained attention and discrimination function in children with attention deficit hyperactivity disorder. *PeerJ, 5,* e2883.

Choudhri, A.F., & others (2018). Twenty-five diagnoses on midline images of the brain: From fetus to child to adult. *Radiographics, 38,* 218–235.

Choukas-Bradley, S., & Prinstein, M.J. (2016). Peer relationships and the development of psychopathology. In M. Lewis & D. Rudolph (Eds.), *Handbook of developmental psychopathology* (3rd ed.). New York: Springer.

Christ, S.L., Kwak, Y.Y., & Lu, T. (2017). The joint impact of parental psychological neglect and peer isolation on adolescents' depression. *Child Abuse and Neglect, 69,* 151–162.

Christen, M., Narváez, D., & Gutzwiller, E. (2018, in press). Comparing and integrating biological and cultural moral progress. *Ethical Theory and Moral Practice.*

Christensen, D.L., & others (2016). *Prevalence and characteristics of autism spectrum disorder among children aged 8 years–Autism and Developmental Disabilities*

Monitoring Network, 11 sites, United States 2012. Atlanta: Centers for Disease Control and Prevention.

Christodoulou, J., Leland, D.S., & Moore, D.S. (2018, in press). Overt and covert attention in infants revealed using steady-state visually evoked potentials. *Developmental Psychology.*

Chu, F.W., & others (2018). Children's early understanding of number predicts their later problem-solving sophistication in addition. *Journal of Experimental Child Psychology, 169,* 73–92.

Chua, A. (2011). *Battle hymn of the tiger mother.* New York: Penguin.

Chung, S.J., Ersig, A.L., & McCarthy, A.M. (2017). The influence of peers on diet and exercise among adolescents: A systematic review. *Journal of Pediatric Nursing, 36,* 44–56.

Chung, S.J., & others (2018, in press). Effect of striatal dopamine depletion on cognition in de novo Parkinson disease. *Parkinsonism and Related Disorders.*

Chung, S.T., Onuzuruike, A.U., & Magge, S.N. (2018). Cardiometabolic risk in obese children. *Annals of the New York Academy of Sciences, 141,* 166–183.

Cicchetti, D. (2018, in press). A multilevel developmental approach to the prevention of psychopathology in children and adolescents. In J.N. Butcher & others (Eds.), *APA handbook of psychopathology.* Washington, DC: American Psychological Association.

Cicchetti, D., & Toth, S.L. (2006). Developmental psychopathology and preventive intervention. In W. Damon & R. Lerner (Eds.), *Handbook of child psychology* (6th ed.). New York: Wiley.

Cicchetti, D., & Toth, S.L. (2016). Child maltreatment and developmental psychopathology: A multi-level perspective. In D. Cicchetti (Ed.), *Developmental psychopathology* (3rd ed.). New York: Wiley.

Cicchetti, D., Toth, S.L., & Rogosch, F.A. (2005). *A prevention program for child maltreatment.* Unpublished manuscript. Rochester, NY: University of Rochester.

Cicek, D., & others (2018). Clinical follow-up data and the rate of development of precocious and rapidly progressive puberty in patients with premature thelarche. *Journal of Pediatric Endocrinology and Metabolism, 31,* 305–312.

Cicirelli, V. (2009). Sibling relationships, later life. In D. Carr (Ed.), *Encyclopedia of the life course and human development.* Boston: Gale Cengage.

Cicirelli, V.G. (2010). Attachment relationships in old age. *Journal of Social and Personal Relationships, 27,* 191–199.

Cillessen, A.H.N., & Bukowski, W.M. (2018). Sociometric perspectives. In W.M. Bukowski & others (Eds.), *Handbook of peer interactions, relationships, and groups* (2nd ed.). New York: Guilford.

Cimarolli, V.R., & others (2017). A population study of correlates of social participation in older adults with age-related vision loss. *Clinical Rehabilitation, 31,* 115–125.

Claes, H.I., & others (2010). Understanding the effects of sildenafil treatment on erection maintenance and erection hardness. *Journal of Sexual Medicine, 7*(6), 2184–2191.

Clark, C.D. (2015). Play interventions and therapy. In J.E. Johnson & others (Eds.), *Handbook of the study of play.* Blue Ridge Summit, PA: Rowman & Littlefield.

Clark, C.D. (2016). *Play and well-being.* New York: Routledge.

Clark, E.V. (1993). *The lexicon in acquisition.* New York: Cambridge University Press.

Clark, E.V. (2017). *Language in children.* New York: Psychology Press.

Clarke-Stewart, A.K., & Miner, J.L. (2008). Child and day care, effects of. In M.M. Haith & J.B. Benson (Eds.), *Encyclopedia of infant and early childhood development.* Oxford, UK: Elsevier.

Clarke-Stewart, A.K., & Parke, R.D. (2014). *Social development* (2nd ed.). New York: Wiley.

Claro, S., Paunesku, D., & Dweck, C.S. (2016). Growth mindset tempers the effect of poverty on academic achievement. *Proceedings of the National Academy of Sciences USA, 113,* 8664–8668.

Cleal, K., Norris, K., & Baird, D. (2018, in press). Telomere length dynamics and the evolution of cancer genome architecture. *International Journal of Molecular Sciences.*

Clearfield, M.W., Diedrich, F.J., Smith, L.B., & Thelen, E. (2006). Young infants reach correctly in A-not-B tasks: On the development of stability and perseveration. *Infant Behavior and Development, 29,* 435–444.

Clements, J.M. (2009). Patient perceptions on the use of advance directives and life-prolonging technology. *American Journal of Hospice and Palliative Care, 26,* 270–276.

Clifton, R.K., Morrongiello, B.A., Kulig, J.W., & Dowd, J.M. (1981). Developmental changes in auditory localization in infancy. In R.N. Aslin, J.R. Alberts, & M.R. Petersen (Eds.), *Development of perception* (Vol. 1). Orlando, FL: Academic Press.

Clifton, R.K., Muir, D.W., Ashmead, D.H., & Clarkson, M.G. (1993). Is visually guided reaching in early infancy a myth? *Child Development, 64,* 1099–1110.

Cnattingius, S., & others (2013). Maternal obesity and risk of preterm delivery. *Journal of the American Medical Association, 309,* 2362–2370.

Coetsee, C., & Terblanche, E. (2018, in press). The effect of three different exercise training modalities on cognitive and physical function in a healthy older population. *European Review of Aging and Physical Activity.*

Cogmed (2013). *Cogmed: Working memory is the engine of learning.* Upper Saddle River, NJ: Pearson.

Cohen, A.A. (2015). Physiological and comparative evidence fails to confirm an adaptive role for aging in evolution. *Current Aging Science, 8,* 14–23.

Cohen, A.O., & Casey, B.J. (2017). The neurobiology of adolescent self-control. In T. Egner (Ed.), *Wiley handbook of cognitive control.* New York: Wiley.

Cohen, J.R., & others (2018, in press). Anxiety and depression during childhood and adolescence: Testing theoretical models of continuity and discontinuity. *Journal of Abnormal Child Psychology.*

Cohen, P. (2012). *In our prime: The invention of middle age.* New York: Scribner.

Cohen, P., Kasen, S., Chen, H., Hartmark, C., & Gordon, K. (2003). Variations in patterns of developmental transitions in the emerging adulthood period. *Developmental Psychology, 39,* 657–669.

Cohen, R., Bavishi, C., & Rozanski, A. (2016). Purpose in life and its relationship to all-cause mortality and cardiovascular events: A meta-analysis. *Psychosomatic Medicine, 78,* 122–133.

Cohen, W.R., Sumersille, M., & Friedman, E.A. (2018). Management of labor: Are the new guidelines justified? *Journal of Midwifery and Women's Health, 63,* 10–13.

Coie, J. (2004). The impact of negative social experiences on the development of antisocial behavior. In J.B. Kupersmidt & K.A. Dodge (Eds.), *Children's peer relations: From development to intervention.* Washington, DC: American Psychological Association.

Coker, T.R., & others (2015). Media violence exposure and physical aggression in fifth-grade children. *Academic Pediatrics, 15,* 82–88.

Colcombe, S.J., & others (2006). Aerobic exercise training increases brain volume in aging humans. *Journals of Gerontology: Medical Sciences, 61A,* 1166–1170.

Cole, M.A., & others (2018, in press). Extracellular matrix regulation of fibroblast function: Redefining our perspective on skin aging. *Journal of Cell Communication and Signaling.*

Cole, P.M. (2016). Emotion and the development of psychopathology. In D. Cicchetti (Ed.), *Developmental psychopathology* (3rd ed.). New York: Wiley.

Cole, P.M., Dennis, T.A., Smith-Simon, K.E., & Cohen, L.H. (2009). Preschoolers' emotion regulation strategy understanding: Relations with maternal socialization and child behavior. *Social Development, 18*(2), 324–352.

Cole, P.M., & Hollenstein, T. (Eds.) (2018). *Emotion regulation.* New York: Routledge.

Cole, P.M., Lougheed, J.P., & Ram, N. (2018). The development of emotion regulation in early childhood. In P.M. Cole & T. Hollenstein (Eds.), *Emotion regulation.* New York: Routledge.

Cole, P.M., & Tan, P.Z. (2007). Emotion socialization from a cultural perspective. In J.E. Grusec & P.D. Hastings (Eds.), *Handbook of socialization.* New York: Guilford.

Cole, T.J., & Mori, H. (2018, in press). Fifty years of child height and weight in Japan and South Korea: Contrasting secular trend patterns analyzed by SITAR. *American Journal of Human Biology.*

Cole, W.G., Robinson, S.R., & Adolph, K.E. (2016). Bouts of steps: The organization of infant exploration. *Developmental Psychobiology, 58,* 341–354.

Coleman, A.M. (2013). Physicians' attitudes toward advance directives: A literature review of variables impacting on physicians' attitudes toward advance directives. *American Journal of Hospice and Palliative Care, 30,* 696–706.

Coleman, P.D. (1986, August). *Regulation of dendritic extent: Human aging brain and Alzheimer's disease.* Paper presented at the meeting of the American Psychological Association, Washington, DC.

Colen, C.G., & Ramey, D.M. (2014). Is breast truly best? Estimating the effects of breastfeeding on long-term health and well-being in the United States using sibling comparisons. *Social Science and Medicine, 109C,* 55–65.

Coley, R.L., & others (2018). Locating economic risks for adolescent mental and behavioral health: Poverty and affluence in families, neighborhoods, and schools. *Child Development, 89,* 360–369.

Collins, W.A., & van Dulmen, M. (2006). The significance of middle childhood peer competence for work and relationships in early childhood. In A.C. Huston & M.N. Ripke (Eds.), *Developmental contexts in middle childhood.* New York: Cambridge University Press.

Comalli, D.M., Persand, D., & Adolph, K.E. (2017). Motor decisions are not black and white: Selecting actions in the "gray zone." *Experimental Brain Research, 235,* 1793–1807.

Comer, J. (1988). Educating poor minority children. *Scientific American, 259,* 42–48.

Comer, J. (2004). *Leave no child behind.* New Haven, CT: Yale University Press.

Comer, J. (2006). Child development: The underweighted aspect of intelligence. In P.C. Kyllonen, R.D. Roberts, & L. Stankov (Eds.), *Extending intelligence.* Mahwah, NJ: Erlbaum.

Comer, J. (2010). Comer School Development Program. In J. Meece & J. Eccles (Eds.), *Handbook of research on schools, schooling, and human development.* New York: Routledge.

Comhaire, F. (2016). Hormone replacement therapy and longevity. *Andrologia, 48,* 65–68.

Committee for Children (2018). *Second Step.* Retrieved January 3, 2018, from www.cfchildren.org/second-step

Committee on the Rights of the Child (2014). *The Convention on the Rights of the Child and its treaty body—The Committee on the Rights of the Child.* Retrieved April 14, 2015, from http://endcorporalpunishment.org/pages/hrlaw/crc_session.html

Common Core State Standards Initiative (2018). *Read the standards.* Retrieved June 12, 2018, from http://www.corestandards.org/read-the-standards/

Common Sense Media (2013). *Zero to eight: Children's media use in America 2013.* San Francisco: Common Sense Media.

Commoner, B. (2002). Unraveling the DNA myth: The spurious foundation of genetic engineering. *Harper's Magazine, 304,* 39–47.

Condition of Education (2016). *Participation in education.* Washington, DC: U.S. Office of Education.

Conlin, S.E., Douglass, & Ouch, S. (2018, in press). Discrimination, subjective wellbeing, and the role of gender: A mediation model of LGB minority stress. *Journal of Homosexuality.*

Conner, T.S., & others (2017). The role of personality traits in young adult fruit and vegetable consumption. *Frontiers in Psychology, 8,* 119.

Connolly, H.L., & others (2018, in press). Sex differences in emotion recognition: Evidence for a small overall female superiority on facial disgust. *Emotion.*

Connolly, J.A., & McIsaac, C. (2009). Romantic relationships in adolescence. In R.M. Lerner & L. Steinberg (Eds.), *Handbook of adolescent psychology* (3rd ed.). New York: Wiley.

Connolly, J.A., Nguyen, H.N., Pepler, D., Craig, W., & Jiang, D. (2013). Developmental trajectories of romantic stages and associations with problem behaviors during adolescence. *Journal of Adolescence, 36,* 1013–1024.

Connolly, M.D., & others (2016). The mental health of transgender youth: Advances in understanding. *Journal of Adolescent Health, 59,* 489–495.

Conry-Murray, C., Kim, J.M., & Turiel, E. (2012, April). *U.S. and Korean children's judgments of gender norm violations.* Paper presented at the Gender Development Research conference, San Francisco.

Consoli, A., & others (2013). Suicidal behaviors in depressed adolescents: Role of perceived relationships in the family. *Child and Adolescent Psychiatry and Mental Health, 7*(1), 8.

Constantinescu, M., & others (2017). Treatment with sildenafil and donepezil improves angiogenesis in experimentally induced critical limb ischemia. *Biomedical Research International, 2017,* 9532381.

Conway, B.N., & others (2018). The obesity epidemic and rising diabetes incidence in a low-income racially diverse southern U.S. cohort. *PLoS One, 13*(1), e190993.

Cook, R.E., & Richardson-Gibbs, A.M. (Eds.) (2018). *Strategies for including children with special needs in early childhood settings* (2nd ed.). Boston: Cengage.

Coontz, S. (2005). *Marriage: A history.* New York: Penguin.

Cooper, C.R. (2011). *Bridging multiple worlds.* New York: Oxford University Press.

Cooper, M., Warland, J., & McCutcheon, H. (2018, in press). Australian midwives' views and experiences of practice and politics to water immersion for labor and birth: A web based survey. *Women and Birth.*

Cooperrider, K., & Goldin-Meadow, S. (2017). When gesturing becomes analogy. *Topics in Cognitive Science, 9,* 719–737.

Cooperrider, K., & Goldin-Meadow, S. (2018). Gesture, language, and cognition. In B. Dancygier (Ed.), *Cambridge handbook of cognitive linguistics.* New York: Cambridge University Press.

Copeland, W.E., & others (2013). Adult psychiatric outcomes of bullying and being bullied by peers in childhood and adolescence. *JAMA Psychiatry, 70,* 419–426.

Copen, C.E., Chandra, A., & Febo-Vasquez, I. (2018). Sexual behavior, sexual attraction, and sexual orientation among adults aged 18–44 in the United States: Data from the 2011–2013 National Survey of Family Growth. *National Health Statistics Reports, 88,* 1–14.

Copen, C.E., Daniels, C.E., & Mosher, W.D. (2013, April 4). First premarital cohabitation in the United States: 2006–2010. National Survey of Family Growth. *National Health Statistics Reports, 64,* 1–16.

Copen, C.E., Daniels, K., Vespa, J., & Mosher, W.D. (2012). First marriages in the United States: Data from the 2006–2010 National Survey of Family Growth. *National Health Statistics Reports, 49,* 1–22.

Coplan, R.J., & others (2018). Peer-based interventions with behaviorally inhibited, withdrawn, and socially anxious children. In W.M. Bukowski & others (Eds.), *Handbook of peer interactions, relationships, and groups* (2nd ed.). New York: Guilford.

Cordier, S. (2008). Evidence for a role of paternal exposure in developmental toxicity. *Basic and Clinical Pharmacology and Toxicology, 102,* 176–181.

Cordova, D., Huang, S., Lally, M., Estrada, Y., & Prado, G. (2014). Do parent-adolescent discrepancies in family functioning increase the risk of Hispanic adolescent HIV risk behaviors? *Family Process, 53,* 348–363.

Cornelissen, K.K., & others (2015). The influence of personal BMI on body size estimations and sensitivity to body size change in anorexia spectrum disorders. *Body Image, 13,* 75–85.

Corona, G., Rastrelli, G., Maseroli, E., Forti, G., & Maggi, M. (2013). Sexual functioning of the aging male. *Best Practices & Research: Clinical Endocrinology and Metabolism, 27,* 581–601.

Correia, C., & others (2016). Global sensory impairment in older adults in the United States. *Journal of the American Geriatrics Society, 64,* 306–313.

Costa, I.B., & others (2017). Change in INSR, APBA2, and IDE gene expressions in brains of Alzheimer's disease patients. *Current Alzheimer Research, 14,* 760–765.

Costa, P.T., & McCrae, R.R. (1998). Personality assessment. In H.S. Friedman (Ed.), *Encyclopedia of mental health* (Vol. 3). San Diego: Academic Press.

Costa, P.T., & McCrae, R.R. (2000). Contemporary personality psychology. In C.E. Coffey and J.L. Cummings (Eds.), *Textbook of geriatric neuropsychiatry.* Washington, DC: American Psychiatric Press.

Cote, J., & Bynner, J.M. (2008). Changes in the transition to adulthood in the UK and Canada: The role of structure and agency in emerging adulthood. *Journal of Youth Studies, 11,* 251–258.

Cotten, S.R., Anderson, W.A., & McCullough, B.M. (2013). Impact of Internet use on loneliness and contact with others among older adults: Cross-sectional analysis. *Journal of Medical Internet Research, 15*(2), e39.

Cottrell, L., & Duggleby, W. (2016). The "good death": An integrative literature review. *Palliative and Supportive Care, 14,* 686–712.

Cottrell, L.A., & others (2017). Constructing tailored parental monitoring strategy profiles to predict adolescent disclosure and risk involvement. *Preventive Medicine Reports, 7,* 147–151.

Coubart, A., & others (2014). Dissociation between small and larger numerosities in newborn infants. *Developmental Science, 17,* 11–22.

Couch, K.A., & others (2017). The distributional impact of social security options. *Research on Aging, 39,* 135–165.

Coulson, S. (2018). Language and the brain. In B. Dancygier (Ed.), *Cambridge handbook of cognitive linguistics.* New York: Cambridge University Press.

Courage, M.L., Bakhtiar, A., Fitzpatrick, C., Kenny, S., & Brandeau, K. (2015). Growing up multitasking: The costs and benefits for cognitive development. *Developmental Review, 35,* 5–41.

Courage, M.L., Edison, S.C., & Howe, M.L. (2004). Variability in the early development of visual self-recognition. *Infant Behavior and Development, 27,* 509–532.

Courtois, G., & others (2018). Effects of binaural spatialization in wireless microphone systems for hearing aids on normal-hearing and hearing-impaired listeners. *Trends in Hearing, 22,* 1331216517753548.

Cousins, L., & Goodyer, I.M. (2015). Antidepressants and the adolescent brain. *Journal of Psychopharmacology, 29,* 545–555.

Cowan, C.P., & Cowan, P.A. (2000). *When partners become parents.* Mahwah, NJ: Erlbaum.

Cowan, P., Cowan, C., Ablow, J., Johnson, V.K., & Measelle, J. (2005). *The family context of parenting in children's adaptation to elementary school.* Mahwah, NJ: Lawrence Erlbaum Associates.

Cox, K.S., Wilt, J., Olson, B., & McAdams, D.P. (2010). Generativity, the Big Five, and psychosocial adaptation in midlife adults. *Journal of Personality, 78,* 1185–1208.

Cox, M.J., & others (2018, in press). Bidirectional relationships between alcohol-specific parental socialization behaviors and adolescent alcohol misuse. *Substance Use and Abuse.*

Coyne, J., & others (2018). The circle of security. In C.H. Zeanah (Ed.), *Handbook of infant mental health* (4th ed.). New York; Guilford.

Coyne, S.M., Padilla-Walker, L.M., & Holmgren, H.G. (2018). A six-year longitudinal study of texting trajectories during adolescence. *Child Development, 89,* 58–65.

Cozza, S.J., & others (2018). Deployment status and child neglect types in the U.S. Army. *Child Maltreatment, 23,* 25–33.

Crain, S. (2012). Sentence scope. In E.L. Bavin (Ed.), *Cambridge handbook of child language.* New York: Cambridge University Press.

Cramer, P. (2017). Childhood precursors of the narcissistic personality. *Journal of Nervous and Mental Diseases, 205,* 679–684.

Crane, J.D., Macneil, L.G., & Tarnopolsky, M.A. (2013). Long-term aerobic exercise is associated with greater muscle strength throughout the life span. *Journals of Gerontology A: Biological Sciences and Medical Sciences, 68,* 631–638.

Crawford, B., & others (2018, in press). DNA methylation and inflammation marker profiles associated with a history of depression. *Human Molecular Genetics.*

Crawford, D., & others (2010). The longitudinal influence of home and neighborhood environments on children's body mass index and physical activity over 5 years: The CLAN study. *International Journal of Obesity, 34,* 1177–1187.

Creighton, G., & others (2018, in press). "I should have . . .": A photovoice study with women who have lost a man to suicide. *American Journal of Men's Health.*

Cremation Association of North America (2018). *Statistics about cremation trends.* Wheeling, IL: Author.

Crimmins, E.M., & Levine, M.E. (2016). Current status of research on trends in morbidity, health, life expectancy, and the compression of morbidity. In M.R. Kaeberlein & G.M. Martin (Eds.), *Handbook of the biology of aging* (8th ed.). New York: Elsevier.

Criss, M.M., & others (2015). Link between monitoring behavior and adolescent adjustment: An analysis of direct and indirect effects. *Journal of Child and Family Studies, 24,* 668–678.

Crocetti, E., & others (2017). Identity processes and parent-child and sibling relationships in adolescence: A five-wave multi-informant longitudinal study. *Child Development, 88,* 210–228.

Crockenberg, S.B. (1986). Are temperamental differences in babies associated with predictable differences in caregiving? In J.V. Lerner & R.M. Lerner (Eds.), *Temperament and social interaction during infancy and childhood.* San Francisco: Jossey-Bass.

Crockenberg, S.B., & Leerkes, E.M. (2006). Infant and maternal behaviors moderate reactivity to novelty to predict anxious behavior at 2.5 years. *Development and Psychopathology, 18,* 17–24.

Croffut, S.E., & others (2018, in press). HIV-positive Malawian women with young children prefer overweight body sizes and link underweight body size with inability to exclusively breastfeed. *Maternal and Child Nutrition.*

Crone, E.A. (2017). *The adolescent brain.* New York: Routledge.

Crone, E.A., & Konijn, E.A. (2018). Media use and brain development during adolescence. *Nature Communications, 9*(1), 588.

Crone, E.A., Peters, S., & Steinbeis, N. (2018). Executive function development in adolescence. In S.A. Wiebe & J. Karbach (Eds.), *Executive function.* New York: Routledge.

Crooks, C.V., & others (2017). Two years of relationship-focused mentoring for First Nations, Metis, and Inuit adolescents: Promoting positive mental health. *Journal of Primary Prevention, 38,* 87–104.

Crooks, R.L., & Baur, K. (2017). *Our sexuality* (13th ed.). Boston: Cengage.

Crosnoe, R. (2011). *Fitting in, standing out.* New York: Cambridge University Press.

Crosnoe, R., Bonazzo, C., & Wu, N. (2015). *Healthy learners: A whole child approach to disparities in early education.* New York: Teachers College Press.

Cross, D., Lester, L., & Barnes, A. (2015). A longitudinal study of the social and emotional predictors and consequences of cyber and traditional bullying victimization. *International Journal of Public Health, 60,* 207–217.

Cross, W.E. (2017). Ecological factors in human development. *Child Development, 88,* 767–769.

Croteau-Chonka, E.C., & others (2016). Examining the relationships between cortical maturation and white matter myelination throughout early childhood. *Neuroimage, 125,* 413–421.

Crouter, A.C. (2006). Mothers and fathers at work. In A. Clarke-Stewart & J. Dunn (Eds.), *Families count.* New York: Cambridge University Press.

Crowley, J.E. (2018, in press). Gray divorce: Explaining midlife marital splits. *Journal of Women and Aging.*

Crowley, K., Callahan, M.A., Tenenbaum, H.R., & Allen, E. (2001). Parents explain more to boys than to girls during shared scientific thinking. *Psychological Science, 12,* 258–261.

Cruz, R.A., & others (2018). Mexican-origin youth substance use trajectories: Associations with cultural and family factors. *Developmental Psychology, 54,* 111–126.

Cruz-Jentoft, A.J., & others (2017). Nutrition, frailty, and sarcopenia. *Aging: Clinical and Experimental Research, 29,* 43–48.

Csikszentmihalyi, M. (1995). *Creativity.* New York: HarperCollins.

Csikszentmihalyi, M. (2000). Creativity: An overview. In A. Kazdin (Ed.), *Encyclopedia of psychology.* Washington, DC, & New York: American Psychological Association and Oxford University Press.

Cucina, J.M., Peyton, S.T., Su, C., & Byle, K.A. (2016). Role of mental abilities and mental tests in explaining school grades. *Intelligence, 54,* 90–104.

Cuevas, K., & Bell, K.A. (2014). Infant attention and early childhood executive function. *Child Development, 85*(2), 397–404.

Cuffe, J.S., & others (2017). Review: Placental derived biomarkers of pregnancy disorders. *Placenta, 54,* 104–110.

Culen, C., & others (2017). Care of girls and women with Turner syndrome: Beyond growth and hormones. *Endocrine Connections, 6,* R39–R51.

Cummings, E.M., & Miller, L.M. (2015). Emotional security theory: An emerging theoretical model for youths' psychological and physiological responses across multiple developmental contexts. *Current Directions in Psychological Science, 24,* 208–213.

Cummings, E.M., & Valentino, K.V. (2015). Developmental psychopathology. In R.M. Lerner (Ed.), *Handbook of child psychology and developmental science* (7th ed.). New York: Wiley.

Cummings, E.M., & others (2017). Emotional insecurity about the community: A dynamic, within-person mediator of child adjustment in contexts of political violence. *Development and Psychopathology, 29,* 27–36.

Cunha, A.B., & others (2016). Effect of short-term training on reaching behavior in infants: A randomized controlled trial. *Journal of Motor Behavior, 48,* 132–142.

Cunningham, M. (2009). Housework. In D. Carr (Ed.), *Encyclopedia of the life course and human development.* Boston: Gale Cengage.

Cunningham, P.J., Green, T.L., & Braun, R.T. (2018). Income disparities in the prevalence, severity, and costs of co-occurring chronic and behavioral health conditions. *Medical Care, 56,* 139–145.

Cunningham, P.M. (2017). *Phonics they use: Words for reading and writing* (7th ed.). Upper Saddle River, NJ: Pearson.

Cunningham, S.A., Kramer, M.R., & Narayan, K.M. (2014). Incidence of childhood obesity in the United States. *New England Journal of Medicine, 370,* 403–411.

Curl, A.L., Bibbo, J., & Johnson, R.A. (2017). Dog walking, the human-animal bond, and older adults' physical health. *Gerontologist, 57,* 930–939.

Curran, K., DuCette, J., Eisenstein, J., & Hyman, I.A. (2001, August). *Statistical analysis of the cross-cultural data: The third year.* Paper presented at the meeting of the American Psychological Association, San Francisco, CA.

Currier, J.M., Holland, J.M., & Neimeyer, R.A. (2006). Sense-making, grief, and the experience of violent loss: Toward a mediational model. *Death Studies, 30,* 403–428.

Cvencek, D., Meltzoff, A.N., & Greenwald, A.G. (2011). Math-gender stereotypes in elementary school children. *Child Development, 82,* 766–779.

Czekalla, C., & others (2017). Impact of body site, age, and gender on the collagen/elastin index by noninvasive in vivo vertical two-photon microscopy. *Skin Pharmacology and Physiology, 30,* 260–267.

D

D'Acunto, C.W., & others (2018). Metallomics for Alzheimer's disease treatment: Use of new generation of chelators combining metal-cation binding and transport properties. *European Journal of Medicinal Chemistry, 150,* 140–155.

D'Souza, H., & Karmiloff-Smith, A. (2018, in press). Neurodevelopmental disorders. *Wiley Interdisciplinary Reviews: Cognitive Science.*

D'Souza, H., & others (2018, in press). Specialization of the motor system in infancy: From broad tuning to selectively specialized purposeful actions. *Developmental Science.*

da Costa Souza, A., & Ribeiro, S. (2015). Sleep deprivation and gene expression. *Current Topics in Behavioral Neurosciences, 25,* 65–90.

Daelmans, B., & others (2017). Early childhood development: The foundation of sustainable development. *Lancet, 389,* (10064), 9–11.

Dagan, O., Facompre, C.R., & Bernard, K. (2018). Adult attachment representations and depressive symptoms: A meta-analysis. *Journal of Affective Disorders, 236,* 274–290.

Dahl, A., & others (2017). Explicit scaffolding increases simple helping in younger infants. *Developmental Psychology, 53,* 407–416.

Dahl, R.E. (2004). Adolescent brain development: A period of vulnerability and opportunity. *Annals of the New York Academy of Sciences, 1021,* 1–22.

Dahl, R.E., & others (2018). Importance of investing in adolescence from a developmental science perspective. *Nature, 554,* 441–450.

Dahlberg, L., Agahi, N., & Lennartsson, C. (2018). Lonelier than ever? Loneliness of older people over two decades. *Archives of Gerontology and Geriatrics, 75,* 96–103.

Dahm, C.C., & others (2018, in press). Adolescent diet quality and cardiovascular disease risk factors and incident cardiovascular disease in middle-aged women. *Journal of the American Heart Association.*

Dai, R., Thomas, A.K., & Taylor, H.A. (2018, in press). Age-related differences in the use of spatial and categorical relationships in a visuo-spatial working memory task. *Memory and Cognition.*

Daiello, L.A., & others (2015). Association of fish oil supplement use with preservation of brain volume and cognitive function. *Alzheimer's and Dementia, 11,* 226–235.

Daien, C.I., & others (2017). Non-pharmaceutical and pharmacological interventions in patients with early arthritis: A systematic literature review informing the 2016 update of EULAR recommendations for the management of early arthritis. *RMD Open, 3*(1), e000404.

Dale, B., & others (2014). Utility of the Stanford-Binet Intelligence Scales, Fifth Edition, with ethnically diverse preschoolers. *Psychology in the Schools, 51,* 581–590.

Dale, P., & Goodman, J. (2004). Commonality and differences in vocabulary growth. In M. Tomasello & D.I. Slobin (Eds.), *Beyond nature-nurture.* Mahwah, NJ: Erlbaum.

Dale, W., & others (2018, in press). Cognitive function and its risk factors among older U.S. adults living at home. *Alzheimer Disease and Associated Disorders.*

Daly, M., Delaney, L., Egan, M., & Baumeister, R.F. (2015). Childhood self-control and unemployment through the life span: Evidence from two British cohort studies. *Psychological Science, 26,* 709–723.

Damoiseaux, J.S. (2017). Effects of aging on functional and structural brain connectivity. *NeuroImage, 160,* 32–40.

Damon, F., & others (2018, in press). Preference for facial averageness: Evidence for a common mechanism in human and macaque infants. *Scientific Reports.*

Damon, W. (2008). *The path to purpose.* New York: Free Press.

Daniels, H. (Ed.) (2017). *Introduction to Vygotsky* (3rd ed.). New York: Routledge.

Danielson, C.K., & others (2017). Clinical decision-making following disasters: Efficient identification of PTSD risk in adolescents. *Journal of Abnormal Child Psychology, 48,* 117–128.

Danilovich, M.K., & others (2018, in press). The impact of Strong for Life on the physical functioning and health of older adults receiving home and community-based services. *Aging and Society.*

Danilovich, M.K., Conroy, D.E., & Hornby, T.G. (2017). Feasibility and impact of high-intensity walking training in frail older adults. *Journal of Aging and Physical Activity, 25,* 533–538.

Danovitch, J.H., & Mills, C.M. (2018). Children's learning from explanations: When and how explanation leads to exploration. In M.M. Saylor & P.A. Ganea (Eds), *Active learning from infancy to childhood.* New York: Springer.

Dao-Fu, D., & others (2016). Cardiac aging. In M.R. Kaeberlein & G.M. Martin (Eds.), *Handbook of the biology of aging* (8th ed.). New York: Elsevier.

Daoulah, A., & others (2017). Divorce and severity of coronary heart disease: A multicenter study. *Cardiology Research and Practice, 2017,* 4751249.

Daoulah, A., & others (2017). Widowhood and severity of coronary artery disease: A multicenter study. *Coronary Artery Disease, 28,* 98–103.

Darcy, E. (2012). Gender issues in child and adolescent eating disorders. In J. Lock (Ed.), *Oxford handbook of child and adolescent eating disorders: Developmental perspectives.* New York: Oxford University Press.

Dardas, L.A., van de Water, B., & Simmons, L.A. (2018, in press). Parental involvement in adolescent depression interventions: A systematic review of randomized clinical trials. *International Journal of Mental Health Nursing.*

Dariotis, J.K., & others (2016). A qualitative evaluation of student learning and skills use in a school-based mindfulness and yoga program. *Mindfulness, 7,* 76–89.

Darnell, A.J., & Schuler, M.S. (2015). Quasi-experimental study of functional family therapy effectiveness for juvenile justice aftercare in a racially and ethnically diverse community sample. *Children and Youth Services Review, 50,* 75–82.

Darwin, C. (1859). *On the origin of species.* London: John Murray.

Datar, A., & Nicosia, N. (2017). The effect of state competitive food and beverage regulations on childhood overweight and obesity. *Journal of Adolescent Health, 60,* 520–527.

Dathe, K., & Schaefer, C. (2018). Drug safety and pregnancy: the German Embryotox Institute. *European Journal of Clinical Pharmacology, 74,* 171–179.

Dato, S., & others (2017). The genetics of human longevity: An intricacy of genes, environment, culture, and microbiome. *Mechanics of Aging and Development, 165*(Pt. B), 147–155.

Davidson, J.G.S., & Gutherie, D.M. (2018, in press). Older adults with a combination of vision and hearing impairment experience higher rates of cognitive impairment, functional dependence, and worse outcomes across a set of quality indicators. *Journal of Aging and Health.*

Davies, G., & others (2011). Genome-wide association studies establish that human intelligence is highly heritable and polygenic. *Molecular Psychiatry, 16,* 996–1005.

Davies, J., & Brember, I. (1999). Reading and mathematics attainments and self-esteem in years 2 and 6—an eight-year cross-sectional study. *Educational Studies, 25,* 145–157.

Davies, P.T., Martin, M.J., & Cummings, E.M. (2018). Interparental conflict and children's social problems: Insecurity and friendship affiliation as cascading mediators. *Developmental Psychology, 54,* 83–97.

Davies, P.T., Martin, M.J., & Sturge-Apple, M.L. (2016). Emotional security theory and developmental psychopathology. In D. Cicchetti (Ed.), *Developmental psychopathology* (3rd ed.). New York: Wiley.

Davies, R., Davies, D., Pearce, M., & Wong, N. (2015). The effect of waterbirth on neonatal mortality and morbidity: A systematic review and meta-analysis. *JBI Database of Systematic Reviews and Implementation Reports, 13,* 180–231.

Davila, J., Capaldi, D.M., & La Greca, A.M. (2016). Adolescent/young adult romantic relationships and psychopathology. In D. Cicchetti (Ed.), *Developmental psychopathology* (3rd ed.). New York: Wiley.

Davis, A.N., & others (2018, in press). The roles of familism and emotion reappraisal in the relations between acculturative stress and prosocial behaviors in Latina/o college students. *Journal of Latina/o Psychology.*

Davis, J.C., & others (2017). Slow processing speed predicts falls in older adults with a falls history: One-year prospective cohort study. *Journal of the American Geriatrics Society, 65,* 916–923.

Davis, K., & Weinstein, E. (2017). Identity development in the digital age: An Eriksonian perspective. In M.F. Wright (Ed.), *Identity, sexuality, and relationships in the digital age.* Hershey, PA: IGI Global.

Davis, L., & Keyser, J. (1997). *Becoming the parent you want to be: A sourcebook of strategies for the first five years.* New York: Broadway.

Davis, M.C., Burke, H.M., Zautra, A.J., & Stark, S. (2013). Arthritis and musculoskeletal conditions. In I.B. Weiner & others (Eds.), *Handbook of psychology* (2nd ed., Vol. 9). New York: Wiley.

Davis, S.W., Kragel, J.E., Madden, D.J., & Cabeza, R. (2012). The architecture of cross-hemispheric communication in the aging brain: Linking behavior to functional and structural connectivity. *Cerebral Cortex, 22,* 232–242.

Dawson-McClure, S., & others (2015). A population-level approach to promoting healthy child development and school success in low-income, urban neighborhoods: Impact on parenting and child conduct problems. *Prevention Science, 16,* 279–290.

Day, N.L., Goldschmidt, L., & Thomas, C.A. (2006). Prenatal marijuana exposure contributes to the prediction of marijuana use at age 14. *Addiction, 101,* 1313–1322.

Dayton, C.J., & Malone, J.C. (2017). Development and socialization of physical aggression in very young boys. *Infant Mental Health, 38,* 150–165.

Dayton, C.J., Walsh, T.B., Oh, W., & Volling, B. (2015). Hush now baby: Mothers' and fathers' strategies for soothing their infants and associated parenting outcomes. *Journal of Pediatric Health Care, 29,* 145–155.

de Abreu, C.N., & Cangelli Filho, R. (2017). Anorexia nervosa and bulimia nervosa—a psychotherapeutic cognitive-constructivist approach. *International Review of Psychiatry, 29,* 248–253.

de Barse, L.M., & others (2017). Infant feeding and child fussy eating: The Generation R Study. *Appetite, 114,* 374–381.

de Boer, B., & Thompson, B. (2018). Biology-culture co-evolution in finite populations. *Scientific Reports, 8*(1), 1209.

De Bruyne, L.K., & Pinna, K. (2017). *Nutrition for health and healthcare* (6th ed.). Boston: Cengage.

De Genna, N.M., Goldschmidt, L., Day N.L., & Cornelius, M.D. (2016). Prenatal and postnatal maternal trajectories of cigarette use predict adolescent cigarette use. *Nicotine and Tobacco Research, 18,* 988–992.

De Giovanni, N., & Marchetti, D. (2012). Cocaine and its metabolites in the placenta: A systematic review of the literature. *Reproductive Toxicology, 33,* 1–14.

de Greeff, J.W., & others (2018, in press). Effects of physical activity on executive functions, attention, and academic performance in preadolescent children: A meta-analytic review. *Journal of Science and Medicine in Sport.*

de Gregorio, C. (2018, in press). Physical training and cardiac rehabilitation in heart failure patients. *Advances in Experimental Medicine and Biology, 1067,* 161–181.

de Haan, M. (2015). Neuroscientific methods with children. In R.M. Lerner (Ed.), *Handbook of child psychology and developmental science* (7th ed.). New York: Wiley.

de Haan, M., & Johnson, M.H. (2016). Typical and atypical human functional brain development. In D. Cicchetti (Ed.), *Developmental psychopathology* (3rd ed.). New York: Wiley.

de Heer, H.D., & others (2017). Let's move together. *Health Education and Behavior, 44,* 141–152.

De La Fuente, M. (2019). Bio-psycho-social bridge: The psychoneuroimmune system in successful aging. In R. Fernandez-Ballesteros & others (Eds.), *Cambridge handbook of successful aging.* New York: Cambridge University Press.

de la Haye, K., & others (2017). The dual role of friendship and antipathy relations in the marginalization of overweight children in their peer networks: The TRAILS study. *PLoS One, 12*(6), e0178130.

de Leo, D. (2018). Ageism and suicide prevention. *Lancet Psychiatry, 5,* 192–193.

de Magalhaes, J.P., & Tacutu, R. (2016). Integrative genomics and aging. In M.R. Kaeberlein & G.M. Martin (Eds.), *Handbook of the biology of aging* (8th ed.). New York: Elsevier.

de Medeiros, T.S., & others (2017). Caffeine intake during pregnancy in different intrauterine environments and its association with infant anthropometric measurements at 3 and 6 months of age. *Maternal and Child Health Journal, 21,* 1297–1307.

de Oliveira, S.R., & others (2018). Association between hemodynamic activity and motor performance in six-month-old full-term and preterm infants: A functional near-infrared spectroscopy study. *Neurophotonics, 5*(1), 1117.

de Villiers, T.J. (2018, in press). Should women be screened for osteoporosis at midlife? *Climacteric.*

De Vitis, M., Berardinelli, F., & Sgura, A. (2018, in press). Telomere length maintenance in cancer: At the crossroads between telomerase and alternative lengthening of telomeres (ALT). *International Journal of Molecular Sciences.*

De, R., & others (2017). Identifying gene-gene interactions that are highly associated with four quantitative lipid traits across multiple cohorts. *Human Genetics, 136,* 165–178.

Dean, D.C., & others (2018, in press). Investigation of brain structure in the 1-month infant. *Brain Structure and Function.*

Dean, E. (2017). Responding to a request to hasten death. *Nursing Standard, 31*(25), 15.

Dean, G.E., & others (2017). Impaired sleep: A multifaceted geriatric syndrome. *Nursing Clinics of North America, 52,* 387–404.

Dearing, E., & others (2016). Can community and school-based supports improve the achievement of first-generation immigrant children attending high-poverty schools? *Child Development, 87,* 883–897.

Deater-Deckard, K. (2013). The social environment and the development of psychopathology. In P.D. Zelazo (Ed.), *Handbook of developmental psychology.* New York: Oxford University Press.

Deaton, A. (2008). Income, health, and well-being around the world: Evidence from the Gallup World Poll. *Journal of Economic Perspectives, 22,* 53–72.

DeCasper, A.J., & Spence, M.J. (1986). Prenatal maternal speech influences newborns' perception of speech sounds. *Infant Behavior and Development, 9,* 133–150.

DeCesare. J.Z., & Jackson, J.R. (2015). Centering-Pregnancy: Practical tips for your practice. *Archives of Gynecology and Obstetrics, 29,* 499–507.

DeCosmi, V., Scaglioni, S., & Agostini, C. (2018, in press). Early taste experiences and later food choices. *Nutrients.*

Dee, D.L., & others (2017). Trends in repeat births and use of postpartum contraception among teens—United States, 2004–2015. *MMWR Morbidity and Mortality Weekly Reports, 66,* 422–426.

Deeg, D.J.H. (2005). The development of physical and mental health from late midlife to early old age. In S.L. Willis & M. Martin (Eds.), *Middle adulthood: A lifespan perspective.* Thousand Oaks, CA: Sage.

Degrelle, S.A., & Fournier, T. (2018). Fetal-sex determination of human placental tissues. *Placenta, 61,* 103–105.

Del Campo, M., & Jones, K.L. (2017). A review of the physical features of the fetal alcohol syndrome disorders. *European Journal of Medical Genetics, 60,* 55–64.

Del Giudice, M. (2011). Sex differences in romantic attachment: A meta-analysis. *Personality and Social Psychology Bulletin, 37,* 193–214.

Del Gobbo, L.C., & others (2015). Contribution of major lifestyle risk factors for incident heart failure in older adults: The Cardiovascular Health Study. *JACC Heart Failure, 3,* 520–528.

Del-Aguila, J.L., & others (2018). Assessment of the genetic architecture of Alzheimer's disease risk in rate of memory decline. *Journal of Alzheimer's Disease, 62,* 745–756.

DeLisi, R. (2015). Piaget's sympathetic but unromantic account of children's play. In J.E. Johnson & others (Eds.), *Handbook of the study of play.* Blue Ridge Summit, PA: Rowman & Littlefield.

Delker, B.C., Bernstein, R.E., & Laurent, H.K. (2018). Out of harm's way: Secure versus insecure-disorganized attachment predicts less adolescent risk taking related to childhood poverty. *Development and Psychopathology, 30,* 283–296.

DeLongis, A., & Zwicker, A. (2017). Marital satisfaction and divorce in couples in stepfamilies. *Current Opinion in Psychology, 13,* 158–161.

Demanchick, S.P. (2015). The interpretation of play: Psychoanalysis and beyond. In J.E. Johnson & others (Eds.), *Handbook of the study of play.* Blue Ridge Summit, PA: Rowman & Littlefield.

Demby, S.L. (2016). Parenting coordination: Applying clinical thinking to the management of post-divorce conflict. *Journal of Clinical Psychology, 72,* 458–468.

Dempster, F.N. (1981). Memory span: Sources of individual and developmental differences. *Psychological Bulletin, 80,* 63–100.

Den Heijer, A.E., & others (2017). Sweat it out? The effects of physical exercise on cognition and behavior in children and adults with ADHD: A systematic literature review. *Journal of Neural Transmission, 124*(Suppl. 1), S3–S26.

Denard, P.J., & others (2010). Back pain, neurogenic symptoms, and physical function in relation to spondylolisthesis among elderly men. *Spine Journal, 10,* 865–887.

Denes, G. (2016). *Neural plasticity across the lifespan.* New York: Psychology Press.

Denford, S., & others (2017). A comprehensive review of reviews of school-based intervention to improve sexual health. *Health Psychology Review, 11,* 33–52.

Deng, Y., & others (2018). Timing of spermarche and menarche among urban students in Guangzhou, China: Trends from 2005 to 2012 and association with obesity. *Scientific Reports, 8*(1), 263.

Denham, S.A., Bassett, H.H., & Wyatt, T. (2015). The socialization of emotional competence. In J.E. Grusec & P.D. Hastings (Eds.), *Handbook of socialization* (2nd ed.). New York: Guilford.

Denham, S.A., & others (2012). Preschoolers' emotion knowledge: Self-regulatory foundations and predictors of school success. *Cognition and Emotion, 26,* 667–679.

Dennis, C.L. (2017). Psychological treatment is one of the several important components to the effective management of postpartum depression. *Evidence Based Nursing, 20*(1), 9.

Deoni, S.C., & others (2016). White matter maturation profiles through early childhood predict general cognitive ability. *Brain Structure and Function, 22,* 1189–1203.

DePaulo, B. (2006). *Singled out.* New York: St. Martin's Press.

DePaulo, B. (2011). Living single: Lightening up those dark, dopey myths. In W.R. Cupach & B.H. Spitzberg (Eds.), *The dark side of close relationships.* New York: Routledge.

Derlan, C.L., & others (2018). Cultural socialization attitudes and behaviors: Examining mothers' centrality, discrimination experiences, and children's effortful control as moderators. *Cultural Diversity and Ethnic Minority Psychology, 24,* 162–172.

Derry, H.M., & others (2015). Yoga and self-induced cognitive problems in breast cancer survivors: A randomized controlled trial. *Psycho-Oncology, 24,* 958–966.

Desilver, D. (2017). *U.S. students' academic achievement still lags that of their peers in many other countries.* Washington, DC: Pew Research Center.

DeSpelder, L.A., & Strickland, A.L. (2005). *The last dance: Encountering death and dying* (7th ed.). New York: McGraw-Hill.

Despres, O., & others (2017). Gamma oscillatory activity is impaired in episodic memory encoding with age. *Neurobiology of Aging, 52,* 53–65.

Dette-Hagenmeyer, D.E., Erzinger, A.G., & Reichle, B. (Eds.) (2016). *Fathers in families.* New York: Psychology Press.

Dettori, E., & Rao Gupta, G. (2018). Gender and the SDGs: Collective impact for change. In J.E. Lansford & P. Banati (Eds.), *Handbook of adolescent development research and its impact on global policy.* New York: Oxford University Press.

Deutsch, A.R., Wood, P.K., & Slutske, W.S. (2018). Developmental etiologies of alcohol use and their relations to parent and peer influences over adolescence and young adulthood: A genetically informed approach. *Alcoholism: Clinical and Experimental Research, 41,* 2151–2162.

Devaney, S.A., Palomaki, G.E., Scott, J.A., & Bianchi, D.W. (2011). Noninvasive fetal sex determination using cell-free fetal DNA: A systematic review and meta-analysis. *Journal of the American Medical Association, 306,* 627–636.

Devine, R.T., & Hughes, C. (2018a, in press). Family correlates of false belief understanding in early childhood: A meta-analysis. *Child Development.*

Devine, R.T., & Hughes, C. (2018b, in press). Let's talk: Parents' mental talk (not mind-mindedness or mind-reading capacity) predicts children's false belief understanding. *Child Development.*

Devinish, B., Hooley, M., & Mellor, D. (2017). The pathways between socioeconomic status and adolescent outcomes: A systematic review. *American Journal of Community Psychology, 59,* 219–238.

Devore, E.E., Grodstein, F., & Schemhammer, E.S. (2016). Sleep duration in relation to cognitive function among older adults: A systematic review of observational studies. *Neuroepidemiology, 46,* 57–78.

DeZolt, D.M., & Hull, S.H. (2001). Classroom and school climate. In J. Worell (Ed.), *Encyclopedia of women and gender.* San Diego: Academic Press.

Di Domenico, F., & others (2018). mTOR in Down syndrome: Role in AB and tau neuropathology and transition to Alzheimer disease-like dementia. *Free Radical Biology and Medicine, 114,* 94–101.

Di Florio, A., & others (2014). Mood disorders and parity—a clue to the etiology of the postpartum trigger. *Journal of Affective Disorders, 152,* 334–349.

Di Giuseppe, D., Bottai, M., Askling, J., & Wolk, A. (2015). Physical activity and risk of rheumatoid arthritis in women: A population-based prospective study. *Arthritis Research and Therapy, 17,* 40

Diamond, A. (1985). Development of the ability to use recall to guide action, as indicated by infants' performance on A-not-B. *Child Development, 56,* 866–883.

Diamond, A. (2013). Executive functions. *Annual Review of Psychology* (Vol. 64). Palo Alto, CA: Annual Reviews.

Diamond, A., & Lee, K. (2011). Interventions shown to aid executive function development in children 4 to 12 years old. *Science, 333,* 959–964.

Diamond, L.M. (2017). Three critical questions for future research on lesbian families. *Journal of Lesbian Studies, 21,* 106–119.

Diamond, L.M., & Alley, J. (2018). The dynamic expression of same-sex sexuality from childhood to young adulthood. In S. Lamb & D. Gilbert (Eds.), *Cambridge handbook of sexuality: Childhood and adolescence.* New York: Cambridge University Press.

Dias, C.C., & others (2018, in press). Reference values and changes in infant sleep-wake behavior during the first 12 months of life: A systematic review. *Journal of Sleep Research.*

Diaz-Rico, L.T. (2018). *Crosscultural, language, and academic development handbook: A complete K-12 reference guide* (6th ed.). Upper Saddle River, NJ: Pearson.

DiBennardo, R., & Gates, G.J. (2014). Research note: U.S. Census same-sex couple data: Adjustments to reduce measurement error and empirical implications. *Population Research and Policy Review, 33,* 603–614.

Dickinson, W.J., & others (2011). Change in stress and social support as predictors of cognitive decline in older adults with and without depression. *International Journal of Geriatric Psychiatry, 26,* 1267–1274.

Diedrich, J.T., Klein, D.A., & Peipert, J.F. (2017). Long-acting reversible contraception in adolescents: A systematic review and meta-analysis. *American Journal of Obstetrics and Gynecology, 364,* e1–e12.

Diego, M.A., Field, T., & Hernandez-Reif, M. (2008). Temperature increases in preterm infants during massage therapy. *Infant Behavior and Development, 31,* 149–152.

Diego, M.A., Field, T., & Hernandez-Reif, M. (2014). Preterm infant weight gain is increased by massage therapy and exercise via different underlying mechanisms. *Early Human Development, 90,* 137–140.

Diener, E. (2018). *Subjective well-being.* Retrieved January 6, 2018, from http://internal.psychology.illinois.edu/~ediener/SWLS.html

Dimaghani, M. (2018). Importance of religion or spirituality and mental health in Canada. *Journal of Religion and Health, 57,* 120–135.

Dimitropoulos, G., & others (2018). Open trial of family-based treatment of anorexia nervosa for transition age of youth. *Journal of the Canadian Academy of Child and Adolescent Psychiatry, 27,* 50–61.

Dimmitt, C., & McCormick, C.B. (2012). Metacognition in education. In K.R. Harris, S. Graham, & T. Urdan (Eds.), *Handbook of educational psychology.* Washington, DC: American Psychological Association.

Ding, Y., & others (2018). Evaluation of basal sex hormone levels for activation of the hypothalamic-pituitary-gonadal axis. *Journal of Pediatric Endocrinology and Metabolism, 31,* 323–329.

Dion, K.L., & Dion, K.K. (1993). Individualistic and collectivistic perspectives on gender and the cultural context of love and intimacy. *Journal of Social Issues, 49,* 53–69.

Dirks, M.A., Dunfield, K.A., & Recchia, H.E. (2018). Prosocial behavior with peers: Intentions, outcomes, and interpersonal adjustment. In W.M. Bukowski & others (Eds.), *Handbook of peer interactions, relationships, and groups* (2nd ed.). New York: Guilford.

Dishion, T.J., & Piehler, T.F. (2009). Deviant by design: Peer contagion in development, interventions, and schools. In K.H. Rubin, W.M. Bukowski, & B. Laursen (Eds.), *Handbook of peer interactions, relationships, and groups.* New York: Guilford.

Dittus, P.J., & others (2015). Parental monitoring and its associations with adolescent sexual risk behavior: A meta-analysis. *Pediatrics, 136,* e1587–e1599.

Diwadkar, V.A., & others (2012). Differences in cortico-striatal-cerebellar activation during working memory in syndromal and nonsyndromal children with prenatal exposure to alcohol. *Human Brain Mapping, 34,* 1931–1945.

Djelantik, A.A., Smid, G.E., Kleber, R.J., & Boelen, P.A. (2017). Symptoms of prolonged grief, post-traumatic stress, and depression after loss in a Dutch community sample: A latent class analysis. *Psychiatry Research, 247,* 276–281.

Docking, R.E., & Stock, J. (Eds.) (2018). *International handbook of positive aging.* New York: Elsevier.

Dodge, K.A. (1983). Behavioral antecedents of peer social status. *Child Development, 54,* 1386–1399.

Dodge, K.A. (2011). Social information processing models of aggressive behavior. In M. Mikulincer & P.R. Shaver (Eds.), *Understanding and reducing aggression, violence, and their consequences.* Washington, DC: American Psychological Association.

Dodson, L.J., & Davies, A.P.C. (2014). Different challenges, different well-being: A comparison of psychological well-being across stepmothers and biological mothers and across four categories of stepmothers. *Journal of Divorce & Remarriage, 55,* 49–63.

Doenyas, C., Yavuz, H.M., & Selcuk, B. (2018). Not just the sum of its parts: How tasks of theory of mind scale relate to executive function over time. *Journal of Experimental Child Psychology, 166,* 485–501.

Doering, J.J., Sims, D.A., & Miller, D.D. (2017). How postpartum women with depressive symptoms manage sleep disruption and fatigue. *Research in Nursing & Health, 40,* 132–142.

Doering, J.J., & others (2017). Sleep quality and quantity in low-income post-partum women. *MCN American Journal of Maternal and Child Nursing, 42,* 166–172.

Dolbin-MacNab, M.L., & Yancura, L.A. (2018). International perspectives on grandparents raising grandchildren. *International Journal of Aging and Human Development, 86,* 3–33.

Dombrowsky, T.A. (2018, in press). Relationship between engagement and level of functional status in older adults. *SAGE Open Medicine.*

Domenech-Abella, J., & others (2018). The impact of socioeconomic status on the association between biomedical well-being and all-cause mortality in older Spanish adults. *Social Psychiatry and Psychiatric Epidemiology, 53,* 259–268.

Donatelle, R.J. (2019). *Health* (13th ed.). Upper Saddle River, NJ: Pearson.

Donatelle, R.J., & Ketcham, P. (2018). *Access to health* (15th ed.). Upper Saddle River, NJ: Pearson.

Dong, X.S., & others (2017). Baby boomers in the United States: Factors associated with working longer and delaying retirement. *American Journal of Industrial Medicine, 60,* 315–328.

Donnellan, M.B., Larsen-Rife, D., & Conger, R.D. (2005). Personality, family history, and competence in early adult romantic relationships. *Journal of Personality and Social Psychology, 88,* 562–576.

Donovan, M.K. (2017). The looming threat to sex education: A resurgence of federal funding for abstinence-only programs? *Guttmacher Policy Review, 20,* 44–47.

Dooley, J., Bass, N., & McCabe, R. (2018, in press). How do doctors deliver a diagnosis of dementia in memory clinics? *British Journal of Psychiatry.*

Doom, J.R., & others (2017). Pathways between childhood/adolescent adversity, adolescent socioeconomic status, and long-term cardiovascular disease risk in young adulthood. *Social Science & Medicine, 188,* 166–175.

Dorfeshan, P., & others (2018). The effects of in vitro maturation technique on the expression of genes involved in embryonic genome activation of human embryos. *Cell Journal, 20,* 90–97.

Dosso, J.A., Herrera, S.V., & Boudreau, J.P. (2017). A study of reaching actions in walking infants. *Infant Behavior and Development, 47,* 112–120.

Dotti Sani, G.M., & Quaranta, M. (2015). The best is yet to come? Attitudes toward gender roles among adolescents in 36 countries. *Sex Roles, 65,* 80–99.

Douglass, S., & Umana-Taylor, A.J. (2017). Examining discrimination, ethnic-racial identity status, and youth public regard among Black, Latino, and White adolescents. *Journal of Research on Adolescence, 27,* 155–172.

Dow, B.J., & Wood, J. (Eds.) (2006). *The SAGE handbook of gender and communication.* Thousand Oaks, CA: Sage.

Dowda, M., & others (2017). Physical activity and changes in adiposity in the transition from elementary to middle school. *Child Obesity, 13*, 53–62.

Dowling, N.A., & others (2017). Early risk and protective factors for problem gambling: A systematic review and meta-analysis of longitudinal studies. *Clinical Psychology Review, 51*, 109–124.

Doyle, C., & Cicchetti, D. (2018). Child maltreatment. In M.H. Bornstein (Ed.), *SAGE encyclopedia of lifespan human development.* Thousand Oaks, CA; Sage.

Dozier, M., & Bernard, K. (2017). Attachment and biobehavioral catchup: Addressing the needs of infants and toddlers exposed to inadequate or problematic caregiving. *Current Opinion in Psychology, 15*, 111–117.

Dozier, M., & Bernard, K. (2018). Attachment and biobehavioral catch-up. In C.H. Zeanah (Ed.), *Handbook of infant mental health* (4th ed.). New York: Guilford.

Dozier, M., Bernard, K., & Roben, C.K.P. (2017). Attachment and biobehavioral catch-up. In H. Steele & M. Steele (Eds.), *Handbook of attachment-based interventions.* New York: Guilford.

Dozier, M., & others (2018). Attachment and biobehavioral catch-up: An evidence-based intervention for vulnerable infants and their families. *Psychotherapy Research, 28*, 18–29.

Dragano, N., & others (2017). Effort-reward imbalance at work and incident coronary heart disease: A multicohort study of 90,164 individuals. *Epidemiology, 28*, 619–626.

Dragoset, L., & others (2017). School improvement grants: Implementation and effectiveness. NCEE 2017-4013. *ERIC,* ED572215.

Drew, D.A., & others (2017). Cognitive decline and its risk factors in prevalent hemodialysis patients. *American Journal of Kidney Diseases, 69*, 780–787.

Dryfoos, J.G. (1990). *Adolescents at risk: Prevalence or prevention.* New York: Oxford University Press.

Dryfoos, J.G., & Barkin, C. (2006). *Growing up in America today.* New York: Oxford University Press.

Du, D., Derks, D., & Bakker, A.B. (2018, in press). Daily spillover from family to work: A test of the work-home resources model. *Journal of Occupational Health Psychology.*

Dubal, D.B., & Rogine, C. (2017). Apolipoprotein E4 and risk factors for Alzheimer disease—let's talk about sex. *JAMA Neurology, 74*, 1167–1168.

Dube, E., Desparois G., & Lafond, J. (2018) Placental lipid transport. *Methods in Molecular Biology, 1710*, 305–316.

Dube, S., & others (2017). Psychological well-being as a predictor of casual sex relationships and experiences among adolescents: A short-term perspective study. *Archives of Sexual Behavior, 46*, 1807–1818.

Dubois, J., & others (2016). Exploring the early organization and maturation of linguistic pathways in the human infant brain. *Cerebral Cortex, 26*, 2283–2298.

Dubol, M., & others (2018). Dopamine transporter and reward anticipation in a dimensional perspective: A multimodal brain imaging study. *Neuropsychopharmacology, 43*, 820–827.

Dubow, E.F., & others (2017). Conducting longitudinal, process-oriented research with conflict-affected youth: Solving the inevitable challenges. *Development and Psychopathology, 29*, 85–92.

Due, T.D., Sandholdt, H., & Waldorff, F.B. (2018, in press). Social relations and loneliness among older patients consulting a general practitioner. *Danish Medical Journal.*

Duell, N., & others (2018). Age patterns in risk taking across the world. *Journal of Youth and Adolescence, 47*, 1052–1072.

Duff, F.J., Reen, G., Plunkett, K., & Nation, K. (2015). Do infant vocabulary skills predict school-age language and literacy outcomes? *Journal of Child Psychology and Psychiatry, 56*, 848–856.

Duggal, N.A., & others (2018, in press). Major features of immunosenescence, including thymic output, are ameliorated by high levels of physical activity in adulthood. *Aging Cell.*

Duke, S.A., Balzer, B.W., & Steinbeck, K.S. (2014). Testosterone and its effects on human male adolescent mood and behavior: A systematic review. *Journal of Adolescent Health, 55*, 315–322.

Dumitrache, C.G., Rubio, L., & Rubio-Herrera, R. (2017). Perceived health status and life satisfaction in old age, and the moderating role of social support. *Aging and Mental Health, 21*, 751–757.

Dumuid, D., & others (2017). Health-related quality of life and lifestyle behavior clusters in school-aged children from 12 countries. *Journal of Pediatrics, 183*, 178–183.

Duncan, G.J., Magnuson, K., & Votruba-Drzal, E. (2017). Moving beyond correlations in assessing the consequences of poverty. *Annual Review of Psychology* (Vol. 68). Palo Alto, CA: Annual Reviews.

Duncan, R., McClelland, M.M., & Acock, A.C. (2017). Relations between executive function, behavioral regulation, and achievement: Moderation by family income. *Journal of Applied Developmental Psychology, 49*, 21–30.

Dunlop, W.L., Bannon, B.L., & McAdams, D.P. (2017). Studying the motivated agent through time: Personal goal development during the adult life span. *Journal of Personality, 85*, 207–219.

Dunn, J. (1984). Sibling studies and the developmental impact of critical incidents. In P.B. Baltes & O.G. Brim (Eds.), *Life-span development and behavior* (Vol. 6). Orlando, FL: Academic Press.

Dunn, J. (2007). Siblings and socialization. In J.E. Grusec & P.D. Hastings (eds.), *Handbook of socialization.* New York: Guilford.

Dunn, J. (2015). Siblings. In J.E. Grusec & P.D. Hastings (Eds.), *Handbook of socialization* (2nd ed.). New York: Guilford.

Dunn, J., & Kendrick, C. (1982). *Siblings.* Cambridge, MA: Harvard University Press.

Dunsmore, J.C., Booker, J.A., & Ollendick, T.H. (2013). Parental emotion coaching and child emotion regulation as protective factors for children with oppositional defiant disorder. *Social Development, 22*(3), 444–466.

Dupere, V., & others (2015). Stressors and turning points in high school and dropout: A stress process, life course framework. *Review of Educational Research, 85*, 591–629.

Dupre, M.E., George, L.K., Liu, G., & Peterson, E.D. (2015). Association between divorce and risks for acute myocardial infarction. *Circulation: Cardiovascular Quality and Outcomes, 8*, 244–251.

Durston, S., & others (2006). A shift from diffuse to focal cortical activity with development. *Developmental Science, 9*, 1–8.

Dutton, H., & others (2018). Obesity in pregnancy: Optimizing outcomes for mom and baby. *Medical Clinics of North America, 102*, 87–106.

Dweck, C.S. (2006). *Mindset.* New York: Random House.

Dweck, C.S. (2015, September 23). Carol Dweck revisits the "growth mindset." *Education Week, 35*(5), 24–26.

Dweck, C.S. (2016, March 11). *Growth mindset, revisited.* Invited address at Leaders to Learn From. Washington, DC: Education Week.

Dweck, C.S., & Master, A. (2009). Self-theories and motivation: Students' beliefs about intelligence. In K.R. Wentzel & A. Wigfield (Eds.), *Handbook of motivation at school.* New York: Routledge.

Dweck, C.S., & Molden, D.C. (2017). Mindsets: Their impact on competence motivation and acquisition. In A.J. Elliott, C.S. Dweck, & D.S. Yeager (Eds.), *Handbook of competence and motivation* (2nd ed.). New York: Guilford.

Dworkin, S.L., & Santelli, J. (2007). Do abstinence-plus interventions reduce sexual risk behavior among youth? *PLoS Medicine, 4*, 1437–1439.

Dwyer, J.W., & Coward, R.T. (1991). A multivariate comparison of the involvement of adult sons versus daughters in the care of impaired parents. *Journals of Gerontology B: Psychological Sciences and Social Sciences, 46*, S259–S269.

E

Eagan, K., & others (2017). *The American college freshman: National norms fall 2016.* Los Angeles: Higher Education Research Institute, UCLA.

Eagly, A.H. (2001). Social role theory of sex differences and similarities. In J. Worrell (Ed.), *Encyclopedia of women and gender.* San Diego: Academic Press.

Eagly, A.H. (2010). Gender roles. In J. Levine & M. Hogg (Eds.), *Encyclopedia of group process and intergroup relations.* Thousand Oaks, CA: Sage.

Eagly, A.H. (2012). Science, feminism, and the investigation of gender. In R.W. Proctor & E.J. Capaldi (Eds.), *Psychology of science: Implicit and explicit reasoning.* New York: Oxford University Press.

Eagly, A.H. (2016). Has the psychology of women stopped playing handmaiden to social values? *Feminism & Psychology, 26*, 282–291.

Eagly, A.H. (2017). Making a difference: Feminist scholarship. In C.B. Gravis & J.W. White (Eds.), *Handbook of the psychology of women.* Washington, DC: APA Books.

Eagly, A.H., & Steffen, V.J. (1986). Gender and aggressive behavior: A meta-analytic review of the social psychological literature. *Psychological Bulletin, 100*, 309–330.

Eagly, A.H., & Wood, W. (2017). Gender identity: Nature and nurture working together. *Evolutionary Studies in Imaginative Culture, 1*, 59–62.

East, P. (2009). Adolescent relationships with siblings. In R.M. Lerner & L. Steinberg (Eds.), *Handbook of adolescent psychology* (3rd ed.). New York: Wiley.

Eastman, M., & others (2018). Profiles of internalizing and externalizing symptoms associated with bullying victimization. *Journal of Adolescence, 65*, 101–110.

Eccles, J.S. (2007). Families, schools, and developing achievement-related motivations and engagement. In J.E. Grusec & P.D. Hastings (Eds.), *Handbook of socialization.* New York: Guilford.

Eccles, J.S., & Roeser, R.W. (2015). School and community influences on human development. In M.H. Bornstein & M.E. Lamb (Eds.), *Developmental science* (7th ed.). New York: Psychology Press.

Echevarria, J.J., Vogt, M.J., & Short, D.J. (2017). *Making content comprehensible for English learners: The SIOP model* (5th ed.). Upper Saddle River, NJ: Pearson.

Eckerman, C., & Whitehead, H. (1999). How toddler peers generate coordinated action: A cross cultural exploration. *Early Education & Development, 10*, 241–266.

Eckler, P., Kalyango, Y., & Paasch, E. (2017). Facebook use and negative body image among U.S. college women. *Women and Health, 57*, 249–267.

Edwards, K.S., & Shin, M. (2017). Media multitasking and implicit learning. *Attention, Perception, and Psychophysics, 79*, 1535–1549.

Edwards, M.L., & Jackson, A.D. (2017). The historical development of obstetric anesthesia and its contributions to perinatology. *American Journal of Perinatology, 34*, 211–216.

Eggebrecht, A.T., & others (2017). Joint attention and brain functional connectivity in infants and toddlers. *Cerebral Cortex, 27*, 1709–1720.

Eggenberger, P., & others (2015). Does multicomponent physical exercise with simultaneous cognitive training boost cognitive performance in older adults? A 6-month randomized controlled trial with a 1-year follow-up. *Clinical Interventions in Aging, 10*, 1335–1349.

Ehninger, D., Neff, F., & Xie, K. (2014). Longevity, aging, and rapamycin. *Cellular and Molecular Life Sciences, 71*, 4325–4346.

Eichorn, D.H., Clausen, J.A., Haan, N., Honzik, M.P., & Mussen, P.H. (Eds.). (1981). *Present and past in middle life.* New York: Academic Press.

Eiferman, R.R. (1971). Social play in childhood. In R. Herron & B. Sutton-Smith (Eds.), *Child's play.* New York: Wiley.

Ein-Dor, T., & others (2018). Epigenetic modification of the oxytocin and glucocorticoid receptor genes is linked to attachment avoidance in young adults. *Attachment and Human Development, 20,* 439–454.

Einziger, T., & others (2018). Predicting ADHD symptoms in adolescence from early childhood temperament traits. *Journal of Abnormal Child Psychology, 46,* 265–276.

Eisenberg, N., Duckworth, A., Spinrad, L., & Valiente, C. (2014). Conscientiousness and healthy aging. *Developmental Psychology, 50,* 1331–1349.

Eisenberg, N., Fabes, R.A., & Spinrad, T.L. (2006). Prosocial development. In W. Damon & R. Lerner (Eds.), *Handbook of child psychology* (6th ed.). New York: Wiley.

Eisenberg, N., & Spinrad, T.L. (2016). Multidimensionality of prosocial behavior: Rethinking the conceptualization and development of prosocial behavior. In L. Padilla-Walker & G. Carlo (Eds.), *Prosocial behavior.* New York: Oxford University Press.

Eisenberg, N., Spinrad, T.L., & Valiente, C. (2016). Emotion-related self-regulation and children's social, psychological, and academic functioning. In L. Balter & C.S. Tamis-LeMonda (Eds.), *Child psychology* (3rd ed.). New York: Routledge.

Eisharkawy, H., Sonny, A., & Chin, K.J. (2017). Localization of epidural space: A review of available technologies. *Journal of Anesthesiology and Clinical Pharmacology, 33,* 16–27.

Eisman, A.B., Stoddard, S.A., Bauermeister, J.A., Caldwell, C.H., & Zimmerman, M.A. (2018). Organized activity participation and relational aggression: The role of positive youth development. *Violence and Victims, 33,* 91–108.

Ekas, N.A., Braungart-Rieker, & Messinger, D.S. (2018). The development of infant emotion regulation: Time is of the essence. In P.M. Cole & T. Hollenstein (Eds.), *Emotion regulation.* New York: Routledge.

Eklund, K., Tanner, N., Stoll, K., & Anway, L. (2015). Identifying emotional and behavioral risk among gifted and nongifted children: A multi-gate, multi-informant approach. *School Psychology Quarterly, 30,* 197–211.

Eliasieh, K., Liets, L.C., & Chalupa, L.M. (2007). Cellular reorganization in the human retina during normal aging. *Investigative Ophthalmology and Visual Science, 48,* 2824–2830.

Eliassen, C.F., Reinvang, I., Selnes, P., Fladby, T., & Hessen, E. (2017). Convergent results from neuropsychology and from neuroimaging in patients with mild cognitive impairment. *Dementia and Geriatric Cognitive Disorders, 43,* 144–154.

Elkind, D. (1976). *Child development and education: A Piagetian perspective.* New York: Oxford University Press.

Ellemers, N. (2018). Gender stereotypes. *Annual Review of Psychology* (Vol. 69). Palo Alto, CA: Annual Reviews.

Elliot, A.J., & others (2018, in press). Lifetime trauma, perceived control, and all-cause mortality: Results from the Midlife in the United States Study. *Health Psychology.*

Elliott, E.M., & others (2011). Working memory in the oldest-old: Evidence from output serial position curves. *Memory and Cognition, 10,* 20–27.

Ellis, W., & Zarbatany, L. (2018, in press). Understanding processes of peer clique influence in late childhood. *Child Development Perspectives.*

eMarketeer.com (2016). *Trends in social media use.* Retrieved November 15, 2016, from eMarketing.com

Ember, M.R., Ember, C.R., & Peregrine, P.N. (2015). *Cultural anthropology* (14th ed.). Upper Saddle River, NJ: Pearson.

Emberson, L.L., & other (2017b). Deficits in top-down sensory prediction in infants at risk due to premature birth. *Current Biology, 27,* 431–436.

Emberson, L.L., & others (2017a). Using fNIRS to examine occipital and temporal responses to stimulus repetition in young infants: Evidence of selective frontal cortex involvement. *Developmental Cognitive Neuroscience, 23,* 26–38.

Emde, R.N., Gaensbauer, T.G., & Harmon, R.J. (1976). Emotional expression in infancy: A biobehavioral study. *Psychological Issues: Monograph Series, 10*(37).

Engels, A.C., & others (2016). Sonographic detection of central nervous system in the first trimester of pregnancy. *Prenatal Diagnosis, 36,* 266–273.

English, T., & Carstensen, L.L. (2014). Selective narrowing of social networks across adulthood is associated with improved emotional experience in life. *International Journal of Behavioral Development, 38,* 195–202.

Eno Persson, J., & others (2018). Prevention of childhood obesity in child health services: Follow-up of the PRIMROSE trial. *Child Obesity, 99,* 99–105.

Ensor, R., Spencer, D., & Hughes, C. (2011). You feel sad? Emotional understanding mediates effects of verbal ability and mother-child mutuality on prosocial behaviors: Findings from 2 to 4 years. *Social Development, 20,* 93–110.

Eo, Y.S., & Kim, J.S. (2018, in press). Parenting stress and maternal-child interactions among preschool mothers from the Philippines, Korea, and Vietnam: A cross-sectional, comparative study. *Journal of Transcultural Nursing.*

Erez, M. (2018). From local to cross-cultural to global work motivation and innovation. In M.J. Gelfand & others (Eds.), *Handbook of advances in culture and psychology* (Vol. 7). New York: Oxford University Press.

Erickson, K.I., Hillman, C.H., & Kramer, A.F. (2015). Physical activity, brain, and cognition. *Current Opinion in the Behavioral Sciences, 4,* 27–32.

Erickson, K.I., & Oberlin, L.E. (2017). Effects of exercise on cognition, brain structure, and brain function in older adults. In R. Cabeza, L. Nyberg, & D.C. Park (Eds.), *Cognitive neuroscience of aging* (2nd ed.). New York: Oxford University Press.

Erickson, K.I., & others (2011). Exercise training increases the size of the hippocampus and improves memory. *Proceedings of the National Academy of Sciences U.S.A., 108,* 3017–3022.

Ericsson, K.A. (2017). Expertise and individual differences: The search for the structure and acquisition of experts' superior performance. *Wiley Interdisciplinary Reviews. Cognitive Science, 8,* 1–2.

Ericsson, K.A., Krampe, R., & Tesch-Romer, C. (1993). The role of deliberate practice in the acquisition of expert performance. *Psychological Review, 100,* 363–406.

Ericsson, K.A., & others (Eds.) (2016). *Cambridge handbook of expertise and expert performance.* New York: Cambridge University Press.

Ericsson, K.A., & others (Eds.) (2018). *Cambridge handbook of expertise and expert performance* (2nd ed.). New York: Cambridge University Press.

Erikson, E.H. (1950). *Childhood and society.* New York: W.W. Norton.

Erikson, E.H. (1968). *Identity: Youth and crisis.* New York. W.W. Norton.

Erskine, H.E., & others (2016). Long-term outcomes of attention deficit/hyperactivity disorder and conduct disorder: A systematic review and meta-analysis. *Journal of the Academy of Child and Adolescent Psychiatry, 55,* 641–650.

Eskola, K., & others (2017). Maintaining family life balance while facing a child's imminent death—a mixed methods study. *Journal of Advanced Nursing, 73,* 2462–2472.

Espinosa, A., & others (2017). Ethnic identity and perceived stress among ethnically diverse immigrants. *Journal of Immigrant and Minority Health, 20,* 155–160.

Esposito, A.G., & others (2018). Bilingual education. In M.H. Bornstein (Ed.), *SAGE encyclopedia of lifespan human development.* Thousand Oaks, CA: Sage.

Esposito, G., & others (2017a). Response to infant cry in clinically depressed and non-depressed mothers. *PLoS One, 12*(1), e0169066.

Esposito, G., & others (2017b). The development of attachment: Integrating genes, brain, behavior, and environment. *Behavioral Brain Research, 325* (Pt. B), 87–89.

Estill, A., & others (2018). The effects of subjective age and aging attitudes on mid- to late-life sexuality. *Journal of Sex Research, 55,* 146–151.

Estrada, E., & others (2017). Separating power and speed components of standardized intelligence measures. *Intelligence, 61,* 159–168.

Estrada, Y., & others (2017). Parent-centered prevention of risky behaviors among Hispanic youths in Florida. *American Journal of Public Health, 107,* 607–613.

Etaugh, C., & Bridges, J.S. (2010). *Women's lives* (2nd ed.). Boston: Allyn & Bacon.

Ethier, K.A., Harper, C.R., Hoo, E., & Ditts, P.J. (2016). The longitudinal impact of perceptions of parental monitoring on adolescent initiation of sexual activity. *Journal of Adolescent Health, 59,* 570–576.

Eun, J.D., & others (2018, in press). Parenting style and mental disorders in a nationally representative sample of U.S. adolescents. *Social Psychiatry and Psychiatric Epidemiology.*

Evans, G.W., & English, G.W. (2002). The environment of poverty. *Child Development, 73,* 1238–1248.

Evans, S.Z., Simons, L.G., & Simons, R.L. (2016). Factors that influence trajectories of delinquency throughout adolescence. *Journal of Youth and Adolescence, 45,* 156–171.

Evans, W.J. (2010). Skeletal muscle loss: Cachexia, sarcopenia, and inactivity. *American Journal of Clinical Nutrition, 91,* S1123–S1127.

Evans-Lacko, S., & others (2017). Childhood bullying victimization is associated with the use of mental health services over five decades: A longitudinal nationally representative study. *Psychological Medicine, 47,* 127–135.

Ezaki, T., & others (2018, in press). Age-related changes in the ease of dynamical transitions in human brain activity. *Human Brain Mapping.*

Ezkurdia, L., & others (2014). The shrinking human protein coding complement: Are there fewer than 20,000 genes? arXiv:1312.7111[q-bio.GN]

F

Fabricius, W.V., Braver, S.L., Diaz, P., & Schenck, C. (2010). Custody and parenting time: Links to family relationships and well-being after divorce. In M.E. Lamb (Ed.), *The role of the father in child development* (5th ed.). New York: Wiley.

Faghihi, F., & Moustafa, A.A. (2017). Combined computational systems biology and computational neuroscience approaches help develop future "cognitive developmental robotics." *Frontiers in Neurobiology, 11,* 63.

Faghiri, A., & others (2018). Changing brain connectivity dynamics: From early childhood to adulthood. *Human Brain Mapping, 39,* 1108–1117.

Fagot, B.I., Rodgers, C.S., & Leinbach, M.D. (2000). Theories of gender socialization. In T. Eckes & H.M. Trautner (Eds.), *The developmental social psychology of gender.* Mahwah, NJ: Erlbaum.

Fagundes, C.P., Gillie, B.L., Derry, H.M., Bennett, J.M., & Kiecolt-Glaser, J.K. (2016). Resilience and immune function in older adults. In G.C. Smith and B. Hayslip (Eds.), *Annual Review of Gerontology and Geriatrics.* New York: Springer.

Fajkowska, M. (2018). Personality traits: Hierarchically organized systems. *Journal of Personality, 86,* 36–54.

Falandry, C. (2019). The connection between cellular senescence and age-related diseases. In R. Fernandez-Ballesteros & others (Eds.), *Cambridge handbook of successful aging.* New York: Cambridge University Press.

Falbo, T., & Poston, D.L. (1993). The academic, personality, and physical outcomes of only children in China. *Child Development, 64,* 18–35.

Falck, R.S., & others (2017). How much will older adults exercise? A feasibility study of aerobic training combined with resistance training. *Pilot and Feasibility Studies, 3,* 2.

Falck-Ytter, T., & others (2018, in press). Reducing orienting to audiovisual synchrony in infancy predicts autism diagnosis at 3 years of age. *Journal of Child Psychology and Psychiatry.*

Falconier, M.K., & others (2015). Stress from daily hassles in couples: Its effects on intradyadic relationship satisfaction and physical and psychological well-being. *Journal of Marital and Family Therapy, 41,* 221–235.

Fali, T., Vallet, H., & Sauce, D. (2018, in press). Impact of stress on aged immune system compartments: Overview from fundamental to clinical data. *Experimental Gerontology.*

Falsetti, L., & others (2018). Interactions between atrial fibrillation, cardiovascular risk factors, and ApoE genotype in promoting cognitive decline in patients with Alzheimer's disease: A prospective cohort study. *Journal of Alzheimer's Disease, 62,* 713–725.

Fang, Y., & others (2018, in press). Information and communicative technology use enhances psychological well-being of older adults: The roles of age, social connectedness, and frailty status. *Aging and Mental Health.*

Fanning, P.A.J., & others (2018). Delineation of spatial working memory profile using a non-verbal eye-tracking paradigm in young children with autism and Williams syndrome. *Child Neuropsychology, 24,* 469–489.

Fantz, R.L. (1963). Pattern vision in newborn infants. *Science, 140,* 286–297.

Farah, M.J. (2017). The neuroscience of socioeconomic status: Correlates, causes, and consequences. *Neuron, 96,* 56–71.

Farajinia, S., & others (2014). Aging of the suprachiasmatic clock. *Neuroscientist, 21,* 44–55.

Faria, A-M., & others (2017). The "I" in QRIS survey: Collecting data on quality improvement activities for early childhood education programs. *ERIC document:* ED573027.

Farioli-Vecchioli, S., & others (2018). The role of physical exercise and omega-3 acids in depressive illness in the elderly. *Current Neuropharmacology, 16,* 308–326.

Faris, M.A.E., & others (2017). Energy drink consumption is associated with reduced sleep quality among college students: A cross-sectional study. *Nutrition and Dietetics, 74,* 268–274.

Farr, R.H. (2017). Does parental sexual orientation matter? A longitudinal follow-up of adoptive families with a school-age child. *Developmental Psychology, 53,* 252–264.

Farr, R.H., & Goldberg, A.E. (2018, in press). Sexual orientation, gender, identity, and adaptation. *Family Court Review.*

Farr, R.H., Oakley, M.K., & Ollen, E.W. (2016). School experiences of young children and their lesbian and gay adoptive parents. *Psychology of Sexual Orientation and Gender Diversity, 3,* 442–447.

Farr, R.H., & Patterson, C.J. (2013). Coparenting among lesbian, gay, and heterosexual couples: Associations with adopted children's outcomes. *Child Development, 84,* 1226–1240.

Farr, R.H., & others (2018, in press). Children's gender-typed behavior from early to middle childhood in adoptive families with lesbian, gay, and heterosexual parents. *Sex Roles.*

Farrell, A.D., Thompson, E.L., & Mehari, K.R. (2017). Dimensions of peer influences and their relationship to adolescents' aggression, other problem behaviors, and prosocial behavior. *Journal of Youth and Adolescence, 46,* 1351–1369.

Fasig, L. (2000). Toddlers' understanding of ownership: Implications for self-concept development. *Social Development, 9,* 370–382.

Fatima, M., Srivastav, S., & Mondal, A.C. (2017). Prenatal stress and depression-associated neuronal development in neonates. *International Journal of Developmental Neuroscience, 60,* 1–7.

Fatima, Y., Doi, S.A.R., & Al Mamun, A. (2018). Sleep problems in adolescence and overweight/obesity in young adults: Is there a causal link? *Sleep Health, 4,* 154–159.

Fatusi, A.O., & Hindin, M.J. (2010). Adolescents and youths in developing countries: Health and development issues in context. *Journal of Adolescence, 33,* 499–508.

Faucher, M.A. (2018, in press). Updates from the literature, September/October 2017. *Journal of Midwifery and Women's Health.*

Faye, P.M., & others (2016). Kangaroo care for low birth weight infants at Albert-Royer National Children's Hospital Center of Dakar. *Archives of Pediatrics, 23,* 268–274.

Feeney, S., Moravcik, E., & Nolte, S. (2019). *Who am I in the lives of children?* (11th ed.). Upper Saddle River, NJ: Pearson.

Feigelman, W., & others (2018). Suicide exposures and bereavement among American adults: Evidence from the 2016 General Social Survey. *Journal of Affective Disorders, 227,* 1–6.

Feist, G.J. (2018). In search of the creative personality. In R.J. Sternberg & J.C. Kaufman (Eds.), *The nature of human creativity.* New York: Cambridge University Press.

Feldkamp, M.L., & others (2017). Etiology and clinical presentation of birth defects: Population based study. *BMJ, 357,* j2249.

Feldman, H.D. (2001, April). *Contemporary developmental theories and the concept of talent.* Paper presented at the meeting of the Society for Research in Child Development, Minneapolis.

Feldman, R., Rosenthal, Z., & Eidelman, A.I. (2014). Maternal-preterm skin-to-skin contact enhances child physiologic organization and cognitive control across the first 10 years of life. *Biological Psychiatry, 75,* 56–64.

Feldman, S.S., Turner, R., & Araujo, K. (1999). Interpersonal context as an influence on sexual timetables of youths: Gender and ethnic effects. *Journal of Research on Adolescence, 9,* 25–52.

Feldman-Winter, L., & others (2018, in press). Weight gain in the first week of life predicts overweight at 2 years: A prospective cohort study. *Maternal and Child Nutrition.*

Feltosa, C.M. (2018, in press). Determination of parameters of oxidative stress in vitro models of neurodegenerative diseases—a review. *Current Clinical Pharmacology.*

Felver, J.C., & others (2017). Contemplative intervention reduces physical interventions in residential psychiatric treatment. *Prevention Science, 18,* 164–173.

Fergus, T.A., & Bardeen, J.R. (2018, in press). The metacognitions questionnaire—30. *Assessment.*

Ferguson, C.J. (2013). Spanking, corporal punishment, and negative long-term outcomes: A meta-analytic review of longitudinal studies. *Clinical Psychology Review, 33,* 196–208.

Ferguson, D.M., Harwood, L.J., & Shannon, F.T. (1987). Breastfeeding and subsequent social adjustment in 6- to 8-year-old children. *Journal of Child Psychology and Psychiatry, 28,* 378–386.

Ferjan Ramirez, N., & others (2017). Speech discrimination in 11-month-old bilingual and monolingual infants: A magnetoencephalography study. *Developmental Science, 20,* e12427.

Fernandez, M., Mollinedo-Gajate, I., & Penagarikano, O. (2018). Neural circuits for social cognition: Implications for autism. *Neuroscience, 370,* 148–162.

Fernandez-Ballesteros, R. (2019, in press). The concept of successful aging and related terms. In R. Fernandez-Ballesteros & others (Eds.), *Cambridge handbook of successful aging.* New York: Cambridge University Press.

Fernandez-Ballesteros, R., & others (Eds.) (2019). *Cambridge handbook of successful aging.* New York: Cambridge University Press.

Ferrazzi, G., & others (2018). An efficient sequence for fetal brain imaging at 3T with enhanced T1 contrast and motion robustness. *Magnetic Resonance Medicine, 80,* 137–146.

Ferreira, D., & others (2015). Cognitive decline before the age of 50 can be detected with sensitive cognitive measures. *Psichothema, 27,* 216–222.

Ferreira, T., & others (2018). Trajectories of parental engagement in early childhood among dual-earner families: Effects on child self-control. *Developmental Psychology, 54,* 731–743.

Field, D. (1999). A cross-cultural perspective on continuity and change in social relations in old age: Introduction to a special issue. *International Journal of Aging and Human Development, 48,* 257–262.

Field, T.M. (2001). Massage therapy facilitates weight gain in preterm infants. *Current Directions in Psychological Science, 10,* 51–55.

Field, T.M. (2007). *The amazing infant.* Malden, MA: Blackwell.

Field, T.M. (2010a). Pregnancy and labor massage. *European Review of Obstetrics and Gynecology, 5,* 177–181.

Field, T.M. (2010b). Postpartum depression effects on early interactions, parenting, and safety practices: A review. *Infant Behavior and Development, 33,* 1–6.

Field, T.M. (2017). Preterm newborn pain research review. *Infant Behavior and Development, 49,* 141–150.

Field, T.M., & others (1986). Tactile/kinesthetic stimulation effects on preterm neonates. *Pediatrics, 77,* 654–658.

Field, T.M., Diego, M., & Hernandez-Reif, M. (2008). Prematurity and potential predictors. *International Journal of Neuroscience, 118,* 277–289.

Field, T.M., Diego, M., & Hernandez-Reif, M. (2011). Preterm infant massage therapy research: A review. *Infant Behavior and Development, 34,* 383–389.

Field, T.M., Hernandez-Reif, M., Diego, M., Feijo, L., Vera, Y., & Gil, K. (2004). Massage therapy by parents improves early growth and development. *Infant Behavior & Development, 27,* 435–442.

Fielder, R.L., Walsh, J.L., Carey, K.B., & Carey, M.P. (2013). Predictors of sexual hookups: A theory-based, prospective study of first-year college women. *Archives of Sexual Behavior, 42,* 1425–1441.

Fileborn, B., & others (2017). The importance of sex and the meaning of sex and sexual pleasure for men aged 60 and older who engage in heterosexual relationships: Findings from a qualitative interview study. *Archives of Sexual Behavior, 46,* 2097–2110.

Finch, C.E. (2009). The neurobiology of middle-age has arrived. *Neurobiology of Aging, 30,* 503–520.

Fincham, F.D., & May, R.W. (2017). Infidelity in romantic relationships. *Current Opinion in Psychology, 13,* 70–74.

Fine, A., & others (2016). Self-control assessments and implications for predicting adolescent offending. *Journal of Youth and Adolescence, 45,* 701–712

Fine, A., & others (2017). Is the effect of justice system attitudes on recidivism stable after youths' first arrests? *Race and legal socialization, 41,* 146–158.

Finelli, J., Zeanah, C.H., & Smyke, A.T. (2018). Attachment disorders in early childhood. In C.H. Zeanah (Ed.), *Handbook of infant mental health* (4th ed.). New York: Guilford.

Fingerhut, A.W., & Peplau, L.A. (2013). Same-sex romantic relationships. In C.J. Patterson & A.R. D'Augelli (Eds.), *Handbook of psychology and sexual orientation.* New York: Oxford University Press.

Fingerman, K.L., & Baker, B. (2006). Socioemotional aspects of aging. In J. Wilmouth & K. Ferraro (Eds.), *Perspectives in gerontology* (3rd ed.). New York: Springer.

Fingerman, K.L., Cheng, Y.P., Tighe, L., Birditt, K.S., & Zarit, S. (2011). Parent-child relationships in young adulthood. In A. Booth & others (Eds.), *Early adulthood in a family context.* New York: Springer.

Fingerman, K.L., & others (2011). Who gets what and why: Help middle-aged adults provide to parents and grown children. *Journal of Gerontology B: Psychological Sciences and Social Sciences, 66,* 87–98.

Fingerman, K.L., & others (2012). The Baby Boomers' intergenerational relationships. *Gerontologist, 52,* 199–209.

Fingerman, K.L., & others (2017). Coresident and non-coresident emerging adults' daily experiences with parents. *Emerging Adulthood, 5,* 337–350.

Fingerman, K.L., & others (2018, in press). A family affair: Family typologies of problems and midlife well-being. *Gerontologist.*

Finke, E.H., Wilkinson, K.M., & Hickerson, B.D. (2017). Social referencing gaze behavior during a videogame task:

Eye tracking evidence from children with and without ASD. *Journal of Autism Spectrum Disorders, 47,* 415-423.

Finkel, D., Andel, R., & Pedersen, N.L. (2018, in press). Gender differences in longitudinal trajectories of change in physical, social, and cognitive/sedentary leisure activities. *Journals of Gerontology B: Psychological Sciences and Social Sciences.*

Finkelstein, E.A., & others (2012). Obesity and severe obesity forecasts through 2030. *American Journal of Preventive Medicine, 42,* 563-570.

Finley, C., & others (2018). Stakeholder education for community-wide health initiatives: A focus on teen pregnancy prevention. *Health Promotion Practice, 19,* 38-50.

Firk, C., & others (2018). Down-regulation of amygdala response to infant crying: A role for distraction in maternal mood regulation. *Emotion, 18,* 412-423.

Fischhoff, B., Bruine de Bruin, W., Parker, A.M., Millstein, S.G., & Halpern-Felsher, B.L. (2010). Adolescents' perceived risk of dying. *Journal of Adolescent Health, 46,* 265-269.

Fisher, G.G., & others (2017). Cognitive functioning, aging, and work: A review and recommendations for research and practice. *Journal of Occupational Health Psychology, 22,* 314-336.

Fisher, H. (2017). Commentary in *Match.com Singles in America 2017.* Retrieved August 17, 2017, from www.singlesinamerica.com

Fitzpatrick, K.K. (2012). Developmental considerations when treating anorexia nervosa in adolescents and young adults. In J. Lock (Ed.), *Oxford handbook of child and adolescent eating disorders: Developmental perspectives.* New York: Oxford University Press.

Fivush, R. (2011). The development of autobiographical memory. *Annual Review of Psychology* (Vol. 62). Palo Alto, CA: Annual Reviews.

Fivush, R., & Haden, C.A. (1997). Narrating and representing experience: Preschoolers' developing autobiographical accounts. In P. van den Broek, P.J. Bauer, & T. Bourg (Eds.), *Developmental spans in event representations and comprehension: Bridging fictional and actual events.* Mahwah, NJ: Erlbaum.

Fladby, T., & others (2017). Detecting at-risk Alzheimer's disease cases. *Journal of Alzheimer's Disease, 60,* 97-105.

Flam, K.K., Sandler, I., Wolchik, S., & Tein, J.Y. (2016). Non-residential father-child involvement, interparental conflict, and mental health of children following divorce: A person-focused approach. *Journal of Youth and Adolescence, 45,* 581-593.

Flanagan, T., & others (2018, in press). Feasibility and acceptability of screening for adverse childhood experiences in prenatal care. *Journal of Women's Health.*

Flannigan, R., & Schlegel, P.N. (2017). Genetic diagnostics of male infertility in clinical practice. *Best Practice and Research: Clinical Obstetrics and Gynecology, 44,* 26-37.

Flaskerud, J.H. (2017). Individual and dynamic: Western views of a good death. *Issues in Mental Health Nursing, 38,* 865-868.

Flavell, J.H. (2004). Theory-of-mind development: Retrospect and prospect. *Merrill-Palmer Quarterly, 50,* 274-290.

Flavell, J.H., Friedrichs, A., & Hoyt, J. (1970). Developmental changes in memorization processes. *Cognitive Psychology, 1,* 324-340.

Flavell, J.H., Green, F.L., & Flavell, E.R. (2000). Development of children's awareness of their own thoughts. *Journal of Cognition and Development, 7,* 97-112.

Flegal, K.M., & others (2016). Trends in obesity among adults in the United States, 2005 to 2014. *JAMA, 315,* 2284-2291.

Flensborg-Madsen, T., & Mortensen, E.L. (2017). Predictors of motor developmental milestones during the first year of life. *European Journal of Pediatrics, 176,* 109-119.

Fletcher, S., & others (2018, in press). Tracking of toddler fruit and vegetable preferences to intake and adiposity later in childhood. *Maternal and Child Health.*

Flicek, P., & others (2013). Ensembl 2013. *Nucleic Acids Research, 41,* D48-D55.

Flint, M.S., Baum, A., Chambers, W.H., & Jenkins, F.J. (2007). Induction of DNA damage, alteration of DNA repair, and transcriptional activation by stress hormones. *Psychoneuroendocrinology, 32,* 470-479.

Flood, S.M., & Genadek, K.R. (2016). Time for each other: Work and family constraints among couples. *Journal of Marriage and the Family, 78,* 142-164.

Florencio, R.S., & others (2018, in press). Plasmatic estradiol concentration in the mid-luteal phase is a good prognostic factor for clinical and ongoing pregnancies, during stimulated cycles of in vitro fertilization. *JBRA Assisted Reproduction.*

Florsheim, P. (2014). *The young parenthood program.* New York: Oxford University Press.

Florsheim, P., Moore, D., & Edgington, C. (2003). Romantic relationships among pregnant and parenting adolescents. In P. Florsheim (Ed.), *Adolescent romantic relations and sexual behavior.* Mahwah, NJ: Erlbaum.

Flouri, E., & Buchanan, A. (2004). Early father's and mother's involvement and child's later educational outcomes. *British Journal of Educational Psychology, 74,* 141-153.

Flouri, E., Midouhas, E., & Joshi, H. (2014). Family poverty and trajectories of children's emotional and behavioral problems: The moderating role of self-regulation and verbal cognitive ability. *Journal of Abnormal Child Psychology, 42,* 1043-1056.

Flynn, J.R. (1999). Searching for justice: The discovery of IQ gains over time. *American Psychologist, 54,* 5-20.

Flynn, J.R. (2007). The history of the American mind in the 20th century: A scenario to explain IQ gains over time and a case for the relevance of g. In P.C. Kyllonen, R.D. Roberts, & L. Stankov (Eds.), *Extending intelligence.* Mahwah, NJ: Erlbaum.

Flynn, J.R. (2011). Secular changes in intelligence. In R.J. Sternberg & S.B. Kaufman (Eds.), *Cambridge handbook of intelligence.* New York: Cambridge University Press.

Flynn, J.R. (2013). *Are we getting smarter?* New York: Cambridge University Press.

Follari, L. (2019). *Foundations and best practices in early childhood education* (4th ed.). Upper Saddle River, NJ: Pearson.

Fonseca-Machado Mde, O., & others (2015). Depressive disorder in Latin women: Does intimate partner violence matter? *Journal of Clinical Nursing, 24,* 1289-1299.

Font, S.A., & Cage, J. (2018). Dimensions of physical punishment and their associations with children's cognitive performance and school adjustment. *Child Abuse and Neglect, 75,* 29-40.

Food and Drug Administration (2018a). *Oxytocin.* Washington, DC: Author.

Food and Drug Administration (2018b). *Fish: What pregnant women and parents should know.* Washington, DC: Author.

Forbes, J.M., & Thorburn, D.R. (2018, in press). Mitochondrial dysfunction in diabetic kidney disease. *Nature Reviews. Nephrology.*

Ford, D.Y. (2012). Gifted and talented education: History, issues, and recommendations. In K.R. Harris, S. Graham, & T. Urdan (Eds.), *APA handbook of educational psychology.* Washington, DC: American Psychological Association.

Ford, D.Y. (2015a). Multicultural issues: Recruiting and retaining Black and Hispanic students in gifted education: Equality versus equity in schools. *Gifted Child Today, 38,* 187-191.

Ford, D.Y. (2015b). Culturally responsive gifted classrooms for culturally different students: A focus on invitational learning. *Gifted Child Today, 38,* 67-69.

Ford, D.Y. (2016). Black and Hispanic students. In L. Corno & E.M. Anderman (Eds.), *Handbook of educational psychology* (3rd ed.). New York: Routledge.

Foroughe, M. (Ed.) (2018). *Emotion focused family therapy with children and caregivers.* New York: Routledge.

Forrest, K.Y.Z., Leeds, M.J., & Ufelle, A.C. (2017). Epidemiology of obesity in the Hispanic adult population in the United States. *Family & Community Health, 40,* 291-297.

Forrest, L.N., & others (2018, in press). Core psychopathology in anorexia nervosa and bulimia nervosa: A network analysis. *International Journal of Eating Disorders.*

Foster, C., & others (2018). Physical activity and family-based obesity treatment: A review of expert recommendations on physical activity in youth. *Clinical Obesity, 8,* 68-79.

Fougare, B., & Cesari, M. (2019, in press). Prevention of frailty. In R. Fernandez-Ballesteros & others (Eds.), *Cambridge handbook of successful aging.* New York: Cambridge University Press.

Fouts, H.N., & Bader, L.R. (2017). Transitions in siblinghood: Integrating developments, cultural, and evolutionary perspectives. In D. Narváez & others (Eds.), *Contexts for young child flourishing.* New York: Oxford University Press.

Fox, E., & Alexander, R.A. (2017). Learning to read. In R.E. Mayer & P.A. Alexander (Eds.), *Handbook of research on learning and instruction* (2nd ed.). New York: Routledge.

Fox, M.K., & others (2010). Food consumption patterns of young preschoolers: Are they starting off on the right path? *Journal of the American Dietetic Association, 110*(Suppl. 12), S52-S59.

Fox, M.K., Pac, S., Devaney, B., & Jankowski, L. (2004). Feeding infants and toddlers study: What foods are infants and toddlers eating? *American Dietetic Association Journal, 104*(Suppl.), S22-S30.

Fozard, J.L. (1992, December 6). Commentary in "We can age successfully." *Parade Magazine,* pp. 14-15.

Fraiberg, S. (1959). *The magic years.* New York: Scribner's.

Fraley, R.C., Roisman, G.I., Booth-LaForce, C., Owen, M.T., & Holland, A.S. (2013). Intrapersonal and genetic origins of adult attachment styles: A longitudinal study from infancy to early adulthood. *Journal of Personality and Social Psychology, 104,* 817-838.

Franchak, J.M., Kretch, K.S., & Adolph, K.E. (2019, in press). See and be seen: Infant-caregiver social looking during locomotor free play. *Developmental Science.*

Francis, J., Fraser, G., & Marcia, J.E. (1989). *Cognitive and experimental factors in moratorium-achievement (MAMA) cycles.* Unpublished manuscript, Department of Psychology, Simon Fraser University, Burnaby, British Columbia.

Frank, J.C., & others (2018). Mental health services for older adults: Creating a system that tells the story. *Policy Brief UCLA Center for Health Policy Research, 2,* 1-8.

Frankenhuis, W.E., & Tiokhin, L. (2018, in press). Bridging evolutionary biology and developmental psychology: Toward an enduring theoretical infrastructure. *Child Development.*

Frankl, V. (1984). *Man's search for meaning.* New York: Basic Books.

Fransson, M., & others (2016). Is middle childhood attachment related to social functioning in young adulthood? *Scandinavian Journal of Psychology, 57,* 108-116.

Franzoza, E., Tsui, E.K., & Baron, S. (2018). Home health aides' perceptions of quality care: Goals, challenges, and implications for a rapidly changing industry. *New Solutions, 27,* 629-647.

Frasquilho, D., & others (2016). Distress and unemployment: The related economic and noneconomic factors in a sample of unemployed adults. *International Journal of Public Health, 61,* 821-828.

Frawley, J.M., & others (2017). Complementary and alternative medicine practitioner use prior to pregnancy predicts use during pregnancy. *Women's Health, 53,* 782-787.

Freberg, L.A. (2019). *Discovering behavioral neuroscience* (4th ed.). Boston: Cengage.

Frederikse, M., & others (2000). Sex differences in inferior lobule volume in schizophrenia. *American Journal of Psychiatry, 157,* 422-427.

Fredriksen-Goldsen, K.I., & others (2017). The unfolding of LGBT lives: Key events associated with health and well-being in later life. *Gerontologist, 57*(Suppl. 1), S15–S29.

Freeman, S., & others (2017). *Biological science* (6th ed.). Upper Saddle River, NJ: Pearson.

Freitas, M., & Rahioul, H. (2018). Late-life attachment. *Geriatric Psychology and Neuropsychiatry, 15,* 56–64.

Freud, S. (1917). *A general introduction to psychoanalysis.* New York: Washington Square Press.

Freund, A.M., & Blanchard-Fields, F. (2014). Age-related differences in altruism across adulthood: Making personal financial gain versus contributing to the public good. *Developmental Psychology, 50*(4), 1125–1136.

Freund, A.M., & Hennecke, M. (2015). On means and end: The role of goal focus in successful goal pursuit. *Current Directions in Psychological Science, 24,* 149–153.

Freund, A.M., Nikitin, J., & Riediger, M. (2013). Successful aging. In I.B. Weiner & others (Eds.), *Handbook of psychology* (2nd ed., Vol. 6). New York: Wiley.

Frey, B.S. (2011). Happy people live longer. *Science, 331,* 542–543.

Frick, M.A., & others (2018). The role of sustained attention, maternal sensitivity, and infant temperament in the development of early self-regulation. *British Journal of Psychology, 109,* 277–298.

Fridman, I., & others (2018, in press). Information framing reduces initial negative attitudes in cancer patients' decisions about hospice care. *Journal of Pain and Symptom Management.*

Fridy, R.L., & others (2018, in press). Pediatricians' knowledge and practices related to long-acting reversible contraceptives for adolescent girls. *Journal of Pediatric and Adolescent Gynecology.*

Friedman, S.L., Melhuish, E., & Hill, C. (2010). Child-care research at the dawn of a new millennium: An update. In G. Bremner & T. Wachs (Eds.), *Wiley-Blackwell handbook of infant development* (2nd ed.). Oxford, UK: Wiley-Blackwell.

Friend, M. (2018). *Special education* (5th ed.). Upper Saddle River, NJ: Pearson.

Frisen, A., & Holmqvist, K. (2010). What characterizes early adolescents with a positive body image? A qualitative investigation of Swedish boys and girls. *Body Image, 7,* 205–212.

Frith, E., & Lorinzi, P.D. (2018). Physical activity is associated with higher cognitive function among adults at risk for Alzheimer's disease. *Complementary Therapy in Medicine, 36,* 46–49.

Frost, D.M. (2011). Stigma and intimacy in same-sex relationships: A narrative approach. *Journal of Family Psychology, 25,* 1–10.

Fry, R. (2016, May 14). *For first time in modern era, living with parents edges out other living arrangements for 18- to 34-year-olds.* Washington, DC: Pew Research Center.

Frydenberg, E. (2019). *Adolescent coping* (3rd ed.). New York: Routledge.

Fu, F., & others (2018, in press). Mothers' grief experiences of losing their only child in the 2008 Sichuan earthquake: A qualitative longitudinal study. *Omega.*

Fuhs, M.W., Nesbitt, K.T., Farran, D.C., & Dong, N. (2014). Longitudinal associations between executive functioning and academic skills across content areas. *Developmental Psychology, 50,* 1698–1709.

Fujiki, M., & Brinton, B. (2017). Pragmatics and social communication in child language disorders. In R. Schwartz (Ed.), *Handbook of child language disorders* (2nd ed.). New York: Routledge.

Fuligni, A.J. (2012). Gaps, conflicts, and arguments between adolescents and their parents. *New Directions for Child and Adolescent Development, 135,* 105–110.

Fullwood, C., & Attrill-Smith, A. (2018, in press). Up-dating: Ratings of perceived dating success are better online than offline. *Cyberpsychology, Behavior, and Social Networks.*

Fulop, T. & others (2019, in press). From inflamm-aging to immunosenescence. In R. Fernandez-Ballesteros &

others (Eds.), *Cambridge handbook of successful aging.* New York: Cambridge University Press.

Fumagalli, M., & others (2018). From early stress to 12-month development in very preterm infants: Preliminary findings on epigenetic mechanisms and brain growth. *PLoS One, 13*(1), e0190602.

Furman, E. (2005). *Boomerang nation.* New York: Fireside.

Furman, L. (2018, in press). Kangaroo care 20 years later: Connecting infants and families. *Pediatrics.*

Furman, W. (2018). The romantic relationships of youth. In W.M. Bukowski & others (Eds.), *Handbook of peer interactions, relationships, and groups* (2nd ed.). New York: Guilford.

Furman, W., Low, S., & Ho, M.J. (2009). Romantic experience and psychosocial adjustment in middle adolescence. *Journal of Clinical Child and Adolescent Psychology, 38,* 75–90.

Furstenberg, F.F. (2007). The future of marriage. In A.S. Skolnick & J.H. Skolnick (Eds.), *Family in transition* (14th ed.). Boston: Allyn & Bacon.

Furth, H.G., & Wachs, H. (1975). *Thinking goes to school.* New York: Oxford University Press.

G

Gabbe, P.T., & others (2018). Beyond the traditional models of group prenatal care: The case for Moms2B. *American Journal of Obstetrics and Gynecology, 218,* 147–148.

Gabrian, M., Dutt, A.J., & Wahl, H.W. (2017). Subjective time perceptions and aging well—a review of concepts and empirical research—a mini-review. *Gerontology, 63,* 350–358.

Gaillardin, F., & Baudry, S. (2018, in press). Influence on working memory and executive function on stair ascent and descent in young and older adults. *Experimental Gerontology.*

Galambos, N.L., Howard, A.L., & Maggs, J.L. (2011). Rise and fall of sleep quality with student experiences across the first year of the university. *Journal of Research on Adolescence, 21,* 342–349.

Gale, C.R., Booth, T., Mottus, R., Kuh, D., & Deary, J.J. (2013). Neuroticism and extraversion in youth predict mental wellbeing and life satisfaction 40 years later. *Journal of Research in Personality, 47,* 687–697.

Galinsky, E. (2010). *Mind in the making.* New York: Harper Collins.

Galinsky, E., & others (2017). Civic science for public use: Mind in the Making and Vroom. *Child Development, 88,* 1409–1418.

Galland, B.C., Taylor, B.J., Edler, D.E., & Herbison, P. (2012). Normal sleep patterns in infants and children: A systematic review of observational studies. *Sleep Medicine Review, 16,* 213–222.

Gallant, S.N. (2016). Mindfulness meditation practice and executive functioning: Breaking down the benefit. *Consciousness and Cognition, 40,* 116–130.

Galliher, R.V., McLean, K.C., & Syed, M. (2017). An integrated developmental model for studying identity content in context. *Developmental Psychology, 53,* 2011–2022.

Gallo, R.B.S., & others (2018). Sequential application of non-pharmacological interventions reduces the severity of labor pain, delays use of pharmacological analgesia, and improves some obstetrics outcomes: A randomized trial. *Journal of Physiotherapy, 64,* 33–40.

Galloway, J.C., & Thelen, E. (2004). Feet first: Object exploration in young infants. *Infant Behavior & Development, 27,* 107–112.

Gallup (2013). *No major change in Americans' exercise habits in 2011.* Washington, DC: Gallup.

Gamito, P., & others (2017). Cognitive training on stroke patients via virtual reality-based serious games. *Disability and Rehabilitation, 39,* 385–388.

Ganapathy, K. (2018). Brain death revisited. *Neurology India, 66,* 308–315.

Ganci, M., Pradel, M., & Hughes, E.K. (2018, in press). Feasibility of a parent education and skills workshop for improving response to family-based treatment of adolescent anorexia nervosa. *International Journal of Eating Disorders.*

Gangamma, R., & Shipman, D. (2018, in press). Transnational intersectionality in family therapy with resettled refugees. *Journal of Marital and Family Therapy.*

Gangisetty, O., Cabrera, M.A., & Murugan, S. (2018). Impact of epigenetics in aging and age related neurodegenerative diseases. *Frontiers in Bioscience, 23,* 1445–1464.

Ganguli, M. (2017). The times they are a-changin': cohort effects in aging, cognition, and dementia. *International Psychogeriatrics, 29,* 353–355.

Ganong, L., & Coleman, M. (2018, in press). Studying stepfamilies: Four eras of scholarship. *Family Process.*

Ganong, L., Coleman, M., & Russell, L. (2015). Children in diverse families. In R.M. Lerner (Ed.), *Handbook of child psychology and developmental science* (7th ed.). New York: Wiley.

Ganong, L., Coleman, M., & Sanner, C. (2018). Stepfamilies. In M.H. Bornstein (Ed.), *SAGE handbook of lifespan human development.* Thousand Oaks, CA: Sage.

Gao, G. (2001). Intimacy, passion, and commitment in Chinese and U.S. American romantic relationships. *International Journal of Intercultural Relations, 25,* 329–342.

Gao, G. (2016). Cross-cultural romantic relationships. *Oxford research encyclopedia of romantic relationships.* New York: Oxford University Press.

Garaschuk, O., Semchyshyn, H.M., & Lushchak, V.I. (2018). Healthy brain aging: Interplay between reactive species, inflammation, and energy supply. *Aging Research Reviews, 43,* 26–45.

Garcia-Gomariz, C., & others (2018). Effects of 2 years of endurance and high-impact training on preventing osteoporosis in postmenopausal women: Randomized clinical trial. *Menopause, 25,* 301–306.

Garcia-Huidobro, D., & others (2018). For whom do parenting interventions to prevent adolescent substance use work? *Prevention Science, 19,* 570–578.

Gardner, H. (1983). *Frames of mind.* New York: Basic Books.

Gardner, H. (1993). *Multiple intelligences.* New York: Basic Books.

Gardner, H. (2002). The pursuit of excellence through education. In M. Ferrari (Ed.), *Learning from extraordinary minds.* Mahwah, NJ: Erlbaum.

Gardner, H. (2016). *Multiple intelligences: Prelude, theory, and aftermath.* In R.J. Sternberg, S.T. Fiske, & J. Foss (Eds.), *Scientists making a difference.* New York: Cambridge University Press.

Gardner, H., Kornhaber, W., & Chen, J-Q. (2018). The theory of multiple intelligences: Psychological and educational perspectives. In R.J. Sternberg (Ed.), *The nature of human intelligence.* New York: Cambridge University Press.

Gardner, M., Brooks-Gunn, J., & Chase-Lansdale, P.L. (2016). The two-generation approach to building human capital: Past, present, and future. In E. Votruba-Drzal & E. Dearing (Eds.), *Handbook of early childhood development programs, practices, and policies.* New York: Wiley.

Gardosi, J., & others (2013). Maternal and fetal risk factors for stillbirth: Population-based study. *British Medical Journal, 346,* f108.

Gareau, S., & others (2016). Group prenatal care results in Medicaid savings with better outcomes: A propensity score analysis of CenteringPregnancy participation in South Carolina. *Maternal and Child Health, 20,* 1384–1393.

Gareri, P., & others (2017). The Citicholinage Study: Citicoline Plus Cholinesterase Inhibitors in Aged Patients Affected with Alzheimer's Disease Study. *Journal of Alzheimer's Disease, 56,* 557–565.

Harris, K.R., & others (2018, in press). Self-regulated strategy development in writing. In C. Bazerman & others (Eds.), *The lifespan development of writing*. Urbana, IL: National Council of English.

Harris, P.L. (2000). *The work of the imagination*. Oxford University Press.

Harris, P.L. (2006). Social cognition. In W. Damon & R. Lerner (Eds.), *Handbook of child psychology* (6th ed.). New York: Wiley.

Harrison, C. (2012). Aging: Telomerase gene therapy increases longevity. *Nature Reviews/Drug Discovery, 11,* 518.

Harrison, M., Brodribb, W., & Hepworth, J. (2018, in press). A qualitative systematic review of maternal infant feeding practices in transitioning from milk to solid foods. *Maternal and Child Nutrition.*

Hart, B., & Risley, T.R. (1995). *Meaningful differences.* Baltimore: Paul H. Brookes.

Hart, C.H., Yang, C., Charlesworth, R., & Burts, D.C. (2003, April*). Early childhood teachers' curriculum beliefs, classroom practices, and children's outcomes: What are the connections?* Paper presented at the biennial meeting of the Society for Research in Child Development, Tampa, FL.

Hart, D., Goel, N., & Atkins, R. (2017). Prosocial tendencies, antisocial behavior, and moral development in childhood. In A. Slater & G. Bremner (Eds.), *Introduction to developmental psychology* (3rd ed.). New York: Wiley.

Hart, D., & Karmel, M.P. (1996). Self-awareness and self-knowledge in humans, great apes, and monkeys. In A. Russori, K. Bard, & S. Parker (Eds.), *Reaching into thought.* New York: Cambridge University Press.

Hart, D., & van Goethem, A. (2017). The role of civic and political participation in successful early adulthood. In L. Padilla-Walker & L. Nelson (Eds.), *Flourishing in emerging adulthood.* New York: Oxford University Press.

Hart, D., & others (2017). Morality and mental health. In C. Markey (Ed.), *Encyclopedia of mental health.* New York: Elsevier.

Hart, W., Adams, J., & Tullett, A. (2016). "It's complicated"—Sex differences in perceptions of cross-aged friendships. *Journal of Social Psychology, 156,* 190–201.

Harter, S. (2006). The self. In W. Damon & R. Lerner (Eds.), *Handbook of child psychology* (6th ed.). New York: Wiley.

Harter, S. (2012). *The construction of the self* (2nd ed.). New York: Wiley.

Harter, S. (2013). The development of self-esteem. In M.H. Kermis (Ed.), *Self-esteem: Issues and answers.* New York: Psychology Press.

Harter, S. (2016). I-self and me-self processes affecting developmental psychopathology and mental health. In D. Cicchetti (Ed.), *Developmental psychopathology* (3rd ed.). New York: Wiley.

Hartshorne, H., & May, M.S. (1928–1930). *Moral studies in the nature of character.* New York: Macmillan.

Hartup, W.W. (1983). The peer system. In P.H. Mussen (Ed.), *Handbook of child psychology* (4th ed., Vol. 4). New York: Wiley.

Hartup, W.W. (1996). The company they keep: Friendships and their developmental significance. *Child Development, 67,* 1–13.

Hartup, W.W. (2009). Critical issues and theoretical viewpoints. In K.H. Rubin, W.M. Bukowski, & B. Laursen (Eds.), *Handbook of peer interactions, relationships, and groups.* New York: Guilford.

Hasbrouck, S.L., & Pianta, R. (2016). Understanding child care quality and implications for dual language learners. In K.E. Sanders & A.W. Guerra (Eds.), *The culture of child care.* New York: Oxford University Press.

Hasmanova Marhankova, M.J. (2016). Women's attitudes toward forming new partnerships in widowhood: The search for "your own someone" and for freedom. *Journal of Women and Aging, 28,* 34–45.

Hassard, J., Teoh, K.R.H., Visockaite, G., Dewe, P., & Cox, T. (2018). The cost of work-related stress to society: A systematic review. *Journal of Occupational Health Psychology, 23,* 1–17.

Hastings, P.D., Miller, J.G., & Troxel, N.R. (2015). Making good: The socialization of children's prosocial development. In J.E. Grusec & P.D. Hastings (Eds.), *Handbook of socialization* (2nd ed.). New York: Guilford.

Hatano, K., Sugimura, K., & Schwartz, S.J. (2018, in press). Longitudinal links between identity consolidation and psychological problems in adolescence: Using bi-factor latent change and cross-lagged effect models. *Journal of Youth and Adolescence.*

Hatoun, J., & others (2018). Tobacco control laws and pediatric asthma. *Pediatrics, 141*(Suppl. 1), S130–S136.

Hawk, S.T., Becht, A., & Branje, S. (2016). "Snooping" as a distinct monitoring strategy: Comparison with overt solicitation and control. *Journal of Research on Adolescence, 26,* 443–458.

Hawkes, C. (2006). Olfaction in neurodegenerative disorder. *Advances in Otorhinolaryngology, 63,* 133–151.

Hawkins, A.J. (2018, in press). Shifting the relationship education field to prioritize youth relationship education. *Journal of Couple and Relationship Therapy.*

Hawkley, L.C., & Kocherginsky, M. (2018). Transitions in loneliness among older adults: A 5-year follow-up in the National Social Life, Health, and Aging Project. *Research on Aging, 40,* 365–387.

Hawley, P.H.l., & Bower, A.R. (2018). Evolution of peer relations: Considering the functional roles of aggression and prosociality. In W.M. Bukowski & others (Eds.), *Handbook of peer interaction, relationships, and groups.* New York: Guilford.

Hay, W.W., & others (2017). *Current diagnosis and treatment pediatrics* (23rd ed.). New York: McGraw-Hill.

Hayashi, A., & Mazuka, R. (2017). Emergence of Japanese infants' prosodic preferences in infant-directed vocabulary. *Developmental Psychology, 53,* 28–37.

Hayatbakhsh, R., & others (2013). Early childhood predictors of early onset of smoking: A birth prospective study. *Addictive Behaviors, 38,* 2513–2519.

Haycraft, A.L. (2018). Pregnancy and the opioid epidemic. *Journal of Psychosocial Nursing and Mental Health Services, 56,* 19–23.

Hayflick, L. (1977). The cellular basis for biological aging. In C.E. Finch & L. Hayflick (Eds.), *Handbook of the biology of aging.* New York: Van Nostrand.

Hayman, K.J., Kerse, N., & Consedine, N.S. (2017). Resilience in context: The special case of advanced age. *Aging and Mental Health, 21,* 577–585.

Hayslip, B., Fruhauf, C.A., & Dolbin-MacNab, M.L. (2018, in press). Grandparents raising grandchildren: What have we learned over the past decade? *Gerontologist.*

Hazan, C., & Shaver, P.R. (1987). Romantic love conceptualized as an attachment process. *Journal of Personality and Social Psychology, 52,* 522–524.

He, M., Walle, E.A., & Campos, J. (2015). A cross-national investigation between infant walking and language development. *Infancy, 20,* 283–305.

Heard, E., & others (2011). Mediating effects of social support on the relationship between perceived stress, depression, and hypertension in African Americans. *Journal of the American Medical Association, 103,* 116–122.

Heberlein, E.C., & others (2016). The comparative effects of group prenatal care on psychosocial outcomes. *Archives of Women and Mental Health, 19,* 259–269.

Hechtman, L., & others (2016). Functional adult outcomes 16 years after childhood diagnosis of attention-deficit/hyperactivity disorder: MTA results. *Journal of the American Academy of Child and Adolescent Psychiatry, 55,* 945–952.

Hegedus, C., & others (2018). Redox control of cancer cell destruction. *Redox Biology, 16,* 74.

Heimann, M., & others (2006). Exploring the relation between memory, gestural communication, and the emergence of language in infancy: A longitudinal study. *Infant and Child Development, 15,* 233–249.

Heinonen, M.T., & others (2015). GIMAP GTPase family genes: Potential modifiers in autoimmune diabetes, asthma, and allergy. *Journal of Immunology, 194,* 5885–5894.

Heinrich, J. (2017). Modulation of allergy risk by breast feeding. *Current Opinion in Clinical Nutrition and Metabolic Care, 20,* 217–221.

Helgeson, V.S. (2012). *Psychology of gender* (4th ed.). Upper Saddle River, NJ: Pearson.

Helgeson, V.S. (2017). *Psychology of gender* (5th ed.). New York: Routledge.

Helgesson, G., & others (2018). Ethical aspects of diagnosis and interventions for children with fetal alcohol spectrum disorder (FASD) and their families. *BMC Medical Ethics, 19*(1), 1.

Hellgren, K., & others (2017). The new Swedish report on shaken baby syndrome is misleading. *Acta Paediatrica, 106,* 1040.

Helm, R.K., McCormick, M., & Reyna, V.F. (2018, in press). Expert decision-making: A fuzzy-trace theory perspective. In L.J. Ball & A. Thompson (Eds.), *International handbook of thinking and reasoning.* New York: Routledge.

Helm, R.K., & Reyna, V.F. (2018, in press). Cognitive and neurobiological aspects of risk. In M. Raue & others (Eds.), *Psychological aspects of risk and risk analysis.* New York: Springer.

Helman, R., Copeland, C., & VanDerhei, J. (2012). The 2012 Retirement Confidence Survey: Job insecurity, debt weigh on retirement confidence, savings. *EBRI Issue Brief, 369,* 5–32.

Henderson, R.M., & others (2018, in press). Maintenance of physical function 1 year after exercise intervention in at-risk older adults: Follow-up from the LIFE Study. *Journals of Gerontology: Biological Sciences and Medical Sciences A.*

Henderson, V.W. (2011). Gonadal hormones and cognitive aging: A midlife perspective. *Women's Health, 7,* 81–93.

Hendricks-Munoz, K.D., & others (2013). Maternal and neonatal nurse perceived value of kangaroo mother care and maternal care partnership in the Neonatal Intensive Care Unit. *American Journal of Perinatology, 30,* 875–880.

Hendrickson, Z.M., & others (2018). Resilience among Nepali widows after the death of a spouse: "That was my past and now I have to see my present." *Quality Health Research, 28,* 466–478.

Hengartner, M.P., & Yamanaka-Altenstein, M. (2017). Personality, psychopathology, and psychotherapy. *Frontiers in Psychology, 8,* 9.

Hennessy, G. (2018). Marijuana and pregnancy. *American Journal of Addiction, 27,* 44–45.

Henretta, J.C. (2010). Lifetime marital history and mortality after age 50. *Journal of Aging and Health, 22*(8), 1198–1212.

Henricks, T.S. (2015a). Classical theories of play. In J.E. Johnson & others (Eds.), *Handbook of the study of play.* Blue Ridge Summit, PA: Rowman & Littlefield.

Henricks, T.S. (2015b). Modern theories of play. In J.E. Johnson & others (Eds.), *Handbook of the study of play.* Blue Ridge Summit, PA: Rowman & Littlefield.

Henslin, J.M. (2017). *Essentials of sociology* (12th ed.). Upper Saddle River, NJ: Pearson.

Heo, J., & others (2018, in press). Cohort-based income gradients in obesity among U.S. adults. *American Journal of Human Biology.*

Herman-Giddens, M.E. (2007). The decline in the age of menarche in the United States: Should we be concerned? *Journal of Adolescent Health, 40,* 201–203.

Hernandez-Segura, A., Nehme J., & Demaria, M. (2018). Hallmarks of cellular senescence. *Trends in Cell Biology, 28,* 436–453.

Hernandez-Zimbron, L.F., & others (2018, in press) Age-related macular degeneration: New paradigms for treatment and management of AMD. *Oxidative Medicine and Cell Longevity.*

Heron, M. (2016). Deaths: Leading causes for 2013. *National Vital Statistics Reports, 65*(2), 1–95.

Hershner, S.D., & Chervin, R.D. (2015). Causes and consequences of sleepiness among college students. *Nature and Science of Sleep, 6,* 73–84.

Herting, M.M., & Sowell, E.R. (2017). Puberty and structural brain development in humans. *Frontiers in Neuroendocrinology, 44,* 122–137.

Hess, J.L., & others (2018, in press). Why is there selective cortical vulnerability in ADHD? Clues from postmortem brain gene expression data. *Molecular Psychiatry.*

Hessel, P., & others (2018, in press). Trends and determinants of the Flynn effect in cognitive functioning among older individuals in 10 European countries. *Journal of Epidemiology and Community Health.*

Hetherington, E.M. (1989). Coping with family transitions: Winners, losers, and survivors. *Child Development, 60,* 1–14.

Hetherington, E.M. (2006). The influence of conflict, marital problem solving, and parenting on children's adjustment in nondivorced, divorced, and remarried families. In A. Clarke-Stewart & J. Dunn (Eds.), *Families count.* New York: Oxford University Press.

Hetherington, E.M., & Kelly, J. (2002). *For better or for worse: Divorce reconsidered.* New York: Norton.

Hetherington, E.M., & Stanley-Hagan, M. (2002). Parenting in divorced and remarried families. In M.H. Bornstein (Ed.), *Handbook of parenting* (2nd ed., Vol. 3). Mahwah, NJ: Erlbaum.

Heward, W.L., Alber-Morgan, S., & Konrad, M. (2017). *REVEL for exceptional children* (11th ed.). Upper Saddle River, NJ: Pearson.

Hewlett, B.S. (1991). *Intimate fathers: The nature and context of Aka Pygmy.* Ann Arbor: University of Michigan Press.

Hewlett, B.S. (2000). Culture, history and sex: Anthropological perspectives on father involvement. *Marriage and Family Review, 29,* 324–340.

Hewlett, B.S., & MacFarlan, S.J. (2010). Fathers, roles in hunter-gatherer and other small-scale cultures. In M.E. Lamb (Ed.) *The role of the father in child development* (5th ed.). New York: Wiley.

Heyman, G.D., Fu, G., & Lee, K. (2013). Selective skepticism: American and Chinese children's reasoning about evaluative feedback. *Developmental Psychology, 49,* 543–553.

High/Scope Resource (2005, Spring). The High/Scope Perry Preschool Study and the man who began it. *High/Scope Resource 9.* Ypsilanti, MI: High/Scope Press.

Highfield, R. (2008, April 30). *Harvard's baby brain research lab.* Retrieved January 24, 2009, from http://www.telegraph.co.uk/science/science-news/3341166/Harvards-baby-brain-research-lab.html

Hill, C.R., & Stafford, E.P. (1980). Parental care of children: Time diary estimate of quantity, predictability, and variety. *Journal of Human Resources, 15,* 219–239.

Hill, K.D., & others (2018). What works in falls prevention in Asia: A systematic review and meta-analysis of randomized controlled trials. *BMC Geriatrics, 18*(1), 3.

Hill, P.C., & Pargament, K.I. (2003). Advances in conceptualization and measurement of religion and spirituality: Implications for physical and mental health research. *American Psychologist, 58,* 64–74.

Hill, P.L., & Roberts, B.W. (2016). Personality and health: Reviewing recent research and setting a directive for the future. In K.W. Schaie & S.L. Willis (Eds.), *Handbook of the psychology of aging* (8th ed.). New York: Elsevier.

Hill, P.L., & others (2016). Purpose in life in emerging adulthood: Development and validation of a new brief measure. *Journal of Positive Psychology, 11,* 237–245.

Hill, T.D., Angel, J.L., Ellison, C.G., & Angel, R.J. (2005). Religious attendance and mortality: An 8-year follow-up of older Mexican Americans. *Journals of Gerontology B: Psychological Sciences and Social Sciences, 60,* S102–S109.

Hill, W.D., & others (2018, in press). A combined analysis of genetically correlated traits identifies 187 loci and a role for neurogenesis and myelination in intelligence. *Molecular Psychiatry.*

Himes, C.L. (2009). Age structure. In D. Carr (Ed.), *Encyclopedia of the life course and human development.* Boston: Gale Cengage.

Hinshaw, H.P. (2018). Attention deficit hyperactivity disorder (ADHD): Controversy, developmental mechanisms, and multiple levels of analysis. *Annual Review of Clinical Psychology, 14,* 291–316.

Hinze, S.W., Lin, J., & Andersson, T.E. (2012). Can we capture the intersections? Older Black women, education, and health. *Women's Health Issues, 22,* e91–e98.

Hipwell, A.E., & others (2018, in press). Police contacts, arrests, and decreasing self-control and personal responsibility among female adolescents. *Journal of Child Psychology and Psychiatry.*

Hirsch, B.J., & Rapkin, B.D. (1987). The transition to junior high school: A longitudinal study of self-esteem, psychological symptomatology, school life, and social support. *Child Development, 58,* 1235–1243.

Hirsch, J.K., & Sirois, F.M. (2016). Hope and fatigue in chronic illness: The role of perceived stress. *Journal of Health Psychology, 21,* 451–456.

Hirsh-Pasek, K., Golinkoff, R.M., Singer, D., & Berk, L. (2009). *A mandate for playful learning in preschool: Presenting the evidence.* New York: Oxford University Press.

Hitchcock, C., & others (2017). Autobiographical episodic-memory-based training for the treatment of mood, anxiety, and stress-related disorders: A systematic review and meta-analysis. *Clinical Psychology Review, 52,* 92–107.

Hjortsvang, K., & Lagattuta, K.H. (2017). Emotional development. In A.E. Wenzel (Ed.), *SAGE encyclopedia of abnormal and clinical psychology.*

Hochberg, C., & others (2012). Association of vision loss in glaucoma and age-related macular degeneration with IADL disability. *Investigative Ophthalmology and Visual Science, 53,* 3201–3206.

Hockenberry, M.J., Wilson, D., & Rodgers, C.C. (2017). *Wong's essentials of pediatric nursing* (10th ed.). Maryland Heights, MO: Mosby.

Hockenberry, S., & Puzzanchera, C. (2017, April). *Juvenile court statistics, 2014.* Washington, DC: National Center for Juvenile Justice.

Hocking, E.C., & others (2018, in press). Adult attachment and drinking context as predictors of alcohol problems and relationship satisfaction in college students. *American Journal of Drug and Alcohol Abuse.*

Hodder, R.K., & others (2018). Association between Australian adolescent alcohol use and alcohol risk and protective factors in 2011 and 2014. *Drug and Alcohol Reviews, 37*(Suppl. 1), S22–S33.

Hoefnagels, M. (2018). *Biology* (4th ed.). New York: McGraw-Hill.

Hoefnagels, M. (2019). *Biology: Essentials* (3rd ed.). New York: McGraw-Hill.

Hoelter, L. (2009). Divorce and separation. In D. Carr (Ed.), *Encyclopedia of the life course and human development.* Boston: Gale Cengage.

Hofer, A., & others (2007). Sex differences in brain activation patterns during processing of positively and negatively balanced emotional stimuli. *Psychological Medicine, 37,* 109–119.

Hoff, E. (2015). Language development. In M.H. Bornstein & M.E. Lamb (Eds.), *Developmental science* (7th ed.). New York: Psychology Press.

Hoff, E., Laursen, B., & Tardif, T. (2002). Socioeconomic status and parenting. In M.H. Bornstein (Ed.), *Handbook of parenting* (2nd ed.). Mahwah, NJ: Erlbaum.

Hoffman, K., Cooper, G., Powell, B., & Benton, C.M. (2017). *Raising a secure child.* New York: Guilford.

Hoffman, P., & Morcom, A.M. (2018). Age-related changes in the neural networks supporting semantic cognition: A meta-analysis of 47 functional neuroimaging studies. *Neuroscience and Biobehavioral Reviews, 84,* 134–150.

Hoffman, S., & Warschburger, P. (2017). Weight, shape, and muscularity concerns in male and female adolescents: Predictors of change and influences on eating disorders. *International Journal of Eating Disorders, 50,* 139–147.

Hoffman, S., & Warschburger, P. (2018). Patterns of body image concerns in adolescence and early adulthood: A latent profile analysis. *Eating Behavior, 29,* 28–34.

Holden, G.W., Vittrup, B., & Rosen, L.H. (2011). Families, parenting, and discipline. In M.K. Underwood & L.H. Rosen (Eds.), *Social development.* New York: Guilford.

Holden, G.W., & others (2017). The emergence of "positive parenting" as a new paradigm: Theory, processes, and evidence. In D. Narváez & others (Eds.), *Contexts for young child flourishing.* New York: Oxford University Press.

Holfeld, B., & Mishna, F. (2018). Longitudinal associations in youth involvement as victimized, bullying, or witnessing bullying. *Cyberpsychology, Behavior, and Social Networking, 21,* 234–239.

Hollams, E.M., de Klerk, N.H., Holt, P.G., & Sly, P.D. (2014). Persistent effects of maternal smoking during pregnancy on lung function and asthma in adolescents. *American Journal of Respiratory and Critical Care Medicine, 189,* 401–407.

Holland, J.M., & others (2014). The unique impact of late-life bereavement and prolonged grief on diurnal cortisol. *Journals of Gerontology B: Psychological Sciences and Social Sciences, 69,* 4–11.

Holler-Wallscheid, M.S., & others (2017). Bilateral recruitment of prefrontal cortex in working memory is associated with task demand but not with age. *Proceedings of the National Academy of Sciences U.S.A., 114,* E830–E839.

Holley, S.R. (2017). Perspectives on contemporary lesbian relationships. *Journal of Lesbian Studies, 21,* 1–6.

Hollister, M. (2011). Employment stability in the U.S. labor market: Rhetoric versus reality. *Annual Review of Sociology* (Vol. 37). Palo Alto, CA: Annual Reviews.

Holmes, T.H., & Rahe, R.H. (1967). The social readjustment rating scale. *Journal of Psychosomatic Research, 11,* 213–218.

Holsen, I., Carlson Jones, D., & Skogbrott Birkeland, M. (2012). Body image satisfaction among Norwegian adolescents and young adults: A longitudinal study of the influence of interpersonal relationships and BMI. *Body Image, 9,* 201–208.

Holt, C.L., & others (2017). Longitudinal effects of religious involvement on religious coping and health behaviors in a national sample of African Americans. *Social Science and Medicine, 187,* 11–19.

Holway, G.V. (2015). Vaginal and oral sex initiation timing: A focus on gender and race/ethnicity. *International Journal of Sexual Health, 27,* 351–367.

Holway, G.V., & Hernandez, S.M. (2018). Oral sex and condom use in a US national sample of adolescents and young adults. *Journal of Adolescent Health, 62,* 402–410.

Holzman, L. (2017). *Vygotsky at work and play* (2nd ed.). New York: Routledge.

Homan, K.J. (2018). Secure attachment and eudaimonic well-being in late adulthood: The mediating role of self-compassion. *Aging and Mental Health, 22,* 363–370.

Hong, S.M., & Hur, Y.I. (2017). Relationship between obesity and depression in Korean adults: Korea National Health and Nutrition Examination Survey, 2014. *Medicine, 96,* e9478.

Hong, X., & others (2015). Normal aging selectivity diminishes alpha lateralization in visual spatial attention. *Neuroimage, 106,* 353–363.

Hoogenhout, M., & Malcolm-Smith, S. (2017). Theory of mind predicts severity level in autism. *Autism, 21,* 242–252.

Hook, P.E., & Haynes, C.W. (2017). Reading and writing in child language disorders. In R. Schwartz (Eds.), *Handbook of child language disorders* (2nd ed.). New York: Routledge.

Hooper, S.Y., & others (2016). *Creating a classroom incremental theory matters, but it is not as straightforward as you might think: Evidence from a multi-level analysis at ten high schools.* Poster presented at the biennial meeting of the Society for Research on Adolescence, Baltimore.

Hoover, J., & others (2018). Into the wild: Building value through moral pluralism. In K. Gray & J. Graham (Eds.), *Atlas of moral psychology.* New York: Guilford.

Hope, D.A. (2009). Contemporary perspectives on lesbian, gay, and bisexual identities: Introduction. *Nebraska Symposium on Motivation, 54,* 1–4.

Hopping-Winn, J., & others (2018, in press). The progression of end-of-life wishes and concordance with end-of-life care. *Journal of Palliative Medicine.*

Hoppmann, C.A., Infuma, F.J., Ram, N., & Gerstorf, D. (2017). Associations among individuals' perceptions of future time, individual resources, and subjective well-being in old age. *Journals of Gerontology B: Psychological Sciences and Social Sciences, 72,* 388–399.

Horgusluoglu, E., Nudelman, K., Nho, K., & Saykin, A.J. (2017). Adult neurogenesis and neurodegenerative diseases: A systems biology perspective. *American Journal of Medical Genetics B: Neuropsychiatric Genetics, 174,* 93–112.

Horn, J.L., & Donaldson, G. (1980). Cognitive development II: Adulthood development of human abilities. In O.G. Brim & J. Kagan (Eds.), *Constancy and change in human development.* Cambridge, MA: Harvard University Press.

Horne, R.S.C. (2018, in press). Cardiovascular autonomic dysfunction in sudden infant death syndrome. *Clinical Autonomic Research.*

Horowitz-Kraus, T., & Hutton, J.S. (2018). Brain connectivity in children is increased by the time they spend in reading books and decreased by the length of exposure to screen-based media. *Acta Paediatrica, 121,* 17–23.

Hosie, A., (2018). Medical assistance in dying—unanswered questions. *JAMA Internal Medicine, 178,* 156.

Hoskin, J. (2018). *Discovering who I am.* New York: Routledge.

Hoskyn, M.J., Iarocci, G., & Young, A.R. (Eds.) (2017). *Executive functions in children's everyday lives.* New York: Oxford University Press.

Hospital for Sick Children & others (2010). *The Hospital for Sick Children's handbook of pediatrics* (11th ed.). London: Elsevier.

Hotta, R., & others (2018, in press). Cognitive function and unsafe driving acts during an on-road test among community-dwelling older adults with cognitive impairments. *Geriatrics and Gerontology International.*

Hou, L., & others (2016). Systems approaches to understanding aging. In M.R. Kaeberlein & G.M. Martin (Eds.), *Handbook of the biology of aging* (8th ed.). New York: Elsevier.

Hou, Y., & Kim, S.Y. (2018). Acculturation-related stressors and individual adjustment in Asian American families. In S.S. Chuang & C. Costigan (Eds.), *An international approach to parenting and parent-child families in immigrant families.* New York: Routledge.

Hou, Y., Kim, S.Y., & Wang, Y. (2016). Parental acculturative stressors and adolescent adjustment through interparental and parent-child relationships in Chinese American families. *Journal of Youth and Adolescence, 45,* 1466–1481.

Houssaini, A., & others (2018, in press). mTOR pathway activation drives lung cell senescence and emphysema. *JCI Insight.*

Howard, M.M., Mehta, N.D., & Powrie, R. (2017). Peripartum depression: Early recognition improves outcomes. *Cleveland Clinic Journal of Medicine, 84,* 388–396.

Howard, S., & others (2017). Perceived social support predicts lower cardiovascular reactivity to stress in older adults. *Biological Psychology, 125,* 70–75.

Howard, S.R., & Dunkel, L. (2018). The genetic basis of delayed puberty. *Neuroendocrinology, 103,* 649–659.

Howe, G.W., Homberger, A.P., Weihs, K., Moreno, F., & Neiderhiser, J.M. (2012). Higher-order structure in the trajectories of depression and anxiety following sudden involuntary unemployment. *Journal of Abnormal Psychology, 121,* 325–338.

Howe, M.J.A., Davidson, J.W., Moore, D.G., & Sloboda, J.A. (1995). Are there early childhood signs of musical ability? *Psychology of Music, 23,* 162–176.

Howell, D.C. (2017). *Fundamental statistics for the behavioral sciences* (9th ed.). Boston: Cengage.

Howes, C. (2016). Children and child care: A theory of relationships within cultural communities. In K. Sanders & A.W. Guerra (Eds.), *The culture of child care.* New York: Oxford University Press.

Hoyer, W.J. (2015). Brain aging: Behavioral, cognitive, and personality consequences. In J.D. Wright (Ed.), *International encyclopedia of the social and behavioral sciences* (2nd ed.). New York: Elsevier.

Hoyer, W.J., & Roodin, P.A. (2009). *Adult development and aging* (6th ed.). New York: McGraw-Hill.

Hoyt, L.T., & others (2018a, in press). Girls' sleep trajectories across the pubertal transition: Emerging racial/ethnic differences. *Journal of Adolescent Health.*

Hoyt, L.T., & others (2018b, in press). Adolescent sleep barriers: Profiles within a diverse sample of urban youth. *Journal of Youth and Adolescence.*

HSBC Insurance (2007). *The future of retirement: The new old age global report.* London: HSBC.

Hsieh, H.H., & Huang, J.T. (2017). Core self-evaluations and job and life satisfaction: The mediating and moderated mediating role of job insecurity. *Journal of Psychology, 151,* 282–298.

Hsin, A., & Xie, Y. (2014). Explaining Asian Americans' academic advantage over whites. *Proceedings of the National Academy of Sciences U.S.A., 111,* 8416–8421.

Hsueh, A.J., & He, J. (2018, in press). Gonadotropins and their receptors: Co-evolution, genetic variants, receptor imaging, and functional antagonists. *Biological Reproduction.*

Hua, L., & others (2016). Four-locus gene interaction between IL13, IL4, FCER1B, and ADRB2 for asthma in Chinese Han children. *Pediatric Pulmonology, 51,* 364–371.

Huang, J-H., DeJong, W., Towvim, L.G., & Schneider, S.K. (2009). Sociodemographic and psychobehavioral characteristics of U.S. college students who abstain from alcohol. *Journal of American College Health, 57,* 395–410.

Huang, L., & others (2018a, in press). Maternal smoking and attention-deficit/hyperactivity disorder in offspring: A meta-analysis. *Pediatrics.*

Huang, L., & others (2018b, in press). The mediating role of the placenta in the relationship between maternal exercise during pregnancy and full-term low birth weight. *Journal of Maternal-Fetal and Neonatal Medicine.*

Huang, L.B., & others (2017). Influencing and protective factors of suicide ideation among older adults. *International Journal of Mental Health Nursing, 26,* 191–199.

Huang, Y., & Spelke, E. (2015). Core knowledge and the emergence of symbols: The case of maps. *Journal of Cognition and Development, 16,* 81–96.

Huang, Y.A., & others (2017). ApoE2, ApoE3, and ApoE4 differentially stimulate APP transcription and AB secretion. *Cell, 168,* 427–441.

Huckle, W.R. (2017). Cell- and tissue-based models for study of placental development. *Progress in Molecular Biology and Translational Science, 145,* 29–37.

Hudson, A., & Jacques, S. (2014). Put on a happy face! Inhibitory control and socioemotional knowledge predict emotion regulation in 5- to 7-year-olds. *Journal of Experimental Child Psychology, 123,* 36–52.

Hudson, N.W., Fraley, R.C., Chopik, W.J., & Hefferman, M.E. (2015). Not all attachment relationships change alike: Normative cross-sectional age trajectories in attachment to romantic partners, friends, and parents across the lifespan. *Journal of Research in Personality, 59,* 44–55.

Hudson, R.B. (2016). Politics and policies of aging in the United States. In L.K. George & K.F. Ferraro (Eds.), *Handbook of aging and the social sciences* (8th ed.). New York: Elsevier.

Hudziak, J., & Archangeli, C. (2017). The future of preschool prevention, assessment, and intervention. *Child and Adolescent Psychiatric Clinics of North America, 26,* 611–624.

Huelsnitz, C.O., & others (2018, in press). Attachment and jealousy: Understanding the dynamic experience of jealousy using the response escalation paradigm. *Personality and Social Psychology Bulletin.*

Huesmann, L.R., Dubow, E.F., Eron, L.D., & Boxer, P. (2006). Middle childhood family-contextual and personal factors as predictors of adult outcomes. In A.G. Huston & M.N. Ripke (Eds.), *Developmental contexts in middle childhood: Bridges to adolescence and adulthood.* New York: Cambridge University Press.

Huffman, J.C., & others (2016). Effects of optimism and gratitude on physical activity, biomarkers, and readmissions after an acute coronary syndrome: The Gratitude Research in Acute Coronary Events Study. *Circulation: Cardiovascular Quality and Outcomes, 9,* 55–63.

Hughes, C., Devine, R.T., & Wang, Z. (2018, in press). Does parental mind-mindedness account for cross-cultural differences in preschoolers' theory of mind? *Child Development.*

Hughes, C., Marks, A., Ensor, R., & Lecce, S. (2010). A longitudinal study of conflict and inner state talk in children's conversations with mothers and younger siblings. *Social Development, 19,* 822–837.

Hughes, E.K., & others (2018, in press). A case series of family-based treatment for adolescents with atypical anorexia nervosa. *International Journal of Eating Disorders.*

Hughes, J.C., Volicer, L., & van der Steen, J.T. (2018). Complexity and gaps: The high-hanging fruit of dementia and palliative care research. *Palliative Medicine, 32,* 591–593.

Hughes, J.N., & Cao, Q. (2018). Trajectories of teacher-student warmth and conflict at the transition to middle school: Effects on academic engagement and achievement. *Journal of School Psychology, 67,* 148–162.

Huo, M., & Fingerman, K.L. (2018). Grandparents. In M.H. Bornstein (Ed.), *SAGE encyclopedia of lifespan human development.* Thousand Oaks, CA: Sage.

Huo, M., & others (2018, in press). Support grandparents give to their adult grandchildren. *Journals of Gerontology B: Psychological Sciences and Social Sciences.*

Huo, M., & others (2018a, in press). Aging parents' daily support exchanges with adult children suffering problems. *Journals of Gerontology B: Psychological Sciences and Social Sciences.*

Huo, M., & others (2018b, in press). Aging parents' disabilities and daily support exchanges with middle-aged children. *Gerontologist.*

Hurrell, K.E., Houwing, F.L., & Hudson, J.L. (2017). Parental meta-emotion philosophy and emotion coaching in families of children and adolescents with an anxiety disorder. *Journal of Abnormal Child Psychology, 45,* 569–582.

Hurst, S.A., & Mauron, A. (2017). Assisted suicide in Switzerland: Clarifying the liberties and claims. *Bioethics, 31* 199–208.

Hustedt, J.T., Friedman, A.H., & Barnett, W.S. (2012). Investments in early education: Resources at the federal and state levels. In R.C. Pianta (Ed.), *Handbook of early childhood education.* New York: Guilford.

Huston, A.C., & Ripke, N.N. (2006). Experiences in middle and late childhood and children's development. In A.C. Huston & M.N. Ripke (Eds.), *Developmental contexts in middle childhood.* New York: Cambridge University Press.

Huston, T.L., & Holmes, E.K. (2004). Becoming parents. In A.L. Vangelisti (Ed.), *Handbook of family communication.* Mahwah, NJ: Erlbaum.

Huttenlocher, P.R., & Dabholkar, A.S. (1997). Regional differences in synaptogenesis in human cerebral cortex. *Journal of Comparative Neurology, 37*(2), 167–178.

Hyde, J.S. (2014). Gender similarities and differences. *Annual Review of Psychology* (Vol. 65). Palo Alto, CA: Annual Reviews.

Hyde, J.S. (2017). Gender similarities. In C.B. Travis & J.W. White (Eds.), *APA handbook of the psychology of women.* Washington, DC: American Psychological Association.

Hyde, J.S., & DeLamater, J.D. (2017). *Understanding human sexuality* (13th ed.). New York: McGraw-Hill.

Hyde, J.S., & Else-Quest, N. (2013). *Half the human experience* (8th ed.). Boston: Cengage.

Hyde, J.S., Lindberg, S.M., Linn, M.C., Ellis, A.B., & Williams, C.C. (2008). Gender similarities characterize math performance. *Science, 321,* 494–495.

Hyson, M.C., Copple, C., & Jones, J. (2006). Early childhood development and education. In W. Damon & R. Lerner (Eds.), *Handbook of child psychology* (6th ed.). New York: Wiley.

I

Igarashi, H., Hooker, K., Coehlo, D.P., & Manoogian, M.M. (2013). "My nest is full": Intergenerational relationships at midlife. *Journal of Aging Studies, 27,* 102–112.

Ihara, M., & Washida, K. (2018). Linking atrial fibrillation with Alzheimer's disease: Epidemiological, pathological, and mechanistic evidence. *Journal of Alzheimer's Disease, 62,* 61–72.

Ihle, A., & others (2015). The association of leisure activities in middle adulthood with cognitive performance in old age: The moderating role of educational level. *Gerontology, 61,* 543–550.

Ihongbe, T.O., Cha, S., & Masho, S.W. (2017). Age of sexual debut and physical dating violence victimization: Sex differences among U.S. high school students. *Journal of School Health, 87,* 200–208.

Ilmakunnas, P., & Ilmakunnas, S. (2018). Health and retirement age: Comparison of expectations and actual retirement. *Scandinavian Journal of Public Health, 46*(Suppl. 19), S18–S31.

Im, Y., Oh, W.O., & Suk, M. (2017). Risk factors for suicide ideation among adolescents: Five-year national data analysis. *Archives of Psychiatric Nursing, 31,* 282–286.

Inderkum, A.P., & Tarokh, L. (2018, in press). High heritability of adolescent sleep-wake behavior on free, but not school days: A long-term twin study. *Sleep.*

Insel, P., & Roth, W.T. (2018). *Core concepts in health* (15th ed.). New York: McGraw-Hill.

Insel, P., & Walton, R. (2018). *Connect core concepts in health, brief* (15th ed.). New York: McGraw-Hill.

International Montessori Council (2006). *Larry Page and Sergey Brin, founders of Google.com, credit their Montessori education for much of their success on prime-time television.* Retrieved June 24, 2006, from www.Montessori.org/enews/barbara_walters.html

Isgut, M., & others (2017). The impact of psychological distress during pregnancy on the developing fetus: Biological mechanisms and the potential benefits of mindfulness interventions. *Journal of Perinatal Medicine, 45,* 999-1011.

Ishi, R., & others (2018, in press). Healthy and pathological brain aging: From the perspectives of oscillations, functional connectivity, and signal complexity. *Neuropsychobiology.*

Ishtiak-Ahmed, K., & others (2018, in press). Social relations at work and incident dementia: 29-years' follow-up of the Copenhagen Male Study. *Journal of Occupational and Environmental Medicine.*

Isidori, A.M., & others (2014). A critical analysis of the role of testosterone in erectile function: From pathophysiology to treatment—a systematic analysis. *European Urology, 65*(1), 99–112.

Islam, B.U., & others (2017). Exploration of various proteins for the treatment of Alzheimer's disease. *Current Drug Metabolism, 18,* 808–813.

Ismaeel, N., & Wang, R. (2017). Testosterone replacement—freedom from symptoms or hormonal shackles? *Sexual Medicine Reviews, 5,* 81–86.

Ismail, F.Y., Fatemi, A., & Johnston, M.V. (2017). Cerebral plasticity: Windows of opportunity for the developing brain. *European Journal of Pediatric Neurology, 21,* 23–48.

Israel, M. (2019). Semantics. In C. Genetti (Ed.), *How languages work* (2nd ed.). New York: Cambridge University Press.

Ito-Jager, S., & others (2017). Attention focus and self-touch in toddlers: The moderating effect of attachment security. *Infant Behavior and Development, 48*(Pt. B), 114–123.

Ivey-Stephenson, A.Z., & others (2017). Suicide trends among and within urbanization by sex, race/ethnicity, age group, and mechanism of death—United States 2001-2015. *MMWR Surveillance Summary, 66*(18), 1–16.

Iwata, S., & others (2012). Qualitative brain MRI at term and cognitive outcomes at 9 years after very preterm birth. *Pediatrics, 129,* e1138-1147.

J

Jabeen, H., & others (2018). Investigating the scavenging of reactive oxygen species by antioxidants via theoretical and experimental methods. *Journal of Photochemistry and Photobiology B, 180,* 268–275.

Jacher, J.E., & others (2017). Pulmonary arterial hypertension: Specialists' knowledge, practices, and attitudes of genetic counseling and genetic testing in the USA. *Pulmonary Circulation, 7,* 372–383.

Jackson, J.J., & Roberts, B.W. (2016). Conscientiousness. In T.A. Widiger (Ed.), *Oxford handbook of the five factor model.* New York: Oxford University Press.

Jackson, J.J., & others (2009). Not all conscientiousness scales change alike: A multimethod, multisample study of age differences in the facets of conscientiousness. *Journal of Personality and Social Psychology, 96,* 446–459.

Jackson, M.I. (2015). Early childhood WIC participation, cognitive development, and academic achievement. *Social Science and Medicine, 126,* 145–153.

Jackson, W.M., & others (2016). Physical activity and cognitive development: A meta-analysis. *Journal of Neurosurgery and Anesthesiology, 28,* 373–380.

Jacobs, J.M., Hammerman-Rozenberg, R., Cohen, A., & Stressman, J. (2008). Reading daily predicts reduced mortality among men from a cohort of community dwelling 70-year-olds. *Journals of Gerontology B: Psychological Sciences and Social Sciences, 63,* S73–S80.

Jacobson, S.W., & others (2017). Heavy prenatal alcohol exposure is related to smaller corpus callosum in newborn MRI scans. *Alcoholism: Clinical and Experimental Research, 41,* 965–975.

Jacoby, N., Overfeld, J., Brinder, E.B., & Heim, C.M. (2016). Stress neurobiology and developmental psychopathology. In D. Cicchetti (Ed.), *Developmental psychopathology* (3rd ed.). New York: Wiley.

Jadhav, A., & Weir, D. (2018, in press). Widowhood and depression in a cross-national perspective: Evidence from the United States, Europe, Korea, and China. *Journals of Gerontology B: Psychological Sciences and Social Sciences.*

JafariNasabian, P., & others (2017). Osteosarcopenic obesity in women: Impact, prevalence, and management challenges. *International Journal of Women's Health, 9,* 33–42.

Jaffee, S., & Hyde, J.S. (2000). Gender differences in moral orientation: A meta-analysis. *Psychological Bulletin, 126,* 703–726.

Jakobsen, I.S., Larsen, K.J., & Horwood, J.L. (2017). Suicide risk assessment in adolescents—C-SSRS, K20, and READ. *Crisis, 38,* 247–254.

Jambon, M., & Smetana, J.G. (2018, in press). Individual differences in prototypical moral and conventional judgments and children's proactive and reactive aggression. *Child Development.*

James, W. (1890/1950). *The principles of psychology.* New York: Dover.

Jang, S., & others (2017). Measurement invariance of the Satisfaction with Life Scale across 26 countries. *Journal of Cross-Cultural Psychology, 48,* 560–576.

Jannini, E.A., & Nappi, R.E. (2018). Couplepause: A new paradigm in treating sexual dysfunction during menopause and andropause. *Sexual Medicine Reviews, 6,* 384–395.

Jansen, J., de Weerth, C., & Riksen-Walraven, J.M. (2008). Breastfeeding and the mother-infant relationship—A review. *Developmental Review, 28,* 503–521.

Janssen, I., & others (2005). Comparison of overweight and obesity prevalence in school-aged youth from 34 countries and their relationships with physical activity and dietary patterns. *Obesity Reviews, 6,* 123–132.

Janssen, J.A., & others (2017). Childhood temperament predictors of adolescent physical activity. *BMC Public Health, 17*(1), 8.

Janssens, A., & others (2017). Adolescent externalizing behavior, psychological control, and rejection: Transactional links and dopaminergic moderation. *British Journal of Developmental Psychology, 35,* 420–438.

Janz, K.F., & Baptista, F. (2018). Bone strength and exercise during youth—the year that was 2017. *Pediatric Exercise Science, 30,* 28–31.

Jaramillo, N., & others (2017). Associations between sex education and contraceptive use among heterosexually active, adolescent males in the United States. *Journal of Adolescent Health, 60,* 534–540.

Jardri, R., & others (2012). Assessing fetal response to maternal speech using a noninvasive functional brain imaging technique. *International Journal of Developmental Neuroscience, 30,* 159–161.

Jaremka, L.M., Derry, H., & Kiecolt-Glaser, J.K. (2016). Psychoneuroimmunology of interpersonal relationships: Both the presence/absence of social ties and relationship quality matter. In D.I. Mostofksy (Ed.), *Handbook of behavioral medicine.* New York: Wiley.

Jarris, P.E., & others (2017). Group prenatal care compared with traditional prenatal care: A systematic review and meta-analysis. *Obstetrics and Gynecology, 129,* 384–385.

Jaruatanasirikul, S., & others (2017). A population-based study of Down syndrome in Southern Thailand. *World Journal of Pediatrics, 13,* 63–69.

Jasinska, K.K., & Petitto, L-A. (2018). Age of bilingual exposure is related to the contribution of phonological and semantic knowledge to successful reading development. *Child Development, 89,* 310–331.

Jasiulionis, M.G. (2018). Abnormal epigenetic regulation of immune system during aging. *Frontiers in Immunology, 9,* 197.

Jaul, E., & Barron, J. (2017). Age-related diseases and clinical and public health implications for the 85 years old and over population. *Frontiers in Public Health, 5,* 335.

Jarvis, S.N., & Okonofua, J.A. (2020). School deferred: When bias affects school leaders. *Social Psychological and Personality Science, 11,* 492–498.

Jaworska, N., & others (2018, in press). Aerobic exercise in depressed youth: A feasibility and clinical outcomes pilot. *Early Intervention in Psychiatry.*

Jenni, O.G., and Carskadon, M.A. (2007). Sleep behavior and sleep regulation from infancy through adolescence: Normative aspects. In O.G. Jenni and M.A. Carskadon (Eds.), *Sleep medicine clinics: Sleep in children and adolescents.* Philadelphia: W.B. Saunders.

Jennifer, R.E. (2018). *International handbook of positive aging.* New York: Routledge.

Jensen, H., & Tubaek, G. (2018, in press). Elderly people need an eye examination before entering nursing homes. *Danish Medical Journal.*

Jensen, L.A. (2018). The cultural-developmental approach to moral psychology: Autonomy, community, and diversity across cultures and age. In M.J. Gelfand & others (Eds.), *Handbook of advances in culture and psychology* (Vol. 7). New York: Oxford University Press.

Jensen, M.M., & others (2015). Prostate stem cell antigen interacts with nicotinic acetylcholine receptors and is affected in Alzheimer's disease. *Neurobiology of Aging, 36,* 1629-1638.

Jensen, T.M., & others (2018, in press). Stepfamily relationship quality and children's internalizing and externalizing problems. *Family Process.*

Jeong, K.S., & others (2017). High maternal blood mercury level is associated with low verbal IQ in children. *Journal of Korean Medical Science, 32,* 1097-1104.

Jeong, Y., & others (2018). Placental transfer of persistent organic pollutants and feasibility of using the placenta as a non-invasive biomonitoring matrix. *Science of the Total Environment, 612,* 1498-1505.

Jeremic, S., & others (2018, in press). Selected anthraquinones as potential free radical scavengers and P-glycoprotein inhibitors. *Organic and Biomedical Chemistry.*

Ji, B.T., & others (1997). Paternal cigarette smoking and the risk of childhood cancer among offspring of nonsmoking mothers. *Journal of the National Cancer Institute, 89,* 238-244.

Ji, J., Negriff, S., Klim, H., & Susman, E.J. (2016). A study of cortisol reactivity and recovery among young adolescents: Heterogeneity and longitudinal stability and change. *Developmental Psychobiology, 58,* 283-302.

Jia, G., Hill, M.A., & Sowers, J.A. (2018). Diabetic cardiomyopathy: An update of mechanisms contributing to this clinical entity. *Circulation Research, 122,* 624-638.

Jia, R., & Schoppe-Sullivan, S.J. (2011). Relations between coparenting and father involvement in families with preschool-age children. *Developmental Psychology, 47,* 106-118.

Jiang, N., & others (2018). Meta-analysis of the efficacy and safety of combined surgery in the management of eyes with coexisting cataract and open angle glaucoma. *International Journal of Ophthalmology, 11,* 279-286.

Jiang, X., & others (2018). Hope and adolescent mental health. In M.W. Gallagher & S.J. Lopez (Eds.), *Oxford handbook of hope.* New York: Oxford University Press.

Jiang, Y., Granja, M.R., & Koball, H. (2017). *Basic facts about low-income children.* New York: National Center for Children in Poverty, Columbia University.

Jiang, Z., & others (2017). Event-related theta oscillatory substrates for facilitation and interference effects of negative emotion on children's cognition. *International Journal of Psychophysiology, 116,* 26-31.

Jiao, S., Ji, G., & Jing, Q. (1996). Cognitive development of Chinese urban only children and children with siblings. *Child Development, 67,* 387-395.

Jin, I., & others (2018). Young infants expect an unfamiliar adult to comfort a crying baby: Evidence from a standard violation-of-expectation task and a novel infant-triggered video task. *Cognitive Psychology, 102,* 1-20.

John, A., & others (2018). Self-harm, suicidal behaviors, and cyberbullying in children and young people: Systematic review. *Journal of Medical Internet Research, 20*(4), e129.

Johns Hopkins University (2006, February 17). *Undergraduate honored for launching health program in India.* Baltimore: Johns Hopkins University News Releases.

Johnson, J.A., Xu, J., & Cox, R.M. (2017). Impact of hearing aid technology on outcomes in daily life III: Localization. *Ear and Hearing, 38,* 746-759.

Johnson, J.A., & others (2018). *Foundations of American education* (17th ed.). Upper Saddle River, NJ: Pearson.

Johnson, J.S., & Newport, E.L. (1991). Critical period effects on universal properties of language: The status of subjacency in the acquisition of a second language. *Cognition, 39,* 215-258.

Johnson, L.S.M. (2017). Death by neurological criteria: Definitions and lay misgivings. *QJM, 110,* 267-270.

Johnson, M.D. (2017). *Human biology* (8th ed.). Upper Saddle River, NJ: Pearson.

Johnson, M.H. (2008, April 30). *Commentary in R. Highfield, Harvard's baby brain research lab.* Retrieved January 24, 2008, from http://www.telegraph.co.uk/ science/science-news/3341166/Harvards-baby-brain-research-lab.html

Johnson, P. (2018). *The emotional needs of young children.* New York: Routledge.

Johnson, S.P. (2010). How infants learn about the visual world. *Cognitive Science, 34,* 1158-1184.

Johnson, S.P. (2011). A constructivist view of object perception in infancy. In L.M. Oakes & others (Eds.), *Infant perception and cognition.* New York: Oxford University Press.

Johnson, S.P. (2013). Object perception. In P.D. Zelazo (Ed.), *Handbook of developmental psychology.* New York: Oxford University Press.

Johnson, S.P., & Hannon, E.E. (2015). Perceptual development. In R.M. Lerner (Ed.), *Handbook of child psychology and developmental science* (7th ed.). New York: Wiley.

Johnston, C., & others (2017). Skin-to-skin care for procedural pain in neonates. *Cochrane Database of Systematic Reviews, 2,* CD008435.

Johnston, L.D., & others (2015). *Monitoring the future: National survey results on drug use, 1974-2014. Vol 2: College students and adults ages 19-55.* Ann Arbor: University of Michigan Institute for Social Research.

Johnston, L.D., & others (2018). *Monitoring the future: National survey results on drug use, 1975-2017.* Ann Arbor, MI: Institute for Social Research, University of Michigan.

Joling, K.J., & others (2018). Quality indicators for community care for older people: A systematic review. *PLoS One, 13*(1), e0190298.

Jolly, C.A. (2005). Diet manipulation and prevention of aging, cancer, and autoimmune disease. *Current Opinions in Clinical Nutrition and Metabolic Care, 8,* 382-387.

Jones, C.R.G., & others (2018). The association between theory of mind, executive function, and the symptoms of autistic spectrum disorder. *Autism Research, 11,* 95-109.

Jones, D.G., & Nie, J.B. (2018, in press). Does Confucianism allow for body donation? *Anatomical Sciences Education.*

Jones, E., & Reynolds, G. (2011). *The play's the thing: Teachers' roles in children's play.* New York: Columbia University Press.

Jones, E.J.H., & others (2017). Parent-delivered early intervention in infants at risk for ASD: Effects on electrophysiological and habituation measures of social attention. *Autism Research, 10,* 961-972.

Jones, L., & others (2017). Nociceptive cortical activity is dissociated from nociceptive behavior in newborn human infants under stress. *Current Biology, 27,* 3846-3851.

Jones, M.C. (1965). Psychological correlates of somatic development. *Child Development, 36,* 899-911.

Jones, T.H., & Kelly, D.M. (2018, in press). Randomized controlled trials—mechanistic studies of testosterone and the cardiovascular system. *Asian Journal of Andrology.*

Jorgensen, M.J., & others (2015). Sexual behavior among young Danes aged 15-29 years: A cross-sectional study of core indicators. *Sexually Transmitted Infections, 91,* 171-177.

Jose, A., O'Leary, K.D., & Moyer, A. (2010). Does premarital cohabitation predict subsequent marital stability and marital quality? A meta-analysis. *Journal of Marriage and the Family, 72,* 105-116.

Joseph, J. (2006). *The missing gene.* New York: Algora.

Jouffre, S., & others (2018, in press). Personalizing patients' advance directives decreases the willingness of intensive care unit residents to stop treatment: A randomized study. *Journal of Palliative Medicine.*

Juang, C., & others (2018, in press). Understanding the mechanisms of change in a lifestyle intervention for older adults. *Gerontologist.*

Juang, L.P., & others (2018, in press). Time-varying associations of parent-adolescent cultural conflict and youth adjustment among Chinese American families. *Developmental Psychology.*

Judd, F.K., Hickey, M., & Bryant, C. (2012). Depression and midlife: Are we overpathologizing the menopause? *Journal of Affective Disorders, 136,* 199-211.

Juhasz, A., & others (2017). How efficient is subthalamic deep brain stimulation in reducing dyskinesia in Parkinson's disease? *European Neurology, 77,* 281-287.

Julvez, J., & others (2016). Maternal consumption of seafood in pregnancy and child neuropsychological development: A longitudinal study based on a population with high consumption levels. *American Journal of Epidemiology, 183,* 169-182.

Jung, C. (1933). *Modern man in search of a soul.* New York: Harcourt Brace.

Jung, E.Y., & others (2017). Amniotic fluid infection, cytokine levels, and mortality and adverse pulmonary, intestinal, and neurologic outcomes in infants at 32 weeks' gestation or less. *Journal of Korean Medical Science, 32,* 480-487.

Jung, S., & others (2017). Location and modality effects in online dating: Rich modality and location-based information cues increase social presence, while moderating the impact of uncertainty reduction strategy. *Cyberpsychology, Behavior, and Social Networking, 20,* 553-560.

Juraska, J.M., & Willing. J. (2017). Pubertal onset as a critical transition for neural development and cognition. *Brain Research, 1654*(Pt. B), 87-94.

K

Kader, F., Ghai, M., & Mahraj, L. (2018, in press). The effects of DNA methylation on human psychology. *Behavioral Brain Research.*

Kagan, J. (1987). Perspectives on infancy. In J.D. Osofsky (Ed.), *Handbook of infant development* (2nd ed.). New York: Wiley.

Kagan, J. (2002). Behavioral inhibition as a temperamental category. In R.J. Davidson, K.R. Scherer, & H.H. Goldsmith (Eds.), *Handbook of affective sciences.* New York: Oxford University Press.

Kagan, J. (2010). Emotions and temperament. In M.H. Bornstein (Ed.), *Handbook of cultural developmental science.* New York: Psychology Press.

Kagan, J. (2013). Temperamental contributions to inhibited and uninhibited profiles. In P.D. Zelazo (Ed.), *Oxford handbook of developmental psychology.* New York: Oxford University Press.

Kagan, J. (2018). Perspectives on two temperamental biases. *Philosophical transactions of the Royal Society of London, Series B: Biological Sciences, 373,* 1744.

Kagan, J.J., Kearsley, R.B., & Zelazo, P.R. (1978). *Infancy: Its place in human development.* Cambridge, MA: Harvard University Press.

Kahlbaugh, P., & Huffman, L. (2017). Personality, emotional qualities of leisure, and subjective well-being in the elderly. *International Journal of Aging and Human Development, 85,* 164-184.

Kahn, N.F., & Halpern, C.T. (2018, in press). Associations between patterns of sexual initiation, sexual partnering, and sexual health outcomes from adolescence to early adulthood. *Archives of Sexual Behavior.*

Kahrs, B.A., Jung, W.P., & Lockman, J.J. (2013). Motor origins of tool use. *Child Development, 84*(3), 810-818.

Kalashnikova, M., Goswami, U., & Burnham, D. (2018, in press). Mothers speak differently to infants at-risk for dyslexia. *Developmental Science.*

Kalat, J.W. (2019). *Biological psychology* (13th ed.). Boston: Cengage.

Kalish, R.A. (1981). *Death, grief, and caring relationships,* Monterey, CA: Brooks/Cole.

Kalsi, D.S. (2015) What is the effect of fasting on the lifespan of neurons? *Aging Research Reviews, 24,* 160-165.

Kamal, M.A., & others (2017). Inhibition of butyrylcholinesterase with fluorobenzylcymserine, an experimental Alzheimer's drug candidate: Validation of enzoinformatics results by classical and innovative enzyme kinetic analyses. *CNS & Neurological Disorders Drug Targets, 16,* 820–827.

Kancherla, V., & Oakley, G.P. (2018). Total prevention of folic acid-preventable spina bifida and anencephaly would reduce child mortality in India: Implications in achieving Target 3.2 of the Sustainable Development Goals. *Birth Defects Research, 110,* 421–428.

Kandler, C., & others (2016). The nature of creativity: The roles of genetic factors, personality traits, cognitive abilities, and environmental sources. *Journal of Personality and Social Psychology, 111,* 230–249.

Kane, R.L., Saliba, D., & Hollmann, P. (2017). The evolving health policy landscape and suggested geriatric tenets to guide future responses. *Journal of the American Geriatrics Society, 65,* 162–165.

Kanesarajah, J., & others (2018). Multimorbidity and quality of life at mid-life: A systematic review of general population studies. *Maturitas, 109,* 53–62.

Kang, X., & others (2017). Post-mortem whole-body magnetic resonance imaging of human fetuses: A comparison of 3-T vs. 1.5-T MR imaging with classical autopsy. *European Radiology, 27,* 3542–3553.

Kann, L., & others (2016a, June 10). Youth Risk Behavior Surveillance—United States, 2015. *MMWR, 65,* 1–174.

Kann, L., & others (2016b, August 12). Sexual identity, sex of sexual contacts, and health-related behaviors among students in grades 9–12—United States and selected sites, 2015. *MMWR Surveillance Summary, 65*(9), 1–202.

Kanniyakonil, S. (2018, in press). New developments in India concerning the policy of passive euthanasia. *Developing World Bioethics.*

Kansky, J., Ruzek, E., & Allen, J. (2018). Observing adolescent relationships: Autonomy processes in parent, peer, and romantic relationships. In B. Soenens, M. Vansteenkiste, & S. Van Petegem (Eds.), *Autonomy in adolescent development.* New York: Routledge.

Kantoch, A., & others (2018, in press). Treatment of cardiovascular diseases among elderly residents of long-term care facilities. *Journal of the American Medical Directors Association.*

Kantrowitz, B., & Namuth, T. (1991, Summer). The good, the bad, and the difference. *Newsweek, 117,* 48–50.

Kaplan, R.M., & Saccuzzo, D.P. (2018). *Psychological testing* (9th ed.). Boston: Cengage.

Karoly, L.A., & Bigelow, J.H. (2005). *The economics of investing in universal preschool education in California.* Santa Monica, CA: RAND Corporation.

Karreman, A., van Tuijl, C., van Aken, M.A., & Dekovic, M. (2008). Parenting, coparenting, and effortful control in preschoolers. *Journal of Family Psychology, 22,* 30–40.

Karthivashan, G., & others (2018). Therapeutic strategies and nano-drug delivery applications in management of aging Alzheimer's disease. *Drug Delivery, 25,* 307–320.

Kaseva, N., & others (2018, in press). Pre-pregnancy overweight or obesity and gestational diabetes as predictors of body composition in offspring twenty years later: Evidence from two birth cohort studies. *International Journal of Obesity.*

Kashdan, T.B., & others (2018). Sexuality leads to boosts in mood and meaning in life with no evidence for the reverse direction: A daily diary investigation. *Emotion, 18,* 563–576.

Kastenbaum, R.J. (2009). *Death, society, and human experience* (10th ed.). Boston: Allyn & Bacon.

Kastenbaum, R.J. (2012). *Death, society, and human experience* (11th ed.). Boston: Allyn & Bacon.

Kato, T., & others (2016). Extremely preterm infants small for gestational age are at risk for motor impairment at 3 years corrected age. *Brain Development, 38,* 188–195.

Katsiaficas, D. (2017). "I know I'm an adult when . . . I can care for myself and others." *Emerging Adulthood, 5,* 392–405.

Katz, L. (1999). *Curriculum disputes in early childhood education.* ERIC Clearinghouse on Elementary and Early Childhood Education, Document EDO-PS-99-13.

Katz-Wise, S.L., & others (2018, in press). Sexual fluidity and social determinants of mental health in gender minority adults in Massachusetts. *Archives of Sexual Behavior.*

Kauffman, J.M., McGee, K., & Brigham, M. (2004). Enabling or disabling? Observations on changes in special education. *Phi Delta Kappan, 85,* 613–620.

Kaufman, S.B., & others (2016). Openness to experience and intellect differentially predict creative achievement in the arts and sciences. *Journal of Personality, 84,* 248–258.

Kaunhoven, R.J., & Dorjee, D. (2017). How does mindfulness modulate self-regulation in pre-adolescent children? An integrative neurocognitive review. *Neuroscience and Biobehavioral Reviews, 74*(Pt. A), 163–184.

Kauppila, T.E., Kauppila, J.H., & Larsson, N.G. (2017). Mammalian mitochondria and aging: An update. *Cell Metabolism, 25,* 57–71.

Kavanaugh, R.D. (2006). Pretend play and theory of mind. In L.L. Balter & C.S. Tamis-LeMonda (Eds.), *Child psychology* (2nd ed.). New York: Psychology Press.

Kavosi, Z., & others (2015). A comparison of mothers' quality of life after normal vaginal, cesarean, and water birth deliveries. *International Journal of Community Based Nursing and Midwifery, 3,* 198–204.

Kavsek, M. (2013). The comparator model of infant visual habituation and dishabituation: Recent insights. *Developmental Psychobiology, 55,* 793–808.

Kawakita, T., & others (2016). Adverse maternal and neonatal outcomes in adolescent pregnancy. *Journal of Pediatric and Adolescent Gynecology, 29,* 130–136.

Kazdin, A.E. (2017). *REVEL for research design in clinical psychology* (5th ed.). Upper Saddle River, NJ: Pearson.

Keating, D.P. (1990). Adolescent thinking. In S.S. Feldman & G.R. Elliott (Eds.), *At the threshold: The developing adolescent.* Cambridge, MA: Harvard University Press.

Keen, R. (2011). The development of problem solving in young children: A critical cognitive skill. *Annual Review of Psychology* (Vol. 62). Palo Alto, CA: Annual Reviews.

Keen, R., Lee, M-H., & Adolph, K.E. (2014). Planning an action: A developmental progression for tool use. *Ecological Psychology, 26,* 98–108.

Keim, M.C., & others (2017). Parent distress and the decision to have another child after an infant's death in the NICU. *Journal of Obstetric, Gynecologic, and Neonatal Nursing, 46,* 446–455.

Keles, S., & others (2016). Depression among unaccompanied minor refugees: The relative contribution of general and acculturation-specific daily hassles. *Ethnicity and Health, 21,* 300–317.

Keller, A., Ford, L., & Meacham, J. (1978). Dimensions of self-concept in preschool children. *Developmental Psychology, 14,* 483–489.

Kelley, C.P., Soboroff, S.D., & Lovaglia, M.J. (2017). The status value of age. *Social Science Research, 66,* 22–31.

Kelley-Moore, J. (2009). Chronic illness, adulthood and later life. In D. Carr (Ed.), *Encyclopedia of the life course and human development.* Boston: Gale Cengage.

Kelly, C., & others (2018, in press). The effectiveness of a classroom-based phonological awareness program for 4-5-year-olds. *International Journal of Speech-Language Pathology.*

Kelly, J.P., Borchert, J., & Teller, D.Y. (1997). The development of chromatic and achromatic sensitivity in infancy as tested with the sweep VEP. *Vision Research, 37,* 2057–2072.

Keltner, K.W. (2013). *Tiger babies strike back.* New York: William Morrow.

Kemmler, W., Engelke, K., & von Stengel, S. (2016). Long-term exercise and bone mineral density changes in postmenopausal women—are there periods of reduced effectiveness? *Journal of Bone and Mineral Research, 31,* 215–222.

Kemmler, W., Kohl, M., & von Stengel, S. (2017). Long-term effects of exercise in postmenopausal women: 16-year results of the Erlangen Fitness and Osteoporosis Prevention study (EFOPS). *Menopause, 24,* 45–51.

Kemp, J., Despres, O., Pebayle, T., & Dufour, A. (2014). Age-related decrease in sensitivity to electrical stimulation is unrelated to skin conductance: An evoked potentials study. *Clinical Neurophysiology, 125,* 602–607.

Kendler, K.S., & others (2017). Divorce and the onset of alcohol use disorder: A Swedish population-based longitudinal cohort and co-relative study. *American Journal of Psychiatry, 174,* 45–58.

Kendler, K.S., Ohlsson, H., Sundquist, K., & Sundquist, J. (2016). The rearing environment and risk for drug use: A Swedish national high-risk adopted and not adopted co-sibling control study. *Psychological Medicine, 46,* 1359–1366.

Kendler, K.S., & others (2018). Prediction of drug abuse recurrence: A Swedish national study. *Psychological Medicine, 48,* 1367–1374.

Kendrick, K., Jutengren, G., & Stattin, H. (2012). The protective role of supportive friends against bullying perpetration and victimization. *Journal of Adolescence, 35*(4), 1069–1080.

Kennedy, K.M., & others (2017). Dynamic range in BOLD modulation: Lifespan aging trajectories and association with performance. *Neurobiology of Aging, 60,* 153–163.

Kennell, J.H. (2006). Randomized controlled trial of skin-to-skin contact from birth versus conventional incubator for physiological stabilization in 1200 g to 2199 g newborns. *Acta Paediatrica* (Sweden), *95,* 15–16.

Kennell, J.H., & McGrath, S.K. (1999). Commentary: Practical and humanistic lessons from the third world for perinatal caregivers everywhere. *Birth, 26,* 9–10.

Kerns, K.A., & Brumariu, L.E. (2016). Attachment in middle childhood. In J. Cassidy & P. Shaver (Eds.), *Handbook of attachment* (3rd ed.). New York: Guilford.

Kerns, K.A., & Seibert, A.C. (2012). Finding your way through the thicket: Promising approaches to assessing attachment in middle childhood. In E. Waters & B. Vaughn (Eds.), *Measuring attachment.* New York: Guilford.

Kershaw, K.N., & others (2014). Associations of stressful life events and social strain with incident cardiovascular disease in the Women's Health Initiative. *Journal of the American Heart Association, 3*(3), e000687.

Kerstis, B., Aslund, C., & Sonnby, K. (2018). More secure attachment to the father and the mother is associated with fewer depressive symptoms in adolescence. *Upsala Journal of Medical Sciences, 123,* 62–67.

Kerstis, B., & others (2016). Association between parental depressive symptoms and impaired bonding with the infant. *Archives of Women's Mental Health, 19,* 87–94.

Keunen, K., Counsell, S.J., & Benders, M.J.N.L. (2017). The emergence of functional architecture during early brain development. *NeuroImage, 160,* 2–14.

Khalsa, A.S., & others (2017). Attainment of '5-2-1-0' obesity recommendations in preschool-aged children. *Preventive Medicine Reports, 8,* 79–87.

Kharitonova, M., Winter, W., & Sheridan, M.A. (2015). As working memory grows: A developmental account of neural bases of working memory capacity in 5- to 8-year-old children and adults. *Journal of Cognitive Neuroscience, 27,* 1775–1788.

Khashan, A.S., Baker, P.N., & Kenny, L.C. (2010). Preterm birth and reduced birthweight in first and second teenage pregnancies: A register-based cohort study. *BMC Pregnancy and Childbirth, 10,* 36.

Khatun, M., & others (2017). Do children born to teenage parents have lower adult intelligence? A prospective birth cohort study. *PloS Once, 12*(3), e0167395.

Khoury, J.E., & Milligan, K. (2018, in press). Comparing executive functioning in children and adolescents with fetal alcohol spectrum disorders and ADHD: A meta-analysis. *Journal of Attention Disorders.*

Khundrakpam, B.S., & others (2018, in press). Exploring individual brain variability during development based on patterns of maturational coupling of cortical thickness: A longitudinal MRI study. *Cerebral Cortex*.

Kiang, L., Witkow, M.R., & Champagne, M.C. (2013). Normative changes in ethnic and American identities and links with adjustment among Asian American adolescents. *Developmental Psychology, 49*, 1713–1722.

Kida, Y., & Goligorsky, M.S. (2016). Sirtuins, cell senescence, and vascular aging. *Canadian Journal of Cardiology, 32*, 634–641.

Kiecolt-Glaser, J.K., & Wilson, S. (2017). Lovesick: Couples' relationships and health. *Annual Review of Clinical Psychology*. Palo Alto, CA: Annual Reviews.

Kiecolt-Glaser, J.K., & others (2014). Yoga's impact on inflammation, mood, and fatigue in breast cancer survivors: A randomized controlled trial. *Journal of Clinical Oncology, 32*, 1040–1049.

Kilic, A., Sayali, Z.C., & Oztekin, I. (2017). Aging slows access to temporal information from working memory. *Journals of Gerontology B: Psychological Sciences and Social Sciences, 72*, 996–1005.

Kilic, S., & others (2012). Environmental tobacco smoke exposure during intrauterine period promotes granulosa cell apoptosis: A prospective, randomized study. *Journal of Maternal-Fetal and Neonatal Medicine, 25*(10), 1904–1908.

Killen, M., & Dahl, A., (2018). Moral judgment: Reflective, interactive, spontaneous, challenging, and always evolving. In K. Gray & J. Graham (Eds.), *The atlas of moral psychology*. New York: Guilford.

Kilwein, T.M., & Looby, A. (2017). Predicting risky sexual behaviors among college student drinkers as a function of event-level drinking motives and alcohol use. *Addictive Behaviors, 76*, 100–105.

Kim, A.S. (2016). Nursing home report card and performance gap. *Health Care Management Review, 25*, 1326–1335.

Kim, B.R., & others (2017). Trajectories of mothers' emotional availability: Relations with infant temperament in predicting attachment security. *Attachment and Human Development, 19*, 38–57.

Kim, E.S., Chopik, W.J., & Smith, J. (2014). Are people healthier if their partners are more optimistic? The dyadic effect of optimism on health among older adults. *Journal of Psychosomatic Research, 76*, 447–453.

Kim, G.R., Jee, S.H., & Pikhart, H. (2018, in press). Role of allostatic load and health behaviors in explaining socioeconomic disparities in mortality: A structural equation modeling approach. *Journal of Epidemiology and Community Health*.

Kim, H.K., & others (2017). All-extremity exercise training improves arterial stiffness in older adults. *Medicine and Science in Sports and Exercise, 49*, 1404–1411.

Kim, J., & Fletcher, J.M. (2018). The influence of classmates on adolescent criminal activities in the United States. *Deviant Behavior, 39*, 275–292.

Kim, J.I., & others (2018). Interaction of DRD4 methylation and phthalate metabolites affects continuous performance test performance in ADHD. *Journal of Attention Disorders*.

Kim, K.H. (2010, May). Unpublished data. School of Education, College of William & Mary, Williamsburg, VA.

Kim, S., & Kochanska, G. (2017). Relational antecedents and social implications of the emotion of empathy: Evidence from three studies. *Emotion, 17*, 981–992.

Kim, S.H., & others (2017). Early menarche and risk-taking behavior in Korean adolescent students. *Asia Pacific-Psychiatry, 59*, 1270–1275.

Kim, S.Y., & others (2018). Culture's influence on stressors, parental socialization, and developmental processes in the mental health of children of immigrants. *Annual Review of Clinical Psychology, 14*, 343–370.

Kimlin, J.A., Black, A.A., & Wood, J.M. (2017). Nighttime driving in older adults: Effects of glare and association with mesopic visual function. *Investigative Ophthalmology and Visual Science, 58*, 2796–2803.

Kimmel, M.S., & Aronson, A. (2018). *Sociology* (3rd ed.). Upper Saddle River, NJ: Pearson.

Kindermann, T.A., & Gest, S.D. (2018). The peer group: Linking conceptualizations, theories, and methods. In W.M. Bukowski & others (Eds.), *Handbook of peer interactions, relationships, and groups* (2nd ed.). New York: Guilford.

King, B.M., & Regan, M. (2019). *Human sexuality today* (9th ed.). Upper Saddle River, NJ: Pearson.

King, C.T., Chase-Lansdale, P.L., & Small, M. (Eds.) (2015). *Two generations, one future: An anthology from the Ascend Fellowship*. Washington, DC: Ascend at the Aspen Institute.

King, J.D., & others (2018, in press). The interpersonal-psychological theory of suicide in adolescents: A preliminary report of changes following treatment. *Suicide and Life-Threatening Behavior*.

King, L.A. (2017). *Psychology: An appreciative experience* (4th ed.). New York: McGraw-Hill.

King, L.A. (2017). *The science of psychology* (4th ed.). New York: McGraw-Hill.

King, L.A. (2018). *Experience psychology* (3rd ed.). New York: McGraw-Hill.

King, L.A. (2019). *Experience psychology* (4th ed.). New York: McGraw-Hill.

King, L.A., & Hicks, J.A. (2007). Whatever happened to "What might have been?" Regrets, happiness, and maturity. *American Psychologist, 62*, 625–636.

King, V., & Scott, M.E. (2005). A comparison of cohabiting relationships among older and younger adults. *Journal of Marriage and the Family, 67*, 271–285.

Kingdon, D., Cardoso, C., & McGrath, J.J. (2016). Research review: Executive function deficits in fetal alcohol spectrum disorders and attention-deficit/hyperactivity disorder—a meta-analysis. *Journal of Child Psychology and Psychiatry, 57*, 116–131.

Kingo, O.S., & Krojgaard, P. (2015). Eighteen-month-olds' memory for short movies of simple shots. *Scandinavian Journal of Psychology, 56*, 151–156.

Kingsbury, A.M., Plotnikova, M., & Naiman, J.M. (2018). Commonly occurring adverse birth outcomes and maternal depression: A longitudinal study. *Public Health, 155*, 45–54.

Kins, E., & Beyers, W. (2010). Failure to launch, failure to achieve criteria for adulthood? *Journal of Adolescent Research, 25*, 743–777.

Kinugawa, K. (2019, in press). Plasticity of the brain and cognition in older adults. In R. Fernandez-Ballesteros & others (Eds.), *Cambridge handbook of successful aging*. New York: Cambridge University Press.

Kiray, H., Lindsay, S.L., Hosseinzadeh, S., & Barnett, S.C. (2016). The multifaceted role of astrocytes in regulating myelination. *Experimental Neurology, 283*, 541–549.

Kircaburun, K., & Griffiths, M.D. (2018, in press). Instagram addiction and the Big Five of personality: The mediating role of self-liking. *Journal of Behavioral Addictions*.

Kirkham, N.Z., Wagner, J.B., Swan, K.A., & Johnson, S.P. (2012). Sound support: Intermodal information facilitates infants' perception of an occluded trajectory. *Infant Behavior and Development, 35*, 174–178.

Kirkorian, H.L., Anderson, D.R., & Keen, R. (2012). Age differences in online processing of video: An eye movement study. *Child Development, 83*, 497–507.

Kisilevsky, B.S., & others (2009). Fetal sensitivity to properties of maternal speech and language. *Infant Behavior and Development, 32*, 59–71.

Kito, M. (2005). Self-disclosure in romantic relationships and friendships among American and Japanese college students. *Journal of Social Psychology, 145*, 127–140.

Kitsantas, A., & Cleary, T.J. (2016). The development of self-regulated learning in secondary school years: A social cognitive instructional perspective. In K.R. Wentzel & D.B. Miele (Eds.), *Handbook of motivation at school* (2nd ed.). New York: Routledge.

Kiviniemi, A.M., & others (2017). Fitness, fatness, physical activity, and autonomic function in midlife. *Medicine and Science in Sports and Exercise, 49*, 2459–2468.

Klaus, M., & Kennell, H.H. (1976). *Maternal-infant bonding*. St. Louis: Mosby.

Klein, A.C. (2018). The *Every Student Succeeds Act: An ESSA Overview*. Retrieved June 12, 2018, from https://www.edweek.org/ew/issues/every-student-succeeds-act/index.html

Klein, M.R., & others (2018, in press). Bidirectional relations between temperament and parenting predict preschool-age children's adjustment. *Journal of Clinical Child and Adolescent Psychology*.

Kleinman, C., & Reizer, A. (2018). Negative caregiving representations and postpartum depression: The mediating roles of parenting efficacy and relationship satisfaction. *Health for Women International, 39*, 79–84.

Kliegman, R.M., Stanton, B., St. Geme, J., & Schor, N. (2016). *Nelson textbook of pediatrics* (20th ed.). New York: Elsevier.

Klinenberg, E. (2013). *Going solo: The extraordinary rise and surprising appeal of living alone*. New York: Penguin.

Klingman, A. (2006). Children and war trauma. In W. Damon & R. Lerner (Eds.), *Handbook of child psychology* (6th ed.). New York: Wiley.

Kloss, J.D., & others (2016). A "Sleep 101" program for college students improves sleep hygiene knowledge and reduces maladaptive beliefs about sleep. *Behavioral Medicine, 42*, 48–56.

Klug, J., & others (2016). Secondary school students' LLL competencies and their relation with classroom structure and achievement. *Frontiers in Psychology, 7*, 680.

Klug, W.S., & others (2017). *Essentials of genetics* (9th ed.). Upper Saddle River, NJ: Pearson.

Knapen, J.E.P., Blaker, N.M., & Van Vugt, M. (2018, in press). The Napoleon complex: When shorter men take more. *Psychological Science*.

Knapp, K., & Morton, J.B. (2017). Executive functioning: A developmental cognitive neuroscience perspective. In M.J., Hoskyn & others (Eds.), *Executive function in children's everyday lives*. New York: Oxford University Press.

Knight, B.G., Rastegar, S., & Kim, S. (2016). Age differences in the connection of mood and cognition: Evidence from mood congruent effects. In K.W. Schaie & S.L. Willis (Eds.), *Handbook of the psychology of aging* (8th ed.). New York: Elsevier.

Knight, L.F., & Hope, D.A.M. (2012). Correlates of same-sex attractions and behaviors among self-identified heterosexual university students. *Archives of Sexual Behavior, 41*, 1199–1208.

Knopfli, B., & others (2016). Marital breakup in later adulthood and self-rated health: A cross-sectional survey in Switzerland. *International Journal of Public Health, 61*, 357–366.

Knowles, E.E., & others (2016). Genome-wide linkage on chromosome 10q26 for a dimensional scale of major depression. *Journal of Affective Disorders, 191*, 123–131.

Knyazev, G.G., & others (2018). Resting state networks mediate the effect of genotype by environment interaction on mental health. *Neuroscience, 369*, 139–151.

Kobayashi, S., & others (2017). Assessment and support during early labor for improving birth outcomes. *Cochrane Database of Systematic Reviews, 4*, CD011516.

Kocahan, S., & Dogan, Z. (2017). Mechanisms of Alzheimer's disease pathogenesis and prevention: The brain, neural pathology, N0methyl-D-aspartate receptors, tau protein, and other risk factors. *Clinical Psychopharmacology and Neuroscience, 15*, 1–8.

Kochanek, K.D., & others (2011). Deaths: Preliminary data, 2009. *National Vital Statistics Reports, 59*(4), 1–51.

Kochanska, G., & Kim, S. (2013). Early attachment organization with both parents and future behavior problems: From infancy to middle childhood. *Child Development, 84*, 283–296.

Kochendorfer, L.B., & Kerns, K.A. (2017). Perceptions of parent-child attachment relationships and friendship qualities: Predictors of romantic relationship involvement and quality in adolescence. *Journal of Youth and Adolescence, 46,* 1009–1021.

Koehn, A.J., & Kerns, K.A. (2018). Parent-child attachment: Meta-analysis of associations with parenting behaviors in middle childhood and adolescence. *Attachment and Human Development.*

Koffer, R., & others (2018, in press). The role of general and daily control beliefs for affective stressor-reactivity across adulthood and old age. *Journals of Gerontology B: Psychological Sciences and Social Sciences.*

Koh, H. (2014). The Teen Pregnancy Prevention Program: An evidence-based public health program model. *Journal of Adolescent Health, 54*(Suppl. 1), S1–S2.

Koh, V., & others (2017). Success rates of 2-site phacoemulsification combined with fornix-based trabeculectomy using mitomycin C for primary angle-closure glaucoma and primary open-angle glaucoma in an Asian population. *Japanese Journal of Ophthalmology, 61,* 245–252.

Kohen, D.E., Lerenthal, T., Dahinten, V.S., & McIntosh, C.N. (2008). Neighborhood disadvantage: Pathways of effects for young children. *Child Development, 79,* 156–169.

Kohlberg, L. (1958). *The development of modes of moral thinking and choice in the years 10 to 16.* Unpublished doctoral dissertation, University of Chicago.

Kohlberg, L. (1986). A current statement of some theoretical issues. In S. Modgil & C. Modgil (Eds.), *Lawrence Kohlberg.* Philadelphia: Falmer.

Kojola, E., & Moen, P. (2016). No more lock-step retirement: Boomers' shifting meanings of work and retirement. *Journal of Aging Studies, 36,* 59–70.

Kok, A.A., & others (2017). The effects of life events and socioeconomic position in childhood and adulthood on successful aging. *Journals of Gerontology B: Psychological Sciences and Social Sciences, 72,* 268–278.

Kok, F.M., Groen, Y., Fuermaier, A.B., & Tucha, O. (2016). Problematic peer functioning in girls with ADHD: A systematic literature review. *PLoS One, 11,* e0165118.

Kok, R., & others (2015). Normal variation in early parental sensitivity predicts child structural brain development. *Journal of the American Academy of Child and Adolescent Psychiatry, 54,* 824–831.

Koksvik, G.H. (2018, in press). Medically timed death as an enactment of good death: An ethnographic study of three European intensive care units. *Omega.*

Koller, S.H., Santana, J.P., & Raffaelli, M. (2018). Poverty, risk, and resilience: The case of street-involved youth. In J.E. Lansford & P. Banati (Eds.), *Handbook of adolescent development research and its impact on global policy.* New York: Oxford University Press.

Kolokotroni, P., Anagnostopoulos, F., & Hantzi, A. (2018, in press). The role of optimism, social constraints, coping, and cognitive processing in psychosocial adjustment among breast cancer survivors. *Journal of Clinical Psychology in Medical Settings.*

Kominiarek, M.A., & Peaceman, A.M. (2017). Gestational weight gain. *American Journal of Obstetrics and Gynecology, 217,* 642–651.

Kondolot, M., & others (2017). Risk factors for overweight and obesity in children 2–6 years. *Journal of Pediatric Endocrinology and Metabolism, 30,* 499–505.

Konrath, S.H., Chopik, W.J., Hsing, C.K., & O'Brien, E. (2014). Changes in adult attachment styles in American college students over time: A meta-analysis. *Personality and Social Psychology Bulletin, 18,* 326–348.

Kontis, V., & others (2017). Future life expectancy in 35 industrialized countries: Projections with a Bayesian model ensemble. *Lancet, 389,* No.10076, 1323–1335.

Koo, Y.J., & others (2012). Pregnancy outcomes according to increasing maternal age. *Taiwan Journal of Obstetrics and Gynecology, 51,* 60–65.

Kopp, F., & Lindenberger, U. (2011). Effects of joint attention on long-term memory in 9-month-old infants: An event-related potentials study. *Developmental Science, 14,* 660–672.

Koppelman, K.L. (2017). *Understanding human differences* (5th ed.). Upper Saddle River, NJ: Pearson.

Korczak, D.J., & others (2018). The longitudinal association between temperament and physical activity in children. *Preventive Medicine, 111,* 342–347.

Koren, C., Simhi, S., Lipman-Schiby, S., & Fogel, S. (2016). The partner in late-life repartnering: Caregiving expectations from an intergenerational perspective. *International Psychogeriatrics, 28,* 1555–1565.

Koren, G., & Ornoy, A. (2018). The role of the placenta in drug transport and fetal drug exposure. *Expert Review of Clinical Pharmacology, 11,* 373–385.

Korja, R., & others (2017). The relations between maternal prenatal anxiety or stress and the child's early negative reactivity or self-regulation: A systematic review. *Child Psychiatry and Human Development, 48,* 851–869.

Koropeckyj-Cox, T. (2009). Loneliness, later life. In D. Carr (Ed.), *Encyclopedia of the life course and human development.* Boston: Gale Cengage.

Korte, J., Drossaert, C.H., Westerhof, G.J., & Bohlmeijer, E.T. (2014). Life review in groups? An explorative analysis of social processes that facilitate or hinder the effectiveness of life review. *Aging and Mental Health, 18,* 376–384.

Kotre, J. (1984). *Outliving the self: Generativity and the interpretation of lives.* Baltimore: Johns Hopkins University Press.

Kotter-Gruhn, D., & Smith, J. (2011). When time is running out: Changes in positive future perception and their relationships to changes in well-being in old age. *Psychology and Aging, 26,* 381–387.

Kouros, C.D., Morris, M.C., & Garber, J. (2016). Within-person changes in individual symptoms of depression predict subsequent depressive episodes in adolescents: A prospective study. *Journal of Abnormal Child Psychology, 44,* 483–494.

Kowalski, R.M., Giumetti, G.W., Schroeder, A.N., & Lattanner, M.R. (2014). Bullying in the digital age: A critical review and meta-analysis of cyberbullying research on youth. *Psychological Bulletin, 140,* 1073–1137.

Koyanagi, A., & others (2018). Chronic physical conditions, multimorbidity, and mild cognitive impairment in low- and middle-income countries. *Journal of the American Geriatrics Society,* 721–727.

Kozhimmanil, K.B., & others (2013). Doula care, birth outcomes, and costs among Medicaid beneficiaries. *American Journal of Public Health, 103*(4), e113–e121.

Kozhimmanil, K.B., & others (2016). Modeling the cost-effectiveness of doula care associated with reductions in preterm birth and cesarean delivery. *Birth, 43,* 20–27.

Kozol, J. (2005). *The shame of the nation.* New York: Crown.

Kraig, E., & others (2018, in press). A randomized control trial to establish the feasibility and safety of rapamycin treatment in an older human cohort: Immunological, physical performance and cognitive effects. *Experimental Gerontology.*

Kramer, H.J., & Lagattuta, K.H. (2018). Social categorization. In M.H. Bornstein (Ed.), *SAGE handbook of lifespan human development.* Thousand Oaks, CA: Sage.

Kramer, L. (2006, July 10). Commentary in "How your siblings make you who you are" by J. Kluger. *Time,* 46–55.

Kramer, L., & Perozynski, L. (1999). Parental beliefs about managing sibling conflict. *Developmental Psychology, 35,* 489–499.

Kramer, L., & Radey, C. (1997). Improving sibling relationships among young children: A social skills training model. *Family Relations, 46,* 237–246.

Krans, E.E., & others (2016). Factors associated with buprenorphine versus methadone use in pregnancy. *Substance Abuse, 37,* 550–557.

Krause, N. (2008). The social foundations of religious meaning in life. *Research on Aging, 30*(4), 395–427.

Krause, N. (2009). Deriving a sense of meaning in late life. In V.L. Bengtson, D. Gans, N.M. Putney, & M. Silverstein (Eds.), *Handbook of theories of aging.* New York: Springer.

Krause, N., & Hayward, R.D. (2016). Religion, health, and aging. In L.K. George & K.F. Ferraro (Eds.), *Handbook of aging and the social sciences* (8th ed.). New York: Elsevier.

Krause, N., Ironson, G., & Hill, P.C. (2017). Volunteer work, religious commitment, and resting pulse rates. *Journal of Religion and Health, 56,* 591–603.

Kretch, K.S., & Adolph, K.E. (2018, in press). The organization of exploratory behaviors in infant locomotor planning. *Developmental Science.*

Kreutzer, M., Leonard, C., & Flavell, J.H. (1975). An interview study of children's knowledge about memory. *Monographs of the Society for Research in Child Development, 40* (Serial No. 159).

Krieger, V., & Amador-Campos, J.A. (2018, in press). Assessment of executive function in ADHD adolescents: Contribution of performance tests and rating scales. *Child Neuropsychology.*

Kriemler, S., & others (2010). Effect of school-based physical activity program (KISS) on fitness and adiposity in primary schoolchildren: Cluster randomized controlled trial. *British Medical Journal, 45,* 923–930.

Kring, A.M. (2000). Gender and anger. In A.H. Fischer (Ed.), *Gender and emotion: Social psychological perspectives.* New York: Cambridge University Press.

Krishnan, P. (2017). Concept analysis of good death in long term care residents. *International Journal of Palliative Nursing, 23,* 29–34.

Krishnan, S., & others (2018). Deep brain stimulation for movement disorders. *Neurology India, 66*(Suppl.), S90–S101.

Krogh-Jespersen, S., Liberman, Z., & Woodward, A.L. (2015). Think fast! The relationship between goal prediction speed and social competence in infants. *Developmental Science, 18,* 815–823.

Krogh-Jespersen, S., & Woodward, A.L. (2016). Infant origins of social cognition. In L. Balter & C. Tamis-LeMonda (Eds.), *Child psychology* (3rd ed.). New York: Psychology Press.

Krogh-Jespersen, S., & Woodward, A.L. (2018, in press). Reaching the goal: Active experience facilitates 8-month-old infants' actions. *Journal of Experimental Child Psychology.*

Kroll-Desrosiers, A.R., & others (2016). Improving pregnancy outcomes through maternity care coordination: A systematic review. *Women's Health Issues, 26,* 87–99.

Krueger, J.I., Vohs, K.D., & Baumeister, R.F. (2008). Is the allure of self-esteem a mirage after all? *American Psychologist, 63,* 64.

Krueger, P.M., & Chang, V.W. (2008). Being poor and coping with stress: Health behaviors and the risk of death. *American Journal of Public Health, 98,* 889–896.

Kruger, J., Blanck, H.M., & Gillespie, C. (2006). Dietary and physical activity behaviors among adults successful at weight loss management. *International Journal of Behavioral Nutrition and Physical Activity, 3,* 17.

Kübler-Ross, E. (1969). *On death and dying.* New York: Macmillan.

Kuebli, J. (1994, March). Young children's understanding of everyday emotions. *Young Children,* 36–48.

Kuersten-Hogan, R. (2017). Bridging the gap across the transition to coparenthood: Triadic interactions and coparenting representations from pregnancy through 12 months postpartum. *Frontiers in Psychology, 8,* 475.

Kuhl, P.K. (2000). A new view of language acquisition. *Proceedings of the National Academy of Sciences, 97*(22), 11850–11857.

Kuhl, P.K. (2007). Is speech learning "gated" by the social brain? *Developmental Science, 10,* 110–120.

Kuhl, P.K. (2009). Linking infant speech perception to language acquisition: Phonetic learning predicts language growth. In J. Colombo, P. McCardle, & L. Freund (Eds.), *Infant pathways to language.* New York: Psychology Press.

Kuhl, P.K. (2011). Social mechanisms in early language acquisition: Understanding integrated brain systems and supporting language. In J. Decety & J. Cacioppo (Eds.), *Handbook of social neuroscience.* New York: Oxford University Press.

Kuhl, P.K. (2012). Language learning and the developing brain: Cross-cultural studies unravel the effects of biology and culture. *Journal of the Acoustical Society of America, 131*(4).

Kuhl, P.K. (2015). Baby talk. *Scientific American, 313,* 64–69.

Kuhl, P.K., & Damasio, A. (2012). Language. In E.R. Kandel & others (Eds.), *Principles of neural science* (5th ed.). New York: McGraw-Hill.

Kuhn, D. (1998). Afterword to Vol. 2: Cognition, perception, and language. In W. Damon (Ed.), *Handbook of child psychology* (5th ed., Vol. 2). New York: Wiley.

Kuhn, D. (2009). Adolescent thinking. In R.M. Lerner & L. Steinberg (Eds.), *Handbook of adolescent psychology* (3rd ed.). New York: Wiley.

Kuhn, D. (2013). Reasoning. In P.D. Zelazo (Ed.), *Handbook of developmental psychology.* New York: Oxford University Press.

Kuhnert, R.L., & others (2017). Gender-differentiated effects of theory of mind, emotion understanding, and social preferences on prosocial behavior development: A longitudinal study. *Journal of Experimental Child Psychology, 154,* 13–27.

Kuiper, J., Broer, J., & van der Wouden, J.C. (2018, in press). Association between physical exercise and psychosocial problems in 96,617 Dutch adolescents in secondary education: A cross-sectional study. *European Journal of Public Health.*

Kulu, H. (2014). Marriage duration and divorce: The seven-year itch or a lifelong itch? *Demography, 51,* 881–893.

Kumar, K., & others (2018). Recent advances in the neurobiology and neuropharmacology of Alzheimer's disease. *Biomedicine and Pharmacology, 98,* 297–307.

Kumar, S.V., Oliffe, J.L., & Kelly, M.T. (2018). Promoting postpartum mental health in fathers: Recommendations for nurse practitioners. *American Journal of Men's Health, 12,* 221–226.

Kumpulainen, S.M., & others (2018). Maternal early pregnancy obesity and depressive symptoms during and after pregnancy. *Psychological Medicine, 17,* 1–11.

Kunzmann, U. (2019, in press). Wisdom: The royal road to personality growth. In R. Fernandez-Ballesteros & others (Eds.), *Cambridge handbook of successful aging.* New York: Cambridge University Press.

Kunzmann, U., & others (2017). Speaking about feelings: Further evidence for multidirectional age differences in anger and sadness. *Psychology and Aging, 32,* 93–103.

Kuo, L.J., & Anderson, R.C. (2012). Effects of early bilingualism on learning phonological regularities in a new language. *Journal of Experimental Child Psychology, 111,* 455–467.

Kuperberg, A. (2014). Age at coresidence, premarital cohabitation, and marriage dissolution: 1985–2009. *Journal of Marriage and Family, 76,* 352–369.

Kuzik, N., & others (2017). Physical activity and sedentary time associations with metabolic health across weight statuses in children and adolescents. *Obesity, 25,* 1762–1769.

Kuznetsov, I.A., & Kuznetsov, A.V. (2018). How the formation of amyloid plaques and neurofibrillary tangles may be related: A mathematical modeling study. *Proceedings. Mathematical, Physical, and Engineering Sciences, 474,* 20170777.

Kvalo, S.E., & others (2017). Does increased physical activity in school affect children's executive function and aerobic fitness? *Scandinavian Journal of Medicine and Science in Sports, 38,* 1833–1844.

Kymre, I.G. (2014). NICU nurses' ambivalent attitudes in skin-to-skin care practice. *International Journal of Qualitative Studies on Health and Well-Being, 9,* 23297.

L

Labayen Goñi, I., & others (2018, in press). Associations between adherence to the Mediterranean diet and cardiorespiratory fitness with total and central obesity in preschool children: The PREFIT project. *European Journal of Nutrition.*

Labella, M.H., & Masten, A.S. (2018). Family influences on the development of aggression and violence. *Current Opinion in Psychology, 19,* 11–16.

Labella, M.H., & others (2018, in press). Risk and adversity, parenting quality, and children's socio-emotional development in families experiencing homelessness. *Child Development.*

Laborte-Lemoyne, E., Currier, D., & Ellenberg, D. (2017). Exercise during pregnancy enhances cerebral maturation in the newborn: A randomized controlled trial. *Journal of Clinical and Experimental Neuropsychology, 39,* 347–354.

Labouvie-Vief, G. (1986, August). *Modes of knowing and life-span cognition.* Paper presented at the meeting of the American Psychological Association, Washington, DC.

Labouvie-Vief, G. (2009). Cognition and equilibrium regulation in development and aging. In V. Bengtson & others (Eds.), *Handbook of theories of aging.* New York: Springer.

Labouvie-Vief, G., Gruhn, D., & Studer, J. (2010). Dynamic integration of emotion and cognition: Equilibrium regulation in development and aging. In M.E. Lamb, A. Freund, & R.M. Lerner (Eds.), *Handbook of life-span development* (Vol. 2). New York: Wiley.

Lacaze-Masmonteil, T., & O'Flaherty, P. (2018). Managing infants born to mothers who have used opioids during pregnancy. *Pediatrics and Child Health, 23,* 220–226.

Lachman, M.E. (2004). Development in midlife. *Annual Review of Psychology* (Vol. 55). Palo Alto, CA: Annual Reviews.

Lachman, M.E. (2006). Perceived control over aging-related declines. *Current Directions in Psychological Science, 15,* 282–286.

Lachman, M.E., Agrigoroaei, S., & Hahn, E.A. (2016). Making sense of control: Change and consequences. In R. Scott & S. Kosslyn (Eds.), *Emerging trends in the social and behavioral sciences.* New York: Wiley.

Lachman, M.E., & Firth, K.M.P. (2004). The adaptive value of feeling in control during midlife. In O.G. Brim, C.D. Ruff, & R.C. Kessler (Eds.), *How healthy are we?* Chicago: University of Chicago Press.

Lachman, M.E., Maier, H., & Budner, R. (2000). *A portrait of midlife.* Unpublished manuscript, Brandeis University, Waltham, MA.

Lachman, M.E., Neupert, S.D., & Agrigoroaei, S. (2011). The relevance of control beliefs for health and aging. In K.W. Schaie & S.L. Willis (Eds.), *Handbook of the psychology of aging* (7th ed.). New York: Elsevier.

Lachman, M.E., Teshale, S., & Agrigoroaei, S. (2015). Midlife as a pivotal period in the life course: Balancing growth and decline at the crossroads of youth and old age. *International Journal of Behavioral Development, 39,* 20–31.

Laciga, J., & Cigler, H. (2017). The Flynn effect in the Czech Republic. *Intelligence, 61,* 7–10.

Ladd, H.C. (2017). No Child Left Behind: A deeply flawed federal policy. *Journal of Policy Analysis and Management, 36,* 461–469.

Ladewig, P.W., London, M.L., & Davidson, M. (2017). *Contemporary maternal-newborn nursing* (9th ed.). Upper Saddle River, NJ: Pearson.

Laflin, M.T., Wang, J., & Barry, M. (2008). A longitudinal study of adolescent transition from virgin to non-virgin status. *Journal of Adolescent Health, 42,* 228–236.

Lafreniere, D., & Mann, N. (2009). Anosmia: Loss of smell in the elderly. *Otolaryngologic Clinics of North America, 42,* 123–131.

Laftman, S.B., & others (2018). Future orientation among students exposed to school bullying and cyberbullying

victimization. *International Journal of Environmental Research and Public Health, 15,* 4.

Lagattuta, K.H. (2014a). *Children and emotion: New insights into developmental affective science.* Basel, Switzerland: Karger.

Lagattuta, K.H. (2014b). Linking past, present, and future: Children's ability to connect mental states and emotions across time. *Child Development Perspectives, 8,* 90–95.

Lagattuta, K.H., & others (2015). Beyond Sally's missing marble: Further development in children's understanding of mind and emotion in middle childhood. *Advances in Child Development and Behavior, 48,* 185–217.

Lahat, A., & others (2014). Early behavioral inhibition and increased error monitoring predict later social phobia symptoms in childhood. *Journal of the American Academy of Child and Adolescent Psychiatry, 53,* 447–455.

Lai, A., & others (2017). An outpatient methadone weaning program by a neonatal intensive care unit for neonatal abstinence syndrome. *Population Health Management, 20,* 397–401.

Lai, T.P., & others (2017). A method for measuring the distribution of the shortest telomeres in cells and tissues. *Nature Communications, 8,* 1356.

Laible, D.J., Thompson, R.A., & Froimson, J. (2015). Early socialization: The influence of close relationships. In J.E. Grusec & P.D. Hastings (Eds.), *Handbook of socialization* (2nd ed.). New York: Guilford.

Laible, D.J., & others (2017). The longitudinal associations among temperament, parenting, and Turkish children's prosocial behaviors. *Child Development, 88,* 1057–1062.

Lam, C.B., & others (2018, in press). The link between coparenting cooperation and child social competence: The moderating role of childhood negative affect. *Journal of Family Psychology.*

Lamb, M.E. (1994). Infant care practices and the application of knowledge. In C.B. Fisher & R.M. Lerner (Eds.), *Applied developmental psychology.* New York: McGraw-Hill.

Lamb, M.E., Bornstein, M.H., & Teti, D.M. (2002). *Development in infancy* (4th ed.). Mahwah, NJ: Erlbaum.

Lamb, M.E., & Lewis, C. (2015). The role of parent-child relationships in child development. In M.H. Bornstein & M.E. Lamb (Eds.), *Developmental science* (7th ed.). New York: Psychology Press.

Lamela, D., & Figueiredo, B. (2016). Co-parenting after marital dissolution and children's mental health: A systematic review. *Journal de Pediatria* (Rio J.), *92,* 331–342.

Lammers, A.J., Zive, D.M., Tolle, S.W., & Fromme, E.K. (2018). The oncology specialist's role in POLST form completion. *American Journal of Hospice and Palliative Care, 35,* 297–303.

Lampard, A.M., Byrne, S.M., McLean, N., & Fursland, A. (2012). The Eating Disorder Inventory-2 perfectionism scale: Factor structure and associations with dietary restraint and weight and shape concern in eating disorders. *Eating Behaviors, 13,* 49–53.

Lampl, M. (1993). Evidence of saltatory growth in infancy. *American Journal of Human Biology, 5,* 641–652.

Lampl, M., & Johnson, M.L. (2011). Infant growth in length follows prolonged sleep and increased naps. *Sleep, 34,* 641–650.

Lampl, M., & Schoen, M. (2018, in press). How long bones grow children: Mechanistic paths to variation in human height growth. *American Journal of Human Biology.*

Lamy, S., & others (2014). Psychosocial and organizational work factors and incidence of arterial hypertension among female healthcare workers: Results of the Organisation des soins et santé des soignants cohort. *Journal of Hypertension, 32,* 1229–1236.

Landberg, M., Dimitrova, R., & Syed, M. (2018). International perspectives on identity and acculturation in emerging adulthood. *Emerging Adulthood, 6,* 3–6.

Landes, S.D., Ardelt, M., Vaillant, G.E., & Waldinger, R.J. (2014). Childhood adversity, midlife generativity, and later life well-being. *Journals of Gerontology B: Psychological Sciences and Social Sciences, 69,* 942–952.

Landi, F., & others (2018, in press). Sarcopenia: An overview on current definitions, diagnosis, and treatment. *Current Protein and Peptide Science.*

Landrum, A.R., Pflaum, A., & Mills, C.M. (2016). Inducing knowledgeability from niceness: Children use social features for making epistemic inferences. *Journal of Cognition and Development, 17,* 699–717.

Lane, A.P., & others (2017). Is occupational complexity associated with cognitive performance or decline? Results from the Australia Longitudinal Study of Aging. *Gerontology, 63,* 550–559.

Lane, H. (1976). *The wild boy of Aveyron.* Cambridge, MA: Harvard University Press.

Lane-Donovan, C., & Herz, J. (2017). ApoE, ApoE receptors, and the synapse in Alzheimer's disease. *Trends in Endocrinology and Metabolism, 28,* 273–284.

Langer, R.D. (2017). The evidence base for HRT: What can we believe? *Climacteric, 20,* 91–98.

Langstrom, N., Rahman, Q., Carlstrom, E., & Lichtenstein, P. (2010). Genetic and environmental effects on same-sex sexual behavior: A population study of twins in Sweden. *Archives of Sexual Behavior, 39,* 75–80.

Lansford, J.E. (2009). Parental divorce and children's adjustment. *Perspectives on Psychological Science, 4,* 140–152.

Lansford, J.E. (2012). Divorce. In R.J.R. Levesque (Ed.), *Encyclopedia of adolescence.* New York: Springer.

Lansford, J.E. (2013). Single- and two-parent families. In J. Hattie & E. Anderman (Eds.), *International guide to student achievement.* New York: Routledge.

Lansford, J.E., & Banati, P. (Eds.) (2018). *Handbook of adolescent development research and its impact on global policy.* New York: Oxford University Press.

Lansford, J.E., & others (2010). Developmental precursors of number of sexual partners from ages 16 to 22. *Journal of Research on Adolescence, 20,* 651–677.

Lansford, J.E., & others (2018, in press). Longitudinal associations between parenting and youth adjustment in twelve cultural groups: Cultural normativeness of parenting as a moderator. *Developmental Psychology.*

Lantagne, A., & Furman, W. (2017). Romantic relationship development: The interplay between age and relationship length. *Developmental Psychology, 53,* 1738–1749.

Lantagne, A., Furman, W., & Novak, J. (2017). "Stay or leave": Predictors of relationship dissolution in emerging adulthood. *Emerging Adulthood, 5,* 241–250.

Lantolf, J. (2017). Materialist dialectics in Vygotsky's methodological approach: Implications for second language education research. In C. Ratner & D. Silva (Eds.), *Vygotsky and Marx.* New York: Routledge.

Lany, J., & others (2018, in press). Infant statistical-learning ability is related to real-time language processing. *Journal of Child Language.*

Laranjo, J., Bernier, A., Meins, E., & Carlson, S.M. (2010). Early manifestations of theory of mind: The roles of maternal mind-mindedness and infant security of attachment. *Infancy, 15,* 300–323.

Larsen, S.B., Hanss, Z., & Kruger, R. (2018, in press). The genetic architecture of mitochondrial dysfunction in Parkinson's disease. *Cell Tissue Research.*

Larson, R.W., & Dawes, N.P. (2015). How to cultivate adolescents' motivation: Effective strategies employed by the professional staff of American youth programs. In S. Joseph (Ed.), *Positive psychology in practice.* New York: Wiley.

Larsson, M., & others (2017). Do pregnant women want to know the sex of the expected child at routine ultrasound and are they interested in sex selection? *Upsala Journal of Medical Sciences, 122,* 254–259.

Larzelere, R.E., & Kuhn, B.R. (2005). Comparing child outcomes of physical punishment and alternative disciplinary tactics: a meta-analysis. *Clinical Child and Family Psychology Review, 8,* 1–37.

Latendresse, G., Elmore, C., & Deneris, A. (2017). Selective serotonin reuptake inhibitors as first-line antidepressant therapy for perinatal depression. *Journal of Midwifery & Women's Health, 62,* 317–328.

Latham, R.M., Mark, K.M., & Oliver, B.R. (2018). Coparenting and children's disruptive behavior: Interacting processes for parenting sense of competence. *Journal of Family Psychology 32,* 151–156.

Lau, E.Y., & others (2017). Sleep and optimism: A longitudinal study of bidirectional causal relationship and its mediating and moderating variables in a Chinese student sample. *Chronobiology International, 34,* 360–372.

Lau, J.S., Adams, S.H., Irwin, C.E., & Ozer, E.M. (2013). Receipt of preventive health services in young adults. *Journal of Adolescent Health, 52,* 42–49.

Lau, J.Y., & Waters, A.M. (2017). Annual research review: An expanded account of information-processing mechanisms in risk for child and adolescent anxiety and depression. *Journal of Child Psychology and Psychiatry, 58,* 387–407.

Laumann, E.O., Glasser, D.B., Neves, R.C., & Moreira, E.D. (2009). A population-based survey of sexual activity, sexual problems, and associated help-seeking behavior patterns in mature adults in the United States of America. *International Journal of Impotence Research, 21,* 171–178.

Laureiro-Martinez, D., Trujillo, C.A., & Unda, J. (2017). Time perspective and age: A review of age-associated differences. *Frontiers in Psychology, 8,* 101.

Laurent, H.K., Wright, D., & Finnegan, M. (2018). Mindfulness-related differences in neural response to own infant negative and positive emotion contexts. *Developmental Cognitive Neuroscience, 30,* 70–76.

Laursen, B. (2018). Peer influence. In W.M. Bukowski & others (Eds.), *Handbook of peer interactions, relationships, and groups* (2nd ed.). New York: Guilford.

Laursen, B., & Adams, R. (2018). Conflict between peers. In W.M. Bukowski & others (Eds.), *Handbook of peer interactions, relationships, and groups* (2nd ed.). New York: Guilford.

Laursen, B., & others (2017). The spread of substance use and delinquency between adolescent twins. *Developmental Psychology, 53,* 329–339.

Laursen, B., Coy, K.C., & Collins, W.A. (1998). Reconsidering changes in parent-child conflict across adolescence: A meta-analysis. *Child Development, 69,* 817–832.

Lautenbacher, S., & others (2017). Age changes in pain perception: A systematic-review and meta-analysis of age effects on pain and tolerance thresholds. *Neuroscience and Biobehavioral Reviews.*

Lavender, J.M., & others (2014). Dimensions of emotion dysregulation in bulimia nervosa. *European Eating Disorders Review, 22,* 212–216.

Lavner, J.A., & Bradbury, T.N. (2013). Newlyweds' optimistic forecasts of their marriage: For better or for worse? *Journal of Family Psychology, 27,* 531–540.

Lavner, J.A., & others (2016). Narcissism and newlywed marriage: Partner characteristics and marital trajectories. *Personality Disorders, 7,* 169–179.

Law, B.H.Y., & others (2018). Analysis of neonatal resuscitation using eye tracking: A pilot study. *Archives of Disease in Childhood: Fetal and Neonatal Edition, 103,* F82–F84.

Law, L.L., & others (2018). Moderate intensity physical activity associates with CSF biomarkers in a cohort at risk for Alzheimer's disease. *Alzheimer's and Dementia, 10,* 188–195.

Layland, E.K., Hill, B.J., & Nelson, L.J. (2018). Freedom to explore the self: How emerging adults use leisure to develop identity. *Journal of Positive Psychology, 13,* 78–91.

Le Page, A., & others (2018, in press). Role of the peripheral innate immune system in the development of Alzheimer's disease. *Experimental Gerontology.*

le Ray, I., & others (2018, in press). Evaluation of a decision tree for efficient antenatal red blood cell antibody screening. *Epidemiology.*

Leaper, C. (2017). Further reflections on Sandra Lipsitz Bem's impact. *Sex Roles, 76,* 759–765.

Leaper, C., & Bigler, R.S. (2018). Societal causes and consequences of gender typing of children's toys. In E.S. Weisgram & L.M. Dinella (Eds.), *Gender typing of children's play.* Washington, DC: APA Books.

Leaper, C., & Smith, T.E. (2004). A meta-analytic review of gender variations in children's language use: Talkativeness, affiliative speech, and assertive speech. *Development Psychology, 40,* 993–1027.

Leary, M.R. (2017). *REVEL for introduction to behavioral research methods* (7th ed.). Upper Saddle River, NJ: Pearson.

Lebel, C., & Deoni, S. (2018, in press). The development of brain white matter microstructure. *NeuroImage.*

Lebenbaum, M., & others (2018). Development and validation of a population based risk algorithm for obesity: The Obesity Population Risk Tool (OPoRT). *PLoS One, 13*(1), e0191169.

Lecce, S., Bianco, F., Devine, R.T., & Hughes, C. (2018). Relations between theory of mind and executive function in middle childhood: A short-term longitudinal study. *Journal of Experimental Child Psychology, 163,* 69–86.

Ledonne, A., & Meruri, N.B. (2017). Current concepts on the physiopathological relevance of dopaminergic receptors. *Frontiers in Cellular Neuroscience, 11,* 27.

Lee, C.C., & others (2018). Babbling development as seen in canonical babbling ratios: A naturalistic evaluation of all-day recordings. *Infant Behavior and Development, 50,* 140–153.

Lee, D., & others (2018, in press). The impact of psychological problems and adverse life events on suicidal ideation among adolescents using nationwide data of a school-based mental health screening test in Korea. *European Child and Adolescent Psychiatry.*

Lee, D.K., & others (2019, in press). The cost of simplifying complex developmental phenomena. *Developmental Science.*

Lee, F., & others (2017). Trends in breastfeeding among infants enrolled in the Special Supplemental Nutrition program for Women, Infants, and Children—New York, 2002–2015. *MMWR: Morbidity and Mortality Weekly Report, 66,* 610–614.

Lee, G., & Ham, O.K. (2018, in press). Behavioral and psychosocial factors associated with suicidal ideation among adolescents. *Nursing and Health Education.*

Lee, I.M., & Skerrett, P.J. (2001). Physical activity and all-cause mortality: What is the dose-response relation? *Medical Science and Sports Exercise, 33*(6 Suppl.), S459–S471.

Lee, J.E., Kahana, B., & Kahana, E. (2017). Successful aging from the viewpoint of older adults: Development of a brief Successful Aging Inventory (SAI). *Gerontology, 63,* 359–371.

Lee, J.H., & others (2014). Five-factor model personality traits as predictors of incident coronary heart disease in the community. *Psychosomatics, 55,* 352–361.

Lee, K., Cameron, C.A., Doucette, J., & Talwar, V. (2002). Phantoms and fabrications: Young children's detection of implausible lies. *Child Development, 73,* 1688–1702.

Lee, K., Quinn, P.C., Pascalis, O., & Slater, A. (2013). Development of face-processing ability in children. In P.D. Zelazo (Ed.), *Handbook of developmental psychology.* New York; Oxford University Press.

Lee, K.S., & Vaillancort, T. (2018, in press). Longitudinal associations among bullying by peers, disordered eating behavior, and symptoms of depression during adolescence. *JAMA Psychiatry.*

Lee, K.Y., & others (2011). Effects of combined radiofrequency radiation exposure on the cell cycle and its regulatory proteins. *Bioelectromagnetics, 32,* 169–178.

Lee, N.C., Hollarek, M., & Krabbendam, L. (2018). Neurocognitive development during adolescence. In J.E. Lansford & P. Banati (Eds), *Handbook of adolescent development research and its impact on global policy.* New York: Oxford University Press.

Lee, R., Zhai, F., Brooks-Gunn, J., Han, W.J., & Waldfogel, J. (2014). Head Start participation and school readiness: Evidence from the Early Childhood Longitudinal Study-Birth Cohort. *Developmental Psychology, 50,* 202-215.

Leerkes, E.M., Parade, S.H., & Gudmundson, J.A. (2011). Mothers' emotional reactions to crying pose risk for subsequent attachment insecurity. *Journal of Family Psychology, 25,* 635-643.

Leerkes, E.M., & others (2017). Further evidence of the limited role of candidate genes in relation to mother-infant attachment. *Attachment and Human Development, 19,* 76-105.

Leerkes, E.M., & others (2017). Maternal physiological dysregulation while parenting poses risks for infant attachment disorganization and behavior problems. *Development and Psychopathology, 29,* 245-257.

Lefkowitz, E.S., & Gillen, M.M. (2006). "Sex is just a normal part of life": Sexuality in emerging adulthood. In J.J. Arnett & J.L. Tanner (Eds.), *Emerging adults in America.* Washington, DC: American Psychological Association.

Leftwich, H.K., & Alves, M.V. (2017). Adolescent pregnancy. *Pediatric Clinics of North America, 64,* 381-388.

Legare, C.H., Clegg, J.M., & Wen, N.J. (2018, in press). Evolutionary developmental psychology: 2017 redux. *Child Development.*

Leger, K.A., & others (2016). Personality and stressor-related affect. *Journal of Personality and Social Psychology, 111,* 917-928.

Lehman, E.B., & others (2010). Long-term stability of young children's eyewitness accuracy, suggestibility, and resistance to misinformation. *Journal of Applied Developmental Psychology, 31,* 145-154.

Lehman, H.C. (1960). The age decrement in outstanding scientific creativity. *American Psychologist, 15,* 128-134.

Lehr, C.A., Hanson, A., Sinclair, M.F., & Christensen, S.I. (2003). Moving beyond dropout prevention towards school completion. *School Psychology Review, 32,* 342-364.

Leinaweaver, J. (2014). Informal kinship-based fostering around the world: Anthropological findings. *Child Development Perspectives, 8,* 131-136.

Lenhart, A. (2015, April 9). *Teens, social media, and technology: Overview 2015.* Washington, DC: Pew Research Center.

Lenhart, A., Smith, A., Anderson, M., Duggan, M., & Perrin, A. (2015, August 6). *Teens, technology, and friendships.* Washington, DC: Pew Research Center.

Leonard, B.E. (2018, in press). Inflammation and depression: A causal or coincidental link to the pathophysiology? *Acta Neuropsychiatrica.*

Lerner, H.G. (1989). *The dance of intimacy.* New York: Harper & Row.

Lerner, R.M., Boyd, M., & Du, D. (2008). Adolescent development. In I.B. Weiner & C.B. Craighead (Eds.), *Encyclopedia of psychology* (4th ed.) Hoboken, NJ: Wiley.

Lerner, R.M., & others (2018). Studying positive youth development in different nations: Theoretical and methodological issues. In J.E. Lansford & P. Banati (Eds.), *Handbook of adolescent development research and its impact on global policy.* New York: Oxford University Press.

Lesaux, N.K., & Siegel, L.S. (2003). The development of reading in children who speak English as a second language. *Developmental Psychology, 39,* 1005-1019.

Leslie, S.J., Cimpian, A., Meyer, M., & Freeland, E. (2015). Expectations of brilliance underlie gender distributions across academic disciplines. *Science, 347,* 262-265.

Leung, R.C., & others (2016). The role of executive functions in social impairment in autism spectrum disorder. *Child Neuropsychology, 22,* 336-344.

Levelt, W.J.M. (1989). *Speaking: From intention to articulation.* Cambridge, MA: MIT Press.

Lever-Duffy, J., & McDonald, J. (2018). *Teaching and learning with technology* (6th ed.). Upper Saddle River, NJ: Pearson.

Levine, T.P., & others (2008). Effects of prenatal cocaine exposure on special education in school-aged children. *Pediatrics, 122,* e83-e91.

Levinson, D.J. (1978). *The seasons of a man's life.* New York: Knopf.

Levinson, D.J. (1996). *The seasons of a woman's life.* New York: Knopf.

Lewanda, A.F., & others (2016). Preoperative evaluation and comprehensive risk assessment for children with Down syndrome. *Pediatric Anesthesia, 26,* 356-362.

Lewis, A.C. (2007). Looking beyond NCLB. *Phi Delta Kappan, 88,* 483-484.

Lewis, B.A., & others (2018). The effect of sleep pattern changes on postpartum depressive symptoms. *BMC Women's Health, 18*(1), 12.

Lewis, D.M.G., & others (2017). Evolutionary psychology—A how-to-guide. *American Psychologist, 72,* 353-373.

Lewis, J.P., & Allen, J. (2017). Alaska native elders in recovery: Linkages between indigenous cultural generativity and sobriety to promote successful aging. *Journal of Cross-Cultural Psychology, 32,* 209-222.

Lewis, L., & others (2018a). The perceptions and experiences of women who achieved and did not achieve waterbirth. *BMC Pregnancy and Childbirth, 18*(1), 23.

Lewis, L., & others (2018b, in press). Obstetric and neonatal outcomes for women intending to use immersion in water for labor and birth in Western Australia (2015-2016): A retrospective audit of clinical outcomes. *Australian and New Zealand Journal of Obstetrics and Gynecology.*

Lewis, M. (2005). Selfhood. In B. Hopkins (Ed.), *The Cambridge encyclopedia of child development.* Cambridge, UK: Cambridge University Press.

Lewis, M. (2007). Early emotional development. In A. Slater & M. Lewis (Eds.), *Introduction to infant development.* Malden, MA: Blackwell.

Lewis, M. (2010). The emergence of consciousness and its role in human development. In W.F. Overton & R.M. Lerner (Eds.), *Handbook of life-span development.* New York: Wiley.

Lewis, M. (2014). *The rise of consciousness and the development of emotional life.* New York: Guilford.

Lewis, M. (2015). Emotional development and consciousness. In R.M. Lerner (Ed.), *Handbook of child psychology and developmental science* (7th ed.). New York: Wiley.

Lewis, M. (2016). Self-conscious emotions: Embarrassment, pride, shame, guilt, and hubris. In L.F. Barrett, M. Lewis, & J.M. Haviland-Jones (Eds.), *Handbook of emotion* (4th ed.). New York: Guilford.

Lewis, M., & Brooks-Gunn, J. (1979). *Social cognition and the acquisition of the self.* New York: Plenum.

Lewis, M., Feiring, C., & Rosenthal, S. (2000). Attachment over time. *Child Development, 71,* 707-720.

Lewis, R.B., Wheeler, J.J., & Carter, S.L. (2017). *REVEL for teaching students with special needs in general education* (9th ed.). Upper Saddle River, NJ: Pearson.

Lewis, T.L., & Maurer, D. (2005). Multiple sensitive periods in human visual development: Evidence from visually deprived children. *Developmental Psychobiology, 46,* 163-183.

Lewis, T.L., & Maurer, D. (2009). Effects of early pattern deprivation on visual development. *Optometry and Vision Science, 86,* 640-646.

Lewis-Morrarty, E., & others (2015). Infant attachment security and early childhood behavioral inhibition interact to predict adolescent social anxiety symptoms. *Child Development, 86,* 598-613.

Li, G., Kung, K.T., & Hines, M. (2017). Childhood gender-typed behavior and adolescent sexual orientation: A longitudinal population-based study. *Developmental Psychology, 53,* 764-777.

Li, J., Tendeiro, J.N., & Stroebe, M. (2018, in press). Guilt in bereavement: Its relationship to complicated grief and depression. *International Journal of Psychology.*

Li, J., Vitiello, M.V., & Gooneratne, N.S. (2018). Sleep in normal aging. *Sleep Medicine Reviews, 13,* 1-11.

Li, J., & others (2016). Heritability of children's dietary intake: A population-based study in China. *Twin Research and Human Genetics, 19,* 472-484.

Li, J., & others (2018, in press). Physical activity in relation to sleep among community-dwelling older adults in China. *Journal of Aging and Physical Activity.*

Li, J.S.Z., & Denchi, E.L. (2018). How stem cells keep telomeres in check. *Differentiation, 100,* 21-25.

Li, J.W., & others (2017). The effect of acute and chronic exercise on cognitive function and academic performance in adolescents: A systematic review. *Journal of Science and Medicine in Sport, 20,* 841-848.

Li, M., & others (2017). Parental expectations and child screen and academic sedentary behaviors in China. *American Journal of Preventive Medicine, 52,* 680-689.

Li, S., & others (2017). Telomere length is positively associated with the expression of IL-6 and MIP-1a in bone marrow mesenchymal stem cells of multiple myeloma. *Molecular Medical Reports, 16,* 2497-2504.

Li, W., Farkas, G., Duncan, G.J., Burchinal, M.R., & Vandell, D.L. (2013). Timing of high quality child care and cognitive, language, and preacademic development. *Developmental Psychology, 49,* 1440-1451.

Li, W., Huang, E., & Gao, S. (2017). Type 1 diabetes mellitus and cognitive impairments: A systematic reiew. *Journal of Alzheimer's Disease, 57,* 29-36.

Li, Y., Allen, J., & Casillas, A. (2017). Relating psychological and social factors to academic performance: A longitudinal investigation of high-poverty middle school students. *Journal of Adolescence, 56,* 179-189.

Li, Y., & others (2018, in press). Genome-wide survey reveals dynamic effects of folate supplement on DNA methylation and gene expression during C2C12 differentiation. *Physiological Genomics.*

Li, Z., Zhang, L., Li, H., Ye, R., Liu, J., & Ren, A. (2013). Maternal severe life events and risk of neural tube defects among rural Chinese. *Birth Defects Research A: Clinical and Molecular Teratology, 97,* 109-114.

Liang, W., & Chikritzhs, T. (2015). Age at first use of alcohol predicts the risk of heavy alcohol use in early adulthood: A longitudinal study in the United States. *International Journal on Drug Policy, 26,* 131-134.

Liang, Y.J., Xi, B., Song, A.Q., Liu, J.X., & Mi, J. (2012). Trends in general and abdominal obesity among Chinese children and adolescents, 1993-2009. *Pediatric Obesity, 7,* 355-364.

Liben, L.S. (1995). Psychology meets geography: Exploring the gender gap on the national geography bee. *Psychological Science Agenda, 8,* 8-9.

Liben, L.S. (2017). Gender development: A constructivist-ecological perspective. In N. Budwig, E. Turiel, & P.D. Zelazo (Eds.), *New perspectives on human development.* New York: Cambridge University Press.

Liben, L.S., & others (2018). Cognitive consequences of gendered toy play. In E.S. Weisgram & L.M. Dinella (Eds.), *Gender typing of children's play.* Washington, DC: APA Books.

Liberati, A., & others (2017). A statistical physics perspective to understand social visual attention in autism spectrum disorder. *Perception, 46,* 889-913.

Liberman, Z., Woodward, A.L., & Kinzler, K.D. (2018, in press). The origins of social categorization. *Trends in Cognitive Science.*

Libertus, K., & Needham, A. (2010). Teach to reach: The effects of active versus passive reading experiences on action and perception. *Vision Research, 50,* 2750-2757.

Lickliter, R. (2018, in press). Developmental evolution. *Wiley Interdisciplinary Reviews. Cognitive Science.*

Liddon, L., Kingerlee, R., & Barry, J.A. (2018). Gender differences in preference for psychological treatment, coping strategies, and barriers to help-seeking. *British Journal of Clinical Psychology, 57,* 42-58.

Lieber, M. (2017). Assessing the mental health impact of the 2011 Great Japan earthquake, tsunami, and radiation disaster on elementary and middle school children in the Fukushima Prefecture of Japan. *PLoS One, 12*(1), e170402.

Liebermann, J. (2017). Chapter 11: Human embryo vitrification. *Methods in Molecular Biology, 1568,* 141–159.

Lillard, A. (2006). Pretend play in toddlers. In C.A. Brownell & C.B. Kopp (Eds.), *Socioemotional development in the toddler year.* New York: Oxford University Press.

Lillard, A. (2015). The development of play. In R.M. Lerner (Ed.), *Handbook of child psychology and developmental science* (7th ed.). New York: Wiley.

Lillard, A.S., & Kavanaugh, R.D. (2014). The contribution of symbolic skills to the development of explicit theory of mind. *Child Development, 85,* 1535–1551.

Lim, J.A., & others (2017). Modulation of mTOR signaling as a strategy for the treatment of Pompe disease. *EMBO Molecular Medicine, 8,* 85203–85213.

Lim, S.H., & others (2018). Enhanced skin pigmentation of anti-wrinkle peptides via molecular modification. *Scientific Reports, 8*(1), 1596.

Lin, F.R., Thorpe, R., Gordon-Salant, S., & Ferrucci, L. (2011). Hearing loss prevalence and risk factors among older adults in the United States. *Journals of Gerontology A: Biological Sciences and Medical Sciences, 66,* 582–590.

Lin, F.V., & others (2017). Identification of successful cognitive aging in the Alzheimer's Disease Neuroimaging Initiative Study. *Journal of Alzheimer's Disease, 59,* 101–111.

Lin, I.F., Brown, S.L., & Hammersmith, A.M. (2017). Marital biography, Social Security receipt, and poverty. *Research on Aging, 39,* 86–110.

Lin, I.F., Brown, S.L., Wright, M.R., & Hammersmith, A.M. (2018, in press). Antecedents of gray divorce: A life course perspective. *Journals of Gerontology B: Psychological Sciences and Social Sciences.*

Lin, L., Zheng, L.J., & Zhang, L.J. (2018, in press). Neuroinflammation, gut microbiome, and Alzheimer's disease. *Molecular Neurobiology.*

Lin, L.Y., & others (2015). Effects of television exposure on developmental skills of young children. *Infant Behavior and Development, 38,* 20–26.

Lind, L., & others (2018, in press). Impact of aging on the strength of cardiovascular risk factors: A longitudinal study over 40 years. *Journal of the American Heart Association.*

Lind, R.R., & others (2018). Improved cognitive performance in preadolescent Danish children after the school-based physical activity program "FIFA 11 for Health" for Europe—A cluster-randomized controlled trial. *European Journal of Sport Science, 18,* 130–139.

Lindahl-Jacobsen, R., & Christensen, K. (2019). Gene-lifestyle interactions in longevity. In R. Fernandez-Ballesteros & others (Eds.), *Cambridge handbook of successful aging.* New York: Cambridge University Press.

Lindau, S.T., & others (2007). A study of sexuality and health among older adults in the United States. *New England Journal of Medicine, 357,* 162–174.

Lindberg, L.D., Maddow-Zimet, I., & Boonstra, H. (2016). Changes in adolescents' receipt of sex education: 2006–2013. *Journal of Adolescent Health, 58,* 621–627.

Lindberg, S.M., Hyde, J.S., Petersen, J.L., & Lin, M.C. (2010). New trends in gender and mathematics performance: A meta-analysis. *Psychological Bulletin, 136,* 1123–1135.

Lindsay, A.C., Wallington, S.F., Muñoz, M.A., & Greaney, M.L. (2018). A qualitative study conducted in the U.S.A. exploring Latino fathers' beliefs, attitudes, and practices related to their young children's eating, physical activity, and sedentary behaviors. *Public Health Nutrition, 21,* 403–415.

Lindsay, A.C., & others (2018). Examining influences of parenting styles and practices on physical activity and sedentary behaviors in Latino children in the United States: Integrative review. *JMR Public Health and Surveillance, 4*(1), e14.

Lindwall, M., & others (2012). Dynamic associations of change in physical activity and change in cognitive function: Coordinated analyses across four studies with up to 21 years of longitudinal data. *Journal of Aging Research. 2012,* Article ID 493598.

Linsell, L., & others (2017). Risk factor models for neurodevelopmental outcomes in children born very preterm or with very low birth weight: A systematic review of methodology and reporting. *American Journal of Epidemiology, 185,* 601–612.

Lintu, N., & others (2016). Determinants of cardiorespiratory fitness in a population sample of girls and boys 6–8 years. *Journal of Physical Activity and Health, 13,* 1149–1155.

Lipowski, M., Lipowska, M., Jochimek, M., & Krokosz, D. (2016). Resilience as a factor protecting youths from risky behavior: Moderating effects of gender and sport. *European Journal of Sport Science, 16,* 246–255.

Lippa, R.A. (2013). Men and women with bisexual identities show bisexual patterns of sexual attraction to male and female "swimsuit models." *Archives of Sexual Behavior, 42,* 187–196.

Lipson, S.K., & Sonneville, K.R. (2017). Eating disorder symptoms among undergraduate and graduate students at 12 U.S. colleges and universities. *Eating Behavior, 24,* 81–88.

Lisha, N.E., & others (2012). Evaluation of the psychometric properties of the Revised Inventory of the Dimensions of Emerging Adulthood (IDEA-R) in a sample of continuation high school students. *Evaluation & the Health Professions, 37,* 156–177.

Lissak, G. (2018). Adverse physiological and psychological effects of screen time on children and adolescents: Literature review and case study. *Environmental Research, 164,* 149–157.

Litz, J., Snyder, W., & Pater, J. (Eds.) (2017). *Oxford handbook of developmental linguistics.* New York: Oxford University Press.

Liu, G., & others (2018). Alzheimer's disease rs11767557 variant regulates EPHA1 gene expression specifically in human whole blood. *Journal of Alzheimer's Disease, 61,* 1077–1088.

Liu, H., & others (2016). A voxel-based morphometric study of age- and sex-related changes in white matter volume in the normal aging brain. *Neuropsychiatric Disease and Treatment, 12,* 453–465.

Liu, L. (2017). Linking telomere regulation to stem cell pluripotency. *Trends in Genetics, 33,* 16–33.

Liu, P.Z., & Nusslock, R. (2018). Exercise-mediated neurogenesis in the hippocampus vis BDNF. *Frontiers in Neuroscience, 12,* 52.

Liu, R., & others (2017). Does CenteringPregnancy group prenatal care affect the birth experience of underserved women? A mixed methods analysis. *Journal of Immigration and Minority Health, 19,* 415–422.

Liu, S., & Spelke, E.S. (2017). Six-month-old infants expect agents to minimize the cost of their actions. *Cognition, 160,* 35–42.

Liu, X., & others (2015). Folic acid supplementation, dietary folate intake, and risk of preterm birth in China. *European Journal of Nutrition, 103,* 501–508.

Liu, Y., & others (2018, in press). The unique role of executive function skills in predicting Hong Kong kindergarteners' reading comprehension. *British Journal of Educational Psychology.*

Lively, W., & Bromley, D. (1973). *Person perception in childhood and adolescence.* New York: Wiley.

Livingston, G. (2014, June 5). Growing number of dads home with the kids. Washington, DC: Pew Research Center.

Livingston, G. (2017). *5 facts on love and marriage in America.* Washington, DC: Pew Research Center.

Llewellyn, R., & others (2017). "Why worry about something you can't control?" Negotiated risk, longevity, and health behaviors. *Health, 21,* 259–277.

Llop, S., & others (2017). Prenatal exposure to mercury and neuropsychological development in young children: The role of fish consumption. *International Journal of Epidemiology, 46,* 827–838.

Lo, C.C., Cheng, T.C., & Simpson, G.M. (2016). Marital status and work-related health limitation: A longitudinal study of young adult and middle-aged Americans. *International Journal of Public Health, 61,* 91–100.

Lo, C.C., & others (2017). Racial/ethnic differences in emotional health: A longitudinal study of immigrants' adolescent children. *Community Mental Health Journal, 53,* 92–101.

Lo, C.K., & others (2017). Risk factors for child physical abuse and neglect among Chinese young mothers. *Child Abuse and Neglect, 67,* 193–206.

Lo, H.H.M., & others (2018b, in press). The effects of family-based mindfulness intervention for ADHD symptomatology in young children and their parents: A randomized controlled trial. *Journal of Attention Disorders.*

Lo, J.C., & others (2016). Self-reported sleep duration and cognitive performance in older adults: A systematic review and meta-analysis. *Sleep Medicine, 17,* 87–98.

Lo, K.Y., & others (2018a, in press). Association of school environment and after-school physical activity with health-related physical fitness among junior high school students. *International Journal of Environmental Research and Public Health.*

Lobo, R.A. (2017). Hormone-replacement therapy: Current thinking. *Nature Reviews. Endocrinology, 13,* 220–231.

Locher, J.L., & others (2016). Calorie restriction in overweight older adults: Do benefits exceed potential risks? *Experimental Gerontology, 86,* 4–13.

Lock, M. (1998). Menopause: Lessons from anthropology. *Psychosomatic Medicine, 60,* 410–419.

Lockhart, G., & others (2017). Prospective relations among low-income African American adolescents' maternal attachment security, self-worth, and risk behaviors. *Frontiers in Psychology, 8,* 33.

Locquet, M., & others (2018, in press). Bone health assessment in older people with or without muscle health impairment. *Osteoporosis International.*

Lohmander, A., & others (2017). Observation method identifies that a lack of canonical babbling can indicate future speech and language problems. *Acta Paediatrica, 106,* 935–943.

Loi, E.C., & others (2017). Using eye movements to assess language comprehension in toddlers born preterm and full-term. *Journal of Pediatrics, 180,* 124–129.

Loizou, E. (2017). Children's sociodramatic play typologies and teacher play involvement within the zone of proximal development. In T. Bruce (Ed.), *Routledge international handbook of early childhood play.* New York: Routledge.

Lojko, D., & others (2015). Atypical features in depression: Association with obesity and bipolar disorder. *Journal of Affective Disorders, 185,* 75–80.

Lomanowska, A.M., & others (2017). Parenting begets parenting: A neurobiological perspective on early adversity and the transmission of parenting styles across generations. *Neuroscience, 342,* 120–139.

London, M.L., & others (2017). *Maternal & child nursing care* (5th ed.). Upper Saddle River, NJ: Pearson.

Longo, F., McPherran Lombardi, C., & Dearing, E. (2017). Family investments in low-income children's achievement and socioemotional functioning. *Developmental Psychology, 53,* 2273–2289.

Lopez-Higes, R., & others (2018). Efficacy of cognitive training in older adults with and without subjective cognitive decline is associated with inhibition efficiency and working memory span, not cognitive reserve. *Frontiers in Aging Neuroscience, 10,* 23.

Loprinzi, P.D. (2015). Dose-response association of moderate-to-vigorous physical activity with cardiovascular biomarkers and all-cause mortality: Considerations of individual sports, exercise, and recreational physical activities. *Preventive Medicine, 81,* 73–77.

Loprinzi, P.D., & Crush, E.A. (2018). Source and size of social support network on sedentary behavior among older adults. *American Journal of Health Promotion, 32,* 28–31.

Loprinzi, P.D., Crush, E., & Joyner, C. (2017). Cardiovascular disease biomarkers on cognitive function in older adults: Joint effects of cardiovascular disease biomarkers and cognitive function on mortality risk. *Preventive Medicine, 94,* 27–30.

Loprinzi, P.D., & Loenneke, J.P. (2016). Lower extremity muscular strength and leukocyte telomere length: Implications of muscular strength in attenuating age-related chronic disease. *Journal of Physical Activity and Health, 13,* 454–457.

Lorenz, K.Z. (1965). *Evolution and the modification of behavior.* The University of Chicago Press.

Lorenzo-Blanco, E.L., & others (2018, in press). Longitudinal trajectories of family functioning among recent immigrant adolescents and parents: Links with adolescent and parent cultural stress, emotional well-being, and behavioral health. *Child Development.*

Loria, H., & Caughy, M. (2017). Prevalence of adverse childhood experiences in low-income Latino immigrant and nonimmigrant children. *Journal of Pediatrics, 192,* 209–215.

Louch, G., & others (2017). A daily diary approach to the examination of chronic stress, daily hassles, and safety perceptions in hospital nursing. *International Journal of Behavioral Medicine, 24,* 946–956.

Lovden, M., Backman, L., & Lindenberger, U. (2017). The link of intellectual engagement to cognitive and brain aging. In R. Cabeza, L. Nyberg, and D. Park (Eds.), *Handbook of cognitive neuroscience of aging* (2nd ed.). New York: Oxford University Press.

Love, J.M., Chazan-Cohen, R., Raikes, H., & Brooks-Gunn, J. (2013). What makes a difference: Early Head Start evaluation findings in a developmental context. *Monographs of the Society for Research in Child Development, 78,* 1–173.

Lovell, J.L., & White, J.L. (2019). *The "troubled adolescent."* New York: Routledge.

Lovely, C., & others (2017). Gene-environment interactions in development and disease. *Wiley Interdisciplinary Review of Developmental Biology, 6,* 1.

Lovgren, M., & others (2018, in press). Spirituality and religious coping are related to cancer-bereaved siblings' long-term grief. *Palliative and Supportive Care.*

Lowenstein, A., Katz, R., & Tur-Sanai, A. (2019, in press). Intergenerational family relationships and successful aging. In R. Fernandez-Ballesteros & others (Eds.), *Cambridge handbook of successful aging.* New York: Cambridge University Press.

Lowry, R., & others (2017). Early sexual debut and associated risk behaviors among sexual minority youth. *American Journal of Preventive Medicine, 52,* 379–384.

Lu, P.H., & others (2011). Age-related slowing in cognitive processing speed is associated with myelin integrity in a very healthy elderly sample. *Journal of Clinical and Experimental Neuropsychology, 33,* 1059–1068.

Lubetkin, E.I., & Jia, H. (2017). Burden of disease associated with lower levels of income among U.S. adults aged 65 and older. *BMJ Open, 7*(1), e013720.

Lucas, J.E., Richter, L.M., & Daelmans, B. (2018). Care for child development: An intervention in support of responsive caregiving and early child development. *Child Care, Health, and Development, 44,* 41–49.

Lucchetti, G., Lucchetti, A.L., & Koenig, H.G. (2011). Impact of spirituality/religiosity on mortality: Comparison with other health interventions. *Explore, 7,* 234–238.

Luchetti, M., Terracciano, A., Stephan, Y., & Sutin, A.R. (2016). Personality and cognitive decline in older adults: Data from a longitudinal sample and meta-analysis. *Journals of Gerontology B: Psychological Sciences and Social Sciences, 71,* 591–601.

Luders, E., & others (2004). Gender differences in cortical complexity. *Nature Neuroscience, 1,* 799–800.

Ludyga, S., & others (2017). An event-related potential investigation of the acute effects of aerobic and coordinative exercise on inhibitory control in children with ADHD. *Developmental Cognitive Neuroscience, 28,* 21–28.

Lukowski, A.F., & Bauer, P. (2014). Long-term memory in infancy and early childhood. In P. Bauer & R. Fivush

(Eds.), *Wiley-Blackwell handbook of children's memory.* New York: Wiley.

Lum, H., & others (2017). Use of medical orders for scope of treatment for heart failure patients during post-acute care in skilled nursing facilities. *Journal of the American Medical Directors Association, 18,* 885–890.

Lund, H.G., Reider, B.D., Whiting, A.B., & Prichard, J.R. (2010). Sleep patterns and predictors of disturbed sleep in a large population of college students. *Journal of Adolescent Health, 46,* 124–132.

Lundin, A., Falkstedt, D., Lundberg, I., & Hemmingsson, T. (2014). Unemployment and coronary heart disease among middle-aged men in Sweden: 39,243 men followed for 8 years. *Occupational and Environmental Medicine, 71,* 183–188.

Lundorff, M., & others (2017). Prevalence of prolonged grief disorder in adult bereavement: A systematic review and meta-analysis. *Journal of Affective Disorders, 212,* 138–149.

Luria, A., & Herzog, E. (1985, April). *Gender segregation across and within settings.* Paper presented at the biennial meeting of the Society for Research in Child Development, Toronto.

Lusby, C.M., & others (2016). Infant EEG and temperament negative affectivity: Coherence of vulnerabilities to mothers' perinatal depression. *Development and Psychopathology, 28,* 895–911.

Luyckx, K., & others (2014). Identity processes and personality traits and types in adolescence: Directionality of effects and developmental trajectories. *Developmental Psychology, 50,* 2144–2153.

Luyckx, K., & others (2017). Identity processes and intrinsic and extrinsic goal pursuits: Directionality of effects in college students. *Journal of Youth and Adolescence, 46,* 1758–1771.

Luyster, F.S., & others (2012). Sleep: A health imperative. *Sleep, 35,* 727–734.

Luyten, P., & Fonagy, P. (2018, in press). The stress-reward-mentalizing model of depression: An integrative developmental cascade approach to child and adolescent depressive disorder based on the research domain criteria (RDoC) approach. *Clinical Psychology Review.*

Lyon, T.D., & Flavell, J.H. (1993). Young children's understanding of forgetting over time. *Child Development, 64,* 789–800.

Lyons, D.M., & others (2010). Stress coping stimulates hippocampal neurogenesis in adult monkeys. *Proceedings of the National Academy of Sciences U.S.A., 107,* 14823–14827.

Lyons, E.M., & others (2018, in press). Stereotype threat effects on learning from a cognitively demanding math lesson. *Cognitive Science.*

Lyons, H., Manning, W.D., Longmore, M.A., & Giordano, P.C. (2015). Gender and casual sexual activity from adolescence to emerging adulthood: Social and life course correlates. *Journal of Sex Research, 52,* 543–557.

Lytle, A., Levy, S.R., & Meeks, S. (2018, in press). Reducing ageism: Education about aging and extended contact with older adults. *Gerontologist.*

M

Ma, C.L., & others (2017). Physical exercise induces hippocampal neurogenesis and prevents cognitive decline. *Behavioral Brain Research, 317,* 332–339.

Ma, F., & others (2018). Promoting honesty in young children through observational learning. *Journal of Experimental Child Psychology, 167,* 234–245.

Maag, J.W. (2018). *Behavior management from theoretical implications* (3rd ed.). Boston: Cengage.

Maalouf, F.T., & Brent, D.A. (2012). Child and adolescent depression intervention overview: What works for whom and how well? *Child and Adolescent Psychiatry Clinics of North America, 21,* 299–312.

Maccalum, F., & Bryant, R.A. (2013). A cognitive attachment model of prolonged grief: Integrating attachments,

memory, and identity. *Clinical Psychology Review, 33,* 713–727.

Maccoby, E.E. (1984). Middle childhood in the context of the family. In *Development during middle childhood.* Washington, DC: National Academy Press.

Maccoby, E.E. (1998). *The two sexes: Growing up apart, coming together.* Cambridge, MA: Harvard University Press.

Maccoby, E.E. (2002). Gender and group processes. *Current Directions in Psychological Science, 11,* 54–58.

Maccoby, E.E. (2015). Historical overview of socialization research and theory. In J.E. Grusec & P.D. Hastings (Eds.), *Handbook of socialization* (2nd ed.). New York: Guilford.

Maccoby, E.E., & Martin, J.A. (1983). Socialization in the context of the family: Parent-child interaction. In P.H. Mussen (Ed.), *Handbook of child psychology* (4th ed., Vol. 4). New York: Wiley.

MacDonald, S.W., DeCarlo, C.A., & Dixon, R.A. (2011). Linking biological and cognitive aging: Toward improving characterizations of developmental time. *Journals of Gerontology B: Psychological Sciences and Social Sciences, 66B*(Suppl. 1), i59–i70e.

MacDonald, S.W.S., Hultch, D., Strauss, E., & Dixon, R. (2003). Age-related slowing of digit symbol substitution revisited: What do longitudinal age changes reflect? *Journals of Gerontology B: Psychological Sciences and Social Sciences, 58B,* P187–P184.

MacDonald, S.W.S., & Stawski, R.S. (2015). Intraindividual variability—an indicator of vulnerability or resilience in adult development and aging? In M. Diehl, I. Hooker, & M. Sliwinski (Eds.), *Handbook of intraindividual variability across the life span.* New York: Routledge.

MacDonald, S.W.S., & Stawski, R.S. (2016). Methodological perspectives for the psychology of aging in a lifespan context. In K.W. Schaie & S.L. Willis (Eds.), *Handbook of the psychology of aging* (8th ed.). New York: Elsevier.

MacDougall, B.J., Robinson, J.D., Kappus, L., Sudikoff, S.N., & Greer, D.M. (2014). Simulation-based training in brain death determination. *Neurocritical Care, 21,* 383–391.

MacFarlane, J.A. (1975). Olfaction in the development of social preferences in the human neonate. In *Parent-infant interaction. Ciba Foundation Symposium,* No. 33. Amsterdam: Elsevier.

Machado, A., & others (2018, in press). ADHD among offenders: Prevalence and relationship with psychopathic traits. *Journal of Attention Disorders.*

Machado, B., & others (2014). Risk factors and antecedent life events in the development of anorexia nervosa: A Portuguese case-control study. *European Eating Disorders Review, 22,* 243–251.

Machalek, D.A., & others (2017). Genetic and environmental factors in invasive cervical cancer: Design and methods of a classical twin study. *Twin Research and Human Genetics, 20,* 10–18.

Maciejewski, P.K., & Prigerson, H.G. (2017). Prolonged, but not complicated, grief is a mental disorder. *British Journal of Psychology, 211,* 189–191.

MacKenzie, A., Hedge, N., & Enslin, P. (2017). Sex education: Challenges and choices. *British Journal of Educational Studies, 65,* 27–44.

MacNeil Vroomen, J.L., & others (2018, in press). Diabetes, heart disease, and dementia: National estimates of functional disability trajectories. *Journal of the American Geriatrics Association.*

MacNeill, L., & others (2018, in press). Trajectories of infants' biobehavioral development: Timing and rate of A-not-B performance gains and EEG maturation. *Child Development.*

Madden, D.J., & others (1999). Aging and recognition memory: Changes in regional cerebral blood flow associated with components of reaction time distributions. *Journal of Cognitive Neuroscience, II,* 511–520.

Madden, D.J., & Parks, E.L. (2017). Age differences in structural connectivity: DTI and WMHs. In R. Cabeza,

L. Nyberg, & D. Park (Eds.), *Handbook of cognitive neuroscience of aging* (2nd ed.). New York: Oxford University Press.

Mader, S., & Windelspecht, M. (2018). *Human biology* (15th ed.). New York: McGraw-Hill.

Mader, S., & Windelspecht, M. (2019). *Biology* (13th ed.). New York: McGraw-Hill.

Madjar, N., Cohen, V., & Shoval, G. (2018). Longitudinal analysis of the trajectories of academic and social motivation across the transition from elementary to middle school. *Educational Psychology, 38,* 221–247.

Madrasi, K., & others (2018, in press). Regulatory perspectives in pharmacometric models of osteoporosis. *Journal of Clinical Pharmacology.*

Magro-Malosso, E.R., & others (2017). Exercise during pregnancy and risk of gestational hypertensive disorders: A systematic review and meta-analysis. *Acta Obstetricia et Gynecologica Scandinavica, 96,* 263–273.

Mah, A., Geeraert, B., & Lebel, C. (2017). Detailing neuroanatomical development in late childhood and early adolescence using NODDI. *PloS One, 12,* e0182340.

Maher, H., Winston, C.N., & Ur, S. (2017). What it feels like to be me: Linking emotional intelligence, identity, and intimacy. *Journal of Adolescence, 56,* 162–165.

Maher, J.P., & others (2013). A daily analysis of physical activity and satisfaction with life in emerging adults. *Health Psychology, 32,* 647–656.

Maher, L.M. (2018). Broca's aphasia and grammatical processing. In A.M. Rayner & L.J. Gonzalez Rothi (Eds.), *Oxford handbook of aphasia and language disorders.* New York: Oxford University Press.

Maid, S., & Power, J.H.T. (2018, in press). Oxidative stress and decreased mitochondrial superoxide dismutase 2 and peroxiredoxin 1 and 4 based mechanism of concurrent activation of AMPK and mTOR in Alzheimer's disease. *Current Alzheimer Research.*

Maillard, P., & others (2012). Effects of systolic blood pressure on white-matter integrity in young adults in the Framington Heart Study: A cross-sectional study. *Lancet Neurology, 11,* 1039–1047.

Maitre, N.L., & others (2017). The dual nature of early-life experience on somatosensory processing in the human infant brain. *Current Biology, 27,* 1048–1054.

Malamitsi-Puchner, A., & Boutsikou, T. (2006). Adolescent pregnancy and perinatal outcome. *Pediatric Endocrinology Review, 3*(1, Suppl.), S170–S171.

Malinowski, P., & others (2017). Mindful aging: The effects of regular brief mindfulness practice on electrophysiological markers of cognitive and affective processing in older adults. *Mindfulness, 8,* 78–84.

Malmberg, L.E., & others (2016). The influence of mothers' and fathers' sensitivity in the first year of life on children's cognitive outcomes at 18 and 36 months. *Child Care, Health, and Development, 42,* 1–7.

Maloy, R.W., Verock, R-E., Edwards, S.A., & Woolf, B.P. (2017). *Transforming learning with new technologies* (3rd ed.). Upper Saddle River, NJ: Pearson.

Mandara, J. (2006). The impact of family functioning on African American males' academic achievement: A review and clarification of the empirical literature. *Teachers College Record, 108,* 206–233.

Mandler, J. (2000). Unpublished review of J.W. Santrock's *Life-Span Development,* 8th ed. (New York: McGraw-Hill).

Mandler, J.M. (2004). *The foundations of mind.* New York: Oxford University Press.

Mandler, J.M. (2009). Conceptual categorization. In D.H. Rakison & L.M. Oakes (Eds.), *Early category and concept development.* New York: Oxford University Press.

Mandler, J.M., & McDonough, L. (1993). Concept formation in infancy. *Cognitive Development, 8,* 291–318.

Manenti, R., Cotelli, M., & Miniussi, C. (2011). Successful physiological aging and episodic memory: A brain stimulation study. *Behavioral Brain Research, 216,* 153–158.

Manfredini, R., & others (2017). Marital status, cardiovascular diseases, and cardiovascular risk factors: A review of the evidence. *Journal of Women's Health, 26,* 624–632.

Manganaro, L., & others (2018). Highlights on MRI of the fetal body. *La Radiologia Medica, 123,* 271–285.

Mann, F.D., & others (2015). Person × environment interactions on adolescent delinquency: Sensation seeking, peer deviance, and parental monitoring. *Personality and Individual Differences, 76,* 129–134.

Manning. R.P., & others (2017). A systematic review of adult attachment and social anxiety. *Journal of Affective Disorders, 211,* 44–59.

Mantzavinosa, V., & others (2017). Biomarkers for Alzheimer's disease diagnosis. *Current Alzheimer Disease., 14,* 1149–1154.

Manuck, S.B., & McCaffery, J.M. (2014). Gene-environment interaction. *Annual Review of Psychology* (Vol. 65). Palo Alto, CA: Annual Reviews.

Manzanares, S., & others (2016). Accuracy of fetal sex determination on ultrasound examination in the first trimester of pregnancy. *Journal of Clinical Ultrasound, 44,* 272–277.

Mao, H.F., & others (2018, in press). Diagnostic accuracy of instrumental activities of daily living for dementia in community-dwelling older adults. *Age and Aging.*

Maoz, H., & others (2018, in press). Theory of mind and empathy in children with ADHD. *Journal of Attention Disorders.*

Maravilla, J.C., & others (2017). Factors influencing repeated adolescent pregnancy: A review and meta-analysis. *American Journal of Obstetrics and Gynecology, 217,* 527–545.

Marcell, J.J. (2003). Sarcopenia: Causes, consequences, and preventions. *Journals of Gerontology A: Biological Sciences and Medical Sciences,* M911–M916.

March of Dimes (2018). *Multiple pregnancy and birth: Considering fertility treatments.* White Plains, NY: Author.

Marchman, V.A., & others (2018, in press). Caregiver talk to young Spanish-English bilinguals: comparing direct observation and parent report measures of dual-language exposure. *Developmental Science.*

Marcia, J.E. (1980). Ego identity development. In J. Adelson (Ed.), *Handbook of adolescent psychology.* New York: Wiley.

Marcia, J.E. (1994). The empirical study of ego identity. In H.A. Bosma, T.L.G. Graafsma, H.D. Grotevant, & D.J. De Levita (Eds.), *Identity and development.* Newbury Park, CA: Sage.

Marcia, J.E. (2002). Identity and psychosocial development in adulthood. *Identity: An International Journal of Theory and Research, 2,* 7–28.

Mares, M-L., & Pan, Z. (2013). Effects of Sesame Street: A meta-analysis of children's learning in 15 countries. *Journal of Applied Developmental Psychology, 34,* 140–151.

Marion, R.M., & others (2017). Common telomere changes during in vivo reprogramming and early stages of tumorigenesis. *Stem Cell Research, 8,* 460–475.

Marioni, R.E., & others (2018, in press). Meta-analysis of epigenome association studies of cognitive abilities. *Molecular Psychiatry.*

Marjanovic-Umek, L., Fekonja-Peklaj, U., & Socan, G. (2017). Early vocabulary, parental education, and the frequency of shared reading as predictors of toddlers' vocabulary and grammar at age 2;7: A Slovenian longitudinal CDI study. *Journal of Child Language, 44,* 457–479.

Markant, J.C., & Thomas, K.M. (2013). Postnatal brain development. In P.D. Zelazo (Ed.), *Handbook of developmental psychology.* New York: Wiley.

Markham, C.M., & others (2010). Connectedness as a predictor of sexual and reproductive health outcomes for youth. *Journal of Adolescent Health, 46*(3, Suppl.), S23–S41.

Markovic, G., Sarabon, N., Greblo, Z., & Krizanic, V. (2015). Effects of feedback-based balance and core resistance training vs. Pilates training on balance and muscle

function in older women: A randomized-controlled task. *Archives of Gerontology and Geriatrics, 61,* 117–123.

Marotta, P. (2017). Exploring relationships between delinquent peer groups, participation in delinquency, substance use, and injecting drug use among the incarcerated: Findings from a national sample of state and federal inmates in the United States. *Journal of Drug Issues.*

Marquez-Gonzalez, M., Cheng, S-T., & Losada, A. (2019, in press). Coping mechanisms through successful aging. In R. Fernandez-Ballesteros & others (Eds.), *Cambridge handbook of successful aging.* New York: Cambridge University Press.

Marrus, N., & others (2018). Walking, gross motor development, and brain functional connectivity in infants and toddlers. *Cerebral Cortex, 28,* 750–763.

Marsh, H., Ellis, L., & Craven, R. (2002). How do preschool children feel about themselves? Unraveling measurement and multidimensional self-concept structure. *Developmental Psychology, 38,* 376–393.

Marsh, H.L., & Legerstee, M. (2017). Awareness of goal-directed behavior during infancy and early childhood, in human- and non-human primates. *Infant Behavior and Development, 48*(Pt. A), 30–37.

Marshall, K.A., & Hale, D. (2018). Elder abuse. *Home Healthcare Now, 36,* 51–52.

Marshall, N.A., & others (2018, in press). Socioeconomic disadvantage and altered corticostriatal circuitry in urban youth. *Human Brain Mapping.*

Marshall, S.L., Parker, P.D., Ciarrochi, J., & Heaven, P.C.L. (2014). Is self-esteem a cause or consequence of social support? A 4-year longitudinal study. *Child Development, 85,* 1275–1291.

Martin, A., & others (2018). Physical activity, diet, and other behavioral interventions for improving cognition and school achievement in children and adolescents with obesity or overweight. *Cochrane Database of Systematic Reviews, 1,* CD009728.

Martin, A.J., & others (2016). Personal best (PB) goal structure, individual PB goals, engagement, and achievement: A study of Chinese- and English-speaking students in Australian schools. *British Journal of Educational Psychology, 86,* 75–91.

Martin, C., Sargrad, S., & Batel, S. (2016). Making the grade: A 50-state analysis of school accountability systems. *ERIC,* ED567858.

Martin, C.L., & Cook, R. (2017). Cognitive perspectives on children's toy choices and play styles. In E. Wigram & L. Dinella (Eds.), *Gender-typing of children's toys.* Washington, DC: American Psychological Association.

Martin, C.L., Fabes, R.A., & Hanish, L.D. (2018). Differences and similarities: The dynamics of same- and other-sex peer relationships. In W.H. Bukowski & others (Eds.), *Handbook of peer interactions, relationships, and groups* (2nd ed.). New York: Guilford.

Martin, C.L., & Ruble, D.N. (2010). Patterns of gender development. *Annual Review of Psychology* (Vol. 61). Palo Alto, CA: Annual Reviews.

Martin, E.M., & Fry, R.C. (2018, in press). Environmental influences on the epigenome: Exposure-associated DNA methylation in human populations. *Annual Review of Public Health.*

Martin, J.A., & others (2015). Births: Final data for 2013. *National Vital Statistics Reports, 54*(1).

Martin, J.A., & others (2017). Births: Final data for 2015. *National Vital Statistics Reports, 66*(1).

Martin, K.B., & Messinger, D.B. (2018). Smile. In M.H. Bornstein (Ed.), *SAGE encyclopedia of lifespan human development.* Thousand Oaks, CA: Sage.

Martin, M.M., & others (2016). Cocaine-induced neurodevelopmental deficits and underlying mechanisms. *Birth Defects Research C: Embryo Today, 108,* 147–173.

Martin-Espinosa, N., & others (2017). Prevalence of high blood pressure and association with obesity in Spanish schoolchildren aged 4–6 years old. *PLoS One, 12*(1), e170926.

Martinez-Brockman, J.L., & others (2018). Impact of Lactation Advice through Texting Can Help (LATCH) trial on time to first contact and exclusive breastfeeding among WIC participants. *Journal of Nutrition Education and Behavior, 50,* 33–42.

Mary, A., & others (2016). Executive and attentional contributions to theory of mind deficit in attention deficit/hyperactivity disorder (ADHD). *Child Neuropsychology, 22,* 345–365.

Marzetti, E., & others (2017). Physical activity and exercise as countermeasures to physical frailty and sarcopenia. *Aging. Clinical and Experimental Research, 29,* 35–42.

Masapollo, M., Polka, L., & Menard, L. (2016). When infants talk, infants listen: Pre-babbling infants prefer listening to speech with infant vocal properties. *Developmental Science, 19,* 318–328.

Mascolo, M.F., & Fischer, K.W. (2007). The co-development of self and socio-moral emotions during the toddler years. In C.A. Brownell & C.B. Kopp (Eds.), *Transitions in early development.* New York: Guilford.

Mascolo, M.F., & Ficher, K.W. (2010). The dynamic development of thinking, feeling, and acting over the life span. In W.F. Overton & R.M. Lerner (Eds.), *Handbook of life-span development* (Vol. 1). New York: Wiley.

Mash, E.J., & Wolf, D.A. (2019). *Abnormal child psychology* (7th ed.). Boston: Cengage.

Mason, A., & others (2017). Family factors and health behavior of thin adolescent boys and girls. *Journal of Advanced Nursing, 7,* 77–189.

Mason, K., & others (2018). *Understanding biology* (2nd ed.). New York: McGraw-Hill.

Mason-Apps, E., & others (2018, in press). Longitudinal predictors of early language in infants with Down syndrome: A preliminary study. *Research in Developmental Disabilities.*

Masoodi, N. (2013). Review: Cholinesterase inhibitors do not reduce progress to dementia from mild cognitive impairment. *Annals of Internal Medicine, 158,* JC2–JC3.

Masten, A.S. (2006). Developmental psychopathology: Pathways to the future. *International Journal of Behavioral Development, 46,* 53.

Masten, A.S. (2016). Faculty profile: Ann Masten. *The Institute of Child Development, further developments.* Minneapolis: School education.

Masten, A.S. (2016). Risk and resilience in development. In P.D. Zelazo (Ed.), *Oxford handbook of developmental psychology.* New York: Oxford University Press.

Masten, A.S. (2001). *Ordinary magic.* New York: Guilford.

Masten, A.S. (2016). Pathways to integrated resilience science. *Psychological Inquiry, 27,* 187–196.

Masten, A.S. (2016a). Resilience in the context of ambiguous loss: A commentary. *Journal of Family Theory and Review, 8,* 287–293.

Masten, A.S. (2016b). Resilience in developing systems: The promise of integrated approaches. *Journal of Developmental Psychology, 13,* 297–312.

Masten, A.S. (2017). Building a transactional science on children and youth affected by political violence and armed conflict: A commentary. *Development and Psychopathology, 29,* 79–84.

Masten, A.S. (2018a, in press). Resilience from a developmental systems perspective. *World Psychiatry.*

Masten, A.S. (2018b). Resilience theory and research on children and families: Past, present, and promise. *Journal of Family Theory and Review, 10,* 12–31.

Masten, A.S., Burt, K., & Coatsworth, J.D. (2006). Competence and psychopathology in development. In D. Cicchetti & D. Cohen (Eds.), *Developmental psychopathology: Risk, disorder, and psychopathology* (2nd ed., Vol. 3). New York: Wiley.

Masten, A.S., & Kalstabakken, A.W. (2018). Developmental perspectives on psychopathology in children and adolescents. In J. Butcher (Ed.), *APA handbook of psychopathology.* Washington, DC: American Psychological Association.

Masten, A.S., & Palmer, A. (2018). Parenting to promote resilience in children. In M.H. Bornstein (Ed.), *Handbook of lifespan human development.* Thousand Oaks, CA: Sage.

Masten, A.S., & others (2008). School success in motion: Protective factors for academic achievement in homeless and highly mobile children in Minneapolis. *Center for Urban and Regional Affairs Reporter, 38,* 3–12.

Masters, A.R., & others (2017). Immune senescence: Significance of the stromal microenvironment. *Clinical and Experimental Immunology, 187,* 6–15.

Mastropieri, M.A., & Scruggs, T.E. (2018). *The inclusive classroom* (6th ed.). Upper Saddle River, NJ: Pearson.

Match.com (2017). *Singles in America 2017.* Retrieved August 16, 2017, from www.singlesinamerica.com

Mateus, V., & others (2018). Contributions of infant vagal regulation at 1 month to subsequent joint attention abilities. *Developmental Psychobiology.*

Mather, M. (2012). The emotion paradox in the human brain. *Annals of the New York Academy of Sciences, 1251,* 33–49.

Matias, M., & Fontaine, M. (2015). Coping with work and family: How do dual-earners interact? *Scandinavian Journal of Psychology, 56,* 212–222.

Matlow, J.N., Jubetsky, A., Aleksa, K., Berger, H., & Koren, G. (2013). The transfer of ethyl glucuronide across the dually perfused human placenta. *Placenta, 34*(4), 369–373.

Matos, K. (2015). *Modern families: Same- and different-sex couples negotiating at home.* New York: Families and Work Institute.

Matsumoto, D., & Juang, L. (2017). *Culture and psychology* (6th ed.). Boston: Cengage.

Maule, M., & Perren, S. (2018). Ignoring children's bedtime crying: The power of Western-oriented beliefs. *Infant Mental Health Journal, 39,* 220–230.

Maunder, R.G., & others (2017). An attachment-based model of the relationship between childhood adversity and somatization in children and adults. *Psychosomatic Medicine, 79,* 506–513.

Maurer, D. (2016). How the baby learns to see: Donald O. Hebb Award lecture, Canadian Society for Brain, Behavior, and Cognitive Science, Ottawa, June 2015. *Canadian Journal of Experimental Psychology, 70,* 195–200.

Maurer, D., & Lewis, T.L. (2013). Sensitive periods in visual development. In P.D. Zelazo (Ed.), *Oxford handbook of developmental psychology.* New York: Oxford University Press.

Maurer, D., Lewis, T.L., Brent, H.P., & Levin, A.V. (1999). Rapid improvement in the acuity of infants after visual input. *Science, 286,* 108–110.

Maurer, D., Mondloch, C.J., & Leis, T.L. (2007). Effects of early visual deprivation on perceptual and cognitive development. In C. von Hofsten & K. Rosander (Eds.), *Progress in Brain Research, 164,* 87–104.

Mayas, J., Parmentier, F.B., Andres, P., & Ballesteros, S. (2014). Plasticity of attentional functions in older adults after non-action video game training: A randomized controlled trial. *PLoS One, 9,* e92269.

Mayer, K.D., & Zhang, L. (2009). Short-and long-term effects of cocaine abuse during pregnancy on heart development. *Therapeutic Advances in Cardiovascular Disease, 3,* 7–16.

Mayerl, H., & others (2017). Exploring differential health effects of work stress: A latent class cluster approach. *PeerJ, 5,* e3106.

Mayo Clinic (2018). *Male hypogonadism.* Rochester, MN: Mayo Clinic.

Mayo Clinic (2018). *Pregnancy and fish: What's safe to eat?* Retrieved January 10, 2018, from www.mayoclinic.com/health/pregnancy-and-fish/PR00158

Mayoral, V.F.S., & others (2018, in press). Cross-cultural adaptation of the Physician Orders for Life-Sustaining Treatment form to Brazil. *Journal of Palliative Medicine.*

Mazul, M.C., Salm Ward, T.C., & Ngui, E.M. (2017). Anatomy of good prenatal care: Perspectives of low income African-American women on barriers and facilitators to prenatal care. *Journal of Racial and Ethnic Health Disparities, 4,* 79–86.

Mazzu-Nascimento, T., & others (2017). Teratogens: A public health issue—a Brazilian overview. *Genetics and Molecular Biology, 40,* 387–397.

McAdams, D.P., Josselson, R., & Lieblich, A. (2006). *Identity and story: Creating self in narrative.* Washington, DC: American Psychological Association.

McAdams, D.P., & Olson, B.D. (2010). Personality development: Continuity and change over the life course. *Annual Review of Psychology* (Vol. 61). Palo Alto, CA: Annual Reviews.

McCabe, K.O., & Fleeson, W. (2016). Are traits useful? Explaining trait manifestations as tools in the pursuit of goals. *Journal of Personality and Social Psychology, 110,* 287–301.

McCarroll, J.E., & others (2017). Characteristics, classification, and prevention of child maltreatment fatalities. *Military Medicine, 182,* e1551–e1557.

McCartney, K. (2003, July 16). Interview with Kathleen McCartney in A. Bucuvalas, "Child care and behavior." *HGSE News,* pp. 1–4. Cambridge, MA: Harvard Graduate School of Education.

McCartney, K., Dearing, E., Taylor, B.A., & Bub, K.L. (2007). Quality child care supports the achievement of low-income children: Direct and indirect pathways through caregiving and the home environment. *Journal of Applied Developmental Psychology, 28,* 411–426.

McCaskey, U., & others (2018). Longitudinal brain development in numerical skills in typically developing children and children with developmental dyscalculia. *Frontiers in Human Neuroscience, 11,* 629.

McClellan, M.D. (2004, February 9). Captain Fantastic: The interview. *Celtic Nation,* pp. 1–9.

McClelland, M.M., Acock, A.C., Piccinin, A., Rhea, S.A., & Stallings, M.C. (2013). Relations between preschool attention span persistence and age 25 educational outcomes. *Early Childhood Research Quarterly, 28,* 314–324.

McClelland, M.M., & others (2017). Self-regulation. In N. Halfon & others (Eds.), *Handbook of life course health development.* New York; Springer.

McCluney, C.L., & others (2018). Structural racism in the workplace: Does perception matter for health inequalities? *Social Science and Medicine, 199,* 106–144.

McClure, E.R., & others (2018). Look at that! Video chat and joint visual attention development among infants and toddlers. *Child Development, 89,* 27–36.

McCormack, T., Hoerl, C., & Butterfill, C. (2012). *Tool use and causal cognition.* New York: Oxford University Press.

McCoy, M.B., & others (2018). Associations between peer counseling and breastfeeding initiation and duration: An analysis of Minnesota participants in the Special Supplemental Nutrition Program for Women, Infants, and Children (WIC). *Maternal and Child Health Journal, 22,* 71–81.

McCrae, R.R., & Costa, P.T. (2006). Cross-cultural perspectives on adult personality trait development. In D.K. Mroczek & T.D. Little (Eds.). *Handbook of personality development.* Mahwah, NJ: Erlbaum.

McCullogh, S. (2016). *Highest C-section rates by country.* Retrieved April 26, 2017, from www.bellybelly.com

McCurdy, A.P., & others (2017). Effects of exercise on mild-to-moderate depressive symptoms in the post-partum period: A meta-analysis. *Obstetrics and Gynecology, 129,* 1087–1097.

McDermott, E.R., & others (2018). Family ethnic socialization predicts better academic outcomes via proactive coping with discrimination and increased self-efficacy. *Journal of Adolescence, 65,* 189–195.

McDonald, K.L., & Asher, S.R. (2018). Peer acceptance, peer rejection, and popularity: Social cognitive and behavioral perspectives. In W.M. Bukowski & others (Eds.), *Handbook of peer interactions, relationships, and groups* (2nd ed.). New York: Guilford.

McElhaney, K.B., & Allen, J.P. (2012). Sociocultural perspectives on adolescent autonomy. In P.K. Kreig, M.S. Schulz, & S.T. Hauser (Eds.), *Adolescence and beyond.* New York: Oxford University Press.

McElvaney, R., Greene, S., & Hogan, D. (2014). To tell or not to tell? Factors influencing young people's informal disclosures of child sexual abuse. *Journal of Interpersonal Violence, 29,* 928–947.

McGarry, J., Kim, H., Sheng, X., Egger, M., & Baksh, L. (2009). Postpartum depression and help-seeking behavior. *Journal of Midwifery and Women's Health, 54,* 50–56.

McGillion, M., & others (2017a). What paves the way to conventional language? The predictive value of babble, pointing, and socioeconomic status. *Child Development, 88,* 156–166.

McGillion, M., & others (2017b). A randomized controlled trial to test the effect of promoting caregiver contingent talk on language development from diverse socioeconomic status backgrounds. *Journal of Child Psychology and Psychiatry, 58,* 1122–1131.

McGough, E.L., & others (2018, in press). Limbic and basal ganglia neuroanatomical correlates of gait and executive function: Older adults with mild cognitive impairment and intact cognition. *American Journal of Physical Medicine and Rehabilitation.*

McGregor, K.K. (2017). Semantics in child language disorders. In R. Schwartz (Ed.), *Handbook of child language disorders* (2nd ed.). New York: Routledge.

McHale, S.M., Updegraff, K.A., & Whiteman, S.D. (2013). Sibling relationships. In G.W. Peterson & K.R. Bush (Eds.), *Handbook of marriage and family* (3rd ed.). New York: Springer.

McLaughlin, C.N., & Broihier, H.T. (2018). Keeping neurons young and foxy: FoxOs promote neuronal plasticity. *Trends in Genetics, 34,* 65–78.

McLaughlin, K. (2003, December 30). Commentary in K. Painter, "Nurse dispenses dignity for dying." *USA Today,* Section D, pp. 1–2.

McLaughlin, K.A., Sheridan, M.A., & Nelson, C.A. (2017). Neglect as a violation of species-expectant experience: Neurodevelopmental consequences. *Biological Psychiatry, 82,* 462–471.

McLean, K.C., Syed, M., Yoder, A., & Greenhoot, A. (2016). The role of domain content in understanding identity development processes. *Journal of Research on Adolescence, 26,* 60–75.

McLean, K.C., & others (2018, in press). Identity development in cultural context: The role of deviating master narratives. *Journal of Personality.*

McLeish, J., & Redshaw, M. (2018). A qualitative study of volunteer doulas working alongside midwives at births in England: Mothers' and doulas' experiences. *Midwifery, 56,* 53–60.

McLimans, K.E., & others (2017). Autotaxin is related to metabolic dysfunction and predicts Alzheimer's disease outcomes. *Journal of Alzheimer's Disease, 56,* 403–413.

McMahon, D.M., Liu, J., Zhang, H., Torres, M.E., & Best, R.G. (2013). Maternal obesity, folate intake, and neural tube defects in offspring. *Birth Defects A: Clinical and Molecular Teratology, 97,* 115–122.

McMillan, J.H. (2018). *Classroom assessment* (7th ed.). Upper Saddle River, NJ: Pearson.

McMurray, B. (2016). Language at three timescales: The role of real-time processes in language development and evolution. *Topics in Cognitive Science, 8,* 393–407.

McNicholas, F., & others (2014). Medical, cognitive, and academic outcomes of very low birth weight infants at 10–14 years in Ireland. *Irish Journal of Medical Science, 183,* 525–532.

McQueen, D.V. (2017). Policy development and decision making in prevention science. In M. Israelashvili & J. Romano (Eds.), *Cambridge handbook of international prevention science.* New York: Cambridge University Press.

McRae, C., Petrov, M.E., Dautovich, N., & Lichstein, K.L. (2016). Late-life sleep and sleep disorders. In K.W. Schaie

& S.L. Willis (Eds.), *Handbook of the psychology of aging* (8th ed.). New York: Elsevier.

Medford, E., & others (2018). Treatment adherence and psychological wellbeing in maternal caregivers of children with phenylketonuria (PKU). *JMD Reports, 39,* 107–116.

Medrano, M., & others (2018, in press). Evidence-based exercise recommendations to reduce hepatic fat content in youth—A systematic review and meta-analysis. *Progress in Cardiovascular Disease.*

Meerlo, P., Sgoifo, A., & Suchecki, D. (2008). Restricted and disrupted sleep: Effects on autonomic function, neuroendocrine stress systems, and stress responsivity. *Sleep Medicine Review, 12,* 197–210.

Meert, K.L., & others (2015). Meaning making during parent-physician bereavement meetings after a child's death. *Health Psychology, 34,* 453–461.

Meeus, W. (2017). Adolescent ethnic identity in social context: A commentary. *Child Development, 88,* 761–766.

Mehta, C.M., & Keener, E. (2017). Oh, the places we'll go: Where will Sandra Bem's work lead us next? *Sex Roles, 76,* 637–642.

Meier, E.A., & others (2016). Defining a good death (successful dying): Literature review and a call for research and public dialogue. *American Journal of Geriatric Psychiatry, 24,* 261–271.

Meins, E., Bureau, J.F., & Ferryhough, C. (2018, in press). Mother-child attachment from infancy to the preschool years: Predicting security and stability. *Child Development.*

Meins, E., & others (2013). Mind-mindedness and theory of mind: Mediating processes of language and perspectival symbolic play. *Child Development, 84,* 1777–1790.

Mejia, S.T., Ryan, L.J., Gonzalez, R., & Smith, J. (2017). Successful aging as the intersection of individual resources, age, environment, and experiences of well-being in daily activities. *Journals of Gerontology B: Psychological Sciences and Social Sciences, 72,* 279–289.

Meldrum, R.C., & others (2017). Reassessing the relationship between general intelligence and self control in childhood. *Intelligence, 60,* 1–9.

Melehan, K.L., & others (2018, in press). Randomized trial of CPAP and Vardenafil on erectile and arterial function in men with obstructive sleep apnea and erectile dysfunction. *Journal of Clinical Endocrinology and Metabolism.*

Melis Yavuz, H., & Selcuk, B. (2018). Predictors of obesity and overweight in preschoolers: The role of parenting styles and feeding practices. *Appetite, 120,* 491–499.

Meltzer, L. (Ed.) (2018). *Executive function in education* (2nd ed.). New York: Guilford.

Meltzer, L.J. (2017). Future directions in sleep and developmental psychopathology. *Journal of Clinical Child and Adolescent Psychology, 46,* 295–301.

Meltzoff, A.N. (1988). Infant imitation and memory: Nine-month-old infants in immediate and deferred tests. *Child Development, 59,* 217–225.

Meltzoff, A.N. (2004). Imitation as a mechanism of social cognition: Origins of empathy, theory of mind, and the representation of action. In U. Goswami (Ed.), *Blackwell handbook of childhood cognitive development.* Malden, MA: Blackwell.

Meltzoff, A.N. (2005). Imitation. In B. Hopkins (Ed.), *Cambridge encyclopedia of child development.* Cambridge: Cambridge University Press.

Meltzoff, A.N. (2007). Infants' causal learning. In A. Gopnik & L. Schulz (Eds.), *Causal learning.* New York: Oxford University Press.

Meltzoff, A.N. (2011). Social cognition and the origins of imitation, empathy, and theory of mind. In U. Goswami (Ed.), *Wiley-Blackwell handbook of childhood cognitive development* (2nd ed.). New York: Wiley.

Meltzoff, A.N. (2017). Elements of a comprehensive theory of infant imitation. *Behavioral and Brain Sciences, 40,* e396.

Meltzoff, A.N., & Brooks, R. (2009). Social cognition: The role of gaze following in early word learning. In

J. Colombo, P. McCardle, & L. Freund (Eds), *Infant pathways to language.* Clifton, NJ: Psychology Press.

Meltzoff, A.N., & Williamson, R.A. (2010). The importance of imitation for theories of social-cognitive development. In J.G. Bremner & T.D. Wachs (Eds.), *Wiley-Blackwell handbook of infant development* (2nd ed.). New York: Wiley.

Meltzoff, A.N., & Williamson, R.A. (2013). Imitation: Social, cognitive, and theoretical perspectives. In P.D. Zelazo (Ed.), *Oxford handbook of developmental psychology.* New York: Oxford University Press.

Meltzoff, A.N., & others (2018a, in press). Infant brain responses to felt and observed touch of hands and feet: An MEG study. *Developmental Science.*

Meltzoff, A.N., & others (2018b, in press). Re-examination of Oostenbroek et al. (2016): Evidence for neonatal imitation of tongue protrusion. *Developmental Science.*

Memari, A., Ziaee, V., Mirfaxeli, F., & Kordi, R. (2012). Investigation of autism comorbidities and associations in a school-based community sample. *Journal of Child and Adolescent Psychiatric Nursing, 25,* 84–90.

Memitz, S.A. (2018, in press). The mental health implications of emerging adult long-term cohabitation. *Emerging Adulthood.*

Mendelson, M., & others (2016). Sleep quality, sleep duration, and physical activity in obese adolescents: Effects of exercise training. *Pediatric Obesity, 11,* 26–32.

Mendes, A. (2016). Nursing care to facilitate and support 'good' grieving. *British Journal of Nursing, 24,* 95.

Mendle, J., Ryan, R.M., & McKone, K.M.P. (2018, in press). Age at menarche, depression, and antisocial behavior in adulthood. *Pediatrics.*

Mendoza Laiz, N., & others (2018). Potential benefits of a cognitive training program in mild cognitive impairment (MCI). *Restorative Neurology and Neuroscience, 36,* 207–213.

Mendoza-Nunez, M., & de la Luz Martinez-Maldonado, N. (2019, in press). Promoting successful aging in the community. In R. Fernandez-Ballesteros & others (Eds.), *Cambridge handbook of successful aging.* New York: Cambridge University Press.

Menesini, E., & Salmivalli, C. (2017). Bullying in schools: The state of the knowledge and effective interventions. *Psychology, Health, and Medicine, 22* (Suppl. 1), S240–S253.

Meng, X., & D'Arcy, C. (2014). Successful aging in Canada: Prevalence and predictors from a population-based sample of older adults. *Gerontology, 60,* 65–72.

Meng, X., Uto, Y., & Hashiya, K. (2017). Observing third-party attentional relationships affects infants' gaze following: An eye-tracking study. *Frontiers in Psychology, 7,* 2065.

Menn, L., & Stoel-Gammon, C. (2009). Phonological development: Learning sounds and patterns. In J. Berko Gleason & N. Ratner (Eds.), *The development of language* (7th ed.). Boston: Allyn & Bacon.

Menon, R., & others (2011). Cigarette smoking induces oxidative stress and atopsis in normal fetal membranes. *Placenta, 32,* 317–322.

Menotti, A., Puddu, P.E., Maiani, G., & Catasta, G. (2015). Lifestyle behavior and lifetime incidence of heart diseases. *International Journal of Cardiology, 401,* 293–299.

Mercer, N., & others (2016). Childhood predictors and adult life success of adolescent delinquency abstainers. *Journal of Abnormal Child Psychology, 44,* 615–624.

Meredith, N.V. (1978). Research between 1960 and 1970 on the standing height of young children in different parts of the world. In H.W. Reece & L.P. Lipsitt (Eds.), *Advances in child development and behavior* (Vol. 12). New York: Academic Press.

Merianos, A.L., Dixon, C.A., & Mahabee-Gittens, E.M. (2017). Tobacco smoke exposure-related illnesses among pediatric emergency department patients. *Journal of Pediatric Health Care, 31,* 161–166.

Merlo, P., & others (2018, in press). Alzheimer café: An approach focused on Alzheimer's patients but with remarkable values on the quality of life of their caregivers. *Aging Clinical and Experimental Research*.

Mermelshtine, R. (2017). Parent-child learning interactions: A review of the literature on scaffolding. *British Journal of Educational Psychology, 87*, 241–254.

Merrill, D.M. (2009). Parent-child relationships: Laterlife. In D. Carr (Ed.), *Encyclopedia of the life course and human development*. Boston: Gale Cengage.

Meschkow, A.M., & others (2018). Risk taking. In M.H. Bornstein (Ed.), *SAGE encyclopedia of lifespan human development*. Thousand Oaks, CA: Sage.

Mesman, J. (2018, in press). Video observations of sensitive caregiving "off the beaten track": Introduction to the special issue. *Attachment and Human Development*.

Messerlian, C., & Basso, O. (2018, in press). Cohort studies in the context of obstetric and gynecologic research: A methodological overview. *Acta Obstetricia et Gynecologica Scandinavica*.

Messiah, S.E., Miller, T.L., Lipshultz, S.E., & Bandstra, E.S. (2011). Potential latent effects of prenatal cocaine exposure on growth and the risk of cardiovascular and metabolic disease in childhood. *Progress in Pediatric Cardiology, 31*, 59–65.

Messinger, D.S., & others (2017). Temporal dependency and the structure of early looking. *PLoS One, 12*, e0169458.

Meyer, L.E. (2017). From article to action: Fostering literacy skills for diverse learners across learning environments. *Young Exceptional Children, 20*, 145–147.

Meyre, D., & others (2018). An evolutionary genetic perspective of eating disorders. *Neuroendocrinology, 106*, 292–306.

Michael, R.T., Gagnon, J.H., Laumann, E.O., & Kolata, G. (1994). *Sex in America*. Boston: Little, Brown.

Michalicova, A., & others (2017). Taupathies–focus on changes at the neurovascular unit. *Current Alzheimer Disease, 14*, 507–520.

Michaud, I., & others (2017). Physical activity and sedentary behavior levels in children and adolescents with type 1 diabetes using insulin pump or injection therapy–The importance of parental activity profile. *Journal of Diabetes and Its Complications, 31*, 381–386.

Mick, P., & others (2018). Associations between sensory loss and social networks, participation, support, and loneliness: Analysis of the Canadian Longitudinal Study of Aging. *Canadian Family Physician, 64*, e33–e41.

Micoch, T., & others (2018). Dietary patterns, cost, and compliance with low-protein diet of phenylketonuria and other inherited metabolic diseases. *European Journal of Clinical Nutrition, 72*, 87–92.

Middleton, R.J., & others (2017). Epigenetic silencing of the human 18 kDA translocator protein in a T cell leukemia cell line. *DNA and Cell Biology, 38*, 103–108.

Mikkola, T.M., & others (2016). Self-reported hearing is associated with time spent out-of-home and withdrawal from leisure activities in older community-dwelling adults. *Aging: Clinical and Experimental Research, 28*, 297–302.

Mikulincer, M., & Shaver, P.R. (2016). *Attachment in adulthood* (2nd ed.). New York: Guilford.

Mila, M., & others (2017). Fragile X syndrome: An overview and update of the FMR1 gene. *Clinical Genetics, 93*, 197–205.

Milic, J., & others (2018, in press). Determinants and predictors of grief severity and persistence: The Rotterdam Study. *Journal of Aging and Health*.

Miller, A.B., & others (2018). Neural correlates of emotion regulation and adolescent suicidal ideation. *Biological Psychology. Cognition, Neuroscience, and Neuroimaging, 3*, 125–132.

Miller, A.C. (2016). Opinions on the legitimacy of brain death among Sunni and Shi'a scholars. *Journal of Religion and Health, 55*, 394–402.

Miller, B. (2017). *Cultural anthropology* (4th ed.). Upper Saddle River, NJ: Pearson.

Miller, C., & Price, J. (2013). *The number of children being raised by gay or lesbian parents*. Unpublished manuscript, Department of Economics, Brigham Young University, Provo, UT.

Miller, D.G., Dresser, R., & Kim, S.Y.H. (2018, in press). Advance euthanasia directives: A controversial case and its ethical implications. *Journal of Medical Ethics*.

Miller, E.B., Farkas, G., & Duncan, G.J. (2016). Does Head Start differentially benefit children with risks targeted by the program's service model? *Early Childhood Research Quarterly, 34*, 1–12.

Miller, F.G., & Appelbaum, P.S. (2018). Physician-assisted death for psychiatric patients—misguided public policy. *New England Journal of Medicine, 378*, 883–885.

Miller, L.M., & Bell, R.A. (2012). Online health information seeking: The influence of age, information trustworthiness, and search challenges. *Journal of Aging and Health, 24*, 525–541.

Miller, M.S. (2018). Save for retirement. *Annals of Emergency Medicine 71*, 252.

Miller, P.H. (2011). Piaget's theory: Past, present, and future. In U. Goswami (Ed.), *Wiley-Blackwell handbook of childhood cognitive development* (2nd ed.). New York: Wiley.

Miller, P.H. (2015). *Theories of developmental psychology* (6th ed.). New York: Worth.

Miller, P.J., & Cho, G.E. (2018). *Self-esteem in time and place*. New York: Academic Press.

Miller, R., Wankerl, M., Stalder, T., Kirschbaum, C., & Alexander, N. (2013). The serotonin transporter gene-linked polymorphic region (5-HTTLPR) and cortisol stress reactivity: A meta-analysis. *Molecular Psychiatry, 18*, 1018–1024.

Miller, S.L., Huppi, P.S., & Mallard, C. (2016). The consequences of fetal growth restriction on brain structure and neurodevelopmental outcome. *Journal of Physiology, 594*, 807–823.

Miller, W.R. (2018, in press). Self-management behaviors of children with spina bifida. *Journal of Neuroscience Nursing*.

Miller-Perrin, C.L., Perrin, R.D., & Kocur, J.L. (2009). Parental, physical, and psychological aggression: Psychological symptoms in young adults. *Child Abuse and Neglect, 33*, 1–11.

Mills, C.M., & Elashi, F.B. (2014). Children's skepticism: Developmental and individual differences in children's ability to detect and explain distorted claims. *Journal of Experimental Child Psychology, 124C*, 1–17.

Mills-Koonce, W.R., Propper, C.B., & Barnett, M. (2012). Poor infant soothability and later insecure-ambivalent attachment: Developmental change in phenotypic markers of risk or two measures of the same construct? *Infant Behavior and Development, 35*, 215–235.

Milne, E., & others (2012). Parental prenatal smoking and risk of childhood acute lymphoblastic leukemia. *American Journal of Epidemiology, 175*, 43–53.

Milner, A., & others (2014). The effects of involuntary job loss on suicide and suicide attempts among young adults: Evidence from a matched case-control study. *Australian and New Zealand Journal of Psychiatry, 48*, 333–340.

Mindell, L.A., & others (2016). Development of infant and toddler sleep patterns: Real-world data from a mobile application. *Journal of Sleep Research*.

Minkler, M., & Fuller-Thompson, E. (2005). African American grandparents raising grandchildren: A national study using the Census 2000 American Community Survey. *Journals of Gerontology B: Psychological Sciences and Social Sciences, 60*, S82–S92.

Minnes, S., & others (2010). The effects of prenatal cocaine exposure on problem behavior in children 4–10 years. *Neurotoxicology and Teratology, 32*, 443–451.

Minnes, S., & others (2016). Executive function in children with prenatal cocaine exposure (12-15 years). *Neurotoxicology and Teratology, 57*, 79–86.

Minnesota Family Investment Program (2009). *Longitudinal study of early MFIP recipients*. Retrieved January 12, 2009, from www.dhs.state.mn.us/main/idcplg?IdcService=GET_DYNAMIC_CONVERSION&RevisionSelectionMethod= LatestReleased&dDocName =id_004113

Minsart, A.F., Buekens, P., Spiegelaere, M., & Englert, Y. (2013). Neonatal outcomes in obese mothers: A population-based analysis. *BMC Pregnancy and Childbirth, 13*, 36.

Mischel, W. (2004). Toward an integrative science of the person. *Annual Review of Psychology* (Vol. 55). Palo Alto, CA: Annual Reviews.

Mischel, W. (2014). *The marshmallow test; Mastering self-control*. New York: Little Brown.

Mischel, W., Cantor, N., & Feldman, S. (1996). Principles of self-regulation: The nature of will power and self-control. In E.T. Higgins & A.W. Kruglanski (Eds.), *Social psychology*. New York: Guilford.

Mischel, W., & Moore, B.S. (1980). The role of ideation in voluntary delay for symbolically presented rewards. *Cognitive Therapy and Research, 4*, 211–221.

Mischel, W., & others (2011). "Willpower" over the life span: Decomposing self-regulation. *Social Cognitive and Affective Neuroscience, 6*, 252–256.

Mishra, G.D., Cooper, R., Tom, S.E., & Kuh, D. (2009). Early life circumstances and their impact on menarche and menopause. *Women's Health, 5*, 175–190.

Mitanchez, D., & others (2015). The offspring of the diabetic mother—short- and long-term implications. *Best Practice and Research: Clinical Obstetrics and Gynecology, 29*, 256–269.

Mitchell, E.A., & Krous, H.F. (2015). Sudden unexpected death in infancy: A historical perspective. *Journal of Pediatrics and Child Health, 5*, 108–112.

Mitchell, M.B., & others (2012). Cognitively stimulating activities: Effects on cognition across four studies with up to 21 years of longitudinal data. *Journal of Aging Research, 2012*. Article ID 461592.

Mitchison, D., & others (2017). Disentangling body image: The relative associations of overvaluation, dissatisfaction, and preoccupation with psychological distress and eating disorder behaviors in male and female adolescents. *International Journal of Eating Disorders, 50*, 118–126.

Mithun, M. (2019). Morphology: What's in a word. In C. Genetti (Ed.), *How languages work* (2nd ed.). New York: Cambridge University Press.

Miyahara, R., & others (2017). Exposure to paternal tobacco smoking increased child hospitalization for lower respiratory infections but not for other diseases in Vietnam. *Scientific Reports, 7*, 45481.

Miyake, S., & others (2017). Community midwifery initiatives in fragile and conflict-affected countries: A scoping review of approaches from recruitment to retention. *Health Policy Planning, 32*, 21–33.

Miyakoshi, K., & others (2013). Perinatal outcomes: Intravenous patient-controlled fentanyl versus no analgesia in labor. *Journal of Obstetrics and Gynecology Research, 39*(4), 783–789.

Miyata, K., & others (2018). Effects of cataract surgery on cognitive function in elderly: Results of Fujiwara-kyo Eye Study. *PLoS One, 13*(2), e0192677.

Miyazaki, K., Song, J.W., & Takahashi, E. (2016). Asymmetry of radial and symmetry of tangential neuronal migration pathways in developing human fetal brains. *Frontiers in Neuroanatomy, 10*, 2.

Mnyani, C.N., & others (2017). Infant feeding knowledge, perceptions, and practices among women with and without HIV in Johannesburg, South Africa: A survey in healthcare facilities. *International Breastfeeding Journal, 12*, 17.

Moen, P. (2007). Unpublished review of J.W. Santrock's *Life-span development* (12th ed.). New York: McGraw-Hill.

Moen, P. (2009a). Careers. In D. Carr (Ed.), *Encyclopedia of the life course and human development*. Boston: Gale Cengage.

Moen, P. (2009b). Dual-career couples. In D. Carr (Ed.), *Encyclopedia of the life course and human development*. Boston: Gale Cengage.

Moharei, F., & others (2018). Evaluating of psychiatric behavior in obese children and adolescents. *Iranian Journal of Child Neurology, 12*, 26–36.

Mok, Y., & others (2018, in press). American Heart Association's Life's Simple 7 at middle age and prognosis after myocardial infarction in later life. *Journal of the American Heart Association.*

Mola, J.R. (2015). Erectile dysfunction in the older adult male. *Urological Nursing, 35*, 87–93.

Molgora, S., & others (2018, in press). Dyadic coping and marital adjustment during pregnancy: A cross-sectional study of Italian couples expecting their first child. *International Journal of Psychology.*

Moline, H.R., & Smith, J.F. (2016). The continuing threat of syphilis in pregnancy. *Current Opinion in Obstetrics and Gynecology, 28*, 101–104.

Mollart, L., & others (2018, in press). Midwives' personal use of complementary and alternative medicine (CAM) influences their recommendations to women experiencing a post-date pregnancy. *Women and Birth.*

Mollborn, S. (2017). Teenage mothers today: What we know and how it matters. *Child Development Perspectives, 11*, 63–69.

Molton, I.R., & Terrill, A.L. (2014). Overview of persistent pain in older adults. *American Psychologist, 69*, 197–207.

Monge, Z.A., & Madden, D.J. (2016). Linking cognitive and visual perceptual decline in healthy aging: The information degradation hypothesis. *Neuroscience and Biobehavioral Reviews, 69*, 166–173.

Monin, J.K., & others (2018, in press). The impact of both spousal caregivers' and care recipients' health on relationship satisfaction in the Caregiver Health Effects Study. *Journal of Health Psychology.*

Monn, A.R., & others (2017). Executive function and parenting in the context of homelessness. *Journal of Family Psychology, 31*, 61–70.

Monroy, C.D., & others (2018, in press). The infant motor system predicts actions based on visual statistical learning. *NeuroImage.*

Monserud, M.A. (2008). Intergenerational relationships and affectual solidarity between grandparents and young adults. *Journal of Marriage and the Family, 70*, 182–195.

Monserud, M.A., & Markides, K.S. (2017). Changes in depressive symptoms during widowhood among older Mexican Americans: The role of financial strain, social support, and religious attendance. *Aging and Mental Health, 21*, 586–594.

Montague, T., & others (2017). Public and professional insights on end-of-life care: Results of the 2016 Health Care in Canada survey. *Healthcare Quarterly, 20*(2), 18–21.

Moon, M. (2016). Aging and society. In L.K. George & K.F. Ferraro (Eds.), *Handbook of aging and the social sciences* (8th ed.). New York: Elsevier.

Moon, R.Y., & others (2017). Impact of a randomized controlled trial to reduce bedsharing on breastfeeding rates and duration for African American infants. *Journal of Community Health, 42*, 707–715.

Mooney-Leber, S.M., & Brummelte, S. (2017). Neonatal pain and reduced maternal care: Early-life stressors interacting to impact brain and behavioral development. *Neuroscience, 342*, 21–36.

Moore, D. (2001). *The dependent gene.* New York: W.H. Freeman.

Moore, D.S. (2013). Behavioral genetics, genetics, and epigenetics. In P.D. Zelazo (Ed.), *Handbook of developmental psychology.* New York: Oxford University Press.

Moore, D.S. (2015). *The developing genome.* New York: Oxford University Press.

Moore, D.S. (2017). Behavioral epigenetics. *Wiley Interdisciplinary Reviews: Systems Biology and Medicine, 9*, 1.

Moore, S.J., & Murphy, G.G. (2016). Age-related alterations in neural plasticity. In M. Kaeberlein & G.M. Martin (Eds.), *Handbook of the biology of aging* (8th ed.). New York: Elsevier.

Moore, S.R., Harden, K.P., & Mendle, J. (2014). Pubertal timing and adolescent sexual behavior in girls. *Developmental Psychology, 50*, 1734–1745.

Moosmann, D.A., & Roosa, M.W. (2015). Exploring Mexican American adolescent romantic relationship profiles and adjustment. *Journal of Adolescence, 43*, 181–192.

Mooya, H., Sichimba, F., & Bakermans-Kranenburg, M. (2016). Infant-mother and infant-sibling attachment in Zambia. *Attachment and Human Development, 18*, 618–635.

Mora, J.C., & Valencia, W.M. (2018). Exercise and older adults. *Clinics in Geriatric Medicine, 34*, 145–162.

Moradi, B., & others (2016). A content analysis of literature on trans people and issues: 2002–2012. *The Counseling Psychologist, 44*, 960–965.

Morbelli, S., & Baucknecht, M. (2018). Amyloid PET imaging: Standardization and integration with other Alzheimer's disease biomarkers. *Methods in Molecular Biology, 1750*, 203–212.

Moreau, D., Kirk, I.J., & Waldie, K.E. (2018, in press). High-intensity training enhances executive function in children in a randomized, placebo-controlled trial. *Elife.*

Morikawa, T., & others (2017). Admission of people with dementia to psychiatric hospitals in Japan: Factors that can shorten their hospitalizations. *Psychogeriatrics, 17*, 341–347.

Morin, A.J.S., & others (2017). Adolescents' body image trajectories: A further test of the self-equilibrium hypothesis. *Developmental Psychology, 53*, 1501–1521.

Morosan, L., & others (2017). Emotion recognition and perspective taking: A comparison between typical and incarcerated male adolescents. *PLoS One, 12*(1), e0170646.

Morra, S., Gobbo, C., Marini, Z., & Sheese, R. (2008). *Cognitive development: Neo-Piagetian perspectives.* Mahwah, NJ: Erlbaum.

Morris, A.S., & others (2013). Effortful control, behavior problems, and peer relations: What predicts academic adjustment in kindergarteners from low-income families? *Early Education Development, 24*, 813–828.

Morris, B.J., & others (2012). A 'snip' in time: What is the best age to circumcise? *BMC Pediatrics, 12*, 20.

Morris, S., & others (2018). Emotion regulation dynamics during parent-child interactions: Implications for research and practice. In P.M. Cole & T. Hollenstein (Eds.), *Emotion regulation.* New York: Routledge.

Morrison, G.S. (2017). *Fundamentals of early childhood education* (8th ed.). Upper Saddle River, NJ: Pearson.

Morrison, G.S. (2018). *Early childhood education today* (14th ed.). Upper Saddle River, NJ: Pearson.

Morrison, R.S. (2013). Models of palliative care delivery in the United States. *Current Opinion in Supportive and Palliative Care, 7*, 201–206.

Morrison, S.C., Fife, T., & Hertlein, K.M. (2017). Mechanisms behind prolonged effects of parental divorce: A phenomenological study. *Journal of Divorce and Remarriage, 58*, 44–63.

Morrison-Beedy, D., & others (2013). Reducing sexual risk behavior in adolescent girls: Results from a randomized trial. *Journal of Adolescent Health, 52*, 314–322.

Morrissey, T.W. (2009). Multiple child-care arrangements and young children's behavioral outcomes. *Child Development, 80*, 59–76.

Morse, A.F., & Cangelosi, A. (2017). Why are there developmental stages in language learning? A developmental robotics model of language development. *Cognitive Science, 41*(Suppl. 1), S32–S51.

Moss, A.H., & others (2017). The quality of POLST completion to guide treatment: A 2-state study. *Journal of the American Medical Directors Association, 8*(9), e5–e10.

Moss, S.A., & Wilson, S.G. (2018). Why are older people often so responsible and considerate even when their future seems limited? A systematic review. *International Journal of Aging and Human Development, 86*, 82–108.

Mossburg, S.E. (2018). Baby boomer retirement: Are you up to the challenge? *Nursing Management, 49*, 13–14.

Motti-Stefanidi, F. (2018). Immigrant and refugee youth positive adaptation and development. In J.E. Lansford & P. Banati (Eds.), *Handbook of adolescent development research and its impact on global policy.* New York: Oxford University Press.

Motti-Stefanidi, F., & Masten, A.S. (2017). A resilience perspective on immigrant youth adaptation and development. In N.J. Cabrera & B. Leyendecker (Eds.), *Positive development of minority children.* New York: Springer.

Moura da Costa, E., & Tuleski, S.C. (2017). Social constructivist interpretation of Vygotsky. In C. Ratner & D. Silva (Eds.), *Vygotsky and Marx.* New York: Routledge.

Mparmpakas, D., & others (2013). Immune system function, stress, exercise, and nutrition profile can affect pregnancy outcome: Lessons from a Mediterranean cohort. *Experimental and Therapeutic Medicine, 5*, 411–418.

Mroczek, D.K., Spiro, A., & Griffin, P.W. (2006). Personality and aging. In J.E. Birren & K.W. Schaie (Eds.). *Handbook of the psychology of aging* (6th ed.). San Diego: Academic Press.

Mroczek, D.K., & others (2015). Emotional reactivity and mortality: Longitudinal findings from the VA Normative Aging Study. *Journals of Gerontology B: Psychological Sciences and Social Sciences, 70*(3), 398–406.

Mrowka, R. (2017). Arterial hypertension. *Acta Physiologica, 219*, 697–699.

Mucke, M., & others (2018). Moderate-to-vigorous physical activity, executive functions, and prefrontal brain oxygenation in children: A functional near-infrared spectroscopy study. *Journal of Sports Sciences, 36*, 630–636.

Mueller, S.C., & others (2017). Evidence for the triadic model of adolescent brain development: Cognitive load and task-relevance of emotion differentially affect adolescents and adults. *Developmental Cognitive Neuroscience, 26*, 91–100.

Muftic, L.R., & others (2018, in press). The mediating effect of self-control on parenting and delinquency: A gendered approach with a multinational sample. *International Journal of Offender Therapy and Comparative Criminology.*

Muijs, D. (2017). Can schools reduce bullying? The relationship between school characteristics and the prevalence of bullying behaviors. *British Journal of Educational Psychology, 87*, 255–272.

Mulder, T.M., & others (2018). Risk factors for child neglect: A meta-analytic review. *Child Abuse and Neglect, 77*, 198–210.

Muller, M.J., & others (2017). Sleep duration of inpatients with a depressive disorder: Associations with age, subjective sleep quality, and cognitive complaints. *Archives of Psychiatric Nursing, 31*, 77–82.

Muller, U., Miller, M., Hutchison, S., & Ten Eycke, K. (2017). Transition to school: Executive function, emergent academic skills, and early school achievement. In M.J. Hoskyn, G. Iarocci, & A.R. Young (Eds.), *Executive functions in children's everyday lives.* New York: Oxford University Press.

Munroe, B.A., & others (2018, in press). Physiological substrates of executive functioning: A systematic review of the literature. *Attention Deficit and Hyperactivity Disorders.*

Muntane, G., & others (2018, in press). Biological processes modulating longevity in primates: A phylogenetic genome-phenome analysis. *Molecular Biology and Evolution.*

Murcia, M., & others (2017). Prenatal mercury exposure and birth outcomes. *Environmental Research, 151*, 11–20.

Murdock, K.K., Horissian, M., & Crichlow-Ball, C. (2017). Emerging adults' text message use and sleep characteristics: A multimethod, naturalistic study. *Behavioral Sleep Medicine, 15*, 228–241.

Murray, H.B., & others (2017). Will I get fat? 22-year weight trajectories of individuals with eating disorders. *International Journal of Eating Disorders, 50*, 739–747.

Mussen, P.H., Honzik, M., & Eichorn, D. (1982). Early adult antecedents of life satisfaction at age 70. *Journal of Gerontology, 37*, 316–332.

Mychasiuk, R., Muhammad, A., & Kolb, B. (2016). Chronic stress induces persistent changes in global DNA methylation and gene expression in the medial frontal cortex, orbitofrontal cortex, and hippocampus. *Neuroscience, 322*, 489–499.

Myers, D.G. (2010). *Psychology* (9th ed.). New York: Worth.

Myers, J., & others (2018, in press). Provider tools for advance care planning and goals of care discussion: A systematic review. *American Journal of Hospice and Palliative Care.*

Myerson, J., Rank, M.R., Raines, F.Q., & Schnitzler, M.A. (1998). Race and general cognitive ability: The myth of diminishing returns in education. *Psychology Science, 9.*

N

Nabe-Nielsen, K., & others (2014). Demand-specific work ability, poor health, and working conditions in middle-aged full-time employees. *Applied Ergonomics, 45*, 1174–1180.

Nagel, B.J., & others (2011). Altered white matter microstructure in children with attention-deficit/hyperactivity disorder. *Journal of the American Academy of Child and Adolescent Psychiatry, 50*, 283–292.

Naicker, K., Galambos, N.L., Zeng, Y., Senthilselvan, A., & Colman, I. (2013). Social, demographic, and health outcomes in the 10 years following adolescent depression. *Journal of Adolescent Health, 52*, 533–538.

Nair, R.L., Roche, K.M., & White, R.M.B. (2018). Acculturation gap distress among Latino youth: Prospective links to family processes and youth depressive symptoms, alcohol use, and academic performance. *Journal of Youth and Adolescence, 47*, 105–120.

Nair, S., & others (2018, in press). Local resting state functional connectivity in autism: Site and cohort variability and the effect of eye status. *Brain Imaging and Behavior.*

Najman, J.M., & others (2009). The impact of episodic and chronic poverty on child cognitive development. *Journal of Pediatrics, 154*, 284–289.

Najman, J.M., & others (2010). Timing and chronicity of family poverty and development of unhealthy behaviors in children: A longitudinal study. *Journal of Adolescent Health, 46*, 538–544.

Nakagawa, T., & others (2018, in press). Subjective well-being in centenarians: A comparison of Japan and the United States. *Aging and Mental Health.*

Nakamichi, K. (2018, in press). Differences in young children's peer preference by inhibitory control and emotion regulation. *Psychological Reports.*

Namgoong, S., & Kim, N.H. (2018, in press). Meiotic spindle formatin in mammalian oocytes: Implications for human infertility. *Biological Reproduction.*

Nansel, T.R., & others (2001). Bullying behaviors among U.S. youth. *Journal of the American Medical Association, 285*, 2094–2100.

Narayan, A.J., & Masten, A.S. (2018, in press). Resilience in the context of violence and trauma: Promotive and protective processes of positive caregiving. In J. Osofsky & B.M. Groves (Eds.), *Violence and trauma in the lives of children.* Santa Barbara, CA: Praeger.

Narayan, A.J., & others (2017). Intergenerational continuity of adverse childhood experiences: Unpacking exposure to maltreatment versus family dysfunction. *American Journal of Orthopsychiatry, 87*, 3–14.

Narváez, D. (2016). *Embodied morality.* New York: Palgrave-McMillan.

Narváez, D. (2017a). Evolution, childrearing, and compassionate morality. In P. Gilbert (Ed.), *Compassion.* New York: London.

Narváez, D. (2017b). The ontogenesis of moral becoming. In A. Fuentes & A. Visala (Eds.). *Verbs, bones, and brains.* Notre Dame, IN: University of Notre Dame Press.

Narváez, D. (2018). Ethogenesis: Evolution, early experience, and moral becoming. In J. Graham & K. Gray (Eds.), *The atlas of moral psychology.* New York: Guilford Press.

Narváez, D., & Gleason, T.R. (2013). Developmental optimism. In D. Narváez & others (2013). *Evolution, early experience, and human development.* New York: Oxford University Press.

National Alliance for Caregiving (2009). *Caregiving in the United States 2009.* Retrieved June 29, 2012, from www.caregiving.org/pdf/research/Caregiving

National Assessment of Educational Progress (2012). *The nation's report card: 2012.* Washington, DC: U.S. Department of Education.

National Association for Gifted Children (2017). *Gifted children.* Washington, DC: Author.

National Association for Sport and Physical Education (2002). *Active start: A statement of physical activity guidelines for children birth to five years.* Reston, VA: National Association for Sport and Physical Education Publications.

National Center for Education Statistics (2002). *Work during college.* Washington, DC: U.S. Office of Education.

National Center for Education Statistics (2017). *Status dropout rates. Digest of Education Statistics.* Washington, DC: U.S. Department of Education.

National Center for Education Statistics (2017). *The condition of education, 2017.* Washington, DC: U.S. Office of Education.

National Center for Health Statistics (2000). *Health United States, 2000, with adolescent health chartbook.* Bethesda, MD: U.S. Department of Health and Human Services.

National Center for Health Statistics (2018). *Death statistics.* Atlanta: Centers for Disease Control and Prevention.

National Center for Health Statistics (2018). *Sexually transmitted diseases.* Atlanta: Centers for Disease Control and Prevention.

National Center on Shaken Baby Syndrome (2012). *Shaken baby syndrome.* Retrieved April, 20, 2011, from www.dontshake.org/

National Clearinghouse on Child Abuse and Neglect (2013, July). *What is child abuse and neglect?* Washington, DC: U.S. Department of Health and Human Services.

National Council on Aging (2000, March). *Myths and realities survey results.* Washington, DC: Author.

National Institute for Early Education Research (2016). *Did state pre-K get back on track in 2015?* Retrieved November 29, 2016, from http://nieer/org

National Institute of Drug Abuse (2018). *Treating opioid use disorder during pregnancy.* Washington, DC: Author.

National Institute of Mental Health (2018). Autism spectrum disorders (pervasive developmental disorders). Retrieved January 12, 2018, from www.nimh.nih.gov/Publicat/autism.clm

National Sleep Foundation (2006). *Sleep in America poll 2006.* Washington, DC: Author.

National Sleep Foundation (2007). *Sleep in America poll 2007.* Washington, DC: Author.

Naughton, A.M., & others (2017). Ask me! Self-reported features of adolescents experiencing neglect or emotional maltreatment: A rapid systematic review. *Child: Care, Health, and Development, 43*, 348–360.

Naumova, O.Y., & others (2016). Epigenetic patterns modulate the connection between developmental dynamics of parenting and offspring psychosocial adjustment. *Child Development, 87*, 98–110.

Ncube, C.N., & Mueller, B.A. (2017). Daughters of mothers who smoke: A population-based cohort study of maternal prenatal tobacco use and subsequent prenatal smoking in offspring. *Pediatric and Perinatal Epidemiology, 31*, 14–20.

Needham, A.W., Barrett, T., & Peterman, K. (2002) A pick-me-up for infants' exploratory skills: Early simulated experiences reaching for objects using "sticky mittens" enhances young infants' object exploration skills. *Infant Behavior and Development, 25*, 279–295.

Needham, A.W., & others (2017). Characteristics of brief sticky mittens training that leads to increases in object exploration. *Journal of Experimental Child Psychology, 164*, 209–224.

Negriff, S., Susman, E.J., & Trickett, P.K. (2011). The development pathway from pubertal timing to delinquency and sexual activity from early to late adolescence. *Journal of Youth and Adolescence, 40*, 1343–1356.

Negru-Subtirica, O., & Pop, E.L. (2018). Reciprocal associations between educational identity and vocational identity in adolescence: A three-wave longitudinal investigation. *Journal of Youth and Adolescence, 47*, 703–716.

Nelson, C.A. (2003). Neural development and lifelong plasticity. In R.M. Lerner, F. Jacobs, & D. Wertlieb (Eds.), *Handbook of applied developmental science* (Vol. 1). Thousand Oaks, CA: Sage.

Nelson, C.A. (2008). Unpublished review of J.W. Santrock's *Topical approach to life-span development,* 5th ed. New York: McGraw-Hill.

Nelson, C.A. (2011). Brain development and behavior. In A.M. Rudolph, C. Rudolph, L. First, G. Lister, & A.A. Gersohon (Eds.), *Rudolph's pediatrics* (22nd ed.). New York: McGraw-Hill.

Nelson, C.A. (2013). Some thoughts on the development and neural bases of face processing. In M. Banaji & S. Gelman (Eds.), *The development of social cognition.* New York: Oxford University Press.

Nelson, G., & Powell, S.R. (2018, in press). A systematic review of longitudinal studies of mathematics difficulty. *Journal of Learning Disabilities.*

Nelson, J.A., Leerkes, E.M., O'Brien, M., Calkins, S.D., & Maracovitch, S. (2012). African American and European American mothers' beliefs about negative emotions and emotion socialization practices. *Parenting, 12*, 22–41.

Nelson, L.J., & others (2007). "If you want me to treat you like an adult, start acting like one!" Comparing the criteria that emerging adults and their parents have for adulthood. *Journal of Family Psychology, 21*, 665–674.

Nelson, S.E., Van Ryzin, M.J., & Dishion, T.J. (2015). Alcohol, marijuana, and tobacco use trajectories from ages 12 to 24 years: Demographic correlates and young adult substance use problems. *Development and Psychopathology, 27*, 253–277.

Nelson, S.K., Kushlev, K., English, T., Dunn, E.W., & Lyubomirsky, S. (2013). In defense of parenthood: Children associated with more joy than misery. *Psychological Science, 24*, 3–10.

Nemet, D. (2016). Childhood obesity, physical activity, and exercise. *Pediatric Exercise Science, 28*, 48–51.

Nene, R.V., & others (2018). Cdc73 suppresses genome instability by mediating telomere homeostasis. *PLoS One, 14*(1), e1007170.

Nergard-Nilssen, T., & Eklund, K. (2018, in press). Evaluation of the psychometric properties of the Norwegian screening test for dyslexia. *Dyslexia.*

Nesi, J., & others (2017). Friends' alcohol-related social networking site activity predicts escalations in adolescent drinking: Mediation by peer norms. *Journal of Adolescent Health, 60*, 641–647.

Netz, Y. (2017). Is the comparison between exercise and pharmacologic treatment of depression in the clinical practice guideline of the American College of Physicians evidence-based? *Frontiers in Pharmacology, 8*, 257.

Nevalainen, T., & others (2017). Obesity accelerates epigenetic aging in middle-aged but not elderly individuals. *Clinical Epigenetics, 9*, 20.

Neville, H.J. (2006). Different profiles of plasticity within human cognition. In Y. Munakata & M.H. Johnson (Eds.), *Attention and Performance XXI: Processes of change in brain and cognitive development.* Oxford, UK: Oxford University Press.

Nevitt, S.J., Jones, A.P., & Howard, J. (2017). Hydroxyurea (hydroxycarbamide) for sickle cell disease. *Cochrane Database of Systematic Reviews, 4*, CD002202.

Newton, E.R., & May, L. (2018, in press). Adaptation of maternal-fetal physiology to exercise in pregnancy: The basis of guidelines for physical activity in pregnancy. *Clinical and Medical Insights: Women's Health.*

Ng, F.F., Pomerantz, E.M., & Deng, C. (2014). Why are Chinese parents more psychologically controlling than American parents? "My child is my report card." *Child Development, 85,* 355–369.

Ng, F.F., Pomerantz, E.M., & Lam, S. (2013). Mothers' beliefs about children's learning in Hong Kong and the United States: Implications for mothers' child-based worth. *International Journal of Behavioral Development, 37,* 387–394.

Ng, M., & others (2017). Environmental factors associated with autism spectrum disorder: A scoping review for the years 2003–2013. *Health Promotion and Chronic Disease Prevention in Canada, 37,* 1–23.

Ng, Q.X., & others (2018). Early life sexual abuse is associated with increased suicide attempts: An updated meta-analysis. *Journal of Psychiatric Research, 99,* 129–141.

Ngantcha, M., & others (2018, in press). Revisiting factors associated with screen time media use: A structural study among school-aged adolescents. *Journal of Physical Activity and Health.*

Nguyen, T.V. (2018, in press). Developmental effects of androgens in the human brain. *Journal of Neuroendocrinology.*

NICHD (2018). *SIDS facts.* Retrieved January 6, 2016, from www.nichd.nih/gov/sids

NICHD Early Child Care Research Network (2001). Nonmaternal care and family factors in early development: An overview of the NICHD study of Early Child Care. *Journal of Applied Developmental Psychology, 22,* 457–492.

NICHD Early Child Care Research Network (2002). Structure→Process→Outcome: Direct and indirect effects of child care quality on young children's development. *Psychological Science, 13,* 199–206.

NICHD Early Child Care Research Network (2003). Does amount of time spent in child care predict socioemotional adjustment during the transition to kindergarten? *Child Development, 74,* 976–1005.

NICHD Early Child Care Research Network (2004). Type of child care and children's development at 54 months. *Early Childhood Research Quarterly, 19,* 203–230.

NICHD Early Child Care Research Network (2005a). *Child care and development.* New York: Guilford.

NICHD Early Child Care Research Network (2005b). Predicting individual differences in attention, memory, and planning in first graders from experiences at home, child care, and school. *Developmental Psychology, 41,* 99–114.

NICHD Early Child Care Research Network (2006). Infant-mother attachment classification: Risk and protection in relation to changing maternal caregiving quality. *Developmental Psychology, 42,* 38–58.

NICHD Early Child Care Research Network (2010). Testing a series of causal propositions relating time spent in child care to children's externalizing behavior. *Developmental Psychology, 46*(1), 1–17.

Nicolaou, E., & others (2018). Changes in verbal and visuospatial working memory from grade 1 to grade 3 in primary school: Population longitudinal study. *Child: Care, Health, and Development, 44,* 392–400.

Nicoteri, J.A., & Miskovsky, M.J. (2014). Revisiting the freshman "15": Assessing body mass index in the first college year and beyond. *Journal of the American Association of Nurse Practitioners, 26,* 220–224.

Nieto, S., & Bode, P. (2018). *Affirming diversity* (7th ed.). Upper Saddle River, NJ: Pearson.

Nikitin, J., & Freund, A.M. (2019, in press). The adaptation process of aging. In R. Fernandez-Ballesteros & others (Eds.), *Cambridge handbook of successful aging.* New York: Cambridge University Press.

Nilsen, E.S., & Bacso, S.A. (2017). Cognitive and behavioral predictors of adolescents' communicative perspective-taking and social relationships. *Journal of Adolescence, 56,* 52–63.

Nilsen, P., & others (2018). Towards evidence-based palliative care in nursing homes in Sweden: A qualitative study informed by the organizational readiness to change theory. *Implementation Science, 13*(1), 1.

Niraula, A., Sheridan, J.F., & Godbout, J.P. (2017). Microglia priming with aging and stress. *Neuropsychopharmacology, 42,* 318–333.

Nisbett, R. (2003). *The geography of thought.* New York: Free Press.

Nisbett, R.E., & others (2012). Intelligence: New findings and theoretical developments. *American Psychologist, 67*(2), 130–159.

Nishina, A., & Bellmore, A. (2018). Inequality and neighborhood effects on peer relations. In W.M. Bukowski & others (Eds.), *Handbook of peer interactions, relationships, and groups* (2nd ed.). New York: Guilford.

Nissim, N.R., & others (2017). Frontal structural neural correlates of working memory performance in older adults. *Frontiers in Aging Neuroscience, 8,* 328.

Niu, M., & others (2017). Fragile X syndrome: Prevalence, treatment, and prevention in China. *Frontiers in Neurology, 8,* 254.

Noble, N. (2018). Symptom management in women undergoing the menopause. *Nursing Standard, 32,* 53–63.

Noll, J.G., & others (2017). Childhood sexual abuse and early timing of puberty. *Journal of Adolescent Health, 60,* 65–71.

Nomoto, M., & others (2009). Inter- and intra-individual variation in L-dopa pharmacokinetics in the treatment of Parkinson's disease. *Parkinsonism and Related Disorders, 15*(Suppl. 1), S21–S24.

Non, A.L., & others (2018, in press). Stress across generations: A qualitative study of stress, coping, and caregiving among Mexican immigrant mothers. *Ethnicity and Health.*

Nora, A., & others (2017). Children show right-lateralized effects of spoken word-form learning. *PLoS One, 12*(2), e0171034.

Nordheim, K.L., & others (2018, in press). Inflammation relates to resistance training-induced hypertrophy in elderly patients. *Medicine and Science in Sports and Exercise.*

Norman, E. (2017). Metacognition and mindfulness: The role of fringe consciousness. *Mindfulness, 8,* 95–100.

Norman, J.F., Holmin, J.S., & Bartholomew, A.N. (2011). Visual memories for perceived length are well preserved in older adults. *Vision Research, 51,* 2057–2062.

Norona, A.N., & Baker, B.L. (2017). The effects of early positive parenting and developmental delay status on child emotion dysregulation. *Journal of Intellectual Disability Research, 61,* 130–143.

Norouzieh, K. (2005). Case management of the dying child. *Case Manager, 16,* 54–57.

North American Menopause Society (2017). *The 2017 hormone position statement of the North American Menopause Society.* Retrieved August 20, 2017, from www.menopause.org

Nosraty, L., Jylha, M., Raittila, T., & Lumme-Sandt, K. (2015). Perceptions by the oldest old of successful aging, vitality 90+ study. *Journal of Aging Studies, 32,* 50–58.

Nottelmann, E.D., & others (1987). Gonadal and adrenal hormone correlates of adjustment in early adolescence. In R.M. Lerner & T.T. Foch (Eds.), *Biological-psychological interactions in early adolescence.* Hillsdale, NJ: Erlbaum.

Nouchi, R., Saito, T., Nouchi, H., & Kawashima, R. (2016). Small acute benefits of 4 weeks processing speed training games on processing speed and inhibition performance and depressive mood in healthy elderly people: Evidence from a randomized trial. *Frontiers in Aging Neuroscience, 8,* 302.

Novack, M.A., & others (2018). Gesture's role in reflecting and fostering conceptual change. In T. Amin & O. Levrini (Eds.), *Converging perspectives on conceptual change.* New York: Routledge.

Novello, L., & Speiser, P.W. (2018). Premature adrenarche. *Pediatric Annals, 47*(1), e7–e11.

Novick, G., & others (2013). Group prenatal care: Model fidelity and outcomes. *American Journal of Obstetrics and Gynecology, 209*(2), 112.e1–112.e6.

Nowson, C.A., & others (2018). The impact of dietary factors on indices of chronic disease in older people: A systematic review. *Journal of Nutrition, Health, and Aging, 22,* 282–296.

Nucci, L. (2006). Education for moral development. In M. Killen & J. Smetana (Eds.), *Handbook of moral development.* Mahwah, NJ: Erlbaum.

Nunes, A.S., & others (2018, in press). Idiosyncratic organization of cortical networks in autism spectrum disorder. *NeuroImage.*

Nye, C., Allemand, M., Gosling, S., Potter, J., & Roberts, B.W. (2016). Personality trait differences between young and middle-aged adults: Measurement artifacts or actual trends? *Journal of Personality, 84,* 473–492.

Nygard, C-H. (2013). *The ability to work peaks in middle age.* Interview. Retrieved September 15, 2013, from http://researchandstudy.uta.fi/2013/094/12/the-ability-to-work-peaks-in-middle-age/

O

O'Brien, J.L., & others (2013). Cognitive training and selective attention in the aging brain: An electrophysiological study. *Clinical Neurophysiology, 124,* 2198–2208.

O'Brien, M., & Moss, P. (2010). Fathers, work, and family policies in Europe. In M.E. Lamb (Ed.), *The role of the father in child development* (5th ed.). New York: Wiley.

O'Brien, M., & others (2014). Women's work and child care: Perspectives and prospects. In E.T. Gershoff, R.S. Mistry, & D.A. Crosby (Eds.), *Societal contexts of child development.* New York: Oxford University Press.

O'Connor, D., & Kelson, E. (2018). Boomer matters: Responding to emotional health needs in an aging society. *Journal of Gerontological Social Work, 61,* 61–77.

O'Connor, D.B., & others (2011). The relationships between sex hormones and sexual function in middle-aged and older European men. *Journal of Clinical Endocrinology and Metabolism, 96,* E1577–E1587.

O'Connor, T.G., & others (2017). Immune and neuroendocrine correlates of temperament in infancy. *Development and Psychopathology, 29,* 1589–1600.

O'Halloran, A.M., & others (2011). Falls and fall efficacy: The role of sustained attention in older adults. *BMC Geriatrics, 11,* 85.

O'Hara, M.W., & Engeldinger, J. (2018, in press). Treatment of postpartum depression: Recommendations for the clinician. *Clinical Obstetrics and Gynecology.*

O'Hara, M.W., & McCabe, F. (2013). Postpartum depression: Current status and future directions. *Annual Review of Clinical Psychology* (Vol. 9). Palo Alto, CA: Annual Reviews.

O'Kearney, R., & others (2017). Emotional abilities in children with oppositional defiant disorder (ODD): Impairment of perspective-taking and understanding mixed emotions with high callous-unemotional traits. *Child Psychiatry and Human Development, 48,* 346–357.

O'Leary, O.F., & others (2018). The vagus nerve modulates BDNF expression and neurogenesis in the hippocampus. *European Neuropsychopharmacology, 28,* 307–316.

Oakley, M., Farr, R.H., & Scherer, D.G. (2017). Same-sex parent socialization: Understanding gay and lesbian parenting practices as cultural socialization. *Journal of GLBT Family Studies, 13,* 56–75.

Oates, K. (2018, in press). The Royal Commission into child sexual abuse: A beginning. *Journal of Pediatrics and Child Health.*

Oberle, E. (2018). Early adolescents' emotional well-being in the classroom: The role of personal and contextual assets. *Journal of School Health, 88,* 101–111.

Obradovic, J., Yousafzai, A.K., Finch, J.E., & Rasheed, M.A. (2016). Maternal scaffolding and home stimulation: Key mediators of early intervention effects on children's cognitive development. *Developmental Psychology, 52*, 1409–1421.

OECD (2014). Life satisfaction. *Society at a glance, 2014: OECD social indicators.* Paris: OECD Publishing.

OECD (2016). *Marriage and divorce rates.* Paris: OECD.

OECD (2017). *OECD health statistics.* Paris: OECD.

Offer, D., Ostrov, E., Howard, K.I., & Atkinson, R. (1988). *The teenage world: Adolescents' self-image in ten countries.* New York: Plenum.

Ogbuanu, I.U., & others (2014). Maternal, fetal, and neonatal outcomes associated with measles during pregnancy: Namibia, 2009–2010. *Clinical Infectious Diseases, 58*, 1086–1092.

Ogden, C.L., Carroll, M.D., Kit, B.K., & Flegal, K.M. (2012, January). Prevalence of obesity in the United States, 2009–2010. *NCHS Data Brief*, 1–9.

Ogden, C.L., Carroll, M.D., Kit, B.K., & Flegal, K.M. (2014). Prevalence of childhood and adult obesity in the United States, 2011–2012. *Journal of the American Medical Association, 311*, 806–814.

Ogden, C.L., & others (2016). Trends in obesity prevalence among children and adolescents in the United States, 1988–1994 through 2013–2014. *JAMA, 315*, 2292–2299.

Ogden, T., & Hagen, K.M. (2019). *Adolescent mental health.* New York: Routledge.

Ogino, T., & others (2017). Predicting the reading skill of Japanese children. *Brain and Development, 39*, 112–121.

Oh, S., & others (2017). Prevalence and correlates of alcohol and tobacco use among pregnant women in the United States: Evidence from the NSDUH 205-2014. *Preventive Medicine, 97*, 93–99.

Oh, S.J., & others (2018). Effects of smartphone-based memory training for older adults with subjective memory complaints: A randomized controlled trial. *Aging and Mental Health, 22*, 526–534.

Ohlin, A., & others (2015). Sepsis as a risk factor for neonatal morbidity in extremely preterm infants. *Acta Paediatrica, 104*, 1070–1076.

Okun, M.A., Yeung, E.W., & Brown, S. (2013). Volunteering by older adults and risk of mortality: A meta-analysis. *Psychology and Aging, 28*, 564–577.

Okuzono, S., & others (2017). Spanking and subsequent behavioral problems in toddlers: A propensity score-matched prospective study in Japan. *Child Abuse and Neglect, 69*, 62–71.

Olderbak, S., & others (2018, in press). Sex differences in facial emotion perception ability across the lifespan. *Cognition and Emotion.*

Olesen, M.V., & others (2017). Electroconvulsive stimulation results in long-term survival of newly generated hippocampal neurons in rats. *Hippocampus, 27*, 52–60.

Oliva, A., & others (2017). Medico-legal perspectives on sudden cardiac death in young athletes. *International Journal of Legal Medicine, 131*, 393–409.

Olsen, D.P. (2016). Ethically relevant differences in advance directives for psychiatric and end-of-life care. *Journal of the American Psychiatric Nurses Association, 22*, 52–59.

Olson, N.C., & others (2018). Associations of activated coagulation factor VII and factor VIIa-antithrombin levels with genome-wide polymorphisms and cardiovascular risk disease. *Journal of Thrombosis and Hemostasis, 16*, 19–30.

Olszewski-Kubilius, P., & Thomson, D. (2013). Gifted education programs and procedures. In I.B. Weiner & others (Eds.), *Handbook of psychology* (2nd ed., Vol. 7). New York: Wiley.

Oltmanns, J., & others (2017). Don't lose your brain at work—the role of recurrent novelty at work in cognitive and brain aging. *Frontiers in Psychology, 8*, 117.

Olweus, D. (2003). Prevalence estimation of school bullying with the Olweus bully/victim questionnaire. *Aggressive Behavior, 29*(3), 239–269.

Omaggio, N.F., Baker, M.J., & Conway, L.J. (2018, in press). Have you ever Googled or been friended by a patient? Social media intersects the practice of genetic counseling. *Journal of Genetic Counseling.*

Onder, G., & others (2018, in press). Accounting for frailty when treating chronic diseases. *European Journal of Internal Medicine.*

Onders, B., & others (2018, in press). Pediatric injuries related to window blinds, shades, and cords. *Pediatrics.*

Onen, S.H., & Onen, F. (2018). Chronic medical conditions and sleep in the older adult. *Sleep Medicine Clinics, 13*, 71–79.

Ong, A.L.C., & Ramasamy, T.S. (2018, in press). Role of Sirtuin1-p53 regulatory axis imaging, cancer, and cellular reprogramming. *Aging Research Reviews.*

Oppenheimer, C.W., Hankin, B.L., & Young, J. (2018, in press). Effect of parenting and peer stressors on cognitive vulnerability and risk for depression among youth. *Journal of Abnormal Child Psychology.*

Ordonez, T.N., & others (2017). Activity station: Effects on global cognition of mature adults and healthy elderly program using electronic games. *Dementia and Neuropsychology, 11*, 186–197.

Oren, E., & others (2017). Self-reported stressful life events during adolescence and subsequent asthma: A longitudinal study. *Journal of Allergy and Clinical Immunology: In Practice, 5*, 427–434.

Oren, N., & others (2018, in press). How attention modulates encoding of dynamic stimuli in older adults. *Behavioral and Brain Research.*

Orkaby, A.R., & others (2018). Preventing cardiovascular disease in older adults: One size does not fit all. *Cleveland Clinic Journal of Medicine, 85*, 55–64.

Orlich, D.C., & Harder, R.J. (2018). *Teaching strategies* (11th ed.). Boston: Cengage.

Orosz, G., & others (2015). Elevated romantic love and jealousy if relationship is declared on Facebook. *Frontiers in Psychology, 6*, 214.

Orpinas, P., McNicholas, C., & Nahapetyan, L. (2015). Gender differences in trajectories of relational aggression perpetration and victimization from middle to high school. *Aggressive Behavior, 41*, 401–412.

Orth, U., Robins, R.W., Meier, L.L., & Conger, R.D. (2017). Refining the vulnerability model of low self-esteem and depression: Disentangling the effects of genuine self-esteem and narcissism. *Journal of Personality and Social Psychology, 110*, 133–149.

Ostan, R., & others (2016). Gender, aging, and longevity in humans: An update of an intriguing/neglected scenario paving the way to a gender-specific medicine. *Clinical Science.*

Ostergaard, S.D., & others (2017). Teenage parenthood and birth rates for individuals with and without attention-deficit/hyperactivity disorder: A nationwide cohort study. *Journal of the American Academy of Child and Adolescent Psychiatry, 56*, 578–584.

Ostfeld, B.M., & others (2018, in press). Prematurity and sudden unexpected infant deaths in the United States. *Pediatrics.*

Ota, M., & Skarabela, B. (2018). Reduplication facilitates early word segmentation. *Journal of Child Language, 45*, 204–218.

Otto, H. (2018). Don't show our emotions! Emotion regulation and attachment in the Cameroonian Nso. In H. Otto & H. Keller (Eds.), *Difference faces of attachment.* New York; Cambridge University Press.

Otto, H., & Keller, H. (Eds) (2018). *Different faces of attachment.* New York: Cambridge University Press.

Owen, K.B., & others (2018). Regular physical activity and educational outcomes in youth: A longitudinal study. *Journal of Adolescent Health, 62*, 334–340.

Owens, J.A., Belon, K., & Moss, P. (2010). Impact of delaying school start time on adolescent sleep, mood, and behavior. *Archives of Pediatric and Adolescent Medicine, 164*, 608–614.

Owsley, C., & others (2016). Comparison of visual function in older eyes in the earliest stages of age-related macular degeneration to those in normal macular health. *Current Eye Research, 41*, 266–272.

Ozcan, L., & others (2018, in press). Effects of taking tadalafil 5 mg once daily on erectile function and total testosterone levels in patients with metabolic syndrome. *Andrologia.*

Ozturk, M.B., Li, Y., & Tergaonkar, V. (2018, in press). Current insights to regulation and role of telomerase in human diseases. *Antioxidants.*

P

Pace, A., & others (2016). The story of language acquisition: From words to world and back again. In L. Alter & C. Tamis-LeMonda (Eds.), *Child psychology: A handbook of contemporary issues* (3rd ed.). New York: Psychology Press.

Padilla-Walker, L.M., & Nelson, L.J. (2017). Flourishing in emerging adulthood: An understudied approach to the third decade of life. In L.M. Padilla-Walker & L. Nelson (Eds.), *Flourishing in emerging adulthood.* New York: Oxford University Press.

Padilla-Walker, L.M., & others (2018). The protective role of parental media monitoring style from early to late adolescence. *Journal of Youth and Adolescence, 47*, 445–459.

Pagani, L.S., Levesque-Seck, F., Archambault, I., & Janosz, M. (2017). Prospective longitudinal associations between household smoke exposure in early childhood and antisocial behavior at age 12. *Indoor Air, 27*, 622–630.

Pakhomov, S.V., & Hemmy, L.S. (2014). A computational linguistic measure of clustering behavior on semantic verbal fluency task predicts risk of future dementia in the Nun Study. *Cortex, 55*, 97–106.

Palmer, C.A., & others (2018, in press). Associations among adolescent sleep problems, emotion regulation, and affective disorders: Findings from a nationally representative sample. *Journal of Psychiatric Research.*

Palmore, E.B. (2004). Research note: Ageism in Canada and the United States. *Journal of Cross Cultural Gerontology, 19*, 41–46.

Pan, B.A., & Uccelli, P. (2009). Semantic development. In J. Berko Gleason & N.B. Ratner (Eds.), *The development of language* (7th ed.). Boston: Allyn & Bacon.

Pan, C.Y., & others (2018, in press). Effects of physical exercise intervention on motor skills and executive functions with ADHD: A pilot study. *Journal of Attention Disorders.*

Pan, Z., & Chang, C. (2012). Gender and the regulation of longevity: Implications for autoimmunity. *Autoimmunity Reviews, 11*, A393–A403.

Pantell, R.H., & others (2018, in press). The child witness in the courtroom. *Pediatrics.*

Paolucci, E.M., & others (2018, in press). Exercise reduces depression and inflammation but intensity matters. *Biological Psychology.*

Papanicolas, I., Wolski, L.R., & Jha, A.K. (2018). Health care spending in the United States and other high-income countries. *JAMA, 319*(10), 1024–1039.

Papastavrou, E., Charlalambous, A., Tsangari, H., & Karayiannis, G. (2012). The burdensome and depressive experience of caring: What cancer, schizophrenia, and Alzheimer's disease caregivers have in common. *Cancer Nursing, 35*, 187–194.

Papernow, P. (2018, in press). Clinical guidelines for working with stepfamilies: What family, couple, and child therapists need to know. *Family Process.*

Papernow, P.L. (2018, in press). Recoupling in mid-life and beyond: From love at last to not so fast. *Family Process.*

Parade, S.H., & others (2018, in press). Family context moderates the association of maternal postpartum depression and stability of infant attachment. *Child Development.*

Parashar, S., & others (2018). DNA methylation signatures of breast cancer in peripheral T-cells. *BMC Cancer, 18*(1), 574.

Parcianello, R.R., & others (2018). Increased cocaine and amphetamine-regulated transcript cord blood levels in the newborns exposed to crack cocaine in utero. *Psychopharmacology, 235,* 215–222.

Parcon, P.A., & others (2018). Apolipoprotein E4 inhibits autophagy gene products through direct, specific binding to CLEAR motifs. *Alzheimer's and Dementia, 25,* 230–242.

Parens, E., & Johnston, J. (2009). Facts, values, and attention-deficit hyperactivity disorder (ADHD): An update on the controversies. *Child and Adolescent Psychiatry and Mental Health, 3,* 1.

Parish-Morris, J., Golinkoff, R.M., & Hirsh-Pasek, K. (2013). From coo to code: A brief story of language development. In P.D. Zelazo (Ed.), *Handbook of developmental psychology.* New York: Oxford University Press.

Park, C.L. (2010). Making sense out of the meaning literature: An integrative review of meaning making and its effect on adjustment to stressful life events. *Psychological Bulletin, 136,* 257–301.

Park, C.L. (2012). Meaning, spirituality, and growth: Protective and resilience factors in health and illness. In A.S. Baum, T.A. Revenson, & J.E. Singer (Eds.), *Handbook of health psychology* (2nd ed.). New York: Sage.

Park, C.L. (2013). Meaning making in cancer survivorship. In P.T.P. Wong (Ed.), *Handbook of meaning* (2nd ed.). Thousand Oaks, CA: Sage.

Park, C.L. (2016). Meaning making in the context of disasters. *Journal of Clinical Psychology, 72,* 1234–1246.

Park, C.L., & Ono, D. (2018, in press). Spiritual well-being and spiritual distress predict adjustment in adolescent and young adult cancer survivors. *Psycho-Oncology.*

Park, C.L., & others (2016). Spiritual peace predicts 5-year mortality in congestive heart failure patients. *Health Psychology, 35,* 203–210.

Park, C.L., & others (2017). Positive and negative religious/spiritual coping and combat exposure in Iraq and Afghanistan veterans. *Psychology of Religion and Spirituality, 9,* 13–20.

Park, D. (2001). Commentary in R. Restak, *The secret life of the brain.* Washington, DC: Joseph Henry Press.

Park, D.C., & Farrell, M.E. (2016). The aging mind in transition: Amyloid deposition and progression toward Alzheimer's disease. In K.W. Schaie & S.L. Willis (Eds.), *Handbook of the psychology of aging* (8th ed.). New York: Elsevier.

Park, D.C., & Festini, S.B. (2017). Theories of memory and aging: A look at the past and a glimpse of the future. *Journals of Gerontology B: Psychological Sciences and Social Sciences, 72,* 82–90.

Park, D.C., & Festini, S.B. (2018). Cognitive health. In M.H. Bornstein (Ed.), *SAGE encyclopedia of lifespan human development.* Thousand Oaks, CA: Sage.

Park, D.C., & others (2014). The impact of sustained engagement on cognitive function in older adults: The Synapse Project. *Psychological Science, 25,* 103–112.

Park, H.S., & others (2018, in press). Physical exercise prevents cognitive impairment by enhancing hippocampal neuroplasticity and mitochondrial function in doxorubicin-induced chemobrain. *Neuropharmacology.*

Park, I.J.K., & others (2018, in press). Coping with racism: Moderators of the discrimination-adjustment link among Mexican-origin adolescents. *Child Development.*

Park, J.S., & others (2018). Variants of cancer susceptibility genes in Korean BRCA1/2 mutation-negative patients with high risk for hereditary breast cancer. *BMC Cancer, 18*(1), 83.

Park, M., & others (2018, in press). Maternal depression trajectories from pregnancy to 3 years postpartum are associated with children's behavior and executive functions at 3 and 6 years. *Archives of Women's Mental Health.*

Park, M.J., Paul Mulye, T., Adams, S.H., Brindis, C.D., & Irwin, C.E. (2006). The health status of young adults in the United States. *Journal of Adolescent Health, 39,* 305–317.

Park, Y.M. (2017). Relationship between child maltreatment, suicidality, and bipolarity: A retrospective study. *Psychiatry Investigation, 14,* 136–140.

Parke, R.D. (2017). Family psychology: Past and future reflections on the field. *Journal of Family Psychology, 31,* 257–260.

Parker, C.B. (February 11, 2016). Stanford project suggests longer, healthier lives possible. *Stanford Report,* 1–4.

Parker, K., & Stepler, R. (2017, September 14). *As U.S. marriage rate hovers at 50%, education gap in marital status widens.* Washington, DC: Pew Research Center.

Parkes, K.R. (2006). Physical activity and self-rated health: Interactive effects of activity in work and leisure domains. *British Journal of Health Psychology, 11,* 533–550.

Parmar, M. (2018, in press). Towards stem cell based therapies for Parkinson's disease. *Development.*

Parrott, A.C., & others (2014). MDMA and heightened cortisol: A neurohormonal perspective on the pregnancy outcomes of mothers who used 'Ecstasy' during pregnancy. *Human Psychopharmacology, 29,* 1–7.

Parsons, C.E., & others (2017). Interpreting infant emotional expressions: Parenthood has differential effects for men and women. *Quarterly Journal of Experimental Psychology, 70,* 554–564.

Pascal, A., & others (2018, in press). Neurodevelopmental outcome in very preterm and very-low-birthweight infants born over the past decade: A meta-analytic review. *Developmental Medicine and Child Neurology.*

Paschall, K.W., & Mastergeorge, A.M. (2018). A longitudinal, person-centered analysis of Head Start mothers' parenting. *Infant Mental Health, 39,* 70–84.

Pasley, K., & Moorefield, B.S. (2004). Stepfamilies. In M. Coleman & L. Ganong (Eds.), *Handbook of contemporary families.* Thousand Oaks, CA: Sage.

Pate, R.R., & others (2015). Prevalence of compliance with a new physical activity guideline for preschool-aged children. *Childhood Obesity, 11,* 45–70.

Patel, R., & others (2018). Prostate cancer susceptibility and growth linked to Y chromosome genes. *Frontiers in Bioscience, 10,* 423–436.

Patel, S., & others (2016). Association of maternal diabetes/glycosuria and pre-pregnancy body mass index with offspring indicators of non-alcoholic fatty liver disease. *BMC Pediatrics, 16,* 47.

Pathman, T., Doydum, A., & Bauer, P.J. (2013). Bringing order to life events: Memory for the temporal order of autobiographical events over an extended period in school-aged children and adults. *Journal of Experimental Child Psychology, 115,* 309–325.

Patlamazoglou, L., Simmonds, J.G., & Snell, T.L. (2018, in press). Same-sex partner bereavement. *Omega.*

Patrick, J.H., Carney, A.K., & Nehrkorn, A.M. (2017). Aging in the context of life events. *International Journal of Aging and Human Development, 84,* 209–212.

Patrick, M.E., & others (2017a). Age-related changes in associations between reasons for alcohol use and high-intensity drinking across young adulthood. *Journal of Studies on Alcohol and Drugs, 78,* 558–570.

Patrick, M.E., & others (2017b). Age-specific prevalence of binge drinking and high-intensity drinking among U.S. young adults: Changes from 2005 to 2015. *Alcoholism: Clinical and Experimental Research, 41,* 1319–1328.

Patrick, M.E., & others (2017c). Patterns of high-intensity drinking among young adults in the United States: A repeated measures latent class analysis. *Addictive Behaviors, 74,* 134–139.

Patterson, C.J., Farr, R.H., & Hastings, P.D. (2015). Socialization in the context of family diversity. In J.E. Grusec & P.D. Hastings (Eds.), *Handbook of socialization* (2nd ed.). New York: Guilford.

Patterson, G.D., & others (2018). Recurrent acute chest syndrome in pediatric sickle cell disease: Clinical features and risk factors. *Journal of Pediatric Hematology/Oncology, 40,* 51–55.

Patterson, J., & others (2018). *Essential skills in family therapy* (3rd ed.). New York: Guilford.

Patton, G.C., & others (2011). Overweight and obesity between adolescence and early adulthood: A 10-year prospective study. *Journal of Adolescent Health, 45,* 275–280.

Paul, C. (2019, in press). Emotions and successful aging. In R. Fernandez-Ballesteros & others (Eds.), *Cambridge handbook of successful aging.* New York: Cambridge University Press.

Paulhus, D.L. (2008). Birth order. In M.M. Haith & J.B. Benson (Eds.), *Encyclopedia of infant and early childhood development.* Oxford, UK: Elsevier.

Paunesku, D., & others (2015). Mind-set interventions are a scaleable treatment for academic underachievement. *Psychological Science, 26,* 784–793.

Paus, T., & others (2007). Morphological properties of the action-observation cortical network in adolescents with low and high resistance to peer influence. *Social Neuroscience 3*(3), 303–316.

Pawluski, J.L., Lonstein, J.S., & Fleming, A.S. (2017). The neurobiology of postpartum period anxiety and depression. *Trends in Neuroscience, 40,* 106–120.

Paxton, S.J., & Damiano, S.R. (2017). The development of body image and weight bias in childhood. *Advances in Child Development and Behavior, 52,* 269–298.

Payer, L. (1991). The menopause in various cultures. In H. Burger & M. Boulet (Eds.), *A portrait of the menopause.* Park Ridge, NJ: Parthenon.

Payne, K. (2015). *The remarriage rate.* Bowling Green, Ohio: Bowling Green State University, National Center for Family and Marriage Research.

Pazoki, R., & others (2018, in press). Genetic predisposition to high blood pressure and lifestyle factors: Associations with midlife blood pressure levels and cardiovascular events. *Circulation.*

Pea, R., & others (2012). Media use, face-to-face communication, media multitasking, and social well-being among 8- to 12-year-old girls. *Developmental Psychology, 48,* 327–336.

Pearson, N., & others (2017). Clustering and correlates of screen time and eating behaviors among young adolescents. *BMC Public Health, 17,* 533.

Peck, T., Scharf, R.J., Conaway, M.R., & DeBoer, M.D. (2015). Viewing as little as 1 hour of TV daily is associated with higher change in BMI between kindergarten and first grade. *Obesity, 23,* 1680–1686.

Pedersen, L.R., & others (2016). Risk factors for myocardial infarction in women and men: A review of the current literature. *Current Pharmaceutical Design, 22,* 3835–3852.

Pedrinolla, A., Schena, F., & Venturelli, M. (2018, in press). Resilience to Alzheimer's disease: The role of physical activity. *Current Alzheimer Research.*

Peek, M.K. (2009). Marriage in later life. In D. Carr (Ed.), *Encyclopedia of the life course and human development.* Boston: Gale Cengage.

Peets, K., Hodges, E.V.E., & Salmivalli, C. (2011). Actualization of social cognitions into aggressive behavior toward disliked targets. *Social Development, 20,* 233–250.

Pei, J., & others (2017). Intervention recommendations and subsequent access to services following clinical assessment for fetal alcohol syndrome disorders. *Research in Developmental Disabilities, 60,* 176–186.

Peixoto, C.E., & others (2017). Interviews of children in a Portuguese special judicial procedure. *Behavioral Sciences & the Law, 35,* 189–203.

Peltola, M.J., Strathearn, L., & Puura, K. (2018). Oxytocin promotes face-sensitive neural responses to infant and adult faces in mothers. *Psychoneuroendocrinology, 91,* 261–270.

Penazzi, L., Bakota, L., & Brandt, R. (2016). Microtubule dynamics in neuronal development, plasticity, and neurodegeneration. *International Review of Cell and Molecular Biology, 321,* 89–169.

Peng, F., & others (2016). A cross-sectional voxel-based morphometric study of age- and sex-related changes in gray matter volume in the normal aging brain. *Journal of Computer Assisted Tomography, 40,* 307–315.

Peng, Z., & others (2017). Efficacy and safety of tadalafil once-a-day versus tadalafil on-demand in patients with erectile dysfunction: A systematic review and meta-analyses. *Urology International, 99,* 343–352.

Penhollow, T.M., Young, M., & Nnaka, T. (2017). Alcohol use, hooking-up, condom use: Is there a sexual double standard? *American Journal of Health Behavior, 41,* 92–103.

Penn, S. (2015). Overcoming the barriers to use of kangaroo care in neonatal settings. *Nursing Children and Young People, 27,* 22–27.

Pepping, C.A., & MacDonald, G. (2018). Adult attachment and long-term singlehood. *Current Opinion in Psychology, 125,* 105–109.

Peregoy, S.F., & Boyle, O.F. (2017). *Reading, writing, and learning ESL* (7th ed.). Upper Saddle River, NJ: Pearson.

Pereira, C., & others (2018, in press). Effects of a 10-week multimodal exercise program on physical and cognitive function of nursing home residents: A psychomotor intervention pilot study. *Aging: Clinical and Experimental Research.*

Pereira-Salgado, A., & others (2018, in press). Religious leaders' perceptions of advance care planning: A secondary analysis of interviews with Buddhist, Christian, Hindu, Islamic, Jewish, Sikh, and Baha'i leaders. *BMC Palliative Care.*

Perelli-Harris, B., & others (2017). The rise in divorce and cohabitation: Is there a link? *Population and Development Review, 43,* 303–329.

Perez, H.C.S., & others (2018, in press). Prolonged grief and cognitive decline: A prospective population-based study in middle-aged and older persons. *American Journal of Geriatric Psychiatry.*

Perez-Edgar, K.E., & Guyer, A.E. (2014). Behavioral inhibition: Temperament or prodrome? *Current Behavioral Neuroscience Reports, 1,* 182–190.

Perez-Escamilla, R., & Moran, V.H. (2017). The role of nutrition in integrated early child development in the 21st century: Contribution from the Maternal and Child Nutrition Journal. *Maternal and Child Nutrition, 13,* 3–6.

Perkisas, S., & Vandewoude, M. (2019, in press). Nutrition and cognition. In R. Fernandez-Ballesteros & others (Eds.), *Cambridge handbook of successful aging.* New York: Cambridge University Press.

Perneczky, R. (2018). Population-based approaches to Alzheimer's disease prevention. In R. Pernecsky & others (Eds.), *Biomarkers for Alzheimer's disease drug development. Methods in Molecular Biology* (Vol. 1750). New York: Humana Press.

Perone, S., Almy, B., & Zelazo, P.D. (2017). Toward an understanding of the neural basis of executive function development. In R.L. Gibb & B. Kolb (Eds.), *The neurobiology of brain and behavioral development* (2nd ed.). New York: Elsevier.

Perone, S., Palanisamy, J., & Carlson, S.M. (2018, in press). Age-related change in brain rhythms from early to middle childhood: Links to executive function. *Developmental Science.*

Perry, N.B., & Calkins, S.D. (2018). Emotion regulation across childhood. In P.M. Cole & T. Hollenstein (Eds.), *Emotion regulation.* New York: Routledge.

Perry, N.B., & others (2017). Self-regulation as a predictor of patterns of change in externalizing behaviors from infancy to adolescence. *Development and Psychopathology, 23,* 1–14.

Perry, R.A., Daniels, L.A., Bell, L., & Magarey, A.M. (2017). Facilitators and barriers to the achievement of healthy lifestyle goals: Qualitative findings from Australian parents enrolled in the PEACH child weight management program. *Journal of Nutrition Education and Behavior, 49,* 43–52.

Perry, S.E., & others (2018). *Maternal child nursing care* (6th ed.). New York: Elsevier.

Peskin, H. (1967). Pubertal onset and ego functioning. *Journal of Abnormal Psychology, 72,* 1–15.

Petersen, A.C., & others (Eds.) (2017). *Positive youth development in global contexts of social and economic change.* New York: Routledge.

Petersen, I.T., & others (2012). Interaction between serotonin transporter polymorphism (5-HTTLPR) and stressful life events in adolescents' trajectories of anxious/depressed symptoms. *Developmental Psychology, 48*(5), 1463–1475.

Petersen, J.L., & Hyde, J.S. (2010). A meta-analytic review of research on gender differences in sexuality, 1973–2007. *Psychological Bulletin, 136,* 21–38.

Peterson, C.B., & others (2017). The effects of psychotherapy treatment on outcome in bulimia nervosa: Examining indirect effects through emotion regulation, self-directed behavior, and self-discrepancy within the mediation model. *International Journal of Eating Disorders, 50,* 636–647.

Peterson, C.C., & others (2016). Peer social skills and theory of mind in children with autism, deafness, or typical development. *Developmental Psychology, 52,* 46–57.

Petrie, J.R., Guzik, T.J., & Touyz, R.M. (2018, in press). Diabetes, hypertension, and cardiovascular disease: Clinical insights and vascular mechanisms. *Canadian Journal of Cardiology.*

Petry, N., & others (2017). The proportion of anemia associated with iron deficiency in low, medium, and high human development index countries: A systematic analysis of national surveys. *Nutrients, 49,* 43–52.

Pew Research Center (2010). *Millennials: Confident, connected, open to change.* Washington, DC: Pew Research Center.

Pew Research Center (2012). *Religion & Public Life Project.* Washington, DC: Pew Research Center.

Pew Research Center (2015). *Five facts about online dating.* Washington, DC: Author.

Peyre, H., & others (2017). Contributing factors and mental health outcomes of first suicide attempt during childhood and adolescence: Results from a nationally representative study. *Journal of Clinical Psychiatry, 78,* e622–e630.

Pham, T.B., & Adesman, A. (2018, in press). Increased risk of sadness and suicidality among victims of bullying experiencing additional threats to physical safety. *International Journal of Adolescent Mental Health.*

Phinney, J.S., & Vedder, P. (2013). Family relationship values of adolescents and parents: Intergenerational discrepancies and adaptation. In J.W. Berry & others (Eds.), *Immigrant youth in cultural transmission.* New York: Psychology Press.

Phull, A.R., & others (2018). Oxidative stress, consequences, and ROS mediated cellular signaling in rheumatoid arthritis. *Chemico-Biological Interactions, 281,* 121–136.

Piaget, J. (1932). *The moral judgment of the child.* New York: Harcourt Brace Jovanovich.

Piaget, J. (1952). *The origins of intelligence in children* (M. Cook, Trans.). New York: International Universities Press.

Piaget, J. (1954). *The construction of reality in the child.* New York: Basic Books.

Piaget, J. (1962). *Play, dreams, and imitation.* New York. W.W. Norton.

Piaget, J., & Inhelder, B. (1969). *The child's conception of space* (F.J. Langdon & J.L. Lunzer, Trans.). New York: W.W. Norton.

Piazza, J.R., Charles, S.T., Sliwinski, M.J., Mogle, J., & Almeida, D.M. (2013). Affective reactivity to daily stressors and long-term risk of reporting chronic physical health condition. *Annals of Behavior Medicine, 45,* 110–120.

Picherot, G., & others (2018, in press). Children and screens: Groupe de Pediatrie Generale guidelines for pediatricians and families. *Archives in Pediatrics.*

Pickard, J.A., & others (2018). Top-down and bottom-up: The role of social information processing and mindfulness as predictors of maternal-infant interaction. *Infant Mental Health Journal, 39,* 44–54.

Pidgeon, T.M., & others (2018, in press). Perceptions of the care received from Australian palliative care services: A caregiver perspective. *Palliative and Supportive Care.*

Piekarski, D.J., & others (2017). Does puberty mark a transition in sensitive periods for plasticity in the associative neocortex? *Brain Research, 1654*(Pt. B), 123–144.

Pietromonaco, P.R., & Beck, L.A. (2018). Adult attachment and physical health. *Current Opinion in Psychology, 25,* 115–120.

Pike, A., & Oliver, B.R. (2017). Child behavior and sibling relationship quality: A cross-lagged analysis. *Journal of Family Psychology, 31,* 250–255.

Piko, B.F., & Balazs, M.A. (2012). Authoritative parenting style and adolescent smoking and drinking. *Addictive Behaviors, 37,* 353–356.

Pinhas, L., & others (2017). Classification of childhood onset eating disorders: A latent class analysis. *International Journal of Eating Disorders, 50,* 657–664.

Pinheiro, M.B., & others (2018). Genetic and environmental influences to low back pain and symptoms of depression and anxiety: A population-based twin study. *Journal of Psychosomatic Research, 105,* 92–98.

Pinker, S. (2015). *Language, cognition, and human nature.* New York: Oxford University Press.

Pinninti, S.G., & Kimberlin, D.W. (2013). Neonatal herpes simplex virus infections. *Pediatric Clinics of North America, 60,* 351–365.

Pino, E.C., & others (2018). Adolescent socioeconomic status and depressive symptoms in later life: Evidence from structural equation models. *Journal of Affective Disorders, 225,* 702–708.

Pinquart, M. (2017). Associations of parenting dimensions and styles with externalizing problems of children and adolescents: An updated meta-analysis. *Developmental Psychology, 53,* 873–932.

Pinquart, M., & Kauser, R. (2018). Do the association of parenting styles with behavior problems and academic achievement vary by culture? Results from a meta-analysis. *Cultural Diversity and Ethnic Minority Psychology, 24,* 75–100.

Pinto Pereira, S.M., van Veldhoven, K., Li, L., & Power, C. (2016). Combined early and adult life risk factor associations for mid-life obesity in a prospective birth cohort: Assessing potential public health impact. *BMJ Open, 6*(4), e011044.

Pinto, T.M., & others (2017). Maternal depression and anxiety and fetal-neonatal growth. *Journal of Pediatrics, 93,* 452–459.

Pipp, S.L., Fischer, K.W., & Jennings, S.L. (1987). The acquisition of self and mother knowledge in infancy. *Developmental Psychology, 23,* 86–96.

Pirillo, A., & others (2018). The interplay of lipids, lipoproteins, and immunity in atherosclerosis. *Current Atherosclerosis Reports, 20*(3), 12.

Pitkänen, T., Lyrra, A.L., & Pulkkinen, L. (2005). Age of onset of drinking and the use of alcohol in adulthood: A follow-up study from age 8–42 for females and males. *Addiction, 100,* 652–661.

Pitman, A.L., & others (2018). The stigma associated with bereavement by suicide and other sudden deaths: A qualitative interview study. *Social Science and Medicine., 198,* 121–129.

Planalp, E.M., & others (2017a). The infant version of the Laboratory Temperament Assessment Battery (Lab-TAB): Measurement properties and implications for concepts of temperament. *Frontiers in Psychology, 8,* 846.

Planalp, E.M., & others (2017b). Genetic and environmental contributions to the development of positive affect in infancy. *Emotion, 17,* 412–420.

Platt, B., Kadosh, K.C., & Lau, J.Y. (2013). The role of peer rejection in adolescent depression. *Depression and Anxiety, 30,* 809–821.

Platt, J.M., & others (2017). Transdiagnostic psychiatric disorder risk associated with early age of menarche: A latent modeling approach. *Comprehensive Psychiatry, 79,* 70–79.

Plourde, K.F., & others (2017). Mentoring interventions and the impact of protective assets on the reproductive health of adolescent girls and young women. *Journal of Adolescent Health, 61,* 131–139.

Plucker, J. (2010, July 19). Commentary in P. Bronson & A. Merryman, *The creativity crisis. Newsweek*, pp. 45–46.

Pluess, M., & Belsky, J. (2009). Differential susceptibility to rearing experience: The case of child care. *Journal of Child Psychology and Psychiatry, 50,* 396–404.

Podrebarac, S.K., & others (2017). Antenatal exposure to antidepressants is associated with altered brain development in very preterm-born neonates. *Neuroscience, 342,* 252–262.

Poehlmann-Tynan, J., & others (2016). A pilot study of contemplative practices with economically disadvantaged preschoolers: Children's empathic and self-regulatory behaviors. *Mindfulness, 7,* 146–158.

Pohlabein, H., & others (2017). Further evidence for the role of pregnancy-induced hypertension and other early life influences in the development of ADHD: Results from the IDEFICS study. *European Child and Adolescent Psychiatry. 26,* 957–967.

Polenick, C.A., Birditt, K.S., & Zarit, S.H. (2018, in press). Parental support of adult children and middle-aged couples' marital satisfaction. *Gerontologist.*

Polenick, C.A., & DePasquale, N. (2018, in press). Predictors of secondary role strains among spousal caregivers of older adults with functional disability. *Gerontologist.*

Polenick, C.A., & others (2018, in press). Relationship quality between older fathers and middle-aged children: Associations with both parties' subjective well-being. *Journals of Gerontology B: Psychological Sciences and Social Sciences.*

Polenova, E., Vedral, A., Brisson, L., & Zinn, L. (2018). Emerging between two worlds. *Emerging Adulthood, 6,* 53–65.

Polka, L., Orena, A.J., Sundara, M., & Worrall, J. (2018, in press). Segmenting words from fluent speech during infancy—challenges and opportunities in a bilingual context. *Developmental Science.*

Pollock, K., & Seymour, J. (2018, in press). Reappraising 'the good death' for populations in the age of aging. *Age and Aging.*

Pomerantz, E.M. (2018). *Center for Parent-Child Studies.* Retrieved January 11, 2018, from http://labs.psychology.illinois.edu/cpcs/

Pomerantz, E.M., Cheung, C.S., & Qin, L. (2012). Relatedness between children and parents: Implications for motivation. In R. Ryan (Ed.), *Oxford handbook of motivation.* New York: Oxford University Press.

Pomerantz, E.M., & Grolnick, W.S. (2017). The role of parenting in children's motivation and competence: What underlies facilitative parenting? In A.S. Elliott, C.S. Dweck, and D.S. Yeager (Eds.), *Handbook of competence and motivation* (2nd ed.). New York: Guilford.

Pomerantz, E.M., & Kempner, S.G. (2013). Mothers' daily person and process praise: Implications for children's intelligence and motivation. *Developmental Psychology, 49,* 2040–2046.

Pomerantz, E.M., Kim, E.M., & Cheung, C.S. (2012). Parents' involvement in children's learning. In K.R. Harris & others (Eds.), *APA educational psychology handbook.* Washington, DC: American Psychological Association.

Pong, S., & Landale, N.S. (2012). Academic achievement of legal immigrants' children: The roles of parents' pre- and post-immigration characteristics in origin-group differences. *Child Development, 83,* 1543–1559.

Poole, L.A., & others (2018). A randomized controlled trial of the impact of a family-based adolescent depression intervention on both youth and parent mental health outcomes. *Journal of Abnormal Child Psychology, 46,* 169–181.

Popadin, K., & others (2018, in press). Slightly deleterious genomic variants and transcriptome perturbations in Down syndrome embryonic selection. *Genome Research.*

Popham, W.J. (2017). *Classroom assessment* (8th ed.). Upper Saddle River, NJ: Pearson.

Porcelli, B., & others (2016). Association between stressful life events and autoimmune diseases: A systematic review and and meta-analysis of retrospective case-control studies. *Autoimmunity Reviews, 15,* 325–334.

Porteri, C. (2018). Advance directives as a tool to respect patients' values and preferences: Discussion on the case of Alzheimer's disease. *BMC Journal of Medical Ethics, 19*(1), 9.

Posner, M. (2018a). Current landscape and historical context. In K. Nobre & S. Kastner (Eds.), *Oxford handbook of attention.* New York: Oxford University Press.

Posner, M. (2018b). Developing attention and self-regulation in childhood. In K. Nobre & S. Kastner (Eds.), *Oxford handbook of attention.* New York: Oxford University Press.

Posner, M.I., & Rothbart, M.K. (2007). *Educating the human brain.* Washington, DC: American Psychological Association.

Posner, M.I., Rothbart, M.K., Sheese, B.E., & Voelker, P. (2014). Developing attention: Behavioral and brain mechanisms. *Advances in Neuroscience, 2014,* 405094.

Possel, P., & others (2018, in press). Associations between social support from family, friends, and teachers and depressive symptoms of adolescents. *Journal of Youth and Adolescence.*

Poulain, T., & others (2018). Cross-sectional and longitudinal associations of screen time and physical activity with school performance at different types of secondary school. *BMC Public Health, 18*(1), 583.

Poulakis, K., & others (2018). Heterogeneous patterns of brain atrophy in Alzheimer's disease. *Neurobiology of Aging, 65,* 95–108.

Poulsen, R.D., & others (2018). How does general anesthesia affect the circadian clock? *Sleep Medicine Reviews, 37,* 35–44.

Powell, L.J., & Carey, S. (2017). Executive function depletion in children and its impact on theory of mind. *Cognition, 164,* 150–162.

Powell, R.E., & others (2018, in press). A multidisciplinary approach to impact acute care utilization in sickle cell disease. *American Journal of Medical Quality.*

Powell, S.D. (2019). *Your introduction to education* (4th ed.). Upper Saddle River, NJ: Pearson.

Powers, K.E., Chavez, R.S., & Heatherton, T.F. (2016). Individual differences in response of dorsomedial prefrontal cortex predict daily social behavior. *Social Cognitive and Affective Neuroscience, 11,* 121–126.

Powers, S.K., & Dodd, S.L. (2017). *Total fitness and wellness* (7th ed.). Upper Saddle River, NJ: Pearson.

Powers, S.K., & Howley, E. (2018). *Exercise physiology* (10th ed.). New York: McGraw-Hill.

Poyatos-Leon, R., & others (2017). Effects of exercise-based interventions on post-partum depression: A meta-analysis of randomized controlled trials. *Birth, 44,* 200–208.

Prenoveau, J.M., & others (2017). Maternal postnatal depression and anxiety and their association with child emotional negativity and behavior problems at two years. *Developmental Psychology, 53,* 50–62.

Pressley, M. (2007). An interview with Michael Pressley by Terri Flowerday and Michael Shaughnessy. *Educational Psychology Review, 19,* 1–12.

Preston, J.D., Reynolds, L.J., & Pearson, K.J. (2018, in press). Developmental origins of health span and life span: A mini-review. *Gerontology.*

Preston, R. (2018). Death on demand? An analysis of physician-administered euthanasia in the Netherlands. *British Medical Bulletin, 125,* 145–155.

Prince, H. (2018). Celebrating indigenous communities' compassionate traditions. *Annals of Palliative Medicine, 7*(Suppl. 1), ABOO5.

Prino, L.E., Longobardi, C., & Settanni, M. (2018, in press). Young adult retrospective reports of adverse childhood experiences: Prevalence of physical, emotional, and sexual abuse in Italy. *Archives of Sexual Behavior.*

Prinstein, M.J., & Giletta, M. (2016). Peer relations and developmental psychopathology. In D. Cicchetti (Ed.), *Developmental psychopathology* (3rd ed.). New York: Wiley.

Prinstein, M.J., & others (2018). Peer status and psychopathology. In W.M. Bukowski & others (Eds.), *Handbook of peer interactions, relationships, and groups* (2nd ed.). New York: Guilford.

Profili, E., & others (2017). School wellness team best practices to promote wellness policy implementation. *Preventive Medicine, 101,* 34–37.

Proulx, C.M., Curl, A.L., & Ermer, A.E. (2018). Longitudinal associations between formal volunteering and cognitive functioning. *Journals of Gerontology B: Psychological Sciences and Social Sciences, 73,* 522–531.

Pruett, M.K., & others (2017). Enhancing father involvement in low-income families: A couples group approach to preventive intervention. *Child Development, 88,* 398–407.

Pufal, M.A., & others (2012). Prevalence of overweight in children of obese patients: A dietary overview. *Obesity Surgery, 22*(8), 1220–1224.

Pugmire, J., Sweeting, H., & Moore, L. (2017). Environmental tobacco smoke exposure among infants, children, and youth people: Now is no time to relax. *Archives of Disease in Childhood, 102,* 117–118.

Pulcini, C.D., & others (2018, in press). Poverty and trends in three common chronic disorders. *Pediatrics.*

Puma, M., & others (2010). *Head Start impact study. Final report.* Washington, DC: Administration for Children & Families.

Pun, J.K.H., & others (2018, in press). Health professional-patient communication practices in East Asia: An integrative review of an emerging field of research and practice in Hong Kong, South Korea, Japan, Taiwan, and Mainland China. *Patient Education and Counseling.*

Putallaz, M., & others (2007). Overt and relational aggression and victimization: Multiple perspectives within the school setting. *Journal of School Psychology, 45,* 523–547.

Puts, M.T., & others (2017). Interventions to prevent or reduce the level of frailty in community-dwelling older adults: A scoping review of the literature and international policies. *Age and Aging, 46,* 383–392.

Q

Qin, J., & others (2015). Impact of arthritis and multiple chronic conditions on selected life domains—United States, 1913. *MMWR Morbidity and Mortality Weekly Report, 64,* 578–582.

Qiu, R., & others (2017). Greater intake of fruits and vegetables is associated with greater bone density and lower osteoporosis risk in middle-aged and elderly adults. *PLoS One, 12*(1), e168906.

Qu, Y., & others (2016). Conceptions of adolescence: Implications for differences in engagement in school over early adolescence in the United States and China. *Journal of Research on Adolescence, 26,* 126–141.

Quereshi, I.A., & Mehler, M.F. (2018). Epigenetic mechanisms underlying nervous system diseases. *Handbook of Clinical Neurology, 147,* 43–58.

Quimby, D., & others (2018, in press). Positive peer association among Black American youth and the roles of ethnic identity and gender. *Journal of Research on Adolescence.*

Quinn, P.C. (2016). What do infants know about cats, dogs, and people? Development of a "like-people" representation for non-human animals. In L. Freund & others (Eds.), *Social neuroscience and human-animal interaction.* Washington, DC: American Psychological Association.

Quinn, P.C., & Bhatt, R.S. (2015). Development of perceptual organization in infancy. In J. Wagemans (Ed.), *Oxford handbook of perceptual organization.* New York: Oxford University Press.

Quinn, P.C., & others (2013). On the developmental origins of differential responding to social category information. In M.R. Banaji & S.A. Gelman (Eds.),

Navigating the social world. New York: Oxford University Press.

Quinones-Camacho, L.E., & Davis, E.L. (2018, in press), Discrete emotion regulation strategy repertoires and parasympathetic physiology characterize psychopathology symptoms in childhood. *Developmental Psychology.*

R

Raajashri, R., & others (2018). Maternal perceptions and factors affecting kangaroo mother care continuum at home: A descriptive study. *Journal of Maternal-Fetal and Neonatal Medicine, 31,* 666-669.

Raby, K.L., & others (2018, in press). The legacy of early abuse and neglect for social and academic competence from childhood to adulthood. *Child Development.*

Radhakrishnan, D., & Goyal, V. (2018). Parkinson's disease: A review. *Neurology India, 66*(Suppl.), S26-S35.

Radhakrishnan, S., & others (2018, in press). Laser peripheral iridotomy in primary angle closure: A report by the American Academy of Ophthalmology. *Ophthalmology.*

Radvansky, G.A., & Ashcraft, M.H. (2018). *Cognition* (7th ed.). Upper Saddle River, NJ: Pearson.

Raemaekers, M., & others (2018, in press). Knowing left from right: Asymmetric functional connectivity during resting state. *Brain Structure and Function.*

Ragavan, M., & others (2018, in press). Chinese, Vietnamese, and Asian Indian parents' perspectives about well-child visits: A qualitative analysis. *Acta Paediatrica.*

Raichlen, D.A., & Alexander, G.E. (2017). Adaptive capacity: An evolutionary neuroscience model linking exercise, cognition, and brain health. *Trends in Neuroscience, 40,* 408-421.

Raikes, H., & others (2006). Mother-child bookreading in low-income families: Correlates and outcomes during the first three years of life. *Child Development, 77,* 924-953.

Rajan, S., & others (2017). Integrating health education in core curriculum classrooms: Successes, challenges, and implications for urban middle schools. *Journal of School Health, 87,* 949-957.

Rajan, T.M., & Menon, V. (2017). Psychiatric disorders and obesity: A review of association studies. *Journal of Postgraduate Medicine, 63,* 182-190.

Rajaraman, P., & others (2011). Early life exposure to diagnostic radiation and ultrasound scans and risk of childhood cancer: Case-control study. *British Medical Journal, 342,* d472.

Rajeh, A., & others (2017). Interventions in ADHD: A comparative review of stimulant medications and behavioral therapies. *Asian Journal of Psychiatry, 25,* 131-135.

Raketic, D., & others (2017). Five-factor model personality profiles: The differences between alcohol and opiate addiction among females. *Psychiatria Danubina, 29,* 74-80.

Rakoczy, H. (2012). Do infants have a theory of mind? *British Journal of Developmental Psychology, 30,* 59-74.

Rakoczy, H., & others (2018). Theory of mind and wisdom: The development of different forms of perspective-taking in late adulthood. *British Journal of Psychology, 109,* 8-24.

Ramaswami, G., & Geschwind, D.H. (2018). Genetics of autism spectrum disorder. *Handbook of Clinical Neurology, 147,* 321-329.

Ramirez-Esparza, N., Garcia-Sierra, A., & Kuhl, P.K. (2017). The impact of early social interactions on later language development in Spanish-English bilingual infants. *Child Development, 85,* 1216-1234.

Ramus, F., & others (2018). Neuroanatomy of developmental dyslexia: Pitfalls and promises. *Neuroscience and Biobehavioral Reviews.*

Rana, B.K., & others (2018). Association of sleep quality on memory-related executive functions in middle age. *Journal of the International Neuropsychology Society, 24,* 67-76.

Randall, W.L. (2013). The importance of being ironic: Narrative openness and personal resilience in later life. *Gerontologist, 53*(1), 9-16.

Rangey, P.S., & Sheth, M. (2014). Comparative effect of massage therapy versus kangaroo mother care on body weight and length of hospital stay in low birth weight infants. *International Journal of Pediatrics, 2014,* 434060.

Rankin, J. (2017). *Physiology in childbearing* (4th ed.). New York: Elsevier.

Rapee, R.M. (2014). Preschool environment and temperament as predictors of social and nonsocial anxiety disorders in middle adolescence. *Journal of the American Academy of Child and Adolescent Psychiatry, 53,* 320-328.

Rapp, S.R., & others (2013). Educational attainment, MRI changes, and cognitive function in older postmenopausal women from the Women's Health Initiative Memory Study. *International Journal of Psychiatry in Medicine, 46,* 121-143.

Rastedt, D.E., Vaughan, R.A., & Foster, J.D. (2017). Palmitoylation mechanisms in dopamine transporter regulation. *Journal of Chemical Neuroanatomy, 84,* 3-9.

Rasulo, D., Christensen, K., & Tomassini, C. (2005). The influence of social relations on mortality in later life: A study on elderly Danish twins. *Gerontologist, 45,* 601-608.

Rathunde, K., & Csikszentmihalyi, M. (2006). The developing person: An experiential perspective. In W. Damon & R. Lerner (Eds.), *Handbook of child psychology* (6th ed.). New York: Wiley.

Rattan, A., & Dweck, C.S. (2018). What happens after prejudice is confronted in the workplace? How mindsets affect minorities' and women's outlook on future social relations. *Journal of Applied Psychology, 103,* 676-687.

Raudsepp, L., & Riso, E.M. (2017). Longitudinal associations between sedentary behavior of adolescent girls, their mothers, and best friends. *Pediatric Exercise Science, 29,* 419-426.

Raver, C.C., & others (2011). CSRP's impact on low-income preschoolers' preacademic skills: Self-regulation as a mediating mechanism. *Child Development, 82,* 362-378.

Raver, C.C., & others (2012). Testing models of children's self-regulation within educational contexts: Implications for measurement. *Advances in Child Development and Behavior, 42,* 245-270.

Raver, C.C., & others (2013). Predicting individual differences in low-income children's executive control from early to middle childhood. *Developmental Science, 16,* 394-408.

Ray, J., & others (2017). Callous-unemotional traits predict self-reported offending in adolescent boys: The mediating role of delinquent peers and the moderating role of parenting practices. *Developmental Psychology, 53,* 319-328.

Razavi, S.M., & others (2017). Comprehensive functional enrichment analysis of male infertility. *Scientific Reports, 7,* 15778.

Razaz, N., & others (2016). Five-minute Apgar score as a marker for developmental vulnerability at 5 years of age. *Archives of Disease in Childhood: Fetal and Neonatal Edition, 101,* F114-F120.

Razza, R.A., Martin, A., & Brooks-Gunn, J. (2012). The implications of early attentional regulation for school success among low-income children. *Journal of Applied Developmental Psychology, 33,* 311-319.

Read, J., & others (2018, in press). How do mental health services respond when child abuse or neglect become known? A literature review. *International Journal of Mental Health Nursing.*

Reader, J.M., Teti, D.M., & Cleveland, M.J. (2017). Cognitions about infant sleep: Interparental differences, trajectories across the first year, and coparenting quality. *Journal of Family Psychology, 31,* 453-463.

Rebok, G.W., & others (2014). Ten-year effects of the Advanced Cognitive Training for Independent and Vital Elderly Cognitive Training Trial on cognition and everyday functioning in older adults. *Journal of the American Geriatrics Society, 62*(1), 16-24.

Recode (2016, June 27). *You are still watching a staggering amount of TV every day.* Retrieved March 6, 2018, from https://www.recode.net/2016/6/27/12041028/tv-hours-per-week-nielsen

Reece, E., & others (2017). Telling the tale and living well: Adolescent narrative identity, personality traits, and well-being across cultures. *Child Development, 88,* 612-628.

Reed, A.E., & Carstensen, L.L. (2015). Age-related positivity effect and its implications for social and health gerontology. In N.A. Pachana (Ed.), *Encyclopedia of geropsychology.* New York: Springer.

Rees, M., & others (2018). Joint opinion paper—"Aging and sexual health" by the European Board & College of Obstetrics and Gynecology (EBCOG) and the European Menopause and Andropause Society (EMAS). *European Journal of Obstetrics, Gynecology, and Reproductive Biology, 220,* 132-134.

Reese, B.M., Haydon, A.A., Herring, A.H., & Halpern, C.T. (2013). The association between sequences of sexual initiation and the likelihood of teenage pregnancy. *Journal of Adolescent Health, 52,* 228-233.

Regalado, M., Sareen, H., Inkelas, M., Wissow, L.S., & Halfon, N. (2004). Parents' discipline of young children: Results from the National Survey of Early Childhood Health. *Pediatrics, 113,* 1952-1958.

Regev, R.H., & others (2003). Excess mortality and morbidity among small-for-gestational-age premature infants: A population based study. *Journal of Pediatrics, 143,* 186-191.

Regnart, J., Truter, I., & Meyer, A. (2017). Critical exploration of co-occurring attention-deficit/hyperactivity disorder, mood disorder, and substance use disorder. *Expert Review of Pharmaco Economics & Outcomes Research, 17,* 275-282.

Reiersen, A.M. (2017). Early identification of autism spectrum disorder: Is diagnosis by age 3 a reasonable goal? *Journal of the American Academy of Child and Adolescent Psychiatry, 56,* 284-285.

Reilly, D. (2012). Gender, culture, and sex-typed cognitive abilities. *PLoS One, 7*(7), e39904.

Rejeski, W.J., & others (2017). Community weight loss to combat obesity and disability in at-risk older adults. *Journals of Gerontology A: Biological Sciences and Medical Sciences, 72,* 1547-1553.

Ren, H., & others (2017). Excessive homework, inadequate sleep, physical inactivity, and screen viewing time are major contributors to high pediatric obesity. *Acta Paediatrica, 106,* 120-127.

Renzulli, J. (2017). Developing creativity across all areas of the curriculum. In R.A. Beghetto & J.C. Kaufman (Eds.), *Nurturing creativity in the classroom* (2nd ed.). New York: Cambridge University Press.

Renzulli, J. (2018). The malleability of creativity: A career in helping students discover and nurture their creativity. In R.J. Sternberg & J.C. Kaufman (Eds.), *The nature of human creativity.* New York: Cambridge University Press.

Reproductive Endocrinology and Infertility Committee & others (2012). Advanced reproductive age and fertility. *Journal of Obstetrics and Gynecology Canada.*

Reuter-Lorenz, P.A., Festini, S.B., & Jantz, T.K. (2016). Executive functions and neurocognitive aging. In K.W. Schaie & S.L. Willis (Eds.), *Handbook of the psychology of aging* (8th ed.). New York: Elsevier.

Reuter-Lorenz, P.A., & Lustig, C. (2017). Working memory and executive functions in the aging brain. In R. Cabeza, L. Nyberg, & D. Park (Eds.), *Handbook of cognitive neuroscience of aging* (2nd ed.). New York: Oxford University Press.

Reutzel, D.R., & Cooter, R.B. (2019). *Teaching children to read* (8th ed.). Upper Saddle River, NJ: Pearson.

Revelas, M., & others (2018, in press). Review and meta-analysis of genetic polymorphisms associated with exceptional human longevity. *Mechanisms of Aging and Development.*

Reyna, V.F. (2018, in press). Neurobiological models of risky decision-making and adolescent substance use. *Current Addiction Reports.*

Reyna, V.F., & Rivers, S.E. (2008). Current theories of risk and rational decision making. *Developmental Review, 28,* 1–11.

Reyna, V.F., & Zayas, V. (Eds.) (2014). *Neuroscience of risky decision making.* Washington, DC: American Psychological Association.

Reyna, V.F., & others (2018, in press). Brain activation covaries with reported criminal behaviors when making risky choices. *Journal of Experimental Psychology: General.*

Reynolds, A.J., Ou, S.R., & Temple, J.A. (2018). A multicomponent, preschool to third grade intervention and educational attainment at 35 years of age. *JAMA Pediatrics, 172,* 247–256.

Reynolds, G.D., & Richards, J.E. (2018, in press). Infant visual attention and stimulus repetition effects on object recognition. *Child Development.*

Rhodes, R.E., & Katz, B. (2017). Working memory plasticity and aging. *Psychology and Aging, 32,* 51–59.

Riaz, A., & others (2018). Fusion of fMRI and non-imaging data for ADHD classification. *Computerized and Medical Imaging Graphics, 65,* 115–128.

Ribeiro, O., & Araujo, L. (2019). Defining 'success' in exceptional longevity. In R.Fernandez-Ballesteros & others (Eds.), *Cambridge handbook of successful aging.* New York: Cambridge University Press.

Richardson, G.A., Goldschmidt, L., Leech, S., & Willford, J. (2011). Prenatal cocaine exposure: Effects on mother- and teacher-rated behavior problems and growth in school-age children. *Neurotoxicology and Teratology, 33,* 69–77.

Richardson, G.A., Goldschmidt, L., & Willford, J. (2008). The effects of prenatal cocaine use on infant development. *Neurotoxicology and Teratology, 30,* 96–106.

Richardson, M.A., & others (2016). Psychological distress among school-aged children with and without intrauterine cocaine exposure: Perinatal versus contextual effects. *Journal of Abnormal Child Psychology, 44,* 547–560.

Richtsmeier, P.T., & Goffman, L. (2017). Perceptual statistical learning over one week in child speech production. *Journal of Communication Disorders, 68,* 70–80.

Rideout, V., Foehr, U.G., & Roberts, D.P. (2010). *Generation M: Media in the lives of 8- to 18-year-olds.* Menlo Park, CA: Kaiser Family Foundation.

Rietjens, J.A.C., & others (2017). Definition and recommendations for advance care planning: An international consensus supported by the European Association of Palliative Care. *Lancet Oncology, 18,* e543–e551.

Riggins, T. (2012). Building blocks of recollection. In S. Ghetti & P.J. Bauer (Eds.), *Origins and development of recollection: Perspectives from psychology and neuroscience.* New York: Oxford University Press.

Rimfeld, K., & others (2017). Phenotypic and genetic evidence for a unifactorial structure of spatial abilities. *Proceedings of the National Academy of Sciences USA, 114,* 2777–2782.

Rimsza, M.E., & Kirk, G.M. (2005). Common medical problems of the college student. *Pediatric Clinics of North America, 52,* 9–24.

Ringe, D. (2019). *An introduction to grammar for language learners.* New York: Cambridge University Press.

Rios, A.C., & Clevers, H. (2018). Imaging organoids: A bright future ahead. *Nature Methods, 15,* 24–26.

Rioux, C., & others (2018, in press). Age of cannabis use onset and adult drug abuse symptoms: A prospective study of common risk factors and indirect effects. *Canadian Journal of Psychiatry.*

Rivas-Drake, D., & Umana-Taylor, A. (2018, in press). Ethnic-racial identity and friendships in adolescence. *Child Development.*

Rivas-Drake, D., & others (2017). Ethnic-racial identity and friendships in early adolescence. *Child Development, 88,* 710–724.

Rix, S. (2011). Employment and aging. In R.H. Binstock & L.K. George (Eds.), *Handbook of aging and the social sciences* (7th ed.). New York: Elsevier.

Rizvi, S.J., & others (2015). Depression and employment status in primary and tertiary care settings. *Canadian Journal of Psychiatry, 60,* 14–22.

Roberts, B.W., & Damian, R.I. (2018). The principles of personality trait development and their relation to psychopathology. In D. Lynam & D. Samuel (Eds.), *Using personality research to inform the personality disorders.* New York: Oxford University Press.

Roberts, B.W., & Hill, P.L. (2017). The sourdough bread model of conscientiousness. In J. Burrus & others (Eds.), *Building better students: Preparation for the workforce.* New York: Oxford University Press.

Roberts, B.W., & Mroczek, D. (2008). Personality trait change in adulthood. *Current Directions in Psychological Science, 17,* 31–35.

Roberts, B.W., & Wood, D. (2006). Personality development in the context of the neo-socioanalytic model of personality. In D. Mroczek & T. Little (Eds.), *Handbook of personality development.* Mahwah, NJ: Erlbaum.

Roberts, B.W., & others (2017). A systematic review of personality trait change through intervention. *Psychological Bulletin, 143,* 117–141.

Roberts, K.L., & Allen, H.A. (2016). Perception and cognition in the aging brain: A brief review of short-term and long-term links between perceptual and cognitive decline. *Frontiers in Aging Neuroscience, 8,* 39.

Roberts, L., Marx, J.M., & Musher-Eizenman, D.R. (2018). Using food as a reward: An examination of parental reward practices. *Appetite, 120,* 318–326.

Roberts, S.D., & others (2018). Children's descriptive-to-prescriptive tendency replicates (and varies) cross-culturally: Evidence from China. *Journal of Experimental Child Psychology, 165,* 148–160.

Robine, J-M. (2019). Successful aging and the longevity revolution. In R. Fernandez-Ballesteros & others (Eds), *Cambridge handbook of successful aging.* New York: Cambridge University Press.

Robinson, A., & Lachman, M.E. (2017). Perceived control and aging: A mini-review and directions for future research. *Gerontology, 63,* 435–442.

Robinson, A.T., & others (2017). Short-term regular aerobic exercise reduces oxidative stress produced by acute high intraluminal pressure in the adipose microvasculature. *American Journal of Physiology: Heart and Circulatory Physiology, 312,* H896–H906.

Robinson, K., Garnier-Villarreal, M., & Hanson, L. (2018). Effectiveness of CenteringPregnancy on breastfeeding initiation among African Americans: A systematic review and meta-analysis. *Journal of Perinatal and Neonatal Nursing, 32,* 116–126.

Robinson, S., & Lachman, M.E. (2017). Perceived control and behavior change: A personalized approach. In F. Infurna & J. Reich (Eds.), *Perceived control: Theory, research, and practice in the first 50 years.* New York: Oxford University Press.

Robinson, S.A., & Lachman, M.E. (2017). Perceived control and aging: A mini-review and directions for future research. *Gerontology, 63,* 435–442.

Roblyer, M.D., & Hughes, J.E. (2019). *Integrating educational technology into teaching* (8th ed.). Upper Saddle River, NJ: Pearson.

Rochlen, A.B., McKelley, R.A., Suizzo, M.-A., & Scaringi, V. (2008). Predictors of relationship satisfaction, psychological well-being, and life-satisfaction among stay-at-home fathers. *Psychology of Men and Masculinity, 9,* 17–28.

Rode, S.S., Chang, P., Fisch, R.O., & Sroufe, L.A. (1981). Attachment patterns of infants separated at birth. *Developmental Psychology, 17,* 188–191.

Rodin, J., & Langer, E.J. (1977). Long-term effects of a control-relevant intervention with the institutionalized

aged. *Journal of Personality and Social Psychology, 35,* 397–402.

Rodriguez Villar, S., & others (2012). Prolonged grief disorder in the next of kin of adult patients who die during or after admission to intensive care. *Chest, 141,* 1635–1636.

Rodrique, K.M., & Bischof, G. (2017). The modifying role of hypertension in cognitive and brain aging. In R. Cabeza, L. Nyberg, & D.C. Park (Eds.), *Cognitive neuroscience of aging* (2nd ed.). New York: Oxford University Press.

Rodrique, K.M., & Kennedy, K.M. (2011). The cognitive consequences of structural changes to the aging brain. In K.W. Schaie & S.L. Willis (Eds.), *Handbook of the psychology of aging* (7th ed.). New York: Elsevier.

Roelfs, D.J., Shor, E., Davidson, K.W., & Schwartz, J.E. (2011). Losing life and livelihood: A systematic review and meta-analysis of unemployment and all-cause mortality. *Social Science & Medicine, 72,* 840–854.

Roese, N.J., & Summerville, A. (2005). What we regret most . . . and why. *Personality and Social Psychology Bulletin, 31,* 1273–1285.

Roeser, R.W. (2016). Beyond all splits: Mindfulness in students' motivation, learning, and self-identity at school. In K.R. Wentzel & D.B. Miele (Eds.), *Handbook of motivation at school.* New York: Routledge.

Roeser, R.W., & Eccles, J.S. (2015). Mindfulness and compassion in human development: Introduction to the special section. *Developmental Psychology, 51,* 1–6.

Roeser, R.W., & Zelazo, P.D. (2012). Contemplative science, education and child development. *Child Development Perspectives, 6,* 143–145.

Roeser, R.W., & others (2014). Contemplative education. In L. Nucci & others (Eds.), *Handbook of moral and character education.* New York: Routledge.

Rogers, E.E., & Hintz, S.R. (2016). Early neurodevelopmental outcomes of extremely preterm infants. *Seminars in Perinatology, 40,* 497–509.

Rogers, M.L., & others (2016). Maternal emotion socialization differentially predicts third-grade children's emotion regulation and lability. *Emotion, 16,* 280–291.

Roggman, L.A., & others (2016). Home visit quality variations in two early Head Start programs in relation to parenting and child vocabulary outcomes. *Infant Mental Health Journal, 37,* 193–207.

Rognum, I.J., & others (2014). Serotonin metabolites in the cerebrospinal fluid in sudden infant death syndrome. *Journal of Neuropathology and Experimental Neurology, 73,* 115–122.

Rohrer, J.M., Egloff, B., & Schmukle, S.C. (2017). Probing birth-order effects on narrow traits using specification-curve analysis. *Psychological Science, 28,* 1821–1832.

Roisman, G.I., & Cicchetti, D. (2017). Attachment in the context of atypical caregiving: Harnessing insights from developmental psychopathology. *Development and Psychopathology, 20,* 331–335.

Roisman, G.I., & others (2016). Strategic considerations in the search for transactional processes. *Development and Psychopathology, 28,* 791–800.

Rojas-Flores, L., & others (2017). Trauma and psychological distress in Latino citizen children following parental detention and deportation. *Psychological Trauma, 9,* 352–361.

Rolfes, S.R., & Pinna, K. (2018). *Understanding normal and clinical nutrition* (11th ed.). Boston: Cengage.

Rolfes, S.R., Pinna, K., & Whitney, E. (2018). *Understanding normal and clinical nutrition* (11th ed.). Boston: Cengage.

Rolland, B., & others (2016). Pharmacotherapy for alcohol dependence: The 2015 recommendations of the French Alcohol Society, issued in partnership with the European Federation of Addiction Societies. *CNS Neuroscience and Therapeutics, 22,* 25–37.

Rollins, B.Y., Savage, J.S., Fisher, J.O., & Birch, L.L. (2016). Alternatives to restrictive feeding practices to promote self-regulation in childhood: A developmental perspective. *Pediatric Obesity, 11,* 326–332.

Romer, D., Reyna, V.F., & Satterthwaite, T.D. (2017). Beyond stereotypes of adolescent risk taking: Placing the adolescent brain in developmental context. *Developmental Cognitive Neuroscience, 26,* 19–34.

Romero, L.M., & others (2017). Efforts to increase implementation of evidence-based clinical practices to improve adolescent-friendly reproductive health services. *Journal of Adolescent Health, 60*(Suppl. 3), S30–S37.

Romo, L.F., Mireles-Rios, R., & Lopez-Tello, G. (2014). Latina mothers' and daughters' expectations for autonomy at age 15 (La Quinceañera). *Journal of Adolescent Research, 29*(2), 279–294.

Roohan, P.J. (2018). Paying outcomes in Medicaid: The time is now. *Journal of Ambulatory Care Management, 41,* 101–102.

Roopnarine, J.L., & Yildirim, E.D. (2018). *Fathering in cultural contexts.* New York: Routledge.

Roring, R.W., Hines, F.G., & Charness, N. (2007). Age differences in identifying words in synthetic speech. *Human Factors, 49,* 25–31.

Rose, A.J., & Smith, R.L. (2018). Gender and peer relationships. In W.M. Bukowski & others (Eds.), *Handbook of peer interactions, relationships, and groups* (2nd ed.). New York: Guilford.

Rose, A.J., & others (2017). Co-rumination exacerbates stress generation among adolescents with depressive symptoms. *Journal of Abnormal Child Psychology, 45,* 985–995.

Rose, S.A., Feldman, J.F., & Jankowski, J.J. (2015). Pathways from toddler information processing to adolescent lexical proficiency. *Child Development, 86,* 1935–1947.

Roseberry, S., Hirsh-Pasek, K., & Golinkoff, R. (2014). Skype me! Socially contingent interactions help toddlers learn language. *Child Development, 85,* 956–970.

Roseberry, S., Hirsh-Pasek, K., Parish-Morris, J., & Golinkoff, R. (2009). Live action: Can young children learn verbs from video? *Child Development, 80,* 1360–1375.

Rosen, L., & others (2018). Protecting children from tobacco smoke exposure: A pilot study of Project Zero exposure. *Pediatrics, 141*(Suppl. 1), S107–S117.

Rosen, M.L., & others (2018). Socioeconomic disparities in academic achievement: A multi-modal investigation of neural mechanisms in children and adolescents. *NeuroImage, 173,* 298–310.

Rosen, R.C., & others (2017). Quality of life and sexual function benefits of long-term testosterone treatment: Longitudinal results from the registry of hypogonadism in men (RHYME). *Journal of Sexual Medicine, 14,* 1104–115.

Rosengard, C. (2009). Confronting the intendedness of adolescent rapid repeat pregnancy. *Journal of Adolescent Health, 44,* 5–6.

Rosenstein, D., & Oster, H. (1988). Differential facial responses to four basic tastes in newborns. *Child Development, 59,* 1555–1568.

Rosenstrom, T., & others (2018). Prediction of alcohol use disorder using personality disorder traits: A twin study. *Addiction, 113,* 15–24.

Ross, J. (2017). You and me: Investigating the role of self-evaluative emotion in preschool prosociality. *Journal of Experimental Child Psychology, 155,* 67–83.

Rossi, A.S. (1989). A life-course approach to gender, aging, and intergenerational relations. In K.W. Schaie & C. Schooler (Eds.), *Social structure and aging.* Hillsdale, NJ: Erlbaum.

Rossler, W., & others (2017). Sleep disturbances in young and middle-aged adults—Empirical patterns and related factors from an epidemiological survey. *Comprehensive Psychiatry, 78,* 83–90.

Rostamian, S., & others (2015). Executive function, but not memory, associates with incident coronary heart disease and stroke. *Neurology, 85,* 783–789.

Rote, W.M., & Smetana, J.G. (2016). Beliefs about parents' right to know: Domain distinctions and associations with change in concealment. *Journal of Research on Adolescence, 26,* 334–344.

Rotenberg, J., & others (2018, in press). Home-based primary care: Beyond extension of the independence at home demonstration. *Journal of the American Geriatrics Society.*

Roth, B., & others (2015). Intelligence and school grades: A meta-analysis. *Intelligence, 53,* 118–137.

Roth, J., Brooks-Gunn, J., Murray, L., & Foster, W. (1998). Promoting healthy adolescents: Synthesis of youth development program evaluations. *Journal of Research on Adolescence, 8,* 423–459.

Rothbart, M.K. (2011). *Becoming who we are.* New York: Guilford.

Rothbart, M.K., & Bates, J.E. (2006). Temperament. In W. Damon & R. Lerner (Eds.), *Handbook of child psychology* (6th ed.). New York: Wiley.

Rothbart, M.K., & Posner, M. (2015). The developing brain in a multitasking world. *Developmental Review, 35,* 42–63.

Rothbaum, F., Poll, M., Azuma, H., Miyake, K., & Welsz, J. (2000). The development of close relationships in Japan and the United States: Paths of symbiotic harmony and generative tension. *Child Development, 71,* 1121–1142.

Rovee-Collier, C. (1987). Learning and memory in children. In J.D. Osofsky (Ed.), *Handbook of infant development* (2nd ed.). New York: Wiley.

Rovee-Collier, C. (2008). The development of infant memory. In N. Cowan & M. Courage (Eds.), *The development of memory in infancy and childhood.* Philadelphia: Psychology Press.

Rovee-Collier, C., & Barr, R. (2010). Infant learning and memory. In U.J.G. Bremner & T.D. Wachs (Ed.), *Wiley-Blackwell handbook of infant development* (2nd ed.). New York: Wiley.

Rovner, P., & others (2018). Induction of the LH surge in premenarchal girls confirms early maturation of the hypothalamic-pituitary-ovarian axis. *Reproductive Sciences, 25,* 33–38.

Rowland, T. (2016). Pediatric exercise science: A brief overview. *Pediatric Exercise Science, 28,* 167–170.

Rowland, T. (2018). Cardiovascular physiology and diseases in youth—the year that was 2017. *Pediatric Exercise Science, 30,* 32–34.

Rozenblat, V., & others (2017). A systematic review and secondary data analysis of the interactions between the serotonin transporter 5-HTTLPR polymorphism and environmental and psychological factors in eating disorders. *Journal of Psychiatric Research, 84,* 62–72.

Rubin, K.H., & Barstead, M. (2018). Social withdrawal and solitude. In M.H. Bornstein (Ed.), *SAGE handbook of lifespan human development.* Thousand Oaks, CA: Sage.

Rubin, K.H., Bukowski, W.M., & Bowker, J. (2015). Children in peer groups. In R.M. Lerner (Ed.), *Handbook of child psychology and developmental science* (7th ed.). New York: McGraw-Hill.

Rubin, K.H., Bukowski, W.M., & Parker, J.G. (2006). Peer interactions, relationships, and groups. In W. Damon & R. Lerner (Eds.), *Handbook of child psychology* (6th ed.). New York: Wiley.

Rubin, K.H., & others (2015). Peer relationships. In M.H. Bornstein & M.E. Lamb (Eds.), *Developmental science* (7th ed.). New York: Psychology Press.

Rubin, K.H., & others (2018). Avoiding and withdrawing from the peer group. In W.M. Bukowski & others (Eds.), *Handbook of peer interaction, relationships, and groups* (2nd ed.). New York: Guilford.

Rubio-Fernandez, P. (2017). Why are bilinguals better than monolinguals at false-belief tasks? *Psychonomic Bulletin and Review, 24,* 987–998.

Ruble, D. (1983). The development of social comparison processes and their role in achievement-related self-socialization. In E. Higgins, D. Ruble, & W. Hartup (Eds.), *Social cognitive development: A social-cultural perspective.* New York: Cambridge University Press.

Ruck, M.D., Peterson-Badali, M., & Freeman, M. (Eds.). (2017). *Handbook of children's rights.* New York: Routledge.

Rudolph, K.D., Troop-Gordon, W., Lambert, S.F., & Natsuaki, M.N. (2014). Long-term consequences of pubertal timing for youth depression: Identifying personal and contextual pathways of risk. *Development and Psychopathology, 26,* 1423–1444.

Rueda, M.R., Posner, M.I., & Rothbart, M.K. (2005). The development of executive attention: Contributions to the emergence of self-regulation. *Developmental Neuropsychology, 28,* 573–594.

Ruffman, T., Slade, L., & Crowe, E. (2002). The relation between children's and mothers' mental state language and theory-of-mind understanding. *Child Development, 73,* 734–751.

Rugg, M.D. (2017). Interpreting age-related differences in memory-related neural activity. In R. Cabeza, L. Nyberg, & D.C. Park (Eds.), *Cognitive neuroscience and aging* (2nd ed.). New York: Oxford University Press.

Ruisch, I.H., & others (2018). Maternal substance use during pregnancy and offspring conduct problems: A meta-analysis. *Neuroscience and Biobehavioral Reviews, 84,* 325–336.

Ruitenberg, M.F., & others (2015). Sequential movement skill in Parkinson's disease: A state-of-the-art. *Cortex, 65C,* 102–112.

Ruitenberg, M.J., & others (2017). Enrichment increases hippocampal neurogenesis independent of blood monocyte-derived microglia presence following high-dose total body irradiation. *Brain Research Bulletin, 132,* 150–159.

Ruiz-Casares, M., & others (2017). Parenting for the promotion of adolescent mental health: A scoping review of programs targeting ethnoculturally diverse families. *Health & Social Care in the Community, 25,* 743–757.

Rumberger, R.W. (1983). Dropping out of high school: The influence of race, sex, and family background. *American Educational Research Journal, 20,* 199–220.

Rupp, D.E., Vodanovich, S.J., & Crede, M. (2005). The multidimensional nature of ageism: Construct validity and group differences. *Journal of Social Psychology, 145,* 335–362.

Rusby, J.C., & others (2018, in press). Influence of parent-youth relationship, parental monitoring, and parent substance use on adolescent substance use onset. *Journal of Family Psychology.*

Russo-Netzer, P., & Moran, G. (2018). Positive growth from adversity and beyond: Insights gained from cross-examination of clinical and non-clinical samples. *American Journal of Orthopsychiatry, 88,* 59–68.

Ryan, A.M., & Shin, H. (2018). Peers, academics, and teachers. In W.M. Bukowski & others (Eds.), *Handbook of peer interactions, relationships, and groups* (2nd ed.). New York: Guilford.

Ryff, C.D. (1984). Personality development from the inside: The subjective experience of change in adulthood and aging. In P.B. Baltes & O.G. Brim (Eds.), *Life-span development and behavior.* New York: Academic Press.

S

Saab, A.S., & Nave, K.A. (2017). Myelin dynamics: Protecting and shaping neurons. *Current Opinion in Neurobiology, 47,* 104–112.

Saad, L. (2014). The "40-hour" workweek is actually longer—by seven hours. Washington, DC: Gallup.

Saarni, C. (1999). *The development of emotional competence.* New York: Guilford.

Saarni, C., Campos, J., Camras, L.A., & Witherington, D. (2006). Emotional development. In W. Damon & R. Lerner (Eds.), *Handbook of child psychology* (6th ed.). New York: Wiley.

Sabir, M., Henderson, C.R., Kang, S.Y., & Pillemer, K. (2016). Attachment-focused integrative reminiscence with older African Americans: A randomized controlled intervention study. *Aging and Mental Health, 20,* 517–528.

Sackett, P.R., & others (2017). Individual differences and their measurement: A review of 100 years of research. *Journal of Applied Psychology, 102*, 254–273.

Sackett, P.R., Borneman, M.J., & Connelly, B.S. (2009). Response to issues raised about validity, bias, and fairness in high-stakes testing. *American Psychologist, 64*, 285–287.

Sadeh, A. (2007). Consequences of sleep loss or sleep disruption in children. *Sleep Medicine, 2*, 513–520.

Sadeh, A. (2008). Sleep. In M.M. Haith & J.B. Benson (Eds.), *Encyclopedia of infant and early childhood development*. Oxford, UK: Elsevier.

Sadker, D.M., & Zittleman, K. (2016). *Teachers, schools, and society* (4th ed.). New York: McGraw-Hill.

Saez de Urabain, I.R., Nuthmann, A., & Johnson, M.H. (2017). Disentangling the mechanisms underlying infant fixation durations in scene perception: A computational account. *Vision Research, 134*, 43–59.

Saffran, J.R., & Kirkham, N.Z. (2018). Infant statistical learning. *Annual Review of Psychology* (Vol. 69). Palo Alto, CA: Annual Reviews.

Saffran, J.R., Werker, J.F., & Werner, L.A. (2006). The infant's auditory world: Hearing, speech, and the beginnings of language. In W. Damon & R. Lerner (Eds.), *Handbook of child psychology* (6th ed.). New York: Wiley.

Saha, S.K., & others (2017). Correlation between oxidative stress, nutrition, and cancer initiation. *International Journal of Molecular Science, 18*, 7.

Saint-Onge, J.M. (2009). Mortality. In D. Carr (Ed.), *Encyclopedia of the life course and human development*. Boston: Gale Cengage.

Salama, R.H., & others (2013). Clinical and biochemical effects of environmental tobacco smoking on pregnancy outcome. *Indian Journal of Clinical Biochemistry, 28*, 368–373.

Salkind, N.J. (2017). *Exploring research* (9th ed.). Upper Saddle River, NJ: Pearson.

Salm Ward, T.C., & Balfour, G.M. (2016). Infant safe sleep interventions, 1990–2015: A review. *Journal of Community Health, 41*, 180–196.

Salmivalli, C., & Peets, K. (2018). Bullying and victimization. In W.M. Bukowski & others (Eds.), *Handbook of peer interactions, relationships, and groups* (2nd ed.). New York: Guilford.

Salmivalli, C., Peets, K., & Hodges, E.V.E. (2011). Bullying. In P.K. Smith & C.H. Hart (Eds.), *Wiley-Blackwell handbook of childhood social development* (2nd ed.). New York: Wiley.

Salthouse, T.A. (2009). When does age-related cognitive decline begin? *Neurobiology of Aging, 30*, 507–514.

Salthouse, T.A. (2012). Consequences of age-related cognitive declines. *Annual Review of Psychology* (Vol. 63). Palo Alto, CA: Annual Reviews.

Salthouse, T.A. (2014). Why are there different age relations in cross-sectional and longitudinal comparisons of cognitive functioning? *Current Directions in Psychological Science, 23*, 252–256.

Salthouse, T.A. (2016). Aging cognition unconfounded by prior test experiences. *Journals of Gerontology B: Psychological Sciences and Social Sciences, 71*, 49–58.

Salthouse, T.A. (2017). Neural correlates of age-related slowing. In R. Cabeza, L. Nyberg, & D.C. Park (Eds.), *Cognitive neuroscience of aging* (2nd ed.). New York: Oxford University Press.

Salthouse, T.A. (2018, in press). Why is cognitive change more negative with increased age? *Neuropsychology.*

Salthouse, T.A., & Skovronek, E. (1992). Within-context assessment of working memory. *Journals of Gerontology, 47*, P110–P117.

Salvatore, J.E., & others (2018). Genetics, the rearing environment, and the intergenerational transmission of divorce: A Swedish National Adoption Study. *Psychological Science, 29*, 370–378.

Salvatore, J.E., Kuo, S.I., Steele, R.D., Simpson, J.A., & Collins, W.A. (2011). Recovering from conflict in romantic relationships: A developmental perspective. *Psychological Science, 22*, 376–383.

Salzwedel, A.P., & others (2017). Thalamocortical functional connectivity and behavioral disruptions in neonates with prenatal cocaine exposure. *Neurotoxicology and Teratology, 56*, 16–25.

Samek, D.R., & others (2017). Antisocial peer affiliation and externalizing disorders: Evidence for gene × environment × development interaction. *Development and Psychopathology, 29*, 155–172.

Sameroff, A.J. (2009). *The transactional model of development: How children and contexts shape each other.* Washington, DC: American Psychological Association.

Sameroff, A.J. (2012). Conceptual issues in studying the development of self-regulation. In S.L. Olson & A.J. Sameroff (Eds.), *Biopsychosocial regulatory processes in the development of childhood behavioral problems.* New York: Cambridge University Press.

Samjoo, I.A., & others (2013). The effect of endurance exercise on both skeletal muscle and systemic oxidative stress in previously sedentary obese men. *Nutrition and Diabetes, 3*, e88.

Sampath, A., Maduro, G., & Schillinger, J.A. (2018, in press). Infant deaths due to herpes simplex virus, congenital syphilis, and HIV in New York City. *Pediatrics.*

Sanchez-Perez, N., & others (2018). Computer-based training in math and working memory improves cognitive skills and academic achievement in primary school children: Behavioral results. *Frontiers in Psychology, 8*, 2327.

Sanchez-Roige, S., & others (2018). Genome-wide association study of delay discounting in 23,217 adult research participants of European ancestry. *Nature Neuroscience, 21*, 16–18.

Sandler, I., & others (2017). Effectiveness trial of the New Beginnings Program for divorcing parents. In M. Israelashvili & J. Romano (Eds.), *Cambridge handbook of international prevention science.* New York: Cambridge University Press.

Sands, A., Thompson, E.J., & Gaysina, D. (2017). Long-term influences of parental divorce on offspring affective disorders: A systematic review and meta-analysis. *Journal of Affective Disorders, 218*, 105–114.

Sangree, W.H. (1989). Age and power: Life-course trajectories and age structuring of power relations in East and West Africa. In D.I. Kertzer & K.W. Schaie (Eds.), *Age structuring in comparative perspective.* Hillsdale, NJ: Erlbaum.

Sanikhani, M., & others (2018, in press). SIRT2 deacetylase represses NFAT transcription factor to maintain cardiac homeostasis. *Journal of Biological Chemistry.*

Sannita, W.G. (2017). Commitment to life and the right to die. *European Journal of Internal Medicine, 41*, e48–e49.

Sanson, A., & Rothbart, M.K. (1995). Child temperament and parenting. In M.H. Bornstein (Ed.), *Handbook of parenting* (Vol. 4). Hillsdale, NJ: Erlbaum.

Santacreu, M., Rodriguez, M.A., & Molina, M.A. (2019, in press). Behavioral health. In R. Fernandez-Ballesteros & others (Eds.), *Cambridge handbook of successful aging.* New York: Cambridge University Press.

Santangeli, L., Sattar, N., & Huda, S.S. (2015). Impact of maternal obesity on perinatal and child outcomes. *Best Practices and Research: Clinical Obstetrics and Gynecology, 29*, 438–448.

Santelli, J., & others (2017). Abstinence-only-until-marriage: An updated review of U.S. policies and programs for their impact. *Journal of Adolescent Health, 61*, 273–280.

Santos, C.E., Komienko, O., & Rivas-Drake, D. (2017). Peer influences on ethnic-racial identity development: A multi-site investigation. *Child Development, 88*, 725–742.

Santos, L.M., & others (2016). Prevention of neural tube defects by fortification of flour with folic acid: A population-based retrospective study in Brazil. *Bulletin of the World Health Organization, 94*, 22–29.

Santrock, J.W., Sitterle, K.A., & Warshak, R.A. (1988). Parent-child relationships in stepfather families. In P. Bronstein & C.P. Cowan (Eds.), *Fatherhood today: Men's changing roles in the family.* New York: Wiley.

Sao Jose, J.M., & Amado, C.A. (2017). On studying ageism in long-term care: A systematic review of the literature. *International Psychogeriatrics, 29*, 373–387.

Sarchiapone, M., & others (2014). Hours of sleep in adolescents and its association with anxiety, emotional concerns, and suicidal ideation. *Sleep Medicine, 15*, 248–254.

Sargent-Cox, K. (2017). Ageism: We are our own worst enemy. *International Psychogeriatrics, 29*, 1–8.

Sarid, O., & others (2018, in press). Daily hassles score associates with the somatic and psychological health of patients with Crohn's disease. *Journal of Clinical Psychology.*

Sarman, I. (2018, in press). Review shows that early fetal alcohol exposure may cause adverse effects even when the mother consumes low levels. *Acta Paediatrica.*

Sarquella-Brugada, G., & others (2016). Sudden infant death syndrome caused by cardiac arrhythmias: Only a matter of genes encoding ion channels? *International Journal of Legal Medicine, 130*, 415–420.

Sassler, S., Michelmore, K., & Qian, Z. (2018, in press). Transitions from sexual relationships into cohabitation and beyond. *Demography.*

Satorres, E., & others (2018, in press). Effectiveness of instrumental reminiscence intervention on improving coping in healthy older adults. *Stress and Health.*

Sauce, B., & Matzel, L.D. (2018). The paradox of intelligence: Heritability and malleability coexist in hidden gene-environment interplay. *Psychological Bulletin, 144*, 26–47.

Sauchelli, A. (2018). Life-extending enhancements in the narrative approach to personal identity. *Journal of Medical Ethics, 44*, 219–225.

Saul, J.S., & Rodgers, R.F. (2018). Adolescent eating disorder risk and the online world. *Child and Adolescent Psychiatric Clinics of North America, 27*, 221–228.

Saunders, N.R., & others (2017). Risk of firearm injuries among children and youth of immigrant families. *Canadian Medical Association Journal, 189*, E452–E458.

Savin-Williams, R.C. (2018). Developmental trajectories and milestones of sexual-minority youth. In J. Gilbert & S. Lamb (Eds.), *Cambridge handbook of sexuality.* New York: Cambridge University Press.

Savin-Williams, R.C. (2017). *Mostly straight: Sexual fluidity among men.* Cambridge, MA: Harvard University Press.

Savulescu, J. (2018, in press). The structure of ethics review: Expert ethics committees and the challenge of voluntary research euthanasia. *Journal of Medical Ethics.*

Sawyer, S.M., & Patton, G.C. (2018). Health and well-being in adolescence: A dynamic profile. In J.E. Lansford & P. Banati (Eds.), *Handbook of adolescent development research and its impact on global policy.* New York: Oxford University Press.

Sawyer, W., & others (2018). *Engaging schooling.* New York: Routledge.

Saxena, M., Srivastava, N., & Banerjee, M. (2018). Cytokine gene variants as predictors of type 2 diabetes. *Current Diabetes Review, 14*, 307–319.

Sbarra, D.A. (2015). Divorce and health: Current trends and future directions. *Psychosomatic Medicine, 77*, 227–236.

Sbarra, D.A., & Borelli, J.L. (2018). Attachment reorganization following divorce: Normative processes and individual differences. *Current Opinion in Psychology, 25*, 71–75.

Sbarra, D.A., Hasselmo, K., & Bourassa, K.J. (2015). Divorce and health: Beyond individual differences. *Current Directions in Psychological Science, 24*, 109–113.

Scaglioni, S., & others (2018, in press). Factors influencing children's eating behaviors. *Nutrients.*

Scales, P.C., & Roehlkepartain, E.C. (2018). The contribution of nonfamily adults to adolescent well-being. In J.E. Lansford & P. Banati (Eds.), *Handbook of adolescent development research and its impact on global policy.* New York; Oxford University Press.

Scarabino, D., & others (2017). Common variants of human TERT and TERC genes and susceptibility to sporadic Alzheimer's disease. *Experimental Gerontology, 88,* 19–24.

Scarabino, D., & others (2017). Leukocyte telomere length in mild cognitive impairment and Alzheimer's disease patients. *Experimental Gerontology, 98,* 143–147.

Scarr, S. (1993). Biological and cultural diversity: The legacy of Darwin for development. *Child Development, 64,* 1333–1353.

Scelfo, J. (2015, February 3). A university recognizes a third gender: neutral. *New York Times.* Retrieved June 18, 2016, from https://www.nytimes.com/2015/02/08/education/edlife/a-university-recognizes-a-third-gender-neutral.html

Schaefer, I.M., Hornick, J.L., & Bovee, J.V.M.G. (2018, in press). The role of metabolic enzymes in mesenchymal tumors and tumor syndromes: Genetics, pathology, and molecular mechanisms. *Laboratory Investigations.*

Schafer, M.J., & others (2015). Calorie restriction suppresses age-dependent hippocampal transcriptional signatures. *PLoS One, 10*(7), e0133923.

Schaffer, H.R. (1996). *Social development.* Cambridge, MA: Blackwell.

Schaffer, M.A., Goodhue, A., Stennes, K., & Lanigan, C. (2012). Evaluation of a public health nurse visiting program for pregnant and parenting teens. *Public Health Nursing, 29,* 218–231.

Schaie, K.W. (1994). The life course of adult intellectual abilities. *American Psychologist, 49,* 304–313.

Schaie, K.W. (1996). *Intellectual development in adulthood: The Seattle Longitudinal Study.* New York: Cambridge University Press.

Schaie, K.W. (2005). *Developmental influences on adult intelligence: The Seattle Longitudinal Study.* New York: Oxford University Press.

Schaie, K.W. (2009). When does age-related cognitive decline begin? Salthouse again reifies the "cross-sectional fallacy." *Neurobiology of Aging, 30,* 528–529.

Schaie, K.W. (2011). Adult intellectual abilities. *Corsini encyclopedia of psychology.* New York: Wiley.

Schaie, K.W. (2011). Historical influences on aging and behavior. In K.W. Schaie & S.L. Willis (Eds.), *Handbook of the psychology of aging* (7th ed.). New York: Elsevier.

Schaie, K.W. (2013). *Developmental influences on adult intelligence: The Seattle Longitudinal Study* (2nd ed.). New York: Oxford University Press.

Schaie, K.W. (2016). Theoretical perspectives for the psychology of aging in a lifespan context. In K.W. Schaie & S.L. Willis (Eds.), *Handbook of the psychology of aging* (8th ed.). New York: Elsevier.

Schaie, K.W., & Willis, S.L. (Eds.) (2016). *Handbook of the psychology of aging* (8th ed.). New York: Elsevier.

Scheuer, H., & others (2017). Reduced fronto-amygdalar connectivity in adolescence is associated with increased depression symptoms over time. *Psychiatry Research, 266,* 35–41.

Schieber, F. (2006). Vision and aging. In J.E. Birren & K.W. Schaie (Eds.), *Handbook of the psychology of aging* (6th ed.). San Diego: Academic Press.

Schiff, R., Nuri Ben-Shushan, Y., & Ben-Artzi, E. (2017). Metacognitive strategies: A foundation for early word spelling and reading in kindergartners with SLI. *Journal of Learning Disabilities, 50,* 143–157.

Schiff, W. (2019). *Nutrition for healthy living* (5th ed.). New York: McGraw-Hill.

Schiffman, S.S. (2007). Smell and taste. In J.E. Birren (Ed.), *Encyclopedia of gerontology* (2nd ed.). San Diego: Academic Press.

Schittny, J.C. (2017). Development of the lung. *Cell & Tissue Research, 367,* 427–444.

Schlam, T.R., Wilson, N.L., Shoda, Y., Mischel, W., & Ayduk, O. (2013). Preschoolers' delay of gratification predicts their body mass 30 years later. *Journal of Pediatrics, 162,* 90–93.

Schlarb, A.A., Friedrich, A., & Clausen, M. (2017). Sleep problems in university students—an intervention. *Neuropsychiatric Disease and Treatment, 13,* 1989–2001.

Schlegel, M. (2000). All work and all play: Developmental psychologist finds a niche in a "smart toy" world. *Monitor on Psychology, 31*(11), 50–51.

Schlosnagle, L., & Strough, J. (2017). Understanding adult age differences in the frequency of problems with friends. *International Journal of Aging and Human Development, 84,* 159–179.

Schmidt, E.L., Burge, W., Visscher, K.M., & Ross, L.A. (2016). Cortical thickness in frontoparietal and cingulo-opercular networks predicts executive function performance in older adults. *Neuropsychology, 30,* 322–331.

Schmitt, S.A., & others (2017). Examining the relations between executive function, math, and literacy during the transition to kindergarten: A multi-analytic approach. *Journal of Educational Psychology, 109,* 1120–1140.

Schneider, W. (2011). Memory development in childhood. In U. Goswami (Ed.), *Wiley-Blackwell handbook of childhood cognitive development* (2nd ed.). New York: Wiley.

Schnittker, J. (2007). Look (closely) at all the lonely people: Age and social psychology of social support. *Journal of Aging and Health, 19,* 659–682.

Schnohr, P., & others (2017). Impact of persistence and non-persistence in leisure time physical activity on coronary heart disease and all-cause mortality: The Copenhagen City Heart Study. *European Journal of Cardiology, 24,* 1615–1623.

Schoeneberger, J. (2012). Longitudinal attendance patterns: Developing high school dropouts. *Clearinghouse, 85,* 7–14.

Schoenfeld, E.A., & others (2017). Does sex really matter? Examining the connections between spouses' non-sexual behaviors, sexual frequency, sexual satisfaction, and marital satisfaction. *Archives of Sexual Behavior, 46,* 489–501.

Schoffstall, C.L., & Cohen, R. (2011). Cyber aggression: The relation of online offenders and offline social competence. *Social Development, 20*(3), 587–604.

Schonert-Reichl, K.A., & others (2015). Enhancing cognitive and socio-emotional development through a simple-to-administer mindfulness-based school program for elementary school children: A randomized controlled trial. *Developmental Psychology, 51,* 52–56.

Schooreel, T., & Verbruggen, M. (2016). Use of family-friendly work arrangements and work-family conflict: Cross-over effects in dual-earner couples. *Journal of Occupational Health Psychology, 21,* 119–132.

Schreiber, K.H., O'Leary, M., & Kennedy, B.K. (2016). The mTOR pathway and aging. In K.W. Schaie & S.L. Willis (Eds.), *Handbook of the psychology of aging* (8th ed.). New York: Elsevier.

Schreuders, E., & others (2018, in press). Friend versus foe: Neural correlates of prosocial decisions for liked and disliked peers. *Cognitive, Affective, and Behavioral Neuroscience, 18,* 127–142.

Schuch, F.B., & others (2017). Physical activity and sedentary behavior in people with major depressive disorder: A systematic review and analysis. *Journal of Affective Disorders, 210,* 139–150.

Schulenberg, J.E., & Patrick, J.E. (2018). Binge drinking. In M.H. Bornstein (Ed.), *SAGE encyclopedia of lifespan human development.* Thousand Oaks, CA: Sage.

Schulenberg, J.E., & others (2017). *Monitoring the Future national survey results on drug use, 1975–2016: Vol. II, college students and adults, aged 19–55.* Ann Arbor, MI: Institute for Social Research, University of Michigan.

Schulster, M.L., Liang, S.E., & Najari, B.B. (2017). Metabolic syndrome and sexual dysfunction. *Current Opinion in Urology, 27,* 435–440.

Schultz, M.L., Kostic, M., & Kharasch, S. (2018, in press). A case of toxic breast-feeding? *Pediatric Emergency Care.*

Schumann, L., & others (2017). Persistence and innovation effects in genetic and environmental factors in negative

emotionality during infancy: A twin study. *PLoS One, 12*(4), e0176601.

Schunk, D.H. (2016). *Learning theories: An educational perspective* (7th ed.). Upper Saddle River, NJ: Prentice Hall.

Schunk, D.H., & Greene, J.A. (Eds.) (2018). *Handbook of self-regulation of learning and performance* (2nd ed.). New York: Routledge.

Schutten, D., Stokes, K.A., & Arnell, K.M. (2017). I want to media multitask and I want to do it now: Individual differences in media multitasking predict delay of gratification and system-1 thinking. *Cognitive Research: Principles and Implications, 2*(1), 8.

Schutze, U. (2017). *Language learning and the brain.* New York: Cambridge University Press.

Schwartz, L.E., Howell, K.H., & Jamison, L.E. (2018, in press). Effect of time since loss on grief, resilience, and depression among bereaved emerging adults. *Death Studies, 42,* 537–547.

Schwartz, M.A., & Scott, B.M. (2018). *Marriages and families* (8th ed.). Upper Saddle River, NJ: Pearson.

Schweinhart, L.J., & others (2005). *Lifetime effects: The High/Scope Perry Preschool Study through age 40.* Ypsilanti, MI: High/Scope Press.

Sciafe, J.C., & others (2017). Reduced resting-state functional connectivity in current and recovered restrictive anorexia nervosa. *Frontiers in Psychology, 8,* 30.

Scialfa, C.T., & Kline, D.W. (2007). Vision. In J.E. Birren (ed.), *Encyclopedia of gerontology* (2nd ed.). San Diego: Academic Press.

Sclar, D.A., & others (2012). Attention deficit/hyperactivity disorder among children and adolescents in the United States: Trends in diagnosis and use of pharmacotherapy by gender. *Clinical Pediatrics, 51,* 584.

Scott, D., & others (2018). Associations of components of sarcopenic obesity with bone health and balance in older adults. *Archives of Gerontology and Geriatrics, 75,* 125–131.

Scott, R.M., & Baillargeon, R. (2017). Early false-belief understanding. *Trends in Cognitive Science, 21,* 237–249.

Scott, S.B., & others (2018). Perceived neighborhood characteristics predict severity and emotional response to daily stressors. *Social Science and Medicine, 200,* 262–270.

Scott-Goodwin, A.C., Puerto, M., & Moreno, I. (2016). Toxic effects of prenatal exposure to alcohol, tobacco, and other drugs. *Reproductive Toxicology, 61,* 120–130.

Sebastiani, P., & Perls, T.T. (2012). The genetics of extreme longevity: Lessons from the New England Centenarian study. *Frontiers in Genetics, 30*(3), 277.

Sebastiani, P., & others (2013). Meta-analysis of genetic variants associated with human exceptional longevity. *Aging, 5,* 653–661.

Sechrist, J., & Fingerman, K.L. (2018). Intergenerational relationships. In M.H. Bornstein (Ed.), *SAGE encyclopedia of lifespan human development.* Thousand Oaks, CA: Sage.

Sedgh, G., & others (2015). Adolescent pregnancy, birth, and abortion rates across countries: Levels and recent trends. *Journal of Adolescent Health, 56,* 223–230.

Seider, S., Jayawickreme, E., & Lerner, R.M. (2017). Theoretical and empirical bases of character development in adolescence: A view of the issues. *Journal of Youth and Adolescence, 46,* 1149–1152.

Seiter, L.N., & Nelson, L.J. (2010). An examination of emerging adulthood in college students and nonstudents in India. *Journal of Adolescent Research, 26,* 506–536.

Selim, A.J., & others (2005). Comprehensive health status assessment of centenarians: Results from the 1999 Large Health Survey of Veteran Enrollees. *Journals of Gerontology A: Biological Sciences and Medical Sciences, 60,* 515–519.

Selkie, E. (2018, in press). When age-based guidance is not enough: The problem of early puberty. *Pediatrics.*

Sen, B. (2010). The relationship between frequency of family dinner and adolescent problem behaviors after adjusting for other characteristics. *Journal of Adolescence, 33*, 187–196.

Senin-Calderon, C., & others (2017). Body image and adolescence: A behavioral impairment model. *Psychiatry Research, 248*, 121–126.

Seo, Y.S., Lee, J., & Ahn, H.Y. (2016). Effects of kangaroo care on neonatal pain in South Korea. *Journal of Tropical Pediatrics, 62*, 246–249.

Serrano-Villar, M., Huang, K.Y., & Calzada, E.J. (2017). Social support, parenting, and social emotional development in young Mexican American and Dominican American children. *Child Psychiatry and Human Development, 48*, 597–609.

Serrat, R., & others (2018, in press). On the quality of adjustment to retirement: The longitudinal role of personality traits and generativity. *Journal of Personality.*

Sethna, V., & others (2018). Father-child interactions at 3 months and 24 months: Contributions to children's cognitive development at 24 months. *Infant Mental Health Journal, 229*, 364–370.

Setterson, R.A. (2009). Neugarten, Bernice. In D. Carr (Ed.), *Encyclopedia of the life course and human development.* Boston: Gale Cengage.

Setterson, R.A., & Trauten, M.E. (2009). The new terrain of old age: Hallmarks, freedoms, and risks. In V.L. Bengtson, D. Gans, N.M. Putney, & M. Silverstein (Eds.), *Handbook of theories of aging.* New York: Springer.

Sewdas, R., & others (2017). Why older workers work beyond the retirement age: A qualitative study. *BMC Public Health, 17*(1), 672.

Sgro, P., & Di Luigi, L. (2017). Sport and male sexuality. *Journal of Endrocrinology Investigation, 40*, 911–923.

Shackleton, B., Crawford, F., & Bachmeier, C. (2017). Apolipoprotein E-mediated modulation of ADAM10 in Alzheimer's disease. *Current Alzheimer Research, 14*, 578–585.

Shah, A.A., & others (2018). Meeting the mental health needs of Hurricane Harvey evacuees. *American Journal of Psychiatry, 175*, 13–14.

Shahoei, R., & others (2017). The effect of perineal massage during the second stage of birth on nulliparous women perineal: A randomization clinical trial. *Electronic Physician, 9*, 5588–5595.

Shalitin, S., & Kiess, W. (2017). Putative effects of obesity on linear growth and puberty. *Hormone Research in Pediatrics, 88*, 101–110.

Shankar, A., McMunn, A., Demakakos, P., Hamer, M., & Steptoe, A. (2017). Social isolation and loneliness: Prospective associations with functional status in older adults. *Health Psychology, 36*, 179–187.

Shapka, J.D., & others (2018). Cyberbullying and cybervictimization within a cross-cultural context: A study of Canadian & Tanzanian adolescents. *Child Development. 89*, 89–99.

Sharma, D., Murki, S., & Oleti, T.P. (2018, in press). Study comparing "kangaroo ward care" with "intermediate intensive care" for improving growth outcome and cost effectiveness: Randomized control trial. *Journal of Maternal-Fetal and Neonatal Medicine.*

Sharma, M., Raghuraman, R., & Sajikumar, S. (2018). Epigenetics: The panacea for cognitive decline? *Aging, 10*, 1–2.

Sharma, R., & others (2015). Effects of increased paternal age on sperm quality, reproductive outcome, and associated epigenetic risks to offspring. *Reproductive Biology and Endocrinology, 13*, 35.

Sharma, R., & others (2015). Normalization of testosterone level is associated with reduced incidence of myocardial infarction and mortality in men. *European Heart Journal, 36*, 2706–2715.

Sharony, R., & others (2018, in press). The impact of third-trimester genetic counseling. *Archives of Gynecology and Obstetrics.*

Shatz, M., & Gelman, R. (1973). The development of communication skills: Modifications in the speech of young children as a function of the listener. *Monographs of the Society for Research in Child Development, 38*(Serial No. 152).

Shaver, P. (1986, August). *Being lonely, falling in love: Perspectives from attachment theory.* Paper presented at the meeting of the American Psychological Association, Washington, DC.

Shaw, P., & others (2007). Attention-deficit/hyperactivity disorder is characterized by a delay in cortical maturation. *Proceedings of the National Academy of Sciences, 104*(49), 19649–19654.

Shaywitz, S.E., Gruen, J.R., & Shaywitz, B.A. (2007). Management of dyslexia, its rationale and underlying neurobiology. *Pediatric Clinics of North America, 54*, 609–623.

Shebloski, B., Conger, K.J., & Widaman, K.F. (2005). Reciprocal links among differential parenting, perceived partiality, and self-worth: A three-wave longitudinal study. *Journal of Family Psychology, 19*, 633–642.

Sheinbaum, T., & others (2015). Attachment style predicts affect, cognitive appraisals, and social functioning in daily life. *Frontiers in Psychology, 6*, 296.

Sheldrick, R.C., Maye, M.P., & Carter, A.S. (2017). Age at first identification of autism spectrum disorder: An analysis of two U.S. surveys. *Journal of the American Academy of Child and Adolescent Psychiatry, 56*, 313–320.

Shenk, D. (2017). What is the Flynn effect, and how does it change our understanding of IQ? *Wiley Interdisciplinary Reviews: Cognitive Science, 8*, 1–2.

Sherman, C.W., Webster, N.J., & Antonucci, T.C. (2016). Dementia caregiving in the context of late life remarriage: Support networks, relationship quality, and well-being. In K.W. Schaie & S.L. Willis (Eds.), *Handbook of the psychology of aging* (8th ed.). New York: Elsevier.

Sherman, L., Steinberg, L., & Chein, J. (2018, in press). Connecting brain responsivity and real-world risk taking: Strengths and weaknesses of current methodological approaches. *Developmental Cognitive Neuroscience.*

Sherwood, C.C., & others (2011). Aging of the cerebral cortex differs between humans and chimpanzees. *Proceedings of the National Academy of Sciences U.S.A., 108*, 13029–13034.

Shi, C., & others (2017). Cdk5-Foxo3 axis: Initially neuroprotective, eventually neurodegenerative in Alzheimer's disease. *Journal of Cell Science, 129*, 1815–1830.

Shin, D.W., & others (2016). End-of-life communication in Korean older adults: With focus on advance care planning and advance directives. *Geriatrics and Gerontology International, 16*, 407–415.

Shiner, S., Many, A., & Maslovitz, S. (2016). Questioning the role of pituitary oxytocin in parturition: Spontaneous onset of labor in women with panhypopituitarism—a case series. *European Journal of Obstetrics and Gynecology and Reproductive Medicine, 197*, 83–85.

Shivarama Shetty, M., & Sajikumar, S. (2017). 'Tagging' along memories in aging: Synaptic tagging and capture mechanisms in the aged hippocampus. *Aging Research Reviews, 55*, 22–35.

Shohayeb, B., & others (2018). Factors that influence adult neurogenesis as potential therapy. *Translational Neurodegeneration 7*, 4.

Shorey, S., & others (2017). First-time fathers' postnatal experiences and support needs: A descriptive qualitative study. *Journal of Advanced Nursing, 73*, 2987–2996.

Shors, T.J. (2009). Saving new brain cells. *Scientific American, 300*, 46–52.

Short, D. (2015, April 7). *Demographic trends in the 50-and-older work force.* Retrieved April 19, 2015, from www.advisorperspectives.com/commentaries/dshort_011314.php

Short, D. (2018). *Demographic trends for the 50-and-older work force.* Retrieved June 28, 2018, from https://seekingalpha.com/article/4136795-demographic-trends-50-older-workforce

Sidtis, J.J., & others (2018). Switching language modes: Complementary brain patterns for formulaic and propositional language. *Brain Connectivity, 8*, 189–196.

Siegel, A.L.M., & Castel, A.D. (2018). Memory for important item-location association in younger and older adults. *Psychology and Aging, 33*, 30–45.

Siegel, R.S., & Brandon, A.R. (2014). Adolescents, pregnancy, and mental health. *Journal of Pediatric and Adolescent Gynecology, 27*(3), 138–150.

Siegler, R., & Braithwaite, D.W. (2017). Numerical development. *Annual Review of Psychology* (Vol. 68). Palo Alto, CA: Annual Reviews.

Siegler, R., & Lortie-Forgues, H. (2017). Hard lessons: Why rational number arithmetic is so difficult for so many people. *Current Directions in Psychological Science, 26*, 346–351.

Siegler, R.S. (2006). Microgenetic analysis of learning. In W. Damon & R. Lerner (Eds.), *Handbook of child psychology* (6th ed.). New York: Wiley.

Siegler, R.S. (2017). Foreword: Build it and they will come. In D.G. Geary & others (Eds.), *Acquisition of complex arithmetic skills and higher order mathematics concepts.* New York: Academic Press.

Siennick, S.E., & others (2017). Risk factors for substance misuse and adolescents' symptoms of depression. *Journal of Adolescent Health, 60*, 50–56.

Sievert, L.L. (2014). Menopause across cultures: Clinical considerations. *Menopause, 21*, 421–423.

Siflinger, B. (2017). The effect of widowhood on mental health—an analysis of anticipation patterns surrounding the death of a spouse. *Health Economics, 28*, 1505–1523.

Sightlines Project (2016). *Seeing our way to living long, living well in 21st century America.* Palo Alto, CA: Stanford University.

Sigman, M. (2017). Introduction: What to do with older prospective fathers: The risks of advanced paternal age. *Fertility and Sterility, 107*, 299–300.

Silber, S. (2017). Chapter 13: Human ovarian tissue vitrification. *Methods in Molecular Biology, 1568*, 177–194.

Silva, C. (2005, October 31). When teen dynamo talks, city listens. *Boston Globe*, pp. B1, B4.

Silva, K., & others (2017). Joint effects of peer presence and fatigue on risk and reward processing in late adolescence. *Journal of Youth and Adolescence, 46*, 1878–1890.

Silva, K., Chein, J., & Steinberg, L. (2016). Adolescents in peer groups make more prudent decisions when a slightly older adult is present. *Psychological Science, 27*, 322–330.

Silverman, J.M., & Schmeidler, J. (2018). The protected survivor model: Using resistant successful cognitive aging to identify protection in the very old. *Medical Hypotheses, 110*, 9–14.

Silverman, M.E., & others (2017). The risk factors for postpartum depression. *Depression and Anxiety, 34*, 178–187.

Silverstein, M. (2009). Caregiving. In D. Carr (Ed.), *Encyclopedia of the life course and human development.* Boston: Gale Cengage.

Sim, Z.L., & Xu, F. (2017). Learning higher-order generalizations through free play: Evidence from 2- and 3-year-old children. *Developmental Psychology, 53*, 642–651.

Simms, N.K., Frausel, R.R., & Richland, E.E. (2018). Working memory predicts children's analogical reasoning. *Journal of Experimental Child Psychology, 166*, 160–177.

Simon, E.J. (2017). *Biology* (2nd ed.). Upper Saddle River, NJ: Pearson.

Simon, K.A., & others (2018, in press). Envisioning future parenthood among bisexual, lesbian, and heterosexual women. *Psychology of Sexual Orientation and Gender Diversity.*

Simon, P., & others (2017). Youth e-cigarette, blunt, and other tobacco use profiles: Does SES matter? *Tobacco Regulatory Science, 3*, 115–127.

Simoni, E., & others (2017). Multitarget drug design strategy in Alzheimer's disease: Focus on cholinergic transmission and amyloid-B aggregation. *Future in Medicinal Chemistry, 9*, 953–963.

Simons, L.G., & others (2016). Mechanisms that link parenting practices to adolescents' risky sexual behavior: A test of six competing theories. *Journal of Youth and Adolescence, 45*, 255–270.

Simpkins, S.D., Fredricks, J.A., Davis-Kean, P.E., & Eccles, J.S. (2006). Healthy mind, healthy habits: The influence of activity involvement in middle childhood. In A.C. Huston & M.N. Ripke (Eds.), *Developmental contexts in middle childhood*. New York: Cambridge University Press.

Simpson, D.M., Leonhardt, N.D., & Hawkins, A.J. (2018). Learning about love: A meta-analytic study of individually-oriented relationship education programs for adolescents and emerging adults. *Journal of Youth and Adolescence, 47*, 477–489.

Simpson, J.A., Collins, W.A., Tran, S., & Haydon, K.C. (2007). Attachment and the experience and expression of emotions in romantic relationships: A developmental perspective. *Journal of Personality and Social Psychology, 92*, 355–367.

Simpson, J.A., & Rholes, W.S. (2017). Adult attachment, stress, and romantic relationships. *Current Opinion in Psychology, 13*, 19–24.

Sims, T., Hogan, C., & Carstensen, L.L. (2015). Selectivity as an emotion regulation strategy: Lessons from older adults. *Current Opinion in Psychology, 3*, 80–84.

Sin, N.L., Sloan, R.P., McKinley, P.S., & Almeida, D.M. (2017). Linking daily stress processes and laboratory-based heart rate variability in a national sample of midlife and older adults. *Psychosomatic Medicine, 83*, 91–100.

Sinclair, E.M., & others (2018). Home literacy environment and shared reading in the newborn period. *Journal of Developmental and Behavioral Pediatrics, 39*, 66–71.

Singarajah, A., & others (2017). Infant attention to same- and other-race faces. *Cognition, 159*, 76–84.

Singer, A.E., & others (2015). Symptom trends in the last year of life from 1998 to 2010: A cohort study. *Annals of Internal Medicine, 162*, 175–183.

Singer, D., Golinkoff, R.M., & Hirsh-Pasek, K. (Eds.) (2006). *Play = learning: How play motivates and enhances children's cognitive and social-emotional growth.* New York: Oxford University Press.

Singer, M.A. (2016). The origins of aging: Evidence that aging is an adaptive phenotype. *Current Aging Science, 9*, 95–115.

Singh, L., & others (2018). Novel word learning in bilingual and monolingual infants: Evidence for a bilingual advantage. *Child Development. 89*, e183–e196.

Singh, M., & others (2018). Deep brain stimulation for movement disorders: Surgical nuances. *Neurology India, 66*(Suppl.), S122–S130.

Singh, N.N., & others (2016). Effects of Samatha meditation on active academic engagement and math performance of students with attention deficit/hyperactivity disorder. *Mindfulness, 7*, 68–75.

Singh, R., Dohlman, T.H., & Sun, G. (2017). Immediately sequential bilateral cataract surgery: Advantages and disadvantages. *Current Opinion in Ophthalmology, 28*, 81–86.

Singh, R., & Mukherjee, P. (2018). Push-out, pull-out, or opting-out? Reasons cited by adolescents for discontinuing education in four low and middle income countries. In J.E. Lansford & P. Banati (Eds.), *Handbook of adolescent development research and its impact on global policy.* New York: Oxford University Press.

Sinnott, J.D. (2003). Postformal thought and adult development: Living in balance. In J. Demick & C. Andreoletti (Eds.), *Handbook of adult development.* New York: Kluwer.

Sirard, J.R., & others (2013). Physical activity and screen time in adolescents and their friends. *American Journal of Preventive Medicine, 44*, 48–55.

Sirrine, E.H., Salloum, A., & Boothroyd, R. (2017). Predictors of continuing bonds among bereaved adolescents. *Omega, 76*, 237–255.

Sirsch, U., Dreher, E., Mayr, E., & Willinger, U. (2009). What does it take to be an adult in Australia? Views of adulthood in Australian adolescents, emerging adults and adults. *Journal of Adolescent Research, 24*, 275–292.

Siverova, J., & Buzgova, R. (2018, in press). The effect of reminiscence therapy on quality of life, attitudes to aging, and depressive symptoms in institutionalized elderly adults with cognitive impairment: A quasi-experimental study. *International Journal of Mental Health Nursing.*

Skaper, S.D., & others (2017). Synaptic plasticity, dementia, and Alzheimer disease. *CNS & Neurological Disorders Drug Targets, 16*, 220–233.

Skinner, B.F. (1938). *The behavior of organisms: An experimental analysis.* New York: Appleton-Century-Crofts.

Skloot, G.S. (2017). The effects of aging on lung structure and function. *Clinics in Geriatric Aging, 33*, 447–457.

Skrzypek, H., & Hui, L. (2017). Noninvasive prenatal testing for fetal aneuploidy and single gene disorders. *Best Practices and Research: Clinical Obstetrics and Gynecology, 42*, 26–38.

Skuse, D., Printzlau, F., & Wolstencroft, J. (2018). Sex chromosome aneuploidies. *Handbook of Clinical Neurology, 147*, 355–376.

Slater, A., Field, T., & Hernandez-Reif, M. (2007). The development of the senses. In A. Slater & M. Lewis (Eds.), *Introduction to infant development* (2nd ed.). New York: Oxford University Press.

Slater, A.M., Bremner, J.G., Johnson, S.P., & Hayes, R. (2011). The role of perceptual processes in infant addition/subtraction events. In L.M. Oakes, C.H. Cashon, M. Casasola, & D.H. Rakison (Eds.), *Early perceptual and cognitive development.* New York: Oxford University Press.

Slaughter, V., & others (2014). Meta-analysis of theory of mind and peer popularity in the preschool and early school years. *Child Development, 86*, 1159–1174.

Sleet, D.A., & Mercy, J.A. (2003). Promotion of safety, security, and well-being. In M.H. Bornstein, L. Davidson, C.L.M. Keyes & K.A. Moore (Eds.), *Well-being.* Mahwah, NJ: Erlbaum.

Sloan, D.H., & others (2017). The influence of relationships on the meaning making process: Patients' perspectives. *Annals of Palliative Medicine, 6*, 220–226.

Slobin, D. (1972, July). Children and language: They learn the same way around the world. *Psychology Today,* 71–76.

Sloutsky, V. (2015). Conceptual development. In R.M. Lerner (Ed.), *Handbook of child psychology and developmental science* (7th ed.). New York: Wiley.

Smaldino, S.E., & others (2018). *Instructional technology and media for learning* (12th ed.). Upper Saddle River, NJ: Pearson.

Small, B.J., Dixon, R.A., McArdle, J.J., & Grimm, K.J. (2012). Do changes in lifestyle engagement moderate cognitive decline in normal aging? Evidence from the Victoria Longitudinal Study. *Neuropsychology, 26*, 144–155.

Small, H. (2011). *Why not? My seventy year plan for a college degree.* Franklin, TN: Carpenter's Son Publishing.

Smarius, L.J., & others (2017). Excessive infant crying doubles the risk of mood and behavioral problems at age 5: Evidence for mediation by maternal characteristics. *European Child and Adolescent Psychiatry, 26*, 293–302.

Smetana, J.G. (2018). The development of autonomy in adolescence: A social-cognitive domain view. In B. Soenens & others (Eds.), *Autonomy in adolescent development.* New York: Routledge.

Smetana, J.G., & Ball, C.L. (2018, in press). Young children's moral judgments: justifications, and emotion attributions in peer relationship contexts. *Child Development*

Smith, A., & Anderson, M. (2018). *Social media use in 2018.* Washington, DC: Pew Research Center.

Smith, A., & Collene, A. (2019). *Wardlaw's contemporary nutrition* (11th ed.). New York: McGraw-Hill.

Smith, A.D. (1996). Memory. In J.E. Birren (Ed.), *Encyclopedia of gerontology* (Vol. 2). San Diego: Academic Press.

Smith, A.E., Hendy, A.M., & Tempest, G.D. (2018, in press). The importance of understanding the underlying physiology of exercise when designing interventions for brain health. *Journal of Physiology.*

Smith, A.J., Abeyta, A.A., Hughes, M., & Jones, R.T. (2015). Persistent grief in the aftermath of mass violence: The predictive roles of posttraumatic stress symptoms, self-efficacy, and disrupted worldview. *Psychological Trauma, 7*, 179–186.

Smith, A.K., & Periyakoli, V.S. (2018, in press). Should we bury "The good death"? *Journal of the American Geriatrics Society.*

Smith, A.R., & others (2017). "I don't want to grow up, I'm a (Gen X, Y, Me) kid": Increasing maturity fears across the decades. *International Journal of Behavioral Development, 41*, 655–662.

Smith, C.A., Armour, M., & Ee, C. (2016). Complementary therapies and medicines and reproductive medicine. *Seminars in Reproductive Medicine, 34*, 67–73.

Smith, E.R., & others (2017). Barriers and enablers of health system adoption of kangaroo care: A systematic review of caregiver perspectives. *BMC Pediatrics, 17*(1), 35.

Smith, J.D., & others (2018, in press). A developmental cascade perspective of pediatric obesity: A conceptual model and scoping review. *Health Psychology Review.*

Smith, K.E., Mason, T.B., & Lavender, J.M. (2018, in press). Rumination and eating disorder psychopathology: A meta-analysis. *Clinical Psychology Review.*

Smith, K.Z., & others (2018, in press). Child maltreatment and physical victimization: Does heavy drinking mediate the relationship? *Child Maltreatment.*

Smith, L.E., & Howard, K.S. (2008). Continuity of paternal social support and depressive symptoms among new mothers. *Journal of Family Psychology, 22*, 763–773.

Smith, R.A., & Davis, S.F. (2016). *The psychologist as detective* (7th ed.). Upper Saddle River, NJ: Prentice Hall.

Smith, R.L., Rose, A.J., & Schwartz-Mette, R.A. (2010). Relational and overt aggression in childhood and adolescence: Clarifying mean-level gender differences and associations with peer acceptance. *Social Development, 19*, 243–269.

Smith, S.G., & others (2018). Social isolation, health literacy, and mortality risk: Findings from the English Longitudinal Study of Aging. *Health Psychology, 37*, 160–169.

Smith, T.E., & others (2016). *Teaching students with special needs in inclusive settings* (7th ed.). Upper Saddle River, NJ: Pearson.

Smith, T.E., & others (2018). *Introduction to contemporary special education* (2nd ed.). Upper Saddle River, NJ: Pearson.

SmithBattie, L., & others (2017). An umbrella review of meta-analyses of interventions to improve outcomes for teen mothers. *Journal of Adolescence, 59*, 97–111.

Smock, P.J., & Gupta, S. (2013). Cohabitation in contemporary North America. In A. Booth, A.C. Crouter, & N.S. Lansdale (Eds.), *Just living together.* New York: Psychology Press.

Smokowksi, P.R., Bacallao, M.L., Cotter, K.L., & Evans, C.B. (2015). The effects of positive and negative parenting practices on adolescent mental health outcomes in a multicultural sample of rural youth. *Child Psychiatry and Human Development, 46*, 333–345.

Smokowski, P.R., Guo, S., Cotter, K.L., Evans, C.B., & Rose, R.A. (2016). Multi-level risk factors and developmental assets associated with aggressive behavior in disadvantaged adolescents. *Aggressive Behavior, 42*, 222–238.

Smokowski, P.R., & others (2017). Family dynamics and aggressive behavior in Latino adolescents. *Cultural Diversity and Ethnic Minority Psychology, 23*, 81–90.

Smoreda, Z., & Licoppe, C. (2000). Gender-specific use of the domestic telephone. *Social Psychology Quarterly, 63*, 238–252.

Smyth, J.M., & others (2018). Everyday stress response targets in the science of behavior change. *Behavior Research and Therapy, 101,* 20-29.

Snarey, J. (1987, June). A question of morality. *Psychology Today,* pp. 6-8.

Snow, C.E., & Kang, J.Y. (2006). Becoming bilingual, biliterate, and bicultural. In W. Damon & R. Lerner (Eds.), *Handbook of child psychology* (6th ed.). New York: Wiley.

Snowdon, D.A. (2003). Healthy aging and dementia: Findings from the Nun Study. *Annals of Internal Medicine, 139,* 450-454.

Snyder, A.C., & Smith, M.A. (2018). Early steps toward understanding neural communication. *Current Opinion in Neurology, 31,* 59-65.

Snyder, W. (2017). Compound word formation. In J. Lidz, W. Snyder, & J. Pater (Eds.), *Oxford handbook of developmental linguistics.* New York: Oxford University Press.

Sobowale, K., & others (2018, in press). Personality traits are associated with academic achievement in medical school: A nationally representative study. *Academic Psychiatry.*

Society for Adolescent Health and Medicine (2017). Abstinence-only-until-marriage policies and programs: An updated position paper of the Society for Adolescent Health and Medicine, 61, 400-403.

Sokol, R.L., Qin, B., & Poti, J.M. (2017). Parenting styles and body mass index: A systematic review of prospective studies among children. *Obesity Reviews, 18,* 281-292.

Sokolowski, M., Wasserman, J., & Wasserman, D. (2016). Polygenic associations of neurodevelopmental genes in suicide attempt. *Molecular Psychiatry, 21,* 1381-1390.

Solomon, J., & George, C. (2016). The measurement of attachment security and related concepts. In J. Cassidy & P.R. Shaver (Eds.), *Handbook of attachment* (3rd ed.). New York: Guilford.

Solomon-Moore, E., & others (2018). Roles of mothers and fathers in supporting child physical activity: A cross-sectional mixed-methods study. *BMJ Open, 8*(1), e019732.

Solovieva, Y., & Quintanar, L. (2017). Play with social roles as a method for psychological development in young children. In T. Bruce & others (Eds.), *Routledge international handbook of early childhood play.* New York: Routledge.

Someya, S., & others (2017). Effects of calorie restriction on the lifespan and healthspan of POLG mitochondrial mutator mice. *PLoS One, 12*(2), e0171159.

Song, Y., & others (2016). Secular trends for age at spermarche among Chinese boys from 11 ethnic minorities, 1995-2001: A multiple cross-sectional study. *BMJ Open, 6*(2), e010518.

Song, Y., & others (2018, in press). T-cell immunoglobin and ITIMdomain contributes to CD8+ T-cell immunosenescence. *Aging Cell.*

Sophian, C. (1985). Perseveration and infants' search: A comparison of two-and three-location tasks. *Developmental Psychology, 21,* 187-194.

Soto, C.J. (2015). Is happiness good for your personality? Concurrent and prospective relations of the Big Five with subjective well-being. *Journal of Personality, 83,* 45-55.

Sousa, S.S., & others (2018, in press). Developmental trajectory of the prefrontal cortex: A systematic review of diffusion tensor imaging studies. *Brain Imaging and Behavior.*

Spangler, G., Johann, M., Ronai, Z., & Zimmermann, P. (2009). Genetic and environmental influence on attachment disorganization. *Journal of Child Psychology and Psychiatry, 50,* 952-961.

Specht, J., Egloff, B., & Schukle, S.C. (2011). Stability and change of personality across the life course: The impact of age and major life events on mean-level and rank-order stability of the Big Five. *Journal of Personality and Social Psychology, 101*(4), 862-882.

Spelke, E.S. (2004). Core knowledge. In N. Kanwisher & J. Duncan (Eds.), *Attention and Performance: Functional neuroimaging of visual cognition* (Vol. 20, pp. 29-56). Oxford, UK: Oxford University Press.

Spelke, E.S. (2011). Natural number and natural geometry. In E. Brannon & S. Dehaene (Eds.), *Space, time, and number in the brain.* New York: Oxford University Press.

Spelke, E.S. (2013). *Developmental sources of social divisions. Neurosciences and the human person: New perspectives on human activities.* Unpublished manuscript, Department of Psychology, Harvard University, Cambridge, MA.

Spelke, E.S. (2016a). Core knowledge and conceptual change: A perspective on social cognition. In D. Barner & A.S. Baron (Eds.), *Core knowledge and conceptual change.* New York: Oxford University Press.

Spelke, E.S. (2016b). Cognitive abilities of infants. In R.J. Sternberg, S.T. Fiske, & J. Foss (Eds.), *Scientists making a difference.* New York: Cambridge University Press.

Spelke, E.S. (2017). Core knowledge. Language and number. *Language learning and development, 132,* 147-170.

Spelke, E.S., Bernier, E.P., & Snedeker, J. (2013). Core social cognition. In M.R. Banaji & S.A. Gelman (Eds.), *Navigating the social world: What infants, children, and other species can teach us.* New York: Oxford University Press.

Spelke, E.S., & Owsley, C.J. (1979). Intermodal exploration and knowledge in infancy. *Infant Behavior and Development, 2,* 13-28.

Spence, A.P. (1989). *Biology of human aging.* Englewood Cliffs, NJ: Prentice Hall.

Sperhake, J., Jorch, G., & Bajanowski, T. (2018). The prone sleeping position and SIDS. Historical aspects and possible pathomechanisms. *International Journal of Legal Medicine, 132,* 181-185.

Sprecher, S., Treger, S., & Sakaluk, J.K. (2013). Premarital sexual standards and sociosexuality: Gender, ethnicity, and cohort differences. *Archives of Sexual Behavior, 42,* 1395-1405.

Springelkamp, H., & others (2017). New insights into the genetics of primary open-angle glaucoma based on a meta-analysis of intraocular pressure and optic disc characteristics. *Human Molecular Genetics, 26,* 438-453.

Sreetharan, S., & others (2017). Ionizing radiation exposure during pregnancy: Effects on postnatal development and life. *Radiation Research, 187,* 647-658.

Sroufe, L.A. (2016). The place of attachment in development. In J. Cassidy & P.R. Shaver (Eds.), *Handbook of attachment* (3rd ed.). New York: Guilford.

Sroufe, L.A., Egeland, B., Carlson, E., & Collins, W.A. (2005). The place of early attachment in developmental context. In K.E. Grossman, K. Krossman, & E. Waters (Eds.), *The power of longitudinal attachment research: From infancy and childhood to adulthood.* New York: Guilford.

Sroufe, L.A., Waters, E., & Matas, L. (1974). Contextual determinants of infant affectional response. In M. Lewis & L. Rosenblum (Eds.), *Origins of fear.* New York: Wiley.

Stadelmann, S., & others (2017). Self-esteem in 8-14-year-old children with psychiatric disorders: Disorder- and gender-specific effects. *Child Psychiatry and Human Development, 48,* 40-52.

Staes, N., & others (2017). FOXP2 variation in great ape populations offers insight into the evolution of communication skills. *Scientific Reports, 7*(1), 16866.

Staff, J., Mont'Alvao, A., & Mortimer, J.T. (2015). Children at work. In R.M. Lerner (Ed.), *Handbook of child psychology and developmental psychology* (7th ed.). New York: Wiley.

Staley, C. (2019). *College success and study skills.* Boston: Cengage.

Stancil, S.L., & others (2018, in press). Contraceptive provision to adolescent females prescribed teratogenic medicines. *Pediatrics.*

Stanford Center for Longevity (2011). *Experts' consensus on brain health.* Retrieved April 30, 2011, from http://longevity.stanford.edu/my mind/cognitiveagingstatement

Stanford Center for Longevity and Max Planck Institute for Human Development (2014). *A consensus on the brain training industry from the scientific community.* Retrieved September 16, 2015, from http://longevity3.stanford.edu.blog/2014/10/15

Stanovich, K.E. (2019). *How to think straight about psychology* (11th ed.). Upper Saddle River, NJ: Pearson.

Stansfield, S.A., & others (2017). Childhood adversity and midlife suicidal ideation. *Psychological Medicine, 47,* 327-340.

Starr, C., Evers, C., & Starr, L. (2018). *Biology* (10th ed.). Boston: Cengage.

Starr, L.R., & others (2012). Love hurts (in more ways than one): Specificity of psychological symptoms as predictors and consequences of romantic activity among early adolescent girls. *Journal of Clinical Psychology, 68*(4), 373-381.

Staszewski, J. (Ed.) (2013). *Expertise and skill acquisition: The impact of William C. Chase.* New York: Taylor & Francis.

statisticbrain (2017). *Online dating statistics.* Retrieved November 4, 2017, from www.statisticbrain.com/online-dating-statistics

Staudinger, U.M. (1996). Psychologische Produktivität und Selbstentfaltung im Alter. In M.M. Baltes & L. Montada (Eds.), *Produktives Leben im Alter.* Frankfurt: Campus.

Stavans, M., & Baillargeon, R. (2018). Four-month-old infants individuate and track simple tools following functional demonstrations. *Developmental Science, 21,* e12500.

Stawski, R.S., Sliwinski, M.J., & Hofer, S.M. (2013). Between-person and within-person associations among processing speed, attention switching, and working memory in younger and older adults. *Experimental Aging Research, 39,* 194-214.

Steck, N., & others (2013). Euthanasia and assisted suicide in selected European countries and U.S. states: Systematic literature review. *Medical Care, 51,* 938-944.

Steckler, C.M., & Hamlin, J.K. (2016). Theories of moral development. In H. Miller (Ed.), *Encyclopedia of theory in psychology.* Thousand Oaks, CA: Sage.

Steckler, C.M., & others (2018, in press). Feeling out a link between feeling and infant sociomoral evaluation. *British Journal of Developmental Psychology.*

Steele, C.M., Spencer, S.J., & Aronson, J. (2002). Contending with group image: The psychology of stereotype and social identity threat. *34,* 379-444.

Steele, H., & Steele, M. (Eds.) (2017). *Handbook of attachment-related interventions.* New York: Guilford.

Steele, J., Waters, E., Crowell, J., & Treboux, D. (1998, June). *Self-report measures of attachment: Secure bonds to other attachment measures and attachment theory.* Paper presented at the meeting of the International Society for the Study of Personal Relationships, Saratoga Springs, NY.

Stefani, A., & others (2017). Subthalamic nucleus deep brain stimulation on motor symptoms of Parkinson's disease: Focus on neurochemistry. *Progress in Neurobiology, 151,* 157-174.

Steffen, E., & Coyle, A. (2017). "I thought they should know. . . that daddy is not completely gone." *Omega, 74,* 363-385.

Steffener, J., Barulli, D., Habeck, C., & Stern, Y. (2014). Neuroimaging explanations of age-related differences in task performance. *Frontiers in Aging Neuroscience, 6,* 46.

Steiger, A.E., Allemand, M., Robins, R.W., & Fend, H.A. (2014). Low and decreasing self-esteem during adolescence predict adult depression two decades later. *Journal of Personality and Social Psychology, 106,* 325-338.

Steinberg, L. (2014). *Age of opportunity.* Boston: Houghton Mifflin Harcourt.

Steinberg, L., & others (2018, in press). Around the world, adolescence is a time of heightened sensation seeking and immature self-regulation. *Developmental Science*.

Steinborn, M.B., & Huestegge, L. (2017). Phone conversation while processing information: Chronometric analysis of load effects in everyday media multitasking. *Frontiers in Psychology, 8,* 896.

Steiner, J.E. (1979). Human facial expressions in response to taste and smell stimulation. In H. Reese & L. Lipsitt (Eds.), *Advances in child development and behavior, 13,* 257–295.

Stenberg, G. (2017). Does contingency in adults' responding influence 12-month-old infants' social referencing? *Infant Behavior and Development, 49,* 9–20.

Stenholm, S., & others (2014). Age-related trajectories of physical functioning in work and retirement: The role of sociodemographic factors, lifestyles, and disease. *Journal of Epidemiology and Community Health, 68,* 503–509.

Stephens, F.B., & Tsintzas, K. (2018, in press). Metabolic and molecular changes associated with the increased skeletal muscle insulin action 24-48 h after exercise in young and old humans. *Biochemical Society Transactions.*

Stepler, R. (2017). *Led by baby boomers, divorce rates climb for America's 50+ population.* Washington, DC: Pew Research Center.

Stepler, R. (2017, April 6). *Number of U.S. adults cohabiting with a partner continues to rise, especially among those 50 and older.* Washington, DC: Pew Research Center.

Steptoe, A., & others (2017). The longitudinal relationship between cortisol responses to mental stress and leukocyte telomere attrition. *Journal of Clinical Endocrinology and Metabolism, 102,* 962–969.

Steptoe, A., Deaton, A., & Stone, A.A. (2015). Subjective well being, health, and aging. *Lancet, 385,* 640–648.

Steric, M., & others (2015). The outcome and course of pregnancies complicated with fetal neural tube defects. *Clinical and Experimental Obstetrics and Gynecology, 42,* 57–61.

Sternberg, R.J. (1986). *Intelligence applied.* San Diego. Harcourt Brace Jovanovich.

Sternberg, R.J. (1988). *The triangle of love.* New York: Basic Books.

Sternberg, R.J. (2004). Individual differences in cognitive development. In U. Goswami (Ed.), *Blackwell handbook of childhood cognitive development.* Malden, MA: Blackwell.

Sternberg, R.J. (2010). Componential models of creativity. In M. Runco & S. Spritzker (Eds.), *Encyclopedia of creativity.* New York: Elsevier.

Sternberg, R.J. (2011). Individual differences in cognitive development. In U. Goswami (Ed.), *Blackwell handbook of childhood cognitive development.* Malden, MA: Blackwell.

Sternberg, R.J. (2012). Human intelligence. In V.S. Ramachandran (Ed.), *Encyclopedia of human behavior* (2nd ed.). New York: Elsevier.

Sternberg, R.J. (2013). Contemporary theories of intelligence. In I.B. Weiner & others (Eds.), *Handbook of psychology* (2nd ed., Vol. 7). New York: Wiley.

Sternberg, R.J. (2014a). Building wisdom and character. In S. Lynn (Ed.), *Health, happiness, and well-being.* Thousand Oaks, CA: Sage.

Sternberg, R.J. (2014b). Teaching about the nature of intelligence. *Intelligence, 42,* 176–179.

Sternberg, R.J. (2015). Successful intelligence: A new model for testing intelligence beyond IQ tests. *European Journal of Education and Psychology, 8,* 76–84.

Sternberg, R.J. (2016a). What does it mean to be intelligent? In R.J. Sternberg & others (Eds.), *Scientists making a difference.* New York: Cambridge University Press.

Sternberg, R.J. (2016b). Theories of intelligence. In S. Pfeiffer (Ed.), *APA handbook of giftedness and talent.* Washington, DC: American Psychological Association.

Sternberg, R.J. (2017). *Cognitive psychology* (7th ed.). Boston: Cengage.

Sternberg, R.J. (2017a). Intelligence and competence in theory and practice. In A.J. Elliot & C.S. Dweck (Eds.), *Handbook of competence and motivation* (2nd ed.). New York: Guilford.

Sternberg, R.J. (2017b). IQ testing. In S. Ayers & others (Eds.), *Cambridge handbook of psychology, health, and medicine* (3rd ed.). New York: Cambridge University Press.

Sternberg, R.J. (2017c, in press). ACCEL: A new model for identifying the gifted. *Roeper Review, 39,* 152–169.

Sternberg, R.J. (2018). Introduction. In R.J. Sternberg & J. Glueck (Eds.), *Cambridge handbook of wisdom.* New York: Cambridge University Press.

Sternberg, R.J. (2018a). Successful theory in theory, research, and practice. In R.J. Sternberg (Ed.), *The nature of intelligence.* New York: Cambridge University Press.

Sternberg, R.J. (2018b). The triangle of intelligence. In R.J. Sternberg & J.C. Kaufman (Eds.), *The nature of human creativity.* New York: Cambridge University Press.

Sternberg, R.J. (2018c). Triarchic theory of intelligence. In B. Frey (Ed.), *SAGE encyclopedia of educational research, measurement, and evaluation.* Thousand Oaks, CA: Sage.

Sternberg, R.J. (2018d). The triarchic theory of successful intelligence. In D.P. Flanagan & P.L. Harrison (Eds.), *Contemporary intellectual assessment* (4th ed.). New York: Guilford Press.

Sternberg, R.J. (2018e, in press). The psychology of creativity. In S. Nalbantian & P.M. Matthews (Eds.), *Secrets of creativity.* New York: Oxford University Press.

Sternberg, R.J. (2018f). The triangle of creativity. In R.J. Sternberg, & J.C. Kaufman (Eds.), *The nature of human creativity.* New York: Cambridge University Press.

Sternberg, R.J., & Glueck, J. (Eds.) (2018). *Cambridge handbook of wisdom.* New York: Cambridge University Press.

Sternberg, R.J., & Hagen, E.S. (2018). Wisdom. In M.H. Bornstein (Ed.), *SAGE encyclopedia of lifespan human development.* Thousand Oaks, CA: Sage.

Sternberg, R.J., & Kaufman, J.C. (2018a). *The nature of human creativity.* New York: Cambridge University Press.

Sternberg, R.J., & Kaufman, J.C. (2018b). Theories and conceptions of giftedness. In S. Pfeiffer (Ed.), *Handbook of giftedness in children* (2nd ed.). New York: Springer.

Sternberg, R.J., & Sternberg, K. (2017). *Cognitive psychology* (7th ed.). Boston: Cengage.

Sternberg, R.J., & Sternberg, K. (Eds.) (2018). *The new psychology of love* (2nd ed.). New York: Cambridge University Press.

Sterns, H., & Huyck, M.H. (2001). The role of work in midlife. In M. Lachman (Ed.), *Handbook of midlife development.* New York: Wiley.

Stevens, C., & Bavelier, D. (2012). The role of selective attention on academic foundations: A cognitive neuroscience perspective. *Developmental Cognitive Neuroscience,* 15 (Suppl. 1), S30–S48.

Stevens, E.A., Walker, M.A., & Vaughn, S. (2017). The effects of reading fluency interventions on the reading fluency and reading comprehension performance of elementary students with learning disabilities: A synthesis of research from 2001 to 2014. *Journal of Learning Disabilities, 50,* 576–590.

Stevens, M., & N'zi, A. (2018). Parent-child interaction therapy. In C.H. Zeanah (Ed.), *Handbook of infant mental health* (4th ed.). New York; Guilford.

Stevenson, H.W. (1995). Mathematics achievements of American students: First in the world by the year 2000: In C.A. Nelson (Ed.), *Basic and applied perspectives on learning, cognition, and development.* Minneapolis: University of Minnesota Press.

Stevenson, H.W. (2000). Middle childhood: Education and schooling. In A. Kazdin (Ed.), *Encyclopedia of psychology.* Washington, DC, & New York: American Psychological Association and Oxford University Press.

Stevenson, H.W., Hofer, B.K., & Randel, B. (1999). *Middle childhood: Education and schooling.* Unpublished manuscript, Dept. of Psychology, University of Michigan, Ann Arbor.

Stevenson, H.W., Lee, S., & Stigler, J.W. (1986). Mathematics achievement of Chinese, Japanese, and American children. *Science, 231,* 693–699.

Stevenson, H.W., & Zusho, A. (2002). Adolescence in China and Japan: Adapting to a changing environment. In B.B. Brown, R.W. Larson, & T.S. Saraswathi (Eds.), *The world's youth.* New York: Cambridge University Press.

Stevenson, H.W., & others (1990). Contexts of achievement. *Monograph of the Society for Research in Child Development, 55*(Serial No. 221).

Stewart, A.J., Ostrove, J.M., & Helson, R. (2001). Middle aging in women: Patterns of personality change from the 30s to the 50s. *Journal of Adult Development, 8,* 23–37.

Stewart, J.G., & others (2017). Cognitive control deficits differentiate adolescent suicide ideators from attempters. *Journal of Clinical Psychology, 78,* e614–e621.

Stice, E., & others (2017). Risk factors that predict future onset of each DSM-5 eating disorder: Predictive specificity in high-risk adolescent females. *Journal of Abnormal Psychology, 126,* 38–51.

Stiel, S., & others (2018). Palliative sedation in Germany: Factors and treatment practices associated with different sedation rate estimates in palliative and hospice care services. *BMC Palliative Care, 17*(1), 48.

Stiggins, R. (2008). *Introduction to student involved assessment for learning* (5th ed.). Upper Saddle River, NJ: Prentice Hall.

Stipek, D. (2005, February 16). Commentary in *USA Today,* p. 10.

Stokes, C.E., & Raley, R.K. (2009). Cohabitation. In D. Carr (Ed.), *Encyclopedia of the life course and human development.* Boston: Gale Cengage.

Stolove, C.A., Galatzer-Levy, I.R., & Bonanno, G.A. (2017). Emergence of depression following job loss prospectively predicts lower rates of reemployment. *Psychiatry Research, 253,* 79–83.

Stone, A.A., Schwartz, J.E., Broderick, J.E., & Deaton, A. (2010). A snapshot of the age distribution of psychological well-being in the United States. *Proceedings of the National Academy of Sciences USA, 107,* 9985–9990.

Strandberg, T. (2019, in press). Preventive effects of physical activity in old people. In R. Fernandez-Ballesteros & others (Eds.), *Cambridge handbook of successful aging.* New York: Cambridge University Press.

Strasser, B., & others (2018). Role of dietary protein and muscular fitness on longevity and aging. *Aging and Disease, 9,* 119–132.

Straus, M.B. (2018). *Treating trauma in adolescents.* New York: Guilford.

Strenze, T. (2007). Intelligence and socioeconomic success: A meta-analytic review of longitudinal research. *Intelligence, 35,* 401–426.

Strickhouser, J.E., Zell, E., & Krizan, Z. (2017). Does personality predict health and well-being? A metasynthesis. *Health Psychology. 36,* 797–810.

Strickland, B., & Chemla, E. (2018). Cross-linguistic regularities and learner biases reflect "core" mechanics. *PLoS One, 13*(1), e0184132.

Strong, D.R., & others (2017). Pre-adolescent receptivity to tobacco marketing and its relationship to acquiring friends who smoke and cigarette smoking initiation. *Annals of Behavioral Medicine, 51,* 730–740.

Stroope, S., McFarland, M.J., & Uecker, J.E. (2015). Marital characteristics and the sexual relationships of U.S. older adults: An analysis of national social life, health, and aging project data. *Archives of Sexual Behavior, 44,* 233–247.

Strough, J., & others (2016). Hour glass half full or half empty? Future time perspective and preoccupation with negative events across the life span. *Psychology and Aging, 31,* 558–573.

Struck, B.D., Brown, E.A., & Madison, S. (2017). Advance care planning in the outpatient geriatric medicine setting. *Primary Care, 44,* 511–518.

Stuart, R.B., & Thielke, S. (2017). Standardizing protection of patients' rights from POLST to MOELI (Medical Orders for End-of-Life Intervention). *Journal of the American Medical Directors Association, 18,* 741–745.

Stubbs, B., Brefka, S., & Denkinger, M.D. (2015). What works to prevent falls in community-dwelling older adults? An umbrella review of meta-analyses of randomized controlled trials. *Physical Therapy, 95,* 1095–1110.

Stuebe, A.M., & Schwartz, E.G. (2010). The risks and benefits of infant feeding practices for women and their children. *Journal of Perinatology, 30,* 155–162.

Stumper, A., & others (2017). Parents' behavioral inhibition moderates association of preschoolers' BI with risk for age 9 anxiety disorders. *Journal of Affective Disorders, 210,* 35–42.

Su, C.H., Dhananjaya, D., & Tarn, W.Y. (2018). Alternative splicing in neurogenesis and brain development. *Frontiers in Molecular Science, 5,* 12.

Su, D., Stimpson, J.P., & Wilson, F.A. (2015). Racial disparities in mortality among middle-aged and older men: Does marriage matter? *American Journal of Men's Health, 9,* 289–300.

Su, L., & others (2018, in press). LPRP: A gene-gene interaction network construction algorithm and its application in breast cancer data analysis. *Interdisciplinary Sciences.*

Suárez-Orozco, C. (2018a, in press). Conferring disadvantage: Behavioral and developmental implications for current children growing up in the shadow of undocumented immigrant status. *Journal of Developmental and Behavioral Pediatrics.*

Suárez-Orozco, C. (2018b, in press). The diverse immigrant experience: What does it mean for teaching? *Educational Studies.*

Suárez-Orozco, C. (2018c, in press). A compassionate perspective on immigrant- and refugee-origin children and youth. In Suárez-Orozco, C. (Ed.). *Humanism and mass migration.* Berkeley, CA: University of California Press.

Suárez-Orozco, C., & Suárez-Orozco, M. (2018, in press). The experience of Latino/a immigrant origin adolescents in the U.S. In J. Bhabha & others (Eds.), *Research handbook on migration and childhood.* Cheltenham, UK: Elgar Publishing.

Sucheston-Campbell, L.E., & others (2018). Genome-wide meta-analyses identifies novel taxane-induced peripheral neuropathy-associated loci. *Pharmacogenetics and Genomics, 28,* 49–56.

Suchow, J.W., Bourgin, D.D., & Griffiths, T.L. (2017). Evolution in mind: Evolutionary dynamics, cognitive processes, and Bayesian inference. *Trends in Cognitive Science, 21,* 522–530.

Sugden, N.A., & Moulson, M.C. (2017). Hey baby, what's "up"? One- and 3-month-olds experience faces primarily upright but non-upright faces offer the best views. *Quarterly Journal of Experimental Psychology, 70,* 959–969.

Sugiura, M. (2016). Functional neuroimaging of normal aging: Declining brain, adapting brain. *Aging Research Reviews, 30,* 61–72.

Suitor, J.J., Gilligan, M., & Pillemer, K. (2016). Stability, change, and complexity in later life families. In L.K. George & K.F. Ferraro (Eds.), *Handbook of aging and the social sciences* (8th ed.). New York: Elsevier.

Suleiman, A.B., & others (2017). Becoming a sexual being: The 'elephant in the room' of adolescent brain development. *Developmental Cognitive Neuroscience, 25,* 209–220.

Sullivan, A.R., & Fenelon, A. (2014). Patterns of widowhood mortality. *Journals of Gerontology B: Psychological Sciences and Social Sciences, 69,* 53–62.

Sullivan, H.S. (1953). *The interpersonal theory of psychiatry.* New York: W.W. Norton.

Sullivan, K., & Sullivan, A. (1980). Adolescent-parent separation. *Developmental Psychology, 16,* 93–99.

Sullivan, M.D., & others (2014). Early stage second-language learning improves executive control: Evidence from ERP. *Brain and Language, 139,* 84–98.

Sullivan, R., & Wilson, D. (2018). Neurobiology of infant attachment. *Annual Review of Psychology* (Vol. 69). Palo Alto, CA: Annual Reviews.

Sullivan, S.P., & others (2018, in press). "It was supposed to be a one-time thing": Experiences of romantic and sexual relationship typologies among young gay, bisexual, and other men who have sex with men. *Archives of Sexual Behavior.*

Sulmasy, D.P. (2018, in press). Italy's new advance directive law: When in Rome. . . . *JAMA Internal Medicine.*

Sumontha, J., Farr, R.H., & Patterson, C.J. (2018, in press). Children's gender development: Associations with parental sexual orientation, division of labor, and gender ideology. *Psychology of Sexual Orientation and Gender Diversity.*

Sun, A., & others (2018, in press). Home-based and technology-centered childhood obesity prevention for Chinese mothers with preschool-aged children. *Journal of Transcultural Nursing.*

Sun, H., & others (2018). Psychoradiologic utility of MR imaging for diagnosis of attention deficit hyperactivity disorder: A radiomics analysis. *Radiology, 287,* 20–30.

Sun, K.L. (2015). *There's no limit: Mathematics teaching for a growth mindset.* Doctoral dissertation, Stanford University, Stanford, CA.

Sun, R., & others (2015). Congenital heart disease: Causes, diagnosis, symptoms, and treatment. *Cellular Biochemistry and Biophysics, 72,* 857–860.

Sun, X., & others (2017). Longitudinal links between work experiences and marital satisfaction in African American dual-earner couples. *Journal of Family Psychology, 31,* 1029–1039.

Sunderam, S., & others (2017). Assisted reproduction technology surveillance—United States 2014. *MMWR Surveillance Summaries, 66*(6), 1–24.

Suo, C., & others (2016). Therapeutically relevant structural and functional mechanisms triggered by physical and cognitive exercise. *Molecular Psychiatry, 21*(11), 1145.

Suri, G., & Gross, J.J. (2012). Emotion regulation and successful aging. *Trends in Cognitive Science, 16,* 409–410.

Susman, E.J., & Dorn, L.D. (2013). Puberty: Its role in development. In I.B. Weiner & others (Eds.), *Handbook of psychology* (3rd ed., Vol. 6). New York: Wiley.

Sutcliffe, K., & others (2012). Comparing midwife-led and doctor-led maternity care: A systematic review of reviews. *Journal of Advanced Nursing, 68*(11), 2376–2386.

Sutin, A.R., Robinson, E., Daly, M., & Terracciarno, A. (2016). Parent-reported bullying and child weight gain between 6 and 15. *Child Obesity, 12,* 482–487.

Svatikova, A., & Kopecky, S.L. (2017). Cholesterol management in the era of PCSK9 inhibitors. *Current Cardiology Reports, 19*(9), 83.

Svensson, Y., Berne, J., & Syed, M. (2018, in press). A narrative approach to the role of others in ethnic identity formation. *Cultural Diversity and Ethnic Minority Psychology.*

Swanson, H.L. (2017). Verbal and visual-spatial working memory: What develops over a life span? *Developmental Psychology, 53,* 971–995.

Sweeney, M.M. (2009). Remarriage. In D. Carr (Ed.), *Encyclopedia of the life course and human development.* Boston: Gale Cengage.

Sweeney, M.M. (2010). Remarriage and stepfamilies: Strategic sites for family scholarship in the 21st century. *Journal of Marriage and the Family, 72,* 667–684.

Swift, A. (2016, June 24). *Euthanasia still acceptable to a majority in U.S.* Washington, DC: Gallup.

Syed, M., Juang, L.P., & Svensson, Y. (2018, in press). Toward a new understanding of ethnic-racial identity development. *Journal of Research on Adolescence.*

Sykes, C.J. (1995). *Dumbing down our kids: Why America's children feel good about themselves but can't read, write, or add.* New York: St. Martin's Press.

Szanto, K., & others (2018, in press). Pathways to late-life suicidal behavior: Cluster analysis and predictive validation of suicidal behavior in a sample of older adults with major depression. *Journal of Clinical Psychiatry.*

Szepsenwol, O., & Simpson, J.A. (2018). Attachment within life history theory: An evolutionary perspective on individual differences in attachment. *Current Opinion in Psychology, 25,* 65–70.

Szutorisz, H., & Hurd, Y.L. (2018). High times for cannabis: Epigenetic imprint and its legacy on brain and behavior. *Neuroscience and Biobehavioral Reviews, 85,* 93–101.

Szwedo, D.E., Hessel, E.T., & Allen, J.P. (2017). Supportive romantic relationships as predictors of resilience against early adolescent maternal negativity. *Journal of Youth and Adolescence, 46,* 454–465.

T

Taga, G., Watanabe, H., & Homae, F. (2018). Spatial variation in the hemoglobin phase of oxygenation and deoxygenation in the developing cortex of infants. *Neurophotonics, 5*(1), 011017.

Taggart, J., Eisen, S., & Lillard, A.S. (2018). Pretense. In M.H. Bornstein & others (Eds.), *The SAGE encyclopedia of lifespan human development.* Thousand Oaks, CA: Sage.

Taige, N.M., & others (2007). Antenatal maternal stress and long-term effects on child neurodevelopment: How and why? *Journal of Child Psychology and Psychiatry, 48,* 245–261.

Takehara, K., & others (2017). Prenatal and postnatal depression and child maltreatment among Japanese fathers. *Child Abuse and Neglect, 70,* 231–239.

Talbot, D., & others (2018, in press). Importance of lipid-related pathways in the association between statins, mortality, and cardiovascular disease risk: The Multi-Ethnic Study of Atherosclerosis. *Pharmacoepidemiology and Drug Safety.*

Tamai, K., & others (2018). Fetal ultrasonographic findings including cerebral hyperechogenicity in a patient with non-lethal form of Raine syndrome. *American Journal of Medical Genetics A, 176,* 682–686.

Tamnes, C.K., & others (2018, in press). Development of the cerebral cortex across adolescence: A multisample study of interrelated longitudinal changes in cortical volume, surface area, and thickness. *Journal of Neuroscience.*

Tan, B.W., Pooley, J.A., & Speelman, C.P. (2016). A meta-analytic review of the efficacy of physical exercise interventions on cognition in individuals with autism spectrum disorders and ADHD. *Journal of Autism and Developmental Disorders, 46,* 3126–3143.

Tan, C.C., & Holub, S.C. (2015). Emotion regulation feeding practices link parents' emotional eating to children's emotional eating: A moderated mediation study. *Journal of Pediatric Psychology, 40,* 657–663.

Tan, M.E., & others (2017). Employment status among the Singapore elderly and its correlates. *Psychogeriatrics, 17,* 155–163.

Tan, P.Z., Armstrong, L.M., & Cole, P.M. (2013). Relations between temperament and anger regulation over early childhood. *Social Development, 22,* 755–772.

Tanajak, P., & others (2017). Vildagliptin and caloric restriction for cardioprotection in pre-diabetic rats. *Journal of Endocrinology, 232,* 189–204.

Tanaka, H. (2017). Aging of competitive athletes. *Gerontology, 63,* 488–494.

Tang, S., & Chow, A.Y. (2017). Subjective and objective traumatic death: Distinct roles in developing complicated grief and depression among older adults in Hong Kong. *International Psychogeriatrics, 29,* 409–417.

Tannen, D. (1990). *You just don't understand: Women and men in conversation.* New York: Ballantine.

Tartaglia, N.R., & others (2017). Autism spectrum disorder in males with sex chromosome aneuploidy: XXY/Klinefelter syndrome, XYY, and XXXY. *Journal of Developmental and Behavioral Pediatrics, 38,* 197–207.

Taverno Ross, S., Dowda, M., Saunders, R., & Pate, R. (2013). Double dose: The cumulative effect of TV viewing at home and in preschool on children's activity patterns and weight status. *Pediatric Exercise Science, 25,* 262–272.

Taylor, A.W., & others (2017). Estimated perinatal HIV infection among infants born in the United States, 2002–2013. *JAMA Pediatrics, 17,* 435–442.

Taylor, H., & others (2016, in press). Neonatal outcomes of waterbirth: A systematic review and meta-analysis. *Archives of Disease in Childhood: Fetal and Neonatal Edition, 101,* F357–F365.

Taylor, H.O., & others (2018). Social isolation, depression, and psychological distress among older adults. *Journal of Aging and Health, 30,* 229–246.

Taylor, L.H. (2017). Supporting elementary children in crisis. *NAMTA Journal, 42,* 193–247.

Taylor, L.K., & others (2017). Complexity of risk: Mixed methods approach to understanding youth risk and insecurity in post-conflict settings. *Journal of Clinical Child and Adolescent Psychology, 32,* 585–613.

Taylor, S.E. (2011a). Affiliation and stress. In S.S. Folkman (Ed.), *Oxford handbook of stress, health, and coping.* New York: Oxford University Press.

Taylor, S.E. (2011b). *Health psychology* (8th ed.). New York: McGraw-Hill.

Taylor, S.E. (2011c). Tend and befriend theory. In A.M. van Lange, A.W. Kruglanski, & E.T. Higgins (Eds.), *Handbook of theories of social psychology.* Thousand Oaks, CA: Sage.

Taylor, S.E. (2015). *Health psychology* (9th ed.). New York: McGraw-Hill.

Taylor, S.E. (2018). *Health psychology* (10th ed.). New York: McGraw-Hill.

Taylor, Z.E., Widaman, K.F., & Robins, R.W. (2018, in press). Longitudinal relations of economic hardship and effortful control to active coping in Latino youth. *Journal of Research on Adolescence.*

Teach for America (2018). *Teach for America.* Retrieved February 6, 2018, from www.teachforamerica.org

Tearne, J.E., & others (2016). Older maternal age is associated with depression, anxiety, and stress symptoms in young adult female offspring. *Journal of Abnormal Psychology, 125,* 1–10.

Tegin, G., & others (2018). E-cigarette toxicity? *Southern Medical Journal, 111,* 35–38.

Teivaanmaki, T., & others (2018, in press). Depressive symptoms are common among rural Malawian adolescents. *Child Care, Health, and Development.*

Telzer, E.H., Rogers, C.R., & Van Hoorn, J. (2017). Neural correlates of social influence on risk taking and substance use in adolescents. *Current Addiction Reports, 4,* 333–341.

Temple, C.A., & others (2018). *All children read: Teaching for literacy* (5th ed.). Upper Saddle River, NJ: Pearson.

Tenenbaum, H., & May, D. (2014). Gender in parent-child relationships. In P. Leman & H. Tenenbaum, *Gender and development (Current Issues in Developmental Psychology).* New York: Psychology Press.

Tenzek, K.E., & Depner, R. (2017). Still searching: A meta-synthesis of a good death from the bereaved family member perspective. *Behavioral Sciences, 7*(2), E25.

Terman, L. (1925). *Genetic studies of genius. Vol. 1: Mental and physical traits of a thousand gifted children.* Stanford, CA: Stanford University Press.

Terracciano, A., & others (2017). Personality traits and risk of cognitive impairment and dementia. *Journal of Psychiatric Research, 89,* 22–27.

Terry, D.F., Nolan, V.G., Andersen, S.L., Perls, T.T., & Cawthon, R. (2008). Association of longer telomeres with better health in centenarians. *Journals of Gerontology A: Biological Sciences and Medical Sciences, 63,* 809–812.

Tesch-Romer, C., & Wahl, H.W. (2017). Toward a more comprehensive concept of successful aging: Disability and care needs. *Journals of Gerontology B: Psychological Sciences and Social Sciences, 72,* 310–318.

Teshale, S.M., & Lachman, M.E. (2016). Managing daily happiness: The relationship between selection, optimization, and compensation strategies and well-being in adulthood. *Psychology and Aging, 31,* 687–692.

Tevendale, H.D., & others (2017). Practical approaches to evaluating progress and outcomes in community-wide teen pregnancy prevention initiatives. *Journal of Adolescent Health, 60*(Suppl. 3), S63–S68.

Tham, E.K., Schneider, N., & Broekman, B.F. (2017). Infant sleep and its relation to cognition and growth: A narrative review. *Nature and Science of Sleep, 9,* 135–149.

Thanh, N.X., & Jonsson, E. (2016). Life expectancy of people with fetal alcohol syndrome. *Journal of Population Therapeutics and Clinical Pharmacology, 23,* e53–e59.

Tharmaratnam, T., & others (2017). Exercise becomes brain: Sustained aerobic exercise enhances hippocampal neurogenesis. *Journal of Physiology, 595,* 7–8.

The, N.S., & others (2010). Association of adolescent obesity with risk of severe obesity in adulthood. *JAMA, 304,* 2042–2047.

Thelen, E., & Smith, L.B. (1998). Dynamic systems theory. In W. Damon & R. Lerner (Eds.), *Handbook of child psychology* (5th ed., Vol. 1.). New York: Wiley.

Thelen, E., & Smith, L.B. (2006). Dynamic development of action and thought. In W. Damon & R. Lerner (Eds.), *Handbook of child psychology* (6th ed.). New York: Wiley.

Thibault, R.T., & others (2018). Treating ADHD with suggestion: Neurofeedback and placebo therapeutics. *Journal of Attention Disorders, 22,* 707–711.

Thoma, S.J., & Bebeau, M. (2008). Moral judgment competency is declining over time: Evidence from 20 years of defining issues test data. Paper presented at the meeting of the American Educational Research Association, New York, NY.

Thomas, A., & Chess, S. (1991). Temperament in adolescence and its functional significance. In R.M. Lerner, A.C. Petersen, & J. Brooks-Gunn (Eds.), *Encyclopedia of adolescence* (Vol. 2). New York: Garland.

Thomas, H.N., Hess, R., & Thurston, R.C. (2015). Correlates of sexual activity and satisfaction in midlife and older women. *Annals of Family Medicine, 13,* 336–342.

Thomas, J.C., & others (2017). Developmental origins of infant emotion regulation: Mediation by temperamental negativity and moderation by maternal sensitivity. *Developmental Psychology, 53,* 611–628.

Thomas, K.A., & Spieker, S. (2016). Sleep, depression, and fatigue in late postpartum. *MCN American Journal of Maternal and Child Nursing, 41,* 104–109.

Thomas, M.L., & others (2018, in press). A new scale for assessing wisdom based on common domains and a neurobiological model: The San Diego Wisdom Scale (SD-WISE). *Journal of Psychiatric Research.*

Thomas, M.S.C., & Johnson, M.H. (2008). New advances in understanding sensitive periods in brain development. *Current Directions in Psychological Science, 17,* 1–5.

Thomas, P.A. (2010). Is it better to give or to receive? Social support and the well-being of older adults. *Journals of Gerontology B: Psychological Sciences and Social Sciences, 65B,* 351–357.

Thompson, A.E., & Voyer, D. (2014). Sex differences in the ability to recognize non-verbal displays of emotion: A meta-analysis. *Cognition and Emotion, 28,* 1164–1195.

Thompson, J.J., & Manore, M. (2018). *Nutrition* (5th ed.). Upper Saddle River, NJ: Pearson.

Thompson, M.P., & Swartout, K. (2018, in press). Epidemiology of suicide attempts among youth transitioning to adulthood. *Journal of Youth and Adolescence.*

Thompson, R., & Murachver, T. (2001). Predicting gender from electronic discourse. *British Journal of Social Psychology, 40,* 193–201.

Thompson, R., & others (2017). Is the use of physical punishment associated with aggressive behaviors in young children? *Academic Pediatrics, 17,* 34–44.

Thompson, R.A. (2006). The development of the person. In W. Damon & R. Lerner (Eds.), *Handbook of child psychology* (6th ed.). New York: Wiley.

Thompson, R.A. (2012). Whither the preoperational child? Toward a life-span moral development theory. *Child Development Perspectives, 6,* 423–429.

Thompson, R.A. (2014). Why are relationships important to children's well-being? In A. Ben Arieh, I. Frones, F. Cases, & J. Korbin (Eds.), *Handbook of child well-being.* New York: Springer.

Thompson, R.A. (2015). Relationships, regulation, and development. In R.M. Lerner (Ed.), *Handbook of child psychology* (7th ed.). New York: Wiley.

Thompson, R.A. (2016). Early attachment and later development: New questions. In J. Cassidy & P.R. Shaver (Eds.), *Handbook of attachment* (3rd ed.). New York: Guilford.

Thompson, R.A. (2019, in press). Emotion dysregulation and early social relationships. In T.P. Beauchaine & S.E. Crowell (Eds.), *Oxford handbook of emotion dysregulation.* New York: Oxford University Press.

Thompson, R.A., & Goodvin, R. (2016). Social support and developmental psychopathology. In D. Cicchetti (Ed.), *Developmental psychopathology* (3rd ed.). New York: Wiley.

Thornton, R. (2017). The acquisition of syntax. In J. Lidz, W. Snyder, & Pater, J. (Eds.), *Oxford handbook of developmental linguistics.* New York: Oxford University Press.

Thorsen, M.L. (2017). The adolescent, family environment, and cohabitation across the transition to adulthood. *Social Science Research, 64,* 249–262.

Thorvaldsson, V., & others (2017). Better cognition in new birth cohorts of 70 year olds, but greater decline thereafter. *Journals of Gerontology B: Psychological Sciences and Social Sciences, 72,* 16–24.

Thurman, A.J., & others (2017). Language skills of males and Fragile X syndrome or nonsyndromic autism spectrum disorder. *Journal of Autism and Developmental Disorders, 47,* 728–743.

Tian, S., & Xu, Y. (2016). Association of sarcopenic obesity with the risk of all-cause mortality: A meta-analysis of prospective cohort studies. *Geriatrics and Gerontology International, 16,* 155–166.

Tieu, L., & others (2018). Children's comprehension of plural predicate conjunction. *Journal of Child Language, 45,* 242–259.

Tiggemann, M., & Slater, A. (2017). Facebook and body image concern in adolescent girls: A prospective study. *International Journal of Eating Disorders, 50,* 80–83.

Timmers, T., & others (2018). Quantification of tau load in Alzheimer's disease clinical trials using positron emission tomography. *Methods in Molecular Biology, 1750,* 221–229.

TIMSS (2015). *TIMSS 2015 and TIMSS advanced 2015 international results.* Chestnut Hill, MA: TIMSS.

Tincoff, R., & Jusczyk, P.W. (2012). Six-month-olds comprehend words that refer to parts of the body. *Infancy, 17*(4), 432–444.

Titzmann, P.F., & Gniewosz, B. (2018). With a little help from my child: A dyad approach to immigrant mothers' and adolescents' sociocultural adaptation. *Journal of Adolescence, 62,* 198–206.

Tkatch, R., & others (2017). A qualitative study to examine older adults' perceptions of health: Keys to aging successfully. *Geriatric Nursing, 38,* 485–490.

Tobin, M., Lambert, S., & McCarthy, J. (2018, in press). Grief, tragic death, and multiple loss in the lives of Irish Traveller community health workers. *Omega.*

Tolani, N., & Brooks-Gunn, J. (2008). Family support, international trends. In M.M. Haith & J.B. Benson

(Eds.), *Encyclopedia of infant and early childhood development*. Oxford, UK: Elsevier.

Tolppanen, A.M., & others (2015). Leisure-time physical activity from mid- to late life, body mass index, and risk of dementia. *Alzheimer's and Dementia, 11,* 434–443.

Tomasello, M. (2014). *A natural history of human thinking.* Cambridge, MA: Harvard University Press.

Tompkins, G.E. (2015). *Literacy in the early grades* (4th ed.). Upper Saddle River, NJ: Pearson.

Tompkins, G.E. (2017). *REVEL for literacy in the 21st century* (7th ed.). Upper Saddle River, NJ: Pearson.

Tompkins, G.E. (2018). *Literacy for the 21st century* (7th ed.). Upper Saddle River, NJ: Pearson.

Tompkins, G.E. (2019). *Teaching writing* (7th ed.). Upper Saddle River, NJ: Pearson.

Tompkins, V., & others (2017). Child language and parent discipline mediate the relation between family income and false belief understanding. *Journal of Experimental Psychology, 158,* 1–18.

Top, N., Liew, J., & Luo, W. (2017). Family and school influences on youths' behavioral and academic outcomes: Cross-level interactions between parental monitoring and character development curriculum. *Journal of Genetic Psychology, 178,* 108–118.

Topa, G., Depolo, M., & Alcover, C.M. (2018). Early retirement: A meta-analysis of its antecedent and subsequent correlates. *Frontiers in Psychology, 8,* 2157.

Topa, G., Lunceford, G., & Boyatzis, R.E. (2018). Financial planning for retirement: A psychosocial perspective. *Frontiers in Psychology, 8,* 2338.

Toro, C.A., Aylwin, C.F., & Lomniczi, A. (2018, in press). Hypothalamic epigenetics driving female puberty. *Journal of Neuroendocrinology.*

Torstveit, L., Sutterlin, S., & Lugo, R.G. (2016). Empathy, guilt proneness, and gender: Relative contributions to prosocial behavior. *European Journal of Psychology, 12,* 260–275.

Toth, B., & others (2017). Large-scale network organization of EEG functional connectivity in newborn infants. *Human Brain Mapping, 38,* 4019–4033.

Tottenham, N. (2017). *The brain's emotional development.* New York: The Dana Foundation.

Toupance, S., & Benetos, A. (2019, in press). Telomere dynamics and aging related diseases. In R. Fernandez-Ballesteros & others (Eds.), *Cambridge handbook of successful aging.* New York: Cambridge University Press.

Toy, W., Nai, Z.L., & Lee, H.W. (2016). Extraversion and agreeableness: Divergent routes to daily satisfaction with social relationships. *Journal of Personality, 84,* 121–134.

Trainor, L.J., & He, C. (2013). Auditory and musical development. In P.D. Zelazo (Ed.), *Handbook of developmental psychology.* New York: Oxford University Press.

Traisrisilp, K., & Tongsong, T. (2015). Pregnancy outcomes of mothers with very advanced age (40 years and more). *Journal of the Medical Association of Thailand, 98,* 117–122.

Tramultola, A., Lanzillotta, C., & Di Domenico, F. (2017). Targeting mTOR to reduce Alzheimer-related cognitive decline: From current hits to future therapies. *Expert Review of Neurotherapy, 17,* 33–45.

Treas, J., & Gurbernskaya, Z. (2016). Immigration, aging, and the life course. In L.K. George & K.F. Ferraro (Eds.), *Handbook of aging and the social sciences* (8th ed.). New York: Elsevier.

Trehub, S.E., Schneider, B.A., Thorpe, L.A., & Judge, P. (1991). Observational measures of auditory sensitivity in early infancy. *Developmental Psychology, 27,* 40–49.

Trejos-Castillo, E., & Trevino-Schafer, N. (Eds.) (2018). *Handbook of foster youth.* New York: Routledge.

Tremblay, R.E., Vitaro, F., & Cote, S.M. (2018). Developmental origins of chronic physical aggression: A bio-psycho-social model for the next generation of preventive interventions. *Annual Review of Psychology, 69,* 383–407.

Trevino, K.M., & others (2018, in press). Bereavement challenges and their relationship to physical and psychological adjustment to loss. *Journal of Palliative Medicine.*

Trickett, P.K., Negriff, S., Ji, J., & Peckins, M. (2011). Child maltreatment and adolescent development. *Journal of Research on Adolescence, 21,* 3–20.

Trivedi, A.N. (2016). Understanding seniors' choices in Medicare Advantage. *Journal of General Internal Medicine, 31,* 151–152.

Troop-Gordon, W. (2017). Peer victimization in adolescence: The nature, progression, and consequences of being bullied within a developmental context. *Journal of Adolescence, 55,* 116–128.

Trotman, G., & others (2015). The effect of Centering Pregnancy versus traditional prenatal care models on improved adolescent health behaviors in the prenatal period. *Journal of Pediatric and Adolescent Gynecology, 28,* 395–401.

Trude, A.C.B., & others (2018, in press). A youth-leader program in Baltimore City recreation centers: Lessons learned and applications. *Health Promotion Practice.*

Tsai, W., & others (2018). Prolonged grief disorder and depression are distinct for caregivers across their first bereavement year. *Psychoncology.*

Tsang, A., & others (2008). Common persistent pain conditions in developed and developing countries: Gender and age differences and comorbidity with depression-anxiety disorders. *Journal of Pain, 9,* 883–891.

Tsang, T.W., & others (2016). Prenatal alcohol exposure, FASD, and child behavior: A meta-analysis. *Pediatrics, 137,* e20152542.

Tsubomi, H., & Wanatabe, K. (2017). Development of visual working memory and distractor resistance in relation to academic performance. *Journal of Experimental Psychology, 154,* 98–112.

Tsurumi, S., Kanazawa, S., & Yamaguchi, M.K. (2018). The development of object-based attention in infants. *Infant Behavior and Development, 52,* 14–21.

Tu, K.N., & others (2018). Osteoporosis: A review of treatment options. *Pharmacy and Therapeutics, 43,* 92–104.

Tullis, J.A. (2017). Death of an ex-spouse: Lessons in family communication about disenfranchised grief. *Behavioral Sciences, 7*(2), e16.

Turecki, G., & Meaney, M.J. (2016). Effects of the social environment and stress on glucocorticoid receptor gene methylation: A systematic review. *Biological Psychiatry, 79,* 87–96.

Turiel, E., & Gingo, M. (2017). Development in the moral domain: Coordination and the need to consider other domains of social reasoning. In N. Budwig, E. Turiel, & P.D. Zelazo (Eds.), *New perspectives on human development.* New York: Cambridge University Press.

Turkeltaub, P.E., Gareau, L., Flowers, D.L., Zeffiro, T.A., & Eden, G.F. (2003). Development of neural mechanisms for reading. *Nature Neuroscience, 6,* 767–773.

Turnbull, A., Rutherford-Turnbull, H., Wehmeyer, M.L., & Shogren, K.A. (2016). *Exceptional lives* (8th ed.). Upper Saddle River, NJ: Pearson.

Turner, S., & others (2017). The relationship between childhood sexual abuse and mental health outcomes among males: Results from a nationally representative United States sample. *Child Abuse and Neglect, 66,* 64–72.

Tweed, E.J., & others (2016). Five-minute Apgar scores and educational outcomes: Retrospective cohort study for 751,369 children. *Archives of Disease in Child, Fetal, and Neonatal Medicine, 101,* F121–F126.

Twenge, J.M., Martin, G.N., & Campbell, W.K. (2018, in press). Decreases in psychological well-being among American adolescents after 2012 and links to screen time during the rise of smartphone technology. *Emotion.*

Tyas, S.L., & others (2007). Transitions to mild cognitive impairments, dementia, and death: Findings from the Nun Study. *American Journal of Epidemiology, 165,* 1231–1238.

Tyrell, F.A., & others (2016). Family influences on Mexican American adolescents' romantic relationships: Moderation by gender and culture. *Journal of Research on Adolescence, 26,* 142–158.

U

U.S. Bureau of Labor Statistics (2008). *Employment of older workers.* Washington, DC: Author.

U.S. Bureau of Labor Statistics (2016). *Volunteering in the United States: 2015.* Washington, DC: Author.

U.S. Census Bureau (2012). *Births, deaths, marriages, divorces: Life expectancy.* Table 102. Washington, DC: Author.

U.S. Census Bureau (2013). *Births, deaths, marriages, divorces: Life expectancy.* Table 102. Washington, DC: Author.

U.S. Census Bureau (2015). *Population statistics.* Washington, DC: Author.

U.S. Census Bureau (2016). *People.* Washington, DC: Author.

U.S. Census Bureau (2017). *Families and living arrangements: 2016.* Washington, DC: Author.

U.S. Census Bureau (2017). *People.* Washington, DC: Author.

U.S. Census Bureau (2018). *Births, deaths, marriages, divorces.* Washington, DC: Author.

U.S. Census Bureau (2018). *People.* Washington, DC: U.S Department of Labor.

U.S. Census Bureau (2018). *Poverty.* Washington, DC: Author.

U.S. Department of Education Office of Civil Rights (2018). *School suspensions.* Retrieved 7/10/2020 from ocdata.ed.gov

U.S. Department of Energy (2001). The human genome project. Washington, DC: Author.

U.S. Department of Health and Human Services (2015). *Child maltreatment: 2013.* Washington, DC: Author.

U.S. Department of Health and Human Services (2018). Folic acid. Retrieved January 9, 2018, from www.cdc.gov/ncbddd/folicacid/

U.S. Department of Health and Human Services (2018). *Health, United States 2017.* Washington, DC: Author.

Ulfsdottir, H., Saltvedt, S., & Georgsson, S. (2018, in press). Waterbirth in Sweden—a comparative study. *Acta Obstetricia et Gynecologica Scandinavica.*

Ullsperger, J.M., & Nikolas, M.A. (2017). A meta-analytic review of the association between pubertal timing and psychopathology in adolescence: Are there sex differences in risk? *Psychological Bulletin, 143,* 903–938.

Umana-Taylor, A.J., & Douglass, S. (2017). Developing an ethnic-racial identity intervention from a developmental perspective: Process, content, and implementation. In N.J. Cabrera & B. Leyendecker (Eds.), *Handbook of positive development of minority children.* New York: Springer.

Umana-Taylor, A.J., & others (2018). A universal intervention program increases ethnic-racial identity exploration and resolution to predict adolescent psychosocial functioning one year later. *Journal of Youth and Adolescence, 47,* 1–15.

Umana-Taylor, A.J., & others (2018). A small-scale randomized efficacy trial of the Identity Project: Promoting adolescents' ethnic-racial identity exploration and resolution. *Child Development, 69,* 862–870.

Umemura, T., & others (2018, in press). Secure base script and psychological dysfunction in Japanese young adults in the 21st century: Using the attachment script assessment. *Developmental Psychology.*

UNAIDS (2011). *AIDS at 30: Nations at a crossroads.* Geneva, Switzerland: United Nations.

UNAIDS (2015). *UNAIDS fact sheet: 2015.* Geneva, Switzerland: United Nations.

UNAIDS (2017). *UNAIDS fact sheet: 2016.* Geneva, Switzerland: United Nations.

Unalmis Erdogan, S., Yanikkerem, E., & Goker, A. (2017). Effects of low back massage on perceived birth pain and satisfaction. *Complementary Therapies in Clinical Practice, 28,* 169–175.

Ungar, M. (2015). Practitioner review: Diagnosing childhood resilience: A systematic diagnosis of adaption in diverse social ecologies. *Journal of Child Psychology and Psychiatry, 56,* 4–17.

UNICEF (2007). *The state of the world's children: 2007.* Geneva, Switzerland: UNICEF.

UNICEF (2018). *The state of the world's children: 2018.* Geneva, Switzerland: UNICEF.

United Nations (2015). *World population aging 2015.* New York: United Nations.

Urqueta Alfaro, A., & others (2018). Joint engagement in infants and its relationship to their visual impairment measurements. *Infant Behavior and Development, 50,* 311–323.

Usher, E.L., & Schunk, D.H. (2018). Social cognitive perspective of self-regulation. In D.H. Schunk & J.A. Greene (Eds.), *Handbook of self-regulation of learning and performance* (2nd ed.). New York: Routledge.

Uwaezuoke, S.N., Eneh, C.I., & Ndu, I.K. (2018, in press). Relationship between exclusive breastfeeding and lower risk of childhood obesity: A narrative review of published evidence. *Clinical Medicine Insights. Pediatrics.*

V

Vacaru, V.S., Sterkenburg, P.S., & Schuengel, C. (2018). Self-concept in institutionalized children with disturbed attachment: The mediating role of exploratory behaviors. *Child: Care, Health, and Development, 44,* 476–484.

Vacca, J.A., & others (2018). *Reading and learning to read* (10th ed.). Upper Saddle River, NJ: Pearson.

Vaillant, G.E. (1977). *Adaptation to life.* Boston: Little, Brown.

Vaillant, G.E. (2002). *Aging well.* Boston: Little, Brown.

Valdiserri, R.O., & others (2018, in press). Unraveling health disparities among sexual and gender minorities: A commentary on the persistent impact of stigma. *Journal of Homosexuality.*

Valera, M.C., Gourdy, P., Tremollieres, F., & others (2015). From the Women's Health Initiative combination of estrogen and selective estrogen receptor modulators to avoid progestin addition. *Maturitas, 82,* 274–277.

Valero, S., & others (2014). Neuroticism and impulsivity: Their hierarchical organization in the personality characterization of drug-dependent patients from a decision tree learning perspective. *Comprehensive Psychiatry, 55,* 1227–1233.

Valgarda, S. (2018). Childhood obesity policies—mighty concerns, meager reactions. *Obesity Reviews, 19,* 295–301.

Valiathan, R., Ashman, M., & Asthana, D. (2016). Effects of aging on the immune system: Infants to elderly. *Scandinavian Journal of Immunology, 83,* 255–266.

Valiente-Palleja, A., & others (2018, in press). Genetic and clinical evidence of mitochondrial dysfunction in autism spectrum disorder and intellectual disability. *Human Molecular Genetics.*

Valimaki, T.H., & others (2016). Impact of Alzheimer's disease on the family caregiver's long-term quality of life: Results from the ALSOVA follow-up study. *Quality of Life Research, 25,* 687–697.

Van Assche, E., & others (2017). Gene-based interaction analysis shows GABAergic genes interacting with parenting in adolescent depressive symptoms. *Journal of Child Psychology and Psychiatry, 58,* 1301–1309.

Van de Vondervoort, J., & Hamlin, J.K. (2018). The infantile roots of sociomoral evaluations. In K. Gray & J. Graham (Eds.), *The atlas of moral psychology.* New York: Guilford.

van den Boomen, C., Munsters, N.M., & Kemner, C. (2018, in press). Emotion processing in the infant brain: The importance of local information. *Neuropsychologia.*

van den Brink, A.M.A., & others (2018). What do nursing home residents with mental-physical multimorbidity

need and who actually knows this? A cross-sectional cohort study. *International Journal of Nursing Studies, 81,* 89–97.

van den Heuvel, M.I., & others (2018). Hubs in the human fetal brain network. *Developmental Cognitive Neuroscience, 30,* 108–115.

van der Flier, W.M., & others (2018). Vascular cognitive impairment. *Nature Reviews: Disease Primers, 4,* 18003.

van der Hulst, H. (2017). Phonological typology. In A.Y. Aikhenvald & R.M.W. Dixon (Eds.), *Cambridge handbook of linguistic typology.* New York: Cambridge University Press.

van Doeselaar, L., Klimstra, T.A., Denissen, J.J.A., Branje, S., & Meeus, W. (2018). The role of identity commitments in depressive symptoms and stressful life events in adolescence and young adulthood. *Developmental Psychology, 54,* 950–962.

Van Elderen, S.S., & others (2016). Brain volume as an integrated marker for the risk of death in a community-based sample: Age gene/environment susceptibility-Reykjavik study. *Journals of Gerontology A: Biological Sciences and Medical Sciences, 71,* 131–137.

van Geel, M., Vedder, P., & Tanilon, J. (2014). Relationship between peer victimization, cyberbullying, and suicide in children and adolescents: A meta-analysis. *JAMA Pediatrics, 168,* 435–442.

Van Hecke, V., & others (2012). Infant responding to joint attention, executive processes, and self-regulation in preschool children. *Infant Development and Behavior, 35,* 303–311.

Van Hedel, K., & others (2015). Marital status, labor force activity, and mortality: A study in the USA and six European countries. *Scandinavian Journal of Public Health, 43,* 469–480.

van Hooft, E.A. (2014). Motivating and hindering factors during the reemployment process: The added value of employment counselors' assessment. *Journal of Occupational Health Psychology, 19,* 1–17.

van Hout, A. (2017). Lexical and grammatical aspect. In J. Lidz, W. Snyder, & J. Peter (Eds.), *Oxford handbook of developmental linguistics.* New York: Oxford University Press.

Van Hulle, C.A., & others (2017). Infant stranger fear trajectories predict anxious behaviors and diurnal cortisol rhythm during childhood. *Development and Psychopathology, 29,* 1119–1130.

Van Lissa, C.J., & others (2015). Divergence between adolescent and parent perceptions of conflict in relationship to adolescent empathy development. *Journal of Youth and Adolescence, 44,* 48–51.

van Renswoude, D.R., & others (2018, in press). Gazepath: An eye-tracking analysis tool that accounts for individual differences and data quality. *Behavior Research Methods.*

Van Ryzin, M.J., Carlson, E.A., & Sroufe, L.A. (2011). Attachment discontinuity in a high-risk sample. *Attachment and Human Development, 13,* 381–401.

Van Skike, C.E., & others (2018, in press). Inhibition of mTOR protects the blood-brain barrier in models of Alzheimer's disease and vascular cognitive impairment. *American Journal of Physiology: Heart and Circulatory Physiology, 314,* H693–H703.

van Tilborg, E., & others (2018). Origin and dynamics of oligodendrocytes in the developing brain: Implications for perinatal white matter injury. *Glia, 66,* 221–238.

Vandell, D.L., & others (2010). Do effects of early child-care extend to age 15 years? From the NICHD Study of Early Child Care and Youth Development. *Child Development, 81,* 737–756.

Vandenberghe, J. (2018). Physician-assisted suicide and psychiatric illness. *New England Journal of Medicine, 378,* 885–887.

Vanhaelen, Q. (2015). Aging as an optimization between cellular maintenance requirements and evolutionary constraints. *Current Aging Science, 8,* 110–119.

Vanicek, T., & others (2017). Altered interregional molecular associations of the serotonin transporter in

attention deficit/hyperactivity disorder assessed with PET. *Human Brain Mapping, 38,* 792–802.

Varahra, A., & others (2018). Exercise to improve functional outcomes in persons with osteoporosis: A systematic review and meta-analysis. *Osteoporosis International, 29,* 265–286.

Vardavas, C.I., & others (2016). The independent role of prenatal and postnatal exposure to active and passive smoking on the development of early wheeze in children. *European Respiratory Journal, 48,* 115–124.

Varga, N.L., & others (2018). Knowledge. In M.H. Bornstein (Ed.), *SAGE encyclopedia of lifespan human development.* Thousand Oaks, CA: Sage.

Varner, M.W., & others (2014). Association between stillbirth and illicit drug use and smoking during pregnancy. *Obstetrics and Gynecology, 123,* 113–125.

Vasa, F., & others (2018). Adolescent tuning of association cortex in human structural brain networks. *Cerebral Cortex, 28,* 281–294.

Vatalaro, A., Szente, J., & Levin, J. (2015). Transformative learning of pre-service teachers during study abroad in Reggio Emilia, Italy: A case study. *Journal of the Scholarship of Teaching and Learning, 15,* 42–55.

Vaughan, O.R., & others (2017). Regulation of placental amino acid transport and fetal growth. *Progress in Molecular Biology and Translational Science, 145,* 217–251.

Veldman, S.L., Palmer, K.K., Okely, A.D., & Robinson, L.E. (2017). Promoting ball skills in preschool-age girls. *Journal of Science and Medicine in Sport, 20,* 50–54.

Veness, C., Prior, M., Eadie, P., Bavin, E., & Reilly, S. (2014). Predicting autism diagnosis by 7 years of age using parent report of infant social communication skills. *Journal of Pediatrics and Child Health, 50,* 693–700.

Venetsanou, F., & Kambas, A. (2017). Can motor proficiency in preschool age affect physical activity in adolescence? *Pediatric Exercise Science, 49,* 254–259.

Venkatesan, U.M., & others (2018, in press). Differential contributions of selective attention and sensory integration to driving performance in healthy aging and Alzheimer's disease. *Journal of the International Neuropsychology Society.*

Venners, S.A., & others (2005). Paternal smoking and pregnancy loss: A prospective study using a biomarker of pregnancy. *American Journal of Epidemiology, 159,* 993–1001.

Verhagen, J., & Leseman, P. (2016). How do verbal short-term memory and working memory relate to the acquisition of vocabulary and grammar? A comparison between first and second language learners. *Journal of Experimental Child Psychology, 141,* 65–82.

Vernon, L., Modecki, K.L., & Barber, B.L. (2018). Mobile phones in the bedroom: Trajectories of sleep habits and subsequent adolescent psychological development. *Child Development, 89,* 66–77.

Vespa, J. (2017, April). The changing economics and demographics of young adulthood: 1975–2016. *Current Population Reports,* P20-579. Washington, DC: U.S. Census Bureau.

Vidal, S., & others (2017). Maltreatment, family environment, and social risk factors: Determinants of the child welfare to juvenile justice transition among maltreated children and adolescents. *Child Abuse and Neglect, 63,* 7–18.

Vignoles, V.L. (2016). Beyond the 'east-west' dichotomy: Global variation in cultural models of selfhood. *Journal of Experimental Psychology: General, 145,* 966–1000.

Vijayakumar, N., & others (2018, in press). Structural brain development: A review of methodological approaches and best practices. *Developmental Cognitive Neuroscience.*

Villamor, E., & Jansen, E.C. (2016). Nutritional determinants of the timing of puberty. *Annual Review of Public Health, 37,* 33–46.

Villeda, S. (2017). Brain and aging. *Annual Review of Neuroscience* (Vol. 40). Palo Alto, CA: Annual Reviews.

Villemagne,V.L., & others (2018, in press). Imaging tau and amyloid-*B* proteinopathies in Alzheimer disease and other conditions. *Nature Reviews: Neurology.*

Vinik, J., Almas, A., & Grusec, J. (2011). Mothers' knowledge of what distresses and comforts their children predicts children's coping, empathy, and prosocial behavior. *Parenting: Science and Practice, 11,* 56–71.

Virta, J.J., & others (2013). Midlife cardiovascular risk factors and late cognitive development. *European Journal of Epidemiology, 28,* 405–416.

Viswanathan, M., & others (2017). *Folic acid supplementation: An evidence review for the U.S. Preventive Services Task Force.* Rockville, MD: U.S. Preventive Services.

Vitaro, F., Boivin, M., & Poulin, F. (2018). The interface of aggression and peer relations in childhood and adolescence. In W.M. Bukowski & others (Eds.), *Handbook of peer interaction, relationships, and groups* (2nd ed.). New York: Guilford.

Vittrup, B., Holden, G.W., & Buck, M. (2006). Attitudes predict the use of physical punishment: A prospective study of the emergence of disciplinary practices. *Pediatrics, 117,* 2055–2064.

Vo, P., & others (2017). Individual factors, neighborhood social context, and asthma at age 5 years. *Journal of Asthma, 54,* 265–272.

Voigt, R.G., & others (2017). Academic achievement in adults with a history of attention-deficit/hyperactivity disorder: A population-based prospective study. *Journal of Developmental and Behavioral Pediatrics, 38,* 1–11.

Volkmar, F.R., Riechow, B., Westphal, A., & Mandell, D.S. (2014). Autism and autism spectrum diagnostic concepts. In F.R. Volkmar & others (Eds.), *Handbook of autism and pervasive developmental disorders.* New York: Wiley.

Volkow, N.D., Compton, W.M., & Wargo, E.M. (2017). The risks of marijuana use during pregnancy. *JAMA, 317,* 129–130.

Volkwein-Caplan, K., & Tahmaseb-McConatha, J. (Eds.) (2018). *Aging, physical activity, and health.* New York: Routledge.

von Bonsdorff, M.B., & others (2011). Work ability in midlife as a predictor of mortality and disability in later life: A 28-year prospective follow-up study. *Canadian Medical Association Journal, 183,* E235–E242.

von Bonsdorff, M.B., & others (2012). Work ability as a determinant of old age disability severity: Evidence from the 28-year Finnish longitudinal study on municipal employees. *Aging: Clinical and Experimental Research, 24,* 354–360.

Voorpostel, M., & Blieszner, R. (2008). Intergenerational solidarity and support between adult siblings. *Journal of Marriage and the Family, 70,* 157–167.

Vorona, R.D., & others (2014). Adolescent crash rates and school start times in two Central Virginia counties, 2009–2011: A follow-up study to a Southeastern Virginia study, 2007–2008. *Journal of Clinical Sleep Medicine, 10,* 1169–1177.

Vosylis, R., Erentaite, R., & Crocetti, E. (2018). Global versus domain-specific identity processes. *Emerging Adulthood, 6,* 32–41.

Votavova, H., & others (2012). Deregulation of gene expression induced by environmental tobacco smoke exposure in pregnancy. *Nicotine and Tobacco Research, 14*(9), 1073–1082.

Votruba-Drzal, E., Coley, R.L., & Chase-Lansdale, P.L. (2004). Child care and low-income children's development: Direct and moderated effects. *Child Development, 75,* 296–312.

Vreeman, R.C., & Carroll, A.E. (2007). A systematic review of school-based interventions to prevent bullying. *Archives of Pediatric and Adolescent Medicine, 161,* 78–88.

Vu, J.A. (2016). The fourth 'R': Relationships: Shifting from risk to resilience. In K.E. Sanders & A.W. Guerra (Eds.), *The culture of child care.* New York: Oxford University Press.

Vujovic, V., & others (2017). Evolutionary developmental robotics: Improving morphology and control of physical robots. *Artificial Life, 23,* 169–185.

Vuolo, M., Staff, J., & Mortimer, J.T. (2012). Weathering the great recession: Psychological and behavioral trajectories in the transition from school to work. *Developmental Psychology, 48,* 1759–1773.

Vurpillot, E. (1968). The development of scanning strategies and their relation to visual differentiation. *Journal of Experimental Child Psychology, 6,* 632–650.

Vygotsky, L.S. (1962). *Thought and language.* Cambridge, MA: MIT Press.

Vysniauske, R., Verburgh, L., Oosterlaan, J., & Molendijk, M.L. (2018, in press). The effects of physical exercise on functional outcomes in the treatment of ADHD. *Journal of Attention Disorders.*

W

Wachs, T.D., & Bates, J.E. (2010). Temperament. In J.G. Bremner & T.D. Wachs (Eds.), *Wiley Blackwell handbook of infant development* (2nd ed.). New York: Wiley.

Wagner, D.A. (2018). *Human development and international development.* New York: Routledge.

Wagner, N.J., Camerota, M., & Propper, C. (2017). Prevalence and perceptions of electronic cigarette use during pregnancy. *Maternal and Child Health Journal, 21,* 1655–1661.

Waismeyer, A., & Meltzer, A.N. (2017). Learning to make things happen: Infants' observational learning of social and physical causative events. *Journal of Experimental Child Psychology, 162,* 58–71.

Waldenstrom, U., Cnattingius, S., Norman, M., & Schytt, E. (2015). Advanced maternal age and stillbirth risk in nulliparous and parous women. *Obstetrics and Gynecology, 126,* 355–362.

Waldinger, R.J., Vaillant, G.E., & Orav, E.J. (2007). Childhood sibling relationships as a predictor of major depression in adulthood: A 30-year prospective study. *American Journal of Psychiatry, 164,* 949–954.

Walker, A. (2019, in press). The promise of active aging. In R. Fernandez-Ballesteros & others (Eds.), *Cambridge handbook of successful aging.* New York: Cambridge University Press.

Walker, L.J. (1982). The sequentiality of Kohlberg's stages of moral development. *Child Development, 53,* 1130–1136.

Walker, L.J. (2004). Progress and prospects in the psychology of moral development. *Merrill-Palmer Quarterly, 50,* 546–557.

Walker, L.J., & Frimer, J.A. (2011). The science of moral development. In M.K. Underwood & L. Rosen (Eds.), *Social development.* New York: Guilford.

Wallace, L.N. (2017). Siblings and adolescent weapon carrying: Contributions of genetics, shared environment, and nonshared environment. *Youth Violence and Juvenile Justice, 15,* 264–280.

Waller, E.M., & Rose, A.J. (2010). Adjustment tradeoffs of co-rumination in mother-adolescent relationships. *Journal of Adolescence, 33,* 487–497.

Waller, K.L., & others (2016). Subjective sleep quality and daytime sleepiness in late midlife and their association with age-related changes in cognition. *Sleep Medicine, 17,* 165–176.

Walsh, R. (2011). Lifestyle and mental health. *American Psychologist, 66*(7), 579–592.

Walton-Fisette, J., & Wuest, D. (2018). *Foundations of physical education, exercise science, and sport* (19th ed.). New York: McGraw-Hill.

Wang, B., & others (2014). The impact of youth, family, peer, and neighborhood risk factors on developmental trajectories of risk involvement from early through middle adolescence. *Social Science Medicine, 106,* 43–52.

Wang, C., & others (2016). Coevolution of adolescent friendship networks and smoking and drinking behaviors with consideration of parental influence. *Psychology of Addictive Behaviors, 30,* 312–324.

Wang, H., Lin, S.L., Leung, G.M., & Schooling, C.M. (2018, in press). Age at onset of puberty and adolescent depression: "Children of 1997" birth cohort. *Pediatrics.*

Wang, L., & Palacios, E.L. (2017). The social and spatial patterning of life stress among immigrants in Canada. *Journal of Immigrant and Minority Health, 19,* 665–673.

Wang, L., & others (2018). Clinical nurses' attitudes towards death and caring for dying patients in China. *International Journal of Palliative Nursing, 24,* 33–39.

Wang, M., & Shi, J. (2016). Work, retirement, and aging. In K.W. Schaie & S.L. Willis (Eds.), *Handbook of the psychology of aging* (8th ed.). New York: Elsevier.

Wang, S.Y., & others (2017). End-of-life care transition patterns in Medicare beneficiaries. *Journal of the American Geriatrics Society, 65,* 1406–1413.

Wang, W., & Parker, K. (2014, September 24). *Record share of Americans have never married.* Washington, DC: Pew Research Center.

Wang, W.Y., & others (2017). Impacts of CD33 genetic variations on the atrophy rates of hippocampus and parahippocampal gyrus in normal aging and mild cognitive impairment. *Molecular Neurobiology, 54,* 1111–1118.

Wang, X., & others (2018, in press). An epigenome-wide study of obesity in African American youth and young adults: Novel findings, replication in neutrophils, and relationship with gene expression. *Clinical Epigenetics.*

Wang, Z.W., Hua, J., & Xu, Y.H. (2015). The relationship between gentle tactile stimulation on the fetus and its temperament 3 months after birth. *Behavioral Neuroscience, 2015,* 371906.

Wangmo, T., Nordstrom, K., & Kressig, R.W. (2017). Preventing elder abuse and neglect in geriatric institutions: Solutions from nursing care providers. *Geriatric Nursing, 38,* 385–392.

Wardlaw, G.M., Smith, A.M., & Collene, A.L. (2018). *Contemporary nutrition* (5th ed.). New York: McGraw-Hill.

Ware, P., & others (2017). Using eHealth technologies: Interests, preferences, and concerns of older adults. *Interactive Journal of Medical Research, 6*(1), e3.

Warner, T.D. (2018). Adolescent sexual risk taking: The distribution of youth behaviors and perceived peer attitudes across neighborhood contexts. *Journal of Adolescent Health, 62,* 226–233.

Warr, P. (2004). Work, well-being, and mental health. In J. Baring, E.K. Kelloway, & M.R. Frone (Eds.), *Handbook of work stress.* Thousand Oaks, CA: Sage.

Warren, S.F., & others (2017). The longitudinal effects of parenting on adaptive behavior in children with Fragile X syndrome. *Journal of Autism and Developmental Disorders, 47,* 768–784.

Washington, T.R., & Tachman, J.A. (2017). Gerontological social work student-delivered respite—A community-university partnership pilot program. *Journal of Gerontological Social Work, 60,* 48–67.

Wataganara, T., & others (2016). Fetal magnetic resonance imaging and ultrasound. *Journal of Perinatal Medicine, 44,* 533–542.

Watamura, S.E., Phillips, D.A., Morrissey, D.A., McCartney, T.W., & Bub, K. (2011). Double jeopardy: Poorer social-emotional outcomes for children in the NICHD SECCYD who experience home and child-care environments that convey risk. *Child Development, 82,* 48–65.

Watanabe, E., Lee, J.S., Mori, K., & Kawakubo, K. (2016). Clustering patterns of obesity-related multiple lifestyle behaviors and their associations with overweight and family environments: A cross-sectional study in Japanese preschool children. *BMJ Open, 6* (11), e012773.

Waterman, A.S. (1985). Identity in the context of adolescent psychology. In A.S. Waterman (Ed.), *Identity in adolescence: Processes and contents.* San Francisco: Jossey-Bass.

Waterman, A.S. (1992). Identity as an aspect of optimal psychological functioning. In G.R. Adams, T.P. Gullotta, & R. Montemayor (Eds.), *Adolescent identity formation.* Newbury Park, CA: Sage.

Waterman, E.A., & Lefkowitz, E. (2018). Sexuality. In M.H. Bornstein (Ed.), *SAGE encyclopedia of lifespan human development*. Thousand Oaks, C.A.: Sage.

Watson, G.L., Arcona, A.P., Antonuccio, D.O., & Healy, D. (2014). Shooting the messenger: The case of ADHD. *Journal of Contemporary Psychotherapy, 44*, 43-52.

Watson, J.A., Randolph, S.M., & Lyons, J.L. (2005). African-American grandmothers as health educators in the family. *International Journal of Aging and Human Development, 60*, 343-356.

Watson, V. (2018). *Transformative schooling*. New York: Routledge.

Wattmwar, K., & others (2017). Increases in the rate of age-related hearing loss in the older old. *JAMA Otolaryngology–Head and Neck Surgery, 143*, 41-45.

Waweru-Silka, W., & others (2017). Brain death determination: The imperative for policy and legal initiative in sub-Saharan Africa. *Global Public Health, 12*, 589-600.

Wawrziczny, E., & others (2017). Modeling the distress of spousal caregivers of people with dementia. *Journal of Alzheimer's disease, 55*, 703-716.

Waxman, S., & Goswami, U. (2012). Acquiring language: Learning the spoken and the written word. In S. Pauen & M. Bornstein (Eds.), *Early childhood development and later outcome*. New York: Cambridge University Press.

Weatherhead, D., & White, K.S. (2017). Read my lips: Visual speech influences word processing in infants. *Cognition, 160*, 103-109.

Weaver, J.M., & Schofield, T.J. (2015). Mediation and moderation of divorce effects on children's behavior problems. *Journal of Family Psychology, 29*, 39-48.

Webb, L.D., & Metha, A. (2017). *Foundations of American education* (8th ed.). Upper Saddle River, NJ: Pearson.

Webber, T.A., & others (2017). Neural outcome processing of peer-influenced risk-taking behavior in late adolescence: Preliminary evidence for gene x environment interactions. *Experimental and Clinical Psychopharmacology, 25*, 31-40.

Weber, D., Dekhtyar, S., & Herlitz, A. (2017). The Flynn effect in Europe—effects of sex and region. *Intelligence, 60*, 39-45.

Webster, J.D., & others (2018). Wisdom and meaning in emerging adulthood. *Emerging Adulthood, 6*, 118-136.

Webster, N.S., & Worrell, F.C. (2008). Academically talented students' attitudes toward service in the community. *Gifted Child Quarterly, 52*, 170-179.

Wechsler, H., Davenport, A., Sowdall, G., Moetykens, B., & Castillo, S. (1994). Health and behavioral consequences of binge drinking in college. *Journal of the American Medical Association, 272*, 1672-1677.

Wedell-Neergaard, A.S., & others (2018). Low fitness is associated with abdominal adiposity and low-grade inflammation independent of BMI. *PLoS One, 13*(1), e0190645.

Weersing, V.R., & others (2016). Prevention of depression in at-risk adolescents: Predictors and moderators of acute effects. *Journal of the American Academy of Child and Adolescent Psychiatry, 55*, 219-226.

Weger, H.W., Cole, M., & Akbulut, V. (2018). Relationship maintenance across platonic and non-platonic cross-sex friendships in emerging adults. *Journal of Social Psychology, 13*, 1-15.

Wegmann, M. (2017). "His skin doesn't match what he wants to do": Children's perceptions of stereotype threat. *American Journal of Orthopsychiatry, 87*, 615-625.

Weikert, D.P. (1993). *Long-term positive effects in the Perry Preschool Head Start Program*. Unpublished data. High/Scope Foundation, Ypsilanti, MI.

Weiler, L.M., & Taussig, H.N. (2018, in press). The moderating effect of risk exposure on an efficacious intervention for maltreated children. *Journal of Clinical Child and Adolescent Psychology*.

Weinraub, M., & others (2012). Patterns of developmental change in infants' nighttime sleep awakenings from 6 through 36 months of age. *Developmental Psychology, 48*(6), 1511-1528.

Weisgram, E.S., & Dinella, L.M. (Eds.) (2018). *Gender typing of children's toys*. Washington, DC: APA Books.

Weisleder, A., & others (2018, in press). Reading aloud and child development: A cluster-randomized trial in Brazil. *Pediatrics*.

Weisman, J., & others (2018, in press). Adolescent sexual behavior and emergency department use. *Pediatric Emergency Care*.

Weissenberger, S., & others (2017). ADHD, lifestyles, and comorbidities: A call for an holistic perspective—from medical to societal intervening factors. *Frontiers in Psychology, 8*, 454.

Wellman, H.M. (2015). *Making minds*. New York: Oxford University Press.

Wellman, H.M., Cross, D., & Watson, J. (2001). Meta-analysis of theory-of-mind development: The truth about false belief. *Child Development, 72*, 655-684.

Wellman, R.J., & others (2018). Socioeconomic status is associated with the prevalence and co-occurrence of risk factors for cigarette smoking initiation during adolescence. *International Journal of Public Health, 63*, 125-136.

Wells, E.M., & others (2011). Body burdens of mercury, lead, selenium, and copper among Baltimore newborns. *Environmental Research, 111*, 411-417.

Wendelken, C., Gerrer, E., Whitaker, K.J., & Bunge, S.A. (2016). Fronto-parietal network reconfiguration supports the development of reasoning ability. *Cerebral Cortex, 26*, 2178-2190.

Wendelken, C., & others (2017). Frontoparietal structural connectivity in childhood predicts development of functional connectivity and reasoning ability: A large-scale investigation. *Journal of Neuroscience, 37*, 8549-8558.

Wentzel, K.R., & Miele, D.B. (Eds.) (2016). *Handbook of motivation at school*. New York: Routledge.

Wentzel, K.R., & Ramani, G. (2016). *Social influences on social-emotional, motivational, and cognitive outcomes in school contexts*. New York: Taylor & Francis.

Werenga, L.M., & others (2018). Unraveling age, puberty, and testosterone effects on subcortical brain development across adolescence. *Psychoneuroendocrinology, 91*, 105-114.

Werneck, A.O., Oyeyemi, A.L., & Silva, D.R. (2018, in press). Physical activity and depression: Is 150 min/week of moderate to vigorous physical activity a necessary threshold for decreasing risk of depression in adults? Different views from the same data. *Social Psychiatry and Psychiatric Epidemiology*.

Werner, N.E., & others (2014). Maternal social coaching quality interrupts the development of relational aggression during early childhood. *Social Development, 23*, 470-486.

Wertz, J., & others (2018). From childhood conduct problems to poor functioning at 18 years: Examining explanations in a longitudinal cohort study. *Journal of the American Academy of Child and Adolescent Psychiatry, 57*, 54-60.

Wesche, R., & Lefkowitz, E. (2018, in press). Normative sexual development and milestones. In S. Hupp & J. Jewell (Eds.), *Encyclopedia of child and adolescent development*. New York: Wiley.

Wesche, R., & others (2018, in press). Evaluation and future plans after casual sexual experiences: Differences across partner type. *Journal of Sex Research*.

West, G.L., & others (2017). Playing Super Mario 6 increases hippocampal gray matter in older adults. *PLoS One, 12*(12), e0187779.

Westerhof, G.J. (2009). Age identity. In D. Carr (Ed.), *Encyclopedia of the life course and human development*. Boston: Gale Cengage.

Westermann, G., Thomas, M.S.C., & Karmiloff-Smith, A. (2011). Neuroconstructivism. In U. Goswami (Ed.), *Wiley-Blackwell handbook of childhood cognitive development* (2nd ed.). New York: Wiley.

Westrate, N.M., & Gluck, J. (2017). Hard-earned wisdom: Exploratory processing of difficult life experience is positively associated with wisdom. *Developmental Psychology, 53*, 800-814.

Whaley, S.E., Jiang, L., Gomez, J., & Jenks, E. (2011). Literacy promotion for families participating in the Women, Infants, and Children program. *Pediatrics, 127*, 454-461.

Wheaton, A.G., & others (2018). Short sleep duration among middle school and high school students—United States, 2015, *MMWR Morbidity and Mortality Weekly Reports, 67*(3), 85-90.

Wheeler, L.A., & others (2017). Mexican-origin youth's risk behavior from adolescence to young adulthood: The role of familism values. *Developmental Psychology, 53*, 126-137.

White, C.L., & others (2018). Advancing care for family caregivers of persons with dementia through caregiver and community partnerships. *Research Involvement and Engagement, 4*, 1.

White, E.R., & others (2018, in press). Freshman year alcohol and marijuana use prospectively predict time to college graduation and subsequent adult roles and independence. *Journal of American College Health*.

White, M.J., & others (2017). Calorie restriction attenuates terminal differentiation of immune cells. *Frontiers in Neuroscience, 7*, 667.

White, R.M., & others (2013). Cultural values, U.S. neighborhood danger, and Mexican American parents' parenting. *Journal of Family Psychology, 27*, 365-375.

White, R.M., & others (2018, in press). Ethnic socialization in neighborhood contexts: Implications for ethnic attitude and identity development among Mexican-origin adolescents. *Child Development*.

White, V., & others (2018, in press). Adolescents' alcohol use and strength of policy relating to youth access, trading hours, and driving under the influence: Findings from Australia. *Addiction*.

Whitehead, B.D., & Popenoe, D. (2003). *The state of our unions*. Piscataway, NJ: The National Marriage Project, Rutgers University.

Whitehouse, H. (2018, in press). Dying for the group: Towards a general theory of extreme self-sacrifice. *Behavioral and Brain Science*.

Whiteman, S.D., McHale, S.M., & Soli, A. (2011). Theoretical perspectives on sibling relationships. *Journal of Family Theory and Review, 3*, 124-139.

Whiting, W.L., & Murdock, K.K. (2016). Emerging adults' sleep patterns and attentional capture: Pivotal role of consistency. *Cognitive Processes, 17*, 155-162.

Whitton, S.W., Stanley, S.M., Markman, H.W., & Johnson, C.A. (2013). Attitudes toward divorce, commitment, and divorce proneness in first marriages and remarriages, 75, 276-287.

Wichmann, S., & others (2017). Cortisol stress response in post-traumatic stress disorder, panic disorder, and major depressive disorder patients. *Psychoneuroendocrinology, 83*, 135-141.

Widman, L., Choukas-Bradley, S., Helms, S.W., & Prinstein, M.J. (2016). Adolescent susceptibility to peer influences in sexual situations. *Journal of Adolescent Health, 58*, 323-329.

Widom, C.S., Czaja, S.J., Bentley, T., & Johnson, M.S. (2012). A prospective investigation of physical health outcomes in abused and neglected children: New findings from a 30-year follow-up. *American Journal of Public Health, 102*(6), 1135-1144.

Wiebe, S.A., & Karbach, J. (Eds.) (2018). *Executive function*. New York: Routledge.

Wigfield, A., Rosenzweig, E.Q., & Eccles, J.S. (2017). Achievement values, interactions, interventions, and future directions. In A.J. Elliott, C.S. Dweck, & D.S. Yeager (Eds.), *Handbook of competence and motivation* (2nd ed.). New York: Guilford.

Wigfield, A., Tonks, S.M., & Klauda, S.L. (2016). Expectancy-value theory. In K.R. Wentzel & D.B. Miele (Eds.), *Handbook of motivation at school*. New York: Routledge.

Wigfield, A., & others (2015). Development of achievement motivation and engagement. In R.M. Lerner

(Ed.), *Handbook of child psychology and developmental science* (7th ed.). New York: Wiley.

Wijndaele, K., & others (2017). Mortality risk reductions from substituting screen time by discretionary activities. *Medicine and Science in Sports and Exercise, 49,* 1111–1119.

Wike, R. (2014, January 14). *French more accepting of infidelity than people in other countries.* Washington, DC: Pew Research Center.

Wikman, A., Wardle, J., & Steptoe, A. (2011). Quality of life and affective well-being in middle-aged and older people with chronic medical illnesses: A cross-sectional population based study. *PLoS One, 7,* e18952.

Wilcox, S., & Occhino, C. (2017). Signed languages. In B. Dancygier (Ed.), *Cambridge handbook of cognitive linguistics.* New York: Cambridge University Press.

Willcox, D.C., Scapagnini, G., & Willcox, B.J. (2014). Healthy aging diets other than Mediterranean: A focus on the Okinawan diet. *Mechanisms of Aging and Development, 136–137,* 148–162.

Williams, B.K., Sawyer, S.C., & Wahlstrom, C.M. (2017). *Marriages, families, and intimate relationships* (4th ed.). Upper Saddle River, NJ: Pearson.

Williams, D.P., & others (2018, in press). Stereotype threat, trait preservation, and vagal activity: Evidence for mechanisms underpinning health disparities in Black Americans. *Ethnicity and Health.*

Williams, K.E., & Sciberras, E. (2016). Sleep and self-regulation from birth to 7 years: A retrospective study of children with and without attention-deficit/hyperactivity disorder at 8 to 9 years. *Journal of Developmental and Behavioral Pediatrics. 37,* 331–350.

Williams, R.D., & others (2018). High-risk driving behaviors among 12th-grade students: Differences between alcohol-only and alcohol mixed with energy drink users. *Substance Use and Misuse, 53,* 137–142.

Williamson, D. (2013). Of years of love, and a long goodbye. Retrieved from www.telegram.com/article/20130929/COLUMN01/309299933

Williamson, J.B., & Beland, D. (2016). The future of retirement security in comparative perspective. In L.K. George & K.F. Ferraro (Eds.), *Handbook of aging and the social sciences* (8th ed.). New York: Elsevier.

Willis, S.L., & Belleville, S. (2016). Cognitive training in later adulthood. In K.W. Schaie & S.L. Willis (Eds.), *Handbook of the psychology of aging* (8th ed.). New York: Elsevier.

Willoughby, B.J., & James, S.L. (2017). *The marriage paradox.* New York: Oxford University Press.

Willoughby, B.J., Hall, S.S., & Goff, S. (2015). Marriage matters, but how much? Marital centrality among young adults. *Journal of Psychology, 149,* 796–817.

Willoughby, M.T., & others (2016). Developmental delays in executive function from 3 to 5 years of age predict kindergarten academic readiness. *Journal of Learning Disabilities, 50,* 359–372.

Willoughby, M.T., Gottfredson, N.C., & Stifter, C.A. (2017). Observed temperament from ages 6 to 36 months predicts parent- and teacher-reported attention deficit/hyperactivity disorder symptoms in first grade. *Development and Psychopathology, 29,* 107–120.

Wilson, D.M., & others (2013). The preferred place of last days: Results of a representative population-based survey. *Journal of Palliative Medicine, 16,* 502–508.

Wilson, G., & Roscigno, V.J. (2018). Race, ageism, and the slide from privileged occupations. *Social Science Research, 69,* 52–64.

Wilson, M.N., & others (2018, in press). Driving under the influence behaviors among high school students who mix alcohol with energy drinks. *Preventive Medicine.*

Wilson, R.S., & others (2015). Conscientiousness, dementia-related pathology, and trajectories of cognitive aging. *Psychology and Aging, 30,* 74–82.

Wilson, R.S., & others (2018, in press). Terminal decline of episodic memory and perceptual speed in a biracial population. *Neuropsychology, Development, and Cognition B: Aging, Neuropsychology, and Cognition.*

Wilson, S.F., & others (2017). Doulas for surgical management of miscarriage and abortion: A randomized controlled trial. *American Journal of Obstetrics and Gynecology, 216,* e1–e44.

Wilson, S.H., & others (2018). Labor analgesia onset with dural puncture epidural versus traditional epidural using a 26-gauge Whitacre needle and 0.125 bupivacaine bolus: A randomized clinical trial. *Anesthesia and Analgesia, 126,* 545–551.

Windle, W.F. (1940). *Physiology of the humantus.* Philadelphia: W.B. Saunders.

Wink, P., & Dillon, M. (2002). Spiritual development across the adult life course: Findings from a longitudinal study. *Journal of Adult Development, 9,* 79–94.

Winne, P.H. (2018). Cognition and metacognition within self-regulated learning. In D.H. Schunk & J.A. Greene (Eds.), *Handbook of self-regulation of learning and performance* (2nd ed.). New York: Cambridge University Press.

Winner, E. (1996). *Gifted children: Myths and realities.* New York: Basic Books.

Winner, E. (2009). Toward broadening our understanding of giftedness: The spatial domain. In F.D. Horowitz, R.F. Subotnik, & D.J. Matthews (Eds.), *The development of giftedness and talent across the life span.* Washington, DC: American Psychological Association.

Winsler, A., Carlton, M.P., & Barry, M.J. (2000). Age-related changes in preschool children's systematic use of private speech in a natural setting. *Journal of Child Language, 27,* 665–687.

Winsper, C., Lereya, T., Zanarini, M., & Wolke, D. (2012). Involvement in bullying and suicide-related behavior at 11 years: A prospective birth cohort study. *Journal of the Academy of Child and Adolescent Psychiatry, 51,* 271–282.

Wise, P.H. (2017). Palliative care doctors should be included in treatment discussions. *BMJ, 356,* 1551.

Wise, P.M. (2006). Aging of the female reproductive system. In E.J. Masoro & S.N. Austad (Eds.), *Handbook of the biology of aging* (6th ed.). San Diego: Academic Press.

Witherington, D.C., Campos, J.J., Harriger, J.A., Bryan, C., & Margett, T.E. (2010). Emotion and its development in infancy. In J.G. Bremner & T.D. Wachs (Eds.), *Wiley-Blackwell handbook of infant development* (2nd ed.). New York: Wiley.

Withers, M., Kharazmi, N., & Lim, E. (2018). Traditional beliefs and practices in pregnancy, childbirth, and postpartum: A review of the evidence from Asian countries. *Midwifery, 56,* 158–170.

Witkin, H.A., & others (1976). Criminality in XYY and XXY men. *Science, 193,* 547–555.

Witkow, M.R., Rickert, N.P., & Cullen, L.E. (2017). Daily school context of adolescents' single best friendship and adjustment. *Journal of Genetic Psychology, 178,* 119–132.

Witte, A.V., & others (2014). Long-chain omega-3 fatty acids improve brain function and structure in older adults. *Cerebral Cortex, 24,* 3059–3068.

Wittig, S.L., & Spatz, D.L. (2008). Induced lactation: Gaining a better understanding. *MCN: The Journal of Maternal Child Nursing, 33,* 76–81.

Wojcicki, J.M. (2017). Time to consider moving beyond exclusive breastfeeding in Southern Africa. *Children, 4,* 1.

Wojcik, M., & Helka, A.M. (2018, in press). Meeting the needs of young adolescents: ABBL anti-bullying program during middle school transition. *Psychological Reports.*

Wolfe, K.L., & others (2018, in press). Hopelessness as a predictor of suicide ideation in depressed male and female adolescent youth. *Suicide and Life-Threatening Behavior.*

Wolff, J.L., Mulcahy, J., Huang, J., Roth, D.L., Covinsky, K., & Kasper, J.D. (2018, in press). Family caregivers of older adults, 1999–2015: Trends in characteristics, circumstances, and role-related appraisal. *Gerontologist.*

Wolford, E., & others (2017). Maternal depressive symptoms during and after pregnancy associated with attention-deficit/hyperactivity disorder symptoms in their 3- to 6-year-old children. *PLoS One, 12,* e0190248.

Wolke, D., & Lereya, S.T. (2015). Long-term effects of bullying. *Archives of Disease in Childhood, 100,* 879–885.

Wolke, D., Lee, K., & Guy, A. (2017). Cyberbullying: A storm in a teacup? *European Child and Adolescent Psychiatry, 26,* 899–908.

Wolters, F.J., & others (2018, in press). Coronary heart disease, heart failure, and the risk of dementia: A systematic review and meta-analysis. *Alzheimer's and Dementia.*

Wombacher, K., & others (2018, in press). "It just kind of happens": College students' rationalizations for blackout drinking. *Health Communication.*

Wood, J.G., & others (2018). Sirt4 is a mitochondrial regulator of metabolism and lifespan in drosophila melanogaster. *Proceedings of the National Academy of Sciences USA, 115,* 1564–1589.

Woodhouse, S.S. (2018, in press). Attachment-based interventions for families with young children. *Journal of Clinical Psychology.*

Woodhouse, S.S., & others (2017). The Circle of Security intervention: Design, research, and intervention. In H. Steele & M. Steele (Eds.), *Handbook of attachment-based interventions.* New York: Guilford.

Woods, B., & others (2018). Reminiscence therapy for dementia. *Cochrane Database of Systematic Reviews, 3,* CD001120.

World Health Organization (2018). *Adolescent pregnancy: Fact sheet.* Geneva, Switzerland: World Health Organization.

Woyka, J. (2017). Consensus statement for non-hormonal-based treatments for menopausal symptoms. *Post Reproductive Health, 23,* 71–75.

Wright, H., Jenks, R.A., & Demeyere, N. (2018, in press). Frequent sexual activity predicts specific cognitive abilities in older adults. *Journals of Gerontology B: Psychological Sciences & Social Sciences.*

Wright, M.R., & Brown, S.L. (2017). Psychological well-being among older adults: The role of partnership status. *Journal of Marriage and the Family, 79,* 833–849.

Wu, D., & others (2018, in press). Verbal responses, depressive symptoms, reminiscence functions, and cognitive emotion in older women receiving individual reminiscence therapy. *Journal of Clinical Nursing.*

Wu, R., & Scerif, G. (2018). Attention. In M.H. Bornstein (Ed.), *SAGE encyclopedia of lifespan human development.* Thousand Oaks, CA: Sage.

Wu, T., Gao, X., Chen, M., & van Dam, R.M. (2009). Long-term effectiveness of diet-plus-exercise interventions vs. diet-only interventions for weight loss: A meta-analysis. *Obesity, 10,* 313–323.

Wu, Z., Schimmele, C.M., & Quellet, N. (2015). Repartnering after widowhood. *Journal of Gerontology B: Psychological Sciences and Social Sciences, 70,* 496–507.

X

Xaverius, P., Alman, C., Holtz, L., & Yarber, L. (2016). Risk factors associated with very low birth weight in a large urban area, stratified by adequacy of prenatal care. *Maternal and Child Health Journal, 20,* 623–629.

Xiao, J., & others (2018). Sarcopenic obesity and health outcomes in patients seeking weight loss treatment. *Clinical Nutrition ESPEN, 23,* 79–83.

Xiao, J., & others (2017). The role of exosomes in the pathogenesis of Alzheimer's disease. *Translational Neurodegeneration, 6,* 3.

Xie, W., Mallin, B.M., & Richards, J.E. (2018, in press). Development of infant sustained attention and its relation to EEG oscillations: An EEG and cortical course analysis study. *Developmental Science.*

Xing, Y.Q., & others (2018). The regulation of FOXO1 and its role in disease progression. *Life Sciences, 193,* 124–131.

Xu, H., Wen, L.M., & Rissel, C. (2014). Associations of maternal influences with outdoor play and screen time of two-year-olds: Findings from the Healthy Beginnings trial. *Journal of Pediatrics and Child Health, 50,* 680-686.

Xu, H., Wen, L.M., Hardy, L.L., & Rissel, C. (2016). Associations of outdoor play and screen time with nocturnal sleep duration and pattern among young children. *Acta Paediatrica, 105,* 297-303.

Xu, J. (2016). Mortality among centenarians in the United States, 2000-2014. *NCHS Data Brief, 233,* 1-8.

Xu, W., & others (2015). Meta-analysis of modifiable risk factors for Alzheimer's disease. *Journal of Neurology, Neurosurgery, and Psychiatry, 86,* 1299-1306.

Xue, F., Holzman, C., Rahbar, M.H., Trosko, K., & Fischer, L. (2007). Maternal fish consumption, mercury levels, and risk of preterm delivery. *Environmental Health Perspectives, 115,* 42-47.

Y

Yackobovitch-Gavan, M., & others (2018, in press). Intervention for childhood obesity based on parents only or parents and child compared with follow-up alone. *Pediatric Obesity.*

Yakoboski, P.J. (2011). Worries and plans as individuals approach retirement. *Benefits Quarterly, 27,* 34-37.

Yan, H., & others (2017). Associations among screen time and unhealthy behaviors, academic performance, and well-being in Chinese-American adolescents. *International Journal of Environmental Research and Public Health, 14,* 6.

Yan, H., & others (2018, in press). Exercise effects on adipose tissue postprandial lipolysis and blood flow in children. *Medicine and Science in Sports and Exercise.*

Yan, Z. (2018, in press). Child and adolescent use of mobile phones: An unparalleled complex developmental phenomenon. *Child Development.*

Yanai, H., & others (2017). Wide-scale comparative analysis of longevity genes and interventions. *Aging Cell, 16,* 1267-1275.

Yang, B., Ren, B.X., & Tang, F.R. (2017). Prenatal irradiation-induced brain neuropathy and cognitive impairment. *Brain Development, 39,* 10-22.

Yang, Y. (2008). Social inequalities in happiness in the United States, 1972-2004: An age-period-cohort analysis. *American Sociological Review, 73,* 204-226.

Yang, Y., & Kozloski, M. (2011). Sex differences in age trajectories of physiological deregulation: Inflammation, metabolic syndrome, and allostatic load. *Journals of Gerontology A: Biological Sciences and Medical Sciences, 66A,* 493-500.

Yang, Y.X., & others (2017). Validity of estimating muscle and fat volume from a single fMRI section in older adults with sarcopenia and sarcopenic obesity. *Clinical Radiology, 72,* e9-e14.

Yaniv-Salem, S., & others (2016). Obesity in pregnancy: What's next? Long-term cardiovascular morbidity in a follow-up period of more than a decade. *Journal of Maternal-Fetal and Neonatal Medicine, 29,* 619-623.

Yanovski, S.Z., & Yanovski, J.A. (2018). Toward precision approaches for the prevention and treatment of obesity. *JAMA, 319,* 223-224.

Yap, M.B., & others (2017). Modifiable parenting factors associated with adolescent alcohol misuse: A systematic review and meta-analysis of longitudinal studies. *Addiction, 112,* 1142-1162.

Yasukochi, Y., & others (2018, in press). Identification of three genetic variants as novel susceptibility loci for body mass index in a Japanese population. *Physiological Genomics.*

Yau, J.C., & Reich, S.M. (2018, in press). "It's just a lot of work": Adolescents' self-presentation norms and practices on Facebook and Instagram. *Journal of Research on Adolescence.*

Yavorsky, J.E., Dush, C.M., & Schoppe-Sullivan, S.J. (2015). The production of inequality: The gender division of labor across the transition to parenthood. *Journal of Marriage and the Family, 77,* 662-679.

Yazigi, A., & others (2017). Fetal and neonatal abnormalities due to congenital rubella syndrome: A review of the literature. *Journal of Maternal-Fetal and Neonatal Medicine, 30,* 274-278.

Yen, H.Y., & Lin, L.J. (2018). A systematic review of reminiscence therapy for older adults in Taiwan. *Journal of Nursing Research, 26,* 138-150.

Yen, Y.F., & others (2018). Association of advance directives completion with the utilization of life-sustaining treatments during end-of-life care in older patients. *Journal of Pain and Symptom Management, 55,* 265-271.

Yeon, S., Bae, H.S., & Joshi, M. (2017). Cross-language transfer of metalinguistic skills: Evidence from spelling English words by Korean students in grades 4, 5, and 6. *Dyslexia, 23,* 428-448.

Yin, H., & others (2018). Relationship of polymorphisms and haplotype in interleukin-16 and adiponectin gene with late-onset Alzheimer's disease risk. *Oncotarget, 8,* 79157-79164.

Yip, D.K., & others (2018, in press). A network approach to exploring the functional basis of gene-gene epistatic interactions in disease susceptibility. *Bioinformatics.*

Yip, P.S., & others (2015). The roles of culture and gender in the relationship between divorce and suicide risk: A meta-analysis. *Social Science and Medicine, 138,* 87-94.

Yolton, K., & others (2010). Associations between secondhand smoke exposure and sleep patterns in children. *Pediatrics, 125,* e261-e268.

Yoo, J., Kim, Y., Cho, E.R., & Jee, S.H. (2017). Biological age as a useful index to predict seventeen-year survival and mortality in Koreans. *BMC Geriatrics, 17*(1), 7.

Yoo, K.B., & others (2016). Association between employment status change and depression in Korean adults. *BMJ Open, 6*(3), e008570.

Yoon, E., & others (2017). East Asian adolescents' ethnic identity and cultural integration: A qualitative investigation. *Journal of Counseling Psychology, 64,* 65-79.

Yoon, S.H., & others (2015). Correlates of self-reported sleep duration in middle-aged and elderly Koreans: From the Health Examinees Study. *PLoS One, 10*(5), e0123510.

Yoshikawa, H., & others (2017). New directions in developmentally informed intervention research for vulnerable populations. *Child Development, 88,* 459-465.

Young, D.R., & others (2018, in press). Associations of overweight/obesity and socioeconomic status with hypertension prevalence across racial and economic groups. *Journal of Clinical Hypertension.*

Young, K.T. (1990). American conceptions of infant development from 1955 to 1984: What the experts are telling parents. *Child Development, 61,* 17-28.

Youyou, W., & others (2017). Birds of a feather do flock together. *Psychological Science, 28,* 276-284.

Yow, W.Q., & others (2018, in press). A bilingual advantage in 54-month-olds' use of referential cues in fast mapping. *Developmental Science.*

Yu, C., & Smith, L.B. (2016). The social origins of sustained attention in one-year-old humans. *Current Biology, 26,* 1235-1240.

Yu, C., & Smith, L.B. (2017). Hand-eye coordination predicts joint attention. *Child Development, 88,* 2060-2078.

Yu, C.Y., & others (2012). Prenatal predictors for father-infant attachment after childbirth. *Journal of Clinical Nursing, 49,* 127-137.

Yu, J., Wu, Y., & Yang, P. (2016). High glucose-induced oxidative stress represses sirtuin deacetylase expression and increases histone acetylation leading to neural tube defects. *Journal of Neurochemistry, 137,* 371-383.

Yu, S., & Hu, G. (2017). Can higher-proficiency L2 learners benefit from working with lower-proficiency partners in peer feedback? *Teaching in Higher Education, 22,* 178-192.

Yu, S., & others (2018). Emerging technologies for home-based semen analysis. *Andrology, 6,* 10-19.

Yu, T., & others (2018, in press). Impact of stressful life events on patients with chronic obstructive pulmonary disease. *Respiration.*

Yuan, B., & others (2017). Autism-related protein MeCP2 regulates FGF13 expression and emotional behaviors. *Journal of Genetics and Genomics, 44,* 63-66.

Z

Zabaneh, D., & others (2017). Fine mapping genetic associations between the HLA region and extremely high intelligence. *Scientific Reports, 7,* 41182.

Zachrisson, H.D., Lekhal, R., Dearing, E., & Toppelberg, C.O. (2013). Little evidence that time in child care causes externalizing problems during early childhood in Norway. *Child Development, 84*(4), 1152-1170.

Zaghloul, S.B., & others (2018). Deep molecular phenotypes link complex disorders and physiological insult to CpG methylation. *Human Molecular Genetics, 27,* 1106-1121.

Zalzali, H., & others (2018, in press). Interplay between p53 and Ink4c in spermatogenesis and fertility. *Cell Cycle.*

Zammit, A.R., & others (2018, in press). Identification of heterogeneous cognitive subgroups in community-dwelling older adults: A latent class analysis of the Einstein Aging Study. *Journal of the International Neuropsychology Society.*

Zamuner, T., Fais, L., & Werker, J.F. (2014). Infants track words in early word-object associations. *Developmental Science, 17,* 481-491.

Zannas, A.S., & others (2012). Stressful life events, perceived stress, and 12-month course of geriatric depression: Direct effects and moderation by the 5-HTTLPR and COMT Val158Met polymorphisms. *Stress, 15*(4), 425-434.

Zanolie, K., & Crone, E.A. (2018, in press). Development of cognitive control across childhood and adolescence. In J. Wixsted (Ed.), *Stevens' handbook of experimental psychology and cognitive neuroscience* (5th ed.). New York: Wiley.

Zanto, T.P., & Gazzaley, A. (2017). Selective attention and inhibitory control in the aging brain. In R. Cabeza, L. Nyberg, & D.C. Park (Eds.), *Cognitive neuroscience and aging* (2nd ed.). New York: Oxford University Press.

Zeifman, D., & Hazan, C. (2008). Pair bonds as attachments: Reevaluating the evidence. In J. Cassidy & P.R. Shaver (Eds.), *Handbook of attachment* (2nd ed.). New York: Guilford.

Zeifman, D.M., & St. James-Roberts, I. (2017). Parenting the crying infant. *Current Opinion in Psychology, 15,* 149-154.

Zelazo, P.D. (2013). Developmental psychology: A new synthesis. In P.D. Zelazo (Ed.), *Oxford handbook of developmental psychology.* New York: Oxford University Press.

Zelazo, P.D., & Muller, U. (2011). Executive function in typical and atypical children. In U. Goswami (Ed.), *Wiley-Blackwell handbook of childhood cognitive development* (2nd ed.). New York: Wiley.

Zeskind, P.S., Klein, L., & Marshall, T.R. (1992). Adults' perceptions of experimental modifications of durations and expiratory sounds in infant crying. *Developmental Psychology, 28,* 1153-1162.

Zettel-Watson, L., & others (2017). Aging well: Processing speed inhibition and working memory related to balance and aerobic endurance. *Geriatrics and Gerontology International, 17,* 108-115.

Zgheib, N.K., & others (2018). Short telomere length is associated with aging, central obesity, poor sleep, and hypertension in Lebanese individuals. *Aging and Disease, 9,* 77-89.

Zhang, D., & others (2017). Is maternal smoking during pregnancy associated with an increased risk of congenital heart defects among offspring? A systematic review and meta-analysis of observational studies. *Journal of Maternal-Fetal and Neonatal Medicine, 30,* 645–657.

Zhang, J., & others (2017). Sleep patterns and mental health correlates in U.S. adolescents. *Journal of Pediatrics, 182,* 137–143.

Zhang, M., & others (2015). Cognitive function in older adults according to current socioeconomic status. *Neuropsychology, Development, and Cognition B: Aging, Neuropsychology, and Cognition, 22,* 534–543.

Zhang, M.W., & Ho, R.C. (2017). Personalized reminiscence therapy M-health application for patients living with dementia: Innovating using open source code repository. *Technology and Health Care, 25,* 153–156.

Zhang, Q., & others (2017). Stem cells for modeling and therapy of Parkinson's disease. *Human Gene Therapy, 28,* 85–98.

Zhang, S., & others (2018, in press). Intra- and inter-individual differences in adolescent depressive mood: The role of relationships with parents and friends. *Journal of Abnormal Child Psychology.*

Zhang, W., & others (2017). Reconsidering parenting in Chinese culture: Subtypes, stability, and change of maternal parenting style during early adolescence. *Journal of Youth and Adolescence, 46,* 1117–1136.

Zhang, X., & others (2018). Transplacental transfer characteristics of organochlorine pesticides in paired maternal and cord sera, and placentas and possible influencing factors. *Environmental Pollution, 233,* 446–454.

Zhang, X.C., & others (2018, in press). Do health-related factors predict major depression? A longitudinal epidemiologic study. *Clinical Psychology and Psychotherapy.*

Zhang, Y., & others (2016). A cross-cultural comparison of climacteric symptoms, self-esteem, and perceived social support between Mosuo women and Han Chinese women. *Menopause, 23,* 784–791.

Zhang, Y., & others (2017). Cross-cultural consistency and diversity in intrinsic functional organization of Broca's region. *NeuroImage, 150,* 177–190.

Zhang, Y., & others (2018, in press). Enriched environment promotes post-stroke neurogenesis through NF-kB mediated secretion of IL-17A from astrocytes. *Brain Research.*

Zhang, Z. (2018, in press). Outdoor activity, depression, and subjective well-being among retirees of China: The mediating role of meaning in life. *Journal of Health Psychology.*

Zheng, B., & others (2017). Selenomethionine promoted hippocampal neurogenesis via the P13K-Akt-GSK3*B*-Wnt pathway in a mouse model of Alzheimer's disease. *Biochemical and Biophysical Research Communications, 485,* 6–15.

Zheng, Y., & others (2017). Associations of weight gain from early to middle adulthood with major health outcomes later in life. *JAMA, 318,* 255–269.

Zhou, Q. (2013). Commentary in S. Smith, "Children of "tiger parents" develop more aggression and depression, research shows." Retrieved July 20, 2013, from http://www.cbsnews.com/news/children-of-tiger-parents-develop-more-aggression-and-depression-research-shows/

Zhou, Q., & others (2013). Asset and protective factors for Asian American children's mental health adjustment. *Child Development Perspectives, 6,* 312–319.

Zhou, Q., Fan, L., & Yin, Z. (2017). Association between family socioeconomic status and depressive symptoms among Chinese adolescents: Evidence from a national household survey. *Psychiatry Research, 259,* 81–88.

Zhou, Y., & others (2017). Big Five personality and adolescent Internet addiction: The mediating role of coping style. *Addictive Behaviors, 64,* 42–48.

Zhou, Y., & others (2017). Prevalence of overweight and obesity in Chinese children and adolescents from 2015. *Annals of Human Biology, 44,* 642–643.

Zhou, Y., & others (2018, in press). Weight changes since age 20 and cardiovascular risk factors in a middle-aged Chinese population. *Journal of Public Health.*

Zhou, Z., & others (2017). CXCR4 antagonist AMD3100 reverses the neurogenesis promoted by

enriched environment and suppresses long-term seizure activity in adult rats of temporal lobe epilepsy. *Behavioral Brain Research, 322*(Pt. A), 83–91.

Zhou, Z., & others (2018). The C-terminal tails of endogenous GluA1 and GluA2 differentially contribute to hippocampal synaptic plasticity and learning. *Nature Neuroscience, 21,* 50–62.

Zhou, Z., & others (2018, in press). Pold3 is required for genomic stability and telomere integrity in embryonic stem cells and meiosis. *Nucleic Acids Research.*

Zhu, Y., & others (2017). Probing impaired neurogenesis in human brain organoids exposed to alcohol. *Integrative Biology, 9,* 968–978.

Zhu, Z., & others (2018). Causal associations between risk factors and common diseases inferred from GWAS summary data. *Nature Communications, 9*(1), 224.

Ziegler, D.A., Janowich, J.R., & Gazzaley, A. (2018). Differential impact of interference on internally- and externally-directed attention. *Scientific Reports, 8*(1), 2498.

Ziermans, T., & others (2017). Formal thought disorder and executive functioning in children and adolescents with autism spectrum disorder: Old leads and new avenues. *Journal of Autism and Developmental Disorders, 47,* 1756–1768.

Zigler, E.F., Gilliam, W.S., & Barnett, W.S. (Eds.) (2011). *The pre-K debates: Controversies and issues.* Baltimore: Paul H. Brookes.

Zigler, E.F., Gilliam, W.S., & Jones, S.M. (2006). *A vision for universal preschool education.* New York: Cambridge University Press.

Zole, E., & Ranka, R. (2018, in press). Mitochondria, its DNA, and telomeres in aging and human population. *Biogerontology.*

Zozuls, K., & others (2016). Developmental changes in the link between gender typicality and peer victimization and exclusion. *Sex Roles, 75,* 243–256.

Zucker, K.J., Lawrence, A.A., & Kreukels, B.P. (2016). Gender dysforia in adults. *Annual Review of Psychology, 12,* 217–247.

Homan, K. J., 417
Hong, S. M., 311
Hong, X., 385
Honzik, M., 311
Hoogenhout, M., 159
Hook, P. E., 202
Hooley, M., 267
Hooper, S. Y., 253
Hoover, J., 173, 234
Hope, D. A., 338
Hope, D. A. M., 315
Hopping-Winn, J., 425
Hoppmann, C. A., 345
Hopwood, C. J., 298
Horgusluoglu, E., 385
Horissian, M., 271
Horn, J. L., 354
Horn, M. C., 367
Hornby, T. G., 387
Horne, R. S. C., 83
Hornick, J. L., 44
Horowitz-Kraus, T., 200
Horwood, J. L., 303
Hosie, A., 426
Hoskin, J., 115
Hoskyn, M. J., 156
Hotta, R., 396
Hou, L., 392
Hou, Y., 8, 290, 297
Houssaini, A., 383
Houwing, F. L., 172
Howard, A. L., 271
Howard, J., 46
Howard, K. S., 74
Howard, M. M., 74
Howard, S., 418
Howard, S. R., 259
Howe, G. W., 323
Howe, M. J. A., 220
Howe, M. L., 124
Howell, D. C., 31
Howell, K. H., 431
Howes, C., 136
Howley, E., 143, 145, 199, 269, 311
Hoyer, W. J., 13, 348, 357, 358, 384, 386, 388
Hoyt, J., 212
Hoyt, L. T., 270
Hritz, A., 155, 156
Hsieh, H. H., 321
Hsin, A., 251
Hsueh, A. J., 258
Hu, G., 150, 152
Hua, J., 96
Hua, L., 44
Huang, C. J., 204
Huang, E., 398
Huang, J. T., 321
Huang, J-H., 312
Huang, K. Y., 177
Huang, L., 59, 65
Huang, L. B., 46, 434
Huang, Y., 101
Huckle, W. R., 52
Huda, S. S., 62
Hudson, A., 171
Hudson, J. L., 172
Hudson, N. W., 129
Hudson, R. B., 414
Hudziak, J., 210
Huelsnitz, C. O., 328
Huesmann, L. R., 242
Huestegge, L., 298
Huffman, J. C., 370
Huffman, L., 413
Hughes, A. C., 131
Hughes, C., 158, 159, 170, 171, 184

Hughes, E. K., 273
Hughes, J. C., 426
Hughes, J. E., 298
Hughes, J. N., 278
Hughes, M., 335
Hui, L., 56
Hull, S. H., 238
Huo, M., 374, 375, 417
Huppi, P. S., 55
Hur, Y. I., 311
Hurd, Y. L., 49
Hurley, K. M., 85, 144
Hurrell, K. E., 172
Hurst, S. A., 426
Hustedt, J. T., 164
Huston, A. C., 239
Huston, T. L., 340
Huttenlocher, P. R., 80, 81, 260
Hutton, J. S., 200
Huyck, M. H., 358
Huynh, V. W., 270
Hyde, J. S., 39, 235–238, 262, 315, 333, 342
Hymel, S., 244
Hyson, M. C., 163

I

Iarocci, G., 156
Igarashi, H., 376
Ihara, M., 405
Ihle, A., 359
Ihongbe, T. O., 263
Ilmakunnas, P., 403
Ilmakunnas, S., 403
Im, Y., 303
Inderkum, A. P., 47
Inhelder, B., 147
Inker, J., 413
Insel, P., 145, 200, 268, 311
Ironson, G., 360
Isgut, M., 62, 63
Ishi, R., 385
Ishtiak-Ahmed, K., 33
Isidori, A. M., 390
Islam, B. U., 404
Ismaeel, N., 353
Ismail, F. Y., 80
Israel, M., 106
Ito-Jager, S., 102
Iverson, S. L., 117
Ivey-Stephenson, A. Z., 302
Iwata, S., 71

J

Jabeen, H., 25, 383
Jacher, J. E., 46
Jackman, H., 163
Jackson, A. D., 67
Jackson, J. J., 145, 413
Jackson, J. R., 64
Jackson, W. M., 199
Jacobs, J. M., 398
Jacobson, S. W., 58
Jacoby, N., 30
Jacques, S., 171
Jadhav, A., 433, 434
JafariNasabian, P., 387, 391
Jaffee, S., 235
Jaffee, S. R., 260
Jager, J., 289
Jakobsen, I. S., 303
Jambon, M., 235, 236
James, S. L., 335
Jamison, L. E., 431

Jang, S., 8
Jankowski, J. J., 155
Jannini, E. A., 353
Janowich, J. R., 394
Jansen, E. C., 259
Jansen, J., 84
Janssen, I., 145
Janssen, J. A., 119
Janssens, A., 242
Jantz, T. K., 401
Janz, K. F., 269
Jaramillo, N., 267
Jardri, R., 95
Jaremka, L. M., 351
Jarris, P. E., 64
Jaruatanasirikul, S., 63
Jasinska, K. K., 223
Jasiulionis, M. G., 384
Jaul, E., 392
Jauniaux, E., 52
Jaworska, N., 269
Jayawickreme, E., 256
Jee, S. H., 384
Jeka, J., 86
Jenks, R. A., 354
Jenni, O. G., 270
Jennifer, R. E., 10
Jennings, S. L., 123
Jensen, H., 387
Jensen, L. A., 306
Jensen, M. M., 385
Jensen, T. M., 241
Jeong, K. S., 62
Jeong, Y., 52
Jeremic, S., 25, 383
Jha, A. K., 414
Ji, G., 185
Ji, J., 30
Jia, G., 348
Jia, H., 5
Jia, R., 181
Jiang, N., 256, 387
Jiang, Y., 9
Jiang, Z., 115
Jiao, S., 185
Jin, I., 100
Jing, Q., 185
Jirstrom, K., 352
Johansson, M., 211
John, A., 303
John, O. P., 372, 373
Johnson, D. R., 372
Johnson, J. A., 246
Johnson, J. A., 246, 388
Johnson, J. S., 223
Johnson, M. D., 16, 37, 40, 42, 424
Johnson, M. H., 101, 199, 223, 261, 262
Johnson, M. L., 78
Johnson, P., 115–117, 131
Johnson, R. A., 392
Johnson, S. P., 94, 98, 275
Johnston, C., 71
Johnston, J., 204
Johnionis, L. D., 271, 272, 312
Johnston, M. V., 80
Joling, K. J., 16
Jolly, C. A., 392
Jones, A. P., 46
Jones, C. R. G., 159, 205
Jones, D. G., 428
Jones, E., 140
Jones, E. J. H., 96, 102
Jones, J., 163
Jones, K. L., 58
Jones, M. C., 259
Jones, T. H., 353, 390

Jonsson, E., 58
Jorch, G., 83
Jorgensen, M. J., 264
Jose, A., 334
Joshi, H., 230
Joshi, M., 222
Josselson, R., 285
Jouffre, S., 425, 426
Joyner, C., 398
Juang, C., 410
Juang, L., 5, 8, 122, 130, 189, 294
Juang, L. P., 285
Judd, F. K., 352
Juhasz, A., 406
Julvez, J., 62
Jung, C., 346
Jung, E. Y., 55, 329
Jung, W. P., 91
Juraska, J. M., 80, 142, 260
Jusczyk, P. W., 96, 108
Jutengren, G., 244

K

Kader, F., 41, 405
Kadosh, K. C., 242, 302
Kagan, J., 116, 117, 119–122, 130
Kagan, J. J., 118
Kahana, B., 421
Kahana, E., 421
Kahlbaugh, P., 413
Kahn, N. F., 263
Kahrs, B. A., 91
Kail, B. L., 419
Kalashnikova, M., 50
Kalat, J. W., 17
Kalish, C. W., 160
Kalish, R. A., 431
Kalmijn, M., 375
Kalsi, D. S., 383
Kalstabakken, A. W., 10, 231, 232
Kalyango, Y., 259
Kamal, M. A., 404
Kambas, A., 143
Kammer, T., 109
Kanazawa, S., 102
Kancherla, V., 62
Kandemir, N., 145
Kandler, C., 319
Kane, R. L., 10
Kanesarajah, J., 349
Kang, J. Y., 224
Kang, X., 56
Kann, L., 262–264, 269, 270, 302
Kanniyakonil, S., 425
Kansky, J., 16
Kantoch, A., 389
Kantrowitz, B., 168
Kaplan, R. M., 29
Karbach, J., 276
Karmel, M. P., 124
Karmiloff-Smith, A., 82
Karoly, L. A., 166
Karreman, A., 181
Karthivashan, G., 404
Kaseva, N., 61
Kashdan, T. B., 315
Kastenbaum, R. J., 429, 430
Kato, T., 71
Katsiaficas, D., 308
Katz, B., 396
Katz, L., 165
Katz, R., 417
Katz-Wise, S. L., 343
Kauffman, J. M., 7, 203, 206
Kaufman, J. C., 211, 219, 220

Kaufman, S. B., 319, 369
Kaunhoven, R. J., 116
Kauppila, J. H., 25
Kauppila, T. E., 25
Kauser, R., 179
Kavanaugh, R. D., 147, 159
Kavosi, Z., 68
Kavsek, M., 102
Kawakita, T., 63
Kazdin, A. E., 34
Kearsley, R. B., 118
Keating, D. P., 277
Keen, R., 91, 93
Keener, E., 343
Keim, M. C., 432
Keles, S., 367
Keller, A., 170
Keller, H., 130
Kelley, C. P., 347
Kelley-Moore, J., 351
Kelly, C., 160
Kelly, D. M., 353, 390
Kelly, J., 241, 341
Kelly, J. P., 94
Kelly, M. T., 74
Kelson, E., 414
Keltner, K. W., 252
Kemmler, W., 391
Kemner, C., 115
Kemp, J., 388
Kempermann, G., 385
Kempner, S. G., 252
Kendig, H. L., 10
Kendler, K. S., 48, 272, 337
Kendrick, C., 185
Kendrick, K., 244
Kennedy, B. K., 392
Kennedy, K. M., 384, 385, 400
Kennell, J. H., 72
Kenny, L. C., 265
Kenny, S., 94
Kerns, K. A., 240, 294
Kerse, N., 5
Kershaw, K. N., 366
Kerstis, B., 74, 288
Ketcham, P., 268
Keunen, K., 54
Khalsa, A. S., 145
Kharasch, S., 84
Kharazmi, N., 68
Kharitonova, M., 209
Khashan, A. S., 265
Khatun, M., 265
Khoury, J. E., 58
Khundrakpam, B. S., 198
Kiang, L., 287
Kida, Y., 383
Kiecolt-Glaser, J. K., 351
Kiess, W., 257, 259
Kilic, A., 396
Kilic, S., 59
Killen, M., 173, 234, 235
Kilwein, T. M., 311
Kim, A. S., 393
Kim, B. R., 130, 263, 350
Kim, E. M., 252
Kim, E. S., 370
Kim, G. R., 384
Kim, J., 300
Kim, J. I., 7, 41, 64, 297
Kim, J. M., 177
Kim, J. S., 189
Kim, K. H., 211
Kim, N. H., 57
Kim, S., 129, 173, 398
Kim, S. K., 391
Kim, S. Y., 8, 290, 297

Kim, S. Y. H., 425
Kimberlin, D. W., 61
Kimlin, J. A., 387
Kimmel, M. S., 297
Kindermann, T. A., 241
King, A. E., 405
King, B. M., 264
King, C. T., 9
King, J. D., 302
King, L. A., 315, 316, 343, 344, 410
King, V., 417
Kingdon, D., 58
Kingerlee, R., 368
Kingo, O. S., 93
Kingsbury, A. M., 63
Kins, E., 306, 307
Kinugawa, K., 5, 17, 385, 394,
    398–401, 421
Kinzler, K. D., 126
Kiray, H., 80
Kirby, M., 353, 390
Kircaburun, K., 369
Kirk, G. M., 310
Kirk, I. J., 199
Kirkham, N. Z., 97, 107
Kirkorian, H. L., 93
Kisilevsky, B. S., 95
Kitayama, S., 368, 371
Kito, M., 332
Kitsantas, A., 279
Kiviniemi, A. M., 348
Klauda, S. L., 278
Klein, A. C., 247
Klein, D. A., 264
Klein, L., 117
Klein, M. R., 132, 180
Kleinman, C., 74
Kliegman, R. M., 141, 198
Kliewer, R., 121
Kline, D. W., 349, 387
Klinenberg, E., 332, 333
Klingman, A., 232
Kloss, J. D., 271
Klug, J., 238
Klug, W. S., 43
Knapen, J. E. P., 38
Knapp, K., 156, 212, 276
Knight, B. G., 398
Knight, L. F., 315
Knopfli, B., 373
Knowles, E. E., 40
Knyazev, G. G., 49, 50
Koball, H., 9
Kobayashi, S., 67
Kocahan, S., 404
Kochanek, K. D., 352
Kochanska, G., 129, 173
Kochendorfer, L. B., 294
Kocherginsky, M., 418
Kocur, J. L., 183
Koehn, A. J., 240
Koenig, H. G., 361
Koffer, R., 367
Koh, H., 265
Koh, V., 387
Kohen, D. E., 248
Kohl, M., 391
Kohlberg, L., 232
Kojola, E., 402
Kok, A. A., 366
Kok, F. M., 203
Kok, R., 142
Koksvik, G. H., 427
Kolb, B., 41
Koller, S. H., 9
Kolokotroni, P., 370, 413
Kominiarek, M. A., 61

Kondolot, M., 195
Konijn, E. A., 277
Konrad, M., 206, 219
Konrath, S. H., 328
Kontis, V., 380
Koo, Y. J., 63
Kopecky, S. L., 350
Kopp, F., 103
Koppelman, K. L., 189
Korczak, D. J., 122
Koren, C., 416
Koren, G., 52, 61
Korja, R., 63
Kornhaber, W., 215, 216
Koropeckyj-Cox, T., 418
Korte, J., 364, 410
Kosidou, K., 302
Kostic, M., 84
Kotter-Gruhn, D., 345
Kouros, C. D., 301
Kowalski, M., 155
Kowalski, R. M., 244
Koyanagi, A., 351, 390, 398
Kozhimmanil, K. B., 67
Kozloski, M., 381
Kozol, J., 226
Krabbendam, L., 11
Kraig, E., 383
Kramer, A. F., 392, 395
Kramer, H. J., 231
Kramer, L., 184
Kramer, M. R., 144, 268
Krampe, R., 220
Krampe, R. T., 357
Krans, E. E., 60
Krause, N., 360, 362
Kressig, R. W., 393
Kretch, K. S., 86, 89, 92, 93, 98, 126
Kreukels, B. P., 343
Kreutzer, M., 212
Kreye, M., 118
Krieger, V., 204
Kriemler, S., 200
Kring, A. M., 238
Krishnan, P., 427
Krishnan, S., 407
Krizan, Z., 369, 370
Krogh-Jespersen, S., 126
Krojgaard, P., 93
Kroll-Desrosiers, A. R., 64
Krous, H. F., 83
Krueger, J. I., 229
Krueger, P. M., 414
Kruger, J., 311
Kruger, R., 383
Kruse, A., 184
Kübler-Ross, E., 429
Kuebli, J., 230
Kuersten-Hogan, R., 132
Kuhl, P. K., 106, 107, 110, 111
Kuhn, B. R., 181
Kuhn, D., 260, 275, 276, 318
Kuhnert, R. L., 171
Kuiper, J., 269
Kulu, H., 336
Kumar, K., 404
Kumar, S. V., 74
Kumpulainen, S. M., 62
Kung, K. T., 175
Kuntzmann, 2019, 4, 5, 397, 398
Kunzmann, U., 397, 411, 421
Kuo, H. W., 201
Kuo, L. J., 223
Kuperberg, A., 334
Kuzik, N., 269
Kuznetsov, A. V., 404
Kuznetsov, I. A., 404

Kvaavik, E., 299
Kvalo, S. E., 212
Kwak, Y. Y., 302
Kwitowski, M. A., 259
Kymre, I. G., 71

L

Labayen Goñi, I., 145
Labella, M. H., 49, 157
Laborte-Lemoyne, E., 65
Labouvie-Vief, G., 318
Lacaze-Masmonteil, T., 60
Lachman, M. E., 346–348, 366–368,
    371, 412, 421
Laciga, J., 217
Ladd, H. C., 247
Ladewig, P. W., 69
Ladhani, S. N., 61
Laflin, M. T., 264
Lafond, J., 52
Lafreniere, D., 388
Laftman, S. B., 244
Lagattuta, K. H., 231
La Greca, A. M., 293
Lahat, A., 120
Lai, A., 30, 60
Laible, D. J., 125, 181, 236
Lam, C. B., 181
Lam, S., 252
Lamb, M. E., 73, 99, 129, 134–136,
    155, 156, 186, 336, 337
Lambert, S., 432
Lamb-Parker, F. G., 164
Lamela, D., 188
Lammers, A. J., 425
Lampard, A. M., 273
Lampl, M., 78
Lamy, S., 322
Landale, N. S., 297
Landberg, M., 285
Landes, S. D., 365
Landi, F., 349
Landrum, A. R., 170
Lane, A. P., 398
Lane, H., 105
Lane-Donovan, C., 405
Langer, E. J., 14, 393, 421, 430
Langer, R. D., 352
Langstrom, N., 316
Lansford, J. E., 7, 9, 187, 188, 239,
    264, 418, 420
Lantagne, A., 292, 293, 328, 330
Lantolf, J., 151
Lany, J., 107
Lanz, M., 306
Lanzillotta, C., 383
Laranjo, J., 159
Larkina, M., 104, 105, 154, 156
Larsen, K. J., 303
Larsen, S. B., 383
Larsen-Rife, D., 370
Larson, D. B., 361
Larson, J., 291
Larson, R. W., 189, 295
Larsson, M., 55
Larsson, N. G., 25
Larzelere, R. E., 181
Latendresse, G., 74
Latham, R. M., 181
Lathrop, A. L., 93
Lau, E. Y., 370
Lau, J. S., 310
Lau, J. Y., 242, 277, 302
Laumann, E. O., 354
Laureiro-Martinez, D., 412

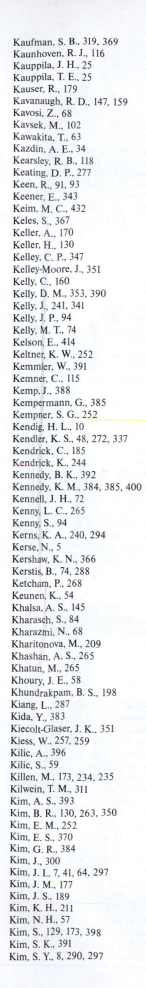

Laurent, H. K., 115, 288
Laursen, B., 190, 191, 241, 245, 289, 290, 300
Lautenbacher, S., 389
Lavender, J. M., 273
Lavner, J. A., 228, 334
Law, B. H. Y., 93
Law, L. L., 405
Lawrence, A. A., 343
Layland, E. K., 285, 306
Leaper, C., 175, 236, 342, 343
Leary, M. R., 28
Lebel, C., 198, 260, 261
Lebenbaum, M., 348
Lecce, S., 159
Ledonne, A., 204
Lee, C. C., 106, 302
Lee, D. K., 86, 89, 98, 100
Lee, F., 145
Lee, G., 302
Lee, G. R., 417
Lee, H. J., 349
Lee, H. W., 369
Lee, I. M., 392
Lee, J., 16, 96, 175, 176, 294
Lee, J. E., 421
Lee, K., 94, 170, 212, 228, 244
Lee, K. S., 243
Lee, K. Y., 41
Lee, M-H., 91
Lee, N. C., 11
Lee, R., 164, 370
Lee, R. M., 115, 116
Lee, S. J., 181
Leeds, M. J., 348
Leerkes, E. M., 115, 118, 130, 326
Lefkowitz, E., 313
Lefkowitz, E. S., 313
Leftwich, H. K., 266
Legare, C. H., 38
Leger, K. A., 369, 370
Legerstee, M., 126
Le Grange, D., 273
Lehman, E. B., 155
Lehman, H. C., 319
Lehr, C. A., 280
Leinaweaver, J., 375
Leinbach, M. D., 176
Leis, T. L., 97
Leland, D. S., 102
Lemola, S., 215, 216
Lenhart, A., 299
Lennartsson, C., 434
Leonard, B. E., 351
Leonard, C., 212
Leong, D. J., 152, 192, 212
Leonhardt, N. D., 330
Le Page, A., 384
le Ray, I., 56
Lereya, S. T., 244
Lerner, H. G., 325
Lerner, R. M., 9, 256, 262
Lesaux, N. K., 224
Leseman, P., 209
Leslie, S. J., 218
Lester, L., 244
Leung, R. C., 159
Levelt, W. J. M., 4
Leventon, S. J., 104
Lever-Duffy, J., 10, 298
Levin, J., 141
Levine, M. E., 381
Levine, T. P., 59
Levinson, D. J., 358, 365, 366
Levy, S. R., 413
Lewanda, A. F., 44
Lewis, A. C., 247

Lewis, B. A., 73
Lewis, C., 124, 129, 134–136, 243
Lewis, D. M. G., 25
Lewis, J. P., 364
Lewis, L., 68
Lewis, M., 116, 124, 129, 171, 327
Lewis, R. B., 206
Lewis, T. L., 97
Lewis-Morrarty, E., 129
Li, G., 175
Li, J., 47, 54, 62, 389, 432
Li, J. S. Z., 382
Li, J. W., 194, 269
Li, W., 138, 398
Li, Y., 296, 382
Liang, S. E., 353
Liang, W., 272
Liang, Y. J., 200
Liao, C. Y., 201
Liao, D. C., 276
Liben, L. S., 8, 134, 177, 235–237
Liberati, A., 93
Liberman, Z., 126
Libertus, K., 91
Lickliter, R., 25, 38, 41, 43
Licoppe, C., 342
Liddon, L., 368
Lieber, M., 232
Liebermann, J., 56
Libermann, A., 285
Liets, L. C., 385
Liew, J., 287
Lifter, K., 108
Lillard, A., 193
Lillard, A. S., 147, 192–194
Lim, E., 68
Lim, J. A., 383
Lim, S. H., 348
Lin, F., 385
Lin, F. R., 388
Lin, I. F., 372, 373, 416
Lin, J., 420
Lin, L., 404
Lin, L. J., 410
Lin, L. Y., 110
Lind, L., 389
Lind, R. R., 199
Lindahl-Jacobsen, R., 17
Lindau, S. T., 390
Lindberg, L. D., 267
Lindberg, S. M., 237
Lindenberger, U., 4, 16, 103, 347, 385, 398, 399, 412
Lindholm-Leary, K., 224
Lindsay, A. C., 143, 177, 287
Lindwall, M., 399
Linsell, L., 70
Lintu, N., 145
Lipowski, M., 264
Lippa, R. A., 315
Lipson, S. K., 310
Lisha, N. E., 307
Lissak, G., 195, 298
Litz, J., 159
Liu, H., 384
Liu, L., 382
Liu, P. Z., 385
Liu, R., 64, 115, 116
Liu, S., 100, 101
Liu, X., 62
Liu, Y., 40, 156, 172
Lively, W., 227
Livingston, G., 134, 313, 335, 337
Llewellyn, R., 230
Llop, S., 62
Lo, C. C., 182, 297, 335, 372
Lo, H. H. M., 204

Lo, J. C., 389
Lo, K. Y., 199
Lobo, R. A., 352
Locher, J. L., 393
Locke, A. M., 352
Lockhart, G., 7, 228, 288
Lockman, J. J., 91
Locquet, M., 349
Loenneke, J. P., 392
Lohmander, A., 106
Loi, E. C., 30
Loizou, E., 192
Lojko, D., 311
Lomanowska, A. M., 133
Lomniczi, A., 259
Longo, F., 239, 240
Longo, M. R., 94
Longobardi, C., 183
Lonstein, J. S., 73
Looby, A., 311
Lopez, K., 205
Lopez-Higes, R., 396, 399
Lopez-Tello, G., 288
Loprinzi, P. D., 359, 392, 398, 421
Lorenz, K. Z., 24
Lorenzo-Blanco, E. L., 297
Loria, H., 250
Lorinzi, P. D., 391
Lortie-Forgues, H., 21
Losada, A., 421
Louch, G., 367
Lougheed, J. P., 115, 125, 172, 230
Lovaglia, M. J., 347
Lovden, M., 16, 385, 398
Love, J. M., 164
Lovell, J. L., 256, 257
Lovely, C., 44
Lovgren, M., 432
Low, S., 293
Lowe, N. K., 67
Lowenstein, A., 417
Lowry, R., 263, 303
Lu, P. H., 385
Lu, T., 302
Lubetkin, E. I., 5
Lucas, J. E., 145
Lucas-Thompson, R., 186
Lucchetti, A. L., 361
Lucchetti, G., 361
Luchetti, M., 369, 413
Luders, E., 237
Ludyga, S., 199
Lugo, R. G., 173
Lukowski, A. F., 211
Lum, H., 425, 426
Lunceford, G., 414
Lund, H. G., 271
Lundin, A., 323
Lundorff, M., 432
Luo, W., 287
Luo, Y., 124
Luria, A., 176
Lusby, C. M., 115
Lushchak, V. I., 385
Lustig, C., 385, 395, 396, 399–401, 421
Lutkenhaus, P., 124
Luyckx, K., 285
Luyster, F. S., 311
Luyten, P., 130, 301
Lyon, T. D., 211
Lyons, D. M., 385
Lyons, E. M., 218
Lyons, H., 313

Lyons, J. L., 375
Lyrra, A. L., 272
Lytle, A., 413

M

Ma, C. L., 385
Ma, F., 170, 174
Maag, J. W., 23
Maalouf, F. T., 302
Maccalum, F., 432
Maccoby, E. E., 132, 133, 176, 179, 240
MacDonald, G., 328
MacDonald, S. W., 345
MacDonald, S. W. S., 13, 33
MacDougall, B. J., 424
MacFarlan, S. J., 134
MacFarlane, J. A., 96
Machado, A., 203, 204
Machado, B., 273
Machado, L., 419
Machalek, D. A., 47
Maciejewski, P. K., 432
MacKenzie, A., 267
Macneil, L. G., 386
MacNeill, L., 100
MacNeil Vroomen, J. L., 404
Madden, D. J., 385–387, 400, 401
Maddow-Zimet, I., 267
Mader, S., 15, 38, 43
Madison, S., 425
Madjar, N., 278
Madrasi, K., 391
Maduro, G., 61
Magge, S. N., 201
Maggs, J. L., 271
Magnuson, K., 7, 9, 248, 296, 297
Magowska, A., 427
Magro-Malosso, E. R., 65
Mah, A., 198
Mahabee-Gittens, E. M., 146
Maher, H., 285
Maher, J. P., 312
Maher, L. M., 109
Mahraj, L., 41, 405
Maid, S., 383
Maier, H., 346
Maillard, P., 350
Maitre, N. L., 133
Malamitsi-Puchner, A., 266
Malcolm-Smith, S., 159
Malinowski, P., 395
Mallard, C., 55
Mallin, B. M., 79, 101, 105
Malmberg, L. E., 135
Malone, J. C., 238
Maloy, R. W., 298
Mandara, J., 103, 105, 240
Mandler, J. M., 105
Manenti, R., 401
Manfredini, R., 335
Manganaro, L., 56
Mann, F. D., 300
Mann, N., 388
Manning, R. P., 328
Manore, M., 84, 143, 200
Mantzavinosa, V., 405
Manuck, S. B., 49
Many, A., 67
Manzanares, S., 56
Mao, H. F., 404
Maoz, H., 204
Maravilla, J. C., 265
Marcell, J. J., 349
Marchetti, D., 59

Morra, S., 208
Morris, A. S., 121
Morris, B. J., 96
Morris, M. C., 301
Morris, P. A., 25
Morris, S., 116, 119, 171, 230
Morrison, G. S., 7, 141, 143, 162, 163, 165, 192, 208, 217
Morrison, R. S., 427
Morrison, S. C., 187
Morrison-Beedy, D., 264
Morrissey, T. W., 135
Morrow-Howell, N., 421
Morse, A. F., 23
Mortelmans, D., 187
Mortensen, E. L., 90
Mortimer, J. T., 322
Morton, J. B., 156, 212, 276
Mosher, W. D., 333, 334
Moss, A. H., 425
Moss, P., 134, 270
Moss, S. A., 4, 14, 411, 421
Mossburg, S. E., 403
Motti-Stefanidi, F., 9, 10
Moulson, M. C., 94, 125
Mounts, E. L., 46
Mouquet-River, C., 85
Moura da Costa, E., 150
Moustafa, A. A., 23
Moyer, A., 334
Mparmpakas, D., 63
Mroczek, D., 371
Mroczek, D. K., 351, 371
Mrowka, R., 349
Mucke, M., 82
Mudrazija, S., 420
Mueller, B. A., 59
Mueller, M. R., 208
Mueller, S. C., 277
Muftic, L. R., 300
Muhammad, A., 41
Muijs, D., 243, 245
Mukherjee, P., 8, 190
Mulder, T. M., 183
Muller, M. J., 172
Muller, U., 156, 212, 350
Munholland, K. A., 128
Muniz Terrera, G., 397
Munn-Chernoff, M. A., 273
Munoz, K. D., 6, 84, 85, 143, 200
Munroe, B. A., 204
Munsters, N. M., 115
Muntane, G., 381
Murachver, T., 342
Murcia, M., 62
Murdock, K. K., 271
Murki, S., 71
Murphy, G. G., 384
Murphy, K., 298
Murphy, P. A., 64
Murray, H. B., 273
Murray, P. J., 263
Murugan, S., 405
Musher-Eizenman, D. R., 144
Mussen, P. H., 311
Mychasiuk, R., 41
Myers, D. G., 50
Myers, J., 425
Myerson, J., 218

Naicker, K., 301
Naiman, J. M., 63
Nair, R. L., 5, 190
Nair, S., 205
Najari, B. B., 353
Najman, J. M., 248, 300
Nakagawa, T., 381
Nakamichi, K., 172
Namgoong, S., 57
Namuth, T., 168
Nansel, T. R., 243
Nappi, R. E., 353
Narayan, A. J., 10, 232
Narayan, K. M., 144, 268
Narváez, D., 173, 234
Naughton, A. M., 182
Naumova, O. Y., 49
Nave, K. A., 80
Nave-Blodgett, J. E., 97
Ncube, C. N., 59
Ndu, I. K., 84
Needham, A., 91
Needham, A. W., 90
Neff, F., 383
Negriff, S., 260
Negru-Subtirica, O., 283
Nehme J., 382
Nehrkorn, A. M., 366
Neimeyer, R. A., 433
Nelson, C. A., 54, 81, 82, 101, 261, 385
Nelson, G., 202
Nelson, J. A., 171
Nelson, L. J., 285, 306–308
Nelson, S. E., 272
Nelson, S. K., 177
Nemet, D., 199, 201
Nene, R. V., 382
Nergard-Nilssen, T., 202
Nesi, J., 241, 291
Netz, Y., 312
Neupert, S. D., 368
Nevalainen, T., 348
Neville, H. J., 223
Nevitt, S. J., 46
Newport, E. L., 223
Newton, E. R., 65
Ng, F. F., 252
Ng, M., 71
Ng, Q. X., 303
Ngantcha, M., 298
Ngnoumen, C., 14, 421
Ngui, E. M., 64
Nguyen, T. V., 258
Nicolaou, E., 209
Nicosia, N., 200
Nicoteri, J. A., 310
Nie, J. B., 428
Nieto, S., 8, 189, 190, 248, 250, 297
Nikitin, J., 412, 421
Nikolas, M. A., 259
Nilsen, E. S., 228
Nilsen, P., 427
Niraula, A., 384
Nisbett, R., 216
Nishina, A., 290
Nissim, N. R., 396
Nitzke, S., 145
Niu, M., 45
Nnaka, T., 313
Noble, N., 352
Noll, J. G., 259
Nolte, S., 162, 166, 192, 208
Nomoto, M., 407
Non, A. L., 190
Nora, A., 80
Nordheim, K. L., 391

Nordstrom, K., 393
Norman, E., 211
Norman, J. F., 395
Norona, A. N., 133, 172
Norouzieh, K., 428
Norris, K., 382
Nosraty, L., 421
Nottelmann, E. D., 258
Nouchi, R., 396
Novack, M. A., 106
Novak, J., 328, 330
Novello, L., 258
Novick, G., 65
Nowson, C. A., 389
Nunes, A. S., 205
Nuri Ben-Shushan, Y., 222, 223
Nusslock, R., 385
Nuthmann, A., 101
Nye, C., 371
Nygard, C-H., 358
N'zi, A., 131

O

Oakley, G. P., 62
Oakley, M., 188
Oakley, M. K., 189, 338
Oates, K., 183
Oberle, E., 228
Oberlin, L. E., 5, 385, 391, 392, 400
Obradovic, J., 133, 217
O'Brien, J. L., 394
O'Brien, M., 134, 185
Occhino, C., 106
O'Connor, D., 414
O'Connor, D. B., 353
O'Connor, T. G., 121
Offer, D., 256
O'Flaherty, P., 60
Ogbuanu, I. U., 61
Ogden, C. L., 144, 200
Ogden, T., 256, 257
Ogino, T., 209
Ogletree, A. M., 328, 329, 342, 416, 418
Oh, S., 59
Oh, S. J., 396
Oh, W. O., 303
O'Halloran, A. M., 395
O'Hara, M. W., 73, 74
Ohlin, A., 71
O'Kearney, R., 228
Okereke, O., 431
Okun, M. A., 419
Okuzono, S., 181
Olderbak, S., 238
O'Leary, K. D., 334
O'Leary, M., 392
O'Leary, O. F., 385
Olesen, M. V., 385
Oleti, T. P., 71
Oliffe, J. L., 74
Oliva, A., 424
Oliver, B. R., 181, 184
Ollen, E. W., 189, 338
Ollendick, T. H., 172
Olsen, D. P., 425
Olson, B. D., 371
Olson, N. C., 40
Olszewski-Kubilius, P., 219
Oltmanns, J., 16, 398
Olweus, D., 245
Omaggio, N. F., 46
Onder, G., 414
Onders, B., 146
Onen, F., 389

Onen, S. H., 389
Ong, A. L. C., 382
Ono, D., 360
Onuzuruike, A. U., 201
Oppenheimer, C. W., 302
Orav, E. J., 374
Ordonez, T. N., 400
Oren, E., 366
Oren, N., 394
Orkaby, A. R., 13, 421
Orlich, D. C., 246
Ornoy, A., 52, 61
Orosova, O., 186
Orosz, G., 329
Orovecz, J. J., 8, 343
Orpinas, P., 238
Orth, U., 228
Ostan, R., 380
Oster, H., 96
Ostergaard, S. D., 203
Ostfeld, B. M., 59
Ostrove, J. M., 365
Ota, M., 107
Otsuki-Clutter, M., 179
Otto, H., 116, 130
Ou, S. R., 190, 249
Ouch, S., 338
Owen, K. B., 269
Owens, J. A., 270
Owsley, C., 388
Owsley, C. J., 100
Oyeyemi, A. L., 312
Ozcan, L., 353, 390
Oztekin, I., 396
Ozturk, M. B., 382

P

Paasch, E., 259
Pace, A., 107, 110, 112
Padilla-Walker, L. M., 194, 287, 306, 308
Pagani, L. S., 146
Pakhomov, S. V., 386
Palacios, E. L., 190
Palanisamy, J., 212
Palmer, A., 10, 231
Palmer, C. A., 270
Palmieri, A., 433
Palmore, E. B., 414
Pan, B. A., 222
Pan, C. Y., 204
Pan, Z., 194, 381
Pantell, R. H., 155
Paolucci, E. M., 312
Papanicolas, I., 414
Papastavrou, E., 406
Papernow, P., 240, 416
Parade, S. H., 118, 122
Parashar, S., 41
Parasuraman, R., 395
Parcianello, R. R., 60
Parcon, P. A., 30
Parens, E., 204
Pargament, K. I., 361
Parish-Morris, J., 107
Park, C. L., 357, 360, 361, 433
Park, D. C., 3, 5, 11, 13, 16, 29, 30, 386, 399, 400, 404
Park, H. S., 43, 287, 385
Park, M., 63
Park, M. J., 302, 310
Park, S., 421
Park, Y. M., 303
Parke, R. D., 134, 185, 186, 188
Parker, C. B., 411

Wood, J. M., 387
Wood, P. K., 272
Wood, W., 175
Woodhouse, S. S., 129, 131, 240
Woods, B., 410
Woodward, A. L., 126
Worrell, F. C., 280
Woyka, J., 353
Wright, D., 115
Wright, H., 354
Wright, H. F., 242
Wright, M. R., 417
Wright, M. W., 417
Wu, D., 23, 410
Wu, N., 280
Wu, R., 102, 105, 153, 208, 275, 277
Wu, T., 311
Wu, Y., 54
Wu, Z., 417
Wuest, D., 143, 145, 199, 268, 269, 311
Wyatt, S., 163
Wyatt, T., 230

X

Xaverius, P., 64
Xiao, J., 349
Xiao, T., 404
Xie, K., 383
Xie, W., 79, 101, 105
Xie, Y., 251
Xing, Y. Q., 30
Xu, F., 192
Xu, H., 195, 200
Xu, J., 381, 388
Xu, W., 405

Xu, Y., 349
Xu, Y. H., 96
Xue, F., 62

Y

Yackobovitch-Gavan, M., 201
Yakoboski, P. J., 403
Yamaguchi, M. K., 102
Yamanaka-Altenstein, M., 368
Yan, H., 199
Yan, Z., 298, 299
Yanai, H., 382
Yancura, L. A., 375
Yang, B., 60
Yang, P., 54
Yang, Y., 14, 381
Yang, Y. X., 348, 349
Yanikkerem, E., 68
Yaniv-Salem, S., 62
Yanovski, J. A., 200
Yanovski, S. Z., 200
Yap, M. B., 267, 272
Yarmohammadian, M. H., 163
Yasukochi, Y., 40
Yau, J. C., 286
Yauk, C. L., 64
Yavorsky, J. E., 132
Yavuz, H. M., 159
Yazigi, A., 61
Yen, H. Y., 410
Yen, Y. F., 425
Yeon, S., 222
Yeung, E. W., 419
Yildirim, E. D., 114, 135
Yin, H., 44
Yin, Z., 296

Yip, D. K., 44
Yip, P. S., 337
Yolton, K., 146
Yoo, J., 4, 13
Yoo, K. B., 323
Yoon, E., 286, 293, 297
Yoon, S. H., 351
Yorgason, J. B., 372
Yoshikawa, H., 9, 190, 217, 297
Young, A. R., 156
Young, D. R., 311
Young, J., 302
Young, K. T., 84
Young, M., 313
Youyou, W., 331
Yow, W. Q., 223, 224
Yu, C., 102, 103
Yu, C. Y., 135
Yu, J., 54
Yu, S., 57, 150, 152, 351
Yuan, B., 206

Z

Zabaneh, D., 44
Zachrisson, H. D., 138
Zagaria, A. B., 421
Zaghlool, S. B., 41, 405
Zalzali, H., 57
Zammit, A. R., 4, 394, 396
Zamuner, T., 107
Zannas, A. S., 49
Zanolie, K., 260, 261
Zanto, T. P., 394
Zarbatany, L., 292
Zarit, S. H., 376
Zayas, V., 275, 277

Zeanah, C. H., 129
Zeichner, A., 238
Zeifman, D., 328
Zeifman, D. M., 117
Zelazo, P. D., 156, 210, 260, 396
Zelazo, P. R., 118
Zell, E., 369, 370
Zerwas, S., 126
Zeskind, P. S., 117
Zettel-Watson, L., 396
Zgheib, N. K., 382
Zhang, D., 59, 109, 252, 270, 383, 385
Zhang, L., 60
Zhang, L. J., 404
Zhang, M., 414
Zhang, M. W., 409
Zhang, S., 52, 245, 311, 385
Zhang, Y., 352
Zhang, Z., 362
Zheng, B., 349, 385
Zheng, L. J., 404
Zhou, Q., 252, 296
Zhou, Y., 80, 200, 350, 369, 382, 385
Zhu, Y., 54
Zhu, Z., 40
Ziegler, D. A., 394
Ziermans, T., 205
Zigler, E. F., 165, 166
Ziliak, J. P., 185, 217
Zimprich, D., 413
Zittleman, K., 247
Zole, E., 383
Zozuls, K., 176
Zucker, K. J., 343
Zusho, A., 179
Zwicker, A., 337

in early adulthood, 310
in early childhood, 146
euthanasia and, 425–426
grief and, 431–432
historical circumstances, changes
    in, 428
Kübler-Ross' stages of dying and,
    429–430
in late adulthood, 390
of life partner, 433–434
making sense of, 433
mourning following, 434–435
perceived control and denial
    and, 430
Debriefing, 34
Deception, in research, 34
Decision making, in adolescence, 277
Declarative memory. *See* Explicit
    memory
Dementia, 403–404
Dendrites, 80, 384
Denial and isolation stage of
    dying, 429
Dependent variables, 31
Depression
    in adolescence, 300–302
    exercise and, 312
    peer relations and, 244, 301–302
    postpartum, 73, 74
    during pregnancy, 63
    socioeconomic status and, 296
    as stage of dying, 429
    suicide and, 302–303
Depth perception, 94, 95
Descriptive research, 30
Development. *See also* Human
    development; Life-span
    development
    characteristics of, 4–6
    explanation of, 2
    nature of, 11–17
    periods of, 12–13
Developmental cascade model, 130
Developmental cognitive
    neuroscience, 11, 198–199
Developmentally appropriate
    practice (DAP), 163–164
Developmental psychologists, 157
Developmental research. *See* Research
Developmental social neuroscience,
    11, 261
Diabetes, 46, 145
Diet. *See* Nutrition
Differential susceptibility model, 123
Difficult child, 120
Direct instruction approach, 246
Disabilities. *See* Children with
    disabilities
Disasters, coping with, 231–232
Discipline, for infants, 134
Disease. *See* Illness and disease;
    specific conditions
Disenfranchised grief, 432
Dishabituation, 92, 102
Divergent thinking, 211
Diversity. *See* Cultural diversity
Divorce. *See also* Remarriage
    among older individuals, 416
    challenges of, 337
    children and, 186–188
    in middle adulthood, 372
    prior cohabitation and, 334
    socioeconomic status and, 188
    stepfamilies and, 240–241
    strategies to deal with, 341
    trends in, 186, 336
DNA, 40–42, 49–50

Domain theory of moral
    development, 235–236
Dominant genes, 43
Dopamine, 406
Doulas, 67
Down syndrome, 44–45
Dropout rate, school, 279–280
Drugs. *See* Medication; Substance
    use/abuse
Dual-career couples, 324
Dual-language education, 224
Dynamic systems theory, 86–87
Dyscalculia, 202
Dysgraphia, 202
Dyslexia, 202

E

Early adulthood
    careers and work in, 320–324
    cognitive development in, 317–320
    creativity in, 319–320
    divorce in, 341
    eating and weight in, 311
    exercise in, 311–312
    explanation of, 12
    friendship in, 329
    gender and relationships, 341–342
    gender classification in, 342–343
    gender communication styles
        in, 341
    health in, 310–311
    key features of, 306–307
    lifestyles in, 332–338
    love and intimacy in, 328–332
    marriage in, 338–339
    parenting in, 339–341
    physical performance and
        development in, 309–310
    sexually transmitted infections in,
        316–317
    sexual orientation and behavior
        in, 313–316
    sleep in, 271
    substance abuse in, 312–313
    transition from high school to
        college in, 308–309
Early bloomers, 293
Early childhood. *See also* Children
    birth order and, 185
    brain development in, 142
    child maltreatment and, 182–183
    cognitive development in, 147–159
    development of self in, 169–170
    educational programs for, 162–163
    emotional development in, 171–172
    executive function in, 156–157
    exercise in, 145
    explanation of, 12
    families and, 177–191
    gender issues in, 174–177
    height and weight in, 141
    illness and death in, 146
    information processing in, 153–159
    language development in, 151,
        159–162
    media and screen time in, 194–195
    memory in, 154–156, 211
    moral development in, 172–174
    motor development in, 142–143
    nutrition in, 143–145
    peer relations in, 191
    play in, 192–194
    sibling relationships and,
        184–185
    theory of mind and, 158–159

Early childhood education
    child-centered kindergarten as, 162
    controversies in, 165–166
    curriculum for, 165–166
    developmentally appropriate and
        inappropriate, 163–164
    disadvantaged children and,
        164–165
    Montessori approach to, 162–163
Early Head Start, 165
Easy child, 120
Eating disorders, 272–274
Eclectic theoretical orientation, 27
Ecological theory, 25–26
Ecological view, of perceptual
    development, 91–92, 97
ED (erectile dysfunction), 353
Education. *See also* Achievement;
    Colleges/universities; Early
    childhood education; Schools
    of children from low-income
        families, 164–165, 247
    of children who are gifted, 221
    of children with disabilities, 206
    cognitive functioning in late
        adulthood and, 397
    constructivist and direct
        instruction approaches to, 246
    contemporary concerns in, 7
    dual-language, 224
    early childhood, 162–166
    ethnic diversity and, 249–250
    family life, 266
    gender and, 8
    intelligence and, 217
    for second-language learners, 224
    service learning, 280
    sex, 267
Education for All Handicapped
    Children Act (1975), 206
Egocentrism
    adolescent, 275–276
    in young children, 147, 170–171
Eight frames of mind theory
    (Gardner), 215
Elaboration, 209
ELLs (English language learners),
    224
Embryonic period, 52
Emerging adulthood, 306
Emotional abuse, 183
Emotional development. *See also*
    Socioemotional development
    in early childhood, 171–172
    in infancy, 115–119
    in middle and late childhood,
        230–232
Emotional expression
    crying as, 117–118
    in early childhood, 171
    fear as, 118
    smiling as, 118
    social referencing as, 118–119
Emotion-coaching parents, 172
Emotion-dismissing parents, 172
Emotions
    biological and environmental
        influences on, 115–116
    explanation of, 115
    expression of, 115–119
    postpartum fluctuations in, 73–74
    regulation of, 119, 171–172
    self-conscious, 171
Empiricists, 97
Empty nest syndrome, 373–374
English language learners (ELLs),
    224

Environmental influences. *See also*
    Nature-nurture issue
    on emotional development,
        115–116
    on giftedness, 220
    on intelligence, 216–217
    on language development,
        110–112
    on overweight, 200
    prenatal development and,
        60–61
    on temperament, 123
Epidural block, 67
Epigenetic view, 48–49
Episodic memory, 395
Equilibration, in cognitive
    development, 99
Erectile dysfunction (ED), 353
Erikson's psychosocial theory
    autonomy vs. shame and doubt
        stage in, 18, 124
    explanation of, 18–19, 27
    generativity vs. stagnation stage
        in, 19, 364–365
    identity vs. identity confusion,
        19, 284
    industry vs. inferiority stage in,
        19, 230
    initiative vs. guilt stage in, 18–19,
        169
    integrity vs. despair stage in, 19,
        409–410
    intimacy vs. isolation and, 19
    trust vs. mistrust stage in, 18,
        123, 127
ESSA (Every Student Succeeds
    Act), 247–248
Estradiol, 258
Estrogen, 258
Ethical issues
    in fetal sex determination, 56
    in research, 34–35
Ethnic identity, 286–287
Ethnicity. *See also* Cultural diversity;
    Culture; *specific groups*
    adolescent pregnancy and, 265
    adolescents and, 296–297
    explanation of, 8
    families and, 189–190
    gifted program
        underrepresentation and,
        219–220
    immigration and, 297
    intelligence tests and, 218
    older adults and, 419–420
    preterm birth and, 69–70
    school dropout rate and,
        279–280
Ethological theory, 24–25, 127
Ethology, 24
Euthanasia, 425–426
Every Student Succeeds Act
    (ESSA), 247–248
Evocative genotype-environment
    correlations, 48
Evolutionary perspective, 37–39
Evolutionary psychology, 38–39
Evolutionary theory of aging, 382
Executive attention, 153, 156
Executive function
    in adolescence, 276–277
    attention deficit hyperactivity
        disorder and, 204–205
    in early childhood, 156–157
    explanation of, 156
    in late adulthood, 396–397
    in middle and late childhood, 212

Exercise
    in adolescence, 268–269
    aerobic, 199, 204, 311
    depression and, 312
    in early adulthood, 311–312
    in early childhood, 145
    in late adulthood, 391–392,
        398, 400
    in middle adulthood, 350
    in middle and late childhood,
        199–200
Exosystem, 26
Experimental research, 30–31, 228
Experiments, 30
Expertise, 209, 357
Explicit memory, 104, 154, 395
Extreme binge drinking, 312
Extremely low birth weight
    newborns, 69
Extremely preterm infants, 69
Eye-tracking studies, in infants, 93
Eye-witness testimony, 155–156

F

False beliefs, 158
Families. See also Divorce; Fathers;
        Marriage; Mothers; Parents
    adolescence and, 287–290, 295
    attachment in, 240
    child maltreatment and, 182–183
    children in divorced, 186–188
    cultural, ethnic and
        socioeconomic variations in,
        189–191, 294–295
    extended, 189
    with gay and lesbian parents,
        188–189
    immigrant, 297
    infant caregiving in, 134–135
    in late adulthood, 415–417
    managing and guiding infant
        behavior in, 133–134
    moral development and, 234–235
    parental management in, 240,
        287–288, 300
    parent-child relationships in,
        239–240
    reciprocal socialization and,
        132–133
    sibling relationships and, 184–185
    single-parent, 189
    stepfamilies, 240–241
    subsystems within, 131–132
    transition to parenthood in, 132
    with two working parents,
        185–186, 324
Family and consumer science
        educators, 266
Family life education, 266
FASD (fetal alcohol spectrum
        disorders), 58–59
Fast mapping, 161
Fathers. See also Families; Parents
    as caregivers, 134–135
    gender development and, 176
    in postpartum period, 74
Fear, in infancy, 118
Feelings. See Emotions
Females. See also Gender/gender
        differences
    achievement and, 237–238
    body image and, 259
    early-maturing, 259–260
    education of, 8
    friendship among, 291, 329

as juvenile delinquents, 299
    prosocial behavior and, 238
Fertilization, 42
Fetal alcohol spectrum disorders
        (FASD), 58–59
Fetal MRI, 56
Fetal period, 52–54
Fetus. See also Prenatal development
    brain development in, 54–55
    determining sex of, 56
    development of, 51–55
    diagnostic tests for, 55–56
    hearing in, 95
    nutritional status of, 62
    transition to newborn from, 69
Fight-or-flight pattern, 368
Fine motor skills
    in early childhood, 143
    in infancy, 90–91
    in middle and late childhood, 199
Fish, during pregnancy, 62–63
5-HTTLPR, 49, 130
Fluid intelligence, 354–355
Folic acid, 62
Formal operational stage (Piaget),
        20–21, 274–275
Fractional magnetic resonance
        imaging (fMRI), 29
Fragile X syndrome, 43–45
Free radicals, 383
Free-radical theory of aging, 383
Freud's psychoanalytic theory,
        17–18, 173
Friendship. See also Peer relations
    in adolescence, 290–291
    in early adulthood, 329
    gender differences in, 291, 329,
        342–343
    in late adulthood, 418
    in middle adulthood, 374
    in middle and late childhood, 245
Frontal lobes, 79
Funerals, 434–435
Fuzzy trace theory, 210

G

Games, 193. See also Play
Gays
    attitudes and behavior of, 316
    dating among, 293
    as parents, 188–189
    same-sex relationships among,
        337–338
    sexual identity and, 262
Gender bias, 235
Gender/gender differences. See also
        Females; Males
    in adolescence, 294
    in aggression, 238
    attention deficit hyperactivity
        disorder and, 203
    autism spectrum disorders and,
        205
    body image and, 259
    in children with working mothers,
        186
    classification of, 343–344
    in cognitive development, 177,
        237–238
    communication styles and, 342
    cultural diversity and, 239
    divorce and, 337
    educational opportunities and, 8
    explanation of, 8, 174
    in friendship, 291, 329, 342–343

in interest in religion, 360
    in intergenerational relationships,
        377
    in juvenile delinquency, 299
    learning disabilities and, 202
    in life expectancy, 380–381, 428
    moral development and, 235
    older adults and, 420
    parental influences on, 175–176
    peer influences on, 176–177
    in physical development, 141,
        236–237
    psychoanalytic theory of, 175
    relationships and, 342–343
    school dropout rate and, 279
    social cognitive theory of, 175
    social influences on, 175
    social role theory of, 175
    social theories of, 175
    in socioemotional development,
        238
    stress and, 368
    temperament and, 122
Gender identity, 174
Gender roles
    culture and, 239
    explanation of, 174–175
Gender schema theory, 177
Gender stereotypes
    explanation of, 236
    function of, 239
    math ability, 254
Gene-gene interaction, 44
Gene-linked abnormalities, 45–46
Generation X, 34
Generativity, 364, 365
Generativity vs. stagnation stage
        (Erikson's theory), 19, 364–365
Genes
    dominant, 43
    explanation of, 40, 41
    longevity, 43
    mitosis, meiosis, and fertilization
        and, 42
    mutated, 42
    recessive, 43
    sex-linked, 43
    sources of variability and, 42–43
    susceptibility, 43
Genetic code, 40
Genetic counselors, 47
Genetic expression, 41
Genetic factors
    autism spectrum disorders and,
        205
    background of, 40–41
    in depression, 301
    eating disorders and, 273
    giftedness and, 220
    intelligence and, 216
    overweight and, 200
Genetics
    behavior, 47–48
    chromosomal abnormalities and,
        44–46
    human genome and, 40, 41
Genetic susceptibility, 57
Gene x environment (G x E)
        interaction, 49
Genital herpes, 61, 317
Genital warts, 317
Genome-wide association method, 40
Genotype, 43
Geriatric nurses, 394
Germinal period, 51–52
Gestures, in infancy, 106
Giftedness, 219–221

Glaucoma, 387
Gonads, 258
Gonorrhea, 317
Goodness of fit, 122–123
Grammar, 221–222. See also
        Language development
Grandparenting, 374–375
Grasping, 90
Grief, 431
Grieving, 431–432
Gross motor skills
    in early childhood, 142–143
    in infancy, 88–90
    in middle and late childhood, 199
Growth. See Physical development;
        specific age groups

H

Habituation, 92, 102
Happiness, age and, 14–15
Head Start, 164–165
Health care
    for older adults, 393, 414–415
    prenatal, 64–65
Health issues. See also Illness and
        disease; specific conditions
    in adolescence, 267–274, 294
    in early adulthood, 310–313
    in early childhood, 146
    in late adulthood, 390–391
    in middle adulthood, 349–351
    in middle and late childhood,
        200–201
    overweight and obesity as,
        200–201
    poverty and, 146
    religion and, 360–361
Health psychologists, 301
Hearing
    in fetus, 95
    in infancy, 95–96
    in late adulthood, 388
    in middle adulthood, 349
Height
    in adolescence, 257
    in early childhood, 141
    in infancy, 78
    in middle adulthood, 348–349
    in middle and late childhood, 198
Hemophilia, 46
Heredity. See Genetic factors
Heredity-environment correlations,
        48–49. See also Nature-nurture
        issue
Heroin, 60
Heteronomous morality (Kohlberg),
        173, 232
Heterosexuality, 314–315
High school
    features of, 279–280
    transition to college from,
        308–309
Hispanics. See Latinos/Latinas
HIV/AIDS. See also Sexually
        transmitted infections (STIs)
    in children, 146
    explanation of, 317
    infants and, 61
    statistics related to, 316–317
    strategies for protection from,
        316–317
Home hospice nurses, 427
Homicide, 271
Homosexuals. See Gays; Lesbians
Hormonal stress theory of aging, 384

Hormones
    genes and, 41
    for infertility, 57
    menopause and, 352
    in middle-aged men, 353
    in postpartum period, 73
    in puberty, 30, 258
    transgender people and, 342–343
Hospice, 427
Human development, 6. *See also*
    Life-span development
Human genome, 40
Human Genome Project, 40–41
Huntington disease, 46
Hypertension, 349–350
Hypothalamus, 258
Hypotheses, 17
Hypothetical-deductive reasoning, 274

I

IDEA (Individuals with Disabilities
    Education Act, 1997), 206
Identity
    cultural and ethnic, 286–287
    developmental changes and,
        284–286
    in early adulthood, 306
    Erikson's view of, 19, 284
    explanation of, 282–283
    gender, 174
    sexual, 262
Identity achievement, 285
Identity diffusion, 284
Identity foreclosure, 284
Identity moratorium, 285
Identity vs. identity confusion
    (Erikson), 19, 284
IEPs (individualized education
    plans), 206
Illness and disease. *See also* Health
    issues; *specific conditions*
    in early childhood, 146
    in middle adulthood, 351
    during pregnancy, 61
Imaginary audience, 275
Imitation
    deferred, 103
    explanation of, 23–24
    in infancy, 103
Immanent justice, 174
Immigrants/immigration
    adolescents as, 290, 297
    families and, 190
    second-language learning and, 224
    undocumented, 297
Implicit memory, 104, 154, 395
Imprinting, 25
Inclusion, 206
Income, 414. *See also*
    Socioeconomic status (SES)
Independence, in infancy, 124–125
Independent variables, 31
Individuality, respect for, 122–123
Individualized education plans
    (IEPs), 206
Individuals with Disabilities Education
    Act (1997, IDEA), 206
Individuals with Disabilities
    Education Improvement Act
    (2004), 206
Indulgent parenting, 178
Industry vs. inferiority stage
    (Erikson's theory), 19, 230
Infancy. *See also* Newborns
    attachment in, 84, 127–131

attention in, 101–102
biological influences on language
    development in, 109–110
brain development in, 78–82
child care for, 135–138
cognitive development in, 98–105
conception formation and
    categorization in, 104–105
conditioning in, 102
emotional development in,
    115–119
explanation of, 12
family and, 131–135
hearing in, 95
height and weight in, 78
HIV/AIDS and, 61
imitation in, 103
independence in, 124–125
intention, goal-directed behavior,
    and cooperation in, 126
language development in, 106–107
locomotion in, 88–89, 126
low birth weight and preterm,
    69–71
memory in, 103–104
motor development in, 86–91
nature-nurture issue and, 97–98
nutrition in, 84–85
patterns of growth in, 77–78
perceptual development in, 91–93
personality development in,
    123–125
reciprocal socialization and,
    132–133
reflexes in, 87–88
sensory and perceptual
    development in, 91–98
sleep in, 82–83
smell sensation in, 96
social orientation in, 125–126
social sophistication and insight
    in, 126
temperament in, 119–123
visual perception in, 93–94
Infantile amnesia, 104
Infertility, 56–57
Infinite generativity, 106
Information processing. *See also*
    Memory; Metacognition;
    Thinking
    in adolescence, 276–277
    in early childhood, 153–159
    in infancy, 105
    in middle adulthood, 357
    in middle and late childhood,
        208–212
    speed of, 357
Information-processing theory, 21–23
Informed consent, 34
Inhibition to the unfamiliar, 120
Initiative vs. guilt stage (Erikson's
    theory), 18–19, 169
Injuries. *See* Accidents
Inner speech, 151
Insecure avoidant babies, 128
Insecure disorganized babies, 129
Insecure resistant babies, 128
Integrity vs. despair stage (Erikson's
    theory), 19, 409–410
Intellectual disability, 218–219
Intelligence
    analytical, 214
    creative, 214
    crystallized, 354–355
    culture and, 218
    environmental influences on,
        216–217

explanation of, 213
extremes of, 218–221
fluid, 354–355
Gardner's eight frames of mind
    theory of, 215
genetics and, 216
in middle adulthood, 354–356
multiple, 215–216
practical, 214
Seattle Longitudinal Study of,
    355–356
triarchic theory of, 214
types of, 215–216
Intelligence quotient (IQ), 213,
    216–218
Intelligence tests
    Binet, 213–214
    culture-fair, 218
    group differences in, 218
    intellectual disabilities and,
        218–219
    IQ, 216–218
    Wechsler, 214
Interactionist view, of language
    development, 112
Intergenerational relationships,
    376–377. *See also* Families
Intermodal perception, 96–97
Internet. *See also* Screen time;
    Technology use
    adolescents' use of, 298–299
    cyberbullying and, 244
Interpersonal intelligence, 215
Interviews, 28–29
Intimacy
    in adolescence, 291
    in early adulthood, 328–329
Intimacy vs. isolation stage
    (Erikson's theory), 19
Intrapersonal intelligence, 215
Intuitive thought substage (Piaget),
    148
In vitro fertilization (IVF), 57
Involution, 73
IQ (intelligence quotient), 213,
    216–218

J

Jigsaw classroom, 250
Joint attention, 102, 103, 126
Junior high school, transition to,
    278
Justice perspective, 235
Juvenile delinquency, 299–300

K

Kangaroo care, 71
Kindergarten, child-centered, 162
Klinefelter's syndrome, 44, 45
Knowledge, memory and, 209
Kohlberg's moral development theory
    critics of, 234–235
    influences on, 233–234
    stages of, 233–235
Kübler-Ross' stages of dying,
    429–430

L

Labor. *See* Childbirth
Laboratory, 28
Lamaze childbirth method, 67

Language
    brain lateralization and, 79
    explanation of, 106
    social aspect of, 151
Language acquisition device (LAD),
    109
Language development
    biological influences on, 109–110
    in early childhood, 159–162
    environmental influences on,
        110–112
    in infancy, 106–107
    interactionist view of, 112
    in middle and late childhood,
        221–224
    play and, 192
    poverty and, 110
    second-language learning and,
        223–224
    strategies to promote, 111–112
    vocabulary and, 107–108
Late adulthood. *See also* Aging
    adult children and, 417
    altruism and volunteerism in, 419
    Alzheimer disease in, 404–406
    attachment in, 417
    attention in, 394–395
    biological theories of aging and,
        381–384
    brain function in, 384–386
    circulatory system and lungs in,
        389
    cognitive activity patterns in,
        398–399
    cognitive functioning in, 394–401
    cognitive neuroscience and,
        400–401
    cognitive skills training and,
        399–400
    culture and, 420
    dementia in, 403–404
    education and, 397
    ethnicity and, 419–420
    executive function in, 396–397
    exercise in, 391–392, 398, 400
    explanation of, 13
    friendship in, 418
    gender and, 420
    health in, 390–391, 398
    health treatment in, 393
    lifestyle diversity in, 415–417
    longevity in, 379–381
    memory in, 395–396
    mental health in, 403–407
    nutrition and weight in, 392–393
    Parkinson disease in, 406–407
    personality in, 413
    retirement in, 402–403
    sensory development in, 387–389
    sexuality in, 389–390
    sleep in, 389
    social policy and, 414–415
    social support and social
        integration in, 418–419
    socioemotional development
        theories and, 409–413
    stereotypes of, 413–414
    successful aging in, 421–422
    wisdom in, 397
    work in, 398, 402
Late bloomers, 293
Late childhood. *See* Adolescence;
    Middle and late childhood
Lateralization, brain, 79
Latinos/Latinas. *See also* Ethnicity
    adolescent pregnancy among, 265
    education and, 249–250

Social work professors and administrators, 420
Sociocultural cognitive theory. *See* Vygotsky's sociocultural cognitive theory
Socioeconomic status (SES)
  child-rearing practices in, 190–191
  delinquency and, 300
  development and, 296
  divorce and, 188
  education and, 164–165, 247
  ethnicity and, 297
  explanation of, 8
  families and, 190–191
  intelligence tests and, 218
  tobacco smoke exposure and, 146
Socioemotional development. *See also* Emotional development; Emotions; Personality/personality development
  in adolescence, 282–304
  aging and theories of, 409–410
  in early adulthood, 326
  in early childhood, 168–196
  in infancy, 114–139
  in middle and late childhood, 226–254
  theories of, 409–413
Socioemotional processes, 11
Socioemotional selectivity theory, 410–412
Spatial intelligence, 215
Speech. *See also* Language development
  child-directed, 110–111
  telegraphic, 108
Spina bifida, 46, 54
Spirituality, in middle adulthood, 360–361
Stability-change issue, 16
Stagnation, 364
Standardized tests, 29
Stanford-Binet tests, 213–214
Stanford Center for Longevity, 399
Stepfamilies, 240–241
Stereotypes
  gender, 236, 239
  of older adults, 413–414
STIs. *See* Sexually transmitted infections
Stranger anxiety, 118
Strange Situation, 128
Stress
  in caregivers, 115–116
  coping with, 231–232
  in families, 190
  gender and, 368
  immigrants and, 297
  in middle adulthood, 367–368
  during pregnancy, 54, 63
  work and, 323
Substance use/abuse. *See also* Alcohol use/abuse; Tobacco/tobacco use

in adolescence, 271–272
in early adulthood, 312–313
during pregnancy, 58–60
Successful aging, 14
Sucking reflex, 87
Sudden infant death syndrome (SIDS), 83
Suicide, in adolescence, 302–303
Supercentenarians, 381
Surveys, 28–29
Susceptibility genes, 43
Sustained attention, 153, 395
Symbolic function substage (Piaget), 147–148
Symbolic play, 193
Synapses, 80–81
Syntax, 160–161
Syphilis, 61, 317

T

Taste
  in infancy, 96
  in late adulthood, 388
Tay-Sachs disease, 46
Teach for America instructors, 249
Technology use
  in adolescence, 298–299
  contemporary concerns and, 10
  in early childhood, 154
  to improve attention, 154
  in late adulthood, 415
  reproductive, 56–57
Telegraphic speech, 108
Television viewing, 194–195
Telomerase, 382
Telomeres, 382
Temperament
  biological influences on, 121–122
  classification of, 119–121
  explanation of, 119
  goodness of fit and, 122–123
Temporal lobes, 79
Tend-and-befriend pattern, 368
Teratogens
  environmental, 60–61
  explanation of, 57
  prescription and nonprescription drugs as, 58
  psychoactive drugs as, 58–60
Teratology, 57
Testosterone, 258, 353
Theories, 17. *See also* Life-span development theories
Theory of mind
  autism and, 159
  developmental changes in, 158–159, 170
  explanation of, 158
  individual differences and, 158–159
Thinking. *See also* Cognitive development
  convergent, 211

creative, 211
critical, 210–211
explanation of, 210
Time out, 181
Tobacco/tobacco use. *See also* Substance use/abuse
  childhood exposure to, 146
  placenta development and, 52
  as teratogen, 59, 64
Toddlers. *See also* Early childhood; Infancy
  executive function in, 156–157
  language development in, 159 (*See also* Language development)
  memory in, 155
  theory of mind in, 158–159
Top-dog phenomenon, 278
Touch
  in infancy, 96
  in late adulthood, 388–389
Transgender, 343
Transitivity, 207–208
Triarchic theory of intelligence, 214
Trimesters, 53, 54
Trust vs. mistrust stage (Erikson's theory), 18, 123, 127
Turner syndrome, 44, 45
Twin studies, 47, 216
Two-word utterances, 108

U

Ultrasound sonography, 55
Umbilical cord, 52, 69
Unconscious thought, 19
Unemployment, 323
Universal preschool education, 166
Universities. *See* Colleges/universities
University professors, 268, 361, 420

V

Verbal intelligence, 215
Very low birth weight newborns, 69
Very preterm infants, 71
Violence, 194–195. *See also* Aggression
Vision
  in infancy, 93–94, 97
  in late adulthood, 387–388
  in middle adulthood, 349
Visual acuity, 93–94
Visual preference method, 92–93
Vocabulary development. *See also* Language development
  in infancy, 107–108
  in middle and late childhood, 221–222
Vocabulary spurt, 108

Vygotsky's sociocultural cognitive theory
  evaluation of, 152–153
  explanation of, 21, 27, 150
  language and thought and, 151
  Piaget's theory vs., 152, 153
  scaffolding and, 150–151
  teaching strategies based on, 151–152
  zone of proximal development and, 150–151

W

Waterbirth, 68
Wechsler scales, 214
Weight. *See also* Obesity; Overweight
  in adolescence, 257
  in early adulthood, 311
  in early childhood, 141
  in infancy, 78
  in middle adulthood, 348–349
  in middle and late childhood, 198
Wernicke's area, 109
Whole-language approach, 222
Widowers, 415, 433–434
Widows, 415, 433–434
Widow-to-Widow program, 434
Wisdom, 397
Women. *See* Females; Gender/gender differences
Work. *See also* Careers
  aging and, 398, 402
  during college, 322–323
  in early adulthood, 321–322
  impact of, 321–322
  in middle adulthood, 358
  occupational outlook and, 323
Working memory
  in late adulthood, 395–396
  in middle adulthood, 357
  in middle and late childhood, 208
Working parents, 185–186
Writing skills, gender and, 237

X

X chromosomes, 43–45
X-linked inheritance, 43
XYY syndrome, 44, 45

Y

Y chromosomes, 43–45

Z

Zone of proximal development (ZPD), 150–151
Zygote, 42, 51